Anderson's Business Law and the Legal Environment

The University at Albany

22nd Edition

David P. Twomey | Marianne M. Jennings

CENGAGE
Learning

Australia • Brazil • Japan • Korea • Mexico • Singapore • Spain • United Kingdom • United States

CENGAGE
Learning·

Anderson's Business Law and the Legal Environment: The University at Albany, 22nd Edition

Source:

Anderson's Business Law and the Legal Environment, Comprehensive Volume, 22nd Edition
David P. Twomey | Marianne M. Jennings

Senior Manager, Student Engagement:

Linda deStefano

Janey Moeller

Manager, Student Engagement:

Julie Dierig

Marketing Manager:

Rachael Kloos

Manager, Production Editorial:

Kim Fry

Manager, Intellectual Property Project Manager:

Brian Methe

Senior Manager, Production and Manufacturing:

Donna M. Brown

Manager, Production:

Terri Daley

For product information and technology assistance, contact us at
Cengage Learning Customer & Sales Support, 1-800-354-9706

For permission to use material from this text or product,
submit all requests online at **cengage.com/permissions**
Further permissions questions can be emailed to
permissionrequest@cengage.com

This book contains select works from existing Cengage Learning resources and was produced by Cengage Learning Custom Solutions for collegiate use. As such, those adopting and/or contributing to this work are responsible for editorial content accuracy, continuity and completeness.

Compilation © 2014 Cengage Learning

ISBN-13: 978-1-305-28677-1
ISBN-10: 1-305-28677-4

WCN: 01-100-101

Cengage Learning
5191 Natorp Boulevard
Mason, Ohio 45040
USA

Cengage Learning is a leading provider of customized learning solutions with office locations around the globe, including Singapore, the United Kingdom, Australia, Mexico, Brazil, and Japan. Locate your local office at:
international.cengage.com/region.

Cengage Learning products are represented in Canada by Nelson Education, Ltd.
For your lifelong learning solutions, visit **www.cengage.com/custom.**
Visit our corporate website at **www.cengage.com.**

Printed in the United States of America

Brief Contents

PART 7: BUSINESS ORGANIZATIONS

CHAPTER 1

The Nature and Sources of Law

learningoutcomes

After studying this chapter, you should be able to

LO.1 Discuss the nature of law

LO.2 List the sources of law

LO.3 Describe the classifications of law

W hy have law? If you have ever been stuck in a traffic jam or jostled in a crowd leaving a stadium, you have observed the need for order to keep those involved moving in an efficient and safe manner. The issues with bloggers' use of others' materials and continuing downloading of music and films without compensation to copyright holders illustrate the need for rules and order in this era of new technology. When our interactions are not orderly, whether at our concerts or through our e-mail, all of us and our rights are affected. The order or pattern of rules that society uses to govern the conduct of individuals and their relationships is called **law**. Law keeps society running smoothly and efficiently.

law – the order or pattern of rules that society establishes to govern the conduct of individuals and the relationships among them.

A. NATURE OF LAW AND LEGAL RIGHTS

Law consists of the body of principles that govern conduct and that can be enforced in courts or by administrative agencies. The law could also be described as a collection or bundle of rights.

1. Legal Rights

right – legal capacity to require another person to perform or refrain from an action.

duty – an obligation of law imposed on a person to perform or refrain from performing a certain act.

A **right** is a legal capacity to require another person to perform or refrain from performing an act. Our rights flow from the U.S. Constitution, state constitutions, federal and state statutes, and ordinances at the local levels, including cities, counties, and boroughs. Within these sources of rights are also duties. A **duty** is an obligation of law imposed on a person to perform or refrain from performing a certain act.

Duties and rights coexist. No right exists in one person without a corresponding duty resting on some other person or persons. For example, if the terms of a lease provide that the premises will remain in a condition of good repair so that the tenant can live there comfortably, the landlord has a corresponding duty to provide a dwelling that has hot and cold running water.

2. Individual Rights

The U.S. Constitution gives individuals certain rights. Those rights include the right to freedom of speech, the right to due process or the right to have a hearing before any freedom is taken away, and the right to vote. There are also duties that accompany individual rights, such as the duty to speak in a way that does not cause harm to others. For example, individuals are free to express their opinions about the government or its officials, but they would not be permitted to yell "Fire!" in a crowded theater and cause unnecessary harm to others. The rights given in the U.S. Constitution are rights that cannot be taken away or violated by any statutes, ordinances, or court decisions. These rights provide a framework for the structure of government and other laws.

3. The Right of Privacy

One very important individual legal right is the right of privacy, which has two components. The first is the right to be secure against unreasonable searches and seizures by the government. The Fourth Amendment of the U.S. Constitution

right of privacy—the right to be free from unreasonable intrusion by others.

guarantees this portion of the **right of privacy**.[1] A police officer, for example, may not search your home unless the officer has a reasonable suspicion (which is generally established through a warrant) that your home contains evidence of a crime, such as illegal drugs. If your home or business is searched unlawfully, any items obtained during that unlawful search could be excluded as evidence in a criminal trial because of the Fourth Amendment's exclusionary rule. **For Example,** in the murder trial of O.J. Simpson, Judge Lance Ito excluded some of the evidence the police had obtained from inside Mr. Simpson's Ford Bronco, which was parked on the street outside his home. Judge Ito ruled that the officers should have first obtained a warrant for the locked vehicle, which was not going to be taken anywhere because Mr. Simpson was out of town at that time.

CASE SUMMARY

Searches of Cars When Drivers Are Cuffed

FACTS: Rodney Gant was arrested for driving with a suspended license and handcuffed in the back seat of the squad car of the arresting officers. After handcuffing Mr. Gant, the arresting officers searched his car and found cocaine in the pocket of a jacket lying on the back seat of Gant's vehicle. Mr. Gant was charged with possession of cocaine (as well as driving with a suspended license).

Mr. Gant's lawyer challenged the search of his client's vehicle on the grounds that there were not exigent circumstances. That is, locked in and handcuffed as he was, there was no emergency or reason to believe that Mr. Gant would spring into action and hide, destroy, or swallow the cocaine. As a result, his lawyer argued that the officers needed a warrant. Without the warrant, his lawyer argued, the cocaine could not be used as evidence in the case.

The cocaine evidence was admitted and Mr. Gant was convicted and appealed. The Court of Appeals of Arizona reversed. The United States Supreme Court granted Arizona's petition for *certiorari*, and subsequently vacated and remanded. The Court of Appeals of Arizona remanded for evidentiary hearing on the legality of the warrantless search. On remand, the trial court found no violation. Defendant appealed again. The Court of Appeals of Arizona reversed the decision and the Supreme Court of Arizona affirmed that reversal. Arizona appealed.

DECISION: The court held that the officers needed to impound the vehicle and obtain a warrant in order to search it. Police may search the passenger compartment of a vehicle after such an arrest only if it is reasonable to believe that the person arrested might somehow access the vehicle at the time of the search or that the vehicle contains evidence of the offense of arrest, which, in this case, was a suspended license. Without a warrant to search the vehicle while its owner was handcuffed, the cocaine that was found was not admissible for purposes of prosecuting Mr. Gant on the cocaine charges. Without the cocaine evidence, unless Mr. Gant confesses, that charge had to be dropped. Searches require warrants or a valid exception to the privacy provided under the Fourth Amendment. Affirmed. [*Arizona v. Gant,* 556 U.S. 332 (2009)]

---

[1] Police officers who record the arrest of a DUI suspect have not violated the suspect's privacy. *State v. Morris,* 214 P.3d 883 (Ut. App. 2009)

A second aspect of the right of privacy protects individuals against intrusions by others. Your private life is not subject to public scrutiny when you are a private citizen. This right is provided in many state constitutions and exists through interpretation at the federal level through the landmark case of *Roe v. Wade*,[2] in which the U.S. Supreme Court established a right of privacy that gives women the right to choose whether to have an abortion.

These two components of the right to privacy have many interpretations. These interpretations are often found in statutes that afford privacy rights with respect to certain types of conduct. **For Example,** a federal statute provides a right of privacy to bank customers that prevents their banks from giving out information about their accounts except to law enforcement agencies conducting investigations. Some laws protect the rights of students. **For Example,** the Family Educational Rights and Privacy Act of 1974 (FERPA, also known as the *Buckley Amendment*) prevents colleges and universities from disclosing students' grades to third parties without the students' permission. From your credit information to your Social Security number, you have great privacy protections.

4. Privacy and Technology

Technology creates new situations that may require the application of new rules of law. Technology has changed the way we interact with each other, and new rules of law have developed to protect our rights. Today, business is conducted by computers, wire transfers of funds, e-mail, electronic data interchange (EDI) order

---

Ethics & the Law

Twitter, Facebook, Google, and Your Job Application

A study by the social monitoring service, Reppler, found the following about employers:

- 91 percent of the employers polled use social networking sites (Twitter, Facebook, and LinkedIn) to screen prospective employees. Some employers even ask for applicants' passwords as a condition of employment.

- 69 percent say they have rejected a job applicant because of something they saw on one of these social platforms.

- 47 percent of employers do their checks of these social networking sites immediately after receiving their job applications.

- 76 percent of employers check Facebook.

- 53 percent check Twitter.

- 48 percent check LinkedIn.

- 68 percent of employers say that they have hired someone because they liked what they saw on these social networking sites.

One employer commented that these searches are so simple that it would be irresponsible to not do them. Experts tell college students to remember that what may seem to be fun can later come back to haunt you when you begin your professional career. Their advice is to watch what you post and what you write. Discuss privacy rights and whether there is any legal issue when information is posted voluntarily on the Internet. Is there an ethical issue with these types of searches?

Source: Shea Bennett, "91% of Employers Use Twitter, Facebook, and LinkedIn to Screen Job Applicants," **www.alltwitter.com**, October 24, 2011.

---

[2] 410 U.S. 113 (1973).

placements, and the Internet. We still expect that our communication is private. However, technology also affords others the ability to eavesdrop on conversations and intercept electronic messages. The law has stepped in to reestablish that the right of privacy still exists even in these technologically nonprivate circumstances. Some laws now make it a crime and a breach of privacy to engage in such interceptions of communications.[3] (See Chapter 11)

E-Commerce & Cyberlaw

A University's Access to Your Computer

Scott Kennedy, a computer system administrator for Qualcomm Corporation in San Diego, California, discovered that somebody had obtained unauthorized access (or "hacked into," in popular parlance) the company's computer network. Kennedy contacted the Federal Bureau of Investigation (FBI). Working together, Kennedy and the FBI were able to trace the intrusion to a computer on the University of Wisconsin at Madison network. They contacted Jeffrey Savoy, the University of Wisconsin computer network investigator, who found evidence that someone using a computer on the university network was in fact hacking into the Qualcomm system and that the user had gained unauthorized access to the university's system as well. Savoy traced the source of intrusion to a computer located in university housing, the room of Jerome Heckenkamp, a computer science graduate student at the university. Savoy knew that Heckenkamp had been terminated from his job at the university computer help desk two years earlier for similar unauthorized activity.

While Heckenkamp was online and logged into the university's system, Savoy, along with detectives, went to Heckenkamp's room. The door was ajar, and nobody was in the room. Savoy entered the room and disconnected the network cord that attached the computer to the network. In order to be sure that the computer he had disconnected from the network was the computer that had gained unauthorized access to the university server, Savoy wanted to run some commands on the computer. Detectives located Heckenkamp, explained the situation, and asked for Heckenkamp's password, which Heckenkamp voluntarily provided. Savoy then ran tests on the computer and copied the hard drive without a warrant. When Heckenkamp was charged with several federal computer crimes, he challenged the university's access to his account and Savoy's steps that night, including the copy of the hard drive, as a breach of his privacy. Was Heckenkamp correct? Was his privacy breached?

[*U.S. v. Heckenkamp*, 482 F.3d 1142 (9th Cir. 2007)]

B. Sources of Law

Several layers of law are enacted at different levels of government to provide the framework for business and personal rights and duties. At the base of this framework of laws is constitutional law.

5. Constitutional Law

constitution–a body of principles that establishes the structure of a government and the relationship of the government to the people who are governed.

Constitutional law is the branch of law that is based on the constitution for a particular level of government. A **constitution** is a body of principles that establishes the structure of a government and the relationship of that government to the people who are governed. A constitution is generally a combination of the written document and the practices and customs that develop with the passage of time and the

---

[3] *Luangkhot v. State,* 722 S.E.2d 193 (Ga. App. 2012).

emergence of new problems. In each state, two constitutions are in force: the state constitution and the federal Constitution.

6. Statutory Law

statutory law – legislative acts declaring, commanding, or prohibiting something.

Statutory law includes legislative acts. Both Congress and the state legislatures enact statutory law. Examples of congressional legislative enactments include the Securities Act of 1933 (Chapter 46), the Sherman Antitrust Act (Chapter 5), the bankruptcy laws (Chapter 35), and consumer credit protection provisions (Chapter 33). At the state level, statutes govern the creation of corporations, probate of wills, and the transfer of title to property. In addition to the state legislatures and the U.S. Congress, all cities, counties, and other governmental subdivisions have some power to adopt ordinances within their sphere of operation. Examples of the types of laws found at this level of government include traffic laws, zoning laws, and pet and bicycle licensing laws.

7. Administrative Law

administrative regulations – rules made by state and federal administrative agencies.

Administrative regulations are rules promulgated by state and federal administrative agencies, such as the Securities and Exchange Commission and the National Labor Relations Board. For example, most of your rights related to your wages, hours worked, and overtime pay have been promulgated by the Department of Labor. These regulations generally have the force of statutes.

8. Private Law

private law – the rules and regulations parties agree to as part of their contractual relationships.

Even individuals and businesses create their own laws, or **private law**. Private law consists of the rules and regulations parties agree to as part of their contractual relationships. **For Example,** landlords develop rules for tenants on everything from parking to laundry room use. Employers develop rules for employees on everything from proper computer use to posting pictures and information on bulletin boards located within the company walls. Homeowner associations have rules on everything from your landscaping to the color of your house paint.

9. Case Law, Statutory Interpretation, and Precedent

Law also includes principles that are expressed for the first time in court decisions. This form of law is called **case law**. Case law plays three very important roles. The first is one of clarifying the meaning of statutes, or providing statutory interpretation. **For Example,** a man who was sentenced to house arrest left his house but still wanted to count the time as part of his sentence.[4] A court decision held that you must actually be in the house to have the time count. The second role that courts play is in creating precedent. When a court decides a new question or problem, its decision becomes a **precedent**, which stands as the law in future cases that involve that particular problem.

case law – law that includes principles that are expressed for the first time in court decisions.

precedent – a decision of a court that stands as the law for a particular problem in the future.

---

[4] *Com. v. Stafford*, 29 A.3d 800 (Pa. Super. 2011).

stare decisis – "let the decision stand"; the principle that the decision of a court should serve as a guide or precedent and control the decision of a similar case in the future.

Using precedent and following decisions is also known as the doctrine of **stare decisis**. However, the rule of *stare decisis* is not cast in stone. Judges have some flexibility. When a court finds an earlier decision to be incorrect, it overrules that decision. **For Example,** in 1954, the U.S. Supreme Court departed from the general rule of *stare decisis* in *Brown v. Board of Education.*[5] In that case, the Court decided that its 1896 decision *Plessy v. Ferguson,*[6] that held separate facilities for blacks were equal to facilities for whites, was incorrect.

The third role courts play is in developing a body of law that is not statutory but addresses long standing issues. Court decisions do not always deal with new problems or make new rules. In many cases, courts apply rules as they have been for many years, even centuries. These time-honored rules of the community are called the

common law – the body of unwritten principles originally based upon the usages and customs of the community that were recognized and enforced by the courts.

common law. For Example, most of law that we still follow today in determining real property rights developed in England, beginning in 1066. Statutes sometimes repeal or redeclare the common law rules. Many statutes depend on the common law for definitions of the terms in the statutes.

10. Other Forms of Law: Treaties and Executive Orders

Law also includes treaties made by the United States and proclamations and executive orders of the president of the United States or of other public officials.

11. Uniform State Laws

To facilitate the national nature of business and transactions, the National Conference of Commissioners on Uniform State Laws (NCCUSL), composed of representatives from every state, has drafted statutes on various subjects for adoption by the states. The best example of such laws is the Uniform Commercial Code (UCC).[7] (See Chapters 23–31, Chapter 34.) The UCC regulates the sale and lease of goods; commercial paper, such as checks; fund transfers; secured transactions in personal property; banking; and letters of credit. Having the same principles of law on contracts for the sale of goods and other commercial transactions in most of the 50 states makes doing business easier and less expensive. Other examples of uniform laws across the states include the Model Business Corporations Act (Chapter 44), the Uniform Partnership Act (Chapter 42), and the Uniform Residential Landlord Tenant Act (Chapter 51). The Uniform Computer Information Transactions Act (UCITA) as well as the Uniform Electronic Transactions Act (UETA) are two uniform laws that have taken contract law from the traditional paper era to the paperless computer age.

---

[5] 349 U.S. 294 (1954).
[6] 163 U.S. 537 (1895).
[7] The UCC has been adopted in every state, except that Louisiana has not adopted Article 2, Sales. Guam, the Virgin Islands, and the District of Columbia have also adopted the UCC. The NCCUSL has adopted amendments to Article 8, Investment Securities (1977 and 1994), and Article 9, Secured Transactions (1999, and as amended 2001). There have been new articles of the UCC: Article 2A, Leases, and Article 4A, Funds Transfers. The United Nations Convention on Contracts for the International Sale of Goods (CISG) has been adopted as the means for achieving uniformity in sale-of-goods contracts on an international level. Provisions of CISG were strongly influenced by Article 2 of the UCC.

C. CLASSIFICATIONS OF LAW

12. Substantive Law vs. Procedural Law

substantive law – the law that defines rights and liabilities.

procedural law – the law that must be followed in enforcing rights and liabilities.

Substantive law creates, defines, and regulates rights and liabilities. The law that determines when a contract is formed is substantive law. **Procedural law** specifies the steps that must be followed in enforcing those rights and liabilities. For example, once that contract is formed, you have rights to enforce that contract, and the steps you take through the court system to recover your damages for a breach of contract are procedural laws. The laws that prohibit computer theft are substantive laws. The prosecution of someone for computer theft follows procedural law.

13. Criminal Law vs. Civil Law

Criminal laws define wrongs against society. **Civil laws** define the rights of one person against another. Criminal law violations carry fines and imprisonment as penalties. Civil laws carry damage remedies for the wronged individual.

Sports & Entertainment Law

MLB and Steroids

On March 17, 2005, former and current major league baseball (MLB) players, Commissioner Bud Selig, and the parents of young baseball players who had taken their own lives after taking steroids testified before the U.S. House of Representatives Government Reform Committee. The House held the hearings to determine whether government regulation of baseball is necessary.

Committee Chair Tom Davis made an opening statement with the following excerpts:

> Fourteen years ago, anabolic steroids were added to the Controlled Substance Act as a Schedule III drug, making it illegal to possess or sell them without a valid prescription. Today, however, evidence strongly suggests that steroid use among teenagers—especially aspiring athletes—is a large and growing problem.
>
> Today we take the committee's first steps toward understanding how we got here, and how we begin turning those numbers around. Down the road, we need to look at whether and how Congress should exercise its legislative powers to further restrict the use and distribution of these substances.
>
> Our specific purpose today is to consider MLB's recently negotiated drug policy; how the testing

policy will be implemented; how it will effectively address the use of prohibited drugs by players; and, most importantly, the larger societal and public health ramifications of steroid use.

Mark McGwire, now a retired MLB player and a record holder, stated during the hearings:

> Asking me, or any other player, to answer questions about who took steroids in front of television cameras will not solve this problem. If a player answers 'no,' he simply will not be believed. If he answers 'yes,' he risks public scorn and endless government investigations. My lawyers have advised me that I cannot answer these questions without jeopardizing my friends, my family, or myself. I intend to follow their advice.*

Give a list of all the laws, rights, and duties you can find in this information.

*http://reform.house.gov/GovReform/Hearings/EventSingle.aspx?
EventID=1637. Click on Mark McGwire

For Example, if you run a red light, you have committed a crime and you will be punished with a fine and points on your license. If you run a red light and strike a pedestrian, you will also have committed a civil wrong of injury to another through your carelessness. Civil laws provide that in addition to taking care of your wrong to society, you must take care of your wrong to the pedestrian and pay damages for the cost of her injuries (see Chapter 8 for more information about recovery of damages for accidents such as this).

14. Law vs. Equity

equity – the body of principles that originally developed because of the inadequacy of the rules then applied by the common law courts of England.

Equity is a body of law that provides justice when the law does not offer an adequate remedy or the application of the law would be terribly unfair. Equity courts developed in England as a means of getting to the heart of a dispute and seeing that justice was done. **For Example,** Christian Louboutin shoes have a distinctive red bottom that is their trademark. Yves Saint Laurent began producing its shoes with a red bottom. Common and statutory law provide for Louboutin to collect damages— the amount the company lost in sales through the copycat efforts of Yves Saint Laurent. However, if the Yves Saint Laurent shoes continue in production, Louboutin is never adequately compensated. Equity provides for an injunction, a court order to stop Yves Saint Laurent from making the red-soled shoes.[8] At one time, the United States had separate law courts and equity courts, but, today, these courts have been combined so that one court applies principles of both law and equity. A party may ask for both legal and equitable remedies in a single court.[9] **For Example,** suppose a homeowner contracts to sell his home to a buyer. If the homeowner then refuses to go through with the contract, the buyer has the legal remedy of recovering damages. The rules of equity go further and could require the owner to convey title to the house, an equitable remedy known as *specific performance.* Equitable remedies may also be available in certain contract breaches (see Chapters 2, 12, and 20).

LawFlix

And Justice for All (1979) (R)

An excellent film that gives an overview of the judicial system in Maryland. Rights, precedent, and the role of lawyers are all topics for satire and analysis in the movie.

---

[8] *Christian Louboutin S.A. v. Yves Saint Laurent America, Inc.,* 778 F. Supp. 2d 445 (S.D.N.Y. 2011).
[9] For example, Jennifer Lopez and Marc Anthony filed suit against the manufacturer of a British company that produces baby carriages for using their images on its Web site and in ads without permission; they asked for $5 million in damages as well as an injunction to stop use of their photos and likenesses in the company's ads. *Lopez v. Silver Cross,* 2009 WL 481386 (CD Cal). The case was settled prior to the dissolution of the Lopez and Anthony marriage. The terms of the settlement are not known, but Silver Cross no longer uses the images of Lopez and Anthony in its ads.

MAKE THE CONNECTION

SUMMARY

Law provides rights and imposes duties. One such right is the right of privacy, which affords protection against unreasonable searches of our property and intrusion into or disclosure of our private affairs.

Law consists of the pattern of rules established by society to govern conduct and relationships. These rules can be expressed as constitutional provisions, statutes, administrative regulations, and case decisions. Law can be classified as substantive or procedural, and it can be described in terms of civil or criminal law. Law provides remedies in equity in addition to damages.

The sources of law include constitutions, federal and state statutes, administrative regulations, ordinances, and uniform laws generally codified by the states in their statutes. The courts are also a source of law through their adherence to case precedent under the doctrine of *stare decisis* and through their development of time-honored principles called the common law.

LEARNING OUTCOMES

After studying this chapter, you should be able to clearly explain:

A. Nature of Law and Legal Rights

L0.1 Discuss the nature of law and legal rights
See *Arizona v. Gant*, p. 5.
See Ethics & the Law on p. 6 for a discussion of employers checking Twitter, Facebook, and LinkedIn for information about potential employees.
See E-Commerce & Cyberlaw, p. 7.

B. Sources of Law

L0.2 List the sources of law
See the *For Example* discussion of landlords developing rules for tenants on everything from parking to laundry room use on p. 8.

See the list and explanation of uniform laws on p. 9.
See the Sports & Entertainment Law discussion of steroids in baseball on p. 10.

C. Classifications of Law

L0.3 Describe the classifications of law
See the discussion of law, equity, procedural, substantive, criminal, and civil on pp. 10–11.
See the Christian Louboutin example on its red-bottomed shoe being copied and footnote 9 with the discussion of the Jennifer Lopez/Marc Anthony suit on p. 11.
Explain uniform state laws.

KEY TERMS

administrative
  regulations
case law
civil law
common law
constitution

criminal law
duty
equity
law
precedent
private law

procedural law
right of privacy
right
stare decisis
statutory law
substantive law

QUESTIONS AND CASE PROBLEMS

1. On January 9, 2007, two Springfield, Missouri, Police Department officers made a traffic stop of a vehicle driven by Claude X. The purpose of the stop was to arrest X's passenger, Melissa Owen, who had a pending warrant for check-kiting. Once the officers made visual contact with Owen, the officers stopped X's car and instructed Owen to get out of the car. Ms. Owen did not bring her belongings with her when she got out of the car. One of the officers called dispatch to verify Owen's warrant and requested backup from a K–9 officer. Another officer arrived at the scene with his service dog, Marko. X was told to get out of the car so that it could be searched. X did get out of the car but then also locked it and refused to allow the officers to search. X was handcuffed for obstruction and the officers took away his keys to the car.

   At that time, Marko searched (sniffed) the exterior of X's car. Marko alerted to the car's rear bumper. The officers began to search the trunk of the vehicle and found containers with drugs in them along with a weighing scale. X's lawyer moved to have the evidence excluded because the drugs were found without a warrant. Should the judge exclude the evidence or is it admissible? Be sure to refer to the *Arizona v. Gant* case on p. 5 in developing your answer and explaining why. [*U.S. v. Claude X,* 648 F.3d 599 (8th Cir.)]

2. The Family Educational Rights and Privacy Act (FERPA) protects students' rights to keep their academic records private. What duties are imposed and upon whom because of this protection of rights? Discuss the relationship between rights and duties.

3. List the sources of law.

4. What is the difference between common law and statutory law?

5. Classify the following laws as substantive or procedural:

   a. A law that requires public schools to hold a hearing before a student is expelled.

   b. A law that establishes a maximum interest rate for credit transactions of 24 percent.

   c. A law that provides employee leave for the birth or adoption of a child for up to 12 weeks.

   d. A law that requires the county assessor to send four notices of taxes due and owing before a lien can be filed (attached) to the property.

6. What do uniform laws accomplish? Why do states adopt them? Give an example of a uniform law.

7. Cindy Nathan is a student at West University. While she was at her 9:00 A.M. anthropology class, campus security entered her dorm room and searched all areas, including her closet and drawers. When Cindy returned to her room and discovered what had happened, she complained to the dorm's senior resident. The senior resident said that this was the university's property and that Cindy had no right of privacy. Do you agree with the senior resident's statement? Is there a right of privacy in a dorm room?

8. Professor Lucas Phelps sent the following e-mail to Professor Marlin Jones: "I recently read the opinion piece you wrote for the *Sacramento Bee* on affirmative action. Your opinion is incorrect, your reasoning and analysis are poor, and I am embarrassed that you are a member of the faculty here at Cal State Yolinda." Professor Jones forwarded the note from Professor Phelps to the provost of the university and asked that Professor Phelps be disciplined for using the university e-mail system for harassment purposes. Professor Phelps objected when the provost contacted him: "He had no right to forward that e-mail to you. That was private correspondence. And you have no right of access to my e-mail. I have privacy rights." Do you agree with Professor Phelps? Was there a breach of privacy?

9. Under what circumstances would a court disregard precedent?

10. What is the difference between a statute and an administrative regulation?

11. The Eminem ad for Chrysler that ran during the Super Bowl in February 2011 was rated as one of the best ads for the game. In May 2011, Audi ran an ad at a German auto show that had the "feel" of the Eminem Chrysler "Lose Yourself" ad.

Subsequently, the German auto show ad made its way onto the Internet.

The German ad caught the attention of Eminem and 8 Mile, Eminem's publishing company. They notified Audi that the ad constituted an unauthorized use of their intellectual property. Explain what rights Eminem and 8 Mile have and how the courts can help.

12. Give examples of areas covered by federal laws. Give examples of areas covered by city ordinances. What are the limitations on these two sources of laws? What could the laws at these two levels not do?

13. What is the principle of *stare decisis?*

14. Explain how Twitter, Facebook, and LinkedIn have resulted in the development of new laws and precedent.

15. During the 2001 baseball season, San Francisco Giants player Barry Bonds hit 73 home runs, a new record that broke the one set by Mark McGwire in 2000 (72 home runs). When Mr. Bonds hit his record-breaking home run, the ball went into the so-called cheap seats. Alex Popov was sitting in those seats and had brought along his baseball glove for purposes of catching any hits that might come into the stands.

Everyone sitting in the area agreed that Mr. Popov's glove touched Bonds's home-run ball. Videotape also shows Mr. Popov's glove on the ball. However, the ball dropped and, following a melee among the cheap-seat fans, Patrick Hayashi ended up with Bonds's home-run ball.

Mr. Popov filed suit for the ball, claiming it as his property. Such baseballs can be very valuable. The baseball from Mr. McGwire's record-breaking home run in 2000 sold for $3 million. List those areas of law that will apply as the case is tried and the owner of the baseball is determined.

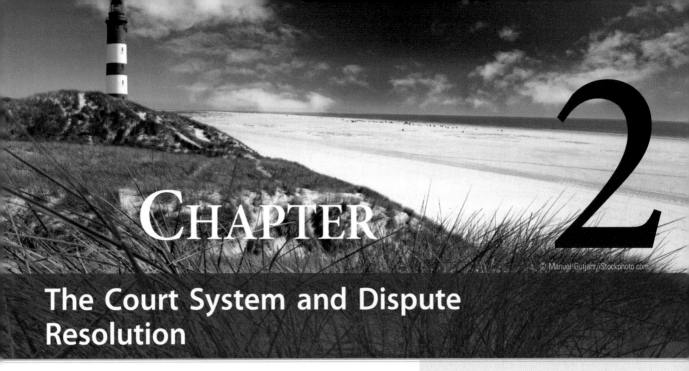

© Manuel Gutjahr/iStockphoto.com

CHAPTER 2

The Court System and Dispute Resolution

learningoutcomes

After studying this chapter, you should be able to

LO.1 Explain the federal and state court systems

LO.2 Describe court procedures

LO.3 List the forms of alternative dispute resolution and distinguish among them

Despite carefully negotiated and well-written contracts and high safety standards in the workplace or in product design and production, businesses can end up in a lawsuit. **For Example,** you could hire the brightest and most expensive lawyer in town to prepare a contract with another party and believe the final agreement is "bulletproof." However, even a bulletproof contract does not guarantee performance by the other party, and you may have to file a suit to collect your damages.

Business disputes can be resolved in court or through alternative dispute resolution. This chapter covers the structure of the court system and the litigation process as well as the forms of alternative dispute resolution.

A. THE COURT SYSTEM

court – a tribunal established by government to hear and decide matters properly brought to it.

A **court** is a tribunal established by government to hear evidence, decide cases brought before it, and, provide remedies when a wrong has been committed. As discussed in Chapter 1, sometimes courts prevent wrongs by issuing the equitable remedy of an injunction. **For Example,** in March 2012, a federal court issued an injunction against Cardinal Health because it was shipping too much oxycodone to pharmacies in Florida, and the FDA had discovered that the prescriptions were fraudulent. The FDA needed to stop the flow of the drug while it pulled the prescriptions.[1]

1. The Types of Courts

jurisdiction – the power of a court to hear and determine a given class of cases; the power to act over a particular defendant.

Each type of court has the authority to decide certain types or classes of cases. The authority of courts to hear cases is called **jurisdiction**. One form of jurisdiction, **subject matter jurisdiction**, covers the type of cases the court has the authority to hear. Courts that have the authority to hear the original proceedings in a case (the trial court) are called courts of **original jurisdiction**. **For Example,** in a court of original jurisdiction witnesses testify, documents are admitted into evidence, and the jury, in the case of a jury trial, hears all the evidence and then makes a decision.

subject matter jurisdiction – judicial authority to hear a particular type of case.

Other types of subject matter jurisdiction give courts the authority over particular legal topic areas. A court with **general jurisdiction** has broad authority to hear general civil and criminal cases. When a general jurisdiction trial court hears criminal cases, it serves as the trial court for those charged with crimes. General trial courts also have the authority to hear civil disputes, such as breach of contract cases and personal injury lawsuits.

original jurisdiction – the authority to hear a controversy when it is first brought to court.

A court with **limited or special jurisdiction** has the authority to hear only particular kinds of cases. **For Example,** many states have courts that can hear only disputes in which the damages are $10,000 or less. Other examples of limited or special jurisdiction courts are juvenile courts, probate courts, and domestic relations courts. States vary in the names they give these courts, but these courts of special or limited jurisdiction have very narrow authority for the types of cases they hear. In the federal court system, limited or special jurisdiction courts include bankruptcy courts and the U.S. Tax Court.

general jurisdiction – the power to hear and decide most controversies involving legal rights and duties.

limited (special) jurisdiction – the authority to hear only particular kinds of cases.

---

[1] *Holiday CVS, L.L.C. v. Holder*, 839 F. Supp. 2d 145 (D.D.C. 2012).

appellate jurisdiction–the power of a court to hear and decide a given class of cases on appeal from another court or administrative agency.

appeal–taking a case to a reviewing court to determine whether the judgment of the lower court or administrative agency was correct. (Parties–appellant, appellee)

reversible error–an error or defect in court proceedings of so serious a nature that on appeal the appellate court will set aside the proceedings of the lower court.

affirm–action taken by an appellate court that approves the decision of the court below.

reverse–the term used when the appellate court sets aside the verdict or judgment of a lower court.

remand–term used when an appellate court sends a case back to trial court for additional hearings or a new trial.

A court with **appellate jurisdiction** reviews the work of a lower court. **For Example,** a trial court may issue a judgment that a defendant in a breach of contract suit should pay $500,000 in damages. That defendant could appeal the decision to an appellate court and seek review of the decision itself or even the amount of the damages.[2] An **appeal** is a review of the trial and decision of the lower court. An appellate court does not hear witnesses or take testimony. An appellate court, usually a panel of three judges, simply reviews the transcript and evidence from the lower court and determines whether there has been **reversible error**. A reversible error is a mistake in applying the law or a mistake in admitting evidence that affected the outcome of the case. An appellate court can **affirm** or **reverse** a lower court decision or **remand** that decision for another trial or additional hearings.

CASE SUMMARY

Law and Order on TV and in the Court

FACTS: Andrea Yates was charged with capital murder in the drowning deaths of her five young children. Mrs. Yates had been in and out of treatment facilities, had been taking antidepressants, and was under the care of several experts for her depression. She was also experiencing postpartum depression when she drowned each of her five children in the bathtub at their family home. She then called her husband to ask him to come home and also called 9-1-1.

She entered a "not guilty by reason of insanity" plea, and 10 psychiatrists and two psychologists testified at the trial about Mrs. Yates's mental condition before, during, and after the deaths of the children.

Dr. Parke Dietz, the psychiatrist for the prosecution, testified that he believed Mrs. Yates knew right from wrong and that she was not insane at the time of the drownings. Dr. Dietz had also served as a consultant for the television series *Law and Order* and testified as follows about one of the shows in the series:

As a matter of fact, there was a show of a woman with postpartum depression who drowned her children in the bathtub and was found insane and it was aired shortly before the crime occurred.

The prosecution used this information about the television show to cross-examine witnesses for Mrs. Yates and also raised its airing in its closing argument to the jury.

The jury found Mrs. Yates guilty. The defense lawyers later discovered that Dr. Dietz was mistaken and that there had been no such *Law and Order* show on postpartum depression. They appealed on the grounds that the evidence was material, prejudiced the jury, and required a new trial.

DECISION: The court held that because Dr. Dietz had testified about the show, that his testimony and the subject matter of the show were a part of the prosecution's examination of defense witnesses, that the prosecution raised the airing of the show in closing arguments, and that the defense had to respond by talking about it meant that the testimony was material. Inasmuch as it was false, there was a reversible error and a retrial was required without the untrue and highly prejudicial evidence. [*Yates v. State,* **171 S.W.3d 215 (Tex. App. 2005)**][3]

---

[2] A case that is sent back for a redetermination of damages is remanded for what is known as *remittur.* For example, an appeal of Oracle's $1.3 billion verdict against SAP was sent back for another determination of damages, with the judge indicating $272 million was in the right range. *Oracle USA, Inc. v. SAP AG,* 2012 WL 29095 (N.D. Cal.).

[3] Mrs. Yates was found to be criminally insane in her 2006 retrial and is now institutionalized.

| **FIGURE 2-1** | ***The Federal Court System*** |

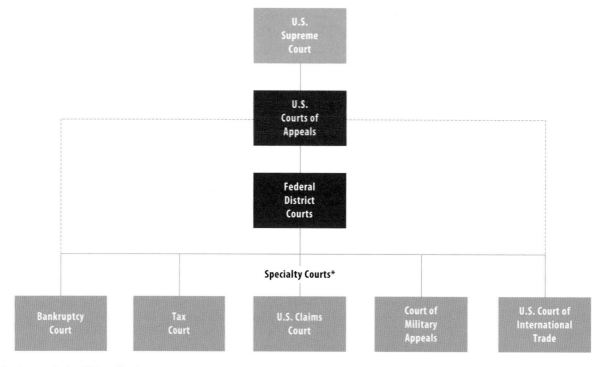

*Appeals often go directly to U.S. Courts of Appeals.

© Cengage Learning

---

2. The Federal Court System

The federal court system consists of three levels of courts. Figure 2-1 illustrates federal court structure.

federal district court – a general trial court of the federal system.

(A) FEDERAL DISTRICT COURTS. The **federal district courts** are the general trial courts of the federal system. They are courts of original jurisdiction that hear both civil and criminal matters. Criminal cases in federal district courts are those in which the defendant is charged with a violation of federal law (the U.S. Code). In addition to the criminal cases, the types of civil cases that can be brought in federal district courts include (1) civil suits in which the United States is a party, (2) cases between citizens of different states that involve damages of $75,000 or more, and (3) cases that arise under the U.S. Constitution or federal laws and treaties.

Federal district courts are organized within each of the states. There are 94 federal districts (each state has at least one federal district and there are 89 federal districts in the United States with the remaining courts found in Puerto Rico, Guam, etc.). Judges and courtrooms are assigned according to the caseload in that geographic area of the state.[4] Some states, such as New York and California, have several federal districts because of the population base and the resulting caseload. Figure 2-2 shows the geographic structure of the federal court system, including the appellate circuits.

The federal system has additional trial courts with limited jurisdiction, differing from the general jurisdiction of the federal district courts. These courts include, for

---

[4] For complete information about the courts and the number of judgeships, go to 28 U.S.C. §§81-144 and 28 U.S.C. §133.

FIGURE 2-2	*The Thirteen Federal Judicial Circuits*

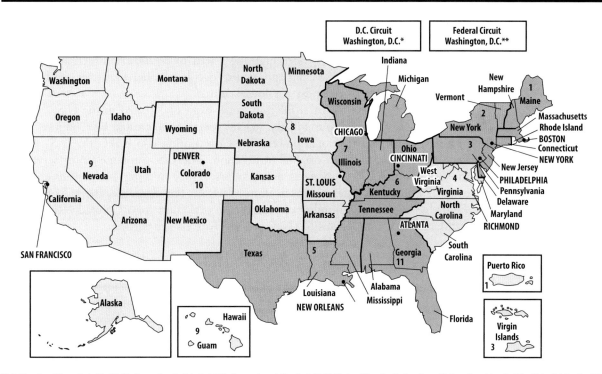

*A sizable portion of the caseload of the D.C. Circuit comes from the federal administrative agencies and offices located in Washington, D.C., such as the Securities and Exchange Commission, the National Labor Relations Board, the Federal Trade Commission, the Secretary of the Treasury, and the Labor Department, as well as appeals from the U.S. District Court of the District of Columbia.

**Rather than being defined by geography like the regional courts of appeals, the Federal Circuit is defined by subject matter, having jurisdiction over such matters as patent infringement cases, appeals from the Court of Federal Claims and the Court of International Trade, and appeals from administrative rulings regarding subject matter such as unfair import practices and tariff schedule disputes.

© Cengage Learning

example, the federal bankruptcy courts, Indian tribal courts, Tax Court, Court of Federal Claims, Court of Veterans Appeals, and the Court of International Trade.

(B) U.S. COURTS OF APPEALS. The final decision in a federal district court can be appealed to a court with appellate jurisdiction. In the federal court system, the federal districts are grouped together geographically into 12 judicial circuits, including one for the District of Columbia. Additionally, a thirteenth federal circuit, called the *Federal Circuit,* hears certain types of appeals from all of the circuits, including specialty cases such as patent appeals. Each circuit has an appellate court called the U.S. Court of Appeals, and the judges for these courts review the decisions of the federal district courts. Generally, a panel of three judges reviews the cases. However, some decisions, called **en banc** decisions, are made by the circuit's full panel of judges. **For Example,** in 2003, the Ninth Circuit heard an appeal on a father's right to challenge the requirement that his daughter recite the Pledge of Allegiance in the public school she attended. The contentious case had so many issues that the Ninth Circuit issued three opinions and the third opinion was issued after the case was heard *en banc.*[5]

en banc–the term used when the full panel of judges on the appellate court hears a case.

---

[5] *Newdow v. U.S. Congress,* 292 F.3d 597 (9th Cir. 2002) (*Newdow I*); *Newdow v. U.S. Congress,* 313 F.3d 500, 502 (9th Cir. 2002) (*Newdow II*); and *Newdow v. U.S. Congress,* 328 F.3d 466, 468 (9th Cir. 2003) (*Newdow III*). The U.S. Supreme Court eventually heard the case. *Elkgrove Unified School District v. Newdow,* 542 U.S. 1 (2004). Another *en banc* hearing occurred at the Ninth Circuit over the issues in the California gubernatorial recall election. The three-judge panel held that the voting methods in California violated the rights of voters and therefore placed a stay on the election. However, the Ninth Circuit then heard the case *en banc* and reversed the decision of the original three-judge panel. The recall election then proceeded.

(c) U.S. SUPREME COURT. The final court in the federal system is the U.S. Supreme Court. The U.S. Supreme Court has appellate jurisdiction over cases that are appealed from the federal courts of appeals as well as from state supreme courts when a constitutional issue is involved in the case or a state court has reversed a federal court ruling. The U.S. Supreme Court does not hear all cases from the federal courts of appeals but has a process called granting a **writ of *certiorari***, which is a preliminary review of those cases appealed to decide whether a case will be heard or allowed to stand as ruled on by the lower courts.[6]

writ of *certiorari*– order by the U.S. Supreme Court granting a right of review by the court of a lower court decision.

The U.S. Supreme Court is the only court expressly created in the U.S. Constitution. All other courts in the federal system were created by Congress pursuant to its Constitutional power. The Constitution also makes the U.S. Supreme Court a court of original jurisdiction. The U.S. Supreme Court serves as the trial court for cases involving ambassadors, public ministers, or consuls and for cases in which two states are involved in a lawsuit. **For Example,** the U.S. Supreme Court has served for a number of years as the trial court for a Colorado River water rights case in which California, Nevada, and Arizona are parties.

3. State Court Systems

(A) GENERAL TRIAL COURTS. Most states have trial courts of general jurisdiction that may be called superior courts, circuit courts, district courts, or county courts. These courts of general and original jurisdiction usually hear both criminal and civil cases. Cases that do not meet the jurisdictional requirements for the federal district courts would be tried in these courts. Figure 2-3 illustrates a sample state court system.

(B) SPECIALTY COURTS. Most states also have courts with limited jurisdiction, sometimes referred to as *specialty courts.* **For Example,** most states have juvenile courts, or courts with limited jurisdiction over criminal matters that involve defendants who are under the age of 18. Other specialty courts or lesser courts in state systems are probate and family law courts.

(c) CITY, MUNICIPAL, AND JUSTICE COURTS. Cities and counties may also have lesser courts with limited jurisdiction, which may be referred to as *municipal courts* or *justice courts.* These courts generally handle civil matters in which the claim made in the suit is an amount below a certain level, such as $5,000 or $10,000. These courts may also handle misdemeanor types of offenses, such as traffic violations or violations of noise ordinances, and the trials for them.

(D) SMALL CLAIMS COURTS. Most states also have **small claims courts** at the county or city level. These are courts of limited jurisdiction where parties with small amounts in dispute may come to have a third party, such as a justice of the peace or city judge, review their disputes and determine how they should be resolved. A true small claims court is one in which the parties are not permitted to be represented by counsel. Rather, the parties present their cases to the judge in an informal manner without the strict procedural rules that apply in courts of general jurisdiction. Small claims courts provide a faster and inexpensive means for resolving a dispute that does not involve a large amount of claimed damages.

small claims courts– courts that resolve disputes between parties when those disputes do not exceed a minimal level; no lawyers are permitted; the parties represent themselves.

---

[6] For example, the Supreme Court refused to grant *certiorari* in a Fifth Circuit case on law school admissions at the University of Texas. However, it granted *certiorari* in a later case involving law school admissions at the University of Michigan. *Gratz v. Bollinger*, 539 U.S. 244 (2003). And the court will hear the issue again, in *Fisher v. University of Texas*, 132 S.Ct. 1536 (2012).

| FIGURE 2-3 | *Sample State Court System* |

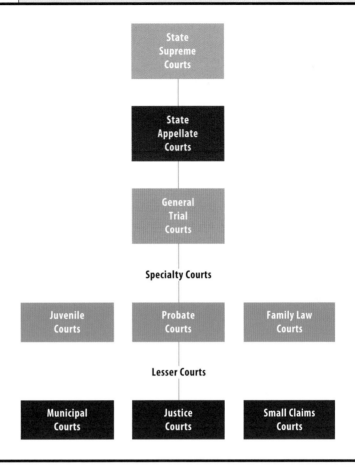

© Cengage Learning

(E) STATE APPELLATE COURTS. Most states also have intermediate-level courts similar to the federal courts of appeals. They are courts with appellate jurisdiction that review the decisions of lower courts in that state. Decisions of the general trial courts in a state would be appealed to these courts.

(F) STATE SUPREME COURTS. The highest court in most states is generally known as the *state supreme court,* but a few states, such as New York, may call their highest court the *court of appeals;* Maine and Massachusetts, for example, call their highest court the *supreme judicial court.* State supreme courts primarily have appellate jurisdiction, but some states' courts do have original jurisdiction, such as in Arizona, where counties in litigation have their trial at the supreme court level. Most state supreme courts also have a screening process for cases. They are required to hear some cases, such as criminal cases in which the defendant has received the death penalty. A decision of a state supreme court is final except in those circumstances in which a federal law or treaty or the U.S. Constitution is involved. Cases with these federal subject matter issues can then be appealed to the U.S. Supreme Court.

B. Court Procedure

Once a party decides to use the court system for resolution of a dispute, that party enters a world with specific rules, procedures, and terms that must be used to have a case proceed.

4. Participants in the Court System

plaintiff–party who initiates a lawsuit.

prosecutor–party who originates a criminal proceeding.

defendant–party charged with a violation of civil or criminal law in a proceeding.

judge–primary officer of the court.

attorney-client privilege–right of individual to have discussions with his/her attorney kept private and confidential.

jury–a body of citizens sworn by a court to determine by verdict the issues of fact submitted to them.

The **plaintiff** is the party that initiates the proceedings in a court of original jurisdiction. In a criminal case in which charges are brought, the party initiating the proceedings would be called the **prosecutor**. The party against whom the civil or criminal proceedings are brought is the **defendant**. A **judge** is the primary officer of the court and is either an elected or an appointed official who presides over the matters brought before the court. Attorneys or lawyers are representatives for the plaintiff and the defendant for purposes of presenting their cases. Lawyers and clients have a privilege of confidentiality known as the **attorney-client privilege**. Lawyers cannot disclose what their clients tell them unless the client is committing, or plans to commit, a crime.

A **jury** is a body of citizens sworn by a court to reach a verdict on the basis of the case presented to them. Jurors are chosen for service based on lists compiled from voter registration and driver's license records.

5. Which Law Applies—Conflicts of Law

When a lawsuit is brought, there is not just the question of where a case will be tried but also of what law will be applied in determining the rights of the parties. The principle that determines when a court applies the law of its own state—the law of the forum—or some foreign law is called *conflict of laws*. Because there are 50 state court systems and a federal court system, as well as a high degree of interstate activity, conflicts of law questions arise frequently.

Some general rules apply. For example, the law of the state in which the court is located governs the case on procedural issues and rules of evidence. In contract litigation, the court applies the law of the state in which the contract was made for determining issues of formation. Performance disputes and damages for nonperformance are generally governed by the law of the state where the contract is to be performed. International contracts follow similar rules. **For Example,** a California court will apply Swiss law to a contract made in Switzerland that is to be performed in that country.

However, it is becoming more common for the parties to specify their choice of law in their contract. In the absence of a law-selecting provision in the contract, there is a growing acceptance of the rule that a contract should be governed by the law of the state that has the most significant contacts with the transaction.

For Example, assume the buyer's place of business and the seller's plant are located in Nebraska, and the buyer is purchasing goods from the seller to resell to Nebraska customers. Many courts will hold that this is a contract governed by the law of Nebraska. In determining which state has the most significant contacts, the court considers the place of contracting, negotiating, and performing; the location of the subject matter of the contract; and the domicile (residence), states of incorporation, and principal place of business of the parties.

6. Initial Steps in a Lawsuit

The following steps in a lawsuit generally apply in cases brought in courts of original jurisdiction. Not every step applies in every case, but understanding litigation steps and terms is important for businesspeople.

(A) COMMENCEMENT OF A LAWSUIT. A lawsuit begins with the filing of a **complaint**. The complaint generally contains a description of the wrongful conduct and a request for damages, such as a monetary amount. **For Example,** a plaintiff in a contract suit would describe the contract, when it was entered into, and when the defendant stopped performance on the contract. A copy of the contract would be attached to the complaint.

complaint – the initial pleading filed by the plaintiff in many actions, which in many states may be served as original process to acquire jurisdiction over the defendant.

(B) SERVICE OF PROCESS. Once the plaintiff has filed the complaint with the proper court, the plaintiff has the responsibility of notifying the defendant that the lawsuit has been filed. The defendant must be served with **process**. Process, often called a *writ, notice,* or *summons,* is delivered to the defendant and includes a copy of the complaint and notification that the defendant must appear and respond to the allegations in the complaint.

process – paperwork served personally on a defendant in a civil case.

(C) THE DEFENDANT'S RESPONSE AND THE PLEADINGS. After the defendant is served with process in the case, the defendant is required to respond to or **answer** the complaint within the time provided under the court's rules. In answering the plaintiff's complaint, the defendant has several options. For example, the defendant could make a **motion to dismiss**, which is a request to the court to dismiss the lawsuit on the grounds that, even if everything the plaintiff said in the complaint were true, there is still no right of recovery. A motion to dismiss is also called a **demurrer**.

answer – what a defendant must file to admit or deny facts asserted by the plaintiff.

motion to dismiss – a pleading that may be filed to attack the adverse party's pleading as not stating a cause of action or a defense.

A defendant could also respond and deny the allegations. **For Example,** in a contract lawsuit, the defendant-seller could say he did not breach the contract but stopped shipment of the goods because the plaintiff-buyer did not pay for the goods in advance as the contract required. A defendant could also **counterclaim** in the answer, which is asking the court for damages as a result of the underlying dispute. **For Example,** the defendant-seller in the contract lawsuit might ask for damages for the plaintiff-buyer's failure to pay as the contract required.

demurrer – a pleading to dismiss the adverse party's pleading for not stating a cause of action or a defense.

counterclaim – a claim that the defendant in an action may make against the plaintiff.

All documents filed in this initial phase of the case are referred to as the **pleadings**. The pleadings are a statement of the case and the basis for recovery if all the facts alleged can be proved.

pleadings – the papers filed by the parties in an action in order to set forth the facts and frame the issues to be tried, although, under some systems, the pleadings merely give notice or a general indication of the nature of the issues.

(D) DISCOVERY. The Federal Rules of Civil Procedure and similar rules in all states permit one party to obtain from the adverse party information about all witnesses, documents, and any other items relevant to the case. **Discovery** requires each side to name its potential witnesses and to provide each side the chance to question those witnesses in advance of the trial. Each party also has the opportunity to examine, inspect, and photograph books, records, buildings, and machines. Even examining the physical or mental condition of a party is part of discovery when it has relevance in the case. The scope of discovery is extremely broad because the rules permit any questions that are likely to lead to admissible evidence.

discovery – procedures for ascertaining facts prior to the time of trial in order to eliminate the element of surprise in litigation.

Deposition.

A **deposition** is the testimony of a witness taken under oath outside the courtroom; it is transcribed by a court reporter. Each party is permitted to question the witness. If a party or a witness gives testimony at the trial that is inconsistent with her

deposition – the testimony of a witness taken out of court before a person authorized to administer oaths.

impeach – using prior inconsistent evidence to challenge the credibility of a witness.

deposition testimony, the prior inconsistent testimony can be used to **impeach** the witness's credibility at trial

Depositions can be taken either for discovery purposes or to preserve the testimony of a witness who will not be available during the trial. Some states now permit depositions to be videotaped. A videotape is a more effective way of presenting deposition testimony than reading that testimony at trial from a reporter's transcript because jurors can see the witness and the witness's demeanor and hear the words as they were spoken, complete with inflection.[7]

Other Forms of Discovery.

interrogatories – written questions used as a discovery tool that must be answered under oath.

request for production of documents – discovery tool for uncovering paper evidence in a case.

Other forms of discovery include medical exams, particularly in cases in which the plaintiff is claiming damages for physical injuries. Written **interrogatories** (questions) and written **requests for production of documents** are discovery requests that can be very time consuming to the answering party and often lead to pretrial legal disputes between the parties and their attorneys as a result of the legal expenses involved.

motion for summary judgment – request that the court decide a case on basis of law only because there are no material issues disputed by the parties.

(E) MOTION FOR SUMMARY JUDGMENT. If a case has no material facts in dispute, either party can file a **motion for summary judgment**. Using affidavits or deposition testimony obtained in discovery, the court can find that there are no factual issues and decide the case as a matter of law. **For Example,** suppose that the parties can agree that they entered into a life insurance contract but dispute whether the policy applies when there is a suicide. The facts are not in dispute; the law on payment of insurance proceeds in the event of a suicide is the issue. Such a case is one that is appropriate for summary judgment.

expert witness – one who has acquired special knowledge in a particular field as through practical experience or study, or both, whose opinion is admissible as an aid to the trier of fact.

(F) DESIGNATION OF EXPERT WITNESSES. In some cases, such as those involving product safety, the parties may want to designate an expert witness. An **expert witness** is a witness who has some special expertise, such as an economist who gives expert opinion on the value of future lost income or a scientist who testifies about the safety of a prescription drug. There are rules for naming expert witnesses as well as for admitting into evidence any studies or documents of the expert.[8] The purpose of these rules is to avoid the problem of what has been called *junk science,* or the admission of experts' testimony and research that has not been properly conducted or reviewed by peers.

7. The Trial

(A) SELECTING A JURY. Jurors drawn for service are questioned by the judge and lawyers to determine whether they are biased or have any preformed judgments about the parties in the case. Jury selection is called *voir dire* **examination**. **For Example,** in the trial of Martha Stewart, the multimedia home and garden diva, it took a great deal of time for the lawyers to question the potential jurors about their prior knowledge concerning the case, which had received nationwide attention and much media coverage. Lawyers have the opportunity to remove jurors who know parties in

voir dire **examination** – the preliminary examination of a juror or a witness to ascertain fitness to act as such.

---

[7] At the civil trial of O.J. Simpson for the wrongful death of Nicole Brown Simpson and Ronald Goldman, Daniel Petrocelli used a videotape of Mr. Simpson's deposition very effectively in impeaching Mr. Simpson's testimony at trial. Daniel Petrocelli, *Triumph of Justice: The Final Judgment on the Simpson Saga* (New York: Crown, 1998).

[8] *Daubert v. Merrell Dow Pharmaceuticals, Inc.,* 509 U.S. 579 (1993).

opening statements –
statements by opposing
attorneys that tell the jury what
their cases will prove.

admissibility – the quality of
the evidence in a case that
allows it to be presented to the
jury.

direct examination –
examination of a witness by his
or her attorney.

cross-examination – the
examination made of a witness
by the attorney for the adverse
party.

redirect examination –
questioning after cross-
examination, in which the
attorney for the witness
testifying may ask the same
witness other questions to
overcome effects of the cross-
examination.

recross-examination – an
examination by the other side's
attorney that follows the
redirect examination.

the case or who indicate they have already formed opinions about guilt or innocence. The attorneys question the potential jurors to determine if a juror should be *challenged for cause* (e.g., when the prospective juror states he is employed by the plaintiff's company). Challenges for cause are unlimited, but each side can also exercise six to eight peremptory challenges.[9] A peremptory challenge is a challenge that is used to strike (remove) a juror for any reason except on racial grounds.[10]

(B) OPENING STATEMENTS. After the jury is chosen, the attorneys for each of the parties make their **opening statements** to the jury. An opening statement, as one lawyer has explained, makes a puzzle frame for the case so jurors can follow the witnesses and place the pieces of the case—the various forms of evidence—within the frame.

(C) THE PRESENTATION OF EVIDENCE. Following the opening statements, the plaintiff presents his case with witnesses and other evidence. A judge rules on the **admissibility** of evidence. Evidence can consist of documents, testimony, expert testimony, medical information from exams, and even physical evidence.

In the case of testimony, the attorney for the plaintiff conducts **direct examination** of his witnesses during his case, and the defense attorney conducts **cross-examination** of the plaintiff's witnesses. The plaintiff's attorney can then ask questions again of his witnesses in what is called **redirect examination**. Finally, the defense attorney may question the plaintiff's witnesses again in **recross-examination**. The defendant presents her case after the plaintiff's case concludes. During the defendant's case, the lawyer for the defendant conducts direct examination of the defendant's witnesses, and the plaintiff's lawyer can then cross-examine the defendant's witnesses.

Thinking Things Through

Why Do We Require Sworn Testimony?

There is a difference between what people say in conversation (and even what company executives say in speeches and reports) and what they are willing to say under oath. Speaking under oath often means that different information and recollections emerge. The oath is symbolic and carries the penalty of criminal prosecution for perjury if the testimony given is false.

The *Wall Street Journal* has reported that the testimony of executives in the Microsoft antitrust trial and their statements regarding their business relationships outside the courtroom are quite different. For example, the following quotations indicate some discrepancies. Eric Benhamou, the chief executive officer (CEO) of Palm, Inc., said:

We believe that the handheld opportunity remains wide open …. Unlike the PC industry, there is no monopoly of silicon, there is no monopoly of software.

However, at the Microsoft trial, another officer of Palm, Michael Mace, offered the following testimony:

We believe that there is a very substantial risk that Microsoft could manipulate its products and its standards in order to exclude Palm from the marketplace in the future.

---

[9] The number of peremptory challenges varies from state to state and may also vary within a particular state depending on the type of case. For example, in Arizona, peremptory challenges are unlimited in capital cases.

[10] *Felkner v. Jackson*, 131 S.Ct. 1305 (2011).

Thinking Things Through

Continued

Likewise, Microsoft has taken different positions inside and outside the courtroom. For example, an attorney for Microsoft stated that Microsoft had "zero deployments of its interactive TV middleware products connected to cable systems in the United States." However, Microsoft's marketing materials provide as follows:

Microsoft's multiple deployments around the world now including Charter-show Microsoft TV is ready to

deploy now and set the standard for what TV can be.*

Explain why the executives had differing statements. For more information on the Microsoft antitrust cases, go to **www.usdoj.gov** or **www.microsoft.com**.

*Rebecca Buckman and Nicholas Kulish, "Microsoft Trial Prompts an Outbreak of Doublespeak," Wall Street Journal, April 15, 2002, B1, B3.

---

directed verdict – a direction by the trial judge to the jury to return a verdict in favor of a specified party to the action.

(D) MOTION FOR A DIRECTED VERDICT. A motion for a **directed verdict** asks the court to grant a verdict because even if all the evidence that has been presented by each side were true, there is either no basis for recovery or no defense to recovery. **For Example,** suppose that a plaintiff company presented evidence that an employee who quit working for the company posted on his Facebook page, "I just wasn't happy there." The company might not feel good about the former employee's post, but there is no false statement and no breach of privacy. The evidence is true, but there is no legal right of recovery. The defendant employee would be entitled to a directed verdict. A directed verdict means that the party has not presented enough evidence to show that there is some right of recovery under the law.

summation – the attorney address that follows all the evidence presented in court and sums up a case and recommends a particular verdict be returned by the jury.

(E) CLOSING ARGUMENTS OR SUMMATION. After the witnesses for both parties have been examined and all the evidence has been presented, each attorney makes a closing argument. These statements are also called **summations**; they summarize the case and urge the jury to reach a particular verdict.

mistrial – a court's declaration that terminates a trial and postpones it to a later date; commonly entered when evidence has been of a highly prejudicial character or when a juror has been guilty of misconduct.

(F) MOTION FOR MISTRIAL. During the course of a trial, when necessary to avoid great injustice, the trial court may declare a **mistrial**. A mistrial requires a do-over, a new jury. A mistrial can be declared for jury or attorney misconduct. **For Example,** if a juror were caught fraternizing with one of the lawyers in the case, objectivity would be compromised and the court would most likely declare a mistrial. See also eCommerce & Cyber Law on p. 30 for more information on juror misconduct and case dismissals.

instruction – summary of the law given to jurors by the judge before deliberation begins.

(G) JURY INSTRUCTIONS AND VERDICT. After the summation by the attorneys, the court gives the jurors **instructions** on the appropriate law to apply to the facts presented. The jury then deliberates and renders its verdict. After the jury verdict, the court enters a judgment. If the jury is deadlocked and unable to reach a verdict, known as a hung jury or a mistrial, the case is reset for a new trial at some future date.

judgment n.o.v. – or *non obstante veredicto* (notwithstanding the verdict), a judgment entered after verdict upon the motion of the losing party on the ground that the verdict is so wrong that a judgment should be entered the opposite of the verdict.

(H) MOTION FOR NEW TRIAL; MOTION FOR JUDGMENT N.O.V. A court may grant a **judgment *non obstante veredicto*** or a **judgment *n.o.v.*** (notwithstanding the verdict) if the verdict is clearly wrong as a matter of law. The court can set aside the verdict and enter a judgment in favor of the other party. Perhaps one of the most famous judgments n.o.v. occurred in Boston in 1997 when a judge reversed the murder conviction of nanny Louise Woodward, who was charged with the murder of one of her young charges.

Ethics & the Law

Injustice, Misconduct, and Senator Stevens

The late Senator Ted Stevens (from Alaska) was tried in the fall of 2008 on charges that he lied on his financial disclosure forms by not disclosing the work a contractor performed on his Alaska home. He was convicted just days before the 2008 federal elections and he lost his Senate seat. However, the verdict and all of the charges were dismissed in 2009 on a motion by the U.S. attorney general, Eric Holder, when the Department of Justice discovered that prosecutors withheld exculpatory evidence, evidence that would have helped Senator Stevens. Sadly, Senator Stevens was killed in a plane crash in 2010. A 525-page report released in 2012 concluded that several prosecutors withheld evidence that Mr. Stevens had asked several times to be billed for the work on his home so that he could pay and make the necessary financial disclosures about its value. Also, one of the witness's background was shaky, something that would have caused his credibility to come into question at the trial. The jury never heard this evidence and neither Senator Stevens nor his lawyers were given the documents and interviews that would have helped his case. No criminal charges will be brought against the prosecutors who withheld the evidence. However, does that mean that their conduct was ethical? What is the obligation of lawyers when they discover evidence that favors the other side in a case?

[*In re Special Proceedings*, 842 F. Supp. 2d 232 (D.D.C. 2012)]

8. Posttrial Procedures

(A) RECOVERY OF COSTS/ATTORNEY FEES. Generally, the prevailing party is awarded costs. Costs include filing fees, service-of-process fees, witness fees, deposition transcript costs, and jury fees. Costs do not include compensation spent by a party for preparing the case or being present at trial, including the time lost from work because of the case and the fee paid to the attorney, although lost wages from an injury are generally part of damages.

Attorney fees may be recovered by a party who prevails if a statute permits the recovery of attorney fees or if the complaint involves a claim for breach of contract and the contract contains a clause providing for recovery of attorney fees.

(B) EXECUTION OF JUDGMENT. After a judgment has been entered or all appeals or appeal rights have ended, the losing party must pay that judgment. The winning party can also take steps to execute, or carry out, the judgment. The **execution** is accomplished by the seizure and sale of the losing party's assets by the sheriff according to a writ of execution or a writ of possession.

execution – the carrying out of a judgment of a court, generally directing that property owned by the defendant be sold and the proceeds first be used to pay the execution or judgment creditor.

garnishment – the name given in some states to attachment proceedings.

Garnishment is a common method of satisfying a judgment. When the judgment debtor is an employee, the appropriate judicial authority in the state garnishes (by written notice to the employer) a portion of the employee's wages on a regular basis until the judgment is paid.

C. ALTERNATIVE DISPUTE RESOLUTION (ADR)

Parties can use means other than litigation to resolve disagreements or disputes. Litigation takes significant time and money, so many businesses use alternative methods for resolving disputes. Those methods include arbitration, mediation, and several other formats. Figure 2-4 provides an overall view of alternative dispute resolution procedures.

9. Arbitration

arbitration – the settlement of disputed questions, whether of law or fact, by one or more arbitrators by whose decision the parties agree to be bound.

In **arbitration**, arbitrators (disinterested persons selected by the parties to the dispute) hear evidence and determine a resolution. Arbitration enables the parties to

FIGURE 2-4   *Dispute Resolution Procedures*

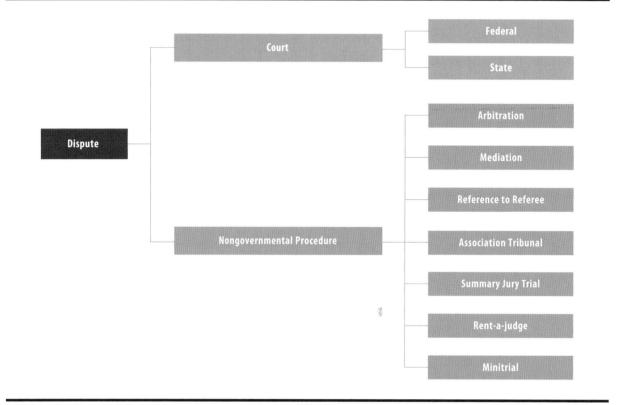

present the facts before trained experts familiar with the industry practices that may affect the nature and outcome of the dispute. Arbitration first reached extensive use in the field of commercial contracts and is encouraged as a means of avoiding expensive litigation and easing the workload of courts.[11]

A number of states have adopted the Uniform Arbitration Act.[12] Under this act and similar statutes, the parties to a contract may agree in advance that all disputes arising under it will be submitted to arbitration. In some instances, the contract will name the arbitrators for the duration of the contract. The uniform act requires a written agreement to arbitrate.[13]

The Federal Arbitration Act[14] provides that an arbitration clause in a contract relating to an interstate transaction is valid, irrevocable, and enforceable. When a contract subject to the Federal Arbitration Act provides for the arbitration of disputes, the parties are bound to arbitrate in accordance with the federal statute even if the agreement to arbitrate would not be binding under state law.

[11] *Warfield v. Beth Israel Deaconess Medical Center, Inc.*, 910 N.E.2d 317 (Mass. 2009). Arbitration has existed in the United States since 1920 when New York passed an arbitration statute. For a look at the history of arbitration, see Charles L. Knapp, "Taking Contracts Private: The Quiet Revolution in Contract Law," 71 *Fordham L. Rev.* 761 (2002).

[12] On August 3, 2000, the National Conference of Commissioners on Uniform State Laws unanimously passed major revisions to the Uniform Arbitration Act (UAA). These revisions were the first major changes in 45 years to the UAA, which is the basis of arbitration law in 49 states, although not all states have adopted it in its entirety. Thirty-five states and the District of Columbia have adopted the 1955 version. Only 13 states have adopted the UAA 2000 revisions. Uniform Laws Annotated, Section 1 (2012); see also Donald L. Carpo & John B. LaRocco, "A Comparison of Litigation, Arbitration, and Mediation," 63 *Dispute Resolution J.* 48 (2008).

[13] *Fawzy v. Fawzy*, 973 A.2d 347 (N.J. 2009).

[14] 9 U.S.C §§114 *et seq.*

(A) **MANDATORY ARBITRATION.** In contrast with statutes that merely regulate arbitration when it is selected voluntarily by the parties, some statutes require that certain kinds of disputes be submitted to arbitration. In some states, by rule or statute, the arbitration of small claims is required.

(B) **FINALITY OF ARBITRATION.** Most parties provide, within their arbitration agreements, that the decision of the arbitrator will be final. Such a clause is binding on the parties, even when the decision seems to be wrong, and can be set aside only if there is clear proof of fraud, arbitrary conduct, or a significant procedural error.[15]

If the arbitration is mandatory under statute or rule, the losing party generally may appeal such arbitration to a court.[16] The appeal proceeds just as though there had never been any prior arbitration. This new court proceeding is called a **trial *de novo*** and is necessary to preserve the constitutional right to a jury trial. As a practical matter, however, relatively few appeals are taken from arbitration decisions.

trial *de novo* – a trial required to preserve the constitutional right to a jury trial by allowing an appeal to proceed as though there never had been any prior hearing or decision.

10. Mediation

In **mediation**, a neutral person acts as a messenger between opposing sides of a dispute, carrying to each side the latest settlement offer made by the other. The mediator has no authority to make a decision, although in some cases the mediator may make suggestions that might ultimately be accepted by the disputing parties.

mediation – the settlement of a dispute through the use of a messenger who carries to each side of the dispute the issues and offers in the case.

The use of mediation has the advantage of keeping discussions going when the disputing parties have developed such fixed attitudes or personal animosity that direct discussion between them has become impossible.

11. MedArb

In this new form of alternative dispute resolution (ADR), the arbitrator is also empowered to act as a mediator. Beyond just hearing a case, the arbitrator acts as a messenger for the parties on unresolved issues.

12. Reference to a Third Person

Many types of transactions provide for **reference to a third person**, in which a third person or a committee makes an out-of-court determination of the rights of persons. **For Example,** employees and an employer may have agreed as a term of the employment contract that claims of employees under retirement plans will be decided by a designated board or committee. In a sales contract, the seller and buyer can select a third person to determine the price to be paid for goods. Construction contracts often include a provision for disputes to be referred to the architect in charge of the construction with the architect's decision being final.

reference to a third person – settlement that allows a nonparty to resolve the dispute.

These referrals often eliminate the disputes or pursuit of remedies. **For Example,** fire insurance policies commonly provide that if the parties cannot agree on the amount of the loss, each will appoint an appraiser, the two appraisers will appoint a third appraiser, and the three will determine the amount of the loss the insurer is required to pay.

---

[15] *Apache Bohai Corp. LDC v. Texaco China BV*, 480 F.3d 397 (5th Cir. 2007).
[16] *U.S. v. Park Place Associates*, 563 F.3d 907 (9th Cir. 2009).

E-Commerce & Cyberlaw

The Googling Juror

Referred to as the "Google Mistrial," a federal judge in Florida declared a mistrial after a juror told that judge that he had been doing research on the Internet on the drug trial in which he was serving. When the judge declared the mistrial, eight other jurors confessed that they had been doing the same thing.

Judges have long warned jurors about using outside sources, including the Internet, but BlackBerries and iPhones have proven to be mighty tempting for jurors. Some jurors are using Facebook to announce when verdicts are coming. One juror even looked up evidence that had been excluded by the judge in the case. When asked why he violated the judge's order, the juror said simply, "Well, I was curious." Another juror contacted the defendant through Facebook, and another mistrial resulted.

A judge in Arkansas is reviewing a request for a reversal of a $12.6 million jury verdict against a company from one of the company's lawyers based on the court's discovery that one of the jurors was using Twitter to send out postings about how the trial was proceeding. An excerpt from the posting follows:

> "Oh, and nobody buy Stoam. It's bad mojo and they'll probably cease to Exist now that their wallet is $12m lighter … So, Jonathan, what did you do today? Oh nothing really, I just gave away TWELVE MILLION DOLLARS of somebody else's money."*

What is the problem with jurors using these electronic tools during their cases?

*John Schwartz, "As Jurors Turn to Google and Twitter, Mistrials Are Popping Up," *New York Times*, March 18, 2009, p. A1.

13. Association Tribunals

association tribunal – a court created by a trade association or group for the resolution of disputes among its members.

Many disputes never reach the courts because both parties to a dispute belong to a group or an association, and the **association tribunal** created by the group or association disposes of the matter. Trade associations commonly require their members to employ out-of-court methods of dispute settlement. **For Example,** the National Association of Home Builders requires its member builders to employ arbitration. The National Automobile Dealers Association provides for panels to determine warranty claims of customers. The decision of such panels is final as to the builder or dealer, but the consumer can still bring a regular lawsuit after losing before the panel. Members of an association must use the association tribunal, which means they cannot bypass the association tribunal and go directly to a law court.[17]

14. Summary Jury Trial

summary jury trial – a mock or dry-run trial for parties to get a feel for how their cases will play to a jury.

A **summary jury trial** is a dry-run or mock trial in which the lawyers present their claims before a jury of six persons. The object is to get the reaction of a sample jury. No evidence is presented before this jury, and it bases its opinion solely on what the lawyers state. The determination of the jury has no binding effect, but it has value in that it gives the lawyers some idea of what a jury might think if there were an actual trial. This type of ADR has special value when the heart of a case is whether something is reasonable under all circumstances. When the lawyers and their clients see how the sample jury reacts, they may moderate their positions and reach a settlement.

15. Rent-A-Judge

rent-a-judge plan – dispute resolution through private courts with judges paid to be referees for the cases.

Under the **rent-a-judge plan**, the parties hire a judge to hear the case. In many states, the parties voluntarily choose the judge as a "referee," and the judge acts under a statute

[17] The securities industry follows this process as well.

authorizing the appointment of referees. Under such a statute, the referee hears all evidence just as though there were a regular trial, and the rented judge's determination is binding on the parties unless reversed on appeal if such an appeal (like a court trial) is permitted under the parties' agreement.

16. Minitrial

minitrial – a trial held on portions of the case or certain issues in the case.

When only part of a case is disputed, the parties may stay within the framework of a lawsuit but agree that only the disputed issues will be taken to trial and submitted to a jury. **For Example,** if there is no real dispute over who is liable but the parties disagree as to the damages, the issue of damages alone may be submitted to the jury. This shortened trial is often called a **minitrial**. A minitrial may use a retired judge to make a decision on just the disputed issues. The parties may also specify whether this decision will be binding on the parties. As a practical matter, the evaluation of a case by a neutral person often brings the opposing parties together to reach a settlement.

17. Judicial Triage

judicial triage – court management tool used by judges to expedite certain cases in which time is of the essence, such as asbestos cases in which the plaintiffs are gravely ill.

The court systems, experiencing heavy caseloads, now practice **judicial triage**. Judges examine cases from a timeliness perspective. For example, in asbestos cases, judges are now evaluating plaintiffs on the basis of "how sick they are" and expediting trials for those plaintiffs who are the most ill from the alleged effects of asbestos that are the subject of their suits. The trials of those who do not have medical documentation of current illness are postponed and placed on the inactive docket until the court can get to them or until the plaintiffs become sick. Using triage, one judge has been able to bring to trial 40 percent of all asbestos cases brought since 1992.[18]

18. Contract Provisions

The parties' contract may pave the way for the settlement of future disputes by including clauses that require the parties to use one of the means of ADR. Other provisions in contracts that serve to keep the parties calm with the hope of resolving differences without a lawsuit include waiting periods before a suit can be filed and obligations to continue performing even as they try to resolve differences and issues.

LawFlix

Class Action (1991) (R)

Here is a good movie to illustrate discovery and the ethics of withholding paperwork.

Twelve Angry Men (1957) G

A movie that shows the jury process, rights of parties in court, jury instructions, and group think, all wrapped up in terrific dialogue.

---

[18] Susan Warren, "Swamped Courts Practice Plaintiff Triage," *Wall Street Journal*, January 27, 2003, B1, B3.

MAKE THE CONNECTION

SUMMARY

Courts have been created to hear and resolve legal disputes. A court's specific power is defined by its jurisdiction. Courts of original jurisdiction are trial courts, and courts that review the decisions of trial courts are appellate courts. Trial courts may have general jurisdiction to hear a wide range of civil and criminal matters, or they may be courts of limited jurisdiction—such as a probate court or the Tax Court—with the subject matter of their cases restricted to certain areas.

The courts in the United States are organized into two different systems: the state and federal court systems. There are three levels of courts, for the most part, in each system, with trial courts, appellate courts, and a supreme court in each. The federal courts are federal district courts, federal courts of appeals, and the U.S. Supreme Court.

In the states, there may be specialized courts, such as municipal, justice, and small claims courts, for trial courts. Within the courts of original jurisdiction, there are rules for procedures in all matters brought before them. A civil case begins with the filing of a complaint by a plaintiff, which is then answered by a defendant. The parties may be represented by their attorneys.

Discovery is the pretrial process used by the parties to find out the evidence in the case. The parties can use depositions, interrogatories, and document requests to uncover relevant information.

The case is managed by a judge and may be tried to a jury selected through the process of *voir dire,* with the parties permitted to challenge jurors on the basis of cause or through the use of their peremptory challenges. The trial begins following discovery and involves opening statements and the presentation of evidence, including the direct examination and cross-examination of witnesses. Once a judgment is entered, the party who has won can collect the judgment through garnishment and a writ of execution.

Alternatives to litigation for dispute resolution are available, including arbitration, mediation, MedArb, reference to a third party, association tribunals, summary jury trials, rent-a-judge plans, minitrials, and judicial triage. Court dockets are relieved and cases consolidated using judicial triage, a process in which courts hear the cases involving the most serious medical issues and health conditions first. Triage is a blending of the judicial and alternative dispute resolution mechanisms.

LEARNING OUTCOMES

After studying this chapter, you should be able to clearly explain:

A. The Court System

L0.1   Explain the federal and state court systems

See Figure 2-1 on p. 18 and accompanying text.
See Figure 2-3 on p. 21 and accompanying text.

B. Court Procedure

L0.2   Describe court procedures
See the discussion of steps in litigation that begins on p. 23.
See the *For Example* discussion of the Martha Stewart *voir dire* example on p. 24.

C. Alternative Dispute Resolution (ADR)

L0.3   List the forms of alternative dispute resolution and distinguish among them
See the discussion of arbitration that begins on p. 27.
See the discussion of other forms of ADR, mediation, minitrials, rent-a-judge, MedArb, judicial triage, and referral to a third party that begins on p. 29.
See the discussion of employee and employer referrals of disputes to a designated board or committee on p. 30.

KEY TERMS

admissibility

affirm

answer

appeal

appellate jurisdiction

arbitration

association tribunal

attorney-client privilege

complaint

counterclaim

court

cross-examination

defendant

demurrer

deposition

direct examination

directed verdict

discovery

en banc

execution

expert witness

federal district courts

garnishment

general jurisdiction

impeach

instructions

interrogatories

judge

judgment *n.o.v.* or judgment *non obstante veredicto*

judicial triage

jurisdiction

jury

limited (special) jurisdiction

mediation

minitrial

mistrial

motion for summary judgment

motion to dismiss

opening statements

original jurisdiction

plaintiff

pleadings

process

prosecutor

recross-examination

redirect examination

reference to a third person

remand

rent-a-judge plan

requests for production of documents

reverse

reversible error

small claims courts

subject matter jurisdiction

summary jury trial

summations

trial *de novo*

voir dire examination

writ of *certiorari*

QUESTIONS AND CASE PROBLEMS

1. List the steps in a lawsuit. Begin with the filing of the complaint, and explain the points at which there can be a final determination of the parties' rights in the case.

2. Explain why a business person would want to use alternative dispute resolution methods. Discuss the advantages. What disadvantages do you see?

3. Ralph Dewey has been charged with a violation of the Electronic Espionage Act, a federal statute that prohibits the transfer, by computer or disk or other electronic means, of a company's proprietary data and information. Ralph is curious. What type of court has jurisdiction? Can you determine which court?

4. Jerry Lewinsky was called for jury duty. When *voir dire* began, Jerry realized that the case involved his supervisor at work. Can Jerry remain as a juror on the case? Why or why not?

5. Carolyn, Elwood, and Isabella are involved in a real estate development. The development is a failure, and Carolyn, Elwood, and Isabella want to have their rights determined. They could bring a lawsuit, but they are afraid the case is so complicated that a judge and jury not familiar with the problems of real estate development would not reach a proper result. What can they do?

6. Larketta Randolph purchased a mobile home from Better Cents Home Builders, Inc., and financed her purchase through Green Tree Financial Corporation. Ms. Randolph signed a standard form contract that required her to buy Vendor's Single Interest insurance, which protects the seller against the costs of repossession in the event of default. The agreement also provided that all disputes arising from the contract would be resolved by binding arbitration. Larketta found that there was an additional $15 in finance charges that were not disclosed in the contract. She and other Green Tree customers filed a class-action suit to recover the fees. Green Tree moved to dismiss the suit because Larketta had not submitted the issue to arbitration. Larketta protests, "But I want the right to go to court!" Does she have that right? What are the

rights of parties under a contract with an arbitration clause? [*Green Tree Financial Corp. v. Randolph*, 531 U.S. 79]

7. John Watson invested $5,000,000 in SmartRead, Inc., a company that was developing an electronic reading device. Within a few months, the $5,000,000 was spent but SmartRead never developed the reading device. John filed suit against directors of SmartRead for their failure to supervise SmartRead's CEO in his operation of the company. The directors used an expert on corporate governance to testify that the directors had done all that they could to oversee the company. The expert did not disclose that he had served as a director of a company and had been found to be negligent in his role there and had been required to pay $370,000 to shareholders. The directors won the case. Is there anything Watson can do?

8. Indicate whether the following courts are courts of original, general, limited, or appellate jurisdiction:

   a. Small claims court

   b. Federal bankruptcy court

   c. Federal district court

   d. U.S. Supreme Court

   e. Municipal court

   f. Probate court

   g. Federal court of appeals

9. The Nursing Home Pension Fund filed suit against Oracle Corporation alleging that Larry Ellison, the company's CEO, misled investors in 2001 about the true financial condition of the company. During the time of the alleged misrepresentation, Mr. Ellison was working with a biographer on his life story and there are videotapes of Mr. Ellison's interviews with his biographer as well as e-mails between the two that discuss Oracle. Could the Nursing Home Pension Fund have access to the tapes and e-mails? Explain how. [*Nursing Home Pension Fund, Local 144 v. Oracle Corp.*, 380 F.3d 1226 (9th Cir.)]

10. Mostek Corp., a Texas corporation, made a contract to sell computer-related products to North American Foreign Trading Corp., a New York corporation. North American used its own purchase order form, on which appeared the statement that any dispute arising out of an order would be submitted to arbitration, as provided in the terms set forth on the back of the order. Acting on the purchase order, Mostek delivered almost all of the goods but failed to deliver the final installment. North American then demanded that the matter be arbitrated. Mostek refused to do so. Was arbitration required? [*Application of Mostek Corp.*, 502 N.Y.S.2d 181 (App. Div.)]

11. Ceasar Wright was a longshoreman in Charleston, South Carolina, and a member of the International Longshoremen's Association (AFL-CIO). Wright used the union hiring hall. The collective bargaining agreement (CBA) of Wright's union provides for arbitration of all grievances. Another clause of the CBA states: "It is the intention and purpose of all parties hereto that no provision or part of this Agreement shall be violative of any Federal or State Law."

    On February 18, 1992, while Wright was working for Stevens Shipping and Terminal Company (Stevens), he injured his right heel and back. He sought permanent compensation from Stevens and settled his claims for $250,000 and another $10,000 in attorney fees. Wright was also awarded Social Security disability benefits.

    In January 1995, Wright, whose doctor had approved his return to work, returned to the hiring hall and asked to be referred for work. Wright did work between January 2 and January 11, 1995, but when the companies realized Wright had been certified as permanently disabled, they deemed him not qualified for longshoreman work under the CBA and refused to allow him to work for them.

    Wright did not file a grievance under the union agreement but instead hired a lawyer and proceeded with a claim under the Americans with Disabilities Act. The district court dismissed the case because Wright had failed to pursue the grievance procedure provided by the CBA. Must Wright pursue the dispute procedure first, or can he go right to court on the basis of his federal rights under the Americans with Disabilities Act? [*Wright v. Universal Maritime Service Corp.*, 525 U.S. 70]

12. Winona Ryder was arrested for shoplifting from Saks Fifth Avenue in California. One of the members of the jury panel for her trial was Peter Guber, a Hollywood executive in charge of the production of three films in which Ms. Ryder starred, including *Bram Stoker's Dracula, The Age of Innocence,* and *Little Women*. If you were the prosecuting attorney in the case, how could you discover such information about this potential juror, and what are your options for excluding him from selection? [Rick Lyman, "For the Ryder Trial, a Hollywood Script," *New York Times,* November 3, 2002, SL-1]

13. Two doctors had a dispute over who was doing how much work at their clinic. Their dispute was submitted to arbitration and the arbitrator held in favor of the less experienced doctor. The senior doctor wants the arbitration set aside. Is it possible for the arbitrator's decision to be set aside?

14. Martha Simms is the plaintiff in a contract suit she has brought against Floral Supply, Inc., for its failure to deliver the green sponge Martha needed in building the floral designs she sells to exclusive home decorators. Martha had to obtain the sponge from another supplier and was late on seven deliveries. One of Martha's customers has been called by Martha's lawyer as a witness and is now on the witness stand, testifying about Martha's late performance and the penalty she charged. The lawyer for Floral Supply knows that Martha's customer frequently waives penalties for good suppliers. How can Floral Supply's lawyer get that information before the jury?

15. What would happen if lawyers for one side withheld evidence in a case? How could the party affected have the problem corrected?

CHAPTER 3

Business Ethics, Social Forces, and the Law

© Manuel Gutjahr/iStockphoto.com

learningoutcomes

After studying this chapter, you should be able to

LO.1 Define business ethics

LO.2 Discuss why ethics are important in business

LO.3 Describe how to recognize and resolve ethical dilemmas

E ach day businesspeople work together on contracts and projects. Their completion of the work is partially the result of the laws that protect contract rights. Much of what businesspeople do, however, is simply a matter of their word. Executives arrive at a 9:00 A.M. meeting because they promised they would be there. An employee meets a deadline for an ad display board because she said she would. Business transactions are completed through a combination of the values of the parties and the laws that reflect those values and the importance of one's word in business.

This chapter takes you behind the rules of law to examine the objectives in establishing rules for business conduct. Ethical principles, social norms, and business needs contribute to the standards that govern businesses and their operations.

A. WHAT IS BUSINESS ETHICS?

ethics – a branch of philosophy dealing with values that relate to the nature of human conduct and values associated with that conduct.

business ethics – balancing the goal of profits with values of individuals and society.

Ethics is a branch of philosophy dealing with values that relate to the nature of human conduct and values associated with that conduct. Balancing the goal of profits with the values of individuals and society is the focus of **business ethics**. Some economists make the point that insider trading is an efficient way to run that market. To an economist, inside information allows those with the best information to make the most money. This view ignores some issues: What about those who trade stock who do not have access to that information? What will happen to the stock market if investors perceive there is not a level playing field? In the U.S. Supreme Court decision *United States v. O'Hagan*[1] on insider trading, Justice Ruth Ginsburg noted, "Investors likely wouldn't invest in a market where trading based on misappropriated nonpublic information is unchecked." The field of business ethics deals with the balance between society's values and the need for businesses to remain profitable.

1. The Law as the Standard for Business Ethics

positive law – law enacted and codified by governmental authority.

Philosophers debate the origin of moral and ethical standards as well as which of those standards should be applied. One view of ethics is simply following what codified or **positive law** requires. The test of whether an act is legal is a common moral standard used frequently in business. Codified law, or law created by governmental authority, is used as the standard for ethical behavior. Absent illegality, all behavior is ethical under this simple standard. The phrase "AS IS," on a contract (see Chapter 25 for further discussion), means by law that there are no warranties for the goods being sold. **For Example,** if a buyer purchases a used car and the phrase "AS IS" is in the contract, the seller has no legal obligation, in most states, if the transmission falls apart the day after the buyer's purchase. Following a positive law standard, the seller who refuses to repair the transmission has acted ethically. However, ethical standards are different. We know there was no legal obligation to fix the transmission, but was it fair that the car fell apart the day after it was purchased?

[1] 521 U.S. 657 (1997).

2. The Notion of Universal Standards for Business Ethics

Another view of ethics holds that standards exist universally and cannot be changed or modified by law. In many cases, universal standards stem from religious beliefs. In some countries today, the standards for business are still determined by religious tenets. **Natural law** imposes higher standards of behavior than those required by positive law and they must be followed even if those higher standards run contrary to codified law. **For Example,** in the early nineteenth century when slavery was legally permissible in the United States, a positive law standard supported slavery. However, slavery violates the natural law principle of individual freedom and would be unethical. **Civil disobedience** is the remedy natural law proponents use to change positive law.

Former Supreme Court Justice Sandra Day O'Connor, who was second in her class at Stanford Law School (the late Chief Justice William Rehnquist was first), was offered a job as a receptionist for a law firm while her male classmates were hired as attorneys. At that time, no law prohibited discrimination against women, so law firms' hiring practices, using only a positive law standard, were ethical. However, if the natural law standard of equality is applied, the refusal to hire Sandra O'Connor as a lawyer, a position for which she was qualified, was a violation of the natural law principle of equality and unethical.

natural law – a system of principles to guide human conduct independent of, and sometimes contrary to, enacted law and discovered by man's rational intelligence.

civil disobedience – the term used when natural law proponents violate positive law.

3. Ethical Theories and Standards

There are many different views about the correct theory or standard we should apply when we face ethical dilemmas. Some of those theories and standards are covered here.

(A) THE CATEGORICAL IMPERATIVE AND IMMANUEL KANT. Philosopher Immanuel Kant does not allow any resolution of an ethical dilemma in which human beings are used as a means by which others obtain benefits. **Kant's categorical imperative** theory, reduced to simplest terms, is that you cannot use others in a way that gives you a one-sided benefit. Everyone must operate under the same usage rules. In Kant's words, "One ought only to act such that the principle of one's act could become a universal law of human action in a world in which one would hope to live." **For Example,** if you hit a car in a parking lot and damaged it but you could be guaranteed that no one saw you do it, would you leave a note on the other car with contact information? If you answered, "No, because that's happened to me 12 times before and no one left me a note," then you are unhappy with universal behaviors but are unwilling to commit to universal standards of honesty and disclosure to remedy those behaviors.

Kant's categorical imperative – a standard of ethics that requires that we avoid one-sided benefit for us as a result of the conduct or decision

International business presents some interesting Kantian dilemmas. For example, there are some U.S. companies that use suppliers in developing nations. Those suppliers have employees in sweatshop atmospheres who work for pennies per hour. The pennies-per-hour wage seems unjust. However, suppose the company was operating under one of its universal principles: Always pay a fair wage to those who work for it. A "fair wage" in that country might be pennies, and the company owner could argue, "I would work for that wage if I lived in that country." The company owner could also argue, "But, if I lived in the United States, I would not work for that wage, would require a much higher wage, and would want benefits, and we do provide that to all of our U.S. workers."

The company has developed its own ethical standard that is universally applicable, and those who own the company could live with it if it was applied to them, but context is everything under the categorical imperative. The basic question is: Are you comfortable living in a world operating under the standards you have established, or would you deem them unfair or unjust?

There is one more part to Kant's theory: You not only have to be fair but also have to want to do it for all the right reasons. Kant wants you to adopt and accept these ethical standards because you do not want to use other people as a means to your enrichment at their expense.

(B) THE CONTRACTARIANS AND JUSTICE. John Locke and John Rawls developed what is sometimes called the **theory of justice** and sometimes referred to as the **social contract**. Rawls and Locke believe that Kant was wrong in assuming that we could all have a meeting of the minds on what were the good rules for society. Locke and Rawls preferred just putting the rules into place with a social contract. Under this theory we imagine what it would be like if we had no rules or laws at all. If we started with a blank slate, or *tabula rasa* as these philosophers would say, rational people would agree—perhaps in their own self-interest, or perhaps to be fair—that certain universal rules must apply. Rational people, thinking through the results and consequences if there were not rules, would develop rules that would result in fairness. **For Example,** we would probably develop rules such as "Don't take my property without my permission" and "I would like the same rights in court that rich people have even if I am not so rich." Locke and Rawls want us to step back from the emotion of the moment and make universal principles that will survive the test of time.

(c) RIGHTS THEORY. The **rights theory** is also known as an **entitlement theory** and is one of the more modern theories of ethics. Robert Nozick is the key modern-day philosopher on this theory, which has two big elements: (1) everyone has a set of rights, and (2) it is up to the governments to protect those rights. **For Example,** there are rights issues related to sweatshops, abortion, slavery, property ownership and use, justice (as in court processes), animal rights, privacy, and euthanasia. Nozick dealt with all the controversial and emotional issues of ethics including everything from human dignity in suffering to third-trimester abortions.

(D) ETHICAL EGOISM THEORY: AYN RAND AND ATLAS. **Ethical egoism** holds that we all act in our own self-interest and that all of us should limit our judgment to our own ethical egos and not interfere with the exercise of ethical egoism by others. This view holds that everything is determined by self-interest. We act as we do and decide to behave as we do because we have determined that it is in our own self-interest.

Ayn Rand, who wrote books about business and business leaders' decisions in ethical dilemmas, such as *The Fountainhead* and *Atlas Shrugged,* was an ethical egoist. These two famous books made Ms. Rand's point about ethical dilemmas: the world would be better if we did not feel so guilty about the choices we make in ethical dilemmas and just acknowledged that it is all self-interest.

(E) THE UTILITARIAN THEORY: BENTHAM AND MILL. **Utilitarians** resolve ethical dilemmas by doing the most good for the most people. For example, suppose that the FBI has just arrested a terrorist who is clearly a leader in a movement that plans to plant bombs in the nation's trains, subways, and airports. This individual has critical information

---

theory of justice – the Locke and Rawlsian standard for ethics that requires that we all agree on certain universal principles in advance.

social contract – the agreement under Locke and Rawls as to what our ethical standards will be.

rights theory – Nozick's theory of ethics that we all have a set of rights that must be honored and protected by government

entitlement theory – another name for Nozick's theory that we all have certain rights that must be honored and protected by government.

Ethical egoism – theory of ethics that we should all act in our own self-interest; the Ayn Rand theory that separates guilt from acting in our own self-interest

Utilitarians – theory of ethics based on doing the most good for the most people in making decisions about upcoming planned attacks but refuses to speak. A utilitarian would want the greatest good for the greatest number and would feel that harsh interrogation methods would be justified to save thousands of lives. Rights theorists would disagree with using torture to obtain the information because human rights must be protected.

Moral relativists—those who make decisions based on circumstances and not on the basis of any predefined standards.

(F) MORAL RELATIVISTS. Moral relativists resolve ethical dilemmas according to time and place. For example, suppose that you live in a neighborhood in which drug dealers are operating a crystal meth lab or crack house, something that is causing violence in your neighborhood. A relativist would feel justified in committing arson to get rid of the drug house. Another classic example would be a parent stealing a loaf of bread to feed a starving child. Moral relativists resolve ethical dilemmas by weighing competing factors at the moment and then taking the lesser of the evils as the solution. **For Example,** Google and other Internet service providers have agreed to do business in China despite the restrictions the Chinese government places on the use of the Internet and the content of search engines. Such restrictions in the United States would be an unconstitutional violation of our First Amendment. In China, however, government control of information is legal. Google and others testified before Congress that some entry, however restricted, was better for the Chinese people than no access at all. Their decision weighed the conflicting values and concluded that they would use the standard of honoring the law of China despite the censorship.

Thinking Things Through

Corrupt Climates: Good or Bad for Business?

As you examine the following list of countries, those in the column labeled "Least Corrupt" (countries in which government officials are least likely to accept bribes) and those in the column marked "Most Corrupt" (countries in which government officials are most likely to accept bribes), can you comment on the business climates in them? What can you conclude about following the cultural practices of paying bribes? Who is harmed when a company pays bribes?

Least Corrupt (Least Likely to Accept Bribes)

- New Zealand
- Denmark
- Finland
- Sweden
- Singapore
- Norway
- Netherlands
- Australia
- Switzerland
- Canada
- Luxembourg
- Hong Kong
- Iceland
- Germany
- Japan
- Austria
- Barbados
- United Kingdom
- Belgium
- Ireland
- Bahamas
- Chile
- Qatar
- United States
- France
- Santa Lucia

Most Corrupt (Most Likely to Accept Bribes)

- Somalia
- Korea (North)
- Myanmar
- Afghanistan
- Uzbekistan
- Turkmenistan
- Sudan
- Iraq
- Haiti
- Venezuela
- Equatorial Guinea
- Burundi
- Libya
- Democratic Republic of Congo
- Chad
- Yemen
- Kyrgyzstan
- Guinea
- Cambodia
- Zimbabwe
- Paraguay
- Papua New Guinea
- Nepal
- Laos
- Kenya

*From 2011 Transparency International annual survey, **http://www.transparency.org**.

(G) PLATO AND ARISTOTLE: VIRTUE ETHICS. Aristotle and Plato taught that solving ethical dilemmas requires training, that individuals solve ethical dilemmas when they develop and nurture a set of virtues. Aristotle encouraged his students to solve ethical dilemmas using virtues such as honesty, justice, and fairness.

4. The Business Stakeholder Standard of Behavior

stakeholders – those who have a stake, or interest, in the activities of a corporation; stakeholders include employees, members of the community in which the corporation operates, vendors, customers, and any others who are affected by the actions and decisions of the corporation.

stakeholder analysis – the term used when a decision-maker views a problem from different perspectives and measures the impact of a decision on various groups.

Businesses have different constituencies, referred to as **stakeholders**, often with conflicting goals for the business. Shareholders, for example, may share economists' view that earnings, and hence dividends, should be maximized. Members of the community where a business is located are also stakeholders in the business and have an interest in preserving jobs. The employees of the business itself are stakeholders and certainly wish to retain their jobs. Balancing the interests of these stakeholders is a standard used in resolving ethical dilemmas in business.

As Figure 3-1 indicates, stakeholder analysis requires a view of an issue from different perspectives in a transparent way. **Stakeholder analysis** measures the impact of a decision on various groups and then asks whether public disclosure of that decision is defensible. The questions provide insight in a variety of situations and ethical dilemmas. **For Example,** if a lender gives a loan to a debtor without checking income, the lapse seems harmless. But, suppose someone purchases that loan believing the debtor met the standards and the lender verified income. The debtor defaults on the loan. The purchaser has to write down or write off the loan. If enough loans that were not documented go into default, you create the kind of ripples in the real estate and stock markets that occurred in late 2008. Stakeholder analysis helps you to see that the decisions we make in business are not made in isolation or limited in their impact. Figure 3-1 summarizes ethical analysis.

In other ethical dilemmas, a business faces the question of taking voluntary action or simply complying with the law. Some experts maintain that the shareholders' interest is paramount in resolving these conflicts among stakeholders. Others maintain that a business must assume some responsibility for social issues and their

---

FIGURE 3-1 | *Guidelines for Analyzing a Contemplated Action*

1. Define the problem from the decision maker's point of view.
2. Identify who could be injured by the contemplated action.
3. Define the problem from the opposing point of view.
4. Would you (as the decision maker) be willing to tell your family, your supervisor, your CEO, and the board of directors about the planned action?
5. Would you be willing to go before a community meeting, a congressional hearing, or a public forum to describe the action?
6. With full consideration of the facts and alternatives, reach a decision about whether the contemplated action should be taken.

resolution. Economist Milton Friedman expresses his views on resolving the conflicts among stakeholders as follows:

> *A corporate executive's responsibility is to make as much money for the shareholders as possible, as long as he operates within the rules of the game. When an executive decides to take action for reasons of social responsibility, he is taking money from someone else—from the stockholders, in the form of lower dividends; from the employees, in the form of lower wages; or from the consumer, in the form of higher prices. The responsibility of the corporate executive is to fulfill the terms of his contract. If he can't do that in good conscience, then he should quit his job and find another way to do good. He has the right to promote what he regards as desirable moral objectives only with his own money.*[2]

Many businesses feel an obligation to solve social problems because those problems affect their stakeholders. **For Example,** programs such as flextime, job sharing, and telecommuting for work are not legal requirements but voluntary options businesses offer their employees to accommodate family needs. These options are a response to larger societal issues surrounding children and their care but may also serve as a way to retain a quality workforce that is more productive without the worry of poor child care arrangements.

Some businesses are also involved in their communities through employees' volunteer work and companies' charitable donations. For example, a painting company in Phoenix donates paint, and its employees work on weekends painting Habitat for Humanity homes and helping churches get their facilities painted. Apple was able to capture future customers through its donations of computers to schools. Many companies also provide support for employees to participate in volunteer programs in their communities.

Ethics & the Law

Hopping Plankers

Plankers are subway riders who hop the turn styles that is they do not pay. Plankers have a pool that they all contribute to with the funds being used to pay their fines if they are arrested for riding for free. Plankers feel public transportation should be free. Discuss which ethical theories and standards the plankers are following. List the stakeholders in the plankers' actions.

B. WHY IS BUSINESS ETHICS IMPORTANT?

Ethics and values represent an important part of business success. Business ethics is important for more than the simple justification that "it's the right thing to do." This section covers the significance of ethics in business success.

5. The Importance of Trust

Capitalism succeeds because of trust. Investors provide capital for a business because they believe the business will provide a return on their investment. Customers are willing to purchase products and services from businesses because they believe the businesses will honor their commitments to deliver quality and then stand behind

---

[2] "Interview: Milton Friedman," *Playboy,* February 1973. ©1973 *Playboy.*

their product or service. Businesses are willing to purchase equipment and hire employees on the assumption that investors will continue to honor their commitment to furnish the necessary funds and will not withdraw their promises or funds. Business investment, growth, and sales are a circle of trust. Although courts provide remedies for breaches of agreements, no economy could grow if it were based solely on positive law and court-mandated performance. It is the reliance on promises, not the reliance on litigation, that produces good business relationships.

6. Business Ethics and Financial Performance

Studies centering on a business's commitment to values and its financial performance suggest that those with the strongest value systems survive and do so successfully. According to the book *Building and Growing a Business Through Good Times and Bad* by Louis Grossman and Marianne Jennings,[3] an in-depth look at companies that paid 100 years of consistent dividends produced a common thread: the companies' commitment to values. All firms studied had focused on high standards for product quality, employee welfare, and customer service.

Poor value choices do have an effect on financial performance. A study of the impact of just breaches of federal law by companies showed that for five years after their regulatory or legal misstep, these companies were still struggling to recover the financial performances they had achieved prior to their legal difficulties.[4]

Over the past few years, there have been devastating stories of companies' fates after ethical lapses. For example, after the congressional hearings revealed that Goldman Sachs took positions in the market that were the opposite of recommendations to its clients, its revenue dropped 18 percent and its share price dropped 32 percent.[5] Columbia Health Care's share price dropped 58 percent and it experienced a 93 percent drop in earnings after it was charged with overbilling for Medicare reimbursements. Its share price dropped from $40 to $18. The nation's largest hospital chain had to spin off 100 hospitals and has paid record fines to settle the charges.[6] When the subprime lender New Century Financial announced that it was finally writing down all the subprime loans it had made that had gone into default but that it had been concealing, it was forced to declare bankruptcy because it was insolvent. On January 1, 2007, New Century had $1.75 billion in market capitalization, but by the middle of March, that figure was $55 million and its stock was delisted by the New York Stock Exchange.

Insurance broker Marsh & McLennan paid $850 million to former clients to settle price-fixing charges brought by then–New York Attorney General Eliot Spitzer. The 134-year-old company saw a drop in both its earnings (64 percent) and its share price (40 percent).[7] The financial crunch resulted in 3,000 employees losing their jobs. AIG, the insurance giant, paid $1.64 billion, to settle charges that it smoothed its earnings over time and was forced to reduce its reported earnings by $1.3 billion.[8] Its $73 share price dropped to $50 before the financial reporting allegations were settled. But AIG continued to underestimate its needed reserves and losses for the subprime mortgage market it had insured. By the fall of 2008, AIG had to be rescued by the federal government with a funds bailout. In 2011, MF Global

---

[3] Greenwood Press (2002).

[4] Melinda S. Baucus and David A. Baucus, "Paying the Piper: An Empirical Examination of Longer-Term Financial Consequences of Illegal Corporate Behavior," 40 *Academic Management Journal* 129 (1997).

[5] Susanne Craig, "Goldman's Safer Position Eats Deeply Into Its Profits," *New York Times*, July 20, 2011, p. B4.

[6] Lucette Lagnado, "Columbia/HCA Warns of Profit Decline," *Wall Street Journal*, September 10, 1987, A3.

[7] Ian McDonald, "After Spitzer Probe, Marsh CEO Tries Corporate Triage," *Wall Street Journal*, August 29, 2005 A1, A5.

[8] Ian McDonald and Liam Pleven, "AIG Reaches Accord with Regulators, Stock Rises but May Still be a Bargain," *Wall Street Journal*, February 10, 2006, C1, C4.

had to declare bankruptcy after its risky bets on Greek bonds resulted in $1.6 billion in losses. Over 1,000 employees lost their jobs and the firm is being liquidated.[9]

Ethics & the Law

AIG Bailout and Bonuses

In March 2009, after it received government assistance, AIG announced the payment of $100 million in bonuses to various executives and managers in the company. There was a great hue and cry from regulators, legislators, and the public. However, AIG maintained it was contractually obligated to pay the bonuses. For a time, AIG had to cover its name on its New York office building because of public protests. The executives who received the bonuses received death threats. Evaluate the ethical issues related to the bonus payments. Evaluate the ethical issues in the public response to those bonuses. Be sure to discuss AIG's argument on the legal requirements for the bonuses.

7. The Importance of a Good Reputation

Richard Teerlink, the CEO of Harley-Davidson, once said, "A reputation, good or bad, is tough to shake.[10] A breach of ethics is costly to a firm not only in the financial sense of drops in earnings and possible fines. A breach of ethics also often carries with it a lasting memory that affects the business and its sales for years to come. **For Example,** the Peanut Corporation of America had to declare bankruptcy in 2009 after government officials discovered that its plant was the source of salmonella poisonings among those customers who had eaten peanut products that used Peanut Corporation's base in their production. Records showed that Peanut Corporation continued to produce the product even after salmonella warnings and questions arose. The company's name and image became so damaged that it could not continue to make sales. When an ethical breach occurs, businesses lose that component of trust important to customers' decisions to buy and invest.

8. Business Ethics and Business Regulation: Public Policy, Law, and Ethics

When business behavior results in complaints from employees, investors, or customers, laws or regulations are often used to change the behavior. **For Example,** the bankruptcy of Lehman Brothers, the near-collapse of Bear Stearns, and the losses at Merrill Lynch and AIG in 2008–2009 all resulted from the subprime mortgage financial derivative investment market, a market that had previously been a relatively regulation-free environment. The companies had billions of dollars of exposure because of their sales and purchases of financial instruments that were tied to the subprime mortgage market that ultimately resulted in high rates of foreclosure and nearly worthless loans. Congress, the Securities and Exchange Commission (SEC), and the Federal Reserve all stepped in to regulate virtually all aspects of mortgage transactions, including the lenders and others who were involved in packaging the loans into financial products.

---

[9] Mike Spector, Aaron Lucchetti, and Liam Pleven, "Corzine Firm's Final Struggles," *Wall Street Journal*, November 5–6, 2011, p. A1.
[10] David K. Wright, *The Harley-Davidson Motor Co.: An Official Ninety-Year History* (Milwaukee: Motorbook International, 1993).

Confusion among consumers about car leasing and its true costs and the fees applicable at the end of the lease terms caused the Federal Reserve (now the Consumer Financial Protection Bureau) to expand its regulation of credit to car leases. Figure 3-2 depicts the relationships among ethics, the social forces of customers and investors, and the laws that are passed to remedy the problems raised as part of the social forces movement.

Businesses that act voluntarily on the basis of value choices often avoid the costs and the sometimes arbitrariness of legislation and regulation. Voluntary change by businesses is less costly and is considered less intrusive.

Businesses that respond to social forces and the movements of the cycle of societal interaction often gain a competitive advantage. Businesses that act irresponsibly and disregard society's views and desire for change speed the transition from value choice to enforceable law. Businesses should watch the cycle of social forces and follow trends there to understand the values attached to certain activities and responses. These values motivate change either in the form of voluntary business activity or legislation. All values that precipitate change have one of several basic underlying goals. These underlying goals are discussed in the following sections.

(A) PROTECTION OF THE STATE. A number of laws exist today because of an underlying goal or value of protection of the state. The U.S Patriot Act and airport security regulations are examples of government programs and regulations created with the protection and security of the state as the goal.

(B) PROTECTION OF THE PERSON. A second social force is protection of the person. Criminal laws are devoted to protection of individuals and their properties. In addition, civil suits permit private remedies for wrongful acts toward people and their property. Over time, the protection of personal rights has expanded to include the rights of privacy and the protection of individuals from defamation. Laws continue to evolve to protect the reputations, privacy, and mental and physical well-being of individuals.

FIGURE 3-2 | *The Endless Cycle of Societal Interaction*

Ethics & the Law

Ethics, Trust, and Markets

The cover of *Fortune* magazine from May 14, 2001, featured a picture of Wall Street financial analyst Mary Meeker and the words, "Can we ever trust again?"[*] The inside story focused on the relationship of underwriters, analysts, and brokerage houses with the high-tech companies whose stocks they were touting and selling, knowing there were questionable accounting practices and a lack of earnings at these companies. When the dot-com market bubble burst, the losses to shareholders were catastrophic. Those in the financial markets had too much at stake to be honest with investors. They did not break the law, however.

In 2002, when companies, such as Enron, WorldCom, and Tyco had to take write-downs because of years of overstating earnings, the market once again looked at analysts, wondering how they had failed to catch the accounting issues. The cover of *Fortune* read, "In Search of the Last Honest Analyst."[**]

During 2007, *Fortune* ran a cover with the pictures of the CEOs of the major Wall Street investment firms (such as Merrill Lynch, Bear Stearns, and Lehman Brothers) who had managed to lose trillions of investors' pension and 401(k) plans to risky investments in subprime mortgages that were marketed as low-risk investments. The cover's headline asked, "What Were They Smoking?"[***] In 2011, following the collapse of Jon Corzine's MF Global hedge fund, a headline read, "Trustee Says More Cash Is Missing at MF Global." The estimated loss to investors at the firm was $1.6 billion.[****]

What do these headlines convey about the importance of trust and its role in markets?

[*]"Can We Ever Trust Again?" *Fortune*, May 14, 2001 (cover).
[**]"In Search of the Last Honest Analyst," *Fortune*, June 10, 2002 (cover).

[***]"What Were They Smoking?" *Fortune*, November 26, 2007 (cover).
[****]Michael J. de la Merced and Ben Protess, "Trustee Says More Cash Is Missing at MF Global," *New York Times*, November 22, 2011, p. B1.

(c) PROTECTION OF PUBLIC HEALTH, SAFETY, AND MORALS. Food-labeling regulations are an example of laws grounded in the value of protecting the safety and health of individuals. Food and restaurant inspections, mandatory inoculation, speed limits on roadways, mandatory smoke detectors and sprinkler systems in hotels, and prohibitions on the sale of alcohol to minors are all examples of laws based on the value of safety for the public. Zoning laws that prohibit the operation of adult bookstores and movie theaters near schools and churches are examples of laws based on moral values.

(d) PROTECTION OF PROPERTY: ITS USE AND TITLE. Someone who steals another's automobile is a thief and is punished by law with fines and/or imprisonment. A zoning law that prohibits the operation of a steel mill in a residential area also provides protection for property. A civil suit brought to recover royalties lost because of another's infringement of one's copyrighted materials is based on federal laws that afford protection for property rights in nontangible or intellectual property (see Chapter 10). Laws afford protection of title for all forms of property. The deed recorded in the land record is the legal mechanism for protecting the owner's title. The copyright on a software program or a song protects the creator's rights in that intellectual property. The title documents issued by a department of motor vehicles afford protection of title for the owner of a vehicle.

Those who have title to property are generally free to use the property in any manner they see fit. However, even ownership has restrictions imposed by law. A business may operate a factory on its real property, but if the factory creates a great deal of pollution, adjoining landowners may successfully establish it as a nuisance (see Chapter 49) that interferes with their use and enjoyment of their land.

Environmental laws also emerged as regulation of land use in response to concerns about legal, but harmful, emissions by companies.

(E) PROTECTION OF PERSONAL RIGHTS. The desire for freedom from economic domination resulted in the free enterprise philosophy that exists in the United States today. Individual freedoms and personal rights continue as a focus of value discussions followed by legislation if those individual rights are violated.

(F) ENFORCEMENT OF INDIVIDUAL INTENT. When we voluntarily enter into a contract, we have a responsibility to fulfill the promises made in that agreement. Principles of honesty and the honoring of commitments are the ethical values at the heart of the parties' conduct in carrying out contracts. If, however, the parties do not keep their promises, the law does enforce transactions through sets of rules governing requirements for them. **For Example,** the law will carry out the intentions of the parties to a business transaction through judicial enforcement of contract rights and damages.

(G) PROTECTION FROM EXPLOITATION, FRAUD, AND OPPRESSION. Many laws have evolved because businesses took advantage of others. Minors, or persons under legal age (see Chapter 14), are given special protections under contract laws that permit them to disaffirm their contracts so they are not disadvantaged by excessive commitments without the benefit of the wisdom of age and with the oppressive presence of an adult party.

The federal laws on disclosure in the sales of securities and shareholder relations (see Chapters 45 and 46) were developed following the 1929 stock market crash when many investors lost all they had because of the lack of candor and information by the businesses in which they were investing.

(H) FURTHERANCE OF TRADE. Some laws are the result of social forces seeking to simplify business and trade. Credit laws, regulations, and protections have made additional capital available for businesses and provided consumers with alternatives to cash purchases. The laws on checks, drafts, and notes have created instruments used to facilitate trade.

(I) PROTECTION OF CREDITORS AND REHABILITATION OF DEBTORS. Mortgages, security interests, and surety relationships (see Chapters 32, 34, and 49) are mechanisms created by law to provide creditors the legal mechanisms for collecting their obligations.

When collection techniques became excessive and exploitative, new laws on debtors' rights were enacted. Debtors' prisons were abolished. Congress mandated disclosure requirements for credit contracts. The Fair Debt Collections Practices Act (see Chapter 33) limited collection techniques. The remedy of bankruptcy was afforded debtors under federal law to provide them an opportunity to begin a new economic life when their existing debts reached an excessive level and could no longer be paid in a timely fashion (see Chapter 35).

(J) STABILITY AND FLEXIBILITY. Because of the desire for stability, courts will ordinarily follow former decisions unless there is a strong reason to depart from them. (See Chapter 1 for more discussion of precedent.) Similarly, when no former case bears on the point involved, a court will try to reach a decision that is a logical extension of some former decision or that follows a former decision by analogy rather than strike out on a new path to reach a decision unrelated to the past.

C. How to Recognize and Resolve Ethical Dilemmas

Business managers often find themselves in circumstances in which they are unclear about right and wrong and are confused about how to resolve the dilemmas they face. A recent survey showed that 98 percent of all Fortune 500 companies have codes of ethics designed to help their employees recognize and resolve ethical dilemmas. Nearly 99 percent of those firms provide their employees some form of training in ethics.[11] Almost 80 percent of companies now have an ethics officer. These codes of ethics provide employees information about categories of behavior that constitute ethical breaches. Regardless of the industry, the type of business, or the size of the company, certain universal categories can help managers recognize ethical dilemmas. Figure 3-3 provides a list of those categories.

9. Categories of Ethical Behavior

(A) Integrity and Truthfulness. A famous anonymous quote on truth is, "Circumstances beyond your control will cause the truth to come out, no matter what." As discussed earlier, trust is a key component of business relationships and of the free enterprise system. Trust begins with the belief that honesty is at the heart of relationships. Many contract remedies in law are based on the failure of the parties to be truthful with each other. **For Example,** if you purchase a home that has been certified as termite free but you discover termites in the home shortly after you move in, someone has not been truthful. If you also discover that two termite inspections were conducted and that the first one, which revealed there were termites, was concealed from you, your trust in both the sellers and their exterminators is diminished.

integrity—the adherence to one's values and principles despite the costs and consequences.

Integrity is the adherence to one's values and principles despite the costs and consequences. **For Example,** an executive contracted with a variety of companies to sell his hard-to-find computer components. When he was approached by one of his largest customers to break a contract with a small customer, the executive refused. The customer assured the executive it would be his last order with the company if he did not get more components. Despite facing the threat of losing a multimillion-

FIGURE 3-3	*Categories of Ethical Behavior*

1. Integrity and truthfulness
2. Promise keeping
3. Loyalty—avoiding conflicts of interest
4. Fairness
5. Doing no harm
6. Maintaining confidentiality

---

[11] Jason Lunday, "The Need for More Effective Standards of Conduct," *Corporate Compliance Insights*, June 8, 2010, **http://www.corporatecomplianceinsights.com/the-need-for-more-effective-standards-of-conduct/**

Ethics & the Law

Lying to Get into a Top School

The University of California at Berkeley has implemented a new step in its admission process. The Haas School of Business has begun running background checks on students who have applied to determine whether the information in their applications is correct. The Wharton School implemented a similar procedure and charges applicants a $35 fee for these background checks.

Of the 100 students admitted to Berkeley in the fall of 2003, 5 students were found to have offered false information on their admissions applications. The most common type of false information

was the job titles they held, and the second most common type was their number of years of work experience. Haas admissions officers indicated that had the students not lied, they otherwise met the GMAT score and GPA standards for admission to Haas.

What risk do the students take in lying on their applications? What are the long-term consequences?

Source: "Cheaters Don't Make the Grade at Berkeley Business School," **www.azcentral.com**, March 14, 2003, AP wire reports.

dollar customer, the executive fulfilled his promises to the small purchasers. The executive kept his word on all of his contracts and demonstrated integrity.

(B) PROMISE KEEPING. If we examined the types of things we do in a day, we will find that most of them are based on promises. We promise to deliver goods either with or without a contract. We promise to pay the dentist for our dental work. We promise to provide someone with a ride. Keeping those promises, regardless of whether there is a legal obligation to do so, is a key component of being an ethical person and practicing ethical business. Keeping promises is also evidence of integrity for example.

(C) LOYALTY—AVOIDING CONFLICTS OF INTEREST. An employee who works for a company owes allegiance to that company. Conduct that compromises that loyalty is a **conflict of interest. For Example,** suppose that your sister operates her own catering business. Your company is seeking a caterer for its monthly management meetings. You are responsible for these meetings and could hire your sister to furnish the lunches for the meetings. Your sister would have a substantial contract, and your problems with meal logistics would be solved. Nearly all companies have a provision in their codes of ethics covering this situation. An employee cannot hire a relative, friend, or even her own company without special permission because it is a conflict of interest. Your loyalty to your sister conflicts with the loyalty to your employer, which requires you to make the best decision at the best price.

A conflict of interest arises when a purchasing agent accepts gifts from suppliers, vendors, or manufacturers' representatives. The purchasing agent has introduced into the buy-sell relationship an element of *quid pro quo,* or the supplier's expectation that the gift will bring about a return from the agent in the form of a contract. Some companies have zero tolerance for conflicts and establish a complete prohibition on employees accepting any gifts from suppliers and manufacturers. **For Example,** Wal-Mart buyers are not permitted to accept even a cup of coffee from potential merchandise suppliers, and Amgen's buyers can go out to dinner with a supplier only if Amgen pays.

(D) DOING NO HARM. Imagine selling a product that your company's internal research shows presents significant health dangers to its users. Selling the product without disclosure of the information is unfair. There is the additional ethical breach of

conflict of interest – conduct that compromises an employee's allegiance to that company.

Sports & Entertainment Law

Identity Theft and MLB

The Washington Nationals signed Esmailyn "Smiley" Gonzalez (aka Carlos Gonzalez), whom they believed to be a 19-year-old phenomenon, for $1.4 million. Mr. Gonzalez turned out to be a 23-year-old who had presented the Nationals with fake identification when he first signed for the minor leagues, with the ID placing his age at 16. After the Nationals signed, they realized that they did not have a wonder player and that his years left for playing were far less than they had figured. "You know, to say I'm disappointed doesn't begin to describe how I feel. I'm angry. I am very angry. We've been defrauded, and make no mistake—this wasn't a college kid with a fake ID that came in and did this. This was a deliberate, premeditated

fraud with a lot more to this story, and we are going to get to the bottom of it. There were many, many people involved in this premeditated fraud."* Some fans and Mr. Gonzalez and his agent did not see any problem because they never misrepresented his skill. They say he was signed because of his skill, not his age. Should the Nationals have been told his real age? Is it fraud or is it an ethical issue? Both? What will the impact be on the sports agent?

*Chico Harlan, "I'm Angry, We've Been Defrauded," *Washington Post*, September 21, 2010. http://voices.washingtonpost.com/nationalsjournal/2010/09/a_new_development_in_the_smile.html

---

physical harm to your customers and users. Ford designed and sold its Pinto with a fundamental flaw in the placement of the car's gas tank. Rear-end collisions in which a Pinto was involved resulted, even at very low speeds, in fires that engulfed the car so quickly that occupants could not always escape from it. An internal memo from engineers at Ford revealed that employees had considered doing an analysis of the risk of the tanks versus the cost of redesign but never did. The late Peter Drucker's advice on ethics for businesses is ***primum non nocere***, or "above all, do no harm." Such a rule might have helped Ford.

primum non nocere – above all do no harm.

(E) Maintaining Confidentiality.   Often the success of a business depends on the information or technology that it holds. If the competitive edge that comes from the business's peculiar niche or knowledge is lost through disclosure, so are its profits. Employees not only owe a duty of loyalty to their employers, but they also owe an obligation of confidentiality. Employees should not use, either personally or through a competitor, information they have obtained through their employer's work or research. Providing customer lists or leads is a breach of employees' obligation of confidentiality.

In addition, managers have responsibilities regarding their employees' privacy. Performance evaluations of individual employees are private and should never be disclosed or revealed, even in one-on-one conversations outside the lines of authority and the workplace.

10. Resolving Ethical Dilemmas

Recognizing an ethical dilemma is perhaps the easiest part of business ethics. Resolution of that dilemma is more difficult. The earlier section on stakeholders offers one model for resolution of ethical dilemmas (see Figure 3-1). Other models have been developed to provide managers analytical methods for resolving dilemmas in a timely fashion.

E-Commerce & Cyberlaw

Piggybacking on Wireless Networks

A new issue that has evolved because of technology could require legal steps to stop it. People are "piggybacking" or tapping onto their neighbors' wireless Internet connection. The original subscriber pays a monthly fee for the service, but without security, people located in the area are able to tap into the wireless network, which bogs down the speed of the service. Once limited to geeks and hackers, the practice is now common among the ordinary folk who just want free Internet service.

One college student said, "I don't think it's stealing. I always find [P]eople out there … aren't protecting their connection, so I just feel free to go ahead and use it."* According to a recent survey, only about 30 percent of the 4,500 wireless networks onto which the surveyors logged were encrypted, and another survey shows that 32 percent of us do engage in Wi-Fi piggybacking.

An apartment dweller said she leaves her connection wide open because "I'm sticking it to the man. I open up my network, leave it wide open for anyone to jump on." One of the users of another's wireless network said, "I feel sort of bad about it, but I do it anyway. It just seems harmless." She said that if she gets caught, I'll just play the dumb card."

Some neighbors offer to pay those with wireless service in exchange for their occasional use rather than paying a wireless company for full-blown service. However, the original subscribers do not really want to run their own Internet service.

Do you think we need new legislation to cover this activity? What do you think of the users' statements? Is their conduct legal? Is it ethical?

*Michael Marriott, "Hey Neighbor, Stop Piggybacking on My Wireless," *New York Times*, March 5, 2006, A1, A23.

(A) BLANCHARD AND PEALE THREE-PART TEST. Dr. Kenneth Blanchard, author of the books on the *One-Minute Manager,* and the late Dr. Norman Vincent Peale developed a model for evaluating ethical breaches that is widely used among Fortune 500 companies.[12] To evaluate situations, ask the following three questions: Is it legal? Is it balanced? How does it make me feel?

In answering the questions on legality, a manager should look to positive law both within and outside the company. If the proposed conduct would violate antitrust laws, the manager's analysis can stop there. If the proposed conduct would violate company policy, the manager's analysis can stop. In the field of business ethics, there is little room for civil disobedience. Compliance with the law is a critical component of a successful ethics policy in any company.

The second question on balance forces the manager to examine the ethical value of fairness. A good follow-up question is, "How would I want to be treated in this circumstance?" Perhaps the decision to downsize must be made, but couldn't the company offer the employees a severance package and outplacement assistance to ease the transition?

The final question of the Blanchard and Peale model is conscience based. Although some managers may employ any tactics to maximize profits, this final question forces a manager to examine the physical impact of a decision: Does it cause sleeplessness or appetite changes? Personalizing business choices often helps managers to see the potential harm that comes from poor ethical choices.

(B) THE FRONT-PAGE-OF-THE-NEWSPAPER TEST. This simple but effective model for ethical evaluation helps a manager visualize the public disclosure of proposed conduct.

[12] Kenneth Blanchard and Norman Vincent Peale, *The Power of Ethical Management* (New York: William Morrow, 1986).

When he temporarily took over as the leader of Salomon Brothers after its bond-trading controversy, Warren Buffett described the newspaper test as follows:

> *Contemplating any business act, an employee should ask himself whether he would be willing to see it immediately described by an informed and critical reporter on the front page of his local paper, there to be read by his spouse, children, and friends. At Salomon, we simply want no part of any activities that pass legal tests but that we, as citizens, would find offensive.*[13]

(C) LAURA NASH MODEL. In her work, business ethicist Laura Nash has developed a series of questions to help businesspeople reach the right decision in ethical dilemmas. These are her questions: Have you defined the problem accurately? How would you define the problem if you stood on the other side of the fence? How did this situation occur in the first place? What is your intention in making this decision? How does the intention compare with the probable results? Whom could your decision or action injure? Can you discuss your decision with the affected parties? Are you confident that your position will be as valid over a long period of time as it seems now? Could you discuss your decision with your supervisor, coworkers, officers, board, friends, and family?

The Nash model requires an examination of the dilemma from all perspectives. Defining the problem and how the problem arose provides the business assistance in avoiding the dilemma again. **For Example,** suppose that a supervisor is asked to provide a reference for a friend who works for her. The supervisor is hesitant because

Ethics & the Law

Pumping Up the SAT Scores for a Good Ranking

Since 2005, Claremont McKenna, ranked #9 on *U.S. News & World Report's* best liberal arts colleges in the country, has been lopping on a few points here and there to its entering students' average SAT score before reporting those numbers to *U.S. News & World Report* and rating organizations such as the Princeton Review. For example, in 2010, its combined median score was reported as 1410, rather than its actual 1400. And its 75th percentile was reported at 1510, when it was, in reality, 1480.

Oops! Turns out the academic world is darn near as competitive as Wall Street when it comes to rankings and ratings. In fact, so competitive are those of the ivory tower that they used the same strategies: cook the books and hope no one notices.

Claremont McKenna's vice president and dean of admissions has been removed from his job title on the college Website. President Pamela B. Gann explained the problem and concluded, "As an institution of higher education with a deep and consistent commitment to the integrity of our academic activities, and particularly, our reporting of institutional data, we take this situation very seriously."

Indeed. Now, if we could just get the rankings and ratings organizations to respond with appropriate outrage. From Robert Franek of the Princeton Review, we have these thoughts, "That is a pretty mild difference in a point score. That said, 10 points, 20 points to a student that isn't getting that score on the SAT could be an important distinction." Yes, but even without the numbers difference, it is an important distinction. Claremont McKenna was not honest, and students who rely on reviews when such an obvious flaw is on the table deserve whatever fate awaits them at an institution that would pull a statistical stunt (however it may have impacted the rankings/ratings). Oh, and Mr. Franek finished with a flourish, "I feel like so many schools have a very clear obligation to college-bound students to report this information honestly." Actually, it would be all schools, not just "so many," and the reporting of correct data is not just a "clear obligation," it is an ethical responsibility.

Daniel E. Slotnik and Richard Pérez-Peña, "College Sats It Exaggerrated SAT Figures for Rating," *New York Times*, Jan. 31, 2012, p. A12.

---

[13] Janet Lowe, *Warren Buffett Speaks: Wit and Wisdom from the World's Greatest Investor* (New York: Wiley, 1997).

the friend has not been a very good employee. The ethical dilemma the manager believes she faces is whether to lie or tell the truth about the employee. The real ethical dilemma is why the supervisor never provided evaluation or feedback indicating the friend's poor performance. Avoiding the problem in the future is possible through candid evaluations. Resolving the problem requires that the supervisor talk to her friend now about the issue of performance and the problem with serving as a reference.

One final aspect of the Nash model that businesspeople find helpful is a question that asks for a perspective on an issue from family and friends. The problem of groupthink in business situations is very real. As businesspeople sit together in a room and discuss an ethical dilemma, they can persuade each other to think the same way. The power of consensus can overwhelm each person's concerns and values. There is a certain fear in bringing up a different point of view in a business meeting. Proper perspective is often lost as the discussion centers around numbers. Therefore, bringing in the views of an outsider is often helpful. **For Example,** when McNeil, the manufacturer of Tylenol, faced the cyanide poisonings from contaminated capsules sold in the Chicago area, it had to make a decision about the existing Tylenol inventory. It was clear to both insiders and outsiders that the poison had not been put in the capsules at McNeil but after delivery to the stores. Despite the huge numbers involved in the recall and the destruction of inventory, the McNeil managers made the decision easily because they viewed the risk to their own families, that is, from the outside. From this standpoint, the issue became a question of human life, not of numbers.[14]

LawFlix

Breaking Away (1979) (PG)

In this story about "cutters" (a nickname for natives of Bloomington, Indiana), a recent high school graduate trains to be a first-class bike rider. He idolizes the Italian world racing team and enters an Indiana race to have the opportunity to compete with them. He does well in the race and manages to catch up and keep pace with the Italian team. As he rides alongside his idols, one of the members of the Italian team places a tire pump in his spoke. His bike crashes, he loses the race and is injured. He becomes disillusioned. Is this experience like business? Do unethical tactics get you ahead? Do nice guys finish last? Are there sanctions for unethical conduct?

Jaws (1975) (PG-13)

The movie that shot Steven Spielberg to directorial legend brings us the classic business dilemma of what to do when you have a high-risk/low-probability event that you know about but about which the public has no knowledge. Do you stop? But what about the economic losses?

Hoosiers (1986) (PG)

Often called the "greatest sports movie ever made," this story of a coach with a history and a small-town team presents several life-defining ethical moments. In one, with advancement to the finals on the table, Coach Norman Dale grapples with whether he should allow one of his injured players to continue when he has no depth on his bench. What do you do when your values are in conflict?

[14] "Brief History of Johnson & Johnson" (company pamphlet, 1992).

LawFlix

Continued

The Family Man (2000) (PG-13)

Nicolas Cage plays a Wall Street billionaire who is suddenly given a suburban life in New Jersey with all of its family life and financial constraints. He is forced to examine who he really is and what is important.

MAKE THE CONNECTION

SUMMARY

Business ethics is the application of values and standards to business conduct and decisions. These values originate in various sources from positive (codified) law to natural law to ethical theories and standards and on to stakeholder values. Business ethics is important because trust is a critical component of good business relationships and free enterprise. A business with values will enjoy the additional competitive advantage of a good reputation and, over the long term, better earnings. When businesses make decisions that violate basic ethical standards, they set into motion social forces and cause the area of abuse to be regulated, resulting in additional costs and

restrictions for business. Voluntary value choices by businesses position them for a competitive advantage.

The categories of ethical values in business are truthfulness and integrity, promise keeping, loyalty and avoiding conflicts of interest, fairness, doing no harm, and maintaining confidentiality.

Resolution of ethical dilemmas is possible through the use of various models that require a businessperson to examine the impact of a decision before it is made. These models include stakeholder analysis, the Blanchard and Peale test, the front-page-of-the-newspaper test, and the Laura Nash model.

LEARNING OUTCOMES

After studying this chapter, you should be able to clearly explain:

A. What Is Business Ethics?

L0.1   Define business ethics
See the discussion of the definition, balancing the goal of profits with the values of individuals and society, on p. 41–42.

B. Why Is Business Ethics Important?

L0.2   Discuss why ethics are important in business

See "The Importance of Trust" on p. 42.
See "Business Ethics and Financial Performance" on p. 43.
See "The Importance of a Good Reputation" on p. 44.

See Ethics & the Law on market trust on p. 46.

C. How to Recognize and Resolve Ethical Dilemmas

LO.3 Describe how to recognize and resolve ethical dilemmas

See "Integrity and Truthfulness" on p. 48.
See "Promise Keeping" on p. 49.
See "Loyalty—Avoiding Conflicts of Interest" on p. 49.

See "Doing No Harm" on p. 49.
See "Maintaining Confidentiality" on p. 50.
See "Resolving Ethical Dilemmas" on p. 50.
See "Blanchard and Peale Three-Part Test" on p. 51.
See "The Front-Page-of-the-Newspaper Test" on p. 51.
See Ethics & the Law on pumping up SAT scores on p. 52.
See "Laura Nash Model" on p. 52.

KEY TERMS

business ethics
civil disobedience
conflict of interest
entitlement theory
ethics
ethical egoism

integrity
Kant's categorical imperative
moral relativists
natural law
positive law
primum non nocere

rights theory
social contract
stakeholder analysis
stakeholders
theory of justice
utilitarians

QUESTIONS AND CASE PROBLEMS

1. Marty Mankamyer, the president of the United States Olympic Committee (USOC), resigned in early February 2003 following reports in *The Denver Post* that indicated she had demanded a commission from a fellow real estate broker in the Colorado Springs area, the home of the USOC, who had sold property to Lloyd Ward, the CEO of the USOC. Mr. Ward had purchased a 1.3-acre lot in Colorado Springs for $475,000 and had paid the listing broker, Brigette Ruskin, a commission.

    Ms. Mankamyer allegedly demanded a portion of the commission from Ms. Ruskin, and Ms. Ruskin sent her a check. Ms. Mankamyer had shown Mr. Ward and his wife properties in the area when they were being considered for the job and when he was considering taking the job. However, Mrs. Ward indicated that Ms. Mankamyer did not identify herself as a real estate agent and that she assumed that Ms. Mankamyer was showing the properties as a "goodwill gesture."[15] What conflicts of interest do you see here?

2. Ann Elkin, who works for Brill Co., has been sent out to conduct two customer evaluations,

which have gone much more quickly than Ann anticipated. Her supervisor does not expect Ann back until after lunch. It is now 10:30 A.M., and Ann would like to run some personal errands and then go to lunch before returning to work at 1:00 P.M. Should Ann take the time? Would you? Why or why not? Be sure to consider the categories of ethical values and apply one or two models before reaching your conclusion.

3. Fred Sanguine is a New York City produce broker. Ned Santini is a 19-year-old college student who works for Sanguine from 4:00 A.M. until 7:00 A.M. each weekday before he attends classes at Pace University. Fred has instructed Ned on the proper packing of produce as follows: "Look, put the bad and small cherries at the bottom. Do the same with the strawberries and blueberries. Put the best fruit on top and hide the bad stuff at the bottom. This way I get top dollar on all that I sell." Ned is uncomfortable about the instructions, but, as he explains to his roommate, "It's not me doing it. I'm just following orders. Besides, I need the job."

    Should Ned just follow instructions? Is the manner in which the fruit is packed unethical?

---

[15] Richard Sandomir, "U.S. Olympic Chief Resigns in a Furor Over Ethics Issues," *New York Times*, February 5, 2003, A1, C17; Bill Briggs, *Realtor Waving Red Flag*, **www.denverpost.com**, February 4, 2003.

Would you do it? Why or why not? Is anyone really harmed by the practice?

4. Alan Gellen is the facilities manager for the city of Milwaukee and makes all final decisions on purchasing items such as chairs, lights, and other supplies and materials. Alan also makes the final decisions for the award of contracts to food vendors at event sites. Grand Beef Franks has submitted a bid to be one of the city's vendors. Alan went to school with Grand Beef's owner, Steve Grand, who phones Alan and explains that Grand Beef owns a condominium in Maui that Alan could use. Steve's offer to Alan is: "All it would cost you for a vacation is your airfare. The condo is fully stocked with food. Just let me know."

   Should Alan take the offer? Would you? Be sure to determine which category of ethical values this situation involves and to apply several models as you resolve the question of whether Alan should accept the invitation.

5. A Dillard's customer brought in a pair of moderately expensive dress shoes, expressing a desire to return them because they just weren't quite right. As the manager processed the order she checked inside the box to be sure that the shoes in the box were the shoes that matched the box – past experience dictated that follow-up on returns. The shoes were the correct ones for the box, but there was another issue. The shoes had masking tape on the bottom – masking tape that was dirty. When the manager returned to the customer she said, "You forgot to remove the masking tape from your shoes." The customer responded, "I only wore them once. That's all I needed them for."

   From Neiman Marcus to Saks to Dillard's, managers have to stay one step ahead of customers, or lessees, who buy, or lease for free, dresses and now shoes for one use with premeditated intent to return the merchandise. Stores now place tags strategically so that the dresses cannot be worn without cutting them off and there are no returns if the tags are cut off on formal wear.

   Ace Hardware and Home Depot have customers who "buy" a special tool, try to use it once, and then return it. The hardware/home improvement stores are left with opened

packaging and used goods by buy-it-temporarily customers.

   List some consequences for this behavior by customers.

6. Adam Smith wrote the following in *The Theory of Moral Sentiments*:

   In the practice of the other virtues, our conduct should rather be directed by a certain idea of propriety, by a certain taste for a particular tenor of conduct, than by any regard to a precise maxim or rule; and we should consider the end and foundation of the rule, more than the rule itself.[16]

   Do you think Adam Smith adhered to positive law as his ethical standard? Was he a moral relativist? Does his quote match stakeholder analysis? What would his ethical posture be on violating the law?

7. A new phenomenon for admissions to MBA programs is hiring consultants to help applicants hone their applications. About 20 percent of those who apply to the top MBA programs have hired consultants at a cost of $150 to $200 per hour to help them say and do the right things to be admitted. The total cost for most who use a consultant is $5,000. The consultants help with personal essays and applications. One admissions officer points out that one function of the consultant is to draw out and emphasize skills that the applicant may not see as important. For example, playing the piano is looked upon favorably because it shows discipline and focus.

   However, admissions committees are becoming adept at spotting the applications via consultant because, as the faculty describe it, these essays and applications have a certain "sameness" to them. The Fuqua School at North Carolina suggests that students simply call the admissions office and get comparable advice for free. Is it ethical to use an admissions consultant? When would you cross a line in using the consultant on the essay?

8. "I was very upset that there's that many dishonest people," said Andrea Reuland, the owner of Trigs Shell Station in Minocqua, Wisconsin.

---

[16] Adam Smith, *The Theory of Moral Sentiments* (Arlington House, 1969; originally published in 1769).

She lost $3 per gallon on 586 gallons of gas sold during a 45-minute period when local residents phoned others to come and get gas because an employee had made a mistake and entered the price at 32.9 cents vs. $3.299 per gallon.

Eighty-seven percent of the people who responded to a survey about the incident said they would have done the same thing as the Minocqua residents.

Describe who is affected by what buyers did by not paying the correct price for the gas. Describe a simple test for resolving an ethical dilemma such as this where you can get something for free or very little.

9. The state of Arizona mandates emissions testing for cars before drivers can obtain updated registrations. The state hires a contractor to conduct the emissions tests in the various emissions-testing facilities around the state. In October 1999, the Arizona attorney general announced the arrest of 13 workers at one of the emissions-testing facilities for allegedly taking payoffs of between $50 and $200 from car owners to pass their cars on the emissions tests when those cars fell below emissions standards and would not have been registered. Nearly half of the staff at the emissions facility were arrested.

Why is it a crime for someone working in a government-sponsored facility to accept a payment for a desired outcome? Do the payoffs to the workers really harm anyone?

10. The president and athletic director at the University of California at Los Angeles (UCLA) fired the school's basketball coach because an expense form he had submitted for reimbursement had the names of two students he said had joined him for a recruiting dinner. The students had not been to the dinner. The coach was stunned because he had been at UCLA for eight years and had established a winning program. He said, "And to throw it all away on a meal?" Do you agree with the coach's assessment? Was it too harsh to fire him for one inaccurate expense form? Did the coach commit an ethical breach?

11. When some runners in the New York City Marathon hit the Queensboro Bridge,

temptation sets in and, rather than finishing the last 10 miles through Harlem and the Bronx, they hop a ride on the subway and head toward the finish line at Central Park. A total of 46 runners used the subway solution to finish the race in the 2008 NYC Marathon. When one runner was questioned about his unusual time, he admitted to using the subway and said, "So I skipped a few boroughs. I didn't do anything illegal." How would you respond to his point that he did not break the law? Why should we worry about some runners?

12. David A. Vise, a Pulitzer Prize winner and a reporter for the *Washington Post*, wrote the book *The Bureau and the Mole*. When the book hit the market, Mr. Vise purchased 20,000 copies via Barnes & Noble.com, taking advantage of both free shipping offered by the publisher and a discounted initial price. Mr. Vise's book had already hit the *New York Times'* bestseller list in the week before the purchases. He used the books he purchased to conduct online sales of autographed copies of the books, and then returned 17,500 books and asked for his money back. However, that return of 17,500 books represented more books than a publisher generally runs for a book. Mr. Vise said that he did not intend to manipulate the market or profit from the transactions. He said his only intent was to "increase awareness of *The Bureau and the Mole*."

Mr. Vise's editor offered to pay Barnes & Noble for any expenses it incurred. Was it ethical to do what Mr. Vise did? Was he within his rights to return the books? What are his remedies? Does Barnes & Noble have any rights?

13. Former Enron Chief Financial Officer Andrew Fastow, in his testimony against his former bosses at their criminal trial for fraud, said, "I thought I was being a hero for Enron. At the time, I thought I was helping myself and helping Enron to make its numbers." Mr. Fastow also added, however, "I lost my moral compass."

Are you able to classify Mr. Fastow into a particular ethical standard or principle?

14. Piper High School in Piper, Kansas, a town located about 20 miles west of Kansas City,

experienced national attention because of questions about students and their term papers for a botany class. Christine Pelton, a high school science teacher, had warned students in her sophomore class not to use papers posted on the Internet for their projects. When their projects were turned in, Ms. Pelton noticed that the writing in some of the papers was well above the students' usual quality and ability. She found that 28 of her 118 students had taken substantial portions of their papers from the Internet. She gave these students a zero grade on their term paper projects with the result that many of the students were going to fail the course for that semester. The students' parents protested, and the school board ordered Ms. Pelton to raise the grades.

She resigned in protest. She received a substantial number of job offers from around the country following her resignation. Nearly half of the high school faculty as well as its principal announced their plans to resign at the end of the year. Several of the parents pointed to the fact that there was no explanation in the Piper High School handbook on plagiarism. They also said that the students were unclear about what could be used, when they had to reword, and when quotations marks were necessary.

The annual Rutgers University survey on academic cheating has revealed that 15 percent of college papers turned in for grades are completely copied from the Internet.

Do you think such copying is unethical? Why do we worry about such conduct? Isn't this conduct just a function of the Internet? Isn't it accepted behavior?

15. Pharmaceutical companies, faced with the uphill battle of getting doctors to take a look at their new products, have created complex systems and programs for enticing doctors to come, sit, and absorb information about the new products.

Following is a list of the various type of benefits and gifts that drug companies have given doctors over the past few years to entice them to consider prescribing their new offerings:

- An event called "Why Cook?" in which doctors were given the chance to review drug studies and product information at a restaurant as their meals were being prepared—they could leave as soon as their meals were ready, and they were treated to appetizers and drinks as they waited

- Events at Christmas tree lots where doctors can come and review materials and pick up a free Christmas tree

- Flowers sent to doctors' offices on Valentine's Day with materials attached

- Manicures as they study materials on new drugs

- Pedicures as they study materials on new drugs

- Free car washes during which they study materials

- Free books with materials enclosed

- Free CDs with materials attached

- Bottles of wine with materials attached

- Events at Barnes & Noble where doctors can browse and pick out a book for themselves for free as long as they also take some materials on a new drug

Some doctors say that they can enjoy dinner on a drug company as often as five times per week. The American Medical Association (AMA) frowns on the "dine-and-dash" format because its rules provide that dinners are acceptable only as long as the doctors sit and learn something from a featured speaker. The AMA also limits gifts to those of a "minimal value" that should be related to their patients, such as note pads and pens with the new drug's name imprinted on them. The chairman of the AMA Committee on Ethics says the following about gifts, "There are doctors who say, 'I always do what's best for my patients, and these gifts and dinners and trips do not influence me.' They are wrong."[17]

In which category of ethical issues do these gifts fall? Do you think doctors act ethically in accepting gifts, meals, and favors? The Food and Drug Administration recently issued rules about such favors and perks. Why?

---

[17] Chris Adams, "Doctors on the Run Can 'Dine 'n' Dash' in Style in New Orleans," *Wall Street Journal*, May 14, 2001, A1, A6.

© Manuel Gutjahr/iStockphoto.com

CHAPTER 4

The Constitution as the Foundation of the Legal Environment

learningoutcomes

After studying this chapter, you should be able to

LO.1 Describe the U.S. Constitution and the Federal System

LO.2 Explain the relationship between the U.S. Constitution and the States

LO.3 Discuss interpreting and amending the Constitution

LO.4 List and describe the significant federal powers

LO.5 Discuss constitutional limitations on governmental power

T his chapter introduces you to the powers of government and to the protections that you have for your rights. The Constitution of the United States establishes the structure and powers of government but also the limitations on those powers. This Constitution forms the foundation of our legal environment.

A. THE U.S. CONSTITUTION AND THE FEDERAL SYSTEM

By establishing a central government to coexist with the governments of the individual states, the U.S. Constitution created a federal system. In a **federal system,** a central government has power to address national concerns, while the individual states retain the power to handle local concerns.

1. What a Constitution Is

A **constitution** is the written document that establishes the structure of the government and its relationship to the people. The U.S. Constitution was adopted in 1789 by the 13 colonies that had won their independence from King George.[1]

2. The Branches of Government

The U.S. Constitution establishes a **tripartite** (three-part) government: a **legislative branch** (Congress) to make the laws, an **executive branch** (the president) to execute or enforce the laws, and a **judicial branch** (courts) to interpret the laws.[2] The national legislature or Congress is a **bicameral** (two-house) body consisting of the Senate and the House of Representatives. Members of the Senate are popularly elected for a term of six years. Members of the House of Representatives are popularly elected for a term of two years. The president is elected by an electoral college whose membership is popularly elected. The president serves for a term of four years and is eligible for reelection for a second term. Judges of the United States are appointed by the president with the approval of the Senate and serve for life, subject to removal only by impeachment because of misconduct. (See Chapter 2 for a discussion of the federal court system.)

B. THE U.S. CONSTITUTION AND THE STATES

The Constitution created certain powers within the national government that would have been exercised by the individual states, which are given their powers by the people of the state. Figure 4-1 illustrates the delegation of powers. Likewise, the states, as the power-granting authorities, reserved certain powers for themselves.

3. Delegated and Shared Powers

(A) DELEGATED POWERS. The powers given by the states to the national government are described as *delegated powers.* Some of these **delegated powers** are given exclusively

---

federal system – the system of government in which a central government is given power to administer to national concerns while individual states retain the power to administer to local concerns.

constitution – a body of principles that establishes the structure of a government and the relationship of the government to the people who are governed.

tripartite – three-part division (of government).

legislative branch – the branch of government (e.g., Congress) formed to make the laws.

executive branch – the branch of government (e.g., the president) formed to execute the laws.

judicial branch – the branch of government (e.g., the courts) formed to interpret the laws.

bicameral – a two-house form of the legislative branch of government.

delegated powers – powers expressly granted the national government by the Constitution.

---

[1] To examine the U.S. Constitution, go to **www.constitution.org** and click on "Founding Documents," or refer to Appendix 2.
[2] *Free Enterprise Fund v. Public Company Accounting Oversight Board*, 130 S. Ct. 3138 (2010).

FIGURE 4-1 | *Governments of the United States*

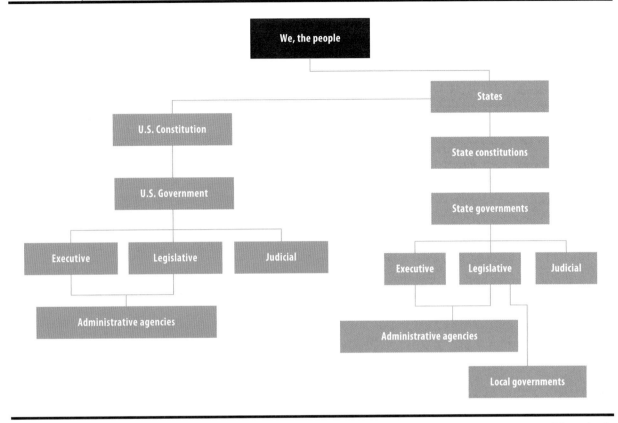

© Cengage Learning

to the national government. **For Example,** the national government alone may declare war or establish a currency.

(B) SHARED POWERS. The powers delegated to the national government that may still be exercised by the states are **shared powers. For Example,** the grant of power to the national government to impose taxes did not destroy the state power to tax. In other cases, a state may provide regulation along with, but subject to the supremacy of, federal law. **For Example,** regulation of the use of navigable waterways within a state is an example of joint state and federal regulation.

shared powers – powers that are held by both state and national governments.

4. Other Powers

(A) STATE POLICE POWER. The states possess the power to adopt laws to protect the general welfare, health, safety, and morals of the people. This authority is called the **police power. For Example,** states may require that businesses be licensed with state agencies to protect persons dealing with the business. State exercise of the police power may not unreasonably interfere with federal powers.

police power – the power to govern; the power to adopt laws for the protection of the public health, welfare, safety, and morals.

(B) PROHIBITED POWERS. The Constitution also prohibits both states and the federal government from doing certain things. **For Example,** neither states nor the national government may adopt *ex post facto* **laws,** which make criminal an act that has

***ex post facto* law** – a law making criminal an act that was lawful when done or that increases the penalty when done. Such laws are generally prohibited by constitutional provisions.

already been committed but was not criminal when it was committed. Laws that increase the penalty for an act already committed above the penalty in force when the act was committed are also *ex post facto* laws.

5. Federal Supremacy

preemption – the federal government's superior regulatory position over state laws on the same subject area.

States cannot enact conflicting state regulation if the congressional intent to regulate exclusively can be inferred from the details of congressional regulation. **Preemption** means that the federal regulatory scheme is controlling.

(A) EXPRESS FEDERAL REGULATION. The Constitution and statutes passed by Congress are the supreme law of the land. They cancel out any conflicting state law.[3] When a direct conflict exists between federal and state statutes, federal law prevails.

In some cases, however, no obvious conflict occurs because the federal statute covers only part of the subject matter. In such cases, the question becomes whether a state law can regulate the areas not regulated by Congress or whether the partial regulation made by Congress preempts, or takes over, the field so as to preclude state legislation.

CASE SUMMARY

The Folk Singer Who Staged a Protest against Preemption

FACTS: Diana Levine, a folk singer from Vermont, suffered from migraine headaches. She was being administered Wyeth Laboratory's Phenergan through a drip IV. Either because the IV needle entered Levine's artery or the drug escaped from the vein into her surrounding tissue, Ms. Levine developed gangrene. Doctors amputated her right hand and eventually her forearm. Levine could no longer work as a professional musician. Levine filed suit against both the clinic that administered the drug and Wyeth. She was awarded $7.4 million and Wyeth appealed on the grounds that the FDA approval of the drug preempted state tort suits by patients.

DECISION: In a 6 to 3 decision that departed from past precedent on preemption, the U.S. Supreme Court held that federal regulation did not preempt Levine's state tort suit against Wyeth. Wyeth argued that it could not change the label to warn against IV use of Phenergan without first obtaining FDA approval for the change. Wyeth also argued that FDA approval of the drug as safe for use was all that was needed. The Court held that Wyeth could move, when necessary, to change the label with the FDA in a timely fashion and that federal regulation did not preempt responsible follow-up by manufacturers with regard to their drugs. [*Wyeth v. Levine*, 555 U.S. 555 (2009)][4]

(B) SILENCE OF CONGRESS. In some situations, the silence of Congress in failing to cover a particular subject area indicates that Congress does not want any law on the matter. However, when national uniformity is essential, the silence of Congress generally means that the subject has been preempted for practical reasons by Congress and that no state law on the subject may be adopted.

---

[3] U.S. Const., Art VI, cl 2. *Cuomo v Clearinghouse Ass'n, LLC*, 557 U.S. 519 (2009).

[4] For an earlier decision that concluded differently on another preemption case involving medical and FDA issues, see *Riegel v. Medtronic*, 552 U.S. 312 (2008). For a decision reached on generic drug manufacturers' liability under state law, see *Pliva v. Mensing*, 131 S.Ct. 2567 (2011).

(c) Effect of Federal Deregulation. The fact that the federal government removes the regulations from a regulated industry does not automatically give the states the power to regulate that industry. If under the silence-of-Congress doctrine the states cannot regulate, they are still barred from regulating after deregulation. **For Example,** deregulation of banks in the 1980s did not mean that the states could step in and regulate those banks.[5]

C. Interpreting and Amending the Constitution

The Constitution as it is interpreted today has changed greatly from the Constitution as originally written. The change has been brought about by interpretation, amendment, and practice.

6. Conflicting Theories

Shortly after the Constitution was adopted, conflict arose over whether it was to be interpreted strictly, so as to give the federal government the least power possible, or broadly, so as to give the federal government the greatest power that the words would permit. These two views may be called the *bedrock view* and the *living-document view*, respectively.

> **bedrock view** – a strict constructionist interpretation of a constitution.
>
> **living-document view** – the term used when a constitution is interpreted according to changes in conditions.

In the **bedrock view,** or strict constructionist or originalist view, the purpose of a constitution is to state certain fundamental principles for all time. In the **living-document view,** a constitution is merely a statement of goals and objectives and is intended to grow and change with time.

Whether the Constitution is to be liberally interpreted under the living-document view or narrowly interpreted under the bedrock view has a direct effect on the Constitution. For the last century, the Supreme Court has followed the living-document view. This view has resulted in strengthening the power of the federal government, permitting the rise of administrative agencies, and expanding the protection of human rights.

One view is not selected to the exclusion of the other. As contradictory as these two views sound, the Constitution remains durable. We do not want a set of New Year's resolutions that will soon be forgotten. At the same time, we know that the world changes, and therefore, we do not want a constitution that will hold us tied in a straitjacket of the past.

In terms of social forces that make the law, we are torn between our desire for stability and our desire for flexibility. We want a constitution that is stable. At the same time, we want one that is flexible.

7. Amending the Constitution

Constitution has been amended in three ways: (1) expressly, (2) by interpretation, and (3) by practice. Figure 4-2 illustrates these three methods of amendment.

(a) Constitutional Method of Amending. Article V of the Constitution gives the procedure to be followed for amending the Constitution. Relatively few changes have been made to the Constitution by this formal process, although thousands of

---

[5] For a discussion of preemption of state regulation of airline advertising when federal regulation of air travel is so pervasive see *New York v. Trans World Airlines*, 556 N.Y.S. 2d 803 (1990) and *Pan American World Airways, Inc. v. Abrams*, 764 F. Supp. 864, 868 (S.D.N.Y. 1991). See also footnote 3 and the *Cuomo* case from 2009.

FIGURE 4-2	*Amending the U.S. Constitution*

*Article V of the U.S. Constitution specifies the procedure for adopting amendments.

© Cengage Learning

proposals have been made. Since the time of its adoption, there have been only 27 amendments to the Constitution.[6]

(B) AMENDMENT BY JUDICIAL INTERPRETATION. The U.S. Supreme Court has made the greatest changes to the written Constitution by interpreting it. Generally, interpretation is used to apply the Constitution to a new situation that could not have been foreseen when the written Constitution was adopted.

(C) AMENDMENT BY PRACTICE. In practice, the letter of the Constitution is not always followed. Departure from the written Constitution began as early as 1793 when George Washington refused to make treaties as required by the Constitution, by and with the consent of the Senate. Washington began the practice of the president's negotiating a treaty with a foreign country and then submitting it to the Senate for approval. This practice has been followed since that time. Similarly, the electoral college was originally intended to exercise independent judgment in selecting the president, but it now automatically elects the official candidate of the party that elected the majority of the members of the electoral college.

8. The Living Constitution

The living Constitution has the following characteristics.

(A) STRONG GOVERNMENT. One of the characteristics of the new Constitution is strong government. Business enterprises are highly regulated and the economy is controlled through monetary policy.

(B) STRONG PRESIDENT. Instead of being merely an officer who carries out the laws, the president has become the political leader of a party, exerting strong influence on the lawmaking process.

(C) ECLIPSE OF THE STATES. Under constitutional interpretations, all levels of government have powers that they never possessed before, but the center of gravity has shifted from the states to the nation. When the Constitution was adopted in 1789, the federal government was to have only the very limited powers specified in Article I, Section 8, of the Constitution. Whatever regulation of business was permissible was to be imposed by the states. Today, the great bulk of the regulation of business is adopted

[6] Gregory Watson, a University of Texas at Austin student who was doing research for a paper for a class on the U.S. Constitution, ran across a 1789 proposed amendment to the Constitution that had never been ratified by the states. Watson wrote a paper and got a "C," but through a successful letter-writing campaign was able to get the 27th Amendment passed. The amendment reads, "No law, varying the compensation for the services of the Senators and Representatives, shall take effect, until an election of Representatives shall have intervened."

by the federal government through Congress or its administrative agencies. As the U.S. economy moved from the local community stage to the nationwide and then international stages, individual states could no longer provide effective regulation of business. Regulation migrated to the central government.

(D) ADMINISTRATIVE AGENCIES. These units of government were virtually unheard of in 1789, and the Constitution made no mention of them. The vast powers of the new Constitution are exercised to a very large degree by administrative agencies. They are in effect a fourth branch of the government, not provided for in the written Constitution. More importantly, the administrative agencies are the ones that come in contact with the majority of businesspersons and citizens.

Agencies have had a significant amount of power delegated to them. The members and heads of the agencies, boards, or commissions are not elected by the voters (see Chapter 6). They are appointed by the president and, at certain levels of appointment in the agency, must be approved by Congress.

D. FEDERAL POWERS

The federal government possesses powers necessary to administer matters of national concern.

9. The Power to Regulate Commerce

The desire to protect commerce from restrictions and barriers set up by the individual states was a prime factor leading to the adoption of the Constitution of 1789. To protect commerce, Congress was given Article I, Section 8, Clause 3—now known as the **commerce clause**—the power "to regulate commerce with foreign nations, and among the several states, and with the Indian tribes."[7]

Until 1937, the Supreme Court held that this provision gave Congress the power to control or regulate only that commerce crossing a state line, such as an interstate railway train or an interstate telegraph message.

(A) THE COMMERCE POWER BECOMES A GENERAL WELFARE POWER. In 1937, the Supreme Court began expanding the concept of interstate commerce. By 1946, the power to regulate interstate commerce had become very broad. By that year, the power had expanded to the point that it gave authority to Congress to adopt regulatory laws that were "as broad as the economic needs of the nation."[8] By virtue of this broad interpretation, Congress can regulate manufacturing, agriculture, mining, stock exchanges, insurance, loan sharking, monopolies, and conspiracies in restraint of trade. The far reach of the interstate commerce power is seen in the Freedom of Access to Clinic Entrances Act,[9] which prohibits obstruction of entrances to clinics, as well as in the commerce clause challenges to the Affordable Health Care Act, also known as Obama Care.[10]

The case that was the beginning point in the transition of the commerce clause was *NLRB v. Jones & Laughlin Steel,* 301 U.S. 1 (1937). The "affectation" doctrine

commerce clause—that section of the U.S. Constitution allocating business regulation between federal and state governments.

---

[7] For more details on the actual language in the U.S. Constitution, go to **www.constitution.org** and click on "Founding Documents," or refer to Appendix 2.
[8] *American Power & Light Co. v. Securities and Exchange Commission,* 329 U.S. 90 (1946).
[9] 18 USC §248.
[10] *United States v. Wilson,* 73 F.3d 675 (7th Cir. 1995), *cert. denied,* 519 U.S. 806 (1996), Florida ex rel. *National Federation of Independent Business v. Sebelius,* 132 S.Ct. 2566 (2012).

expanded the authority of the federal government under the commerce clause. At that time, the Court concluded, "If it is interstate commerce that feels the pinch, it does not matter how local the squeeze."

(B) THE COMMERCE CLAUSE TODAY. Today, judicial review of the commerce clause typically finds some connection between the legislation and congressional authority. However, in the past five years, the U.S. Supreme Court has found some areas Congress may not regulate and has placed some limitations on the commerce clause. These constraints on the commerce clause focus on the nature of the underlying activity being regulated. So long as the federal regulation relates to economic/ commercial activity, it is constitutional. If, however, the underlying activity is not economic and has only an economic impact, the Supreme Court has imposed restrictions on congressional authority under the commerce clause. **For Example,** in U.S. v. Morrison, 529 U.S. 598 (2000), the Supreme Court held that the Violence Against Women Act was unconstitutional because the underlying activity being regulated was violence, an activity that was not economic. Regulation of economic activity is required in order to survive constitutional scrutiny under the Commerce Clause.

CASE SUMMARY

If I Don't Buy Something, Is That Economic Activity Congress Can Regulate?

FACTS: Congress passed the Patient Protection and Affordable Care Act (also known as Obama Care) in order to increase the number of Americans covered by health insurance and decrease the cost of health care. One key provision in the law was the individual mandate, which requires most Americans to maintain "minimum essential" health insurance coverage. Attorneys general and businesses from several states challenged this requirement (and other provisions of the law) as being unconstitutional under the Commerce Clause. From a series of federal decisions from the courts below, some finding the law constitutional and others not, the affected parties appealed to the U.S. Supreme Court. The court granted *certiorari* and their cases were consolidated for review.

DECISION: The court faced a new commerce clause issue of whether the federal government could require citizens to purchase a good or service because the lack of health insurance affected commerce. In the 5-4 decision, the court concluded, "The individual mandate, however, does not regulate existing commercial activity. It instead compels individuals to *become* active in commerce by purchasing a product, on the ground that their failure to do so affects interstate commerce. Construing the Commerce Clause to permit Congress to regulate individuals precisely *because* they are doing nothing would open a new and potentially vast domain to congressional authority. Every day individuals do not do an infinite number of things. In some cases they decide not to do something; in others they simply fail to do it. Allowing Congress to justify federal regulation by pointing to the effect of inaction on commerce would bring countless decisions an individual could *potentially* make within the scope of federal regulation, and—under the Government's theory—empower Congress to make those decisions for him." [*National Federation of Independent Business v. Sebelius,* 132 S.Ct. 2566 (2012)] (Note: the law was still upheld)

(C) THE COMMERCE POWER AS A LIMITATION ON STATES. The federal power to regulate commerce not only gives Congress the power to act but also prevents states from acting in any way that interferes with federal regulation or burdens interstate commerce. **For Example,** if the federal government establishes safety device regulations for interstate carriers, a state cannot require different devices.

CASE SUMMARY

Minors in Maine and a Major Commerce Clause Decision

FACTS: Maine passed a law that prohibited anyone other than a Maine-licensed tobacco retailer from accepting an order for delivery of tobacco. The law required the retailer to arrange for delivery with a special receipt showing that someone over the age of 18 had received and signed for the tobacco products delivered. Out-of-state shippers and tobacco sellers challenged the law as one that favored Maine tobacco retailers. The state of Maine argued that its law was passed to prevent the public health hazard of minors becoming addicted to tobacco. The federal district court granted summary judgment for the shippers, and the court of appeals affirmed. The state of Maine appealed.

DECISION: In a 9 to 0 decision, the Court held that the Maine law may have been passed with health benefits in mind, but it clearly gave Maine businesses an economic benefit. In addition, other states had managed to fight teen smoking using programs other than discrimination between in-state and out-of-state tobacco retailers. [*Rowe v. New Hampshire Motor Transport Association* 552 U.S. 364 (2008)]

States may not use their tax power for the purpose of discriminating against interstate commerce. **For Example,** a state cannot impose a higher tax on goods imported from another state than it imposes on the same kind of goods produced in its own territory.

State regulations designed to advance local interests may conflict with the commerce clause. Such regulations are invalid. For example, suppose a state has a health concern about having milk properly processed. One way to address the concern is to require all milk to be processed in-state. Such a regulation clearly favors that state's businesses and imposes a great burden on out-of-state milk producers. Such a regulation would be an unconstitutional exercise of state power because the state could simply require all milk sellers to be licensed. Licensing would allow the state to check the milk-processing procedures of all firms and accomplish the safety goal without imposing such a burden on out-of-state firms.[11]

CASE SUMMARY

Whining about Wine

FACTS: Michigan and New York regulate the sale and importation of alcoholic beverages, including wine, through a three-tier distribution system. Separate licenses are required for producers, wholesalers, and retailers. Both New York and Michigan prohibit out-of-state wine producers from selling their wines directly to consumers there. In-state wineries can sell directly to consumers. The impact of the prohibition on the out-of-state wine producers is that they are required to pay wholesaler fees and thus cannot compete with in-state wine producers on direct-to-consumer sales.

The wine producers challenging the New York and Michigan statutes are small wineries that rely on direct consumer sales as an important part of their businesses. If they did business through wholesalers in the state, the price of their wines would have to be increased to a level that would be noncompetitive.

The district court granted summary judgment for the state of Michigan. The Sixth Circuit Court of Appeals reversed on the grounds that the out-of-state restrictions violated the commerce clause. The state of Michigan appealed. In the New York case, the district court found that the

[11] *Minnesota v. Clover Leaf Creamery,* 449 U.S. 456 (1981).

CASE SUMMARY

Continued

out-of-state restrictions violated the commerce clause, and the Second Circuit Court of Appeals reversed and upheld the New York statute as constitutional. The out-of-state wine producers appealed.

DECISION: State laws violate the commerce clause if they treat in-state and out-of-state economic interests differently with the result that one benefits and the other is burdened. The mere fact that a wine producer is not a resident of the state should not foreclose access to markets there. The Michigan statutes prohibiting out-of-state wineries from shipping wine directly to in-state consumers, but permitting in-state wineries to do so if licensed, discriminated against interstate commerce. New York statutes imposing additional burdens on out-of-state wineries seeking to ship wine directly to New York consumers discriminated against interstate commerce. The effect of both statutes was to favor in-state wine producers and create the economic Balkanization that the commerce clause was intended to prevent. Both statutes violated the commerce clause. [*Granholm v. Heald*, 544 U.S. 460 (2005)]

10. The Financial Powers

The financial powers of the federal government include the powers to tax and to borrow, spend, and coin money.

(A) THE TAXING POWER. The federal Constitution provides that "Congress shall have power to lay and collect taxes, duties, imposts and excises, to pay the debts and provide for the common defence and general welfare of the United States."[12] Subject to the express and implied limitations arising from the Constitution, the states may impose such taxes as they desire and as their own individual constitutions and statutes permit. In addition to express constitutional limitations, both national and local taxes are subject to the unwritten limitation that they be imposed for a public purpose. Taxes must also be apportioned. A business cannot be taxed for all of its revenues in all 50 states. There must be apportionment of taxes, and there must be sufficient connection with the state.[13]

CASE SUMMARY

A Quill in Your State Means Taxes in the Coffer

FACTS: Quill is a Delaware corporation with offices and warehouses in Illinois, California, and Georgia. None of its employees works or lives in North Dakota, and Quill owns no property in North Dakota.

Quill sells office equipment and supplies; it solicits business through catalogs and flyers, advertisements in national periodicals, and telephone calls. Its annual national sales exceed $200 million, of which almost $1 million are made to about 3,000 customers in North Dakota. The sixth-largest vendor of office supplies in the state, it delivers all of its merchandise to its North Dakota customers by mail or common carriers from out-of-state locations.

North Dakota requires every "retailer maintaining a place of business in" the state to collect the tax from the consumer and remit it to the state. In 1987, North Dakota amended its statutory definition of the term "retailer" to include "every person who engages in regular or systematic

---

[12] U.S. Const., Art 1, §8, cl 1. To read more of the U.S. Constitution, refer to Appendix 2, or go to **www.constitution.org** and click on "Founding Documents."
[13] *Polar Tankers, Inc. v. City of Valdez, Alaska*, 557 U.S. 1 (2009).

CASE SUMMARY

Continued

solicitation of a consumer market in the state." State regulations in turn define "regular or systematic solicitation" to mean three or more advertisements within a 12-month period.

Quill argued that North Dakota does not have the power to compel it to collect a use tax from its North Dakota customers. North Dakota filed suit to require Quill to pay taxes (as well as interest and penalties) on all such sales made after July 1, 1987. The trial court ruled in Quill's favor.

The North Dakota Supreme Court reversed, and Quill appealed.

DECISION: The Court held that the issue is one of whether the company has intentionally placed itself within a state. Whether it does so with offices and salespeople or deluges the citizens with catalogs is irrelevant. So long as the company has voluntarily placed itself within the state, the taxation is neither unfair nor unconstitutional. However, the Court also held that under the Commerce Clause the exercise of the taxing authority placed an undue burden on commerce and retailers such as Quill and that the standard of presence in the state through property or personnel was required to impose taxes. The decision was reversed. [*Quill v. North Dakota*, **504 U.S. 298 (1992)**]

(B) **THE SPENDING POWER.** The federal government may use tax money and borrowed money "to pay the debts and provide for the common defence and general welfare of the United States."[14]

(C) **THE BANKING POWER.** The Constitution is liberally interpreted to allow the federal government to create banks and to regulate banks created under state laws. **For Example,** the Federal Reserve System is responsible for this regulatory oversight of banks.

E. CONSTITUTIONAL LIMITATIONS ON GOVERNMENT

The constitutional limitations discussed in the following sections afford protections of rights for both persons and businesses.

11. Due Process

The power of government is limited by both the Fifth and Fourteenth Amendments to the Constitution. Those amendments respectively prohibit the national government and state governments from depriving any person "of life, liberty, or property without due process of law."[15]

due process clause — a guarantee of protection against the loss of property or rights without the chance to be heard.

(A) **WHEN DUE PROCESS RIGHTS ARISE.** As a result of liberal interpretation of the Constitution, the **due process clause** now provides a guarantee of protection against the loss of property or rights without the chance to be heard. These amendments also guarantee that all citizens are given the same protections. **For Example,** the Supreme Court has extended the due process clause to protect the record or standing of a student.[16] A student cannot lose credit in a course or be suspended or expelled without some form of a hearing.

quasi-judicial proceedings — forms of hearings in which the rules of evidence and procedure are more relaxed but each side still has a chance to be heard.

Because there are so many areas in which due process rights exist and require a chance to be heard, speeding up due process has resulted in the creation of **quasi-judicial**

---

[14] U.S. Const., Art 1, §8, cl 1. See **www.constitution.org**, or Appendix 2.

[15] For more information on the language of the Fifth and Fourteenth Amendments, see the U.S. Constitution in Appendix 2, or go to **www.constitution.org**.

[16] That is, a student cannot be expelled without a chance to have his or her side of the story reviewed.

E-Commerce & Cyberlaw

Internet and Interstate

Collection of sales tax from Internet stores has been a stickler of an issue for businesses, state revenue officials, and the U.S. Supreme Court. All three were grappling with how to collect, what to collect, and whether anybody had any authority to collect. Internet sales represent a large, untapped source of revenue. A study from the Center for Business and Economic Research at the University of Tennessee estimates the lost tax revenue from untaxed Internet sales as $30 billion in 2011.

The merchants involved fell into several different legal groups in terms of their theories on whether tax was owed and whether they should just pay it, with or without the states having the authority to tax:

1. Those stores with physical presences in states (Wal-Mart and J.C. Penney) that just collected sales tax as if they were collecting it in a store in that state where the Internet purchaser was located

2. Those stores without a physical presence (Amazon) that did collect taxes, particularly in those states known for taking a hard-line approach

3. Those stores without a physical presence that do not collect taxes and maintain that it is unconstitutional to do so

4. Those stores with or without a physical presence that have collected taxes but held them until everyone could figure out the legal status of the companies.

What are the constitutional issues in this taxation question?

Note: Amazon.com filed suit in 2011 in nine states challenging their laws on collection of taxes from Amazon when it has no physical presence in those states. In July, 2012, some of the suits were settled. Amazon collected taxes now in Kentucky, New York, North Dakota, Texas, and Washington, and it will collect taxes in eight more states.

Source: Stu Woo, "Amazon Battles States Over Sales Tax," *Wall Street Journal*, August 3, 2011, p. A1.

proceedings. In these types of proceedings, the parties need not go through the complex, lengthy, and formal procedures of a trial (described in Chapter 2). Rather, these proceedings have a hearing officer or administrative law judge (see Chapter 6) who conducts an informal hearing in which the rules of evidence and procedure are relaxed.

For Example, a student taking a grade grievance beyond a faculty member's decision will generally have his case heard by a panel of faculty and students as established by college or university rules. An employer appealing its unemployment tax rate will have the appeal heard by an administrative law judge.

(B) WHAT CONSTITUTES DUE PROCESS? Due process does not require a trial on every issue of rights. Shortcut procedures, such as grade grievance panels, have resulted as a compromise for providing the right to be heard along with a legitimate desire to be expeditious in resolving these issues.

12. Equal Protection of the Law

The Constitution prohibits the states and the national government from denying any person the equal protection of the law.[17] This guarantee prohibits a government from treating one person differently from another when there is no reasonable ground for classifying them differently.

(A) REASONABLE CLASSIFICATION. Whether a classification is reasonable depends on whether the nature of the classification bears a reasonable relation to the wrong to be remedied or to the object to be attained by the law. The judicial trend is to permit

---

[17] U.S. Constitution, Fourteenth Amendment as to the states; modern interpretation of due process clause of the Fifth Amendment as to national government. Congress adopted the Civil Rights Act to implement the concept of equal protection.

the classification to stand as long as there is a rational basis for the distinction made.[18] Whether a rational basis exists is determined by answering whether the lawmaking body has been arbitrary or capricious.

The equal protection clause is the basis of many of the U.S. Supreme Court's most complicated decisions. **For Example,** during the 2000 presidential election, the U.S. Supreme Court faced an issue of equal protection with regard to the challenge then–vice president and presidential candidate Al Gore made to the undervotes in Florida's ballots. However, then–presidential candidate George W. Bush argued that counting the undervotes in some counties and not in others and applying different standards for counting or not counting the infamous dimpled chads, hanging chads, and other undervotes was unconstitutional because it deprived other Florida voters of equal protection because each vote is intended to count equally. Recounts in only some counties while using varying standards resulted in some counties being given greater weight in Florida's presidential election. The U.S. Supreme Court agreed in a 7–2 decision that the recounts were unconstitutional on equal protection grounds.[19] However, the justices split 5–4 on the correct remedy for the unconstitutional recounts.

(B) Improper Classification. Laws that make distinctions in the regulation of business, the right to work, and the right to use or enjoy property on the basis of race, national origin, or religion are invalid. Also invalid are laws that impose restrictions on some, but not all, persons without any justification for the distinction.[20] **For Example,** a state statute taxing out-of-state insurance companies at a higher rate than in-state insurance companies violates the equal protection clause.[21]

13. Privileges and Immunities

The U.S. Constitution declares that "the citizens of each state shall be entitled to all privileges and immunities of citizens in the several states."[22] The so-called **privileges and immunities clause** means that a person going into another state is entitled to make contracts, own property, and engage in business to the same extent as the citizens of that state. **For Example,** a state cannot bar someone who comes from another state from engaging in local business or from obtaining a hunting or fishing license merely because the person is not a resident of that state.

14. Protection of the Person

The Constitution has no general provision declaring that the government shall not impair rights of persons. The Constitution does not mention the phrase "unalienable right" that was part of the Declaration of Independence.[23] However, the Bill of Rights, the first 10 amendments to the Constitution, does provide protections for freedom of speech, jury trials, and freedom of religion and association.[24] The Bill of Rights provides for the due process protections discussed

privileges and immunities clause – a clause that entitles a person going into another state to make contracts, own property, and engage in business to the same extent as citizens of that state.

[18] *Ileto v. Glock, Inc.*, 565 F.3d 1126 (9th Cir. 2006).

[19] *Bush v. Gore*, 531 U.S. 98 (2000).

[20] *Associated Industries of Missouri v. Lohman*, 511 U.S. 641 (1994).

[21] *Metropolitan Life Ins. Co. v. Ward*, 470 U.S. 869 (1985).

[22] U.S. Const., Art IV, §2, cl 1. See **www.constitution.org** and click on "Founding Documents" to access more language of the Constitution, or see Appendix 2.

[23] The term *unalienable right* is employed in reference to natural right, fundamental right, or basic right. Apart from the question of scope of coverage, the adjective *unalienable* emphasizes the fact that the people still possess the right rather than having surrendered or subordinated it to the will of society. The word *alien* is the term of the old common law for transferring title or ownership. Today, we would say *transfer* and, instead of saying unalienable rights, would say *nontransferable* rights. Unalienable rights of the people were therefore rights that the people not only possessed but also could not give up even if they wanted to. Thus, these rights are still owned by everyone. It is important to note that the Declaration of Independence actually uses the word "unalienable" when describing the rights eventually placed in the Constitution as Amendments I–X, the Bill of Rights, not "inalienable."

[24] *North Coast Women's Care Medical Group, Inc. v. San Diego County Superior Court*, 189 P.3d 959 (Ca. 2008).

earlier as well as those that prohibit unlawful searches and seizures. The Second Amendment provides for the right to keep and bear arms, an issue that has resulted in some conflicting decisions that the U.S. Supreme Court has begun to address.[25]

During the last six decades, the Supreme Court has been interpreting the rights in these amendments and has been finding constitutional protection for a wide array of rights of the person that are not expressly protected by the Constitution. **For Example,** judicial interpretations have concluded that the Constitution provides for the right of privacy, the right to marry the person one chooses,[26] protection from unreasonable zoning, protection of parental control, protection from discrimination because of poverty, and protection from gender discrimination.[27]

15. The Bill of Rights and Businesses as Persons

The Bill of Rights provides protections for individuals and also for corporations. **For Example,** the Fourth Amendment (see Chapter 8) provides protections against unreasonable searches. Individuals enjoy that protection in their homes, and corporations enjoy that protection with their files, offices, and business records. Businesses also enjoy freedom of speech protections under the First Amendment. The First Amendment provides that "Congress shall make no law … abridging the freedom of speech …"[28]

The U.S. Supreme Court has clarified the free speech rights of business through classification of the types of business speech. One form of business or commercial speech is advertising. This form of speech in which businesses tout their products is subject to regulation and restriction on form, content, and placement, and such regulation has been deemed constitutional. (See Chapters 25 and 33 for more information on the regulation of advertising.) However, there are other forms of commercial speech. Businesses do have the right to participate in political processes such as creating political action committees and supporting or opposing ballot initiatives. Businesses often take positions and launch campaigns on ballot initiatives that will affect the taxes they will be required to pay. The courts are often balancing the power of corporate political speech, regulation of ads, and the right of corporations as citizens to speak.

CASE SUMMARY

The Case That Caused a Dust-Up between the President and a Justice

FACTS: In January 2008, Citizens United released a film entitled *Hillary: The Movie (Hillary),* a 90-minute documentary about then-senator Hillary Clinton, who was a candidate in the Democratic Party's 2008 presidential primary elections. Most of the commentators in the film were quite critical of Senator Clinton. *Hillary* was released in theaters and on DVD, but Citizens United wanted to increase distribution by making it available through video-on-demand.

Citizens United produced two 10-second ads and one 30-second ad for *Hillary.* Each ad included a short, pejorative statement about Senator Clinton, followed by the name of the movie and the movie's Web site address. Citizens United wanted to run the advertisements on broadcast and cable television. The Federal Election Commission (FEC) wanted to stop Citizens

---

[25] *District of Columbia v. Heller,* 554 U.S. 570 (2008).

[26] *Akron v. Akron Center for Reproductive Health, Inc.,* 462 U.S. 416 (1983); but see *Colorado v. Hill, cert.* granted, 527 US 1068 (2000). See also Snyder v. Phelps, 131 S.Ct. 1207 (2011). For more on commercial speech, see *Greater New Orleans Broadcasting Association, Inc., v. U.S.* 527 U.S. 173 (1999) and *U.S. v. Philip Morris USA Inc.,* 566 F.3d 1095 (D.C. Cir. 2009).

[27] In some cases, the courts have given the due process and equal protection clauses a liberal interpretation in order to find a protection of the person. *Davis v. Passman,* 442 U.S. 228 (1979) (due process); *Grutter v. Bollinger,* 530 U.S. 306 (2003) (equal protection).

[28] To read the full language of the First Amendment, go to Appendix 2, or to **www.constitution.org** and click on "Founding Documents."

CASE SUMMARY

Continued

United from running the ads and Citizens United brought suit, seeking a preliminary injunction against the FEC. The District Court denied Citizens United a preliminary injunction and granted the FEC summary judgment. Citizens United requested and was granted *certiorari*.

DECISION: The court held that the restrictions on running ads were unconstitutional as a prior restraint on speech as well as discrimination between and among speakers. The court held that requirements on disclosure of funding for ads was constitutional, an alternative to a ban on speech that was reasonable and allowed citizens to make their own determinations about the quality/bias of the speech (ads). President Obama spoke harshly of the decision in his State of the Union address in 2011, and Justice Samuel Alito mouthed, "Not true," in response to the president's remarks. [*Citizens United v. Federal Election Commission*, **558 U.S. 310 (2010)**]

Thinking Things Through

Sweating It Out on Free Speech

In 1996, Nike was inundated with allegations about its labor practices in shoe factories around the world. Nike responded to the negative reports and allegations with a series of releases, advertisements, and op-ed pieces in newspapers around the country. *New York Times* columnist Bob Herbert wrote two columns that were sharply critical of Nike's conditions in plants throughout Asia. The columns compared then-CEO Philip Knight's compensation with the $2.20 per day wages of Nike workers in Indonesia.

After the columns appeared, CEO Knight wrote a letter to the editor in response to them. In that letter, he wrote, "Nike has paid, on average, double the minimum wage as defined in countries where its products are produced under contract. History shows that the best way out of poverty for such countries is through exports of light manufactured goods that provide the base for more skilled production."*

Marc Kasky filed suit against Nike in California, alleging that the op-ed pieces and letters in response to negative op-ed pieces about

*Roger Parloff, "Can We Talk?" *Fortune*, September 2, 2002, 102–110.

Nike violated the False Advertising Act of California. The act permits state agencies to take action to fine corporate violators of the act as well as to obtain remedies such as injunctions to halt the ads.

Nike challenged the suit on the grounds that such an interpretation and application of the advertising regulation violated its rights of free speech. The lower court agreed with Kasky and held that the advertising statute applied to Nike's defense of its labor practices, even on the op-ed pages of newspapers. The California Supreme Court, 45 P.3d 243 (Cal. 2002), ruled that Nike could be subject to regulatory sanctions for false advertising. Nike appealed to the U.S. Supreme Court. Should Nike's editorial be protected by the First Amendment? Discuss where this type of speech fits.

The opinion handed down in this case is only one sentence: "The writ of *certiorari* is dismissed as improvidently granted." 539 U.S. 645 (2003). Nike settled the case. Is this letter protected speech? Does the California statute, as applied to Nike's op-ed letters, violate the First Amendment?

LawFlix

The Candidate (1972) (PG)

The movie depicts an idealist running for office who finds himself caught in the political process of fundraising, image-building, and winning. A number of scenes with speeches, fundraising, and principles in conflict provide excellent discussion issues with respect to government structure, the First Amendment, and campaign contributions.

MAKE THE CONNECTION

SUMMARY

The U.S. Constitution created the structure of our national government and gave it certain powers. It also placed limitations on those powers. It created a federal system with a tripartite division of government and a bicameral national legislature.

The national government possesses some governmental powers exclusively, while both the states and the federal government share other powers. In areas of conflict, federal law is supreme.

The U.S. Constitution is not a detailed document. It takes its meaning from the way it is interpreted. In recent years, liberal interpretation has expanded the powers of the federal government. Among the powers of the federal government that directly affect business

are the power to regulate commerce; the power to tax and to borrow, spend, and coin money; and the power to own and operate businesses.

Among the limitations on government that are most important to business are the requirements of due process and the requirement of equal protection of the law. In addition, government is limited by the rights given to individuals such as freedom of speech, freedom of religion, and equal protection. The equal protection concept of the U.S. Constitution prohibits both the federal government and the state governments from treating one person differently from another unless there is a legitimate reason for doing so and unless the basis of classification is reasonable.

LEARNING OUTCOMES

After studying this chapter, you should be able to clearly explain:

A. The U.S. Constitution and the Federal System

L0.1   Describe the U.S. Constitution and the Federal System

See the discussion of the **tripartite** (three-part) government on p. 60.

B. The U.S. Constitution and the States

L0.2   Explain the relationship between the U.S. Constitution and the States

See the discussion of the federal system on p. 60.

See Figure 4-1 for an illustration of the delegation of powers.

C. Interpreting and Amending the Constitution

L0.3   Discuss interpreting and amending the Constitution

See the discussion of the bedrock and constructionist views on p. 63.

D. Federal Powers

L0.4   List and describe the significant federal powers

See the discussion of the commerce power on p. 65.

See the discussion of the taxing power on p. 68.

See the discussion of the banking power on p. 69.

E. Constitutional Limitations on Government

L0.5   Discuss constitutional limitations on governmental power

See the discussion of the Bill of Rights on p. 72.

See the discussion of the Fourth Amendment on p. 72.

See the discussion of due process starting on p. 69.

See the *For Example* discussion of a student taking a grade grievance beyond a faculty member's decision on p. 70.

KEY TERMS

bedrock view
bicameral
commerce clause
constitution
delegated powers
due process clause

executive branch
ex post facto laws
federal system
judicial branch
legislative branch
living-document view

police power
preemption
privileges and immunities clause
quasi-judicial proceedings
shared powers
tripartite

QUESTIONS AND CASE PROBLEMS

1. Federal law requires most interstate truckers to obtain a permit that reflects compliance with certain federal requirements. The 1965 version of the law authorized states to require proof that a truck operator had such a permit. By 1991, 39 states had demanded such proof, requiring a $10 per truck registration fee and giving each trucker a stamp to affix to a multistate "bingo card" carried in the vehicle. Finding this scheme inefficient and burdensome, Congress created the current Single State Registration System (SSRS), which allows a trucking company to fill out one set of forms in one state, thereby registering in every participating state through which its trucks travel.

   A subsection of Michigan's Motor Carrier Act imposes on truck companies operating in interstate commerce an annual fee of $100 for each self-propelled motor vehicle operated by or on behalf of the motor carrier. The American Truckers Association (ATA) and others challenged the $100 fee as preempted by the extensive federal regulation of interstate trucking and trucking companies. The ATA and others appealed to the U.S. Supreme Court. What should the U.S. Supreme Court do? Be sure to discuss what portion of the Constitution applies to this issue. [*American Trucking Associations, Inc. v. Michigan Public Service Com'n*, 545 U.S. 429]

2. J.C. Penney, a retail merchandiser, has its principal place of business in Plano, Texas. It operates retail stores in all 50 states, including 10 stores in Massachusetts, and a direct mail catalog business. The catalogs illustrated merchandise available for purchase by mail order. The planning, artwork, design, and layout for these catalogs were completed and paid for outside of Massachusetts, primarily in Texas, and Penney contracted with independent printing companies located outside Massachusetts to produce the catalogs. The three major catalogs were generally printed in Indiana, while the specialty catalogs were printed in South Carolina and Wisconsin. Penney supplied the printers with paper, shipping wrappers, and address labels for the catalogs; the printers supplied the ink, binding materials, and labor. None of these materials was purchased in Massachusetts. Printed catalogs, with address labels and postage affixed, were transported by a common carrier from the printer to a U.S. Postal Service office located outside Massachusetts, where they were sent to Massachusetts addressees via third- or fourth-class mail. Any undeliverable catalogs were returned to Penney's distribution center in Connecticut.

   Purchases of catalog merchandise were made by telephoning or returning an order form to Penney at a location outside Massachusetts, and the merchandise was shipped to customers from a Connecticut distribution center. The Massachusetts Department of Revenue audited Penney in 1995 and assessed a use tax, penalty, and interest on the catalogs that had been shipped into Massachusetts. The position of the department was that there was a tax due of $314,674.62 on the catalogs that were used by Penney's Massachusetts customers. Penney said such a tax was unconstitutional in that it had no control or contact with the catalogs in the state. Can the state impose the tax? Why or why not? [*Commissioner of Revenue v. J.C. Penney Co., Inc.*, 730 N.E.2d 266 (Mass)]

3. Alfonso Lopez, Jr., a 12th-grade student at Edison High School in San Antonio, Texas, went to school carrying a concealed .38-caliber handgun and five bullets. School officials, acting on an anonymous tip, confronted Lopez. Lopez admitted that he had

the gun. He was arrested and charged with violation of federal law, the Gun-Free School Zones Act of 1990. Lopez moved to dismiss his indictment on the grounds that the provision of the Gun-Free School Zones Act with which he was charged was unconstitutional in that it was beyond the power of Congress to legislate controls over public schools. The district court found the statute to be a constitutional exercise of congressional authority.

Lopez was found guilty and sentenced to two years in prison. He appealed and challenged his conviction on the basis of the commerce clause. The Court of Appeals agreed with Lopez, found the Gun-Free School Zones Act an unconstitutional exercise of congressional authority, and reversed the conviction. The U.S. Attorney appealed. Who should win at the U.S. Supreme Court and why? [*United States v. Lopez*, 514 U.S. 549]

4. The University of Wisconsin requires all of its students to pay, as part of their tuition, a student activity fee. Those fees are used to support campus clubs and activities. Some students who objected to the philosophies and activities of some of the student clubs filed suit to have the fees halted. What constitutional basis do you think they could use for the suit? [*Board of Regents of Wisconsin System v. Southworth*, 529 U.S. 217]

5. The Crafts' home was supplied with gas by the city gas company. Because of some misunderstanding, the gas company believed that the Crafts were delinquent in paying their gas bill. The gas company had an informal complaint procedure for discussing such matters, but the Crafts had never been informed that such a procedure was available. The gas company notified the Crafts that they were delinquent and that the company was shutting off the gas. The Crafts brought an action to enjoin the gas company from doing so on the theory that a termination without any hearing was a denial of due process. The lower courts held that the interest of the Crafts in receiving gas was not a property interest protected by the due process clause and that the procedures the gas company followed satisfied the requirements of due

process. The Crafts appealed. Were they correct in contending that they had been denied due process of law? Why or why not? [*Memphis Light, Gas and Water Division v. Craft*, 436 U.S. 1]

6. In 2002, the Williamson family, riding in their 1993 Mazda minivan, was struck head-on by another vehicle. Thanh Williamson was sitting in a rear aisle seat, wearing a lap belt; she died in the accident. Delbert and Alexa Williamson were wearing lap-and-shoulder belts; they survived. Thanh's estate brought suit in a California state court to recover from Mazda for her wrongful death. The basis of the suit was that Mazda should have installed lap-and-shoulder belts on all seats, including the rear aisle seats, and that Thanh died because Mazda equipped her seat with only a lap belt instead. Federal safety requirements do not require lap-and-shoulder belts except for seats located next to doors and windows. Middle seats (aisle) can have a lap belt only. Mazda asked for a dismissal on the grounds that allowing Thanh's estate to recover would contradict federal law and that federal law preempts state tort laws on product liability. The trial court dismissed the suit as preempted by federal law, and the Court of Appeal affirmed. The U.S. Supreme Court granted *certiorari*. What should the court decide and why? [*Williamson v. Mazda Motor of America, Inc.* 131 S. Ct. 1131]

7. Montana imposed a severance tax on every ton of coal mined within the state. The tax varied depending on the value of the coal and the cost of production. It could be as high as 30 percent of the price at which the coal was sold. Montana mine operators and some out-of-state customers claimed that this tax was unconstitutional as an improper burden on interstate commerce. Decide. [*Commonwealth Edison Co. v. Montana*, 453 U.S. 609]

8. Ollie's Barbecue is a family-owned restaurant in Birmingham, Alabama, specializing in barbecued meats and homemade pies, with a seating capacity of 220 customers. It is located on a state highway 11 blocks from an interstate highway and a somewhat greater distance from railroad and bus stations. The restaurant caters to a family and white-collar trade, with a take-out service for

"Negroes." (Note: This term is used by the Court in its opinion in the case.) In the 12 months preceding the passage of the Civil Rights Act, the restaurant purchased locally approximately $150,000 worth of food, $69,683 or 46 percent of which was meat that it bought from a local supplier who had procured it from outside the state. Ollie's has refused to serve Negroes in its dining accommodations since opening in 1927, and since July 2, 1964, it has been operating in violation of the Civil Rights Act. A lower court concluded that if it were required to serve Negroes, it would lose a substantial amount of business. The lower court found that the Civil Rights Act did not apply because Ollie's was not involved in "interstate commerce." Will the commerce clause permit application of the Civil Rights Act to Ollie's? [*Katzenbach v. McClung*, 379 U.S. 294]

9. Ellis was employed by the city of Lakewood. By the terms of his contract, he could be discharged only for cause. After working for six years, he was told that he was going to be discharged because of his inability to generate safety and self-insurance programs, because of his failure to win the confidence of employees, and because of his poor attendance. He was not informed of the facts in support of these conclusions and was given the option to resign. He claimed that he was entitled to a hearing. Is he entitled to one? Why or why not? [*Ellis v. City of Lakewood*, 789 P.2d 449 (Colo. App.)]

10. The Federal Food Stamp Act provided for the distribution of food stamps to needy households. In 1971, section 3(e) of the statute was amended to define households as limited to groups whose members were all related to each other. This was done because of congressional dislike for the lifestyles of unrelated hippies who were living together in hippie communes. Moreno and others applied for food stamps but were refused them because the relationship requirement was not satisfied. An action was brought to have the relationship requirement declared unconstitutional. Is it constitutional? Discuss why or why not. [*USDA v. Moreno*, 413 U.S. 528]

11. New Hampshire adopted a tax law that in effect taxed the income of nonresidents working in New Hampshire only. Austin, a nonresident who worked in New Hampshire, claimed that the tax law was invalid. Was he correct? Explain. [*Austin v. New Hampshire*, 420 U.S. 656]

12. Gladys Mensing and other patients took the generic version of metoclopramide over a long period a time, which resulted in serious neurological damage. Ms. Mensing and others filed suit against the generic manufacturers under the Louisiana Products Liability Act. They alleged that despite mounting evidence of the connection between long-term use of metoclopramide and neurological damage, the manufacturers did not change their labels to provide warnings. The generic drug manufacturers argued that federal statutes and FDA regulations require generic manufacturers to use the same safety standards and labeling as their brand-name counterparts. They argued that it was impossible to simultaneously comply with both federal law and any state tort-law duty that required them to use a different label. What section of the U.S. Constitution will be used to resolve this issue? How will the court decide whether the manufacturers can be held liable? [*PLIVA, Inc. v. Mensing*, 131 S.Ct. 2567]

13. California passed a law that prohibited the sale or rental of "violent video games." The act defined violent video games as games "in which the range of options available to a player includes killing, maiming, dismembering, or sexually assaulting an image of a human being, if those acts are depicted" in a manner that "[a] reasonable person, considering the game as a whole, would find appeals to a deviant or morbid interest of minors." The association of video game manufacturers and developers brought suit, challenging the California statute as an unconstitutional violation of their First Amendment right and a violation of their due process rights because it is so vague. What should the U.S. Supreme Court hold on the constitutionality of the statute and why? [*Brown v. Entertainment Merchants Ass'n*, 131 S.Ct. 2729]

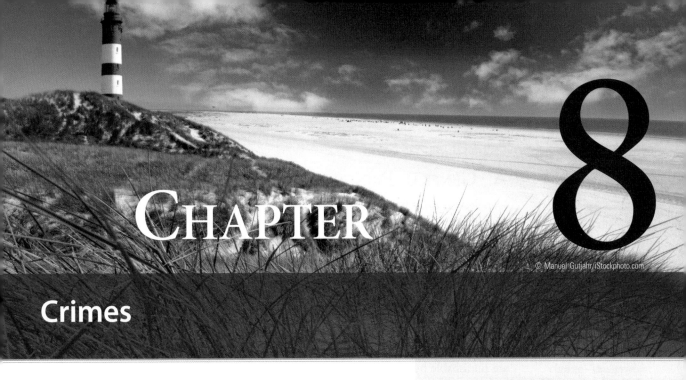

© Manuel Gutjahr/iStockphoto.com

CHAPTER 8

Crimes

learningoutcomes

After studying this chapter, you should be able to

LO.1 Discuss the nature and classification of crimes

LO.2 Describe the basis of criminal liability

LO.3 Identify who is responsible for criminal acts

LO.4 Explain the penalties for crimes and the sentencing for corporate crimes

LO.5 List examples of white-collar crimes and their elements

LO.6 Describe the common law crimes

LO.7 Discuss crimes related to computers

LO.8 Describe the rights of businesses charged with crimes and the constitutional protections afforded them

S ociety sets certain standards of conduct and punishes a breach of those standards as a crime. This chapter introduces the means by which government protects people and businesses from prohibited conduct.

A. General Principles

Detailed criminal codes and statutes define crimes and specify their punishment. Crimes vary from state to state but still show the imprint of a common law background through similar elements and structure.

1. Nature and Classification of Crimes

crime – violation of the law that is punished as an offense against the state or government.

misdemeanor – criminal offense with a sentence of less than one year that is neither treason nor a felony.

felony – criminal offense that is punishable by confinement in prison for more than one year or by death, or that is expressly stated by statute to be a felony.

A **crime** is conduct that is prohibited and punished by a government. Crimes are classified as *common law* or *statutory* according to their origin. Offenses punishable by less than one year in prison are called **misdemeanors**. More serious crimes are called **felonies**, including serious business crimes such as bribery and embezzlement, which are punishable by confinement in prison for more than one year. Misdemeanors include weighing goods with uninspected scales or operating without a sales tax license. An act may be a felony in one state and a misdemeanor in another.[1]

2. Basis of Criminal Liability

A crime generally consists of two elements: (1) a mental state (scienter or intent) and (2) an act or omission. Harm may occur as a result of a crime, but harm is not an essential element of a crime.

(A) Mental State. Mental state, or intent, does not require an awareness or knowledge of guilt. In most crimes, the voluntary commission of the act is sufficient for proving mental state. Ignorance that a law is being broken does not mean there is not mental state. **For Example,** dumping waste without a permit is still a criminal act even when the party releasing the waste did not know about the permit requirement.

(B) Act or Omission. Specific statutes define the conduct that, when coupled with sufficient mental state, constitutes a crime. **For Example,** writing a check knowing you do not have the funds available is a crime. Likewise, the failure to file your annual income tax returns is also a crime.

3. Responsibility for Criminal Acts

In some cases, persons who did not necessarily commit the criminal act itself are still held criminally responsible for acts committed by others.

(A) Corporate Liability. Corporations are held responsible for the acts of their employees. A corporation may also be held liable for crimes based on the failure of its employees to act. In the past decade, some of the nation's largest corporations have paid fines for crimes based on employees' failure to take action or for the

---

[1] Some states further define crimes by seriousness with different degrees of a crime, such as first-degree murder, second-degree murder, and so on. Misdemeanors may be differentiated by giving special names to minor misdemeanors.

CASE SUMMARY

Making Stuff Up for the Grand Jury

FACTS: Kathryn Erickson was the general manager of the Uintah Special Services District (USSD), an entity created to use federal-mineral-lease revenues for road projects. She, along with her secretary, Cheryl McCurdy, administered the USSD from a small office in Vernal, Utah. Ms. Erickson's authority was limited and she was not permitted to enter into or modify contracts for or to expend more than $1,000 of USSD funds, without board approval.

Mitchell Construction was a major contractor for USSD. In 1998, USSD awarded Mitchell Construction a contract to haul gravel from a site called Hamaker Bottoms and another contract to carry out small asphalt-paving projects. Both contracts were to be completed within the 1998 construction year.

During 1999 and 2000 Mitchell Construction continued to perform work on the projects covered by its 1998 contracts with USSD, despite their expiration. It submitted invoices to USSD and was paid for this work.

In June 1999 a federal grand jury began to investigate contracting irregularities at USSD and the Uintah County Road Department and issued a *subpoena duces tecum* to USSD requesting copies of "project contracts, invoices" between USSD and contractors.

While the office was preparing the response for the grand jury subpoena, Ms. McCurdy saw Ms. Erickson prepare a handwritten change order for the Hamaker Bottoms contract and saw Ms. Erickson and Gilman N. Mitchell both sign it. The change order, which was backdated to January 13, 1999, extended the contract through December 31, 2000.

Ms. McCurdy later discovered that two other change orders had been created and backdated. She spent a day copying documents for the grand jury and recording, on a handwritten list, all of the documents that she had copied. However, she left Ms. Erickson in the office while she was working on the list in order to go home for dinner. Ms. Erickson called her and told her not to come back because all the copying was done. Later, Ms. McCurdy found on Ms. Erickson's desk a photocopy of the grand jury document list and saw that two entries not in her handwriting had been added. These entries were for change orders for contracts between Mitchell Construction and USSD. Ms. McCurdy reported the change to the government.

Ms. Erickson and Mr. Mitchell were each indicted by a grand jury in the U.S. District Court for the District of Utah on three counts of obstruction of justice by knowingly falsifying a document with the knowledge and intent that the grand jury would rely on it.

The jury returned a verdict of guilty against both Ms. Erickson and Mr. Mitchell on all three counts. The two appealed.

DECISION: The court affirmed the decision. There are three requirements for conviction of obstruction of justice: (1) There must be a pending judicial proceeding; (2) the defendant must have knowledge or notice of the pending proceeding; and (3) the defendant must have acted corruptly with the specific intent to obstruct or impede the administration of justice. The two had backdated the documents in order to cover up the fact that the contracts had expired. They had continued the contracts without authority and authorized or received payments above the $1,000 limit. They were responding to a grand jury subpoena and gave it false change orders. They did so in order to protect Ms. Erickson's job and Mr. Mitchell's company's contracts and relationship with USSD. [*U.S. v. Erickson,* **561 F.3d 1150 (10th Cir. 2009)**]

actions they did take. **For Example,** Siemens, an international company, paid the largest fine in the history of the Foreign Corrupt Practices Act for paying bribes in order to win contracts in countries around the world, a total of $1.6 billion in fines, including $350 million in the United States.

(B) OFFICERS AND AGENTS OF CORPORATIONS. One of the main differences between nonbusiness and business crimes is that more people in a company can be convicted for the same business crime. For nonbusiness crimes, only those who are actually involved in the act itself can be convicted of the crime. For business crimes, however, managers of firms whose employees commit criminal acts can be held liable if the managers authorized the conduct of the employees or knew about their conduct and did nothing or failed to act reasonably in their supervisory positions to prevent the employees from engaging in criminal conduct. **For Example,** the former security chief for Massey Mines was sentenced to three years in prison after being found guilty of notifying employees in advance of the arrival of federal mine inspectors at the company's mines.[2]

(C) FEDERAL LAWS TARGETING OFFICER AND DIRECTOR CRIMINAL RESPONSIBILITY. Following the Michael Milken and Ivan Boesky junk bond era on Wall Street in 1988, the Insider Trading and Securities Fraud Act of 1988 increased the criminal penalties for officers and directors who violated the law tenfold. In addition, the "white-collar kingpin" law imposed mandatory minimum sentences for corporate officers. Sarbanes-Oxley, which followed the 2000-era dot-com failures increased penalties for officers and directors from 5 years to 20 years, along with an increase in fines by 20 times. Under The Dodd-Frank Wall Street Reform and Consumer Protection Act, the types of white-collar executives covered under criminal laws increased to include brokers, insurers, and any financial services firms.

So-called "honest services" fraud has been refined by Dodd-Frank and court decisions.[3] Executives can no longer be convicted on the basis that something went wrong at their company. Proof of fraud requires something more than an officer just being an officer at the company—there must be active engagement in operations that led to the officer's committing fraud.

CASE SUMMARY

Rats in the Warehouse and a CEO with a Fine

FACTS: Acme Markets, Inc., was a national food retail chain headquartered in Philadelphia. John R. Park was president of Acme, which, in 1970, employed 36,000 people and operated 16 warehouses.

In 1970, the Food and Drug Administration (FDA) forwarded a letter to Park describing, in detail, problems with rodent infestation in Acme's Philadelphia warehouse facility. In December 1971, the FDA found the same types of conditions in Acme's Baltimore warehouse facility. In January 1972, the FDA's chief of compliance for its Baltimore office wrote to Park about the inspection:

> We note with much concern that the old and new warehouse areas used for food storage were actively and extensively inhabited by live rodents. Of even more concern was the observation that such reprehensible conditions obviously existed for a prolonged period of time without any detection, or were completely ignored.
>
> We trust this letter will serve to direct your attention to the seriousness of the problem and formally advise you of the urgent need to initiate whatever measures are necessary to prevent recurrence and ensure compliance with the law.

[2] Ken Maher, "Ex-Massey Official Gets Three Years," *Wall Street Journal*, March 1, 2012, p. A3.
[3] *Skilling v. U.S.* 130 S.Ct. 2896 (2010).

CASE SUMMARY

Continued

After Park received the letter, he met with the vice president for legal affairs for Acme and was assured that he was "investigating the situation immediately and would be taking corrective action."

When the FDA inspected the Baltimore warehouse in March 1972, there was some improvement in the facility, but there was still rodent infestation. Acme and Park were both charged with violations of the federal Food, Drug and Cosmetic Act. Acme pleaded guilty. Park was convicted and fined $500; he appealed.

DECISION: Officers of a corporation can be held criminally liable for the conduct of others within the company if it can be shown that the officers knew of the issue and failed to take the steps necessary to eliminate the criminal activity. In this case, Park had been warned and had been given several opportunities to remedy the problem. Part of his responsibility as an officer is following up to be certain that tasks he has assigned are completed. Failure to follow through can be a basis for criminal liability. [*United States v. Park,* 421 U.S. 658 (1975)]

(D) PENALTY FOR CRIME: FORFEITURE. When a defendant is convicted of a crime, the court may also declare that the defendant's rights in any property used or gained from a crime (an instrument of that crime) be confiscated. Some types of instruments of the crime are automatically forfeited, such as the tools of a crime. **For Example,** the U.S. government confiscated from confessed $50-billion-Ponzi schemer, Bernie Madoff, everything from his yacht to his bank accounts to his seat on NASDAQ. Confiscation is, in effect, an increased penalty for the defendant's crime.

(E) PENALTIES FOR BUSINESS AND WHITE-COLLAR CRIMES. Most common law criminal penalties were created with "natural" persons in mind, as opposed to "artificial" or corporate persons. A $100,000 fine may be significant to an individual but to a corporation with $3 billion in assets and hundreds of millions in income, such a fine could be viewed as a minimal cost of doing business.

As a result of these fine amount realities, corporate penalties and processes have been reformed. Congress, prosecutors, and the courts are in a continual processes of developing penalties for corporations and white-collar crimes so that the result is both a deterrent effect as well as changes in cultures of corporations to prevent additional violations.

(E)(1) COMPUTING NEW PENALTIES FOR CORPORATIONS. Criminal penalties have been increased to allow judges to fine corporations according to how much a bad decision would cost. For example, if a company develops a faulty product, net earnings could decline 10 to 20 percent. Criminal penalties can be assessed as a percentage of net income.

Rather than using fixed-amount fines for corporations, statutes and courts apply percentage of revenue penalties. **For Example,** a bad decision on a product line would cost a company 10 percent to 20 percent of its earnings. A criminal penalty could be imposed in the same percentage fashion with the idea that the company simply made a bad legal decision that should be reflected in earnings.

(E)(2) CORPORATE INTEGRITY AGREEMENTS. Using a corporate integrity agreement (CIA), judges are able to, in effect, place corporations on probation. Under CIAS, companies are assigned monitors who are on-site and follow up to be sure the company is not committing any further violations. **For Example,** because of environmental law violations, ConEd was assigned a monitor from the National

Resources Defense Council to observe the company's activities. CIAS do not require an admission of guilt, but generally require the payment of a fine and an agreement to "stay clean" for three to five years.

(E)(3) FEDERAL SENTENCING GUIDELINES. Another change in penalties for business and white-collar crimes has been the requirement for mandatory prison sentences for officers and directors who are convicted of crimes committed as they led their corporations. The human element of the corporation is then punished for the crimes that the business committed. The U.S. Sentencing Commission, established by Congress in 1984, has developed both federal sentencing guidelines and a carrot-and-stick approach to fighting business crime. If the managers of a company are involved and working to prevent criminal misconduct in the company and a crime occurs, the guidelines permit sentence reductions for the managers' efforts. If the managers do not adequately supervise conduct and do not encourage compliance with the law, the guidelines require judges to impose harsher sentences and fines. The guidelines, referred to as the **Federal Sentencing Guidelines** (or the *U.S. Sentencing Guidelines*), apply to federal crimes such as securities fraud, antitrust violations, racketeering, theft (embezzlement), Medicare fraud, and other business crimes. The sentencing guidelines permit a judge to place a guilty company on probation, with the length of the probation controlled by whether the company had prevention programs in place.

Federal Sentencing Guidelines – federal standards used by judges in determining mandatory sentence terms for those convicted of federal crimes.

(E)(4) MANDATORY SENTENCES FOR OFFICERS OF CORPORATIONS WHO MASTERMIND CRIMES. Following the collapse of companies such as Enron, WorldCom, and Adelphia, the U.S. Sentencing Commission (USSC) piloted the passage of the 2001 Economic Crime Package: Consolidation, Clarification, and Certainty. Amended guidelines, post-Enron, address the increased corporate and white-collar criminal penalties enacted under Sarbanes-Oxley (SOX) (see (E)(5) for more discussion of SOX), and consider the seriousness of the offense, the company's history of violations, its cooperation in the investigation, the effectiveness of its compliance program (often called an *ethics program*), and the role of senior management in the wrongdoing. Corporate managers found to have masterminded any criminal activity must be sentenced to prison time.[4] Figure 8-1 is a summary of the current penalties for federal crimes. Under a U.S. Supreme Court decision in 2005, *U.S. v. Booker,* judges may only use the guidelines as just that, guidelines; the sentencing ranges are no longer mandatory for judges.[5] Going outside those ranges, however, is carefully reviewed by appellate courts.[6] Federal judges can consider only evidence presented at trial in making their sentencing determinations. They can consider evidence of prior convictions, but only if that evidence was presented at trial or if the defendant has a chance to present evidence about those convictions at the sentencing.[7]

White-Collar Crime Penalty Enhancement Act of 2002 – federal reforms passed as a result of the collapses of companies such as Enron; provides for longer sentences and higher fines for both executives and companies.

(E)(5) SARBANES-OXLEY REFORMS TO CRIMINAL PENALTIES. Part of SOX, passed by Congress following the collapses of Enron and WorldCom corporations, was the **White-Collar Crime Penalty Enhancement Act of 2002**.[8] This act increases penalties substantially. **For Example,** the penalties for mail and wire fraud are increased from a maximum of 5 years to a maximum of 20 years. Penalties for violation of pension laws increased from 1 year to 10 years and the fines increased from $5,000 to $100,000.[9] In addition, many

---

[4] *U.S. v. Booker,* 543 U.S. 220 (2005).
[5] *U.S. v. Skilling,* 554 F.3d 529 (5th Cir. 2009).
[6] *Gall v. U.S.,* 552 U.S. 38 (2007).
[7] Miriam H. Baer, "Choosing Punishment," 92 *Boston Univ. Law Rev.* 577 (2010).
[8] 18 U.S.C. §1314 *et seq.*
[9] 18 U.S.C. §§1341 and 1343; 29 U.S.C. §1131.

FIGURE 8-1	*Roster of White-Collar Criminal Charges*

COMPANY/PERSON	ISSUE	STATUS
Andrew Fastow, former CFO of Enron (2004)	Multimillion-dollar earnings from serving as principal in SPEs of Enron created to keep debts off the company books; significant sales of shares during the time frame preceding company collapse	Resigned as CFO; appeared before Congress and took the Fifth Amendment; entered guilty plea to securities and wire fraud; sentence of 6 years; reduced to five years and 3 months; completed at the end of 2012
Galleon Group (hedge fund 2011) A Goldman Sachs director who fed information to Galleon Group was also convicted of insider trading.	Insider trading charges	Twenty-three executives, including CEO, convicted or entered guilty pleas; Galleon's $3.7 billion fund liquidated; CEO sentenced to 11 years
Bernie Ebbers (2005) Former CEO, WorldCom	Fraud	Convicted; sentenced to 25 years
Computer Associates (2004)	Criminal investigation for securities fraud and obstruction following $2.2 billion restatement in sales	Company paid $225 million fine; former CEO entered guilty plea to felony charges; sentenced to 11 years; Company changed name to CA, Inc.
Countrywide Mortgage (2009)	Insider trading; securities fraud	Former CEO Angelo Mozilo charged with insider trading, CFO and COO charged with failure to disclose firm's relaxed lending standards; settled cases for fines
Enron (2001)	Earnings overstated through mark-to-market accounting; off-the-book/special-purpose entities (SPEs) carried significant amounts of Enron debt not reflected in the financial statements; significant offshore SPEs (881 of 3,000 SPEs were offshore, primarily in Cayman Islands)	Company in bankruptcy; impetus for SOX; CFO Andrew Fastow and others entered guilty pleas; Jeffrey Skilling, former CEO, found guilty
HealthSouth (2003)	$2.7 billion accounting fraud; overstatement of revenues	16 former executives indicted; 5 plead guilty; see Richard Scrushy
KPMG (2006)	Tax shelter fraud	Settled by paying a penalty of $456 million fine in lieu of indictment; 16 former partners and employees indicted; most charges dismissed
L. Dennis Kozlowski, former CEO of Tyco (2003)	Accused of improper use of company funds	Indicted in New York for failure to pay sales tax on transactions in fine art; hung jury on charges of looting Tyco; convicted on retrial with 15–25-year sentence; denied parole in 2012
Bernard Madoff (2009)	Ran a $50-billion Ponzi scheme through Madoff Securities	Entered guilty plea to all charges and refused to cooperate with investigators; 150-year sentence (at age of 71 in 2009, it is the equivalent of a life sentence)
Martha Stewart, CEO of Martha Stewart Living, Omnimedia, Inc., and close friend of Dr. Waksal (2003)	Sold 5,000 shares of ImClone one day before public announcement of negative FDA action on Erbitux	Indicted and convicted, along with her broker at Merrill Lynch, of making false statements and conspiracy; served sentence and probation
Richard Scrushy (2003)	Indicted for fraud and bribery for HealthSouth accounting fraud	Acquitted of all charges related to HealthSouth; convicted of bribing former governor of Alabama
Stanford Securities (2012)	$9 billion Ponzi scheme	CEO convicted of mail, wire, and securities fraud; Laura Pendergest-Holt, the former chief investment officer, entered a guilty plea to obstruction of an SEC investigation.

Thinking Things Through

Can a Pharmacy's License Be Revoked for Too Many Cash Sales of Oxycodone?

The Drug Enforcement Administration (DEA) has moved to revoke the controlled medication licenses of two pharmacies because the pharmacies were filling prescriptions for oxycodone (the painkiller) in excess of their monthly allowances for controlled substances. In addition, the DEA alleges that the pharmacies' corporate entities failed to conduct on-site inspections and failed to notice that 42 to 58 percent of all the sales of the substances were cash sales, something that is considered a red flag in the sale and distribution of controlled substances. In addition, the number of prescriptions filled continued to escalate.

The two pharmacies won an injunction against the revocation in federal district court. However, the DEA is hoping to persuade the judge to lift the injunction once it is able to show that the corporations should have known there was a problem. The rate of cash sales at these pharmacies was eight times the national rate for filling prescriptions with cash. Pharmacists at the drug stores, in interviews with the DEA agents, indicated that the customers paying cash for the oxycodone were "shady," and that they suspected that some of the prescriptions were not legitimate. One of the companies adjusted (increased) the levels of

shipment of oxycodone to the pharmacies five times. In one on-site visit by a DEA agent, the following information emerged: one of every three cars that came to the drive-thru window had a prescription for oxycodone; many patients living at the same address had the same prescriptions for oxycodone from the same doctor.

Both companies, CVS and Cardinal Health, have indicated in court filings that they have changed their practices and provided training to pharmacy personnel so that they can spot these types of illegal prescriptions and report suspicious activity. Both pharmacy companies have terminated customers, meaning that they will no longer fill prescriptions for those customers.

The DEA seeks to hold the corporations responsible because of the lack of on-site presence and the failure to follow the numbers for sales and distribution at the pharmacies. Can the corporation be held liable when it was not actually participating in the distribution of the oxycodone?

Source: Timothy W. Martin and Devlin Barrett, "Red Flags Ignored, DEA Says," *Wall Street Journal*, February 21, 2012. p. B1.

federal statutes now require executives to reimburse their companies for any money earned as a result of illegal activity. **For Example,** the former CEO of UnitedHealth Group Inc. was required to pay back $448 billion in profits he had made from stock options that were granted illegally.[10]

(E)(6) CREATIVE PENALTIES FOR WHITE-COLLAR CRIME. Federal judges are developing new types of sentences in order to use those convicted to convince business people to avoid criminal conduct. **For Example,** in 2009, a federal judge required an executive who entered a guilty plea to spend his two years of probation writing a book about what he did and offer guidance to business executives so that they can avoid his missteps. He was required to publish and distribute the book.[11] In 2010, a federal agency agreed to defer penalties if an officer agreed to travel around the country and speak to comapneis and executives about the mistakes he had made in order to help them understand the need for vigilance in stopping missteps that lead to crimes.

4. Indemnification of Crime Victims

Penalties are paid to the government. Typically, the victim of a crime does not benefit from the criminal prosecution and conviction of the wrongdoer, although courts can order that restitution be paid to victims.

---

[10] S. Almashat et al., "Rapidly Increasing Criminal and Civil Monetary Penalties Against the Pharmaceutical Industry: 1991 to 2010," *Public Citizen's Health Research Group*, December 16, 2010, *available at* **http://www.citizen.org/documents/rapidlyincreasingcriminalandcivilpenalti**

[11] Natasha Singer, "Judge Orders Former Bristol-Myers Executive to Write Book," *New York Times*, June 9, 2009, p. B3.

The Victims of Crime Act of 1984 creates a federal Crime Victims Fund.[12] Using the fines paid into the federal courts as well as other monies, the federal government makes grants to the states to assist them in financing programs to provide assistance for victims of crime.[13] The Victim and Witness Protection Act of 1982 authorizes the sentencing judge in a federal district court to order, in certain cases, that the defendant make restitution (restoration) to the victim or pay the victim the amount of medical expenses or loss of income caused by the crime.[14]

Victims may also be entitled to bring civil actions for recovery of the damages they experience because a crime is committed. **For Example,** a company or individual violating federal antitrust laws is liable to the victim for three times the damages actually sustained.

B.   White-Collar Crimes

white-collar crimes – crimes that do not use nor threaten to use force or violence or do not cause injury to persons or property.

White-collar crime is generally considered business crime, the type committed generally in the course of doing business and usually involving some form of deceit used to get gains.

5. Conspiracies

conspiracy – agreement between two or more persons to commit an unlawful act.

The crime of conspiracy is committed before the actual crime; it is the planning of the crime. A **conspiracy** is an agreement between two or more persons to commit an unlawful act or to use unlawful means to achieve an otherwise lawful result. Some conspiracy statutes do require that those charged must have done something to carry out the agreement before the crime of conspiracy is committed.

6. Crimes Related to Production, Competition, and Marketing

(A) Improper Use of Interstate Commerce. The shipment of improper goods or the transmission of improper information in interstate commerce is a federal crime. **For Example,** knowingly shipping food with salmonella would be a violation of the federal law that prohibits shipping adulterated foods, drugs, or cosmetics in interstate commerce.

The Communications Act of 1934, as amended, makes it a crime to manufacture or sell devices knowing their primary use is to unscramble satellite telecasts without having paid for the right to do so.[15]

(B) Securities Crimes. To protect the investing public, both state and federal laws have regulated the issuance and public sale of stocks and bonds. These statutes and the crimes associated with sales of securities are covered in Chapter 46.

7. Money Laundering

The federal government has adopted a Money Laundering Control Act (MLCA).[16] The act prohibits the knowing and willful participation in a financial transaction when

---

[12] 18 U.S.C. §3771. The act was amended in 2004 to include a type of bill of rights for crime victims, including assistance through the newly created Office for Victims of Crime.

[13] 18 U.S.C. §1401 *et seq.*

[14] 18 U.S.C. §3579, as amended by 18 U.S.C. §18.18; see *Hughey v. United States,* 495 U.S. 411 (1990). Some states likewise provide for payment into a special fund. Ex parte *Lewis,* 556 So.2d 370 (Ala. 1989). In 2002, Congress passed another victims' compensation statute, with this one providing relief and assistance to the victims of terrorist attacks in the United States. 42 U.S.C. §10603b.

[15] 47 U.S.C. §705(d)(1), (e)(4), 47 U.S.C. §605 (d)(1), (e)(4); *United States v. Harrell,* 983 F.2d 36 (5th Cir. 1993); but see *DIRECTV, Inc. v. Robson,* 420 F.3d 740 (6th Cir. 2000).

[16] 18 U.S.C. §§1956–1957 (2000). *U.S. v. Prince,* 214 F.3d 740 (6th Cir. 2000).

the transaction is designed to conceal or disguise the source of the funds. The so-called *USA Patriot Act* that was passed on October 26, 2001, less than two months after the destruction of the World Trade Center and the damage to the Pentagon on September 11, 2001, includes a substantial number of changes and amendments to the MLCA and the Bank Secrecy Act (BSA).[17] Both statutes have been used as means to control bribery, tax evasion, and money laundering. Their changes and amendments were designed to curb the funding of terrorist activities in the United States.

The Patriot Act expands the coverage of the law from banks and financial institutions to anyone involved in financial transactions, which includes securities brokers; travel agents; those who close real estate transactions; insurance companies; loan or finance companies; casinos; currency exchanges; check-cashing firms; auto, plane, and boat dealers; and branches and agencies of foreign banks located in the United States. The amendments make even small businesses subject to the requirements of disclosure under MLCA and BSA, such as reporting cash transactions in excess of $10,000.

In addition, the types of accounts covered have been expanded. The accounts covered are not only securities accounts but also money market accounts. Furthermore, banks are now more actively involved in supervising accounts and following through on government information furnished to the bank on suspicious transactions and activities as well as individuals. Banks are required to implement new policies to prevent the types of transactions tagged by the government and conduct internal investigations for suspicious transactions. Because of the required close-watch provisions of these laws, banks and others covered under the federal statutes have developed anti-money-laundering programs. These programs must include a "Know Your Customer" training segment that teaches employees how to spot suspicious customers and transactions.

8. Racketeering

Racketeer Influenced and Corrupt Organizations (RICO) Act – federal law, initially targeting organized crime, that has expanded in scope and provides penalties and civil recovery for multiple criminal offenses, or a pattern of racketeering.

Congress passed the **Racketeer Influenced and Corrupt Organizations (RICO) Act**[18] in 1970 as part of the Organized Crime Control Act. The law was designed primarily to prevent individuals involved in organized crime from investing money obtained through racketeering in legitimate businesses. However, the broad language of the act, coupled with a provision that allows individuals and businesses to sue for treble damages, has resulted in an increasing number of lawsuits against ordinary business persons not associated with organized crime.

(A) Criminal and Civil Applications. RICO authorizes criminal and civil actions against persons who use any income derived from racketeering activity to invest in, control, or conduct an enterprise through a pattern of *racketeering activity*.[19] In criminal and civil actions under RICO, a pattern of racketeering activity must be established by

---

[17] 31 U.S.C. §531(h).

[18] 18 U.S.C. §§1961–1968.

[19] §1961. Definitions:

   (1) "Racketeering activity" means any act or threat involving murder, kidnapping, gambling, arson, robbery, bribery, extortion, dealing in obscene matter, dealing in a controlled substance or listed chemical, or sports bribery; counterfeiting; theft from interstate shipment; embezzlement from pension and welfare funds; extortionate credit transactions; fraud; wire fraud; mail fraud; procurement of citizenship or nationalization unlawfully; reproduction of naturalization or citizenship papers; obstruction of justice; tampering with a witness, victim, or an informant; retaliating against a witness, victim, or an informant; false statement in application and use of passport; forgery or false use of passport; fraud and misuse of visas, permits, and other documents; racketeering; unlawful welfare fund payments; laundering of monetary instruments; use of interstate commerce facilities in the commission of murder-for-hire; sexual exploitation of children; interstate transportation of stolen motor vehicles; interstate transportation of stolen property; trafficking in counterfeit labels of phonorecords, computer programs or computer program documentation, or packaging and copies of motion pictures or other audiovisual works; criminal infringement of a copyright; trafficking in contraband cigarettes; and white slave traffic.

proving that at least two acts of racketeering activity—so-called *predicate acts*—have been committed within 10 years.[20] Conviction under RICO's criminal provisions may result in a $25,000 fine and up to 20 years' imprisonment as well as forfeiture of the property involved. A successful civil plaintiff may recover three times the actual damages suffered and attorney fees.[21]

(B) EXPANDING USAGE. Civil RICO actions have been successful against business entities, such as accounting firms, labor unions, insurance companies, commercial banks, and stock brokerage firms. However, under the Private Securities Litigation Reform Act of 1995, securities fraud was eliminated as a **predicate act**, or a qualifying underlying offense, for private RICO actions, absent a prior criminal conviction.[22]

> **predicate act**—qualifying underlying offense for RICO liability.

9. Bribery

Bribery is the act of giving money, property, or any benefit to a particular person to influence that person's judgment in favor of the giver.[23] At common law, the crime was limited to doing such acts to influence a public official.

The giving and the receiving of a bribe constitute separate crimes. In addition, the act of trying to obtain a bribe may be a crime of solicitation of bribery in some states, while in other states bribery is broadly defined to include solicitation of bribes.

10. Commercial Bribery

Commercial bribery is a form of bribery in which an agent for another is paid or given something of value in order to make a decision on behalf of his or her principal that benefits the party paying the agent. **For Example,** a napkin supplier who pays a restaurant agent $500 in exchange for that agent's decision to award the restaurant's napkin contract to that supplier has engaged in commercial bribery.[24]

11. Extortion and Blackmail

Extortion and *blackmail* are crimes in which money is exchanged for either specific actions or restraint in taking action.

(A) EXTORTION. When a public officer makes an illegal demand, the officer has committed the crime of **extortion**. **For Example,** if a health inspector threatens to close down a restaurant on a false sanitation law charge unless the restaurant pays the inspector a sum of money, the inspector has committed extortion. (If the restaurant voluntarily offers the inspector the money to prevent the restaurant from being shut down because of actual violations of the sanitation laws, the crime committed would be bribery.)

> **extortion**—illegal demand by a public officer acting with apparent authority.

(B) BLACKMAIL. In jurisdictions where extortion is limited to the conduct of public officials, a nonofficial commits **blackmail** by making demands that would be extortion if made by a public official. Ordinarily, blackmail is the act of threatening

> **blackmail**—extortion demands made by a nonpublic official.

---

[20] Brian Slocum, "RICO and the Legislative Supremacy Approach to Federal Criminal Lawmaking," 31 *Loyola Univ. Chicago Law Journal* 639 (2000).

[21] *Criminal RICO: 18 U.S.C. 1961–1968: A Manual for Federal Prosecutors.* Washington, D.C.: U.S. Dept. of Justice, Criminal Division, Organized Crime and Racketeering Section, [2009].

[22] 15 U.S.C. §78(a), (n)–(t).

[23] *In re Mangone,* 923 N.Y.S.2d 679 (2011).

[24] Connecticut's commercial bribery statute is a good example. It provides: *A person is guilty of commercial bribery when he confers, or agrees to confer, any benefit upon any employee, agent or fiduciary without the consent of the latter's employer or principal, with intent to influence his conduct in relation to his employer's or principal's affairs.* CGSA §53a-160 (2012). Other examples of commercial bribery statues can be found at Minn. Stat Ann §609.86 (Minnesota 2012); NH Rev Stat §638:8 (New Hampshire 2010); Alaska Stat §11.45.670 (Alaska 2012); and Ala. Code §13A-11-120 (Alabama 2012). Mississippi prohibits commercial bribery as well as sports bribery, which is paying the agent of a sports team in order to influence the outcome of a sporting event. Miss. Code Ann §97-9-10 (2010).

someone with publicity about a matter that would damage the victim's personal or business reputation.

12. Corrupt Influence

Legislative bodies have increasingly outlawed certain practices that exert a corrupting influence on business transactions.

(A) IMPROPER POLITICAL INFLUENCE. At the federal and state levels, it is a crime for one who holds public office to hold a financial interest in or to receive money from an enterprise that seeks to do business with the government. Such conduct is a conflict of interest between the official's duty to citizens and his or her personal financial interests. **For Example,** the former governor of Illinois, Rod Blagojevich, was convicted of seeking funds, fundraisers, and positions in exchange for political favors. To keep officials' conduct transparent, lobbyists must register in Washington, D.C.,[25] and adhere to statutory limits on gifts and contributions to political campaigns. Public officials must file annual disclosure forms about their financial positions as well as provide a disclosure of all gifts and their value.

Foreign Corrupt Practices Act (FCPA) – federal law that makes it a felony to influence decision makers in other countries for the purpose of obtaining business, such as contracts for sales and services; also imposes financial reporting requirements on certain U.S. corporations.

grease payments – (facilitation payments) legal payments to speed up or ensure performance of normal government duties.

facilitation payments – (grease payments) legal payments to speed up or ensure performance of normal government duties.

(B) FOREIGN CORRUPT PRACTICES ACT. The **Foreign Corrupt Practices Act (FCPA)** is a federal criminal statute that applies to businesses whose principal offices are in the United States; it is an antibribery and anticorruption statute covering these companies' international operations.[26] The FCPA prohibits making, authorizing, or promising payments or gifts of money or anything of value with the intent to corrupt. This prohibition applies to payments or gifts designed to influence official acts of foreign officials, parties, party officials, candidates for office, nongovernmental organizations (NGOs), or any person who transmits the gift or money to these types of persons.[27]

The FCPA does not prohibit **grease** or **facilitation payments**. These are payments made only to get officials to perform their normal duties or to perform them in a timely manner. Facilitation payments are those made to (1) secure a permit or a license, (2) obtain paper processing, (3) secure police protection, (4) provide phone, water, or power services, or (5) obtain any other similar action.

13. Counterfeiting

Counterfeiting is making, with fraudulent intent, a document or coin that appears to be genuine but is not because the person making it did not have the authority to make it. It is a federal crime to make, to possess with intent to transfer, or to transfer counterfeit coins, bank notes, or obligations or other securities of the United States. Various states also have statutes prohibiting the making and passing of counterfeit coins and bank notes. These statutes often provide, as does the federal statute, a punishment for the mutilation of bank notes or the lightening (of the weight) or mutilation of coins.

---

[25] Foreign Agents Registration Act, 22 U.S.C. §611 *et seq.*, as amended.
[26] 15 U.S.C. §78dd-1 *et seq.*
[27] A state-owned electric utility is considered an instrumentality of government. *United States v. Aguilar*, 783 F. Supp. 2d 1108 (C.D. Cal. 2011)

Ethics & the Law

Am I My Company's Keeper?

Think about the following statements by the former CEOs of companies that had accounting fraud.

CEO	QUOTE
Ken Lay, Enron	"Enron was an enormous corporation. How could I have known everything going on everywhere in the company?"
Richard Scrushy, HealthSouth	"You have to rely; you have to trust people. You have to believe. You have to delegate . . . I signed off on the information based on what was provided to me. And what I was told."
Bernie Ebbers, WorldCom	"Bernie Ebbers did not know about the accounting decisions of Scott Sullivan to reassign billions of dollars."
John Rigas, Adelphia	"John Rigas had a right to trust and rely on professionals and his own staff to get the financials right."

Are the CEOs responsible for knowing what goes on at their companies? Are they able to find out what is happening? Are they criminally responsible? Are they ethically responsible?

Source: Mike France, "The New Accountability," *BusinessWeek,* July 25, 2004. p. 30 at p. 32.

14. Forgery

Forgery consists of the fraudulent making or material altering of an instrument, such as a check, that attempts to create or changes a legal liability of another person.[28] Ordinarily, **forgery** consists of signing another's name with intent to defraud, but it may also consist of making an entire instrument or altering an existing one. It may result from signing a fictitious name or the offender's own name with the intent to defraud.

forgery – fraudulently making or altering an instrument that apparently creates or alters a legal liability of another.

The issuing or delivery of a forged instrument to another person constitutes the crime of **uttering** a forged instrument. Sending a forged check through the channels of commerce or of bank collection constitutes an uttering of a forged instrument. The act of depositing a forged check into the forger's bank account by depositing it in an automatic teller machine constitutes uttering within the meaning of a forgery statute.[29]

uttering – crime of issuing or delivering a forged instrument to another person.

15. Perjury

Perjury consists of knowingly giving false testimony in a judicial proceeding after having been sworn to tell the truth. Knowingly making false answers on any form filed with a government typically constitutes perjury or is subjected to the same punishment as perjury. In some jurisdictions, the false answers given in a situation other than in court or the litigation process is called the crime of *false swearing.* The penalties for perjury were increased substantially under SOX.

16. False Claims and Pretenses

Many statutes make it a crime to submit false claims or to obtain goods by false pretenses.

[28] Misrepresenting the nature of a document in order to obtain their signature on it is forgery. *State v. Martinez,* 74 Cal. Rptr. 3d 409 (2008).
[29] *Warren v. State,* 711 S.E.2d 108 (Ga. App. 2011).

(A) FALSE CLAIMS. The federal false statement statute makes it a crime to knowingly and willfully make a false material statement about any matter within the jurisdiction of any department or agency of the United States. **For Example,** it is a crime for a contractor to make a false claim against the United States for payment for work that was never performed. It is also a crime to make false statements about income and assets on a student's application for federal financial aid.

(B) OBTAINING GOODS BY FALSE PRETENSES. Almost all states have statutes that forbid obtaining money or goods under false pretenses.[30] An intent to defraud is an essential element of obtaining property by false pretenses.[31]

Examples of false pretense include delivering a check knowing that there is insufficient money in the bank account to cover the check.[32] False representations as to future profits in a business are also forms of false pretenses. Identity theft can be prosecuted under false pretenses statutes.[33]

Failing to perform on a contract is not a false pretense crime unless the contract had been entered into with the intent of not performing it.[34]

(C) UNAUTHORIZED USE OF AUTOMATED TELLER MACHINE. Obtaining money from an automated teller machine (ATM) by the unauthorized use of the depositor's ATM card is a federal crime.

(D) FALSE INFORMATION SUBMITTED TO BANKS. Knowingly making false statements in a loan application to a federally insured bank is a federal crime.[35] It is also a crime for a landowner to put a false value on land transferred to a bank as security for a loan.[36] **For Example,** many of the initial criminal charges in the subprime mortgage market collapse have involved mortgage brokers and appraisers who misrepresented property value or applicants' income in their mortgage applications for federally insured loans.

17. Bad Checks

Under a bad check statute, it is a crime to use or pass a check with the intent to defraud with the knowledge that there are insufficient funds in the bank to pay the check when it is presented for payment. Knowledge that the bad check will not be paid when presented to the bank is an essential element of the crime. The bad check statutes typically provide that if the check is not made good within a specified number of days after payment by the bank is refused, it is presumed that the defendant acted with the intent to defraud.[37] For more information on checks, see Chapters 28 and 31.

18. Credit Card Crimes

It is a crime to steal a credit card and, in some states, to possess the credit card of another person without that person's consent. Using a credit card without the permission of the card owner is the crime of obtaining goods or services by false pretenses or with the intent to defraud. Likewise, a person who continues to use a credit card with the knowledge that it has been canceled is guilty of the crime of

[30] *Mass. v. Cheromcka,* 850 N.E.2d 1088 (Mass. App. 2006).
[31] *State v. Moore,* 903 A.2d 669 (Conn. App. 2006).
[32] *U.S. v. Tudeme,* 457 F.3d 577 (Fed. App. 2006).
[33] *State v. Parker,* 2009 WL 1065988 (Ariz. App. 2009).
[34] *Higginbotham v. State,* 356 S.W.3d 584 (Tex. App. 2011).
[35] 18 U.S.C. §1014. See *United States v. Autorino,* 381 F.3d 48 (2nd Cir. 2004).
[36] *U.S. v. Rizk,* 660 F.3d 1125 (9th Cir. 2011).
[37] *McMillan v. First Nat. Bank of Berwick,* 978 A.2d 370 (Pa. Super. 2009).

obtaining goods by false pretenses. Federal law also makes it a crime to use counterfeit credit cards for purposes of obtaining goods, services, or cash. The statute now covers the use of credit card numbers on the Internet in order to obtain goods and services.[38]

19. Embezzlement

Embezzlement is the fraudulent conversion of another's property or money by a person to whom it has been entrusted.[39] Employees who take or sell their employer's property or funds for personal use have committed the crime of embezzlement. An agent employee commits embezzlement when he receives and keeps payments from third persons—payments the agent should have turned over to the principal.

For Example, when an insured gives money to an insurance agent to pay the insurance company but the insurance agent uses the money to pay premiums on the policies of other persons, the agent is guilty of embezzlement. Generally, the intent to return the property or money embezzled or does in fact do so is no defense.

20. Obstruction of Justice: Sarbanes-Oxley (SOX)

Another SOX provision clarifies what constitutes obstruction of justice and increases the penalties for such an act. The new section makes it a felony for anyone, including company employees, auditors, attorneys, and consultants,

> *to alter, destroy, mutilate, conceal, cover up, falsify or make a false entry with the "intent to impede, obstruct, or influence the investigation or proper administration of any matter within the jurisdiction of any department or agency of the United States."*[40]

The statute goes on to address audit records specifically and requires auditors to retain their work papers related to a client's audit for at least five years. Any destruction of documents prior to that time constitutes a felony and carries a penalty of up to 20 years. The statute was passed in response to the conduct of Arthur Andersen, the audit firm for the collapsed Enron Corporation. Many of the firm's audit papers on Enron were destroyed, but the firm and partner-in-charge escaped criminal liability because the government could not establish that the senior managers in Andersen were aware of the shredding.[41]

21. Corporate Fraud: SOX

SOX also created a new form of mail and wire fraud. Ordinarily, mail or wire fraud consists of the use of the mail or telephones for purposes of defrauding someone of money and/or property. However, the SOX form of mail or wire fraud is based on new requirements imposed on corporate officers to certify their financial statements when they are issued. If a corporate officer fails to comply with all requirements for financial statement certification or certifies financial statements that

---

[38] 18 U.S.C. §1029. Fines for credit card fraud were increased in 2002 to levels between $50,000 and $100,000 per offense.
[39] *State v. Henry,* 73 So.3d 958 (La. App. 2011); *Stern v. Epps,* 464 Fed.Appx. 388 (5th Cir. 2012).
[40] 18 U.S.C. §1519. *U.S. v. Hunt,* 526 F.3d 739 (11th Cir. 2008).
[41] *Arthur Andersen LLP v. U.S.,* 544 U.S. 696 (2005). The obstruction conviction of the firm was reversed because of insufficient proof of the firm's actual knowledge of document destruction.

Sports & Entertainment Law

The NBA Referee, Gambling, and Some Tossed Games

Tim Donaghy, a referee for the NBA, entered a guilty plea to two federal felony charges in connection with his bets and tips on NBA games. The charges were conspiracy to engage in wire fraud and transmitting betting information via interstate commerce. Mr. Donaghy picked teams to win in games he was scheduled to referee. Mr. Donaghy committed the equivalent of insider trading on Wall Street by providing outsiders with information about games, players, and referees. He got $5,000 from his tippees for correct picks.

Mr. Donaghy began betting on games in 2003, but in December 2006 began passing along inside information to others who were also charged in the conspiracy. The communication was in code via cell phone. Mr. Donaghy explained at his sentencing that he had a gambling addiction problem and took medication under the treatment of a psychiatrist.

The NBA Commissioner, David Stern, referred to Mr. Donaghy as a "rogue referee," but said that the gambling charges were a wake-up call for the NBA and that it must not be "complacent."*

Mr. Donaghy's missteps were discovered as the federal government was conducting an investigation into the Gambino crime family, based in Brooklyn.

*Roscoe Nance, "Scandal Is a 'Wakeup Call,' Stern Says," *USA Today*, August 16, 2007 p. 1C.

Commissioner Stern said that the NBA would be looking at the checks and balances that the NFL has built into its system including Las Vegas travel prohibitions on referees. The NFL also has significant background checks and ongoing monitoring of its referees.

Mr. Donaghy ran a basketball clinic for developmentally disabled boys in Springfield, PA (Mr. Donaghy's hometown) for almost a decade. He was a graduate of Villanova and had worked his way up to being one of the NBA's top referees, coming through the ranks of refereeing in both high school and the Continental Basketball Association. Mr. Donaghy had a wife and four children. His salary with the NBA during 2006 was $260,000. Mr. Donaghy was sentenced to 15 months in prison. After serving 11 months of his prison term, Mr. Donaghy was released to a halfway house, but was sent back to prison to finish out his term because of violations of the terms of his partial release. He wrote a book about his actions, *Personal Foul: A First-Person Account of the Scandal That Rocked the NBA*.

Why do you think Mr. Donaghy was engaged in gambling? Doesn't his civic activity paint a different picture of his character? Mr. Donaghy said in an interview about his book that what he did was no different from Wall Streeters who engaged in insider trading except, "I didn't affect the economy." How would you analyze his comparison?

contain false material information, the officer and company have committed corporate fraud with penalties that range from fines of $1,000,000 and/or 10 years to $5,000,000 and/or 20 years for willful violation of the certification requirements.

22. The Common Law Crimes

In contrast to white-collar crimes, *common law crimes* are crimes that involve the use of force or the threat of force or cause injury to persons or damage to property. The following sections discuss crimes of force and crimes against property that affect businesses.

(A) LARCENY. *Larceny* is the wrongful or fraudulent taking of the personal property of another by any person with fraudulent intent. Shoplifting is a common form of larceny. In many states, shoplifting is made a separate crime. In some states, all forms of larceny and robbery are consolidated into a statutory crime of theft. At common law, there was no crime known as theft.

(B) ROBBERY. *Robbery* is the taking of personal property from the presence of the victim by use of force or fear. Most states have aggravated forms of robbery, such as robbery with a deadly weapon. Snatching a necklace from the neck of the victim involves sufficient force to constitute robbery. When the unlawful taking is not by force or fear, as when the victim does not know that the property is being taken, the offense is larceny, but it cannot be robbery.

Some statutes may be aimed at a particular kind of robbery. **For Example,** carjacking is a federal crime under the Anti-Car Theft Act of 1992.[42]

(c) Burglary. At common law, *burglary* was the breaking and entering during the night into the dwelling house of another with the intent to commit a felony. Inserting the automatic teller card of another, without their knowledge or permission, into an automatic teller machine set in the wall of the bank may constitute an entry into the bank for the purpose of committing burglary.[43] Some states word their burglary statutes, however, so that there is no burglary in this automatic teller case. This act would be covered by other criminal statutes.

Modern statutes have eliminated many of the elements of the common law definition so that under some statutes it is now immaterial when or whether there was an entry to commit a felony. The elements of breaking and entering are frequently omitted. Under some statutes, the offense is aggravated and the penalty is increased, depending on the place where the offense was committed, such as a bank building, freight car, or warehouse. Related statutory offenses, such as the crime of possessing burglars' tools, have been created.

(d) Arson. At common law, *arson* was the willful and malicious burning of another's dwelling. The law was originally designed to protect human life, although arson has been committed just with the burning of the building even if no one is actually hurt. In most states, arson is a felony, so if someone is killed in the resulting fire, the offense is considered a felony-murder. Under the felony-murder rule, homicide, however unintended, occurring in the commission of a felony is automatically classified as murder. Virtually every state has created a special offense of burning to defraud an insurer.

(e) Riots and Civil Disorders. Damage to property in the course of a riot or civil disorder is ordinarily covered by other types of crimes such as the crime of larceny or arson. In addition, the act of assembling as a riotous mob and engaging in civil disorders is generally some form of crime in itself under either common law concepts of disturbing the peace or modern antiriot statutes, even without destruction or theft of property. However, statutes on civil disorders must be carefully drawn to avoid infringing on constitutionally protected free speech.

C. Criminal Law and the Computer

In some situations, ordinary crimes cover computer crimes situations. In other situations, new criminal law statutes are required.

23. What Is a Computer Crime?

computer crimes – wrongs committed using a computer or with knowledge of computers.

Generally, the term **computer crime** is used to refer to a crime that can be committed only by a person having some knowledge of the operation of a computer.

---

[42] 18 U.S.C. §2119. See *U.S. v. Bell*, 608 F. Supp. 2d 1257 (Kan. 2009).
[43] *People v. Cardwell*, 137 Cal. Rptr.3d 525 (2012).

Just as stealing an automobile requires knowledge of how to operate and drive a car, so the typical computer crime requires the knowledge of how the computer works.

Because the more serious and costly wrongs relating to computers do not fit into the ordinary definitions of crime, there are now computer-specific criminal statutes: Computer crimes can be committed against the computer, using the computer, or through the computer.

24. The Computer as Victim

A traditional crime may be committed by stealing or intentionally damaging a computer.

(A) THEFT OF HARDWARE. When a computer itself is stolen, the ordinary law relating to theft crimes should apply. Theft of a computer is subject to the same law as the theft of a truck or a desk.

(B) THEFT OF SOFTWARE. When a thief takes software, whether in the form of a program written on paper or a program on a disk or memory stick, something has been taken, but it is not tangible property as larceny requires. Virtually every state makes stealing software a crime. Chapter 11 provides more information on crimes, software, and the Internet.

(C) INTENTIONAL DAMAGE. The computer may be the "victim" of a crime when it is intentionally destroyed or harmed. In the most elementary form of damage, the computer could be harmed if it was smashed with an ax or destroyed in an explosion or a fire. In such cases, the purpose of the intentional damage is to cause the computer's owner the financial loss of the computer and the destruction of the information that is stored in it.

Intentional damage can result from more subtle means. Gaining access to the computer and then erasing or altering the data is also the crime of intentional damage. Likewise, interfering with the air conditioning so computers are damaged or malfunction would also be covered under intentional damage statutes. Planting a bug or virus in the software, causing the program to malfunction or to give incorrect output, is a form of intentional damage. Angry employees, former employees, and competitors have all been convicted of intentional damage.

25. Unauthorized Use of Computers

The unlawful use of a computer belonging to someone else is also a crime in some states. There are specific statutes at the state and federal levels that make it unlawful to use government computers without permission. One of the issues that is critical in criminal prosecution is whether the use was, in fact, "unauthorized." With Wi-Fi networks, the ease of access and openess has proven to be a challenge in prosecution for unauthorized use.[44]

26. Computer Raiding

Taking information from a computer without the consent of the owner is a crime. Whether theft is accomplished by instructing the computer to make a printout of

---

[44] U.S.C. §1030(e)(6); for an article summarizing the issues, see Orin S. Kerr, "Cybercrime's Scope: Interpreting 'Access' and 'Authorization' in Computer Misuse Statutes", 78 *N.Y.U. L. Rev.* 1596, 1632-37 (2003).

stored information or by tapping into its data bank by electronic means is not important. In some states, taking information is known as the crime of "computer trespass."[45]

Both Congress and state legislatures have adopted statutes that make it a crime to gain unauthorized access to a computer or use information so gained to cause harm to the computer or its rightful user.[46] Again, the presence of Wi-Fi when there are unsecured users has complicated prosecutions for taking information.

27. Diverted Delivery by Computer

In many industries, a computer controls the delivery of goods. The person in charge of that computer or someone unlawfully gaining access to it may cause the computer to direct delivery to an improper place. That is, instead of shipping goods to the customers to whom they should go, the wrongdoer diverts the goods to a different place, where the wrongdoer or a confederate receives them.

Instructing the computer to give false directions can cause this fraudulent diversion of goods. Because the computer allows changes in delivery of goods through a mere keystroke, the depth of diversion cases is great. **For Example,** in one case, several hundred loaded freight cars disappeared. In another case, a loaded oil tanker was diverted to unload into a fleet of tank trucks operated by an accomplice of the computer operator.

E-Commerce & Cyberlaw

They Were Bullies: Mean Girls in Cyberspace

It has been called the MySpace suicide case. On May 14, 2008, a federal grand jury indicted Lori Drew, 49, of Missouri, the so-called cyber bully. Ms. Drew had created a MySpace site for Josh Evans, a fictitious teen boy she used as a means of getting information from Megan Meier, a 13-year-old girl with whom Ms. Drew's daughter had had a falling-out. Josh pretended to be interested in Megan, but then said that she was "fat" and that the world would be a better place without her. Megan hanged herself within an hour of receiving the final comments from "Josh."

Ms. Drew was charged with one count of conspiracy and two counts of accessing computers without authorization and was convicted of three lesser charges. However, the judge dismissed the charges because of issues related to the meaning of the term "unauthorized use" and whether the federal statutes could be applied to what Ms. Drew did.

When the indictment was made public, Salvador Hernandez, assistant director of the FBI in Los Angeles, said, "Whether we characterize this tragic case as 'cyber-bullying,' cyberabuse, or illegal computer access, it should serve as a reminder that our children use the Internet for social interaction and that technology has altered the way they conduct their daily activities. As adults, we must be sensitive to the potential dangers posed by the use of the Internet by our children."*

Some states have now passed specific statutes to make cyber-bullying a crime.

Why would the judge not find a criminal violation? Is it a crime to bully over the Internet?

U.S. v. Lori Drew, 259 F.R.D. 449 (C.D. Cal. 2009).

---

[45] *Washington v. Riley*, 846 P.2d 1365 (Wash. 1993).
[46] The Counterfeit Access Device and Computer Fraud Act of 1984, 18 U.S.C. §1030 *et seq.*; Computer Fraud and Abuse Act of 1986, 18 U.S.C. §1001; Electronic Communications Privacy Act of 1986, 18 U.S.C. §2510; Computer Fraud Act of 1987, 15 U.S.C. §§272, 278, 40 U.S.C. §759; National Information Infrastructure Protection Act, 18 U.S.C. §1030 (protecting confidentiality and integrity on the Internet).

28. Economic Espionage by Computer

Economic Espionage Act (EEA) – federal law that makes it a felony to copy, download, transmit, or in any way transfer proprietary files, documents, and information from a computer to an unauthorized person.

The **Economic Espionage Act (EEA)** is a federal law[47] passed in response to several cases in which high-level executives took downloaded proprietary information from their computers to their new employers. The EEA makes it a felony to steal, appropriate, or take a trade secret as well as to copy, duplicate, sketch, draw, photograph, download, upload, alter, destroy, replicate, transmit, deliver, send, mail, or communicate a trade secret. The penalties for EEA violations are up to $500,000 and 15 years in prison for individuals and $10 million for organizations. When employees take new positions with another company, their former employers are permitted to check the departing employees' computer e-mails and hard drives to determine whether the employees have engaged in computer espionage.

29. Electronic Fund Transfer Crimes

The Electronic Fund Transfers Act (EFTA)[48] makes it a crime to use any counterfeit, stolen, or fraudulently obtained card, code, or other device to obtain money or goods in excess of a specified amount through an electronic fund transfer system. The EFTA also makes it a crime to ship in interstate commerce devices or goods so obtained or to knowingly receive goods that have been obtained by means of the fraudulent use of the transfer system.

Ethics & the Law

Ethics and the Tobacco Class-Action Lawyer

Class-action lawyer Dickie Scruggs was portrayed in the 1999 movie "The Insider," which starred Russell Crowe as Jeffrey Wigand, the tobacco industry whistle-blower who obtained a $206 billion settlement from the tobacco companies (Mr. Scruggs's fee for the case was $1 billion). Almost a decade after the movie that made him a hero came out, Scruggs entered a guilty plea to bribery and was sentenced to five years in prison for his role in an attempt to bribe a federal judge.

Mr. Scruggs was representing insurance claimants against insurers for their damages from Hurricane Katrina. The judge presiding over the case contacted the FBI about a bribery attempt. One of the four lawyers working with Scruggs was approached by the FBI and agreed to wear a wire to catch Scruggs. The content of the tapes revealed both *actus reus* and *scienter*. Zachary Scruggs, Dickie's son, also entered a guilty plea. All of the remaining lawyers involved in the bribery scheme entered guilty pleas as well.

Those in the legal profession said they did not understand Scruggs's actions because he had the skill to win any case. "He didn't need to cheat," was the comment of a representative from the American Trial Lawyers Association. Scruggs's words at his sentencing were poignant: "I could not be more ashamed to be where I am today, mixed up in a judicial bribery scheme…. I realized I was getting mixed up in it. And I will go to my grave wondering why. I have disappointed everyone in my life—my wife, my family, my son, particularly…. I deeply regret my conduct. It is a scar and a stain on my soul that will be there forever."

Source: Abha Bhattarai, "Class-Action Lawyer Given 5 Years in a Bribery Case," *New York Times*, June 28, 2008, B3.

30. Circumventing Copyright Protection Devices Via Computer

The Digital Millennium Copyright Act (DMCA)[49] makes it a federal offense to circumvent or create programs to circumvent encryption devices that copyright

[47] 18 U.S.C. §1831.
[48] 15 U.S.C. §1693(n).
[49] 17 U.S.C. §512(2010).

holders place on copyrighted material to prevent unauthorized copying.
For Example, circumventing the encryption devices on software or CDs or DVDs is a violation of the DMCA.

For Example, Dmitry Sklyarov, a Russian computer programmer, was the first person to be charged with a violation of the DMCA. Mr. Sklyarov was arrested in early 2002 at a computer show after giving a speech in Las Vegas at the Defcon convention on his product that he had developed to permit the circumvention of security devices on copyrighted materials. His program unlocks password-protected e-books and PDF files. He gave his speech and was returned to Russia in exchange for his agreement to testify in a case that will determine the constitutionality of DMCA.

The No Electronic Theft Act makes it a federal criminal offense to willfully infringe copyrighted material worth more than $1,000 using the Internet or other electronic devices even if the infringer does not profit from others' use of the material. **For Example,** sending along copyrighted articles on the Internet to friends, without permission from the site, would be a violation even though there is no profit.

31. Spamming

More states are addressing the use of computers to send unsolicited e-mails. For 2011, there were 7 trillion pieces of spam sent over the Internet. Criminal regulation began with very narrowly tailored statutes such as one in Washington that made it a crime to send an e-mail with a misleading title line. The specific criminal statutes on spamming are evolving, and Virginia became the first state to pass a criminal antispamming law. The statute prohibits sending "unsolicited bulk electronic mail" or spam and makes the offense a felony based on the level of activity.[50] Thirty-six states and the federal government now have some form of spamming regulation.[51] The penalties range from fines to imprisonment.

D. CRIMINAL PROCEDURE RIGHTS FOR BUSINESSES

The U.S. Constitution guarantees the protection of individual and corporate rights within the criminal justice system.

32. Fourth Amendment Rights for Businesses

(A) SEARCH AND SEIZURE: WARRANTS. The **Fourth Amendment** of the U.S. Constitution provides that "the right of the people to be secure in their persons, houses, papers, and effects, against unreasonable searches and seizures, shall not be violated." This amendment protects individual privacy by preventing unreasonable searches and seizures. Before a government agency can seize the property of individuals or businesses, it must obtain a valid **search warrant** issued by a judge or magistrate, based on probable cause, unless an exception to this warrant requirement applies. In other words, there must be good reason to search the location named. The Fourth Amendment applies equally to individuals and corporations. If an improper search is conducted, evidence obtained during the

Fourth Amendment–privacy protection in the U.S. Constitution; prohibits unauthorized searches and seizures.

search warrant–judicial authorization for a search of property where there is the expectation of privacy.

[50] *Gordon v. Virtumundo, Inc.,* 575 F.3d 1040 (9th Cir. 2009).
[51] Controlling the Assault of Non-Solicited Pornography and Marketing (CAN-SPAM), 15 U.S.C. §7701.

course of that search may be inadmissible in the criminal proceedings for the resulting criminal charges.[52]

(B) EXCEPTIONS TO THE WARRANT REQUIREMENT. Exceptions to the warrant requirement are emergencies, such as a burning building, and the "plain-view" exception, which allows law enforcement officials to take any property that anyone can see, for no privacy rights are violated when items and property are left in the open for members of the public to see. **For Example,** you have an expectation of privacy in the garbage in your garbage can when it is in your house. However, once you move that garbage can onto the public sidewalk for pickup, you no longer have the expectation of privacy because you have left your garbage out in plain view of the public.

Another exception allows officers to enter when they are needed to give aid because of an ongoing criminal act. **For Example,** officers who are able to see a fight through the windows of a house and resulting injuries can enter to render help. Another exception would be that the person who lives in the property to be searched has given permission for the search.

CASE SUMMARY

Low-Flying Aircraft Bearing Federal Agents with Cameras

FACTS: Dow Chemical (petitioner) operates a 2,000-acre chemical plant at Midland, Michigan. The facility, with numerous buildings, conduits, and pipes, is visible from the air. Dow has maintained ground security at the facility and has investigated flyovers by other, unauthorized aircraft. However, none of the buildings or manufacturing equipment is concealed.

In 1978, the Environmental Protection Agency (EPA) conducted an inspection of Dow. The EPA requested a second inspection, but Dow denied the request. The EPA then employed a commercial aerial photographer to take photos of the plant from 12,000, 3,000, and 1,200 feet. The EPA had no warrant, but the plane was always within navigable air space when the photos were taken.

When Dow became aware of the EPA photographer, it brought suit in federal district court and challenged the action as a violation of its Fourth Amendment rights. The district court found that the EPA had violated Dow's rights and issued an injunction prohibiting further use of the aircraft. The Court of Appeals reversed and Dow appealed.

DECISION: The Court ruled against Dow, finding that the EPA did not need explicit statutory provisions to use methods of observation commonly available to the public. There was no expectation of privacy in an area that was not covered. [***Dow Chemical Co. v. United States,* 476 U.S. 1819 (1986)**]

(C) BUSINESS RECORDS AND SEARCHES. In many business crimes, the records that prove a crime was committed are not in the hands of the person who committed that crime. Accountants, attorneys, and other third parties may have the business records in their possession. In addition to the Fourth Amendment issues involved in seizing these records (a warrant is still required), there may be protections for the business defendants. The next section covers those protections.

---

[52] See, *Arizona v. Gant,* 556 U.S. 332 (2009) in which the U.S. Supreme Court held that evidence obtained searching the vehicle of a suspect who is handcuffed and locked in a police car cannot be used. A search warrant is needed when the suspect has no access to the evidence to destroy it.

(D) PROTECTIONS FOR PRIVILEGED RECORDS AND DOCUMENTS. All states recognize an attorney-client privilege, which means that an individual's conversations with her lawyer and the notes of those conversations are not subject to seizure unless the privilege is waived. In many of the prosecutions of companies, the Justice Department has asked companies to waive the attorney/client privilege so that it can have access to information that is then used to find other companies that may have participated in criminal activity. Some states recognize an accountant-client privilege and other privileges, such as those between priest and parishioner or doctor and patient. A privileged relationship is one in which the records and notes resulting from the contact between individuals cannot be seized even with a warrant (with some exceptions).

33. Fifth Amendment Self-Incrimination Rights for Businesses

Fifth Amendment – constitutional protection against self-incrimination; also guarantees due process.

(A) SELF-INCRIMINATION. The words "I take the Fifth" are used to invoke the constitutional protections against self-incrimination provided under the **Fifth Amendment** that prevents compelling a person to be a witness against himself. **For Example,** Mark McGwire, the former St. Louis baseball player, invoked the Fifth Amendment in his testimony during Congressional hearings on steroid use. Edith O'Brien, a lawyer for the collapsed investment fund, MF Global, refused to answer questions before Congress, claiming her right against self-incrimination. The Fifth Amendment protection applies only to individuals; corporations are not given Fifth Amendment protection. A corporation cannot prevent the disclosure of its books and records on the grounds of self-incrimination. The officers and employees of a corporation can assert the Fifth Amendment, but the records of the corporation belong to the corporation, not to them.

CASE SUMMARY

A Man's Home Is His Castle, but His Wife Can Still Turn on Him

FACTS: Scott Randolph and his wife, Janet, separated in late May 2001, when she left their Americus, Georgia, home and went to stay with her parents in Canada, taking their son and some belongings. In July, she returned to the Americus house with the child. No one is sure whether she had returned to reconcile or whether she had come to gather her remaining possessions.

On July 6, 2001, Janet called police and told them that there were "items of drug evidence" in the house. Sergeant Murray asked Scott Randolph for permission to search the house, which he refused.

The sergeant turned to Janet for consent to search, which she readily gave. She led the officer upstairs to a bedroom that she identified as Scott's, where the sergeant noticed a section of a drinking straw with a powdery residue he suspected was cocaine. He then left the house to get an evidence bag from his car and to call the district attorney's office, which instructed him to stop the search and apply for a warrant. When Sergeant Murray returned to the house, Janet Randolph withdrew her consent. The police took the straw and the Randolphs to the police station. After getting a search warrant, the police returned to the house and seized further evidence of drug use, which served as the basis of Scott's indictment for possession of cocaine.

Scott Randolph moved to suppress the evidence, as products of a warrantless search. The trial court denied the motion, ruling that Janet had common authority to consent to the search.

CASE SUMMARY

Continued

The Court of Appeals of Georgia reversed, and the Georgia Supreme Court sustained the reversal. The state of Georgia appealed, and the U.S. Supreme Court granted *certiorari*.

DECISION: The Court held that "a man's home is his castle" and that when he objects to a search, his spouse could not overrule his decision. Co-ownership of property does not necessarily mean that individuals are willing to waive their rights of privacy for purposes for warrantless searches. The dissent argued that sharing necessarily means waiving privacy. The fact that they are betrayed by a spouse, roommate, or others does not affect the consent exception to the Fourth Amendment because underlying that protection is the right to privacy and that right has been waived through the shared ownership or living arrangement. [*Gerogia v. Randolph* 547 U.S. 103 (2006)]

Miranda warnings – warnings required to prevent self-incrimination in a criminal matter.

(B) MIRANDA RIGHTS. The famous **Miranda warnings** come from a case interpreting the extent of Fifth Amendment rights. In *Miranda v. Arizona*,[53] the U.S. Supreme Court ruled that certain warnings must be given to persons who face custodial interrogation for the purposes of possible criminal proceedings. The warnings consist of an explanation to individuals that they have the right to remain silent; that if they do speak, anything they say can be used against them; that they have the right to have an attorney present; and that if they cannot afford an attorney, one will be provided for them. Failure to give the *Miranda* warnings means that any statements, including a confession, obtained while the individual was being interrogated cannot be used as evidence against that individual. The prosecution will have to rely on evidence other than the statements made in violation of *Miranda,* if such evidence exists.

34. Due Process Rights for Businesses

due process – the constitutional right to be heard, question witnesses, and present evidence.

Also included in the Fifth Amendment is the language of due process. **Due process** is the right to be heard, question witnesses, and present evidence before any criminal conviction can occur. Due process in criminal cases consists of an initial appearance at which the charges and the defendant's rights are outlined; a preliminary hearing or grand jury proceeding in which the evidence is determined to be sufficient to warrant a trial; an arraignment for entering a plea and setting a trial date when the defendant pleads innocent; a period of discovery for obtaining evidence; and a trial at which witnesses for the prosecution can be cross-examined and evidence presented to refute the charges. In addition to these procedural steps, the **Sixth Amendment**

Sixth Amendment – the U.S. constitutional amendment that guarantees a speedy trial.

guarantees that the entire process will be completed in a timely fashion because this amendment guarantees a speedy trial.

[53] 384 U.S. 436 (1966).

CASE SUMMARY

I Confess, but without *Miranda* You Can't Use It against Me

FACTS: Dickerson confessed to robbing a bank at a field office of the Federal Bureau of Investigation (FBI). At the time he confessed, he was not a suspect, was free to leave, and was not in custody. He was not, however, given his *Miranda* warnings before the FBI agents interrogated him about the robbery. Dickerson's lawyer moved to have his confession excluded from his trial because it was obtained in violation of *Miranda.* The federal district court suppressed the confession. The Court of Appeals reversed, noting that while the warnings had not been given, the confession was clearly voluntary. Dickerson appealed.

DECISION: The U.S. Supreme Court held that the confession could not be used because Dickerson had not been given his warnings. The judicial decision is complex because it focuses on the difference between questioning in custody and the need to give *Miranda* warnings even when there is no custody of the person. The majority of the Court ruled that *Miranda* warnings must still be given as a way to prevent those being questioned from unknowingly waiving their rights. [***Dickerson v. U.S.,*** **530 U.S. 428 (2000)**]

LawFlix

Double Jeopardy (2000) R

Ashley Judd plays a woman on the run for false charges of killing her husband. But her husband faked his death and then she finds and kills him – can she be tried again?

Columbo (Seasons 1–6)

Detective Columbo is the bumbling, brilliant sleuth who crosses a few Fourth and Fifth Amendment lines here and there.

MAKE THE CONNECTION

SUMMARY

When a person does not live up to the standards set by law, this punishable conduct, called *crime,* may be common law or statutory in origin. Crimes are classified as *felonies,* which generally carry greater sentences and more long-term consequences, and *misdemeanors.*

Employers and corporations may be criminally responsible for their acts and the acts of their employees. The federal sentencing guidelines provide parameters for sentences for federal crimes and allow judges to consider whether the fact that a business promotes compliance with the law is a reason to reduce a sentence.

White-collar crimes include those relating to financial fraud. Sarbanes-Oxley reforms increased the penalties for financial fraud and added fraudulent financial statement certification as a crime. Other white-collar crimes include bribery, extortion, blackmail, and corrupt influence in politics and in business. Also included as white-collar crimes are counterfeiting, forgery, perjury, making false claims against the government, obtaining goods or money by false pretenses, using bad checks, false financial reporting, and embezzlement. The common law crimes include those that involve injury to person and/or property, such as arson and murder.

Statutes have expanded the area of criminal law to meet situations in which computers are involved. Both federal and state statutes make the unauthorized taking of information from a computer a crime. The diversion of deliveries of goods and the transfer of funds, the theft of software, and the raiding of computers are made crimes to some extent by federal laws. Newer federal statutes that apply to computers are the Economic Espionage Act, which prohibits downloading or copying information via computer to give to a competitor, and the Digital Millennium Copyright Act that prohibits circumventing or designing programs to circumvent encryption devices.

Criminal procedure is dictated by the Fourth, Fifth, and Sixth Amendments. The Fourth Amendment protects against unreasonable searches, the Fifth Amendment protects against self-incrimination and provides due process, and the Sixth Amendment guarantees a speedy trial.

LEARNING OUTCOMES

After studying this chapter, you should be able to clearly explain:

A. General Principles

L0.1   Discuss the nature and classification of crimes
See the discussion of crimes and misdemeanors on p. 142.

L0.2   Describe the basis of criminal liability
See the *For Example,* discussion of dumping waste and intent on p. 142.
See *U.S. v. Erickson* on p. 143.

L0.3   Identify who is responsible for criminal acts
See *U.S. v. Park* on p. 144.
See Thinking Things Through on p. 148.
See Ethical Issue on p. 153, Am I My Company's Keeper?

L0.4   Explain the penalties for crimes and the sentencing for corporate crimes
See the discussion of the sentencing guidelines and the various cases related to them on p. 146.

B. White-Collar Crimes

L0.5   List examples of white-collar crimes and their elements
See the discussion that begins on p. 149.
See the Sports & Entertainment Law discussion of the NBA referee on p. 156.

L0.6   Describe the common law crimes
See the discussion that begins on p. 156.
See the E-Commerce & Cyberlaw discussion of cyber-bullying on p. 159.

C. Criminal Law and the Computer

L0.7   Discuss crimes related to computers
See the discussion that begins on p. 157.

D. Criminal Procedure Rights for Businesses

L0.8   Describe the rights of businesses charged with crimes and the constitutional protections afforded them
See the *Dow* case on p. 162.
See the *Dickerson* case on p. 165.

KEY TERMS

blackmail	due process	facilitation payments
computer crime	Economic Espionage Act (EEA)	Federal Sentencing Guidelines
conspiracy	embezzlement	felonies
crime	extortion	Fifth Amendment

Foreign Corrupt Practices Act
 (FCPA)
forgery
Fourth Amendment
grease payments
Miranda warnings

misdemeanors
predicate act
Racketeer Influenced and Corrupt
 Organizations (RICO) Act
search warrant
Sixth Amendment

uttering
white-collar crime
White-Collar Crime Penalty
 Enhancement Act of 2002

QUESTIONS AND CASE PROBLEMS

1. Bernard Flinn operated a business known as Harvey Investment Co., Inc./High Risk Loans. Flinn worked as a loan broker, matching those who came to him with lenders willing to loan them money given their credit history and the amount involved. From 1982 through 1985, Flinn found loans for five people. Indiana requires that persons engaged in the business of brokering loans obtain a license from the state. Flinn was prosecuted for brokering loans without having a license. He raised the defense that he did not know that a license was required and that, accordingly, he lacked the criminal intent to broker loans without having a license. Does Flinn have a good defense?
[*Flinn v. Indiana,* 563 N.E.2d 536 (Ind.)]

2. H. J., Inc., and other customers of Northwestern Bell Corp. alleged that Northwestern Bell had furnished cash and tickets for air travel, plays, and sporting events and had offered employment to members of the Minnesota Public Utilities Commission in exchange for favorable treatment in rate cases before the commission. A Minnesota statute makes it a felony to bribe public officials. H. J. and other customers brought suit against Northwestern for violating the criminal bribery statute. Can the customers bring a criminal action?
[*H. J., Inc. v. Northwestern Bell Corp.,* 420 N.W.2d 673 (Minn. App.)]

3. Baker and others entered a Wal-Mart store shortly after 3:00 A.M. by cutting through the metal door with an acetylene torch. They had moved some of the merchandise in the store to the rear door, but the police arrived before the merchandise could be taken from the store. Baker was prosecuted for larceny. He raised the defense that he was not guilty of larceny because no merchandise had ever left the store. Is there enough intent and action for a crime?
[*Tennessee v. Baker,* 751 S.W.2d 154 (Tenn. App.)]

4. Gail drove her automobile after having had dinner and several drinks. She fell asleep at the wheel and ran over and killed a pedestrian. Prosecuted for manslaughter, she raised the defense that she did not intend to hurt anyone and because of the drinks did not know what she was doing. Was this a valid defense?

5. Dr. Doyle E. Campbell, an ophthalmologist, established his practice in southern Ohio in 1971. Many of Dr. Campbell's patients are elderly people who qualify for federal Medicare benefits and state Medicaid benefits. Under the existing financing system, a doctor who treats a Medicare patient is required to submit a "Medicare Health Insurance Claim Form" (HCFA Form 1500). The doctor is required to certify that "the services shown on this form were medically indicated and necessary for the health of the patient and were personally rendered by me or were rendered incident to my professional service by my employees." Claims Dr. Campbell submitted for his elderly patients ranged from $900 to $950, of which $530 to $680 were covered by the Medicare program. The government alleged that Dr. Campbell billed Medicare for several treatments that were either not performed or not necessary. Dr. Campbell was charged with fraud for the paperwork he submitted. Has he committed a crime? [*United States v. Campbell,* 845 F.2d 1374 (6th Cir.)]

6. In the late 1980s, Life Energy Resources, Ltd. (LER), a New York corporation, was a multilevel marketing network. LER's marketing plan provided that members of the general public could purchase its products only through an official LER distributor or by becoming LER distributors themselves. Each potential distributor had to be sponsored by an existing distributor and

was required to sign a distributorship agreement with LER stating that he or she would not make medical claims or use unofficial literature or marketing aids to promote LER products.

Ballistrea and his partner Michael Ricotta were at the top of the LER distribution network. Two products sold by LER were the REM SuperPro Frequency Generator (REM) and the Lifemax Miracle Cream (Miracle Cream). The REM, which sold for $1,350 to distributors, was a small box powered by electricity that ran currents through the feet and body of the user.

Ballistrea and Ricotta distributed literature and audiotapes to many potential downstream distributors and customers—some of whom were undercover government agents—touting the REM and the Miracle Cream. Other literature claimed that the Miracle Cream could alleviate the discomforts of premenstrual syndrome and reverse the effects of osteoporosis. The Food and Drug Administration charged Ballistrea and Ricotta with violating federal law for making medical claims concerning LER products. Their defense is that they never sold any of the products. They simply earned commissions as part of the marketing scheme and could not be held criminally liable on the charges. Are they correct? [*United States v. Ballistrea*, 101 F.3d 827 (2d Cir.)]

7. Carriage Homes, Inc. was a general contractor that built multifamily residential and land-development projects in Minnesota. John Arkell was Carriage Homes' chief executive officer, president, and sole shareholder. Carriage Homes built Southwinds, a condominium development of 38 residential units in Austin, Minnesota. The foundation elevations of some of the Southwinds units were lower than permitted under the State Building Code, causing storm water to pool in the units' driveways and garages. The city of Austin's development director sent Arkell a series of seven letters in 1999 and 2001 concerning the elevation problems, and Arkell gave the letters to the project managers, who failed to resolve the problems.

Minnesota makes a violation of the State Building Code a misdemeanor. On May 30, 2001, the state charged Carriage Homes and Arkell with three misdemeanor counts each, alleging a violation of the Uniform Building Code (UBC).

Carriage Homes pleaded guilty and was sentenced to a $1,000 fine. But Arkell pleaded not guilty, asserting that he could not be held criminally responsible for the violation. After a bench trial, the district court found Arkell guilty. He was sentenced to pay a fine, pay restitution to the condominium owners, and serve 90 days in jail, with 80 days stayed pending his compliance with sentencing conditions. Mr. Arkell appealed on the grounds that the employees and subcontractors had simply not followed his orders and he was not responsible for their failures. Is he correct? [*State v. Arkell*, 657 N.W.2d 883 (Minn. App. 2003)]

8. James Durham runs an art gallery. He has several paintings from unknown artists that he has listed for sale. The paintings always sell at his weekly auction for $20,000 to $50,000 above what James believes them to be worth. James learns that the bidders at the auctions are employed by an olive distributor located near the shipping yards of the city. What concerns should Durham have about the art, the bidders and the large purchase prices?

9. Jennings operated a courier service to collect and deliver money. The contract with his customers allowed him a day or so to deliver the money that had been collected. Instead of holding collections until delivered, Jennings made short-term investments with the money. He always made deliveries to the customers on time, but because he kept the profit from the investments for himself, Jennings was prosecuted for embezzlement. Was he guilty? [*New York v. Jennings*, 504 N.E.2d 1079 (N.Y.)]

10. In April 2006, a DC-9 aircraft landed in the port city of Ciudad del Carmen, located 500 miles east of Mexico City. When the plane's crew began directing security personnel away from the plane, the suspicious activity piqued the curiosity of local law enforcement officials. They decided to search the plane and found 128 suitcases packed with over 56 tons of cocaine. The cocaine was to have been delivered to Toluca, near Mexico City. In investigating the plane and individual involved, law enforcement agents discovered that the plane had been purchased with money that had been laundered through two U.S. banks, Wachovia Corp. and Bank of America Corp. Neither bank

was actually aware that the money was being used to purchase a plane that would then be used for drug trafficking. Are the banks still criminally liable for breaking the rules? Explain why or why not. What if the banks were aware of large sums of money being run through particular customers' accounts? Would that knowledge make a difference?

11. Grabert ran Beck's, an amusement center in Louisiana. He held a license for video gambling machines. Louisiana makes it illegal to allow a minor to play a video gambling machine. A mother came into Grabert's center carrying her 23-month-old baby in her arms. She sat at the video poker machine with her child on her lap and proceeded to play. State troopers witnessed the baby pushing the buttons on the machine at least three times. The Department of Public Safety and Corrections revoked Grabert's video gaming license because a minor had been allowed to play the machines, and Grabert sought judicial review. The trial court reversed, and the department appealed. Has Grabert committed the crime of allowing a minor to engage in gaming? Is this the crime of allowing a minor to gamble? [*Grabert v. Department of Public Safety & Corrections*, 680 So.2d 764 (La. App.) *cert.* denied; *Grabert v. State through Dept. of Public Safety and Corrections*, 685 So.2d 126 (La.)]

12. The Banco Central administered a humanitarian plan for the government of Ecuador. Fernando Banderas and his wife presented false claims that the bank paid. After the fraud was discovered, the bank sued Banderas and his wife for damages for fraud and treble damages under the Florida version of RICO. Banderas and his wife asserted that they were not liable for RICO damages because there was no proof that they were related to organized crime and because the wrong they had committed was merely ordinary fraud. They had not used any racketeering methods. Is involvement with organized crime a requirement for liability under RICO? [*Banderas v. Banco Central del Ecuador*, 461 So.2d 265 (Fla. App.)]

13. Kravitz owned 100 percent of the stock of American Health Programs, Inc. (AHP). To obtain the Philadelphia Fraternal Order of Police as a customer for AHP, Kravitz paid money bribes to persons who he thought were officers of that organization but who in fact were federal undercover agents. He was prosecuted for violating RICO. He was convicted, and the court ordered the forfeiture of all of Kravitz's shares of AHP stock. Can a forfeiture be ordered? [*United States v. Kravitz*, 738 F.2d 102 (3d Cir.)]

14. Howell made long-distance telephone calls through the telephone company's computer-controlled switching system to solicit funding for a nonexistent business enterprise. What crimes did Howell commit? [*New Mexico v. Howell*, 895 F.2d 232 (N.M. App.)]

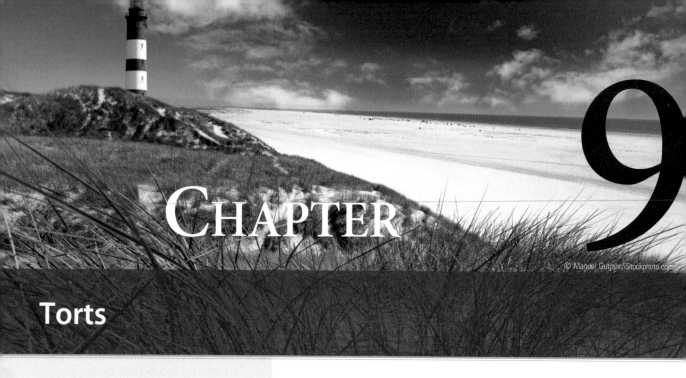

CHAPTER 9

Torts

© Manuel Gutjahr/iStockphoto.com

learningoutcomes

After studying this chapter, you should be able to

LO.1 Explain the difference between torts and crimes

LO.2 Identify the possible tort theories applicable to transmission of disease cases

LO.3 Distinguish between an assault and a battery

LO.4 Explain the three different torts of invasion of privacy

LO.5 Explain the torts of defamation and defenses

LO.6 Explain the elements of negligence and defenses

LO.7 Explain the tort of strict liability and why very few defenses are avaliable

T he law of torts permits individuals and companies to recover from other individuals and companies for wrongs committed against them. Tort law provides rights and remedies for conduct that meets the elements required to establish that a wrong has occurred.

A. General Principles

Civil, or noncriminal, wrongs that are not breaches of contract are governed by tort law. This chapter covers the types of civil wrongs that constitute torts and the remedies available for those wrongs.

1. What Is a Tort?

tort – civil wrong that interferes with one's property or person.

Tort comes from the Latin term *tortus,* which means "crooked, dubious, twisted." Torts are actions that are not straight but are crooked, or civil, wrongs. A tort is an interference with someone's person or property. **For Example,** entering someone's house without his or her permission is an interference and constitutes the tort of trespass. Causing someone's character to be questioned is a wrong against the person and is the tort of defamation. The law provides protection against these harms in the form of remedies awarded after the wrongs are committed. These remedies are civil remedies for the acts of interference by others.

2. Tort and Crime Distinguished

A *crime* is a wrong that arises from a violation of a public duty, whereas a *tort* is a wrong that arises from a violation of a private duty. A crime is a wrong of such a serious nature that the appropriate level of government steps in to prosecute and punish the wrongdoer to deter others from engaging in the same type of conduct. However, whenever the act that is committed as a crime causes harm to an identifiable person, that person may recover from the wrongdoer for monetary damages to compensate for the harm. For the person who experiences the direct harm, the act is called a *tort*; for the government, the same act is called a *crime.*

When the same act is both a crime and a tort, the government may prosecute the wrongdoer for a violation of criminal law, and the individual who experiences the direct harm may recover damages. **For Example,** O. J. Simpson was charged by the state of California with the murder of his ex-wife, Nicole Brown Simpson, and her friend Ron Goldman. A criminal trial was held in which O. J. Simpson was acquitted. Simpson was subsequently sued civilly by the families of Nicole Simpson and Ron Goldman for the tort of wrongful death. The jury in the civil case found Simpson civilly liable and the court ordered him to pay nearly $20 million in damages plus interest. Only $382,000 of this judgment has actually been paid to the families.

3. Types of Torts

intentional tort – civil wrong that results from intentional conduct.

There are three types of torts: intentional torts, negligence, and strict liability. **Intentional torts** are those that occur when wrongdoers engage in intentional conduct. **For Example,** striking another person in a fight is an intentional act and would be the tort of battery and possibly also the crime of battery. Your arm striking another person's nose in a fast-moving crowd of people at a rock concert is not a tort or crime because your arm was pushed unintentionally by the force of the crowd. If you stretched out your arms in that crowd or began to swing your arms about and struck another person, you would be behaving carelessly in a crowd of people; and, although you may not have committed an intentional tort, it is possible that your careless conduct constitutes the tort of **negligence**. Careless actions, or actions taken without thinking through their consequences, constitute negligence. The harm to the other person's nose may not have been intended, but there is liability for these accidental harms under negligence. **For Example,** if you run a red light, hit another car, and injure its driver, you did not intend the result. However, your careless behavior of disregarding a traffic signal resulted in the injury, and you would have liability for your negligence to that driver.

> **negligence** – failure to exercise due care under the circumstances in consequence of which harm is proximately caused to one to whom the defendant owed a duty to exercise due care.

In transmission of disease cases, depending on the facts, both intentional torts and negligence theories may apply. A person who knows or should know that he or she has herpes and fails to disclose that fact, or misrepresents that he or she is disease-free, may be liable to a sexual partner. The torts theories may include negligence, battery, intentional infliction of emotional distress, and fraud. In most cases, the three words "I have herpes" is fair notice of the danger of infection.[1] However, saying it is okay to have sex because the individual was not having an outbreak of the disease is actionable. **For Example,** Thomas R. disclosed to his girlfriend that he had herpes but nevertheless told her that it was "okay" to have sex with him because he was not then experiencing an outbreak of the disease. The jury's finding of negligence and fraudulent concealment in the transmission of the disease was upheld by the appeals court, and the plaintiff was awarded compensatory damages as well as $2.75 million in punitive damages.[2]

> **strict liability** – civil wrong for which there is absolute liability because of the inherent danger in the underlying activity, for example, the use of explosives.

Strict liability is another type of tort that imposes liability without regard to whether there was any intent to harm or any negligence occurred. Strict liability is imposed without regard to fault. Strict or absolute liability is imposed because the activity involved is so dangerous that there must be full accountability. Nonetheless, the activity is necessary and cannot be prohibited. The compromise is to allow the activity but ensure that its dangers and resulting damages are fully covered through the imposition of full liability for all injuries that result. **For Example,** contractors often need to use dynamite to take a roadway through a mountainside or demolish a building that has become a hazard. When the dynamite is used, noise, debris, and possibly dangerous pieces of earth and building will descend on others' land and possibly on people. In most states, contractors are held strictly liable for the resulting damage from the use of dynamite. The activity is necessary and not illegal, but those who use dynamite must be prepared to compensate those who are injured as a result.

Other areas in which there is strict liability for activity include the storage of flammable materials and crop dusting. The federal government and the states have pure food laws that impose absolute liability on manufacturers who fail to meet the statutory standards for their products. Another area of strict liability is *product liability,* which is covered in Chapter 25.

---

[1] *R.A.P. v. B.J.P.,* 428 N.W.2d 103, 108 (Minn. App. 1988).
[2] *Behr v. Redmond,* 123 Cal. Rptr. 3d 97 (Cal. App. 2011).

B. Intentional Torts

4. Assault

An *assault* is intentional conduct that threatens a person with a well-founded fear of imminent harm coupled with the present ability to carry out the threat of harm. **For Example,** the angry assertion "I'm going to kick your butt" along with aggressive movement in the direction of the victim with the intent to carry out the threat is an assault, even though a third person intervenes to stop the intended action. Mere words, however, although insulting, are ordinarily insufficient to constitute an assault.

5. Battery

A *battery* is the intentional, wrongful touching of another person without that person's consent. Thus, a threat to use force is an assault, and the actual use of force is the battery. The single action of striking an individual can be both a crime and a tort. A lawsuit for the tort of battery provides a plaintiff with the opportunity to recover damages resulting from the battery. The plaintiff must prove damages, however.

CASE SUMMARY

An Exchange of Unpleasantries ...

FACTS: Moore and Beye had an altercation after a public meeting regarding airport expansion. Moore owns a ranch near the airport and staunchly opposes expansion. Beye owns a flying service and avidly supports expansion. Moore and Beye exchanged unpleasantries while leaving the meeting. Beye then punched Moore on the left side of the jaw. Moore stumbled but caught himself before falling. He then exclaimed to the crowd, "You saw that. You are my witnesses. I've been assaulted. I want that man arrested." Ravalli County deputies took Beye into custody, and the state charged him with misdemeanor assault. Moore visited the hospital complaining of back and neck pain two days later and contended that he had injured his back while reeling from Beye's punch. He filed a civil complaint against Beye for damages. Moore's evidence mostly concerned his alleged back injury. Beye did not contest that he had punched Moore. His evidence countered that Moore's back problems had existed before the altercation. The judge instructed the jury that Beye had committed a battery as a matter of law and directed that they answer the question, "Was Moore damaged as a result of the battery?" The jury voted 11 to 1 that the battery did not injure Moore, and Moore appealed.

DECISION: Judgment for Beye. Beye presented the testimony of several eyewitnesses and a medical expert that Moore had sustained no damages. Although Moore presented considerable evidence to the contrary, it was not the court's function to agree or disagree with the verdict. Beye presented sufficient evidence to uphold the jury's verdict. [*Moore v. Beye,* **122 P.3d 1212 (Mont. 2005)**]

6. False Imprisonment

false imprisonment— intentional detention of a person without that person's consent; called the *shopkeeper's tort* when shoplifters are unlawfully detained.

False imprisonment is the intentional detention of a person without that person's consent.[3] The detention need not be for any specified period of time, for any detention against one's will is false imprisonment. False imprisonment is often called

[3] *Forgie-Buccioni v. Hannaford Bros. Inc.,* 413 F.3d 175 (1st Cir. 2005).

the *shopkeeper's tort* because so much liability has been imposed on store owners for their unreasonable detention of customers suspected of shoplifting. Requiring a customer to sit in the manager's office or not allowing a customer to leave the store can constitute the tort of false imprisonment. Shop owners do, however, need the opportunity to investigate possible thefts in their stores. As a result, all states have some form of privilege or protection for store owners called a *shopkeeper's privilege*.

The **shopkeeper's privilege** permits the store owner to detain a suspected shoplifter based on reasonable suspicion for a reasonable time without resulting liability for false imprisonment to the accused customer.[4] The privilege applies even if the store owner was wrong about the customer being a shoplifter, so long as the store owner acted based on reasonable suspicions and treated the accused shoplifter in a reasonable manner.

shopkeeper's privilege – right of a store owner to detain a suspected shoplifter based on reasonable cause and for a reasonable time without resulting liability for false imprisonment.

CASE SUMMARY

A Can of Mousse: A Tote Bag of Trouble

FACTS: Patricia Holguin went to Sally's Beauty Supply Store carrying her "eco-friendly canvas shopping tote," a large bag that is conspicuous when used. Upon entering the store, there were no posted signs stating that shopping totes were not allowed. She picked up a can of mousse that was not exactly what she wanted and started to carry it in her tote toward the front counter to ask the cashier a question about it. As she walked toward the front of the store the assistant manager approached her and asked what was in the bag. She was detained by this manager, who told her that once she put the hair mousse in her tote bag, she was shoplifting. Holguin's lawsuit for false imprisonment against the store was dismissed with prejudice by the trial court. This court held that once she placed the merchandise in her bag, the store had probable cause to believe she was shoplifting and had a statutory conditional privilege to detain her, free from civil liability for false imprisonment, because she "willfully concealed merchandise." Holguin appealed.

DECISION: The court of appeals reversed the district court's decision. In general, merchants and their employees have a conditional privilege to detain a person free from civil liability based on probable cause, or reasonable grounds to believe that the individual "willfully concealed" merchandise without paying for it, provided the detention is for a reasonable time and conducted in a reasonable manner. "Willfully concealed," however, requires more than merely putting merchandise out of sight. In self-service stores customers have implied permission to pick up, handle, move, try on, replace, and carry about merchandise within the store. There must be circumstances which reflect that the purpose of the concealment is adverse to the store's right to be paid before the conclusion can be drawn that the merchandise was "willfully concealed" under the statute providing the conditional privilege to detain a customer. Placing the can of mousse in a reusable, personal canvas shopping bag to carry to the front of the store to ask a question, without more, did not constitute "willful concealment." [***Holguin v. Sally's Beauty Supply, Inc.,*** 264 P.3d 732 (N. Mex. App. 2011)]

7. Intentional Infliction of Emotional Distress

The **intentional infliction of emotional distress** (IIED) is a tort involving conduct that goes beyond all bounds of decency and produces mental anguish in the harmed individual. This tort requires proof of outrageous conduct and resulting emotional

intentional infliction of emotional distress – tort that produces mental anguish caused by conduct that exceeds all bounds of decency.

[4] *Limited Stores, Inc. v. Wilson-Robinson,* 876 S.W.2d 248 (Ark. 1994); see also *Wal-Mart Stores, Inc. v. Binns,* 15 S.W.3d 320 (Ark. 2000).

distress in the victim. **For Example,** Erica Schoen, a 16-year employee of Freightliner, returned to work on light duty after surgery for a work-related shoulder injury. She was assigned to work out of the nurse's station under two employees who intentionally worked her beyond her restrictions, assigned her to humiliating work, repeatedly called her worthless, and used her as a personal servant—ordering her to get snacks, sodas, and lunches for them and not reimbursing her. After five months of this treatment, Erica brought the matter to the human resources manager, who told her, in part, "Nobody wants you. You're worthless. We build trucks down here…." Erica became hysterical and thereafter required psychiatric care. The jury awarded $250,000 for IIED, and it was upheld on appeal because the repetitive misconduct and its duration, ratified by the human resource manager, was intolerable.[5]

8. Invasion of Privacy

invasion of privacy—tort of intentional intrusion into the private affairs of another.

The right of privacy is the right to be free of unreasonable intrusion into one's private affairs. The tort of **invasion of privacy** actually consists of three different torts: (1) intrusion into the plaintiff's private affairs (for example, planting a microphone in an office or home); (2) public disclosure of private facts (for example, disclosing private financial information, such as a business posting returned checks from customers near its cash register in a public display); and (3) appropriation of another's name, likeness, or image for commercial advantage. This form of invasion of privacy is generally referred to as the *right of publicity.* The elements of this tort are (1) appropriation of the plaintiff's name or likeness for the value associated with it, and not in an incidental manner or for a newsworthy purpose, (2) identification of the plaintiff in the publication, and (3) an advantage or benefit to the defendant. The right to publicity is designed to protect the commercial interest of celebrities in their identities.

For Example, popular and critically acclaimed rock and roll musician Don Henley, the founder and member of the band The Eagles, successfully sued a department store chain that ran an international newspaper advertisement for its Henley shirt, which stated in large letters as the focus of the ad "This is Don's henley." The ad (1) used the value associated with the famous name Don Henley to get consumers to read it, (2) the plaintiff was identifiable in the ad, and (3) the ad was created with the belief that use of the words "Don's henley" would help sell the product.[6]

CASE SUMMARY

Cashing in on Catherine's Vacation

FACTS: Catherine Bosley worked as a television news anchor for WKBN, Channel 27, in Youngstown, Ohio. While on vacation with her husband in Florida, she participated in a "wet t-shirt" contest that was videotaped without her consent by DreamGirls, Inc., and licensed to Marvad Corp., which runs a Web site for adult entertainment through a subscription service on the Internet. Marvad used depictions of her in advertisements to promote the materials and

[5] *Schoen v. Freightliner LLC,* 199 P.3d 332 (Or. App. 2008).
[6] *Henley v. Dillard Department Stores,* 46 F. Supp. 2d 587 (N.D. Tex. 1999).

CASE SUMMARY

Continued

services it markets. Web site searches related to Catherine Bosley in 2004 were the most popular search on the World Wide Web. Due to the publicity, she resigned from her position at WKBN and was prevented from seeking other employment. Bosley sought an injunction under the right of publicity theory against the defendants from using her image in any manner that promotes the sale of their goods or services. The defendants contended that an injunction would violate their First Amendment rights.

DECISION: Judgment for Bosley. The First Amendment does not immunize defendants from damages for infringement of the right of publicity. No significant editorial comment or artistic expression involving First Amendment protections applies in this case. If any "speech" interest is involved, it is commercial speech. At its core, the defendants are selling Bosley's image for a profit without her consent. It is in violation of her right of publicity, which protects one's right to be free from the appropriation of one's persona. The injunction sought was granted. [*Bosley v. Wildwett.com*, **310 F. Supp. 2d 914 (N.D. Ohio 2004)**]

Some states refer to the right of publicity as a cause of action for *commercial misappropriation of a name or likeness,* and provide two vehicles a plaintiff can use to protect the economic value of one's name, a common law action or a statutory remedy. The *Schlein* case involved a breach of contract action and an action for commercial misappropriation of his name.

CASE SUMMARY

The Name Game: We Are Discontinuing Your Royalty on the "Schlein Ultra," Dr. Schlein

FACTS: Orthopedic Systems, Inc. (OSI), and Dr. Schlein entered into a contract, whereby OSI would manufacture and sell an unpatented product originally designed by Dr. Schlein called the "Schlein Shoulder Positioner," to be used in arthroscopic shoulder surgery. The contract called for a 5% royalty of the list price less discounts. Over the years OSI's marketing brochures thanked "Allen P. Schlein M.D. for his assistance in the development of the product." OSI paid royalty checks from January 1991 to January 2005, when OSI paid its last royalty payment for the period ending December 2004. In January 2005, OSI sent a letter to Dr. Schlein stating that in light of the fact that there is no patent protection on the product, it would be discontinuing the royalty. From January 2005 until July 29, 2005, OSI continued to market and sell the product using Dr. Schlein's name. OSI sued Dr. Schlein for declaratory relief and reformation of the royalty contract. Dr. Schlein cross-complained for breach of contract and commercial misappropriation of his name. The jury awarded Dr. Schlein $616,043 for failure to pay royalties under the contract. OSI earned $1,220,000 in profits attributed to the use of Dr. Schlein's name during the period from January 1, 2005 to July 31, 2005, after which OSI stopped using Schlein's name. The trial court declined to award the profits to Schlein, and both parties appealed.

DECISION: The statutory remedy of Section 3444(a) requires the payment of the greater of $750, or the actual damages suffered as a result of the unauthorized use, and any profits for the unauthorized use that are attributable to use and are not taken into account in computing actual

CASE SUMMARY

Continued

damages. The legislative history for the minimum $750 award was intended to fill the gap that existed in the common law tort of invasion of privacy as applied to noncelebrities whose names lacked commercial value on the open market. Unlike sports and entertainment stars, noncelebrities often could not prove damages under the common law; therefore, the statute established a concrete remedy for the little man with a minimum payment. An interpretation that limits damages to $750 as an alternative to all other damages would be contrary to the spirit of the statute. Judgment for Dr. Schlein who is entitled as well to the $1,220,000 profits as a result of OSI's unauthorized use of his name. [***Orthopedic Systems, Inc. v. Schlein,*** **135 Cal. Rptr. 3d 200 (Cal. App. 2011)**]

9. Defamation

defamation – untrue statement by one party about another to a third party.

slander – defamation of character by spoken words or gestures.

libel – written or visual defamation without legal justification.

Defamation is an untrue statement by one party about another to a third party. **Slander** is oral or spoken defamation, and **libel** is written (and in some cases broadcast) defamation. The elements for defamation are (1) a statement about a person's reputation, honesty, or integrity that is untrue; (2) publication (accomplished when a third party hears or reads the defamatory statement); (3) a statement directed at a particular person; and (4) damages that result from the statement.[7]

For Example, a false statement by the owner of a business that the former manager was fired for stealing when he was not would be defamation, and the former manager's damages could be his inability to find another position because of the statement's impact on his reputation.

In cases in which the victim is a public figure, such as a Hollywood celebrity or a professional sports player, another element is required, the element of malice, which means that what was said or written was done with the knowledge that the information was false or with reckless disregard for whether it was true or false.

CASE SUMMARY

"I'm a Great Builder," Trump Said, Nonresponsively

FACTS: Timothy O'Brien, the author of *Trump Nation, the Art of Being the Donald,* and his publisher were sued by Donald Trump for defamation. In writing the book in 2005, O'Brien reinterviewed three anonymous sources who lowered their estimates of Trump's net worth at that time to between $150 million and $250 million because of the decreased value of Trump's casino holding at the time he was writing the book. O'Brien, who interviewed Trump, wrote:

---

[7] Regarding damages, where one publishes a slander that imputes to another a communicable disease, or would adversely affect that person's fitness for the proper conduct of a lawful business, trade, or profession, the words are actionable in themselves, and the law implies compensatory damages. Once compensatory damages are established the jury will assess punitive damages to punish the party who committed the wrong and to deter others from committing similar wrongs in the future. See *Tanner v. Ebbole,* 2011 WL 4425540 (Ala. App. 2011) where the jury returned "nominal" compensatory damages of $1 and punitive damages of $100,000 against Paul Averette, the owner of a competing tattoo business, for slanderous statements to several patrons that his competitor Chassity Ebbole had hepatitis, syphilis, gonorrhea, and AIDS and that she used "nasty needles."

CASE SUMMARY

Continued

So I asked around for guidance. Three people with direct knowledge of Donald's finances, people who had worked closely with him for years, told me that they thought his net worth was somewhere between $150 million and $250 million. By anyone's standards this still qualified Donald as comfortably wealthy, but none of these people thought he was remotely close to being a billionaire.

That passage was followed by:

Donald dismissed this as naysaying. "You can go ahead and speak to guys who have four-hundred-pound wives at home who are jealous of me, but the guys who really know me know I'm a great builder," he told me.

This and other statements underestimating Trump's wealth according to Trump's lawsuit were false statements that tended to harm his reputation in the eyes of the community. From summary judgment in favor of O'Brien and the publisher, Trump appealed.

DECISION: Judgment for O'Brien and the publisher. In order to establish a prima facie case of defamation, a plaintiff must show that a defendant communicated to a third person a false statement about the plaintiff that tended to harm the plaintiff's reputation in the eyes of the community or to cause others to avoid him. Because there is no doubt that Trump is a public figure, to be actionable, the alleged defamatory statements by O'Brien must have been published with "actual malice" or reckless disregard for the truth. There is no evidence to support Trump's conclusion that the confidential sources utilized by O'Brien were fictitious. The issue is not whether the book contained false statements or whether O'Brien had ill will toward him as Trump contends, but, rather, whether the book contained defamatory statements made with actual malice. The record does not support this contention. [*Trump v. O'Brien,* **29 A.3d 1090 (N.J. Super. 2011)**]

---

absolute privilege – complete defense against the tort of defamation, as in the speeches of members of Congress on the floor and witnesses in a trial.

The defenses to defamation include the truth. If the statement is true, even if it is harmful to the victim, it is not the tort of defamation.[8]

Some statements are privileged, and this privilege provides a full or partial defense to the tort of defamation. **For Example,** members of Congress enjoy an **absolute privilege** when they are speaking on the floor of the Senate or the House because public policy requires a free dialogue on the issues pending in a legislative body. The same absolute privilege applies to witnesses in court proceedings to encourage witnesses with information to come forward and testify. Where a witness granted immunity from prosecution testifies before a governmental agency, the witness is entitled to immunity from defamation lawsuits. **For Example,** Roger Clemens sued his former trainer, Brian McNamee, for defamation, contending that McNamee falsely stated to a congressional committee that Clemens had used steroids during his professional baseball career. This defamation claim was dismissed because McNamee's statements were entitled to absolute immunity on the reasoning that the proper administration of justice requires full disclosure from witnesses without fear of retaliatory lawsuits.[9]

---

[8] See *Stark v. Zeta Phi Beta Sorority Inc.*, 587 F. Supp. 2d 170 (D. D.C. 2008).

[9] *Clemens v. McNamee*, 608 F. Supp. 2d 811 (S.D. Tex. 2009). On June 18, 2012, Clemens was acquitted of all six counts of lying to Congress.

qualified privilege – media privilege to print inaccurate information without liability for defamation, so long as a retraction is printed and there was no malice.

The media enjoy a **qualified privilege** for stories that turn out to be false. Their qualified privilege is a defense to defamation so long as the information was released without malice and a retraction or correction is made when the matter is brought to their attention.

A *qualified privilege* to make a defamatory statement in the workplace exists when the statement is made to protect the interests of the private employer on a work-related matter, especially when reporting actual or suspected wrongdoing. **For Example,** Neda Lewis was fired from her job at Carson Oil Company for allegedly stealing toilet paper. The employee in charge of supplies noticed toilet paper was regularly missing from the ladies room, and one evening from a third-floor window overlooking the parking lot, she observed that the plaintiff's bag contained two rolls of toilet paper. She reported the matter to the executive secretary, who reported it to both the president and the CEO of the firm, who decided to fire her. Two other employees were also informed. The employer was able to successfully raise the defense of a qualified privilege to Ms. Lewis' defamation action for "false accusations of theft" since all of the employees involved were participants in the investigation and termination of the employee.[10]

A new statutory privilege has been evolving with respect to letters of recommendation and references given by employers for employees who are applying for jobs at other companies. Most companies, because of concerns about liability for defamation, will only confirm that a former employee did work at their firm and will provide the time period during which the person was employed. However, many employees who had histories that should have been revealed for safety reasons have been hired because no negative information was released. Numerous states now have statutes that provide employers a qualified privilege with respect to references and recommendations. So long as the employer acts in good faith in providing information, there is no liability for defamation to the former employee as a result of the information provided.

10. Product Disparagement

slander of title – malicious making of false statements as to a seller's title.

trade libel – written defamation about a product or service.

product disparagement – false statements made about a product or business.

Although the comparison of products and services is healthy for competition, false statements about another's products constitute a form of slander called **slander of title** or libel called **trade libel**; collectively, these are known as **product disparagement**, which occurs when someone makes false statements about another business, its products, or its abilities.[11] The elements of product disparagement are (1) a false statement about a particular business product or about its service in terms of honesty, reputation, ability, or integrity; (2) communication of the statement to a third party; and (3) damages.

11. Wrongful Interference with Contracts

contract interference – tort in which a third party interferes with others' freedom to contract.

The tort of **contract interference** or (tortious interference with contracts) occurs when parties are not allowed the freedom to contract without interference from third parties. While the elements required to establish the tort of contract interference are complex, a basic definition is that the law affords a remedy when a third party

---

[10] *Lewis v. Carson Oil Co.*, 127 P.3d 1207 (Or. App. 2006).

[11] *Sannerud v. Brantz*, 879 P.2d 341 (Wyo. 1994). See *Suzuki Motor Corp. v. Consumers Union*, 230 F.3d 1110 (9th Cir. 2003), *cert denied* 540 U.S. 983 (2003), for an example of the complexity of a product disparagement action.

intentionally causes another to break a contract already in existence.[12] **For Example,** Nikke Finke, a newspaper reporter who had a contract with the *New York Post* to write stories about the entertainment industry for the *Post's* business section, wrote two articles about a lawsuit involving a literary agent and the Walt Disney Company over merchandising rights to the Winnie-the-Pooh characters. Finke reported that the trial court sanctioned Disney for engaging in "misuse of the discovery process" and acting in "bad faith" and ordered Disney to pay fees and costs of $90,000. Disney's president, Robert Iger, sent a letter to the *Post's* editor-in-chief, Col Allan, calling Finke's reporting an "absolute distortion" of the record and "absolutely false." Approximately two weeks after the Pooh articles were published, the *Post* fired Finke; her editor told her she was being fired for the Pooh articles. She sued Disney on numerous tort theories, including interference with her contract with the *Post*. Disney sought to have the complaint dismissed, which motion was denied by the court. The Court of Appeals concluded that Finke demonstrated a reasonable probability of proving that Iger's allegations that she made false statements in her article were themselves false; and it concluded that a jury could find Disney liable for intentional interference with contractual relations based on circumstantial evidence and negligent interference with contractual relations because it was reasonably foreseeable to Disney that the nature of its accusations against Finke would result in her termination from employment.[13]

12. Trespass

trespass – unauthorized action with respect to person or property.

A **trespass** is an unauthorized action with respect to land or personal property. A *trespass to land* is any unpermitted entry below, on, across, or above the land of another. **For Example,** Joyce Ameral's home abuts the mid-way point of the 240-yard, par-4 ninth hole of the public Middlebrook Country Club. Balls sliced and hooked by golfers have damaged her windows and screens, dented her car, and made her deck too dangerous for daytime use. Her landscapers are forced to wear hard hats when cutting her lawn. In her lawsuit against the country club owner, the court ruled that the projection of golf balls onto Ameral's property constituted a continuing trespass and it enjoined the trespass.[14]

A *trespass to personal property* is the invasion of personal property without the permission of the owner. **For Example,** the use of someone's car without that person's permission is a trespass to personal property.

C. NEGLIGENCE

The widest range of tort liability today arises in the field of negligence. Accidents happen! Property is damaged, and/or injuries result. The fact that an individual suffers an injury does not necessarily mean that the individual will be able to recover damages for the injury. **For Example,** Rhonda Nichols was shopping in the outdoor garden center at a Lowe's Home Center when a "wild bird" flew into the back of her head, causing injuries. Her negligence lawsuit against Lowe's was dismissed

---

[12] See *Ventas, Inc. v. HCP, Inc.*, 647 F.3d 291 (6th Cir. 2011); *ASDI, Inc. v. Beard Research, Inc.*, 11 A.3d 749 (Del. 2010).
[13] *Finke v. The Walt Disney Co.*, 2 Cal. Rptr. 3d 436 (Cal. App. 2003).
[14] *Ameral v. Pray*, 831 N.E.2d 915 (Mass. App. 2005).

because the owner did not have a duty to protect her from a wild bird attack because it was not reasonably foreseeable.[15] Jane Costa was passively watching a Boston Red Sox baseball game at Fenway Park when a foul ball struck her in the face, causing severe and permanent injuries. Her negligence lawsuit against the Boston Red Sox was unsuccessful because it was held that the owners had no duty to warn Ms. Costa of the obvious danger of foul balls being hit into the stands.[16] Although cases involving injury to spectators at baseball games in other jurisdictions have turned on other tort doctrines, injured fans, like Ms. Costa, are left to bear the costs of their injuries. Only when an injured person can demonstrate the following four elements of negligence is a right to recover established: (1) a duty, (2) breach of duty, (3) causation, and (4) damages.[17] Several defenses may be raised in a negligence lawsuit.

13. Elements of Negligence

(A) DUTY TO EXERCISE REASONABLE CARE. The first element of negligence is a *duty*. There is a general duty of care imposed to act as a reasonably prudent person would in similar circumstances. **For Example,** Gustavo Guzman worked for a sub-contractor as a chicken catcher at various poultry farms where a Tyson Foods employee, Brian Jones, operated a forklift and worked with the catchers setting up cages to collect birds for processing at a Tyson plant. Contrary to Tyson's instructions "never to allow catchers to move behind the forklift or otherwise out of sight," Brian moved his forklift and struck Guzman, who suffered a serious spinal injury. A general contractor, Tyson Foods, owes a duty to exercise reasonable care to a subcontractor's employee, Gustavo Guzman.[18]

malpractice – when services are not properly rendered in accordance with commonly accepted standards; negligence by a professional in performing his or her skill.

Professionals have a duty to perform their jobs at the level of a reasonable professional. For a professional such as an accountant, doctor, lawyer, dentist, or architect to avoid liability for **malpractice**, the professional must perform his or her skill in the same manner as, and at the level of, other professionals in the same field.

Those who own real property have a duty of care to keep their property in a condition that does not create hazards for guests. Businesses have a duty to inspect and repair their property so that their customers are not injured by hazards, such as spills on the floor or uneven walking areas. When customer safety is a concern, businesses have a duty to provide adequate security, such as security patrols in mall parking lots.

(B) BREACH OF DUTY. The second element of negligence is the breach of duty imposed by statute or by the application of the reasonable person standard. The defendant's conduct is evaluated against what a reasonable person would have done under the circumstances. That is, when there is sufficient proof to raise a jury question, the jury decides whether the defendant breached the duty to the injured person from a reasonable person's perspective.[19] **For Example,** the jury in Guzman's lawsuit against Tyson Foods (the *Tyson* case), after weighing all of the facts and

[15] *Nichols v. Lowe's Home Center, Inc.,* 407 F. Supp. 2d 979 (S.D. Ill. 2006).

[16] *Costa v. Boston Red Sox Baseball Club,* 809 N.E.2d 1090 (Mass. App. 2004).

[17] *Alfred v. Capital Area Soccer League, Inc.,* 669 S.E.2d 277 (N.C. App. 2008).

[18] *Tyson Foods Inc. v. Guzman,* 116 S.W.3d 233 (Tex. App. 2003). But see *Pippin v. Hill-Rom Co., Inc.,* 615 F.3d 886 (8th Cir. 2010), where a shipper's failure to load cargo onto an independent truck driver's trailer, as required by the transportation contract, did not give rise to a cause of action for negligence, where the driver was injured loading the truck by himself. The shipper owed no duty to the driver, who chose to load the truck by himself.

[19] A breach of duty may be established by the very nature of the harm to the plaintiff. The doctrine of *res ipsa loquitur* ("the event speaks for itself") provides a rebuttable presumption that the defendant was negligent when a defendant owes a duty to the plaintiff, the nature of the harm caused the plaintiff is such that it ordinarily does not happen in the absence of negligence, and the instrument causing the injury was in the defendant's exclusive control. An example of the doctrine is a lawsuit against a surgeon after a surgical device is discovered in a former patient months after the surgery by another physician seeking the cause of the patient's continuing pain subsequent to the operation.

circumstances, determined that Tyson's employee's operation of the forklift constituted a breach of Tyson's duty of care to Guzman.

(c) CAUSATION. A third element of negligence is *causation,* the element that connects the duty and the breach of duty to the injuries to the plaintiff.
For Example, in Guzman's lawsuit, the forklift operator's careless conduct was the cause in fact of this worker's injuries. A "but for" test for causation is used. *But for* Tyson employee Brian Jones' negligent conduct in moving the forklift under the circumstances surrounding the accident, Guzman would not have been injured.

Once the cause in fact is established, the plaintiff must establish *proximate cause.* That is, it must establish that the harm suffered by the injured person was a foreseeable consequence of the defendant's negligent actions. Foreseeability requires only the general danger to be foreseeable. In the *Tyson* case, the court determined that while there was some evidence that a jury could possibly infer that Tyson could not foresee an accident similar to the one involving Guzman, the evidence was legally sufficient to support the jury's finding that Tyson's negligence was foreseeable and the cause in fact of Guzman's injuries.

The landmark *Palsgraf v. Long Island Rail Road Co.* case established a limitation on liability for unforeseeable or unusual consequences following a negligent act.

CASE SUMMARY

The Scales Tipped on Causation

FACTS: Helen Palsgraf lived in Brooklyn. On a summer's day, she purchased tickets to travel to Rockaway Beach on the Long Island Rail Road (LIRR) with her two daughters. She was standing on a platform on the LIRR's East New York station when two men ran to catch another train. One of the men made it onto the train, but the other man, who was carrying a package, was unsteady as the train was about to pull out of the station. The LIRR conductor pulled him up, while the LIRR platform guard pushed him in the train, but in the process, he dropped the package. It contained fireworks and exploded! The concussion from the explosion caused the scales located next to Mrs. Palsgraf to fall over, striking and injuring her. Mrs. Palsgraf sued LIRR for the negligence of the two employees who had assisted the passenger with the package to board the train. A jury awarded her $6,000, which was upheld 3-2 by the Appellate Division. Thereafter the state's highest court considered the railroad's appeal.

DECISION: Recovery for negligence is not available unless there has been some violation of a right. Helen Palsgraf was too remote in distance from the accident for any invasion of rights. To reach a different decision would mean that there could be no end to those who might be harmed. By helping someone onto a moving train, the train employees can anticipate that the passenger himself might be injured, that other passengers might be injured, and that those around the immediate scene might be injured. But Mrs. Palsgraf was too remote for her injuries to be reasonably foreseeable as a consequence of the action of helping a passenger onto a moving train. She was 25 to 30 feet away from the scene, and the explosion cannot be called the proximate cause of her concussion and other injuries. [***Palsgraf v. Long Island R.R. Co.,*** **162 N.E. 99 (N.Y. 1928)]**

(D) DAMAGES. The plaintiff in a personal injury negligence lawsuit must establish the actual losses caused by the defendant's breach of duty of care and is entitled to be made whole for all losses. The successful plaintiff is entitled to compensation for (1) past and future pain and suffering (mental anguish), (2) past and future physical impairment, (3) past and future medical care, and (4) past and future loss of earning capacity. Life and work life expectancy are critical factors to consider in assessing damage involving permanent disabilities with loss of earning capacity. Expert witnesses are utilized at trial to present evidence based on worklife tables and present value tables to deal with these economic issues. The jury considers all of the evidence in the context of the elements necessary to prove negligence and all defenses raised, and it renders a verdict. **For Example,** in the *Tyson* case, the defendant presented evidence and argued that Gustavo Guzman was himself negligent regarding the accident. The jury found that both parties were negligent and attributed 80 percent of the fault to Tyson and 20 percent to Guzman (this is called *comparative negligence* and is discussed in the following section). The jury awarded Guzman $931,870.51 in damages ($425,000.00 for past physical pain and mental anguish, $150,000.00 for future physical pain and mental anguish, $10,000.00 for past physical impairment, $10,000.00 for future physical impairment, $51,870.51 for past medical care, $5,000.00 for future medical care, $70,000.00 for past lost earning capacity, and $210,000.00 for future lost earning capacity). After deducting 20 percent of the total jury award for Guzman's own negligence, the trial court's final judgment awarded Guzman $745,496.41.

In some situations, the independent actions of two defendants occur to cause harm. **For Example,** Penny Shipler was rendered a quadriplegic as a result of a Chevrolet S-10 Blazer rollover accident. She sued the driver Kenneth Long for negligence and General Motors for negligent design of the Blazer's roof. She was awarded $18.5 million in damages. Because two causes provided a single indivisible injury, the two defendants were held jointly and severally liable.[20] Under *joint and several liability,* each defendant may be held liable to pay the entire judgment. However, should one defendant pay the entire judgment, that party may sue the other for "contribution" for its proportionate share.

In some cases in which the breach of duty was shocking, plaintiffs may be awarded *punitive damages.* However, punitive (also called *exemplary*) damages are ordinarily applied when the defendant's tortious conduct is attended by circumstances of fraud, malice, or willful or wanton conduct.[21]

14. Defenses to Negligence

(A) CONTRIBUTORY NEGLIGENCE. A plaintiff who is also negligent gives the defendant the opportunity to raise the defense of **contributory negligence**, which the defendant establishes by utilizing the elements of negligence previously discussed, including the plaintiff's duty to exercise reasonable care for his or her own safety, the breach of that duty, causation, and harm. Under common law, the defense of contributory negligence, if established, is a complete bar to recovery of damages from the defendant.

The *Hardesty case* involves the application of the contributory negligence defense.

contributory negligence – negligence of the plaintiff that contributes to injury and at common law bars from recovery from the defendant although the defendant may have been more negligent than the plaintiff.

---

[20] *Shipler v. General Motors Corp.,* 710 N.W.2d 807 (Neb. 2006).
[21] See *Eden Electrical, Ltd. v. Amana Co.,* 370 F.3d 824 (8th Cir. 2004); and *University of Colorado v. American Cyanamid Co.,* 342 F.3d 1298 (Fed. Cir. 2003).

CASE SUMMARY

Keep Your Eye on the Ball in Sports: Keep Your Eye on the 300-Pound Boxes in Trucking

FACTS: Lawrence Hardesty is an over-the-road tractor-trailer truck driver who picked up a load of stadium seating equipment for the NFL stadium under construction in Baltimore. The equipment was packaged in large corrugated cardboard boxes weighing several hundred pounds. The shipper, American Seating Co., loaded the trailer while Hardesty remained in the cab of his truck doing "paperwork" and napping. Considerable open space existed between the boxes and the rear door of the trailer. The evidence showed that Hardesty failed to properly examine the load bars used to secure the boxes from movement during transit. When Hardesty arrived at the Baltimore destination, he opened the rear trailer door and boxes at the end of the trailer fell out and injured him. Hardesty brought a personal injury negligence action against the shipper. American Seating Co. responded that Hardesty was contributorily negligent, thus barring his negligence claim.

DECISION: Judgment for American Seating Co. because the claim is barred by Hardesty's contributory negligence. His decision to ignore the loading process by remaining in his truck, oblivious to the manner and means of the loading of the trailer, coupled with his own failure to examine the load bars sufficiently to confirm that they would "adequately secure" the cargo, together with his decision, in the face of his prior omissions, to open the doors of the trailer upon his arrival in Baltimore while standing within the zone of danger created by the possibility (of which he negligently failed to inform himself) of injury from cargo falling out of the trailer, cohered to rise to the level of a cognizable breach of duty—contributory negligence. [*Hardesty v. American Seating Co.*, 194 F. Supp. 2d 447 (D. Md. 2002)]

The contributory negligence defense has given way to the defense of comparative negligence in most states.

(B) COMPARATIVE NEGLIGENCE. Because contributory negligence produced harsh results with no recovery of damages for an injured plaintiff, most states have adopted a fairer approach to handling situations in which both the plaintiff and the defendant are negligent; it is called *comparative negligence*. Comparative negligence is a defense that permits a negligent plaintiff to recover some damages but only in proportion to the defendant's degree of fault.[22] **For Example,** in the *Tyson* case, both the defendant and the plaintiff were found to be negligent. The jury attributed 80 percent of the fault for the plaintiff's injury to Tyson and 20 percent of the fault to the plaintiff, Guzman. While Guzman's total damages were $931,870, they were reduced by 20 percent, and the final judgment awarded Guzman was $745,496.

Some comparative negligence states refuse to allow the plaintiff to recover damages if the plaintiff's fault was more than 50 percent of the cause of the harm.[23]

(C) ASSUMPTION OF THE RISK. The assumption of the risk defense has two categories. *Express assumption of the risk* involves a written exculpatory agreement under which a plaintiff acknowledges the risks involved in certain activities and releases the defendant from prospective liability for personal injuries sustained as a result of the

---

[22] *City of Chicago v. M/V Morgan*, 375 F.3d 563 (7th Cir. 2004).
[23] *Davenport v. Cotton Hope Plantation*, 482 S.E.2d 569 (S.C. App. 1997).

defendant's negligent conduct. Examples include ski lift tickets, white water rafting contracts, permission for high school cheerleading activities, and parking lot claim checks. In most jurisdictions these agreements are enforceable as written. However, in some jurisdictions they may be considered unenforceable because they violate public policy. **For Example,** Gregory Hanks sued the Powder Ridge Ski Resort for negligence regarding serious injuries he sustained while snowtubing at the defendant's facility. He had signed a release which explicitly provided that the snowtuber: *["fully] assume[s] all risks associated with [s]nowtubing,* even if due to the NEGLIGENCE" of the defendants [emphasis in original]. The Supreme Court of Connecticut found that the release was unenforceable because it violated the public policy by shifting the risk of negligence to the weaker bargainer.[24]

Implied primary assumption of the risk arises when a plaintiff has impliedly consented, often in advance of any negligence by the defendant, to relieve a defendant of a duty to the plaintiff regarding specific known and appreciated risks. It is a subjective standard, one specific to the plaintiff and his or her situation. **For Example,** baseball mom Delinda Taylor took her two boys to a Seattle Mariners baseball game and was injured during the pregame warm-up when a ball thrown by José Mesa got past Freddie Garcia, striking Taylor in the face and causing serious injuries. The defendant baseball team successfully raised the affirmative defense of implied primary assumption of the risk by showing that Mrs. Taylor had full subjective understanding of the specific risk of getting hit by a thrown baseball, and she voluntarily chose to encounter that risk.[25] Riding in a motorcycle procession on a Los Angeles freeway qualifies as an application of the implied primary assumption of the risk doctrine regarding involvement in a traffic collision.[26]

A number of states have either abolished the defense of assumption of the risk, reclassifying the defense as comparative negligence so as not to completely bar a plaintiff's recovery of damages, or have eliminated the use of the assumption of the risk terminology and handle cases under the duty, breach of duty, causation, and harm elements of negligence previously discussed.[27]

(D) IMMUNITY. Governments are generally immune from tort liability.[28] This rule has been eroded by decisions and in some instances by statutes, such as the Federal Tort Claims Act. Subject to certain exceptions, this act permits the recovery of damages from the United States for property damage, personal injury, or death action claims arising from the negligent act or omission of any employee of the United States under such circumstances that the United States, if a private person, would be liable to the claimant in accordance with the law of the place where the act or omission occurred. A rapidly growing number of states have abolished governmental immunity, although many still recognize it.

Until the early 1900s, charities were immune from tort liability, and children and parents and spouses could not sue each other. These immunities are fast disappearing. **For Example,** if a father's negligent driving of his car causes injuries to his minor child passenger, the child may recover from the father for his injuries.[29]

[24] *Hanks v. Powder Ridge*, 885 A.2d 734 (Conn. 2005).
[25] *Taylor v. Baseball Club of Seattle*, 130 P.3d 835 (Wash. App. 2006).
[26] *Amezcua v. Los Angeles Harley-Davidson*, 132 Cal. Rptr. 3d 567 (Cal. App. 2011).
[27] See, for example, *Costa v. The Boston Red Sox Baseball Club*, 809 N.E.2d 1090 (Mass. App. 2004), where the court cites state precedent that "... the abolishment of assumption of the risk as an affirmative defense did not alter the plaintiff's burden ... to prove the defendant owed [the plaintiff] a duty of care ... and thus left intact the open and obvious damages rule, which operates to negate the existence of a duty to care."
[28] *Kirby v. Macon County*, 892 S.W.2d 403 (Tenn. 1994).
[29] *Cates v. Cates*, 588 N.E.2d 330 (Ill. App. 1992); see also *Doe v. McKay*, 700 N.E.2d 1018 (Ill. 1998).

Sports & Entertainment Law

Liability for Injuries under the Sports Exception Doctrine

Charles "Booby" Clark played football for the Cincinnati Bengals as a running back on offense. Dale Hackbart played defensive free safety for the Denver Broncos. As a consequence of an interception by the Broncos, Hackbart became an offensive player, threw a block, and was watching the play with one knee on the ground when Clark "acting out of anger and frustration, but without a specific intent to injure," stepped forward and struck a blow to the back of Hackbart's head and neck, causing a serious neck fracture. Is relief precluded for injuries occurring during a professional football game? The answer is no. While proof of mere negligence is insufficient to establish liability during such an athletic contest, liability must instead be premised on heightened proof of reckless or intentional conduct on the part of the defendant. In the *Hackbart* case, the court determined that if the evidence established that the injury was the result of acts of Clark that were in reckless disregard of Hackbart's safety, Hackbart is entitled to damages.* Why didn't Hackbart pursue recovery under negligence law, contending that Clark had a general duty of care to act as a reasonably prudent person would in similar circumstances? Because football and other contact sports contain within the rules of the games inherent *unreasonable* risks of harm, a negligence theory is not applicable. What contact sports do you believe qualify under this "sports exception" doctrine for which proof of negligence is insufficient to establish liability for injuries sustained during the athletic contest? Is softball a contact sport for players? What about coaching or officiating decisions made in the middle of a fast-moving game?**

PGA golfer Walter Mallin sued PGA golfer John Paesani for injuries that Mallin sustained while competing in a PGA golf tournament when Paesani drove a golf ball that struck Mallin in the head on his right temple. Paesani contends that the "sports exception" doctrine applies and the negligence case must be dismissed. How would you decide this case?***

*Hackbart v. Cincinnati Bengals, Inc., 601 F.2d 516 (10th Cir. 1979).

**See Guillo v. DeKamp Junction, Inc., 959 N.E.2d 215 (Ill. App. 2011).
***Mallin v. Paesani, 892 A.2d 1043 (Conn. Super, 2005).

D. Strict Liability

The final form of tort liability is known as *strict liability*. When the standards of strict liability apply, very few defenses are available. Strict liability was developed to provide guaranteed protection for those who are injured by conduct the law deems both serious and inexcusable.

Thinking Things Through

Torts and Public Policy

Over a decade ago, a jury awarded 81-year-old Stella Liebeck nearly $3 million because she was burned after she spilled a cup of McDonald's coffee on her lap. Based on these limited facts, a national discussion ensued about a need for tort reform, and to this day "Stella Awards" are given on Web sites for apparently frivolous or excessive lawsuits. Consider the following additional facts and the actual damages awarded Stella Liebeck. Decide whether her recovery was just.

● McDonald's coffee was brewed at 195 to 205 degrees.

● McDonald's quality assurance manager "was aware of the risk [of burns] ... and had no plans to turn down the heat."

Thinking Things Through

Continued

- Mrs. Liebeck spent seven days in the hospital with third degree burns and had skin grafts. Gruesome photos of burns of the inner thighs, groin, and buttocks were entered as evidence.

- The compensatory damages were $200,000, which were reduced to $160,000 because Mrs. Liebeck was determined to be 20 percent at fault.

- The jury awarded $2.7 million in punitive damages. The trial court judge reduced this amount to $480,000.

- The total recovery at the trial court for Mrs. Liebeck was $640,000. Both parties appealed, and a settlement was reached at what is believed to be close to the $640,000 figure.

Tort remedies have evolved because of public policy incentives for the protection of individuals from physical, mental, and economic damage. Tort remedies provide economic motivation for individuals and businesses to avoid conduct that could harm others.

The amount of the compensation and the circumstances in which compensation for torts should be paid are issues that courts, juries, and legislatures review. Many legislatures have examined and continue to review the standards for tort liability and damages.

The U.S. Supreme Court devoted several decisions in recent years to dealing with excessive punitive damages in civil litigation, and it has set "guideposts" to be used by courts in assessing punitive damages.* In *State Farm Mutual Automobile Insurance Co. v. Campbell*, compensatory damages for the plaintiffs at the trial court level were $1 million, and punitive damages, based in part on evidence that State Farm's nationwide policy was to underpay claims regardless of merit to enhance profits, were assessed at $145 million. The Supreme Court concluded that the facts of *Campbell* would likely justify a punitive damages award only at or near the amount of compensatory damages. Thus, even those who act very badly as State Farm Insurance did have a constitutionally protected right under the Due Process Clause of the Fourteenth Amendment to have civil law damages assessed in accordance with the Supreme Court's guideposts.

BMW of North America v. Gore, 517 U.S. 559 (1996); *Cooper Industries v. Leatherman Tool Group, Inc.*, 532 U.S. 424 (2001); *State Farm Insurance v. Campbell*, 538 U.S. 408 (2003); *Exxon Shipping Co. v. Baker*, 128 S. Ct. 2605, 2621 (2008).

15. What Is Strict Liability?

Strict liability is an absolute standard of liability imposed by the law in circumstances the courts or legislatures have determined require a high degree of protection. When strict liability is imposed, the result is that the company or person who has caused injury or damages by the conduct will be required to compensate for those damages in an absolute sense. Few, if any, defenses apply in a situation in which the law imposes a strict liability standard. **For Example,** as noted earlier in the chapter, engaging in ultrahazardous activities, such as using dynamite to excavate a site for new construction, results in strict liability for the contractor performing the demolition. Any damages resulting from the explosion are the responsibility of that contractor, so the contractor is strictly liable.

16. Imposing Strict Liability

Strict liability arises in a number of different circumstances, but the most common are in those situations in which a statutory duty is imposed and in product liability. **For Example,** at both the state and federal levels, there are requirements for the use, transportation, and sale of radioactive materials, as well as the disposal of biomedical materials and tools. Any violation of these rules and regulations would result in strict liability for the company or person in violation.

Product liability, while more fully covered in Chapter 25, is another example of strict liability. A product that is defective through its design, manufacture, or instructions and that injures someone results in strict liability for the manufacturer.

LawFlix

Class Action (1991) (R)

This movie depicts the magnitude of damages and recovery when multiple injuries occur. The film provides insights on tort reform and the ethics of lawyers. You can learn about the magnitude of discovery and evidence.

Notting Hill (1999) (PG-13)

A story of famous star gets guy, dumps guy, gets guy back, dumps guy again, and then guy dumps famous star, and on and on. But, the guy owns a bookstore that sells travel books and he has a shoplifter. Hugh Grant, as the guy, illustrates perfection in exercising the shopkeeper's privilege.

MAKE THE CONNECTION

SUMMARY

A *tort* is a civil wrong that affords recovery for damages that result. The three forms of torts are intentional torts, negligence, and strict liability. A tort differs from a crime in the nature of its remedy. Fines and imprisonment result from criminal violations, whereas money damages are paid to those who are damaged by conduct that constitutes a tort. An action may be both a crime and a tort, but the tort remedy is civil in nature.

Selected intentional torts are false imprisonment, defamation, product disparagement, contract interference or tortious interference, and trespass. False imprisonment is the detention of another without his or her permission. False imprisonment is often called the *shopkeeper's tort* because store owners detain suspected shoplifters. Many states provide a privilege to store owners if they detain shoplifting suspects based on reasonable cause and in a reasonable manner. Defamation is slander (oral) or libel (written) and consists of false statements about another that damage the person's reputation or integrity. Truth is

an absolute defense to defamation, and there are some privileges that protect against defamation, such as those for witnesses at trial and for members of Congress during debates on the floor. There is a developing privilege for employers when they give references for former employees. Invasion of privacy is intrusion into private affairs; public disclosure of private facts; or appropriation of someone's name, image, or likeness for commercial purposes.

To establish the tort of negligence, one must show that there has been a breach of duty in the form of a violation of a statute or professional competency standards or of behavior that does not rise to the level of that of a reasonable person. That breach of duty must have caused the foreseeable injuries to the plaintiff, and the plaintiff must be able to quantify the damages that resulted. Possible defenses to negligence include contributory negligence, comparative negligence, and assumption of risk.

Strict liability is absolute liability with few defenses.

LEARNING OUTCOMES

After studying this chapter, you should be able to clearly explain:

A. General Principles

L0.1   Explain the difference between torts and crimes

See the discussion on wrongs that are a violation of a private duty as torts, and wrongs that are a violation of a public duty of crimes, p. 171.
See the O.J. Simpson example of his acquittal of the crime of murder and his civil liability for the torts of wrongful death on p. 171.

L0.2   Identify the possible tort theories applicable to transmission of disease cases
See the transmission of herpes example on p. 172.

B. Intentional Torts

L0.3   Distinguish between an assault and a battery

See the "kick your butt" threat example of an assault on p. 173.

L0.4   Explain the three different torts of invasion of privacy
See the discussion of the intrusion into a person's private affairs, public disclosure of private facts, and right to publicity torts beginning on p. 175.
See the *Schlein* case involving commercial misappropriation of one's name on pp. 176–177.

L0.5   Explain the torts of defamation and defenses
See the discussion of slander, libel, and trade libel beginning on p. 177.
See the discussion of the requirement of the enhanced element of malice for cases in which the victim is a public figure, p. 177.

C. Negligence

L0.6   Explain the elements of negligence and defenses

See the discussion of the elements of negligence: duty, breach of duty, and causation and damages beginning on p. 181.
See the discussion of the defenses of contributory negligence, comparative negligence, assumption of risk, and immunity beginning on p. 183.

D. Strict Liability

L0.7   Explain the tort of strict liability and why very few defenses are avaliable
See the dynamite excavation example, holding the contractor liable for any damages with no defenses because of the hazardous activity, p. 187.

KEY TERMS

absolute privilege
contract interference
contributory negligence
defamation
false imprisonment
intentional infliction of
 emotional distress

intentional torts
invasion of privacy
libel
malpractice
negligence
product disparagement
qualified privilege

shopkeeper's privilege
slander
strict liability
tort
trade libel
trespass

QUESTIONS AND CASE PROBLEMS

1. Christensen Shipyards built a 155-foot yacht for Tiger Woods at its Vancouver, Washington, facilities. It used Tiger's name and photographs relating to the building of the yacht in promotional materials for the shipyard without seeking his permission. Was this a right of publicity tort because Tiger could assert that his name and photos were used to attract attention to the shipyard to obtain commercial advantage? Did the shipyard have a First Amendment right to present the truthful facts regarding their building of the yacht and the owner's identity as promotional materials? Does the fact that the yacht was named *Privacy* have an impact on this case? Would it make a difference as to the outcome of this case if the contract for building the yacht had a clause prohibiting the use of Tiger's name or photo without his permission?

2. ESPN held its Action Sports and Music Awards ceremony in April, at which celebrities in the fields of extreme sports and popular music such as rap and heavy metal converged. Well-known musicians Ben Harper and James Hetfield were there, as were popular rappers Busta Rhymes and LL Cool J. Famed motorcycle stuntman Evel Knievel, who is commonly thought of as the "father of extreme sports," and his wife Krystal were photographed. The photograph depicted Evel, who was wearing a motorcycle jacket and rose-tinted sunglasses, with his right arm around Krystal and his left arm around another young woman. ESPN published the photograph on its "extreme sports" Web site with a caption that read "Evel Knievel proves that you're never too old to be a pimp." The Knievels brought suit against ESPN, contending that the photograph and caption were defamatory because they accused Evel of soliciting prostitution and implied that Krystal was a prostitute. ESPN contends that the caption was a figurative and slang usage and was not defamatory as a matter of law. Decide. [*Knievel v. ESPN*, 393 F3.d 1068 (9th Cir.)]

3. While snowboarding down a slope at Mammoth Mountain Ski Area (Mammoth), 17-year-old

David Graham was engaged in a snowball fight with his 14-year-old brother. As he was "preparing to throw a snowball" at his brother, David slammed into Liam Madigan, who was working as a ski school instructor for Mammoth, and injured him. Madigan sued Graham for damages for reckless and dangerous behavior. The defense contended that the claim was barred under the doctrine of assumption of the risk, applicable in the state, arising from the risk inherent in the sport that allows for vigorous participation and frees a participant from a legal duty to act with due care. Decide. [*Mammoth Mountain Ski Area v. Graham*, 38 Cal. Rptr. 3d 422 (Cal. App.)]

4. Following a visit to her hometown of Coalinga, Cynthia wrote "An Ode to Coalinga" (Ode) and posted it in her online journal on MySpace.com. Her last name did not appear online. Her page included her picture. The Ode opens with "The older I get, the more I realize how much I despise Coalinga" and then proceeds to make a number of extremely negative comments about Coalinga and its inhabitants. Six days later, Cynthia removed the Ode from her journal. At the time, Cynthia was a student at UC Berkeley, and her parents and sister were living in Coalinga. The Coalinga High School principal, Roger Campbell, submitted the Ode to the local newspaper, the *Coalinga Record*, and it was published in the Letters to the Editor section, using Cynthia's full name. The community reacted violently to the Ode, forcing the family to close its business and move. Cynthia and her family sued Campbell and the newpaper on the right-of-privacy theory of public disclosure of private facts. What are the essential element of this theory? Was Cynthia and her family's right of privacy violated? [*Moreno v. Hanford Sentinel, Inc.*, 91 Cal. Rptr. 3d 858 (Cal. App.)]

5. JoKatherine Page and her 14-year-old son Jason were robbed at their bank's ATM at 9:30 P.M. one evening by a group of four thugs. The thieves took $300, struck Mrs. Page in the face with a gun, and ran. Mrs. Page and her son filed suit against the bank for its failure to provide

adequate security. Should the bank be held liable? [*Page v. American National Bank & Trust Co.,* 850 S.W.2d 133 (Tenn.)]

6. A Barberton Glass Co. truck was transporting large sheets of glass down the highway. Elliot Schultz was driving his automobile some distance behind the truck. Because of the negligent way that the sheets of glass were fastened in the truck, a large sheet fell off the truck, shattered on hitting the highway, and then bounced up and broke the windshield of Shultz's car. He was not injured but suffered great emotional shock. He sued Barberton to recover damages for this shock. Barberton denied liability on the ground that Schultz had not sustained any physical injury at the time or as the result of the shock. Should he be able to recover? [*Schultz v. Barberton Glass Co.,* 447 N.E.2d 109 (Ohio)]

7. Mallinckrodt produces nuclear and radioactive medical pharmaceuticals and supplies. Maryland Heights Leasing, an adjoining business owner, claimed that low-level radiation emissions from Mallinckrodt damaged its property and caused a loss in earnings. What remedy should Maryland Heights have? What torts are involved here? [*Maryland Heights Leasing, Inc. v. Mallinckrodt, Inc.,* 706 S.W.2d 218 (Mo. App.)]

8. An owner abandoned his van in an alley in Chicago. In spite of repeated complaints to the police, the van was allowed to remain in the alley. After several months, it was stripped of most of the parts that could be removed. Jamin Ortiz, age 11, was walking down the alley when the van's gas tank exploded. The flames from the explosion set fire to Jamin's clothing, and he was severely burned. Jamin and his family brought suit brought against the city of Chicago to recover damages for his injuries. Could the city be held responsible for injuries caused by property owned by someone else? Why or why not? [*Ortiz v. Chicago,* 398 N.E.2d 1007 (Ill. App.)]

9. Carrigan, a district manager of Simples Time Recorder Co., was investigating complaints of mismanagement of the company's Jackson office. He called at the home of Hooks, the secretary of that office, who expressed the opinion that part of the trouble was caused by the theft of parts and equipment by McCall, another employee. McCall was later discharged and sued Hooks for slander. Was she liable? [*Hooks v. McCall,* 272 So.2d 925 (Miss.)]

10. Defendant no. 1 parked his truck in the street near the bottom of a ditch on a dark, foggy night. Iron pipes carried in the truck projected nine feet beyond the truck in back. Neither the truck nor the pipes carried any warning light or flag, in violation of both a city ordinance and a state statute. Defendant no. 2 was a taxicab owner whose taxicab was negligently driven at an excessive speed. Defendant no. 2 ran into the pipes, thereby killing the passenger in the taxicab. The plaintiff brought an action for the passenger's death against both defendants. Defendant no. 1 claimed he was not liable because it was Defendant no. 2's negligence that had caused the harm. Was this defense valid? [*Bumbardner v. Allison,* 78 S.E.2d 752 (N.C.)]

11. Carl Kindrich's father, a member of the Long Beach Yacht Club before he died, expressed a wish to be "buried at sea." The Yacht Club permitted the Kindrich family the use of one of its boats, without charge, for the ceremony, and Mr. Fuller—a good friend of Carl's father—piloted the boat. Portable stairs on the dock assisted the attendees in boarding. Upon returning, Fuller asked for help to tie up the boat. The steps were not there, and Carl broke his leg while disembarking to help tie up the boat. Carl sued the Yacht Club for negligence in failing to have someone on the dock to ensure that the portable steps were available. The Yacht Club contended that it was not liable because Carl made the conscious decision to jump from the moving vessel to the dock, a primary assumption of risk in the sport of boating. The plaintiff contended that he was not involved in the sport of boating, and at most his actions constituted minimal comparative negligence, the type which a jury could weigh in conjunction with the defendant's negligence in assessing damages. Decide. [*Kindrich v. Long Beach Yacht Club,* 84 Cal. Rptr. 3d 824 (Cal. App.)]

12. Hegyes was driving her car when it was negligently struck by a Unjian Enterprises truck. She was injured, and an implant was placed in her body to counteract the injuries. She sued Unjian, and the case was settled. Two years later Hegyes became pregnant. The growing fetus pressed against the implant, making it necessary for her doctor to deliver the child 51 days prematurely by Cesarean section. Because of its premature birth, the child had a breathing handicap. Suit was brought against Unjian Enterprises for the harm sustained by the child. Was the defendant liable? [*Hegyes v. Unjian Enterprises, Inc.,* 286 Cal. Rptr. 85 (Cal. App.)]

13. Kendra Knight took part in a friendly game of touch football. She had played before and was familiar with football. Michael Jewett was on her team. In the course of play, Michael bumped into Kendra and knocked her to the ground. He stepped on her hand, causing injury to a little finger that later required its amputation. She sued Michael for damages. He defended on the ground that she had assumed the risk. Kendra claimed that assumption of risk could not be raised as a defense because the state legislature had adopted the standard of comparative negligence. What happens if contributory negligence applies? What happens if the defense of comparative negligence applies?

14. A passenger on a cruise ship was injured by a rope thrown while the ship was docking. The passenger was sitting on a lounge chair on the third deck when she was struck by the weighted end of a rope thrown by an employee of Port Everglades, where the boat was docking. These ropes, or heaving lines, were being thrown from the dock to the second deck, and the passenger was injured by a line that was thrown too high.

    The trial court granted the cruise line's motion for directed verdict on the ground there was no evidence that the cruise line knew or should have known of the danger. The cruise line contended that it had no notice that this "freak accident" could occur. What is the duty of a cruise ship line to its passengers? Is there liability here? Does it matter that an employee of the port city, not the cruise lines, caused the injury? Should the passenger be able to recover? Why or why not? [*Kalendareva v. Discovery Cruise Line Partnership,* 798 So.2d 804 (Fla. App.)]

15. Blaylock was a voluntary psychiatric outpatient treated by Dr. Burglass, who became aware that Blaylock was violence prone. Blaylock told Dr. Burglass that he intended to do serious harm to Wayne Boynton, Jr., and shortly thereafter he killed Wayne. Wayne's parents then sued Dr. Burglass on grounds that he was liable for the death of their son because he failed to give warning or to notify the police of Blaylock's threat and nature. Was a duty breached here? Should Dr. Burglass be held liable? [*Boynton v. Burglass,* 590 So.2d 446 (Fla. App.)]

© Manuel Gutjahr/iStockphoto.com

CHAPTER 12

Nature and Classes of Contracts: Contracting on the Internet

learningoutcomes

After studying this chapter, you should be able to

LO.1 Explain the meaning and importance of privity of a contract

LO.2 Describe the way in which a contract arises

LO.3 Distinguish between bilateral and unilateral contracts

LO.4 Explain the reasoning behind quasi-contract recovery

LO.5 Explain how Internet contracts involve the same types of issues as offline contracts.

P ractically every business transaction affecting people involves a contract.

A. NATURE OF CONTRACTS

This introductory chapter will familiarize you with the terminology needed to work with contract law. In addition, the chapter introduces quasi contracts, which are not true contracts but obligations imposed by law.

1. Definition of a Contract

contract – a binding agreement based on the genuine assent of the parties, made for a lawful object, between competent parties, in the form required by law, and generally supported by consideration.

A **contract** is a legally binding agreement.[1] By one definition, "a contract is a promise or a set of promises for the breach of which the law gives a remedy, or the performance of which the law in some way recognizes as a duty."[2] Contracts arise out of agreements, so a contract may be defined as an agreement creating an obligation.

The substance of the definition of a contract is that by mutual agreement or assent, the parties create enforceable duties or obligations. That is, each party is legally bound to do or to refrain from doing certain acts.

2. Elements of a Contract

The elements of a contract are (1) an agreement (2) between competent parties (3) based on the genuine assent of the parties that is (4) supported by consideration, (5) made for a lawful objective, and (6) in the form required by law, if any. These elements will be considered in the chapters that follow.

3. Subject Matter of Contracts

The subject matter of a contract may relate to the performance of personal services, such as contracts of employment to work developing computer software or to play professional football. A contract may provide for the transfer of ownership of property, such as a house (real property) or an automobile (personal property), from one person to another.

4. Parties to a Contract

promisor – person who makes a promise.

promisee – person to whom a promise is made.

obligor – promisor.

obligee – promisee who can claim the benefit of the obligation.

privity – succession or chain of relationship to the same thing or right, such as privity of contract, privity of estate, privity of possession.

privity of contract – relationship between a promisor and the promisee.

The person who makes a promise is the **promisor**, and the person to whom the promise is made is the **promisee**. If the promise is binding, it imposes on the promisor a duty or obligation, and the promisor may be called the **obligor**. The promisee who can claim the benefit of the obligation is called the **obligee**. The parties to a contract are said to stand in **privity** with each other, and the relationship between them is termed **privity of contract**. **For Example,** when the state of North Carolina and the architectural firm of O'Brien/Atkins Associates executed a contract for the construction of a new building at the University of North Carolina, Chapel Hill, these parties were

---

[1] The Uniform Commercial Code defines *contract* as "the total legal obligation which results from the parties' agreement as affected by [the UCC] and any other applicable rules of law." U.C.C. §1–201(11).

[2] Restatement (Second) of Contracts §1.

in privity of contract. However, a building contractor, RPR & Associates, who worked on the project did not have standing to sue on the contract between the architect and the state because the contractor was not in privity of contract.[3]

In written contracts, parties may be referred to by name. More often, however, they are given special names that better identify each party. For example, consider a contract by which one person agrees that another may occupy a house upon the payment of money. The parties to this contract are called *landlord* and *tenant*, or *lessor* and *lessee*, and the contract between them is known as a *lease*. Parties to other types of contracts also have distinctive names, such as *vendor* and *vendee* for the parties to a sales contract, *shipper* and *carrier* for the parties to a transportation contract, and *insurer* and *insured* for the parties to an insurance policy.

A party to a contract may be an individual, a partnership, a limited liability company, a corporation, or a government.[4] One or more persons may be on each side of a contract. Some contracts are three-sided, as in a credit card transaction, which involves the company issuing the card, the holder of the card, and the business furnishing goods and services on the basis of the credit card.

If a contract is written, the persons who are the parties and who are bound by it can ordinarily be determined by reading what the document says and seeing how it is signed. A contract binds only the parties to the contract. It cannot impose a duty on a person who is not a party to it. Ordinarily, only a party to a contract has any rights against another party to the contract.[5] In some cases, third persons have rights on a contract as third-party beneficiaries or assignees. A person cannot be bound, however, by the terms of a contract to which that person is not a party. **For Example,** in approximately 1995 Jeff and Mark Bass signed Marshall B. Mathers III, better known as rapper Eminem, to an exclusive record deal with FBT Productions LLC (FBT), their production company. In 2000 Aftermath Records entered into a direct contractual relationship with Eminem, transferring Eminem's recording services from FBT directly to Aftermath. Under the contract FBT became a "passive income participant," retaining a right to royalty income from Eminem's recordings. A dispute occurred regarding percentages of royalties due. Aftermath entered into an agreement with Eminem in 2009, setting the royalties for Eminem's *Recovery* and *Relapse* albums, asserting that all royalties, including royalties owed FBT were dictated by this 2009 agreement. FBT was not a party to the 2009 agreement and as such cannot be bound by it. A contract cannot bind a nonparty. Therefore, Aftermath was required to pay FBT royalties for the two albums at a higher rate in accordance with an earlier agreement.[6]

5. How a Contract Arises

A contract is based on an agreement. An agreement arises when one person, the **offeror**, makes an offer and the person to whom the offer is made, the **offeree**, accepts. There must be both an offer and an acceptance. If either is lacking, there is no contract.

offeror—person who makes an offer.

offeree—person to whom an offer is made.

[3] *RPR & Associates v. O'Brien/Atkins Associates, P.A.*, 24 F. Supp. 2d 515 (M.D. N.C. 1998). See also *Roof Techs Int. Inc. v. State*, 57 P.3d 538, (Kan. App. 2002), where a layer of litigation was avoided regarding lawsuits involving the renovation of the Farrell Library at Kansas State University. The state was the only party in privity of contract with the architectural firm and would thus have to bring claims against the architectural firm on behalf of all of the contractors. Two subcontractors, the general contractor, and the owner of the library, the state of Kansas, used a settlement and liquidation agreement assigning all of the state's claims against the architect to the general contractor.
[4] See *Purina Mills, LLC v. Less*, 295 F. Supp. 2d 1017 (N.D. Iowa 2003) in which the pig-seller plaintiff, which converted from a corporation to a limited liability company (LLC) while the contract was in effect, was a proper party in interest and could maintain a contract action against defendant buyers.
[5] *Hooper v. Yakima County*, 904 P.2d 1193 (Wash. App. 1995).
[6] *F.B.T. Productions, LLC v. Aftermath Records*, 2011 WL 5174766 (C.D. Cal. Oct. 31, 2011).

6. Intent to Make a Binding Agreement

Because a contract is based on the consent of the parties and is a legally binding agreement, it follows that the parties must have an intent to enter into an agreement that is binding. Sometimes the parties are in agreement, but their agreement does not produce a contract. Sometimes there is merely a preliminary agreement, but the parties never actually make a contract, or there is merely an agreement as to future plans or intentions without any contractual obligation to carry out those plans or intentions.

7. Freedom of Contract

In the absence of some ground for declaring a contract void or voidable, parties may make such contracts as they choose. The law does not require parties to be fair, or kind, or reasonable, or to share gains or losses equitably.

B. Classes of Contracts

Contracts may be classified according to their form, the way in which they were created, their binding character, and the extent to which they have been performed.

CPA

8. Formal and Informal Contracts

Contracts can be classified as formal or informal.

(A) Formal Contracts. **Formal contracts** are enforced because the formality with which they are executed is considered sufficient to signify that the parties intend to be bound by their terms. Formal contracts include (1) **contracts under seal** where a person's signature or a corporation's name is followed by a scroll, the word *seal*, or the letters *L.S.*;[7] (2) contracts of record, which are obligations that have been entered before a court of record, sometimes called a **recognizance**; and (3) negotiable instruments.

CPA

(B) Informal Contracts. All contracts other than formal contracts are called **informal** (or simple) **contracts** without regard to whether they are oral or written. These contracts are enforceable, not because of the form of the transaction but because they represent agreement of the parties.

9. Express and Implied Contracts

Simple contracts may be classified as express *contracts* or *implied contracts* according to the way they are created.

(A) Express Contracts. An **express contract** is one in which the terms of the agreement of the parties are manifested by their words, whether spoken or written.

(B) Implied Contracts. An **implied contract** (or, as sometimes stated, a *contract implied in fact*) is one in which the agreement is shown not by words, written or spoken, but by the acts and conduct of the parties.[8] Such a contract arises when (1) a person renders services under circumstances indicating that payment for them is expected and

formal contracts – written contracts or agreements whose formality signifies the parties' intention to abide by the terms.

contract under seal – contract executed by affixing a seal or making an impression on the paper or on some adhering substance such as wax attached to the document.

recognizance – obligation entered into before a court to do some act, such as to appear at a later date for a hearing. Also called a *contract of record.*

informal contract – simple oral or written contract.

express contract – agreement of the parties manifested by their words, whether spoken or written.

implied contract – contract expressed by conduct or implied or deduced from the facts.

---

[7] Some authorities explain *L.S.* as an abbreviation for *locus sigilium* (place for the seal).
[8] *Lindquist Ford, Inc. v. Middleton Motors, Inc.*, 557 F.3d 469, 481 (7th Cir. 2009). See also *Dynegy Marketing and Trade v. Multiut Corp.*, 648 F.3d 506 (7th Cir. 2011).

| FIGURE 12-1 | *Contractual Liability* |

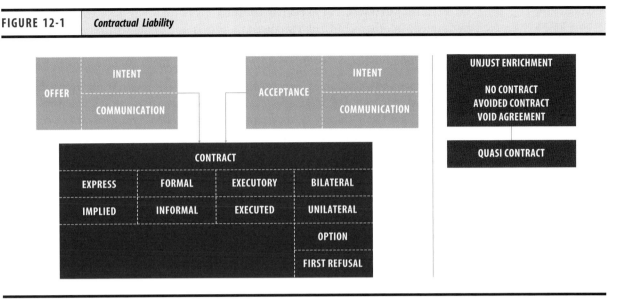

© Cengage Learning

(2) the other person, knowing such circumstances, accepts the benefit of those services. **For Example,** when a building owner requests a professional roofer to make emergency repairs to the roof of a building, an obligation arises to pay the reasonable value of such services, although no agreement has been made about compensation.

An implied contract cannot arise when there is an existing express contract on the same subject.[9] However, the existence of a written contract does not bar recovery on an implied contract for extra work that was not covered by the contract.

CPA 10. Valid and Voidable Contracts and Void Agreements

Contracts may be classified in terms of enforceability or validity.

valid contract – agreement that is binding and enforceable.

(A) VALID CONTRACTS. A **valid contract** is an agreement that is binding and enforceable.

voidable contract – agreement that is otherwise binding and enforceable but may be rejected at the option of one of the parties as the result of specific circumstances.

(B) VOIDABLE CONTRACTS. A **voidable contract** is an agreement that is otherwise binding and enforceable, but because of the circumstances surrounding its execution or the lack of capacity of one of the parties, it may be rejected at the option of one of the parties. **For Example,** a person who has been forced to sign an agreement that that person would not have voluntarily signed may, in some instances, avoid the contract.

void agreement – agreement that cannot be enforced.

(C) VOID AGREEMENTS. A **void agreement** is without legal effect. An agreement that contemplates the performance of an act prohibited by law is usually incapable of enforcement; hence it is void. Likewise, it cannot be made binding by later approval or ratification.

11. Executed and Executory Contracts

Contracts may be classified as *executed contracts* and *executory contracts* according to the extent to which they have been performed.

---

[9] *Pepsi-Cola Bottling Co. of Pittsburgh, Inc., v. PepsiCo, Inc.,* 431 F.3d 1241 (10th Cir. 2000).

executed contract – agreement that has been completely performed.

(A) EXECUTED CONTRACTS. An **executed contract** is one that has been completely performed. In other words, an executed contract is one under which nothing remains to be done by either party.[10] A contract may be executed immediately, as in the case of a cash sale, or it may be executed or performed in the future.

executory contract – agreement by which something remains to be done by one or both parties.

(B) EXECUTORY CONTRACTS. In an **executory contract**, something remains to be done by one or both parties.[11] **For Example,** on July 10, Mark agreed to sell to Chris his Pearl drum set for $600, the terms being $200 upon delivery on July 14, with $200 to be paid on July 21, and the final $200 being due July 28. Prior to the July 14 delivery of the drums to Chris, the contract was entirely executory. After the delivery by Mark, the contract was executed as to Mark and executory as to Chris until the final payment was received on July 28.

12. Bilateral and Unilateral Contracts

In making an offer, the offeror is in effect extending a promise to do something, such as pay a sum of money, if the offeree will do what the offeror requests. Contracts are classified as *bilateral* or *unilateral*. Some bilateral contracts look ahead to the making of a later contract. Depending on their terms, these are called *option contracts* or *first-refusal contracts*.

CPA

bilateral contract – agreement under which one promise is given in exchange for another.

(A) BILATERAL CONTRACT. If the offeror extends a promise and asks for a promise in return and if the offeree accepts the offer by making the promise, the contract is called a **bilateral contract**. One promise is given in exchange for another, and each party is bound by the obligation. **For Example,** when the house painter offers to paint the owner's house for $3,700 and the owner promises to pay $3,700 for the job, there is an exchange of promises, and the agreement gives rise to a bilateral contract.

unilateral contract – contract under which only one party makes a promise.

(B) UNILATERAL CONTRACT. In contrast with a bilateral contract, the offeror may promise to do something or to pay a certain amount of money only when the offeree does an act.[12] Examples of where **unilateral contracts** commonly appear are when a reward is offered, a contest is announced, or changes are made and disseminated in an employee manual. The offeree does not accept the offer by express agreement, but rather by performance.

CASE SUMMARY

Unilateral Contract: Pretty Good Bonus!

FACTS: Aon Risk Services, Inc. (ARS Arkansas), and Combined Insurance Companies are subsidiaries of Aon Corporation. The parent corporation issued an "Interdependency Memo" dated February 2000, which encouraged ARS brokerage offices to place insurance business with Aon-affiliated companies. It also set up a bonus pool for revenues generated under the plan, with Combined agreeing to pay "30% of annualized premium on all life products over 15-year term plus 15% 1st year for all other products." John Meadors saw the memo in February 2000, and believed it would entitle him to this compensation over and above his employment contract.

[10] *Marsh v. Rheinecker*, 641 N.E.2d 1256 (Ill. App. 1994).
[11] *DiGennaro v. Rubbermaid, Inc.*, 214 F. Supp. 2d 1354 (S.D. Fla. 2002).
[12] See *Young v. Virginia Birth-Related Neurological Injury Compensation Program*, 620 S.E.2d 131 (Va. App. 2005).

CASE SUMMARY

Continued

Meadors put Combined in touch with Dillard's Department Stores and on March 24, 2000, Dillard's and Combined executed a five-year agreement whereby Dillard's employees could purchase life, disability, and other insurance policies through workplace enrollment. When Meadors did not receive bonus-pool money generated by the transaction, he sued his employer for breach of a unilateral contract. The employer's defense was that the memo was not sufficiently definite to constitute an offer.

DECISION: Judgment for Meadors for $2,406,522.60. A unilateral contract is composed of an offer that invites acceptance in the form of actual performance. For example, in the case of a reward, the offeree accepts by performing the particular task, such as the capture of the fugitive for which the reward is offered. In this case the offer contained in the Interdependency Memo set out specific percentages of provisions that would go into the bonus pool, and required that the pool be distributed annually. It was sufficiently definite to constitute an offer. Meadors was responsible for the production of the Dillard's account, and was entitled to the bonus promised in the memo. [*Aon Risk Services Inc. v. Meadors*, 267 S.W.3d 603 (Ark. App. 2007)]

---

option contract – contract to hold an offer to make a contract open for a fixed period of time.

(C) OPTION AND FIRST-REFUSAL CONTRACTS. The parties may make a contract that gives a right to one of them to enter into a second contract at a later date. If one party has an absolute right to enter into the later contract, the initial contract is called an **option contract**. Thus, a bilateral contract may be made today giving one of the parties the right to buy the other party's house for a specified amount. This is an option contract because the party with the privilege has the freedom of choice, or option, to buy or not buy. If the option is exercised, the other party to the contract must follow the terms of the option and enter into the second contract. If the option is never exercised, no second contract ever arises, and the offer protected by the option contract merely expires.

right of first refusal – right of a party to meet the terms of a proposed contract before it is executed, such as a real estate purchase agreement.

In contrast with an option contract, a contract may merely give a **right of first refusal**. This imposes only the duty to make the first offer to the party having the right of first refusal.

13. Quasi Contracts

In some cases, a court will impose an obligation even though there is no contract.[13] Such an obligation is called a **quasi contract**, which is an obligation imposed by law.

quasi contract – court-imposed obligation to prevent unjust enrichment in the absence of a contract.

(A) PREVENTION OF UNJUST ENRICHMENT. A quasi contract is not a true contract reflecting all of the elements of a contract set forth previously in this chapter. The court is not seeking to enforce the intentions of the parties contained in an agreement. Rather, when a person or enterprise receives a benefit from another, even in the absence of a promise to pay for the benefit, a court may impose an obligation to pay for the reasonable value of that benefit, to avoid *unjust enrichment*. The spirit behind the law of unjust enrichment is to apply the law "outside the box" and fill in the cracks where common civil law and statutes fail to achieve justice.[14]

---

[13] *Thayer v. Dial Industrial Sales, Inc.*, 85 F. Supp. 2d 263 (S.D.N.Y. 2000).
[14] *Hernandez v. Lopez*, 103 Cal. Rptr.3d 376, 381 (Cal. App. 2009).

FIGURE 12-2 | *Contract*

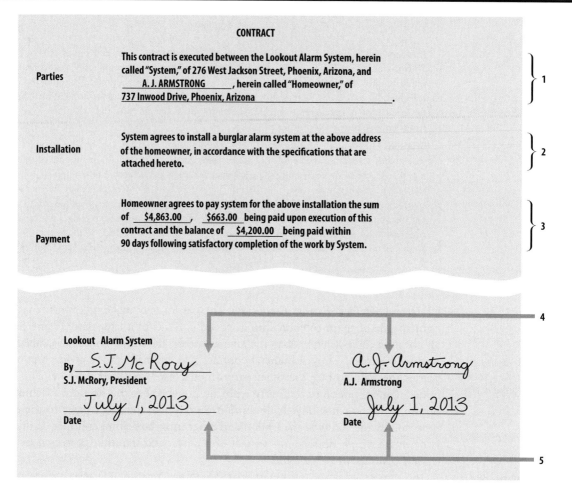

Note that this contract includes the following important information: (1) the name and address of each party, (2) the promise or consideration of the seller, (3) the promise or consideration of the buyer, (4) the signature of the two parties, and (5) the date.

A successful claim for unjust enrichment usually requires (1) a benefit conferred on the defendant, (2) the defendant's knowledge of the benefit, and (3) a finding that it would be unjust for the defendant to retain the benefit without payment. The burden of proof is on the plaintiff to prove all of the elements of the claim. **For Example,** Hiram College sued Nicholas Courtad for $6,000 plus interest for tuition and other expenses. Because no evidence of a written contract was produced, the court considered it an unjust enrichment claim by the college. Courtad had attended classes for a few weeks and had not paid his tuition due to a problem with his financial aid package. Because he did not receive any credit hours toward a degree, which is the ultimate benefit of attending college, the court found that he did not receive a benefit and that a finding of unjust enrichment was not appropriate.[15]

[15] *Hiram College v. Courtad*, 834 N.E.2d 432 (Ohio App. 2005).

Sometimes a contract may be unenforceable because of a failure to set forth the contract in writing in compliance with the statute of frauds. In other circumstances, no enforceable contract exists because of a lack of definite and certain terms. Yet in both situations, one party may have performed services for the benefit of the other party and the court will require payment of the reasonable value of services to avoid the unjust enrichment of the party receiving the services without paying for them. These damages are sometimes referred to as *restitution damages*. Some courts refer to this situation as an action or recovery in **quantum meruit** (as much as he or she deserved).

quantum meruit – as much as deserved; an action brought for the value of the services rendered the defendant when there was no express contract as to the purchase price.

For Example, Arya Group, Inc. (Arya), sued the entertainer Cher for unjust enrichment. In June 1996, Cher negotiated an oral agreement with Arya to design and construct a house on her Malibu property for $4,217,529. The parties' oral agreement was set forth in a written contract with an August 1997 date and was delivered to Cher in October 1997. She never signed it. However, between June 1996 and November 1997, Arya performed and received payment for a number of services discharged under the unsigned contract. In August 1997, Cher requested Arya to meet with a home designer named Bussell who had previously worked with Cher on a Florida project, and Arya showed Bussell the plans and designs for the Malibu property and introduced her to his subcontractors. In November 1997, Cher terminated her agreement with Arya without paying the balance then due, as asserted by Arya, of $415,169.41. Arya claims that Cher and Bussell misappropriated the plans and designs Arya had prepared. Cher and the other defendants demurred to Arya's unjust enrichment complaint, pointing out that construction contracts must be evidenced in a writing signed by both parties under state law in order to be enforceable in a court of law. The appeals court determined that Arya's noncompliance with the state law requiring a signed written contract did not absolutely foreclose Arya from seeking damages for unjust enrichment if he could prove the assertions in the complaint that Cher was a sophisticated homeowner with previous involvement in residential construction who had legal representation in negotiating the agreement with Arya, and that Cher would be unjustly enriched if she were not required to compensate Arya for the reasonable value of the work already performed.[16]

CASE SUMMARY

No Free Rides

FACTS: PIC Realty leased farmland to Southfield Farms. After Southfield harvested its crop, it cultivated the land in preparation for the planting in the following year. However, its lease expired, so it did not plant that crop. It then sued PIC for reimbursement for the reasonable value of the services and materials used in preparing the land because this was a benefit to PIC. There was evidence that it was customary for landlords to compensate tenants for such work.

DECISION: Southfield was entitled to recover the reasonable value of the benefit conferred upon PIC. This was necessary in order to prevent the unjust enrichment of PIC. [*PIC Realty Corp. v. Southfield Farms, Inc.*, 832 S.W.2d 610 (Tex. App. 1992)]

[16] *Arya Group, Inc. v. Cher*, 91 Cal. Rptr. 2d 815 (Cal. App. 2000). See also *Fischer v. Flax*, 816 A.2d 1 (2003).

A situation may arise over the mistaken conference of a benefit. **For Example,** Nantucket Island has a few approved colors for houses in its historic district. Using the approved gray color, Martin Kane and his crew began painting Sheldon Adams's house in the historic district as the result of a mistaken address. Adams observed the initiation of the work from his office across the street but did nothing to stop the painters. At the end of the day when the work was done, Adams refused to pay for the work, saying, "I signed no contract and never approved this work." The law deems it inequitable that Adams should have received the benefit of this work, having observed the benefit being conferred and knowing that the painters expected payment. Adams would be unjustly enriched if he were allowed to retain the benefit without payment for the reasonable value of the work. If Adams did not have knowledge that the work was being done and thus that payment was expected, quasi-contractual liability would not be imposed.

The mistake that benefits the defendant may be the mistake of a third party.

(B) Preclusion by an Express Contract. Courts award relief based on quasi-contractual principles, implying by law a contract where one did not exist in fact. Thus, where an express contract exists, it precludes an unjust enrichment claim.

CASE SUMMARY

When in Doubt, Write It Out

FACTS: Facing financial turbulence, Philippine Airlines (PAL) sought to renegotiate its aircraft lease contract (ALC) with World Airlines (WA). WA refused to negotiate with PAL. PAL retained John Sununu, the former Governor of New Hampshire and the former Chief of Staff to President George H. W. Bush and Sununu's partner Victor Frank to represent it. Sununu and Frank sent a contract proposal to PAL, which included a proposed "success fee" of $600,000 if they persuaded WA to accept a modification of the lease contract. PAL gave Sununu and Frank a verbal go-ahead but did not sign the proposed contract. Thereafter PAL sent a contract that was different from that proposed by Sununu and Frank, containing a success fee of 4 percent of savings if they were able to reach a settlement to reduce the remaining obligation of PAL to WA in accordance with either of two very specific settlement offers. Caught up in the actual intense settlement negotiations with WA on behalf of PAL Sununu and Frank signed the contract. Thereafter, they were successful in obtaining an amendment to the lease contract, saving PAL $12.8 million. PAL refused to pay a success fee of $520,000 because the actual settlement did not meet the contractual criteria, which was limited to just the two specific settlement offers. Sununu and Frank sued PAL for unjust enrichment and other contract theories.

DECISION: Judgment for PAL. Sununu and Frank conferred a benefit on PAL through their efforts to persuade WA to negotiate with PAL; and PAL accepted and retained the benefit for the renegotiated lease. There can be no claim, however, for unjust enrichment when an express contract exists between two parties. A court awards relief based on quasi-contractual principles, implying by law a contract, only where one did not exist in fact. The court stated:

> To grant PAL's summary judgment motion is not to condone its conduct. The airline can rightly be accused of stinginess for enforcing the formalistic terms of the contract in spite of the plaintiffs' earnest efforts on its behalf.... PAL may have violated Sununu and Frank's trust, but it did not violate the law.

CASE SUMMARY

Continued

... Sununu and Frank seem to have done their best to serve their client, but they made a reckless bet by trusting PAL. They were accustomed to handshake deals in which personal relationships count for more than legal documents, so they made little effort to put their understanding with PAL on paper. When they ran into a client who didn't play by the same rules, they paid the price.

The lesson is one that should be taught in law and business schools across America: When in doubt, write it out.

[*Sununu v. Philippine Airlines, Inc.*, 792 F. Supp. 2d 39 (D. D.C. 2011)]

Thinking Things Through

Twelve Years of Litigation

Brown University accepted the bid of Marshall Contractors, Inc. (Marshall), to build the Pizzitola Sports Facility on its Providence, Rhode Island, campus. The parties intended to execute a formal written contract. Brown decided to pay $7,157,051 for the project, but Marshall sought additional payment for items it deemed extras and not contemplated in its bid. Because the parties were unable to agree on the scope of the project as compared to the price Brown was willing to pay, they never executed the formal written contract. Nevertheless, in the context of this disagreement over terms and price, construction began in May 1987. When the parties could not resolve their disagreements as the project neared completion in January 1989, Marshall sued Brown University, seeking to recover the costs for what it deemed "changes." Brown asserted that an implied-in-fact contract existed for all work at the $7,157,051 figure because the contractor went ahead with the project knowing the money Brown would pay. The litigation ended up in the Supreme Court of Rhode Island, and in 1997, the court concluded that no express or implied-in-fact contract had ever been reached by the parties concerning the scope of the project and what costs were to be included in the price stipulated by Brown. The case was remanded to the trial court for a new trial. After a trial on the theories of *quantum meruit* and unjust enrichment, a jury awarded Marshall $1.2 million dollars, which was some $3.1 million less than Marshall sought. Brown University appealed, and on November 21, 2001, the Supreme Court of Rhode Island affirmed the jury verdict for the contractor, determining that the proper measure of damages on unjust enrichment and *quantum meruit* theories was "the reasonable value of the work done."*

In May 1987 when the parties could not reach agreement enabling the execution of a formal written contract, thinking things through at that point in time should have exposed the potential for significant economic uncertainties to both parties in actually starting the building process under such circumstances. In the spring of 1987 when all parties were unable to reach agreement, mediation or expedited arbitration by construction experts may well have resolved the controversy and yielded an amicable written contract with little or no delay to the project. Instead, the unsettled cost issues during the building process could have had an adverse impact on the "job chemistry" between the contractor and the owner, which may have adversely affected the progress and quality of the job. The 12 years of litigation that, with its economic and human resource costs, yielded just $1.2 million for the contractor was a no-win result for both sides. A primary rule for all managers in projects of this scope is to make sure the written contracts are executed before performance begins! Relying on "implied-in-fact" or quasi-contract legal theories is simply a poor management practice.

*ADP Marshall, Inc. v. Brown University, 784 A2d 309 (R.I. 2001).

(c) EXTENT OF RECOVERY. When recovery is allowed in quasi contract, the plaintiff recovers the reasonable value of the benefit conferred on the defendant,[17] or the fair and reasonable[18] value of the work performed, depending on the jurisdiction and the circumstances of the case itself. The customary method of calculating damages in construction contract cases is actual job costs plus an allowance for overhead and profits minus amount paid.[19]

C. CONTRACTING ON THE INTERNET

Doing business online for consumers is very similar to doing business through a catalog purchase or by phone. Before placing an order, a buyer is commonly concerned about the reputation of the seller. The basic purchasing principle of *caveat emptor* still applies: buyer beware! The Internet provides valuable tools to allow a buyer to research the reputation of the seller and its products. Online evaluations of companies and their products can be found at Web sites, such as Consumer Reports (**www.consumerreports.org**), Consumers Digest (**www .consumersdigest.com**), or the Better Business Bureau (**www.bbb.org**). E-consumers may have access to categorized histories of comments by other e-consumers, such as Planet Feedback ratings at **www.planetfeedback.com**.

The intellectual property principles set forth in Chapter 10—as well as the contractual principles, the law of sales, and privacy laws you are about to study—all apply to e-commerce transactions. When you are purchasing an item online, you must carefully read all of the terms and conditions set forth on the seller's Web site when assessing whether to make a contemplated purchase. The proposed terms may require that any disputes be litigated in a distant state or be resolved through arbitration with restricted remedies, or there may be an unsatisfactory return policy, warranty limitations, or limitation of liability. Generally, the Web site terms become the contract of the parties and are legally enforceable.

The laws you have studied that prevent deceptive advertising by brick-and-mortar businesses also apply to Internet sites.[20] If an in-state site is engaging in false advertising, you may be able to exercise consumer protection rights through your state's attorney general's office, or you may find some therapeutic relief by reporting the misconduct to the Internet Scambusters site (**www.scambusters.com**).

From a seller's perspective, it is exceedingly helpful to have as much information as possible on your potential customers' buying habits. Federal law prohibits the collection of personal information from children without parental consent, and some states restrict the unauthorized collection of personal information. European Union countries have strict laws protecting the privacy of consumers. Sellers intending to collect personal information should obtain the consent of their customers, make certain that children are excluded, and make sure that the information is stored in a secure environment.

Advanced encryption technology has made the use of credit card payments through the Internet very safe. No computer system connected to the Internet is

---

[17] *Ramsey v. Ellis*, 484 N.W.2d 331 (Wis. 1992).

[18] *ADP Marshall, Inc. v. Brown University*, 784 A.2d 309 (R.I. 2001).

[19] *Miranco Contracting, Inc. v. Perel*, 871 N.Y.S.2d 310 (A.D. 2008).

[20] See *MADCAP I, LLC v. McNamee*, 712 N.W.2d 16 (Wis. App. 2005) in which the court found genuine issues of material fact as to whether a business Web site falsely represented the size and nature of its business to induce the public to purchase products and services described on its Web site in violation of the state's fraudulent representations statute.

totally secure however. In the worst-case scenario, credit card issuers will not charge a user for more than the first $50 of unauthorized activity.

Internet contracts involve the same types of issues that are addressed in contracts offline but with certain technology-related nuances. The parties to the e-contracts must still negotiate their obligations in clear and unambiguous language, including such terms as quantity, quality, and price as well as warranties, indemnification responsibilities, limitations on liability, and termination procedures. The federal Electronic Signatures in Global and National Commerce Act (E-Sign) and the Uniform Electronic Transactions Act (UETA) mandate parity between paper and electronic contracts. The basic legal rules that govern contracts offline are the very same rules that govern online contracts, and basic civil procedure rules apply.

For Example, California buyer Paul Boschetto bought a 1964 Ford Galaxy that had been advertised on eBay to be "in awesome condition" from a Milton, Wisconsin resident, J. Hansing, for $34,106. On delivery Boschetto discovered that the car had rust, extensive dents, and would not start. His lawsuit against Hansing in U.S. District Court in California was dismissed for lack of personal jurisdiction.[21] (The formation of a contract with a nonresident defendant was not, standing alone, sufficient to create personal jurisdiction in California.)

Boxes identifying special Internet e-commerce topics are strategically placed throughout these chapters.

LawFlix

Paper Moon (1973) (PG)

In this movie for which Tatum O'Neal was given an Oscar, the ongoing issue between Annie and her alleged father is her recoupment of the money she says he promised. Discuss the contract issues (voidable [minor], formation, unilateral vs. bilateral, express, informal, etc.).

MAKE THE CONNECTION

SUMMARY

A contract is a binding agreement between two or more parties. A contract arises when an offer is accepted with contractual intent (the intent to make a binding agreement).

Contracts may be classified in a number of ways according to form, the way in which they were created, validity, and obligations. With respect to form, a contract may be either informal or formal, such as those under seal or those appearing on the records of courts. Contracts may be classified by the way they were created as those that are expressed by words— written or oral—and those that are implied or deduced from conduct. The question of validity requires distinguishing between contracts that are valid, those that are voidable, and those that are not contracts at all but are merely void agreements. Contracts can be distinguished on the basis of the obligations created as executed contracts, in which

---

[21] *Boschetto v. Hansing*, 539 F.3d 1011 (9th Cir. 2008).

everything has been performed, and executory contracts, in which something remains to be done. The bilateral contract is formed by exchanging a promise for a promise, so each party has the obligation of thereafter rendering the promised performance. In the unilateral contract, which is the doing of an act in exchange for a promise, no further performance is required of the offeree who performed the act.

In certain situations, the law regards it as unjust for a person to receive a benefit and not pay for it.

In such a case, the law of quasi contracts allows the performing person to recover the reasonable value of the benefit conferred on the benefited person even though no contract between them requires any payment. Unjust enrichment, which a quasi contract is designed to prevent, sometimes arises when there was never any contract between the persons involved or when there was a contract, but for some reason it was avoided or held to be merely a void agreement.

LEARNING OUTCOMES

After studying this chapter, you should be able to clearly explain:

A. Nature of Contracts

L0.1   Explain the meaning and importance of privity of a contract

See the example of the subcontractor, RPR & Associates, who worked on a project but could not sue the owner for payment, pp. 244–245.
See the example involving rapper Eminem, FBT, and Aftermath Records, where FBT was not a party to the contract and thus not bound by it, p. 245.

L0.2   Describe the way in which a contract arises

See the discussion on offer and acceptance on p. 245.

B. Classes of Contracts

L0.3   Distinguish between bilateral and unilateral contracts

See the example of the Nantucket painters on p. 252.
See the *AON Risk Services* case where an insurance agent won his case based on a unilateral contract theory, pp. 248–249.

L0.4   Explain the reasoning behind quasi-contract recovery

See the example whereby Cher had to pay a home designer for certain work even though there was no contract, p. 251.

C. Contracting on the Internet

L0.5   Explain how Internet contracts involve the same types of issues as offline contracts

See the eBay example on p. 255.

KEY TERMS

bilateral contract
contract
contract under seal
executed contract
executory contract
express contract
formal contract
implied contract
informal contract

obligee
obligor
offeree
offeror
option contract
privity
privity of contract
promisee
promisor

quantum meruit
quasi contract
recognizance
right of first refusal
unilateral contracts
valid contract
void agreement
voidable contract

QUESTIONS AND CASE PROBLEMS

1. What is a contract?

2. Fourteen applicants for a city of Providence, Rhode Island, police academy training class each received from the city a letter stating that it was a "conditional offer of employment" subject to successful completion of medical and psychological exams. The 14 applicants passed the medical and psychological exams. However, these applicants were replaced by others after the city changed the selection criteria. Can you identify an offer and acceptance in this case? Can you make out a bilateral or unilateral contract? [*Ardito et al. v. City of Providence,* 213 F. Supp. 2d 358 (D.R.I.)]

3. Compare an implied contract with a quasi contract.

4. The Jordan Keys law firm represented the Greater Southeast Community Hospital of Washington, D.C., in a medical malpractice suit against the hospital. The hospital was self-insured for the first $1,000,000 of liability and the St. Paul Insurance Co. provided excess coverage up to $4,000,000. The law firm was owed $67,000 for its work on the malpractice suit when the hospital went into bankruptcy. The bankruptcy court ordered the law firm to release its files on the case to St. Paul to defend under the excess coverage insurance, and the Jordan Keys firm sued St. Paul for its legal fees of $67,000 expended prior to the bankruptcy under an "implied-in-fact contract" because the insurance company would have the benefit of all of its work. Decide. [*Jordan Keys v. St. Paul Fire,* 870 A.2d 58 (D.C.)]

5. Beck was the general manager of Chilkoot Lumber Co. Haines sold fuel to the company. To persuade Haines to sell on credit, Beck signed a paper by which he promised to pay any debt the lumber company owed Haines. He signed this paper with his name followed by "general manager." Haines later sued Beck on this promise, and Beck raised the defense that the addition of "general manager" showed that Beck, who was signing on behalf of Chilkoot, was not personally liable and did not intend to be bound by the

paper. Was Beck liable on the paper? [*Beck v. Haines Terminal and Highway Co.,* 843 P.2d 1229 (Alaska)]

6. *A* made a contract to construct a house for *B.* Subsequently, *B* sued *A* for breach of contract. *A* raised the defense that the contract was not binding because it was not sealed. Is this a valid defense? [*Cooper v. G. E. Construction Co.,* 158 S.E.2d 305 (Ga. App.)]

7. Edward Johnson III, the CEO and principal owner of the world's largest mutual fund company, Fidelity Investments, Inc., was a longtime tennis buddy of Richard Larson. In 1995, Johnson asked Larson, who had construction experience, to supervise the construction of a house on Long Pond, Mount Desert Island, Maine. Although they had no written contract, Larson agreed to take on the project for $6,700 per month plus lodging. At the end of the project in 1997, Johnson made a $175,000 cash payment to Larson, and he made arrangements for Larson to live rent-free on another Johnson property in the area called Pray's Meadow in exchange for looking after Johnson's extensive property interests in Maine. In the late summer of 1999, Johnson initiated a new project on the Long Pond property. Johnson had discussions with Larson about doing this project, but Larson asked to be paid his former rate, and Johnson balked because he had already hired a project manager. According to Johnson, at a later date he again asked Larson to take on the "shop project" as a favor and in consideration of continued rent-free use of the Pray's Meadow home. Johnson stated that Larson agreed to do the job "pro bono" in exchange for the use of the house, and Johnson acknowledged that he told Larson he would "take care" of Larson at the end of the project, which could mean as much or as little as Johnson determined. Larson stated that Johnson told him that he would "take care of" Larson if he would do the project and told him to "trust the Great Oracle" (meaning Johnson, the highly successful businessperson). Larson sought payment in March 2000 and asked Johnson for "something on account" in April. Johnson offered

Larson a loan. In August during a tennis match, Larson again asked Johnson to pay him. Johnson became incensed, and through an employee, he ended Larson's participation in the project and asked him to vacate Pray's Meadow. Larson complied and filed suit for payment for work performed at the rate of $6,700 per month. Did Larson have an express contract with Johnson? What legal theory or theories could Larson utilize in his lawsuit? How would you decide this case if you believed Larson's version of the facts? How would you decide the case if you believed Johnson's version of the facts? [*Larson v. Johnson*, 196 F. Supp. 2d 38 (D. Me. 2002)]

8. While Clara Novak was sick, her daughter Janie helped her in many ways. Clara died, and Janie then claimed that she was entitled to be paid for the services she had rendered her mother. This claim was opposed by three brothers and sisters who also rendered services to the mother. They claimed that Janie was barred because of the presumption that services rendered between family members are gratuitous. Janie claimed that this presumption was not applicable because she had not lived with her mother but had her own house. Was Janie correct? [*In re Estate of Novak*, 398 N.W.2d 653 (Minn. App.)]

9. Dozier and his wife, daughter, and grandson lived in the house Dozier owned. At the request of the daughter and grandson, Paschall made some improvements to the house. Dozier did not authorize these, but he knew that the improvements were being made and did not object to them. Paschall sued Dozier for the reasonable value of the improvements, but Dozier argued that he had not made any contract for such improvements. Was he obligated to pay for such improvements?

10. When Harriet went away for the summer, Landry, a house painter, painted her house. He had a contract to paint a neighbor's house but painted Harriet's house by mistake. When Harriet returned from vacation, Landry billed her for $3,100, which was a fair price for the work. She refused to pay. Landry claimed that she had a quasi-contractual liability for that amount.
Was he correct?

11. Margrethe and Charles Pyeatte, a married couple, agreed that she would work so that he could go to law school and that when he finished, she would go back to school for her master's degree. After Charles was admitted to the bar and before Margrethe went back to school, the two were divorced. She sued Charles, claiming that she was entitled to quasi-contractual recovery of the money that she had paid for Charles's support and law school tuition. He denied liability. Was she entitled to recover for the money she spent for Charles's maintenance and law school tuition? [*Pyeatte v. Pyeatte*, 661 P.2d 196 (Ariz. App.)]

12. Carriage Way was a real estate development of approximately 80 houses and 132 apartments. The property owners were members of the Carriage Way Property Owners Association. Each year, the association would take care of certain open neighboring areas, including a nearby lake, that were used by the property owners. The board of directors of the association would make an assessment or charge against the property owners to cover the cost of this work. The property owners paid these assessments for a number of years and then refused to pay any more. In spite of this refusal, the association continued to take care of the areas in question. The association then sued the property owners and claimed that they were liable for the benefit that had been conferred on them. Were the owners liable? [*Board of Directors of Carriage Way Property Owners Ass'n v. Western National Bank*, 487 N.E.2d 974 (Ill. App.)]

13. When improvements or buildings are added to real estate, the real estate tax assessment is usually increased to reflect the increased value of the property. Frank Partipilo and Elmer Hallman owned neighboring tracts of land. Hallman made improvement to his land, constructing a new building and driveway on the tract. The tax assessor made a mistake about the location of the boundary line between Partipilo's and Hallman's land and thought the improvements were made on Partipilo's property. Instead of increasing the taxes on Hallman's land, the assessor wrongly increased the taxes on Partipilo's land. Partipilo paid the increased taxes for three years. When he

learned why his taxes had been increased, he sued Hallman for the amount of the increase that Partipilo had been paying. Hallman raised the defense that he had not done anything wrong and that the mistake had been the fault of the tax assessor. Decide. [*Partipilo v. Hallman*, 510 N.E.2d 8 (Ill.App.)]

14. When a college student complained about a particular course, the vice president of the college asked the teacher to prepare a detailed report about the course. The teacher did and then demanded additional compensation for the time spent in preparing the report. He claimed that the college was liable to provide compensation on an implied contract. Was he correct? [*Zadrozny v. City Colleges of Chicago*, 581 N.E.2d 44 (Ill. App.)]

15. Smith made a contract to sell automatic rifles to a foreign country. Because the sale of such weapons to that country was illegal under an act of Congress, the U.S. government prosecuted Smith for making the contract. He raised the defense that because the contract was illegal, it was void and there is no binding obligation when a contract is void; therefore, no contract for which he could be prosecuted existed. Was he correct?

CPA QUESTIONS

1. Kay, an art collector, promised Hammer, an art student, that if Hammer could obtain certain rare artifacts within two weeks, Kay would pay for Hammer's postgraduate education. At considerable effort and expense, Hammer obtained the specified artifacts within the two-week period. When Hammer requested payment, Kay refused. Kay claimed that there was no consideration for the promise. Hammer would prevail against Kay based on:

   a. Unilateral contract.

   b. Unjust enrichment.

   c. Public policy.

   d. Quasi contract.

© Manuel Gutjahr/iStockphoto.com

CHAPTER 13

Formation of Contracts: Offer and Acceptance

learningoutcomes

After studying this chapter, you should be able to

LO.1 Decide whether an offer contains definite and certain terms

LO.2 Explain the exceptions the law makes to the requirement of definiteness

LO.3 Explain all the ways an offer can be terminated

LO.4 Explain what constitutes the acceptance of an offer

LO.5 Explain the implications of failing to read a clickwrap agreement

A *contract* consists of enforceable obligations that have been voluntarily assumed. Thus, one of the essential elements of a contract is an agreement. This chapter explains how the basic agreement arises, when there is a contract, and how there can be merely unsuccessful negotiations without a resulting contract.

A. REQUIREMENTS OF AN OFFER

offer – expression of an offeror's willingness to enter into a contractual agreement.

An **offer** expresses the willingness of the offeror to enter into a contractual agreement regarding a particular subject. It is a promise that is conditional upon an act, a forbearance (a refraining from doing something one has a legal right to do), or a return promise.

CPA 1. Contractual Intention

To make an offer, the offeror must appear to intend to create a binding obligation. Whether this intent exists is determined by objective standards.[1] This intent may be shown by conduct. **For Example,** when one party signs a written contract and sends it to the other party, such action is an offer to enter into a contract on the terms of the writing.

There is no contract when a social invitation is made or when an offer is made in obvious jest or excitement. A reasonable person would not regard such an offer as indicating a willingness to enter into a binding agreement. The test for a valid, binding offer is whether it induces a reasonable belief in the offeree that he or she can, by accepting it, bind the offeror, as developed in the *Wigod* case.

CASE SUMMARY

A Valid Offer!

FACTS: The U.S. Department of the Treasury implemented the federal Home Affordable Mortgage Program (HAMP) to help homeowners avoid foreclosure amidst the sharp decline in the nation's housing market in 2008. In 2009, Wells Fargo Bank issued Lori Wigod a four-month "trial" loan modification under a Trial Period Plan (TPP). After the trial period, if the borrower complied with all of the terms of the TPP agreement, including making all required payments and providing all required documentation, and if the borrower's representations remained true and correct, the servicer, Well Fargo, had to offer a permanent mortgage modification. Wigod alleged that she complied with these requirements and that Wells Fargo refused to grant a permanent modification. Wells Fargo contended that the TPP contained no valid offer.

DECISION: Judgment for Wigod. A person can prevent his submission from being treated as an offer by using suitable language conditioning the formation of a contract on some further step, such as approval by corporate headquarters. It is when the promisor conditions a promise on *his*

---

[1] *Glass Service Co. v. State Farm Mutual Automobile Ins. Co.,* 530 N.W.2d 867 (Minn. App. 1995).

CASE SUMMARY

Continued

own future action or approval that there is no binding offer. Here, the TTP spelled out two conditions precedent to Wells Fargo's obligation to offer a permanent modification. Wigod had to comply with the requirements of the TPP, and her financial representations had to be true and accurate. These conditions had to be satisfied by the promisee (Wigod). Here a reasonable person in Wigod's position would read the TPP as a default offer that she could accept so long as she satisfied the two conditions. [*Wigod v. Wells Fargo Bank*, 673 F.3d 547 (7th Cir. 2012)]

(A) **INVITATION TO NEGOTIATE.** The first statement made by one of two persons is not necessarily an offer. In many instances, there may be a preliminary discussion or an invitation by one party to the other to negotiate or to make an offer. Thus, an inquiry by a school as to whether a teacher wished to continue the following year was merely a survey or invitation to negotiate and was not an offer that could be accepted. Therefore, the teacher's affirmative response did not create a contract.

Ordinarily, a seller sending out circulars or catalogs listing prices is not regarded as making an offer to sell at those prices. The seller is merely indicating a willingness to consider an offer made by a buyer on those terms. The reason for this rule is, in part, the practical consideration that because a seller does not have an unlimited supply of any commodity, the seller cannot possibly intend to make a contract with everyone who sees the circular. The same principle is applied to merchandise that is displayed with price tags in stores or store windows and to most advertisements. An advertisement in a newspaper is ordinarily considered an invitation to negotiate and is not an offer that can be accepted by a reader of the paper.[2] However, some court decisions have construed advertisements as offers that called for an act on the part of the customer thereby forming a unilateral contract, such as the advertisement of a reward for the return of lost property.

Quotations of prices, even when sent on request, are likewise not offers unless the parties have had previous dealings or unless a trade custom exists that would give the recipient of the quotation reason to believe that an offer was being made. Whether a price quotation is to be treated as an offer or merely an invitation to negotiate is a question of the intent of the party giving the quotation.[3]

(B) **AGREEMENT TO MAKE A CONTRACT AT A FUTURE DATE.** No contract arises when the parties merely agree that at a future date they will consider making a contract or will make a contract on terms to be agreed on at that time. In such a case, neither party is under any obligation until the future contract is made. Unless an agreement is reached on all material terms and conditions and nothing is left to future negotiations, a contract to enter a contract in the future is of no effect. **For Example,** Hewitt Associates provided employee benefits administrative services to Rollins, Inc. under a contract negotiated in 2001 to run through 2006. Prior to its expiration, the

---

[2] *Zanakis-Pico v. Cutter, Dodge, Inc.*, 47 P.2d 1222 (Haw. 2002).
[3] Statutes prohibiting false or misleading advertising may require adherence to advertised prices.

parties negotiated—seeking to agree to a multiyear extension of the 2001 agreement. They agreed to all of the material terms of the contract, except that Rollins balked at a $1.8 million penalty clause. Rollins's employees told Hewitt that the extension "was going to be signed." However, Rollins did not sign and the 2001 agreement expired. Hewitt's contention that the agreement was enforceable at the moment Rollins told Hewitt it was going to sign the new agreement was rejected by the court, stating that an agreement to reach an agreement is a contradiction in terms and imposes no obligation on the parties. [4]

2. Definiteness

An offer, and the resulting contract, must be definite and certain. [5] If an offer is indefinite or vague or if an essential provision is lacking, [6] no contract arises from an attempt to accept it. The reason is that courts cannot tell what the parties are to do. Thus, an offer to conduct a business for as long as it is profitable is too vague to be a valid offer. The acceptance of such an offer does not result in a contract that can be enforced. Statements by a bank that it was "with" the debtors and would "support" them in their proposed business venture were too vague to be regarded as a promise by the bank to make necessary loans to the debtors.

CASE SUMMARY

What Is the Meaning of an Agreement for a "Damn Good Job"?

FACTS: Larry Browneller made an oral contract with Hubert Plankenhorn to restore a 1963 Chevrolet Impala convertible. The car was not in good condition. Hubert advised the owner that his work would not yield a car of "show" quality because of the condition of the body, and he accordingly believed that the owner merely wanted a presentable car. Larry, on the other hand, having told Hubert that he wanted a "damn good job," thought this statement would yield a car that would be competitive at the small amateur car shows he attended. When the finished car had what Larry asserted were "waves" in the paint as a result of an uneven surface on the body, Larry brought suit against Hubert for breach of the oral contract.

DECISION: There was clearly a misunderstanding between the parties over the quality of work that could and would be obtained. *Quality* was a material term of the oral contract between the parties, on which there was no shared understanding. Accordingly, a court will not find an individual in breach of a term of the contract where the term did not exist. [***In re Plankenhorn,* 228 B.R. 638 (N.D. Ohio 1998)**]

The fact that minor, ministerial, and nonessential terms are left for future determination does not make an agreement too vague to be a contract. [7]

[4] *Hewitt Associates, LLC v. Rollins, Inc.,* 669 S.E.2d 551 (Ga. App. 2008).
[5] *Norton v. Correctional Medicare, Inc.,* 2010 WL 4103016 (N.D.N.Y. Oct. 18, 2010).
[6] *Peace v. Doming Holdings Inc.,* 554 S.E.2d 314 (Ga. App. 2001).
[7] *Hsu v. Vet-A-Mix, Inc.,* 479 N.W.2d 336 (Iowa App. 1991). But see *Ocean Atlantic Development Corp. v. Aurora Christian Schools, Inc.,* 322 F.3d 983 (7th Cir. 2003), where letter offers to purchase (OTP) real estate were signed by both parties, but the offers conditioned the purchase and sale of each property upon the subsequent execution of a purchase and sale agreement. The court held that the parties thus left themselves room to walk away from the deal under Illinois law, and the OTPs were not enforced.

CASE SUMMARY

Offer to Purchase Is Controlling Legal Document

FACTS: John McCarthy executed an offer to purchase (OTP) real estate on a preprinted form generated by the Greater Boston Real Estate Board. The OTP contained a description of the property, the price to be paid, deposit requirements, limited title requirements, and the time and place for closing. The OTP required the parties to execute the applicable Standard Form Purchase and Sale Agreement recommended by the Greater Boston Real Estate Board that, when executed, was to be the agreement between the parties. An unnumbered paragraph immediately above the signature line stated: "NOTICE: This is a legal document that creates binding obligations. If not understood, consult an attorney." The seller, Ann Tobin, signed the OTP. While lawyers for the parties exchanged drafts of a purchase and sale agreement, a much higher offer for the property was made to Tobin by the Diminicos. Because she had not yet signed the purchase and sale agreement, Tobin accepted the Diminicos's offer and executed a purchase and sales agreement with them. Before that deal closed, McCarthy filed an action for specific performance of the OTP. McCarthy contended he and Tobin intended to be bound by the OTP and that the execution of a PSA was merely a formality. Tobin contended the OTP language contemplated the execution of a final written document, thus clearly indicating that the parties had not agreed to all material aspects of the transaction, and thus the parties did not intend to be bound until the PSA was signed. From a judgment for Tobin and the Diminicos, McCarthy appealed.

DECISION: Judgment for McCarthy. Although the provisions of the purchase and sale agreement can be the subject of negotiation, norms exist for their customary resolution. The inference that the OTP was legally binding is bolstered by the notice printed on the form. McCarthy and Tobin were alerted to the fact that the OTP "creates binding obligations." The OTP employed familiar contractual language. It stated that McCarthy "hereby offers to buy" the property, and Tobin's signature indicates that "this Offer is hereby accepted." The OTP also details the amount to be paid and when, describes the property bought, and specifies for how long the offer was open. This was a firm offer, the acceptance of which bound Tobin to sell and McCarthy to buy the subject property. [*McCarthy v. Tobin*, 706 N.E.2d 629 (Mass. 1999)]

Thinking Things Through

The Rules of Negotiations

Business agreements are often reached after much discussion, study, and posturing by both sides. Many statements may be made by both sides about the price or value placed on the subject of the transaction. Withholding information or presenting selective, self-serving information may be perceived by a party to the negotiations as protective self-interest. Does the law of contracts apply a duty of good faith and fair dealing in the negotiation of contracts? Does the Uniform Commercial Code provide for a general duty of good faith in the negotiation of contracts? Are lawyers under an ethical obligation to inform opposing counsel of relevant facts? The answer to all of these questions is no.

The Restatement (Second) of Contracts applies the duty of good faith and fair dealing to the performance and enforcement of contracts,

not their negotiation*; so also does the UCC.** The American Bar Association's Model Rules of Professional Conduct, Rule 4.1 Comment 1 requires a lawyer to be "truthful" when dealing with others on a client's behalf, but it also states that generally a lawyer has "no affirmative duty to inform an opposing party of relevant facts."*** Comment 2 to Rule 4.1 contains an example of a "nonmaterial" statement of a lawyer as "estimates of price or value placed on the subject of a transaction."

The legal rules of negotiations state that—in the absence of fraud, special relationships, or statutory or contractual duties—negotiators are

*Restatement (Second) of Contracts §105, comment (c).
**Uniform Commercial Code §1-203.
***American Bar Association Model Rule of Professional Conduct 4.1(a) Comment 1.

Thinking Things Through

Continued

not obligated to divulge pertinent information to the other party to the negotiations. The parties to negotiations themselves must demand and analyze pertinent information and ultimately assess the fairness of the proposed transaction. Should a party conclude that the elements of a final proposal or offer are excessive or dishonest, that party's legal option is to walk away from the deal. Generally, the party has no basis to bring a lawsuit for lack of good faith and fair dealing in negotiations.

However, THINKING THINGS THROUGH, the ethical standards for negotiations set forth in Chapter 3 indicate that establishing a reputation for trustworthiness, candor, and reliability often leads to commercial success for a company's continuing negotiations with its customers, suppliers, distributors, lenders, unions, and employees.*

*For a contrary example, consider the following story. The Atlanta Braves baseball team's general manager Frank Wren negotiated with free agent baseball player Rafael Furcal's agent Paul Kinzer. When all terms had been negotiated, Kinzer asked for a written terms-of-agreement sheet signed by the Braves, which to Wren meant an agreement had been reached. Kinzer took the sheet to the L.A. Dodgers, who then reached an agreement to sign the shortstop. Braves President John Schuerholz said, "The Atlanta Braves will no longer do business with that company—ever. I told Arn Tellem that we can't trust them to be honest and forthright." "Braves GM Blasts Furcal's Agents," Associated Press, *The Boston Globe*, December 20, 2008, C-7.

The law does not favor the destruction of contracts because that would go against the social force of carrying out the intent of the parties.[8] Consequently, when it is claimed that a contract is too indefinite to be enforced, a court will do its best to find the intent of the parties and thereby reach the conclusion that the contract is not too indefinite. **For Example,** boxing promoter Don King had both a Promotional Agreement and a Bout Agreement with boxer Miguel Angel Gonzalez. The Bout Agreement for a boxing match with Julio Cesar Chavez gave King the option to promote the next four of Gonzalez's matches. The contract made clear that if Gonzalez won the Chavez match, he would receive at least $75,000 for the next fight unless the parties agreed otherwise, and if he lost, he would receive at least $25,000 for the subsequent fight unless otherwise agreed. The agreement did not explicitly state the purse for the subsequent match in the event of a draw. The Chavez match ended in a draw, and Gonzalez contended that this omission rendered the contract so indefinite that it was unenforceable. The court disagreed, stating that striking down a contract as indefinite and in essence meaningless is at best a last resort. The court held that although the contract was poorly drafted, the Promotional Agreement contained explicit price terms for which a minimum purse for fights following a draw may be inferred.[9] A court may not, however, rewrite the agreement of the parties in order to make it definite.

(A) DEFINITE BY INCORPORATION. An offer and the resulting contract that by themselves may appear "too indefinite" may be made definite by reference to another writing. **For Example,** a lease agreement that was too vague by itself was made definite because the parties agreed that the lease should follow the standard form with which both were familiar. An agreement may also be made definite by reference to the prior dealings of the parties and to trade practices.

---

[8] *Mears v. Nationwide Mut., Inc. Co.,* 91 F.3d 1118 (8th Cir. 1996).
[9] *Gonzalez v. Don King Productions, Inc.,* 17 F. Supp. 2d 313 (S.D.N.Y. 1998); see also *Echols v. Pelullo,* 377 F.3d 272 (3rd Cir. 2004).

FIGURE 13-1	*Offer and Acceptance*

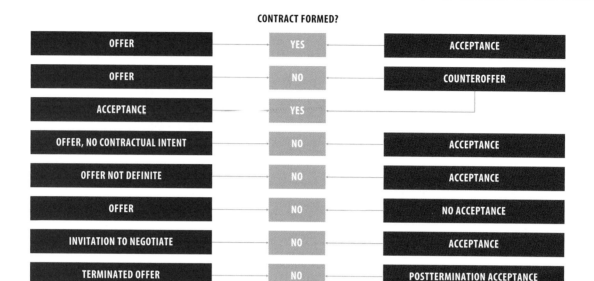

(B) IMPLIED TERMS. Although an offer must be definite and certain, not all of its terms need to be expressed. Some omitted terms may be implied by law. **For Example,** an offer "to pay $400" for a certain Movado timepiece does not state the terms of payment. A court, however, would not condemn this provision as too vague but would hold that it required that cash be paid and that the payment be made on delivery of the watch. Likewise, terms may be implied from conduct. As an illustration, when borrowed money was given to the borrower by a check on which the word *loan* was written, the act of the borrower in endorsing the check constituted an agreement to repay the amount of the check.

(C) "BEST EFFORTS" CLAUSES. While decades ago it was generally accepted that a duty defined only in terms of "best efforts" was too indefinite to be enforced, such a view is no longer widely held. **For Example,** Thomas Hinc, an inventor, executed a contract with Lime-O-Sol Company (LOS) for LOS to produce and distribute Hinc's secret ingredient Stain Remover. Under the contract, Hinc was to receive $10 per gallon sold. The contract contained a clause obligating both parties to use their "best efforts" to market the product "in a manner that seems appropriate." Ultimately, LOS never produced, marketed, or sold Stain Remover for the duration of the contract. The court rejected the defense that the "best efforts" provision was vague and unenforceable stating "[b]est efforts, as commonly understood, means, at the very least *some* effort. It certainly does not mean *zero* effort—the construction LOS urges here to escape any obligation under its contract." [10]

(D) DIVISIBLE CONTRACTS. When the agreement consists of two or more parts and calls for corresponding performances of each part by the parties, the agreement is a **divisible contract**. Thus, in a promise to buy several separate articles at different

divisible contract–agreement consisting of two or more parts, each calling for corresponding performances of each part by the parties.

[10] *Hinc v. Lime-O-Sol Company,* 382 F.3d 716 (7th Cir. 2004).

prices at the same time, the agreement may be regarded as separate or divisible promises for the articles.

(E) EXCEPTIONS TO DEFINITENESS. The law has come to recognize certain situations in which the practical necessity of doing business makes it desirable to have a contract, yet the situation is such that it is either impossible or undesirable to adopt definite terms in advance. In these cases, the indefinite term is often tied to the concept of good-faith performance or to some independent factor that will be definitely ascertainable at some time in the future. The indefinite term might be tied to market price, cost to complete, production, or sales requirements. Thus, the law recognizes binding contracts in the case of a **requirements contract**—that is, a contract to buy all requirements of the buyer from the seller.[11] **For Example,** an agreement between Honeywell International Inc. and Air Products and Chemicals Inc. whereby Air Products would purchase its total requirements of wet process chemicals from Honeywell was held to be an enforceable requirements contract.[12] The law also recognizes as binding an **output contract**—that is, the contract of a producer to sell the entire production or output to a given buyer. These are binding contracts even though they do not state the exact quantity of goods that are to be bought or sold.

> **requirements contract** – contract to buy all requirements of the buyer from the seller.

> **output contract** – contract of a producer to sell its entire production or output to a given buyer.

CASE SUMMARY

GM—In the Driver's Seat on Quantity and Timing!

FACTS: Automodular entered into a series of purchase orders that obligated Delphi to purchase and Automodular to provide all of Delphi's requirements deliverable to the original equipment manufacturer (OEM), General Motors. Automodular receives directions from the OEM's final assembly plants, regardless of whether Automodular is under contract to the OEM or Delphi. The purchase orders ("Contracts") incorporated Delphi's terms that the Buyer, GM, could require Automodular to implement changes to the specifications or design of the goods or to the scope of any services covered by the Contracts. GM informed Automodular that it needed fewer components and directed Automodular to, among other requirements, reduce shifts, change the assembly line speed, and change the length of workers' shifts. As a result, Automodular requested a price increase per unit assembled from Delphi because Automodular believed that such an increase was warranted pursuant to the Contract's change-in-scope provision. Delphi, however, refused to negotiate any price increase and the matter was litigated.

DECISION: Judgment for Delphi. In a requirements contract, the parties do not fix a quantity term, but instead, the quantity will be the buyer's needs of a specific commodity over the contract's life. Section 2.5 of the Contract states in relevant part that "[d]eliveries will be made in the quantities, on the dates, and at the times specified by Buyer in this Contract or any subsequent releases or instructions Buyer issues under this Contract," and that "[i]f the requirements of Buyer's customers or market, economic or other conditions require changes in delivery schedules, Buyer may change the rate of scheduled shipments or direct temporary suspension of scheduled shipments without entitling [Automodular] to a price adjustment or other compensation." This provision demonstrates the intent of the parties to allow the buyer to effectively control the timing and quantity of deliveries without entitling Automodular to an adjustment in price. [*In re Delphi Corp.,* **2009 WL 803598 (S.D.N.Y. 2009)**]

---

[11] *Simcala v. American Coal Trade, Inc.,* 821 So.2d 197 (Ala. 2001).
[12] *Honeywell International Inc. v. Air Products and Chemicals, Inc.,* 872 A.2d 944 (Sup. Ct. Del. 2005).

CPA ## 3. Communication of Offer to Offeree

An offer must be communicated to the offeree. Otherwise, the offeree cannot accept even though knowledge of the offer has been indirectly acquired. Internal management communications of an enterprise that are not intended for outsiders or employees do not constitute offers and cannot be accepted by them. Sometimes, particularly in the case of unilateral contracts, the offeree performs the act called for by the offeror without knowing of the offer's existence. Such performance does not constitute an acceptance. Thus, without knowing that a reward is offered for information leading to the arrest of a particular criminal, a person may provide information that leads to the arrest of the criminal. In most states, if that person subsequently learns of the reward, the reward cannot be recovered.[13]

Not only must the offer be communicated but also it must be communicated by the offeror or at the offeror's direction.

CPA ## B. TERMINATION OF OFFER

An offeree cannot accept a terminated offer. Offers may be terminated by revocation, counteroffer, rejection, lapse of time, death or disability of a party, or subsequent illegality.

CPA ## 4. Revocation of Offer by Offeror

Ordinarily, an offeror can revoke the offer before it is accepted. If this is done, the offeree cannot create a contract by accepting the revoked offer. **For Example,** Bank of America (BOA) contended that it had reached a valid settlement agreement on December 17, 2010, with Jonathan Davidoff concerning his lawsuit against BOA seeking damages for slander of credit and breach of contract. At 3:08 P.M. on December 17, 2010, Davidoff revoked his offer to settle the matter. A few minutes later BOA counsel sent by e-mail the settlement agreements signed by the defendants and asked if Mr. Davidoff would "rescind his rejection." Davidoff clearly revoked the settlement offer prior to BOA's delivery of acceptance of the offer and no contract was formed.[14]

An ordinary offer may be revoked at any time before it is accepted even though the offeror has expressly promised that the offer will be good for a stated period and that period has not yet expired.

The fact that the offeror expressly promised to keep the offer open has no effect when no consideration was given for that promise.

(A) WHAT CONSTITUTES A REVOCATION? No particular form or words are required to constitute a revocation. Any words indicating the offeror's termination of the offer are sufficient. A notice sent to the offeree that the property that is the subject of the offer has been sold to a third person is a revocation of the offer. A customer's order for goods, which is an offer to purchase at certain prices, is revoked by a notice to the seller of the cancellation of the order, provided that such notice is communicated before the order is accepted.

---

[13] With respect to the offeror, it should not make any difference, as a practical matter, whether the services were rendered with or without knowledge of the existence of the offer. Only a small number of states have adopted this view, however.

[14] *Davidoff v. Bank of America,* 2011 WL 999564 (S.D. Fla. Oct. 18, 2010).

(B) COMMUNICATION OF REVOCATION. A revocation of an offer is ordinarily effective only when it is made known to the offeree.[15] Until it is communicated to the offeree, directly or indirectly, the offeree has reason to believe that there is still an offer that may be accepted, and the offeree may rely on this belief. A letter revoking an offer made to a particular offeree is not effective until the offeree receives it. It is not a revocation when the offeror writes it or even when it is mailed or dispatched. A written revocation is effective, however, when it is delivered to the offeree's agent or to the offeree's residence or place of business under such circumstances that the offeree may be reasonably expected to be aware of its receipt.

It is ordinarily held that there is a sufficient communication of the revocation when the offeree learns indirectly of the offeror's revocation. This is particularly true in a land sale when the seller-offeror, after making an offer to sell the land to the offeree, sells the land to a third person and the offeree indirectly learns of such sale. The offeree necessarily realizes that the seller cannot perform the original offer and therefore must be considered to have revoked it.

If the offeree accepts an offer before it is effectively revoked, a valid contract is created.

(C) OPTION CONTRACTS. An *option contract* is a binding promise to keep an offer open for a stated period of time or until a specified date. An option contract requires that the promisor receive consideration—that is, something, such as a sum of money—as the price for the promise to keep the offer open. In other words, the option is a contract to refrain from revoking an offer.

(D) FIRM OFFERS. As another exception to the rule that an offer can be revoked at any time before acceptance, statutes in some states provide that an offeror cannot revoke an offer prior to its expiration when the offeror makes a firm offer. A **firm offer** is an offer that states that it is to be irrevocable, or irrevocable for a stated period of time. Under the Uniform Commercial Code, this doctrine of firm offer applies to a merchant's signed, written offer to buy or sell goods but with a maximum of three months on its period of irrevocability.[16]

firm offer–offer stated to be held open for a specified time, which must be so held in some states even in the absence of an option contract, or under the UCC, with respect to merchants.

5. Counteroffer by Offeree

The offeree rejects the offer when she ignores the original offer and replies with a different offer.[17] If the offeree purports to accept an offer but in so doing makes any change to the terms of the offer, such action is a **counteroffer** that rejects the original offer. An "acceptance" that changes the terms of the offer or adds new terms is a rejection of the original offer and constitutes a counteroffer.[18]

counteroffer–proposal by an offeree to the offeror that changes the terms of, and thus rejects, the original offer.

Ordinarily, if *A* makes an offer, such as to sell a used automobile to *B* for $3,000, and *B* in reply makes an offer to buy at $2,500, the original offer is terminated. *B* is in effect indicating refusal of the original offer and in its place is making a different offer. Such an offer by the offeree is known as a *counteroffer*. No contract arises unless the original offeror accepts the counteroffer.

Counteroffers are not limited to offers that directly contradict the original offers. Any departure from or addition to the original offer is a counteroffer even though the original offer was silent on the point added by the counteroffer.

---

[15] *MD Drilling and Blasting, Inc. v. MLS Construction, LLC,* 889 A.2d 850 (Conn. App. 2006).
[16] U.C.C. §2-205.
[17] *Bourque v. FDIC,* 42 F.3d 704 (1st Cir. 1994).
[18] *McLaughlin v. Heikkila,* 697 N.W.2d 231 (Minn. App. 2005).

6. Rejection of Offer by Offeree

If the offeree rejects the offer and communicates this rejection to the offeror, the offer is terminated. Communication of a rejection terminates an offer even though the period for which the offeror agreed to keep the offer open has not yet expired. It may be that the offeror is willing to renew the offer, but unless this is done, there is no longer any offer for the offeree to accept.

7. Lapse of Time

When the offer states that it is open until a particular date, the offer terminates on that date if it has not yet been accepted. This is particularly so when the offeror declares that the offer shall be void after the expiration of the specified time. Such limitations are strictly construed. **For Example,** Landry's Restaurant Minnesota Inc. extended a written, signed offer to Starlite L.P. to lease Starlite's real estate for a period of 20 years. The written offer stated that if a fully executed acceptance of the lease is not returned to Landry's Minnesota Inc. within six days of the written offer dated April 30, 1998, "the offer to lease … shall be deemed withdrawn and this lease shall be deemed null and void." Starlite signed and returned the lease agreement on May 11, 1998, five days after the May 6 deadline. Landry's Minnesota occupied the property and built a restaurant on it but vacated the property after nine years. Starlite sued the restaurant's parent corporation, Landry's Restaurants Inc., as guarantor of the lease, seeking payment for past due and ongoing rent. Starlite's lawsuit was not successful as no valid lease agreement existed because no contract could be properly formed when acceptance occurred after the written offer had expired.[19]

If the offer contains a time limitation for acceptance, an attempted acceptance after the expiration of that time has no effect and does not give rise to a contract.[20] When a specified time limitation is imposed on an option, the option cannot be exercised after the expiration of that time, regardless of whether the option was exercised within what would have been held a reasonable time if no time period had been specified.

If the offer does not specify a time, it will terminate after the lapse of a reasonable time. What constitutes a reasonable time depends on the circumstances of each case—that is, on the nature of the subject matter, the nature of the market in which it is sold, the time of year, and other factors of supply and demand. If a commodity is perishable or fluctuates greatly in value, the reasonable time will be much shorter than if the subject matter is of a stable value. An offer to sell a harvested crop of tomatoes would expire within a very short time. When a seller purports to accept an offer after it has lapsed by the expiration of time, the seller's acceptance is merely a counteroffer and does not create a contract unless the buyer accepts that counteroffer.

8. Death or Disability of Either Party

If either the offeror or offeree dies or becomes mentally incompetent before the offer is accepted, the offer is automatically terminated. **For Example,** Chet Wilson offers to sell his ranch to Interport, Inc., for $2.5 million. Five days later, Chet

---

[19] *Starlite Limited Partnership v. Landry's Restaurants, Inc.*, 780 N.W.2d 396 (Minn. App. 2010).
[20] *Century 21 Pinetree Properties, Inc. v. Cason*, 469 S.E.2d 458 (Ga. App. 1996).

is killed in an aviation accident. Interport, Inc., subsequently writes to Chet Wilson Jr., an adult, that his father's offer is accepted. No contract is formed because the offer made by Chet died with him.

CPA ## 9. Subsequent Illegality

If the performance of the contract becomes illegal after the offer is made, the offer is terminated. **For Example,** if an offer is made to sell six semiautomatic handguns to a commercial firing range for $550 per weapon but a new law prohibiting such sales is enacted before the offer is accepted, the offer is terminated.

CPA # C. ACCEPTANCE OF OFFER

acceptance – unqualified assent to the act or proposal of another; as the acceptance of a draft (bill of exchange), of an offer to make a contract, of goods delivered by the seller, or of a gift or deed.

An **acceptance** is the assent of the offeree to the terms of the offer. Objective standards determine whether there has been an agreement of the parties.

10. What Constitutes an Acceptance?

No particular form of words or mode of expression is required, but there must be a clear expression that the offeree agrees to be bound by the terms of the offer. If the offeree reserves the right to reject the offer, such action is not an acceptance.[21]

11. Privilege of Offeree

Ordinarily, the offeree may refuse to accept an offer. If there is no acceptance, by definition there is no contract. The fact that there had been a series of contracts between the parties and that one party's offer had always been accepted before by the other does not create any legal obligation to continue to accept subsequent offers.

CPA ## 12. Effect of Acceptance

The acceptance of an offer creates a binding agreement or contract,[22] assuming that all of the other elements of a contract are present. Neither party can subsequently withdraw from or cancel the contract without the consent of the other party. **For Example,** James Gang refused to honor an oral stock purchase agreement he made with Moshen Sadeghi under terms he assented to and that were announced on the record to a court as a mutual settlement of a dispute. Gang was not allowed subsequently to withdraw from the agreement, because it was an enforceable contract.[23]

CPA ## 13. Nature of Acceptance

An *acceptance* is the offeree's manifestation of intent to enter into a binding agreement on the terms stated in the offer. Whether there is an acceptance depends on whether the offeree has manifested an intent to accept. It is the objective or outward appearance that is controlling rather than the subjective or unexpressed intent of the offeree.[24]

[21] *Pantano v. McGowan,* 530 N.W.2d 912 (Neb. 1995).
[22] *Ochoa v. Ford,* 641 N.E.2d 1042 (Ind. App. 1994).
[23] *Sadeghi v. Gang,* 270 S.W.3d 773 (Tex. App. 2008).
[24] *Cowan v. Mervin Mewes, Inc.,* 546 N.W.2d 104 (S.D. 1996).

In the absence of a contrary requirement in the offer, an acceptance may be indicated by an informal "okay," by a mere affirmative nod of the head, or in the case of an offer of a unilateral contract, by performance of the act called for.

The acceptance must be absolute and unconditional. It must accept just what is offered.[25] If the offeree changes any terms of the offer or adds any new term, there is no acceptance because the offeree does not agree to what was offered.

When the offeree does not accept the offer exactly as made, the addition of any qualification converts the "acceptance" into a counteroffer, and no contract arises unless the original offeror accepts such a counteroffer.

CPA   ## 14. Who May Accept?

Only the person to whom an offer is directed may accept it. If anyone else attempts to accept it, no agreement or contract with that person arises.

If the offer is directed to a particular class rather than a specified individual, anyone within that class may accept it. If the offer is made to the public at large, any member of the public at large having knowledge of the existence of the offer may accept it.

When a person to whom an offer was not made attempts to accept it, the attempted acceptance has the effect of an offer. If the original offeror is willing to accept this offer, a binding contract arises. If the original offeror does not accept the new offer, there is no contract.

CASE SUMMARY

There's No Turning Back

FACTS: As a lease was about to expire, the landlord, CRA Development, wrote the tenant, Keryakos Textiles, setting forth the square footage and the rate terms on which the lease would be renewed. Keryakos sent a reply stating that it was willing to pay the proposed rate but wanted different cancellation and option terms in the renewal contract. CRA rejected Keryakos's terms, and on learning this, Keryakos notified CRA that it accepted the terms of its original letter. CRA sought to evict Keryakos from the property, claiming that no lease contract existed between it and Keryakos.

DECISION: The lease contract is governed by ordinary contract law. When the tenant offered other terms in place of those made by the landlord's offer, the tenant made a counteroffer. This had the effect of rejecting or terminating the landlord's offer. The tenant could not then accept the rejected offer after the tenant's counteroffer was rejected. Therefore, there was no contract. [*Keryakos Textiles, Inc. v. CRA Development, Inc.*, 563 N.Y.S.2d 308 (App. Div. 1990)]

CPA   ## 15. Manner and Time of Acceptance

The offeror may specify the manner and time for accepting the offer. When the offeror specifies that there must be a written acceptance, no contract arises when the offeree makes an oral acceptance. If the offeror calls for acceptance by a specified time and date, a late acceptance has no legal effect, and a contract is not formed. Where no time is specified in the offer, the offeree has a reasonable period of time to accept the offer. After the time specified in the offer or a reasonable period of time

[25] *Jones v. Frickey*, 618 S.E.2d 29 (Ga. App. 2005).

expires (when no time is specified in the offer), the offeree's power to make a contract by accepting the offer "lapses."

When the offeror calls for the performance of an act or of certain conduct, the performance thereof is an acceptance of the offer and creates a unilateral contract.

When the offeror has specified a particular manner and time of acceptance, generally, the offeree cannot accept in any other way. The basic rule applied by the courts is that the offeror is the master of the offer!26

CPA

(A) **SILENCE AS ACCEPTANCE.** In most cases, the offeree's silence and failure to act cannot be regarded as an acceptance. Ordinarily, the offeror is not permitted to frame an offer in such a way as to make the silence and inaction of the offeree operate as an acceptance. Nor can a party to an existing contract effect a modification of that agreement without the other party's actual acceptance or approval. **For Example,** H. H. Taylor made a contract with Andy Stricker, a civil engineer, to design a small hotel. The parties agreed on an hourly rate with "total price not to exceed $7,200," and required that additional charges be presented to Taylor prior to proceeding with any changes. Andy was required to dedicate more hours to the project than anticipated but could not present the additional charges to Taylor because Taylor would not return his phone calls. He billed Taylor $9,035 for his services. Taylor's failure to act in not returning phone calls is not a substitute for the assent needed to modify a contract. Stricker is thus only entitled to $7,200. 27

(B) **UNORDERED GOODS AND TICKETS.** Sometimes a seller writes to a person with whom the seller has not had any prior dealings, stating that unless notified to the contrary, the seller will send specified merchandise and the recipient is obligated to pay for it at stated prices. There is no acceptance if the recipient of the letter ignores the offer and does nothing. The silence of the person receiving the letter is not an acceptance, and the sender, as a reasonable person, should recognize that none was intended.

This rule applies to all kinds of goods, books, magazines, and tickets sent through the mail when they have not been ordered. The fact that the items are not returned does not mean that they have been accepted; that is, the offeree is required neither to pay for nor to return the items. If desired, the recipient of the unordered goods may write "Return to Sender" on the unopened package and put the package back into the mail without any additional postage. The Postal Reorganization Act provides that the person who receives unordered mailed merchandise from a commercial sender has the right "to retain, use, discard, or dispose of it in any manner the recipient sees fit without any obligation whatsoever to the sender."28 It provides further that any unordered merchandise that is mailed must have attached to it a clear and conspicuous statement of the recipient's right to treat the goods in this manner.

CPA   16. Communication of Acceptance

Acceptance by the offeree is the last step in the formation of a bilateral contract. Intuitively, the offeror's receipt of the acceptance should be the point in time when the contract is formed and its terms apply. When the parties are involved in face-to-face negotiations, a contract is formed upon the offeror's receipt of the

26 See *1-800 Contacts, Inc. v. Weigner*, 127 P.3d 1241 (Utah App. 2005).
27 *Stricker v. Taylor*, 975 P.2d 930 (Or. App. 1999).
28 Federal Postal Reorganization Act §3009.

E-Commerce & Cyberlaw

Contract Formation on the Internet

It is not possible for an online service provider or seller to individually bargain with each person who visits its Web site. The Web site owner, therefore, as offeror, places its proposed terms on its Web site and requires visitors to assent to these terms in order to access the site, download software, or purchase a product or service.

In a written contract, the parties sign a paper document indicating their intention to be bound by the terms of the contract. Online, however, an agreement may be accomplished by the visitor-offeree simply typing the words "I Accept" in an onscreen box and then clicking a "send" or similar button that indicates acceptance. Or the individual clicks an "I Agree" or "I Accept" icon or check box. Access to the site is commonly denied those who do not agree to the terms. Such agreements have come to be known as *clickwrap* agreements and in the case of software license agreements, *SLAs*. The agreements contain fee schedules and other financial terms and may contain terms such as a notice of the proprietary nature of the material contained on the site and of any limitations on the use of the site and the downloading of software. Moreover, the clickwrap agreements may contain limitations on liability, including losses associated with the use of downloaded software or products or services purchased from the site.

To determine whether a clickwrap agreement is enforceable, courts apply traditional principles of contract law and focus on whether the plaintiffs had reasonable notice of and manifested assent to the clickwrap agreement. Failure to read an enforceable clickwrap agreement, as with any binding contract, will not excuse compliance with its terms.

In *Specht v. Netscape Communications Corp.*,* the Internet users were urged to click on a button to download free software, but the offer did not make clear to the user that clicking the download button would signify assent to restrictive contractual terms and conditions. The court, in its 2002 decision, declined to enforce this clickwrap agreement. Internet sellers and service providers generally learned from the *Specht* decision, and most clickwrap agreements now provide sufficient notice and means for clear assent. For example, in *Feldman v. Google, Inc.*,** decided in 2007, the user was unsuccessful in challenging the terms of Google's "AdWords" Program clickwrap agreement. In order to activate an AdWords account, the user had to visit a Web page that displayed the agreement in a scrollable text box. The text of the agreement was immediately visible to the user, as was a prominent admonition in boldface to read the terms and conditions carefully, and with instructions to indicate assent if the user agreed to the terms.

Unlike the impermissible agreement in *Specht*, the user here had to take affirmative action and click the "Yes, I agree to the above terms and conditions" button in order to proceed to the next step. Clicking "Continue" without clicking the "Yes" button would have returned the user to the same Web page. If the user did not agree to all of the terms, he could not have activated his account, placed ads, or incurred charges.

*306 F.3d 17 (2d Cir. 2002).
**Feldman v. Google, Inc., 513 F. Supp. 2d 229 (E.D. Pa. 2007). See also A.V. v. Iparadigms, LLC, 554 F. Supp. 2d 473 (E.D. Va. 2008).

acceptance. When the offeror hears the offeree's words of acceptance, the parties may shake hands, signifying their understanding that the contract has been formed.

CPA   **(A) MAILBOX RULE.** When the parties are negotiating at a distance from each other, special rules have developed as to when the acceptance takes effect based on the commercial expediency of creating a contract at the earliest period of time and the protection of the offeree. Under the so-called *mailbox rule,* a properly addressed, postage-paid mailed acceptance takes effect when the acceptance is placed into the control of the U.S. Postal Service[29] or, by judicial extension, is placed in the control of a private third-party carrier such as Federal Express or United Parcel Service.[30] That is, the acceptance is effective upon dispatch even before it is received by the offeror.

[29] See *Adams v. Lindsell,* 106 Eng. Rep. 250 (K.B. 1818). Common law jurisdictions have unanimously adopted the mailbox rule, as has the Restatement (Second) of Contracts §63, and the U.C.C [see U.C.C §1-201(26),(38)].

[30] But see *Baca v. Trejo,* 902 N.E.2d 1108 (Ill App. 2009) whereby an Illinois Court determined that a statute deeming a document to be filed with a state court on the date shown by the U.S. Postal Service cancellation mark—the mailbox rule—does not apply to documents consigned to a private carrier, UPS. The court reasoned that courts should not have the task of deciding which carriers are acceptable.

CASE SUMMARY

When the Mailbox Bangs Shut

FACTS: The Thoelkes owned land. The Morrisons mailed an offer to the Thoelkes to buy their land. The Thoelkes agreed to this offer and mailed back a contract signed by them. While this letter was in transit, the Thoelkes notified the Morrisons that their acceptance was revoked. Were the Thoelkes bound by a contract?

DECISION: The acceptance was effective when mailed, and the subsequent revocation of the acceptance had no effect. [*Morrison v. Thoelke*, **155 So. 2d 889 (Fla. App. 1963)**]

The offeror may avoid the application of this rule by stating in the offer that acceptance shall take effect upon receipt by the offeror.

CPA **(B) DETERMINING THE APPLICABLE MEANS OF COMMUNICATION.** The modern rule on the selection of the appropriate medium of communication of acceptance is that unless otherwise unambiguously indicated in the offer, it shall be construed as inviting acceptance in any manner and by any medium reasonable under the circumstances.[31] A medium of communication is normally reasonable if it is one used by the offeror or if it is customary in similar transactions at the time and place the offer is received. Thus, if the offeror uses the mail to extend an offer, the offeree may accept by using the mail. Indeed, acceptance by mail is ordinarily reasonable when the parties are negotiating at a distance even if the offer is not made by mail.

CASE SUMMARY

Just Be Reasonable

FACTS: Maria Cantu was a special education teacher under a one-year contract with the San Benito School District for the 1990–1991 school year. On Saturday, August 18, just weeks before fall-term classes were to begin, she hand delivered a letter of resignation to her supervisor. Late Monday afternoon the superintendent put in the mail a properly stamped and addressed letter to Cantu accepting her offer of resignation. The next morning at 8:00, before the superintendent's letter reached her, Cantu hand delivered a letter withdrawing her resignation. The superintendent refused to recognize the attempted rescission of the resignation.

DECISION: Cantu was wrong. The resignation became binding when the acceptance of the resignation was mailed. The fact that the offer to resign had been delivered by hand did not require that the offer be accepted by a hand delivery of the acceptance. The use of mail was reasonable under the circumstances, and therefore the mailing of the acceptance made it effective. [*Cantu v. Central Education Agency*, **884 S.W.2d 563 (Tex. App. 1994)**]

CPA **(C) TELEPHONE AND ELECTRONIC COMMUNICATION OF ACCEPTANCE.** Although telephonic communication is very similar to face-to-face communication, most U.S. courts, nevertheless, have applied the mailbox rule, holding that telephoned acceptances are effective where and when dispatched.

[31] Restatement (Second) of Contracts §30; U.C.C. §2-206(1) (a).

The courts have yet to address the applicability of the mailbox rule to e-mail. However, when the offeree's server is under the control of an independent entity, such as an online service provider, and the offeree cannot withdraw the message, it is anticipated that the courts will apply the mailbox rule, and acceptance will take effect on proper dispatch. In the case of companies that operate their own servers, the acceptance will take effect when the message is passed onto the Internet.

Facsimile transmissions are substantially instantaneous and could be treated as face-to-face communications. However, it is anticipated that U.S. courts, when called upon to deal with this issue, will apply the mailbox acceptance upon-dispatch rule as they do with telephoned acceptances.

(D) EFFECTS OF THE MAILBOX RULE. If an offer requires that acceptance be communicated by a specific date and the acceptance is properly dispatched by the offeree on the final date, the acceptance is timely and the contract is formed, even though the offeror actually receives the acceptance well after the specified date has passed. **For Example,** by letter dated February 18, 1999, Morton's of Chicago mailed a certified letter to the Crab House accepting the Crab House's offer to terminate its restaurant lease. The Crab House, Inc., sought to revoke its offer to terminate the lease in a certified letter dated February 18, 1999 and by facsimile transmission to Morton's dated February 19, 1999. On February 22, 1999, the Crab House received Morton's acceptance letter; and on the same date Morton's received Crab House's letter revoking the offer to terminate the lease. Acceptance of an offer is effective upon dispatch to the Postal Service, and the contract springs into existence at the time of the mailing. Offers, revocations, and rejections are generally effective only upon the offeree's receipt. Morton's dispatch of its acceptance letter on February 18 formed an agreement to terminate the lease, and the fax dispatched on February 19 was too late to revoke the offer to terminate the lease. [32]

17. Auction Sales

At an auction sale, the statements made by the auctioneer to draw forth bids are merely invitations to negotiate. Each bid is an offer, which is not accepted until the auctioneer indicates that a particular offer or bid is accepted. Usually, this is done by the fall of the auctioneer's hammer, indicating that the highest bid made has been accepted.[33] Because a bid is merely an offer, the bidder may withdraw the bid at any time before it is accepted by the auctioneer.

Ordinarily, the auctioneer who is not satisfied with the amounts of the bids that are being made may withdraw any article or all of the property from the sale. Once a bid is accepted, however, the auctioneer cannot cancel the sale. In addition, if it had been announced that the sale was to be made "without reserve," the property must be sold to the person making the highest bid regardless of how low that bid may be.

In an auction "with reserve," the auctioneer takes bids as agent for the seller with the understanding that no contract is formed until the seller accepts the transaction.[34]

[32] *Morton's of Chicago v. Crab House Inc.*, 746 N.Y.S.2d 317 (2002). *Kass v. Grais*, 2007 WL 2815498 (N.Y. Sup. Sept. 4, 2007).
[33] *Dry Creek Cattle Co. v. Harriet Bros. Limited Partnership*, 908 P.2d 399 (Wyo 1995).
[34] *Marten v. Staab*, 543 N.W.2d 436 (Neb. 1996). Statutes regulate auctions and auctioneers in all states. For example, state of Maine law prohibits an auctioneer from conducting an auction without first having a written contract with the consignor of any property to be sold, including (1) whether the auction is with reserve or without reserve, (2) the commission rate, and (3) a description of all items to be sold. See *Street v. Board of Licensing of Auctioneers*, 889 A.2d 319 ([Me.] 2006).

LawFlix

Funny Farm (1988) (PG)

Near the end of this Chevy Chase movie, two couples face a formation issue as one couple attempts to purchase a home. An offer, presented around a friendly kitchen table setting, is declined by the sellers. Do the buyers' threats to sue the sellers have any legal basis? While the buyers had made a special trip to see the land and felt that since they were offering more than the asking price that they had a contract, the sellers were free to reject the offer. Listing a house for a price is not an offer; it is an invitation for an offer.

MAKE THE CONNECTION

SUMMARY

Because a contract arises when an offer is accepted, it is necessary to find that there was an offer and that it was accepted. If either element is missing, there is no contract.

An offer does not exist unless the offeror has contractual intent. This intent is lacking if the statement of the person is merely an invitation to negotiate, a statement of intention, or an agreement to agree at a later date. Newspaper ads, price quotations, and catalog prices are ordinarily merely invitations to negotiate and cannot be accepted.

An offer must be definite. If an offer is indefinite, its acceptance will not create a contract because it will be held that the resulting agreement is too vague to enforce. In some cases, an offer that is by itself too indefinite is made definite because some writing or standard is incorporated by reference and made part of the offer. In some cases the offer is made definite by implying terms that were not stated. In other cases, the indefinite part of the offer is ignored when that part can be divided or separated from the balance of the offer.

Assuming that there is in fact an offer that is made with contractual intent and that it is sufficiently definite, it still does not have the legal effect of an offer unless it is communicated to the offeree by or at the direction of the offeror.

In some cases, there was an offer but it was terminated before it was accepted. By definition, an attempted acceptance made after the offer has been

terminated has no effect. The offeror may revoke the ordinary offer at any time. All that is required is the showing of the intent to revoke and the communication of that intent to the offeree. The offeror's power to revoke is barred by the existence of an option contract under common law or a firm offer under the Uniform Commercial Code. An offer is also terminated by the express rejection of the offer or by the making of a counteroffer, by the lapse of the time stated in the offer or of a reasonable time when none is stated, by the death or disability of either party, or by a change of law that makes illegal a contract based on the particular offer.

When the offer is accepted, a contract arises. Only the offeree can accept an offer, and the acceptance must be of the offer exactly as made without any qualification or change. Ordinarily, the offeree may accept or reject as the offeree chooses.

The acceptance is any manifestation of intent to agree to the terms of the offer. Ordinarily, silence or failure to act does not constitute acceptance. The recipient of unordered goods and tickets may dispose of the goods or use the goods without such action constituting an acceptance. An acceptance does not exist until the words or conduct demonstrating assent to the offer is communicated to the offeror. Acceptance by mail takes effect at the time and place when and where the letter is mailed or the fax is transmitted.

In an auction sale, the auctioneer asking for bids makes an invitation to negotiate. A person making a bid is making an offer, and the acceptance of the highest bid by the auctioneer is an acceptance of that offer and gives rise to a contract. When the auction sale is without reserve, the auctioneer must accept the highest bid. If the auction is not expressly without reserve, the auctioneer may refuse to accept any of the bids.

LEARNING OUTCOMES

After studying this chapter, you should be able to clearly explain:

A. Requirements of an Offer

L0.1 Decide whether an offer contains definite and certain terms

See the *Plankenhorn* case for the meaning of a "damn good job" on p. 263.
See the legal impact of a party's statement that the contract "was going to be signed" in the *Hewitt* example on pp. 262–263.
See the *Wigod* case that discusses the test for a valid, binding offer, pp. 261–262.

B. Termination of an Offer

L0.2 Explain the exceptions the law makes to the requirement of definiteness

See the *Delphi* case on requirements contracts, p. 267.

L0.3 Explain all the ways an offer can be terminated

See the discussion of revocation, counteroffer, rejection, lapse of time, death or disability of a party, or subsequent illegality, starting on p. 268.

See the *Davidoff* example of a revocation communicated to the offeree prior to acceptance, p. 268.
See the *Landry's Restaurants* example that illustrates the effect of an "acceptance" signed just a few days after the written offer had expired, p. 270.

C. Acceptance of an Offer

L0.4 Explain what constitutes the acceptance of an offer

See the *Sadeghi* example where acceptance of an offer created a binding contract, p. 271.
See the *Keryakos Textiles* case on the impact of a counteroffer, p. 272.

L0.5 Explain the implications of failing to read a clickwrap agreement

See the *Feldman* case as an example of an enforceable clickwrap agreement containing notice and manifested assent, p. 274.

KEY TERMS

acceptance
counteroffer
divisible contract

firm offer
offer
output contract

requirements contract

QUESTIONS AND CASE PROBLEMS

1. Bernie and Phil's Great American Surplus store placed an ad in the *Sunday Times* stating, "Next Saturday at 8:00 A.M. sharp, 3 brand new mink coats worth $5,000 each will be sold for $500 each! First come, First served." Marsha Lufklin was first in line when the store opened and went directly to the coat department, but the coats identified in the ad were not available for sale. She identified herself to the manager and pointed out that she was first in line in conformity with the store's advertised offer and that she was ready to pay the $500 price set forth in the store's offer. The manager responded that a newspaper ad is just an invitation to negotiate and that the store decided to withdraw "the mink coat promotion." Review the text on unilateral contracts in Section 12(B) of Chapter 12. Decide.

2. Brown made an offer to purchase Overman's house on a standard printed form. Underneath Brown's signature was the statement: "ACCEPTANCE ON REVERSE SIDE." Overman did not sign the offer on the back but sent Brown a letter accepting the offer. Later, Brown refused to perform the contract, and Overman sued him for breach of contract. Brown claimed there was no contract because the offer had not been accepted in the manner specified by the offer. Decide. [*Overman v. Brown,* 372 N.W.2d 102 (Neb.)]

3. Katherine mailed Paul an offer with definite and certain terms and that was legal in all respects stating that it was good for 10 days. Two days later she sent Paul a letter by certified mail (time stamped by the Postal Service at 1:14 P.M.) stating that the original offer was revoked. That evening Paul e-mailed acceptance of the offer to Katherine. She immediately phoned him to tell him that she had revoked the offer that afternoon, and he would surely receive it in tomorrow's mail. Was the offer revoked by Katherine?

4. Nelson wanted to sell his home. Baker sent him a written offer to purchase the home. Nelson made some changes to Baker's offer and wrote him that he, Nelson, was accepting the offer as amended. Baker notified Nelson that he was dropping out of the transaction. Nelson sued Baker for breach of contract. Decide. What social forces and ethical values are involved? [*Nelson v. Baker,* 776 S.W.2d 52 (Mo. App.)]

5. Lessack Auctioneers advertised an auction sale that was open to the public and was to be conducted with reserve. Gordon attended the auction and bid $100 for a work of art that was worth much more. No higher bid, however, was made. Lessack refused to sell the item for $100 and withdrew the item from the sale. Gordon claimed that because he was the highest bidder, Lessack was required to sell the item to him. Was he correct?

6. Willis Music Co. advertised a television set at $22.50 in the Sunday newspaper. Ehrlich ordered a set, but the company refused to deliver it on the grounds that the price in the newspaper ad was a mistake. Ehrlich sued the company. Was it liable? Why or why not? [*Ehrlich v. Willis Music Co.,* 113 N.E.2d 252 (Ohio App.)]

7. When a movement was organized to build Charles City College, Hauser and others signed pledges to contribute to the college. At the time of signing, Hauser inquired what would happen if he should die or be unable to pay. The representative of the college stated that the pledge would then not be binding and that it was merely a statement of intent. The college failed financially, and Pappas was appointed receiver to collect and liquidate the assets of the college corporation. He sued Hauser for the amount due on his pledge. Hauser raised the defense that the pledge was not a binding contract. Decide. What ethical values are involved? [*Pappas v. Hauser,* 197 N.W.2d 607 (Iowa)]

8. *A* signed a contract agreeing to sell land he owned but reserved the right to take the hay from the land until the following October. He gave the contract form to *B*, a broker. *C*, a prospective buyer, agreed to buy the land and signed the contract but crossed out the provision regarding the hay crop. Was there a binding contract between *A* and *C*?

9. A. H. Zehmer discussed selling a farm to Lucy. After a 40-minute discussion of the first draft of a contract, Zehmer and his wife, Ida, signed a second draft stating: "We hereby agree to sell to W. O. Lucy the Ferguson farm complete for $50,000 title satisfactory to buyer." Lucy agreed to purchase the farm on these terms. Thereafter, the Zehmers refused to transfer title to Lucy and claimed they had made the contract for sale as a joke. Lucy brought an action to compel performance of the contract. The Zehmers claimed there was no contract. Were they correct? [*Lucy v. Zehmer,* 84 S.E.2d 516 (Va. App.)]

10. Wheeler operated an automobile service station, which he leased from W. C. Cornitius, Inc. The lease ran for three years. Although the lease did not contain any provision for renewal, it was in fact renewed six times for successive three-year terms. The landlord refused to renew the lease for a seventh time. Wheeler brought suit to compel the landlord to accept his offer to renew the lease. Decide. [*William C. Cornitius, Inc. v. Wheeler,* 556 P.2d 666 (Or.)]

11. Buster Cogdill, a real estate developer, made an offer to the Bank of Benton to have the bank

provide construction financing for the development of an outlet mall, with funds to be provided at prime rate plus two percentage points. The bank's president Julio Plunkett thanked Buster for the proposal and said, "I will start the paperwork." Did Cogdill have a contract with the Bank of Benton? [*Bank of Benton v. Cogdill*, 454 N.E.2d 1120 (Ill. App.)]

12. Ackerley Media Group, Inc., claimed to have a three-season advertising Team Sponsorship Agreement (TSA) with Sharp Electronics Corporation to promote Sharp products at all Seattle Supersonics NBA basketball home games. Sharp contended that a valid agreement did not exist for the third season (2000–2001) because a material price term was missing, thus resulting in an unenforceable "agreement to agree." The terms of the TSA for the 2000–2001 third season called for a base payment of $144,200 and an annual increase "not to exceed 6% [and] to be mutually agreed upon by the parties." No "mutually agreed" increase was negotiated by the parties. Ackerley seeks payment for the base price of $144,200 only. Sharp contends that since no price was agreed upon for the season, the entire TSA is unenforceable, and it is not obligated to pay for the 2000–2001 season. Is Sharp correct? [*Ackerley Media Group, Inc. v. Sharp Electronics Corp.*, 170 F. Supp. 2d 445 (S.D.N.Y.)]

13. L. B. Foster invited Tie and Track Systems Inc. to submit price quotes on items to be used in a railroad expansion project. Tie and Track responded by e-mail on August 11, 2006, with prices for 9 items of steel ties. The e-mail concluded, "The above prices are delivered/ Terms of Payment—to be agreed/Delivery—to be agreed/We hope you are successful with your bid. If you require any additional information please call." Just 3 of the 9 items listed in Tie and Track's price quote were "accepted" by the project. L. B. Foster demanded that Tie and Track provide the items at the price listed in the quote. Tie and Track refused. L. B. Foster sued for breach of contract. Did the August 11 e-mail constitute an offer, acceptance of which could bind the supplier to a contract? If so, was there a valid acceptance? [*L. B. Foster v. Tie and Track Systems, Inc.*, 2009 WL 900993 (N.D. Ill.)]

14. On August 15, 2003, Wilbert Heikkila signed an agreement with Kangas Realty to sell eight parcels of Heikkila's property. On September 8, 2003, David McLaughlin met with a Kangas agent who drafted McLaughlin's offer to purchase three of the parcels. McLaughlin signed the offer and gave the agent checks for each parcel. On September 9 and 10, 2003, the agent for Heikkila prepared three printed purchase agreements, one for each parcel. On September 14, 2003, David's wife, Joanne McLaughlin, met with the agent and signed the agreements. On September 16, 2003, Heikkila met with his real estate agent. Writing on the printed agreements, Heikkila changed the price of one parcel from $145,000 to $150,000, the price of another parcel from $32,000 to $45,000, and the price of the third parcel from $175,000 to $179,000. Neither of the McLaughlins signed an acceptance of Heikkila's changes to the printed agreements before Heikkila withdrew his offer to sell. The McLaughlins learned that Heikkila had withdrawn his offer on January 1, 2004, when the real estate agent returned the checks to them. Totally shocked at Heikkila's conduct, the McLaughlins brought action to compel specific performance of the purchase agreement signed by Joanne McLaughlin on their behalf. Decide. [*McLaughlin v. Heikkila*, 697 N.W.2d 231 (Minn. App.)]

CPA QUESTIONS

1. Able Sofa, Inc., sent Noll a letter offering to sell Noll a custom-made sofa for $5,000. Noll immediately sent a telegram to Able purporting to accept the offer. However, the telegraph company erroneously delivered the telegram to Abel Soda, Inc. Three days later, Able mailed a

letter of revocation to Noll, which was received by Noll. Able refused to sell Noll the sofa. Noll sued Able for breach of contract. Able:

a. Would have been liable under the deposited acceptance rule only if Noll had accepted by mail.

b. Will avoid liability since it revoked its offer prior to receiving Noll's acceptance.

c. Will be liable for breach of contract.

d. Will avoid liability due to the telegraph company's error (Law, #2, 9911).

2. On September 27, Summers sent Fox a letter offering to sell Fox a vacation home for $150,000. On October 2, Fox replied by mail agreeing to buy the home for $145,000. Summers did not reply to Fox. Do Fox and Summers have a binding contract?

a. No, because Fox failed to sign and return Summers's letter.

b. No, because Fox's letter was a counteroffer.

c. Yes, because Summers's offer was validly accepted.

d. Yes, because Summers's silence is an implied acceptance of Fox's letter (Law, #2, 0462).

3. On June 15, Peters orally offered to sell a used lawn mower to Mason for $125. Peters specified that Mason had until June 20 to accept the offer. On June 16, Peters received an offer to purchase the lawn mower for $150 from Bronson, Mason's neighbor. Peters accepted Bronson's offer. On June 17, Mason saw Bronson using the lawn mower and was told the mower had been sold to Bronson. Mason immediately wrote to Peters to accept the June 15 offer. Which of the following statements is correct?

a. Mason's acceptance would be effective when received by Peters.

b. Mason's acceptance would be effective when mailed.

c. Peters's offer had been revoked and Mason's acceptance was ineffective.

d. Peters was obligated to keep the June 15 offer open until June 20. (Law, #13, 3095).

© Manuel Gutjahr/iStockphoto.com

CHAPTER 14

Capacity and Genuine Assent

learningoutcomes

After studying this chapter, you should be able to

LO.1 Define contractual capacity

LO.2 Explain the extent and effect of avoidance of a contract by a minor

LO.3 Distinguish unilateral mistakes and mutual mistakes

LO.4 Explain the difference between intentional misrepresentation, negligent misrepresentation, and puffery

LO.5 Explain the difference between undue influence and duress

A. Contractual Capacity

1. CONTRACTUAL CAPACITY DEFINED
2. MINORS
3. MENTALLY INCOMPETENT PERSONS
4. INTOXICATED PERSONS

B. Mistake

5. UNILATERAL MISTAKE
6. MUTUAL MISTAKE
7. MISTAKE IN THE TRANSCRIPTION OR PRINTING OF THE CONTRACT: REFORMATION

C. Deception

8. INTENTIONAL MISREPRESENTATION
9. FRAUD
10. NEGLIGENT MISREPRESENTATION
11. NONDISCLOSURE

D. Pressure

12. UNDUE INFLUENCE
13. DURESS

A *contract* is a binding agreement. This agreement must be made between parties who have the capacity to do so. They must also truly agree so that all parties have really consented to the contract. This chapter explores the elements of contractual capacity of the parties and the genuineness of their assent.

A. CONTRACTUAL CAPACITY

Some persons lack contractual capacity, a lack that embraces both those who have a status incapacity, such as minors, and those who have a factual incapacity, such as persons who are insane.

1. Contractual Capacity Defined

contractual capacity – ability to understand that a contract is being made and to understand its general meaning.

Contractual capacity is the ability to understand that a contract is being made and to understand its general meaning. However, the fact that a person does not understand the full legal meaning of a contract does not mean that contractual capacity is lacking. Everyone is presumed to have capacity unless it is proven that capacity is lacking or there is status incapacity.[1] **For Example,** Jacqueline, aged 22, entered into a contract with Sunrise Storage Co. but later claimed it was not binding because she did not understand several clauses in the printed contract. The contract was binding. No evidence supported her claim that she lacked capacity to contract or to understand its subject. Contractual capacity can exist even though a party does not understand every provision of the contract.

(A) STATUS INCAPACITY. Over the centuries, the law has declared that some classes of persons lack contractual capacity. The purpose is to protect these classes by giving them the power to get out of unwise contracts. Of these classes, the most important today is the class identified as minors.

Until recent times, some other classes were held to lack contractual capacity in order to discriminate against them. Examples are married women and aliens.

CASE SUMMARY

We Really Mean Equal Rights

FACTS: An Alabama statute provided that a married woman could not sell her land without the consent of her husband. Montgomery made a contract to sell land she owned to Peddy. Montgomery's husband did not consent to the sale. Montgomery did not perform the contract and Peddy sued her. The defense was raised that the contract was void and could not be enforced because of the statute. Peddy claimed that the statute was unconstitutional.

DECISION: The statute was unconstitutional. Constitutions, both federal and state, guarantee all persons the equal protection of the law. Married women are denied this equal protection when they are treated differently than married men and unmarried women. The fact that such unequal treatment had once been regarded as proper does not justify its modern continuation. [***Peddy v. Montgomery***, 345 So. 2d 988 (Ala. 1991)]

[1] *In re Adoption of Smith*, 578 So 2d 988 (La. App. 1991).

Still other classes, such as persons convicted of and sentenced for a felony, were held to lack contractual capacity in order to punish them. Today, these discriminatory and punitive incapacities have largely disappeared. Married women have the same contractual capacity as unmarried persons.

By virtue of international treaties, the discrimination against aliens has been removed.

(b) Factual Incapacity. A *factual incapacity* contrasts with incapacity imposed because of the class or group to which a person belongs. A factual incapacity may exist when, because of a mental condition caused by medication, drugs, alcohol, illness, or age, a person does not understand that a contract is being made or understand its general nature. However, mere mental weakness does not incapacitate a person from contracting. It is sufficient if the individual has enough mental capacity to understand, to a reasonable extent, the nature and effect of what he is doing.[2]

2. Minors

Minors may make contracts.[3] To protect them, however, the law has always treated minors as a class lacking contractual capacity.

(a) Who Is a Minor? At common law, any person, male or female, under 21 years of age was a minor. At common law, minority ended the day before the twenty-first birthday. The "day before the birthday" rule is still followed, but the age of majority has been reduced from 21 years to 18 years.

CPA **(b) Minor's Power to Avoid Contracts.** With exceptions that will be noted later, a contract made by a minor is voidable at the election of the minor. **For Example,** Adorian Deck, a minor, created a Twitter feed titled "@OMGFacts." The feed collected and republished interesting and trivial facts from other sources on the Internet. It was subscribed to by over 300,000 Twitter users, including some celebrities. Spatz, Inc. entered into a joint venture with Deck as described in a written contract signed by both parties, under which Spatz would expand the Twitter feed into a suite of Internet products, including a Website and a Youtube.com video channel. In an "OMG-moment" prior to his 18th birthday, Deck notified Spatz, Inc. that he wished to disaffirm the parties' agreement. This disaffirmation by a minor rescinded the entire contract, rendering it a nullity.[4] The minor may affirm or ratify the contract on attaining majority by performing the contract, by expressly approving the contract, or by allowing a reasonable time to lapse without avoiding the contract.

CPA *(1) What Constitutes Avoidance?*
A minor may avoid or *disaffirm* a contract by any expression of an intention to repudiate the contract. Any act inconsistent with the continuing validity of the contract is also an avoidance.

CPA *(2) Time for Avoidance.*
A minor can disaffirm a contract only during minority and for a reasonable time after attaining majority. After the lapse of a reasonable time, the contract is deemed ratified and cannot be avoided by the minor.

---

[2] *Fisher v. Schefers,* 656 N.W.2d 591 (Minn. App. 2003).
[3] *Buffington v. State Automobile Mut. Ins. Co.,* 384 S.E.2d 873 (Ga. App. 1989).
[4] *Deck v. Spatz, Inc.,* 2011 WL 775067 (E.D. Cal. Sept. 27, 2011).

CPA

(3) Minor's Misrepresentation of Age.

Generally, the fact that the minor has misrepresented his or her age does not affect the minor's power to disaffirm the contract. Some states hold that such fraud of a minor bars contract avoidance. Some states permit the minor to disaffirm the contract in such a case but require the minor to pay for any damage to the property received under the contract.

In any case, the other party to the contract may disaffirm it because of the minor's fraud.

CPA

(c) RESTITUTION BY MINOR AFTER AVOIDANCE. When a minor disaffirms a contract, the question arises as to what the minor must return to the other contracting party.

(1) Original Consideration Intact.

When a minor still has what was received from the other party, the minor, on avoiding the contract, must return it to the other party or offer to do so. That is, the minor must put things back to the original position or, as it is called, restore the **status quo ante**.

status quo ante – original positions of the parties.

(2) Original Consideration Damaged or Destroyed.

What happens if the minor cannot return what has been received because it has been spent, used, damaged, or destroyed? The minor's right to disaffirm the contract is not affected. The minor can still disaffirm the contract and is required to return only what remains. The fact that nothing remains or that what remains is damaged does not bar the right to disaffirm the contract. In states that follow the common law rule, minors can thus refuse to pay for what has been received under a contract or can get back what had been paid or given even though they do not have anything to return or return property in a damaged condition. There is, however, a trend to limit this rule.

(D) RECOVERY OF PROPERTY BY MINOR ON AVOIDANCE. When a minor disaffirms a contract, the other contracting party must return the money received. Any property received from the minor must also be returned. If the property has been sold to a third person who did not know of the original seller's minority, the minor cannot get the property back. In such cases, however, the minor is entitled to recover the property's monetary value or the money received by the other contracting party.

CPA

(E) CONTRACTS FOR NECESSARIES. A minor can disaffirm a contract for necessaries but must pay the reasonable value for furnished necessaries.

(1) What Constitutes Necessaries?

Originally, **necessaries** were limited to those things absolutely necessary for the sustenance and shelter of the minor. Thus limited, the term would extend only to food, clothing, and lodging. In the course of time, the rule was relaxed to extend generally to things relating to the health, education, and comfort of the minor. Thus, the rental of a house used by a married minor is a necessary.

necessaries – things indispensable or absolutely necessary for the sustenance of human life.

(2) Liability of Parent or Guardian.

When a third person supplies the parents or guardian of a minor with goods or services that the minor needs, the minor is not liable for these necessaries because the third person's contract is with the parent or guardian, not with the minor.

When necessary medical care is provided a minor, a parent is liable at common law for the medical expenses provided the minor child. However, at common law, the child can be held contractually liable for her necessary medical expenses when the parent is unable or unwilling to pay.

CASE SUMMARY

The Concussion and Legal Repercussions

FACTS: Sixteen-year-old Michelle Schmidt was injured in an automobile accident and taken to Prince George's Hospital. Although the identities of Michelle and her parents were originally unknown, the hospital provided her emergency medical care for a brain concussion and an open scalp wound. She incurred hospital expenses of $1,756.24. Ms. Schmidt was insured through her father's insurance company. It issued a check to be used to cover medical expenses. However, the funds were used to purchase a car for Ms. Schmidt. Since she was a minor when the services were rendered, she believed that she had no legal obligation to pay. After Ms. Schmidt attained her eighteenth birthday and failed to pay the hospital, it brought suit against her.

DECISION: Judgment for the hospital. The prevailing modern rule is that minors' contracts are voidable except for necessaries. The doctrine of necessaries states that a minor may be held liable for necessaries, including medical necessaries when parents are unwilling to pay. The court concluded that Ms. Schmidt's father demonstrated a clear unwillingness to pay by using the insurance money to purchase a car rather than pay the hospital. The policy behind the necessaries exception is for the benefit of minors because the procurement of such is essential to their existence, and if they were not permitted to bind themselves, they might not be able to obtain the necessaries. [*Schmidt v. Prince George's Hospital*, **784 A.2d 1112 (Md. 2001)**]

CPA **(F) RATIFICATION OF FORMER MINOR'S VOIDABLE CONTRACT.** A former minor cannot disaffirm a contract that has been ratified after reaching majority.[5]

CPA **(1) What Constitutes Ratification?**
Ratification consists of any words or conduct of the former minor manifesting an intent to be bound by the terms of a contract made while a minor.

CPA **(2) Form of Ratification.**
Generally, no special form is required for ratification of a minor's voidable contract, although in some states a written ratification or declaration of intention is required.

CPA **(3) Time for Ratification.**
A person can disaffirm a contract any time during minority and for a reasonable time after that but, of necessity, can ratify a contract only after attaining majority. The minor must have attained majority, or the ratification would itself be regarded as voidable.

(G) CONTRACTS THAT MINORS CANNOT AVOID. Statutes in many states deprive a minor of the right to avoid an educational loan;[6] a contract for medical care; a contract made

---

[5] *Fletcher v. Marshall*, 632 N.E.2d 1105 (Ill. App. 1994).
[6] A Model Student Capacity to Borrow Act makes educational loans binding on minors in Arizona, Mississippi, New Mexico, North Dakota, Oklahoma, and Washington. This act was reclassified from a uniform act to a model act by the Commissioners on Uniform State Law, indicating that uniformity was viewed as unimportant and that the matter was primarily local in character.

while running a business; a contract approved by a court; a contract made in performance of a legal duty; and a contract relating to bank accounts, insurance policies, or corporate stock.

(H) LIABILITY OF THIRD PERSON FOR A MINOR'S CONTRACT. The question arises as to whether parents are bound by the contract of their minor child. The question of whether a person cosigning a minor's contract is bound if the contract is avoided also arises.

(1) Liability of Parent.
Ordinarily, a parent is not liable on a contract made by a minor child. The parent may be liable, however, if the child is acting as the agent of the parent in making the contract. Also, the parent is liable to a seller for the reasonable value of necessaries supplied by the seller to the child if the parent had deserted the child.

(2) Liability of Cosigner.
When the minor makes a contract, another person, such as a parent or a friend, may sign along with the minor to make the contract more acceptable to the third person.

With respect to the other contracting party, the cosigner is bound independently of the minor. Consequently, if the minor disaffirms the contract, the cosigner remains bound by it. When the debt to the creditor is actually paid, the obligation of the cosigner is discharged.

If the minor disaffirms a sales contract but does not return the goods, the cosigner remains liable for the purchase price.

3. Mentally Incompetent Persons

A person with a mental disorder may be so disabled as to lack capacity to make a contract. An individual seeking to avoid the consequences of a contract due to incompetency must demonstrate that at the time the agreement was executed he or she was suffering from a mental illness or defect, which rendered the party incapable of comprehending the nature of the transaction, or that by reason of mental illness the party was unable to control his or her conduct.[7] **For Example,** a guardian established that Ms. Brunson suffered from a mental illness at the time the challenged mortgage documents were executed, and the contract was set aside by the court.[8] However, where a guardian's evidence was insufficient to demonstrate that at the time two mortgage transactions occurred, one in 1999 for $212,000 and a second in 2003 for $7,628.08, that Mr. and Mrs. Haedrich were incompetent or that Washington Mutual Bank knew or was put on notice of their purported incapacity, the court refused to vacate the judgments of foreclosure.[9]

(A) EFFECT OF INCOMPETENCY. An incompetent person may ordinarily avoid a contract in the same manner as a minor. Upon the removal of the disability (that is, upon becoming competent), the formerly incompetent person can either ratify or disaffirm the contract.

A mentally incompetent person or his estate is liable for the reasonable value of all necessaries furnished that individual.

---

[7] *Horrell v. Horrell*, 900 N.Y.S. 2d 666 (2d Dept. 2010).
[8] *In re Doar*, 900 N.Y.S. 2d 593 (Sup. Ct. Queens Co., Dec. 18, 2009).
[9] *JP Morgan Chase Bank v. Haedrich*, 918 N.Y.S. 2d 398 (Sup. Ct. Nassau County, Oct. 15, 2010).

A current trend in the law is to treat an incompetent person's contract as binding when its terms and the surrounding circumstances are reasonable and the person is unable to restore the other contracting party to the status quo ante.

CASE SUMMARY

Friends Should Tell Friends about Medical Leaves

FACTS: Wilcox Manufacturing Group, Inc., did business under the name of Superior Automation Co., and Howard Wilcox served as Superior's president. As part of a loan "lease agreement" of $50,000 executed on December 5, 2000, Superior was to repay Marketing Services of Indiana (MSI) $67,213.80 over the course of 60 months. Wilcox gave a personal guarantee for full and prompt payment. Wilcox had been a patient of psychiatrist Dr. Shaun Wood since May 21, 1999, and was diagnosed as suffering from bipolar disorder during the period from June 2000 to January 2001. On June 9, 2000, Wilcox told Dr. Wood he was having problems functioning at work, and Dr. Wood determined that Wilcox was experiencing lithium toxicity, which lasted for 10 months, during which time he suffered from impaired cognitive functions that limited his capacity to understand the nature and quality of his actions and judgments. Superior made monthly payments though to October 28, 2003, and the balance owed at that time was $33,031.37. MSI sued Wilcox personally and the corporation for breach of contract. The defendants raise the defense of lack of capacity and contend that they are not liable on the loan signed by the corporate president when he was incapacitated.

DECISION: Judgment for MSI. The acts or deeds of a person of unsound mind whose condition has not been judicially ascertained and who is not under guardianship are voidable and not absolutely void. The acts are subject to ratification or disaffirmance on removal of the disability. The latest Wilcox could have been experiencing the effects of lithium toxicity was October 2001. Wilcox thus regained his capacity by that date. No attempt was made to disaffirm the contract. Rather, monthly payments continued to be made for a year and one-half before the payments ceased. The contract was thus ratified by the conduct of the president of Superior after he recovered his ability to understand the nature of the contract. [*Wilcox Manufacturing, Inc., v. Marketing Services of Indiana, Inc.*, **832 N.E.2d 559 (Ind. App. 2005)**]

(B) APPOINTMENT OF GUARDIAN. If a court appoints a guardian for the incompetent person, a contract made by that person before the appointment may be ratified or, in some cases, disaffirmed by the guardian. If the incompetent person makes a contract after a guardian has been appointed, the contract is void and not merely voidable.

4. Intoxicated Persons

The capacity of a party to contract and the validity of the contract are not affected by the party's being impaired by alcohol at the time of making the contract so long as the party knew that a contract was being made.

If the degree of intoxication is such that a person does not know that a contract is being made, the contract is voidable by that person. On becoming sober, the individual may avoid or rescind the contract. However, an unreasonable delay in taking steps to set aside a known contract entered into while intoxicated may bar the intoxicated person from asserting this right.[10]

---

[10] *Diedrich v. Diedrich*, 424 N.W.2d 580 (Minn. App. 1988).

Excessive intoxication is a viable defense to contracts arising between casinos and their patrons. Thus, when a casino comes to court to enforce a marker debt against a patron, it seeks to enforce a contractual debt, and the patron is entitled to raise the common law defense that his capacity to contract was impaired by voluntary intoxication.[11]

The courts treat impairment caused by the use of drugs the same as impairment caused by the excessive use of alcohol.

CPA B. MISTAKE

The validity of a contract may be affected by the fact that one or both of the parties made a mistake. In some cases, the mistake may be caused by the misconduct of one of the parties.

5. Unilateral Mistake

A *unilateral mistake*—that is, a mistake by only one of the parties—as to a fact does not affect the contract when the mistake is unknown to the other contracting party.[12] When a contract is made on the basis of a quoted price, the validity of the contract is not affected by the fact that the party furnishing the quotation made a mathematical mistake in computing the price if there was no reason for the other party to recognize that there had been a mistake.[13] The party making the mistake may avoid the contract if the other contracting party knew or should have known of the mistake.

CASE SUMMARY

Bumper Sticker: "Mistakes Happen!" (or words to that effect)

FACTS: Lipton-U City, LLC (Lipton), and Shurgard Storage Centers discussed the sale of a self-storage facility for approximately $7 million. Lipton became concerned about an existing environmental condition and as a result, the parties agreed to a lease with an option to buy rather than an outright sale. The contract specified a 10-year lease with an annual rent starting at $636,000 based on a property valuation of $7 million. Section 2.4 of the contract contained the purchase option. Shurgard representatives circulated an e-mail with a copy to Lipton representatives that a purchase option price would be based on six months of *annualized* net operating income. When the lease was submitted to Lipton, inexplicably any language regarding multiplying by 2 or annualizing the net income was omitted. Donn Lipton announced to his attorneys that the lease reflected his successful negotiation of a purchase option based on six months of *unannualized* net operating income. Eight months after signing the lease, Lipton sought to exercise the purchase option under Section 2.4 and stated a price of $2,918,103. Shurgard rejected the offer and filed suit for rescission, citing the misunderstanding about the price terms.

DECISION: Judgment for Shurgard. Under state law, if a material mistake made by one party is known to the other party or is of such a character or circumstances that the other party should

---

[11] See *Adamar of New Jersey v. Luber*, 2011 WL1325978 (D. N.J. Mar. 30, 2011).
[12] *Truck South Inc. v. Patel*, 528 S.E.2d 424 (S.C. 2000).
[13] *Procan Construction Co. v. Oceanside Development Corp.*, 539 N.Y.S.2d 437 (App. Div. 2d 1989).

CASE SUMMARY

Continued

know of it, the mistaken party has a right to rescission. Lipton knew or should have known of the mistake of the lessor (Shurgard) in believing that the purchase price would be based on a full year of net operating income rather than six months of net operating income. Lipton was notified by e-mail that the six-month figure was to be annualized and knew that the property was valued at approximately $7 million. [*Shurgard Storage Centers v. Lipton-U City, LLC.,* **394 F.3d 1041 (8th Cir. 2005)**]

6. Mutual Mistake

When both parties enter into a contract under a mutually mistaken understanding concerning a basic assumption of fact or law on which the contract is made, the contract is voidable by the adversely affected party if the mistake has a material effect on the agreed exchange.[14]

A contract based on *a mutual mistake in judgment* is not voidable by the adversely affected party. **For Example,** if both parties believe that a colt is not fast enough to develop into a competitive race horse and effect a sale accordingly, when the animal later develops into the winner of the Preakness as a three-year-old, the seller cannot rescind the contract based on mutual mistake because the mutual mistake was a mistake in judgment. In contrast, when two parties to a contract believe a cow to be barren at the time they contract for its sale, but before delivery of the animal to the buyer, it is discovered that the assumption was mistaken, such is a mutual mistake of fact making the contract void.[15]

7. Mistake in the Transcription or Printing of the Contract: Reformation

reformation – remedy by which a written instrument is corrected when it fails to express the actual intent of both parties because of fraud, accident, or mistake.

In some instances, the parties make an oral agreement, and in the process of committing it to writing or printing it from a manuscript, a phrase, term, or segment is inadvertently left out of the final, signed document. The aggrieved party may petition the court to **reform** the contract to reflect the actual agreement of the parties. However, the burden of proof is heightened to clear and convincing evidence that such a mistake was made. **For Example,** Jewell Coke Co. used an illustration to explain a complex pricing formula in its negotiations with the ArcelMittal steel mill in Cleveland, Ohio, for a long-term contract for the supply of blast furnace coke. The multiplier in the illustration was the actual intent of the parties, according to ArcelMittal, but during the drafting process the multiplier was accidently inverted, resulting in an overpayment of $100,000,000 when discovered, and which potentially could result in an overpayment of over $1 billion over the life of the contract. If proven, the court will reform the contract to reflect the intentions of the parties at the time the contract was made.[16]

---

[14] See *Browning v. Howerton,* 966 P.2d 367 (Wash. App. 1998).
[15] See *Sherwood v. Walker,* 66 Mich. 568 (1887).
[16] *ArcelMittal Cleveland, Inc. v. Jewell Coke Co.,* 750 F. Supp. 2d 839 (N.D. Ohio 2010).

| FIGURE 14-1 | *Avoidance of Contract* |

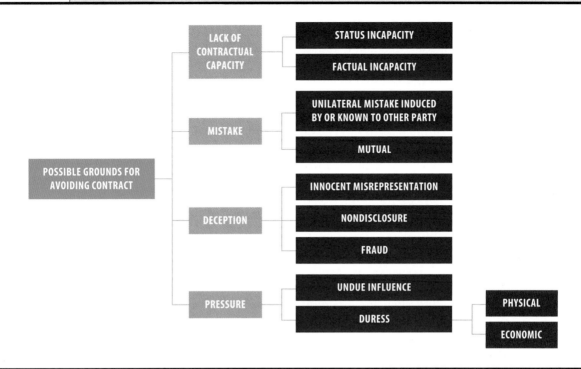

C. DECEPTION

One of the parties may have been misled by a fraudulent statement. In such situations, there is no true or genuine assent to the contract, and it is voidable at the innocent party's option.

8. Intentional Misrepresentation

Fraud is a generic term embracing all multifarious means that human ingenuity can devise and that are resorted to by one individual to get advantage over another. It is classified in the law as a *tort*. However, where a party is induced into making a contract by a material misrepresentation of fact, this form of fraudulent activity adversely affects the genuineness of the assent of the innocent party, and this type of fraud is the focus of our discussion in the chapters on contracts.

9. Fraud

fraud – making of a false statement of a past or existing fact, with knowledge of its falsity or with reckless indifference as to its truth, with the intent to cause another to rely thereon, and such person does rely thereon and is harmed thereby.

Fraud is the making of a material misrepresentation (or false statement) of fact with (1) knowledge of its falsity or reckless indifference to its truth, (2) the intent that the listener rely on it, (3) the result that the listener does so rely, and (4) the consequence that the listener is harmed.[17]

---

[17] *Maack v. Resource Design & Construction, Inc.*, 875 P.2d 570 (Utah 1994); *Bortz v. Noon*, 729 A.2d 555 (Pa. 1999).

To prove fraud, there must be a material misrepresentation of fact. Such a misrepresentation is one that is likely to induce a reasonable person to assent to a contract. **For Example,** Traci Hanson-Suminski purchased a used Honda Civic from Arlington Acura for $10,899. On a test drive with salesperson Mike Dobin, Traci noticed a vibration in the steering wheel and asked if the car had been in an accident. Dobin said, "No, it's fine." The dealer put new tires on the car and Traci bought it. Traci testified that she would not have purchased the car if she had known it had been in an accident. Eight months later when she sought to trade the car for another car, she was shown a Carfax Vehicle History Report which indicated the car had been in an accident. The dealer testified that all its sales associates are trained to respond to questions about vehicle history with "I don't know." It asserted that Dobin's statement was mere puffery. The court found that Dobin's statement was a material misrepresentation of the car's history, inducing the plaintiff to purchase the car. It rejected outright the dealer's assertion of puffery, which it defined as meaningless superlatives that no reasonable person would take seriously.[18]

(A) STATEMENT OF OPINION OR VALUE. Ordinarily, matters of opinion of value or opinions about future events are not regarded as fraudulent. Thus, statements that a building was "very good," it "required only normal maintenance," and the "deal was excellent" were merely matters of opinion. Therefore, a court considered the sophistication and expertise of the parties and the commercial setting of the transaction and enforced the contract "as is." The theory is that the person hearing the statement recognizes or should recognize that it is merely the speaker's personal opinion, not a statement of fact. A statement that is mere sales talk cannot be the basis of fraud liability. **For Example,** CEO Bernard Ellis sent a memo to shareholders of his Internet-related services business some four days before the expiration of a lockup period during which these shareholders had agreed not to sell their stock. In the memo, he urged shareholders not to sell their stock on the release date because in the event of a massive sell-off "our stock could plummet." He also stated, "I think our share price will start to stabilize and then rise as our company's strong performance continues." Based on Ellis's "strong performance" statement, a major corporate shareholder did not sell. The price of the stock fell from $40 a share to 29 cents a share over the subsequent nine-month period. The shareholder sued Ellis for fraud, seeking $27 million in damages. The court held that the first half of the sentence in question was framed as a mere opinion as to future events and thus was nonactionable; and as to the characterization of the company's performance as "strong," such a self-congratulatory comment constituted mere puffery on which no reasonable investor would rely.[19]

A statement of opinion may be fraudulent when the speaker knows of past or present facts that make the opinion false. **For Example,** Biff Williams, the sales manager of Abrasives International (AI), sold an exclusive dealership selling AI products to Fred Farkas for $100,000 down and a 3 percent royalty on all gross proceeds. Williams told Farkas, "You have the potential to earn $300,000 to $400,000 a year in this territory." He later added, "We have four dealerships making that kind of money today." Farkas was thus persuaded by the business potential of the territory and executed the purchase contract. He later found out AI had a total of

---

[18] *Hanson-Suminski v. Rohrman Midwest Motors Inc.*, 858 N.E.2d 194 (Ill. App. 2008).
[19] *Next Century Communications v. Ellis*, 318 F.3d 1023 (11th Cir. 2003).

just four distributorships at that time, and the actual earnings of the highest producer was $43,000. Assertions of opinions about the future profit potential alone may not amount to fraud, but the assertion of present fact—that four dealerships were presently earning $300,000 to $400,000 a year—was a material misstatement of fact that made the forecast sales potential for Farkas's territory a material misstatement of fact as well. Because there were reliance and damages, Farkas can rescind the contract based on fraud and recover all damages resulting from it.[20]

(B) Reliance on Statement. A fraudulent statement made by one party has no importance unless the other party relies on the statement's truth. **For Example,** after making thorough tests of Nagel Company's pump, Allstate Services Company ordered 100 pumps. It later sued Nagel on the ground that advertising statements made about the pumps were false. Allstate Services cannot impose fraud liability on Nagel for the advertisements, even if they were false, because it had not relied on them in making the purchase but had acted on the basis of its own tests.

If the alleged victim of the fraud knew that the statements were false because the truth was commonly known, the victim cannot rely on the false statements. When the statements of a seller are so "indefinite and extravagant" that reasonable persons would not rely on them, the statements cannot be the basis of a claim of fraud.[21] Trusting the honesty of salespersons or their disarming statements, an individual may knowingly agree in writing that no representations have been made to him or her, while at the same time believing and relying upon representation, which in fact have been made and in fact are false, but for which the individual would not have made the agreement. However, purchasers cannot assert justifiable reliance on statements made by sellers that directly contradict clear and specific terms of their written contracts.

CASE SUMMARY

Are Disclaimer of Reliance Clauses a License to Lie?

FACTS: David Sarif and seven other purchasers (Purchasers) each bought a unit at the 26-story Twelve Atlantic Station (Twelve) condominiums in 2005 and 2006. They sued the developers and the brokers for fraud in the inducement and negligent misrepresentation. They alleged that at the time of their purchases, the developers were advertising "spectacular city views" of Atlanta while they had already undertaken to develop the 46-story Atlantic Station tower directly across the street, and that their brokers were advising the Purchasers that any future development to the south of Twelve would be low- to mid-rise office buildings. Purchasers allege that they paid substantial premiums for their views of the city from the southside of the building, which is now blocked by the 46-story building. Each Purchaser signed an agreement containing a provision

[20] The Federal Trade Commission and state agencies have franchise disclosure rules that will penalize the franchisor in this case. See Chapter 41.
[21] *Eckert v. Flair Agency, Inc.,* 909 P.2d 1201 (Okla App. 1995) (seller's statement that house would never be flooded again). But see *Italian Cowboy Partners, Ltd. v. Prudential Insurance,* 341 S.W. 3d 323 (Tex. 2011) where a split decision of the Texas Supreme Court determined that the following contract language was not a disclaimer of reliance to negate the "justifiable reliance" element of a fraud claim.

Tenant acknowledges that neither Landlord nor Landlord's agents, employees or contractors have made any representations or promises with respect to the Site, the Shopping Center or this lease except as expressly set forth herein.

The court determined that the property manager's representations to the future tenant that the building was problem free; no problems had been experienced by the prior tenant; and the building was a perfect restaurant site were false statements of fact known to be false when made. Testimony indicated that the manager herself had personally experienced a sewer gas odor in the prior tenant's restaurant she described as "almost unbearable" and "ungodly."

CASE SUMMARY

Continued

stating that "[t]he views from and natural light available to the Unit may change over time due to, among other circumstances, additional development and the removal or addition of landscaping"; a disclaimer at the top of the first page as required by the Georgia Condominium Act stating that "ORAL REPRESENTATIONS CANNOT BE RELIED UPON AS CORRECTLY STATING THE REPRESENTATIONS OF SELLER"; an express disclaimer in which Purchasers affirmed that they did not rely upon any representations or statements of the brokers; and a comprehensive merger clause.

DECISION: Set forth in the written contract of the parties, all of the Purchasers signed agreements that expressly stated that views may change over time, and oral representations of the sellers could not be relied on. Justifiable reliance is an essential element of a fraud or negligent misrepresentation claim. Since the Purchasers are estopped from relying on representations outside their agreements, they cannot sustain a case that requires justifiable reliance. [***Novare Group, Inc. v. Sarif,*** 718 S.E.2d 304 (Ga. 2011)]

(c) **PROOF OF HARM.** For an individual to recover damages for fraud, proof of harm to that individual is required. The injured party may recover the actual losses suffered as a result of the fraud as well as punitive damages when the fraud is gross or oppressive. The injured party has the right to have the court order the rescission or cancellation of the contract that has been induced by fraud.[22]

10. Negligent Misrepresentation

While fraud requires the critical element of a known or recklessly made falsity, a claim of negligent misrepresentation contains similar elements except it is predicated on a negligently made false statement. That is, the speaker failed to exercise due care regarding material information communicated to the listener but did not intend to deceive. When the negligent misrepresentation of a material fact that the listener relies on results in harm to the listener, the contract is voidable at the option of the injured party. If fraud is proven, as opposed to misrepresentation, recovery of punitive damages in addition to actual damages can occur. Because it may be difficult to prove the intentional falsity required for fraud, it is common for a lawsuit to allege both a claim of fraud and a claim of negligent misrepresentation. **For Example,** Marshall Armstrong worked for Fred Collins, owner of Collins Entertainment, Inc., a conglomerate that owns and operates video games. Collins Entertainment's core product video poker was hurt by a court ruling that prohibited cash payouts, which adversely affected its business and resulted in a debt of $13 to $20 million to SouthTrust bank. Chief operating officer Armstrong, on his own time, came up with the idea of modifying bingo machines as a new venture. To exploit this idea, Collins agreed to form a corporation called Skillpins Inc., that was unencumbered by the SouthTrust debt and to give Armstrong a 10 percent ownership interest. After a period, with some 300 Skillpins machines producing income, Armstrong discovered the revenues from the new venture on the debt-laden Collins

---

[22] *Paden v. Murray,* 523 S.E.2d 75 (Ga. App. 2000).

Entertainment profit and loss statement, not that of Skillpins, Inc. Armstrong's suit for both fraud and intentional misrepresentation was successful. In addition to actual damages, he received $1.8 million in punitive damages for fraud.[23]

11. Nondisclosure

Under certain circumstances, nondisclosure serves to make a contract voidable, especially when the nondisclosure consists of active concealment.

(A) GENERAL RULE OF NONLIABILITY. Ordinarily, a party to a contract has no duty to volunteer information to the other party. **For Example,** if Fox does not ask Tehan any questions, Tehan is not under any duty to make a full statement of material facts. Consequently, the nondisclosure of information that is not asked for does not impose fraud liability or impair the validity of a contract.

CASE SUMMARY

Welcome to the Seesaw: Buyer versus Seller

FACTS: Dalarna Management Corporation owned a building constructed on a pier on a lake. There were repeated difficulties with rainwater leaking into the building, and water damage was visible in the interior of the building. Dalarna made a contract to sell the building to Curran. Curran made several inspections of the building and had the building inspected twice by a licensed engineer. The engineer reported there were signs of water leaks. Curran assigned his contract to Puget Sound Service Corporation, which then purchased the building from Dalarna. Puget Sound spent approximately $118,000 attempting to stop the leaks. Puget Sound then sued Dalarna for damages, claiming that Dalarna's failure to disclose the extent of the water leakage problem constituted fraud.

DECISION: Judgment for Dalarna. Curran was aware there was a water leakage problem, and therefore the burden was on the buyer to ask questions to determine the extent of the problem. There was no duty on the seller to volunteer the extent of the water damage merely because it had been a continuing problem that was more than just a simple leak. The court reached this conclusion because the law "balances the harshness of the former rule of caveat emptor [let the buyer beware] with the equally undesirable alternative of courts standing in loco parentis [in the place of a parent] to parties transacting business." [***Puget Sound Service Corp. v. Dalarna Management Corp.***, 752 P.2d 1353 (Wash. App. 1988)]

(B) EXCEPTIONS. The following exceptions to the general rule of nonliability for nondisclosure exist.

(1) Unknown Defect or Condition.

A duty may exist in some states for a seller who knows of a serious defect or condition to disclose that information to the other party where the defect or condition is unknown to the other person and is of such a nature that it is unlikely that the other person would discover it. However, a defendant who had no knowledge of the defect cannot be held liable for failure to disclose it.[24]

---

[23] *Armstrong v. Collins*, 621 S.E.2d 368 (S.C. App. 2005).
[24] *Nesbitt v. Dunn*, 672 So 2d 226 (La. App. 1996).

confidential relationship –
relationship in which, because of the legal status of the parties or their respective physical or mental conditions or knowledge, one party places full confidence and trust in the other.

(2) Confidential Relationship.

If parties stand in a **confidential relationship**, failure to disclose information may be regarded as fraudulent. **For Example,** in an attorney-client relationship,[25] the attorney has a duty to reveal anything that is material to the client's interest when dealing with the client. The attorney's silence has the same legal consequence as a knowingly made false statement that there was no material fact to be told the client.

(3) Active Concealment.

Nondisclosure may be more than the passive failure to volunteer information. It may consist of a positive act of hiding information from the other party by physical concealment, or it may consist of knowingly or recklessly furnishing the wrong information. Such conduct constitutes fraud. **For Example,** when Nigel wanted to sell his house, he covered the wooden cellar beams with plywood to hide extensive termite damage. He sold the house to Kuehne, who sued Nigel for damages on later discovering the termite damage. Nigel claimed he had no duty to volunteer information about the termites, but by covering the damage with plywood, he committed active fraud as if he had made a false statement that there were no termites.

D. Pressure

What appears to be an agreement may not in fact be voluntary because one of the parties entered into it as the result of undue influence or physical or economic duress.

CPA

12. Undue Influence

An aged parent may entrust all business affairs to a trusted child; a disabled person may rely on a nurse; a client may follow implicitly whatever an attorney recommends. The relationship may be such that for practical purposes, one person is helpless in the hands of the other. When such a confidential relationship exists, it is apparent that the parent, the disabled person, or the client is not exercising free will in making a contract suggested by the child, nurse, or attorney but is merely following the will of the other person. Because of the great possibility of unfair advantage, the law presumes that the dominating person exerts **undue influence** on the other person whenever the dominating person obtains any benefit from a contract made with the dominated person. The contract is then voidable. It may be set aside by the dominated person unless the dominating person can prove that, at the time the contract was made, no unfair advantage had been taken.

undue influence – influence that is asserted upon another person by one who dominates that person.

The class of confidential relationships is not well defined. It ordinarily includes the relationships of parent and child, guardian and ward, physician and patient, and attorney and client, and any other relationship of trust and confidence in which one party exercises a control or influence over another.

Whether undue influence exists is a difficult question for courts (ordinarily juries) to determine. The law does not regard every influence as undue.

An essential element of undue influence is that the person making the contract does not exercise free will. In the absence of a recognized type of confidential relationship, such as that between parent and child, courts are likely to take the

---

[25] *In re Boss Trust*, 487 N.W.2d 256 (Minn. App. 1992).

attitude that the person who claims to have been dominated was merely persuaded and there was therefore no undue influence.

CASE SUMMARY

Cards and Small Talk Sometimes Make the Sale

FACTS: John Lentner owned the farm adjacent to the Schefers. He moved off the farm to a nursing home in 1999. In the fall of 2000, Kristine Schefers visited Lentner at the nursing home some 15 times, engaging in small talk and watching him play cards. In the spring of 2001, Lentner agreed to sell his farm to Kristine and her husband Thomas for $50,000 plus $10,000 for machinery and tools. Kristine drove Lentner to the bank to get the deed from his safe deposit box. She also took him to the abstractor who drafted the transfer documents. Soon after the sale, Earl Fisher was appointed special conservator of Lentner. Fisher sought to set aside the transaction, asserting that Kristine's repeated visits to the nursing home and her failure to involve Lentner's other family members in the transaction unduly influenced Lentner.

DECISION: Judgment for Thomas and Kristine Schefers. Undue influence is shown when the person making the contract ceased to act of his own free volition and became a mere puppet of the wielder of that influence. Mere speculation alone that Lentner was a "puppet" acting according to the wishes of Schefers is insufficient to set aside the sale. Undue influence was not established. [*Fisher v. Schefers*, 656 N.W.2d 592 (Minn. App. 2003)]

CPA 13. Duress

physical duress – threat of physical harm to person or property.

economic duress – threat of financial loss.

duress – conduct that deprives the victim of free will and that generally gives the victim the right to set aside any transaction entered into under such circumstances.

A party may enter into a contract to avoid a threatened danger. The danger threatened may be a physical harm to person or property, called **physical duress**, or it may be a threat of financial loss, called **economic duress**.

(A) PHYSICAL DURESS. A person makes a contract under **duress** when there is such violence or threat of violence that the person is deprived of free will and makes the contract to avoid harm. The threatened harm may be directed either at a near relative of the contracting party or against the contracting party. If a contract is made under duress, the resulting agreement is voidable at the victim's election.

Agreements made to bring an end to mass disorder or violence are ordinarily not binding contracts because they were obtained by duress.

One may not void a contract on grounds of duress merely because it was entered into with great reluctance and proves to be very disadvantageous to that individual.[26]

(B) ECONOMIC DURESS. Economic duress is a condition in which one is induced by a wrongful act or threat of another to make a contract under circumstances that deprive one of the exercise of his own free will.[27] **For Example,** Richard Case, an importer of parts used to manufacture high-quality mountain bicycles, had a contractual duty to supply Katahdin Manufacturing Company's needs for specifically manufactured stainless steel brakes for the 2013 season. Katahdin's president, Bill Read, was in constant contact with Case about the delay in delivery of the parts and the adverse consequences it was having on Katahdin's relationship with its retailers.

---

[26] *Miller v. Calhoun/Johnson Co.*, 497 S.E.2d 397 (Ga. App. 1998).
[27] *Hurd v. Wildman, Harrold, Allen, and Dixon*, 707 N.E.2d 609 (Ill. App. 1999).

Near the absolute deadline for meeting orders for the 2013 season, Case called Read and said, "I've got the parts in, but I'm not sure I'll be able to send them to you because I'm working on next year's contracts, and you haven't signed yours yet." Case's 2014 contract increased the cost of parts by 38 percent. Read signed the contract to obtain the delivery but later found a new supplier and gave notice to Case of this action. The defense of economic duress would apply in a breach of contract suit brought by Case on the 2014 contract because Case implicitly threatened to commit the wrongful act of not delivering parts due under the prior contract, and Katahdin Company had no means available to obtain parts elsewhere to prevent the economic loss that would occur if it did not receive those parts.

LawFlix

Jerry Maguire (1996) (R)

Consider the marriage proposal, its validity, and Dorothy's later statement, "I did this. I made this happen. And the thing is, I can do something about it." What was Maguire's state of mind at the time of the proposal? Consider its possible hypothetical nature and the issues of whether it was a joke and the possible presence of undue influence (the young boy).

Matilda (1996)(PG)

A brilliant little girl with a strong moral compass who tries to instruct her family on many things erudite and her father specifically on what constitutes misrepresentation in selling used cars.

MAKE THE CONNECTION

SUMMARY

An agreement that otherwise appears to be a contract may not be binding because one of the parties lacks contractual capacity. In such a case, the contract is ordinarily voidable at the election of the party who lacks contractual capacity. In some cases, the contract is void. Ordinarily, contractual incapacity is the inability, for mental or physical reasons, to understand that a contract is being made and to understand its general terms and nature. This is typically the case when it is claimed that incapacity exists because of insanity, intoxication, or drug use. The incapacity of minors arises because society discriminates in favor of that class to protect them from unwise contracts.

The age of majority is 18. Minors can disaffirm most contracts. If a minor received anything from the other party, the minor, on avoiding the contract,

must return what had been received from the other party if the minor still has it.

When a minor disaffirms a contract for a necessary, the minor must pay the reasonable value of any benefit received.

Minors only are liable for their contracts. Parents of a minor are not liable on the minor's contracts merely because they are the parents. Frequently, an adult enters into the contract as a coparty of the minor and is then liable without regard to whether the minor has avoided the contract.

The contract of an insane person is voidable to much the same extent as the contract of a minor. An important distinction is that if a guardian has been appointed for the insane person, a contract made by the insane person is void, not merely voidable.

An intoxicated person lacks contractual capacity if the intoxication is such that the person does not understand that a contract is being made.

The consent of a party to an agreement is not genuine or voluntary in certain cases of mistake, deception, or pressure. When this occurs, what appears to be a contract can be avoided by the victim of such circumstances or conduct.

As to mistake, it is necessary to distinguish between unilateral mistakes that are unknown to the other contracting party and those that are known. Mistakes that are unknown to the other party usually do not affect the binding character of the agreement. A unilateral mistake of which the other contracting party has knowledge or has reason to know makes the contract avoidable by the victim of the mistake.

The deception situation may be one of negligent misrepresentation or fraud. The law ordinarily does not attach any significance to nondisclosure. Contrary to this rule, there is a duty to volunteer information when a confidential relationship exists between the possessor of the knowledge and the other contracting party.

When concealment goes beyond mere silence and consists of actively taking steps to hide the truth, the conduct may be classified as fraud. A statement of opinion or value cannot ordinarily be the basis for fraud liability.

The voluntary character of a contract may be lacking because the agreement had been obtained by pressure. This may range from undue influence through the array of threats of extreme economic loss (called *economic duress*) to the threat of physical force that would cause serious personal injury or damage to property (called *physical duress*). When the voluntary character of an agreement has been destroyed by deception, or pressure, the victim may avoid or rescind the contract or may obtain money damages from the wrongdoer.

LEARNING OUTCOMES

After studying this chapter, you should be able to clearly explain:

A. Contractual Capacity

L0.1 Define contractual capacity
See the example where Jacqueline, age 22, did not understand parts of a storage contract, p. 283.

L0.2 Explain the extent and effect of avoidance of a contract by a minor.
See the *Adorian Deck* example where the creator of a Twitter feed, a minor, disaffirmed his joint venture contract, p. 284.
See the *Prince George's Hospital* case where a minor had to pay for medical necessaries, p. 286.

B. Mistake

L0.3 Distinguish unilateral mistakes and mutual mistakes
See the *Shurgard Storage* case where the "other party" should have known of the unilateral mistake, p. 289.
See the *Jewell Coke Co.* example of a remedy for a billion dollar mistake, p. 290.

See the example of the mutual mistake of fact regarding the fertility of a cow on p. 290.

C. Deception

L0.4 Explain the difference between intentional misrepresentation, negligent misrepresentation, and puffery
See the example of the purchase of the used Honda where the misrepresentation was found to be fraud not puffery on p. 292.
See the *Novare Group, Inc.* decision on the enforceability of disclaimer-of-liability clauses, pp. 293–294.

D. Pressure

L0.5 Explain the difference between undue influence and duress
See the *Fisher v. Schefers* undue influence litigation, p. 297.
See the Katahdin bicycle example on economic duress, p. 297.

KEY TERMS

confidential relationship
contractual capacity
duress
economic duress

fraud
necessaries
physical duress
reformation

status quo ante
undue influence

QUESTIONS AND CASE PROBLEMS

1. Lester purchased a used automobile from MacKintosh Motors. He asked the seller if the car had ever been in a wreck. The MacKintosh salesperson had never seen the car before that morning and knew nothing of its history but quickly answered Lester's question by stating: "No. It has never been in a wreck." In fact, the auto had been seriously damaged in a wreck and, although repaired, was worth much less than the value it would have had if there had been no wreck. When Lester learned the truth, he sued MacKintosh Motors and the salesperson for damages for fraud. They raised the defense that the salesperson did not know the statement was false and had not intended to deceive Lester. Did the conduct of the salesperson constitute fraud?

2. Helen, age 17, wanted to buy a Harley-Davidson "Sportster" motorcycle. She did not have the funds to pay cash but persuaded the dealer to sell the cycle to her on credit. The dealer did so partly because Helen said that she was 22 and showed the dealer an identification card that falsely stated her age as 22. Helen drove the motorcycle away. A few days later, she damaged it and then returned it to the dealer and stated that she disaffirmed the contract because she was a minor. The dealer said that she could not because (1) she had misrepresented her age and (2) the motorcycle was damaged. Can she avoid the contract?

3. Paden signed an agreement dated May 28 to purchase the Murrays' home. The Murrays accepted Paden's offer the following day, and the sale closed on June 27. Paden and his family moved into the home on July 14, 1997. Paden had the home inspected prior to closing. The report listed four minor repairs needed by the home, the cost of which was less than $500. Although these repairs had not been completed at the time of closing, Paden decided to go through with the purchase. After moving into the home, Paden discovered a number of allegedly new defects, including a wooden foundation, electrical problems, and bat infestation. The sales agreement allowed extensive rights to inspect the property. The agreement provided:

> Buyer…shall have the right to enter the property at Buyer's expense and at reasonable times…to thoroughly inspect, examine, test, and survey the Property…. Buyer shall have the right to request that Seller repair defects in the Property by providing Seller within 12 days from Binding Agreement Date with a copy of inspection report(s) and a written amendment to this agreement setting forth the defects in the report which Buyer requests to be repaired and/or replaced…. If Buyer does not timely present the written amendment and inspection report, Buyer shall be deemed to have accepted the Property "as is."

Paden sued the Murrays for fraudulent concealment and breach of the sales agreement. If Mr. Murray told Paden on May 26 that the house had a concrete foundation, would this be fraud? Decide. [*Paden v. Murray*, 523 S.E.2d 75 (Ga. App.)]

4. High-Tech Collieries borrowed money from Holland. High-Tech later refused to be bound by the loan contract, claiming the contract was not binding because it had been obtained by duress. The evidence showed that the offer to make the loan was made on a take-it-or-leave-it basis. Was the defense of duress valid? [*Holland v. High-Tech Collieries, Inc.*, 911 F. Supp. 1021 (N.D. W.Va.)]

5. Thomas Bell, a minor, went to work in the Pittsburgh beauty parlor of Sam Pankas and

agreed that when he left the employment, he would not work in or run a beauty parlor business within a 10-mile radius of downtown Pittsburgh for a period of two years. Contrary to this provision, Bell and another employee of Pankas's opened a beauty shop three blocks from Pankas's shop and advertised themselves as Pankas's former employees. Pankas sued Bell to stop the breach of the noncompetition, or restrictive, covenant. Bell claimed that he was not bound because he was a minor when he had agreed to the covenant. Was he bound by the covenant? [*Pankas v. Bell*, 198 A.2d 312 (Pa.)]

6. Aldrich and Co. sold goods to Donovan on credit. The amount owed grew steadily, and finally Aldrich refused to sell any more to Donovan unless Donovan signed a promissory note for the amount due. Donovan did not want to but signed the note because he had no money and needed more goods. When Aldrich brought an action to enforce the note, Donovan claimed that the note was not binding because it had been obtained by economic duress. Was he correct? [*Aldrich & Co. v. Donovan*, 778 P.2d 397 (Mont.)]

7. James Fitl purchased a 1952 Mickey Mantle Topps baseball card from baseball card dealer Mark Strek for $17,750 and placed it in a safe deposit box. Two years later, he had the card appraised, and he was told that the card had been refinished and trimmed, which rendered it valueless. Fitl sued Strek and testified that he had relied on Strek's position as a sports card dealer and on his representations that the baseball card was authentic. Strek contends that Fitl waited too long to give him notice of the defects that would have enabled Strek to contact the person who sold him the card and obtain relief. Strek asserts that he therefore is not liable. Advise Fitl concerning possible legal theories that apply to his case. How would you decide the case? [See *Fitl v. Strek*, 690 N.W.2d 605 (Neb.)]

8. Willingham proposed to obtain an investment property for the Tschiras at a "fair market price," lease it back from them, and pay the Tschiras a guaranteed return through a management contract. Using a shell corporation, The Wellingham Group bought a commercial property in Nashville for $774,000 on December 14, and the very same day sold the building to the Tschiras for $1,985,000. The title insurance policy purchased for the Tschiras property by Willingham was for just $774,000. Willingham believes that the deal was legitimate in that they "guaranteed" a return on the investment. The Tschiras disagree. In a lawsuit against Willingham, what theory will the Tschiras rely on? Decide. [*Tschiras v. Willingham*, 133 F.3d 1077 (6th Cir.)]

9. Blubaugh was a district manager of Schlumberger Well Services. Turner was an executive employee of Schlumberger. Blubaugh was told that he would be fired unless he chose to resign. He was also told that if he would resign and release the company and its employees from all claims for wrongful discharge, he would receive about $5,000 in addition to his regular severance pay of approximately $25,000 and would be given job-relocation counseling. He resigned, signed the release, and received about $40,000 and job counseling. Some time thereafter, he brought an action claiming that he had been wrongfully discharged. He claimed that the release did not protect the defendants because the release had been obtained by economic duress. Were the defendants protected by the release? [*Blubaugh v. Turner*, 842 P.2d 1072 (Wyo.)]

10. Sippy was thinking of buying Christich's house. He noticed watermarks on the ceiling, but the agent showing the house stated that the roof had been repaired and was in good condition. Sippy was not told that the roof still leaked and that the repairs had not been able to stop the leaking. Sippy bought the house. Some time later, heavy rains caused water to leak into the house, and Sippy claimed that Christich was liable for damages. What theory would he rely on? Decide. [*Sippy v. Christich*, 609 P.2d 204 (Kan. App.)]

11. Pileggi owed Young money. Young threatened to bring suit against Pileggi for the amount due. Pileggi feared the embarrassment of being sued and the possibility that he might be thrown into bankruptcy. To avoid being sued, Pileggi executed a promissory note to pay Young the

amount due. He later asserted that the note was not binding because he had executed it under duress. Is this defense valid? [*Young v. Pileggi*, 455 A.2d 1228 (Pa. Super.)]

12. Office Supply Outlet, Inc., a single-store office equipment and supply retailer, ordered 100 model RVX-414 computers from Compuserve, Inc. A new staff member made a clerical error on the order form and ordered a quantity that was far in excess of what Office Supply could sell in a year. Office Supply realized the mistake when the delivery trucks arrived at its warehouse. Its manager called Compuserve and explained that it had intended to order just 10 computers. Compuserve declined to accept the return of the extra machines. Is the contract enforceable? What additional facts would allow the store to avoid the contract for the additional machines?

13. The Printers International Union reached agreement for a new three-year contract with a large regional printing company. As was their practice, the union negotiators then met with Sullivan Brothers Printers, Inc., a small specialty shop employing 10 union printers, and Sullivan Brothers and the union agreed to follow the contractual pattern set by the union and the large printing company. That is, Sullivan Brothers agreed to give its workers all of the benefits negotiated for the employees of the large printing company. When the contract was typed, a new benefit of 75 percent employer-paid coverage for a dental plan was inadvertently omitted from the final contract the parties signed. The mistake was not discovered until six months after the contract took effect. Sullivan Brothers Printers, Inc. is reluctant to assume the additional expense. It contends that the printed copy, which does not cover dental benefits, must control. The union believes that clear and convincing evidence shows an inadvertent typing error. Decide.

14. The city of Salinas entered into a contract with Souza & McCue Construction Co. to construct a sewer. City officials knew unusual subsoil conditions (including extensive quicksand) existed that would make performance of the contract unusually difficult. This information was not disclosed when city officials advertised for bids. The advertisement for bids directed bidders to examine carefully the site of the work and declared that the submission of a bid would constitute evidence that the bidder had made an examination. Souza & McCue was awarded the contract, but because of the subsoil conditions, it could not complete on time and was sued by Salinas for breach of contract. Souza & McCue counterclaimed on the basis that the city had not revealed its information on the subsoil conditions and was thus liable for the loss. Was the city liable? [*City of Salinas v. Souza & McCue Construction Co.*, 424 P.2d 921 (Cal. App. 3d)]

15. Vern Westby inherited a "ticket" from Anna Sjoblom, a survivor of the sinking of the *Titanic*, which had been pinned to the inside of her coat. He also inherited an album of postcards, some of which related to the *Titanic*. The ticket was a one-of-a-kind item in good condition. Westby needed cash and went to the biggest antique dealer in Tacoma, operated by Alan Gorsuch and his family, doing business as Sanford and Sons, and asked about the value of these items. Westby testified that after Alan Gorsuch examined the ticket, he said, "It's not worth nothing." Westby then inquired about the value of the postcard album, and Gorsuch advised him to come back later. On Westby's return, Gorsuch told Westby, "It ain't worth nothing." Gorsuch added that he "couldn't fetch $500 for the ticket." Since he needed money, Westby asked if Gorsuch would give him $1,000 for both the ticket and the album, and Gorsuch did so.

Six months later, Gorsuch sold the ticket at a nationally advertised auction for $110,000 and sold most of the postcards for $1,200. Westby sued Gorsuch for fraud. Testimony showed that Gorsuch was a major buyer in antiques and collectibles in the Puget Sound area and that he would have had an understanding of the value of the ticket. Gorsuch contends that all elements of fraud are not present since there was no evidence that Gorsuch intended that Westby rely on the alleged representations, nor did Westby rely on such. Rather, Gorsuch asserts, it was an arm's-length transaction and Westby had access to the same information as Gorsuch. Decide. [*Westby v. Gorsuch*, 50 P.3d 284 (Wash. App.)]

CPA QUESTIONS

1. A building subcontractor submitted a bid for construction of a portion of a high-rise office building. The bid contained material computational errors. The general contractor accepted the bid with knowledge of the errors. Which of the following statements best represents the subcontractor's liability?

   a. Not liable, because the contractor knew of the errors.

   b. Not liable, because the errors were a result of gross negligence.

   c. Liable, because the errors were unilateral.

   d. Liable, because the errors were material (5/95, Law, #17, 5351).

2. Egan, a minor, contracted with Baker to purchase Baker's used computer for $400. The computer was purchased for Egan's personal use. The agreement provided that Egan would pay $200 down on delivery and $200 thirty days later. Egan took delivery and paid the $200 down payment. Twenty days later, the computer was damaged seriously as a result of Egan's negligence. Five days after the damage occurred and one day after Egan reached the age of majority, Egan attempted to disaffirm the contract with Baker. Egan will:

   a. Be able to disaffirm despite the fact that Egan was *not* a minor at the time of disaffirmance.

   b. Be able to disaffirm only if Egan does so in writing.

   c. Not be able to disaffirm because Egan had failed to pay the balance of the purchase price.

   d. Not be able to disaffirm because the computer was damaged as a result of Egan's negligence (11/93, Law, #21, 4318).

© Manuel Gutjahr/iStockphoto.com

CHAPTER 15

Consideration

learningoutcomes

After studying this chapter, you should be able to

LO.1 Explain what constitutes consideration

LO.2 Distinguish between a "preexisting legal obligation" and "past consideration"

LO.3 Explain why promises based on moral obligations lack consideration

LO.4 List the exceptions to the requirement of consideration

LO.5 Explain the "fundamental idea" underlying promissory estoppel

W ill the law enforce every promise? Generally, a promise will not be enforced unless something is given or received for the promise.

A. GENERAL PRINCIPLES

As a general rule, one of the elements needed to make an agreement binding is consideration.

1. Consideration Defined and Explained

consideration—promise or performance that the promisor demands as the price of the promise.

Consideration is what each party to a contract gives up to the other in making their agreement.

(A) **BARGAINED-FOR EXCHANGE.** *Consideration* is the bargained-for exchange between the parties to a contract. In order for consideration to exist, something of value must be given or promised in return for the performance or promise of performance of the other.[1] The value given or promised can be money, services, property, or the forbearance of a legal right.

For Example, Beth offers to pay Kerry $100 for her used skis, and Kerry accepts. Beth has promised something of value, $100, as consideration for Kerry's promise to sell the skis, and Kerry has promised Beth something of value, the skis, as consideration for the $100. If Kerry offered to *give* Beth the used skis and Beth accepted, these parties would have an agreement but not an enforceable contract because Beth did not provide any consideration in exchange for Kerry's promise of the skis. There was no *bargained-for exchange* because Kerry was not promised anything of value from Beth.

(B) **BENEFIT-DETRIMENT APPROACH.** Some jurisdictions analyze consideration from the point of view of a *benefit-detriment approach,* defining *consideration* as a benefit received by the promisor or a detriment incurred by the promisee.

As an example of a unilateral contract analyzed from a benefit-detriment approach to consideration, Mr. Scully, a longtime summer resident of Falmouth, states to George Corfu, a college senior, "I will pay you $3,000 if you paint my summer home." George in fact paints the house. The work of painting the house by George, the promisee, was a legal detriment to him. Also, the painting of the house was a legal benefit to Scully, the promisor. There was consideration in this case, and the agreement is enforceable.

2. Gifts

Promises to make a gift are unenforceable promises under the law of contracts because of lack of consideration, as illustrated previously in the scenario of Kerry promising to give her used skis to Beth without charge. There was no bargained-for exchange because Kerry was not promised anything of value from Beth. A completed gift, however, cannot be rescinded for lack of consideration.[2]

---

[1] *Brooksbank v. Anderson,* 586 N.W.2d 789 (Minn. App. 1998).
[2] *Homes v. O'Bryant,* 741 So.2d 366 (Miss. App. 1999).

Charitable subscriptions by which individuals make pledges to finance the construction of a college building, a church, or another structure for charitable purposes are binding to the extent that the donor (promisor) should have reasonably realized that the charity was relying on the promise in undertaking the building program. Some states require proof that the charity has relied on the subscription.[3]

CASE SUMMARY

You Can't Back Out Now

FACTS: Salsbury was attempting to establish a new college, Charles City College. Salsbury obtained a pledge from Northwestern Bell Telephone Company to contribute to the college. When the company did not pay, Salsbury sued the company. The company raised the defense that there was no consideration for its promise and that nothing had been done by the college in reliance on the promise.

DECISION: Judgment for Salsbury. As a matter of public policy, a promise of a charitable contribution is binding even though there is no consideration for the promise and without regard for whether the charity had done any acts in reliance on the promise. The company was therefore liable on its promise to contribute. [*Salsbury v. Northwestern Bell Telephone Co.*, **221 N.W.2d 609 (Iowa 1974)**]

An agreement to give property for the consideration of love and affection does not transfer the property to the donee nor secure for the donee a right to sue to compel the completion of the contract. Love and affection alone have not been recognized as consideration for a contract.

CASE SUMMARY

What's Love Got to Do with It...

FACTS: Amber Williams and Frederick Ormsby lived together in a nonmarital relationship in a house deeded to Ormsby in 2004. The couple separated and attended couples counseling. Amber refused to move back into the house unless Frederick granted her a one-half interest in the property. On June 2, 2005, they signed a document purportedly making themselves equal partners in the home. Amber ended the relationship in September 2007, and she sought specific performance of the June 2, 2005 contract giving her a half-interest in the property. Frederick defended that "love and affection is insufficient consideration for a contract."

DECISION: Judgment for Ormsby. The only consideration offered by Amber for the June 2, 2005 agreement was her resumption of a romantic relationship with Frederick. Essentially this agreement amounts to a gratuitous promise by Frederick to give Amber an interest in property based solely on the consideration of love and affection. This June 2005 document is not an enforceable contract because it fails for want of consideration. [*Williams v. Ormsby*, **966 N.E.2d 255 (Ohio 2012)**]

---

[3] *King v. Trustees of Boston University*, 647 N.E.2d 1176 (Ma. 1995).

3. Adequacy of Consideration

Ordinarily, courts do not consider the adequacy of the consideration given for a promise. The fact that the consideration supplied by one party is slight when compared with the burden undertaken by the other party is immaterial. It is a matter for the parties to decide when they make their contract whether each is getting a fair return. In the absence of fraud or other misconduct, courts usually will not interfere to make sure that each side is getting a fair return.

CASE SUMMARY

Who's to Say?

FACTS: On the death of their aunt, a brother and sister became the owners of shares of stock of several corporations. They made an agreement to divide these shares equally between them, although the sister's shares had a value approximately seven times those of the brother. The brother died before the shares were divided. The sister then claimed that the agreement to divide was not binding because the consideration for her promise was not adequate.

DECISION: The value of stock cannot be determined precisely. It may change with time. In addition, the value that one person may see can be different than that seen by another. The court therefore will not make a comparison of the value that each party was to receive under the agreement. It was sufficient that a promise was exchanged for a promise. The adequacy of the consideration would not be examined. This sister was therefore bound by her promise to divide the shares. [*Emberson v. Hartley,* 762 P.2d 364 (Wash. App. 1988)]

Because the adequacy of consideration is ignored, it is immaterial that consideration is so slight that the transaction is in part a "gift." However, the Internal Revenue Service may view a given transaction as part consideration, part gift, and assess a gift tax as appropriate.

The fact that the consideration turns out to be disappointing does not affect the binding character of the contract. Thus, the fact that a business purchased by a group of investors proves unprofitable does not constitute a failure of consideration that releases the buyers from their obligation to the seller.

CASE SUMMARY

Expectations versus Consideration

FACTS: Aqua Drilling Company made a contract to drill a well for the Atlas Construction Company. It was expected that this would supply water for a home being constructed by Atlas. Aqua did not make any guarantee or warranty that water would be produced. Aqua drilled the well exactly as required by the contract, but no water was produced. Atlas refused to pay. It asserted that the contract was not binding on the theory that there had been a failure of consideration because the well did not produce water.

DECISION: The contract was binding. Atlas obtained the exact performance required by the contract. While Atlas had expected that water would be obtained, Aqua did not make any guarantee or warranty that this would be so. Hence, there was no failure of consideration. [*Atlas Construction Co., Inc. v. Aqua Drilling Co.,* 559 P.2d 39 (Wyo. 1977)]

4. Forbearance as Consideration

forbearance – refraining from doing an act.

In most cases, consideration consists of the performance of an act such as providing a service, or the making of a promise to provide a service or goods, or paying money.[4] Consideration may also consist of **forbearance**, which is refraining from doing an act that an individual has a legal right to do, or it may consist of a promise of forbearance. In other words, the promisor may desire to buy the inaction or a promise of inaction of the other party.

The giving up of any legal right can be consideration for the promise of the other party to a contract. Thus, the relinquishment of a right to sue for damages will support a promise for the payment of money given in return for the promise to relinquish the right, if such is the agreement of the parties.

The promise of a creditor to forbear collecting a debt is consideration for the promise of the debtor to modify the terms of the transaction.

5. Illusory Promises

illusory promise – promise that in fact does not impose any obligation on the promisor.

In a bilateral contract, each party makes a promise to the other. For a bilateral contract to be enforceable, there must be *mutuality of obligation*. That is, both parties must have created obligations to the other in their respective promises. If one party's promise contains either no obligation or only an apparent obligation to the other, this promise is an **illusory promise**. The party making such a promise is not bound because he or she has made no real promise. The effect is that the other party, who has made a real promise, is also not bound because he or she has received no consideration. It is said that the contract fails for lack of mutuality.

For Example, Mountain Coal Company promises to sell Midwest Power Company all the coal it may order for $48 per ton for the year 2013, and Midwest Power agrees to pay $48 for any coal it orders from Mountain Coal. Mountain Coal in its promise to Midwest Power has obligated itself to supply all coal ordered at a stated price. However, Midwest Power's promise did not obligate it to buy any coal whatsoever from Mountain Coal (note that it was not a requirements contract). Because Midwest has no obligation to Mountain Coal under its promise, there is no mutuality of obligation, and Midwest cannot enforce Mountain Coal's promise when the market price of coal goes to $55 a ton in the winter of 2013 as the result of severe weather conditions.

Consider as well the example of the Jacksonville Fire soccer team's contract with Brazilian soccer star Edmundo. Edmundo signed a contract to play for the Jacksonville franchise of the new International Soccer League for five years at $25 million. The extensive document signed by Edmundo set forth the details of the team's financial commitment and the details of Edmundo's obligations to the team and its fans. On page 4 of the document, the team inserted a clause reserving the right "to terminate the contract and team obligations at any time in its sole discretion." During the season, Edmundo received a $40 million five-year offer to play for Manchester United of the English Premier League, which he accepted. Because Jacksonville had a free way out of its obligation by the unrestricted cancellation provision in the contract, it thus made its promises to Edmundo illusory. Edmundo was not bound by the Jacksonville contract as a result of a lack of mutuality and was free to sign with Manchester United.

---

[4] *Prenger v. Baumhoer*, 914 S.W.2d 413 (Mo. App. 1996).

(A) CANCELLATION PROVISIONS. Although a promise must impose a binding obligation, it may authorize a party to cancel the agreement under certain circumstances on giving notice by a certain date. Such a provision does not make this party's promise illusory, for the party does not have a free way out and is limited to living up to the terms of the **cancellation provision**. **For Example,** actress Zsa Zsa Gabor made a contract with Hollywood Fantasy Corporation to appear at a fantasy vacation in San Antonio, Texas, on May 2–4, for a $10,000 appearance fee plus itemized (extravagant) expenses. The last paragraph of the agreement stated: "It is agreed that if a significant acting opportunity in a film comes up, Ms. Gabor will have the right to cancel her appearance in San Antonio by advising Hollywood Fantasy in writing by April 15, 1991." Ms. Gabor sent a telegram on April 15, 1991, canceling her appearance. During the May 2 through 4 period, Ms. Gabor's only acting activity was a 14-second cameo role during the opening credits of *Naked Gun 2½*. In a lawsuit for breach of contract that followed, the jury saw this portion of the movie and concluded that Ms. Gabor had not canceled her obligation on the basis of a "significant acting opportunity," and she was held liable for breach of contract.[5]

(B) CONDITIONAL PROMISES. A *conditional promise* is a promise that depends on the occurrence of a specified condition in order for the promise to be binding. **For Example,** Mary Sparks, in contemplation of her signing a lease to take over a restaurant at Marina Bay, wanted to make certain that she had a highly qualified chef to run the restaurant's food service. She made a contract with John "Grumpy" White to serve as executive chef for a one-year period at a salary of $150,000. The contract set forth White's responsibilities and was conditioned on the successful negotiation of the restaurant lease with Marina Bay Management. Both parties signed it. Although the happening of the condition was within Mary's control because she could avoid the contract with Grumpy White by not acquiring the restaurant lease, she limited her future options by the contract with White. Her promise to White was not illusory because after signing the contract with him, if she acquired the restaurant lease, she was bound to hire White as her executive chef. Before signing the contract with White, she was free to sign any chef for the position. The contract was enforceable.

cancellation provision – crossing out of a part of an instrument or a destruction of all legal effect of the instrument, whether by act of party, upon breach by the other party, or pursuant to agreement or decree of court.

CPA B. SPECIAL SITUATIONS

The following sections analyze certain common situations in which a lawsuit turns on whether the promisor received consideration for the promise sued on.

6. Preexisting Legal Obligation

Ordinarily, doing or promising to do what one is already under a legal obligation to do is not consideration.[6] Similarly, a promise to refrain from doing what one has no legal right to do is not consideration. This preexisting duty or legal obligation can be based on statute, on general principles of law, on responsibilities of an office held, or on a preexisting contract.

---

[5] *Hollywood Fantasy Corp. v. Gabor*, 151 F.2d 203 (5th Cir. 1998).
[6] *Willamette Management Associates, Inc. v. Palczynski*, 38 A.3d 1212 (Conn. App. 2012).

For Example, Officer Mary Rodgers is an undercover police officer in the city of Pasadena, California, assigned to weekend workdays. Officer Rodgers promised Elwood Farnsworth that she would diligently patrol the area of the Farnsworth estate on weekends to keep down the noise and drinking of rowdy young persons who gathered in this area, and Mr. Farnsworth promised to provide a $500 per month gratuity for this extra service. Farnsworth's promise is unenforceable because Officer Rodgers has a preexisting official duty as a police officer to protect citizens and enforce the antinoise and public drinking ordinances.

CPA (A) COMPLETION OF CONTRACT. Suppose that a contractor refuses to complete a building unless the owner promises a payment or bonus in addition to the sum specified in the original contract, and the owner promises to make that payment. The question then arises as to whether the owner's promise is binding. Most courts hold that the second promise of the owner is without consideration.

CASE SUMMARY

You're Already Under Contract

FACTS: Crookham & Vessels had a contract to build an extension of a railroad for the Little Rock Port Authority. It made a contract with Larry Moyer Trucking to dig drainage ditches. The ditch walls collapsed because water would not drain off. This required that the ditches be dug over again. Larry Moyer refused to do this unless extra money was paid. Crookham & Vessels agreed to pay the additional compensation, but after the work was done, it refused to pay. Larry Moyer sued for the extra compensation promised.

DECISION: Judgment against Moyer. Moyer was bound by its contract to dig the drainage ditches. Its promise to perform that obligation was not consideration for the promise of Crookham & Vessels to pay additional compensation. Performance of an obligation is not consideration for a promise by a party entitled to that performance. The fact that performance of the contract proved more difficult or costly than originally contemplated does not justify making an exception to this rule. [*Crookham & Vessels, Inc. v. Larry Moyer Trucking, Inc.,* **699 S.W.2d 414 (Ark. App. 1985)**]

If the promise of the contractor is to do something that is not part of the first contract, then the promise of the other party is binding. **For Example,** if a bonus of $5,000 is promised in return for the promise of a contractor to complete the building at a date earlier than that specified in the original agreement, the promise to pay the bonus is binding.

CPA *(1) Good-Faith Adjustment*
A current trend is to enforce a second promise to pay a contractor a higher amount for the performance of the original contract when there are extraordinary circumstances caused by unforeseeable difficulties and when the additional amount promised the contractor is reasonable under the circumstances.

CASE SUMMARY

"You Had a Preexisting Legal Obligation," Said the Public Guardian, Mr. Angel.

FACTS: John Murray was director of finance of the city of Newport. A contract was made with Alfred Maher to remove trash. Later, Maher requested that the city council increase his compensation. Maher's costs were greater than had been anticipated because 400 new dwelling units had been put into operation. The city council voted to pay Maher an additional $10,000 a year. After two such annual payments had been made, Angel and other citizens of the city sued Murray and Maher for a return of the $20,000. They said that Maher was already obligated by his contract to perform the work for the contract sum, and there was, accordingly, no consideration for the payment of the increased compensation. From a decision in favor of the plaintiffs, the city and Maher appealed.

DECISION: Judgment for the city and Maher. When a promise modifying an original contract is made before the contract is fully performed on either side due to unanticipated circumstances that prompt the modification, and the modification is fair and equitable, such a good faith adjustment will be enforced. The unanticipated increase in the number of new units from 20 to 25 per year to 400 units in the third year of this five-year contract, which prompted the additional yearly payments of $10,000, was a voluntary good faith adjustment. It was not a "hold up" by a contractor refusing to complete an unprofitable contract unless paid additional compensation, where the preexisting duty rule would apply. [*Angel v. Murray*, 322 A.2d 630 (R.I. 1974)]

(2) Contract for Sale of Goods

When the contract is for the sale of goods, any modification made in good faith by the parties to the contract is binding without regard to the existence of consideration for the modification.

CPA

(B) **COMPROMISE AND RELEASE OF CLAIMS.** The rule that doing or promising to do what one is already legally bound to do is not consideration applies to a part payment made in satisfaction of an admitted or *liquidated debt*. Thus, a promise to pay part of an amount that is admittedly owed is not consideration for a promise to discharge the balance. It will not prevent the creditor from demanding the remainder later. **For Example,** John owes Mark $100,000, which was due on March 1, 2010. On March 15, John offers to pay back $80,000 if Mark will agree to accept this amount as the discharge of the full amount owed. Mark agrees to this proposal, and it is set forth in writing signed by the parties. However, Mark later sues for the $20,000 balance. Mark will be successful in the lawsuit because John's payment of the $80,000 is not consideration for Mark's promise to discharge the full amount owed because John was doing only what he had a preexisting legal duty to do.

If the debtor pays the part payment before the debt is due, there is consideration because, on the day when the payment was made, the creditor was not entitled to demand any payment. Likewise, if the creditor accepts some article (even of slight value) in addition to the part payment, consideration exists.

A debtor and creditor may have a bona fide dispute over the amount owed or whether any amount is owed. Such is called an *unliquidated debt*. In this case, payment by the debtor of less than the amount claimed by the creditor is consideration for the latter's agreement to release or settle the claim. It is generally regarded as sufficient if the claimant believes in the merit of the claim.[7]

(c) Part-Payment Checks. When there is a good-faith dispute about the amount of a debt and the debtor tenders a check that states on its face "paid in full" and references the transaction in dispute, but the amount of the check is less than the full amount the creditor asserts is owed, the cashing of the check by the creditor discharges the entire debt.

(d) Composition of Creditors. In a **composition of creditors**, the various creditors of one debtor mutually agree to accept a fractional part of their claims in full satisfaction of the claims. Such agreements are binding and are supported by consideration. When creditors agree to extend the due date of their debts, the promise of each creditor to forbear is likewise consideration for the promise of other creditors to forbear.

composition of creditors – agreement among creditors that each shall accept a part payment as full payment in consideration of the other creditors doing the same.

7. Past Consideration

A promise based on a party's past performance lacks consideration.[8] It is said that **past consideration** is no consideration. **For Example,** Fred O'Neal came up with the idea for the formation of the new community bank of Villa Rica and was active in its formation. Just prior to the execution of the documents creating the bank, the organizers discussed that once the bank was formed, it would hire O'Neal, giving him a three-year contract at $65,000 the first year, $67,000 the second year, and $70,000 the third. In a lawsuit against the bank for breach of contract, O'Neal testified that the consideration he gave in exchange for the three-year contract was his past effort to organize the bank. The court stated that past consideration generally will not support a subsequent promise and that the purported consideration was not rendered to the bank, which had not yet been established when his promotion and organization work took place.[9] The presence of a bargained-for exchange is not present when a promise is made in exchange for a past benefit.[10]

past consideration – something that has been performed in the past and which, therefore, cannot be consideration for a promise made in the present.

8. Moral Obligation

In most states, promises made to another based on "moral obligation" lack consideration and are not enforceable.[11] They are considered gratuitous promises and unenforceable. **For Example,** while on a fishing trip, Tom Snyder, a person of moderate means, met an elderly couple living in near-destitute conditions in a rural area of Texas. He returned to the area often, and he regularly purchased groceries for the couple and paid for their medical needs. Some two years later, the couple's son, David, discovered what Tom had been doing and promised to reimburse Snyder for what he had furnished his parents. This promise, based on a moral obligation, is unenforceable. A "past consideration" analysis also renders David's promise as unenforceable.

[7] *F. H. Prince & Co. v. Towers Financial Corp.,* 656 N.E.2d 142 (Ill. App. 1995).
[8] *Smith v. Locklear,* 906 So.2d 1273 (Fla. App. 2005).
[9] *O'Neal v. Home Town Bank of Villa Rica,* 514 S.E.2d 669 (Ga. App. 1999).
[10] But see *United Resource Recovery Corp v. Ranko Venture Management Inc.,* 854 F. Supp. 2d 645 (S.D.N.Y. 2008) where a past work agreement was unenforceable because it was based on past consideration—however, the individual could recover under a signed consulting agreement for which no compensation had been paid. See also *Travis v. Paepke,* 3 So.3d 131 (Miss. App. 2009).
[11] *Production Credit Ass'n of Manaan v. Rub,* 475 N.W.2d 532 (N.D. 1991). As to the Louisiana rule of moral consideration, see *Thomas v. Bryant,* 596 So.2d 1065 (La. App. 1992).

Ethics & the Law

Alan Fulkins, who owns a construction company that specializes in single-family residences, is constructing a small subdivision with 23 homes. Tretorn Plumbing, owned by Jason Tretorn, was awarded the contract for the plumbing work on the homes at a price of $4,300 per home.

Plumbing contractors complete their residential projects in three phases. Phase one consists of digging the lines for the plumbing and installing the pipes that are placed in the foundation of the house. Phase two consists of installing the pipes within the walls of the home, and phase three is installing of the surface plumbing, such as sinks and tubs. However, industry practice dictates that the plumbing contractor receive one-half of the contract amount after completion of phase one.

Tretorn completed the digs of phase one for Fulkins and received payment of $2,150. Tretorn then went to Fulkins and demanded an additional $600 per house to complete the work. Fulkins said, "But you already have a contract for $4,300!" Tretorn responded, "I know, but the costs are killing me. I need the additional $600."

Fulkins explained the hardship of the demand, "Look, I've already paid you half. If I hire someone else, I'll have to pay them two-thirds for the work not done. It'll cost me $5,000 per house."

Tretorn responded, "Exactly. I'm a bargain because the additional $600 I want only puts you at $4,900. If you don't pay it, I'll just lien the houses and then you'll be stuck without a way to close the sales. I've got the contract all drawn up. Just sign it and everything goes smoothly."

Should Fulkins sign the agreement? Does Tretorn have the right to the additional $600? Was it ethical for Tretorn to demand the $600? Is there any legal advice you can offer Fulkins?

FIGURE 15-1 | *Consideration and Promises*

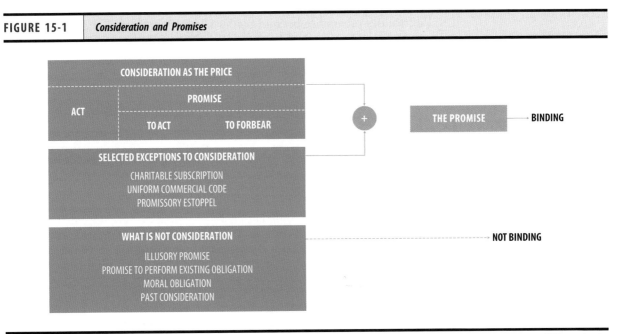

© Cengage Learning

C. EXCEPTIONS TO THE LAWS OF CONSIDERATION

The ever-changing character of law clearly appears in the area of consideration as part of the developing law of contracts.

9. Exceptions to Consideration

By statute or decision, traditional consideration is not required in these situations:

(A) Charitable Subscriptions. Where individuals made pledges to finance the construction of buildings for charitable purposes, consideration is lacking according to technical standards applied in ordinary contract cases. For public policy reasons, the reliance of the charity on the pledge in undertaking the project is deemed a substitute for consideration.

(B) Uniform Commercial Code. In some situations, the Uniform Commercial Code abolishes the requirement of consideration. **For Example,** under the Code, consideration is not required for (1) a merchant's written, firm offer for goods stated to be irrevocable, (2) a written discharge of a claim for an alleged breach of a commercial contract, or (3) an agreement to modify a contract for the sale of goods.[12]

(C) Promissory Estoppel. Under the doctrine of **promissory estoppel**, a promisor may be prevented from asserting that his or her promise is unenforceable because the promisee gave no consideration for the promise. This doctrine, sometimes called the *doctrine of detrimental reliance,* is applicable when (1) the promisor makes a promise that lacks consideration, (2) the promisor intends or should reasonably expect that the promisee will rely on the promise, (3) the promisee in fact relies on the promise in some definite and substantial manner, and (4) enforcement of the promise is the only way to avoid injustice.[13]

Damages recoverable in a case of promissory estoppel are not the profits that the promisee expected, but only the amount necessary to restore the promisee to the position he or she would have been in had the promisee not relied on the promise.[14]

Legal difficulties often arise because parties take certain things for granted. Frequently, they will be sure that they have agreed to everything and that they have a valid contract. Sometimes, however, they do not. The courts are then faced with the problem of leaving them with their broken dreams or coming to their rescue when promissory estoppel can be established.

promissory estoppel – doctrine that a promise will be enforced although it is not supported by consideration when the promisor should have reasonably expected that the promise would induce action or forbearance of a definite and substantial character on the part of the promised and injustice can be avoided only by enforcement of the promise.

CASE SUMMARY

Brits Rescued by Promissory Estoppel

FACTS: Portman Lamborghini, Ltd. (Portman), was owned by Chaplake Holdings, Ltd., a United Kingdom company, which was owned by David Jolliffe and David Lakeman as equal shareholders. Between 1984 and 1987, Portman sold approximately 30 new Lamborghinis each year through its exclusive concession contract with the car maker. It was then the largest Lamborghini dealer in the world since Lamborghini's production was just 250 cars per year. These cars sold at a retail price between $200,000 and $300,000. In 1987, Chrysler Corporation bought Lamborghini, and its chairman, Lee Iacocca, presented a plan to escalate production to 5,000 units within five years. The plan included the introduction of a new model, the P140, with a retail price of $70,000. Between 1987 and 1991, *all* of the Chrysler/Lamborghini top executives with whom Jolliffe and Lakeman and their top advisors came in contact provided the same message to them: Chrysler was committed to the Expansion Plan, and in order for Portman to retain its exclusive U.K. market, it must expand its operational capacity from 35 cars in 1987 to 400 cars by 1992. Accordingly, Portman acquired additional financing, staff, and facilities and

[12] U.C.C. §2-209(1).
[13] *Neuhoff v. Marvin Lumber and Cedar Co.,* 370 F.3d 197 (1st Cir. 2004).
[14] *Medistar Corp. v. Schmidt,* 267 S.W.3d 150 (Tex. App. 2008).

CASE SUMMARY

Continued

built a new distribution center. An economic downturn in the United States and major development and production problems at Lamborghini led Chrysler to reduce its expansion investment by two-thirds. Factory production delays eroded Portman's profitability and success, and it entered into receivership in April 1992. Suit was brought on behalf of the Portman and Chaplake entities on a promissory estoppel theory against Chrysler, a Delaware corporation.

DECISION: Judgment for Portman and Chaplake on the promissory estoppel theory. (1) A promise was made by Chrysler that the Lamborghini line would expand tenfold and that Portman would retain its exclusivity deal *only* if it expanded its operational capacity. (2) The promisor, Chrysler, should have reasonably expected that Portman would rely on this promise. (3) Lakeman and Jolliffe were given the same message and promise by *all* of the top executives involved, and it was therefore not unreasonable for them to rely upon the promises made by these executives and to undertake the detriment of major expansion activity that would have been unnecessary but for the Expansion Plan and the role they were promised. (4) The prevention of injustice is the "fundamental idea" underlying the doctrine of promissory estoppel, and injustice can be avoided in this case only by the enforcement of Chrysler's promise. Portman is entitled to £ 569,321 for its costs to implement its Expansion Plan, and Chaplake is entitled to £ 462,686 for its investment in Portman's expansion. [***Chrysler Corp. v. Chaplake Holdings, Ltd.,*** **822 A.2d 1024 (Del. 2003)**]

LawFlix

Baby Boom (1987) (PG)

Review the scene near the end of the movie when Diane Keaton is presented with an offer for the purchase of her company, Country Baby. List the elements of consideration that Food Giant is paying for the company. Explain what Ms. Keaton's consideration is in exchange.

MAKE THE CONNECTION

SUMMARY

A promise is not binding if there is no consideration for the promise. Consideration is what the promisor requires as the price for his promise. That price may be doing an act, refraining from the doing of an act, or merely promising to do or to refrain. In a bilateral contract, it is necessary to find that the promise of each party is supported by consideration. If either promise is not so supported, it is not binding, and the agreement of the parties is not a contract. Consequently, the agreement cannot be enforced. When a promise is the consideration, it must be a binding promise. The binding character of a promise is not affected by the circumstance that there is a condition precedent to the performance promised. A promise to do what one is already obligated to do is not consideration, although some exceptions are made. Such exceptions include the rendering of a partial performance or a modified performance accepted as a good-faith adjustment to a changed situation, a compromise and release of claims, a part-payment check, and a compromise of creditors. Because consideration is the price that is given to obtain the promise, past benefits conferred on the promisor cannot be consideration.

A promise to refrain from doing an act can be consideration. A promise to refrain from suing or asserting a particular claim can be consideration. When consideration is forbearance to assert a claim, it is immaterial whether the claim is valid as long as the claim has been asserted in the good-faith belief that it was valid.

When the promisor obtains the consideration specified for the promise, the law is not ordinarily concerned with the value or adequacy of that consideration.

Under the doctrine of promissory estoppel a court may enforce a promise lacking consideration where it is the only way to avoid injustice.

LEARNING OUTCOMES

After studying this chapter, you should be able to clearly explain:

A. General Principles—Consideration

LO.1   Explain what constitutes consideration
See the *Williams v. Ormsby* case, which determined that love and affection is not recognized as consideration, p. 306.
See the "bargained for exchange" example involving Beth and Kerry, p. 305.
See the "benefit-detriment" approach to consideration example, p. 305.
See the discussion on forbearance as consideration on p. 308.

B. Special Situations

LO.2   Distinguish between a "preexisting legal obligation" and "past consideration"
See the preexisting duty example involving Officer Rodgers on p. 310.
See the *Angel v. Murray* case involving a good-faith adjustment exception to the preexisting duty rule, p. 311.

See the example involving Fred O'Neal where he found out the past consideration is no consideration rule, p. 312.

LO.3   Explain why promises based on moral obligations lack consideration
See the example of the gratuitous deeds of Tom Snyder on p. 312.

C. Exceptions to The Laws of Consideration

LO.4   List the exceptions to the requirement of consideration
See the discussion on charitable subscriptions, the UCC, and promissory estoppel on p. 314.

LO.5   Explain the "fundamental idea" underlying promissory estoppel
See the *Chaplake Holdings* case where the court enforced Chrysler's promise in order to correct an injustice, pp. 314–315.

KEY TERMS

cancellation provision	forbearance	past consideration
composition of creditors	illusory promise	promissory estoppel
consideration		

QUESTIONS AND CASE PROBLEMS

1. Sarah's house caught on fire. Through the prompt assistance of her neighbor Odessa, the fire was quickly extinguished. In gratitude, Sarah promised to pay Odessa $1,000. Can Odessa enforce this promise?

2. William E. Story agreed to pay his nephew, William E. Story II, a large sum of money (roughly equivalent to $50,000 in 2007 dollars) "if he would refrain from drinking liquor, using tobacco, swearing, and playing cards or billiards for money until he should come to be 21 years of age." William II had been using tobacco and occasionally drank liquor but refrained from using these stimulants over several years until he was 21 and also lived up to the other requirements of his uncle's offer. Just after William II's 21st birthday, Story acknowledged that William II had fulfilled his part of the bargain and advised that the money would be invested for him with interest. Story died, and his executor, Sidway, refused to pay William II because he believed the contract between Story and William II was without consideration. Sidway asserted that Story received no benefit from William II's performance and William II suffered no detriment (in fact, by his refraining from the use of liquor and tobacco, William II was not harmed but benefited, Sidway asserted). Is there any theory of consideration that William II can rely on? How would you decide this case? [*Hamer v. Sidway,* 124 N.Y. 538]

3. Dale Dyer, who was employed by National By-Products, Inc., was seriously injured at work as the result of a job-related accident. He agreed to give up his right to sue the employer for damages in consideration of the employer's giving him a lifetime job. The employer later claimed that this agreement was not binding because Dyer's promise not to sue could not be consideration for the promise to employ on the ground that Dyer in fact had no right to sue. Dyer's only remedy was to make a claim under workers' compensation. Was the agreement binding? [*Dyer v. National By-Products, Inc.,* 380 N.W.2d 732 (Iowa)]

4. Charles Sanarwari retained Stan Gissel to prepare his income tax return for the year 2006. The parties agreed on a fee of $400. Charles had done a rough estimate based on last year's return and believed he would owe the IRS approximately $2,000. When Stan's work was completed, it turned out that Charles would receive a $2,321 tax refund. Stan explained how certain legitimate advantages were used to reduce Charles's tax obligation. Charles paid for Stan's services and was so pleased with the work that he promised to pay Stan an additional $400 for the excellent job on the tax return when he received his tax refund. Thereafter, Stan and Charles had a falling out over a golf tournament where Charles was late for his tee time and Stan started without him, causing Charles to lose an opportunity to win the club championship. Stan was not paid the $400 promised for doing an excellent job on the tax return, and he sued Charles as a matter of principle. Decide.

5. Medistar is a real estate development company specializing in the development of medical facilities. Dr. Schmidt, the team physician for the San Antonio Spurs basketball team, sought to develop "The Texas Center for Athletes" medical center next to the Spurs facility and urged Medistar to obtain the real estate and develop the project on his group's behalf. Medistar spent more than $1 million and thousands of man-hours on the project from 2000 to July 12, 2004 when Dr. Schmidt's new group of investors purchased the property next to the Spur's facility for the project; subsequently, Medistar was informed that it would have no role in the project. Medistar asserts that it relied on Dr. Schmidt's assurances that it would be the developer of the project—and after four years and the $1 million in time and expenses it spent, it is unconscionable to be excluded from the project. Dr. Schmidt and associates contend that Medistar has presented no contractual agreement tying it to any legal obligation to Medistar. Is there a viable legal theory available to Medistar? If so what is the remedy? [*Medistar v. Schmidt,* 267 S.W.3d 150 (Tex. App.)]

6. Fedun rented a building to Gomer, who did business under the name of Mike's Cafe. Later, Gomer was about to sell the business to Brown and requested Fedun to release him from his liability under the lease. Fedun agreed to do so. Brown sold the business shortly thereafter. The balance of the rent due by Gomer under the original lease agreement was not paid, and Fedun sued Gomer on the rent claim. Could he collect after having released Gomer? [*Fedun v. Mike's Cafe*, 204 A.2d 776 (Pa. Super.)]

7. Alexander Proudfoot Co. was in the business of devising efficiency systems for industry. It told Sanitary Linen Service Co. that it could provide an improved system for Sanitary Linen that would save Sanitary Linen money. It made a contract with Sanitary Linen to provide a money-saving system. The system was put into operation, and Proudfoot was paid the amount due under the contract. The system failed to work and did not save money. Sanitary Linen sued to get the money back. Was it entitled to do so? [*Sanitary Linen Service Co. v. Alexander Proudfoot Co.*, 435 F.2d 292 (5th Cir.)]

8. Sears, Roebuck and Co. promised to give Forrer permanent employment. Forrer sold his farm at a loss to take the job. Shortly after beginning work, he was discharged by Sears, which claimed that the contract could be terminated at will. Forrer claimed that promissory estoppel prevented Sears from terminating the contract. Was he correct? [*Forrer v. Sears, Roebuck & Co.*, 153 N.W.2d 587 (Wis.)]

9. Kemp leased a gas filling station from Baehr. Kemp, who was heavily indebted to Penn-O-Tex Oil Corp., transferred to it his right to receive payments on all claims. When Baehr complained that the rent was not paid, he was assured by the corporation that the rent would be paid to him. Baehr did not sue Kemp for the overdue rent but later sued the corporation. The defense was raised that there was no consideration for the promise of the corporation. Decide. [*Baehr v. Penn-O-Tex Corp.*, 104 N.W.2d 661 (Minn.)]

10. Bogart owed several debts to Security Bank & Trust Co. and applied to the bank for a loan to pay the debts. The bank's employee stated that

he would take the application for the loan to the loan committee and "within two or three days, we ought to have something here, ready for you to go with." The loan was not made. The bank sued Bogart for his debts. He filed a counterclaim on the theory that the bank had broken its contract to make a loan to him and that promissory estoppel prevented the bank from going back on what the employee had said. Was this counterclaim valid?

11. Kelsoe worked for International Wood Products, Inc., for a number of years. One day Hernandez, a director and major stockholder of the company, promised Kelsoe that the corporation would give her 5 percent of the company's stock. This promise was never kept, and Kelsoe sued International for breach of contract. Had the company broken its contract? [*Kelsoe v. International Wood Products, Inc.*, 588 So.2d 877 (Ala.)]

12. Kathy left her classic 1978 Volkswagen convertible at Freddie's Service Station, requesting a "tune-up." When she returned that evening, Freddie's bill was $374. Kathy stated that Firestone and Sears advertise tune-ups for $70, and she asked Freddie, "How can you justify this bill?" Freddie responded, "Carburator work." Kathy refused to pay the bill and left. That evening, when the station closed, she took her other set of keys and removed her car, after placing a check in the station's mail slot. The check was made out to Freddie's Service Station for $200 and stated on its face: "This check is in full payment of my account with you regarding the tune-up today on my 1978 Volkswagen convertible." Freddie cashed the check in order to meet his business expenses and then sued Kathy for the difference owed. What result?

13. On the death of their mother, the children of Jane Smith gave their interests in their mother's estate to their father in consideration of his payment of $1 to each of them and his promise to leave them the property on his death. The father died without leaving them the property. The children sued their father's second wife to obtain the property in accordance with the agreement. The second wife claimed that the agreement was not a binding contract because

the amount of $1 and future gifts given for the children's interests were so trivial and uncertain. Decide.

14. Radio Station KSCS broadcast a popular music program. It announced that it would pay $25,000 to any listener who detected that it did not play three consecutive songs. Steve Jennings listened to and heard a program in which two songs were followed by a commercial program. He claimed the $25,000. The station refused to pay on the ground that there was no consideration for its promise to pay that amount. Was the station liable? [*Jennings v. Radio Station KSCS,* 708 S.W.2d 60 (Tex. App.)]

15. Hoffman wanted to acquire a franchise for a Red Owl grocery store. (Red Owl was a corporation that maintained a system of chain stores.) An agent of Red Owl informed Hoffman and his wife that if they would sell their bakery in Wautoma, acquire a certain tract of land in Chilton (another Wisconsin city), and put up $6,000, they would be given a franchise. In reliance on the agent's promise, Hoffman sold his business and acquired the land in Chilton, but he was never granted a franchise. He and his wife sued Red Owl. Red Owl raised the defense that there had been only an assurance that Hoffman would receive a franchise, but because there was no promise supported by consideration, there was no binding contract to give him a franchise. Decide. [*Hoffman v. Red Owl Stores, Inc.,* 133 N.W.2d 267 (Wis.)]

© Manuel Gutjahr/iStockphoto.com

Chapter 16

Legality and Public Policy

learningoutcomes

After studying this chapter, you should be able to

LO.1 Explain the general contract principles on "illegality"

LO.2 Explain the implied obligation on all parties of good faith and fair dealing

LO.3 Understand that it is only in unusual situations that a contract provision will be unenforceable because it is unconscionable

LO.4 Explain the rationale for requiring licenses to carry on as a business, trade, or profession

LO.5 Distinguish between noncompete clauses after the sale of a business and noncompete clauses in employment contracts court will not enforce a contract if it is illegal, contrary to public policy, or unconscionable.

A. General Principles

An agreement is illegal either when its formation or performance is a crime or a tort or when it is contrary to public policy or unconscionable.

1. Effect of Illegality

Ordinarily, an illegal agreement is void. When an agreement is illegal, the parties are usually not entitled to the aid of the courts. Examples of illegal contracts where the courts have left the parties where they found them include a liquor store owner not being allowed to bring suit for money owed for goods (liquor) sold and delivered on credit in violation of statute and an unlicensed home improvement contractor not being allowed to enforce his contract for progress payments due him. If the illegal agreement has not been performed, neither party can sue the other to obtain performance or damages. If the agreement has been performed, neither party can sue the other to obtain damages or to set the agreement aside.[1]

CASE SUMMARY

The Illegal Paralegal

FACTS: Brian Neiman was involved in the illegal practice of law for over seven years. Having been found guilty of illegally practicing law, he sought to collect disability benefits under his disability insurance policy with Provident Life due to an alleged bipolar disorder, the onset of which occurred during the pendency of criminal and bar proceedings against him. Neiman contends that his bipolar disorder prevents him from working as a paralegal. Provident contends that Neiman should not be indemnified for the loss of income generated from his illegal practice of law.

DECISION: Because all of Neiman's income was derived from the unlawful practice of law in the seven years preceding his claim, as a matter of public policy, a court will not enforce a disability benefits policy that compensates him for his loss of income he was not entitled to earn. Neiman's own wrongdoing caused the contract to be void. Accordingly, Neiman was *in pari delicto* [equally guilty], if not more at fault than the insurance company, in causing the contract to be void and will recover neither benefits nor the premiums he paid. The court must leave the parties where it found them. [***Neiman v. Provident Life & Accident Insurance Co.***, **217 F. Supp. 2d 1281 (S.D. Fla. 2002)**]

Even if a contract appears to be legal on its face, it may be unenforceable if it was entered into for an illegal purpose. **For Example,** if zoning regulations in the special-purpose district of Washington, D.C., require that only a professional can lease space in a given building, and the rental agent suggests that two nonprofessionals take out the lease in their attorney's name, but all parties realize

[1] *Sabia v. Mattituck Inlet Marina, Inc.,* 805 N.Y.S.2d 346 (A.D. 2005).

that the premises will be used only by the nonprofessionals, then the lease in question is illegal and unenforceable.[2]

2. Exceptions to Effect of Illegality

To avoid hardship, exceptions are made to the rules stated in Section 1.

(A) Protection of One Party. When the law that the agreement violates is intended to protect one of the parties, that party may seek relief. **For Example,** when, in order to protect the public, the law forbids the issuance of securities by certain classes of corporations, a person who has purchased them may recover the money paid.

(B) Unequal Guilt. When the parties are not ***in pari delicto***—equally guilty—the least guilty party is granted relief when public interest is advanced by doing so. **For Example,** when a statute is adopted to protect one of the parties to a transaction, such as a usury law adopted to protect borrowers, the person to be protected will not be deemed to be *in pari delicto* with the wrongdoer when entering into a transaction that the statute prohibits.

in pari delicto – equally guilty; used in reference to a transaction as to which relief will not be granted to either party because both are equally guilty of wrongdoing.

3. Partial Illegality

An agreement may involve the performance of several promises, some of which are illegal and some legal. The legal parts of the agreement may be enforced provided that they can be separated from the parts that are illegal.

When the illegal provision of a contract may be ignored without defeating the contract's basic purpose, a court will merely ignore the illegal provision and enforce the balance of the contract. Consequently, when a provision for the payment of an attorney's fee in a car rental agreement was illegal because a local statute prohibited it, the court would merely ignore the fee provision and enforce the balance of the contract.[3]

If a contract is susceptible to two interpretations, one legal and the other illegal, the court will assume that the legal meaning was intended unless the contrary is clearly indicated.

4. Crimes and Civil Wrongs

An agreement is illegal, and therefore void, when it calls for the commission of any act that constitutes a crime. To illustrate, one cannot enforce an agreement by which the other party is to commit an assault, steal property, burn a house, or kill a person. A contract to obtain equipment for committing a crime is illegal and cannot be enforced. Thus, a contract to manufacture and sell illegal slot machines is void.

An agreement that calls for the commission of a civil wrong is also illegal and void. Examples are agreements to slander a third person; defraud another; infringe another's patent, trademark, or copyright; or fix prices.

5. Good Faith and Fairness

Every contract has an implied obligation that neither party shall do anything that will have the effect of destroying or injuring the right of the other party to receive the

---

[2] *McMahon v. A, H, & B,* 728 A.2d 656 (D.C. 1999).
[3] *Harbour v. Arelco, Inc.,* 678 N.E.2d 381 (Ind. 1997).

good faith – absence of knowledge of any defects or problems.

fruits of the contract. This means that in every contract there exists an implied covenant of **good faith** and fair dealing. **For Example,** Katy Lesser entered into a 10-year lease of retail space to operate a natural food store in South Burlington, Vermont. Her business prospered and in April of 1999 she signed a lease for additional space. For five years, the landlord continually rebuffed her efforts to meet and discuss plans to renovate the 1999 space to expand the grocery store, motivated solely by a desire to pressure the tenant to pay a portion of his legal fees in an unrelated zoning case. The court found that the landlord breached the obligation of good faith and fair dealing, causing the 1999 space to be essentially unusable from 1999 to 2004. The court awarded the tenant the rent she paid for this period less a storage fee adjustment.[4]

6. Unconscionable Clauses

Ordinarily, a court will not consider whether a contract is fair or unfair, is wise or foolish, or operates unequally between the parties. **For Example,** the Kramper Family Farm agreed to sell 17.59 acres of land to Dakota Industrial Development, Inc. (DID), for $35,000 per acre if the buyer constructed a paved road along the property by December 31. The contract also provided that if the road was not completed by the date set forth in the contract, the price per acre would be $45,000. When the road was not completed by the December 31 date, Family Farm sued DID for the additional $10,000 per acre. DID defended that to apply the contract according to its plain language would create an unconscionable result and was an unenforceable penalty provision contrary to public policy. The court refused to allow DID to escape its contractual obligations on the pretext of unconscionability and public policy arguments. The parties are at liberty to contract as they see fit, the court concluded, and generally, a court will not inquire into the adequacy of consideration inasmuch as the value of property is a matter of personal judgment by the parties to the contract. In this case, the price consisted of either $45,000 per acre, or $35,000 per acre with the road by a certain date.[5]

However, in certain unusual situations, the law may hold a contract provision unenforceable because it is too harsh or oppressive to one of the parties. This principle may be applied to invalidate a clause providing for the payment by one party of an excessive penalty on the breaking of a contract or a provision inserted by the dominant party that it shall not be liable for the consequences of intentional torts, fraud, or gross negligence. This principle is extended in connection with the sale of goods to provide that "if the court … finds the contract or any clause of the contract to have been unconscionable at the time it was made, the court may refuse to enforce the contract, or it may enforce the remainder of the contract without the unconscionable clause, or it may so limit the application of any unconscionable clause as to avoid any unconscionable result."[6]

(A) WHAT CONSTITUTES UNCONSCIONABILITY? A provision in a contract that gives what the court believes is too much of an advantage over a buyer may be held void as unconscionable.

[4] *Century Partners, LP v. Lesser Goldsmith Enterprises,* 958 A.2d 627 (Vt. 2008).
[5] *Kramper Family Farm v. Dakota Industrial Development, Inc.,* 603 N.W.2d 463 (Neb. App. 1999).
[6] U.C.C. §2-302(1).

(B) Determination of Unconscionability. Some jurisdictions analyze unconscionability as having two separate elements: procedural and substantive. Both elements must be present for a court to refuse to enforce a contract provision. Other jurisdictions analyze unconscionability by considering the doctrine of adhesion and whether the clause in question is unduly oppressive.

Procedural unconscionability has to do with matters of freedom of assent resulting from inequality of bargaining power and the absence of real negotiations and meaningful choice or a surprise resulting from hiding a disputed term in an unduly long document or fine print. Companywide standardized form contracts imposed on a take-it-or-leave-it basis by a party with superior bargaining strength are called **contracts of adhesion**, and they may sometimes be deemed procedurally unconscionable.

Substantive unconscionability focuses on the actual terms of the contract itself. Such unconscionability is indicated when the contract terms are so one-sided as to shock the conscience or are so extreme as to appear unconscionable according to the mores and business practices of the time and place.

The U.S. Supreme Court has made clear that arbitration is an acceptable forum for the resolution of employment disputes between employees and their employers, including employment-related claims based on federal and state statutes.[7] The controlling arbitration agreement language is commonly devised and implemented by the employer. Under the Federal Arbitration Act (FAA), the employer can obtain a court order to stay court proceedings and compel arbitration according to the terms of the controlling arbitration agreement. The Supreme Court also made clear that in agreeing to arbitration of a statutory claim, a party does not forgo substantive rights afforded by the statute. In a growing number of court decisions, in effect employers are finding that courts will not enforce arbitration agreements in which the employer has devised an arbitration agreement that functions as a thumb on the employer's side of the scale.[8]

When a court finds that a contract or any clause of a contract was unconscionable at the time it was made, it may enforce the remainder of the contract without the unconscionable clause or refuse to enforce the entire agreement if the agreement is permeated by unconscionability. **For Example,** Sandra Menefee sued Geographic Expeditions, Inc. (GeoEx), for the wrongful death of her son while on a GeoEx expedition up Mount Kilimanjaro. GeoEx moved to compel arbitration under the parties' limitation of liability contract. The arbitration provision was found by the court to be procedurally and substantively unconscionable. GeoEx contended that the court should have severed the objectionable provisions and enforced the remainder of the arbitration clause. The court refused to do so because GeoEx designed its arbitration clause to impose arbitration not simply as an alternative to litigation, but as an inferior forum that would give it an advantage. In addition to limiting the plaintiffs' recovery, the agreement required them to indemnify GeoEx for its legal costs and fees if they pursued any claims covered by the release agreement, compounded by the requirement that plaintiffs pay half of any mediation fees and mediate and arbitrate in San Francisco, GeoEx's choice of venue, far from the plaintiffs' home in Colorado.[9]

contract of adhesion— contract offered by a dominant party to a party with inferior bargaining power on a take-it-or-leave-it basis.

[7] *Gilmer v. Interstate/Johnson Lane Corp.,* 500 U.S. 20 (1991); *Circuit City Stores, Inc. v. Adams,* 532 U.S. 105 (2001).
[8] See *Vassi/Kouska v. Woodfield Nissan Inc.,* 830 N.E.2d 619 (Ill. App. 2005).
[9] *Lhotka v. Geographic Expeditions, Inc.,* 104 Cal. Rptr. 3d 844 (Cal. App. 2010).

B. Agreements Affecting Public Welfare

Agreements that may harm the public welfare are condemned as contrary to public policy and are not binding. Agreements that interfere with public service or the duties of public officials, obstruct legal process, or discriminate against classifications of individuals may be considered detrimental to public welfare and, as such, are not enforceable.

7. Agreements Contrary to Public Policy

A given agreement may not violate any statute but may still be so offensive to society that the courts feel that enforcing the contract would be contrary to public policy.

public policy – certain objectives relating to health, morals, and integrity of government that the law seeks to advance by declaring invalid any contract that conflicts with those objectives even though there is no statute expressly declaring such a contract illegal.

Public policy cannot be defined precisely but is loosely described as protection from that which tends to be injurious to the public or contrary to the public good or which violates any established interest of society. Contracts that may be unenforceable as contrary to public policy frequently relate to the protection of the public welfare, health, or safety; to the protection of the person; and to the protection of recognized social institutions. **For Example,** a woman entered into a services contract with a male in exchange for financial support. The record disclosed, however, that the association between the parties was one founded upon the exchange of money for sex. The court determined that the agreement for financial support in exchange for illicit sexual relations was violative of public policy and thus was unenforceable.[10] Courts are cautious in invalidating a contract on the ground that it is contrary to public policy because courts recognize that, on the one hand, they are applying a very vague standard and, on the other hand, they are restricting the freedom of the contracting parties to contract freely as they choose.[11]

8. Gambling, Wagers, and Lotteries

lottery – any plan by which a consideration is given for a chance to win a prize; it consists of three elements: (1) there must be a payment of money or something of value for an opportunity to win, (2) a prize must be available, and (3) the prize must be offered by lot or chance.

Gambling contracts are illegal. Largely as a result of the adoption of antigambling statutes, wagers or bets are generally illegal. Private **lotteries** involving the three elements of prize, chance, and consideration (or similar affairs of chance) are also generally held illegal. In many states, public lotteries (lotteries run by a state government) have been legalized by statute. Raffles are usually regarded as lotteries.

CASE SUMMARY

Horseplay Prohibited

FACTS: Robert Bovard contracted to sell American Horse Enterprises, Inc., to James Ralph. When Ralph did not make payments when due, Bovard brought suit against him. The trial judge raised the question whether the contract was void for illegality. American Horse Enterprises was predominantly engaged in manufacturing devices for smoking marijuana and tobacco, and to a lesser degree in manufacturing jewelry. When the contract was made, there was no statute prohibiting the manufacture of any of these items, but there was a statute making it illegal to possess, use, or transfer marijuana.

---

[10] *Anonymous v. Anonymous*, 740 N.Y.S.2d 341 (App. Div. 2002).
[11] *Beacon Hill Civic Ass'n v. Ristorante Toscano, Inc.*, 662 N.E.2d 1015 (Mass. 1996).

CASE SUMMARY

Continued

DECISION: Although the question of illegality had not been raised by the parties, the trial judge had the duty to question the validity of the contract when it appeared that the contract might be illegal. Although there was no statute expressly making the contract illegal, the statute prohibiting the possession and sale of marijuana manifested a public policy against anything that would further the use of marijuana. It was therefore against public policy to make the devices used in smoking marijuana or to sell a business that engaged in such manufacture. The sales contract was therefore contrary to public policy and void and could not be enforced. [*Bovard v. American Horse Enterprises, Inc.,* 247 Cal. Rptr. 340 (Cal. App. 1988)]

In some states, bingo games, lotteries, and raffles are legalized by statute when the funds raised are used for a charitable purpose.

Sales promotion schemes calling for the distribution of property according to chance among the purchasers of goods are held illegal as lotteries without regard to whether the scheme is called a *guessing contest,* a *raffle,* or a *gift.*

Giveaway plans and games are lawful so long as it is not necessary to buy anything or give anything of value to participate. If participation is free, the element of consideration is lacking, and there is no lottery.

An activity is not gambling when the result is solely or predominantly a matter of skill. In contrast, it is gambling when the result is solely a matter of luck. Rarely is any activity 100 percent skill or 100 percent luck.

C. REGULATION OF BUSINESS

Local, state, and national laws regulate a wide variety of business activities and practices.

9. Effect of Violation

Whether an agreement made in connection with business conducted in violation of the law is binding or void depends on how strongly opposed the public policy is to the prohibited act. Some courts take the view that the agreement is not void unless the statute expressly specifies this. In some instances, a statute expressly preserves the validity of the contract. **For Example,** if someone fails to register a fictitious name under which a business is conducted, the violator, after registering the name as required by statute, is permitted to sue on a contract made while illegally conducting business.

10. Statutory Regulation of Contracts

To establish uniformity or to protect one of the parties to a contract, statutes frequently provide that contracts of a given class must follow a statutory model or must contain specified provisions. **For Example,** statutes commonly specify that particular clauses must be included in insurance policies to protect the persons insured and their beneficiaries. Other statutes require that contracts executed in connection with credit buying and loans contain particular provisions designed to protect the debtor.

Consumer protection legislation gives the consumer the right to rescind the contract in certain situations. Laws relating to truth in lending, installment sales, and home improvement contracts commonly require that an installment-sale contract specify the cash price, the down payment, the trade-in value (if any), the cash balance, the insurance costs, and the interest and finance charges.

CPA

11. Licensed Callings or Dealings

Statutes frequently require that a person obtain a license, certificate, or diploma before practicing certain professions, such as law and medicine.[12] A license may also be required before carrying on a particular business or trade, such as that of a real estate broker, stockbroker, hotel keeper, or pawnbroker.

If a license is required to protect the public from unqualified persons, a contract made by an unlicensed person is unenforceable. **For Example,** a corporation that does not hold a required real estate broker's license cannot sue to recover fees for services as a broker. An unlicensed insurance broker who cannot recover a fee because of the absence of a license cannot evade the statutory requirement by having a friend who is a licensed broker bill for the services and collect the payment for him.

CASE SUMMARY

How Much for a Brokerage License? How Much Commission Was Lost?

FACTS: Thompson Halbach & Associates, Inc., an Arizona corporation, entered into an agreement with Meteor Motors, Inc., the owner of Palm Beach Acura, to find a buyer for the dealership, and Meteor agreed to pay a 5 percent commission based on the closing price of the sale. Working out of Scottsdale, Arizona, Thompson solicited potential Florida purchasers for the Florida business by phone, fax, and e-mail. Among those contacted was Craig Zinn Automotive Group, which ultimately purchased Palm Beach Acura from Meteor Motors for $5,000,000. Thompson was not paid its $250,000 commission and brought suit against Meteor for breach of contract. Meteor defended that Thompson was an unlicensed broker and that a state statute declares a contract for a commission with an unlicensed broker to be invalid. Thompson responded that the Florida state statue did not apply because it worked out of Scottsdale.

DECISION: Judgment for Meteor. The Florida statute clearly applies to a foreign broker who provides brokerage activities in Florida. Thompson solicited potential Florida purchasers for the Florida business and that purchaser was a Florida corporation. [*Meteor Motors v. Thompson Halbach & Associates*, 914 So.2d 479 (Fla. App. 2005)]

In some states an unlicensed contractor can neither enforce a home improvement contract against an owner, nor seek recovery in *quantum meruit*. **For Example,** a contractor who performed work on Adam Gottbetter's apartment in New York City and was not paid for its work was barred from pursuing its claim against the owner.[13]

---

[12] *Hakimi v. Cantwell*, 855 N.Y.S.2d 273 (App. Div. 2008).
[13] *Orchid Construction Corp. v. Gottbetter*, 932 N.Y.S.2d 100 (A.D. 2011).

CPA

12. Contracts in Restraint of Trade

An agreement that unreasonably restrains trade is illegal and void on the ground that it is contrary to public policy. Such agreements take many forms, such as a combination to create a monopoly or to obtain a corner on the market or an association of merchants to increase prices. In addition to the illegality of the agreement based on general principles of law, statutes frequently declare monopolies illegal and subject the parties to various civil and criminal penalties.[14]

CPA

13. Agreements Not to Compete

In the absence of a valid restrictive covenant, the seller of a business may compete with the buyer, or an ex-employee may solicit customers of the former employer.

A noncompetition covenant may be held invalid because of vagueness concerning the duration and geographic area of the restriction.[15] Moreover, if the agreement not to compete is not properly executed in accordance with state law, it will not be enforced. **For Example,** Holly Martinez worked for Avis Rent-A-Car at the New Bern, North Carolina, airport. When hired, she printed her name on the top of the form containing an agreement not to compete but did not sign it. On December 17, she resigned her position to return to school, saying that she planned to get a part-time job. The next day, she began working for Hertz Rent-A-Car at the counter adjacent to the Avis counter. Avis was unsuccessful in obtaining a restraining order to prevent Holly from working for its competitor because the agreement was not signed as required by state law.[16]

CPA

(A) SALE OF BUSINESS. When a going business is sold, it is commonly stated in the contract that the seller shall not go into the same or a similar business again within a certain geographic area or for a certain period of time, or both. In early times, such agreements were held void because they deprived the public of the service of the person who agreed not to compete, impaired the latter's means of earning a livelihood, reduced competition, and exposed the public to monopoly. To modern courts, the question is whether, under the circumstances, the restriction imposed on one party is reasonably necessary to protect the other party. If the restriction is reasonable, it is valid and enforceable. **For Example,** when Scott Gaddy, the majority stockholder of GWC Insurance Brokers, sold his business to Alliant for $4.1 million he agreed to refrain from competing in the insurance business in California for five years. Under California law, contracts not to compete are void, except for noncompetition covenants in connection with the sale of a business. The reason for the exception is to prevent the seller from depriving the buyer of the full value of the acquisition, including the sold company's goodwill. The court enforced the covenant against Gaddy.[17]

(B) EMPLOYMENT CONTRACT. Restrictions to prevent competition by a former employee are held valid when reasonable and necessary to protect the interest of the former employer. **For Example,** a noncompete clause executed by Dr. Samuel Keeley that prohibited his "establishing a competing cardiovascular surgery practice within a 75-mile radius of Albany, Georgia, for a period of two years following the date of

---

[14] Sherman Antitrust Act, 15 U.S.C. §§1–7; Clayton Act, 15 U.S.C. §§12–27; Federal Trade Commission Act, 15 U.S.C. §§41–58.
[15] *Vukovich v. Coleman*, 789 N.E.2d 520 (Ind. App. 2003).
[16] *New Hanover Rent-A-Car, Inc. v. Martinez*, 525 S.E.2d 487 (N.C. App. 2000).
[17] 72 Cal. Rptr. 3d 259 (Cal. App. 2008).

termination" was upheld in court and did not include more territory than necessary to protect the professional corporation's business interests.[18]

Public policy requires that noncompetition covenants be strictly construed in favor of freedom of action of the employee.[19] A restrictive covenant is not binding when it places a restriction on the employee that is broader than reasonably necessary to protect the employer. **For Example,** Illinois manufacturer Arcor's noncompete clause, which had a restricted area of "the United States and Canada" precluding competition by a former employee for a one-year period, was found to be unenforceable as an industrywide ban that constituted a "blanket prohibition on competition."[20] In determining the validity of a restrictive covenant binding an employee, the court balances the aim of protecting the legitimate interests of the employer with the right of the employee to follow gainful employment and provide services required by the public and other employers.

Thinking Things Through

Noncompete Clauses, Cause for Concern?

Some 10 states do not enforce noncompete clauses in employment contracts, according to the research of Matt Marx who has dedicated his doctoral studies at Harvard to this topic. The states are (from west to east): California, Washington, Nevada, Montana, North Dakota, Minnesota, Oklahoma, West Virginia, and Connecticut. (New York and Oregon have significantly limited their applicability). Marx had naively signed a two-year noncompete agreement out of MIT at SpeechWorks, a voice recognition start-up, and when he wanted to leave and continue in the voice recognition field, his options were to sit out the two-year noncompete period or go to work at a California firm, which he did. He is now researching whether enforcing noncompetes in a state can spur inventors, engineers, and entrepreneurs to move elsewhere to pursue development of their ideas.*

Does a state's innovation suffer when noncompete clauses handcuff employees to an employer, or force employees to take an unpaid leave for the noncompete period before continuing in their field with a new or start-up employer? THINKING THINGS THROUGH, prospective employees should carefully consider the impact noncompetes would have on their lives, and if they must sign one, carefully negotiate its duration and scope.**

*See Scott Kirsner, "Why 'Noncompete' Means 'Don't Thrive,'" *Boston Globe*, December 30, 2007, E-1; Scott Kirsner, "Start-ups Stifled by Noncompetes," *Boston Globe*, June 21, 2009, G-1.
**For a comprehensive study of the strength of noncompetition enforcement rankings by state, see Norman D. Bishara, "Fifty Ways to Leave Your Employer: Relative Enforcement of Covenants Not to Compete, Trends and Implications for Employee Mobility Policy," 13 *U. Pa. J. Bus. L.* 751 (2011).

(c) EFFECT OF INVALIDITY. When a restriction of competition agreed to by the parties is invalid because its scope as to time or geographic area is too great, how does this affect the contract? Some courts trim the restrictive covenant down to a scope they deem reasonable and require the parties to abide by that revision.[21] This rule is nicknamed the "blue-pencil rule." **For Example,** Julie Murray signed a noncompete agreement, which was validly assigned to the purchaser of the Accounting Center of Lucas County, Inc. When the new owner changed from an hourly wage to commission pay for her tax preparation work, she objected and was terminated. The court found the 24-month noncompete restriction exceeded what was reasonable to

---

[18] *Keeley v. CSA, P.C.*, 510 S.E.2d 880 (Ga. App. 1999).
[19] Noncompetition covenants are not valid in California. However, confidentiality agreements protecting trade secrets are enforceable in that state.
[20] *Arcor, Inc. v. Haas*, 842 N.E.2d 265 (Ill. App. 2005).
[21] *Unisource Worldwide, Inc. v. Valenti*, 196 F. Supp. 2d 269 (E.D.N.Y. 2002).

protect the employer's legitimate business interests, and modified the time period to one year.[22] In the *Arcor* case, the court refused to "blue pencil" the covenant because to render the clause reasonable, the court would in effect be writing a new agreement, which is inappropriate.[23]

Ethics & the Law

William Stern and his wife were unable to have children because the wife suffered from multiple sclerosis and pregnancy posed a substantial health risk. Stern's family had been killed in the Holocaust, and he had a strong desire to continue his bloodline.

The Sterns entered into a surrogacy contract with Mary Beth Whitehead through the Infertility Center of New York (ICNY). William Stern and the Whiteheads (husband and wife) signed a contract for Mary Beth to be artificially inseminated and carry Stern's child to term, for which Stern was to pay Mary Beth $10,000 and ICNY $7,500.

Mary Beth was successfully artificially inseminated in 1985, and Baby M was born on March 27, 1986. To avoid publicity, the parents of Baby M were listed as "Mr. and Mrs. Whitehead," and the baby was called Sara Elizabeth Whitehead. On March 30, 1986, Mary Beth turned Baby M over to the Sterns at their home. They renamed the little girl Melissa.

Mary Beth became emotionally distraught and was unable to eat or sleep. The Sterns were so frightened by her behavior that they allowed her to take Baby M for one week to help her adjust. The Whiteheads took the baby and traveled throughout the East, staying in 20 different hotels and motels. Florida authorities found Baby M with Mary Beth's parents and returned her to the Sterns.

Mary Beth said the contract was one to buy a baby and was against public policy and therefore void. She also argued that the contract violated state laws on adoption and the severance of parental rights. The Sterns brought an action to have the contract declared valid and custody awarded to them.

Should the contract be valid or void? What types of behavior would be encouraged if the contract were declared valid? Is it ethical to "rent a womb"? Is it ethical to sell a child? See *In re Baby M*, **537 A.2d 15 (N.J. 1988).**

Other courts refuse to apply the blue-pencil rule and hold that the restrictive covenant is void or that the entire contract is void.[24] There is also authority that a court should refuse to apply the blue-pencil rule when the restrictive covenant is manifestly unfair and would virtually keep the employee from earning a living.

CASE SUMMARY

Overlybroad and Unenforceable

FACTS: Justin Shaffer while an employee of the Home Paramount Pest Control Companies Inc. (Home Paramount) signed an employment agreement (the Provision) providing that:

> *The Employee will not engage directly or indirectly or concern himself/herself in any manner whatsoever in the carrying on or conducting the business of exterminating, pest control, termite control and/or fumigation services as an owner, agent, servant, representative, or employee, and/or as a member of a partnership and/or as an officer, director or stockholder of any corporation, or in any manner whatsoever, in any city, cities, county or counties in the state(s) in which the Employee works and/or in which the*

[22] *Murray v. Accounting Center of Lucas County, Inc.*, 898 N.E.2d 89 (Ohio App. 2008).

[23] *Arcor, Inc. v. Haas*, 842 N.E.2d 265 (Ill. App. 2005).

[24] *SWAT 24 v. Bond*, 759 So.2d 1047 (La. App. 2000). Under California law, any "contract by which anyone is restrained from engaging in a lawful profession, trade or business is to that extent void." Cal B&P Code §16600. A noncompete provision is permitted, however, when "necessary to protect the employer's trade secrets." See *Lotona v. Aetna U.S. Healthcare Inc.*, 82 F. Supp. 2d 1089 (C.D. Cal. 1999), where Aetna was liable for wrongful termination when it fired a California employee for refusing to sign a noncompete agreement.

CASE SUMMARY

Continued

Employee was assigned during the two (2) years next preceding the termination of the Employment Agreement and for a period of two (2) years from and after the date upon which he/she shall cease for any reason whatsoever to be an employee of [Home Paramount].

Shaffer resigned from Home Paramount in 2009 and became an employee of Connor's Termite and Pest Control Inc. Home Paramount sued Shaffer and Connor's, claiming that Shaffer's employment by Connor's violated the provision. The defendants contended the provision was overboard and unenforceable.

DECISION: A noncompetition provision is enforceable if it "is narrowly drawn to protect the employer's legitimate business interest, is not unduly burdensome on the employee's ability to earn a living, and is not against public policy." The employer bears the burden of proving each of these factors. When evaluating whether the employer has met that burden a court considers together the "function, geographic scope, and duration" elements of the restriction. In this case, the provision prohibits Shaffer from working for Connor's or any other business in the pest control industry in any capacity. It bars him from engaging even indirectly, or concerning himself in any manner whatsoever, in the pest control business, even as a passive stockholder of a publicly traded international conglomerate with a pest control subsidiary. The clear overbreadth of the function here cannot be saved by the narrow tailoring of geographic scope and duration. The provision is therefore unenforceable. [***Home Paramount Pest Control Companies, Inc. v. Shaffer*, 718 S.E.2d 762 (Va. 2011)]**

14. Usurious Agreements

usury – lending money at an interest rate that is higher than the maximum rate allowed by law.

Usury is committed when money is loaned at a higher rate of interest than the law allows. Most states prohibit by statute charging more than a stated amount of interest. These statutes provide a maximum annual contract rate of interest that can be exacted under the law of a given state. In many states, the usury law does not apply to loans made to corporations.

Thinking Things Through

Legality and Public Policy

Karl Llewellyn, the principal drafter of the law that governs nearly all sales of goods in the United States—the Uniform Commercial Code (UCC)—once wrote, "Covert tools are never reliable tools." He was referring to unfairness in a contract or between the contracting parties.

The original intent of declaring certain types of contracts void because of issues of imbalance was based in equity. Courts stepped in to help parties who found themselves bound under agreements that were not fair and open in both their written terms and the communications between the parties. One contracts scholar wrote that the original intent could be described as courts stepping in to help "presumptive sillies like sailors and heirs…" and others who, if not crazy, are "pretty peculiar."

However, as the sophistication of contracts and commercial transactions increased, the importance of accuracy, honesty, and fairness increased. Unconscionability is a contracts defense that permits courts to intervene where contracts, if enforced, would "affront the sense of decency." UNCONSCIONABILITY is a term of ethics or moral philosophy used by courts to prevent exploitation and fraud.

When a lender incurs expenses in making a loan, such as the cost of appraising property or making a credit investigation of the borrower, the lender will require the borrower to pay the amount of such expenses. Any fee charged by a lender that goes beyond the reasonable expense of making the loan constitutes "interest" for the purposes of determining whether the transaction is usurious.[25]

Penalites for violating usury laws vary from state to state, with a number of states restricting the lender to the recovery of the loan but no interest whatsoever; other states allow recovery of the loan principal and interest up to the maximum contract rate. Some states also impose a penalty on the lender such as the payment of double the interest paid on a usurious loan.

CASE SUMMARY

Would You Recommend Karen Canzoneri as an Investment Advisor?

FACTS: Karen Canzoneri entered into two agreements with Howard Pinchuck. Under the first agreement, Canzoneri advanced $50,000 to be repaid at 12 percent per month for 12 consecutive months "as an investment profit." The second agreement required "$36,000 to be repaid on or before 6/1/01 with an investment profit of $36,000, total being $72,000." The annualized rate of return for the first transaction was 144 percent and for the second transaction was 608 percent. The civil penalty for violating the state's maximum interest rate of 25 percent per annum is forfeiture of the entire principal amount. Canzoneri contends that the transactions were investments not subject to the usury law.

DECISION: Judgment for Pinchuck. The four elements of a usurious transaction are present: (1) the transaction was a loan, (2) the money loaned required that it be returned, (3) an interest rate higher than allowed by law was required, and (4) a corrupt intention to take more than the legal rate for the use of the money loaned exists. Even though the terms called for "profit," not "interest," the courts looked to the substance, not the form of the transaction. [***Pinchuck v. Canzoneri*, 920 So.2d 713 (Fla. App. 2006)**]

LawFlix

Midnight Run (1988) (R)

Is the contract Robert DeNiro has for bringing in Charles Grodin, an embezzler, legal? Discuss the issues of consideration and ethics as the bail bondsman puts another bounty hunter on the case and DeNiro flees from law enforcement agents in order to collect his fee. And finally, discuss the legality of DeNiro's acceptance of money from Grodin and his release of Grodin at the end of the movie.

---

[25] *Lentimo v. Cullen Center Bank and Trust Co.,* 919 S.W.2d 743 (Tex. App. 1996).

MAKE THE CONNECTION

SUMMARY

When an agreement is illegal, it is ordinarily void and no contract arises from it. Courts will not allow one party to an illegal agreement to bring suit against the other party. There are some exceptions to this, such as when the parties are not equally guilty or when the law's purpose in making the agreement illegal is to protect the person who is bringing suit. When possible, an agreement will be interpreted as being lawful. Even when a particular provision is held unlawful, the balance of the agreement may be saved so that the net result is a contract minus the clause that was held illegal.

The term *illegality* embraces situations in unconscionable contract clauses in which the courts hold that contract provisions are unenforceable because they are too harsh or oppressive to one of the parties to a transaction. If the clause is part of a standard form contract drafted by the party having superior bargaining power and is presented on a take-it-or-leave-it basis (a contract of adhesion) and the substantive terms of the clause itself are unduly oppressive, the clause will be found to be unconscionable and not enforced.

Whether a contract is contrary to public policy may be difficult to determine because public policy is not precisely defined. That which is harmful to the public welfare or general good is contrary to public policy. Contracts condemned as contrary to public policy include those designed to deprive the weaker party of a benefit that the lawmaker desired to provide, agreements injuring public service, and wagers and private lotteries. Statutes commonly make the wager illegal as a form of gambling. The private lottery is any plan under which, for a consideration, a person has a chance to win a prize.

Illegality may consist of the violation of a statute or administrative regulation adopted to regulate business. An agreement not to compete may be illegal as a restraint of trade except when reasonable in its terms and when it is incidental to the sale of a business or to a contract of employment.

The charging by a lender of a higher rate of interest than allowed by law is usury. Courts must examine transactions carefully to see whether a usurious loan is disguised as a legitimate transaction.

LEARNING OUTCOMES

After studying this chapter, you should be able to clearly explain:

A. General Principles

L0.1 Explain the general contract principles on "illegality"

See the unenforceable illegal lease to nonprofessionals example on pp. 321–322.
See the example where a contract to manufacture and sell illegal slot machines is void, p. 322.

L0.2 Explain the implied obligation on all parties of good faith and fair dealing

See the example of the Vermont landlord who deprived a tenant of her rights under a lease, p. 323.

B. Agreements Affecting Public Welfare

L0.3 Understand that it is only in unusual situations that a contract provision will be unenforceable because it is unconscionable

See the *Kramper Family Farm* example where the court refused to consider whether the contract was fair or unfair, wise or foolish, p. 323.
But see the *Geographic Expeditions* case that illustrates an unconscionable arbitration clause, p. 324.

C. Regulation of Business

L0.4 Explain the rationale for requiring licenses to carry on as a business, trade, or profession

See the discussion requiring licenses to protect the public from unqualified persons, p. 327.

L0.5 Distinguish between noncompete clauses in the sale of a business and noncompete clauses in employment contracts

See the example where the California court enforced a five-year noncompete clause against the seller of a business, p. 328.

See the example involving Julie Murray's noncompete clause and why it was modified from 24 months to one year, pp. 329–330.

See the *Home Paramount Pest Control* case that illustrates a trend barring enforcement of overlybroad noncompetition clauses, pp. 330–331.

KEY TERMS

contracts of adhesion	*in pari delicto*	public policy
good faith	lotteries	usury

QUESTIONS AND CASE PROBLEMS

1. When are the parties to an illegal agreement *in pari delicto?*

2. John Iwen sued U.S. West Direct because of a negligently constructed yellow pages advertisement. U.S. West Direct moved to stay litigation and compel arbitration under the yellow pages order form, which required advertisers to resolve all controversies through arbitration, but allowed U.S. West (the publisher) to pursue judicial remedies to collect amounts due it. Under the arbitration provision, Iwen's sole remedy was a pro rata reduction or refund of the cost of the advertisement. The order form language was drafted by U.S. West Direct on a take-it-or-leave-it basis and stated in part:

   > *Any controversy or claim arising out of or relating to this Agreement, or breach thereof, other than an action by Publisher for the collection of amounts due under this Agreement, shall be settled by final, bind-ing arbitration in accordance with the Commercial Arbitration rules of the American Arbitration Association.*

   If forced to arbitration, Iwen would be unable to recover damages for the negligently constructed yellow pages ad, nor could he recover damages for infliction of emotional distress and punitive damages related to his many efforts to adjust the matter with the company, which were ignored or rejected. Must Iwen have his case resolved through arbitration rather than a court of law? [*Iwen v. U.S. West Direct*, 977 P.2d 989 (Mont.)]

3. Sutcliffe Banton, dba Nemard Construction, furnished labor and materials (valued at $162,895) for improving Vicky Deafeamkpor's New York City residential property. She paid only $41,718, leaving $121,987 unpaid. Banton sued her and the jury awarded $90,000 in damages. Deafeamkpor moved for an order setting aside the jury's verdict because Banton was not properly licensed by New York City. Under NYC Code an unlicensed contractor may neither enforce a home improvement contract against an owner or recover in *quantum meruit.* The jury heard all the evidence regarding the materials and labor expended on Deafeamkpor's residence and concluded that the plaintiff performed satisfactory work valued at $90,000 for which he was not paid. Should the court allow the owner to take advantage of Banton and his employees and suppliers? What public policy would support such an outcome? Decide. [*Nemard Construction Corp. v. Deafeamkpor*, 863 N.Y.S.2d 846]

4. Eugene McCarthy left his position as director of sales for Nike's Brand Jordan division in June 2003 to become vice president of U.S. footwear sales and merchandising at Reebok, one of Nike's competitors. Nike sought a preliminary injunction to prevent McCarthy from working for Reebok for a year, invoking a noncompete agreement McCarthy had signed in Oregon in 1997 when Nike had promoted him to his earlier position as a regional footwear sales manager. The agreement stated in pertinent part:

During EMPLOYEE'S employment by NIKE... and for one (1) year thereafter, ("the Restriction Period"), EMPLOYEE will not directly or indirectly... be employed by, consult for, or be connected in any manner with, any business engaged anywhere in the world in the athletic footwear, athletic apparel or sports equipment and accessories business, or any other business which directly competes with NIKE or any of its subsidiaries or affiliated corporations.

McCarty contends that such a contract is a restraint of trade and should not be enforced. Nike contends that the agreement is fair and should be enforced. Decide. [*Nike, Inc. v. McCarthy*, 379 F.3d 576 (9th Cir.)]

5. Ewing was employed by Presto-X-Co., a pest exterminator. His contract of employment specified that he would not solicit or attempt to solicit customers of Presto-X for two years after the termination of his employment. After working several years, his employment was terminated. Ewing then sent a letter to customers of Presto-X stating that he no longer worked for Presto-X and that he was still certified by the state. Ewing set forth his home address and phone number, which the customers did not previously have. The letter ended with the statement, "I thank you for your business throughout the past years." Presto-X brought an action to enjoin Ewing from sending such letters. He raised the defense that he was prohibited only from soliciting and there was nothing in the letters that constituted a seeking of customers. Decide. What ethical values are involved? [*Presto-X-Co. v. Ewing*, 442 N.W.2d 85 (Iowa)]

6. The Minnesota adoption statute requires that any agency placing a child for adoption make a thorough investigation and not give a child to an applicant unless the placement is in the best interests of the child. Tibbetts applied to Crossroads, Inc., a private adoption agency, for a child to adopt. He later sued the agency for breach of contract, claiming that the agency was obligated by contract to supply a child for adoption. The agency claimed that it was required only to use its best efforts to locate a child and was not required to supply a child to Tibbetts unless it found him to be a suitable parent. Decide. [*Tibbetts v. Crossroads, Inc.*, 411 N.W.2d 535 (Minn. App.)]

7. Siddle purchased a quantity of fireworks from Red Devil Fireworks Co. The sale was illegal, however, because Siddle did not have a license to make the purchase, which the seller knew because it had been so informed by the attorney general of the state. Siddle did not pay for the fireworks, and Red Devil sued him. He defended on the ground that the contract could not be enforced because it was illegal. Was the defense valid? [*Red Devil Fireworks Co. v. Siddle*, 648 P.2d 468 (Wash. App.)]

8. Onderdonk entered a retirement home operated by Presbyterian Homes. The contract between Onderdonk and the home required Onderdonk to make a specified monthly payment that could be increased by the home as the cost of operations increased. The contract and the payment plan were thoroughly explained to Onderdonk. As the cost of operations rose, the home continually raised the monthly payments to cover these costs. Onderdonk objected to the increases on the ground that the increases were far more than had been anticipated and that the contract was therefore unconscionable. Was his objection valid?

9. Smith was employed as a salesman for Borden, Inc., which sold food products in 63 counties in Arkansas, 2 counties in Missouri, 2 counties in Oklahoma, and 1 county in Texas. Smith's employment contract prohibited him from competing with Borden after leaving its employ. Smith left Borden and went to work for a competitor, Lady Baltimore Foods. Working for this second employer, Smith sold in 3 counties of Arkansas. He had sold in 2 of these counties while he worked for Borden. Borden brought an injunction action against Smith and Lady Baltimore to enforce the noncompete covenant in Smith's former contract. Was Borden entitled to the injunction? [*Borden, Inc. v. Smith*, 478 S.W.2d 744 (Ark.)]

10. All new employees of Circuit City Stores were required to sign a Dispute Resolution Agreement

(DRA) mandating that employees submit all employment-related disputes to arbitration. Under the DRA Circuit City was not obligated to arbitrate its claims against employees and may bring lawsuits against employees. Remedies are limited under the DRA, including one year back pay limit and a two-year front pay limit, with cap on punitive damages of an amount up to the greater of the amount of back pay and front pay awarded or $5,000. In a civil lawsuit under state law a plaintiff is entitled to all forms of relief. The DRA requires that employees split the cost of the arbitrator's fees with the employer. An individual is not required to pay for the services of a judge. Adams filed a sexual harassment case against his employer in state court. Circuit City filed a petition in federal court to compel arbitration. Decide. [*Circuit City Stores, Inc. v. Adams*, 274 F.3d 889 (9th Cir.)]

11. Vodra was employed as a salesperson and contracting agent for American Security Services. As part of his contract of employment, Vodra signed an agreement that for three years after leaving this employment, he would not solicit any customer of American. Vodra had no experience in the security field when he went to work for American. To the extent that he became known to American's customers, it was because of being American's representative rather than because of his own reputation in the security field. After some years, Vodra left American and organized a competing company that solicited American's customers. American sued him to enforce the restrictive covenant. Vodra claimed that the restrictive covenant was illegal and not binding. Was he correct? [*American Security Services, Inc. v. Vodra*, 385 N.W.2d 73 (Neb.)]

12. Potomac Leasing Co. leased an automatic telephone system to Vitality Centers. Claudene Cato signed the lease as guarantor of payments. When the rental was not paid, Potomac Leasing brought suit against Vitality and Cato. They raised the defense that the rented equipment was to be used for an illegal purpose—namely, the random sales solicitation by means of an automatic telephone in violation of state statute; that this purpose was known to Potomac

Leasing; and that Potomac Leasing could therefore not enforce the lease. Was this defense valid? [*Potomac Leasing Co. v. Vitality Centers, Inc.*, 718 S.W.2d 928 (Ark.)]

13. The English publisher of a book called *Cambridge* gave a New York publisher permission to sell that book any place in the world except in England. The New York publisher made several bulk sales of the book to buyers who sold the book throughout the world, including England. The English publisher sued the New York publisher and its customers for breach of the restriction prohibiting sales in England. Decide.

14. A state law required builders of homes to be licensed and declared that an unlicensed contractor could not recover compensation under a contract made for the construction of a residence. Although Annex Construction, Inc., did not have a license, it built a home for French. When he failed to pay what was owed, Annex sued him. He raised the defense that the unlicensed contractor could not recover for the contract price. Annex claimed that the lack of a license was not a bar because the president of the corporation was a licensed builder and the only shareholder of the corporation, and the construction had been properly performed. Was Annex entitled to recover?

15. Yarde Metals, Inc., owned six season tickets to New England Patriots football games. Gillette Stadium, where the games are played, had insufficient men's restrooms in use for football games at that time, which was the subject of numerous newspaper columns. On October 13, 2002, a guest of Yarde Metals, Mikel LaCroix, along with others, used available women's restrooms to answer the call of nature. As LaCroix left the restroom, however, he was arrested and charged with disorderly conduct. The Patriots organization terminated all six of Yarde's season ticket privileges, incorrectly giving as a reason that LaCroix was ejected "for throwing bottles in the seating section." Yarde sued, contending that "by terminating the plaintiff's season tickets for 2002 and for the future arbitrarily, without cause and based on

false information," the Patriots had violated the implicit covenant of good faith and fair dealing of the season tickets contract. The back of each Patriots ticket states:

> *This ticket and all season tickets are revocable licenses. The Patriots reserve the*

> *right to revoke such licenses, in their sole discretion, at any time and for any reason.*

How would you decide this case? [*Yarde Metals, Inc. v. New England Patriots Ltd.*, 834 N.E.2d 1233 (Mass. App.)]

CPA QUESTIONS

1. West, an Indiana real estate broker, misrepresented to Zimmer that West was licensed in Kansas under the Kansas statute that regulates real estate brokers and requires all brokers to be licensed. Zimmer signed a contract agreeing to pay West a 5 percent commission for selling Zimmer's home in Kansas. West did not sign the contract. West sold Zimmer's home. If West sued Zimmer for nonpayment of commission, Zimmer would be:

   a. Liable to West only for the value of services rendered.

   b. Liable to West for the full commission.

   c. Not liable to West for any amount because West did not sign the contract.

   d. Not liable to West for any amount because West violated the Kansas licensing requirements (5/92, Law, #25).

2. Blue purchased a travel agency business from Drye. The purchase price included payment for Drye's goodwill. The agreement contained a covenant prohibiting Drye from competing with Blue in the travel agency business. Which of the following statements regarding the covenant is *not* correct?

   a. The restraint must be *no* more extensive than is reasonably necessary to protect the goodwill purchased by Blue.

   b. The geographic area to which it applies must be reasonable.

   c. The time period for which it is to be effective must be reasonable.

   d. The value to be assigned to it is the excess of the price paid over the seller's cost of all tangible assets (11/87, Law, #2).

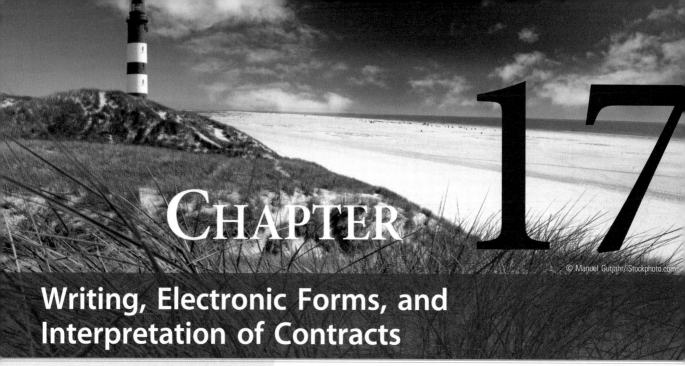

CHAPTER 17

© Manuel Gutjahr/iStockphoto.com

Writing, Electronic Forms, and Interpretation of Contracts

learningoutcomes

After studying this chapter, you should be able to

LO.1   Explain when a contract must be evidenced by a writing

LO.2   Explain the effect of noncompliance with the statute of frauds

LO.3   Explain the parol evidence rule and the exceptions to this rule

LO.4   Understand the basic rule of contract construction that a contract is enforced according to its terms

LO.5   State the rules for interpreting ambiguous terms in a contract

W hen must a contract be written? What is the effect of a written contract? These questions lead to the statute of frauds and the parol evidence rule.

A. Statute of Frauds

A *contract* is a legally binding agreement. Must the agreement be evidenced by a writing?

1. Validity of Oral Contracts

In the absence of a statute requiring a writing, a contract may be oral or written. Managers and professionals should be more fully aware that their oral communications, including telephone conversations and dinner or breakfast discussions, may be deemed legally enforceable contracts. **For Example,** suppose that Mark Wahlberg, after reviewing a script tentatively entitled *The Bulger Boys*, meets with Steven Spielberg to discuss Mark's playing mobster James "Whitey" Bulger in the film. Steven states, "You *are* 'Whitey,' Marky! The nuns at Gate of Heaven Grammar School in South Boston—or maybe it was St. Augustine's—they don't send for the Boston Police when they are troubled about drug use in the schools; they send for you to talk to the kids. Nobody messes with you, and the kids know it. This is true stuff, I think, and this fugitive's brother Bill comes out of the Southie projects to be president of U Mass." Mark likes the script. Steven and Mark block out two months of time for shooting the film this fall. They agree on Mark's usual fee and a "piece of the action" based on a set percentage of the net income from the film. Thereafter, Mark's agent does not like the deal. He believes there are better scripts for Mark. Incredibly brutal things are coming out about "Whitey" and his ties to drug dealers that tarnish the script. And with Hollywood accounting, a percentage of the "net" take is usually of little value. However, all of the essential terms of a contract have been agreed on, and such an oral agreement would be legally enforceable. As set forth in the following text, no writing is required for a services contract that can be performed within one year after the date of the agreement.

Certain contracts, on the other hand, must be evidenced by a writing to be legally enforceable. These contracts are covered by the **statute of frauds**.[1]

Because many oral contracts are legally enforceable, it is a good business practice in the preliminary stages of discussions to stipulate that no binding agreement is intended to be formed until a written contract is prepared and signed by the parties.

statute of frauds – statute that, in order to prevent fraud through the use of perjured testimony, requires that certain kinds of transactions be evidenced in writing in order to be binding or enforceable.

---

[1] The name is derived from the original Statute of Frauds and perjuries, which was adopted in 1677 and became the pattern for similar legislation in America. The 17th section of that statute governed the sale of goods, and its modern counterpart is §2-201 of the U.C.C. The 4th section of the English statute provided the pattern for U.S. legislation with respect to contracts other than for the sale of goods described in this section of the chapter. The English statute was repealed in 1954 except as to land sale and guarantee contracts. The U.S. statutes remain in force, but the liberalization by U.C.C. §2-201 of the pre-Code requirements with respect to contracts for the sale of goods lessens the applicability of the writing requirement. Additional movement away from the writing requirement is seen in the 1994 Revision of Article 8, Securities, which abolishes the statute of frauds provision of the original U.C.C. §8-319 and goes beyond by declaring that the one-year performance provision of the statute of frauds is not applicable to contracts for securities. U.C.C. §8-113 [1994 Revision].

2. Contracts That Must be Evidenced by a Writing

The statute of frauds requires that certain kinds of contracts be evidenced by a writing or they cannot be enforced. This means that either the contract itself must be in writing and signed by both parties or there must be a sufficient written memorandum of the oral contract signed by the person being sued for breach of contract. A *part performance* doctrine or exception to the statute of frauds may exist when the plaintiff's part performance is "unequivocally referable" to the oral agreement.[2]

(A) AGREEMENT THAT CANNOT BE PERFORMED WITHIN ONE YEAR AFTER THE CONTRACT IS MADE. A writing is required when the contract, by its terms or subject matter, cannot be performed within one year after the date of the agreement. An oral agreement to supply a line of credit for two years cannot be enforced because of the statute of frauds.

CASE SUMMARY

Not a Good Move, Doctor

FACTS: Despite not having an executed employment agreement, Dr. William Bithoney sold his home in New York and moved to Atlanta in early October in anticipation of his October 15 start work date as an executive at Grady Memorial Hospital. But the night before his anticipated start, he was informed that Grady's governing body, the Fulton-DeKalb Hospital Authority, did not approve his hiring and would not permit him to commence work. He sued the Authority for breach of an oral contract for severance, claiming that he and Grady's CEO, Otis Story, had agreed that he would receive "a severance payment of 15 months salary if Grady terminated his employment without cause." Bithoney had received a draft employment contract from Grady, which included a provision that, in the event Bithoney was terminated without cause, he would receive "full severance payment," which would be "payable for 15 months from the effective date of said termination."

DECISION: Judgment for the hospital. If the oral severance agreement were to be paid in a lump sum after termination, the oral agreement would not fall within the statute of frauds. Because the draft employment agreement provided that the severance "shall be payable for 15 months from the effective date of said termination," it was found to be a 15-month payment term barred by the statute of frauds. [***Bithoney v. Fulton-DeKalb Hospital Authority,*** **721 S.E.2d 577 (Ga. App. 2011)**]

The year runs from the time the oral contract is made rather than from the date when performance is to begin. In computing the year, the day on which the contract was made is excluded.

No *part performance* exception exists to validate an oral agreement not performable within one year. **For Example,** Babyback's Foods negotiated a multiyear oral agreement to comarket its barbecue meat products with the Coca-Cola Co. nationwide and arranged to have several coolers installed at area grocery stores in Louisville under the agreement. Babyback's faxed to Coca-Cola a contract that summarized the oral agreement but Coca-Cola never signed it. Because Coca-Cola

---

[2] *Carey & Associates v. Ernst*, 802 N.Y.S.2d 160 (A.D. 2005).

FIGURE 17-1	*Hurdles in the Path of a Contract*

WRITING REQUIRED

STATUTE OF FRAUDS	EXCEPTIONS
MORE THAN ONE YEAR TO PERFORM SALE OF LAND ANSWER FOR ANOTHER'S DEBT OR DEFAULT PERSONAL REPRESENTATIVE TO PAY DEBT OF DECEDENT FROM PERSONAL FUNDS PROMISE IN CONSIDERATION OF MARRIAGE SALE OF GOODS FOR $500 OR MORE MISCELLANEOUS	PART PERFORMANCE PROMISOR BENEFIT DETRIMENTAL RELIANCE

PAROL EVIDENCE RULE	EXCEPTIONS
EVERY COMPLETE, FINAL WRITTEN CONTRACT	INCOMPLETE CONTRACT AMBIGUOUS TERMS FRAUD, ACCIDENT, OR MISTAKE TO PROVE EXISTENCE OR NONBINDING CHARACTER OF CONTRACT MODIFICATION OF CONTRACT ILLEGALITY

© Cengage Learning

did not sign and no part performance exception exists for an oral agreement not performable within one year, Babyback's lawsuit was unsuccessful.[3]

When no time for performance is specified by the oral contract and complete performance could "conceivably occur" within one year, the statute of frauds is not applicable to the oral contract.[4]

When a contract may be terminated at will by either party, the statute of frauds is not applicable because the contract may be terminated within a year. **For Example,** David Ehrlich was hired as manager of Gravediggaz pursuant to an oral management agreement that was terminable at will by either Ehrlich or the group. He was entitled to receive 15 percent of the gross earnings of the group and each of its members, including rap artist Robert Diggs, professionally known as RZA, for all engagements entered into while he was manager under this oral agreement. Such an at-will contract is not barred by the statute of frauds.[5]

---

[3] *Coca-Cola Co. v. Babyback's International Inc.*, 841 N.E.2d 557 (Ind. 2006).
[4] *El Paso Healthcare System v. Piping Rock Corp.*, 939 S.W.2d 695 (Tex. App. 1997).
[5] See *Ehrlich v. Diggs*, 169 F. Supp. 2d 124 (E.D.N.Y. 2001). See also *Sterling v. Sterling*, 800 N.Y.S.2d 463 (A.D. 2005), in which the statute of frauds was no bar to an oral partnership agreement, deemed to be at will, that continued for an indefinite period of time.

(1) Oral Extension of a Contract.

A contract in writing, but not required to be so by the statute of frauds because it is terminable at will, may be varied by a new oral contract, even if the original written contract provided that it should not be varied except by writing. However, the burden of proof on the party asserting the oral modification is a heavy one. The modification must be shown by "clear, unequivocal and convincing evidence, direct or implied." **For Example,** John Boyle is the sole shareholder of numerous entertainment-related companies called the Cellar Door Companies, valued at some $106,000,000. Through these companies, he controls much of the large concert business at outdoor amphitheaters in Virginia and North Carolina. Bill Reid worked for Boyle beginning in 1983 as president of one of Boyle's companies. Boyle conducted financial affairs with an "air of informality." Reid proposed to Boyle the need for an amphitheater in Virginia Beach, and Boyle promised him a "33 percent interest" "if he pulled it off." As a result of Reid's efforts, the 20,000-seat Virginia Beach Amphitheater opened in 1996. The Supreme Court of Virginia determined that clear and convincing evidence did support the oral modification of Reid's written contract, including the following excerpt from the Court's opinion:

> *Thomas J. Lyons, Jr., Boyle's friend for over 35 years, testified on behalf of Reid. Lyons and his wife attended a concert in July 1996 at the newly constructed Virginia Beach Amphitheater as guests of Boyle and his wife. Lyons complimented Boyle for the excellent work and effort that Reid had undertaken in making the amphitheater a reality. According to Lyons, Boyle stated: "Well that's why he's my partner… that's why he owns 35 percent in this—in the Amphitheater or this project." After Lyons finished his testimony, the chancellor remarked on the record that Boyle stood up from his seat and "hugged" Lyons, even though Lyons had just provided testimony detrimental to Boyle.*

Reid was thus entitled to a judgment equivalent to the value of his interest in the project, $3,566,343. [6]

(B) **AGREEMENT TO SELL OR A SALE OF AN INTEREST IN LAND.** All contracts to sell land, buildings, or interests in land, such as mortgages, must be evidenced by a writing. [7] Leases are also interests in land and must be in writing, except in some states where leases for one year or less do not have to be in writing. [8] **For Example,** if Mrs. O'Toole orally agrees to sell her house to the Gillespies for $250,000 and, thereafter, her children convince her that she could obtain $280,000 for the property if she is patient, Mrs. O'Toole can raise the defense of the statute of frauds should she be sued for breach of the oral agreement. Under the *part performance doctrine,* an exception exists by which an oral contract for the sale of land will be enforced by a court of equity in a suit for specific performance if the buyer has taken possession of the land under an oral contract and has made substantial improvements, the value of which cannot easily be ascertained, or has taken possession and paid part of the purchase price.

---

[6] *Reid v. Boyle*, 527 S.E.2d 137 (Va. 2000).

[7] *Magnum Real Estate Services, Inc. v. Associates, LLC*, 874 N.Y.S.2d 435 (A.D. 2009).

[8] See, however, *BBQ Blues Texas, Ltd. v. Affiliated Business*, 183 S.W.3d 543 (Tex. App. 2006), in which Eddie Calagero of Affiliated Business and the owners of BBQ Blues Texas, Ltd., entered an oral commission agreement to pay a 10 percent commission if he found a buyer for the restaurant, and he did so. The oral agreement was held to be outside the statute of frauds because the activity of finding a willing buyer did not involve the transfer of real estate. The second contract between the buyer and seller of the restaurant, which involved transfer of a lease agreement, was a separate and distinct agreement over which Calagero had no control.

(c) PROMISE TO ANSWER FOR THE DEBT OR DEFAULT OF ANOTHER. If an individual *I* promises a creditor *C* to pay the debt of *D* if *D* does not do so, *I* is promising to answer for the debt of another. Such a promise is sometimes called a **suretyship** contract, and it must be in writing to be enforceable. *I*, the promisor, is obligated to pay only if *D* does not pay. *I*'s promise is a *collateral* or *secondary* promise, and such promises must be in writing under the statute of frauds.[9]

suretyship – undertaking to pay the debt or be liable for the default of another.

(1) Main Purpose of Exception.

When the main purpose of the promisor's promise to pay the debt of another is to benefit the promisor, the statute of frauds is not applicable, and the oral promise to pay the debt is binding.

For Example, an individual *I* hires a contractor *C* to repair *I*'s building, and the supplier *S* is unwilling to extend credit to *C*. In an oral promise by *I* to pay *S* what is owed for the supplies in question if *C* does not pay, *I* is promising to pay for the debt of another, *C*. However, the *main purpose* of *I*'s promise was not to aid *C* but to get his own house repaired. This promise is not within the statute of frauds.[10]

CASE SUMMARY

"I Personally Guarantee" Doesn't Mean I'm Personally Liable, Does It?

FACTS: Joel Burgower owned Material Partnerships Inc. (MPI), which supplied Sacos Tubulares del Centro, S.A. de C.V. (Sacos), a Mexican bag manufacturer, essential materials to make its products. When MPI was not paid for shipments, it insisted that Jorge Lopez, Sacos's general manager, personally guarantee all past and future obligations to MPI. In a letter to Burgower dated September 25, 1998, Lopez wrote:

> I... want to certify you [sic] that I, personally, guaranty all outstanding [sic] and liabilities of Sacos Tubulares with Material Partnerships as well as future shipments.

Lopez drafted the letter himself and signed it over the designation "Jorge Lopez Venture, General Manager."

After receiving the September 25th letter, MPI resumed shipping product to Sacos, sending additional shipments valued at approximately $200,000. MPI subsequently received one payment of approximately $60,000 from Sacos. When Sacos did not pay for the additional shipments, MPI stopped shipping to it. The Sacos plant closed, and MPI brought suit in a Texas court against Lopez, claiming he was individually liable for the corporate debt of more than $900,000 under the terms of the personal guarantee. Lopez contended that he signed the letter in his capacity as general manager of Sacos as a corporate guarantee and that it was not an enforceable personal guarantee. MPI contended that the letter was a clear personal guarantee.

DECISION: The essential terms of a guarantee agreement required by the statute of frauds were present in this case. Lopez stated in his September 25th letter that "I, personally, guaranty," manifesting an intent to guarantee, and described the obligation being guaranteed as "all outstandings and liabilities of Sacos," as well as "future shipments." Lopez's signature over his corporate office does not render the document ambiguous because the clear intent was expressed in the word "personally." [*MPI v. Jorge Lopez Ventura,* **102 S.W.2d 252 (Tex. App. 2003)**]

---

[9] See *Martin Printing, Inc. v. Sone*, 873 A.2d 232 (Conn. App. 2005), in which James Kuhe, in writing, personally guaranteed Martin Printing, Inc., to pay for printing expenses of *Pub Links Golfer Magazine*, if his corporation, Abbey Inc., failed to do so. When Abbey, Inc., failed to pay, the court enforced Kuhe's promise to pay.

[10] See *Christian v. Smith*, 759 N.W.2d 447 (Neb. 2008).

personal representative – administrator or executor who represents decedents under UPC.

executor, executrix – person (man, woman) named in a will to administer the estate of the decedent.

administrator, administratrix – person (man, woman) appointed to wind up and settle the estate of a person who has died without a will.

decedent – person whose estate is being administered.

(D) PROMISE BY THE EXECUTOR OR ADMINISTRATOR OF A DECEDENT'S ESTATE TO PAY A CLAIM AGAINST THE ESTATE FROM PERSONAL FUNDS. The **personal representative** (**executor** or **administrator**) has the duty of handling the affairs of a deceased person, paying the debts from the proceeds of the estate and distributing any balance remaining. The executor or administrator is not personally liable for the claims against the estate of the **decedent**. If the personal representative promises to pay the decedent's debts with his or her own money, the promise cannot be enforced unless it is evidenced by a writing.

If the personal representative makes a contract on behalf of the estate in the course of administering the estate, a writing is not required. The representative is then contracting on behalf of the estate. Thus, if the personal representative employs an attorney to settle the estate or makes a burial contract with an undertaker, no writing is required.

(E) PROMISES MADE IN CONSIDERATION OF MARRIAGE. Promises to pay a sum of money or give property to another in consideration of marriage must be in writing under the statute of frauds.

For Example, if Mr. John Bradley orally promises to provide Karl Radford $20,000 on Karl's marriage to Mr. Bradley's daughter Michelle—and Karl and Michelle marry—the agreement is not enforceable under the statute of frauds because it was not in writing.

Prenuptial or *antenuptial* agreements are entered into by the parties before their marriage. After full disclosure of each party's assets and liabilities, and in some states, income,[11] the parties set forth the rights of each partner regarding the property and, among other things, set forth rights and obligations should the marriage end in a separation or divorce. Such a contract must be in writing.

For Example, when Susan DeMatteo married her husband M. J. DeMatteo in 1990, she had a 1977 Nova and $5,000 in the bank. M. Joseph DeMatteo was worth as much as $112 million at that time, and he insisted that she sign a prenuptial agreement before their marriage. After full disclosure of each party's assets, the prenuptial agreement was signed and videotaped some five days before their marriage ceremony. The agreement gave Susan $35,000 a year plus cost-of-living increases, as well as a car and a house, should the marriage dissolve. After the couple divorced, Susan argued before the state's highest court that the agreement was not "fair or reasonable" because it gave her less than 1 percent of her former husband's wealth. The court upheld the agreement, however, pointing out that Susan was fully informed about her fiancé's net worth and was represented by counsel.[12] When there is full disclosure and representation, prenuptial agreements, like other contracts, cannot be set aside unless they are unconscionable, which in a domestic relations setting means leaving a former spouse unable to support herself or himself.

(F) SALE OF GOODS. As will be developed in Chapter 23, Nature and Form of Sales, contracts for the sale of goods priced at $500 or more must ordinarily be in writing under UCC §2-201.[13]

---

[11] See FLA. STAT. §732–702 (2).
[12] *DeMatteo v. DeMatteo*, 762 N.E.2d 797 (Mass. 2002). See also *Waton v. Waton*, 887 So.2d 419 (Fla. App. 2004).
[13] As will be presented in Chapter 23, under Revised Article 2, §2-201, the $500 amount is increased to $5,000. This revision has not yet been adopted by any states.

(G) PROMISSORY ESTOPPEL. The statute of frauds may be circumvented when the party seeking to get around the statute of frauds is able to prove an enhanced promissory estoppel. While one element of a routine promissory estoppel case requires that the promisee rely on the promise in some definite and substantial manner, an enhanced level of reasonable reliance is necessary in order to have enhanced promissory estoppel, along with proof of an unconscionable injury or unjust enrichment.

For Example, an Indiana bakery, Classic Cheesecake Inc., was able to interest several hotels and casinos in Las Vegas in buying its products. On July 27, 2004, its principals sought a loan from a local branch office of J. P. Morgan Chase Bank in order to establish a distribution center in Las Vegas. On September 17, local bank officer Dowling told Classic that the loan was a "go." When credit quality issues surfaced, Dowling continued to make assurances that the loan would be approved. On October 12, however, she told Classic that the loan had been turned down. Classic claimed that the bank's breach of its oral promise to make the loan and Classic's detrimental reliance on the promise caused it to lose more than $1 million. The Indiana statute of frauds requires agreements to lend money to be in writing. Classic contended that the oral agreement in this case must be enforced on the basis of promissory estoppel and the company's unconscionable injury. Judge Posner of the Seventh Circuit upheld the dismissal of the claim, writing (in part):

> …*For the plaintiff to treat the bank loan as a certainty because they were told by the bank officer whom they were dealing with that it would be approved was unreasonable, especially if, as the plaintiffs' damages claim presupposes, the need for the loan was urgent. Rational businessmen know that there is many a slip 'twixt cup and lips,' that a loan is not approved until it is approved, that if a bank's employee tells you your loan application will be approved that is not the same as telling you it has been approved, and that if one does not have a loan commitment in writing yet the need for the loan is urgent one had better be negotiating with other potential lenders at the same time….*[14]

CPA

3. Note or Memorandum

The statute of frauds requires a writing to evidence those contracts that come within its scope. This writing may be a note or memorandum as distinguished from a contract.[15] The statutory requirement is, of course, satisfied if there is a complete written contract signed by both parties.

(A) SIGNING. The note or memorandum must be signed by the party sought to be bound by the contract. **For Example,** in the previous scenario involving Mark Wahlberg and Steven Spielberg, suppose the parties agreed to do the film according to the same terms but agreed to begin shooting the film a year from next April, and Mark wrote the essential terms on a napkin, dated it, and had Steven sign it "to make sure I got it right." Mark then placed the napkin in his wallet for his records. Because the contract could not be performed within one year after the date of the agreement, a writing would be required. If Steven thereafter decided not to pursue the film, Mark could enforce the contract against him because the napkin-note had been signed by the party to be bound or "sought to be charged," Steven. However, if Mark later decided not to appear in the film, the agreement to do the film could not

---

[14] *Classic Cheesecake Co. Inc. v. J. P. Morgan Chase Bank,* 546 F.3d 839 (7th Cir. 2008).
[15] *McLinden v. Coco,* 765 N.E.2d 606 (Ind. App. 2002).

be enforced against Mark because no writing existed signed by Mark, the party sought to be charged.

Some states require that the authorization of an agent to execute a contract coming within the statute of frauds must also be in writing. In the case of an auction, it is usual practice for the auctioneer to be the agent of both parties for the purpose of signing the memorandum.

E-Commerce & Cyberlaw

Electronic Signatures in the Internet Age

A SIGNATURE authenticates a writing by identifying the signers through their distinctive marks. The act of signing a document calls to the attention of the signing parties the legal significance of their act and expresses authorization and assent to the body of the signed writing. An ELECTRONIC SIGNATURE, including technology having digital or wireless capabilities, means any electronic sound, symbol, or process attached to, or logically associated with, a contract or other electronic record and executed with the intent to sign the record. An ELECTRONIC RECORD means any contract or other record created or stored in an electronic medium and retrievable in a perceivable form.

Conducting business electronically over the Internet has many advantages for consumers, businesses, and governments by allowing the instant purchase of goods, information, and services, and the reduction of sales, administrative, and overhead expenses. To facilitate the expansion of electronic commerce and place electronic signatures and electronic contracts on an equal footing with written signatures and paper contracts, Congress enacted a federal electronic signatures law.

Under the Electronic Signatures in Global and National Commerce Act (E-Sign),* electronically signed contracts cannot be denied legal effect because the signatures are in electronic form, nor can they be denied legal effect because they are delivered electronically. Contracts or documents requiring a notarized signature can be satisfied by the electronic signatures of the notaries coupled with the enclosure of all other required information as part of the record.

One of the goals of E-Sign was to spur states to enact the Uniform Electronic Transactions Act (UETA). Under E-Sign, a state may "modify, limit or supersede" the provisions of the federal act by enacting UETA "as approved and recommended for enactment in all the states" by the National Conference of Commissioners on Uniform State Laws or enacting a law that is consistent with E-Sign.** Thus, for those states that enacted the official version of UETA or one consistent with E-Sign,

the federal law is superseded by the state law. UETA is similar to E-Sign. It specifies that e-signatures and e-records can be used in contract formation, in audits, and as evidence. Selective differences between E-Sign and UETA are identified below. **For Example,** inventor Stewart Lamle sued toy maker Mattel, Inc., for breach of contract. The U.S. Court of Appeals for the Federal Circuit remanded the case for trial after resolving the motions before it. The facts reveal that after a June 11, 1997, meeting of the parties, Mattel employee Mike Bucher sent an e-mail dated June 26 to Lamle, which set forth the terms agreed to in principle at the meeting with the salutation "Best regards, Mike Bucher" appearing at the end of the e-mail. The court resolved the issue of whether an e-mail is a writing "subscribed by the party to be charged or the party's agent" in Lamle's favor. The court stated that under the UETA, the e-signature satisfies the state's (California's) Statute of Frauds. Because the e-mail was sent in 1997 prior to the effective date on the UETA, January 1, 2000, an evaluation of state common law was necessary. The court stated that it could see no meaningful difference between a typewritten signature on a telegram, which is sufficient to be a signature under state law, and the typed signature on the June 26 e-mail. It concluded that the e-mail satisfies the Statute of Frauds, assuming that there was a binding oral agreement on June 11. ***

(a) General Rule of Parity. E-Sign provides for parity of electronic and paper signatures, contracts, and records. Electronic signatures and contracts satisfy the statute of frauds to the same extent they would if embodied as paper contracts with handwritten signatures. Internet contracts are neither more nor less valid, legal, and binding than are offline paper contracts. The rules are the same! The UETA is comparable to E-Sign in that it treats e-signatures and e-records as if they were handwritten.****

(b) Identity Verification. Neither E-Sign nor UETA is a digital signature law in that neither requires security procedures or a

---

*Pub. L. 106-229, 114 Stat. 464, 15 U.S.C. §7001.

**§102(a) and 102(a)(2). Forty-eight states and the District of Columbia have enacted the UETA in some form.

***Lamle v. Mattel, Inc., 394 F.3d 1355 (Fed. Cir. 2005); see also Payoutone v. Coral Mortgage Bankers, 602 F. Supp. 2d 1219 (D. Colo. 2009).

****UETA §7(a) and 7(b).

E-Commerce & Cyberlaw

Continued

certification authority for the verification of electronic signatures. The parties themselves determine how they will verify each other's identity. Some options are a credit card, a password or PIN, public-key cryptographic exchange of digital signatures, or biometric signatures.

(c) Exceptions. The E-Sign Act exempts documents and records on trust and estate law so that it does not cover wills, codicils, and testamentary trusts or commercial law matters such as checks, negotiable instruments, and letters of credit. The act also does not cover court documents and cancellation of health and life insurance. Generally, the UETA also does not apply to these documents and records set forth previously.

(d) Consumer Protection and Notice and Consent Requirements. Consumer protection laws remain intact under E-Sign. Protections exist for consumers to consent to receiving electronic contracts, records, and documents; and businesses must tell consumers of their right to receive hardcopy documents.

Consumers must consent to receiving documents electronically or confirm consent electronically. For example, a consumer and a business may have negotiated terms of a contract by telephone and agreed to execute their agreement by e-mail. The consumer is then sent an e-mail that contains a consent disclosure, which contains a hypertext markup language (HTML) link the consumer can use to test her ability to view the contract in HTML. The consumer then returns the e-mail message to the business, thereby confirming electronically her consent to use this electronic means.

The UETA, like E-Sign, defers to existing substantive law regarding consumer protection.

(e) Time and Place of Sending and Receipt. E-Sign does not contain a provision addressing basic contract requirements such as sending and delivery, leaving such matters to existing contract law. However, the UETA provides that an electronic record is sent when it (1) is properly directed to an information processing system designated or used by the recipient to receive such records and from which the recipient may recover that record; (2) is in a form that the recipient's system is able to process; and (3) enters an information processing system that is in the control of the recipient but outside the control of the sender. An electronic record is received when (1) it enters an information processing system designated or used by the recipient to receive such records and from which the recipient is able to obtain the record and (2) it is in a form that the recipient's system can process.*

(f) Errors. Unlike E-Sign, which leaves matters relating to errors to be resolved by existing state contract law, UETA creates a system for dealing with errors. For example, when Marv Hale clicks on "buy" to make an online purchase of 12 bottles of Napa Valley Supreme Chardonnay at $12.90 per bottle, the computer will produce the equivalent of an invoice that includes the product's name, description, quantity, and price to enable Marv to avoid possible error when forming the electronic contract. This procedure gives the buyer an opportunity to identify and immediately correct an error. When such a procedure is not in effect and an error is later discovered, prompt notice to the other party can cure the error under Section 10 of the UETA.**

*UETA §15.
**UETA §10(2)(A)-(C).

The signature may be an ordinary one or any symbol that is adopted by the party as a signature. It may consist of initials, figures, or a mark. In the absence of a local statute that provides otherwise, a signature may be made by pencil, pen, typewriter, print, or stamp. As will be discussed, electronic signatures have parity with on-paper signatures.

(B) CONTENT. The note or memorandum must contain all of the essential terms of the contract so the court can determine just what was agreed. If any essential term is missing, the writing is not sufficient. A writing evidencing a sale of land that does not describe the land or identify the buyer does not satisfy the statute of frauds.

The subject matter must be identified either within the writing itself or in other writings to which it refers. A deposit check given by the buyer to the seller does not take an oral land sales contract out of the statute of frauds. This is so because the check does not set forth the terms of the sale.

The note or memorandum may consist of one writing or of separate papers, such as letters, or a combination of such papers. Separate writings cannot be considered together unless they are linked. Linkage may be express reference in each writing to the other or by the fact that each writing clearly deals with the same subject matter.

4. Effect of Noncompliance

The majority of states hold that a contract that does not comply with the statute of frauds is not enforceable.[16] If an action is brought to enforce the contract, the defendant can raise the defense that the alleged contract is not enforceable because it is not evidenced by a writing, as required by the statute of frauds.

(A) RECOVERY OF VALUE CONFERRED. In most instances, a person who is prevented from enforcing a contract because of the statute of frauds is nevertheless entitled to recover from the other party the value of any services or property furnished or money given under the oral contract. Recovery is not based on the terms of the contract but on a quasi-contractual obligation. The other party is to restore to the plaintiff what was received in order to prevent unjust enrichment at the plaintiff's expense. **For Example,** when an oral contract for services cannot be enforced because of the statute of frauds, the person performing the work may recover the reasonable value of the services rendered.

(B) WHO MAY RAISE THE DEFENSE OF NONCOMPLIANCE? Only a party to the oral contract may raise a defense that it is not binding because there is no writing that satisfies the statute of frauds. Third persons, such as an insurance company or the Internal Revenue Service, cannot claim that a contract is void because the statute of frauds was not satisfied.

B. PAROL EVIDENCE RULE

When the contract is evidenced by a writing, may the contract terms be changed by the testimony of witnesses?

5. Exclusion of Parol Evidence

The general rule is that parol or extrinsic evidence will not be allowed into evidence to add to, modify, or contradict the terms of a written contract that is fully integrated or complete on its face.[17] Evidence of an alleged earlier oral or written agreement within the scope of the fully integrated written contract or evidence of an alleged contemporaneous oral agreement within the scope of the fully integrated written contract is inadmissible as *parol evidence.*

Parol evidence is admissible, however, to show fraud, duress, or mistake and under certain other circumstances to be discussed in the following paragraphs.

The **parol evidence rule** is based on the theory that either there never was an oral agreement or, if there was, the parties abandoned it when they reached the stage in negotiations of executing their written contract. The social objective of the parol evidence rule is to give stability to contracts and to prevent the assertion of terms

parol evidence rule–rule that prohibits the introduction into evidence of oral or written statements made prior to or contemporaneously with the execution of a complete written contract, deed, or instrument, in the absence of clear proof of fraud, accident, or mistake causing the omission of the statement in question.

---

[16] The U.C.C. creates several statutes of frauds of limited applicability, in which it uses the phrase "not enforceable": §1-206 (sale of intangible personal property); §2-201 (sale of goods); and §8-319 (sale of securities).
[17] *Mayday v. Grathwohl,* 805 N.W.2d 285 (Minn. App. 2011).

that did not exist or did not survive the bargaining of the parties so as to reach inclusion in the final written contract.

For Example, *L* (landlord), the owner of a new development containing a five-store mall, discusses leasing one of the stores to *T* (tenant), who is viewing the property with his sister *S*, a highly credible poverty worker on leave from her duties in Central America. *L*, in the presence of *S*, agrees to give *T* the exclusive right to sell coffee and soft drinks in the five-store mall. Soon *L* and *T* execute a detailed written lease for the store, which makes no provision for *T*'s exclusive right to sell soft drinks and coffee in the mall. Subsequently, when two of the mall's new tenants begin to sell soft drinks and coffee, *T* brings suit against *L* for the breach of the oral promise granting him exclusive rights to sell soft drinks and coffee. *T* calls *S* as his first witness to prove the existence of the oral promise. *L*, through his attorney, will object to the admission of any evidence of a prior oral agreement that would add to or amend the fully integrated written lease, which set forth all restrictions on the landlord and tenant as to uses of the premises. After study of the matter, the court, based on the parol evidence rule, will not hear testimony from either *S* or *T* about the oral promise *L* made to *T*. In order to preserve his exclusive right to sell the drinks in question, *T* should have made certain that this promise was made part of the lease. His lawsuit will not be successful.

6. When the Parol Evidence Rule Does Not Apply

The parol evidence rule will not apply in certain cases. The most common of these are discussed in the following paragraphs.

ambiguous – having more than one reasonable interpretation.

(A) Ambiguity. If a written contract is **ambiguous** or may have two or more different meanings, parol evidence may generally be admitted to clarify the meaning.[18]

Parol evidence may also be admitted to show that a word used in a contract has a special trade meaning or a meaning in the particular locality that differs from the common meaning of that word.

(B) Fraud, Duress, or Mistake. A contract apparently complete on its face may have omitted a provision that should have been included. Parol evidence may be admitted to show that a provision was omitted as the result of fraud, duress, or mistake and to further show what that provision stated. Parol evidence is admissible to show that a provision of the written contract was a mutual mistake even though the written provision is unambiguous. When one party claims to have been fraudulently induced by the other to enter into a contract, the parol evidence rule does not bar proof that there was a fraud. **For Example,** the parol evidence rule does not bar proof that the seller of land intentionally misrepresented that the land was zoned to permit use as an industrial park. Such evidence does not contradict the terms of the contract but shows that the agreement is unenforceable.[19]

(C) Modification of Contract. The parol evidence rule prohibits only the contradiction of a complete written contract. It does not prohibit proof that the contract was thereafter modified or terminated.

---

[18] *Berg v. Hudesman*, 801 P.2d 222 (Wash. 1990). This view is also followed by U.C.C. §2-202(a), which permits terms in a contract for the sale of goods to be "explained or supplemented by a course of dealing or usage of trade… or by course of performance." Such evidence is admissible not because there is an ambiguity but "in order that the true understanding of the parties as to the agreement may be reached." Official Code Comment to §2-202.

[19] *Edwards v. Centrex Real Estate Corp.*, 61 Cal. Rptr. 518 (Cal. App. 1997).

CASE SUMMARY

All Sail and No Anchor

FACTS: On April 2, 1990, Christian Bourg hired Bristol Boat Co., Inc., and Bristol Marine Co. (defendants) to construct and deliver a yacht on July 1, 1990. However, the defendants did not live up to their promises and the contract was breached. On October 22, 1990, the defendants executed a written settlement agreement whereby Bourg agreed to pay an additional sum of $135,000 for the delivery of the yacht and to provide the defendants a loan of $80,000 to complete the construction of the vessel. Referencing the settlement agreement, the defendants at the same time executed a promissory note obliging them to repay the $80,000 loan plus interest in annual installments due on November 1 of each year, with the final payment due on November 1, 1994. The court stated in presenting the facts: "However, like the yacht itself, the settlement agreement soon proved to be just another hole in the water into which the plaintiff threw his money." Bourg sued the defendants after they failed to make certain payments on the note, and the court granted a motion for summary judgment in favor of Bourg for $59,081. The defendants appealed.

DECISION: Judgment for Bourg. Because the defendants' affidavit recites that an alleged oral side agreement was entered into at the same time as the settlement agreement and promissory note— the oral side agreement allegedly stated "that the note would be paid for by services rendered by the defendants"—the oral side agreement would have constituted a contemporaneous modification that would merge into the integrated promissory note and settlement agreement and thus be barred from admission into evidence under the parol evidence rule. Although parties to an integrated written contract can modify their understanding by a subsequent oral pact, to be legally effective, there must be evidence of mutual assent to the essential terms of the modification and adequate consideration. Here the defendants adduced no competent evidence of either mutual assent to particular terms or a specific consideration that would be sufficiently definite to constitute an enforceable subsequent oral modification to the parties' earlier written agreements. Thus, legally this alleged oral agreement was all sail and no anchor. [*Bourg v. Bristol Boat Co.,* **705 A.2d 969 (R.I. 1998)**]

C. Rules of Construction and Interpretation

In interpreting contracts, courts are aided by certain rules.

7. Intention of the Parties

When persons enter into an agreement, it is to be presumed that they intend for their agreement to have some effect. A court will strive to determine the intent of the parties and to give effect to it. A contract, therefore, is to be enforced according to its terms.[20] A court cannot remake or rewrite the contract of the parties under the pretense of interpreting.[21]

No particular form of words is required, and any words manifesting the intent of the parties are sufficient. In the absence of proof that a word has a peculiar meaning or that it was employed by the parties with a particular meaning, a common word is given its ordinary meaning.

---

[20] See *Greenwald v. Kersh*, 621 S.E.2d 463 (Ga. App. 2005).
[21] *Abbot v. Schnader, Harrison, Segal & Lewis, LLP*, 805 A.2d 547 (Pa. Super. 2002).

(A) MEANING OF WORDS. Ordinary words are to be interpreted according to their ordinary meaning.[22] **For Example,** when a contract requires the gasoline dealer to pay the supplier for "gallons" supplied, the term *gallons* is unambiguous and does not require that an adjustment of the gallonage be made for the temperature.[23] When a contract calls for a businessperson to pay a builder for the builder's "costs," the term *costs* is unambiguous, meaning actual costs, not a lesser amount based on the builder's bid.[24]

If there is a common meaning to a term, that meaning will be followed even though the dictionary may contain additional meanings. If technical or trade terms are used in a contract, they are to be interpreted according to the area of technical knowledge or trade from which the terms are taken.

(B) INCORPORATION BY REFERENCE. The contract may not cover all of the agreed terms. The missing terms may be found in another document. Frequently, the parties executing the contract for storage will simply state that a storage contract is entered into and that the contract applies to the goods listed in the schedule attached to and made part of the contract. Likewise, a contract for the construction of a building may involve plans and specifications on file in a named city office. The contract will simply state that the building is to be constructed according to those plans and specifications that are "incorporated herein and made part of this contract." When there is such an **incorporation by reference**, the contract consists of both the original document and the detailed statement that is incorporated in it.

> **incorporation by reference** – contract consisting of both the original or skeleton document and the detailed statement that is incorporated in it.

When a contract refers to another document, however, the contract must sufficiently describe the document or so much of it as is to be interpreted as part of the contract.

CASE SUMMARY

Specificity Required

FACTS: Consolidated Credit Counseling Services, Inc. (Consolidated), sued Affinity Internet, Inc., doing business as SkyNet WEB (Affinity), for breach of its contract to provide computer and Web-hosting services. Affinity moved to compel arbitration, and Consolidated argued that the contract between the parties did not contain an arbitration clause. The contract between the parties stated in part: "This contract is subject to all of SkyNet WEB's terms, conditions, user and acceptable use policies located at **http://www.skynetweb.com/company/legal/legal.php**." By going to the Web site and clicking to paragraph 17 of the User Agreement, an arbitration provision can be found. The contract itself, however, makes no reference to an agreement to arbitrate, nor was paragraph 17 expressly referred to or described in the contract. Nor was a hard copy of the information on the Web site either signed by or furnished to Consolidated.

DECISION: Judgment for Consolidated. Mere reference to another document is not sufficient to incorporate that document into the contract absent specificity describing the portion of the writing to apply to the contract. [*Affinity Internet v. Consolidated Credit*, **920 So.2d 1286 (Fla. App. 2006)**]

---

[22] *Thorton v. D.F.W. Christian Television, Inc.*, 925 S.W.2d 17 (Tex. App. 1995).
[23] *Hopkins v. BP Oil, Inc.*, 81 F.3d 1070 (11th Cir. 1996).
[24] *Batzer Construction, Inc. v. Boyer*, 125 P.3d 773 (Or. App. 2006).

8. Whole Contract

The provisions of a contract must be construed as a whole in such a way that every part is given effect.

Every word of a contract is to be given effect if reasonably possible. The contract is to be construed as a whole, and if the plain language of the contract thus viewed solves the dispute, the court is to make no further analysis.[25]

CASE SUMMARY

When You Permanently Reduced the Shipping Spots to Zero, You "Terminated" the Contract, Silly

FACTS: C.A. Acquisition Newco LLC is a successor in interest to Cyphermint, Inc. ("CI"), a New York corporation specializing in software development for self-service kiosks. DHL Express (USA), Inc., is an Ohio corporation with a principal place of business in Florida. It is a division of DHL International GmBH, a Deutsche Post Company and express carrier of documents and freight. Until 2008, DHL provided express pick-up and delivery, including same-day air delivery of letters and packages throughout the United States.

DHL entered into an agreement with Cyphermint, hoping to expand its customer base by offering domestic shipping services in retail locations, such as Walgreens and OfficeMax, via kiosks, or "Shipping Spots." Customers were able to use the kiosks' touch screen to pay for shipping costs and print shipping labels. The contract provided for an initial three-year term (August 1, 2006, through July 31, 2009) that automatically renewed for two more years unless either party gave notice of its election not to renew 90 days before the end of the initial contract. Under the contract, Cyphermint agreed to provide interactive software, enabling customers to use DHL's services from the shipping spots. Section 10.5 of the contract governs termination fees:

> *There shall be no termination fees for any termination by either party, irrespective of the reason for such termination, except for a "Material Breach" or as provided pursuant to the "Statement of Work" (SOW).*

The SOW contains the following provision concerning termination fees:

> *Should DHL terminate this agreement for any reason other than a material breach by Cyphermint before its termination date DHL agrees to compensate CI in the amount of $50,000 per month for each month remaining in the initial term.*

In November 2008, DHL decided to end all domestic delivery service within the United States. CI requested early termination fees under Section 10.5 of the contract of $413,333.33. DHL refused to pay, contending that Section 2.8 of the contract gave DHL the discretion to control the number and placement of the shipping spots, and when it ended U.S. domestic operations, it exercised its discretion to reduce shipping spots to zero.

DECISION: Judgment for CI. In reviewing a document, a court must consider the document as a whole, rather than attempting to isolate certain parts of it. Even if the court were to accept DHL's argument that Section 2.8 gave it blanket authority to reduce or eliminate the shipping spot project altogether, the outcome would remain the same. The relevant provision in the contract provides for termination fees without regard to whether the termination was authorized. The only restriction placed on the recovery of such fees is that they will not be available in the case of a material breach by Cyphermint. DHL failed to explain how reducing the shipping spots to zero was in any way different from "terminating" the contract. [***C.A. Acquisition Newco, LLC v. DHL Express (USA), Inc.,*** **795 F. Supp. 2d 140 (D. Mass. 2011)**]

[25] *Covensky v. Hannah Marine Corp.,* 903 N.E.2d 422 (Ill. App. 2009).

9. Contradictory and Ambiguous Terms

One term in a contract may conflict with another term, or one term may have two different meanings. It is then necessary for the court to determine whether there is a contract and, if so, what the contract really means.

CASE SUMMARY

Who Pays the Piper?

FACTS: Olander Contracting Co., developer Gail Wachter, and the City of Bismarck, North Dakota, entered into a water and sewer construction contract including, among other things, connecting a 10-inch sewer line from Wachter's housing development to the city's existing 36-inch concrete sewer main and installing a manhole at the connection, to be paid for by Wachter. Olander installed the manhole, but it collapsed within a few days. Olander installed a second manhole, with a large base supported by pilings, but it too failed a few days after it was installed. Olander then placed a rock bedding under the city's sewer main, replaced 78 feet of the existing concrete pipe with PVC pipe, and installed a manhole a third time on a larger base. Olander sued Wachter and the City of Bismarck for damages of $456,536.25 for extra work it claims it was required to perform to complete its contract. Both defendants denied they were responsible for the amount sued under the contract. The jury returned a special verdict, finding that Olander performed "extra work/ unforeseen work... for which it is entitled to be compensated in excess of the contract price" in the amount of $220,849.67, to be paid by the City of Bismarck. Appeals were taken.

DECISION: Judgment for Olander. The trial judge properly made the initial determination that the contract language was ambiguous. That is, the language used by the parties could support good arguments for the positions of both parties. This resolved a question of law. Once this determination had been made, the judge allowed extrinsic evidence from all parties as to what they meant when they negotiated the contract. This evidence related to the questions of fact, which were left to the jury. Testimony was taken from the parties who negotiated the contract, and testimony was also heard about the role of each of the parties in the actual construction of the manhole, the cause for the collapses, and why the contractor had to replace the city's existing concrete pipe with PVC pipe and the city's role in making this determination. The jury then fulfilled its role answering the question whether or not Olander had performed extra work in the affirmative, concluding that the city was required to pay for it. [*Olander Contracting v. Wachter*, 643 N.W.2d 29 (2002)]

If the language within the four corners of the contract is unambiguous, the parties' intentions are determined from the plain meaning of the words, used in the contract, as a matter of law, by the judge. A contract term or provision is *ambiguous* if it is capable of more than one reasonable interpretation, because of the uncertain meaning of terms or missing terms. A finding of ambiguity is justified only if the language of the contract reasonably supports the competing interpretations.[26] It is the role of the judge—a question of law—to initially determine whether a contract is ambiguous. If the contract is ambiguous, it is the role of the jury—a question of fact—to determine which party's position is correct with the aid of extrinsic evidence.

---

[26] *QEP Energy Co. v. Sullivan*, 444 Fed. Appx. 284 (10th Cir. 2011).

(A) **NATURE OF WRITING.** When a contract is partly a printed form or partly type-written and partly handwritten and the written part conflicts with the printed or typewritten part, the written part prevails. When there is a conflict between a printed part and a typewritten part, the latter prevails. Consequently, when a clause typewritten on a printed form conflicts with what is stated by the print, the conflicting print is ignored and the typewritten clause controls. This rule is based on the belief that the parties had given greater thought to what they typed or wrote for the particular contract as contrasted with printed words already in a form designed to cover many transactions. Thus, a typewritten provision to pay 90 cents per unit overrode a preprinted provision setting the price as 45 cents per unit.

When there is a conflict between an amount or quantity expressed both in words and figures, as on a check, the amount or quantity expressed in words prevails. Words control because there is less danger that a word will be wrong than a number.

(B) **AMBIGUITY.** A contract is ambiguous when the intent of the parties is uncertain and the contract is capable of more than one reasonable interpretation.[27] The background from which the contract and the dispute arose may help in determining the intention of the parties. **For Example,** when suit was brought in Minnesota on a Canadian insurance policy, the question arose whether the dollar limit of the policy referred to Canadian or U.S. dollars. The court concluded that Canadian dollars were intended. Both the insurer and the insured were Canadian corporations; the original policy, endorsements to the policy, and policy renewals were written in Canada; over the years, premiums had been paid in Canadian dollars; and a prior claim on the policy had been settled by the payment of an amount computed on the basis of Canadian dollars.

(C) **STRICT CONSTRUCTION AGAINST DRAFTING PARTY.** An ambiguous contract is interpreted strictly against the party who drafted it.[28] **For Example,** an insurance policy containing ambiguous language regarding coverage or exclusions is interpreted against the insurer and in favor of the insured when two interpretations are reasonably possible. This rule is a secondary rule that may be invoked only after all of the ordinary interpretive guides have been exhausted. The rule basically assigns the risk of an unresolvable ambiguity to the party creating it.[29]

10. Implied Terms

In some cases, a court will imply a term to cover a situation for which the parties failed to provide or, when needed, to give the contract a construction or meaning that is reasonable.

The court often implies details of the performance of a contract not expressly stated in the contract. In a contract to perform work, there is an implied promise to use such skill as is necessary to properly perform the work. When a contract does not specify the time for performance, a reasonable time is implied.

In every contract, there is an implied obligation that neither party shall do anything that will have the effect of destroying or injuring the right of the other party to receive the fruits of the contract. This means that in every contract there

---

[27] *Kaufman & Stewart v. Weinbrenner Shoe Co.,* 589 N.W.2d 499 (Minn. App. 1999).
[28] *Idaho Migrant Council, Inc. v. Warila,* 89 P.2d 39 (Wyo. 1995).
[29] *Premier Title Co. v. Donahue,* 765 N.E.2d 513 (Ill. App. 2002).

good faith – absence of knowledge of any defects or problems.

exists an implied covenant of **good faith** and fair dealing. When a contract may reasonably be interpreted in different ways, a court should make the interpretation that is in harmony with good faith and fair dealing. **For Example,** when a contract is made subject to the condition that one of the parties obtain financing, that party must make reasonable, good-faith efforts to obtain financing. The party is not permitted to do nothing and then claim that the contract is not binding because the condition has not been satisfied. Likewise, when a contract requires a party to obtain government approval, the party must use all reasonable means to obtain it.[30]

The Uniform Commercial Code imposes an obligation of good faith in the performance or enforcement of every contract.[31]

11. Conduct and Custom

The conduct of the parties and the customs and usages of a particular trade may give meaning to the words of the parties and thus aid in the interpretation of their contract.

(a) Conduct of the Parties. The conduct of the parties in carrying out the terms of a contract is the best guide to determine the parties' intent. When performance has been repeatedly tendered and accepted without protest, neither party will be permitted to claim that the contract was too indefinite to be binding. **For Example,** a travel agent made a contract with a hotel to arrange for trips to the hotel. After some 80 trips had already been arranged and paid for by the hotel at the contract price without any dispute about whether the contract obligation was satisfied, any claim by the travel agent that it could charge additional fees must be rejected.

usage of trade – language and customs of an industry.

(b) Custom and Usage of Trade. The customs and **usages of trade** or commercial activity to which the contract relates may be used to interpret the terms of a contract.[32] **For Example,** when a contract for the construction of a building calls for a "turn-key construction," industry usage is admissible to show what this means: a construction in which all the owner needs to do is to turn the key in the lock to open the building for use and in which all construction risks are assumed by the contractor.[33]

Custom and usage, however, cannot override express provisions of a contract that are inconsistent with custom and usage.

12. Avoidance of Hardship

As a general rule, a party is bound by a contract even though it proves to be a bad bargain. If possible, a court will interpret a contract to avoid hardship. Courts will, if possible, interpret a vague contact in a way to avoid any forfeiture of a party's interest.

When hardship arises because the contract makes no provision for the situation that has occurred, the court will sometimes imply a term to avoid the hardship.

---

[30] *Kroboth v. Brent,* 625 N.Y.S.2d 748 (A.D. 1995).
[31] U.C.C. §§1-201(19), 1-203.
[32] *Affiliated FM Ins. Co. v. Constitution Reinsurance Corp.,* 626 N.E.2d 878 (Mass. 1994).
[33] *Blue v. R.L. Glossen Contracting, Inc.,* 327 S.E.2d 582 (Ga. App. 1985).

LawFlix

The Santa Clause (1996) (PG)

When Scott Calvin (Tim Allen) tries on a Santa suit, he discovers that he has assumed all of Santa's responsibility. Calvin tries to challenge his acceptance of the terms of the agreement. Analyze the problems with offer, acceptance, and terms in very fine print (a magnifying glass is required). Do the terms of the suit contract apply when Calvin did not know them at the time he put on the suit?

MAKE THE CONNECTION

SUMMARY

An oral agreement may be a contract unless it is the intention of the parties that they should not be bound by the agreement without a writing executed by them. Certain contracts must be evidenced by a writing, however, or else they cannot be enforced. The statutes that declare this exception are called *statutes of frauds.* Statutes of frauds commonly require that a contract be evidenced by writing in the case of (1) an agreement that cannot be performed within one year after the contract is made, (2) an agreement to sell any interest in land, (3) a promise to answer for the debt or default of another, (4) a promise by the executor or administrator of a decedent's estate to pay a claim against the estate from personal funds, (5) a promise made in consideration of marriage, and (6) a contract for the sale of goods for a purchase price of $500 or more.

To evidence a contract to satisfy a statute of frauds, there must be a writing of all essential terms. The writing must be signed by the defendant against whom suit is brought for enforcement of the contract.

If the applicable statute of frauds is not satisfied, the oral contract cannot be enforced. To avoid unjust enrichment, a plaintiff barred from enforcing an oral contract may in most cases recover from the other contracting party the reasonable value of the benefits conferred by the plaintiff on the defendant.

When there is a written contract, the question arises whether that writing is the exclusive statement of the parties' agreement. If the writing is the complete and final statement of the contract, parol evidence as to matters agreed to before or at the time the writing was signed is not admissible to contradict the writing. This is called the *parol evidence rule.* In any case, the parol evidence rule does not bar parol evidence when (1) the writing is ambiguous, (2) the writing is not a true statement of the agreement of the parties because of fraud, duress, or mistake, or (3) the existence, modification, or illegality of a contract is in controversy.

Because a contract is based on the agreement of the parties, courts must determine the intent of the parties manifested in the contract. The intent that is to be enforced is the intent as it reasonably appears to a third person. This objective intent is followed.

In interpreting a contract, ordinary words are to be given their ordinary meanings. If trade or technical terms have been used, they are interpreted according to their technical meanings. The court must consider the whole contract and not read a particular part out of context. When different writings are executed as part of the same transaction, or one writing refers to or incorporates another, all of the writings are to be read together as the contract of the parties.

When provisions of a contract are contradictory, the court will try to reconcile or eliminate the conflict. If this cannot be done, the conclusion may be that there is no contract because the conflict makes the agreement indefinite as to a material matter. In some cases, conflict is solved by considering the form of conflicting terms. Handwriting prevails over typing and a printed form, and typing prevails over a printed form. Ambiguity will be eliminated in some cases by the admission of parol evidence or by interpreting the

provision strictly against the party preparing the contract, particularly when that party has significantly greater bargaining power.

LEARNING OUTCOMES

After studying this chapter, you should be able to clearly explain:

A. Statute of Frauds

LO.1 Explain when a contract must be evidenced by a writing
See the discussion and examples beginning on p. 339.

LO.2 Explain the effect of noncompliance with the statute of frauds
See the *Bithoney* case where a doctor's oral contract for severance was barred by the statute of frauds, p. 340
See the example in which an oral contract cannot be enforced because it is not in writing, but the plaintiff may recover the reasonable value of the services rendered, p. 348.

B. Parol Evidence Rule

LO.3 Explain the parol evidence rule and the exceptions to this rule
See the example in which the tenant is not allowed to call a witness to testify about a prior oral agreement that

would add to and alter the written lease, p. 349.
See the exceptions based on ambiguity, fraud, duress, and mistake discussed on p. 349.

C. Rules of Construction and Interpretation

LO.4 Understand the basic rule of contract construction that a contract is enforced according to its terms
See the example of the interpretation of the word "costs" on p. 351.
See the *DHL Express* case that illustrates the judicial common sense of interpreting the contract as a whole rather than a strained construction contrary to the contract's intent, p. 352.

LO.5 State the rules for interpreting ambiguous terms in a contract
See the discussion on the nature of the writing beginning on p. 354.

KEY TERMS

administrator
ambiguous
decedent
executor

good faith
incorporation by reference
parol evidence rule
personal representative

statute of frauds
suretyship
usages of trade

QUESTIONS AND CASE PROBLEMS

1. Kelly made a written contract to sell certain land to Brown and gave Brown a deed to the land. Thereafter, Kelly sued Brown to get back a 20-foot strip of the land. Kelly claimed that before making the written contract, it was agreed that Kelly would sell all of his land to Brown to make it easier for Brown to get a building permit, but after that was done, the 20-foot strip would be reconveyed to Kelly. Was Kelly entitled to the

20-foot strip? What ethical values are involved? [*Brown v. Kelly*, 545 So.2d 518 (Fla. App.)]

2. Martin made an oral contract with Cresheim Garage to work as its manager for two years. Cresheim wrote Martin a letter stating that the oral contract had been made and setting forth all of its terms. Cresheim later refused to recognize the contract. Martin sued Cresheim for breach of

the contract and offered Cresheim's letter in evidence as proof of the contract. Cresheim claimed that the oral contract was not binding because the contract was not in writing and the letter referring to the contract was not a contract but only a letter. Was the contract binding?

3. Lawrence loaned money to Moore, who died without repaying the loan. Lawrence claimed that when he mentioned the matter to Moore's widow, she promised to pay the debt. She did not pay it, and Lawrence sued her on her promise. Does she have any defense? [*Moore v. Lawrence*, 480 S.W.2d 941 (Ark.)]

4. Jackson signed an agreement to sell 79 acres of land to Devenyns. Jackson owned 80 acres and was apparently intending to keep for himself the acre on which his home was located. The written agreement also stated that "Devenyns shall have the option to buy on property _____," but nothing was stated in the blank space. Devenyns sued to enforce the agreement. Was it binding? [*In re Jackson's Estate*, 892 P.2d 786 (Wyo.)]

5. Boeing Airplane Co. contracted with Pittsburgh–Des Moines Steel Co. for the latter to construct a supersonic wind tunnel. R.H. Freitag Manufacturing Co. sold materials to York-Gillespie Co., which subcontracted to do part of the work. To persuade Freitag to keep supplying materials on credit, Boeing and the principal contractor both assured Freitag that he would be paid. When Freitag was not paid by the subcontractor, he sued Boeing and the contractor. They defended on the ground that the assurances given Freitag were not written. Decide. What ethical values are involved? [*R.H. Freitag Mfg. Co. v. Boeing Airplane Co.*, 347 P.2d 1074 (Wash.)]

6. Louise Pulsifer owned a farm that she wanted to sell and ran an ad in the local newspaper. After Russell Gillespie agreed to purchase the farm, Pulsifer wrote him a letter stating that she would not sell it. He sued her to enforce the contract, and she raised the defense of the statute of frauds. The letter she had signed did not contain any of the terms of the sale. Gillespie, however, claimed that the newspaper ad could be combined with her letter to satisfy the statute of frauds. Was he

correct? [*Gillespie v. Pulsifer*, 655 S.W.2d 123 (Mo.)]

7. In February or March, Corning Glass Works orally agreed to retain Hanan as management consultant from May 1 of that year to April 30 of the next year for a present value fee of $200,000. Was this agreement binding? Is this decision ethical? [*Hanan v. Corning Glass Works*, 314 N.Y. S.2d 804 (A.D.)]

8. Catherine (wife) and Peter (husband) Mallen had lived together unmarried for some four years when Catherine got pregnant and a marriage was arranged. Peter asked Catherine to sign a prenuptial agreement. Although his financial statement attached to the agreement did not state his income at $560,000 per year, it showed he was wealthy, and she had lived with him for four years and knew from their standard of living that he had significant income. Catherine contends that failure to disclose Peter's income was a nondisclosure of a material fact when the agreement was drawn up and that accordingly the agreement is not valid. Peter contends that he fully disclosed his net worth and that Catherine was well aware of his significant income. Further, he contends that disparities in the parties' financial status and business experience did not make the agreement unconscionable. Decide. [*Mallen v. Mallen*, 622 S.E.2d 812 (Ga. Sup. Ct.)]

9. Panasonic Industrial Co. (PIC) created a contract making Manchester Equipment Co., Inc. (MECI), a nonexclusive wholesale distributor of its products. The contract stated that PIC reserved the unrestricted right to solicit and make direct sales of the products to anyone, anywhere. The contract also stated that it contained the entire agreement of the parties and that any prior agreement or statement was superseded by the contract. PIC subsequently began to make direct sales to two of MECI's established customers. MECI claimed that this was a breach of the distribution contract and sued PIC for damages. Decide. What ethical values are involved? [*Manchester Equipment Co. Inc. v. Panasonic Industrial Co.*, 529 N.Y.S.2d 532 (App. Div.)]

10. A contract made for the sale of a farm stated that the buyer's deposit would be returned "if for any

reason the farm cannot be sold." The seller later stated that she had changed her mind and would not sell, and she offered to return the deposit. The buyer refused to take the deposit back and brought suit to enforce the contract. The seller contended that the "any reason" provision extended to anything, including the seller's changing her mind. Was the buyer entitled to recover? [*Phillips v. Rogers*, 200 S.E.2d 676 (W. Va.)]

11. Integrated, Inc., entered into a contract with the state of California to construct a building. It then subcontracted the electrical work to Alec Fergusson Electrical Contractors. The subcontract was a printed form with blanks filled in by typewriting. The printed payment clause required Integrated to pay Fergusson on the 15th day of the month following the submission of invoices by Fergusson. The typewritten part of the contract required Integrated to pay Fergusson "immediately following payment" (by the state) to the general contractor. When was payment required? [*Integrated, Inc. v. Alec Fergusson Electrical Contractors*, 58 Cal. Rptr. 503 (Cal. App.)]

12. Norwest Bank had been lending money to Tresch to run a dairy farm. The balance due the bank after several years was $147,000. The loan agreement stated that Tresch would not buy any new equipment in excess of $500 without the express consent of the bank. Some time later, Tresch applied to the bank for a loan of $3,100 to purchase some equipment. The bank refused to make the loan because it did not believe the new equipment would correct the condition for which it would be bought and would not result in significant additional income. Tresch then sued the bank, claiming that its refusal to make the loan was a breach of the implied covenant of good faith and fair dealing. Decide. [*Tresch v. Norwest Bank of Lewistown*, 778 P.2d 874 (Mont.)]

13. Physicians Mutual Insurance Co. issued a policy covering Brown's life. The policy declared that it did not cover any deaths resulting from "mental disorder, alcoholism, or drug addiction." Brown was killed when she fell while intoxicated. The insurance company refused to pay because of the quoted provision. Her executor, Savage, sued the insurance company. Did the insurance company have a defense? [*Physicians Mutual Ins. Co. v. Savage*, 296 N.E.2d 165 (Ind. App.)]

14. The Dickinson Elks Club conducted an annual Labor Day golf tournament. Charbonneau Buick-Pontiac offered to give a new car as a prize to anyone making "a hole in one on hole no. 8." The golf course of the club was only nine holes. To play 18 holes, the players would go around the course twice, although they would play from different tees or locations for the second nine holes. On the second time around, what was originally the eighth hole became the seventeenth hole. Grove was a contestant in the tournament. He scored 3 on the no. 8 hole, but on approaching it for the second time as the seventeenth hole, he made a hole in one. He claimed the prize car from Charbonneau. The latter claimed that Grove had not won the prize because he did not make the hole in one on the eighth hole. Decide. [*Grove v. Charbonneau Buick-Pontiac, Inc.*, 240 N.W.2d 8533 (N.D.)]

15. Tambe Electric Inc. entered into a written agreement with Home Depot to provide copper wire to Tambe at a price set forth in the writing, and allowing the contractor the option of paying for the wire over a period of time. Home Depot did not fulfill this written agreement and Tambe sued for $68,598, the additional cost it had to subsequently pay to obtain copper wire for its work. Home Depot defended that it had made an oral condition precedent requiring payment in full by Tambe at the time it accepted the price quoted in the written agreement. Decide. [*Tambe Electric v. Home Depot*, 856 N.Y.S.2d 373]

CPA QUESTIONS

1. Which of the following statements is true with regard to the statute of frauds?

   a. All contracts involving consideration of more than $500 must be in writing.

   b. The written contract must be signed by all parties.

   c. The statute of frauds applies to contracts that can be fully performed within one year from the date they are made.

   d. The contract terms may be stated in more than one document.

2. With regard to an agreement for the sale of real estate, the statute of frauds:

   a. Requires that the entire agreement be in a single writing.

   b. Requires that the purchase price be fair and adequate in relation to the value of the real estate.

   c. Does *not* require that the agreement be signed by all parties.

   d. Does *not* apply if the value of the real estate is less than $500.

3. In negotiations with Andrews for the lease of Kemp's warehouse, Kemp orally agreed to pay one-half of the cost of the utilities. The written lease, later prepared by Kemp's attorney, provided that Andrews pay all of the utilities. Andrews failed to carefully read the lease and signed it. When Kemp demanded that Andrews pay all of the utilities, Andrews refused, claiming that the lease did not accurately reflect the oral agreement. Andrews also learned that Kemp intentionally misrepresented the condition of the structure of the warehouse during the negotiations between the parties. Andrews sued to rescind the lease and intends to introduce evidence of the parties' oral agreement about sharing the utilities and the fraudulent statements made by Kemp. Will the parol evidence rule prevent the admission of evidence concerning each of the following?

	Oral agreement regarding who pays the utilities	Fraudulent statements by Kemp
a.	Yes	Yes
b.	No	Yes
c.	Yes	No
d.	No	No

CHAPTER 18

© Manuel Gutjahr/iStockphoto.com

Third Persons and Contracts

learningoutcomes

After studying this chapter, you should be able to

LO.1 Explain the two types of intended third-party beneficiaries

LO.2 Explain why an incidental beneficiary does not have the right to sue as a third-party beneficiary

LO.3 Define an assignment

LO.4 Explain the general rule that a person entitled to receive money under a contract may generally assign that right to another person

LO.5 List the nonassignable rights to performance

A. Third-Party Beneficiary Contracts

Generally, only the parties to a contract may sue on it. However, in some cases a third person who is not a party to the contract may sue on the contract.

CPA

intended beneficiary – third person of a contract whom the contract is intended to benefit.

third-party beneficiary – third person whom the parties to a contract intend to benefit by the making of the contract and to confer upon such person the right to sue for breach of contract.

1. Definition

When a contract is intended to benefit a third person, such a person is an **intended beneficiary** and may bring suit on and enforce the contract. In some states, the right of the intended **third-party beneficiary** to sue on the contract is declared by statute. **For Example,** Ibberson Co., the general contractor hired by AgGrow Oils, LLC to design and build an oilseed processing plant, contracted with subcontractor Anderson International Corp. to supply critical seed processing equipment for the project. Anderson's formal proposal to Ibberson identified the AgGrow Oils Project, and the proposal included drawings of the planned AgGrow plant. Under state law, this contract made between the contractor and subcontractor for the express benefit of the third-party AgGrow Oils could be enforced by the intended third-party beneficiary AgGrow Oils. The project was a failure. AgGrow was successful in the lawsuit against Anderson under the Anderson-Ibberson contract, having the standing to sue as an intended third-party beneficiary of that contract.[1]

(A) Creditor Beneficiary. The intended beneficiary is sometimes classified as a *creditor beneficiary* when the promisee's primary intent is to discharge a duty owed to the third party.[2] **For Example,** when Max Giordano sold his business, Sameway Laundry, to Harry Phinn, he had three years of payments totaling $14,500 owing to Davco, Inc., on a commercial Davco shirt drying and pressing machine purchased in 2006. Max (the promisee) made a contract with Harry to sell the business for a stipulated sum. A provision in this contract selling the business called for Harry (the promisor) to make the Davco machine payments when due over the next three years. Should Harry fail to make payments, Davco, Inc., as an intended creditor beneficiary under the contract between Max and Harry, would have standing to sue Harry for breach of the payment provision in the contract.

CPA

(B) Donee Beneficiary. The second type of intended beneficiary is a *donee beneficiary* to whom the promisee's primary intent in contracting is to give a benefit. A life insurance contract is such an intended third-party beneficiary contract. The promisee-insured pays premiums to the insurer under the contract of insurance so that, upon the death of the insured, the promisor-insurer would pay the sum designated in the contract to the beneficiary. The beneficiary's rights vest upon the insured's death, and the beneficiary can sue the insurance company upon the insured's death even though the insurance company never made any agreement directly with the beneficiary.

(C) Necessity of Intent. A third person does not have the status of an intended third-party beneficiary unless it is clear at the time the contract was formed that the parties intended to impose a direct obligation with respect to the third person.[3] In

---

[1] *AgGrow Oils, LLC v. National Union Fire Ins.,* 420 F.3d 751 (8th Cir. 2005).
[2] The Restatement (Second) of Contracts §302 substitutes "intended beneficiary" for the terms "creditor" and "donee" beneficiary. However, some courts continue to use the classifications of creditor and donee third-party beneficiaries. Regardless of the terminology, the law continues to be the same. See *Continental Casualty v. Zurich American Insurance,* 2009 WL 455285 (D.C. Or. 2009).
[3] *American United Logistics, Inc. v. Catellus,* 319 F.3d 921 (7th Cir. 2003).

determining whether there is intent to benefit a third party, the surrounding circumstances as well as the contract may be examined.[4] There is a strong presumption that the parties to a contract intend to benefit only themselves.[5]

CASE SUMMARY

The Pest Control Case

FACTS: Admiral Pest Control had a standing contract with Lodging Enterprises to spray its motel every month to exterminate pests. Copeland, a guest in the motel, was bitten by a spider. She sued Admiral on the ground that she was a third-party beneficiary of the extermination contract.

DECISION: Judgment against Copeland. There was no intent manifested in the contract that guests of the motel were beneficiaries of the contract. The contract was made by the motel to protect itself. The guests were incidental beneficiaries of that contract and therefore could not sue for its breach. [*Copeland v. Admiral Pest Control Co.*, 933 P.2d 937 (Okla. App. 1996)]

(D) **DESCRIPTION.** It is not necessary that the intended third-party beneficiary be identified by name. The beneficiary may be identified by class, with the result that any member of that class is a third-party beneficiary. **For Example,** a contract between the promoter of an automobile stock car race and the owner of the racetrack contains a promise by the owner to pay specified sums of money to each driver racing a car in certain races. A person driving in one of the designated races is a third-party beneficiary and can sue the owner on the contract for the promised compensation.

2. Modification or Termination of Intended Third-Party Beneficiary Contract

Can the parties to the contract modify or terminate it so as to destroy the right of the intended third-party beneficiary? If the contract contains an express provision allowing a change of beneficiary or cancellation of the contract without the consent of the intended third-party beneficiary, the parties to the contract may destroy the rights of the intended beneficiary by acting in accordance with that contract provision.[6]

For Example, Roy obtained a life insurance policy from Phoenix Insurance Company that provided the beneficiary could be changed by the insured. Roy named his son, Harry, as the beneficiary. Later, Roy had a falling out with Harry and removed him as beneficiary. Roy could do this because the right to change the beneficiary was expressly reserved by the contract that created the status of the intended third-party beneficiary.

---

[4] See *Becker v. Crispell-Snyder, Inc.*, 763 N.W.2d 192 (Wis. App. 2009) for an example of complex circumstances surrounding a third-party beneficiary contract. The town of Somers, Wisconsin, entered into a contract with engineering firm Crispell-Snyder (C-S) because it needed an engineering firm to oversee a new subdivision to be developed by the Beckers. Under this contract C-S would submit bills to the town for overseeing the development, and the town would pay C-S through a line of credit from the Beckers. The court held that the Beckers were third-party beneficiaries entitled to sue C-S for overcharging change orders.

[5] *Barney v. Unity Paving, Inc.*, 639 N.E.2d 592 (Ill. App. 1994).

[6] A common form of reservation is the life insurance policy provision by which the insured reserves the right to change the beneficiary. Section 142 of the Restatement (Second) of Contracts provides that the promisor and the promise may modify their contract and affect the right of the third-party beneficiary thereby unless the agreement expressly prohibits this or the third-party beneficiary has changed position in reliance on the promise or has manifested assent to it.

In addition, the rights of an intended third-party beneficiary are destroyed if the contract is discharged or ended by operation of law, for example, through bankruptcy proceedings.

3. Limitations on Intended Third-Party Beneficiary

Although the intended third-party beneficiary rule gives the third person the right to enforce the contract, it obviously gives no more rights than the contract provides. That is, the intended third-party beneficiary must take the contract as it is. If there is a time limitation or any other restriction in the contract, the intended beneficiary cannot ignore it but is bound by it.

If the contract is not binding for any reason, that defense may be raised against the intended third-party beneficiary suing on the contract.[7]

CPA   4. Incidental Beneficiaries

Not everyone who benefits from the performance of a contract between other persons is entitled to sue as a third-party beneficiary. If the benefit was intended, the third person is an intended beneficiary with the rights described in the preceding sections. If the benefit was not intended, the third person is an *incidental beneficiary*. **For Example,** real estate developer Ocean Atlantic Corp. purchased a series of bonds from American Southern Insurance Co. for the purpose of guaranteeing the performance of public improvement in a subdivision it was developing in Yorkville, Illinois. The bonds representing the surety contract between Ocean Atlantic and American Southern were issued in favor of the City of Yorkville. Ocean Atlantic hired subcontractor Aurora Blacktop, Inc., to perform several improvements, but the project stalled and Aurora was never paid for its work. Aurora lacked standing as a third-party beneficiary to enforce the subdivision bonds against American Southern because the contractual obligations ran only to the city. Aurora was deemed an incidental beneficiary rather than a third-party beneficiary.[8]

Whether or not a third party is an *intended* or *incidental* beneficiary, therefore, comes down to determining whether or not a reasonable person would believe that the promisee intended to confer on the beneficiary an enforceable benefit under the contract in question. The intent must be clear and definite or expressed in the contract itself or in the circumstances surrounding the contract's execution.

CASE SUMMARY

Third Party Must Be Identified in the Four Corners of the Contract

FACTS: Novus International, Inc., manufactures a poultry-feed supplement named Alimet at its plant in Chocolate Bayou, Texas. A key component of Alimet is the chemical MMP. Novus contracted with Union Carbide to secure MMP from Carbide's plant in Taft, Louisiana.

---

[7] *XL Disposal Corp. v. John Sexton Contractors Co.,* 659 N.E.2d 1312 (Ill. App. 1995).
[8] *City of Yorkville v. American Southern Insurance Co.,* 654 F.3d 713 (7th Cir. 2011).

CASE SUMMARY

Continued

Sometime later, Carbide entered into a major rail-transportation contract with the Union Pacific Railroad (UP). The rail contract consisted of nearly 100 pages. Exhibit 2 of the contract delineated inbound and outbound shipments to and from all of Carbide's Texas and Louisiana facilities. Among the hundreds of shipments listed in Exhibit 2 were three outbound MMP shipments from Taft, Louisiana, to Chocolate Bayou, Texas. These shipments were described as "Taft outbound liquid chemicals." Due to difficulties that arose from its merger with the Southern Pacific Railroad, UP experienced severe disruptions in its rail service over parts of two years and was unable to transport sufficient MMP to Chocolate Bayou. As a result, Novus had to utilize more expensive methods of transportation to obtain Alimet. It sued UP to recover the increased costs of premium freight resulting from UP's breach of its rail contract with Carbide. UP asserts that Novus did not have standing to sue; and Novus contends that it had standing to sue as an intended third-party beneficiary.

DECISION: Judgment for UP. Third-party beneficiary claims succeed or fail according to the provisions of the contact upon which suit is brought. The intention to confer a direct benefit on a third party must be clearly and fully spelled out in the four corners of the contract. Otherwise, enforcement of the contract by a third party must be denied. After reviewing the rail contract, no intent to confer a direct benefit on Novus is evident. Novus is never named in the contract, and all obligations flow between UP and Carbide. Nor is it stated anywhere in the contract that the parties are contracting for the benefit of Carbide's customers. Novus, thus, is an incidental beneficiary without standing to sue. [*Union Pacific Railroad v. Novus International, Inc.*, 113 S.W.3d 418 (Tex. App. 2003)]

---

right – legal capacity to require another person to perform or refrain from an action.

duty – obligation of law imposed on a person to perform or refrain from performing a certain act.

assignment – transfer of a right; generally used in connection with personal property rights, as rights under a contract, commercial paper, an insurance policy, a mortgage, or a lease. (Parties—assignor, assignee.)

obligor – promisor.

debtor – buyer on credit (i.e., a borrower).

obligee – promisee who can claim the benefit of the obligation.

assignor – party who assigns contract rights to a third party.

assignee – third party to whom contract benefits are transferred.

B. ASSIGNMENTS

The parties to a contract have both rights and duties. Can rights be transferred or sold to another person or entity? Can duties be transferred to another person?

5. Definitions

Contracts create **rights** and **duties** between the parties to the contract. An **assignment** is a transfer of contractual rights to a third party. The party owing a duty or debt under the contract is the **obligor** or **debtor**, and the party to whom the obligation is owed is the **obligee**. The party making the assignment is the **assignor**. The third party to whom the assignment is made is the **assignee**. **For Example,** Randy Marshall and Marilee Menendez own Huntington Beach Board (HBB) Company, LLC, a five-employee start-up company making top-of-the line surfboards. Marilee was able to sell 100 Duke Kahanamoku–inspired "longboards" to Watersports, Inc., a large retail sporting goods chain, for $140 per board. However, the best payment terms she could obtain were payment in full in 90 days. A contract containing these terms was executed, and the goods were delivered. To meet internal cash flow needs, HBB assigned its right to receive the $14,000 payment from the buyer to West Coast Financial Associates (Associates) and received $12,800 cash from Associates on execution of the assignment documents. Notice was given at that time to Watersports, Inc., of the assignment. The right to receive the payment due in 90 days under the sales contract has thus been transferred by the

FIGURE 18-1 | *Surfboard Transaction Diagram*

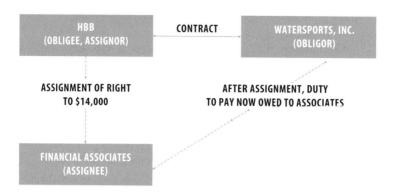

© Cengage Learning

seller HBB (assignor) to the third party, Associates (the assignee), to whom the buyer, Watersports, Inc. (obligor), now owes the duty of payment. Under the law of assignments, Associates, the assignee, now has direct rights against the obligor, Watersports, Inc. (See Figure 18-1.)

6. Form of Assignment

Generally, an assignment may be in any form. Statutes, however, may require that certain kinds of assignments be in writing or be executed in a particular form. Any words, whether written or spoken, that show an intention to transfer or assign will be given the effect of an assignment.[9]

7. Notice of Assignment

An assignment, if otherwise valid, takes effect the moment it is made. The assignee should give immediate notice of the assignment to the obligor, setting forth the obligor's duty to the assignee, in order to prevent improper payment.[10]

CASE SUMMARY

When You Find Yourself in a Hole, NationsBank, Stop Digging

FACTS: L & S General Contractors, LLC (L & S), purchased a book-entry certificate of deposit (CD 005) in the principal amount of $100,000 from NationsBank, N.A. L & S later assigned CD 005 to Credit General Insurance Company (Credit General) as collateral security for performance and payment bonds on a Howard Johnson construction project. Credit General forwarded to NationsBank a written notice of the assignment that stated, "Please hold this account as assigned to use until demanded or released by us." NationsBank recorded the assignment and executed a written acknowledgment. When CD 005 matured, L & S rolled over

---

[9] *JBM Investments, LLC v. Callahan Industries, Inc.*, 667 S.E.2d 429 (Ga. App. 2008).

[10] In some cases, an assignee will give notice of the assignment to the obligor in order to obtain priority over other persons who claim the same right or in order to limit the defenses that the obligor may raise against the assignee. U.C.C. §9-318.

CASE SUMMARY

Continued

the proceeds into a short-term certificate of deposit (CD 058) and, upon maturity, rolled over the proceeds of CD 058 into another short-term certificate of deposit (CD 072).

The bank book entries of CD 058 and CD 072 recorded L & S as the only principal/payee and did not reflect Credit General's assignment interest. NationsBank admitted its failure to show Credit General as assignee on the rollover book entries for CD 058 and CD 072 was a mistake.

Upon maturity, L & S withdrew the proceeds of CD 072 without the knowledge or consent of Credit General. Later Credit General made written demand on NationsBank for the proceeds of CD 005, and NationsBank informed Credit General that CD 005 had been redeemed and refused payment. Credit General sued NationsBank for wrongful payment of proceeds. NationsBank argues that the assignment was limited in time to the completion of the Howard Johnson project.

DECISION: Judgment for the assignee, Credit General. Upon notice and acknowledgment of the assignment, NationsBank incurred a legal duty to pay the account proceeds only to the assignee, Credit General, in whom the account was vested by the terms of the assignment. The assignment was absolute and unambiguous on its face and clearly was not limited as NationsBank proposes. The assignment language controls. [*Credit General Insurance Co. v. NationsBank*, 299 F.3d 943 (8th Cir. 2002)]

If the obligor is notified in any manner that there has been an assignment and that any money due must be paid to the assignee, the obligor's obligation can be discharged only by making payment to the assignee.

If the obligor is not notified that there has been an assignment and that the money due must be paid to the assignee, any payment made by the obligor to the assignor reduces or cancels that portion of the debt. The only remedy for the assignee is to sue the assignor to recover the payments that were made by the obligor.

The Uniform Consumer Credit Code (UCCC) protects consumer-debtors making payments to an assignor without knowledge of the assignment[11] and imposes a penalty for using a contract term that would destroy this protection of consumers.[12]

8. Assignment of Right to Money

Assignments of contracts are generally made to raise money. **For Example,** an automobile dealer assigns a customer's credit contract to a finance company and receives cash for it. Sometimes assignments are made when an enterprise closes and transfers its business to a new owner.

A person entitled to receive money, such as payment for goods sold to a buyer or for work done under a contract, may generally assign that right to another person.[13] A **claim** or **cause of action** against another person may be assigned. Isaac Hayes, an Academy Award®–winning composer, producer, and the original voice of Chef in

claim–right to payment.

cause of action–right to damages or other judicial relief when a legally protected right of the plaintiff is violated by an unlawful act of the defendant.

[11] U.C.C.C. §2.412.
[12] U.C.C.C. §5.202.
[13] *Pravin Banker Associates v. Banco Popular del Peru*, 109 F.3d 850 (2d Cir. 1997).

the television series South Park, assigned his copyright interests in several musical works in exchange for royalties from Stax Records.[14] A contractor entitled to receive payment from a building's owner can assign that right to a bank as security for a loan or can assign it to anyone else.

For Example, Celeste owed Roscoe Painters $5,000 for painting her house. Roscoe assigned this claim to the Main Street Bank. Celeste later refused to pay the bank because she had never consented to the assignment. The fact that Celeste had not consented is irrelevant. Roscoe was the owner of the claim and could transfer it to the bank. Celeste, therefore, is obligated to pay the assignee, Main Street Bank.

(A) FUTURE RIGHTS. By the modern rule, future and expected rights to money may be assigned. Thus, prior to the start of a building, a building contractor may assign its rights to money not yet due under an existing contract's payment on completion-phase schedule.

(B) PURPOSE OF ASSIGNMENT. The assignment of the right to money may be a complete transfer of the right that gives the assignee the right to collect and keep the money. In contrast, the assignment may be held for security. In this case, the assignee may hold the money only as a security for some specified obligation.

(C) PROHIBITION OF ASSIGNMENT OF RIGHTS. A clear and specific contractual prohibition against the assignment of rights is enforceable at common law. However, the UCC favors the assignment of contracts, and express contractual prohibitions on assignments are ineffective against (1) the assignment of rights to payment for goods or services, including accounts receivable,[15] and (2) the assignment of the rights to damages for breach of sales contracts.[16]

9. Nonassignable Rights

If the transfer of a right would materially affect or alter a duty or the rights of the obligor, an assignment is not permitted.[17]

(A) ASSIGNMENT INCREASING BURDEN OF PERFORMANCE. When the assignment of a right would increase the burden of the obligor in performing, an assignment is ordinarily not permitted. To illustrate, if the assignor has the right to buy a certain quantity of a stated article and to take such property from the seller's warehouse, this right can be assigned. However, if the sales contract stipulates that the seller should deliver to the buyer's premises and the assignee's premises are a substantial distance from the assignor's place of business, the assignment would not be given effect. In this case, the seller would be required to give a different performance by providing greater transportation if the assignment were permitted.

(B) PERSONAL SERVICES. Contracts for personal services are generally not assignable. **For Example,** were golf instructor David Ledbetter to sign a one-year contract to provide instruction for professional golfer Davis Love III, David Ledbetter could not assign his first assistant to provide the instruction, nor could Davis Love assign a protégé to receive instruction from Ledbetter. Professional athletes and their agents

---

[14] *Hayes v. Carlin America, Inc.*, 168 F. Supp. 2d 154 (S.D.N.Y 2001).
[15] U.C.C. §9-318(4). This section of the U.C.C. is applicable to most common commercial assignments.
[16] U.C.C. §2-210(2).
[17] *Aslakson v. Home Savings Ass'n*, 416 N.W.2d 786 (Minn. App. 1987) (increase of credit risk).

FIGURE 18-2 | *Limitations on Transfer of Rights and Duties*

ASSIGNMENT OF RIGHT TO MONEY	ASSIGNMENT OF RIGHT TO PERFORMANCE	DELEGATION OF DUTIES
GENERALLY NO LIMITATION	INCREASE OF BURDEN PERSONAL SERVICES CREDIT TRANSACTION	PERSONAL OR NONSTANDARDIZED PERFORMANCE

© Cengage Learning

commonly deal with assignment or trading rights of the athletes in their contracts with professional sports franchises.

There is a split among jurisdictions regarding whether employee noncompetition covenants are assignable to the new owner of a business absent employee consent. That is, some courts permit a successor employer to enforce an employee's noncompetition agreement as an assignee of the original employer. However, a majority of states that have considered this issue have concluded that restrictive covenants are personal in nature and not assignable. **For Example,** in September 2000, Philip Burkhardt signed a noncompetition agreement with his employer, NES Trench Shoring. On June 30, 2002, United Rentals Purchased NES with all contracts being assigned to United Rentals. Burkhardt stayed on with the new owner for five weeks and thereafter went to work for Traffic Control Services, a direct competitor of United. United was unsuccessful in its action to enforce the noncompetition covenant Burkhardt had signed with NES. Burkhardt's covenant with NES did not contain a clause allowing the covenant to be assigned to a new owner, and the court refused to enforce it, absent an express clause permitting assignment.[18]

(c) Credit Transaction. When a transaction is based on extending credit, the person to whom credit is extended cannot assign any rights under the contract to another. **For Example,** Jack Aldrich contracted to sell his summer camp on Lake Sunapee to Pat Norton for $200,000, with $100,000 in cash due at the closing and the balance due on an installment basis secured by a mortgage on the property to be executed by Norton. Several days later, Norton found a more desirable property, and her sister Meg was very pleased to take over the Sunapee contract. Pat assigned her rights to Meg. Jack Aldrich, having received a better offer after contracting with Pat, refused to consent to the assignment. In this situation, the assignment to Meg is prohibited because the assignee, Meg, is a different credit risk even though the property to serve as security remained unchanged.

CPA ## 10. Rights of Assignee

Unless restricted by the terms of the assignment or applicable law, the assignee acquires all the rights of the assignor.[19]

---

[18] *Traffic Control Sources, Inc. v. United Rentals Northwest, Inc.,* 87 P.3d 1054 (Nev. 2004).
[19] *Puget Sound National Bank v. Washington Department of Revenue,* 868 P.2d 127 (Wash. 1994).

An assignee stands exactly in the position of the assignor. The assignee's rights are no more or less than those of the assignor. If the assigned right to payment is subject to a condition precedent, that same condition exists for the assignee. **For Example,** when a contractor is not entitled to receive the balance of money due under the contract until all bills of suppliers of materials have been paid, the assignee to whom the contractor assigns the balance due under the contract is subject to the same condition. As set forth previously, in some states the assignee of a business purchasing all of the assets and rights of the business has the right to enforce a confidentiality and noncompetition agreement against a former employee of the assignor, just as though it were the assignor.[20]

11. Continuing Liability of Assignor

The making of an assignment does not relieve the assignor of any obligation of the contract. In the absence of a contrary agreement, an assignor continues to be bound by the obligations of the original contract. **For Example,** boatbuilder Derecktor NY's assignment of obligations to a Connecticut boatbuilder did not release it from all liabilities under its boatbuilding contract with New York Water Taxi (NYWT); and NYWT was allowed to proceed against Derecktor NY for breach of contract–design and breach of contract–workmanship.[21]

When a lease is assigned, the assignee becomes the principal obligor for rent payments, and the leasee becomes a surety toward the lessor for the assignee's performance. **For Example,** Tri-State Chiropractic (TSC) held a five-year lease on premises at 6010 East Main Street in Columbus, Ohio. Without the leasor's consent, TSC assigned that lease to Dr. T. Wilson and Buckeye Chiropractic, LLC, prior to the expiration of the lease. TSC continues to be liable for rent as surety during the term of the lease, even if the leasor (owner) had consented to the assignment or accepted payment from the assignee.[22] In order to avoid liability as a surety, TSC would have to obtain a discharge of the lease by **novation**, in which all three parties agree that the original contract (the lease) would be discharged and a new lease between Dr. Wilson and the owner would take effect. A novation allows for the discharge of a contractual obligation by the substitution of a new contract involving a new party.[23]

novation – substitution for an old contract with a new one that either replaces an existing obligation with a new obligation or replaces an original party with a new party.

12. Liability of Assignee

It is necessary to distinguish between the question of whether the obligor can assert a particular defense against the assignee and the question of whether any person can sue the assignee. Ordinarily, the assignee is not subject to suit by virtue of the fact that the assignment has been made.

(A) CONSUMER PROTECTION LIABILITY OF ASSIGNEE. The assignee of the right to money may have no direct relationship to the original debtor except with respect to receiving payments. Consumer protection laws in most states, however, may subject the assignee to some liability for the assignor's misconduct.

[20] *Artromick International, Inc. v. Koch,* 759 N.E.2d 385 (Ohio App. 2001).
[21] *New York Trans Harbor, LLC v. Derecktor Shipyards,* 841 N.Y.S.2d 821 (2007).
[22] *Schottenstein Trustees v. Carano,* 2000 WL 1455425 (Ohio. App. 2000).
[23] *Willamette Management Association, Inc. v. Palczynski,* 38 A.3d 1212 (Conn. App. 2012).

CASE SUMMARY

The Pool and the Agreement Will Not Hold Any Water

FACTS: Homeowner Michael Jackson entered into a contract with James DeWitt for the construction of an in-ground lap pool. The contract provided for a 12 ft. by 60 ft. pool at an estimated cost of $21,000. At the time the contract was signed, Jackson paid DeWitt $11,400 in cash and financed $7,500 through a Retail Installment Security Agreement (RISA). Associates Financial Services Company (Associates) provided DeWitt with all of the forms necessary to document the financing of the home improvements. Consumer requests for financing were subject to Associates's approval, which was given for Jackson's lap pool. When the RISA was completed, DeWitt assigned it to Associates. Jackson made two monthly payments of $202.90 and a final payment of $7,094.20 while the lap pool was still under construction. When the pool was filled, it failed to hold water and Jackson had the pool and deck removed. Jackson sued DeWitt for breach of contract. He asserted that all valid claims and defenses he had against DeWitt were also valid against the assignee, Associates. Jackson sought the return of the $7,500 he had financed from Associates. The trial court held that because Jackson had paid the entire balance of the loan before Associates knew of Jackson's claim, he could not obtain relief from Associates under the consumer protection law, section ATCP 110.06 of the Wisconsin Administrative Code. Jackson appealed this decision.

DECISION: Judgment for Jackson. As one commentator has noted, "ch. ATCP 110 deals with virtually a laundry list of unfair or deceptive home improvement practices that have resulted from substantial financial losses to home owners over the years. Jeffries, 57 MARQ. L. REV at 578." Associates is an assignee of a "home improvement contract" that is governed by section ATCP 110.06. The regulation provides that "[e]very assignee of a home improvement contract takes subject to all claims and defenses of the buyer or successors in interest." Therefore, as the assignee of the RISA, Associates is subject to any claims without regard to the negotiability of the contract. [*Jackson v. DeWitt*, 592 N.W.2d 262 (Wis. App. 1999)]

(B) **DEFENSES AND SETOFFS.** The assignee's rights are no greater than those of the assignor.[24] If the obligor could successfully defend against a suit brought by the assignor, the obligor will also prevail against the assignee.

The fact that the assignee has given value for the assignment does not give the assignee any immunity from defenses that the other party, the obligor, could have asserted against the assignor. The rights acquired by the assignee remain subject to any limitations imposed by the contract.

13. Warranties of Assignor

implied warranty – warranty that was not made but is implied by law.

When the assignment is made for a consideration, the assignor is regarded as providing an **implied warranty** that the right assigned is valid. The assignor also warrants that the assignor is the owner of the claim or right assigned and that the assignor will not interfere with the assignee's enforcement of the obligation.

14. Delegation of Duties

delegation of duties – transfer of duties by a contracting party to another person who is to perform them.

A **delegation of duties** is a transfer of duties by a contracting party to another person who is to perform them. Under certain circumstances, a contracting party

---

[24] *Shoreline Communications, Inc. v. Norwich Taxi, LLC*, 797 A.2d 1165 (Conn. App. 2002).

FIGURE 18-3 | *Can a Third Person Sue on a Contract?*

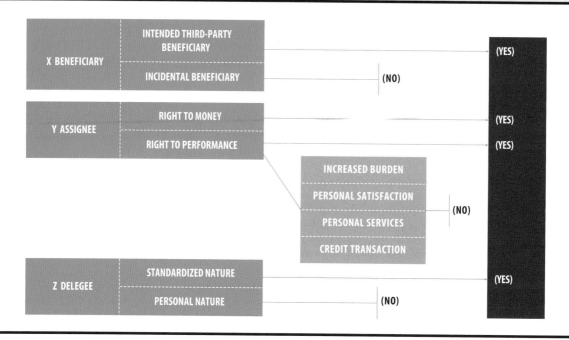

© Cengage Learning

may obtain someone else to do the work. When the performance is standardized and nonpersonal, so that it is not material who performs, the law will permit the **delegation** of the performance of the contract. In such cases, however, the contracting party remains liable in the case of default of the person doing the work just as though no delegation had been made.[25]

delegation – transfer to another of the right and power to do an act.

CASE SUMMARY

Who's Liable for $871,069 In Damages? Not Me. I Wasn't Even There!

FACTS: The Emersons contracted with Martin Winters, the owner of Winters Roofing Company, to install a new roof on their home. When the new roof leaked, Winters agreed to fix the problems. Without the knowledge of the Emersons, Winters hired a subcontractor, Bruce Jacobs, to perform the repair work. Jacobs's use of a propane torch in repairing the roof resulted in a fire that caused $871,069 in damages to the house and personal property. Federal Insurance Co. sued Winters to recover sums it paid the Emersons for damages resulting from the fire. Winters defended that Federal had sued the wrong party because Winters did not participate in the repair work but had subcontracted the work out to Jacobs and was neither at the job site nor supervised Jacobs's work.

DECISION: Judgment for the plaintiff. Winters, based on his contract with the Emersons, had an implied duty under the contract to install the roof properly, skillfully, diligently, and in a workmanlike manner. The delegation of these duties to Jacobs did not serve to release Winters from liability implicit in the original content. [*Federal Insurance Co. v. Winters*, 354 S.W. 3d 287 (Tenn. 2011)]

[25] *Orange Bowl Corp. v. Warren,* 386 S.E.2d 293 (S.C. App. 1989).

A contract may prohibit a party owing a duty of performance under a contract from delegating that duty to another.[26] **For Example,** Tom Joyce of Patriot Plumbing Co. contracts to install a new heating system for Mrs. Lawton. A notation on the sales contract that Tom Joyce will do the installation prohibits Patriot Plumbing from delegating the installation to another equally skilled plumber or to another company if a backlog of work occurs at Patriot Plumbing.

If the performance of a party to a contract involves personal skill, talents, judgment, or trust, the delegation of duties is barred unless consented to by the person entitled to the performance. Examples include performance by professionals such as physicians, dentists, lawyers, consultants, celebrities, artists, and craftpersons with unusual skills.

(A) INTENTION TO DELEGATE DUTIES. An assignment of rights does not in itself delegate the performance of duties to the assignee. In the absence of clear language in the assignment stating that duties are or are not delegated, all circumstances must be examined to determine whether there is a delegation. When the total picture is viewed, it may become clear what was intended. The fact that an assignment is made for security of the assignee is a strong indication there was no intent to delegate to the assignee the performance of any duty resting on the assignor.[27]

CASE SUMMARY

Duties Were Delegated Too, Dude

FACTS: Smith, who owned the Avalon Apartments, a condominium, sold individual apartments under contracts that required each purchaser to pay $15 a month extra for hot and cold water, heat, refrigeration, taxes, and fire insurance. Smith assigned his interest in the apartment house under various contracts to Roberts. When Roberts failed to pay the taxes on the building, the purchasers of the individual apartments sued to compel Roberts to do so.

DECISION: Judgment against Roberts. In the absence of a contrary indication, it is presumed that an assignment of a contract delegates the performance of the duties as well as transfers the rights. Here, there was no indication that a package transfer was not intended, and the assignee was therefore obligated to perform in accordance with the contract terms. [*Radley v. Smith and Roberts*, **313 P.2d 465 (Utah 1957)**]

(B) DELEGATION OF DUTIES UNDER THE UCC. With respect to contracts for the sale of goods, "an assignment of 'the contract' or of 'all my rights under the contract' or an assignment in similar general terms is an assignment of rights and, unless the language or the circumstances (as in an assignment for security) indicate the contrary, it is a delegation of performance of the duties of the assignor, and its acceptance by the assignee constitutes a promise … to perform those duties. This promise is enforceable by either the assignor or the other party to the original contract."[28]

---

[26] See *Physical Distribution Services, Inc. v. R. R. Donnelley*, 561 F.3d 792 (8th Cir. 2009).
[27] *City National Bank of Fort Smith v. First National Bank and Trust Co. of Rogers*, 732 S.W.2d 489 (Ark. App. 1987).
[28] U.C.C. §2-210(4).

MAKE THE CONNECTION

SUMMARY

Ordinarily, only the parties to contracts have rights and duties with respect to such contracts. Exceptions are made in the case of third-party beneficiary contracts and assignments.

When a contract shows a clear intent to benefit a third person or class of persons, those persons are called *intended third-party beneficiaries*, and they may sue for breach of the contract. A third-party beneficiary is subject to any limitation or restriction found in the contract. A third-party beneficiary loses all rights when the original contract is terminated by operation of law or if the contract reserves the right to change the beneficiary and such a change is made.

In contrast, an incidental beneficiary benefits from the performance of a contract, but the conferring of this benefit was not intended by the contracting parties. An incidental beneficiary cannot sue on the contract.

An assignment is a transfer of a right; the assignor transfers a right to the assignee. In the absence of a local statute, there are no formal requirements for an assignment. Any words manifesting the intent to transfer are sufficient to constitute an assignment. No consideration is required. Any right to money may be assigned, whether the assignor is entitled to the money at the time of the assignment or will be entitled or expects to be entitled at some time in the future.

A right to a performance may be assigned except when (1) it would increase the burden of performance, (2) the contract involves the performance of personal services, or (3) the transaction is based on extending credit.

When a valid assignment is made, the assignee has the same rights—and only the same rights—as the assignor. The assignee is also subject to the same defenses and setoffs as the assignor had been.

The performance of duties under a contract may be delegated to another person except when a personal element of skill or judgment of the original contracting party is involved. The intent to delegate duties may be expressly stated. The intent may also be found in an "assignment" of "the contract" unless the circumstances make it clear that only the right to money was intended to be transferred. The fact that there has been a delegation of duties does not release the assignor from responsibility for performance. The assignor is liable for breach of the contract if the assignee does not properly perform the delegated duties. In the absence of an effective delegation or the formation of a third-party beneficiary contract, an assignee of rights is not liable to the obligee of the contract for its performance by the assignor.

Notice is not required to effect an assignment. When notice of the assignment is given to the obligor together with a demand that future payments be made to the assignee, the obligor cannot discharge liability by payment to the assignor.

When an assignment is made for a consideration, the assignor makes implied warranties that the right assigned is valid and that the assignor owns that right and will not interfere with its enforcement by the assignee.

LEARNING OUTCOMES

After studying this chapter, you should be able to clearly explain:

A. Third-Party Beneficiary Contracts

L0.1 Explain the two types of intended third-party beneficiaries

See the Sameway Laundry example that illustrates how the "intended creditor beneficiary" can sue the buyer, p. 362. See the text discussion explaining that a life insurance contract is an "intended" donee third-party beneficiary contract, p. 362.

L0.2 Explain why an incidental beneficiary does not have the right to sue as a third-party beneficiary

See the *City of Yorkville* example, in which a subcontractor was an incidental beneficiary with no standing to sue on performance bonds because the obligation ran only to the city, p. 364.

B. Assignments

L0.3 Define an assignment

See the text discussion explaining that an assignment is the transfer of contractual rights to a third party, p. 365. See the *Huntington Beach Board* example that discusses the assignee's direct rights against the obligor, pp. 365–366.

L0.4 Explain the general rule that a person entitled to receive money under a contract may generally assign that right to another person

See the example of an automobile dealer assigning a customer's credit contract to a finance company in order to raise cash to buy more inventory, p. 367.

L0.5 List the nonassignable rights to performance

See the text discussion regarding increase of burden, personal services, and credit transactions beginning on p. 368.

KEY TERMS

assignee	delegation of duties	obligee
assignment	delegation	obligor
assignor	duties	rights
cause of action	implied warranty	third-party beneficiary
claim	intended beneficiary	
debtor	novation	

QUESTIONS AND CASE PROBLEMS

1. Give an example of a third-party beneficiary contract.

2. A court order required John Baldassari to make specified payments for the support of his wife and child. His wife needed more money and applied for Pennsylvania welfare payments. In accordance with the law, she assigned to Pennsylvania her right to the support payments from her husband. Pennsylvania then increased her payments. Pennsylvania obtained a court order directing John, in accordance with the terms of the assignment from his wife, to make the support-order payments directly to the Pennsylvania Department of Public Welfare. John refused to pay on the ground that he had not been notified of the assignment or the hearing directing him to make payment to the assignee. Was he correct? [*Pennsylvania v. Baldassari*, 421 A.2d 306 (Pa. Super.)]

3. Lee contracts to paint Sally's two-story house for $2,500. Sally realizes that she will not have sufficient money, so she transfers her rights under this agreement to her neighbor Karen, who has a three-story house. Karen notifies Lee that Sally's

contract has been assigned to her and demands that Lee paint Karen's house for $2,500. Is Lee required to do so?

4. Assume that Lee agrees to the assignment of the house-painting contract to Karen as stated in question 3. Thereafter, Lee fails to perform the contract to paint Karen's house. Karen sues Sally for damages. Is Sally liable?

5. Jessie borrows $1,000 from Thomas and agrees to repay the money in 30 days. Thomas assigns the right to the $1,000 to Douglas Finance Co. Douglas sues Jessie. Jessie argues that she had agreed to pay the money only to Thomas and that when she and Thomas had entered into the transaction, there was no intention to benefit Douglas Finance Co. Are these objections valid?

6. Washington purchased an automobile from Smithville Motors. The contract called for payment of the purchase price in installments and contained the defense preservation notice required by the Federal Trade Commission regulation. Smithville assigned the contract to Rustic Finance Co. The car was always in need of repairs, and by the time it was half paid for, it would no longer run. Washington canceled the contract. Meanwhile, Smithville had gone out of business. Washington sued Rustic for the amount she had paid Smithville. Rustic refused to pay on the grounds that it had not been at fault. Decide.

7. Helen obtained an insurance policy insuring her life and naming her niece Julie as beneficiary. Helen died, and about a year later the policy was found in her house. When Julie claimed the insurance money, the insurer refused to pay on the ground that the policy required that notice of death be given to it promptly following the death. Julie claimed that she was not bound by the time limitation because she had never agreed to it, as she was not a party to the insurance contract. Is Julie entitled to recover?

8. Lone Star Life Insurance Co. agreed to make a long-term loan to Five Forty Three Land, Inc., whenever that corporation requested one. Five Forty Three wanted this loan to pay off its short-term debts. The loan was never made, as it was never requested by Five Forty Three, which owed the Exchange Bank & Trust Co. on a short-term debt. Exchange Bank then sued Lone Star for breach of its promise on the theory that the Exchange Bank was a third-party beneficiary of the contract to make the loan. Was the Exchange Bank correct? [*Exchange Bank & Trust Co. v. Lone Star Life Ins. Co.,* 546 S.W.2d 948 (Tex. App.)]

9. The New Rochelle Humane Society made a contract with the city of New Rochelle to capture and impound all dogs running at large. Spiegler, a minor, was bitten by some dogs while in her schoolyard. She sued the school district of New Rochelle and the Humane Society. With respect to the Humane Society, she claimed that she was a third-party beneficiary of the contract that the Humane Society had made with the city. She claimed that she could therefore sue the Humane Society for its failure to capture the dogs that had bitten her. Was she entitled to recover? [*Spiegler v. School District of the City of New Rochelle,* 242 N.Y.S.2d 430]

10. Zoya operated a store in premises rented from Peerless. The lease required Zoya to maintain liability insurance to protect Zoya and Peerless. Caswell entered the store, fell through a trap door, and was injured. She then sued Zoya and Peerless on the theory that she was a third-party beneficiary of the lease requirement to maintain liability insurance. Was she correct? [*Caswell v. Zoya Int'l,* 654 N.E.2d 552 (Ill. App.)]

11. Henry was owed $10,000 by Jones Corp. In consideration of the many odd jobs performed for him over the years by his nephew, Henry assigned the $10,000 claim to his nephew Charles. Henry died, and his widow claimed that the assignment was ineffective so that the claim was part of Henry's estate. She based her assertion on the ground that the past performance rendered by the nephew was not consideration. Was the assignment effective?

12. Industrial Construction Co. wanted to raise money to construct a canning factory in Wisconsin. Various persons promised to subscribe the needed amount, which they agreed

to pay when the construction was completed. The construction company assigned its rights and delegated its duties under the agreement to Johnson, who then built the cannery. Vickers, one of the subscribers, refused to pay the amount that he had subscribed on the ground that the contract could not be assigned. Was he correct?

13. The Ohio Department of Public Welfare made a contract with an accountant to audit the accounts of health care providers who were receiving funds under the Medicaid program. Windsor House, which operated six nursing homes, claimed that it was a third-party beneficiary of that contract and could sue for its breach. Was it correct? [*Thornton v. Windsor House, Inc.,* 566 N.E.2d 1220 (Ohio)]

CPA QUESTIONS

1. On August 1, Neptune Fisheries contracted in writing with West Markets to deliver to West 3,000 pounds of lobster at $4.00 a pound. Delivery of the lobsters was due October 1, with payment due November 1. On August 4, Neptune entered into a contract with Deep Sea Lobster Farms that provided as follows: "Neptune Fisheries assigns all the rights under the contract with West Markets dated August 1 to Deep Sea Lobster Farms." The best interpretation of the August 4 contract would be that it was:

   a. Only an assignment of rights by Neptune.

   b. Only a delegation of duties by Neptune.

   c. An assignment of rights and a delegation of duties by Neptune.

   d. An unenforceable third-party beneficiary contract.

2. Graham contracted with the city of Harris to train and employ high school dropouts residing in Harris. Graham breached the contract. Long, a resident of Harris and a high school dropout, sued Graham for damages. Under the circumstances, Long will:

   a. Win, because Long is a third-party beneficiary entitled to enforce the contract.

   b. Win, because the intent of the contract was to confer a benefit on all high school dropouts residing in Harris.

   c. Lose, because Long is merely an incidental beneficiary of the contract.

   d. Lose, because Harris did not assign its contract rights to Long.

3. Union Bank lent $200,000 to Wagner. Union required Wagner to obtain a life insurance policy naming Union as beneficiary. While the loan was outstanding, Wagner stopped paying the premiums on the policy. Union paid the premiums, adding the amounts paid to Wagner's loan. Wagner died, and the insurance company refused to pay the policy proceeds to Union. Union may:

   a. Recover the policy proceeds because it is a creditor beneficiary.

   b. Not recover the policy proceeds because it is a donee beneficiary.

   c. Not recover the policy proceeds because it is not in privity of contract with the insurance company.

   d. Not recover the policy proceeds because it is only an incidental beneficiary.

© Manuel Gutjahr/iStockphoto.com

CHAPTER 19

Discharge of Contracts

learningoutcomes

After studying this chapter, you should be able to

LO.1 List the three types of conditions that affect a party's duty to perform

LO.2 Explain the on-time performance rule

LO.3 Explain the adequacy of performance rules

LO.4 Explain four ways a contract can be discharged by agreement of the parties

LO.5 State the effect on a contract of the death or disability of one of the contracting parties

LO.6 Explain when impossibility or impracticability may discharge a contract

A. Conditions Relating to Performance
   1. CLASSIFICATIONS OF CONDITIONS

B. Discharge by Performance
   2. NORMAL DISCHARGE OF CONTRACTS
   3. NATURE OF PERFORMANCE
   4. TIME OF PERFORMANCE
   5. ADEQUACY OF PERFORMANCE

C. Discharge by Action of Parties
   6. DISCHARGE BY UNILATERAL ACTION
   7. DISCHARGE BY AGREEMENT

D. Discharge by External Causes
   8. DISCHARGE BY IMPOSSIBILITY
   9. DEVELOPING DOCTRINES
   10. TEMPORARY IMPOSSIBILITY
   11. DISCHARGE BY OPERATION OF LAW

I n the preceding chapters, you studied how a contract is formed, what a contract means, and who has rights under a contract. In this chapter, attention is turned to how a contract is ended or discharged. In other words, what puts an end to the rights and duties created by a contract?

A. CONDITIONS RELATING TO PERFORMANCE

As developed in the body of this chapter, the ordinary method of discharging obligations under a contract is by performance. Certain promises may be less than absolute and instead come into effect only upon the occurrence of a specified event, or an existing obligation may be extinguished when an event happens. These are conditional promises.

1. Classifications of Conditions

condition – stipulation or prerequisite in a contract, will, or other instrument.

When the occurrence or nonoccurrence of an event, as expressed in a contract, affects the duty of a party to the contract to perform, the event is called a **condition**. Terms such as *if, provided that, when, after, as soon as, subject to,* and *on the condition that* indicate the creation of a condition.[1] Conditions are classified as *conditions precedent, conditions subsequent,* and *concurrent conditions.*

condition precedent – event that if unsatisfied would mean that no rights would arise under a contract.

(A) CONDITION PRECEDENT. A **condition precedent** is a condition that must occur before a party to a contract has an obligation to perform under the contract. **For Example,** a condition precedent to a contractor's (MasTec's) obligation to pay a subcontractor (MidAmerica) under a "pay-if-paid" by the owner (PathNet) clause in their subcontract agreement is the receipt of payment by MasTec from PathNet. The condition precedent—payment by the owner—did not occur due to bankruptcy, and therefore MasTec did not have an obligation to pay MidAmerica.[2]

CASE SUMMARY

A Blitz on Offense?

FACTS: Richard Blitz owns a piece of commercial property at 4 Old Middle Street. On February 2, 1998, Arthur Subklew entered into a lease with Blitz to rent the rear portion of the property. Subklew intended to operate an auto sales and repair business. Paragraph C of the lease was a zoning contingency clause that stated, "Landlord [plaintiff] will use Landlord's best efforts to obtain a written verification that Tenant can operate [an] Auto Sales and Repair Business at the demised premises. If Landlord is unable to obtain such commitment from the municipality, then this agreement shall be deemed null and void and Landlord shall immediately return deposit

[1] *Harmon Cable Communications v. Scope Cable Television, Inc.,* 468 N.W.2d 350 (Neb. 1990).
[2] *MidAmerica Construction Management, Inc. v. MasTec North America, Inc.,* 436 F.3d 1257 (10th Cir. 2006). But see *International Engineering Services, Inc. v. Scherer Construction Co.,* 74 So.3d 53 (Fla. App. 2011), where a "pay-when-paid" provision was found to be ambiguous, resulting in the general contractor being liable for the payment to the subcontractor.

CASE SUMMARY

Continued

monies to Tenant." The zoning board approved the location only as a general repair business. When Subklew refused to occupy the premises, Blitz sued him for breach of contract.

DECISION: Judgment for Subklew. A condition precedent is a fact or event that the parties intend must exist before there is right to a performance. If the condition is not fulfilled, the right to enforce the contract does not come into existence. Blitz's obligation to obtain written approval of a used car business was a condition precedent to the leasing agreement. Since it was not obtained, Blitz cannot enforce the leasing agreement. [*Blitz v. Subklew*, **810 A.2d 841** (**Conn. App. 2002**)]

condition subsequent – event whose occurrence or lack thereof terminates a contract.

(B) CONDITION SUBSEQUENT. The parties to a contract may agree that a party is obligated to perform a certain act or pay a certain sum of money, but the contract contains a provision that relieves the obligation on the occurrence of a certain event. That is, on the happening of a **condition subsequent**, such an event extinguishes the duty to thereafter perform. **For Example,** Chad Newly served as the weekend anchor on *Channel 5 News* for several years. The station manager, Tom O'Brien, on reviewing tapes in connection with Newly's contract renewal, believed that Newly's speech on occasion was slightly slurred, and he suspected that it was from alcohol use. In the parties' contract discussions, O'Brien expressed his concerns about an alcohol problem and offered help. Newly denied there was a problem. O'Brien agreed to a new two-year contract with Newly at $167,000 for the first year and $175,000 for the second year with other benefits subject to "the condition" that the station reserved the right to make four unannounced drug-alcohol tests during the contract term; and should Newly test positive for drugs or alcohol under measurements set forth in the contract, then all of Channel 5's obligations to Newly under the contract would cease. When Newly subsequently failed a urinalysis test three months into the new contract, the happening of this event extinguished the station's obligation to employ and pay him under the contract. Conditions subsequent are strictly construed, and where ambiguous, are construed against forfeiture.[3]

Sports & Entertainment Law

Endorsement Contracts

Sports marketing involves the use of famous athletes to promote the sale of products and services in our economy. Should an athlete's image be tarnished by allegations of immoral or illegal conduct, a company could be subject to financial losses and corporate embarrassment. Endorsement contracts may extend for multiyear periods, and should a "morals" issue arise, a company would be well served to have had a broad morals clause in its contract that would allow the company at its sole discretion to summarily terminate the endorsement contract. Representatives of athletes, on the other hand, seek narrow contractual language that allows for termination of endorsement contracts only upon the indictment for a crime, and they seek the right to have an arbitrator, as opposed to the employer, make the determination as to whether the morals clause was violated. NBA player Latrell Spreewell's endorsement contract with Converse Athletic

---

[3] *Cardone Trust v. Cardone*, 8 A.3d 1 (N.H. 2010).

Sports & Entertainment Law

Continued

Shoe Co. was terminated by the company following his altercation with his coach P.J. Carlisimo; John Daly's endorsement contract with Callaway Golf was terminated by the company when he violated his good conduct clause that restricted gambling and drinking activities; and six-time Pro Bowl football player Chad Johnson (aka "Ochocinco") lost his endorsement deal with Zico Coconut Water after he was arrested in a domestic battery case involving his wife. And, Nike,

RadioShack and other sponsors ended their relationships with cyclist Lance Armstrong after a report detailing doping charges was issued by the U.S. Anti-Doping Agency.

Can the courts be utilized to resolve controversies over whether a "morals clause" has been violated? If so, is the occurrence of a morals clause violation a condition precedent or a condition subsequent?

(C) **Concurrent Condition.** In most bilateral contracts, the performances of the parties are *concurrent conditions.* That is, their mutual duties of performance under the contract are to take place simultaneously. **For Example,** concerning a contract for the sale and delivery of certain goods, the buyer must tender to the seller a certified check at the time of delivery as set forth in the contract, and the seller must tender the goods to the buyer at the same time.

B. Discharge by Performance

When it is claimed that a contract is discharged by performance, questions arise as to the nature, time, and sufficiency of the performance.

2. Normal Discharge of Contracts

A contract is usually discharged by the performance of the terms of the agreement. In most cases, the parties perform their promises and the contract ceases to exist or is thereby discharged. A contract is also discharged by the expiration of the time period specified in the contract.[4]

3. Nature of Performance

Performance may be the doing of an act or the making of payment.

tender–goods have arrived, are available for pickup, and buyer is notified.

(A) **Tender.** An offer to perform is known as a **tender**. If performance of the contract requires the doing of an act, the refusal of a tender discharges the party offering to perform and is a basis for that party to bring a lawsuit.

A valid tender of payment consists of an unconditional offer of the exact amount due on the date when due. A tender of payment is not just an expression of willingness to pay; it must be an actual offer to perform by making payment of the amount owed.

(B) **Payment.** When the contract requires payment, performance consists of the payment of money.

---

[4] *Washington National Ins. Co. v. Sherwood Associates,* 795 P.2d 665 (Utah App. 1990).

(1) Application of Payments.

If a debtor owes more than one debt to the creditor and pays money, a question may arise as to which debt has been paid. If the debtor specifies the debt to which the payment is to be applied and the creditor accepts the money, the creditor is bound to apply the money as specified.[5] Thus, if the debtor specifies that a payment is to be made for a current purchase, the creditor may not apply the payment to an older balance.

(2) Payment by Check.

Payment by commercial paper, such as a check, is ordinarily a conditional payment. A check merely suspends the debt until the check is presented for payment. If payment is then made, the debt is discharged; if not paid, the suspension terminates, and suit may be brought on either the debt or the check. Frequently, payment must be made by a specified date. It is generally held that the payment is made on time if it is mailed on or before the final date for payment.

CASE SUMMARY

The Mailed-Check Payment

FACTS: Thomas Cooper was purchasing land from Peter and Ella Birznieks. Cooper was already in possession of the land but was required to pay the amount owed by January 30; otherwise, he would have to vacate the property. The attorney handling the transaction for the Birznieks told Cooper that he could mail the payment to him. On January 30, Cooper mailed to the attorney a personal check drawn on an out-of-state bank for the amount due. The check arrived at the Birznieks' attorney's office on February 1. The Birznieks refused to accept the check on the grounds that it was not a timely payment and moved to evict Cooper from the property.

DECISION: Because of the general custom to regard a check mailed to a creditor as paying the bill that is owed, payment was made by Cooper on January 30 when he mailed the check. Payment was therefore made within the required time even though received after the expiration of the required time. [*Birznieks v. Cooper*, 275 N.W.2d 221 (Mich. 1979)]

4. Time of Performance

When the date or period of time for performance is specified in the contract, performance should be made on that date or within that time period.

(A) No Time Specified. When the time for performance is not specified in the contract, an obligation to perform within a reasonable time is implied.[6] The fact that no time is specified neither impairs the contract on the ground that it is indefinite nor allows an endless time in which to perform. What constitutes a reasonable time is determined by the nature of the subject matter of the contract and the facts and circumstances surrounding the making of the contract.

(B) When Time Is Essential. If performance of the contract on or within the exact time specified is vital, it is said that "time is of the essence." Time is of the essence when

---

[5] *Oakes Logging, Inc. v. Green Crow, Inc.,* 832 P.2d 894 (Wash. App. 1992).
[6] *First National Bank v. Clark,* 447 S.E.2d 558 (W. Va. 1994).

the contract relates to property that is perishable or that is fluctuating rapidly in value. When a contract fixes by unambiguous language a time for performance and where there is no evidence showing that the parties did not intend that time should be of the essence, failure to perform within the specified time is a breach of contract entitling the innocent party to damages. **For Example,** Dixon and Gandhi agreed that Gandhi would close on the purchase of a motel as follows: "Closing Date. The closing shall be held … on the date which is within twenty (20) days after the closing of Nomura Financing." Gandhi did not close within the time period specified, and Dixon was allowed to retain $100,000 in prepaid closing costs and fees as liquidated damages for Gandhi's breach of contract.[7]

(c) WHEN TIME IS NOT ESSENTIAL. Unless a contract so provides, time is ordinarily not of the essence, and performance within a reasonable time is sufficient. In the case of the sale of property, time is not regarded as of the essence when there has not been any appreciable change in the market value or condition of the property and when the person who delayed does not appear to have done so for the purpose of speculating on a change in market price.

(d) WAIVER OF ESSENCE OF TIME LIMITATION. A provision that time is of the essence may be waived. It is waived when the specified time has expired but the party who could complain requests the delaying party to take steps necessary to perform the contract.

5. Adequacy of Performance

When a party renders exactly the performance called for by the contract, no question arises as to whether the contract has been performed. In other cases, there may not have been a perfect performance, or a question arises as to whether the performance satisfies the standard set by the contract.

CPA

substantial performance— equitable rule that if a good-faith attempt to perform does not precisely meet the terms of the agreement, the agreement will still be considered complete if the essential purpose of the contract is accomplished.

(a) SUBSTANTIAL PERFORMANCE. Perfect performance of a contract is not always possible when dealing with construction projects. A party who in good faith has provided **substantial performance** of the contract may sue to recover the payment specified in the contract.[8] However, because the performance was not perfect, the performing party is subject to a counterclaim for the damages caused the other party. When a building contractor has substantially performed the contract to construct a building, the contractor is responsible for the cost of repairing or correcting the defects as an offset from the contract price.[9]

The measure of damages under these circumstances is known as "cost of completion" damages.[10] If, however, the cost of completion would be unreasonably disproportionate to the importance of the defect, the measure of damages is the diminution in value of the building due to the defective performance.

Whether there is substantial performance is a question of degree to be determined by all of the facts, including the particular type of structure involved, its intended purpose, and the nature and relative expense of repairs.

For Example, a certain building contractor (BC) and a certain owner (O) made a contract to construct a home overlooking Vineyard Sound on Martha's Vineyard according to plans and specifications that clearly called for the use of General

[7] *Woodhull Corp. v.Saibaba Corp.,* 507 S.E.2d 493 (Ga. App. 1998).
[8] *Gala v. Harris,* 77 So.3d 1065 (La. App. 2012).
[9] Substantial performance is not a defense to a breach of contract claim, however. See *Bentley Systems Inc. v. Intergraph Corp.,* 922 So.2d 61 (Ala. 2005).
[10] *Hammer Construction Corp. v. Phillips,* 994 So.2d 1135 (Fla. App. 2008).

| FIGURE 19-1 | *Causes of Contract Discharge* |

© Cengage Learning

Plumbing Blue Star piping. The contract price was $1,100,000. Upon inspecting the work before making the final $400,000 payment and accepting the building, O discovered that BC had used Republic piping throughout the house. O explained to BC that his family had made its money by investing in General Plumbing, and he, therefore, would not make the final payment until the breach of contract was remedied. BC explained that Republic pipes were of the same industrial grade and quality as the Blue Star pipes. Moreover, BC estimated that it would cost nearly $300,000 to replace all of the pipes because of the destruction of walls and fixtures necessary to accomplish such a task. BC may sue O for $400,000 for breach of contract, claiming he had substantially performed the contract, and O may counterclaim for $300,000, seeking an offset for the cost of remedying the breach. The court will find in favor of the contractor and will not allow the $300,000 offset but will allow a "nominal" offset of perhaps $100 to $1,000 for the amount by which the Republic pipes diminished the value of the building. To have required the pipes to be replaced would amount to economic waste.[11]

When a contractor does not substantially perform its obligations under a contract, not only will the contractor not prevail in a breach of contract claim against a homeowner for extra work beyond the contract price but the contractor is liable for the reasonable cost of making the contractor's work conform to the contract. **For Example,** Superior Wall and Paver, LLC sued homeowners Pamela and Mark Gacek for $14,350 it claimed was still owed Superior as extra work, for concrete pavers it installed in the driveway of their residence. The Gaceks had previously paid the $45,000 contract price. The Gackes counterclaimed for $60,500 for the reasonable cost of making the contractor's work conform to the contract. The evidence established that Superior did not install a proper base of 3" to 4" of crushed limestone before installing the pavers as required by the contract, which caused the pavers to move, creating gaps between the pavers and causing water to flow into the garage. To correct the problem the pavers needed to be removed and the area excavated and replaced with a crushed limestone base before again installing the pavers. Superior claimed it had substantially performed the contract as a fully usable driveway, and the proper remedy, if any, was the diminution of the market value of the Gaceks' property due to any defective performance. Superior asserted the cost of redoing the entire job would be economic waste. The court determined that Superior had not substantially performed the contract and awarded the homeowners the cost of making Superior's work conform to the contract by having the job redone, rejecting Superior's assertion of economic waste.[12]

In most jurisdictions, the willfulness of the departure from the specifications of the contract does not by itself preclude some recovery for the contractor on the "cost of completion" basis but rather is a factor in consideration of whether there was substantial performance by the contractor.[13]

(B) Fault of Complaining Party. A party cannot complain that a performance was defective when the performance follows the terms of the contract required by the complaining party. Thus, a homeowner who supplied the specifications for poured cement walls could not hold a contractor liable for damages when the walls that were poured in exact compliance with those specifications proved defective.

(C) Performance to the Satisfaction of the Contracting Party or a Third Party. Sometimes an agreement requires performance to the satisfaction, taste, or judgment of the other party to the contract. When the contract specifically stipulates that the performance must satisfy the contracting party, the courts will ordinarily enforce the plain meaning of the language of the parties and the work must satisfy the contracting party—subject, of course, to the requirement that dissatisfaction be made in good faith. **For Example,** the Perrones' written contract to purchase the Hills' residence contained a clause making performance subject to inspection to the

---

[11] See *Jacob & Youngs, Inc. v. Kent,* 230 N.Y. 239 (1921).
[12] *Superior Wall and Paver, LLC. v. Gacek,* 73 So.3d (Ala. App. 2011).
[13] But see *USX Corp. v. M. DeMatteo Construction Co.,* 315 F.3d 43 (1st Cir. 2002), for application of a common law rule that prohibits a construction contractor guilty of a willful breach of contract from maintaining any suit on the contract against the other party.

Perrones' satisfaction. During the house inspection, the inspector found a piece of wood in a crawl space that appeared to have been damaged by termites and had possibly been treated some 18 years before with chlordane. At the end of the inspection Mr. Perrone indicated that he would perform on the contract. Thereafter, he went on the Internet and found that chlordane is a highly toxic pesticide now banned from use as a termite treatment. As a result, the Perrones rescinded the contract under the buyer satisfaction clause. The Hills sued, believing that speculation about a pesticide treatment 18 years ago was absurd. They contended that the Perrones had breached the contract without a valid reason. The court decided for the Perrones, since they exercised the "satisfaction clause" in good faith.[14] Good-faith personal satisfaction is generally required when the subject matter of the contract is personal, such as interior design work, tailoring, or the painting of a portrait.

With respect to things mechanical or routine performances, courts require that the performance be such as would satisfy a reasonable person under the circumstances.

When work is to be done subject to the approval of an architect, engineer, or another expert, most courts apply the reasonable person test of satisfaction.

C. DISCHARGE BY ACTION OF PARTIES

Contracts may be discharged by the joint action of both contracting parties or, in some cases, by the action of one party alone.

6. Discharge by Unilateral Action

Ordinarily, a contract cannot be discharged by the action of either party alone. In some cases, however, the contract gives one of either party the right to cancel the contract by unilateral action, such as by notice to the other party. Insurance policies covering loss commonly provide that the insurer may cancel the policy upon giving a specified number of days' notice.

(A) CONSUMER PROTECTION RESCISSION. A basic principle of contract law is that once made, a contract between competent persons is a binding obligation. Consumer protection legislation introduces into the law a contrary concept—that of giving the consumer a chance to think things over and to rescind the contract. Thus, the federal Consumer Credit Protection Act (CCPA) gives the debtor the right to rescind a credit transaction within three business days when the transaction would impose a lien on the debtor's home. **For Example,** a homeowner who mortgages his or her home to obtain a loan may cancel the transaction for any reason by notifying the lender before midnight of the third full business day after the loan is made.[15]

A Federal Trade Commission regulation gives the buyer three business days in which to cancel a home-solicited sale of goods or services costing more than $25.[16]

---

[14] *Hill v. Perrones*, 42 P.3d 210 (Kan. App. 2002).
[15] If the owner is not informed of this right to cancel, the three-day period does not begin until that information is given. Consumer Credit Protection Act §125, 15 U.S.C. §1635(a), (e), (f).
[16] C.F.R. §429.1.

7. Discharge by Agreement

A contract may be discharged by the operation of one of its provisions or by a subsequent agreement. Thus, there may be a discharge by (1) the terms of the original contract, such as a provision that the contract should end on a specified date; (2) a mutual cancellation, in which the parties agree to end their contract; (3) a mutual **rescission**, in which the parties agree to annul the contract and return both parties to their original positions before the contract had been made; (4) the **substitution** of a new contract between the same parties; (5) a novation or substitution of a new contract involving a new party;[17] (6) an **accord and satisfaction**; (7) a release; or (8) a **waiver**.

(A) SUBSTITUTION. The parties may decide that their contract is not the one they want. They may then replace it with another contract. If they do, the original contract is discharged by substitution.[18]

(B) ACCORD AND SATISFACTION. When the parties have differing views as to the performance required by the terms of a contract, they may agree to a different performance. Such an agreement is called an *accord*. When the accord is performed or executed, there is an accord and satisfaction, which discharges the original obligation. To constitute an accord and satisfaction, there must be a bona fide dispute, a proposal to settle the dispute, and performance of the agreement.

> **rescission** – action of one party to a contract to set the contract aside when the other party is guilty of a breach of the contract.
>
> **substitution** – substitution of a new contract between the same parties.
>
> **accord and satisfaction** – agreement to substitute for an existing debt some alternative form of discharging that debt, coupled with the actual discharge of the debt by the substituted performance.
>
> **waiver** – release or relinquishment of a known right or objection.

CASE SUMMARY

A Full Court Press to No Avail

FACTS: In September 2002, La Crosse Litho Supply, LLC (La Crosse) entered into a distribution agreement with MKL Pre-Press Electronics (MKL) for the distribution of a printing system. La Crosse purchased a 7000 System unit from MKL for its end user Printing Plus. MKL technicians were to provide service and training for the unit. The 7000 System at Printing Plus failed on three occasions, and ultimately repairs were unsuccessful. On September 30, 2003, La Crosse canceled the distribution agreement. On October 2, 2003, La Crosse sent a letter to MKL's sales vice president Bill Landwer setting forth an itemized accounting of what it owed MKL Pre-Press with deductions for the purchase price of the failed 7000 System and other offsets. MKL sent a subsequent bill for repairs and services, to which La Crosse objected and stated that it would not pay. MKL's attorney sent a demand letter for $26,453.31. La Crosse's president, Randall Peters, responded by letter dated December 30, 2003, explaining that with an offset for training and warranty work it had performed, "we are sending you the final payment in the amount of $1,696.47." He added, "[w]ith this correspondence, we consider all open issues between La Crosse Litho Supply and MKL Pre-Press closed." Enclosed with the letter was a check for $1,696.47 payable to MKL Pre-Press. In the remittance portion of the check, under the heading "Ref," was typed "FINAL PAYM." The check was endorsed and deposited on either January 26 or 27, 2004. MKL sued La Crosse for $24,756.84. La Crosse defended that the tender and subsequent deposit of the check for $1,696.47 constituted an accord and satisfaction. Jill Fleming, MKL's office manager, stated that it was her duty to process checks and that she did not read Peters' letter. From a judgment for La Crosse, MKL appealed.

---

[17] *Eagle Industries, Inc. v. Thompson*, 900 P.2d 475 (Or. 1995). In a few jurisdictions, the term *novation* is used to embrace the substitution of any new contract, whether between the original parties or not.

[18] *Shawnee Hospital Authority v. Dow Construction, Inc.*, 812 P.2d 1351 (Okla. 1990).

CASE SUMMARY

Continued

DECISION: Judgment for La Crosse. There was an honest dispute as to the amount owed, as evident from the exchange of letters. La Crosse tendered an amount with the explicit understanding that it was the "final payment" of all demands, and the creditor MKL's acceptance and negotiation of a check for that amount constitutes an accord and satisfaction. Ms. Fleming had the authority to endorse checks and deposit them, and her doing so can and should be imputed to her employer, thereby constituting an accord and satisfaction. [*MKL Pre-Press Electronics v. La Crosse Litho Supply, LLC*, 840 N.E.2d 687 (Ill. App. 2005)]

D. DISCHARGE BY EXTERNAL CAUSES

Circumstances beyond the control of the contracting parties may discharge the contract.

8. Discharge by Impossibility

To establish impossibility a party must show (1) the unexpected occurrence of an intervening act; (2) that the risk of the unexpected occurrence was not allocated by agreement or custom; and (3) that the occurrence made performance impossible. The doctrine of impossibility relieves nonperformance only in extreme circumstances.[19] The party asserting the defense of impossibility bears the burden of proving "a real impossibility and not a mere inconvenience or unexpected difficulty."[20] Moreover, courts will generally only excuse nonperformance where performance is objectively impossible—that is, incapable performance by anyone. Financial inability to perform a contract that a party voluntarily entered into will rarely, if ever, excuse nonperformance. **For Example,** Ms. Robinson was employed by East Capital Community Development Group under a written employment contract for one year, but was terminated early for lack of funding. The contract did not reference that her continued employment was contingent on continued grant funding. The contract was objectively capable of performance. The defense of impossibility was rejected by the court.[21]

(A) DESTRUCTION OF PARTICULAR SUBJECT MATTER. When parties contract expressly for, or with reference to, a particular subject matter, the contract is discharged if the subject matter is destroyed through no fault of either party. When a contract calls for the sale of a wheat crop growing on a specific parcel of land, the contract is discharged if that crop is destroyed by blight.

On the other hand, if there is merely a contract to sell a given quantity of a specified grade of wheat, the seller is not discharged when the seller's crop is destroyed by blight. The seller had made an unqualified undertaking to deliver wheat of a specified grade. No restrictions or qualifications were imposed as to the source. If the seller does not deliver the goods called for by the contract, the contract is broken, and the seller is liable for damages.

---

[19] *Island Development Corp. v. District of Columbia*, 933 A.2d 340, 350 (D.C. 2007).
[20] *Bergmann v. Parker*, 216 A.2d 581 (D.C. 1966).
[21] *East Capital View Community Development Corp. v. Robinson*, 941 A.2d 1036 (D.C. 2008).

(B) CHANGE OF LAW. A contract is discharged when its performance is made illegal by a subsequent change in the law. Thus, a contract to construct a nonfireproof building at a particular place is discharged by the adoption of a zoning law prohibiting such a building within that area. Mere inconvenience or temporary delay caused by the new law, however, does not excuse performance.

(C) DEATH OR DISABILITY. When the contract obligates a party to render or receive personal services requiring peculiar skill, the death, incapacity, or illness of the party that was either to render or receive the personal services excuses both sides from a duty to perform. It is sometimes said that "the death of either party is the death of the contract."

The rule does not apply, however, when the acts called for by the contract are of such a character that (1) the acts may be as well performed by others, such as the promisor's personal representatives, or (2) the contract's terms contemplate continuance of the obligations after the death of one of the parties. **For Example,** Lynn Jones was under contract to investor Ed Jenkins to operate certain Subway sandwich shops and to acquire new franchises with funding provided by Jenkins. After Jenkins's death, Jones claimed he was no longer bound under the contract and was free to pursue franchise opportunities on his own. The contract between Jones and Jenkins expressed that it was binding on the parties' "heirs and assigns" and that the contract embodied property rights that passed to Jenkins's widow. The agreement's provisions thus established that the agreement survived the death of Jenkins, and Jones was therefore obligated to remit profits from the franchise he acquired for himself after Jenkins's death.[22]

(D) ACT OF OTHER PARTY. Every contract contains "an implied covenant of good faith and fair dealing." As a result of this covenant, a promisee is under an obligation to do nothing that would interfere with the promisor's performance. When the promisee prevents performance or otherwise makes performance impossible, the promisor is discharged from the contract. Thus, a subcontractor is discharged from any obligation when it is unable to do the work because the principal contractor refuses to deliver the material, equipment, or money required by the subcontract. When the default of the other party consists of failing to supply goods or services, the duty may rest on the party claiming a discharge of the contract to show that substitute goods or services could not be obtained elsewhere.

9. Developing Doctrines

Commercial impracticability and frustration of purpose may excuse performance.

(A) COMMERCIAL IMPRACTICABILITY. The doctrine of *commercial impracticability* was developed to deal with the harsh rule that a party must perform its contracts unless it is absolutely impossible. However, not every type of impracticability is an excuse for nonperformance. **For Example,** I. Patel was bound by his franchise agreement with Days Inn, Inc., to maintain his 60-room inn on old Route 66 in Lincoln, Illinois, to at least minimum quality assurance standards. His inn failed five consecutive quality inspections over two years, with the inspector noting damaged guest rooms, burns in the bedding, and severely stained carpets. Patel's defense when his franchise was canceled after the fifth failed inspection was that bridge

---

[22] *Jenkins Subway, Inc. v. Jones*, 990 S.W.2d 713 (Tenn. App. 1998).

repairs on the road leading from I-55 to his inn had adversely affected his business and made it commercially impractical to live up to the franchise agreement. The court rejected his defense, determining that while the bridge work might have affected patronage, it had no effect on his duty to comply with the quality assurance standards of his franchise agreement.[23] Commercial impracticability is available only when the performance is made impractical by the subsequent occurrence of an event whose nonoccurrence was a basic assumption on which the contract was made.[24]

The defense of commercial impractability will not relieve sophisticated business entities from their contractual obligations due to an economic downturn, even one as drastic and severe as the recent recession. **For Example,** real estate developer Beemer Associates was not excused under this doctrine of commercial impracticability from performance of its construction loan payment obligation of $5,250,000 plus interest and fees where unanticipated changes in the financial and real estate markets made it unable to secure tenants at the expected rate.[25] Economic downturns and other market shifts do not constitute unanticipated circumstances in a market economy.[26]

(B) FRUSTRATION OF PURPOSE DOCTRINE. Because of a change in circumstances, the purpose of the contract may have no value to the party entitled to receive performance. In such a case, performance may be excused if both parties were aware of the purpose and the event that frustrated the purpose was unforeseeable.[27]

For Example, National Southern Bank rents a home near Willowbend Country Club on the southeastern shore of North Carolina for $75,000 a week to entertain business guests at the Ryder Cup matches scheduled for the week in question. Storm damage from Hurricane David the week before the event caused the closing of the course and the transfer of the tournament to another venue in a different state. The bank's duty to pay for the house may be excused by the doctrine of *frustration of purpose,* because the transfer of the tournament fully destroyed the value of the home rental, both parties were aware of the purpose of the rental, and the cancellation of the golf tournament was unforeseeable.

CASE SUMMARY

Relief for Broken Dreams

FACTS: John J. Paonessa Company made a contract with the state of Massachusetts to reconstruct a portion of highway. Paonessa then made a contract with Chase Precast Corporation to obtain concrete median barriers for use in the highway. Thereafter, the state highway department decided that such barriers would not be used. Paonessa therefore had no reason to go through with the contract to purchase the barriers from Chase because it could not use them and could not get paid for them by the state. Chase sued Paonessa for the profit Chase would have made on the contract for the barriers.

---

[23] *Days Inn of America, Inc. v. Patel,* 88 F. Supp. 2d 928 (C.D. Ill. 2000).

[24] See Restatement (Second) of Contracts §261; U.C.C. §2-615.

[25] *LSREF2 Baron, LLC v. Beemer,* 2011 WL 6838163 (M.D. Fla. Dec. 29, 2011).

[26] *Flathead-Michigan I, LLC v. Peninsula Dev., LLC,* 2011 WL 940048 (E.D. Mich. March 16, 2011).

[27] The defense of frustration of purpose, or commercial frustration, is very difficult to invoke because the courts are extremely reluctant to allow parties to avoid obligations to which they have agreed. See *Wal-Mart Stores, Inc. v. AIG Life Insurance Co.,* 872 A.2d 611 (Del. Ch. 2005), denying application of the commercial frustration doctrine when the supervening event, the invalidation of hundreds of millions in tax deductions by the IRS, was reasonably foreseeable and could have been provided for in the contract.

CASE SUMMARY

Continued

DECISION: Judgment for Paonessa. The change to the highway construction plan made by the State Department of Highways made the barriers worthless. There was accordingly a frustration of the purpose for which the contract had been made to purchase the barriers. Therefore, the contract for the median barriers was discharged by such frustration of purpose and did not bind Paonessa. [*Chase Precast Corp. v. John J. Paonessa Co., Inc.,* 566 N.E.2d 603 (Mass. 1991)]

(c) COMPARISON TO COMMON LAW RULE. The traditional common law rule refuses to recognize commercial impracticability or frustration of purpose. By the common law rule, the losses and disappointments against which commercial impracticability and frustration of purpose give protection are merely the risks that one takes in entering into a contract. Moreover, the situations could have been guarded against by including an appropriate condition subsequent in the contract. A condition subsequent declares that the contract will be void if a specified event occurs.[28] The contract also could have provided for a readjustment of compensation if there was a basic change of circumstances. The common law approach also rejects these developing concepts because they weaken the stability of a contract.

An indication of a wider recognition of the concept that "extreme" changes of circumstances can discharge a contract is found in the Uniform Commercial Code. The UCC provides for the discharge of a contract for the sale of goods when a condition that the parties assumed existed, or would continue, ceases to exist.[29]

(D) FORCE MAJEURE. To avoid litigation over impossibility and impractability issues, modern contracting parties often contract around the doctrine of impossibility, specifying the failures that will excuse performance in their contracts. The clauses in which they do this are called *force majeure*—uncontrollable event—clauses. And they are enforced by courts as written.

CASE SUMMARY

WEPCO Was Not Railroaded, It Was *Force Majeured!*

FACTS: WEPCO, an electric utility, sued the Union Pacific Railroad Co. alleging that the railroad breached the *force majeure* provision of the parties' long-term coal-hauling contract, which ran from 1999 to 2005. The provision at issue provides that if the railroad is prevented by "an event of Force Majeure" from reloading its empty cars (after it has delivered coal to WEPCO) with iron ore destined for Geneva, Utah, it can charge the higher rate that the contract makes applicable to shipments that do not involve backhauling. The rate for coal shipped from one of the Colorado coal mines to WEPCO was specified as $13.20 per ton if there was a backhaul shipment but $15.63 if there was not. The iron ore that the railroad's freight trains would have

---

[28] *Wermer v. ABI,* 10 S.W.3d 575 (Mo. App. 2000).
[29] U.C.C. §2-615.

CASE SUMMARY

Continued

picked up in Minnesota was intended for a steel mill in Utah. The steel company was bankrupt when the parties signed the contract. In November 2001 the steel mill shut down, and closed for good in February 2004. Two months later the railroad wrote WEPCO to declare "an event of Force Majeure" and that henceforth it would be charging WEPCO the higher rate applicable to shipments without a backhaul. WEPCO sued the railroad for breach of the force majeure provision in the contract.

DECISION: Judgment for the railroad. The provision dealt with the foreseeable situation of the steel mill shutdown and the possibility of hauling back to the mine empty coal cars, thereby generating no revenue. The contract clause is enforced as written. [*Wisconsin Electric Power Co. v. Union Pacific Railroad Co.*, 557 F.3d 504 (7th Cir. 2009)]

10. Temporary Impossibility

Ordinarily, a temporary impossibility suspends the duty to perform. If the obligation to perform is suspended, it is revived on the termination of the impossibility. If, however, performance at that later date would impose a substantially greater burden on the party obligated to perform, some courts discharge the obligor from the contract.

After the September 11, 2001, terrorist attack on the World Trade Center, New York City courts followed wartime precedents that had developed the law of temporary impossibility. Such impossibility, when of brief duration, excuses performance until it subsequently becomes possible to perform rather than excusing performance altogether. Thus, an individual who was unable to communicate her cancellation of travel 60 days prior to her scheduled travel as required by her contract, which needed to occur on or before September 14, 2001, could expect relief from a cancellation penalty provision in the contract based on credible testimony of attempted phone calls to the travel agent on and after September 12, 2001, even though the calls did not get through due to communication problems in New York City.[30]

(A) WEATHER. Acts of God, such as tornadoes, lightning, and floods, usually do not terminate a contract even though they make performance difficult. Thus, weather conditions constitute a risk that is assumed by a contracting party in the absence of a contrary agreement. Consequently, extra expense sustained by a contractor because of weather conditions is a risk that the contractor assumes in the absence of an express provision for additional compensation in such a case. **For Example,** Danielo Contractors made a contract to construct a shopping mall for the Rubicon Center, with construction to begin November 1. Because of abnormal cold and blizzard conditions, Danielo was not able to begin work until April 1 and was five months late in completing the construction of the project. Rubicon sued Danielo for breach of contract by failing to perform on schedule. Danielo is liable. Because the contract

---

[30] See *Bugh v. Protravel International, Inc.*, 746 N.Y.S.2d 290 (Civ. Ct. N.Y.C. 2002).

included no provision covering delay caused by weather, Danielo bore the risk of the delay and resulting loss.

Modern contracts commonly contain a "weather clause" and reflect the parties' agreement on this matter. When the parties take the time to discuss weather issues, purchasing insurance coverage is a common resolution.

11. Discharge by Operation of Law

operation of law – attaching of certain consequences to certain facts because of legal principles that operate automatically as contrasted with consequences that arise because of the voluntary action of a party designed to create those consequences.

A contract is discharged by **operation of law** by (1) an alteration or a material change made by a party, (2) the destruction of the written contract with intent to discharge it, (3) bankruptcy, (4) the operation of a statute of limitations, or (5) a contractual limitation.

(A) BANKRUPTCY. As set forth in the chapter on bankruptcy, even though all creditors have not been paid in full, a discharge in **bankruptcy** eliminates ordinary contract claims against the debtor.

CPA

bankruptcy – procedure by which one unable to pay debts may surrender all assets in excess of any exemption claim to the court for administration and distribution to creditors, and the debtor is given a discharge that releases him from the unpaid balance due on most debts.

statute of limitations – statute that restricts the period of time within which an action may be brought.

(B) STATUTE OF LIMITATIONS. A **statute of limitations** provides that after a certain number of years have passed, a contract claim is barred. The time limitation provided by state statutes of limitations varies widely. The time period for bringing actions for breach of an oral contract is two to three years. The period may differ with the type of contract—ranging from a relatively short time for open accounts (ordinary customers' charge accounts) to four years for sales of goods.[31] A somewhat longer period exists for bringing actions for breach of written contracts (usually four to ten years). **For Example,** Prate Installations, Inc., sued homeowners Richard and Rebecca Thomas for failure to pay for a new roof installed by Prate. Prate had sent numerous invoices to the Thomases over a four-year period seeking payment to no avail. The Thomases moved to dismiss the case under a four-year limitation period. However, the court concluded that the state's ten-year limitations period on written contracts applied.[32] The maximum period for judgments of record is usually 10 to 20 years.

A breach of contract claim against a builder begins to run when a home's construction is substantially complete. **For Example,** a breach of contract claim against home builder Stewart Brockett was time barred under a state's six-year statute of limitations for breach of contract actions inasmuch as the home in question was substantially completed in September 2001 and the breach of contract action commenced on June 17, 2008.[33]

(C) CONTRACTUAL LIMITATIONS. Some contracts, particularly insurance contracts, contain a time limitation within which suit must be brought. This is in effect a private statute of limitations created by the agreement of the parties.

A contract may also require that notice of any claim be given within a specified time. A party who fails to give notice within the time specified by the contract is barred from suing on the contract.

A contract provision requiring that suit be brought within one year does not violate public policy, although the statute of limitations would allow two years in the absence of such a contract limitation.[34]

---

[31] U.C.C. §2-725(1).
[32] *Prate Installations, Inc. v. Thomas,* 842 N.E.2d 1205 (Ill. App. 2006).
[33] *New York Central Mutual Fire Insurance Co. v. Gilder Oil Co.,* 936 N.Y.S. 2d 815 (Sup.Ct. A.D. 2011).
[34] *Keiting v.Skauge,* 543 N.W.2d 565 (Wis. App. 1995).

LawFlix

Uncle Buck (1989) (PG-13)

John Candy plays ne'er-do-well Uncle Buck who promises to go to work at his girlfriend's tire store and marry her. When his brother calls in the middle of the night seeking help with his children, Buck tells his girlfriend (Chenise) that he can no longer honor his promise because he must go to the suburbs to care for his brother's children while his brother and sister-in-law travel to Indiana to be with his sister-in-law's very ill father. Discuss Buck's excuse. Is it impossibility? Does the change in circumstances excuse Buck?

MAKE THE CONNECTION

SUMMARY

A party's duty to perform under a contract can be affected by a condition precedent, which must occur before a party has an obligation to perform; a condition subsequent, that is, a condition or event that relieves the duty to thereafter perform; and concurrent conditions, which require mutual and often simultaneous performance.

Most contracts are discharged by performance. An offer to perform is called a *tender of performance*. If a tender of performance is wrongfully refused, the duty of the tenderer to perform is terminated. When the performance called for by the contract is the payment of money, it must be legal tender that is offered. In actual practice, it is common to pay and to accept payment by checks or other commercial paper.

When the debtor owes the creditor on several accounts and makes a payment, the debtor may specify which account is to be credited with the payment. If the debtor fails to specify, the creditor may choose which account to credit.

When a contract does not state when it is to be performed, it must be performed within a reasonable time. If time for performance is stated in the contract, the contract must be performed at the time specified if such time is essential (is of the essence). Ordinarily, a contract must be performed exactly in the manner specified by the contract. A less-than-perfect performance is allowed if it is a substantial performance and if damages are allowed the other party.

A contract cannot be discharged by unilateral action unless authorized by the contract itself or by statute, as in the case of consumer protection rescission.

Because a contract arises from an agreement, it may also be terminated by an agreement. A contract may also be discharged by the substitution of a new contract for the original contract; by a novation, or making a new contract with a new party; by accord and satisfaction; by release; or by waiver.

A contract is discharged when it is impossible to perform. Impossibility may result from the destruction of the subject matter of the contract, the adoption of a new law that prohibits performance, the death or disability of a party whose personal action was required for performance of the contract, or the act of the other party to the contract. Some courts will also hold that a contract is discharged when its performance is commercially impracticable or there is frustration of purpose. Temporary impossibility, such as a labor strike or bad weather, has no effect on a contract. It is common, though, to include protective clauses that excuse delay caused by temporary impossibility.

A contract may be discharged by operation of law. This occurs when (1) the liability arising from the contract is discharged by bankruptcy, (2) suit on the contract is barred by the applicable statute of limitations, or (3) a time limitation stated in the contract is exceeded.

LEARNING OUTCOMES

After studying this chapter, you should be able to clearly explain:

A. Conditions Relating to Performance

L0.1 List the three types of conditions that affect a party's duty to perform
See the "pay-if-paid" condition-precedent example on p. 379.
See the TV anchor's "failed urinalysis test" condition-subsequent example on p. 380.

B. Discharge by Performance

L0.2 Explain the on-time performance rule
See the "mailed payment" example on p. 382.
See the "time is of the essence" example on p. 383.

L0.3 Explain the adequacy of performance rules
See the application of the substantial performance rule to the nonconforming new home piping example, pp. 383–385.

See the effect of failure to substantially perform a contract in the *Superior Wall and Paver* case, p. 385.

C. Discharge by Action of Parties

L0.4 Explain four ways a contract can be discharged by agreement of the parties
See the text discussion on rescission, cancellation, substitution, and novation on p. 387.

D. Discharge by External Causes

L0.5 State the effect on a contract of the death or disability of one of the contracting parties
See the Subway Sandwich Shops example on p. 389.

L0.6 Explain when impossibility or impracticability may discharge a contract
See the Ryder Cup frustration-of-purpose example on p. 390.

KEY TERMS

accord and satisfaction
bankruptcy
condition
condition precedent
condition subsequent

operation of law
rescission
statute of limitations
substantial performance
substitution

tender
waiver

QUESTIONS AND CASE PROBLEMS

1. CIT entered into a sale/leaseback contract with Condere Tire Corporation for 11 tire presses at Condere's tire plant in Natchez, Mississippi. Condere ceased making payments on these presses owned by CIT, and Condere filed for Chapter 11 bankruptcy. CIT thereafter contracted to sell the presses to Specialty Tires Inc., for $250,000. When the contract was made, CIT, Condere, and Specialty Tire believed that CIT was the owner of the presses and was entitled to immediate possession. When CIT attempted to gain access to the presses to have them shipped, Condere changed its position and refused to allow the equipment to be removed from the plant. When the presses were not delivered, Specialty sued CIT for damages for nondelivery of the presses, and CIT asserted the defense of impracticability. Decide. [*Specialty Tires, Inc. v. CIT*, 82 F. Supp. 2d 434 (W.D. Pa.)]

2. Lymon Mitchell operated a Badcock Home Furnishings dealership, under which as dealer he was paid a commission on sales and Badcock retained title to merchandise on display. Mitchell sold his dealership to another and to facilitate the sale, Badcock prepared a summary of

commissions owed with certain itemized offsets it claimed that Mitchell owed Badcock. Mitchell disagreed with the calculations, but he accepted them and signed the transfer documents closing the sale on the basis of the terms set forth in the summary and was paid accordingly. After pondering the offsets taken by Badcock and verifying the correctness of his position, he brought suit for the additional funds owed. What defense would you expect Badcock to raise? How would you decide the case? Explain fully. [*Mitchell v. Badcock Corp.,* 496 S.E.2d 502 (Ga. App.)]

3. American Bank loaned Koplik $50,000 to buy equipment for a restaurant about to be opened by Casual Citchen Corp. The loan was not repaid, and Fast Foods, Inc., bought out the interest of Casual Citchen. As part of the transaction, Fast Foods agreed to pay the debt owed to American Bank, and the parties agreed to a new schedule of payments to be made by Fast Foods. Fast Foods did not make the payments, and American Bank sued Koplik. He contended that his obligation to repay $50,000 had been discharged by the execution of the agreement providing for the payment of the debt by Fast Foods. Was this defense valid? [*American Bank & Trust Co. v. Koplik,* 451 N.Y.S.2d 426 (A. D.)]

4. Metalcrafters made a contract to design a new earth-moving vehicle for Lamar Highway Construction Co. Metalcrafters was depending on the genius of Samet, the head of its research department, to design a new product. Shortly after the contract was made between Metalcrafters and Lamar, Samet was killed in an automobile accident. Metalcrafters was not able to design the product without Samet. Lamar sued Metalcrafters for damages for breach of the contract. Metalcrafters claimed that the contract was discharged by Samet's death. Is it correct?

5. The Tinchers signed a contract to sell land to Creasy. The contract specified that the sales transaction was to be completed in 90 days. At the end of the 90 days, Creasy requested an extension of time. The Tinchers refused to grant an extension and stated that the contract was terminated. Creasy claimed that the 90-day clause was not binding because the contract did not state that time was of the essence. Was the contract terminated? [*Creasy v. Tincher,* 173 S.E.2d 332 (W. Va.)]

6. Christopher Bloom received a medical school scholarship created by the U.S. Department of Health and Human Services to increase the number of doctors serving rural areas. In return for this assistance, Bloom agreed to practice four years in a region identified as being underserved by medical professionals. After some problem with his postgraduation assignment, Bloom requested a repayment schedule from the agency. Although no terms were offered, Bloom tendered to the agency two checks totaling $15,500 and marked "Final Payment." Neither check was cashed, and the government sued Bloom for $480,000, the value of the assistance provided. Bloom claimed that by tendering the checks to the agency, his liability had been discharged by an accord and satisfaction. Decide. [*United States v. Bloom,* 112 F.3d 200 (7th Cir.)]

7. Dickson contracted to build a house for Moran. When it was approximately 25 percent to 40 percent completed, Moran would not let Dickson work any more because he was not following the building plans and specifications and there were many defects. Moran hired another contractor to correct the defects and finish the building. Dickson sued Moran for breach of contract, claiming that he had substantially performed the contract up to the point where he had been discharged. Was Dickson correct? [*Dickson v. Moran,* 344 So.2d 102 (La. App.)]

8. A lessor leased a trailer park to a tenant. At the time, sewage was disposed of by a septic tank system that was not connected with the public sewage system. The tenant knew this, and the lease declared that the tenant had examined the premises and that the landlord made no representation or guarantee as to the condition of the premises. Some time thereafter, the septic tank system stopped working properly, and the county health department notified the tenant that he was required to connect the septic tank system with the public sewage system or else the

department would close the trailer park. The tenant did not want to pay the additional cost involved in connecting with the public system. The tenant claimed that he was released from the lease and was entitled to a refund of the deposit that he had made. Was he correct? [*Glen R. Sewell Street Metal v. Loverde,* 451 P.2d 721 (Cal. App.)]

9. Oneal was a teacher employed by the Colton Consolidated School District. Because of a diabetic condition, his eyesight deteriorated so much that he offered to resign if he would be given pay for a specified number of "sick leave" days. The school district refused to do this and discharged Oneal for nonperformance of his contract. He appealed to remove the discharge from his record. Decide. What ethical values are involved? [*Oneal v. Colton Consolidated School District,* 557 P.2d 11 (Wash. App.)]

10. Northwest Construction, Inc., made a contract with the state of Washington for highway construction. Part of the work was turned over under a subcontract to Yakima Asphalt Paving Co. The contract required that any claim be asserted within 180 days. Yakima brought an action for damages after the expiration of 180 days. The defense was that the claim was too late. Yakima replied that the action was brought within the time allowed by the statute of limitations and that the contractual limitation of 180 days was therefore not binding. Was Yakima correct?

11. The Metropolitan Park District of Tacoma gave Griffith a concession to run the district's parks. The agreement gave the right to occupy the parks and use any improvements found therein. The district later wished to set this agreement aside because it was not making sufficient money from the transaction. While it was seeking to set the agreement aside, a boathouse and a gift shop in one of the parks were destroyed by fire. The district then claimed that the concession contract with Griffith was discharged by impossibility of performance. Was it correct? [*Metropolitan Park District of Tacoma v. Griffith,* 723 P.2d 1093 (Wash.)]

12. Suburban Power Piping Corp., under contract to construct a building for LTV Steel Corp., made a subcontract with Power & Pollution Services, Inc., to do some of the work. The subcontract provided that the subcontractor would be paid when the owner (LTV) paid the contractor. LTV went into bankruptcy before making the full payment to the contractor, who then refused to pay the subcontractor on the ground that the "pay-when-paid" provision of the subcontract made payment by the owner a condition precedent to the obligation of the contractor to pay the subcontractor. Was the contractor correct? [*Power & Pollution Services, Inc. v. Suburban Power Piping Corp.,* 598 N.E.2d 69 (Ohio App.)]

13. Ellen borrowed money from Farmers' Bank. As evidence of the loan, she signed a promissory note by which she promised to pay to the bank in installments the amount of the loan together with interest and administrative costs. She was unable to make the payments on the scheduled dates. She and the bank then executed a new agreement that gave her a longer period of time for making the payments. However, after two months, she was unable to pay on this new schedule. The bank then brought suit against her under the terms of the original agreement. She raised the defense that the original agreement had been discharged by the execution of the second agreement and could not be sued on. Decide.

14. Beeson Company made a contract to construct a shopping center for Sartori. Before the work was fully completed, Sartori stopped making the payments to Beeson that the contract required. The contract provided for liquidated damages of $1,000 per day if Beeson failed to substantially complete the project within 300 days of the beginning of construction. The contract also provided for a bonus of $1,000 for each day Beeson completed the project ahead of schedule. Beeson stopped working and sued Sartori for the balance due under the contract, just as though it had been fully performed. Sartori defended on the ground that Beeson had not substantially completed the work. Beeson proved that Sartori had been able to rent most of the stores in the

center. Was there substantial performance of the contract? If so, what would be the measure of damages? [*J.M. Beeson Co. v. Sartori*, 553 So.2d 180 (Fla. App.)]

15. New Beginnings provides rehabilitation services for alcohol and drug abuse to both adults and adolescents. New Beginnings entered into negotiation with Adbar for the lease of a building in the city of St. Louis, and subsequently entered into a three-year lease. The total rent due for the three-year term was $273,000. After the lease was executed, the city denied an occupancy permit because Alderman Bosley and residents testified at a hearing in vigorous opposition to the presence of New Beginnings in the neighborhood. A court ordered the permit issued. Alderman Bosley thereafter contacted the chair of the state's appointment committee and asked her to pull the agency's funding. He received no commitment from her on this matter. After a meeting with the state director of Alcohol and Drug Abuse where it was asserted that the director said the funding would be pulled if New Beginnings moved into the Adbar location, New Beginnings's board decided not to occupy the building. Adbar brought suit for breach of the lease, and New Beginnings asserted it was excused from performance because of commercial impracticability and frustration of purpose. Do you believe the doctrine of commercial impracticability should be limited in its application so as to preserve the certainty of contracts? What rule of law applies to this case? Decide. [*Adbar v. New Beginnings*, 103 S.W.2d 799 (Mo. App.)]

CPA QUESTIONS

1. Parc hired Glaze to remodel and furnish an office suite. Glaze submitted plans that Parc approved. After completing all the necessary construction and painting, Glaze purchased minor accessories that Parc rejected because they did not conform to the plans. Parc refused to allow Glaze to complete the project and refused to pay Glaze any part of the contract price. Glaze sued for the value of the work performed. Which of the following statements is correct?

   a. Glaze will lose because Glaze breached the contract by not completing performance.

   b. Glaze will win because Glaze substantially performed and Parc prevented complete performance.

   c. Glaze will lose because Glaze materially breached the contract by buying the accessories.

   d. Glaze will win because Parc committed anticipatory breach.

2. Ordinarily, in an action for breach of a construction contract, the statute of limitations time period would be computed from the date the contract is:

   a. Negotiated.

   b. Breached.

   c. Begun.

   d. Signed.

3. Which of the following will release all original parties to a contract but will maintain a contractual relationship?

	Novation	Substituted contract
a.	Yes	Yes
b.	Yes	No
c.	No	Yes
d.	No	No

© Manuel Gutjahr/iStockphoto.com

CHAPTER 20

Breach of Contract and Remedies

learningoutcomes

After studying this chapter, you should be able to

LO.1 Explain what constitutes a breach of contract and an anticipatory breach of contract

LO.2 Describe the effect of a waiver of a breach

LO.3 Explain the range of remedies available for breach of contract

LO.4 Explain when liquidated damages clauses are valid and invalid

LO.5 State when liability-limiting clauses and releases are valid

W

hat can be done when a contract is broken?

A. WHAT CONSTITUTES A BREACH OF CONTRACT?

The question of remedies does not become important until it is first determined that a contract has been violated or breached.

1. Definition of Breach

breach – failure to act or perform in the manner called for in a contract.

A **breach** is the failure to act or perform in the manner called for by the contract. When the contract calls for performance, such as painting an owner's home, the failure to paint or to paint properly is a *breach of contract*. If the contract calls for a creditor's forbearance, the creditor's action in bringing a lawsuit is a breach of the contract.

2. Anticipatory Breach

When the contract calls for performance, a party may make it clear before the time for performance arrives that the contract will not be performed. This is referred to as an **anticipatory breach**.

anticipatory breach – promisor's repudiation of the contract prior to the time that performance is required when such repudiation is accepted by the promisee as a breach of the contract.

anticipatory repudiation – repudiation made in advance of the time for performance of the contract obligations.

(A) ANTICIPATORY REPUDIATION. When a party expressly declares that performance will not be made when required, this declaration is called an **anticipatory repudiation** of the contract. To constitute such a repudiation, there must be a clear, absolute, unequivocal refusal to perform the contract according to its terms. **For Example,** Procter & Gamble (P&G) sought payment on four letters of credit issued by a Serbian bank, Investbanka. P&G presented two letters by June 8, prior to their expiration dates, with the necessary documentation for payment to Beogradska Bank New York, Investbanka's New York agent. A June 11 letter from Beogradska Bank broadly and unequivocally stated that the bank would not pay the letters of credit. Two additional letters of credit totaling $20,000 issued by Investbanka that expired by June 30 were not thereafter submitted to the New York agent bank by P&G. However, a court found that the bank had anticipatorily breached its obligations under those letters of credit by its broad renouncements in the June 11 letter, and judgments were rendered in favor of P&G. [1]

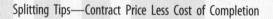

CASE SUMMARY

Splitting Tips—Contract Price Less Cost of Completion

FACTS: Hartland Developers, Inc., agreed to build an airplane hangar for Robert Tips of San Antonio for $300,000, payable in three installments of $100,000, with the final payment due upon the completion of the building and the issuance of a certificate of completion by the engineer representing Tips. The evidence shows that Tips's representative, Mr. Lavelle,

[1] *Procter & Gamble v. Investbanka,* 2000 WL 520630 (S.D.N.Y. 2000).

CASE SUMMARY

Continued

instructed Hartland to cease work on the building because Tips could no longer afford to make payments. Hartland ceased work as instructed before the final completion of the building, having been paid $200,000 at the time. He sued Tips for breach of contract. On May 6, 1996, the trial court allowed Hartland the amount owing on the contract, $100,000, less the cost of completing the building according to the contract, $65,000, plus attorney fees and prejudgment interest. Tips appealed, pointing out, among other assertions, that he was required to spend $23,000 to provide electrical outlets for the hangar, which were contemplated in the contract.

DECISION: Judgment for Tips, subject to offsets. The trial judge based his damages assessment on anticipatory repudiation of contract. The evidence that Tips's representative, Lavelle, instructed Hartland to cease work on the project because Tips no longer could afford to make payments was sufficient to support this finding. However, Tips is entitled to an offset for electrical connections of $23,000 under a breach of contract theory. [*Tips v. Hartland Developers, Inc.,* **961 S.W.2d 618 (Tex. App. 1998)**]

A refusal to perform a contract that is made before performance is required unless the other party to the contract does an act or makes a concession that is not required by the contract, is an anticipatory repudiation of the contract.[2]

A party making an anticipatory repudiation may retract or take back the repudiation if the other party has not changed position in reliance on the repudiation. However, if the other party has changed position, the party making the anticipatory repudiation cannot retract it. **For Example,** if a buyer makes another purchase when the seller declares that the seller will not perform the contract, the buyer has acted in reliance on the seller's repudiation. The seller will therefore not be allowed to retract the repudiation.

(B) ANTICIPATORY REPUDIATION BY CONDUCT. The anticipatory repudiation may be expressed by conduct that makes it impossible for the repudiating party to perform subsequently. **For Example,** while the Town of Mammoth Lakes, California, was claiming a willingness to move forward with a hotel/condominium project under its contract with the developer, in actuality, the evidence established that town officials refused to move forward and actively sought to undermine the developer's rights under the development contract. The court affirmed a judgment of $30 million in damages and attorneys' fees.[3]

B. WAIVER OF BREACH

The breach of a contract may have no importance because the other party to the contract waives the breach.

[2] *Chamberlain v. Puckett Construction,* 921 P.2d 1237 (Mont. 1996).
[3] *Mammoth Lakes Land Acquisition, LLC v. Town of Mammoth Lakes,* 120 Cal. Rptr. 3d 797 (Cal. Ct. of App. 3d Dist. 2010).

3. Cure of Breach by Waiver

The fact that one party has broken a contract does not necessarily mean that there will be a lawsuit or a forfeiture of the contract. For practical business reasons, one party may be willing to ignore or waive the breach. When it is established that there has been a **waiver** of a breach, the party waiving the breach cannot take any action on the theory that the contract was broken. The waiver, in effect, erases the past breach. The contract continues as though the breach had not existed.

The waiver may be express or it may be implied from the continued recognition of the existence of the contract by the aggrieved party.[4] When the conduct of a party shows an intent to give up a right, it waives that right.[5]

waiver – release or relinquishment of a known right or objection.

4. Existence and Scope of Waiver

It is a question of fact whether there has been a waiver.

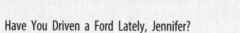

CASE SUMMARY

Have You Driven a Ford Lately, Jennifer?

FACTS: In 1995, Northland Ford Dealers, an association of dealerships, offered to sponsor a "hole in one" contest at Moccasin Creek Country Club. A banner announced that a hole in one would win a car but gave no other details, and the local dealer parked a Ford Explorer near the banner. Northland paid a $4,602 premium to Continental Hole-In-One, Inc., to ensure the award of the contest prize. The insurance application stated in capital letters that "ALL AMATEUR MEN AND WOMEN WILL UTILIZE THE SAME TEE." And Continental established the men/women yardage for the hole to be 170 yards, but did not make this known to the participants. Jennifer Harms registered for the tournament and paid her entrance fee. At the contest hole, she teed off from the amateur women's red marker, which was a much shorter distance to the pin than the 170 yards from the men's marker—and she made a hole in one. When she inquired about the prize, she was told that because of insurance requirements, all amateurs had to tee off from the amateur men's tee box, and because she had not done so, she was disqualified. Harms, a collegiate golfer at Concordia College, returned there to complete her last year of athletic eligibility and on graduation sued Northland for breach of contract. Northland contends that under NCAA rules, accepting a prize or agreeing to accept a prize would have disqualified Harms from NCAA competition. It also asserts that her continuation of her NCAA competition evinced intent to waive acceptance of the car.

DECISION: Judgment for Harms. Northland must abide by the rules it announced, not by the ones it left unannounced that disqualified all amateur women from the contest. This was a vintage unilateral contract with performance by the offeree as acceptance. Harms earned the prize when she sank her winning shot. Waiver is a volitional relinquishment, by act or word, of a known existing right conferred in law or contract. Harms could not disclaim the prize; it was not hers to refuse. She was told her shot from the wrong tee disqualified her. One can hardly relinquish what was never conferred. Northland's waiver defense is devoid of merit. [*Harms v. Northland Ford Dealers,* **602 N.W.2d 58 (S.D. 1999)**]

(A) EXISTENCE OF WAIVER. A party may express or declare that the breach of a contract is waived. A waiver of a breach is more often the result of an express forgiving of a

---

[4] *Huger v. Morrison,* 809 So.2d 1140 (La. App. 2002).
[5] *Stronghaven Inc. v. Ingram,* 555 S.E.2d 49 (Ga. App. 2001).

breach. Thus, a party allowing the other party to continue performance without objecting that the performance is not satisfactory waives the right to raise that objection when sued for payment by the performing party.

For Example, a contract promising to sell back a parcel of commercial property to Jackson required Jackson to make a $500 payment to Massey's attorney on the first of the month for five months, December through April. It was clearly understood that the payments would be "on time without fail." Jackson made the December payment on time. New Year's Day, a holiday, fell on a Friday, and Jackson made the second payment on January 4. He made $500 payments on February 1, March 1, and March 31, respectively, and the payments were accepted and a receipt issued on each occasion. However, Massey refused to convey title back to Jackson because "the January 4 payment was untimely and the parties' agreement had been breached." The court held that the doctrine of waiver applied due to Massey's acceptance of the late payment and the three subsequent payments without objection, and the court declared that Jackson was entitled to possession of the land.[6]

(B) Scope of Waiver. The waiver of a breach of contract extends only to the matter waived. It does not show any intent to ignore other provisions of the contract.

(c) Antimodification Clause. Modern contracts commonly specify that the terms of a contract shall not be deemed modified by waiver as to any breaches. This means that the original contract remains as agreed to. Either party may therefore return to, and insist on, compliance with the original contract.

In the example involving Jackson and Massey's contract, the trial court reviewed the contract to see whether the court was restricted by the contract from applying the waiver. It concluded: "In this case, the parties' contract did not contain any terms that could prevent the application of the doctrine of waiver to the acceptance of late payments."[7]

5. Reservation of Rights

It may be that a party is willing to accept a defective performance but does not wish to surrender any claim for damages for the breach. **For Example,** Midwest Utilities, Inc., accepted 20 carloads of Powder River Basin coal (sometimes called *Western coal*) from its supplier, Maney Enterprises, because its power plants were in short supply of coal. Midwest's requirements contract with Maney called for Appalachian coal, a low-sulfur, highly efficient fuel, which is sold at a premium price per ton. Midwest, in accepting the tendered performance with a **reservation of rights**, gave notice to Maney that it reserved all rights to pursue damages for the tender of a nonconforming shipment.

reservation of rights – assertion by a party to a contract that even though a tendered performance (e.g., a defective product) is accepted, the right to damages for nonconformity to the contract is reserved.

remedy – action or procedure that is followed in order to enforce a right or to obtain damages for injury to a right.

C. Remedies for Breach of Contract

One or more **remedies** may be available to the innocent party in the case of a breach of contract. There is also the possibility that arbitration or a streamlined out-of-court alternative dispute resolution procedure is available or required for determining the rights of the parties.

---

[6] *Massey v. Jackson*, 726 So.2d 656 (Ala. App. 1998).
[7] *Id.* at 659.

FIGURE 20-1 | *What Follows the Breach*

© Cengage Learning

6. Remedies Upon Anticipatory Repudiation

When an anticipatory repudiation of a contract occurs, the aggrieved person has several options. He may (1) do nothing beyond stating that performance at the proper time will be required, (2) regard the contract as having been definitively broken and bring a lawsuit against the repudiating party without waiting to see whether there will be proper performance when the performance date arrives, or (3) regard the repudiation as an offer to cancel the contract. This offer can be accepted or rejected. If accepted, there is a discharge of the original contract by the subsequent cancellation agreement of the parties.

7. Remedies in General and the Measure of Damages

Courts provide a *quasi-contractual* or *restitution* remedy in which a contract is unenforceable because it lacked definite and certain terms or was not in compliance with the statute of frauds, yet one of the parties performed services for the other. The measure of damages in these and other quasi-contract cases is the reasonable value of the services performed, not an amount derived from the defective contract.

In cases when a person retains money or when a contemplated contract is not properly formed and no work is performed, the party retaining the benefit is obligated to make restitution to the person conferring the benefit. **For Example,** Kramer Associates, Inc. (KAI), a Washington D.C., consulting firm, accepted $75,000 from a Ghana-based corporation, Ikam, Ltd., to secure financing for a Ghana development project. No contract was ever executed, and KAI did virtually nothing to secure financing for the project. Restitution of the $75,000 was required.[8]

When there is a breach of contract, the regular remedy is an award of *monetary damages*. In unusual circumstances, when monetary damages are inadequate, the injured party may obtain **specific performance**, whereby the court will order that the contract terms be carried out.

The measure of monetary damages when there has been a breach of contract is the sum of money that will place the injured party in the same position that would have been attained if the contract had been performed.[9] That is, the injured party will be given the *benefit of the bargain* by the court. As seen in the *Tips v. Hartland Developers* case, the nonbreaching party, Hartland, was awarded the contract price less the cost of completion of the project, which had the effect of giving the builder the benefit of the bargain.

> **specific performance** – action brought to compel the adverse party to perform a contract on the theory that merely suing for damages for its breach will not be an adequate remedy.

8. Monetary Damages

Monetary damages are commonly classified as compensatory damages, nominal damages, and punitive damages. **Compensatory damages** compensate the injured party for the damages incurred as a result of the breach of contract. Compensatory damages have two branches, *direct damages* and *consequential* (or *special*) *damages*.

Injured parties that do not sustain an actual loss because of a breach of contract are entitled to a judgment of a small sum of money such as $1; these damages are called **nominal damages**.

Damages in excess of actual loss, imposed for the purpose of punishing or making an example of the defendant, are known as **punitive damages** or *exemplary damages*. In contract actions, punitive damages are not ordinarily awarded.[10]

> **compensatory damages** – sum of money that will compensate an injured plaintiff for actual loss.

> **nominal damages** – nominal sum awarded the plaintiff in order to establish that legal rights have been violated although the plaintiff in fact has not sustained any actual loss or damages.

> **punitive damages** – damages, in excess of those required to compensate the plaintiff for the wrong done, that are imposed in order to punish the defendant because of the particularly wanton or willful character of wrongdoing; also called *exemplary damages*.

(A) DIRECT AND CONSEQUENTIAL DAMAGES. Direct damages (sometimes called *general damages*) are those that naturally flow from the given type of breach of contract involved and include *incidental damages*, which are extra expenditures made by the injured party to rectify the breach or mitigate damages. **Consequential damages** (sometimes called *special damages*) are those that do not necessarily flow from the type of breach of contract involved but happen to do so in a particular case as a result of the injured party's particular circumstances.[11]

> **direct damages** – losses that are caused by breach of a contract.

> **consequential damages** – damages the buyer experiences as a result of the seller's breach with respect to a third party, also called *special damages*.

---

[8] *Kramer Associates, Inc. v. IKAM, Ltd.*, 888 A.2d 247 (D.C. 2005).
[9] *Leingang v. City of Mandan*, 468 N.W.2d 397 (N.D. 1991).
[10] A party who is not awarded actual damages but wins nominal damages can be considered a "prevailing party" for the purposes of a contractual attorney fee-shifting provision. *Brock v. King*, 629 S.E.2d 829 (Ga. App. 2006).
[11] See *Powell Electrical Systems, Inc. v. Hewlett Packard Co.*, 356 S.W.3d 113 (Tex. App. 2011).

CASE SUMMARY

Who Pays the Expenses?

FACTS: Jerry Birkel was a grain farmer. Hassebrook Farm Service, Inc., made a contract with Jerry to sell to him and install a grain storage and drying bin. Jerry traded in his old dryer to the seller. The new equipment did not work properly, and Jerry had to pay other persons for drying and storing his grain. Jerry sued Hassebrook for damages and claimed the right to be repaid what he had paid to others for drying and storage.

DECISION: Jerry was entitled to recover what he had paid others for drying and storage. Because Jerry had traded in his old dryer to the seller, it was obvious to the seller that if the new equipment did not work properly, Jerry would be forced to pay for alternative drying and storage to prevent the total loss of his crops. The cost of such an alternative was therefore within the seller's contemplation when the contract was made, and so the buyer could recover this cost as an element of damages for the seller's breach of contract. [*Birkel v. Hassebrook Farm Service, Inc.*, 363 N.W.2d 148 (Neb. 1985)]

Consequential damages may be recovered only if it was reasonably foreseeable to the defendant that the kind of loss in question could be sustained by the nonbreaching party if the contract were broken.

For Example, in early August, Spencer Adams ordered a four-wheel-drive GMC truck with a rear-end hydraulic lift for use on his Aroostook County, Maine, potato farm. The contract price was $58,500. He told Brad Jones, the owner of the dealership, that he had to have the truck by Labor Day so he could use it to bring in his crop from the fields before the first frost, and Brad nodded that he understood. The truck did not arrive by Labor Day as promised in the written contract. After a two-week period of gradually escalating recriminations with the dealership, Adams obtained the same model GMC truck at a dealership 40 minutes away in Houlton but at the cost of $60,500. He was also able to rent a similar truck from the Houlton dealer for $250 for the day while the new truck was being prepared. Farmhands had used other means of harvesting, but because of the lack of the truck, their work was set back by five days. As a result of the delays, 30 percent of the crop was still in the fields when the first frost came, causing damages expertly estimated at $320,000. The *direct damages* for the breach of contract in this case would be the difference between the contract price for the truck of $58,500 and the market price of $60,500, or $2,000. These direct damages naturally flow from the breach of contract for the purchase of a truck. Also, the *incidental damages* of $250 for the truck rental are recoverable direct damages. The $320,000 loss of the potato crop was a consequence of not having the truck, and this sum is arguably recoverable by Spencer Adams as *consequential or special damages*. Adams notified Brad Jones of the reason he needed to have the truck by Labor Day, and it should have been reasonably foreseeable to Jones that loss of a portion of the crop could occur if the truck contract was breached. However, because of Spencer Adams's obligation to mitigate damages (as discussed below), it is unlikely that Adams will recover the full consequential damages. Truck rental availability or the lack of availability within the rural area, alternative tractor usage, and the actual harvesting methods used by Adams all relate to the mitigation issue to be resolved by the jury.

(B) MITIGATION OF DAMAGES. The injured party is under the duty to mitigate damages if reasonably possible.[12] In other words, damages must not be permitted to increase if an increase can be prevented by reasonable efforts. This means that the injured party must generally stop any performance under the contract to avoid running up a larger bill. The duty to mitigate damages may require an injured party to buy or rent elsewhere the goods that the wrongdoer was obligated to deliver under the contract. In the case of breach of an employment contract by the employer, the employee is required to seek other similar employment. The wages earned from other employment must be deducted from the damages claimed. The discharged employee, however, is not required to take employment of less-than-comparable work.

(1) Effect of Failure to Mitigate Damages.

The effect of the requirement of mitigating damages is to limit recovery by the nonbreaching party to the damages that would have been sustained had this party mitigated the damages where it was possible to do so. **For Example,** self-described "sports nut" Gary Baker signed up for a three-year club-seat "package" that entitled him and a companion to tickets for 41 Boston Bruins hockey games and 41 Boston Celtics basketball games at the New Boston Garden Corporation's Fleet Center for approximately $18,000 per year. After one year, Baker stopped paying for the tickets, thinking that he would simply lose his $5,000 security deposit. Baker, a CPA, tried to work out a compromise settlement to no avail. New Boston sued Baker for breach of contract, seeking the balance due on the tickets of $34,866. At trial, Baker argued to the jury that although he had breached his contract, New Boston had an obligation to mitigate damages, for example, by treating his empty seats and those of others in the same situation as "rush seats" shortly before game time and selling them at a discount. New Boston argued that just as a used luxury car cannot be returned for a refund, a season ticket cannot be canceled without consequences. The jury accepted Baker's position on mitigation and reduced the amount owed New Boston by $21,176 to $13,690.[13]

9. Rescission

When one party commits a material breach of the contract, the other party may rescind the contract; if the party in default objects, the aggrieved party may bring an action for rescission. A breach is *material* when it is so substantial that it defeats the object of the parties in making the contract.[14]

An injured party who rescinds a contract after having performed services may recover the reasonable value of the performance rendered under restitutionary or quasi-contractual damages. Money paid by the injured party may also be recovered. **For Example,** the Sharabianlous signed a purchase agreement to buy a building owned by Berenstein Associates for $2 million. Thereafter the parties learned of environmental contamination on the property. Faced with uncertainty about the scope of the problem and the cost of the cleanup, the deal fell through and litigation ensued. The trial court rescinded the agreement based on mutual

---

[12] *West Pinal Family Health Center, Inc. v. McBride*, 785 P.2d 66 (Ariz. 1989).

[13] Sacha Pfeiffer, "Disenchanted Fan Scores Win in Ticket Fight," *Boston Globe*, August 28, 1999, at B4.

[14] *Greentree Properties, Inc. v. Kissee*, 92 S.W.3d 289 (Mo. App. 2003).

mistake of fact because neither party knew the full extent of the environmental hazard at the property. Damages available to parties upon mistake are more limited than those available in cases in which rescission is based on fault. The Sharabianlous were awarded $61,423.82 in expenses and an order returning their $115,000 deposit.[15]

The purpose of rescission is to restore the injured party to the position occupied before the contract was made. However, the party seeking restitutionary damages must also return what this party has received from the party in default.

For Example, Pedro Morena purchased real estate from Jason Alexander after Alexander had assured him that the property did not have a flooding problem. In fact, the property regularly flooded after ordinary rainstorms. Morena was entitled to the return of the purchase price and payment for the reasonable value of the improvements he made to the property. Alexander was entitled to a setoff for the reasonable rental value of the property during the time Morena was in possession of this property.

10. Action for Specific Performance

Under special circumstances, an injured party may obtain the equitable remedy of specific performance, which compels the other party to carry out the terms of a contract. Specific performance is ordinarily granted only if the subject matter of the contract is "unique," thereby making an award of money damages an inadequate remedy. Contracts for the purchase of land will be specifically enforced.[16]

Specific performance of a contract to sell personal property can be obtained only if the article is of unusual age, beauty, unique history, or other distinction. **For Example,** Maurice owned a rare Revolutionary War musket that he agreed to sell to Herb. Maurice then changed his mind because of the uniqueness of the musket. Herb can sue and win, requesting the remedy of specific performance of the contract because of the unique nature of the goods.

When the damages sustained by the plaintiff can be measured in monetary terms, specific performance will be refused. Consequently, a contract to sell a television station will not be specifically enforced when the buyer had made a contract to resell the station to a third person; the damages caused by the breach of the first contract would be the loss sustained by being unable to make the resale, and such damages would be adequate compensation to the original buyer.[17]

Ordinarily, contracts for the performance of personal services are not specifically ordered. This is because of the difficulty of supervision by the court and the restriction of the U.S. Constitution's Thirteenth Amendment prohibiting involuntary servitude except as criminal punishment.

11. Action for an Injunction

When a breach of contract consists of doing an act prohibited by the contract, a possible remedy is an **injunction** against doing the act. **For Example,** when the obligation in an employee's contract is to refrain from competing after resigning

injunction – order of a court of equity to refrain from doing (negative injunction) or to do (affirmative or mandatory injunction) a specified act. Statute use in labor disputes has been greatly restricted.

[15] *Sharabianlou v. Karp*, 105 Cal. Rptr. 3d 300 (Cal. App. 2010).
[16] *English v. Muller*, 514 S.E.2d 195 (Ga. 1999).
[17] *Miller v. LeSea Broadcasting, Inc.*, 87 F.3d 224 (7th Cir. 1996).

from the company and the obligation is broken by competing, a court may order or enjoin the former employee to stop competing. Similarly, when a vocalist breaks a contract to record exclusively for a particular label, she may be enjoined from recording for any other company. This may have the indirect effect of compelling the vocalist to record for the plaintiff.

12. Reformation of Contract by a Court

At times, a written contract does not correctly state the agreement already made by the parties. When this occurs, either party may seek to have the court reform or correct the writing to state the agreement actually made.

A party seeking reformation of a contract must clearly prove both the grounds for reformation and what the agreement actually was. This burden is particularly great when the contract to be reformed is written. This is so because the general rule is that parties are presumed to have read their written contracts and to have intended to be bound by them when they signed the contracts.

When a unilateral mistake is made and it is of such consequence that enforcing the contract according to its terms would be unreasonable, a court may reform the contract to correct the mistake.

CASE SUMMARY

Will a Court Correct a Huge Mistake?

FACTS: New York Packaging Corp. (NYPC) manufactured plastic sheets used by Owens Corning (OC) at its asphalt plants throughout the country as dividers to separate asphalt containers and prevent them from sticking to one another. Janet Berry, a customer service representative at Owens Corning, called and received a price from NYPC of "$172.50 per box," with a box containing 200 plastic sheets. Ms. Berry put the information into OC's computer systems, which in turn generated a purchase order. She mistakenly believed that the unit of measurement designated as "EA" on the purchase order was per box when it in fact was per sheet. As a result, the purchase orders likewise reflected a price of $172.50 per sheet rather than per box. The computer automatically calculated the total price of the purchase order and faxed it to NYPC as $1,078,195, without Ms. Berry seeing the huge total price. NYPC filled the order, which included overrun sheets, and billed OC $1,414,605.60. NYPC sought payment at the contract price of $172.50 per sheet. It points out that the purchase order contained a "no oral modification" clause and, by its terms, the order was binding when NYPC accepted. The buyer contends that NYPC is attempting to take advantage of this huge and obvious mistake and that the contract should be reformed.

DECISION: Ms. Berry made a unilateral mistake that was, or should have been, known by NYPC. OC used the sheets after its offer to return them to NYPC was refused. Therefore, the contract could not be rescinded. The drafting error in this case was so huge that to enforce the written contract would be unconscionable. Accordingly, the unit of measurement is amended to read "per box" rather than "EA"; the "Order Qty" is amended to read "41 boxes of 200 sheets per box"; and the overall price is modified to read $7,072.50, not $1,078,195. [*In re Owens Corning et al., Debtors in Possession*, 291 B.R. 329 (2003)]

D. Contract Provisions Affecting Remedies and Damages

The contract of the parties may contain provisions that affect the remedies available or the recovery of damages.

13. Limitation of Remedies

The contract of the parties may limit the remedies of the aggrieved parties.
For Example, the contract may give one party the right to repair or replace a defective item sold or to refund the contract price. The contract may require both parties to submit any dispute to arbitration or another streamlined out-of-court dispute resolution procedure.

14. Liquidated Damages

The parties may stipulate in their contract that a certain amount should be paid in case of a breach. This amount is known as liquidated damages and may be variously measured by the parties. When delay is possible, **liquidated damages** may be a fixed sum, such as $1,000 for each day of delay. When there is a total default, damages may be a percentage of the contract price or the amount of the down payment.

liquidated damages – provision stipulating the amount of damages to be paid in the event of default or breach of contract.

liquidated damages clause – specification of exact compensation in case of a breach of contract.

(A) VALIDITY. To be valid, a **liquidated damages clause** must satisfy two requirements: (1) The situation must be one in which it is difficult or impossible to determine the actual damages and (2) the amount specified must not be excessive when compared with the probable damages that would be sustained.[18] The validity of a liquidated damages clause is determined on the basis of the facts existing when the clause was agreed to.

CASE SUMMARY

Can We Freeze the Damages?

FACTS: Manny Fakhimi agreed to buy an apartment complex for $697,000 at an auction from David Mason. Fakhimi was obligated to put up 10 percent of the agreed-to price at the auction as a deposit. The agreement signed by Fakhimi allowed Mason to keep this deposit should Fakhimi fail to come up with the remaining 90 percent of the auction price as liquidated damages for the default. Shortly after the auction, Fakhimi heard a rumor that the military base located near the apartment complex might be closing. Fakhimi immediately stopped payment on the check and defaulted on the agreement. Mason sued Fakhimi for the liquidated damages specified in the sales contract.

DECISION: Because of the difficulty of forecasting the loss that might be caused by the breach of a real estate purchase contract, it is held that a liquidated damage clause of 10 percent of the sale price is valid and is not a penalty. The fact that the damages sustained thereafter were less than 10 percent does not convert the 10 percent into an unreasonable forecast. The 10 percent clause remained valid as it would have remained had the damages on resale been more than 10 percent. [*Mason v. Fakhimi*, 865 P.2d 333 (Neb. 1993)]

---

[18] *Southeast Alaska Construction Co. v. Alaska*, 791 P.2d 339 (Alaska 1990).

(B) EFFECT. When a liquidated damages clause is held valid, the injured party cannot collect more than the amount specified by the clause. The defaulting party is bound to pay such damages once the fact is established that there has been a default. The injured party is not required to make any proof as to damages sustained, and the defendant is not permitted to show that the damages were not as great as the liquidated sum.

(c) INVALID CLAUSES. If the liquidated damages clause calls for the payment of a sum that is clearly unreasonably large and unrelated to the possible actual damages that might be sustained, the clause will be held to be void as a penalty. **For Example,** a settlement agreement between 27 plaintiffs seeking recovery for injuries resulting from faulty breast implants and the implants' manufacturer, Dow Corning Corp., called for seven $200,000 payments to each plaintiff. The agreement also called for a $100 per day payment to each plaintiff for any time when the payments were late as "liquidated damages." The court held that the $100 per day figure was not a reasonable estimate of anticipated damages. Rather, it was an unenforceable "penalty" provision.[19]

When a liquidated damages clause is held invalid, the effect is merely to erase the clause from the contract, and the injured party may proceed to recover damages for breach of the contract. Instead of recovering the liquidated damages amount, the injured party will recover whatever actual damages he can prove. **For Example,** Richard Goldblatt and his wife Valerie breached a five-year restrictive covenant in a settlement agreement with the medical devices corporation that Goldblatt had cofounded, C.P. Motion, Inc. A liquidated damages provision in the settlement agreement that obligated Goldblatt and his wife to pay $250,000 per breach of the restrictive covenant was unenforceable as a penalty clause. The appeals court set aside a $4,969,339 judgment against the Goldblatts, determining that the parties could have agreed to arrive at actual damages by calculating a percentage of lost profits of specific lost clients or reclaiming any profits gained by the breaching parties. Because the liquidated damages clause was a penalty provision, C.P. Motion, Inc., may only recover the actual damages filed and proven at trial.[20]

15. Attorneys' Fees

Attorneys' fees are a very significant factor in contract litigation. In Medistar Corporation's suit against Dr. David Schmidt, the jury awarded it $418,069 in damages under its promissory estoppel claim and in addition thereto the trial court judge allowed Medistar to recover $408,412 for its attorneys' fees. A state statute allows recovery of attorneys' fees for the prevailing party in a breach of partnership claim. On appeal the recovery of $408,412 in attorneys' fees was reversed since the jury awarded zero damages on Medistars' breach of partnership claim. The net result after payment of attorneys' fees—and not counting attorneys' fees for the appeal— was $9657 for Medistar, after four years of "successful" litigation.[21]

---

[19] *Bear Stearns v. Dow Corning Corp.*, 419 F.3d 543 (6th Cir. 2005). See *RKR Motors Inc. v. Associated Uniform Rentals*, 995 So.2d 588 (Fla. App. 2008).

[20] *Goldblatt v. C. P. Motion, Inc.*, 77 So.3d 798 (Fla. App. 2011).

[21] *Medistar Corp. v. Schmidt*, 267 S.W.3d 150 (Tex. App. 2008).

The so-called "American rule" states that each party is responsible for its own attorneys' fees in the absence of an express contractual or statutory provision to the contrary.[22] Even in the event of a valid contractual provision for attorneys' fees, a trial court has the discretion to exercise its equitable control to allow only such sum as is reasonable, or the court may properly disallow attorneys' fees altogether on the basis that such recovery would be inequitable. **For Example,** although Evergreen Tree Care Services was awarded some monetary damages in its breach of contract suit against JHL, Inc., it was unsuccessful in its claim for attorneys' fees under a provision for attorneys' fees in the contract because the trial court exercised its equitable discretion, finding that both parties to the litigation came to court with "unclean hands," and that Evergreen failed to sufficiently itemize and exclude fees to discovery abuses.[23]

16. Limitation of Liability Clauses

A contract may contain a provision stating that one of the parties shall not be liable for damages in case of breach. Such a provision is called an **exculpatory clause**, or when a monetary limit to damages for breach of contract is set forth in the contract, it may be referred to as a **limitation-of-liability clause**.

exculpatory clause – provision in a contract stating that one of the parties shall not be liable for damages in case of breach; also called a *limitation-of-liability clause.*

limitation-of-liability clause – provision in a contract stating that one of the parties shall not be liable for damages in case of breach; also called an *exculpatory clause.*

(A) **CONTENT AND CONSTRUCTION.** If an exculpatory clause or a limitation-of-liability clause limits liability for damages caused only by negligent conduct, liability is neither excluded nor limited if the conduct alleged is found to be grossly negligent, willful, or wanton. **For Example,** Security Guards Inc. (SGI) provided services to Dana Corporation, a truck frame manufacturer under a contract that contained a limitation-of-liability clause capping losses at $50,000 per occurrence for damages "caused solely by the negligence" of SGI or its employees. When a critical alarm was activated by a fire in the paint shop at 5:39 P.M., the SGI guard on duty did not follow appropriate procedures, which delayed notification to the fire department for 15 minutes. Royal Indemnity Co., Dana's insurer, paid Dana $16,535,882 for the fire loss and sued SGI for $7 million, contending that the SGI guard's actions were grossly negligent and caused the plant to suffer increased damages. The court held that if SGI were to be found grossly negligent, the liability would not be limited to $50,000, and a jury could find damages far exceeding that amount.[24]

(B) **VALIDITY.** As a general rule, experienced businesspersons are free to allocate liability in their contracts as they see fit. They have freedom to contract—even to make bad bargains or relinquish fundamental rights. However, courts in most states will not enforce a contract provision that *completely exonerates* a party from gross negligence or intentional acts.

(C) **RELEASES.** Release forms signed by participants in athletic and sporting events declaring that the sponsor, proprietor, or operator of the event shall not be liable for injuries sustained by participants because of its negligence are generally binding.[25] The *Cheley Colorado Camps* decision is such a case.

---

[22] *Centimark v. Village Manor Associates, Ltd.,* 967 A.2d 550 (Conn. App. 2009).

[23] *Stafford v. JHL, Inc.,* 194 P.3d 315 (Wyo. 2008). See also *FNBC v. Jennessey Group, LLC,* 759 N.W.2d 808 (Iowa App. 2008).

[24] *Royal Indemnity Co. v. Security Guards, Inc.,* 255 F. Supp. 2d 497 (E.D. Pa. 2003).

[25] But see *Woodman v. Kera, LLC,* 760 N.W.2d 641 (Mich. App. 2008) where the Court of Appeals of Michigan held that a preinjury waiver signed by a parent on behalf of a five-year-old child was invalid.

CASE SUMMARY

How to Handle a Risky Business

FACTS: Chelsea Hamill attended Camp Cheley for three years. Before attending camp each summer her parents signed a liability/risk release form. In July 2004, when Hamill was 15 years old, she fell off a Cheley horse and broke her arm. Chelsea brought a negligence and gross negligence lawsuit against the summer camp. Hamill's mother testified at her deposition that she voluntarily signed the release after having "skimmed" it. At her deposition, the mother testified as follows:

> Attorney: And, you know, you knew that someone such as Christopher Reeve had been tragically injured falling off a horse?
> Ms. Hamill: Yes.
> Attorney: Did you personally know Mr. Reeve?
> Ms. Hamill: Yes.
> Attorney: And so you were aware that there were significant risks associated with horseback riding?
> Ms. Hamill: Yes.
> Attorney: And you were aware that your daughter was going to be doing a significant amount of horseback riding?
> Ms. Hamill: Yes.

Hamill's mother's interpretation of the release was that prospective negligent claims were not waived. The camp disagreed. The release stated in part:

> I, on behalf of myself and my child, hereby release and waive *any claim of liability against Cheley* ... occurring to my child while he/she participates in any and all camp programs and activities.
> I give my permission for my child to participate in all camp activities, including those described above. I acknowledge and assume the risks involved in these activities, and for any damages, illness, *injury or death* ... resulting from such risks for myself and my child.

> *(Emphasis Added.)*

DECISION: Judgment for Camp Cheley. The release did not need to include an exhaustive list of particularized injury scenarios to be effective. Hamill's mother had more than sufficient information to allow her to assess the extent of injury possible in horseback riding and to make an "informed" decision before signing the release. The mother was informed of the intent to release "all claims," including prospective negligence claims. While exculpatory agreements are not a bar to civil liability for gross negligence, the record is devoid of evidence of gross negligence. [*Hamill v. Cheley Colorado Camps, Inc.*, 262 P.3d 945 (Colo. App. 2011)]

LawFlix

The Goodbye Girl (1977) (PG)

Richard Dreyfuss plays Elliott Garfield, a struggling Shakespearean actor who lands in New York with a sublease on an apartment still occupied by divorcee Marsha Mason and her daughter. The two work out living arrangements, split rent and food, and deal with the issue of whether Mason has any rights. Review all aspects of contracts as the characters discuss subleases, rent payment, living arrangements, and food costs.

MAKE THE CONNECTION

SUMMARY

When a party fails to perform a contract or performs improperly, the other contracting party may sue for damages caused by the breach. What may be recovered by the aggrieved person is stated in terms of being direct or consequential damages. Direct damages are those that ordinarily will result from the breach. Direct damages may be recovered on proof of causation and amount. Consequential damages can be recovered only if, in addition to proving causation and amount, it is shown that they were reasonably within the contemplation of the contracting parties as a probable result of a breach of the contract. The right to recover consequential damages is lost if the aggrieved party could reasonably have taken steps to avoid such damages. In other words, the aggrieved person has a duty to mitigate or reduce damages by reasonable means.

In any case, the damages recoverable for breach of contract may be limited to a specific amount by a liquidated damages clause.

In a limited number of situations, an aggrieved party may bring an action for specific performance to compel the other contracting party to perform the acts called for by the contract. Specific performance by the seller is always obtainable for the breach of a contract to sell land or real estate on the theory that such property has a unique value. With respect to other contracts, specific performance will not be ordered unless it is shown that there was some unique element present so that the aggrieved person would suffer a damage that could not be compensated for by the payment of money damages.

The aggrieved person also has the option of rescinding the contract if (1) the breach has been made concerning a material term and (2) the aggrieved party returns everything to the way it was before the contract was made.

Although there has been a breach of the contract, the effect of this breach is nullified if the aggrieved person by word or conduct waives the right to object to the breach. Conversely, an aggrieved party may accept a defective performance without thereby waiving a claim for breach if the party makes a reservation of rights. A reservation of rights can be made by stating that the defective performance is accepted "without prejudice," "under protest," or "with reservation of rights."

LEARNING OUTCOMES

After studying this chapter, you should be able to clearly explain:

A. What Constitutes a Breach of Contract

LO.1 Explain what constitutes a breach of contract and an anticipatory breach of contract

See the illustration of a painting contractor's failure to properly paint a house, p. 400.

See the *Tips* case in which damages are assessed for anticipatory repudiation of a contract, pp. 400–401.

See the *Mammoth Lakes* example involving anticipatory repudiation by conduct, p. 401.

B. Waiver of Breach

LO.2 Describe the effect of a waiver of a breach
See the application of the waiver doctrine as applied in the Massey example on p. 403.

C. Remedies for Breach of Contract

LO.3 Explain the range of remedies available for breach of contract
See Figure 20-1, "What Follows the Breach," on p. 404.
See the *Spencer Adams* example involving a range of monetary damages on p. 406.

See the *Pedro Morena* example involving rescission of a contract on p. 408.

See the rare Revolutionary War musket example of specific performance, p. 408.

D. Contract Provisions Affecting Remedies and Damages

LO.4   Explain when liquidated damages clauses are valid and invalid

See the Dow Corning faulty breast implants settlement agreement example

in which liquidated damages of a $100 per day late payment were found to be unenforceable penalty provision, p. 411.

LO.5   State when liability-limiting clauses and releases are valid

See the *Cheley Camps* case that illustrates how the camp successfully raised a signed parental exculpatory release as a defense in a horseback riding injury case, p. 413.

KEY TERMS

anticipatory breach
anticipatory repudiation
breach
compensatory damages
consequential damages
direct damages

exculpatory clause
injunction
limitation-of-liability clause
liquidated damages
liquidated damages clause
nominal damages

punitive damages
remedies
reservation of rights
specific performance
valid
waiver

QUESTIONS AND CASE PROBLEMS

1. The Forsyth School District contracted with Textor Construction, Inc., to build certain additions and alter school facilities, including the grading of a future softball field. Under the contract, the work was to be completed by August 1. Various delays occurred at the outset of the project attributable to the school district, and the architect's representative on the job, Mr. Hamilton, told Textor's vice president, William Textor, not to be concerned about a clause in the contract of $250 per day liquidated damages for failure to complete the job by August 1. Textor sued the school district for breach of contract regarding payment for the grading of the softball field, and the District counterclaimed for liquidated damages for 84 days at $250 per day for failure to complete the project by the August 1 date. What legal basis exists for Textor to defend against the counter-claim for failure to complete the job on time? Was it ethical for the school district to bring this counterclaim based on the facts before you? [*Textor Construction, Inc. v. Forsyth R-III School District*, 60 S.W.3d 692 (Mo. App.)]

2. Anthony makes a contract to sell a rare painting to Laura for $100,000. The written contract specifies that if Anthony should fail to perform the contract, he will pay Laura $5,000 as liquidated damages. Anthony fails to deliver the painting and is sued by Laura for $5,000. Can she recover this amount?

3. Rogers made a contract with Salisbury Brick Corp. that allowed it to remove earth and sand from land he owned. The contract ran for four years with provision to renew it for additional four-year terms up to a total of 96 years. The contract provided for compensation to Rogers based on the amount of earth and sand removed. By an unintentional mistake, Salisbury underpaid Rogers the amount of $863 for the months of November and December 1986. Salisbury offered this amount to Rogers, but he refused to accept it and claimed that he had been underpaid in other months. Rogers claimed that he was entitled to rescind the contract. Was he correct? [*Rogers v. Salisbury Brick Corp.*, 882 S. E.2d 915 (S.C.)]

4. A contractor departed from the specifications at a number of points in a contract to build a house. The cost to put the house in the condition called for by the contract was approximately $14,000. The contractor was sued for $50,000 for breach of contract and emotional distress caused by the breach. Decide.

5. Protein Blenders, Inc., made a contract with Gingerich to buy from him the shares of stock of a small corporation. When the buyer refused to take and pay for the stock, Gingerich sued for specific performance of the contract on the ground that the value of the stock was unknown and could not be readily ascertained because it was not sold on the general market. Was he entitled to specific performance? [*Gingerich v. Protein Blenders, Inc.*, 95 N.W.2d 522 (Iowa)]

6. The buyer of real estate made a down payment. The contract stated that the buyer would be liable for damages in an amount equal to the down payment if the buyer broke the contract. The buyer refused to go through with the contract and demanded his down payment back. The seller refused to return it and claimed that he was entitled to additional damages from the buyer because the damages that he had suffered were more than the amount of the down payment. Decide. [*Waters v. Key Colony East, Inc.*, 345 So.2d 367 (Fla. App.)]

7. Kuznicki made a contract for the installation of a fire detection system by Security Safety Corp. for $498. The contract was made one night and canceled at 9:00 the next morning. Security then claimed one-third of the purchase price from Kuznicki by virtue of a provision in the contract that "in the event of cancellation of this agreement… the owner agrees to pay $33^{1/3}$ percent of the contract price, as liquidated damages." Was Security Safety entitled to recover the amount claimed? [*Security Safety Corp. v. Kuznicki*, 213 N.E.2d 866 (Mass.)]

8. FNBC is a business brokerage firm that assits in the purchase and sale of businesses. Jennings and Hennessey were independent contractors working for FNBC. They left FNBC, and FNBC sued them for breach of their contracts with FNBC.

The trial court issued a permanent injunction prohibiting the former contractors from using proprietary information and the court awarded attorneys' fees under a clause in the contract that would obligate Jennings and Hennessey to indemnify FNBC against claims "brought by persons not a party to the provision." Jennings and Hennessey appealed the decision on attorneys' fees. Decide. [*FNBC v. Jennessey Group, LLC*, 759 N.W.2d 808 (Iowa App.)]

9. Melodee Lane Lingerie Co. was a tenant in a building that was protected against fire by a sprinkler and alarm system maintained by the American District Telegraph Co. (ADT). Because of the latter's fault, the controls on the system were defective and allowed the discharge of water into the building, which damaged Melodee's property. When Melodee sued ADT, its defense was that its service contract limited its liability to 10 percent of the annual service charge made to the customer. Was this limitation valid? [*Melodee Lane Lingerie Co. v. American District Telegraph Co.*, 218 N.E.2d 661 (N.Y.)]

10. JRC Trading Corp (JRC) bought computer software and hardware from Progressive Data Systems (PDS) for $167,935, which it paid in full, to track movement of its trucks with inventory and to process transactions. The purchase agreement also called for a $7,500 per year licensing fee for an 18-year period, and it stated that in the event of default PDS could "accelerate and declare all obligations of Customer as a liquidated sum." A dispute arose between the parties, and when the case was litigated the only actual contract charges owed PDS were the license fees of $7,500 for two years. The application of the liquidated damages clause would yield an additional $120,000 cash for PDS for the future fees for 16 years without any reduction for expenses or the present cash value for the not-yet-earned fees. JRC contends that actual damages were clearly ascertainable and that the liquidated damages clause was a penalty provision that should not be enforced. Progressive argued that the court must interpret the contract as written, stating that the court has no power to

rewrite the contract. Decide. [*Jefferson Randolf Corp. v. PDS*, 553 S.E.2d 304 (Ga. App.)]

11. Ken Sulejmanagic, aged 19, signed up for a course in scuba diving taught by Madison at the YMCA. Before the instruction began, Ken was required to sign a form releasing Madison and the YMCA from liability for any harm that might occur. At the end of the course, Madison, Ken, and another student went into deep water. After Ken made the final dive required by the course program, Madison left him alone in the water while he took the other student for a dive. When Madison returned, Ken could not be found, and it was later determined that he had drowned. Ken's parents sued Madison and the YMCA for negligence in the performance of the teaching contract. The defendants raised the defense that the release Ken signed shielded them from liability. The plaintiffs claimed that the release was invalid. Who was correct? [*Madison v. Superior Court*, 250 Cal. Rptr. 299 (Cal. App.)]

12. Wassenaar worked for Panos under a three-year contract stating that if the contract were terminated wrongfully by Panos before the end of the three years, he would pay as damages the salary for the remaining time that the contract had to run. After three months, Panos terminated the contract, and Wassenaar sued him for pay for the balance of the contract term. Panos claimed that this amount could not be recovered because the contract provision for the payment was a void penalty. Was this provision valid? [*Wassenaar v. Panos*, 331 N.W.2d 357 (Wis.)]

13. Soden, a contractor, made a contract to build a house for Clevert. The sales contract stated that "if either party defaults in the performance of this contract," that party would be liable to the other for attorneys' fees incurred in suing the defaulter. Soden was 61 days late in completing the contract, and some of the work was defective.

In a suit by the buyer against the contractor, the contractor claimed that he was not liable for the buyer's attorneys' fees because he had made only a defective performance and because "default" in the phrase quoted meant "nonperformance of the contract." Was the contractor liable for the attorneys' fees? [*Clevert v. Soden*, 400 S.E.2d 181 (Va.)]

14. Protection Alarm Co. made a contract to provide burglar alarm security for Fretwell's home. The contract stated that the maximum liability of the alarm company was the actual loss sustained or $50, whichever was the lesser, and that this provision was agreed to "as liquidated damages and not as a penalty." When Fretwell's home was burglarized, he sued for the loss of approximately $12,000, claiming that the alarm company had been negligent. The alarm company asserted that its maximum liability was $50. Fretwell claimed that this was invalid because it bore no relationship to the loss that could have been foreseen when the contract was made or that in fact "had been sustained." Decide.

15. Shepherd-Will made a contract to sell Emma Cousar:

> *5 acres of land adjoining property owned by the purchaser and this being formerly land of Shepherd-Will, Inc., located on north side of Highway 223. This 5 acres to be surveyed at earliest time possible at which time plat will be attached and serve as further description on property.*

Shepherd-Will owned only one 100-acre tract of land that adjoined Emma's property. This tract had a common boundary with her property of 1,140 feet. Shepherd-Will failed to perform this contract. Emma sued for specific performance of the contract. Decide. [*Cousar v. Shepherd-Will, Inc.*, 387 S.E.2d 723 (S.C. App.)]

CPA QUESTIONS

1. Master Mfg., Inc., contracted with Accur Computer Repair Corp. to maintain Master's computer system. Master's manufacturing process depends on its computer system operating properly at all times. A liquidated damages clause in the contract provided that

Accur pay $1,000 to Master for each day that Accur was late responding to a service request. On January 12, Accur was notified that Master's computer system had failed. Accur did not respond to Master's service request until January 15. If Master sues Accur under the liquidated damages provision of the contract, Master will:

a. Win, unless the liquidated damage provision is determined to be a penalty.

b. Win, because under all circumstances liquidated damages provisions are enforceable.

c. Lose, because Accur's breach was *not* material.

d. Lose, because liquidated damage provisions violate public policy (5/93, Law, #25).

2. Jones, CPA, entered into a signed contract with Foster Corp. to perform accounting and review services. If Jones repudiates the contract prior to the date performance is due to begin, which of the following is *not* correct?

a. Foster could successfully maintain an action for breach of contract after the date performance was due to begin.

b. Foster can obtain a judgment ordering Jones to perform.

c. Foster could successfully maintain an action for breach of contract prior to the date performance is due to begin.

d. Foster can obtain a judgment for the monetary damages it incurred as a result of the repudiation (5/89, Law, #35).

3. Which of the following concepts affect(s) the amount of monetary damages recoverable by the nonbreaching party when a contract is breached?

	Forseeability of damages	Mitigation of damages
a.	Yes	Yes
b.	Yes	No
c.	No	Yes
d.	No	No

© Manuel Gutjahr/iStockphoto.com

CHAPTER 23

Nature and Form of Sales

learningoutcomes

After studying this chapter, you should be able to

LO.1 Define a sale of goods and explain when UCC Article 2 applies to contracts

LO.2 Distinguish between an actual sale of goods and other types of transactions in goods

LO.3 Describe how contracts are formed under Article 2, and list the differences in formation standards between the UCC and common law

LO.4 Explain when a contract for the sale of goods must be in writing

LO.5 List and explain the exceptions to the requirement that certain contracts be in writing

LO.6 Discuss the purpose of the United Nations Convention on Contracts for the International Sale of Goods

Chapters 12 through 20 examined the common law of contracts. That source of contract law applies to contracts whose subject matter is land or services. However, there is another source of contract law, **Article 2** of the Uniform Commercial Code (UCC).

Article 2 was revised substantially by the National Conference of Commissioners on Uniform State Laws (NCCUSL) and the American Law Institute (ALI) in August 2003. Because no state has adopted Revised Article 2, its future remains a question. Revised Article 2 is covered only briefly in this chapter and Chapters 24–27.

UCC Article 2 governs the sale of everything from boats to televisions to compact discs and applies to contracts for the sale of goods. Article 2 exists as a result of the work of businesspeople, commercial transactions lawyers, and legal experts who together have developed a body of contract law suitable for the fast pace of business. Article 2 continues to be refined and modified to ensure seamless laws for transactions in goods across the country.[1]

Article 2 – section of Uniform Commercial Code that governs contracts for the sale of goods.

A. NATURE OF SALES

A *sale of goods* is defined under Article 2 as transfer of title to tangible personal property for a price.[2] This price may be a payment of money, an exchange of other property, or the performance of services.

The parties to a sale are the person who owns the goods, the seller or vendor, and the person to whom the title is transferred, the buyer or vendee.

CPA

1. Subject Matter of Sales

goods – anything movable at the time it is identified as the subject of a transaction.

Goods, as defined under the UCC, consist of all forms of tangible personal property, including specially manufactured goods—everything from a fan to a painting to a yacht.[3] Article 2 does not cover (1) investment securities, such as stocks and bonds, the sale of which is regulated by Article 8 of the UCC; (2) insurance policies, commercial paper, such as checks, and promissory notes because they are regulated under Articles 3 and 4 of the UCC; and (3) real estate, such as houses, factories, farms, and land itself.[4]

---

[1] The UCC Article 2 (prior to the 2003 revisions) has been adopted in 49 states plus the Virgin Islands and the District of Columbia. Louisiana adopted only Article 1; 1990 Revision of Article 3; 1990 Amendments to Article 4; Article 4A (Funds Transfers); 1995 Revision of Articles 5 and 7; 1994 Revision of Article 8; and 2000 Revision of Article 9. The newest revisions of Article 2 were reconciled in July, 2003. The changes in Revised Article 2 are noted briefly throughout this chapter and Chapters 24–27.

[2] UCC §2-105(1). *General Mills Operations, LLC v. Five Star Custom Foods, Ltd.*, 798 F. Supp. 2d 1148 (D. Minn. 2011); *M K Intern., Inc. v. Central Oil & Supply Corp.*, 87 So.3d 165 (La.App. 2012).

[3] *State v. Cardwell*, 718 A.2d 594 (Conn. 1998) (concert tickets are goods); *In re Grede Foundries, Inc.*, 435 B.R. 593 (W.D. Wisc. 2010) (electricity is a good); *Leal v. Holtvogh*, 702 N.E.2d 1246 (Ohio App. 1998) (transfer of part interest in a horse is a good); *Bergeron v. Aero Sales*, 134 P.3d 964 (Or. App. 2006) (jet fuel is a good); *Rite Aid Corp. v. Levy-Gray*, 894 A.2d 563 (Md. 2006) (prescription drug is a good); *Willis Mining v. Noggle*, 509 S.E.2d 731 (Ga. App. 1998) (granite blocks are goods); *Sterling Power Partners, L.P. v. Niagra Mohawk Power Corp.*, 657 N.Y.S.2d 407 (1997) (electricity is a good); *Gladhart v. Oregon Vineyard Supply Co.*, 994 P.2d 134 (Or. App. 1999) (grape plants bought from nursery are goods); *Dantzler v. S.P. Parks, Inc.*, 40 UCC Rep.Serv.2d 955 E.D. Pa. 1988) (purchase of ticket to amusement ride is not transaction in goods); *Rossetti v. Busch Entm't Corp.*, 87 F. Supp. 2d (E.D. Pa. 2000) (computer software programs are goods); and *Saxton v. Pets Warehouse, Inc.*, 691 N.Y.S.2d 872 (1999) (dog is a good).

[4] However, Article 2 does apply to the sale of rare coins. *Bowers and Merena Auctions, LLC, v. James Lull*, 386 B.R. 261, 65 UCC Rep. Ser. 2d 194 (Haw. 2008).

(A) **NATURE OF GOODS.** Article 2 applies not only to contracts for the sale of familiar items of personal property, such as automobiles or chairs, but also to the transfer of commodities, such as oil, gasoline, milk, and grain.[5]

(B) **EXISTING AND FUTURE GOODS.** Goods that are already manufactured or crops already grown and owned by the seller at the time of the transaction are called **existing goods**. All other goods are called **future goods**, which include both goods that physically exist but are not owned by the seller and goods that have not yet been produced, as when a buyer contracts to purchase custom-made office furniture.

existing goods–goods that physically exist and are owned by the seller at the time of a transaction.

future goods–goods that exist physically but are not owned by the seller and goods that have not yet been produced.

2. Sale Distinguished from Other Transactions

Other types of transactions in goods are not covered by Article 2 because they are not transfers of title to the goods.

bailment–relationship that exists when personal property is delivered into the possession of another under an agreement, express or implied, that the identical property will be returned or will be delivered in accordance with the agreement. (Parties—bailor, bailee)

(A) **BAILMENT.** A **bailment** is not a sale because only possession is transferred to a **bailee**. Title to the property is not transferred. (For more information on bailments, their nature, and the rights of the parties, see Chapter 21.) A lease of goods, such as an automobile, is governed by Article 2A of the UCC, which is covered later in Section D of this chapter.

bailee–person who accepts possession of a property.

(B) **GIFT.** A **gift** is a gratuitous (free) transfer of the title to property. The Article 2 definition of a sale requires that the transfer of title be made for a price. Gifts are not covered under Article 2.[6]

gift–title to an owner's personal property voluntarily transferred by a party not receiving anything in exchange.

(C) **CONTRACT FOR SERVICES.** A contract for services, such as a contract for painting a home, is not a sale of goods and is not covered under Article 2 of the UCC. Contracts for services are governed by common law principles.

(D) **CONTRACT FOR GOODS AND SERVICES.** If a contract calls for both rendering services and supplying materials to be used in performing the services, the contract is classified according to its dominant element. **For Example,** a homeowner may purchase a security system. The homeowner is paying for the equipment that is used in the system as well as for the seller's expertise and installation of that system. Is the homeowner's contract governed by Article 2, or is it a contract for services and covered under the common law of contracts?

If the service element dominates, the contract is a service contract and is governed by common law rather than Article 2. If the goods make up the dominant element of the contract, then the parties' rights are determined under Article 2.[7] In the home security system contract example, the question requires comparing the costs of the system's parts versus the costs of its installation. In some contracts, the equipment costs are minimal, and installation is key for the customer. In more sophisticated security systems, the installation is a small portion of the overall contract price, and the contract would be governed by the UCC.[8]

---

[5] UCC §2-105(1)–(2). *Venmar Ventilation, Inc. v. Von Weise USA, Inc.*, 68 UCC Serv. 2d 373 (D. Minn. 2009); *Marcus Dairy, Inc. v. Rollin Dairy Corp.*, 67 UCC Rep. Serv. 2d 777 (D. Conn. 2008).

[6] The adoption of a dog from an animal shelter is not the sale of goods. *Slodov v. Animal Protective League*, 628 N.E.2d 117 (Oh. App. 1993).

[7] Trees and shrubs as part of a landscaping contract are sales of goods. *Kaitz v. Landscape Creations, Inc.*, 2000 Mass.App.Div. 140, 2000 WL 694274 (Mass.App.Div.), 42 UCC Rep.Serv.2d 691.

[8] *TK Power, Inc. v. Textron, Inc.*, 433 F. Supp. 2d 1058 (N.D. Cal. 2006), see also *Lesiak v. Central Valley Ag Co-op., Inc.*, 808 N.W.2d 67 (Neb. 2012) (a contract for the sale and application of herbicide was primarily a contract for the sale of the herbicide and was governed by the UCC).

CASE SUMMARY

Dirt Is Cheap, But It Is Still a Good

FACTS: Paramount, a civil engineering firm and general contractor, submitted a bid to construct runway improvements at the Atlanta Hartsfield–Jackson International Airport. Paramount included DPS's quote for supplying the fill dirt for the project in its bid. DPS's written quote described its work as "furnish[ing] and haul[ing]/deliver[ing] borrow dirt from DPS's location to the job site," and specifically excluded the provision of "traffic control, dust control, security and escort services" from the scope of work. The quote provides that the dirt would be delivered for a price of "$140/Truck Load."

After Paramount was awarded the airport project, it contacted DPS about the amount of dirt and numbers of trucks that it would need for the airport project. DPS believed that the parties had a contract, and it sent a letter to Paramount confirming that it was "holding approximately 45,000 [cubic yards] of borrow dirt ready to be hauled in to your project once we receive [the] 10–day notice from you." Paramount did not respond.

Over the next two months, DPS sent other letters to Paramount, but Paramount did not respond. After executives from the two companies met, Paramount sent the following:

> [Y]ou insisted that we give commitment to you for buying the dirt before you will give us price [for other work]. This really was a surprise to us. … Also please note that we have never committed to buy all the fill materials from you. In the last meeting you were informed that we intend to purchase some materials from you and it may be through other subcontractors. Our decisions will be conveyed to you as soon as possible.

Ultimately, Paramount bought the dirt it needed from another vendor. DPS sued Paramount for breach of contract. The jury found for DPS. Paramount appealed arguing that the UCC did not apply and a more formal contract was needed.

DECISION: The court held that the sale of dirt was the predominant purpose of the contract. The price was based on the quantity of dirt delivered and the language used was for sale of dirt, not hauling of dirt. Further, the seller severed the dirt from the land, something that means the seller was selling a good. The UCC applied, and there was a valid contract. [***Paramount Contracting Co. v. DPS Industries, Inc.*, 709 S.E.2d 288 (Ga.App. 2011)**]

One of the critical issues under Article 2 that has resulted from technological advances is whether Article 2 covers computer software included with the sale of a computer, thus subjecting software manufacturers to warranty liability and the damage provisions of the UCC.[9] Whether software would be covered under Article 2 was the most spirited debate in the 2003 revision process.[10] Under the final draft, Revised Article 2 does not cover "information," but information is not defined. Several state legislatures have addressed this issue by modifying their versions of the UCC with a section that establishes that "goods" does not cover the sale of "information" not associated with "goods."[11]

---

[9] *Multi-Tech Systems, Inc. v. Floreat, Inc.,* 47 UCC Rep. Serv. 2d 924 (D. Minn. 2002).

[10] Section 2-103(1)(k) of Revised Article 2 defines goods as follows: *all things movable at the time of identification to a contract for sale. The term includes future goods, specially manufactured goods, the unborn young of animals, growing crops, and other identified things attached to realty as described in §2-107. The term does not include information, the money in which the price is to be paid, investment securities under Article 8, the subject matter of foreign exchange transactions and choses in action.*

[11] Up through 2002, the UCC revisions included provisions on computer information. However, the original amendments to Section 2-102 (4) and (5) never made their way into the final version of UCC 2-102. We are left only with the comment partially quoted here. The comment basically says "it depends" as to whether Article 2 applies, with the dependency on the nature of the contract.

CPA

3. Formation of Sales Contracts

(A) NECESSARY DETAIL FOR FORMATION. To streamline business transactions, Article 2 of the UCC does not have standards as rigid as the formation standards of common law contracts.

Under the UCC, a contract can be formed even though one or more terms are left open so long as the parties clearly intend to contract.[12] The minimum terms required for formation of an agreement under the UCC are the subject matter and quantity (if there is more than one).[13] **For Example,** an agreement that described "the sale of my white Scion" would be sufficient, but an agreement to purchase "some white Scions" would require a quantity in order to qualify for formation.[14] Other provisions under Article 2 can cover any missing terms so long as the parties are clear on their intent to contract. Article 2 has provisions that cover price, delivery, time for performance, payment, and other details of performance in the event the parties agree to a sale but have not discussed or reduced to writing their desires in these areas.[15]

(B) THE MERCHANT VERSUS NONMERCHANT PARTIES. Because Article 2 applies to all transactions in goods, it is applicable to sales by both **merchants** and nonmerchants,[16] including consumers. In most instances, the UCC treats all buyers and sellers alike. However, some sections in Article 2 are applicable only to merchants, and as a result, there are circumstances in which merchants are subject to different standards and rules. Generally, these areas of different treatment reflect the UCC's recognition that merchants are experienced, have special knowledge of the relevant commercial practices, and often need to have greater flexibility and speed in their transactions. The sections that have different rules for merchants and nonmerchants are noted throughout Chapters 24–27.

merchant – seller who deals in specific goods classified by the UCC.

CPA

(C) OFFER. Just as in common law, the **offer** is the first step in formation of a sales contract under Article 2.[17] The common law contract rules on offers are generally applicable in sales contract formation with the exception of the **firm offer**[18] provision, which is a special rule on offers applicable only to merchants: A firm offer by a merchant cannot be revoked if the offer (1) expresses an intention that it will be kept open, (2) is in a writing, and (3) is signed by the merchant.[19]

offer – expression of an offeror's willingness to enter into a contractual agreement.

firm offer – offer stated to be held open for a specified time, under the UCC, with respect to merchants.

The period of irrevocability in a merchant's firm offer cannot exceed three months. If no specific time is given in the merchant's firm offer for its duration, it remains irrevocable only for a reasonable time. A firm offer need not have consideration to be irrevocable for a period of three months. **For Example,** a rain check given by a store on advertised merchandise is a merchant's firm offer. The rain check guarantees that you will be able to purchase two bottles of Windex at $1.99 each for a period specified in the rain check.

---

[12] 5 UCC §2-204(3); *Cargill v. Jorgenson Farms*, 719 N.W.2d 226 (Minn. App. 2006). This provision on formation assumes that the agreement the parties do have provides "a reasonably certain basis for giving an appropriate remedy." Price quotations are not considered offers. *Ace American Ins. Co. v. Wendt, LLP*, 724 F. Supp. 2d 899 (N.D. Ill. 2010).

[13] See also, *H.P.B.C., Inc. v. Nor-Tech Powerboats, Inc.*, 946 So.2d 1108 (Fla. App. 2006).

[14] *Griffith v. Clear Lakes Trout Co., Inc.*, 200 P.3d 1162, 67 UCC Rep. Ser. 2d 883 (Idaho 2009).

[15] For information on terms, see UCC §§2-305 (price), 2-307 to 2-308 (delivery), 2-310 (payment), and 2-311 (performance).

[16] *Merchant* is defined in UCC §2-104(1). An operator of a turkey farm is not a merchant with regard to heaters used on turkey farms, only for the turkeys themselves. *Jennie-O-Foods, Inc. v. Safe-Glo Prods. Corp.*, 582 N.W.2d 576 (Minn. App. 1998).

[17] A purchase order is generally considered an offer, but it must have enough information to meet the minimum standards for an offer. *Biotech Pharmacal, Inc. v. International Business Connections, LLC*, 184 S.W.3d 447 (Ark. Ct. App. 2004). *Westlaw E.C. Styberg Engineering Co. v. Eaton Corp.*, 492 F.3d 912 (7th Cir. 2007).

[18] Firm offers are covered in UCC §2-205.

[19] A quotation is a firm offer. *Rich Products Corp. v. Kemutec, Inc.*, 66 F. Supp. 2d 937 (E.D. Wis. 1999), but *see Boydstun Metal Works, Inc. v. Cottrell, Inc.*, 519 F. Supp. 2d 1119 (D. Or. 2007).

For nonmerchants' offers and offers in which the parties want firm offer periods that exceed three months, there must be consideration. In these situations, the parties must create an option contract just like those used in common law contracts (see Chapters 12 and 13).

acceptance – unqualified assent to the act or proposal of another; as the acceptance of an offer to make a contract.

(D) ACCEPTANCE—MANNER. Unlike the common law rules on acceptance, which control with great detail the method of **acceptance**, the UCC rules on acceptance are much more flexible. Under Article 2, an acceptance of an offer may be in any manner and by any medium that is reasonable under the circumstances.[20] Acceptance can occur through written communication or through performance, as when a seller accepts an offer for prompt shipment of goods by simply shipping the goods.[21] However, just as under common law, Article 2 requires that if the offer specifies the manner or medium of acceptance, the offer can be accepted only in that manner.

CPA

mailbox rule – timing for acceptance tied to proper acceptance.

(E) ACCEPTANCE—TIMING. The timing rules of the common law for determining when a contract has been formed are used to determine the formation of a contract under Article 2 with one slight modification. The **mailbox rule** applies under the UCC not just for the use of the same method of communication as that used by the offeror, but also applies when the offeree uses any reasonable method of communication. Under the common law, the offeree had to use the same method of communication in order to have the mailbox rule of acceptance apply. However, a UCC offeree can use any reasonable method for communicating acceptance and still enjoy the priority timing of the mailbox rule, something that makes an acceptance effective when it is sent. **For Example,** suppose that Feather-Light Brownies sent a letter offer to Cane Sugar Suppliers offering to buy 500 pounds of confectioner's sugar at $1 per pound. Cane Sugar Suppliers faxes back an acceptance of the letter offer. Cane Sugar Suppliers' acceptance is effective when it sends the fax.

Ethics & the Law

Restocking at Overstock

Cynthia Hines purchased an ElectroluxOxygen 3 Ultra Canister vacuum from Overstock.com, an online retailer that sells closeout goods. Ms. Hines returned the vacuum and was refunded her full amount, less a $30 restocking fee. She filed suit for breach of contract because she said that Overstock.com advertises that you can return merchandise at no cost and that Overstock.com did not disclose the restocking fee.

However, Overstock.com states that its Web site includes the following, "All retail purchases from Overstock are conducted through Overstock's Internet website. When an individual accesses the website, he or she accepts Overstock's terms. conditions and policies, which govern all of Overstock's customer purchases."

However, users were not required to click on the terms and conditions or to scroll all the way through the terms and conditions in order to use the site. It was possible, then, for a user to miss all the terms, such as a restocking fee.

Evaluate whether the restocking fee was part of the contract. Was it ethical for Overstock.com to impose the terms without users being aware of those terms? Discuss whether Overstock.com should have done more to disclose the restocking charge or put the notice in a different place.*

*Hines v. Overstock.com, Inc., 668 F. Supp. 2d 362 (E.D.N.Y. 2009)

---

[20] UCC §2-206(1). Governs acceptance methods. See *Ardus Medical, Inc. v. Emanuel County Hospital Authority*, 558 F. Supp. 2d 1301 (D. Ga. 2008).

[21] UCC §2-206(1)(b). Shipment of coal in response to an offer is acceptance. *Central Illinois Public Service Co. v. Atlas Minerals, Inc.*, 146 F.3d 448 (7th Cir. 1998). When the buyer and the seller have exchanged two purchase orders and three invoices that set forth price per pound of resin, quantity of resin, place and time of shipment, delivery charges, and the buyer's obligation to pay interest, they have formed a contract. *Bro-Tech Corp. v. Purity Water Co. of San Antonio, Inc.*, 681 F. Supp. 2d 791 (W.D. Tex. 2010).

mirror image rule – common law contract rule on acceptance that requires language to be absolutely the same as the offer, unequivocal and unconditional.

(F) ACCEPTANCE—LANGUAGE. Under the common law, the **mirror image rule** applies to acceptances. To be valid acceptances under common law, the language of the acceptance must be absolute, unconditional, and unequivocal; that is, the acceptance under common law must be the mirror image of the offer in order for a contract to be formed. However, the UCC has liberalized this rigid rule and permits formation even in circumstances when the acceptance includes terms that vary from the offer. The following sections explain the UCC rules on differing terms in acceptances. These rules for additional terms in acceptance were eliminated under Revised Article 2.[22]

(1) Additional Terms in Acceptance—Nonmerchants.

Under Article 2, unless an offer expressly specifies that an offer to buy or sell goods must be accepted exactly as made, the offeree may accept an offer and at the same time propose an additional term or terms. The additional term or terms in the acceptance does not result in a rejection as it would under common law. A contract is formed with the terms of the original offer. The additional terms are proposals for addition to the contract and may or may not be accepted by the other party.[23] **For Example,** Joe tells Susan, "I'll sell you my X-box for $150," and Susan responds, "I'll take it. The "Call of Duty" game is included." Susan has added an additional term in her acceptance. At this point, Joe and Susan have a contract for the sale of the X-box for $150. Whether the "Call of Duty" game is included is up to Joe; Joe is free to accept Susan's proposal or reject it, but his decision does not control whether he has a contract. There is a contract because Susan has made a definite statement of acceptance. To avoid being bound by a contract before she is clear on the terms, Susan should make an inquiry before using the language of acceptance, such as "Would you include the "Call of Duty" game as part of the sale?" Susan's inquiry is not an acceptance and leaves the original offer still outstanding, which she is free to accept or reject.

(2) Additional Terms in Acceptance—Merchants.

battle of the forms – merchants' exchanges of invoices and purchase orders with differing boilerplate terms.

Under Article 2, the use of additional terms in acceptances by merchants is treated slightly differently. The different treatment of merchants in acceptances is the result of a commercial practice known as the **battle of the forms**, which results because a buyer sends a seller a purchase order for the purchase of goods. The seller sends back an invoice to the buyer. Although the buyer and seller may agree on the front of their documents that the subject matter of their contracts is 500 treadmills, the backs of their forms have details on the contracts, often called *boilerplate language*, that will never match. Suppose, for example, that the seller's invoice adds a payment term of "10 days same as cash." Is the payment term now a part of the parties' agreement? The parties have a meeting of the minds on the subject matter of the contract but now have a slight difference in performance terms.

Under Article 2, in a transaction between merchants, the additional term or terms sent back in an acceptance become part of the contract if the additional term or terms do not materially alter the offer and the offeror does not object in a timely fashion.[24] **For Example,** returning to the Joe and Susan example, suppose that they are both now secondary market video game merchants negotiating for the sale and

---

[22] However, Revised Article 2 has not been adopted widely by the states.
[23] See the Ethics & Law feature on Restocking and Overstock.com.
[24] UCC §2-207(2).

FIGURE 23-1	*Terms in Contracts under UCC Article §2-207*

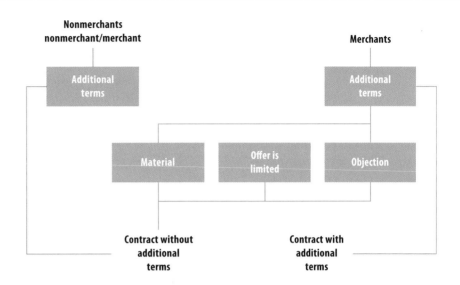

© Cengage Learning

purchase of a used X-box. They would have a contract, and the "Call of Duty" game would be included as part of the sale. Joe could, however, avoid the problem by adding a limitation to his offer, such as "This offer is limited to these terms." With that limitation, Susan would have a contract, but the contract would not include the "Call of Duty" game. Joe could also object immediately to Susan's proposal for the "Call of Duty" game and still have a contract without this additional term.[25]

If the proposed additional term in the acceptance is material, a contract is formed, but the material additional term does not become a part of the contract.[26] **For Example,** if Susan added to her acceptance the statement, "Game system carries one-year warranty," she has probably added a material term because the one-year warranty for a used game system would be unusual in the secondary market and costly for Joe.[27] Again, Joe can avoid this problem by limiting his offer so as to strike any additional terms, whether material or immaterial.

The most significant changes under Revised Article 2 deal with §2-207. Because there were so many confusing circumstances with additional terms, the effect of the new §2-207 is to leave the issues of what is or is not included in a contract to the courts. However, because so many businesses and individuals are using the Internet to contract, they are working out their terms through ongoing and immediate exchanges and questions. The result has been a significant reduction in the number of §2-207 cases.[28]

Figure 23-1 is a graphic picture of the rules on acceptance and contract terms under current Article 2 when additional terms are proposed.

[25] *Oakley Fertilizer, Inc. v. Continental Ins. Co.,* 276 S.W.3d 342 (Mo. App. 2009). Revised UCC Article 2 makes changes in the way these additional terms operate. When there is a record of an agreement, with no objection, the terms in the record are the terms of the contract.

[26] Damage limitations clauses are considered material. *Belden Inc. v. American Electronic Components, Inc.,* 885 N.E.2d 751 (Ind. App. 2008). Forum selection clauses are also material. *Hugo Boss Fashions, Inc. v. Sam's European Tailoring, Inc.,* 742 N.Y.S.2d 1 (2002).

[27] A statute of limitations of one year added to the acceptance of an offer is considered a material change because it limits so severely the amount of time for bringing suit on the contract. *American Tempering, Inc. v. Craft Architectural Metals Corp.,* 483 N.Y.S.2d 304 (1985).

[28] Francis J. Mootz III, "After the Battle of the Forms: Commercial Contracting in the Electronic Age," 4 *Journal of Law & Policy for the Information Society* 271, Summer, 2008.

Even without all the UCC provisions on contract terms, an offeror may expressly or by conduct agree to a term added by the offeree to its acceptance of the offer. The offeror may agree orally or in writing to the additional term. There can be acceptance of the additional term by conduct of the parties if the parties just perform their obligations under the contract with knowledge that the term has been added by the offeree.[29]

CASE SUMMARY

The Helium That Tanked

FACTS: On July 3, 2007, SVC–West, L.P. (SVC) did time-share presentations at hotels and ordered helium tanks quite often for balloons. SVC placed a rush order with C9 Ventures (C9) for eight helium-filled tanks used to inflate festive balloons. C9 accepted the order and later that day delivered the tanks.

On the reverse of the invoice was an indemnification provision requiring SVC to indemnify C9 for any loss arising out of the use or possession of the helium-filled tanks. C9 later picked up the tanks, and, weeks later, SVC paid the invoice. SVC had obtained helium-filled tanks from C9 on prior occasions.

The invoice was on a single piece of paper, on the reverse side of which was a section entitled "INDEMNITY/HOLD HARMLESS" (boldface omitted), which stated in part: "Customer agrees to indemnify[,] defend and hold harmless C9 ... from and against any and all liability, claims, judgments, attorneys fees and cost of ... every[ ] kind and nature, including, but not limited to injuries or death to persons and damage to property, arising out of the use, maintenance, instruction, operation, possession, ownership or Rental & Decor of the items rented, however cause[d], except claims or litigation arising through the solo [sic] gross negligence or willful misconduct of C9...." The reverse side of the invoice also included a section entitled "LEGAL FEES," which provided, in essence, that in an action to enforce "this Rental & Decor Agreement," the prevailing party would be entitled to recover attorney fees.

Before then, C9 had presented the same or similar invoice to SVC 10 times, but had received the signature of an SVC employee only six times. SVC never attempted to substitute its own form agreement for C9's form.

C9 typically delivered the tanks in the morning when no SVC guests were present, but on July 3, C9's employee, Ernesto Roque, did not arrive at the SVC premises to make the delivery until about 5:00 P.M. Roque asked SVC employee, Zayra Renteria, where to place the eight helium-filled tanks. Renteria, who was expecting the delivery during her shift, instructed Roque to bring the tanks up to the mezzanine level of the resort, at which point she would inform him where to place them. Roque wrote the following on the invoice, "[N]obody would sign all running around in lobby nobody knew who . . . After accident nobody got signatures." Roque stacked five to seven tanks against the walls next to the service elevator. He was in the process of bringing up another tank when a young boy, whose parents were attending the time-share presentation, ran up to the tanks and hugged one of them, pulling it over. The tank, which was about five feet tall and weighed 130 pounds, fell on the boy's hand. He was hospitalized and underwent surgery for his injuries.

SVC and C9 each paid the boy's family to settle a lawsuit brought to recover for his injuries. C9 filed a cross-complaint against SVC to enforce the indemnification provision on the back of the unsigned invoice. The trial court found for C9 and SVC appealed.

DECISION: The question: Is the indemnification provision on the back of the unsigned invoice enforceable against SVC? SVC and C9 entered into an oral contract when C9 accepted SVC's

[29] *Panike & Sons Farms, Inc. v. Smith*, 212 P.3d 992 (Idaho 2009).

CASE SUMMARY

Continued

telephone order for eight helium-filled tanks. Under section 2-207, additional terms proposed in an acceptance or confirmation may become terms of the contract in certain situations. The oral contract between SVC and C9, however, was a lease of personal property (the helium-filled tanks), and not a sale of goods under the California Uniform Commercial Code.

The terms on the back of the unsigned invoice would have become part of the parties' oral contract only if SVC agreed to those terms. SVC did not agree to those terms by course of dealing or course of performance, or under basic contract law.

However, even if this were a transaction in goods governed by the California Uniform Commercial Code then the issue turns on whether SVC is a merchant. If SVC is not a merchant, the terms of the invoice are considered to be mere proposals for additional terms, which SVC did not accept. However, an indemnification provision is deemed a material alteration to an agreement as a matter of law, so an indemnification provision on the back of the invoice would not, under section 2-207, become part of the contract between SVC and C9.

Reversed. [*C9 Ventures v. SVC-West, L.P.*, 202 Cal.App.4th 1483, 136 Cal.Rptr.3d 550 (Cal. App. 2012)]

(3) Conflicting Terms in Acceptance.

In some situations, the offeree has not added a different term from the original offer but has instead proposed terms that contradict the terms of the offer. **For Example,** a buyer's purchase order may require the seller to offer full warranty protection, whereas the seller's invoice may include a disclaimer of all warranties. The buyer's purchase order may include a clause that provides "payment in 30 days same as cash," whereas the seller's invoice may include a term that has "10 days same as cash." Once again, it is clear that the parties intended to enter into a contract, and the subject matter is also clear. The task for Article 2 becomes one of establishing the rules that determine the terms of a contract when both sides have used different forms. However, if there are conflicting terms on the basic requirements (such as price) for formation, the courts may conclude that the parties have not met minds.[30]

When a term of an acceptance conflicts with a term of an offer but it is clear that the parties intended to be bound by a contract, the UCC still recognizes the formation of a contract. The terms that are conflicting cancel each other and are ignored. The contract then consists of the terms of the offer and acceptance that agree. **For Example,** if one party's contract form provided for full warranty protection and the other party's form provided for no warranty protection, the terms cancel each other out, and the parties' contract includes only those warranties provided under Article 2 (see Chapter 25 for a discussion of those warranties).

(G) DEFENSES TO FORMATION. Article 2 incorporates the common law defenses to formation of contracts by reference to the common law defenses in §1-103 (see Chapter 14 for a full discussion of those defenses). **For Example,** a party to a

---

[30] *Howard Const. Co. v. Jeff-Cole Quarries, Inc.*, 669 S.W.2d 221 (Mo. App. 1984), where the acceptance changed the price, there was not an acceptance but a counteroffer.

contract who can establish that the other party engaged in fraud to get the contract formed may cancel the contract and recover for losses that result from any damages for goods already delivered or payment already made.

(1) Unconscionability.

The UCC includes an additional contract defense for parties to a sale contract called *unconscionability.*[31] This section permits a court to refuse to enforce a sales contract that it finds to be **unconscionable**, which is generally defined as grossly unfair.[32] A court may also find a clause or portions of a contract to be unconscionable and refuse to enforce those clauses or sections.[33]

unconscionable – unreasonable, not guided or restrained by conscience and often referring to a contract grossly unfair to one party because of the superior bargaining powers of the other party.

(2) Illegality.

At common law, a contract is void if its subject matter itself is illegal, such as a contract for hire to murder someone. Under the UCC, a contract for the sale of heroin would be void. Likewise, a contract for the sale of a recalled or banned toy would be void.

(3) The Effect of Illegal Sale.

An illegal sale or contract to sell cannot be enforced. As a general rule, courts will not aid either party in recovering money or property transferred under an illegal agreement.

4. Terms in the Formed Contract

As noted earlier, contracts can be formed under Article 2 with terms of performance still missing or open. A contract is formed with just the quantity agreed on, but there are issues that must be resolved if the contract is to be completed. Article 2 has provisions for such missing terms.

CPA

(A) PRICE. If the price for the goods is not expressly fixed by the contract, the price may be an open term, whereby the parties merely indicate how the price should be determined at a later time. In the absence of any reference to price, the price will be a reasonable price at the time of the delivery of the goods, which is generally the market price.[34]

Parties often use formulas for determining price in sales of goods. The price itself is missing from the contract until the formula is applied at some future time. The so-called **cost plus** formula for determining price has been used a great deal, particularly in commercial contracts. Under this formula, the buyer pays the seller the seller's costs for manufacture or obtaining the goods plus a specified percentage as profit.

cost plus – method of determining the purchase price or contract price equal to the seller's or contractor's costs plus a stated percentage as the profit.

The UCC allows contracts that expressly provide that one of the parties may determine the price. In such a case, that party must act in good faith, another requirement under the UCC that applies to merchants and nonmerchants in the formation and performance of their contracts.[35]

---

[31] UCC §2-302. Teri J. Dobbins, "Losing Faith: Extracting the Implied Covenant of Good Faith from (Some) Contracts, 84 *Oregon Law Rev* 227 (2005). *U.S. Welding, Inc. v. Battelle Energy Alliance, LLC,* 728 F. Supp. 2d 1110 (D.Idaho 2010).

[32] Disparity in bargaining power is an issue but is not controlling. In *Intrastate Piping & Controls, Inc. v. Robert-James Sales, Inc.,* 39 UCC Rep. Serv. 2d 347 (Ill. Cir. Ct. 1999), a clause limiting remedies to replacement of defective pipe with no additional damages was upheld because while the seller was a large, national business and the buyer a small, local business, the contract merely incorporated industry practice in terms of remedies.

[33] An example would be voiding exorbitant interest charges but enforcing the underlying sale.

[34] UCC §2-305(1) provides, "the price is a reasonable price at the time for delivery."

[35] Good faith requires that the party act honestly and, in the case of a merchant, also requires that the party follow reasonable commercial standards of fair dealing that are recognized in the trade. UCC §§1-201(1)(a), 2-103(1)(b).

CPA

output contract – contract of a producer to sell its entire production or output to a buyer.

requirements contract – contract in which the buyer buys its needs (requirements) from the seller.

(B) OUTPUT AND REQUIREMENTS CONTRACTS. The **output contract** and the **requirements contract**[36] do not specify the quantity to be sold or purchased. Instead, the contract amount is what the seller produces or the buyer requires. **For Example,** a homeowner may contract to purchase propane fuel for her winter heating needs. The propane company agrees to sell her the amount of propane she needs, which will vary from year to year according to the winter weather, her time at home, and other factors. Although the open quantity in contracts such as these introduces an element of uncertainty, such sales contracts are valid but subject to two limitations: (1) The parties must act in good faith and (2) the quantity offered or demanded must not be unreasonably disproportionate to prior output or requirements or to a stated estimate. With these restrictions, the homeowner will obtain all of the propane she needs for heating but could not use her particularly beneficial price under her open-quantity contract to purchase additional propane to sell to others.

(C) INDEFINITE DURATION TERM. When the sales contract is a continuing contract, such as one calling for periodic delivery of coal, but no time is set for the life of the contract, the contract runs for a reasonable time. It may be terminated by notice from either party to the other party.

CPA

(D) CHANGES IN TERMS: MODIFICATION OF CONTRACT. An agreement to modify a contract for the sale of goods is binding even though the modification is not supported by consideration.[37] The modification is valid so long as the agreement is voluntary. **For Example,** suppose that Chester's Drug Store has agreed to purchase 300 bottles of vitamins from Pro-Life, Inc., at a price of $3.71 per bottle. Pro-Life has experienced substantial cost increases from its suppliers and asks Chester to pay $3.74 per bottle. Chester is not required to agree to such a price increase because it has a valid contract for the lower price. If Chester agrees to the price increase, however, the agreement for the higher price is valid despite the lack of additional consideration on the part of Pro-Life. Chester may agree to the higher price because Pro-Life's price is still much lower than its competitors and Chester has a longstanding relationship with Pro-Life and values its customer service. However, Pro-Life could not threaten to cut off Chester's supply in order to obtain the price increase because that would be a breach of contract and would also be duress that would invalidate Chester's consent to the higher price. (See Chapter 14 for a discussion of duress.)

parol evidence rule – rule that prohibits the introduction in evidence of oral or written statements made prior to or contemporaneously with the execution of a complete written contract, deed, or instrument, in the absence of fraud, accident, or mistake.

(E) CONTRADICTING TERMS: PAROL EVIDENCE RULE. The **parol evidence rule** (see Chapter 17 for a complete discussion) applies to the sale of goods, with the slight modification that a writing is not presumed to represent the entire contract of the parties unless the court specifically decides that it does.[38] If the court so decides, parol evidence is not admissible to add to or contradict the terms of the writing. **For Example,** suppose that Ralph Rhodes and Tana Preuss negotiate the sale of Ralph's 1965 Mustang to Tana. During their discussions, Ralph agrees to pay for an inspection and for new upholstery for the car. However, Tana and Ralph sign a simple sales contract that includes only a description of the Mustang and the price. Tana cannot enforce the two provisions because she failed to have them written into their final agreement. The parol evidence rule requires the parties to be certain that

---

[36] UCC §2-306; *XTO Energy Inc. v. Smith Production Inc.*, 282 S.W.3d 672 (Tex. App. 2009); *ABC Metals & Recycling Co., Inc. v. Highland Computer Forms, Inc.*, 771 N.W.2d 651 (Iowa App. 2009).
[37] UCC §2-209(1); *Horbach v. Kacz Marek*, 934 F. Supp. 981 (N.D. Ill. 1996), aff'd, 388 F.3d 969 (7th Cir. 2002).
[38] UCC §2-202.

everything they want is in their agreement before they sign. The courts cannot referee disputes over collateral agreements the parties fail to put in writing.

If the court decides that the writing was not intended to represent the entire contract, the writing may be supplemented by additional extrinsic evidence, including the proof of additional terms as long as these terms are not inconsistent with the written terms. Parol evidence may also be admitted to interpret contract terms or show what the parties meant by their words. The parol evidence rule also does not prohibit the proof of fraud, misrepresentation, and any other defenses in formation.

(F) INTERPRETING CONTRACT TERMS: COURSE OF DEALING AND USAGE OF TRADE. The patterns of doing business the parties develop through their prior contractual transactions, or **course of dealing**, become part of their contract.[39] These patterns may be used to find what was intended by the express provisions in their contract and to supply otherwise missing terms. **For Example,** if the parties had 10 previous agreements and payment was always made on the 30th day following delivery, that conduct could be used to interpret the meaning of a clause "payment due in 30 days" when the start of the 30 days is not specifically agreed to in the contract.

> **course of dealing** – pattern of performance between two parties to a contract.

In addition, the customs of the industry, or **usage of trade**, are adopted by courts in their interpretation of contract terms. **For Example,** suppose that a contract provides for the sale of mohair. There are two types of mohair: adult and kid. Because adult mohair is cheaper and easier to find, industry custom provides that unless the parties specifically place the term *kid* with the term *mohair* in the contract, the contract is one for the sale of adult mohair. Under Article 2, the court need not find that a contract is ambiguous or incomplete in order to examine the parties' pattern of previous conduct as well as industry custom.[40]

> **usage of trade** – language and customs of an industry.

5. Bulk Transfers

Bulk transfer law, Article 6 of the UCC, was created to deal with situations in which sellers of businesses fail to pay the creditors of the business and instead use the proceeds of the sale for their own use.

In 1989, the NCCUSL recommended that UCC Article 6 be repealed because it was obsolete and had little value in the modern business world. At the same time, the commissioners adopted a revised version of Article 6 (Alternative B) for adoption by those states that desired to retain the concept for bulk sales. Rather than relying on the bulk sales law, the trend is for suppliers to use UCC Article 9, Secured Transactions, for protection (see Chapter 34).

B. FORM OF SALES CONTRACT

A contract for the sale of goods may be oral or written. However, under the UCC, certain types of contracts must be evidenced by a record or they cannot be enforced in court.

---

[39] UCC §2-208. Under Revised Article 2, §2-208 is eliminated for those states that have adopted Revised Article 1 because Revised Article 1 contains the definition for course of performance.

[40] Revised §2-202 provides different rules for the use of extrinsic evidence but still includes "course of performance, course of dealing, or usage of trade" as sources for interpretation of contract terms.

CPA

6. Amount

Whenever the sales price of goods is $500 or more, the sales contract must be evidenced by a record to be enforceable. Under Revised Article 2, this amount has been increased to $5,000.[41] The section of the UCC that establishes this requirement is known as the **statute of frauds**. (For more details on the statute of frauds and its role in common law contracts, see Chapter 17.)

statute of frauds – statute that, to prevent fraud through the use of perjured testimony, requires that certain kinds of contracts be in writing to be binding or enforceable.

7. Nature of the Writing Required

The requirement for a record for a contract may be satisfied by a complete written contract signed by both parties. Under Article 2, so that the state laws will be consistent with federal laws on electronic signatures (see Chapter 11), the requirement of a writing has been changed to the requirement of a "record." Under Article 2, two merchants can reduce their agreement to a record in much simpler fashion because the detail required under common law is not required to satisfy the UCC standards.

(A) TERMS. To satisfy the UCC statute of frauds, the record must indicate that there has been a completed transaction covering certain goods. Specifically, the record must (1) indicate that a sale or contract to sell has been made and (2) state the quantity of goods involved.[42] Any other missing terms may be supplied by reference to Code sections (discussed earlier) or shown by parol evidence.

(B) SIGNATURE. The record must be signed or authenticated by the person who is being held to the contract or by the authorized agent of that person. Whatever form of authentication is being used must be put in place in the record with the intention of authenticating the record. The authentication may consist of initials or may be a printed, stamped, electronic, or typewritten signature placed with the intent to authenticate.[43] **For Example,** when you enter into a contract as part of an online transaction, you are generally asked to check a box that states that you understand you are entering into a contract. Once you check that box, a pop-up appears that explains that you are about to charge your credit card or account and that you have agreed to the purchase. These steps are used to authenticate your electronic version of a signature.

The UCC statute of frauds does provide an important exception to the signature requirement for merchants that enables merchants to expedite their transactions. This exception allows merchants to create a confirmation memorandum of their oral agreement as evidence of an agreement. A merchant's *confirmation memorandum* is a letter, memo, or electronic document signed or authenticated by one of the two merchant parties to an oral agreement.[44] This memorandum can be used by either party to enforce the contract. **For Example,** suppose that Ralph has orally agreed to purchase 1,000 pounds of T-bone steak from Jane for $5.79 per pound. Jane sends Ralph a signed memo that reads, "This is to confirm our telephone conversation earlier today. I will sell you 1,000 pounds of T-bone @ $5.79 per pound." Either Ralph or Jane can use the memo to enforce the contract.

---

[41] Under Revised Article 2, the new amount of $5,000 is found at UCC Rev Art 2, §2-201.
[42] *Kelly-Stehney & Assoc., Inc. v. McDonald's Indus. Products, Inc.*, 693 N.W.2d 394 (Mich. 2005).
[43] UCC §§1-201(39), 2-201; *CQ, Inc. v. TXU Min. Co., LP*, 565 F.3d 268 (5th Cir. 2009). Revised Article 2 permits electronic forms and signature and "record" includes e-mail, EDI transmissions, faxes, and printouts of screen pages reflecting transactions.
[44] *Siesta Sol, LLC v. Brooks Pharmacy, Inc.*, 617 F. Supp. 2d 38 (D. R.I. 2007); In re *Sunbelt Grain WKS, LLC*, 406 B.R. 918 (D. Kan. 2009).

A confirming memo, in various forms of communication, sent by one merchant to another results in a binding and enforceable contract that satisfies the statute of frauds. Such a confirmation binds the nonsigning or nonauthenticating merchant, just as if he had signed the letter or a contract. A merchant can object when he receives the confirmation memo, but he must do so immediately because the confirming memo takes effect in 10 days if there is no objection.[45] This confirmation procedure makes it necessary for merchants to watch their communications and all forms of correspondence and to act within 10 days of receiving a confirmation.

CASE SUMMARY

It's Elementary: A Crayon-Scrawled Contract Is Good Enough for the Statute of Frauds

FACTS: Michelle Rosenfeld, an art dealer, went to artist Jean-Michel Basquiat's apartment on October 25, 1982. While she was there, Basquiat agreed to sell her three paintings for $4,000 each, and she picked out three. Basquiat asked for a cash deposit of 10 percent; Rosenfeld left the loft but returned later with $1,000 in cash, which she paid to Basquiat. When she asked for a receipt, he insisted on drawing up a contract and got down on the floor and wrote it out in crayon on a large piece of paper, remarking that someday this contract would be worth money. The handwritten document listed the three paintings, bore Rosenfeld's signature and Basquiat's signature, and stated: "$12,000—$1,000 DEPOSIT ¼ Oct 25 82." Rosenfeld later returned to Basquiat's loft to discuss delivery, but Basquiat convinced her to wait for at least two years so that he could show the paintings at exhibitions. After Basquiat's death, the estate argued that there was no contract because the statute of frauds made the agreement unenforceable. The estate contended that a written contract for the sale of goods must include the date of delivery. From a judgment in favor of the estate, Rosenfeld appealed.

DECISION: The contract for the sale of three paintings is governed by the UCC, and its statute of frauds applies to "transactions in goods for $500 which must be in writing or they are unenforceable. All that is required for a writing is that it provide some basis for believing that there is a real transaction." The writing supplied in this case indicated the price, the date, the specific paintings involved, and that Rosenfeld paid a deposit. It also bore the signatures of the buyer and seller and satisfied the requirements of UCC §2-201. Because the writing, scrawled in crayon by Jean-Michel Basquiat on a large piece of paper, easily satisfied the requirements of §2-201 of the UCC, the alleged contract is valid. [*Rosenfeld v. Basquiat*, **78 F.3d 84 (2nd Cir. 1996)**]

(c) PURPOSE OF EXECUTION. A writing or record can satisfy the statute of frauds even though it was not made for that purpose. For example, if a buyer writes to the seller to complain that the goods have not been delivered, there is proof of the contract because the buyer's complaint indicates that there was some kind of understanding or an acknowledgment that there was a sale of those goods.

(d) PARTICULAR WRITINGS. Formal contracts, bills of sale, letters, and telegrams are common forms of writings that satisfy the record requirement.[46] E-mails, faxes, EDI communications, and verifications through screen printouts will generally satisfy the

---

[45] A confirmation memo is not effective when there is no underlying agreement or the parties did not agree on the terms. *Cargill Inc. v. Jorgenson Farms*, 719 N.W.2d 226 (Minn. App. 2009).

[46] Contract terms can be pieced together from invoices sent over the period of the agreement and that the buyer paid. *Fleming Companies, Inc. v. Krist Oil Co.*, 324 F. Supp. 2d 933 (W.D. Wi. 2001).

requirement as to record and authentication so long as they meet minimum formation standards and comply with the requirement of the UCC to specify any quantity. Two or more records grouped together may constitute a record that will be sufficient to satisfy the UCC statute of frauds.[47]

CASE SUMMARY

A Real Basket Case

FACTS: The Greenbrier Basket Company (GBC), a goods distributor, was selling woven baskets to The Pampered Chef (TPC). The ordering process would begin with TPC e-mailing GBC an offer to fill an order. GBC would then go to TPC's Web site and fill out the purchase order using TPC's purchase order management system and would click on the Accept P.O. button at the end of the terms and conditions field.

TPC sent Mark Beal (a GBC employee) an e-mail with an attachment showing him how to use TPC's purchase order management system, including the following:

> *Clicking on the Accept P.O. button will cause the terms and conditions of the purchase order to pop-up. The user should review these terms and conditions and click the Accept P.O. button at the bottom of the pop-up screen.... If the purchase order is not acceptable in it's [sic] current form, the user may click on the Reject and Request Changes button. This causes a pop-up window to appear where the user may enter a free-form text describing the reason for rejecting the purchase order and request changes that would make the purchase order acceptable.*

Clause 17 of the Terms and Conditions in TPC's purchase management order system provided that all disputes on contracts would be resolved in federal district court in Illinois.

When disputes over orders and payments arose, GBC filed suit against TPC in Kansas for breach of contract. TPC moved to dismiss the suit for improper venue.

DECISION: TPC's e-mails containing purchase order information constituted an offer to buy baskets. The e-mails consisted of information about the quantity of baskets to be bought, price, shipment information, and delivery dates. They also provided that to accept the P.O., GBC should go via Internet to TPC's Web site.

GBC was under a duty to read and understand the terms and conditions prior to clicking the Accept P.O. button because this was the formal acceptance required by TPC's offer to purchase baskets. Failure to read or understand the terms and conditions is not a valid reason to set those provisions aside.

A meeting of the minds requirement is proved when the minds of the parties met on the same matter and agreed upon the terms of the contract. GBC agreed upon these terms and conditions published on TPC's Web site by clicking the Accept P.O. button.

The case was dismissed in Kansas and transferred to Illinois. [**Home Basket Co., LLC v. Pampered Chef, Ltd., 55 UCC Rep. Serv. 2d 792 (D. Kan. 2005)**]

8. Effect of Noncompliance

A sales agreement that does not satisfy the statute of frauds cannot be enforced. However, the oral contract itself is not unlawful and may be voluntarily performed by the parties.

---

[47] *ReMapp Intern. Corp. v. Comfort Keyboard Co., Inc.*, 560 F.3d 628 (7th Cir. 2009). Letters grouped together satisfy UCC §2-201. *Pepsi-Cola Co. v. Steak 'N Shake, Inc.*, 981 F. Supp. 1149 (S.D. Ind. 1997). Letters and faxes also satisfy the writing requirement. *Den Norske Stats Oljeselskap*, 992 F. Supp. 913 (S.D. Tex. 1998), aff'd, 161 F.3d 8 (5th Cir. 1998).

9. Exceptions to Requirement of a Writing

The absence of a writing does not always mean that a sales contract is unenforceable. Article 2 provides some exceptions for the enforceability of certain oral contracts.

CPA   **(A) SPECIALLY MANUFACTURED GOODS.** No record is required when the goods are specially made for the buyer and are of such an unusual nature that they are not suitable for sale in the ordinary course of the seller's business. **For Example,** a manufacturer who builds a stair lift for a two-story home cannot resell the $8,000 device to someone else because it is specially built for the stairs in the buyer's home. The manufacturer could enforce the oral contract against the buyer despite the price being in excess of $500 ($5,000 under Revised Article 2).

For this nonresellable goods exception to apply, the seller must have made a substantial beginning in manufacturing the goods or, if a distributor is the seller, in procuring them before the buyer indicates she will not honor the oral contract.[48]

The stair lift manufacturer, for example, must have progressed to a point beyond simply ordering materials for construction of the lift because those materials could be used for any lift.

CPA   **(B) RECEIPT AND ACCEPTANCE.** An oral sales contract may be enforced if it can be shown that the goods were delivered by the seller and were both received and accepted by the buyer even if the amount involved is over $500 ($5,000 Revised) and there is no record. The receipt and acceptance of the goods by the buyer makes the contract enforceable despite the statute of frauds issue. The buyer must actually receive and accept the goods. If only part of the goods have been received and accepted, the contract may be enforced only insofar as it relates to those goods received and accepted.[49] **For Example,** suppose that Wayne ordered 700 baseball jackets at a price of $72 each from Pamela. The order was taken over the telephone, and Wayne emphasized urgency. Pamela shipped the 320 jackets she had on hand and assured Wayne the remainder would be finished during the next two weeks. Wayne received the 320 jackets and sold them to a golf tournament sponsor. Wayne refused to pay Pamela because the contract was oral. Wayne must pay for the 320 jackets, but Pamela will not be able to recover for the remaining 380 jackets she manufactured.

CPA   **(C) PAYMENT.** An oral contract may be enforced if the buyer has made full payment. In the case of partial payment for divisible units of goods, a contract may be enforced only with respect to the goods for which payment has been made and accepted. In the Pamela and Wayne example, if the circumstances were changed so that Pamela agreed to ship only if Wayne sent payment, then Pamela, upon accepting the payment, would be required to perform the contract for the amount of payment received. If partial payment is made for indivisible goods, such as an automobile, a partial payment avoids the statute of frauds and is sufficient proof to permit enforcement of the entire oral contract.

(D) ADMISSION. An oral contract may be enforced against a party if that party admits in pleadings, testimony, or otherwise in court that a contract for sale was made. The contract, however, is not enforceable beyond the quantity of goods admitted.[50]

---

[48] *Golden State Porcelain Inc. v. Swid Powell Design Inc.*, 37 UCC Rep. Serv. 2d (N.Y. 1999). Where manufacture has not begun, this exception to the statute of frauds does not apply. *EMSG Sys. Div., Inc. v. Miltope Corp.*, 37 UCC Rep. Serv. 2d 39 (E.D.N.C. 1998).

[49] *Allied Grape Growers v. Bronco Wine Co.*, 249 Cal.Rptr. 872 (Ct. App. 1988).

[50] *Delta Stat, Inc. v. Michael's Carpet World*, 666 S.E.2d 331 (Va. 2008).

Thinking Things Through

Chipping Away at the Contract Terms for Wood Chips

Beginning in the mid-1980s GP and WHI entered into a series of one-year contracts under which WHI supplied wood chips to GP's particle board plant in Gaylord, Michigan. The contract was automatically renewed unless either party gave written notice 60 days before the end of the term. The contracts also permitted either party to terminate a contract at any time with 90 days' notice.

WHI and GP signed a new contract on May 20, 2005 (2005 contract). The contract had a three-year term and a provision for subsequent renewal. It included an early termination clause that permitted either party to terminate the contract after 90 days notice. The contract also contained a clause stating that GP intended to purchase 125,000 tons of wood chips per year but was not required to purchase any minimum quantity.

During the negotiations for the 2005 contract, GP represented that the early termination clause and nonbinding volume clauses were merely generic requirements from GP's legal department and would have no effect on GP's performance. WHI also alleges that both before and after the 2005 contract was signed, GP represented (1) that the

early termination clause was subordinate to the clause stating GP's intent to purchase 125,000 tons of wood chips per year, (2) that GP would not exercise the early termination provision during the contract's initial three-year term, and (3) that the contract would be automatically renewed unless WHI defaulted.

In March 2006, GP informed WHI that it was closing the Gaylord plant. It also terminated the 2005 contract and suspended further deliveries of wood chips to the plant. The parties dispute the date on which the decision to close the Gaylord plant was made. WHI alleges that GP knew it would close the plant by October 2004, but repeatedly represented to WHI that there were no plans to close the plant.*

WH1 filed suit for breach of contract. GP has responded that the negotiation terms are irrelevant because they were not part of the contract terms and they could not be used as evidence for a breach of contract suit. Who is correct? Is there a breach? Or is there a written contract that does not contain protection for WH1 in the event of a plant closure?

*Woodland Harvesting, Inc. v. Georgia Pacific Corporation, 693 F. Supp. 2f 732 (E.D. Mich. 2010)

10. Noncode Requirements

In addition to the UCC requirements for contracts that must be evidenced by a record, other statutes may impose requirements. **For Example,** state consumer protection legislation commonly requires that there be a detailed contract and that a copy of it be given to the consumer.

11. Bill of Sale

bill of sale–writing signed by the seller reciting that the personal property therein described has been sold to the buyer.

Regardless of the requirement of the statute of frauds, the parties may wish to execute a writing as evidence or proof of the sale. Through custom, this writing has become known as a **bill of sale**, but it is neither a bill nor a contract. It is merely a receipt or writing signed by the seller reciting the transfer to the buyer of the title to the described property. A bill of sale can be used as proof of an otherwise oral agreement.

C. Uniform Law for International Sales

Contracts for the International Sale of Goods (CISG)–uniform international contract code contracts for international sale of goods.

The United Nations Convention on **Contracts for the International Sale of Goods (CISG)** applies to contracts between parties in the United States and parties in the other nations that have ratified the convention.[51] The provisions of this convention

[51] 52 Fed. Reg. 6262 (1987). While the list of adopting countries is always increasing, those countries involved in NAFTA, GATT, and the European Union (EU) (see Chapter 7) have adopted the CISG. For complete text, commentary, and case law on CISG, go to **www.cisg.law.pace.edu**.

or international agreement have been strongly influenced by Article 2 of the UCC. The international rules of the convention automatically apply to contracts for the sale of goods if the buyer and seller have places of business in different countries that have ratified the convention. The parties may, however, choose to exclude the convention provisions in their sales contract.

12. Scope of the CISG

The CISG does not govern all contracts between parties in the countries that have ratified it. The CISG does not apply to goods bought for personal, family, or household use.[52] The CISG also does not apply to contracts in which the predominant part of the obligations of the party who furnishes the goods consists of the supply of labor or other services. The CISG has five chapters and 101 articles, and the articles have no titles to them. There is a limited body of case law interpreting the CISG because so many of the decisions under the CISG come through arbitration and other forms of dispute resolution, typical of international commercial arrangements.

D. LEASES OF GOODS

Leases of goods represent a significant part of both contract law and the economy. There are more than $628 billion worth of lease transactions in the United States each year, an amount equal to roughly one-third of all capital investment each year in the United States.[53] One-fourth of all vehicles in the United States are leased. Article 2A of the UCC codifies the law of leases for tangible movable goods. Article 2A applies to any transaction, regardless of form, that creates a lease of personal property or fixtures. Many of the provisions of Article 2 were carried over but changed to reflect differences in style, leasing terminology, or leasing practices.[54] As a practical matter, leases will be of durable goods, such as equipment and vehicles of any kind, computers, boats, airplanes, and household goods and appliances. A **lease** is "a transfer of the right to possession and use of goods for a term in return for consideration."[55]

lease – agreement between the owner of property and a tenant by which the former agrees to give possession of the property to the latter for payment of rent. (Parties—landlord or lessor, tenant or lessee)

13. Types of Leases

Article 2A regulates consumer leases, commercial leases, finance leases, nonfinance leases, and subleases. These categories may overlap in some cases, such as when there is a commercial finance lease.

consumer lease – lease of goods by a natural person for personal, family, or household use.

(A) CONSUMER LEASE. A **consumer lease** is made by a merchant lessor regularly engaged in the business of leasing or selling the kinds of goods involved. A consumer lease is made to a natural person (not a corporation) who takes possession of the goods primarily for personal, family, or household use. Each state places a cap on the amount considered a consumer lease. Section 2A-103(f) simply provides that the

---

[52] The UNIDROIT Principles are often used as guidelines for resolving issues in international consumer contracts. M. J. Bonell, "The CISG, European Contract Law and the Development of a World Contract Law," 56 *American Journal of Comparative Law*, 1–28 (2008).

[53] *Equipment Leasing & Finance Foundation Economic Outlook* (2012).

[54] Forty-nine states (Louisiana has not adopted Article 2A), the District of Columbia, and the Virgin Islands have adopted all or some portions of Article 2A. Not all states have adopted the 1997 version of Article 2A, and some have adopted only selected portions of the 1997 version.

[55] UCC §2A-103(1)(j). The definition of what constitutes a lease is the subject of continuing examination by the UCC Article 2A drafters and the American Law Institute.

state should place its own amount in this section with the admonition to place the cap at a level that ensures that vehicle leases will be covered under the law. During the period from 2002 to 2007, there were a number of suits brought by individuals injured in auto accidents against the leasing companies of the drivers who were driving their leased autos at the time they caused an accident. Many states were holding the leasing companies liable for those accidents because they were title holders of the cars. As a result, leasing companies stopped doing business in certain states because of the liability exposure.

In response, the federal government passed legislation that preempted all state laws and limited the liability of vehicle leasing companies to a basic level of liability that was limited to mandatory insurance coverage standards.[56]

(B) COMMERCIAL LEASE. When a lease does not satisfy the definition of a consumer lease, it may be called a **nonconsumer** or a **commercial lease. For Example,** a contractor's one-year rental of a truck to haul materials is a commercial lease.

(C) FINANCE LEASE. A **finance lease** is a three-party transaction involving a lessor, a lessee, and a supplier. Instead of going directly to a supplier for goods, the customer goes to a financier and tells the financier where to obtain the goods and what to obtain. The financier then acquires the goods and either leases or subleases the goods to its customer. The financier-lessor is in effect a paper channel, or conduit, between the supplier and the customer-lessee. The customer-lessee must approve the terms of the transaction between the supplier and the financier-lessor.[57]

14. Form of Lease Contract

The lease must be evidenced by a record if the total of the payments under the lease will be $1,000 or more. The record must be authenticated by the party against whom enforcement is sought. The record must describe the leased goods, state the term of the lease, and indicate that a lease contract has been formed.[58]

15. Warranties

Under Article 2A, the lessor, except in the case of finance leases, makes all usual warranties that are made by a seller in a sale of goods. In a finance lease, however, the real parties in interest are the supplier, who supplies the lessor with the goods, and the lessee, who leases the goods. The lessee looks to the supplier of the goods for warranties. Any warranties, express or implied, made by the supplier to the lessor are passed on to the lessee, who has a direct cause of action on them against the supplier regardless of the lack of privity.[59] **For Example,** if a consumer leased an auto and the auto had a defective steering mechanism that resulted in injury to the consumer, the consumer would have a cause of action against the auto manufacturer.

nonconsumer lease–lease that does not satisfy the definition of a consumer lease; also known as a *commercial lease.*

commercial lease–any nonconsumer lease.

finance lease–three-party lease agreement in which there is a lessor, a lessee, and a financier.

[56] See, e.g., *Oliveira v. Lombardi*, 794 A.2d 453 (R.I. 2002). The federal law did not affect all of the suits that were pending at the time of the passage of the federal law. Those suits were permitted to proceed as long as they had been filed by the end of 2005. Those suits have concluded. Future recovery will be limited to mandatory policy requirements.
[57] UCC §2A-103(1)(g). One of the evolving issues in lease financing is the relationship of the parties, the use of liens, and the role of Article 9 security interests (see Chapter 34). The NCCUSL has created Uniform Certificate of Title Act (UCOTA) that makes the interrelationships of lien laws, Article 2, and Article 9 clear. UCOTA was available for adoption by the states in 2006. As of 2012, only three states had adopted the law.
[58] UCC §2-201(b).
[59] UCC §2A-209.

E-Commerce & Cyberlaw

The Deal with Dell

Dell Computer customers purchased computers through the Dell Web site. There were "Terms and Conditions" on the Web site that included terms and conditions such as the requirement that contract disputes be submitted to arbitration in Illinois and the sales tax provisions related to the purchase of computers and service contracts.

Dell maintains that customers have three separate opportunities to review the terms and conditions agreement: (1) by selecting a hyperlink on the Dell Web site, (2) by reading the terms that were included in the acknowledgment/invoice that was sent to customers after they placed their orders, or (3) by reviewing the copy of the terms Dell included in the packaging of its computer products. The court found that the terms and conditions had to be understood PRIOR to the purchase and that the "Terms and Conditions" tab was not conspicuous on the Dell Web site. From this case and other materials in the chapter, you learn that there are best practices for Internet contracting: (1) Require customers to click on terms and conditions PRIOR to buying; (2) Require customers to physically scroll down through the terms before being allowed to purchase; (3) Notify customers along the way as they are loading their electronic carts that there are terms and conditions and place click points for them to study those terms and conditions; and (4) Posting terms and conditions on your Web site is not enough for those terms and conditions to be part of the contract.

16. Default

The lease agreement and provisions of Article 2A determine whether the lessor or lessee is in default. If either the lessor or the lessee is in default under the lease contract, the party seeking enforcement may obtain a judgment or otherwise enforce the lease contract by any available judicial or nonjudicial procedure. Neither the lessor nor the lessee is entitled to notice of default or notice of enforcement from the other party. Both the lessor and the lessee have rights and remedies similar to those given to a seller in a sales contract.[60] If the lessee defaults, the lessor is entitled to recover any rent due, future rent, and incidental damages.[61] (See Chapter 27 for more information on remedies.)

LawFlix

Beethoven (1992)(G)

Charles Grodin plays a fussy father who has founded and runs an air freshener company. Part of the plot centers on an investment in the company by some venture capitalists who are interested in using Grodin's company as a supplier. There are contract negotiations as well as issues of warranty and liability.

---

[60] UCC §§2A-501, 2A-503; *Mitchell v. Ford Motor Credit Co.*, 702 F. Supp. 2d 1356 (M.D. Fla. 2010).
[61] UCC §2A-529.

MAKE THE CONNECTION

SUMMARY

Contracts for services and real estate are governed by the common law. Contracts for the sale of goods are governed by Article 2 of the UCC. *Goods* are defined as anything movable at the time they are identified as the subject of the transaction. Goods physically existing and owned by the seller at the time of the transaction are *existing goods*.

A *sale of goods* is the transfer of title to tangible personal property for a price. A *bailment* is a transfer of possession but not title and is therefore not a sale. A *gift* is not a sale because no price is paid for the gift. A contract for services is an ordinary contract and is not governed by the UCC. If a contract calls for both the rendering of services and the supplying of goods, the contract is classified according to its dominant element.

The common law contract rules for intent to contract apply to the formation of contracts under the UCC. However, several formation rules under the UCC differ from common law contract rules. A merchant's firm offer is irrevocable without the payment of consideration. The UCC rules on additional terms in an acceptance permit the formation of a contract despite the changes. These proposals for new terms are not considered counteroffers under the UCC. The terms that are included are determined by detailed rules. If the transaction is between nonmerchants, a contract is formed without the additional terms, which the original offeror is free to accept or reject. If the transaction is between merchants, the additional terms become part of the contract if those terms do not materially alter the offer and no objection is made to them. There is no distinction between merchant and nonmerchant for additional terms under Revised Article 2 and the terms issues is left to the courts.

The same defenses available to formation under common law are incorporated in Article 2. In addition, the UCC recognizes unconscionability as a defense to formation.

The UCC does not require the parties to agree on every aspect of contract performance for the contract to be valid. Provisions in Article 2 will govern the parties' relationship in the event their agreement does not cover all terms. The price term may be expressly fixed by the parties. The parties may make no provision as to price, or they may indicate how the price should be determined later. In output or requirements contracts, the quantity that is to be sold or purchased is not specified, but such contracts are nevertheless valid. A sales contract can be modified even though the modification is not supported by consideration. The parol evidence rule applies to a sale of goods in much the same manner as to ordinary contracts. However, the UCC permits the introduction of evidence of course of dealing and usage of trade for clarification of contract terms and performance.

The UCC's statute of frauds provides that a sales contract for $500 ($5,000 under Revised Article 2) or more must be evidenced by a record. The UCC's merchant's confirmation memorandum allows two merchants to be bound to an otherwise oral agreement by a memo or letter signed by only one party that stands without objection for 10 days. Several exceptions to the UCC statute of frauds exist: when the goods are specially made or procured for the buyer and are nonresellable in the seller's ordinary market; when the buyer has received and accepted the goods; when the buyer has made either full or partial payment; and when the party against whom enforcement is sought admits in court pleadings or testimony that a contract for sale was made.

Uniform rules for international sales are applicable to contracts for sales between parties in countries that have ratified the CISG. Under the CISG, a contract for the sale of goods need not be in any particular form and can be proven by any means.

Article 2A of the UCC regulates consumer leases, commercial leases, finance leases, nonfinance leases, and subleases of tangible movable goods. A lease subject to Article 2A must be in writing if the lease payments will total $1,000 or more.

LEARNING OUTCOMES

After studying this chapter, you should be able to clearly explain:

A. Nature and Legality

L0.1 Define a sale of goods and explain when UCC Article 2 applies to contracts
> See *Paramount Contracting Co. v. DPS Industries, Inc.*, on p. 469.

L0.2 Distinguish between an actual sale of goods and other types of transactions in goods
> See footnotes 3 and 4 for examples.

L0.3 Describe how contracts are formed under Article 2, and list the differences in formation standards between the UCC and common law
> See the *For Example,* discussion of Joe and Susan's X-box transaction on p. 472.
> See the *Greenbrier* basket case on p. 481.
> See the *C9 v. SVC* case on pp. 474–475.

B. Form of Sales Contract

L0.4 Explain when a contract for the sale of goods must be in writing
> See the *Basquiat* case on p. 480.

L0.5 List and explain the exceptions to the requirement that certain contracts be in writing
> See the *For Example,* discussion of Wayne and the baseball jackets on p. 482.

C. Uniform Law for International Sales

L0.6 Discuss the purpose of the United Nations Convention on Contracts for the International Sale of Goods
> See the discussion of the CISG on pp. 483–484.

KEY TERMS

acceptance
Article 2
bailee
bailment
battle of the forms
bill of sale
commercial lease
consumer lease
Contracts for the International
  Sale of Goods (CISG)

cost plus
course of dealing
existing goods
finance lease
firm offer
future goods
gift
goods
lease
mailbox rule

merchants
mirror image rule
nonconsumer lease
offer
output contract
parol evidence rule
requirements contract
statute of frauds
unconscionable
usage of trade

QUESTIONS AND CASE PROBLEMS

1. Triple H Construction Co. contracted with Hunter's Run Stables, Inc., to erect a horse barn and riding arena on Hunter's Run's property in Big Flats, New York. Hunter's Run got a guarantee in its contract with Triple H that "such design with the span so shown will support its weight and will withstand natural forces including but not limited to snow load and wind." Hunter's Run also got the following guarantee from Rigidply, the manufacturer of the rafters: "Rigidply ... hereby guarantees that the design to be used for the construction of a horse barn by Triple H ... will support the weight of such barn and to snow load and wind as per drawings." The barn was completed in 1983 and collapsed under the weight of snow in 1994. Hunter's Run has sued Triple H for UCC Article 2 remedies. Does Article 2 apply? [*Hunter's Run Stables, Inc. v. Triple H, Inc.*, 938 F. Supp. 166 (W.D.N.Y.)]

2. R-P Packaging manufactured cellophane wrapping material that was used by Kern's Bakery in packaging its product. Kern's decided to change its system for packaging cookies from a tied bread bag to a tray covered with printed cellophane wrapping. R-P took measurements to determine the appropriate size for the cellophane

wrapping and designed the artwork to be printed on the wrapping. After agreeing that the artwork was satisfactory, Kern placed a verbal order for the cellophane at a total cost of $13,000. When the printed wrapping material was received, Kern complained that it was too short for the trays and the art work was not centered. The material, however, conformed exactly to the order placed by Kern. Kern returned the material to R-P by overnight express. R-P sued Kern. Kern claimed that because there was no written contract, the suit was barred by the statute of frauds. What result? [*Flowers Baking Co. v. R-P Packaging, Inc.*, 329 S.E.2d 462 (Va.)]

3. Smythe wrote to Lasco Dealers inquiring about the price of a certain freezer. Lasco wrote her a letter, signed by its credit manager, stating that Smythe could purchase the freezer in question during the next 30 days for $400. Smythe wrote back the next day ordering a freezer at that price. Lasco received Smythe's letter the following day, but Lasco wrote a response letter stating that it had changed the price to $450. Smythe claims that Lasco could not change its price. Is she correct?

4. Mrs. Downing was fitted for dentures by a dentist, Dr. Cook. After she received her dentures, Mrs. Downing began experiencing mouth pain that she attributed to Dr. Cook's manufacture of dentures that did not fit her properly. Mrs. Downing filed suit against Dr. Cook for breach of warranty under Article 2 of the UCC. Dr. Cook defended on the grounds that his denture work was a service and therefore not covered under Article 2 warranties. The trial court found for Mrs. Downing, and Dr. Cook appealed. Is Dr. Cook correct? Are the dentures a contract for services or goods? [*Cook v. Downing*, 891 P.2d 611 (Oka. App.)] Would silicone breast implants be covered by the UCC Article 2 warranties? Does implantation of silicone gel implants constitute a sale of goods by the surgeon? [*In re Breast Implant Product Liability Litigation*, 503 S.E.2d 445 (S.C.)]

5. Meyers was under contract with Henderson to install overhead doors in a factory that Henderson was building. Meyers obtained the disassembled doors from the manufacturer. His contract with Henderson required Meyers to furnish all labor, materials, tools, and equipment to satisfactorily complete the installation of all overhead doors. Henderson felt the doors were not installed properly and paid less than one-half of the contract price after subtracting his costs for correcting the installation. Because of a business sale and other complications, Meyers did not sue Henderson for the difference in payment until five years later. Henderson raised the defense that because the contract was for the sale of goods, it was barred by the Code's four-year statute of limitations. Meyers claimed that it was a contract for services and that suit could be brought within six years. Who is correct? Why? [*Meyers v. Henderson Construction Co.*, 370 A.2d 547 (N.J. Super.)]

6. Valley Trout Farms ordered fish food from Rangen. Both parties were merchants. The invoice that was sent with the order stated that a specified charge—a percentage common in the industry—would be added to any unpaid bills. Valley Trout Farms did not pay for the food and did not make any objection to the late charge stated in the invoice. When sued by Rangen, Valley Trout Farms claimed that it had never agreed to the late charge and therefore was not required to pay it. Is Valley Trout Farms correct? [*Rangen, Inc. v. Valley Trout Farms, Inc.*, 658 P.2d 955 (Idaho)]

7. LTV Aerospace Corp. manufactured all-terrain vehicles for use in Southeast Asia. LTV made an oral contract with Bateman under which Bateman would supply the packing cases needed for the vehicles' overseas shipment. Bateman made substantial beginnings in the production of packing cases following LTV's specifications. LTV thereafter stopped production of its vehicles and refused to take delivery of any cases. When Bateman sued for breach of contract, LTV argued that the contract could not be enforced because there was no writing that satisfied the statute of frauds. Was this a valid defense? [*LTV Aerospace Corp. v. Bateman*, 492 S.W.2d 703 (Tex. App.)]

8. Syrovy and Alpine Resources, Inc., entered into a "Timber Purchase Agreement." Syrovy agreed to

sell and Alpine agreed to buy all of the timber produced during a two-year period. The timber to be sold, purchased, and delivered was to be produced by Alpine from timber on Syrovy's land. Alpine continued harvesting for one year and then stopped after making an initial payment. Syrovy sued Alpine. Alpine alleged there was no contract because the writing to satisfy the statute of frauds must contain a quantity term. Decide. [*Syrovy v. Alpine Resources, Inc.*, 841 P.2d 1279 (Wash. App.)]

9. A subcontractor agreed to remove and dispose of cabinets from a public housing project. When a dispute arose, one party argued that the UCC applied, and the other argued that it was the common law contract. Explain who is correct and why. [*J.O. Hooker's Sons v. Roberts Cabinet*, 683 So. 2d 396]

10. Fastener Corp. sent a letter to Renzo Box Co. that was signed by Ronald Lee, Fastener's sales manager, and read as follows: "We hereby offer you 200 type #14 Fastener bolts at $5 per bolt. This offer will be irrevocable for ten days." On the fifth day, Fastener informed Renzo it was revoking the offer, alleging that there was no consideration for the offer. Could Fastener revoke? Explain.

11. Richard, a retailer of video equipment, telephoned Craft Appliances and ordered a $1,000 videotape recorder for his business. Craft accepted Richard's order and sent him a copy of the purchase memorandum that stated the price, quantity, and model ordered and that was stamped "order accepted by Craft." Richard, however, did not sign or return the purchase memorandum and refused to accept delivery of the recorder when Craft delivered it to him three weeks later. Craft sued Richard, who raised the statute of frauds as a defense. Will Richard prevail? Why or why not?

12. REMC furnished electricity to Helvey's home. The voltage furnished was in excess of 135 volts and caused extensive damage to his 110-volt household appliances. Helvey sued REMC for breach of warranty. Helvey argued that providing electrical energy is not a transaction in goods but a furnishing of services, so that he had six years to sue

REMC rather than the UCC's four-year statute of limitations, which had expired. Was it a sale of goods or a sale of services? Identify the ethical principles involved in this case. [*Helvey v. Wabash County REMC*, 278 N.E.2d 608 (Ind. App.)]

13. U.S. Surgical manufactures medical surgical instruments and markets the instruments to hospitals. The packaging for U.S. Surgical's disposable medical instruments is labeled "for single use only." As an example, one label contains the following language: "Unless opened or damaged, contents of package are sterile. DO NOT RESTERILIZE. For multiple use during a SINGLE surgical procedure. DISCARD AFTER USE."

    Orris provides a service to the hospitals that purchase U.S. Surgical's disposable instruments. After the hospitals use or open the instruments, Orris cleans, resterilizes, and/or resharpens the instruments for future use and returns them to the hospitals from which they came.

    U.S. Surgical filed suit asserting that reprocessing, repackaging, and reuse of its disposable instruments constituted a violation of its patent and trademark rights. Orris says that U.S. Surgical did not prohibit hospitals from reusing the instruments and it was not doing anything that violated the contracts U.S. Surgical had with the hospitals. U.S. Surgical says the language on the packaging was an additional terms that the hospitals accepted by opening the packages and using the instruments. Who is correct? [*U.S. Surgical Corp. v. Orris, Inc.*, 5 F. Supp. 2d 1201 (D. Kan.); aff'd, 185 F.3d 885 (10th Cir.) and 230 F.3d 1382 (Fed. Cir.)]

14. Flora Hall went to Rent-A-Center in Milwaukee and signed an agreement to make monthly payments of $77.96 for 19 months in exchange for Rent-A-Center's allowing her to have a Rent-A-Center washer and dryer in her home. In addition, the agreement required Hall to pay tax and a liability waiver fee on the washer and dryer. The total amount she would pay under the agreement was $1,643.15. The agreement provided that Hall would return the washer and dryer at the end of the 19 months, or she could, at that time, pay $161.91 and own the washer

and dryer as her own. Is this a sales contract? Is this a consumer lease? At the time Hall leased her washer and dryer, she could have purchased a set for about $600. What do you think about the cost of her agreement with Rent-A-Center? Is it unconscionable? Refer to Chapter 33, and determine whether any other consumer laws apply. Must this contract be in writing? [*Rent-A-Center, Inc. v. Hall*, 510 N.W.2d 789 (Wis.)]

15. Click2Boost, Inc. (C2B) entered into an Internet marketing agreement with the New York Times (NYT) on May 10, 2002, for C2B to solicit subscribers for home delivery of the New York Times newspaper through "pop up ads" at Internet Web sites with which C2B maintained "[m]arketing [a]lliances." The agreement required NYT to pay C2B a fee or commission for each home delivery subscription C2B submitted to NYT. NYT paid C2B more than $1.5 million in subscription submission fees from May 2002 to September 2003, but most of the subscriptions were ended, so NYT terminated the C2B agreement on September 16, 2003.

In October 2003, Wall Street Network (WSN) took over C2B and filed suit for breach of contract against NYT. WSN said that NYT had breached the agreement by terminating it before September 30, 2003, because the contract was one for goods and C2B had furnished those goods. WSN wanted damages under the UCC for breach of a contract because the pop-up ads were sold independently as goods. NYT argued that the contract was one for services for furnishing subscribers, something C2B did not do successfully. WSN countered that the customers generated from the pop-up ads were what was being sold, just like selling a list of names, something that would be considered a good. The trial court granted the NYT summary judgment and WSN appealed. Should WSN win the case? Why or why not? [*Wall Street Network, Ltd. v. New York Times Company*, 164 Cal. App. 4th 1171, 80 Cal. Rptr. 3d 6, 66 UCC Rep. Serv. 2d 261]

CPA QUESTIONS

1. Webstar Corp. orally agreed to sell Northco, Inc., a computer for $20,000. Northco sent a signed purchase order to Webstar confirming the agreement. Webstar received the purchase order and did not respond. Webstar refused to deliver the computer to Northco, claiming that the purchase order did not satisfy the UCC statute of frauds because it was not signed by Webstar. Northco sells computers to the general public, and Webstar is a computer wholesaler. Under the UCC Sales Article, Webstar's position is:

   a. Incorrect, because it failed to object to Northco's purchase order.

   b. Incorrect, because only the buyer in a sale-of-goods transaction must sign the contract.

   c. Correct, because it was the party against whom enforcement of the contract is being sought.

   d. Correct, because the purchase price of the computer exceeded $500.

2. On May 2, Lace Corp., an appliance wholesaler, offered to sell appliances worth $3,000 to Parco, Inc., a household appliances retailer. The offer was signed by Lace's president and provided that it would not be withdrawn before June 1. It also included the shipping terms: "F.O.B.—Parco's warehouse." On May 29, Parco mailed an acceptance of Lace's offer. Lace received the acceptance June 2. Which of the following is correct if Lace sent Parco a telegram revoking its offer and Parco received the telegram on May 25?

   a. A contract was formed on May 2.

   b. Lace's revocation effectively terminated its offer on May 25.

   c. Lace's revocation was ineffective because the offer could not be revoked before June 1.

   d. No contract was formed because Lace received Parco's acceptance after June 1.

3. Bond and Spear orally agreed that Bond would buy a car from Spear for $475. Bond paid Spear a $100 deposit. The next day, Spear received an offer of $575, the car's fair market value. Spear immediately notified Bond that Spear would not sell the car to Bond and returned Bond's $100. If Bond sues Spear and Spear defends on the basis of the statute of frauds, Bond will probably:

   a. Lose, because the agreement was for less than the fair market value of the car.

   b. Win, because the agreement was for less than $500.

   c. Lose, because the agreement was not in writing and signed by Spear.

   d. Win, because Bond paid a deposit.

4. Cookie Co. offered to sell Distrib Markets 20,000 pounds of cookies at $1.00 per pound, subject to certain specified terms for delivery. Distrib replied in writing as follows: "We accept your offer for 20,000 pounds of cookies at $1.00 per pound, weighing scale to have valid city certificate." Under the UCC:

   a. A contract was formed between the parties.

   b. A contract will be formed only if Cookie agrees to the weighing scale requirement.

   c. No contract was formed because Distrib included the weighing scale requirement in its reply.

   d. No contract was formed because Distrib's reply was a counteroffer.

5. Under the Sales Article of the UCC, which of the following requirements must be met for a writing to be an enforceable contract for the sale of goods?

   a. The writing must contain a term specifying the price of the goods.

   b. The writing must contain a term specifying the quantity of the goods.

   c. The writing must contain the signatures of all parties to the writing.

   d. The writing must contain the signature of the party seeking to enforce the writing.

6. Card communicated an offer to sell Card's stereo to Bend for $250. Which of the following statements is correct regarding the effect of the communication of the offer?

   a. Bend should immediately accept or reject the offer to avoid liability to Card.

   b. Card is not obligated to sell the stereo to Bend until Bend accepts the offer.

   c. Card is required to mitigate any loss Card would sustain in the event Bend rejects the offer.

   d. Bend may not reject the offer for a reasonable period of time.

CHAPTER 24

Title and Risk of Loss

© Manuel Gutjahr/iStockphoto.com

learningoutcomes

After studying this chapter, you should be able to

LO.1 Explain when title and risk of loss pass with respect to goods

LO.2 Determine who bears the risk of loss when goods are damaged or destroyed

LO.3 Explain why it is important to know when risk of loss and title pass in transactions for the sale of goods

LO.4 Describe the passage of title and risk in special situations, such as a bailment, sale or return, or a sale on approval

LO.5 Classify the various circumstances in which title can be passed to a bona fide purchaser

493

n most sales, the buyer receives the proper goods and makes payment, and the transaction is completed. However, problems may arise during performance that can result in issues of liability. For example, what if the goods are lost in transit? Must the buyer still pay for those lost goods? Can the seller's creditors take goods from the seller's warehouse when they are packed for shipment to buyers? The parties can include provisions in their contract to address these types of problems. If their contract does not cover these types of problems, however, then specific rules under Uniform Commercial Code (UCC) Article 2 apply. These rules are covered in this chapter.

In businesses today, the management of issues of risk and title as goods flow through commerce is called *supply chain management*. Effective managers know the law and the rules of risk of loss and title so that they can negotiate risk-reducing contracts and be certain that they have all necessary arrangements and paperwork to move goods through streams of commerce.

A. Identifying Types of Potential Problems and Transactions

The types of problems that can arise in supply chain management include damage to the goods in transit, claims by creditors of buyers and sellers while the goods are in transit, and questions relating to whose insurance will cover what damage and when such coverage applies.

1. Damage to Goods

One potential problem occurs if the goods are damaged or totally destroyed without any fault of either the buyer or the seller. With no goods and a contract performance still required, the parties have questions: Must the seller bear the loss and supply new goods to the buyer? Or is it the buyer's loss so that the buyer must pay the seller the purchase price even though the goods are damaged or destroyed?[1] What liability does a carrier have when goods in its possession are damaged? The fact that there may be insurance does not avoid this question because the questions of whose insurer is liable and the extent of liability still remain.

CPA   2. Creditors' Claims

Another potential problem that can arise affecting the buyer's and seller's rights occurs when creditors of the seller or buyer seize the goods under the belief that their debtor has title. The buyer's creditors may seize them because they believe them to be the buyer's. The seller's creditors may step in and take goods because they believe the goods still belong to the seller, and the buyer is left with the dilemma of

---

[1] UCC §2-509 provides for the allocation of the risk of loss in those situations where the goods are destroyed and neither party has breached the contract.

whether it can get the goods back from the creditors. The question of title or ownership is also important in connection with a resale of the goods by the buyer and in determining the parties' liability for, or the computation of, inventory or personal property taxes.

CPA 3. Insurance

insurable interest – the right to hold a valid insurance policy on a person or property.

Until the buyer has received the goods and the seller has been paid, both the seller and the buyer have an economic interest in the sales transaction. A question that can arise is whether either or both have enough of an interest in the goods to allow them to insure them, in other words, do they have an **insurable interest**? There are certain steps that must take place and timing requirements that must be met before that insurable interest can arise. Once buyers have an insurable interest in goods that are the subject matter of their contracts, they have the right to obtain insurance and can submit claims for losses on the goods.

B. DETERMINING RIGHTS: IDENTIFICATION OF GOODS

identification – point in the transaction when the buyer acquires an interest in the goods subject to the contract.

The **identification** of the goods to the contract is a necessary step to provide the buyer an insurable interest. How goods that are the subject matter of a contract are identified depends on the nature of both the contract and the goods themselves.[2] Identification is also the first step for passage of title and risk of loss.

CPA 4. Existing Goods

existing goods – goods that physically exist and are owned by the seller at the time of a transaction.

identified – term applied to particular goods selected by either the buyer or the seller as the goods called for by the sales contract.

Existing goods are goods physically in existence at the time of the contract and owned by the seller. When particular goods have been selected by either the buyer or the seller, or both, as being the goods called for by the sales contract, the goods are **identified**. **For Example,** when you go into a store, point to a particular item, and tell the clerk, "I'll take that one," your sales transaction relates to existing goods that are now identified. This step of identification provides you with certain rights in those goods because of your contract as well as Article 2 protections for buyers when goods are identified.[3]

CPA 5. Future Goods

future goods – goods that exist physically but are not owned by the seller as well as goods that have not yet been produced.

Future goods are those not yet owned by the seller or not yet in existence. **For Example,** suppose that your company is sponsoring a 10-K run and will furnish the t-shirts for the 10,000 runners expected to participate in the race. You have contacted Sporting Tees, Inc., to produce the t-shirts with the name of the race and your company logo on the shirts. The shirts are future goods because you are contracting for goods that will be produced.

Future goods are identified when they are shipped, marked, or otherwise designated by the seller as goods to which the contract refers.[4] The t-shirts cannot be

---

[2] UCC §2-501(1)(a). *Capital One Financial Corp., and Subsidiaries v. C.I.R.*, 659 F.3d 316 (4th Cir. 2011).
[3] *Duddy v. Government Employees Insurance Co., Inc.*, 23 A.2d 436 (N.J. App. 2011).
[4] UCC §2-501(1)(b). Specially manufactured goods are fully identified when the goods are made.

identified until Sporting Tees has manufactured them and designated them for your company. The earliest that the shirts can be identified is when they come off the production line and are designated for your company. Prior to identification of these goods, the buyer has only a future interest at the time of the contract and has few rights with respect to them.[5]

6. Fungible Goods

fungible goods – homogeneous goods of which any unit is the equivalent of any other unit.

Fungible goods are goods that, when mixed together, are indistinguishable. **For Example,** crops such as soybeans and dairy products such as milk are fungible goods. A seller who has 10,000 cases of cling peaches has fungible, unidentified goods. Like future goods, these fungible goods are identified when they are shipped, marked, or otherwise designated for the buyer.[6] The seller's act of tagging, marking, labeling, or in some way indicating to those responsible for shipping the goods that certain goods are associated with a particular contract or order means that identification has occurred.

7. Effect of Identification

Once goods that are the subject matter of a contract have been identified, the buyer holds an *insurable interest* in them. Once the buyer's economic interest in and the identity of the goods are clear, the buyer's insurance company has an obligation to provide coverage for any mishaps that could occur until the contract is performed completely.

Identification is also significant because the questions surrounding passage of title and risk of loss cannot be resolved until the goods have been identified. Identification is the first step in resolving questions about liability for damaged goods and rights of the parties and third parties, including creditors, in the goods. UCC §2-401(1) provides, "Title to goods cannot pass under a contract for sale prior to their identification to the contract."

C. DETERMINING RIGHTS: PASSAGE OF TITLE

When title to goods passes to the buyer (following identification) depends on whether there is a document of title, whether the seller is required to ship the goods, and what the terms of that shipping agreement are. In the absence of an agreement by the parties as to when title will pass, several Article 2 rules govern the timing for passage of title.

8. Passage of Title Using Documents of Title

document of title – document treated as evidence that a person is entitled to receive, hold, and dispose of the document and the goods it covers.

A **document of title** is a means whereby the parties can facilitate the transfer of title to the goods without actually moving them or provide a means for a creditor to take an interest in the goods. The use of a document of title also provides a simple answer

---

[5] *In re Highside Pork, LLC,* 450 B.R. 173 (N.D. Iowa 2011).

[6] Farm products, such as corn, are fungible goods. However, contracts for future crops are not contracts for the sale of goods because there are no goods identified as yet for such contracts. *Top of Iowa Co-Op v. Sime Farms, Inc.,* 608 N.W.2d 454 (Iowa 2000).

to the question of when title to the goods passes from seller to buyer in a sales transaction. Title to the goods passes when the document of title is transferred from the seller to the buyer.[7]

Documents of title are governed under Article 7 of the UCC, the final section of the UCC to undergo major revisions in the last decade of the twentieth century. The purpose of the 2003 revisions to Article 7 was to address the issues that have arisen because of electronic filing of documents of title. Article 7 adoptions have just begun with 40 states passing the new Article 7 by 2011.[8]

Article 7 now addresses the commercial reality of electronic tracking and the use of electronic records as documents of title. Under Article 7, the definition of a document of title now includes electronic documents of title.

bill of lading – document issued by a carrier acknowledging the receipt of goods and the terms of the contract of transportation.

warehouse receipt – receipt issued by the warehouser for stored goods; regulated by the UCC, which clothes the receipt with some degree of negotiability.

The discussion of documents of title here is limited to commercial transactions, transport, and storage. Many forms of documents of title are not covered under Article 7. For example, all states have some form of title system required for the transfer of title to motor vehicles.[9] Those systems govern title passage for automobiles. The two primary forms of documents of title under Article 7 used to pass title to goods are **bills of lading** (issued by a carrier) and **warehouse receipts.**[10] Details on these documents and the rights of the parties are found in Chapter 22.

CPA

9. Passage of Title in Nonshipment Contracts

Unless the parties to the contract agree otherwise, UCC Article 2 does not require that the seller deliver the contracted-for goods to the buyer. In the absence of a provision in the contract, the place of delivery is the seller's place of business or the seller's residence if the seller is not a merchant. When there is no specific agreement for shipment or delivery of the goods and there is no document of title and the goods to the contract have been identified, title passes to the buyer at the time the contract is entered into by the buyer and seller.[11]

10. Passage of Title in Warehouse Arrangements

When the goods to a contract are in a warehouse or the possession of a third party (not the seller), the title to the goods passes from the seller to the buyer when the buyer receives the document of title or, if there is no document of title, any other paperwork required for the third party or warehouse to turn over the goods and the goods are available for the buyer to take. When goods are in the possession of a warehouse, the parties have certain duties and rights. Those rights and duties were covered in Chapter 22.

11. Passage of Title in Bailments and Other Forms of Possession

As a general rule, a seller can sell only what the seller owns. However, some issues of passage of title can arise in specific circumstances. Those circumstances are covered in the following sections.

---

[7] UCC §2-401(3).

[8] The revisions to Article 7 and their history can be found at **www.nccusl.org**. The adopting states are Alabama, Alaska, Arizona, Arkansas, California, Colorado, Connecticut, Delaware, Florida, Georgia, Hawaii, Idaho, Illinois, Indiana, Iowa, Kansas, Louisiana, Maine, Maryland, Minnesota, Mississippi, Montana, Nebraska, Nevada, New Hampshire, New Mexico, North Carolina, North Dakota, Oklahoma, Oregon, Pennsylvania, Rhode Island, South Dakota, Tennessee, Texas, Utah, Virginia, and West Virginia.

[9] Other types of transportation, such as a boat, may not require a title document to be transferred, and title passes at the time of contracting. However, where there are title statutes, they preempt UCC provisions. *Ladd v. NBD Bank*, 550 N.W.2d 826 (Mich. App. 1996). See also *Pierce v. First Nat'l Bank*, 899 S.W.2d 365 (Tex. App. 1995).

[10] UCC §7-202(1) provides, "A warehouse receipt need not be in any particular form. Under Revised Article 7, it can be in electronic form."

[11] *In re Aleris Intern., Inc.*, 456 B.R. 35 (D.Del. 2011).

CPA

(A) STOLEN PROPERTY. Neither those who find stolen property nor thieves can pass title to goods. A thief simply cannot pass good title to even a good-faith purchaser. Anyone who has purchased stolen goods must surrender them to the true owner. The fact that the negligence of the owner made the theft possible or contributed to losing the goods does not bar the owner from recovering the goods or money damages from the thief, the finder, or a good-faith purchaser. It does not matter that the thief may have passed the goods along through several purchasers. Title cannot be cleansed by distance between the thief and the good-faith purchaser. The good-faith purchaser always takes the goods subject to the claim by the owner. The public policy reason for this protection of true owners is to deter theft. Knowing there is no way to sell the goods should deter those who steal and caution those who buy goods to check title and sources.

(B) ESTOPPEL. If an owner has acted in a way that misleads others, the owner of personal property may be prevented, or **estopped,** from asserting ownership. The owner would be barred from denying the right of another person to sell the property. **For Example,** a minor buys a car and puts it in his father's name so that he can obtain lower insurance rates. If the father then sells the car to a good-faith purchaser, the son would be estopped from claiming ownership.

estoppel – principle by which a person is barred from pursuing a certain course of action or of disputing the truth of certain matters.

CPA

(C) AUTHORIZATION. In certain circumstances, persons who just possess someone else's property may sell the property and pass title. Lienholders can sell property when debtors default. **For Example,** if you store your personal property in a storage locker and fail to pay rent, the owner of the storage locker holds a lien on your personal property and could sell it to pay the rent due on your storage unit. Good title passes to the buyer from such a sale. All states have some form of statute giving those who find property the authority to sell the property after certain time periods have passed or when the owner cannot be found.

voidable title – title of goods that carries with it the contingency of an underlying problem.

(D) VOIDABLE TITLE. If the buyer has a **voidable title**—for example, when the goods were obtained by fraud—the seller can rescind the sale. However, if the buyer resells the property to a good-faith purchaser before the seller has rescinded the transaction, the subsequent purchaser acquires valid title. It is immaterial whether the buyer with the voidable title had obtained title by criminal fraud.[12]

CASE SUMMARY

Fat Boy Hoodwinked by a Yacht Thief

FACTS: On August 23, 1995, Eric T. Small purchased a 37-foot (37') Sea Ray 370 Sundancer Yacht from Gulfwind Marine for $251,000.00. Sea Ray had engraved the vessel's hull identification number ("HIN") into the fiberglass on the vessel's transom. The vessel's HIN was SER4860F596 Sea Ray. Northern issued a Master Mariner yacht policy to Small providing insurance coverage for the Sea Ray yacht for theft or loss for $200,000.00.

---

[12] "Criminal fraud" is the language of Revised Article 2, adopted to increase the scope of the original term *larceny* and intended to encompass all forms of criminal activity that might lead to the possession or entrustment of goods. Revised Article 2 also covers all conduct punishable under criminal law.

CASE SUMMARY

Continued

On February 27, 2001, Daniel Dey, a Florida resident, stole the Sea Ray yacht while it was moored at her slip at Gulfwind Marina in Venice, Florida. A police report was filed, and Northern paid Small a total loss of $200,000.00 for the vessel.

Subsequently, Dey altered the Sea Ray yacht's HIN to SERF3571C298 and made other changes to the vessel to disguise the theft and manufacture date. Dey then advertised a 1998 Sea Ray for sale on an Internet Web site. On August 5, 2002, Dey signed a bill of sale conveying the Sea Ray yacht to Fat Boy, a Delaware limited liability company, for $127,500.00. No boat dealer, retailer, distributor, or seller was involved in the transaction.

Fat Boy gave a ship mortgage on the Sea Ray yacht to Carolina First. Carolina First filed the preferred ship mortgage on the Sea Ray yacht.

George Lee and Paul Degenhart, the lawyer for and principal in Fat Boy, became concerned that the Sea Ray yacht may have been manufactured in 1996, not 1998. Lee and Degenhart confronted Dey about the incorrect model year of the Sea Ray yacht. Dey admitted the alteration to make the boat seem to be a 1998, not 1996, model.

Fat Boy and Lee then attempted to trade the Sea Ray yacht to a vessel dealer for another vessel that Lee wanted to purchase. The dealer determined that the vessel had been stolen and told Small. Small contacted Lee and Fat Boy to get back his yacht, but Lee refused.

In June, 2004, the Sea Ray yacht was seized by the U.S. Marshal Service and Northern filed suit to get the yacht back. Fat Boy and Carolina First also claimed title and interest in the yacht.

DECISION: The Sea Ray yacht rightfully belongs to Northern. Small did not have knowledge of or consent to Dey's "sale" of the vessel to Fat Boy. Small did not sell the vessel to Fat Boy or Lee. Dey did not have valid title to the Sea Ray yacht when he issued a bill of sale to Fat Boy. The "sale" of the Sea Ray yacht between Dey and Fat Boy was not consummated through a boat dealer, retailer, distributor, or seller of like goods. Dey is not a boat dealer, retailer, distributor, or seller of like goods. Neither Lee nor Fat Boy ever possessed valid title to the Sea Ray yacht. A purchaser cannot obtain clear title from a thief to defeat the original owner. The most a bona fide purchaser for value can obtain from a thief is superior title to everyone except the original owner. [*Northern Insurance Company of New York v. 1996 Sea Ray Model 370DA Yacht*, 453 F. Supp. 2d 905 (D.S.C. 2006)]

(E) BAILMENTS OR SALE BY AN ENTRUSTEE. A bailee can pass good title to a good-faith purchaser even when the sale was not authorized by the owner and the bailee has no title to the goods but is in the business of selling those particular types of goods.[13] **For Example,** if Gunnell's Jewelry sells and repairs watches and Julie has left her watch with Gunnell's for repair, she has created a bailment. If Gunnell's Jewelry sells Julie's watch by mistake (because Gunnell's is both a new and old watch dealer) to David, a good-faith purchaser, David has valid title to the watch. Julie will have a cause of action against Gunnell's for conversion, and in some states, if Gunnell's sold the watch knowing that it belonged to Julie, the sale could constitute a crime, such as larceny. However, all of these legal proceedings will involve Gunnell's, Julie, and possibly a government prosecution, but not David who will take good title to the watch.

---

[13] *Wells Fargo Bank Northwest, N.A. v. RPK Capital VXI, L.L.C.*, 360 S.W.3d 691 (Tex. App. 2012). In re *Excalibur Machine Co., Inc.*, 404 B.R. 834 (W.D. Pa. 2009).

Thinking Things Through

The Katrina Pillows Donated to Help but Sold for Profit

Tempur-Pedic (TP) manufactures, markets, and distributes mattresses, pillows, cushions, slippers, and other similar products. Mattresses sold in the ordinary course of business by authorized TP distributors are enclosed in a hypo-allergenic cover, sealed in a plastic bag, and packed in cardboard boxes labeled with the TP's registered trademarks. Goods designated for charitable donations are packaged differently.

In 2005, TP decided to make a donation of approximately $15 million in mattress, slipper, and pillow inventory to Gulf Coast residents victimized by Hurricane Katrina. The donation was made to Waste to Charity, Inc. (WTC) with the condition that the donations not be resold, that there were no warranties on the products, that TP be given credit for the donations, and that WTC not portray the TP products in any negative way. If WTC wanted to sell the goods, it had to seek TP's permission.

After the donation, TP was notified by one of its dealers that its products were being sold from a truck in a parking lot in Nashville, TN, and that truckloads of TP mattresses, pillows, and slippers were being sold for $30,000. A TP representative traveled to Nashville and identified the goods as those that had been donated to WTC. The TP representative tried to take the goods, but the owner of the truck said he had purchased the TP products in good faith from WTC and had no way of knowing WTC did not have the authority to sell the products. Who has title to the TP products? Is the good-faith argument relevant? Who will get the mattresses? Does it make a difference if the buyer purchased a TP mattress in a parking lot? *[Tempur-Pedic Intern., Inc. v. Waste to Charity, Inc.,* 483 F. Supp. 2d 766 (W.D. Ark. 2007).]

Ethics & the Law

The Fake Seated Woman

David Bakalar was in possession of a drawing by Egon Schiele (the Drawing) as a result of a $670,000 successful bid at an art auction. Although the Drawing was untitled by the artist, one of the descriptive titles by which it is known is "Seated Woman with Bent Left Leg (Torso)." However, Milos Vavra and Leon Fischer, who are heirs to the estate of Franz Friedrich Grunbaum, have documentation showing that the Drawing was part of Grunbaum's estate that was restored to him and his heirs after the fall of Nazi Germany. Records from the Nazi period show that the Drawing and much of Grunbaum's other property was seized by the Nazi government without compensation. Milos and Leon say that the Drawing was, therefore, stolen property and must be returned to its rightful owner. The auction house and Mr. Bakalar claim that they are both bona fide purchasers and had no knowledge of the Drawing's history. Further, they note that a government taking is different from stealing property in that there is legal documentation that accompanied the seizure of the Drawing. Describe how the UCC title provisions would apply in this situation and what the result would be. What are the ethical issues in allowing the Drawing and other art work taken by the Nazis to become part of the commercial art market? What are the ethical issues if the Drawing is given back to the heirs? *[Bakalar v. Vavra,* 619 F.3d 136 (2nd Cir. 2010)]

In the case of an entrustee who is not a merchant, such as a prospective customer trying out an automobile, there is no transfer of title to the buyer from the entrustee. Similarly, there is no transfer of title when a mere bailee, such as a repairer who is not a seller of goods of that kind, sells the property of a customer.

12. Delivery and Shipment Terms

If delivery is required under the terms of the parties' agreement, the seller is normally required only to make shipment, and the seller's part of the contract is completed by placing the goods in the possession of a carrier for shipment. However, the parties may agree to various shipping provisions that do affect the passage of title under Article 2.[14] Those terms are covered in the following sections and Figure 24-1 provides a summary.

(A) FOB PLACE OF SHIPMENT. *FOB* is a shipping term that is an acronym for free on board.[15] If a contract contains a delivery term of **FOB place of shipment,** then the seller's obligation under the contract is to deliver the goods to a carrier for shipment. **For Example,** if the contract between a New York buyer and a Los Angeles seller provides for delivery as FOB Los Angeles, then the seller's responsibility is to place the goods in the possession of a Los Angeles carrier and enter into a contract to have the goods shipped to New York.

FOB place of shipment – contract that requires the seller to arrange for shipment only.

CPA

(B) FOB PLACE OF DESTINATION. If a contract contains a delivery term of **FOB place of destination,** then the seller's responsibility is to get the goods to the buyer. **For Example,** if the contract between the New York buyer and the Los Angeles seller is FOB New York, then the seller is responsible for getting the goods to New York. An FOB destination contract holds the seller accountable throughout the journey of the goods across the country.

FOB place of destination – shipping contract that requires seller to deliver goods to buyer.

CPA

(C) FAS. **FAS** is a shipping term that means free alongside ship; it is the equivalent of FOB for boat transportation.[16] **For Example,** a contract between a London buyer and a Norfolk, Virginia, seller that is FAS Norfolk requires only that the seller deliver the goods to a ship in Norfolk.

FAS – free alongside the named vessel.

CPA

(D) CF, CIF, AND COD. **CF** is an acronym for cost and freight, and **CIF** is an acronym for cost, insurance, and freight.[17] Under a CF contract, the seller gets the goods to a carrier, and the cost of shipping the goods is included in the contract price. Under a CIF contract, the seller must get the goods to a carrier and buy an insurance policy in

CF – cost and freight.

CIF – cost, insurance, and freight.

FIGURE 24-1	*Delivery and Shipping Terms*

COD	Cash on delivery (payment term, not shipment term)
CF	Cost plus freight lump sum; price includes cost and freight
	Risk: buyer on delivery to carrier
	Title: buyer on delivery to carrier
	Cost, insurance and freight expenses: seller pays; includes cost
	Of freight in contract price
CIF	Lump sum; price includes cost, insurance, and freight
	Risk: buyer on delivery to carrier
	Title: buyer on delivery to carrier
	Expenses: included in contract price (seller buys insurance in
	Buyer's name and pays freight)
FOB	Free on board
FAS	Free alongside ship (FOB for boats)

© Cengage Learning

[14] UCC §2-401(2). When a seller simply ships goods in response to a telephone order and there is no paperwork to indicate shipping terms, the contract is one of shipment (FOB place of shipment). *In re Jasper Seating, Inc.*, 967 A.2d 350 (N.J. Super. 2009).
[15] UCC §2-319.
[16] UCC §2-319.
[17] UCC §§2-320 and 2-321.

the buyer's name to cover the goods while in transit. The costs of the freight and the insurance policy are included in the contract price.

COD–cash on delivery.

Often contracts for the sale of goods provide for **COD.** The acronym stands for cash on delivery. Even though the term includes the word *delivery,* COD is not a shipping term but a payment term that requires the buyer to pay in order to gain physical possession of the goods.

13. Passage of Title in Shipment Contracts

When the parties have shipment and delivery terms in their contract, the type of shipment contract the parties have agreed to controls when title to the goods has passed and, as a result, the rights of creditors of the buyer and seller in those goods.

Revised Article 2 provides for the same results on passage of title in shipment contracts as under Article 2, but the FOB terms are not specifically delineated under the Revised Article 2. (See Figure 24-2.) Revised Article 2 simply uses the generic language of shipment contracts and those shipment contracts in which the seller is required to get the goods to a particular destination.

CPA   **(A) PASSAGE OF TITLE IN A SHIPMENT-ONLY CONTRACT (FOB SHIPMENT).** Title to the goods passes from the seller to the buyer in an FOB shipment contract or under a shipment contract for Revised Article 2 when the seller delivers the goods to the

---

FIGURE 24-2   │   *Passage of Title under Article 2 and Revised Article 2*

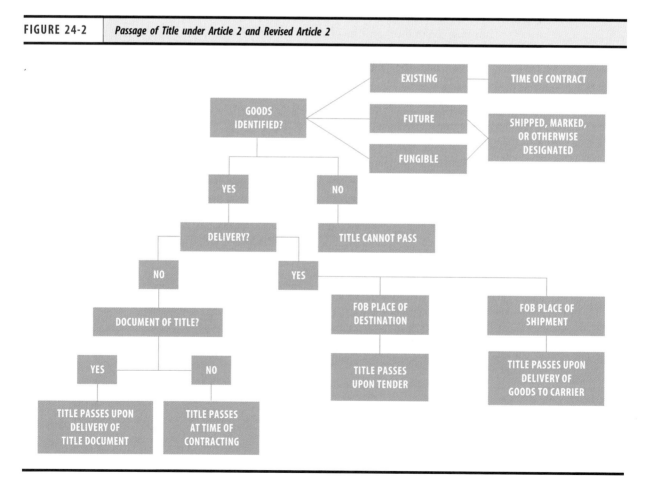

carrier.[18] The title to the goods no longer rests with the Los Angeles seller once the goods are delivered to the carrier if the contract is just a shipment contract only (an FOB Los Angeles contract). **For Example,** if the Internal Revenue Service received authorization to collect taxes by seizing the seller's property, it could not take those goods once they were delivered to the carrier. Under a shipment contract (an FOB shipment contract), the buyer owns the goods once they are in the hands of the carrier.

CPA

tender – goods have arrived, are available for pickup, and buyer is notified.

(B) PASSAGE OF TITLE IN A DESTINATION CONTRACT (FOB PLACE OF DESTINATION). Title to the goods passes from the seller to the buyer in an FOB destination contract when the goods are tendered to the buyer at the destination. **Tender** occurs when the goods have arrived and are available for the buyer to pick up and the buyer has been notified of their availability. **For Example,** when the contract contains an FOB destination provision requiring the seller to deliver to New York, title to the goods passes to the New York buyer when the goods have arrived in New York, they are available for pickup, and the buyer has been notified of their arrival. Thus, the IRS could seize the goods during shipment if the contract is FOB New York because title remains with the seller until actual tender. In the preceding example, the seller's obligation is complete when the goods are at the rail station in New York and the buyer has been notified that she may pick them up at any time during working hours.[19]

CPA

D. DETERMINING RIGHTS: RISK OF LOSS

risk of loss – in contract performance, the cost of damage or injury to the goods contracted for.

Identification determines insurability, and title determines rights of such third parties as creditors. **Risk of loss** determines who must pay under a contract in the event the goods that are the subject of the contract are damaged or destroyed during the course of performance.

CASE SUMMARY

The Taiwan Burlington Express

FACTS: Burlington Express issued a negotiable bill of lading to the seller of goods (Lite-On) being shipped from Taiwan to the United States. Under the contractual terms of the bill of lading, Burlington Express was not to deliver the goods to the buyer (consignee) until the buyer presented the negotiable bill of lading. Burlington Express delivered the goods to the buyer without having the buyer turn over the negotiable bill of lading.

Burlington Express maintained that the shipping contract was FOB Taiwan, which meant that title passed to the buyer upon loading in Taiwan, making the bill of lading irrelevant. The court entered summary judgment for Lite-On for the full value of the goods that Burlington had turned over to the nonpaying buyer, a value of $101,602.80. Burlington appealed.

DECISION: The court ruled that Burlington was bound by its bill of lading contractual terms and that the bill of lading controlled any passing of title to the buyer and for the risk of loss passing at the point of loading. The appellate court affirmed the holding for the judgment for Lite-On. Sadly, however, by the time the appellate process concluded, the Lite-On buyer had entered bankruptcy, and Lite-On was able to recover very little of its judgment. [*Lite-On Peripherals, Inc. v. Burlington Air Express, Inc.*, 255 F.3d 1189 (9th Cir. 2001)]

---

[18] UCC §2-401(2).
[19] In re *Sunbelt Grain WKS, LLC, Bkrtcy.*, 406 B.R. 918 (D. Kan. 2009).

14. Risk of Loss in Nonshipment Contracts

As noted earlier, Article 2 has no provision for delivery in the absence of an agreement. The rules for passage of risk of loss from the seller to the buyer in a nonshipment contract make a distinction between a merchant seller and a nonmerchant seller. If the seller is a merchant, the risk of loss passes to the buyer on actual receipt of the goods from the merchant.[20] If the seller is a nonmerchant, the risk of loss passes when the seller makes the goods available to the buyer or upon tender. **For Example,** if John buys a refrigerator at Kelvinator Appliances and then leaves it there while he goes to borrow a pickup truck, the risk of loss has not yet passed to John. He may have had title at the time he entered into the contract for the existing goods, and the goods are identified, but the risk of loss will not pass to John until he has actually received the refrigerator. His receipt will not occur until the refrigerator is placed in the back of his pickup truck. John is fully protected if anything happens to the refrigerator until then. If John buys the refrigerator from his neighbor at a garage sale, the risk of loss passes at the same time that title passes, or at the time of contracting.

15. Risk of Loss in Shipment Contracts

If the parties have agreed to delivery or shipment terms as part of their contract, the rules for risk of loss are different.[21]

CPA

(A) CONTRACT FOR SHIPMENT TO BUYER (FOB PLACE OF SHIPMENT). In a contract for shipment only, or FOB place of shipment, the risk of loss passes to the buyer at the same time as title does: when the goods are delivered to the carrier, that is, at the time and place of shipment. After the goods have been delivered to the carrier, the seller has no liability for, or insurable interest in, the goods unless the seller has reserved a security interest in them. **For Example,** if the Los Angeles seller has a shipment contract (an FOB Los Angeles contract), once the goods are in the hands of the carrier, the risk belongs to the buyer or the buyer's insurer. If the goods are hijacked outside Kansas City, the New York buyer must still pay the Los Angeles seller for the goods according to the contract price and terms.

E-Commerce & Cyberlaw

Supply Chain and Risk Management

In today's sophisticated supplier and transportation relationships, buyers, sellers, and carriers can pinpoint exactly where goods are and when they have been delivered, and all parties have access to that information online. In many contracts, the parties can avert problems or breaches by monitoring closely the progress of the shipment. The computer interconnection of the supply chain permits faster and better communication among the parties when problems under the contract or in shipment arise. The shipment can be tracked from the time of delivery to the carrier through its route to final signature upon its arrival.

---

[20] UCC §2-509 *Capshaw v. Hickman,* 880 N.E.2d 118 (Oh. App. 2007).
[21] UCC §2-509. *OneBeacon Ins. Co. v. Haas Industries, Inc.,* 634 F.3d 1092 (9th Cir. 2011)

CPA

(B) CONTRACT FOR DELIVERY AT DESTINATION (FOB PLACE OF DESTINATION). When the contract requires the seller to deliver the contract goods at a particular destination (FOB place of destination), the risk of loss does not pass to the buyer until the carrier tenders the goods at the destination. **For Example,** if the contract is FOB New York and the goods are hijacked in Kansas City, the seller is required to find substitute goods and perform under the contract because the risk of loss does not pass to the buyer until the goods arrive in New York and are available to the notified buyer.[22]

16. Damage to or Destruction of Goods

In the absence of a contract provision, Article 2 provides for certain rights for the parties in the event of damage to or destruction of goods that are the subject matter in a contract.

(A) DAMAGE TO IDENTIFIED GOODS BEFORE RISK OF LOSS PASSES. Goods that were identified at the time the contract was made may be damaged or destroyed without the fault of either party before the risk of loss has passed. If so, the UCC provides, "if the loss is total the contract is avoided."[23] The loss may be partial, or the goods may have so deteriorated that they do not conform to the contract. In this case, the buyer has the option, after inspecting the goods, to either avoid the contract or accept the goods subject to an allowance or a deduction from the contract price. There is no breach by the seller, so the purpose of the law is simply to eliminate the legal remedies, allow the buyer to choose to take the goods, and have the insurers involved cover the losses.[24]

(B) DAMAGE TO IDENTIFIED GOODS AFTER RISK OF LOSS PASSES. If partial damage or total destruction occurs after the risk of loss has passed to the buyer, it is the buyer's loss. The buyer may be able to recover the amount of the damages from the carrier, an insurer, the person in possession of the goods (such as a warehouse), or any third person causing the loss.[25] However, the carrier is permitted to limit its liability for damages on valuable goods such as artwork. Without special insurance and absent any negligence by the seller in making shipping arrangements, a buyer who holds the risk of loss will still be bound to pay the seller the full amount.

CASE SUMMARY

FedEx, Candelabras, and Damages in Shipment

FACTS: Yehouda Hanasab, president and sole shareholder of King Jewelry, Inc., bought a pair of marble and brass statues with candelabras from Elegant Reflections, a purveyor of jewelry and object d'art located in Florida, for $37,500.00. Elegant Reflections was to ship the goods to King under FOB place of shipment terms. Elegant Reflections hired Raymond Reppert, a "professional packager and crater" with 12 years experience, to package, crate, and ship the statues and candelabras to King. Reppert packaged and crated the statues with directional markings and signs stating "Fragile—Handle with Care." Reppert paid FedEx $684.50 (transportation charge in the amount of $485.04, declared value charge in the amount of $185.00, and fuel surcharge in the

---

[22] *APL Co. Pte. Ltd. v. UK Aerosols Ltd., Inc.*, 452 F. Supp. 2d 939 (N.D. Cal. 2006).

[23] UCC §613(a).

[24] *Great Southern Wood Preserving, Inc. v. American Home Assur. Co.*, 505 F. Supp. 2d 1287 (M.D. Ala. 2007). *Design Data Corp. v. Maryland Casualty Co.*, 503 N.W.2d 552 (Neb. 1993).

[25] For a discussion of parties' rights, see *Learning Links, Inc. v. United Parcel Services of America, Inc.* 2006 WL 785274 (S.D.N.Y.), *Spray-Tek, Inc. v. Robbins Motor Transp., Inc.*, 426 F. Supp. 2d 875 (W.D. Wis. 2006), and *Dominion Resource Services, Inc. v. 5K Logistics, Inc.*, 2010 WL 2721355 (E.D. Va.)

CASE SUMMARY

Continued

amount of $14.55) to ship the candelabras. However, both candelabras were broken in transit, something King discovered then they arrived in King's offices. FedEx's airbill limits damages to $500. King sought recovery from Elegant and/or FedEx and Reppert.

DECISION: The standard airbill holding FedEx harmless for any damage to artwork was sufficiently plain and conspicuous to give reasonable notice of its meaning and, thus, effectively limited the carrier's liability for damage to the sculptures: A conspicuous notice limiting coverage for artwork appeared on the front of the airbill and directed the shipper to easily understood terms on the back; a service bill incorporated into the airbill expressly provided that the artwork was covered only up to $500; and the shipper had considerable experience in shipping goods. In an FOB place of shipment contract, the seller is not liable unless the buyer can show negligence in packing. King did not establish that Elegant or Reppert was negligent. King received $500.00. [*King Jewelry Inc. v. Federal Express Corporation*, **166 F. Supp. 2d 1280 (C.D. Cal. 2001)**]

(c) **DAMAGE TO UNIDENTIFIED GOODS.** As long as the goods are unidentified, no risk of loss passes to the buyer. If any goods are damaged or destroyed during this period, the loss is the seller's. The buyer is still entitled to receive the goods described by the contract. The seller is therefore liable for breach of contract if the proper goods are not delivered.

The only exceptions to these general rules on damage or destruction arise when the parties have expressly provided in the contract that the destruction of the seller's inventory, crop, or source of supply releases the seller from liability, or when it is clear that the parties contracted for the purchase and sale of part of the seller's supply to the exclusion of any other possible source of such goods. In these cases, destruction of, or damage to, the seller's supply is a condition subsequent that discharges the contract.

17. Effect of Seller's Breach in Risk of Loss

When the seller breaches the contract by sending the buyer goods that do not conform to the contract and the buyer rejects them, the risk of loss does not pass to the buyer. If there has been a breach, the risk of loss remains with the seller even though the risk, according to the contract terms or the Article 2 rules discussed earlier, would ordinarily have passed to the buyer.

Figures 24-3 and 24-4 provide a summary of all the risk provisions for parties in a sales transaction.

E. DETERMINING RIGHTS: SPECIAL SITUATIONS

18. Returnable Goods Transactions

The parties may agree that the goods to be transferred under the contract can be returned to the seller. This type of arrangement in which goods may be returned is classified as one of the following: (1) a sale on approval, (2) a sale or return, or (3) a consignment sale. In the first two types of transactions, the buyer is allowed to return the goods as an added inducement to purchase. The consignment sale is used when the seller is actually the owner's agent for the purpose of selling goods.[26]

[26] *Berry v. Lucas*, 150 P.3d 424 (Or. App. 2006).

FIGURE 24-3	*Risk of Loss*

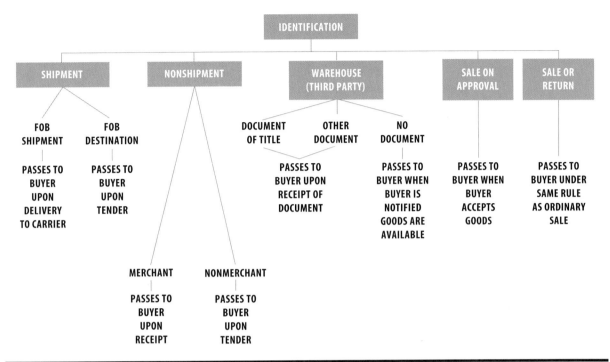

© Cengage Learning

FIGURE 24-4	*Risk of Loss—Revised Article 2*

© Cengage Learning

CPA

sale on approval – term indicating that no sale takes place until the buyer approves or accepts the goods.

(A) SALE ON APPROVAL. In a **sale on approval**, no sale takes place (meaning there is no transfer of title) until the buyer approves, or accepts, the goods. Title and risk of loss remain with the seller until there is an approval. Because the buyer is not the "owner" of the goods before approval, the buyer's creditors cannot attach or take the goods before the buyer's approval of the goods.

The buyer's approval may be shown by (1) express words, (2) conduct, or (3) lapse of time. Trying out or testing the goods does not constitute approval or acceptance. Any use that goes beyond trying out or testing, such as repairing the goods or giving them away as a present, is inconsistent with the seller's continued ownership. These types of uses show approval by the buyer. **For Example,** a buyer may order a home gym through a television ad. The ad allows buyers to try the room full of equipment for 30 days and then promises, "If you are not completely satisfied, return the home gym and we'll refund your money." The offer is one for a sale on approval. If the buyer does not return the home gym equipment or contact the seller within 30 days, the sale is complete.

The contract may give the buyer a fixed number of days for approval. The expiration of that period of time, without any action by the buyer, constitutes an approval. Also during this time, the buyer's creditors cannot take the goods pursuant to a judgment or lien. If no time is stated in the contract, the lapse of a reasonable time without action by the buyer constitutes an approval. If the buyer gives the seller notice of disapproval, the lapse of time thereafter has no effect.

If the buyer does not approve the goods, the seller bears the risk of and expense for their return.

sale or return – sale in which the title to the property passes to the buyer at the time of the transaction but the buyer is given the option of returning the property and restoring the title to the seller.

(B) SALE OR RETURN. A **sale or return** is a completed sale with an option for the buyer to return the goods. Revised Article 2 provides a new distinction between sale on approval and sale or return but with the same basic rules on title and risk of loss.

In a sale or return transaction, title and risk of loss pass to the buyer as in the case of the ordinary or absolute sale. Until the actual return of the goods is made, title and risk of loss remain with the buyer. The buyer bears the expense for and risk of return of the goods. In a sale or return, so long as the goods remain in the buyer's possession, the buyer's creditors may treat the goods as belonging to the buyer.

19. Consignments and Factors

consignment – bailment made for the purpose of sale by the bailee. (Parties–consignor, consignee)

consignor – (1) person who delivers goods to the carrier for shipment; (2) party with title who turns goods over to another for sale.

consignee – (1) person to whom goods are shipped; (2) dealer who sells goods for others.

factor – bailee to whom goods are consigned for sale.

Under a **consignment,** the owner of the goods entrusts them to a dealer for the purpose of selling them. The seller is the **consignor,** and the dealer is the **consignee.** The dealer-consignee is often referred to as a **factor,** a special type of bailee (see Chapter 22) who sells consigned goods just as if the goods were her own. The dealer-consignee is paid a fee for selling the goods on behalf of the seller-consignor. A consignment sale is treated as a sale or return under Article 2, and the dealer-consignee has full authority to sell the goods for the consignor and can pass title to those goods. While the goods are in the possession of the consignee, they are subject to the claims of the seller's creditors.[27]

20. Self-Service Stores

In the case of goods in a self-service store, the reasonable interpretation of the circumstances is that the store, by its act of putting the goods on display on its shelves, makes an offer to sell such goods for cash and confers on a prospective customer a license to carry the goods to the cashier to make payment. Most courts

---

[27] This clarification of creditors' rights in consignments came from Revised Article 9 (see Chapter 34). Revised Article 2 was changed to make the sale or return rights of creditors consistent with Revised Article 9. Prior to these changes, and under current Article 2, whether the seller's creditor could seize the goods depended upon the filing of an Article 9 security interest.

hold that there is no transfer of title until the buyer makes payment to the cashier. Other courts hold that a contract to sell is formed when the customer accepts the seller's offer by taking the item from the shelf. In other words, a sale actually occurs when the buyer takes the item from the shelf. Title passes at that moment to the buyer even though the goods have not yet been paid for.

CPA ## 21. Auction Sales

When goods are sold at an auction in separate lots, each lot is a separate transaction, and title to each passes independently of the other lots. Title to each lot passes when the auctioneer announces by the fall of the hammer or in any other customary manner that the lot in question has been sold to the bidder.

"With reserve" auctions are those that give the auctioneer the right to withdraw the goods from the sale process if the bids are not high enough. If an auction is held "without reserve," the goods must be sold regardless of whether the auctioneer is satisfied with the levels of the bids.

LawFlix

RV (2006)(PG)

Robin Williams leases an RV and drives his family from California to Colorado. Along the way, the RV ends up damaged, in a lake, and generally greatly depreciated in value. The issues of bailment, liability, risk, and title are serious companions to the funny story line of family life and the RV culture.

MAKE THE CONNECTION

SUMMARY

All along the supply chain of a business are issues of risk and title that are often complicated by additional questions about damage to goods in transit, the claims of creditors to goods that are in process under a contract, and insurance. Unless the parties specifically agree otherwise, the solution to these problems depends on the nature of the transaction between the seller and the buyer.

The first issue to be addressed in answering questions of risk, title, and loss is whether the goods are identified. Existing goods are identified at the time the contract is entered into. Future goods, or goods not yet owned by the seller or not yet in existence (as in goods to be manufactured by the seller), are identified when they are shipped, marked, or otherwise designated for the buyer. Without identification, title and risk of loss cannot pass from buyer to seller, nor can the buyer hold an insurable interest.

Once identification has occurred, the issue of title, and hence creditor's rights, can be addressed. If there are identified goods but there is no document of title associated with the goods, then title to the goods passes from the seller to the buyer at the time of the contract.

Sellers can have their goods covered by a document of title. The most common types of documents of title are bills of lading and warehouse receipts. These documents of title, if properly transferred, transfer title to both the document and the underlying goods.

While the seller has no obligation under UCC Article 2 to deliver the goods to the buyer, the parties can agree on delivery as part of their contract. Several common delivery terms are used in supply chain management. *FOB* is "free on board," and its meaning depends on the location that follows the term. *FOB place of shipment* requires the seller to deliver the goods to the carrier. In an FOB place of shipment contract, title to the goods passes from the seller to the buyer when the goods are delivered to the carrier. *FOB place of destination* requires the seller to get the goods to the buyer or a location specified by the buyer and tender the goods there. *FAS* is "free alongside ship," which means free on board for shipment by sea. *CF* is "cost and freight" and requires the seller to deliver the goods to the carrier and make a contract for their shipment. *CIF* is "cost, insurance, and freight" and requires the seller to deliver the goods to the carrier, make a contract for shipment, and purchase insurance for the goods in transit. *COD* means "cash on delivery" and requires the buyer to pay for the goods before taking possession of them.

Ordinarily, sellers cannot pass any title greater than that which they possess. In some cases, however, the law permits a greater title to be transferred even though the transferor may hold voidable title or be in possession of the goods only as in a bailment. These exceptions protect good-faith purchasers.

Risk of loss is an issue for buyers, sellers, and insurers. When risk of loss passes from seller to buyer is controlled, again, by the terms of the contract. In a contract in which there is no agreement on delivery, the risk of loss passes to the buyer upon receipt of the goods if the seller is a merchant and upon tender if the seller is a nonmerchant. Under Revised Article 2, the risk of loss in nonshipment contracts always passes upon receipt, regardless of whether the contract involves a merchant or nonmerchant. If there is an agreement for delivery and the contract provides for shipment only, or FOB place of shipment, then risk of loss passes from seller to buyer when the goods are delivered to the carrier. If the contract provides for delivery to a particular location, or FOB place of destination, then the risk of loss passes from the seller to the buyer when the goods are tendered to the buyer.

Some types of arrangements, such as sales on approval, sales or returns, and consignments or factor arrangements, have specific rules for passage of title and risk of loss. Also, if there is a breach of the contract and the seller ships goods different from those ordered, the breach prevents the risk of loss from passing from the seller to the buyer.

LEARNING OUTCOMES

After studying this chapter, you should be able to clearly explain:

A. Identifying Types of Potential Problems and Transactions

LO.1   Explain when title and risk of loss pass with respect to goods

See *Northern Insurance Company of New York v. 1996 Sea Ray Model 370DA Yacht* on pp. 498–499.

B. Determining Rights: Identification of Goods

LO.2   Determine who bears the risk of loss when goods are damaged or destroyed

See *King Jewelry Inc. v. Federal Express Corporation* on p. 506.

C. Determining Rights: Passage of Title

LO.3   Explain why it is important to know when risk of loss and title pass in transactions for the sale of goods

See *Lite-On Peripherals, Inc. v. Burlington Air Express, Inc.* on p. 503.

D. Determining Rights: Risk of Loss

LO.4   Describe the passage of title and risk in special situations, such as a bailment, sale or return, or a sale on approval

See the *For Example,* discussion of Gunnell's Jewelry on p. 499.

See the *For Example,* discussion of a home gymnasium that is purchased from TV on p. 508.

E. Determining Rights: Special Situations

L0.5   Classify the various circumstances in which title can be passed to a bona fide purchaser

See Thinking Things Through, *Tempur-Pedic Intern., Inc. v. Waste to Charity, Inc.*, on p. 500.

KEY TERMS

bills of lading
CF
CIF
COD
consignee
consignment
consignor
document of title
estoppel

existing goods
factor
FAS
FOB place of destination
FOB place of shipment
fungible goods
future goods
identification
identified

insurable interest
risk of loss
sale on approval
sale or return
tender
voidable title
warehouse receipts

QUESTIONS AND CASE PROBLEMS

1. Schock, the buyer, negotiated to purchase a mobile home that was owned by and located on the sellers' property. On April 15, 1985, Schock appeared at the Ronderos' (the sellers') home and paid them the agreed-on purchase price of $3,900. Schock received a bill of sale and an assurance from the Ronderos that the title certificate to the mobile home would be delivered soon. Also on April 15 and with the permission of the sellers, Schock prepared the mobile home for removal. His preparations included the removal of skirting around the mobile home's foundation, the tie-downs, and the foundation blocks, leaving the mobile home to rest on the wheels of its chassis. Schock intended to remove the mobile home from the Ronderos' property a week later, and the Ronderos had no objection to having the mobile home remain on their premises until that time. Two days later, the mobile home was destroyed by high winds as it sat on the Ronderos' property. Schock received a clear certificate of title to the mobile home in the mail. Thereafter, Schock sued the Ronderos for return of his money on the ground that when the mobile home was destroyed, the risk of loss remained with the Ronderos. Who should win the lawsuit? [*Schock v. Ronderos*, 394 N.W.2d 697 (N.D.)]

2. John C. Clark, using the alias Thomas Pecora, rented a 1994 Lexus from Alamo Rent-A-Car on December 21, 1994. Clark did not return the car and, using falsified signatures, obtained a California so-called "quick" title.

   Clark advertised the car for sale in the *Las Vegas Review Journal*. Terry and Vyonne Mendenhall called the phone number in the ad and reached Clark. He told them that he lived at a country club and could not have people coming to his house to look at the car. He instead drove the car to their house for their inspection the next morning. The car title was in the name of J. C. Clark Enterprises. The Mendenhalls bought the car for $34,000 in cash. They made some improvements on the car and registered it in Utah. On February 24, 1995, Alamo reported the car stolen. On March 21, 1995, the Nevada Department of Motor Vehicles seized the car from the Mendenhalls. The car was returned to Alamo and the Mendenhalls filed suit. The lower court found for the Mendenhalls, and Alamo appealed. Who gets the car and why? [*Alamo Rent-A-Car v. Mendenhall*, 937 P.2d 69 (Nev.)]

3. Felix DeWeldon is a well-known sculptor and art collector. He owned three paintings valued at $26,000 that he displayed in his home in Newport, Rhode Island. In 1991, he declared bankruptcy and DeWeldon, Ltd., purchased all of DeWeldon's personal property from the bankruptcy trustee. Nancy Wardell, the sole

shareholder of DeWeldon, Ltd., sold her stock to Byron Preservation Trust, which then sold Felix an option to repurchase the paintings. At all times, the paintings were on display in DeWeldon's home.

In 1994, DeWeldon's son Byron told Robert McKean that his father was interested in selling the paintings. After viewing them, McKean then purchased the paintings for $50,000. DeWeldon, Ltd., brought suit to have the paintings returned, claiming McKean did not have title because Byron did not have the authority to sell the paintings. Will McKean get the paintings? [*DeWeldon, Ltd. v. McKean*, 125 F.3d 24 (1st Cir)]

4. Helen Thomas contracted to purchase a pool heater from Sunkissed Pools. As part of the $4,000 contract, Sunkissed agreed to install the pool heater, which was delivered to Thomas's home and left in the driveway. The heater was too heavy for Thomas to lift, and she was forced to leave it in the driveway because no one from Sunkissed responded to her calls about its installation. Subsequently, the heater disappeared from the driveway. Sunkissed maintained that the risk of loss had passed to Thomas. Thomas maintained that the failure to install the heater as promised is a breach of contract. Who should bear the risk for the stolen pool heater? [*In re Thomas*, 182 B.R. 774 (Bankr. S.D. Fla.)]

5. Around June 2005, PPI purchased three pallets of computer wafers from Omneon Video Graphics. PPI requested that Omneon ship the wafers directly to the City University of New York, the end purchaser of the goods. Omneon and PPI agreed that Omneon would ship the wafers FOB Omneon's dock. Somewhere between the loading dock and City University, one pallet of the wafers disappeared. Who bears the loss for the lost pallet and why? [*OneBeacon Ins. Co. v. Hass Industries, Inc.*, 634 F.3d 1092 (9th Cir. 2011)]

6. Using a bad check, B purchased a used automobile from a dealer. B then took the automobile to an auction at which the automobile was sold to a party who had no knowledge of its history. When B's check was dishonored, the dealer brought suit against the party who purchased the automobile at the auction. Was the dealer entitled to reclaim the automobile? [*Greater Louisville Auto Auction, Inc. v. Ogle Buick, Inc.*, 387 S.W.2d 17 (Ky.)]

7. Coppola, who collected coins, joined a coin club, First Coinvestors, Inc. The club would send coins to its members, who were to pay for them or return them within 10 days. What was the nature of the transaction? [*First Coinvestors, Inc. v. Coppola*, 388 N.Y.S.2d 833]

8. Would buying a car from a mechanic who works at a car dealership qualify as purchasing a car in the ordinary course of business? [*Steele v. Ellis*, 961 F. Supp. 1458 (D. Kan.)]

9. Does a pawnbroker who purchases property in good faith acquire good title to that property? Can the pawnbroker pass good title? [*Fly v. Cannon*, 813 S.W.2d 458 (Tenn.App.)]

10. Larsen Jewelers sold a necklace to Conway on a layaway plan. Conway paid a portion of the price and made additional payments from time to time. The necklace was to remain in the possession of Larsen until payment was fully made. The Larsen jewelry store was burglarized, and Conway's necklace and other items were taken. Larsen argued that Conway must bear the risk of loss. Conway sought recovery of the full value of the necklace. Decide. [*Conway v. Larsen Jewelry*, 429 N.Y.S.2d 378]

11. Future Tech International, Inc., is a buyer and distributor of Samsung monitors and other computer products. In 1993, Future Tech determined that brand loyalty was important to customers, and it sought to market its own brand of computer products. Future Tech, a Florida firm, developed its own brand name of MarkVision and entered into a contract in 1994 with Tae II Media, a Korean firm. The contract provided that Tae II Media would be the sole source and manufacturer for the MarkVision line of computer products.

The course of performance on the contract did not go well. Future Tech alleged that from the time the ink was dry on the contract, Tae II Media had no intention of honoring its commitment to supply computers and computer products to Future Tech. Future Tech alleged that Tae II Media entered into the contract with the purpose of limiting Future Tech's competitive ability because Tae II Media had its own Tech Media brand of computers and computer products.

Future Tech, through threats and demands, was able to have the first line of MarkVision products completed. Tae II Media delivered the computers to a boat but, while in transit, ordered the shipping line (Maersk Lines) to return the computers. The terms of their contract provided for delivery "FOB Pusan Korea." Future Tech filed suit, claiming that Tae II Media could not take the computer products because title had already passed to Future Tech. Is this interpretation of who has title correct? [*Future Tech Int'l, Inc. v. Tae II Media, Ltd.*, 944 F. Supp. 1538 (S.D. Fla.)]

12. Bakker Brothers of Idaho agreed to buy Charles E. Graff's 1989 onion seed crop. The contract required that the onion seeds have an 85 percent germination rate. Despite careful testing and advice from experts, Bakker Brothers could not get a germination rate on the seed tested higher than 62 to 69 percent. Bakker Brothers rejected the seed, notified Graff, and awaited instructions. Graff gave no instructions and the seed spoiled.

Graff sought to recover the contract price from Bakker Brothers because the risk of loss had passed. The trial court granted summary judgment for Bakker Brothers, and Graff appealed. Was the trial court decision correct? Explain why or why not. [*Graff v. Bakker Brothers of Idaho, Inc.*, 934 P.2d 1228 (Wash. App.)]

13. Without permission, Grissom entered onto land owned by another and then proceeded to cut and sell the timber from the land. On learning that the timber had been sold, the owner of the land brought an action to recover the timber from the purchaser. The purchaser argued that he was a good-faith purchaser who had paid value and therefore was entitled to keep the timber. Decide. [*Baysprings Forest Products, Inc. v. Wade*, 435 So.2d 690 (Miss.)]

14. Brown Sales ordered goods from Eberhard Manufacturing Co. The contract contained no agreement about who would bear the risk of loss. There were no shipping terms. The seller placed the goods on board a common carrier with instructions to deliver the goods to Brown. While in transit, the goods were lost. Which party will bear the loss? Explain. [*Eberhard Manufacturing Co. v. Brown*, 232 N.W.2d 378 (Mich. App.)]

CPA QUESTIONS

1. Bond purchased a painting from Wool, who is not in the business of selling art. Wool tendered delivery of the painting after receiving payment in full from Bond. Bond informed Wool that Bond would be unable to take possession of the painting until later that day. Thieves stole the painting before Bond returned. The risk of loss:

   a. Passed to Bond at Wool's tender of delivery.

   b. Passed to Bond at the time the contract was formed and payment was made.

   c. Remained with Wool, because the parties agreed on a later time of delivery.

   d. Remained with Wool, because Bond had not yet received the painting.

2. Which of the following statements applies to a sale on approval under the UCC Sales Article?

   a. Both the buyer and seller must be merchants.

   b. The buyer must be purchasing the goods for resale.

   c. Risk of loss for the goods passes to the buyer when the goods are accepted after the trial period.

   d. Title to the goods passes to the buyer on delivery of the goods to the buyer.

3. If goods have been delivered to a buyer pursuant to a sale or return contract, the:

   a. Buyer may use the goods but not resell them.

b. Seller is liable for the expenses incurred by the buyer in returning the goods to the seller.

c. Title to the goods remains with the seller.

d. Risk of loss for the goods passes to the buyer.

4. Cey Corp. entered into a contract to sell parts to Deck, Ltd. The contract provided that the goods would be shipped "FOB Cey's warehouse." Cey shipped parts different from those specified in the contract. Deck rejected the parts. A few hours after Deck informed Cey that the parts were rejected, they were destroyed by fire in Deck's warehouse. Cey believed that the parts were conforming to the contract. Which of the following statements is correct?

a. Regardless of whether the parts were conforming, Deck will bear the loss because the contract was a shipment contract.

b. If the parts were nonconforming, Deck had the right to reject them, but the risk of loss remains with Deck until Cey takes possession of the parts.

c. If the parts were conforming, risk of loss does not pass to Deck until a reasonable period of time after they are delivered to Deck.

d. If the parts were nonconforming, Cey will bear the risk of loss, even though the contract was a shipment contract.

5. Under the Sales Articles of the UCC, when a contract for the sale of goods stipulates that the seller ship the goods by common carrier "FOB purchaser's loading dock," which of the parties bears the risk of loss during shipment?

a. The purchaser, because risk of loss passes when the goods are delivered to the carrier.

b. The purchaser, because title to the goods passes at the time of shipment.

c. The seller, because risk of loss passes only when the goods reach the purchaser's loading dock.

d. The seller, because risk of loss remains with the seller until the goods are accepted by the purchaser.

6. When do title and risk of loss for conforming goods pass to the buyer under a shipment contract covered by the Sales Article of the UCC?

a. When the goods are identified and designated for shipment.

b. When the goods are given to a common carrier.

c. When the goods arrive at their destination.

d. When the goods are tendered to the buyer at their destination.

© Manuel Gutjahr/iStockphoto.com

CHAPTER 25

Product Liability: Warranties and Torts

learningoutcomes

After studying this chapter, you should be able to

LO.1 List the theories of product liability

LO.2 Identify who may sue and who may be sued when a defective product causes harm

LO.3 Define and give examples of an express warranty

LO.4 List and explain the types of implied warranties

LO.5 Explain warranty protections under federal law

LO.6 State what constitutes a breach of warranty

LO.7 Describe the extent and manner in which implied warranties may be disclaimed under the UCC and the CISG

W hat happens when goods do not work? Who can recover for injury caused by defective goods? What can you do when the goods are not as promised or pictured?

A. GENERAL PRINCIPLES

When defective goods result in damages or injury to the buyer or other parties, the UCC and tort law provide remedies.

1. Theories of Liability

Two centuries ago, a buyer was limited to recovery from a seller for breach of an express guarantee or for negligence or fraud. After the onset of mass production and distribution, however, these remedies had little value. A guarantee was good, but in the ordinary sales transaction no one stopped to get a guarantee. Few customers remembered to ask the manager of the supermarket to give a guarantee that the loaf of bread purchased was fit to eat. Further, negligence and fraud have become difficult to prove in a mass production world. How can one prove there was a problem in the production process for a can of soup prepared months earlier?

To give buyers protection from economic loss and personal injuries, the concept of warranty liability developed. **Warranties** are either express or implied and can be found in the UCC. There have been changes in warranty liability under the Revised UCC, but because of its limited adoption they are mentioned only briefly. Many courts have decided that still broader protection beyond the UCC contract remedies is required and have created the additional concept of **strict tort liability** for defective goods.

There are five theories in law for what is often called *product liability*, or the protection of buyers that also allows them recovery for injury and economic loss: express warranty, implied warranty, negligence, fraud, and strict tort liability. Any statutory remedies under consumer law or employment law are additional means of recovery. The plaintiff does not have a choice of all theories in every case; the facts of the case dictate the choices the plaintiff has available for possible theories of recovery.

2. Nature of Harm

A defective product can cause harm to person, property, or economic interests. **For Example,** the buyer of a truck may be injured when, through a defect, the truck goes out of control and plunges down the side of a hill. Passengers in the truck, bystanders, or the driver of a car hit by the truck may also be injured. The defective truck may cause injury to a total stranger who seeks to rescue one of the victims. Property damage could occur if the buyer's truck careens off the road into a fence or even a house and causes damages. Another driver's car may be damaged. Commercial and economic interests of the buyer are affected by the fact that the truck is defective. Even if there is no physical harm, the defective truck is not as valuable as it

warranty – promise either express or implied about the nature, quality, or performance of the goods.

strict tort liability – product liability theory that imposes absolute liability upon the manufacturer, seller, or distributor of goods for harm caused by defective goods.

would have been. The buyer who has paid for the truck on the basis of its value as it should have been has sustained an economic loss. If the buyer is required to rent a truck from someone else or loses an opportunity to haul freight for compensation, the fact that the truck was defective also causes economic or commercial loss.

CPA

3. Who Is Liable in Product Liability

Until the early part of the twentieth century, only the parties to a sales contract could recover from each other on product liability issues. A seller was liable to the buyer, but the seller was not liable to others because they were not in **privity of contract** with the seller or in a direct contract relationship with the seller. This requirement of privity of contract has now been widely rejected.[1]

privity of contract – relationship between a promisor and the promisee.

(A) WHO CAN RECOVER UNDER UCC WARRANTIES. Today, not only the buyer but also customers and employees of the buyer and even third persons or bystanders may recover because of harm caused by a defective product. Most states have abolished the requirement of **privity** when the person injured by a product is a member of the buyer's family or household or is a guest of the buyer and has sustained personal injury because of the product.[2] A few states require privity of contract, particularly when the plaintiff does not sustain personal injury or property damage and seeks to recover only economic loss.[3]

privity – succession or chain of relationship to the same thing or right, such as privity of contract, privity of estate, privity of possession.

UCC section 2-318 provides alternatives for who can recover for breach of warranty. Alternative A extends warranty protection to "any individual who is in the family or household of the immediate buyer or the remote purchaser or who is a guest in the home of either…." Alternative B covers "any individual who may reasonably be expected to use, consume, or be affected by the goods." Alternative C covers the same groups as Alternative B but adds that the protections provided cannot be disclaimed.

(B) WHO IS LIABLE UNDER UCC WARRANTIES. Someone who is injured by a defective product can recover from the seller, the manufacturer of the product, and generally even the manufacturer of the component part of the product that caused the harm.[4] **For Example,** when a person is struck by an automobile because the driver has lost control because of the car's defective brakes, the person who was struck and injured may seek recovery from the seller and the manufacturer of the car. The maker of the brake assembly or system that the car manufacturer installed in the car may also be liable.

---

[1] UCC §2-318, Alternative A. The Code gives the states the option of adopting the provision summarized in this chapter or of making a wide abolition of the requirement of privity by adopting Alternative B or C of §2-318. As of October 2012, these states/areas had adopted the versions of §2-318 (not Revised Article 2) as follows: Alternative A adopted in Alaska, Arizona, Arkansas, Connecticut, District of Columbia, Florida, Georgia, Idaho, Illinois, Indiana, Kentucky, Maryland, Michigan, Mississippi, Missouri, Montana, Nebraska, Nevada, New Jersey, New Mexico, North Carolina, Ohio, Oklahoma, Oregon, Pennsylvania, Tennessee, Washington, West Virginia, and Wisconsin. Alternative B adopted in Alabama, Colorado, Delaware, Kansas, South Carolina, South Dakota, Vermont, and Wyoming. Alternative C adopted in Hawaii, Iowa, Minnesota, North Dakota, Vermont, and Utah.

[2] Lack of privity is not a defense in a suit for breach of warranty. *Hyundai Motor America, Inc. v. Goodin*, 822 N.E.2d 947 (Ind. 2005). Revised Article 2 expands warranty protection (§§2-408 and 2-409).

[3] *Praxair, Inc. v. General Insulation Co.* 611 F. Supp. 2d 318 (W.D.N.Y. 2009).

[4] However, see *Barnett v. Leiserv*, 968 F. Supp. 690 (N.D. Ga. 1997), where the child of the person who bought coffee for a friend could not recover for burns from coffee spilled on her by the friend. The court also noted that a child who spills coffee on himself could not recover either. Where the coffee maker at the retail store where the coffee was purchased is not defective, the case is one in negligence and requires proof of breach of duty but does not require privity. *McMahon v. Bunn-O-Matic Corp.*, 150 F.3d 651 (7th Cir. 1998).

B. EXPRESS WARRANTIES

A warranty may be express or implied. Both express and implied warranties operate as though the defendant had made an express promise or statement of fact. Both express and implied warranties are governed primarily by the UCC.

CPA

express warranty – statement by the defendant relating to the goods, which statement is part of the basis of the bargain.

4. Definition of Express Warranty

An **express warranty** is a statement of fact or promise of performance relating to the goods that becomes a basis of the buyer's bargain.[5]

"Basis of the bargain" means that the buyer has purchased the goods because of what the seller has stated about those goods. A statement by the seller regarding the quality, capacity, or other characteristic of the goods is an express warranty. **For Example,** express warranties in sellers' statements are "This cloth is all wool," "This paint is for household woodwork," and "This engine can produce 50 horsepower." A representation that an airplane is a 2007 model is an express warranty. "This computer monitor has a glare-proof screen" is another example of an express warranty.

The manufacturer of the goods cannot isolate itself from claims that are communicated through retailers. **For Example,** WorldWide Wholesalers could purchase Pop-Tarts from Kellogg's. Kellogg's makes warranties to WorldWide Wholesalers directly through their contract relationship, one of privity. WorldWide Wholesalers then sells those Pop-Tarts to grocery stores, convenience stores, and perhaps even to commercial food distributors who then sell them to cafeterias in schools and nursing homes. WorldWide's buyers are remote purchasers. The warranty is not lost through the distribution chain.

5. Form of Express Warranty

No particular group of words is necessary to constitute an express warranty. A seller need not state that a warranty is being made or that one is intended. It is sufficient that the seller asserts a fact that becomes a basis of the bargain or transaction between the parties. UCC §2-313(2) provides, "It is not necessary to the creation of an express warranty that the seller use formal words such as 'warrant' or 'guarantee' or that the seller have a specific intention to make a warranty."[6] If a warranty is a critical part of the bargain for the buyer, it cannot be disclaimed (see p. 2) 526.

An express warranty can be written or printed as well as oral. The words on the label of a can and in a newspaper ad for "boned chicken" constitute an express warranty that the can contains chicken that is free of bones.

Descriptions of goods, such as the illustrations in a seller's catalog, are express warranties. The express warranty given is that the goods will conform to the catalog illustrations.

---

[5] UCC §2-313; *Miles v. Raymond Corp.*, 612 F. Supp. 2d 913 (N.D. Oh. 2005). *Samsung Electronics America, Inc. v. Blu-Ray Class Action Litigation*, 2008 WL 5451024, 67 UCC Rep. Serv.2d 794 (D.N.J. 2008). In the UCC Revised Article 2, the "basis of the bargain" requirement is changed to "become part of the agreement." UCC §2-313(1)(a). Also, §2-404 is the new express warranty section.
[6] UCC §2-313(2).

6. Seller's Opinion or Statement of Value

A statement about the value of goods or the seller's opinion or commendation of the goods does not create a warranty.[7] Section 2-313(1)(b) provides, "an affirmation merely of the value of the goods or a statement purporting to be merely the seller's opinion or commendation of goods does not create a warranty."[8] A buyer cannot hold a seller liable for sales talk. **For Example,** sales talk or puffery by a seller that his cloth is "the best piece of cloth on the market" or that her glassware is "as good as anyone else's" is merely an opinion that the buyer cannot ordinarily treat as a warranty. Statements made by a cosmetics seller that its products are "the future of beauty" and are "just the product for [the plaintiff]" are sales talk arising in the ordinary course of merchandising. They do not constitute warranties.

The UCC does permit an exception to the sales talk liability exemption when the circumstances are such that a reasonable person would rely on such a statement. If the buyer has reason to believe that the seller has expert knowledge of the conditions of the market, and the buyer requests the seller's opinion as an expert, the buyer is entitled to accept as a fact the seller's statement of whether a particular good is the best obtainable. The opinion statement could be reasonably regarded as forming part of the basis of the bargain. A statement by a florist that bulbs are of first-grade quality may be a warranty.[9]

7. Warranty of Conformity to Description, Sample, or Model

When the contract is based in part on the understanding that the seller will supply goods according to a particular description or that the goods will be the same as the sample or a model, the seller is bound by an express warranty that the goods conform to the description, sample, or model.[10] Section 2-313 of the UCC provides, "Any sample or model which is made part of the basis of the bargain creates an express warranty that the whole of the goods shall conform to the sample or model."[11] **For Example,** a blender sitting out in a store is a warranty that the blenders in the boxes below are the same. A model of a mobile home is an express warranty that the mobile home being sold contains the same features.

8. Federal Regulation of Express Warranties

A seller who makes a written express warranty for a consumer product costing more than $10 must conform to certain standards imposed by federal statute[12] and by regulations of the Federal Trade Commission (FTC).[13] The seller is not required to make any express warranty. However, if the seller does make an express warranty in a consumer sale, it must be stated in ordinary, understandable language and must be

---

[7] Id.; *Giles v. Wyeth, Inc.*, 500 F. Supp. 2d 1063 (S.D. Ill. 2007); *In re Ford Motor Co. E-350 Van Products Liability Litigation*, 2008 WL 4126264, 66 UCC Rep. Serv.2d 726 (D.N.J. 2008).

[8] UCC §2-313(1)(b).

[9] Likewise, a statement by an art gallery owner that a "painting is by Francis Bacon" is an express warranty. *Rogath v. Siebenmann*, 129 F.3d 902 (7th Cir. 1997). See also *Forbes v. General Motors Corp.*, 935 So.2d 869 (Miss. 2006).

[10] *Harlan v. Roadtrek Motorhomes, Inc.*, 2009 WL 928309, 68 UCC Rep. Serv.2d 750 (S.D. Cal. 2009).

[11] UCC §2-313(1)(c).

[12] The Magnuson-Moss Act, or Federal Consumer Product Warranty Law, can be found at 15 U.S.C. §2301 *et seq.*

[13] 16 C.F.R. §700.1 *et seq.*

made available for inspection before purchasing so that the consumer may comparison shop.[14]

(A) FULL WARRANTIES. If the seller or the label states that a full warranty is made, the seller is obligated to fix or replace a defective product within a reasonable time without cost to the buyer. If the product cannot be fixed or if a reasonable number of repair attempts are unsuccessful, the buyer has the choice of a cash refund or a free replacement. No unreasonable burden may be placed on a buyer seeking to obtain warranty service. **For Example,** a manufacturer offering a full warranty cannot require that the buyer pay the cost of sending the product to or from a warranty service point. A warrantor making a full warranty cannot require the buyer to return the product to a warranty service point if the product weighs over 35 pounds, to return a part for service unless it can be easily removed, or to fill out and return a warranty registration card shortly after purchase to make the warranty effective. If the manufacturer imposes any of these requirements, the warranty is not a "full warranty" under federal law and must be labeled a *limited warranty*. A **full warranty** runs with the product and lasts for its full term regardless of who owns the product.

full warranty – obligation of a seller to fix or replace a defective product within a reasonable time without cost to the buyer.

(B) LIMITED WARRANTIES. A **limited warranty** is any warranty that does not meet the requirements for a full warranty. **For Example,** a warranty is limited if the buyer must pay any cost for repair or replacement of a defective product, if only the first buyer is covered by the warranty, or if the warranty covers only part of the product. A limited warranty must be conspicuously described as such by the seller.[15]

limited warranty – any warranty that does not provide the complete protection of a full warranty.

(C) INTERNATIONAL PRODUCT SAFETY LAWS IN THE UNITED STATES. In 2008, in response to the lead paint discovered in toys imported from China, Congress passed the **Consumer Product Safety Improvement Act (CPSIA),** which promulgated new standards for product safety.[16] Under CPSIA, the products most affected are those for children under the age of 12. The act provides no discretion for lead levels; it prohibits lead in products for children under 12. Because of the outsourcing issues that resulted in the toys with lead paint making their way into the United States, the CPSIA requires accredited third-party laboratory testing, product tracking, labels, registration, and new warnings in ads and on Web sites about the manufacturing sources of toys. CPSIA increases to $100 million the penalties the Consumer Product Safety Commission can assess.

Consumer Product Safety Improvement Act – federal law that sets standards for the types of paints used in toys; a response to the lead paint found in toys made in China; requires tracking for international production; increases penalties

9. Effect of Breach of Express Warranty

If an express warranty is false, there is a breach of warranty. The warrantor is then liable. It is no defense that the seller or manufacturer who made the express warranty honestly believed that the warranty was true, had exercised due care in manufacturing or handling the product, or had no reason to believe that the warranty was false.

---

[14] Federal warranty language rules apply only in consumer sales, or sales for personal or home use, not in business purchases. There are also state laws that can limit express warranties to the first purchaser. *McMahon v. Advance Stores Co. Inc.*, 705 S.E.2d 131 (W. Va. 2010).

[15] The federal regulations here do not preempt Article 2 warranty coverage. *Wyeth v. Levine*, 555 U.S. 555 (2009). However, FDA regulations can preempt recovery against generic manufacturers of drugs who must use FDA-approved labeling only and not include additional warnings. *PLIVA, Inc. v. Mensing*, 131 S.Ct. 2567 (2011).

[16] 15 U.S.C. §1278a

CASE SUMMARY

Fake Tiffany Lamps for $56,200 and a Disclaimer

FACTS: Richard W. La Trace attended an auction at B & B Antiques, Auction & Realty, a business owned and operated by Ray Webster, Deborah Webster, Bo Webster, and Laura Webster (collectively "the Websters"). La Trace purchased five lamps that were identified at the auction as "Tiffany" lamps and one lampshade that was also identified at the auction as a "Tiffany" product. La Trace spent a total of $56,200 on the lamps.

La Trace contacted Fontaine's Auction Gallery in Pittsfield, Massachusetts, to inquire about selling the lamps in an auction. Fontaine's sent Dean Lowry, an expert in Tiffany products, to examine La Trace's lamps and Lowry determined that the lamps were not authentic Tiffany products but were, in fact, reproductions. La Trace filed suit against the Websters and B & B for fraudulent suppression, fraudulent misrepresentation, breach of warranty, breach of contract, negligence, and wantonness.[17] The Websters claimed they thought the lamps were authentic and pointed out that their sales brochure and "Conditions of Auction" document contained the following disclaimer:

> *1. All property is sold AS IS WHERE IS, and we make NO guarantees, warranties or representations, expressed or implied, with respect to the property or the correctness of the catalog or other description of authenticity of authorship, physical condition, size, quality, rarity, importance, provenance, exhibitions, literature or historical relevance of the property or otherwise. No statement anywhere, whether oral or written, shall be deemed such a guarantee, warranty or representation.*

On a motion for summary judgment, the court found for the Websters, indicating that La Trace trusted blindly and should not have done so. La Trace appealed.

DECISION: The Websters' description of the lamps as "Tiffany" products became part of the basis of the bargain because the representations took place during the auction and were not accompanied by any qualifying statements indicating that the authenticity of the lamps was in doubt. Because it is assumed under the UCC that the object of every UCC-regulated sale is describable, the core description is nondisclaimable by a seller, being the basic foundation upon which every sales contract is made. The lamps here were sold with the core description of being Tiffany products. Although disclaimers in a sales brochure and a "Conditions of Auction" document may have been effective to prevent the formation of any express warranties that might otherwise have arisen in those documents, nothing in the language indicated that the disclaimer in the documents was effective to prevent a seller from making express warranties in the future. Judgment for La Trace. [*La Trace v. Webster***, 17 So.3d 1210 (Ala. Civ. App. 2008)**]

C. IMPLIED WARRANTIES

Whenever a sale of goods is made, certain warranties are implied unless they are expressly excluded. Implied warranties differ depending on whether the seller is a merchant.

---

[17] B & B was dismissed from the case because it had not yet been properly formed as an LLC. See Chapter 41 for more information on forming a business entity properly.

10. Definition of Implied Warranty

implied warranty – warranty that was not made but is implied by law.

An **implied warranty** is one that was not expressly made by the seller but that is implied in certain circumstances by law. An implied warranty arises automatically from the fact that a sale has been made regardless of the seller's conduct.

Express warranties arise because they form part of the basis on which the sale has been made. Implied warranties can exist independent of express warranties. When both express and implied warranties exist, they are interpreted as consistent, if possible. If the warranties cannot be applied together, then the express warranty prevails over any implied warranty except that an implied warranty of fitness for a particular purpose prevails over an express warranty.

11. Implied Warranties of Sellers

Sellers give different types of implied warranties.

CPA

(A) WARRANTY OF TITLE. Every seller, by the mere act of selling, makes an implied warranty that the seller's title to the goods is good and that the seller has the right to transfer title to the goods.[18]

warranty of title – implied warranty that title to the goods is good and transfer is proper.

The **warranty of title** may be disclaimed either by using the words, "There is no warranty of title," or by certain circumstances.[19] If a buyer has reason to know that the seller does not claim to hold the title or that the seller is limited in what can be promised, the warranty of title is disclaimed. **For Example,** no warranty of title arises when the seller makes the sale in a representative capacity, such as a sheriff, an auctioneer, or an administrator of a decedent's estate. Similarly, no warranty arises when the seller makes the sale as a creditor disposing of a debtor's collateral (security). The damages for warranty of title are often the purchase price because the buyer may have to surrender the goods to their rightful owner.[20]

warranty against encumbrances – warranty that there are no liens or other encumbrances to goods except those noted by seller.

(B) WARRANTY AGAINST ENCUMBRANCES. Every seller makes an implied **warranty against encumbrances,** that is, that the goods will be delivered free from any security interest or any other lien or encumbrance of which the buyer at the time of the sales transaction had no knowledge. If the seller sells an automobile to the buyer and then delivers a car with an outstanding lien on it that was unknown to the buyer at the time of the sale, there is a breach of the warranty against encumbrances.

CPA

(C) WARRANTY OF FITNESS FOR A PARTICULAR PURPOSE.[21] A buyer may intend to use the goods for a particular or unusual purpose, as contrasted with the ordinary use for which they are customarily sold. If the seller states that the goods will be fit for the buyer's purpose with the buyer relying on the seller's skill or judgment to select or furnish suitable goods, and the seller, at the time of contracting, knows or has reason to know of both the buyer's particular purpose and the buyer's reliance on the seller's judgment, then the seller has created an implied warranty of fitness for a particular purpose.[22] **For Example,** when the seller represents to a buyer that the two hamsters

[18] UCC §2-312. The key change in the language in Revised Article 2 is that the seller warrants that the buyer will not be subjected to unreasonable litigation.
[19] *Quality Components Corp. v. Kel-Keef Enterprises, Inc.,* 738 N.E.2d 524 (Ill. App. 2000).
[20] *Mayberry v. Volkswagen of America, Inc.,* 692 N.W.2d 226 (Wis. 2005).
[21] UCC §2-315. The warranty does not apply when the injury is not caused by any function represented for the product. For example, a buyer could not recover when she hit her head on a wall-mounted fire extinguisher, for the representations were that it would work for home fires, not about mounting it in the home. *Hayes v. Larsen Mfg. Co., Inc.,* 871 F. Supp. 56 (D. Me. 1996).
[22] UCC §2-315. *Nationwide Agribusiness Ins. Co. v. SMA Elevator Const. Inc.,* 816 F. Supp. 2d 631 (N.D. Iowa 2011).

being sold are of the same gender and can safely occupy the same cage with no offspring, an implied warranty of fitness has been given. When the buyer makes the purchase without relying on the seller's skill and judgment, no warranty of fitness for a particular purpose arises.[23]

CPA ## 12. Additional Implied Warranties of Merchant Sellers

A seller who deals in goods of the kind in question is classified as a merchant by the UCC and is held to a higher degree of responsibility for the product than one who is merely making a casual sale.

(A) WARRANTY AGAINST INFRINGEMENT. Unless otherwise agreed, every merchant seller warrants that the goods will be delivered free of the rightful claim of any third person by way of patent, copyright, or trademark infringement.

For Example, if a buyer purchases videos from a seller who is later discovered to be a bootlegger of the films on the videos, the buyer has a cause of action against the seller for any damages he experiences for perhaps renting out the bootlegged videos. Under Revised Article 2, the seller can disclaim the warranty against infringement.

E-Commerce & Cyberlaw

"Wii" Were Hurt

Nintendo's "Wii" video game system features games with simulation of tennis and boxing. To play the game, the players use a motion-sensitive controller in their hand. When playing the game, some players, in making the motions necessary for the sport, have lost control of their controllers. The controllers have crashed into other objects, including television sets, and then injured the players. Players who have been so injured brought a class action suit against Nintendo for a defective wrist strap on the controllers, designed to keep the controllers from flying out of control. Although the class action was not certified, the court held that there could be remedies on an individual basis for problems with the design of the physical equipment used with computers. [*Elvig v. Nintendo of America, Inc.*, 696 F. Supp. 2d 1207 (D.Colo. 2010)].

implied warranty of merchantability – group of promises made by the seller, the most important of which is that the goods are fit for the ordinary purposes for which they are sold.

(B) WARRANTY OF MERCHANTABILITY OR FITNESS FOR NORMAL USE. A merchant seller makes an **implied warranty of the merchantability** of the goods sold.[24] This warranty is a group of promises, the most important of which is that the goods are fit for the ordinary purposes for which they are sold. This warranty, unless disclaimed, is given in every sale of goods by a merchant. Section 2-314 provides, "Unless excluded or modified, a warranty that the goods shall be merchantable is implied in a contract for their sale if the seller is a merchant with respect to goods of that kind."[25]

---

[23] *Berge Helene Ltd. v. GE Oil & Gas, Inc.*, 830 F. Supp. 2d 235 (S.D. Tex. 2011). Manufacturing to buyer's specifications precludes recovery for breach of the warranty of fitness for a particular purpose. *Simmons v. Washing Equipment Technologies* 857 N.Y.S.2d 412 (2008).

[24] UCC §2-314; *Lawson v. Hale*, 902 N.E.2d 267 (Ind. App. 2009); *Trujillo v. Apple Computer, Inc.*, 581 F. Supp. 2d 935 (N.D. Ill. 2008); limited battery life is not a breach of the implied warranty of merchantability.

[25] UCC §2-314. Revised Article 2 makes only one change as follows: "(c) are fit for the ordinary purposes for which [deleted word *such* here] goods [added following phrase] *of that description* are used... ." The comment explains the change: "The phrase 'goods of that description' rather than 'for which such goods are used' is used in subsection (2)(c). This emphasizes the importance of the agreed description in determining fitness for ordinary purposes."

CASE SUMMARY

When the AV Guys Get It Wrong

FACTS: From February through July 2004, Oheka Management, Inc. purchased an audiovisual system from Home Theatre Interiors for $86,000, which included installation of said audiovisual equipment. The system was required to be operational for an event scheduled for July 18, 2004 at Oheka.

Home Theater Interiors did not properly install or maintain the system. Ohkea was left with no alternative but to hire other technicians to complete the set-up and to repair any improper servicing and installations.

Home Theater Interiors argues that it was Oheka's architect, Richard Diller, who caused the problems with the system and its installation. Additionally, Home Theater maintains that because there was no signed contract for the system, Home Theater could not breach it or any warranties. However, the unsigned contract discussed the variety of audiovisual equipment that Oheka purchased from Home Theatre, as well as the installation that Home Theatre would perform. The unsigned contract contained a warranty for on-site parts and labor for this job which was to run for one year's time from date of purchase. Oheka moved for summary judgment for breach of warranty and breach of contract.

DECISION: The court held that the contract was covered under UCC despite its service component. The court also held that an unsigned contract was not controlling. The parties behaved as if there were a contract and the fact that there was no signature does not mean there was no contract or warranties. Exceptions to the documentation requirement for contracts include both parties behaving as if a contract exists. The court also held that Home Theater Interiors gave an implied warranty of merchantability—that a home theater should do the things it was designed to do, including being a working system in the room. [*Oheka Management, Inc. v. Home Theater Interiors, LLC*, 2007 WL 3325861 (N.Y. Supp.)]

13. Implied Warranties in Particular Sales

Particular types of sales may involve special considerations in terms of the seller's liability and the buyer's rights.

(A) SALE ON BUYER'S SPECIFICATIONS. When the buyer furnishes the seller with exact specifications for the preparation or manufacture of goods, the same warranties arise as in the case of any other sale of such goods by the particular seller. No warranty of fitness for a particular purpose can arise, however. It is clear that the buyer is purchasing on the basis of the buyer's own decision and is not relying on the seller's skill and judgment. Similarly, the manufacturer is not liable for loss caused by a design defect.[26]

(B) SALE OF SECONDHAND OR USED GOODS. Under the UCC, there is a warranty of merchantability in the sale of both new and used goods unless it is specifically disclaimed. However, with respect to used goods, what is considered "fit for normal use" under the warranty of merchantability will be a lower standard. Some courts still follow their pre-Code law under which no warranties of fitness arise in the sale of used goods.

---

[26] *Hallday v. Sturm, Ruger, & Co., Inc.*, 792 A.2d 1145 (Md. App. 2002).

CPA

(c) Sale of Food or Drink. The implied warranty of merchantability also applies to the purchase of food in grocery stores and restaurants. The food sold must be of average quality and fit for its ordinary purpose, which is consumption by humans.[27] **For Example,** the types of restaurant and grocery store cases brought under the warranty of merchantability include those in which the buyer or customer finds foreign substances such as grasshoppers in a can of baked beans.[28]

The application of this warranty to food cases becomes more complex when it is not a nail in a can of crabmeat, but crab shell in a can of crabmeat, or a cherry pit in the cherries of a McDonald's cherry pie. Some courts refuse to impose warranty liability if the thing in the food that caused the harm was naturally present, such as crab shell in crabmeat, prune stones in stewed prunes, or bones in canned fish. Other courts reject this foreign substance/natural substance liability test. They hold that there is liability if the seller does not deliver to the buyer goods of the character that the buyer reasonably expected. Under this view, there is a breach of the implied warranty of fitness for normal use if the buyer reasonably expected the food to be free of harm-causing natural things, such as shells and bones that could cause harm.[29]

CASE SUMMARY

Digging for Teeth among the Clams

FACTS: On April 11, 1996, Sandra Mitchell was having dinner at T.G.I. Friday's restaurant (hereinafter "Friday's"). Ms. Mitchell was eating a fried clam strip when she bit into a hard substance that she believed to be a piece of a clam shell. She experienced immediate pain and later sought dental treatment. Some time later, the crown of a tooth came loose. It was determined that the crown could not be reattached, and the remaining root of the tooth was extracted.

Ms. Mitchell filed a product liability action against Friday's, which served the meal, and Pro Source Distributing, the supplier of the fried clams. Both Friday's and Pro Source filed motions for summary judgment, which the trial court granted without explanation. Ms. Mitchell appealed.

DECISION: Two tests can be used for determining whether there should be recovery. One is the "foreign-natural test;" in this case, a clam shell is a natural part of eating clams. The other test is the "reasonable expectation test," and the court ruled that someone eating clams, even fried clams, should reasonably expect that shells might be part of the experience.

The possible presence of a piece of oyster shell in or attached to an oyster is so well known to anyone who eats oysters that all should reasonably anticipate and guard against eating such a piece of shell. The court held that, as a matter of law, one who eats clams can reasonably anticipate and guard against eating a piece of shell. [*Mitchell v. T.G.I. Friday's,* **748 N.E.2d 89 (Ohio App. 2000)**]

---

[27] *Summers v. Max & Erma's Restaurant, Inc.,* 2008 WL 3822437, 66 UCC Rep. Serv. 2d 664 (Ohio App. 2008).
[28] *Metty v. Shurfine Central Corporation,* 736 S.W.2d 527 (Mo. 1987).
[29] A new type of test for the food cases is called the "duty risk analysis" rule, in which the court examines the injury in light of the risk that comes from the failure to process the items out of the food and weighs that risk with the cost of the processing. *Porteous v. St. Ann's Cafe´ & Deli,* 713 So.2d 454 (La. 1998). Note that the case is from Louisiana, the nation's non-UCC state.

14. Necessity of Defect

To impose liability for breach of the implied warranty of merchantability, the buyer must show that the product is defective and that defect caused harm. A product may be defective because there is (1) a manufacturing defect, (2) a design defect, (3) inadequate instruction on how to use the product, or (4) inadequate warning against dangers involved in using the product.

For Example, if the manufacturer's blueprint shows that there should be two bolts at a particular place and the factory puts in only one bolt, there is a manufacturing defect. If the two bolts are put in but the product breaks because four bolts are required to provide sufficient strength, there is no manufacturing defect, but there is a design defect. A product that is properly designed and properly manufactured may be dangerous because the user is not given sufficient instructions on how to use the product. Also, a product is defective if there is a danger that is not obvious and there is no warning at all or a warning that does not describe the full danger.[30]

15. Warranties in the International Sale of Goods

The warranties of both merchantability and fitness for a particular purpose exist under the Convention on Contracts for the International Sale of Goods (CISG). In most cases, the provisions are identical to those of the UCC. Sellers, however, can expressly disclaim the convention's warranties without mentioning merchantability or making the disclaimer conspicuous.

Thinking Things Through

What's Foreign to You ...

Based on the discussion and the *T. G. I. Friday's* case, decide which of the following would be considered a breach of the implied warranty of merchantability:

Customer ordered "pecan chicken" from T.G.I. Friday's, described on the menu as chicken with "a breaded mixture of pecans and bread crumbs." He broke a tooth when he bit into a pecan shell that was in the breading. *[Carlton v. T.G.I. Friday's, 2006 WL 5129475 (Ohio Com. Pl.)]*

Customer suffered an injury to the throat as a result of a bone in a chicken sandwich getting stuck in his throat. *[Ruvolo v. Homovich, 778 N.E.2d 661 (Ohio App. 2002)]*

Customer bit into a Baby Ruth candy bar, manufactured by Standard Brands, that contained a "snake bone (vertebrae)" and the customer experienced severe psychological difficulty. *[Gates v. Standard Brands Inc., 719 P.2d 130 (Wash. App. 1986)]*

Standard Candy manufacturers the Goo Goo Cluster candy bar, featuring peanuts from Jimbo's. James Newton purchased a Goo Goo, and when he bit into it, he bit down on an undeveloped peanut. The result was a broken tooth. *[Newton v. Standard Candy Co., 2008 WL 752599 (D.Neb.)]*

CPA D. DISCLAIMER OF WARRANTIES

The seller and the buyer may ordinarily agree that there will be no warranties. In some states, disclaimers of warranties are prohibited for reasons of public policy or consumer protection.

---

[30] *Red Hill Hosiery Mill, Inc. v. Magnetek, Inc.* 582 S.E.2d 632 (N.C. Ct. App. 2003). Following government standards does not mean a product is without defect.

16. Validity of Disclaimer

Warranties may be disclaimed by agreement of the parties, subject to the limitation that such a provision must not be unconscionable, must be conspicuous, and in certain cases must use certain language.[31]

(A) CONSPICUOUSNESS. A disclaimer provision is made conspicuous when it appears in a record under a conspicuous heading that indicates there is an exclusion or modification of warranties. A heading cannot be relied on to make such a provision conspicuous when the heading is misleading and wrongfully gives the impression there is a warranty. **For Example,** the heading "Vehicle Warranty" is misleading if the provision that follows contains a limitation of warranties. A disclaimer that is hidden in a mass of materials or records handed to the buyer is not conspicuous and is not effective to exclude warranties. Similarly, an inconspicuous disclaimer of warranties under a posted notice of "Notice to Retail Buyers" has no effect.

When a disclaimer of warranties fails because it is not conspicuous, the implied warranties apply to the buyer.[32]

(B) UNCONSCIONABILITY AND PUBLIC POLICY. An exclusion of warranties made in the manner specified by the UCC is not unconscionable. In some states, warranty disclaimers are invalid because they are contrary to public policy or because they are prohibited by consumer protection laws.

17. Particular Language for Disclaimers

To waive the warranty of merchantability, the record must contain the following language: "The seller undertakes no responsibility for the quality of the goods except as otherwise provided in this contract."[33] The required language for waiving the warranty of fitness for a particular purpose is as follows: "The seller assumes no responsibility that the goods will be fit for any particular purpose for which you may be buying these goods, except as otherwise provided in the contract."[34]

In consumer contracts, the use of terms such as "as is" can also disclaim both of these warranties, as it does for merchant transactions, but the disclaimers must be in the record and must be conspicuously set forth in that record.

Figure 25-1 provides a summary of the warranties under Article 2 and the methods for making disclaimers.

18. Exclusion of Warranties by Examination of Goods

For an inspection of goods by the buyer to constitute a waiver, the seller must demand that the buyer inspect the goods as part of the contracting process. The seller may not use inspection as a defense to warranty issues if that demand was not made at the time the parties contracted.[35]

19. Post-sale Disclaimer

Frequently, a statement purporting to exclude or modify warranties appears for the first time in a written contract sent to confirm or memorialize an oral contract made

---

[31] UCC §2-316; In re *Rafter Seven Ranches LP*, 546 F.3d 1194 (10th Cir. 2008).
[32] A warranty disclaimer written in all caps just below the signature line is conspicuous. *Semitekol v. Monaco Coach Corp.*, 582 F. Supp. 2d 1009 (N.D. III. 2008).
[33] UCC §2-316(2). If the seller undertakes to repair the goods after their exclusion, the waiver becomes null. *Sabbath v. Martin*, 2009 WL 3449096 (La. App. 2009).
[34] *Id.*
[35] Revised UCC §2-316(3)(b).

FIGURE 25-1 | *UCC Warranties*

NAME OF WARRANTY	CREATION	RESTRICTION	DISCLAIMER
EXPRESS	AFFIRMATION OF FACT, PROMISE OF PERFORMANCE (INCLUDES SAMPLES, MODELS, DESCRIPTIONS)	MUST BE PART OF THE BASIS OF THE BARGAIN	CANNOT MAKE A DISCLAIMER INCONSISTENT WITH AN EXPRESS WARRANTY
IMPLIED WARRANTY OF MERCHANTABILITY	GIVEN IN EVERY SALE OF GOODS BY A MERCHANT ("FIT FOR ORDINARY PURPOSES")	ONLY GIVEN BY MERCHANTS	MUST USE STATUTORY LANGUAGE DISCLAIMER OF "AS IS" OR "WITH ALL FAULTS"; MUST BE CONSPICUOUS IN THE RECORD
IMPLIED WARRANTY OF FITNESS FOR A PARTICULAR PURPOSE	SELLER KNOWS OF BUYER'S RELIANCE FOR A PARTICULAR USE (BUYER IS IGNORANT)	SELLER MUST HAVE KNOWLEDGE; BUYER MUST RELY ON SELLER	(1) MUST HAVE A RECORD (2) MUST BE CONSPICUOUS (3) ALSO DISCLAIMED WITH "AS IS" OR "WITH ALL FAULTS"
TITLE	GIVEN IN EVERY SALE	DOES NOT APPLY IN CIRCUMSTANCES WHERE APPARENT WARRANTY IS NOT GIVEN	MUST SAY "THERE IS NO WARRANTY OF TITLE"
MAGNUSON-MOSS (FEDERAL CONSUMER PRODUCT WARRANTY LAW)	ONLY CONSUMER PRODUCTS OF $10 OR MORE	MUST LABEL "FULL" OR "LIMITED"	

earlier. The exclusion or modification may likewise appear in an invoice, a bill, or an instruction manual delivered to the buyer at or after the time the goods are received. Such postsale disclaimers have no effect on warranties that arose at the time of the sale.

E. OTHER THEORIES OF PRODUCT LIABILITY

In addition to recovery for breach of an express guarantee, an express warranty, or an implied warranty, a plaintiff in a given product liability case may be able to recover for negligence, fraud, or strict tort liability.

CPA

20. Negligence

negligence—failure to exercise due care under the circumstances that results in harm proximately caused to one owed a duty to exercise due care.

A person injured because of the defective condition of a product may be entitled to recover from the seller or manufacturer for the damages for **negligence.** The injured person must be able to show that the seller was negligent in the preparation or manufacture of the article or failed to provide proper instructions and warnings of dangers. An action for negligence rests on common law tort principles. Negligence does not require privity of contract.

21. Fraud

The UCC expressly preserves the pre-Code law governing fraud. A person defrauded by a distributor's or manufacturer's false statements about a product generally will be able to recover damages for the harm sustained because of such misrepresentations. False statements are fraudulent if the party who made them did so with knowledge that they were false or with reckless indifference to their truthfulness.

CPA

22. Strict Tort Liability

Strict tort liability exists without regard to whether the person injured is a purchaser, a consumer, or a third person, such as a bystander.[36] It is no defense that privity of contract does not exist between the injured party and the defendant. Likewise, it is no defense that the defect was found in a component part purchased from another manufacturer.[37] **For Example,** defective tires sold on a new car were probably purchased from a tire supplier by the auto manufacturer. However, the manufacturer is not excused from liability.

Strict tort liability requires that the defect in the product exist at the time it left the control of the manufacturer or distributor. The defective condition is defined in the same way as under negligence: defective by manufacturing error or oversight, defective by design, or defective by the failure to warn.[38] There is liability if the product is defective and unreasonably dangerous and has caused harm. It is immaterial whether the seller was negligent or whether the user was contributorily negligent. Knowledge of the defect is not a requirement for liability. Assumption of risk by the injured party, on the other hand, is a defense available to the seller.[39]

CASE SUMMARY

"Towing the Line" on Warnings

FACTS: Ginger Smith was a passenger on a Ronald Smith's boat on West Point Lake, Alabama. Ronald Smith (no relation to Ginger) was operating the boat, which was towing Ms. Smith's son, Shane McClellan, on an inflatable inner tube behind the boat. Shane McClellan weighed 150 pounds at the time and the tube itself weighed 5 to 10 pounds. The inner tube was tied to

---

[36] The concept of strict tort liability was judicially declared in *Greenman v. Yuba Power Products*, 377 P.2d 897 (Cal. 1963). This concept has been incorporated in the Restatement (Second) and (Third) of Torts as §402A.
[37] *Ford v. Beam Radiator, Inc.*, 708 So.2d 1158 (La. App. 1998).
[38] *Lewis v. Ariens*, 751 N.E.2d 862 (Mass. 2011).
[39] *Clark v. Mazda Motor Corp.*, 68 P.3d 207 (Ok. 2003).

CASE SUMMARY

Continued

the boat by a 50-foot Model 51650 polypropylene line that was manufactured by Lehigh Consumer Products, LLC, but carried the label of The Coleman Company (defendants) pursuant to a licensing arrangement and was purchased at a nearby Wal-Mart store. While Shane McClellan was being towed on the inner tube, the line snapped, and the end connected to the boat flew back toward the boat and hit Ms. Smith in the eye, causing the loss of that eye.

The packaging of the line contained several statements. A paper insert identifies it as a "50 ft × 5/16 in UTILITY LINE." Just below that appears the phrase "Ideal for use on boat or dock." Still farther down the insert, and in an all-caps font smaller than that used in the first statement, appears, divided over two lines, "175 LBS WORKING LOAD LIMIT/STAYS AFLOAT." A longer cautionary message appears at the bottom of the insert. It states:

> *Avoid using a knot, splicing is preferable. Knots reduce the strength of the rope up to 40%. Do not use this product where personal safety could be endangered. Never stand in line with a rope under tension. Such a rope, particularly nylon rope, may recoil (snap back). Misuse can result in serious injury or death.*

Ms. Smith filed suit against Coleman, Wal-Mart, and Ronald Smith. (Wal-Mart and Smith were dismissed from the case.) Coleman moved for summary judgment because of the warnings.

DECISION: The court concluded that the statements on the package were warnings despite the fact that there was no labeling such as "WARNING" in that area of the packaging. The content of the warnings was also sufficient. Two of the three warnings were quite specific, and both were violated by Mr. Smith. Mr. Smith tied knots in the rope in order to attach it to the boat and the inner tube. Both Mr. Smith and Ms. Smith were onboard the open boat towing the inner tube behind it; in the ordinary use of language, they were both standing "in line with a rope under tension."

The court held that it is difficult to conceive how the rope could ever be used for towing someone behind an open boat without both the person being towed and persons onboard the boat violating the warning against standing in line with a rope under tension.

The statement that the line was "ideal for use on boat or dock" does not constitute an express warranty. Statements "that are mere sales talk or 'puffery' do not give rise to express warranties," while "representations of fact" may give rise to such warranties. The word "ideal" seems closer to the description of an item as "in good shape," something that Alabama courts have found to constitute "puffery,"....

The final warranty claim for breach of an implied warranty of fitness for a particular purpose was not established. The Smiths clearly did not "rely on the seller's skill or judgment to select or furnish suitable goods." Rather, Mr. Smith selected and purchased the utility line for himself at a Wal-Mart store. Summary judgment was granted for the defendants. [**Smith v. Coleman Co., 71 UCC Rep. Serv. 2d 131 (M.D. Ala. 2010)**]

23. Cumulative Theories of Liability

The theories of product liability are not mutually exclusive. A given set of facts may give rise to two or more theories of liability. **For Example,** suppose that a manufacturer advertises, "Coaches! Protect your players' eyes! Shatterproof sunglasses for baseball." If the glasses shattered and injured a player, an express warranty, implied warranty, implied warranty for a particular purpose, and strict tort liability could apply for recovery.

CASE SUMMARY

A Steely Force in Baseball

FACTS: While pitching in an American Legion baseball game on July 25, 2003, 18-year-old Brandon Patch was struck in the head by a batted ball that was hit using Hillerich & Bradsby's (H & B) model CB–13 aluminum bat. Tragically, Brandon died from his injuries.

The Patches brought suit against H & B for the wrongful death of their son on the grounds that the CB–13 aluminum bat was in a defective condition because of the enhanced risks associated with its use: It increased the velocity speed of a batted ball when it left the bat, thus decreasing infielders' reaction times, and resulted in a greater number of high-energy batted balls in the infield. Some studies note that the average time needed for a pitcher to react to a batted ball is .4 seconds. Analysis of the sound recording from the game confirmed that the reaction time available to Brandon to turn away or defend himself was only .376 of a second.

Before trial, the District Court granted H & B's motion for summary judgment on Patches' manufacturing defect claim, but denied summary judgment on Patches' design defect and failure-to-warn claims. The trial court excluded H & B's assumption of the risk defense. The jury concluded that the model CB–13 aluminum bat was not designed defectively, but determined that the bat was in a defective condition due to H & B's failure to warn of the enhanced risks associated with its use. The jury awarded the Patches an $850,000 verdict on their failure-to-warn claim. H & B appealed.

DECISION: Brandon was still a user or consumer for purposes of strict tort liability, where privity is not an issue. H & B could be held liable for the failure to warn because, although difficult to reach so many, the standard is one tied to the degree of danger. The warning could come through public notices and ads or just general information on the use of aluminum bats. Although Brandon assumed the risks inherent in baseball, the risks with aluminum bats are much greater and required disclosure before that assumption could be assumed. [***Patch v. Hillerich & Bradsby Co.***, **257 P.3d 383 (Mont. 2011)**]

Ethics & the Law

The Paintball Gun From the Pawn Shop

John Clark purchased a paintball gun at a pawn shop and then participated in a community sport of shooting paintball guns at cars. While John and his friend were riding around their small town with their paintball guns, they spotted Chris and shot his car. Chris Rico then aimed his Brass Eagle paintball gun at the car John was riding in, but instead hit John in the eye. John required surgery on his eye that evening and filed suit against Brass Eagle under a theory of strict tort liability. Brass Eagle responded by stating that its gun was not defective and that the young men had ignored warnings about the need to wear eye protection when using the guns. John said he purchased his gun used and was not given all the packaging and instructions. Brass Eagle says that its gun was not defective and that it functioned as it was supposed to. John says the guns are inherently dangerous. Who should be responsible for the injury? Are paintball guns defective if they can harm individuals? How should the courts allocate the risk and loss on products such as these? [*Clark v. Brass Eagle, Inc.*, 866 So.2d 456 (Miss. 2004)]

MAKE THE CONNECTION

SUMMARY

Five theories protect parties from loss caused by nonconforming goods: (1) express warranty, (2) implied warranty, (3) negligence, (4) fraud, and (5) strict tort liability.

Theories of product liability are not mutually exclusive. A given set of facts may give rise to liability under two or more theories.

The requirement of privity of contract (that is, the parties to the sales contract for warranty liability) has been widely rejected. The law is moving toward the conclusion that persons harmed because of an improper product may recover from anyone who is in any way responsible. The requirement of privity has been abolished by most states, and remote buyers as well as their families, members of their households, and guests are covered under the UCC warranties.

Warranties may be express or implied. The types of implied warranties are the warranty of title, the implied warranty of merchantability, and the implied warranty of fitness for a particular purpose. The warranty of title provides that the transfer is lawful, the title is good, and there are no infringement issues. Under Revised Article 2, the warranty of title also protects the buyer against unreasonable litigation. The warranty of merchantability is given by merchants and warrants that the goods are of average quality and will do what those types of goods commonly can do. The implied warranty of fitness for a particular purpose is given in those circumstances in which the buyer relies on the seller's expertise and the seller is aware of that reliance and offers a recommendation on the types of goods.

Express warranties arise from statements of fact and promises of performance made by the seller to the buyer that become a part of the basis for the buyer contracting. Express warranties arise from samples, models, and descriptions.

Warranties may be disclaimed by agreement of the parties provided the disclaimer is not unconscionable. Merchants can have oral disclaimers, but for consumers, warranty disclaimers must be in a record and must be conspicuous. Also for consumers, certain language must be used to disclaim each type of warranty. However, for both merchants and nonmerchants, the use of terms such as "as is" or "with all faults" can disclaim both the warranty of merchantability and the implied warranty of fitness for a particular purpose (although for consumers, there must still be a record and the language must be conspicuous).

The warranties of merchantability and fitness exist under the CISG. However, disclaimers under the CISG need not mention merchantability, nor must such disclaimers be conspicuous.

The strict tort liability plaintiff must show that there was a defect in the product at the time it left the control of the defendant. No negligence need be established on the part of the defendant, nor is the plaintiff's contributory negligence a defense. If negligence is established, however, knowledge by the seller can result in punitive damages. The defendant may show that the injured party assumed the risk.

LEARNING OUTCOMES

After studying this chapter, you should be able to clearly explain:

A. General Principles

L0.1 List the theories of product liability
See the five theories discussed in the "Theories of Liability" section on p. 516.

L0.2 Identify who may sue and who may be sued when a defective product causes harm
See the discussion of privity on p. 517.

B. Express Warranties

L0.3 Define and give examples of an express warranty
See *La Trace v. Webster* on p. 521.
See *Smith v. Coleman* on pp. 529–530.

C. Implied Warranties

L0.4 List and explain the types of implied warranties
See *Oheka Management, Inc. v. Home Theater Interiors* on p. 524.
See *Mitchell v. T.G.I. Friday's* on p. 525.

L0.5 Explain warranty protections under federal law
See the discussion of the Consumer Product Safety Improvement Act (CPSIA) on p. 520.

L0.6 State what constitutes a breach of warranty
See *Patch v. Hillerich & Bradsby Co.* on p. 531.

D. Disclaimer of Warranties

L0.7 Describe the extent and manner in which implied warranties may be disclaimed under the UCC and the CISG

E. Other Theories of Product Liability

See the *For Example*, discussion of the use of the term "Vehicle Warranty" in the "Conspicuousness" section on p. 527.
See the "Ethics & the Law" discussion of paintball guns on p. 531.

KEY TERMS

Consumer Product Safety Improvement Act (CPSIA)
express warranty
full warranty
implied warranty of the merchantability

implied warranty
limited warranty
negligence
privity of contract
privity

strict tort liability
warranties
warranty against encumbrances
warranty of title

QUESTIONS AND CASE PROBLEMS

1. Maria Gonzalez lived in a rental unit with her sons in Queens, New York. The hot water supplied to their apartment was heated by a Morflo water heater, which had a temperature control device on its exterior manufactured by Robertshaw and sold to Morflo. Maria Garcia, the owner of the Gonzalezes' apartment, had purchased and installed the water heater. The Morflo heater was located in the basement of the apartment house, which was locked and inaccessible to tenants.

Extensive warnings were on the water heater itself and in the manual given to Garcia at the time of her purchase. The warning on the Robertshaw temperature device read: "CAUTION: Hotter water increases the risk of scald injury." The heater itself contained a picture of hot water coming from a faucet with the word "DANGER" printed above it. In addition, the water heater had a statement on it: "Water temperature over 120 degrees Fahrenheit can cause severe burns instantly or death from scalds. Children, disabled, and elderly are at highest risk of being scalded. Feel water before bathing or showering. Temperature limiting valves are available, see manual."

In the Morflo manual, the following warning appeared:

> *DANGER! The thermostat is adjusted to its lowest temperature position when shipped from the factory. Adjusting the thermostat past the 120 degree Fahrenheit bar on the temperature dial will increase the risk of scald injury. The normal position is approximately 120 degrees Fahrenheit.*
>
> *DANGER: WARNING: Hot water can produce first degree burns in 3 seconds at 140 degrees Fahrenheit (60 degrees Celsius), in 20 seconds at 130 degrees Fahrenheit (54 degrees Celsius), in 8 minutes at 120 degrees Fahrenheit (49 degrees Celsius).*

On October 1, 1992, 15-month-old Angel Gonzalez was being bathed by his 15-year-old brother, Daniel. When the telephone rang, Daniel left Angel alone in the bathtub. No one else was at home with the boys, and Daniel left the water running. Angel was scalded by the water that came from the tap. Angel and his mother brought suit against Morflo and Robertshaw, alleging defects in the design of the water heater and the failure to warn. Should they recover? [*Gonzalez v. Morflo Industries, Inc.*, 931 F. Supp. 159 (E.D.N.Y.)]

2. Paul Parrino purchased from Dave's Professional Wheelchair Service a wheelchair manufactured by 21st Century Scientific, Inc. The sales brochure from 21st Century Scientific stated that the wheelchair would "serve [the buyer] well for many years to come." Parrino had problems with the wheelchair within a few years and filed suit against Dave's and 21st Century for breach of express warranty. Both defended on the grounds that the statement on years of service was puffery, not an express warranty. Are they right? [*Parrino v. Sperling*, 648 N.Y.S.2d 702]

3. Jane Jackson purchased a sealed can of Katydids, chocolate-covered pecan caramel candies manufactured by NestlT. Shortly after, Jackson bit into one of the candies and allegedly broke a tooth on a pecan shell embedded in the candy. She filed a complaint, asserting breach of implied warranty. How would you argue on behalf of the company? How would you argue on behalf of Jackson? In your answer, discuss both the reasonable expectation test and the foreign substance/natural substance test. [*Jackson v. NestlT-Beich, Inc.*, 589 N.E.2d 547 (Ill. App.)]

4. Webster ordered a bowl of fish chowder at the Blue Ship Tea Room. She was injured by a fish bone in the chowder, and she sued the tea room for breach of the implied warranty of merchantability. The evidence at trial showed that when chowder is made, the entire boned fish is cooked. Should she recover? [*Webster v. Blue Ship Tea Room*, 198 N.E.2d 309 (Mass.)]

5. Andy's Sales (owned by Andy Adams) sold a well-built trampoline to Carl and Shirley Wickers. The Wickerses later sold the trampoline to Herbert Bryant. While using the trampoline, Herbert's 14-year-old nephew, Rex, sustained injuries that left him a quadriplegic. Rex's guardian filed suit for breach of express warranty and merchantability. The sales brochure for the round trampoline described it as "safe" because it had a "uniform bounce" and "natural tendency to work the jumper toward the center." The Wickerses had purchased an oval-shaped trampoline. Discuss Rex's ability to recover. Is privity an issue? [*Bryant v. Adams*, 448 S.E.2d 832 (N.C. App.)]

6. Advent purchased ink from Borden. On the labels of the ink drums delivered to Advent, Borden had imprinted in one-sixteenth-inch type in all caps:

> *SELLER MAKES NO WARRANTY, EXPRESS OR IMPLIED, CONCERN- ING THE PRODUCT OR THE*

MERCHANTABILITY OR FITNESS
THEREOF FOR ANY PURPOSE CON-
CERNING THE ACCURACY OF ANY
INFORMATION PROVIDED BY
BORDEN.

This language was printed beneath the
following:

BORDEN PRINTING INKS—"ZERO
DEFECTS: THAT'S OUR GOAL"

All of the printing was in boldface type. The
disclaimer was also printed on the sales invoice
and on the reverse side of the Borden form, but
there was nothing on the front to call attention
to the critical nature of the terms on the back
because there were simply capital letters reading
"SEE REVERSE SIDE." All of the terms on
the back were in boldface and although the
disclaimer was the first of 19 paragraphs, nothing
distinguished it from the other 18 paragraphs of
detailed contract terms.

Advent said that Borden failed to age the black
ink that it purchased with the result that the ink
separated in Advent's printing machines. Advent
refused to pay for the ink and wrote to Borden
explaining that it would not tender payment
because the ink was defective and demanding
that Borden reimburse it for its lost profits from
the downtime of printing machines. The trial
court held that Borden had disclaimed any and
all warranties on the ink and Advent appealed.
What would you decide about the disclaimer and
why? [*Borden, Inc. v. Advent Ink Co.*, 701 A.2d
255 (Pa. Sup.)]

7. Avery purchased a refrigerator from a retail store.
The written contract stated that the refrigerator
was sold "as is" and that the warranty of
merchantability and all warranties of fitness were
excluded. This was stated in large capital letters
printed just above the line on which Avery
signed her name. The refrigerator worked properly
for a few weeks and then stopped. The store refused
to do anything about it because of the exclusion
of the warranties made by the contract. Avery
claimed that this exclusion was not binding because
it was unconscionable. Was Avery correct? [*Avery v.
Aladdin Products Div., Nat'l Service Industries, Inc.*,
196 S.E.2d 357 (Ga. App.)]

8. James Jelinek purchased Hytest BMR Sorghum
Sudan grass seed, which was produced and
marketed by Land O'Lakes. Land O'Lakes
warranted the seed to be free from defects and
expressly warranted that by using normal farming
practices and proper maintenance, Mr. Jelinek
would obtain yields of 4 1/2 tons per acre. The
seed resulted in reduced yields and an inferior
quality crop. As a result, Mr. Jelinek was not able
to sell his crop and had significant economic
losses. Mr. Jelinek filed suit for breach of express
warranty. Is the promise of a crop yield an
express warranty? Explain your answer. [*Jelinek v.
Land O'Lakes, Inc.*, 797 N.W.2d 289 (Neb.
App.)]

9. Brianna Kriefall, a child, died after she ate meat
at a Sizzler restaurant that was later found to
contain *E. coli*. Her family brought suit against
Sizzler USA to recover for the loss of their
daughter. Is Sizzler liable for the death? Explain
your answer. What would be the liability of
Sizzler's meat supplier in the case? [*Estate of
Kriefall v. Sizzler USA Franchise, Inc.*, 801
N.W.2d 781 (Wis. App.)]

10. Zogarts manufactured and sold a practice device
for beginning golfers. According to statements on
the package, the device was completely safe, and a
player could never be struck by the device's golf
ball. Hauter was hit by the ball while using the
device. He sued Zogarts, which denied liability
on the ground that the statements were merely
matters of opinion, so liability could not be based
on them. Was this a valid defense? [*Hauter v.
Zogarts*, 534 P.2d 377 (Cal.)]

11. GE Oil & Gas, Inc., is a company that
manufactures gas compressors. Berge Helene
owns a large barge that it leases to oil companies
for purposes of storing and producing petroleum
offshore. GE Oil & Gas sold Berge Helene gas
compressors that were to be used on the barge.
Berge Helene representatives asked GE
representatives, as they were negotiating the
contract for the compressors, whether the
compressors could withstand the movement and
vibration that would occur on the front of the
barge once it was out in the ocean. GE's
representatives assured those from Berge Helene

that the compressors were self-stabilizing. Once out in the ocean, the gas compressors on the hull exploded once the vibrations began. Berge Helene brought suit against GE for the resulting crew injuries and damage to the barge. Could Berge Helene recover and, if so, what theory of product liability would apply? [*Berge Helene Ltd. v. GE Oil & Gas, Inc.*, 830 F. Supp. 2d 235 (S.D. Tex.)]

12. After watching a male horse owned by Terry and Manita Darby perform at a horse show, Ashley Sheffield contacted the Darbys about buying him. The Darbys assured her that the horse had no problems and would make a good show horse for use in competition. In the presence of and in consultation with her father (who raised horses for a business), Sheffield rode the horse and decided to purchase him for $8,500.

    Within three weeks, Sheffield and her trainer discerned that the horse was lame. Sheffield sued the Darbys for fraud and for breach of express and implied warranties, and the court entered summary judgment in favor of the Darbys on all claims. Sheffield appealed. Was the court correct in granting summary judgment? Was there a breach of an express warranty? [*Sheffield v. Darby*, 535 S.E.2d 776 (Ga. App.)]

13. On July 27, 2000, Sheldorado Aluminum Products, Inc., installed an aluminum awning on the back of Marie Villette's home for use as a carport. On January 11, 2001, the awning collapsed on top of Ms. Villette's new Mercedes automobile. Ms. Villette brought suit against Sheldorado, seeking recovery of the $3,000 she had paid to them for the awning.

    There was no formal written contract between the parties; the only writing was a one-page order/bill designated a "contract," dated July 11, 2000, and signed by Ms. Villette and apparently by Jack Finklestein, Sheldorado's salesman. No advertising or promotional material was presented by either party. Ms. Villette testified to no express warranty or representation on the transaction, and none appears in the writing. Sheldorado acknowledges that no instructions or

warnings were given to Ms. Villette as to care, maintenance, or use of the awning.

When the awning collapsed, Sheldorado took the position that the cause was an accumulation of snow and high winds and that it bore no responsibility for the loss. Its only response to the incident was to refer Ms. Villette to the insurer on their homeowner's policy.

Does Ms. Villette have any rights that would allow her to collect damages? Apply the UCC to answer this question. [*Villette v. Sheldorado Aluminum Products, Inc.*, 2001 WL 881055 (N.Y. Supp.), 45 UCC Rep Serv. 2d 470 (N.Y. Ci. Ct.)]

14. Drehman Paving & Flooring Co. installed a brick floor at Cumberland Farms that its salesman promised would be "just like" another floor Cumberland had installed several years earlier. The bricks in the new floor came loose because Drehman had failed to install expansion joints. Expansion joints were not included in the second floor contract but were part of the first. Can Cumberland recover? Under what theory? [*Cumberland Farms, Inc. v. Drehman Paving & Flooring Co.*, 520 N.E.2d 1321 (Mass. Ct. App.)]

15. Brian Felley went to the home of Tom and Cheryl Singleton on June 8 to look at a used car that the Singletons had advertised for sale in the local paper. The car was a 1991 Ford with 126,000 miles on it. Following a test drive and the Singletons' representation that the car was "in good mechanical condition," Felley purchased the car for $5,800. By June 18, 1997, Felley had the car in the shop and had paid $942.76 to have its clutch fixed. By July 9, 1997, Felley also had paid $971.18 for a new brake job. By September 16, 1997, Felley had paid another $429.09 for further brake work.

Felley brought suit for breach of express warranty. An auto expert testified that the clutch and brakes were defective when Felley bought the car. Was an express warranty breached? Why or why not? [*Felley v. Singleton*, 705 N.E.2d 930 (Ill. App.)]

CPA QUESTIONS

1. Under the UCC Sales Article, the warranty of title may be excluded by:

   a. Merchants or nonmerchants, provided the exclusion is in writing.

   b. Nonmerchant sellers only.

   c. The seller's statement that it is selling only such right or title that it has.

   d. Use of an "as is" disclaimer.

2. Which of the following factors result(s) in an express warranty with respect to a sale of goods?

   I. The seller's description of the goods is part of the basis of the bargain.

   II. The seller selects goods knowing the buyer's intended use.

      a. I only

      b. II only

      c. Both I and II

      d. Neither I nor II

3. Morgan is suing the manufacturer, wholesaler, and retailer for bodily injuries caused by a power saw Morgan purchased. Which of the following statements is correct under the theory of strict liability?

   a. The manufacturer will avoid liability if it can show it followed the custom of the industry.

   b. Morgan may recover even if he cannot show any negligence was involved.

   c. Contributory negligence on Morgan's part will always be a bar to recovery.

   d. Privity will be a bar to recovery insofar as the wholesaler is concerned if the wholesaler did not have a reasonable opportunity to inspect.

4. On May 2, Handy Hardware sent Ram Industries a signed purchase order that stated, in part: "Ship for May 8 delivery 300 Model A-X socket sets at current dealer price. Terms 2/10/ net 30." Ram received Handy's purchase order on May 4. On May 5, Ram discovered that it had only 200 Model A-X socket sets and 100 Model W-Z socket sets in stock. Ram shipped the Model A-X and Model W-Z sets to Handy without explanation concerning the shipment. The sockets were received by Handy on May 8. Assuming a contract exists between Handy and Ram, which of the following implied warranties would result?

   I. Implied warranty of merchantability

   II. Implied warranty of fitness for a particular purpose

   III. Implied warranty of title

      a. I only

      b. III only

      c. I and III only

      d. I, II, and III

© Manuel Gutjahr/iStockphoto.com

CHAPTER 26

Obligations and Performance

learningoutcomes

After studying this chapter, you should be able to

LO.1 List the steps that can be taken when a party to a sales contract feels insecure about the other party's performance

LO.2 Explain the obligations of the seller and the buyer in a sales contract

LO.3 Identify the types of actions and conduct that constitute acceptance

LO.4 Explain the excuses that exist for nonperformance by one party

C ontracts for the sale of goods impose both obligations and requirements for performance on the parties.

A. GENERAL PRINCIPLES

Each party to a sales contract is bound to perform according to the terms of the contract. Each is likewise under a duty to exercise **good faith** in the contract's performance and to do nothing that would impair the other party's expectation that the contract will be performed.

good faith – absence of knowledge of any defects or problems.

CPA

1. Obligation of Good Faith

Every contract or duty within the Uniform Commercial Code (UCC) imposes an obligation of good faith in its performance or enforcement.[1] The UCC defines good faith as "honesty in fact in the conduct or transaction concerned."[2] In the case of a merchant seller or buyer of goods, the UCC carries the concept of good faith further. The UCC imposes the additional requirement that merchants observe "reasonable commercial standards of fair dealing in the trade."[3] Section 1-203 of the UCC provides, "Every contract or duty within this Act imposes an obligation of good faith in its performance or enforcement."[4]

2. Time Requirements of Obligations

In a cash sale that does not require delivery of the goods, the duties of the seller and buyer are concurrent. Each one has the right to demand that the other perform at the same time. That is, as the seller hands over the goods, the buyer hands over the purchase money. If either party refuses to act, the other party has the right to withhold performance. In self-service stores, the performance occurs simultaneously—the buyer pays as the items are bagged at checkout.

In other types of contracts, there may be blocks of time between when the parties enter into an agreement and when performance, either delivery or payment, is due. During those time periods, buyers may become concerned about the ability of a seller experiencing a labor strike to complete production of the goods ordered in the contract. A seller may feel that a buyer who is experiencing credit difficulties may not be able to pay for the goods. Article 2 covers these periods of time and the conduct of the parties after the contract is entered into but before performance is due.

---

[1] UCC §1-201(20); *C & E Services, Inc. v. Ashland Inc.*, 601 F. Supp. 2d 262 (D.D.C. 2009).
[2] UCC §1-202; Selling the goods and then claiming a breach does not constitute good faith. *Rad Concepts, Inc. v. Wilks Precision Instrument Co., Inc.*, 891 A.2d 1148 (Md. App. 2005).
[3] UCC §1-303; *Greenwood Products, Inc. v. Greenwood Forest Products, Inc.*, 273 P.3d 116 (Or. 2012); *Swanson v. Beco Const. Co., Inc.*, 175 P.3d 748 (Idaho 2007).
[4] UCC §1-203.

3. Repudiation of the Contract

repudiation – result of a buyer or seller refusing to perform the contract as stated.

anticipatory repudiation – repudiation made in advance of the time for performance of the contract obligations.

If the seller or the buyer refuses to perform the contract when the time for performance arises, a **repudiation** of the contract results. Often, before the time for performance arrives, a party to the contract may inform the other that she will not perform the terms of the contract. This repudiation made in advance of the time for performance is called an **anticipatory repudiation**.[5] Under Revised Article 2, repudiation occurs when the party furnishes a *record* (as noted in other chapters, a term that allows for e-mails) including "language that a reasonable party would interpret to mean that the other party will not or cannot make a performance still due under the contract" or when the party exhibits "voluntary, affirmative conduct that would appear to a reasonable party to make a future performance by the other party impossible."[6]

4. Adequate Assurance of Performance

This time between contracting and actual performance may see some developing events that cause the parties concern about the ability of each to perform.[7] **For Example,** if the seller's warehouse is destroyed by fire, the buyer might conclude that the seller might not be able to make a delivery scheduled for the following month. Whenever a party to a sales contract has reasonable grounds to be concerned about the future performance of the other party, a demand may be made in a record for *assurance* that the contract will be performed.[8] **For Example,** a seller who is concerned about a buyer's ability to pay for goods could demand an updated credit report, financial statement, or even additional security or payment.

(A) **FORM OF ASSURANCE.** The person on whom demand for assurance is made must give "such assurance of due performance as is adequate under the circumstances of the particular case."[9] The UCC does not specify the exact form of assurance. If the party on whom demand is made has an established reputation, a reaffirmation of the contract obligation and a statement that it will be performed may be sufficient to assure a reasonable person that it will be performed. In contrast, if the party's reputation or economic position at the time is such that mere words and promises would not give any real assurance, it may be necessary to have a third person (or an insurance company) guarantee performance or to put up property as security for performance.

(B) **FAILURE TO GIVE ASSURANCE.** If adequate assurance is not given within 30 days from the time of demand, the demanding party may treat the contract as repudiated. The party demanding assurances may then proceed as if there were a breach and may pursue damage remedies. The nonbreaching party also has the right to enter into a substitute contract with a third person to obtain goods contracted for under the now-broken contract.

---

[5] UCC §2-610; *In re Mayco Plastics, Inc.*, 389 B.R. 7 (Bankr. E.D. Mich. 2008).

[6] UCC §2-610. The loss of a grain dealer's license is an anticipatory repudiation of his contract to sell grains for farmers. *Timmerman v. Grain Exchange, LLC*, 915 N.E.2d 113 (Ill. App. 2009).

[7] UCC §2-609.

[8] *GFSI, Inc. v. J-Loong Trading, Ltd.*, 505 F. Supp. 2d 935 (D. Kan. 2007).

[9] UCC §2-609(4).

CASE SUMMARY

So, Are We Good on This Contract, or What?

FACTS: On April 1, 2004, Advanced Body Care Solutions, LLC ("Advanced") and Thione International, Inc. ("Thione"), entered into an agreement that required Advanced to make minimum purchases of "Thione Antioxidant Complex," which reduces free radical damage to the body, and Thione's "Free Radical Monitor Test Kit," which is a test kit for at-home use to monitor the body's free radicals. Ampoules are small glass tubes that contain a clear liquid reagent, which tests for the presence of free radicals in a urine sample.

In exchange, Advanced received "the license and authority" "to advertise, promote, market, sell and otherwise distribute" the Dietary Supplement and the Test Kit on an exclusive basis. The agreement was to remain in effect for a minimum of five years: April 1, 2004 to March 31, 2009.

On May 26, 2004, Advanced placed an order for 25,000 ampoules, for which it paid $41,250. It received about 20,000 ampoules on September 1. It was immediately apparent that 200–300 of the 20,000 were broken, and about 1,000 were pink, indicating that they were defective. The following day, Dr. Stephen Perry, Advanced's liaison with Thione, sent an e-mail to Dr. Mark Hersh, the CEO and chief scientist of Thione, stating that, "Carl [Pradelli, Advanced's managing member,] received some vials that are pink," and inquiring, "Do we have a production issue?"

As of March 2005, Thione had not yet identified the source of the problem with the first shipment of 20,000 ampoules, and Advanced had placed no subsequent orders. On March 18, Pradelli sent Hersh a summary of Advanced's marketing efforts. Following five pages on that subject was a section of the letter entitled "The Lingering Black Cloud" that stressed that Advanced's "biggest concern" was the defective ampoules and that it could not launch any additional marketing initiatives until satisfied that the problem was permanently solved.

During the summer of 2006, Advanced and Thione attempted to renegotiate the Licensing Agreement. The renegotiation efforts failed.

On September 26, 2006, Advanced filed suit against Thione for damages, claiming that Thione had breached the Licensing Agreement and an implied warranty by providing Advanced with defective ampoules. Thione counterclaimed for breach of the Agreement by Advanced of its minimum purchase obligations and claiming lost profits.

The district court entered judgment for Thione for $2.5 million and denied the purchaser's post-judgment motions. Advanced appealed.

DECISION: On appeal, the court held that there was sufficient evidence to support the jury's finding that Thione did not breach the installment contract as a whole. The court also held that a reasonable jury could have concluded that Advanced's e-mail inquiry to Thione and subsequent expression of marketing and quality concerns did not constitute a writing demanding adequate assurance of due performance. The e-mail was an inquiry and not an expression that the contract was hanging in the balance. Further, Advanced took no further steps to resolve the issue. Finally, the court held that the damage award was justified because Advanced had breached the contract. [*Advanced Bodycare Solutions, LLC v. Thione International, Inc.*, 615 F.3d 1352 (11th Cir. 2010)]

B. DUTIES OF THE PARTIES

The obligations of the parties to a sales contract include (1) the seller's duty to deliver the goods, (2) the buyer's duty to accept the goods, and (3) the buyer's duty to pay for the goods.

5. Seller's Duty to Deliver

The seller has the duty to deliver the goods according to the terms of the contract.

(A) PLACE, TIME, AND MANNER OF DELIVERY. The terms of the contract determine whether the seller is to send the goods or the buyer is to call for them and whether the goods are to be transported from the seller to the buyer or the transaction is to be completed by the delivery of documents without the movement of the goods. In the absence of a provision in the contract or a contrary course of performance or usage of trade, the place of delivery is the seller's place of business if the seller has one; otherwise, it is the seller's residence. (See Chapter 24 for more details on delivery and shipping terms.)[10] However, if the subject matter of the contract consists of identified goods that are known by the parties to be in some other place, that place is the place of delivery. If no time for shipment or delivery is stated, delivery or shipment is required within a reasonable time.

When a method of transportation called for by the contract becomes unavailable or commercially unreasonable, the seller must make delivery by means of a commercially reasonable substitute if available.

(B) QUANTITY DELIVERED. The buyer has the right to insist that all the goods be delivered at one time. If the seller delivers a smaller or larger quantity than what is stipulated in the contract, the buyer may refuse to accept the goods.[11]

6. Buyer's Duty upon Receipt of Goods

The buyer must accept goods that conform to the contract, and the refusal to do so is a breach of the contract. However, the buyer has certain rights prior to acceptance.

CPA

(A) RIGHT TO EXAMINE GOODS—THE BUYER'S RIGHT OF INSPECTION.[12] To determine whether the goods in fact conform to the contract, the buyer has the right to examine the goods when tendered by the seller. An exception to this rule occurs when goods are sent COD. In a COD shipment, the buyer has no right to examine the goods until payment is made.

The buyer's right of inspection includes the right to remove goods from cartons and to conduct tests. **For Example,** a buyer who is purchasing potatoes for use in making potato chips has the right to peel and test a portion of the potatoes to determine whether they are the appropriate type for "chipping."

(B) RIGHT TO REFUSE OR RETURN THE GOODS—THE BUYER'S RIGHT OF REJECTION.[13] If the goods the seller has tendered do not conform to the contract in any way, the buyer can *reject* the goods. **For Example,** the buyer may reject a mobile home when it does not contain an air conditioner with the capacity specified by the contract. The buyer may reject the goods if they are not perfect.[14] The standard for rejection does not require that the defect in the goods or the breach be material. **For Example,** a small pressure mark on an ottoman is not material; the ottoman will function just as well. However, the buyer still has the right to reject the ottoman because it has a defect.

---

[10] UCC §2-308.

[11] UCC §2-307; Failure to deliver right amounts at the right time allows the buyer to repudiate the contract. *Traxys North America, LLC v. Concept Mining, Inc.,* 808 F. Supp. 2d 853 (W.D. Va. 2011).

[12] UCC §2-601.

[13] UCC §2-602; *In re S.M. Acquisition Co.,* 319 B.R. 553 (N.D. Ill. 2005).

[14] *Precision Mirror & Glass v. Nelms,* 797 N.Y.S.2d 720 (2005).

The buyer has the right to reject the full shipment, accept the full shipment and seek damages for the goods' diminished value (see Chapter 27), or accept any commercial units and reject the remainder. Commercial units are defined by trade and industry according to the customary size of cartons or containers for the goods shipped. Envelopes come in **commercial units** of boxes of 500. Computer CDs often come in packages of 20 or 50. Rejection by a buyer would be not of individual envelopes or disks but of boxes. **For Example,** if Donna purchased a package of 20 CDs and 4 of the 20 CDs were defective, Donna would return the box of 20 CDs for a new box. Rejection and acceptance in commercial units prevent the problems created when a seller has to open other units and mix and match goods in each.

commercial unit – standard of the trade for shipment or packaging of a good.

After rejecting the goods, the buyer may not exercise any right of ownership over the goods.

The buyer's rejection must be made within a reasonable time after the delivery or tender of the goods. The buyer must notify the seller of the rejection and, in transactions with merchants particularly, provide the seller with the reason for the rejection.[15]

CPA

(c) Cure of Defective Tender or Delivery. The buyer's rejection is not an end to the transaction. The seller is given a second chance, or a **right to cure**, to make a proper tender of conforming goods.[16]

right to cure – second chance for a seller to make a proper tender of conforming goods.

This right of cure means that the buyer must give notice of rejection and the reason for that rejection, if the seller has the right, but not necessarily the intent, to cure. That is, the seller has the right to cure if the seller is able to make the cure within the time remaining under the contract. If the time for making delivery under the contract has not expired, the seller need only give the buyer **seasonable** (timely) notice of the intention to make a proper delivery within the time allowed by the contract. Under Revised Article 2, the seller also has the right of cure if the time for making the delivery has expired through the allowance of additional reasonable time in which to make a substitute conforming tender. Such additional time is allowed if (1) the seller so notifies the buyer and (2) the seller had acted reasonably in making the original tender, believing that it would be acceptable to the buyer.[17] Under Revised UCC, installment contracts are also governed under this rule.

seasonable – timely.

acceptance – unqualified assent to the act or proposal of another, such as the acceptance of a draft (bill of exchange), of an offer to make a contract, of goods delivered by the seller, or of a gift or deed.

7. Buyer's Duty to Accept Goods

Assuming that the buyer has no grounds to reject the goods after inspection, the next step in the performance of the contract is the buyer's **acceptance** of the goods.

CPA

(a) What Constitutes Acceptance of Goods.[18] Acceptance of goods means that the buyer, pursuant to a contract, has, either expressly or by implication, taken the goods permanently. The buyer's statement of acceptance is an express acceptance. A buyer can accept goods by implication if there is no rejection after a reasonable opportunity to inspect them or within a reasonable time after the buyer has inspected them. Another form of acceptance by implication is conduct by the buyer

---

[15] UCC §2-602(1); *Adams v. Wacaster Oil Co., Inc.*, 98 S.W. 3d 832 (Ark. App. 2003).
[16] *Inter-Americas Ins. Corp., Inc. v. Imaging Solutions Co.*, 185 P.3d 963 (Kan. App. 2008).
[17] This right to cure after the time for performance has expired exists in nonconsumer contracts only.
[18] UCC §2-606; *Stenzel v. Dell, Inc.*, 870 A.2d 133 (Me. 2005).

that is inconsistent with rejection, as when a buyer uses or sells the delivered goods.[19]

A buyer accepts goods by making continued use of them and by not attempting to return them. A buyer also accepts goods by modifying them because such action is inconsistent with a rejection or with the continued ownership of the goods by the seller.[20]

CASE SUMMARY

The Pasta Ties

FACTS: Country Pasta, located in Polson, Montana, makes noodles. Viking manufactures, fabricates, and services industrial packaging equipment. In 2006, Gary Ivory, the production manager at Country Pasta, contacted Robb Leonhard, one of the owners of Viking, to discuss a quotation for a more automatic pasta bagging system. Country Pasta wanted a system in which the pasta bags would be weighed more accurately and in which the bags would be closed or tied more automatically. Ivory provided Leonhard with a sample of Country Pasta's product in the bag it was using at the time and indicated what he wanted the product to look like. Leonhard then sent Ivory photographs of a bag of Country Pasta's product with a tin-tie on it and stated, "this is basically what your look is going to be." Viking included the photographs on the second page of the quotation.

On July 13, 2007, Country Pasta accepted Viking's quotation to purchase a pasta packaging system. The quotation shows photos of the equipment and of Country Pasta bags closed with a tin-tie. The items related to the tin-tie applicator were priced at $47,173. The total purchase price for the product packaging system was $178,074.

The quotation called for a "checkout," or a pre-shipment inspection, by Country Pasta "prior to shipment." In April 2008, Ivory and Scott Knutson went to Viking's facility to perform the checkout of the packaging system. The tin-ties on the finished bags did not regularly close up during this demonstration; however, Viking worked on the packaging system, and told Country Pasta that the system was "working better." Country Pasta approved the shipment and the packaging system was delivered to Country Pasta before June 17, 2008. Ivory helped unpack and set up the equipment; he did not notice any defects.

The contract provided that "if requested by the customer, [Viking] will provide a service technician for installation of the quoted equipment." The contract did not include free installation but estimated that two days of installation and training for Country Pasta employees would cost $3,373. The contract also provided that "[a]n installation will be considered complete when all systems purchased from [Viking] perform per the Product Performance Specifications."

From June 17, 2008, through June 25, 2008, Viking technician Tim Parrish worked on installing the equipment and training Country Pasta's employees in Montana. During this visit, Parrish discovered that Country Pasta workers would drop or tap bags full of pasta on a table in order to settle the noodles to allow for a twist tie to be applied to the bag. Parrish made adjustments to the machinery, including adding a shelf to assist in the settling of the noodles. Despite these efforts, the tin-tie applicator was not functioning properly at the time he left. Viking and Country Pasta agreed to split the cost of a second visit by Parrish.

Parrish returned to Country Pasta in July 2008 with Steve Almberg, a representative from Weigh Right, the manufacturer of the scale. Parrish and Almberg improved the operation of the scale and bagger by making modifications to Country Pasta's equipment feeding the scale and bagger.

---

[19] *Fabrica de Tejidos Imperial v. Brandon Apparel Group, Inc.*, 218 F. Supp. 2d 974 (N.D. Ill. 2002).
[20] UCC §2-606(1)(a), (b), and (c).

CASE SUMMARY

Continued

A Country Pasta memorandum regarding a meeting with Parrish on July 10, 2008, notes the improvements with the scale and bagger, but states that "[t]here is no way the current tin-tie system will work with our product." Parrish left Montana and was not asked to return to Montana to continue working on the applicator.

On December 4, 2008, five months after delivery of the packaging system, and four months after Parrish's final visit, Kellogg sent an e-mail to Viking stating that Country Pasta wanted a refund for the tin-tie applicator and the associated conveyor in the amount of $47,173. At that time, Country Pasta had outstanding invoices due to Viking in the amount of $34,110.22. Viking brought suit against Country Pasta, seeking the outstanding amount. Country Pasta counterclaimed, alleging breach of contract.

After a trial to the court, judgment for money damages was entered in favor of Viking. Country Pasta's counterclaim alleging breach of contract by Viking and alleging Country Pasta's revocation of acceptance of the tin-tie applicator and conveyor were dismissed. Country Pasta appealed.

DECISION: Country Pasta knew that the machine was not going to work when it came to getting the ties on the pasta bags as it wanted them to look. However, for five months after that, Country Pasta took no action other than to ask for a refund on the tying portion of the equipment, not for damages for a breach of contract. The machinery was one commercial unit and could not be rejected in pieces. In addition, the proposal makes it clear that the sale was for the equipment and that the installation and fine-tuning was beyond the scope of the proposal. Also, Country Pasta used the equipment for too long before deciding to revoke its acceptance. There were no grounds for rejection because there was nothing in the proposal to indicate a breach. If there were grounds for revocation, Country Pasta waited too long to revoke the acceptance.

The key elements of the decision are as follows:

1. The system did not fail to meet any identifiable product performance specifications;
2. The entire integrated system was one commercial unit;
3. The buyer's conduct constituted acceptance of goods;
4. The e-mail that the buyer's owner sent to the seller and that sought a refund for the cost of the system's tin-tie applicator was not sent within a reasonable time and, thus, did not constitute a valid rejection; and
5. The buyer did not revoke its acceptance of the system within a reasonable time.

Affirmed. [*Viking Packaging Technologies, Inc. v. Vassallo Foods, Inc.*, **804 N.W.2d 507 (Wis. App. 2011)**]

CPA

(B) REVOCATION OF ACCEPTANCE. Even after acceptance of the goods, the performance under the contract may not be finished if the buyer exercises the right to revoke acceptance of the goods.[21] The buyer may revoke acceptance of the goods when they do not conform to the contract, the defect is such that it substantially impairs the value of the contract to the buyer, and either the defect is such that the buyer could not discover the problem or the seller has promised to correct a problem the buyer was aware of and pointed out to the seller prior to acceptance.[22]

---

[21] UCC §2-608; *Fode v. Capital RV Center, Inc.*, 575 N.W.2d 682 (N.D. 1998); *Barrett v. Brian Bemis Auto World*, 408 F. Supp. 2d 539 (N.D. Ill. 2005).
[22] Repeated requests for service satisfy the requirement for notifying the seller. *Cliffstar Corp. v. Elmar Industries, Inc.*, 678 N.Y.S.2d 222 (1998). But continued use without notification presents problems for establishing rejection. In re *Rafter Seven Ranches*, 546 F.3d 1194 (10th Cir. 2008).

For Example, a buyer who purchased an emergency electric power generator found that the generator produced only about 65 percent of the power called for by the contract. This amount of power was insufficient for the operation of the buyer's electrical equipment. The seller's repeated attempts to improve the generator's output failed. The buyer, despite having used the generator for three months, could revoke his acceptance of it because its value was substantially impaired and he continued to keep it and use it only because of the seller's assurances that it would be repaired.

substantial impairment – material defect in a good.

Substantial impairment is a higher standard than the one of "fails to conform in any respect" for rejection. Substantial impairment requires proof of more than the mere fact that the goods do not conform to the contract. The buyer is not required to show that the goods are worthless but must prove that their use to the buyer is substantially different from what the contract promised.

E-Commerce & Cyberlaw

Rejection in Cyberspace

Rejection of computers and software presents novel issues for the UCC provisions on rejection because use of the goods is not so easily defined or distinguished by a bright line. With software, for example, the buyer can use the software as a means of conducting an inspection of the goods. However, fully loading the software constitutes acceptance, and the buyer would then step into the UCC provisions on revocation of acceptance, as opposed to rejection. If the software causes the buyer's computer to "crash" every 10 minutes, the buyer has grounds for either rejection or revocation of acceptance. The buyer could also agree to allow the seller to modify the software to prevent the "crashing" problems. Once the buyer decides to reject the software or revoke acceptance of it, he or she cannot continue to use the software, for such

use is inconsistent with the claim that the goods (the software) fail to conform to the contract.*

A buyer is also permitted to test a computer for purposes of inspection and rejection. If, however, the buyer rejects the computer system, it cannot continue to use the system, and allowing third parties to make alterations to the system to help it function better constitutes acceptance.**

*Cooperative Resources, Inc. v. Dynasty Software, Inc., 39 UCC Rep. Serv.2d 101 (N.H. Dist. Ct. 1998).
**Softa Group, Inc. v. Scarsdale Development, 632 N.E.2d 13 (Ill. App. 1993) (using a computer the buyer claims was "defective from inception" is inconsistent with rejection and the required basis for a rejection). Licitra v. Gateway, Inc., 734 N.Y.S.2d 389 (2001). Online retailers have their own rules for rejection. For example, Zappo's offers free returns, but the buyer must comply with the online return processes. There are also time limits placed on revocation of acceptance, such as on Amazon. All goods must be returned within six months of purchase. The online retailers have spelled out the time limits to make rejection and revocation of acceptance requirements clear and not subject to UCC interpretation of reasonableness.

A revocation of acceptance is not a cancellation of the contract with the seller. After revocation of acceptance, the buyer can choose from the remedies available for breach of contract or demand that the seller deliver conforming goods. (See Chapter 27 for more information on remedies for breach.)

(c) NOTIFICATION OF REVOCATION OF ACCEPTANCE. To revoke acceptance properly, the buyer must take certain steps. The buyer must give the seller notice of revocation. The revocation of acceptance is effective when the buyer notifies the seller. The buyer need not actually return the goods to make the notification or the revocation effective.

CASE SUMMARY

Jackson Hole Traders: The Retailer Looking for a Loophole

FACTS: Catherine Joseph, who does business as Metro Classics, sold clothing to Jackson Hole Traders, a corporation owned by David and Elizabeth Speaks. Jackson Hole Traders is located in Jackson, Wyoming, and sells clothing for men and women through a retail store and mail-order catalog business. The clothing Joseph sold was specially manufactured for Jackson Hole Traders and had a total contract price of $50,000 with net 30 terms.

When the clothing items were shipped between July and September 1994, approximately 900 items were sent. Elizabeth Speaks complained about the quality of some of the clothing items when they arrived and was given a credit of $1,096 for returned merchandise. However, Jackson Hole Traders did not pay $33,000 of the total Joseph bill despite its being well past the net 30-day period for payment. When Joseph demanded payment, Elizabeth Speaks boxed up approximately 350 items of the clothing and sent them back, demanding a credit for revocation of acceptance. Joseph filed suit for payment, alleging that it was too late for revocation of acceptance. The trial court found for Joseph, and the Speakses appealed.

DECISION: The Speakses breached the contract when they failed to pay for the garments that had been sent to them and that they had accepted for resale. They could not revoke acceptance after so much time had passed and they had offered the goods for sale. They sent the goods back not because they were defective but because they were unable to make the payments or sell the merchandise. [*Jackson Hole Traders, Inc. v. Joseph*, **931 P.2d 244 (Wyo. 1997)**]

The notice of revocation of acceptance must be given within a reasonable time after the buyer discovers or should have discovered the problems with the goods. The right of revocation is not lost if the buyer gives the seller a longer period of time to correct the defects in the goods.[23] Even the lapse of a year will not cost the buyer the right of revocation of acceptance if the seller has been experimenting during that time trying to correct the problems with the goods.

(D) BUYER'S RESPONSIBILITIES UPON REVOCATION OF ACCEPTANCE. After a revocation of acceptance, the buyer must hold the goods and await instructions from the seller. If the buyer revokes acceptance after having paid the seller in advance, the buyer may retain possession of the goods as security for the refund of the money that has been paid.

Thinking Things Through

ICE, Turbines, Iran, and Impracticability

Turbines Ltd. sells and maintains helicopters. Transupport, Inc. sells spare parts and turbine engines. Monarch Aviation contacted Turbines in search of a "First Stage" turbine nozzle. Turbines did not have the nozzle but, in checking with Transupport, discovered that it did. Turbines sent a purchase order to Transupport for the nozzle for $30,000.

Transupport tried to ship the nozzle directly to Turbines' client in Malaysia. However, Customs seized the nozzle because it was on the "United States Munitions List." There was a resulting dispute about the seizure as the parties tried to get it classified as a "dual-use" item.

Immigration and Customs Enforcement (ICE) told Turbines that it was keeping the nozzle because it was likely to end up in Iran. Following this disclosure, Turbines learned that the wife of one of the owners of Transupport was arrested on charges of conspiracy, money laundering, and export of arms and munitions. Turbines eventually returned the nozzle to Transupport. Transupport filed suit for breach of contract. Turbines maintains that it could not perform the contract because of the events that happened after shipment. Is Turbines correct?

Was the standard of commercial impracticability met? [*Turbines Ltd. v. Transupport, Inc.*, **808 N.W.2d 643 (Neb. 2012)**]

[23] A buyer who took her pop-up camper in for repairs but was then given a different camper without being told about it was entitled to revoke her acceptance. *Head v. Phillips Camper Sales & Rental, Inc.*, 593 N.W.2d 595 (Mich. Ct. App. 1999).

Ethics & the Law

The Return Season

At Saks Fifth Avenue, they call it the "return season." Return season occurs within the week following a major fundraising formal dance. Women who have purchased formal evening wear return the dresses after the dance. The dresses have been worn, and the tags have been cut, but the women return the dresses with requests for a full refund. Neiman Marcus also experiences the same phenomenon of returns.

Some stores have implemented a policy that formal evening wear may not be returned if the tags are cut from it. Others require a return within a limited period of seven days. Others offer an exchange only after five days.

Are the women covered by a right of rejection under Article 2? What do you think of the conduct of the women? Is it simply revocation of acceptance? Is there good faith on the part of the women?

8. Buyer's Duty to Pay

The buyer must pay the amount stated in the sales contract for accepted goods.

(A) TIME OF PAYMENT. The sales contract may require payment in advance or may give the buyer credit by postponing the time for payment.[24]

(B) FORM OF PAYMENT. Unless otherwise agreed, payment by the buyer requires payment in cash. The seller may accept a check or a promissory note from the buyer. If the check is not paid by the bank, the purchase price remains unpaid. A promissory note payable at a future date gives the buyer credit by postponing the time for payment.

The seller can refuse to accept a check or a promissory note as payment for goods but must give the buyer reasonable time in which to obtain legal tender with which to make payment.

CASE SUMMARY

Poor Payment Pattern on Potato Contracts

FACTS: Sun Valley Potatoes, Inc. (Sun Valley) is a fresh packer of potatoes. Magic Valley Foods, Inc. (Magic Valley) is a processor of potatoes. Sun Valley and Magic Valley entered into three written contracts wherein Sun Valley agreed to sell and deliver and Magic Valley agreed to purchase potatoes. Sun Valley provided nine weekly invoices, but none of those invoices were paid according to the following term in all of the contracts: "net thirty (30) days on amounts delivered on a weekly basis." As of August 9, 1995, Sun Valley had delivered 108,169 cwt. (at the contract price of $1.13 cwt.) of potatoes to Magic Valley. Magic Valley, on the other hand, had withheld payments totaling $236,904.44. Sun Valley ceased its deliveries because it had not been paid for a total of 24 invoices. Magic Valley had to shut down its plant for 14 days and it filed suit against Sun Valley for breach of contract. The district court concluded that because Sun Valley had not insisted on strict compliance with the 30-day payment rule, it could not unilaterally repudiate the contract due to late payments. The district court also ruled that Magic Valley was entitled to offset the $236,904.44 it owed Sun Valley against the $231,660.60 it incurred as a result of its processing plant being down for 14 days and the loss of profits associated therewith. Sun Valley appealed.

[24] UCC §2-310.

CASE SUMMARY

Continued

DECISION: The court held that Sun Valley did not waive its right to timely payment under the contract. Because Magic Valley had made arrangements with other suppliers for delivery of potatoes, it was aware that its position with Sun Valley was tenuous and that it might lose the deliveries. The court also noted that if Magic Valley was worried, it should have sought assurances from Sun Valley about deliveries. However, seeking assurances would have brought the nonpayment issue to the forefront of the parties' relationship. The court found that Magic Valley was the party in breach of the agreement and that Sun Valley's response of no further deliveries was an appropriate response to a breach. [*Magic Valley Foods, Inc. v. Sun Valley Potatoes, Inc.*, 10 P.3d 734 (Idaho 2000)]

CPA

9. When Duties Are Excused

commercial impracticability – situation that occurs when costs of performance rise suddenly and performance of a contract will result in a substantial loss.

Under Article 2, the doctrine of commercial impracticability is available as a defense to performance of a contract. The doctrine of **commercial impracticability** is the modern commercial law version of the common law doctrine of impossibility. If a party to a contract can establish that there has been an occurrence or a contingency not anticipated by the parties and not a basic assumption in their entering into a contract, the party can be excused from performance.

The standard for commercial impracticability is objective, not subjective. Additional cost alone is not grounds for application of commercial impracticability.[25]

For Example, if a farmer has contracted to sell 2 tons of peanuts to an airline and the crop fails, the farmer is not excused on the grounds of commercial impracticability. So long as peanuts are available for the farmer to buy, even at a higher price, and then sell to the buyer to satisfy their contract terms, the farmer is not excused. Commercial impracticability refers to those circumstances in which peanuts are not available anywhere because the entire peanut harvest was destroyed rather than just the individual farmer's crop.

CASE SUMMARY

Just a Bunch of Garbage, Especially When There Are No Dump Trucks

FACTS: Ecology Services, Inc. (ESI) entered into a contract in late 2002 with Montgomery County, Maryland for refuse removal services. On a GranTurk "Order Form" dated November 25, 2003, GranTurk agreed to sell the county 12 split rear loaders to be installed on ESI's chassis for a cost of $77,675.13 each. GranTurk subcontracted with G & H for the task of installing the loaders on the chassis. G & H agreed to deliver the first (6) units to GranTurk on or before April

[25] UCC §2-615(a).

15th (provided the chassis arrived prior to March 15th) and the last (6) units on or before May 15th (provided the chassis arrive before April 15th). G & H agreed to a $100 per day late penalty clause.

There was a steel shortage and ESI and GranTurk had difficulties and additional costs in obtaining the steel necessary for the production of the trucks for the county. Following several delays and no deliveries of the garbage trucks, the county filed suit seeking damages of $500,000. As the suit progressed, ESI delivered nine of the trucks, but, by the time of the trial, three trucks had not yet been delivered. ESI and GranTurk argued that they were excused from timely performance because of the worldwide steel shortage and were only liable for the $100 per day late-fee damages provided for in the contract. The parties moved for summary judgment.

DECISION: The court held that a shortage of a component part for production is not by itself grounds for commercial impracticability. Other issues that must be examined include whether the shortage could have been anticipated and whether steel was available but more costly. The court also noted that additional cost is also not in and of itself grounds for commercial impracticability. The court held that a trial was required to determine what the damages for the county were and the full extent of the shortage and ESI's and GranTurk's efforts to find steel. [*Ecology Services Inc. v. GranTurk Equipment, Inc.*, 443 F. Supp. 2d 756 (D. Md. 2006)]

MAKE THE CONNECTION

SUMMARY

Every sales contract imposes an obligation of good faith in its performance. Good faith means honesty in fact in the conduct or transaction concerned. For merchants, the UCC imposes the additional requirement of observing "reasonable commercial standards of fair dealing in the trade."

In the case of a cash sale where no transportation of the goods is required, both the buyer and the seller may demand concurrent performance.

A buyer's or a seller's refusal to perform a contract is called a *repudiation*. A repudiation made in advance of the time for performance is called an *anticipatory repudiation* and is a breach of the contract. If either party to a contract feels insecure about the performance of the other, that party may demand by a record adequate assurance of performance. If that assurance is not given, the demanding party may treat the contract as repudiated.

The seller has a duty to deliver the goods in accordance with the terms of the contract. This duty does not require physical transportation; it requires that the seller permit the transfer of possession of the goods to the buyer.

With the exception of COD contracts, the buyer has the right to inspect the goods upon tender or delivery. Inspection includes the right to open cartons and conduct tests. If the buyer's inspection reveals that the seller has tendered nonconforming goods, the buyer may reject them. Subject to certain limitations, the seller may then offer to replace the goods or cure the problems the buyer has noted.

The buyer has a duty to accept goods that conform to the contract, and refusal to do so is a breach of contract. The buyer is deemed to have accepted goods either expressly or by implication through conduct inconsistent with rejection or by lapse of time. The buyer must pay for accepted goods in accordance with the terms of the contract. The buyer can reject goods in commercial units, accept the goods and collect damages for their problems, or reject the full contract shipment. The buyer must give notice of rejection to the seller and cannot do anything with the goods that would be inconsistent with the seller's ownership rights. The buyer should await instructions from the seller on what to do with the goods.

Even following acceptance, the buyer may revoke that acceptance if the problems with the goods substantially impair their value and the problems were either not easily discoverable or the buyer kept the goods based on the seller's promises to repair them and make them whole. Upon revocation of acceptance, the buyer should await instructions from the seller on what steps to take.

Performance can be excused on the grounds of commercial impracticability, but the seller must show objective difficulties that have created more than cost increases.

LEARNING OUTCOMES

After studying this chapter, you should be able to clearly explain:

A. General Principles

L0.1 List the steps that can be taken when a party to a sales contract feels insecure about the other party's performance
> See *Magic Valley Foods, Inc. v. Sun Valley Potatoes, Inc.* on p. 548.

B. Duties of the Parties

L0.2 Explain the obligations of the seller and the buyer in a sales contract
> See the Viking Packaging Technologies case on pp. 544–546.

L0.3 Identify the types of actions and conduct that constitute acceptance
> See *Jackson Hole Traders, Inc. v. Joseph* on pp. 547–548.
> See ICE, Turbines, Iran, and Commercial Impracticability on p. 547.

L0.4 Explain the excuses that exist for nonperformance by one party
> See *Ecology Services, Inc. v. GranTurk Equipment* on p. 550.

KEY TERMS

acceptance	commercial units	right to cure
anticipatory repudiation	good faith	seasonable
commercial impracticability	repudiation	substantial impairment

QUESTIONS AND CASE PROBLEMS

1. In 1992, Donna Smith telephoned Clark, the manager of Penbridge Farms, in response to an advertisement Clark had placed in the July issue of the *Emu Finder* about the availability for sale of proven breeder pairs. Clark told Smith he had a breeder pair available. Clark sold the pair to Smith for $16,500. Some months later, after Smith had had a chance to inspect the pair, she discovered that Clark had sold her two males. Smith immediately notified Clark and revoked her acceptance of the animals. Clark said the revocation was too late. Was it? [*Smith v. Penbridge Associates, Inc.*, 655 A.2d 1015 (Pa. Super.)]

2. On January 3, 1991, Central District Alarm (CDA) and Hal-Tuc entered into a written sales agreement providing that CDA would sell and install new security equipment described on an equipment list attached to the contract. This list

included a Javelin VCR. When the system was installed, CDA installed a used JVC VCR instead of a new Javelin VCR. Hal-Tuc called CDA the day after the installation and complained that the equipment was not the Javelin brand, and that the VCR was a used JVC VCR. CDA told Hal-Tuc that the equipment was not used and that a JVC VCR was better than a Javelin. Hal-Tuc telephoned CDA personnel over a two-week period during which they denied that the equipment was used.

After two weeks of calls, CDA's installation manager went to the store to see the equipment and admitted that it was used. No one from CDA advised Hal-Tuc in advance that it was installing used equipment temporarily until the right equipment arrived. CDA offered to replace it with a new Javelin VCR as soon as one arrived, which would take one or two months. Hal-Tuc asked CDA to return its deposit and take the equipment back, but CDA refused. Hal-Tuc put all the equipment in boxes and stored it. CDA filed a petition against Hal-Tuc for damages for breach of contract. Hal-Tuc filed a counterclaim, alleging fraud. CDA asserted it had the right to cure by tendering conforming goods after Hal-Tuc rejected the nonconforming goods. Was CDA correct? [*Central District Alarm, Inc. v. Hal-Tuc, Inc.*, 866 S.W.2d 210 (Mo. App.)]

3. Bobby Murray Chevrolet, Inc., submitted a bid to the Alamance County Board of Education to supply 1,200 school bus chassis to the district. Bobby Murray was awarded the contract and contracted with General Motors (GM) to purchase the chassis for the school board.

Between the time of Bobby Murray's contract with GM and the delivery date, the Environmental Protection Agency (EPA) enacted new emission standards for diesel vehicles, such as school buses. Under the new law, the buses Bobby Murray ordered from GM would be out of compliance, as would the buses Bobby Murray specified in its bid to the school board.

GM asked for several extensions to manufacture the buses within the new EPA guidelines. The school board was patient and gave several extensions, but then, because of its

need for buses, purchased them from another supplier after notifying Bobby Murray of its intent to do so. The school board had to pay an additional $150,152.94 for the buses from its alternative source and sued Bobby Murray for that amount. Bobby Murray claimed it was excused from performance on the grounds of commercial impracticability. Is Bobby Murray correct? Does the defense of commercial impracticability apply in this situation? Be sure to compare this case with other cases and examples in the chapter. [*Alamance County Board of Education v. Bobby Murray Chevrolet, Inc.*, 465 S.E.2d 306 (N.C. App.); rev. denied, 467 S.E.2d 899 (N.C.)]

4. The Home Shopping Club ordered 12,000 Care Bear lamps from Ohio International, Ltd. When the lamps arrived, they had poor painting and staining, elements were improperly glued and could come loose (a danger to the children with the lamps in their rooms), and they overheated very easily (another danger for children and a fire hazard). Home Shopping Network notified International and gave it three months to remedy the problems and provide different lamps. After three months, Home Shopping Network returned all lamps and notified International that it was pulling out of the contract. Could they do so, or had too much time passed? [*Home Shopping Club, Inc. v. Ohio International, Ltd.*, 27 UCC Rep. Serv. 2d 433 (Fla. Cir. Ct.)]

5. Lafer Enterprises sold Christmas decorations to B. P. Development & Management Corp., the owners and operators of the Osceola Square Mall. The package of decorations was delivered to Osceola Square Mall prior to Thanksgiving 1986 for a total cost of $48,775, which B. P. would pay in three installments. Cathy Trivigno, a manager at B. P. who supervised the installation of the decorations, indicated that she and the Osceola Square Mall merchants were not satisfied with the quality of the decorations, but they needed to be in place for the day after Thanksgiving (the start of the holiday shopping season). B. P. complained to Lafer about the quality of the decorations but had the decorations installed. B. P. paid the first installment to Lafer

but then stopped payment on the last two checks. B. P. claimed it had rejected the decorations. Lafer claimed breach for nonpayment because B. P. had used the decorations. Did B. P. accept the decorations? [*B. P. Dev. & Management Corp. v. Lafer Enterprises, Inc.*, 538 So.2d 1379 (Fla. App.)]

6. Westinghouse Electric Corporation entered into uranium supply contracts with 22 electric utilities during the late 1960s. The contract prices ranged from $7 to $10 per pound. The Arab oil embargo and other changes in energy resources caused the price of uranium to climb to between $45 and $75 per pound. Supply tightened because of increased demand.

   In 1973, Westinghouse wrote to the utilities and explained that it was unable to perform on its uranium sales contracts. The utilities needed uranium. Westinghouse did not have sufficient funds to buy the uranium it had agreed to supply, assuming that it could find a supply. One utility executive commented, after totaling up all 22 supply contracts, that Westinghouse could not have supplied the uranium even under the original contract terms. He said, "Westinghouse oversubscribed itself on these contracts. They hoped that not all the utilities would take the full contract amount."

   Westinghouse says it is impossible for it to perform. The utilities say they are owed damages because they must still find uranium somewhere. What damages would the law allow? What ethical issues do you see in the original contracts and in Westinghouse's refusal to deliver? Should we excuse parties from contracts because it is so expensive for them to perform? [*In re Westinghouse Uranium Litigation*, 436 F. Supp. 990 (E.D. Va.)]

7. Steel Industries, Inc., ordered steel from Interlink Metals & Chemicals. The steel was to be delivered from a Russian mill. There were political and other issues in Russia, and the mill was shut down. Interlink did not deliver the steel to Steel Industries, claiming that it was excused from performance because it could not get the steel from the Russian mill. What would Interlink have to establish to show that it was excused from performing under the doctrine of commercial impracticability? [*Steel Industries, Inc. v. Interlink Metals & Chemicals, Inc.*, 969 F. Supp. 1046 (E.D. Mich.)]

8. Spaulding & Kimball Co. ordered from Aetna Chemical Co. 75 cartons of window washers. The buyer received them and sold about a third to its customers but later refused to pay for them, claiming that the quality was poor. The seller sued for the price. Would the seller be entitled to the contract price? Refer to the *Weil v. Murray* case described in problem 12 regarding the Degas painting for some insight. [*Aetna Chemical Co. v. Spaulding & Kimball Co.*, 126 A. 582 (Vt.)]

9. Nuco Plastics, Inc., was developing production molds for Universal Plastics, Inc. During the course of the development of the molds, Universal changed specifications and required the use of different materials. Nuco raised the price from $235 per 1,000 parts to $400 per 1,000 parts. Universal refused to pay the additional amount and ended the contract. Nuco was not paid for the molds it had produced and sued for breach of contract and damages. Universal maintained that Nuco had repudiated the contract by raising the price. Is an attempt to raise the price on a contract a repudiation of the contract? [*Nuco Plastics, Inc. v. Universal Plastics, Inc.*, 601 N.E.2d 152 (Ohio App.)]

10. Economy Forms Corp. sold concrete-forming equipment to Kandy. After using the equipment for more than six months, Kandy notified Economy that the equipment was inadequate. Economy Forms alleged that Kandy had accepted the goods. Kandy denied liability. Was there an acceptance? Why or why not? [*Economy Forms Corp. v. Kandy, Inc.*, 391 F. Supp. 944 (N.D. Ga.)]

11. Hornell Brewing Company is a supplier and marketer of alcoholic and nonalcoholic beverages, including the popular iced tea drink, Arizona. In 1992, Stephen A. Spry and Don Vultaggio, Hornell's chairman of the board, made an oral agreement for Spry to be the exclusive distributor of Arizona products in Canada. The initial arrangement was an oral agreement, and in

response to Spry's request for a letter that he needed to secure financing, Hornell provided a letter that confirmed the distributorship.

During 1993 and 1994, Hornell shipped beverages on 10-day credit terms, but between December 1993 and February 1994, Spry's credit balances grew from $20,000 to $100,000, and a $31,000 check from Spry was returned for insufficient funds.

In March 1994, Hornell demanded that Spry obtain a line and/or letter of credit to pay for the beverages to place their relationship on a more secure footing. An actual line of credit never came about. Hornell did receive a partial payment by a wire transfer on May 9, 1994. Spry ordered 30 trailer loads of "product" from Hornell at a total purchase price of $390,000 to $450,000. Hornell learned from several sources, including its regional sales manager Baumkel, that Spry's warehouse was empty; that he had no managerial, sales, or office staff; that he had no trucks; and that his operation was a sham.

On May 10, 1994, Hornell wrote to Spry, telling him that it would extend up to $300,000 of credit to him, net 14 days cash "based on your prior representation that you have secured a $1,500,000 U.S. line of credit." Spry did not respond to this letter. After some months of futile negotiations by counsel, Hornell filed suit. Has there been a breach? What are the parties' rights? [*Hornell Brewing Co., Inc. v. Spry*, 664 N.Y.S.2d 698 (Sup. Ct.)]

12. Mark Murray and Ian Peck are art dealers who own separate art galleries located in New York. Robert and Jean Weil reside in Montgomery, Alabama, and are art collectors. Murray and Sam Lehr, a business acquaintance of his, traveled to Montgomery to see the various paintings in the Weils' collection, including a painting by Edgar Degas titled *Aux Courses*, which Murray examined under ultraviolet light. Murray later telephoned Weil and told him that he had spoken with someone who might be interested in purchasing the Degas.

On November 3, 1997, the director of Murray's gallery, Stephanie Calman, traveled to the Weils' home in Alabama. Calman, on behalf of

Murray, and Robert Weil executed an agreement that provided for consignment of the Degas to Murray's gallery "for a private inspection in New York for a period of a week" from November 3, "to be extended only with the express permission of the consignor." Calman returned to New York with the painting the same day.

Murray then showed the Degas to Peck. Peck expressed an interest in purchasing the Degas after seeing it, and the price of $1,125,000 was discussed.

On November 26, 1997, Murray signed an agreement drafted by Weil and retyped on Murray's letterhead. Weil signed the agreement on December 1, 1997.

Neither Murray nor anyone else ever paid Weil the $1 million. Nonetheless, Murray maintained possession of the Degas from November 3, 1997, through March 25, 1998, when Weil requested its return.

The Weils filed suit, seeking the price for the painting via summary judgment. Are the Weils entitled to recover? Explain why or why not. [*Weil v. Murray*, 161 F. Supp. 2d 250 (S.D.N.Y.)]

13. Trefalcon (a commercial arm of the government of Ghana) entered into a contract with Supply Commission as a purchaser of residual fuel oil (RFO). Supply Commission agreed, among other things, to supply Trefalcon with RFO at competitive prices as reserves permitted. Approximately six weeks into the agreement, on May 3, 1974, Supply Commission wrote a letter to Trefalcon proposing a method for pricing the refined fuel it would sell to Trefalcon.

A dispute arose six months later when Supply Commission first began to raise the price of RFO to account for escalations. In an effort to continue the contract, the parties orally agreed to a so-called Standstill Agreement, pursuant to which Ghana temporarily would forgo payment of escalations. By May 12, 1975, Trefalcon had paid only the base price for each of the 26 residual fuel cargoes it had received.

On May 26, 1975, J.V.L. Mensah, a representative of Supply Commission, sent a letter to Trefalcon demanding payment of $7,885,523.12 for escalation charges and declaring that no further oil would be sold until payment in full was made. After receiving the Mensah letter, Trefalcon tendered two payments to Bank of Ghana—one in the amount of $1,617,682.29 (tendered June 10, 1975), the other in the amount of $1,185,000 (tendered June 27, 1975).

With full payment still outstanding in July 1975, Supply Commission canceled the contract and sought damages for breach following the failure to provide assurances. Will Supply Commission recover? [*Reich v. Republic of Ghana*, 2002 WL 142610 (S.D.N.Y.)]

14. Harry Ulmas made a contract to buy a new car from Acey Oldsmobile. He was allowed to keep his old car until the new car was delivered. The sales contract gave him a trade-in value of $650 on the old car but specified that the car would be reappraised when it was actually brought to the dealer. When Ulmas brought the trade-in to the dealer, an Acey employee took it for a test drive and said that the car was worth between $300 and $400. Acey offered Ulmas only $50 for his trade-in. Ulmas refused to buy from Acey and purchased from another dealer, who appraised the trade-in at $400. Ulmas sued for breach of contract on the grounds of violation of good faith. Was he right? [*Ulmas v. Acey Oldsmobile, Inc.*, 310 N.Y.S.2d 147 (N.Y. Civ.)]

15. Cornelia and Ed Kornfeld contracted to sell a signed Picasso print to David Tunick, Inc. The print, entitled *Le Minotauromachie*, was signed "Pablo Picasso." The signature on the print was discovered to be a forgery, and the Kornfelds offered Tunick a substitute Picasso print. Tunick refused the Kornfelds' substituted performance and demanded a return of the contract price. The Kornfelds refused on the grounds that their cure had been refused. Was the substitute print an adequate cure? [*David Tunick, Inc. v. Kornfeld*, 838 F. Supp. 848 (S.D.N.Y.)]

CPA QUESTIONS

1. Under the sales article of the UCC, which of the following statements is correct?

   a. Obligations of the parties to the contract must be performed in good faith.

   b. Merchants and nonmerchants are treated alike.

   c. The contract must involve the sale of goods for a price of more than $500.

   d. None of the provisions of the UCC may be disclaimed by agreement.

2. Rowe Corp. purchased goods from Stair Co. that were shipped COD. Under the sales article of the UCC, which of the following rights does Rowe have?

   a. The right to inspect the goods before paying.

   b. The right to possession of the goods before paying.

   c. The right to reject nonconforming goods.

   d. The right to delay payment for a reasonable period of time.

3. Bibbeon Manufacturing shipped 300 designer navy blue blazers to Custom Clothing Emporium. The blazers arrived on Friday, earlier than Custom had anticipated and on an exceptionally busy day for its receiving department. They were perfunctorily examined and sent to a nearby warehouse for storage until needed. On the following Monday, upon closer examination, it was discovered that the quality of the blazer linings was inferior to that specified in the sales contract. Which of the following is correct insofar as Custom's rights?

   a. Custom can reject the blazers upon subsequent discovery of the defects.

   b. Custom must retain the blazers since it accepted them and had an opportunity to inspect them upon delivery.

   c. Custom's only course of action is rescission.

   d. Custom had no rights if the linings were merchantable quality.

4. Parker ordered 50 cartons of soap from Riddle Wholesale Company. Each carton contained 12 packages of soap. The terms were: $8.00 per carton 2/10, net/30, FOB buyer's delivery platform, delivery June 1. During transit approximately one-half the packages were damaged by the carrier. The delivery was made on May 28. Answer the following with "Yes" or "No."

a. Riddle had the risk of loss during transit.

b. If Parker elects to accept the undamaged part of the shipment, he will be deemed to have accepted the entire shipment.

c. To validly reject the goods, Parker must give timely notice of rejection to Riddle within a reasonable time after delivery.

d. If Riddle were notified of the rejection on May 28, Riddle could cure the defect by promptly notifying Parker of intention to do so and making a second delivery to Parker of conforming goods by June 1.

e. The statute of frauds is inapplicable to the transaction in the facts given.

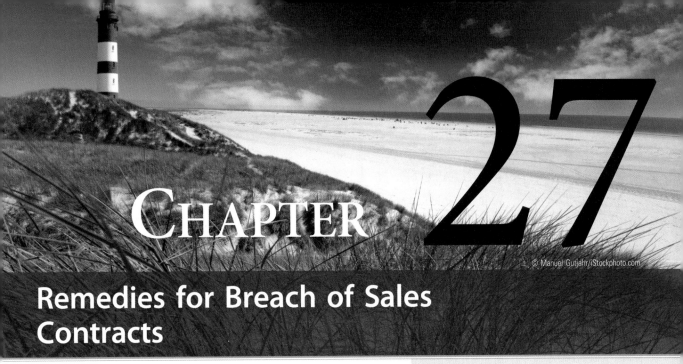

© Manuel Gutjahr/iStockphoto.com

CHAPTER 27

Remedies for Breach of Sales Contracts

learningoutcomes

After studying this chapter, you should be able to

LO.1 List the remedies of the seller when the buyer breaches a sales contract

LO.2 List the remedies of the buyer when the seller breaches a sales contract

LO.3 Determine the validity of clauses limiting damages

I f one of the parties to a sale fails to perform the contract, the nonbreaching party has remedies under Article 2 of the Uniform Commercial Code (UCC). In addition, the parties may have included provisions on remedies in their contract.

A. STATUTE OF LIMITATIONS

Judicial remedies have time limitations. After the expiration of a particular period of time, the party seeking a remedy can no longer resort to the courts. The UCC **statute of limitations** applies to actions brought for remedies on the breach of a sales contract.[1] When a suit is brought on the basis of a tort theory, such as negligence, fraud, or strict tort liability, other general statutes of limitations apply.

statute of limitations – statute that restricts the period of time within which an action may be brought.

CPA

1. Time Limits for Suits under the UCC

An action for breach of a sales contract must be commenced within four years after the time of the **breach**.[2] The statute of limitations can be reduced as between merchants to as little as one year but cannot be reduced in consumer contracts.

breach – failure to act or perform in the manner called for in a contract.

When a cause of action arises depends on the nature of the breach. The UCC has three measurements for determining when a breach occurs. The basic rule is that the time begins to run when the breach occurs, but that rule has exceptions that include special timing rules for repudiation, infringement, breach of warranty, and future performance.

A buyer seeking damages because of a breach of the sales contract must give the seller notice of the breach within a reasonable time after the buyer discovers or should have discovered it.[3]

2. Time Limits for Other Suits

When a party seeks recovery on a non-Code theory, such as on the basis of strict tort liability, fraud, or negligence, the UCC statute of limitations does not apply. The action is subject to each state's tort statute of limitations. Tort statutes of limitations are found in individual state statutes, and the time limitations vary by state. However, the tort statutes of limitations tend to be shorter than the UCC statute of limitations.

B. REMEDIES OF THE SELLER

When the buyer breaches a sales contract, the seller has different remedies available that are designed to afford the seller compensation for the losses caused by the buyer's breach.[4] Revised Article 2 allows the remedies provided to be used together, and although the various remedies may be called out in separate sections, there is no requirement that a party elect only one of the remedies. In many cases of breach, only a combination of the various remedies can make the nonbreaching party whole again.

---

[1] UCC §2-703.

[2] The cause of action arises as soon as the breach occurs even if the party is unaware of the breach at that time.

[3] UCC §2-607(3)(a).

[4] Under Revised Article 2 (§2-803), the overall policy change on remedies relates to the parties' expectations. The revision allows courts to deny a remedy if one party thereby benefits to more than a full performance position.

3. Seller's Lien

In the absence of an agreement for the extension of credit to the buyer for the purchase of goods, and until the buyer pays for the goods or performs whatever actions the contract requires, the seller has the right to retain possession of the goods.[5]

CPA   4. Seller's Remedy of Stopping Shipment

When the buyer has breached the contract prior to the time the goods have arrived at their destination, the seller can stop the goods from coming into the buyer's possession. This remedy is important to sellers because it eliminates the need for sellers to try to recover goods from buyers who have indicated they cannot or will not pay.

A seller has the right to stop shipment if the buyer has received goods on credit and the seller learns that the buyer is insolvent, the buyer has not provided assurances as requested, or the seller has grounds to believe performance by the buyer will not occur.[6] Also, the right to retrieve the goods in the case of a credit buyer's insolvency continues for "a reasonable time after the buyer's receipt of the goods."

CPA   5. Resale by Seller

When the buyer has breached the contract, the seller may resell any of the goods the seller still holds. After the resale, the seller is not liable to the original buyer on the contract and does not have to surrender any profit obtained on the resale. On the other hand, if the proceeds are less than the contract price, the seller may recover the loss from the original buyer.[7] Under Revised UCC, the failure of the seller to resell the goods does not mean the seller cannot recover under the other remedies available under Article 2.

The seller must give reasonable notice to the breaching buyer of the intention to resell the goods. Such notice need not be given if the goods are perishable or could decline rapidly in value. The seller must conduct any method of resale under standards of commercial reasonableness.[8]

6. Cancellation by Seller

When the buyer materially breaches the contract, the seller may cancel the contract. Such a cancellation ends the contract and discharges all unperformed obligations on both sides. Following cancellation, the seller has any remedy with respect to the breach by the buyer that is still available.

7. Seller's Action for Damages under the Market Price Formula

When the buyer fails to pay for accepted goods, the seller may resell the goods, as discussed earlier, or bring a contract action to recover damages. One formula for a seller's damages is the difference between the market price at the time and place of the tender of the goods and the contract price.[9] Under Revised Article 2, in the case of an anticipatory repudiation, the measurement of damages is the difference between the contract price and the market price "at the expiration of a commercially reasonable

---

[5] UCC §2-703.
[6] UCC §2-705.
[7] UCC §2-706(1), (6); *In re Circuit City Stores, Inc.,* 441 B.R. 496 (E.D. Va. 2010).
[8] *In re Lakewood Engineering & Mfg. Co., Inc.,* 459 B.R. 306 (N.D. Ill. 2011).
[9] UCC §2-708. *SEC America, LLC v. Marine Elec. Systems, Inc.,* 39 A.3d 1054 (Vt. 2011).

time after the seller learned of the repudiation" but not later than the time of tender. Whether the seller chooses to resell or recover the difference between the contract price and the market price is the seller's decision. The flexibility in the remedies under the UCC is provided because certain goods have very high market fluctuations. **For Example,** suppose that Sears has agreed to purchase 10 refrigerators from Whirlpool at a price of $1,000 each, but then Sears notifies Whirlpool that it will not be buying the refrigerators after all. Whirlpool determines the market price at the time of tender to be $850 per refrigerator. The best Whirlpool can find from an alternate buyer after a search is $800. Whirlpool can select the resale remedy ($1,000 − $800, or $200 in damages) to adequately compensate for the change in the market price between the time of tender and the time damages are sought.

CPA ## 8. Seller's Action for Lost Profits

If the market and resale price measures of damages do not place the seller in the same position in which the seller would have been had the buyer performed, the seller is permitted to recover lost profits.[10] The recovery of lost profits reimburses the seller for costs incurred in gearing up for contract performance.[11] **For Example,** suppose that a buyer has ordered 200 wooden rocking horses from a seller-manufacturer. Before production on the horses begins, the buyer breaches. The seller has nothing to resell, and the goods have not been identified to even permit a market value assessment. Nonetheless, the seller has geared up for production, counted on the contract, and perhaps bypassed other contracts in order to perform. An appropriate remedy for the seller of the rocking horses would be the profits it would have made had the buyer performed.

Some courts also follow the lost volume doctrine that allows sellers to recover for the profits they would have made if the buyer had completed the transaction.[12] **For Example,** suppose that Maytag has a contract to sell 10 washing machines for $600 each to Lakewood Apartment Managers. Lakewood breaches the agreement and refuses to take or pay for the washing machines. Maytag is able to resell them to Suds 'n Duds Laundromat for $600 each. The price is the same, but, the theory of lost volume profits is that Maytag could have sold 20 washers, not just 10, if Lakewood had not breached. Maytag's profit on each machine is $200. Lost volume profits in this situation would be 10 times the $200, or $2,000.

CPA ## 9. Other Types of Damages

incidental damages – incurred by the nonbreaching party as part of the process of trying to cover (buy substitute goods) or sell (selling subject matter of contract to another); includes storage fees, commissions, and the like.

So far, the discussion of remedies has focused on the damages that result because the seller did not sell the goods. However, the seller may incur additional expenses because of the breach. Some of those expenses can be recovered as damages. UCC §2-710 provides that the seller can also recover, as **incidental damages**, any commercially reasonable charges, expenses, or commissions incurred[13] in recovering damages.[14] **For Example,** the seller may recover expenses for the transportation, care, and storage of the goods after the buyer's breach, as well as any costs incurred

---

[10] Revised Article 2 greatly expands the availability of lost profits.
[11] UCC §2-709.
[12] *Sunrich v. Pacific Foods of Oregon*, 2004 WL 1124495 (D. Or. 2004); *Collins Entertainment Corp. v. Coats and Coats Rental Amusement*, 629 S.E.2d 635 (S.C. 2006).
[13] UCC §2-710.
[14] UCC §2-710; *WPS, Inc. v. Expro Americas, LCC*, 369 S.W.3d 384 (Tex. App. 2012).

in the return or resale of the goods. Such damages are in addition to any others that may be recovered by the seller.

10. Seller's Action for the Purchase Price

If goods are specially manufactured and the buyer refuses to take them, it is possible for the seller to recover as damages the full purchase price and keep the goods.[15] **For Example,** a printing company that has printed catalogs for a retail mail-order merchant will not be able to sell the catalogs to anyone else. The remedy for the seller is recovery of the purchase price.[16]

11. Seller's Nonsale Remedies

In addition to the seller's traditional sales remedies, many sellers enter into other transactions that provide protection from buyer breaches. One such protection is afforded when the seller obtains a security interest from the buyer under UCC Article 9. A **secured transaction** is a pledge of property by the buyer-debtor that enables the seller to take possession of the goods if the buyer fails to pay the amount owed. (See Chapter 34.) Figure 27-1 is a summary of the remedies available to the seller under Article 2.

secured transaction–credit sale of goods or a secured loan that provides special protection for the creditor.

FIGURE 27-1 | *Seller's Remedies under Article 2*

REMEDY	STOP DELIVERY	RESALE PRICE	MARKET PRICE	ACTION FOR PRICE	LOST PROFIT
SECTION NUMBER	2–703	2–706 2–710	2–708 2–710	2–709 2–708	2–708(2)
WHEN AVAILABLE	Insolvency Advance breach by buyer	Buyer fails to take goods	Buyer fails to take goods	Specially manufactured goods	Anticipatory repudiation Breach
NATURE OF REMEDY	Stop delivery of any size shipment or recover goods if buyer insolvent	Contract price – Resale price + Incidental damages – Expenses saved + Consequential damages	Contract price – Market price + Incidental damages – Expenses saved + Consequential damages	Contract price + Incidental damages – Expenses saved + Consequential damages	Profits + Incidental damages – Salvage value + Consequential damages

---

[15] *Hyosung America, Inc. v. Sumagh Textile Co., Ltd.,* (2nd Cir. 1998). *Barrington Group, Ltd., Inc. v. Classic Cruise Holdings S De RL,* 435 Fed.Appx. 382, 2011 WL 3364383 (5th Cir. 2011).
[16] UCC §2-709(1)(a) and (b).

C. Remedies of the Buyer

When the seller breaches a sales contract, the buyer has a number of remedies under Article 2 of the UCC. Additional remedies based on contract or tort theories of product liability may also be available. (See Chapter 25.)

12. Rejection of Improper Tender

As discussed in Chapter 26, if the goods tendered by the seller do not conform to the contract in some way, the buyer may reject them. However, the rejection is the beginning of the buyer's remedies. Following rejection, the buyer can proceed to recover under the various formulas provided for buyers under the UCC.

13. Revocation of Acceptance

The buyer may revoke acceptance of the goods when they do not conform to the contract, the defect substantially impairs the value of the contract to the buyer, and the buyer either could not discover the problem or kept the goods because of a seller's promise of repair (see Chapter 26). Again, following revocation of acceptance, the buyer has various remedies available under the UCC.

CPA
14. Buyer's Action for Damages for Nondelivery—Market Price Recovery

If the seller fails to deliver the goods as required by the contract or repudiates the contract, the buyer is entitled to collect from the seller damages for breach of contract. Under Revised Article 2, the buyer is entitled to recover the difference between the market price at the time of tender and the contract price; this is a change from the previous Article 2 that measured damages at the time the buyer learned of the breach.[17]

CPA
15. Buyer's Action for Damages for Nondelivery—Cover Price Recovery

A buyer may also choose, as a remedy for the seller's nondelivery of goods that conform to the contract, to purchase substitute goods or cover.[18] If the buyer acts in good faith, the measure of damages for the seller's nondelivery or repudiation is then the difference between the cost of cover and the contract price.[19]

The buyer need only make a reasonable cover purchase as a substitute for the contract goods. The goods purchased need not be identical to the contract goods.

---

[17] UCC §2-713.

[18] UCC §2-712; *Irwin Indus. Tool Co. v. Worthington Cylinders Wisconsin, LLC,* 747 F. Supp. 2d 568 (W.D.N.C. 2010). Buyers are also entitled to recover any deposits paid [*Selectouch Corp. v. Perfect Starch, Inc.,* 111 S.W.3d 830, 51 UCC Rep. Serv. 2d 1070 (Tex. App. 2004)].

[19] UCC §2-712(1) and (2). See *New West Charter Middle School v. Los Angeles Unified School Dist.,* 114 Cal. Rptr. 3d 504 (Cal. App. 2010).

For Example, if the buyer could secure only 350 five-speed blenders when the contract called for 350 three-speed blenders, the buyer's cover would be reasonable despite the additional expense of the five-speed blenders.

CASE SUMMARY

Cashing in for the Defective Cashews

FACTS: Schutzman sells roasted and salted nuts. Nutsco is a New Jersey wholesaler of cashews that imports the nuts from Brazil and then packs and sells them in the United States.

In 2006, Nutsco used food broker Jim Warner to broker a contract between Nutsco and Schutzman, whereby Nutsco promised to deliver twelve 35,000-pound loads of super large, whole, first-quality ("SLW-1") cashews. The contract also included an option allowing Schutzman to buy four loads of large, whole, first-quality ("LW-1") cashews, if exercised by a certain date.

Schutzman later wanted to order more cashews. Warner amended the contract to add two additional loads. In March 2007, Warner sent a copy of the revised Contract Confirmation adding the two extra loads (loads 13 and 14) to both Nutsco and Schutzman.

Nutsco delivered 10 loads of SLW-1 cashews to Schutzman. After receiving the tenth load, however, Schutzman roast tested the cashews and determined that they did not qualify as "first quality" under specifications of the Association of Food Industries, Inc. (AFI), because of a high level of scorching. Nutsco represents to the market that if it is going to sell SLW-1 cashews, the cashews will meet AFI standards for SLW-1.

Warner showed the poor results of the roast test to Patricio Assis's (at Nutsco) attention. At Warner's request, Schutzman provided six cases of cashews from the tenth load for evaluation by Nutsco. Nutsco concluded after its own analysis that the raw cashews did not meet AFI Specifications for first-quality cashews.

After Nutsco delivered the tenth load, Patricio Assis began arguing that the parties' contract only provided for 12 loads of SLW-1 cashews and that Nutsco was not responsible for providing the two additional loads because there was no signed contract for the additional loads. Market prices for SLW-1 cashews by now $2 per pound higher than the price that Nutsco had under their contract. Schutzman initially agreed to keep the load and pay the contract price on the condition that Nutsco deliver all remaining loads, including loads 13 and 14. Patricio Assis would not agree to this arrangement. Warner then attempted to circumvent Patricio Assis and contacted Francisco Assis Neto directly. Jim Warner advised Mr. Neto in an e-mail that Schutzman would pay for the scorched tenth load, but wanted delivery of five loads of cashews (loads 10-14). While waiting for a reply, Schutzman stored the tenth load in its refrigerated warehouse.

Jim Warner sent an e-mail to Patricio Assis reminding him that Schutzman was waiting for Nutsco to pick up the rejected tenth load of cashews. After five months, Mr. Assis traveled to Wisconsin to inspect the load and then arranged to have the load picked up.

Schutzman did not pay for the rejected tenth load of SLW-1 cashews that Nutsco retrieved. Schutzman did pay all invoices for the nine preceding loads it received and accepted. Schutzman paid a reduced price on two of the invoices after Warner agreed that it could apply $1,750 and $1,284 in credit against these invoices.

Schutzman paid to purchase loads of SLW-1 cashews from other wholesalers. Schutzman purchased five loads to replace the remaining loads it had expected Nutsco to provide under their contract. Schutzman paid $5.45 per pound for these loads, or $367,850 more for the five loads than it would have paid under the contract with Nutsco. Schutzman filed suit for damages in this amount.

CASE SUMMARY

Continued

DECISION: The court held that there was a contract for shipment of 14 loads of cashews. The court also held that Schutzman did not convert the below-par tenth load of cashews and that Schutzman was entitled to damages for the difference between its contract price with Nutsco and the more-than-doubled price it was required to pay for cover. The court also held that Warner, the agent, at least had apparent authority to negotiate the additional shipments of cashews. [*A. L. Schutzman Company, Inc. v. Nutsco, Inc.*, 2009 WL 5064052 (E.D.Wis. 2009)]

CPA ## 16. Other Types of Damages

The buyer is also entitled to collect incidental damages in situations in which he must find substitute goods. Those incidental damages could include additional shipping expenses or perhaps commissions paid to find the goods and purchase them. Buyers often also experience **consequential damages**, which are those damages the buyer experiences with respect to a third party as a result of the seller's breach. Revised UCC provides consequential damages for sellers and buyers. The seller's section provides, "Consequential damages resulting from the buyer's breach include any loss resulting from general or particular requirements and needs of which the buyer at the time of contracting had reason to know and which could not reasonably be prevented by resale or otherwise."[20]

For Example, a seller's failure to deliver the goods may cause the buyer's production line to come to a halt. The buyer might then breach on its sales and delivery contracts with its buyers. In the case of a government contract, the buyer may have to pay a penalty for being late. These types of damages are consequential ones and can be recovered if the seller knew about the consequences or they were foreseeable. Under Revised Article 2, consequential damages cannot be recovered from a consumer.

consequential damages— damages the buyer experiences as a result of the seller's breach with respect to a third party.

Thinking Things Through

The Rolls Royce Engine That Grounded Planes

Qantas Airlines grounded all of its Airbus 380 jetliners after one of those jets experienced an in-air emergency when one of the Rolls Royce engines on the jumbo jet exploded. The jet landed safely, but all of Qantas's fleet was grounded for inspection of the engines. Qantas filed suit against Rolls Royce for the damages resulting from the losses due to the grounded planes. What would be the basis for the suit? What form of damages is Qantas seeking?

Meraiah Foley and Nicola Clark, "Qantas Goes to Court Over A380 Engines, Facing Added Tests," *New York Times*, Dec. 3, 2010, p. B7.

[20] UCC §2-710.

17. Action for Breach of Warranty

A remedy available to a buyer when goods are delivered but fail to conform to warranties is an action for breach of warranty.

CASE SUMMARY

A Chance of Cloudy Meatballs

FACTS: General Mills Operations, LLC purchased "Big Meatballs Cooked Italian," which is used in General Mills' Progresso Italian–Style Wedding Soup, from Five Star Custom Foods, Ltd.

General Mills sent purchase orders to Five Star. The Purchase Order Terms and Conditions were on the back of every purchase order, including the meatball orders faxed to Five Star. General Mills also mailed a copy of the 2004 version of its Terms and Conditions to Five Star's Customer Service Manager on February 4, 2004.

The Terms and Conditions included the following:

5. GOODS: The Goods shall conform in all respects to the description on the face of this Order, and or [General Mills'] then current specifications furnished to [Five Star]. The Goods ... shall be new, of first class commercial type ... This warranty is in addition to and not in lieu of, any other warranties or guarantees made by [Five Star] or created or implied as a matter of law.

Additionally, the purchase order states that "[t]he goods must conform to all current General Mills' specifications as furnished to Seller." General Mills mailed a copy of the ingredient specifications for its meatballs to Five Star. Five Star acknowledged receipt of the specifications, which included the following:

The Beef or Beef By–Product in this ingredient must be sourced from countries or regions where USDA recognized BSE controls are in place in accordance with the recommendations of the World Animal Health Organization.

One of Five Star's beef suppliers was Westland Meat Packing Company. Westland's beef was used in two orders of meatballs supplied to General Mills. In February 2008, the Food Safety Inspection Service (FSIS) issued a recall of all products containing beef produced by Westland between February 1, 2006, and February 15, 2008. The recall was due to Westland's supposed failure to contact FSIS when it identified nonambulatory disabled, or "downer," cows that became nonambulatory after passing inspections but before slaughter. In such situations, regulations at the time required the producer to notify FSIS and to call a public-health veterinarian to conduct an examination. Westland's alleged failure to consistently do this was deemed noncompliant, and the recall followed. There is no evidence, however, that any of the Westland beef supplied to Five Star or incorporated into General Mills' meatballs came from downer cattle.

When Five Star learned of the recall, it traced the Westland beef that it had incorporated into its products and notified General Mills of the recall on February 8, 2008. Five Star identified two purchase orders of meatballs, totaling 32,460 pounds, which contained Westland beef.

General Mills was required to identify and destroy all soup containing the recalled meatballs in its inventory, as well as soup that it had already sold to grocery stores and other customers. The recall cost General Mills more than $1,000,000.

CASE SUMMARY

Continued

General Mills filed suit in January 2010, asserting claims for breach of contract, breach of express warranties, breach of the implied warranty of merchantability, breach of the implied warranty of fitness for a particular purpose, and negligence. (Five Star filed a Third–Party Complaint asserting claims against Cattleman's Choice, Inc. d/b/a Westland). Both General Mills and Five Star moved for summary judgment.

DECISION: The court held the following:

There was no evidence of an actual defect in the meatball product as required to prove breach of express or implied warranties. Five Star breached the contract with General Mills, since it failed to receive the benefit of its bargain. Five Star was on notice of the terms and conditions since they had been incorporated by reference into the purchase agreement with General Mills. The contract terms were not inconspicuous, illegible, or hidden in boilerplate language; and the placement of the terms and conditions on the back of General Mills purchase order did not render terms unenforceable, under Minnesota law, since they did not materially alter the parties' agreement. General Mills was entitled to the cost of the recall ($1,000,000) plus attorneys' fees. [*General Mills Operations, LLC v. Five Star Custom Foods, LTD*, 789 F. Supp. 2d 1148 (D. Minn. 2011)]

(A) NOTICE OF BREACH. If the buyer has accepted goods that do not conform to the contract or there has been a breach of any warranties given, the buyer must notify the seller of the breach within a reasonable time after the breach is discovered or should have been discovered.[21]

(B) MEASURE OF DAMAGES. If the buyer has given the necessary notice of breach, the buyer may recover damages measured by the loss resulting in the normal course of events from the breach. If suit is brought for breach of warranty, the measure of damages is the difference between the value of the goods as they were at the time of tender and the value that they would have had if they had been as warranted. Under Revised Article 2, the buyer is also entitled to any of the other damage remedies necessary to make the buyer whole.

(C) NOTICE OF THIRD-PARTY ACTION AGAINST BUYER. When a buyer elects the remedy of resale and sells the contract goods to a third party, that third party has the right of suit against the buyer for breach of warranty. In such a case, it is the buyer's option whether to give the seller notice of the action and request that the seller defend that action.

---

[21] *Dunleavey v. Paris Ceramics, USA, Inc.*, 819 A.2d 945 (Super. Ct. 2002); *Muehlbauer v. General Motors Corp.*, 431 F. Supp. 2d 847 (N.D. Ill. 2006).

18. Cancellation by Buyer

The buyer may cancel or rescind the contract if the seller fails to deliver the goods, if the seller has repudiated the contract, or if the goods have been rightfully rejected or their acceptance revoked.[22] A buyer who cancels the contract is entitled to recover as much of the purchase price as has been paid, including the value of any property given as a trade-in as part of the purchase price. The fact that the buyer cancels the contract does not destroy the buyer's cause of action against the seller for breach of that contract. The buyer may recover from the seller not only any payment made on the purchase price but also damages for the breach of the contract. The damages represent the difference between the contract price and the cost of cover.[23]

CASE SUMMARY

The Alpha Chi Omega Battle of the Sweaters

FACTS: Emily Lieberman and Amy Altomondo were members of the Alpha Chi Omega (AXO) sorority at Bowling Green State University. They negotiated with Johnathan James Furlong for the purchase of custom-designed sweaters for themselves and their sorority sisters for a total price of $3,612. Lieberman and Altomondo paid Furlong a $2,000 deposit.

When Lieberman and Altomondo saw the sweaters, they realized that Furlong had made color and design alterations in the lettering imprinted on the sweaters as part of their custom design. Altomondo, as president of AXO, called Furlong and told him that the sweaters were unacceptable and offered to return them. Furlong refused, stating that any changes were immaterial. Altomondo refused to pay the balance due and demanded the return of the $2,000 deposit. Furlong filed suit for breach of contract.

DECISION: The sorority rejected the sweaters within a reasonable time after delivery and notified the seller. The seller breached the contract. The sorority is entitled to cancel the contract, recover the amounts it paid, and hold the sweaters until recovery. The sweaters were altered without authorization and there is a breach of contract. Finally, and alternatively, Furlong should have entered into a contract that gave him discretion to make design changes without AXO's consent. These sweaters, as Furlong himself admits (and describes), were to be "custom-designed" for AXO. Thus, they were to be printed according to AXO's specifications, not according to Furlong's discretion.

The sorority is entitled to a full refund of its deposit and any additional damages it experienced in defending this suit and seeking to collect the amounts it is due. [***Furlong v. Alpha Chi Omega Sorority***, 657 N.E.2d 866 (Ohio. Mun. Ct. 1993)]

The right of the buyer to cancel or rescind the sales contract may be lost by a delay in exercising the right. A buyer who, with full knowledge of the defects in the goods, makes partial payments or performs acts of ownership of the goods

---

[22] UCC §2-720.
[23] UCC §2-712(1), (2); *GFSI, Inc. v. J-Loong Trading, Ltd.*, 505 F. Supp. 2d 935 (D. Kan. 2007).

inconsistent with the decision to cancel may lose certain remedy provisions or be limited in recovery under Article 2.

19. Buyer's Resale of Goods

When the buyer has possession of the goods after rightfully rejecting them or after rightfully revoking acceptance, the buyer is treated as a seller in possession of goods after default by a buyer. When the seller has breached, the buyer has a security interest in the goods to protect the claim against the seller for breach and may proceed to resell the goods. From the proceeds of the sale, the aggrieved buyer is entitled to deduct any payments made to the seller and any expenses reasonably incurred in the inspection, receipt, transportation, care and custody, and resale of the goods.[24]

CPA ## 20. Action for Specific Performance

Under Article 2, specific performance is a remedy available only to buyers in those circumstances in which the goods are specially manufactured, unique, or rare, such as antiques or goods with sentimental value for the buyer. **For Example,** a buyer with a contract to buy a chair from Elvis Presley's home would be entitled to a specific performance remedy of delivery of the chair. Distributors have been granted specific performance against suppliers to deliver goods covered by supply contracts because of the unique dependence of the supply chain and the assumed continuous feeding of that chain.

Specific performance will not be granted, however, merely because the price of the goods purchased from the seller has gone up. In such a case, the buyer can still purchase the goods in the open market. The fact that it will cost more to cover can be compensated for by allowing the buyer to recover the cost increase from the seller.

21. Nonsale Remedies of the Buyer

In addition to the remedies given the buyer under UCC Article 2, the buyer may have remedies based on contract or tort theories of liability.

The pre-Code law on torts still applies in UCC Article 2 transactions. The seller may therefore be held liable to the buyer for any negligence, fraud, or strict tort liability that occurred in the transaction. (See Chapter 25.)

A defrauded buyer may both avoid the contract and recover damages. The buyer also has the choice of retaining the contract and recovering damages for the losses caused by the fraud.[25]

Figure 27-2 provides a summary of the remedies available to buyers under Article 2.

---

[24] UCC §2-715(1); *Gordon v. Gordon*, 929 So. 2d 981 (Miss. App. 2006).
[25] *Sherwin Alumina L.P. v. AluChem, Inc.*, 512 F. Supp. 2d 957 (S.D. Tex. 2007).

FIGURE 27-2	*Buyer's Remedies under Article 2*		
REMEDY	SPECIFIC PERFORMANCE (REPLEVIN IDENTIFICATION)	COVER	MARKET PRICE
SECTION NUMBER	2–711	2–712 2–715	2–708 2–710
WHEN AVAILABLE	Rare or unique goods	Seller fails to deliver or goods are defective (rejection) or revocation of acceptance	Seller fails to deliver or goods are defective (rejection or revocation of acceptance)
NATURE OF REMEDY	Buyer gets goods + incidental damages + consequential damages	Cover price – Contract price + Incidental damages + Consequential damages – Expenses saved	Market price – Contract price + Incidental damages + Consequential damages – Expenses saved

© Cengage Learning

D. Contract Provisions on Remedies

The parties to a sales contract may modify the remedies provided under Article 2 or limit those remedies.

22. Limitation of Damages

CPA

liquidated damages – provision stipulating the amount of damages to be paid in the event of default or breach of contract.

(A) Liquidated Damages. The parties may specify the exact amount of damages that may be recovered in case of breach. A **liquidated damages** clause in a contract can be valid if it meets the standards of Article 2. Under Revised Article 2, the enforceability of a liquidated damages clause in a consumer contract is determined by comparing the amount of the liquidated damages specified with the anticipated or actual harm, the difficulties of proof of loss, and the availability of an otherwise adequate remedy. For nonconsumer contracts, the enforceability of a liquidated damages clause depends on whether the amount is reasonable in light of the anticipated or actual harm.

CASE SUMMARY

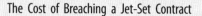

The Cost of Breaching a Jet-Set Contract

FACTS: On August 21, 1992, Miguel A. Diaz Rodriguez (Diaz) entered into a contract with Learjet to buy a model 60 jet aircraft for $3,000,000 with a $250,000 deposit made on execution of the contract; $750,000 payment on September 18, 1992; $1,000,000 180 days before delivery of the aircraft; and the balance due on delivery of the aircraft. Diaz paid the $250,000 deposit but made no other payments.

In September 1992, Diaz said he no longer wanted the aircraft and asked for the deposit to be returned. Learjet informed Diaz that the $250,000 deposit was being retained as liquidated damages because their contract provided as follows:

> *Learjet may terminate this Agreement as a result of the Buyer's failure to make any progress payment when due. If this Agreement is terminated by Learjet for any reason stipulated in the previous sentence, Learjet shall retain all payments theretofore made by the Buyer as liquidated damages and not as a penalty and the parties shall thenceforth be released from all further obligations hereunder. Such damages include, but are not limited to, loss of profit on this sale, direct and indirect costs incurred as a result of disruption in production, training expense advance and selling expenses in effecting resale of the Airplane.*

After Diaz breached the contract, Circus Circus Enterprises purchased the Learjet Diaz had ordered with some changes that cost $1,326. Learjet realized a $1,887,464 profit on the sale of the aircraft to Circus Circus, which was a larger profit than Learjet had originally budgeted for the sale to Diaz.

Diaz filed suit seeking to recover the $250,000 deposit. The district court granted summary judgment to Learjet, and Diaz appealed. The case was remanded for a determination of the reasonableness of the liquidated damages. The district court upheld the $250,000 as reasonable damages, and Diaz appealed.

DECISION: The lower court's judgment was affirmed. Diaz challenged the reasonableness of the liquidated damages clause. The $250,000 deposit as a liquidated damages clause in a contract in this price range was not unreasonable. Also, the seller was the one that lost its profits on a second sale that it would have made had Diaz not breached. The "lost volume" provision of the UCC permits nonbreaching sellers to recover the lost profits on a contract in which the other remedy sections do not compensate for the breach by the buyer. The evidence indicates that the lost profit from the Diaz contract would have been approximately $1.8 million. [***Rodriguez v. Learjet, Inc.,*** **946 P.2d 1010 (Kan. App. 1997)**]

(B) **EXCLUSION OF DAMAGES.** The sales contract may provide that in case of breach, no damages may be recovered or no consequential damages may be recovered. When goods are sold for consumer use and personal injuries are sustained, such total exclusions are unconscionable and unenforceable. Such a contract limitation is not enforceable in other types of contracts (nonconsumer) unless the party seeking to enforce it is able to prove that the limitation of liability was commercially reasonable and fair rather than oppressive and surprising. As discussed in Chapter 25, limitations on damages for personal injuries resulting from breaches of warranty are not enforceable.

CPA 23. Down Payments and Deposits

A buyer can make a deposit with the seller or an initial or down payment at the time of making the contract. If the contract contains a valid provision for liquidation of damages and the buyer defaults, the seller must return any part of the down payment or deposit in excess of the amount specified by the liquidated damages clause. In the absence of such a liquidated damages clause and in the absence of proof of greater damages, the seller's damages are computed as 20 percent of the purchase price or $500, whichever is smaller.

24. Limitation of Remedies

The parties may limit the remedies that are provided by the Code in the case of breach of contract. A seller may specify that the only remedy of the buyer for breach of warranty will be the repair or replacement of the goods or that the buyer will be limited to returning the goods and obtaining a refund of the purchase price, subject to the restrictions discussed in Chapter 25.

25. Waiver of Defenses

A buyer can be barred from claiming a breach of the contract by the seller if the sales contract expressly states that the buyer will not assert any defenses against the seller.

Thinking Things Through

The Gun-Totin' Harley Buyer and His Damages

Wiley Sharbino purchased a 2003 Harley Davidson motorcycle from Cooke Family Enterprises, LLC, d/b/a Renegade Harley-Davidson. He gave a gun as a down payment and financed the remaining amount of the purchase price. Within two days of purchase, the motorcycle sustained a broken drive belt. When Sharbino took the motorcycle back, Renegade told him that "the drive sprockets on the transmission and the rear wheel of the motorcycle were mismatched, causing the drive belt to break." The problem could not be fixed without changing the appearance of the motorcycle. Sharbino said he would not have purchased the motorcycle if he had known of the problem.

Renegade took back the motorcycle and told Sharbino to pick up his gun at the office where the dealership had kept it in a safe. Sharbino still filed suit seeking as damages the sales price plus interest, reasonable expenses related to the sale and preservation of the motorcycle, and attorney fees. Renegade said that the rescission of the agreement and return of Sharbino's "down payment" made him whole and that he had no other damages. Who is correct? Is rescission and the restoring of the party to his original position enough to compensate for a breach? [*Sharbino v. Cooke Family Enterprises, Inc.,* 6 So. 3d 1026 (La. App. 3d Cir. 2009)]

Ethics & the Law

Don't Stop Believing

What are the ethical obligations of sales people who are out selling their companies' products when they know that their companies are in trouble financially? Or that their companies are going to stop making a particular product? Is there a duty to disclose this information or are these risks that are inherent in business and contracts? [*NutraSoya Foods, Inc. v. Sunrich, LLC,* 641 F.3d 282 (8th Cir. 2010)]

26. Preservation of Defenses

Consumer protection law prohibits the waiver of defenses in consumer contracts.

(A) PRESERVATION NOTICE. Consumer defenses are preserved by a Federal Trade Commission (FTC) regulation. This regulation requires that the papers signed by a consumer contain a provision that expressly states that the consumer reserves any defense arising from the transaction.[26] A defense of the consumer arising from the original transaction may be asserted against any third person who acquires rights by assignment in the contract (see Chapter 33).

(B) PROHIBITION OF WAIVER. When the FTC preservation notice is included in the contract that is obtained by, or transferred to, a third party, a waiver of defenses cannot be made. If the preservation notice is not included, the seller has committed an unfair trade practice.

E. REMEDIES IN THE INTERNATIONAL SALE OF GOODS

The United Nations Convention on Contracts for the International Sale of Goods (CISG) provides remedies for breach of a sales contract between parties from nations that have approved the CISG.

27. Remedies of the Seller

Under the CISG, if the buyer fails to perform any obligations under the contract, the seller may require the buyer to pay the price, take delivery, and perform other obligations under the contract. The seller may also declare the contract void if the failure of the buyer to perform obligations under the contract amounts to a fundamental breach of contract.

E-Commerce & Cyberlaw

Consequential Damages and Software

Computer systems and software often do not function as intended or have some glitches when installed at a company. For example, suppose that a software company sold to a utility a software package that was represented as one that would simplify the utility's billing processes. The program is installed and tested, and some changes are made as a result of trial runs. When the program is fully implemented and all customers and bills are run through the new system, there is a complete breakdown. The bills cannot be produced or sent to customers, and the utility company is without cash flow. Without bills going out, no payments are coming in, and the utility must borrow from a high-interest line of credit at an interest cost of $400,000 per month. What damages could the utility collect? Could the software manufacturer limit its liability?

---

[26] 316 C.F.R. §433.1: It is an unfair or deceptive trade practice to take or receive a consumer credit contract that fails to contain such a preservation notice.

28. Remedies of the Buyer

Under the CISG, a buyer may reject goods only if the tender is a fundamental breach of the contract. This standard of materiality of rejection is in contrast to the UCC requirement of perfect tender. Under the CISG, a buyer may also reduce the price when nonconforming goods are delivered even though no notice of nonconformity is given. However, the buyer must have a reasonable cause for failure to give notice about the nonconformity.

MAKE THE CONNECTION

SUMMARY

The law provides a number of remedies for the breach of a sales contract. Remedies based on UCC theories generally are subject to a four-year statute of limitations, with Revised UCC adding an extension of one additional year (making it five years) in cases in which the breach is discovered in year four. If the remedy sought is based on a non-UCC theory, a tort or contract statute of limitations established by state statute will apply.

Remedies of the seller may include (1) a lien on the goods until the seller is paid, (2) the right to resell the goods, (3) the right to cancel the sales contract, (4) the right to recover the goods from the carrier and the buyer, and (5) the right to bring an action for damages or, in some cases, for the purchase price. The seller may also have remedies because of secured transactions.

Remedies of the buyer may include (1) the rejection of nonconforming goods, (2) the revocation of acceptance, (3) an action for damages for nondelivery of conforming goods, (4) an action for breach of warranty, (5) the cancellation of the sales contract, (6) the right to resell the goods, (7) the right to bring an action for conversion, recovery of goods, or specific performance, and (8) the right to sue for damages and cancel if the seller has made a material breach of the contract.

The parties may modify their remedies by a contractual provision for liquidated damages, for limitations on statutory remedies, or for waiver of defenses. When consumers are involved, this freedom of contract is to some extent limited for their protection.

Under the CISG, the seller may require the buyer to pay the price, take delivery, and perform obligations under the contract, or the seller may avoid the contract if there is a fundamental breach.

A buyer may reject goods under the CISG only if there is a fundamental breach of contract. The buyer may also reduce the price of nonconforming goods.

LEARNING OUTCOMES

After studying this chapter, you should be able to clearly explain:

A. Statute of Limitations
B. Remedies of the Seller
L0.1 List the remedies of the seller when the buyer breaches a sales contract
See the *For Example,* discussion of the Whirlpool refrigerators on p. 560.

C. Remedies of the Buyer
L0.2 List the remedies of the buyer when the seller breaches a sales contract
See the Thinking Things Through discussion of the Qantas airline suit for recovery for the losses from its grounded fleet on p. 564.

See *Furlong v. Alpha Chi Omega Sorority* on p. 567.

D. Contract Provisions on Remedies

LO.3 Determine the validity of clauses limiting damages

See *Rodriguez v. Learjet, Inc.* on p. 570.

See *Schutzman v. Nutsco* case on pp. 563–564.

See the E-Commerce & Cyberlaw discussion of software damages on p. 572.

See *General Mills Operations, LLC v. Five Star Custom Foods, LTD* on pp. 565–566.

E. Remedies in the International Sale of Goods

KEY TERMS

breach

consequential damages

incidental damages

liquidated damages

secured transaction

statute of limitations

QUESTIONS AND CASE PROBLEMS

1. Firwood Manufacturing Co. had a contract to sell General Tire 55 model 1225 postcure inflators (PCIs). PCIs are $30,000 machines used by General Tire in its manufacturing process. The contract was entered into in 1989, and by April 1990 General Tire had purchased 22 PCIs from Firwood. However, General Tire then closed its Barrie, Michigan, plant. Firwood reminded General Tire that it still had the obligation to purchase the 33 remaining PCIs. General Tire communicated to Firwood that it would not be purchasing the remaining ones. Firwood then was able, over a period of three years, to sell the remaining PCIs. Some of the PCIs were sold as units, and others were broken down and sold to buyers who needed parts. Firwood's sales of the remaining 33 units brought in $187,513 less than the General Tire contract provided, and Firwood filed suit to collect the resale price difference plus interest. Can Firwood recover? Why or why not? [*Firwood Manufacturing Co., Inc. v. General Tire, Inc.*, 96 F.3d 163 (6th Cir.)]

2. Soon after Gast purchased a used auto from a Chevrolet dealer, he experienced a series of mechanical problems with the car. Gast refused to make further payments on the bank note that had financed the purchase. The bank took possession of the automobile and sold it. Gast then brought an action against the dealer, alleging that he had revoked his acceptance.

Was Gast correct? Explain your answer. [*Gast v. Rodgers-Dingus Chevrolet*, 585 So.2d 725 (Miss.)]

3. Formetal Engineering submitted to Presto a sample and specifications for precut polyurethane pads to be used in making air-conditioning units. Formetal paid for the goods as soon as they were delivered but subsequently discovered that the pads did not conform to the sample and specifications in that there were incomplete cuts, color variances, and faulty adherence to the pad's paper backing. Formetal then informed Presto of the defects and notified Presto that it would reject the pads and return them to Presto, but they were not returned for 125 days. Presto argued that it was denied the right to cure because the goods were not returned until some 125 days after Formetal promised to do so. Was there a breach of the contract? Did the buyer (Formetal) do anything wrong in seeking its remedies? [*Presto Mfg. Co. v. Formetal Engineering Co.*, 360 N.E.2d 510 (Ill. App.)]

4. Lam entered into contracts with Dallas Semiconductor to build six machines, referred to in its contracts as Tools A–F.

   The contracts were entered into in 2000 and in 2001, but Maxim Integrated acquired Dallas Semiconductor in 2001. The employees at Dallas who were in charge of the contracts continued to assure Lam that everything was on track. Lam representatives also had meetings with Maxim representatives. However, those discussions broke down and after Lam issued a demand letter for which there was no response, he filed suit for breach of contract. Lam was able to sell the machines to other customers for an equal or greater price. Lam asked for total damages in the amount of $13,860,847, representing lost profits on all six tools, plus lost profits on the extended warranties and training packages for the tools. Is Lam entitled to such recovery? [*Lam Research Corp. v. Dallas Semiconductor Corp.*, 2006 WL 1000573, 59 UCC Rep.2d 716 (Cal. App.)]

5. McNeely entered into a contract with Wagner to pay $250,000 as a lump sum for all timber present in a given area that Wagner would remove for McNeely. The contract estimated that the volume in the area would be 780,000 board feet. Wagner also had provisions in the contract that made no warranties as to the amount of lumber and that he would keep whatever timber was not harvested if McNeely ended the contract before the harvesting was complete. The $250,000 was to be paid in three advances. McNeely paid two of the three advances but withheld the third payment and ended the contract because he said there was not enough timber. Wagner filed suit for the remaining one-third of the payment. McNeely said Wagner could not have the remaining one-third of the payment as well as the transfer; he had to choose between the two remedies. Is he correct? [*Wagner v. McNeely*, 38 UCC 2d 1176 (Or)]

6. Brown Machine Company, a division of Kvaerner U.S., Inc., entered into a contract to supply a machine and tools to Hakim Plast, a food container–producing company based in Cairo, Egypt, to enable Hakim to meet its growing demand for plastic containers. The plastic containers were for customers to use in the ice cream distribution industry. It was understood that the equipment would be ready for delivery before the busy summer ice cream season. Brown Machine was not able to meet the twice extended deadline. It attempted to obtain another extension, but Hakim Plast refused without additional consideration. Brown refused to provide the requested consideration. Hakim

Plast declared the contract breached on September 25, 1994. Brown then sold the equipment and brought suit for breach of contract, requesting damages for the loss of the sale. Hakim Plast countersued for Brown's breach seeking out-of-pocket expenses and consequential damages for loss of business. Discuss who breached the contract and determine what possible damages might be recovered. [*Kvaerner U.S., Inc. v. Hakim Plast Co.*, 74 F. Supp. 2d (E.D. Mich.)]

7. Sonya Kaminski purchased from Billy Cain's Cornelia dealership a truck that was represented to her to be a 1989 Chevrolet Silverado pickup. However, subsequent incidents involving repair of the truck and its parts, as well as a title history, revealed that the truck was a GMC rather than a Chevrolet. Sales agents at the Cornelia dealership misrepresented the truck's character and sold the truck to Kaminski as a Chevrolet.

Kaminski filed suit for intentional fraud and deceit under the Georgia Fair Business Practices Act (FBPA) and for breach of express warranty. The jury awarded Kaminski $2,823.70 for breach of express warranty and $50,000 punitive (exemplary) damages. The judge added damages under the FBPA of $10,913.29 in actual damages and $9,295 in attorney fees and court costs. The dealership appealed. Must the dealership pay the damages? Why or why not? [*Billy Cain Ford Lincoln Mercury, Inc. v. Kaminski*, 496 SE2d 521 (Ga App)]

8. Mrs. Kirby purchased a wheelchair from NMC/Continue Care. The wheelchair was customized for her and her home. When the wheelchair arrived, it was too wide to fit through the doorways in her home. What options does Mrs. Kirby have? [*Kirby v. NMC Continue Care*, 993 P.2d 951 (Wyo)]

9. Wolosin purchased a vegetable and dairy refrigerator case from Evans Manufacturing Corp. When Evans sued Wolosin for the purchase price, Wolosin claimed damages for breach of warranty. The sales contract provided that Evans would replace defective parts free of charge for one year; it also stated, "This warranty is in lieu of any and all other warranties stated or

inferred, and of all other obligations on the part of the manufacturer, which neither assumes nor authorizes anyone to assume for it any other obligations or liability in connection with the sale of its products." Evans claimed that it was liable only for replacement of parts. Wolosin claimed that the quoted clause was not sufficiently specific to satisfy the limitation-of-remedies requirement of UCC §2-719. Provide some insight on this issue for the parties by discussing damage limitation clauses under the UCC. [*Evans Mfg. Corp. v. Wolosin*, 47 Luzerne County Leg. Reg. 238 (Pa)]

10. McInnis purchased a tractor and scraper as new equipment of the current model year from Western Tractor & Equipment Co. The written contract stated that the seller disclaimed all warranties and that no warranties existed except those stated in the contract. Actually, the equipment was not the current model but that of the prior year. The equipment was not new but had been used for 68 hours as a demonstrator model, after which the hour meter had been reset to zero. The buyer sued the seller for damages. The seller's defense was based on the ground that all liability for warranties had been disclaimed. Was this defense valid? [*McInnis v. Western Tractor & Equipment Co.*, 388 P.2d 562 (Wash)]

11. Elmore purchased a car from Doenges Brothers Ford. The car had been placed with the dealership by a dealership employee as part of a consignment arrangement. Elmore was unable to obtain title to the car because the Environmental Protection Agency had issues with the car's compliance with emissions equipment requirements. Elmore was unable to drive the car. He brought suit because he was forced to sell the car for $10,300 less than he paid because of the title defect, and the fact that only a salvage dealer would purchase it. Because he lost his transportation, he was out of work for eight months and experienced a $20,000 decline in income. What damages could Elmore recover under the UCC? [*Elmore v. Doenges Bros. Ford, Inc.*, 21 P.3d 65 (Okla. App.)]

12. Stock Solution is a "stock photo agency" that leases photographic transparencies produced by professional photographers for use in media advertising. Between October 1, 1994, and May 31, 1995, Stock Solution delivered Axiom 107 color transparencies to be used in Axiom's advertising. The contracts provided that in the event the transparencies were not returned by the specified "return date," Axiom would pay the following fees: (1) an initial "service charge" of $30, (2) "holding fee[s]" in the amount of "$5.00 per week per transparency", (3) "service fees" at a rate of "one and one-half percent per month" on unpaid balances of invoices beginning 30 days after invoice date, and (4) reimbursement for loss or damage of each "original transparency" in the amount of $1,500.

Axiom failed to return 37 of the 107 transparencies in breach of the contracts. Of the 37 missing transparencies, 36 were original color transparencies and 1 was a duplicate color transparency. Stock Solution filed suit seeking damages (1) for the 36 missing original color transparencies, the agreed liquidated value of $54,000 plus sales tax of $3,294; (2) for the 1 missing duplicate color transparency, $1 plus sales tax of $0.06; (3) holding fees on the 37 missing transparencies in the amount of $23,914.83; (4) service fees and charges as provided for in the contracts; and (5) attorney fees.

Discuss whether the liquidated damage clause was enforceable under the law. [*Bair v. Axiom Design, LLC*, 20 P.3d 388 (Utah)]

13. Ramtreat Metal Technology provided for a "double your money back" remedy in its contracts for the sale of its metal drilling assemblies. A buyer filed suit seeking consequential damages and cost of replacement. Ramtreat said that its clause was a limitation of remedies. Could Ramtreat limit its remedies to "double your money back"? [*Adcock v. Ramtreat Metal Technology, Inc.*, 44 UCC Rep. Serv. 2d 1026 (Wash App)]

14. Joseph Perna purchased a 1981 Oldsmobile at a traffic auction conducted by Locascio. The car had been seized pursuant to action taken by the New York City Parking Violation Bureau against Jose Cruz. Perna purchased the car for $1,800 plus tax and towing fees "subject to the terms

and conditions of any and all chattel mortgages, rental agreements, liens, conditional bills of sale, and encumbrances that may be on the motor vehicle of the above judgment debtor." The Olds had 58,103 miles on it at the time of Perna's purchase. On May 7, 1993, Perna sold the car to Elio Marino, a coworker, for $1,200. The vehicle had about 65,000 miles on it at the time of this sale.

During his period of ownership, Marino replaced the radiator ($270), repaired the power steering and valve cover gasket ($117), and replaced a door lock ($97.45). He registered and insured the vehicle. In February 1994, Marino's son was stopped by the police and arrested for driving a stolen vehicle. The son was kept in jail until his arraignment, but the charges were eventually dropped. The Oldsmobile was never returned to Marino, who filed suit for breach of contract because he had been given a car with a defective title. He asked for damages that included the costs of getting his son out of jail and having the theft charges dropped. Is he entitled to those damages? [*Marino v. Perna*, 629 N.Y.S. 2d 669 (N.Y. Cir.)]

15. Stephan's Machine & Tool, Inc., purchased a boring mill from D&H Machinery Consultants. The mill was a specialized type of equipment and was essential to the operation of Stephan's plant. The purchase price was $96,000, and Stephan's had to borrow this amount from a bank to finance the sale. The loan exhausted Stephan's borrowing capacity. The mill was unfit, and D&H agreed to replace it with another one. D&H did not keep its promise, and Stephan's sued it for specific performance of the contract as modified by the replacement agreement. Is specific performance an appropriate remedy? Discuss. [*Stephan's Machine & Tool, Inc. v. D&H Machinery Consultants, Inc.*, 417 N.E.2d 579 (Ohio App.)]

CPA QUESTIONS

1. On April 5, 1987, Anker, Inc., furnished Bold Corp. with Anker's financial statements dated March 31, 1987. The financial statements contained misrepresentations that indicated that Anker was solvent when in fact it was insolvent. Based on Anker's financial statements, Bold agreed to sell Anker 90 computers, "F.O.B.—Bold's loading dock." On April 14, Anker received 60 of the computers. The remaining 30 computers were in the possession of the common carrier and in transit to Anker. If, on April 28, Bold discovered that Anker was insolvent, then with respect to the computers delivered to Anker on April 14, Bold may:

   a. Reclaim the computers upon making a demand.

   b. Reclaim the computers irrespective of the rights of any third party.

   c. Not reclaim the computers since 10 days have elapsed from their delivery.

   d. Not reclaim the computers since it is entitled to recover the price of the computers.

2. February 15, Mazur Corp. contracted to sell 1,000 bushels of wheat to Good Bread, Inc., at $6.00 per bushel with delivery to be made on June 23. On June 1, Good advised Mazur that it would not accept or pay for the wheat. On June 2, Mazur sold the wheat to another customer at the market price of $5.00 per bushel. Mazur had advised Good that it intended to resell the wheat. Which of the following statements is correct?

   a. Mazur can successfully sue Good for the difference between the resale price and the contract price.

   b. Mazur can resell the wheat only after June 23.

   c. Good can retract its anticipatory breach at any time before June 23.

   d. Good can successfully sue Mazur for specific performance.

3. Lazur Corp. entered into a contract with Baker Suppliers, Inc., to purchase a used word processor from Baker. Lazur is engaged in the business of

selling new and used word processors to the general public. The contract required Baker to ship the goods to Lazur by common carrier pursuant to the following provision in the contract: "FOB Baker Suppliers, Inc., loading dock." Baker also represented in the contract that the word processor had been used for only 10 hours by its previous owner. The contract included the provision that the word processor was being sold "as is," and this provision was in a larger and different type style than the remainder of the contract. Assume that Lazur refused to accept the word processor even though it was in all respects conforming to the contract and that the contract is otherwise silent. Under the UCC Sales Article:

a. Baker can successfully sue for specific performance and make Lazur accept and pay for the word processor.

b. Baker may resell the word processor to another buyer.

c. Baker must sue for the difference between the market value of the word processor and the contract price plus its incidental damages.

d. Baker cannot successfully sue for consequential damages unless it attempts to resell the word processor.

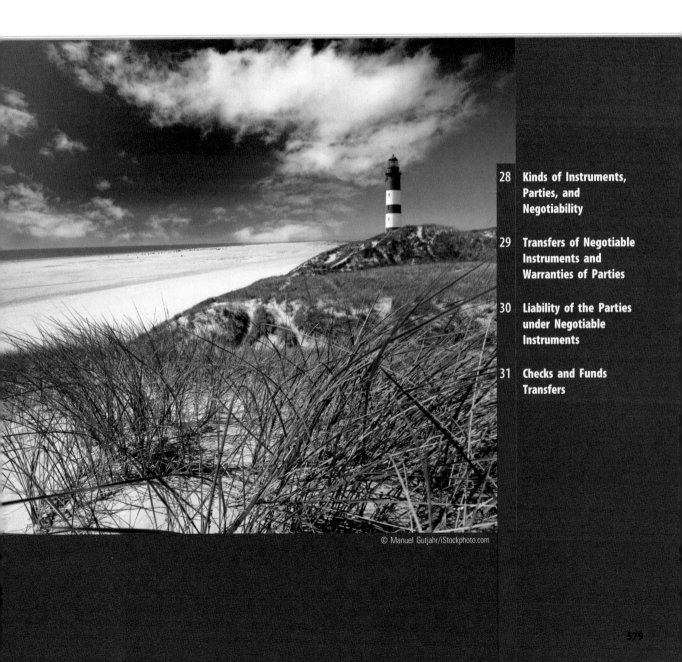

PART 4

Negotiable Instruments

© Manuel Gutjahr/iStockphoto.com

© Manuel Gutjahr/iStockphoto.com

CHAPTER 28

Kinds of Instruments, Parties, and Negotiability

learningoutcomes

After studying this chapter, you should be able to

LO.1 Explain the importance and function of negotiable instruments

LO.2 Name the parties to negotiable instruments

LO.3 Describe the concept of negotiability and distinguish it from assignability

LO.4 List the requirements for a negotiable instrument

commercial paper – written, transferable, signed promise or order to pay a specified sum of money; a negotiable instrument.

F or convenience and as a way to facilitate transactions, businesses began to accept certain kinds of paper called **commercial paper** or negotiable instruments as substitutes for money or as a means of offering credit. Negotiable commercial paper is special paper created for the special purpose of facilitating transfer of funds and payment. In addition, the use of this special paper for special purposes can create additional rights in a special person status known as a *holder in due course*. Although the details on holders in due course are covered in Chapters 29 and 30, it is important to understand that one of the purposes of the use of special paper is to allow parties to achieve the special status of holder in due course and its protections and rights. Taking each component of negotiable instruments in step-by-step sequences, from their creation to the rights associated with each, and to their transfer, helps in understanding how commercial paper is used for special purposes in order to create rights for special persons.

A. TYPES OF NEGOTIABLE INSTRUMENTS AND PARTIES

Article 3 of the Uniform Commercial Code (UCC) defines the types of negotiable instruments and the parties for each.[1] Article 3 of the UCC was last amended in 2002 with those reforms adopted in some states and under consideration in others.[2] Those changes are explained in each of the relevant sections.

1. Definition

negotiable instruments – drafts, promissory notes, checks, and certificates of deposit that, in proper form, give special rights as "negotiable commercial paper."

Section 3-104(a)(1) and (2) of the UCC defines a **negotiable instrument** as "an unconditional promise or order to pay a fixed amount of money, … if it (1) is payable to bearer or order…; (2) is payable on demand or at a definite time; and (3) does not state any other undertaking or instruction … to do any act in addition to the payment of money…."[3] A *negotiable instrument* is a record of a signed promise or order to pay a specified sum of money.[4] The former requirement that the instrument be in writing to be valid has been changed to incorporate requirements of UETA (Uniform Electronic Transactions Act) and E-Sign (Electronic Signatures in Global and National Commerce Act of 2000). Many lenders now use electronic promissory notes.[5] In addition, we now have electronic checks, or those check withdrawals from your account that you authorize over the phone or via the Internet.

Instruments are negotiable when they contain certain elements required by the UCC. These elements are listed and explained in Section 5 of this chapter. However, even those instruments that do not meet the requirements for negotiability may still be referred to by their UCC names or classifications.

[1] The law covering negotiable instruments has been evolving and changing. The latest version of Article 3 was adopted in 1990. The 1990 version of Article 3 had been adopted in all 50 states by August 1999. States with variations are Alabama, Georgia, Montana, Ohio, South Dakota, and Wisconsin. The earlier version was called UCC-Commercial Paper, and the 1990 version is called UCC-Negotiable Instruments.
[2] As of April 2012, 49 states and the District of Columbia had adopted the 2002 changes to Article 3.
[3] UCC §3-104(a)(1) and (2).
[4] See UCC §3-104.
[5] Electronic Signatures in Global and National Commerce Act, 15 U.S.C. §7001 (Supp. 2011).

CPA

2. Kinds of Instruments

There are two categories of negotiable instruments: (1) promises to pay, which include promissory notes and certificates of deposit,[6] and (2) orders to pay, including drafts and checks.

(A) PROMISSORY NOTES. A **promissory note** is a written promise made and signed by the maker to pay a *sum certain* in money to the holder of the instrument.[7] (See Figure 28-1.)

(B) CERTIFICATES OF DEPOSIT. A **certificate of deposit (CD)** is a promise to pay issued by a bank.[8] Through a CD, a bank acknowledges the customer's deposit of a specific sum of money and promises to pay the customer that amount plus interest when the certificate is surrendered.

(C) DRAFTS. A **draft, or bill of exchange**, is an order by one party to pay a sum of money to a second party. (See Figure 28-2.) The party who gives the order is called the *drawer*, and the party on whom the order to pay is drawn is the *drawee*.[9] The party to whom payment is to be made is the *payee*. The drawer may also be named as the payee, as when a seller draws a draft naming a buyer as the drawee. The draft is then used as a means to obtain payment for goods delivered to that buyer. A drawee is not bound to pay a draft simply because the drawer has placed his name on it. However, the drawee may agree to pay the draft by accepting it, which then attaches the drawee's liability for payment.

(D) CHECKS. Under UCC §3-104(f), *check* means "a draft, other than a documentary draft, payable on demand and drawn on a bank."[10] A **check** is an order by a depositor (the drawer) on a bank or credit union (the drawee) to pay a sum of money to the order of another party (the payee).[11]

promissory note – unconditional promise in writing made by one person to another, signed by the maker engaging to pay on demand, or at a definite time, a sum certain in money to order or to bearer. (Parties—maker, payee)

certificate of deposit (CD) – promise-to-pay instrument issued by a bank.

draft or bill of exchange – an unconditional order in writing by one person upon another, signed by the person giving it, and ordering the person to whom it is directed to pay upon demand or at a definite time a sum certain in money to order or to bearer.

check – order by a depositor on a bank to pay a sum of money to a payee; a bill of exchange drawn on a bank and payable on demand.

FIGURE 28-1	*Promissory Note*

> **MARCH 31, 2013**
>
> Six months after date debtor undersigned hereby promises to pay to the order of Galactic Games, Inc., three thousand six hundred dollars with interest at the rate of 5.9%. This note is secured by the Video Arcade game purchased with its funds.
>
> In the event of default, all sums due hereunder may be collected. Debtor agrees to pay all costs of collection including, but not limited to, attorney fees, costs of repossession, and costs of litigation.
>
> /s/ JOHN R. HALDEHAND
>
> VIDEO ARCADE, INC.

© Cengage Learning

[6] UCC §3-104(j).
[7] *IFC Credit Corp. v. Specialty Optical Systems, Inc.*, 252 S.W.3d 761 (Tex. App. 2008).
[8] UCC §3-104(j).
[9] UCC §3-103(a)(2)–(3).
[10] UCC §3-104(f).
[11] *Id.*

FIGURE 28-2	*Draft*

TO: _Topa Fabrics, Inc._
1700 W. Lincoln
Marina Del Rey, CA

March 17, 20 _13_

Thirty days from date   PAY TO THE ORDER OF
Malden Mills, Inc.

THE SUM OF   _sixteen thousand and ⁿᵒ/100_   DOLLARS

ACCEPTED BY: _Aaron Johnson_
                                                     Malden Mills, Inc.

DATE

© Cengage Learning

---

cashier's check – draft drawn by a bank on itself.

teller's check – draft drawn by a bank on another bank in which it has an account.

traveler's check – check that is payable on demand provided it is countersigned by the person whose specimen signature appears on the check.

money order – draft issued by a bank or a nonbank.

In addition to the ordinary checks just described, there are also cashier's checks, teller's checks, traveler's checks, and bank money orders. A **cashier's check** is a draft drawn by a bank on itself. UCC §3-104(g) defines a cashier's check as "a draft with respect to which the drawer and drawee are the same bank or branches of the same bank."[12] A **teller's check** is a draft drawn by a bank on another bank in which it has an account.[13] A **traveler's check** is a check that is payable on demand, provided it is countersigned by the person whose signature was placed on the check at the time the check was purchased.[14] Money orders are issued by both banks and nonbanks. A **money order** drawn by a bank is also a check.[15]

3. Parties to Instruments

A note has two original parties: the *maker* and the *payee*.[16] A draft or a check has three original parties: the *drawer*, the *drawee*, and the *payee*. The names given to the parties to these instruments are important because the liability of the parties varies depending on the parties' roles. The rights and liabilities of the various parties to negotiable instruments are covered in Chapters 29 and 30.

A **party** to an instrument may be a natural person, an artificial person such as a corporation, or an unincorporated enterprise such as a government agency.

party – person involved in a legal transaction; may be a natural person, an artificial person (e.g., a corporation), or an unincorporated enterprise (e.g., a governmental agency).

(A) MAKER. The **maker** is the party who writes or creates a promissory note, thereby promising to pay the amount specified in the note.

maker – party who writes or creates a promissory note.

(B) DRAWER. The **drawer** is the party who writes or creates a draft or check.

drawer – person who writes out and creates a draft or bill of exchange, including a check.

(C) DRAWEE. The **drawee** is the party to whom the draft is addressed and who is ordered to pay the amount of money specified in the draft. The bank is the drawee

drawee – person to whom the draft is addressed and who is ordered to pay the amount of money specified in the draft.

---

[12] UCC §3-104(g).
[13] UCC §3-104(h).
[14] UCC §3-104(i).
[15] *Com. v. Pantalion*, 957 A.2d 1267 (Pa. Super. 2008). Some items are held to be checks for purposes other than Article 3 negotiability. For example, in *In re Armstrong* 291 F.3d 517 (8th Cir. 2002), the court held that gambling markers were checks for purposes of the state's "bad check" law.
[16] UCC §3-103(a)(5).

on a check, and the credit union is the drawee on a share draft. Again, a drawee on a draft has no responsibility under the draft until it has accepted that instrument.

payee–party to whom payment is to be made.

(D) PAYEE. The **payee** is the person named in the instrument to receive payment. **For Example,** on a check with the words "Pay to the order of John Jones," the named person, John Jones, is the payee.

The payee has no rights in the instrument until the drawer or the maker has delivered it to the payee. Likewise, the payee is not liable on the instrument in any way until the payee transfers the instrument to someone else.

(E) ACCEPTOR. When the drawee of a draft has indicated by writing or record a willingness to pay the amount specified in the draft, the drawee has accepted liability and is called the **acceptor**.[17]

acceptor–drawee who has accepted the liability of paying the amount of money specified in a draft.

(F) SECONDARY OBLIGOR (ACCOMMODATION PARTY). When a party who is not originally named in an instrument allows her name to be added to it for the benefit of another party in order to add strength to the collectability of the instrument, that party becomes a secondary obligor (formerly called an **accommodation party**) and assumes a liability role.[18] Revised Article 3 now refers to drawer, indorsers, and accommodation parties as "secondary obligors."[19]

accommodation party– person who signs an instrument to lend credit to another party to the paper.

CPA

B. NEGOTIABILITY

negotiability–quality of an instrument that affords special rights and standing.

An instrument is a form of contract that, if negotiable, affords certain rights and protections for the parties. **Negotiability** is the characteristic that distinguishes commercial paper and instruments from ordinary contracts or what makes such paper and instruments special paper.[20] That an instrument is negotiable means that certain rights and protections may be available to the parties to the instrument under Article 3. A **nonnegotiable instrument's** terms are enforceable, but the instrument is treated simply as a contract governed by contract law.[21]

nonnegotiable instrument– contract, note, or draft that does not meet negotiability requirements of Article 3.

4. Definition of Negotiability

If an instrument is negotiable, it is governed by Article 3 of the UCC, and it may be transferred by negotiation. This form of transfer permits the transferee to acquire rights greater than those afforded assignees of contracts under contract law. The quality of negotiability in instruments creates opportunities for transfers and financings that streamline payments in commerce. Transfers can be made with assurance of payment without the need for investigation of the underlying contract. The process of negotiation is covered in Chapter 29. For more information on the rights of assignees of contracts, refer to Chapter 18.

---

[17] UCC §3-103(a)(1).
[18] UCC §3-419; *In re TML, Inc.*, 291 B.R. 400, 50 UCC Rep. Serv.2d 511 (W.D. Mich. 2003).
[19] Revised Article 3, §3-103(12), has the following definition of a secondary obligor on an instrument: "an indorser, a drawer, an accommodation party, or any other party to the instrument that has a right of recourse against another party to the instrument...." This definition was changed to be consistent with the Restatement of Surety.
[20] UCC §3-104.
[21] Loan-and-supply contract is not a negotiable instrument. *Quality Oil, Inc. v. Kelley Partners, Inc.*, 657 F.3d 609 (7th Cir. 2011). A note payable when "lessee is granted possession of the premises" is not a negotiable instrument, but it is an enforceable contract. *Schiffer v. United Grocers, Inc.*, 989 P.2d 10 (Or. 1999). A deed of trust is not a negotiable instrument. *Arnold v. Palmer*, 686 S.E.2d 725 (W.Va. 2009).

E-Commerce & Cyberlaw

The Check Is in the Internet

The Check Clearing for the 21st Century Act ("Check 21") allows banks to use electronic images of checks as full and complete records of transactions, the same status formerly used only for paper checks that had been canceled. You can also pay your monthly credit card bills by preauthorizing your credit card company to withdraw the amount you specify from your account. With the bank's routing number and your account number, the company can obtain payment on the due date or any date you authorize. PayPal allows you to do the same with your bank account when you purchase items on the Internet. Paperless payment is on the increase.

CPA

5. Requirements of Negotiability

To be negotiable, an instrument (1) must be evidenced by a record[22] and (2) must be signed (authenticated under Revised Article 3) by the maker or the drawer, (3) must contain an unconditional promise or order to pay, (4) must pay a sum certain, (5) must be payable in money, (6) must be payable on demand or at a definite time, and (7) must be payable to order or bearer, using what are known as words of negotiability.[23]

(A) A RECORD (WRITING). A negotiable instrument must be evidenced by a record. The requirement of a *record*, under Revised Article 3, is satisfied by handwriting, typing, printing, electronic record, and any other method of making a record. A negotiable instrument may be partly printed and partly typewritten. No particular form is required for an instrument to satisfy the record requirement, although customers of banks may agree to use the banks' forms as part of their contractual agreement with their banks. Telephonic checks are a complete record for purposes of Article 3 rights and obligations.

(B) AUTHENTICATED (SIGNED) BY THE MAKER OR DRAWER. The instrument must be authenticated (signed under old Article 3) by the maker or the drawer. When a signature is used as authentication, it usually appears at the lower right-hand corner of the face of the instrument, but there is no requirement for where the signature must be placed on the instrument.[24]

The authentication may consist of the full name or of any symbol placed with the intent to authenticate the instrument. Other means of authentication that are valid as signatures include initials, figures, and marks. Electronic security devices can be used as a means of authentication for electronic records. A person signing a trade name or an assumed name is liable just as if the signer's own name had been used.

(1) Agent.

An authentication may be made by the drawer or the maker or by his or her authorized agent. **For Example,** Eileen Smith, the treasurer of Mills Company, could sign a note for her company as an **agent**. No particular form of authorization

---

[22] Revised Article 3. Existing Article 3 requires a writing, but the revisions reflect electronic transactions and the federal mandate for recognizing electronic transactions as valid and on equal footing with paper transactions. The definition of a record is found in Revised UCC §3-103(a)(14), which provides that *record* "means information that is inscribed on a tangible medium or which is stored in an electronic or other medium and is retrievable in perceivable form."

[23] UCC §3-104.

[24] According to Revised UCC §3-103, *authenticate* means (a) to sign or (b) to execute or otherwise adopt a symbol, or encrypt or similarly process a record in whole or in part, with the present intent of the authenticating person to identify the person and adopt or accept a record.

for an agent to authenticate an instrument is required. An authenticating agent should disclose on the instrument (1) the identity of the principal and (2) the fact that the authentication was done in a representative capacity. When this information appears on the face of the instrument, an authorized agent is not liable on it.

The representative capacity of an officer of an organization can be shown by the authentication of the officer along with the title of the office and the organization's name.[25] **For Example,** a signature of "James Shelton, Treasurer, NorWest Utilities, Inc.," or "NorWest Utilities, Inc., by James Shelton, Treasurer," on a note is enough to show Shelton's representative capacity. NorWest Utilities, not Shelton, would be liable on the note.

(2) Absence of Representative Capacity or Identification of Principal.

representative capacity – action taken by one on behalf of another, as the act of a personal representative on behalf of a decedent's estate, or action taken both on one's behalf and on behalf of others, as a shareholder bringing a representative action.

If an instrument fails to show the **representative capacity** of the person who is authenticating or fails to identify the person, then the individual who authenticates the instrument is personally liable on the instrument to anyone who acquires superior rights, such as the rights of a holder in due course (see Chapter 30). Because the instrument is a final agreement, the parol evidence rule applies, and the party who authenticated is not permitted to introduce extrinsic evidence that might clarify his or her representative capacity. The party who authenticated, in order to avoid personal liability, must indicate on the face of the instrument his or her role in the principal, such as president or vice president. (For more information about the parol evidence rule, see Chapter 17.)

However, an agent is not personally liable on a check that is drawn on the bank account of the principal and authenticated by him or her, even though the agent failed to disclose his or her representative capacity on the check. **For Example,** a check that is already imprinted with the employer's name is not the check of the employee, regardless of whether the employee only authenticates with his or her name or also adds a title such as "Payroll Clerk" or "Treasurer" near the signature.

(c) Promise or Order to Pay. A promissory note must contain a promise to pay money. A mere acknowledgment of a debt, such as a record stating "I.O.U.," is not a promise. A draft or check must contain an order or command to pay money.

(d) Unconditional Promise or Order. For an instrument to be negotiable, the promise or order to pay must be unconditional.[26]

For Example, when an instrument makes the duty to pay dependent on the completion of the construction of a building, the promise is conditional and the instrument is nonnegotiable. The instrument is enforceable as a contract, but it is not a negotiable instrument given all the rights and protections afforded under Article 3.

An order for the payment of money out of a particular fund is negotiable. The instrument can refer to a particular account or merely indicate a source of reimbursement for the drawee, such as "Charge my expense account." Nor is an instrument conditional when payment is to be made only from an identified fund if the issuer is a government or governmental unit or agency, or when payment is to be made from the assets of a partnership, unincorporated association, trust, or estate.[27] However, the fund noted must in fact exist because payment from a fund to be

---

[25] UCC §3-402. *In re Bedrock Marketing, LLC*, 404 B.R. 939 (D.Utah 2009) and *Arntz v. Valdez*, 2011 WL 3433018, 163 Wash.App. 1003 (Wash. App. 2011).

[26] UCC §3-109(c).

[27] A check issued by a debtor in bankruptcy for payment of court-ordered obligations is not conditional because of the involvement of the court or ongoing conditions on debtor's payments. *In re Blasco*, 352 B.R. 888 (Bankr. N.D. Ala. Div. 2006).

created by a future event would be conditional. **For Example,** making an instrument "payable from the account I'll establish when the sale of my house occurs" is conditional because the fund's creation is tied to an event whose time of occurrence is unknown.

The standards for negotiability do not require that the issuer of the instrument be personally obligated to pay it.[28] An instrument's negotiability is not destroyed by a reference to a related document. Section 3-106(b) provides, "A promise or order is not made conditional (i) by a reference to another writing for a statement of rights with respect to collateral, prepayment, or acceleration."[29] **For Example,** if a note includes the following phrase, "This note is secured by a mortgage on the property located at Hilding Lane," the note is still negotiable.[30]

CASE SUMMARY

The Sticky Note That Was a Reminder of Personal Liability

FACTS: Northwest Harvest Products, Inc., fell behind on payments on its account with Major Products Company, Inc. Major requested a note for the debt, and Northwest sent a $78,445.24 note. The chief executive officer of Northwest at that time signed the note "Donald H. Eoll CEO," attached a Post-It fax transmittal memo indicating that the note came from Donald Eoll at Northwest, and sent the note via facsimile. The note was not paid, and Major sued both Eoll and Northwest for the debt. Only the facsimile copy of the note was presented at trial, and the trial court found that the writing on the Post-It note, coupled with the signature, identified Northwest as the principal on the note. The trial court held that Eoll was not personally liable for the debt because he signed the note as an agent for Northwest. Major appealed.

DECISION: The court held that Eoll was personally liable on the note. The Post-It note was separate from the document and anything that Eoll and Major wanted to be part of the promissory note should have been written on the promissory note. Without the Post-it, there is no indication of capacity on the promissory note, which leaves Eoll liable personally on that note. Reversed. [***Major Products Co., Inc. v. Northwest Harvest Products, Inc.,*** **979 P.2d 905 (Wash. App. 1999)]**

Thinking Things Through

When Your John Hancock Is Enough

Work through the following examples of signatures on negotiable instruments and capacity, and determine whether there would be personal liability on the part of the company executives signing the instruments personal liability.

1. Donald Schaffer owned and operated Grafton Janitorial Service, Inc. On October 6, 1998, Mr. Schaffer obtained a $25,000 line of credit for his company from First Merit Bank by executing a promissory note, which he signed both as "Donald J. Schaffer,

---

[28] UCC §3-110(c)(1)–(2) (1990); *Ocwen Loan Servicing, LLC v. Branaman*, 554 F. Supp. 2d 645 (N.D. Miss. 2008).

[29] UCC §3-106(b).

[30] Reference to a bill of lading does not affect negotiability. *Regent Corp., U.S.A. v. Azmat Bangladesh, Ltd.*, 686 N.Y.S.2d 24 (1999); However, a reference to a standby agreement does affect negotiability. *In re Sabertooth, LLC*, 443 B.R. 671 (E.D. Pa. 2011).

Thinking Things Through

Continued

President" and "Donald J. Schaffer, Cosigner." The note contains no guarantee provision, and Mr. Schaffer did not sign the note in the capacity as a guarantor. [*Schaffer v. First Merit Bank, N.A.,* **927 N.E.2d 15 (Ohio App. 2009)**]

2. A corporate guaranty was signed as follows:
THE PRODUCERS GROUP OF FLA., INC. a Florida corporation, by the following officers solely on behalf of the corporation:

/s/ Eddie Beverly, as its President

CORPORATE PRESIDENT Eddie Beverly

/s/ Stephen Edman, as its Secretary

CORPORATE SECRETARY Steve Edman

/s/ John Bauder, as its Treasurer

CORPORATE TREASURER John Bauder

Are the officers personally liable on the gzuaranty? [*Tampa Bay Economic Development Corp. v. Edman,* **598 So.2d 172 (Fla. App. 1992)**]

---

money – medium of exchange.

(E) PAYMENT IN MONEY. A negotiable instrument must be payable in money. **Money** is defined to include any medium of exchange adopted or authorized by the United States, a foreign government, or an intergovernmental organization. The parties to an instrument are free to decide which currency will be used for payment even though their transaction may occur in a different country.[31] **For Example,** two parties in the United States are free to agree that their note will be paid in pesos.

If the order or promise is not for money, the instrument is not negotiable. **For Example,** an instrument that requires the holder to take stock or goods in place of money is nonnegotiable. The instrument is enforceable as a contract, but it cannot qualify as a negotiable instrument for purposes of Article 3 rights.

sum certain – amount due under an instrument that can be computed from its face with only reference to interest rates.

(F) SUM CERTAIN. Negotiable instruments must include a statement of a **sum certain**, or an exact amount of money. Without a definite statement as to how much is to be paid under the terms of the instrument, there is no way to determine how much the instrument is worth.

There are some minor variations from sum certain requirement. **For Example,** an instrument is not nonnegotiable because its interest rate provisions include changes in the rate at maturity or because it provides for certain costs and attorney fees to be recovered by the holder in the event of enforcement action or litigation.[32]

In most states, the sum payable under an instrument is certain even though it calls for the payment of a floating or variable interest rate.[33] An instrument is negotiable even though it provides for an interest rate of 1 percent above the prime rate of a named bank. It is immaterial that the exact amount of interest that will be paid cannot be determined at the time the paper is issued because the rate may later change. It is also immaterial that the amount due on the instrument cannot be determined without looking at records outside of the face of the instrument.[34]

---

[31] UCC §3-107. *Means v. Clardy,* 735 S.W.2d 6 (Mo. App. 1987) (payment in cabinets makes a note nonnegotiable).

[32] UCC §3-106. *In re MCB Financial Group, Inc.,* 461 B.R. 914 (N.D. Ga. 2011).

[33] While revised Article 3 permits variable and market rates, notes entered into before the revised act was adopted will be governed under old Article 3; *YYY Corp. v. Gazda,* 761 A.2d 395 (N.H. 2000), *Barnsley v. Empire Mortgage, Ltd. Partnership,* 720 A.2d 63 (N.H. 1998), but see *Bankers Trust (Delaware) v. 236 Beltway Inv.,* 865 F. Supp. 1186 (E.D. Va. 1994)

[34] *SCADIF, S.A. v. First Union Nat. Bank,* 208 F. Supp. 2d 1352 (S.D. Fla. 2002), aff'd, 344 F.3d 1123 (11th Cir. 2003). See also *Bankers Trust v. 236 Beltway Investment,* 865 F. Supp. 1186 (E.D. Va. 1994).

(G) TIME OF PAYMENT. A negotiable instrument must be payable on demand or at a definite time.[35] If an instrument is payable "when convenient," it is nonnegotiable because the day of payment may never arrive. An instrument payable only upon the happening of a particular event that may or may not happen is not negotiable. **For Example,** a provision in a note to pay the sum certain when a person marries is not payable at a definite time because that particular event may never occur. It is immaterial whether the contingency in fact has happened because from an examination of the instrument alone, it still appears to be subject to a condition that might not occur.

(1) Demand.

An instrument is *payable on demand* when it expressly states that it is payable "on demand," at sight, or on presentation. UCC §3-108(a) provides "A promise or order is 'payable on demand' if (i) it states that it is payable on demand or at sight, or otherwise indicates that it is payable at the will of the holder, or (ii) it does not state any time of payment."[36] Presentation occurs when a holder demands payment. Commercial paper is deemed to be payable on demand when no time for payment is stated in the instrument.[37]

(2) Definite Time.

definite time – time of payment computable from the face of the instrument.

The time of payment is a **definite time** if an exact time or times are specified or if the instrument is payable at a fixed time after sight or acceptance or at a time that is readily ascertainable. The time of payment is definite even though the instrument provides for prepayment, for acceleration, or for extensions at the option of a party or automatically on the occurrence of a specified contingency.

CASE SUMMARY

Whenever...Paying When You Can Does Not a Negotiable Instrument Make

FACTS: Gary Vaughn signed a document stating that Fred and Martha Smith were loaning him $9,900. As to when the loan was to be repaid, the document stated, "when you can." Approximately 18 months later, the Smiths sued Vaughn for the entire amount, claiming default on the note as well as unjust enrichment. The Smiths moved for summary judgment. They contended that Vaughn was immediately liable for the entire amount but that they were willing to work out a repayment schedule. Vaughn also moved for summary judgment, arguing that he did not have to repay the Smiths because he did not have the ability to do so. The trial court denied the Smiths' motion and granted Vaughn's. The Smiths appealed.

DECISION: The court held the following: a promissory note that calls for a borrower to repay "when you can" was not payable on demand and was not a negotiable instrument. However, an issue of fact remained as to when a debt payable "when you can" became payable. There were other issues of fact such as whether there was unjust enrichment and whether it was reasonable for the borrower to repay the debt. The language implied that there was an open-ended agreement. The parties might have a contract, but the Smiths could not demand payment as if the instrument were a demand negotiable instrument. Reversed for further factual determinations. [*Smith v. Vaughn*, 882 N.E.2d 941 (Ohio App. 2007)]

---

[35] UCC §3-108.
[36] UCC §3-108(a).
[37] UCC §3-112; *Universal Premium Acceptance Corp. v. York Bank's Trust Co.*, 69 F.3d 695 (3d Cir. 1995); *State v. McWilliams*, 178 P. 3d 121 (Mont. 2008).

(3) Missing Date.

An instrument that is not dated is deemed dated on the day it is issued to the payee. Any holder may add the correct date to the instrument.

(4) Effect of Date on a Demand Instrument.

The date on a demand instrument controls the time of payment, and the paper is not due before its date. Consequently, a check that is postdated ceases to be demand paper and is not properly payable before the date on the check. A bank making earlier payment does not incur any liability for doing so unless the drawer has given the bank a postdated check notice.

(H) Words of Negotiability: Payable to Order or Bearer. An instrument that is not a check must be **payable to order** or **bearer**.[38] This requirement is met by such phrases as "Pay to the order of John Jones," "Pay to John Jones or order," "Pay to bearer," and "Pay to John Jones or bearer." The use of the phrase "to the order of John Jones" or "to John Jones or order" shows that the person executing the instrument had no intention of restricting payment of the instrument to John Jones. These phrases indicate that there is no objection to paying anyone to whom John Jones orders the paper to be paid. Similarly, if the person executing the instrument originally wrote that it will be paid "to bearer" or "to John Jones or bearer," there is no restriction on the payment of the paper to the original payee. However, if the instrument is not a check and it is payable on its face "to John Jones," the instrument is not negotiable.[39] Whether an instrument is bearer or order paper is important because the two instruments are transferred in different ways and because the liability of the transferors can be different.

payable to order – term stating that a negotiable instrument is payable to the order of any person described in it or to a person or order.

bearer – person in physical possession of commercial paper payable to bearer, a document of title directing delivery to bearer, or an investment security in bearer form.

Ethics & the Law

Medicaid Eligibility and Article 3 Negotiability

Kenneth Wilson was hospitalized from January 7, 2007, until his death on February 22, 2007. During the hospitalization, Kenneth's wife, Doris, sold her 100% stock ownership in the Brothers Delivery Service (her husband's company) to her son. The agreement provided that Kenneth, Jr. would pay $62,531 in 60 installments of $1.041.82, starting March 1, 2007. Kenneth Jr. did not sign the promissory note for these terms. Doris never signed the purchase agreement. Doris then applied for Medicaid benefits in order to cover the costs of her husband's hospitalization. Eligibility for Medicaid requires a determination that there are insufficient personal assets to pay the bill. The Division of Social Services concluded that Doris was the owner of a promissory note, a liquid asset, that could be sold to pay the medical bills. Coverage was denied due to excessive resources. Doris argues that there is no negotiable note because the requirements for negotiability are not met. The appellate court agreed because the underlying contract had not been signed by Doris and because there was not, as yet, a promissory note. The purchase agreement did not have words of negotiability and there was no definite time for payment because the note did not yet exist. Discuss whether Doris attained Medicaid eligibility through a legal loophole. Does she actually have assets that could be used to pay at least part of the debt? Should legal definitions allow us to escape an obligation to pay? **[*Estate of Wilson v. Division of Social Services*, 685 S.E.2d 135 (N.C. App. 2009)]**

---

[38] *Unlimited Adjusting Group, Inc. v. Wells Fargo Bank*, 94 Cal. Rptr.3d 672 (Cal. App. 2009).
[39] UCC §3-108.

CASE SUMMARY

The Goal Was a Hockey Team AND a Negotiable Instrument

FACTS: William Kidd served as managing director of Limeco Corporation. Beginning in 2001, negotiations began between Kidd/Limeco (defendants) and R.W. Whitaker and Monty Fletcher (plaintiffs) in connection with what later became a failed effort to purchase a hockey team in Tupelo. Whitaker and Fletcher loaned Limeco $750,000. Whitaker and Fletcher claim that Kidd concealed the fact that Limeco had no assets. Whitaker also loaned Kidd an additional $100,000, with the understanding that Kidd and Limeco would be responsible for paying back the loan that Whitaker had taken out from the Peoples Bank & Trust Company in Tupelo in order to make the loan to Kidd.

On July 1, 2002, the parties entered into what they referred to as promissory notes (referred to as the "Fletcher note" and the "Whitaker note") to memorialize the terms of the loan agreements they had made in early 2002. Both Fletcher and Whitaker, in an effort to secure what they thought were promissory notes, were granted a continuing lien on Limeco's monies, securities, and/or other property for the entire amount of the promissory notes (each in the amount of $375,000).

On December 11, 2003, Whitaker and Fletcher filed separate complaints against Limeco and Kidd for recovery of the more than $850,000 that had never been repaid. The trial court found that the suit had to be dismissed because it was brought after the contracts' statute of limitations had expired. Whitaker and Fletcher argued that the notes were negotiable instruments and that their fraud claim was valid because of the six-year statute of limitations that applied with regard to negotiable instruments.

DECISION: The court held that words of negotiability are an absolute requirement for a negotiable instrument. Without those words, the note is simply a contract, and a suit on a contract required that it be filed within three years. Because Whitaker and Fletcher were over the three years, their suit had to be dismissed. If they had had the words of negotiability, then the suit could have proceeded because it was brought well within the time limits. [*Whitaker v. Limeco Corp.,* **32 So.3d 429 (Miss. 2010)**]

(1) Order Paper.

order paper – instrument payable to the order of a party.

An instrument is payable to order, or **order paper**, when by its terms it is payable to the order of any person described in it ("Pay to the order of K. Read") or to a person or order ("Pay to K. Read or order").

(2) Bearer Paper.

bearer paper – instrument with no payee, payable to cash or payable to bearer.

An instrument is payable to bearer, or **bearer paper**, when it is payable (1) to bearer or the order of bearer, (2) to a specified person or bearer, or (3) to "cash," "the order of cash," or any other designation that does not purport to identify a person or when (4) the last or only indorsement is a blank indorsement (an indorsement that does not name the person to whom the instrument is negotiated). An instrument that does not identify any payee is payable to bearer.[40]

Whether an instrument is bearer or order paper is important for determining how the instrument is transferred (see Chapter 28) and what the liability of the parties under the instrument is. Review Figure 28-3 for more background.

[40] UCC §3-104(d).

CASE SUMMARY

I May Be a Thief, But under Article 3 Bearer Paper Rules, I Am Not a Forger

FACTS: Joshua Herrera found a purse in a dumpster near San Pedro and Kathryn Streets in Albuquerque. Herrera took the purse with him to a friend's house. Either Herrera or his friend called the owner of the purse and the owner retrieved the purse at some point. After the purse was returned to the owner, Herrera returned to the dumpster where he found a check and some other items. The check Herrera found was written out to "Cash" and he thought this meant that he "could get money for [the] check."

When he presented the check to the teller at a credit union to cash it, the teller instructed him to put his name on the payee line next to "Cash." Herrera added "to Joshua Herrera" next to the word "Cash" on the payee line of the check and indorsed the check.

Herrera had pleaded guilty to one count of forgery but moved to have the indictment dismissed on the grounds that adding his name to a bearer instrument was not forgery. He appealed the denial of the motion to dismiss the indictment.

DECISION: The court held that the instrument that Herrera originally found was bearer paper. By adding his named "to Joshua Herrera" to the "Pay to" line after "Cash" did not change the character of the instrument from bearer to order paper. At best, the addition of the words created an ambiguity and under the code interpretations should continue to be treated as bearer paper. Since he did not alter the nature of the instrument or convert it to a different instrument, he could not be charged with forgery. [***New Mexico v. Herrera***, 18 P.3d 326 (N.M. App. 2001); ***cert.*** den. 20 P.3d 810 (N.M. 2001)]

6. Factors Not Affecting Negotiability

postdate – to insert or place on an instrument a later date than the actual date on which it was executed.

Omitting a date of execution or antedating or **postdating** an instrument has no effect on its negotiability.

collateral – property pledged by a borrower as security for a debt.

Provisions relating to **collateral**, such as specifying the collateral as security for the debt or a promise to maintain, protect, or give additional collateral, do not affect negotiability. **For Example,** the phrase "This note is secured by a first mortgage" does not affect negotiability.

FIGURE 28-3	*Bearer versus Order Paper*

"Pay to the order of ABC Corp."	ORDER
"Pay to the order of Bearer."	BEARER
"Pay to the order of ABC Corp. or Bearer"	BEARER
"Pay to the order of ABC Corp., Bearer"	ORDER
"Pay to the order of John Jones" (note)	ORDER
"Pay to the order of John Jones" (check)	ORDER
"Pay to John Jones" (note)	NONNEGOTIABLE
"Pay to John Jones" (check)	NEGOTIABLE/ORDER
"Pay to the order of John Jones or Bearer"	BEARER
"Pay to cash"	BEARER
"Pay to the order of cash"	BEARER

7. Ambiguous Language

ambiguous – having more than one reasonable interpretation.

The following rules are applied when **ambiguous** language exists in words or descriptions:

1. Words control figures where conflict exists.

2. Handwriting supersedes conflicting typewritten and printed terms.

3. Typewritten terms supersede preprinted terms.

4. If there is a failure to provide for the payment of interest or if there is a provision for the payment of interest but no rate is mentioned, the judgment rate at the place of payment applies from the date of the instrument.[41]

8. Statute of Limitations

Article 3 of the UCC establishes a three-year statute of limitations for most actions involving negotiable instruments. This limitation also applies to actions for the conversion of such instruments and for breach of warranty. There is a six-year statute of limitations for suits on certificates of deposit and accepted drafts.

MAKE THE CONNECTION

SUMMARY

An instrument or piece of commercial paper is a transferable, signed promise or order to pay a specified sum of money that is evidenced by a record. An instrument is negotiable when it contains the terms required by the UCC.

Negotiable instruments have two categories: (1) promises to pay and (2) orders to pay. Checks and drafts are orders to pay. Notes and certificates of deposits are promises to pay. In addition to ordinary checks, there are cashier's checks and teller's checks. A bank money order is a check even though it bears the words *money order.*

The original parties to a note are the maker and the payee. The original parties to a draft are the drawer, the drawee, and the payee. The term *party* may refer to a natural person or to an artificial person, such as a corporation. Indorsers and accommodation parties are considered secondary obligors.

The requirements of negotiability are that the instrument (1) be evidenced by a record, (2) be signed (authenticated) by the maker or the drawer, and (3) contain a promise or order (4) of an unconditional character (5) to pay in money (6) a sum certain (7) on demand or at a definite time (8) to order or bearer. A check may be negotiable without being payable to order or bearer.

If an instrument meets the requirements of negotiability, the parties have the rights and protections of Article 3. If it does not meet the requirements of negotiability, the rights of the parties are governed under contract law.

---

[41] *In re Blasco*, 352 B.R. 888 (N.D. Ala. 2006).

LEARNING OUTCOMES

After studying this chapter, you should be able to clearly explain:

A. Types of Negotiable Instruments and Parties

L0.1 Explain the importance and function of negotiable instruments

See the discussion of negotiability on p. 585.
See *New Mexico v. Herrera* on p. 593.

L0.2 Name the parties to negotiable instruments

See the list of parties to instruments starting on p. 584.

B. Negotiability

L0.3 Describe the concept of negotiability and distinguish it from assignability

See *Whitaker v. Limeco Corp.* on p. 592 for what can happen if an instrument is not negotiable.

L0.4 List the requirements for a negotiable instrument

See the list of negotiability requirements on p. 586.
See *Smith v. Vaughn* on p. 590.

KEY TERMS

acceptor	definite time	order paper
accommodation party	draft, or bill of exchange	party
ambiguous	drawee	payable to order
bearer	drawer	payee
bearer paper	maker	postdating
cashier's check	money	promissory note
certificate of deposit (CD)	money order	representative capacity
check	negotiability	sum certain
collateral	negotiable instrument	teller's check
commercial paper	nonnegotiable instrument	traveler's check

QUESTIONS AND CASE PROBLEMS

1. Harold H. Heidingsfelder signed a credit agreement as vice president of J. O. H. Construction Co. for a line of credit with Pelican Plumbing Co. The credit agreement contained the following language:

   In consideration of an open account privilege, I hereby understand and agree to the above terms. Should it become necessary to place this account for collection I shall personally obligate myself and my corporation, if any, to pay the entire amount due including service charges (as outlined above terms) thirty-three and one-third (33¹/₃%) attorney's fees, and all costs of collection, including court costs.
   Signed [Harold H. Heidingsfelder]
   Company J. O. H. Construction Co., Inc.

   When J. O. H. Construction failed to make payment, Pelican, claiming it was a holder of a negotiable instrument, sued Heidingsfelder to hold him personally liable for his failure to indicate a representative capacity on the credit agreement. He claims that a credit application is not a negotiable instrument and that he could not be held personally liable. Is he right? [*Pelican Plumbing Supply, Inc. v. J. O. H. Construction Co., Inc.*, 653 So.2d 699 (La.)]

2. Abby Novel signed a note with the following on it: "Glen Gallwitz 1-8-2002 loaned me $5,000 at 6% interest a total of $10,000.00." The note did not contain a payment schedule or a time for repayment.

Abby used the $10,000 as start-up money for her business and says that she orally agreed to repay the loan out of the proceeds from her first 1,000-product sales. Abby did not make any payments. Glen passed away and his son, as executor of his estate, demanded that Abby repay the $10,000 plus 6% interest for a total of $14,958 (the amount due as of April 2010). The trial court granted judgment for the estate. Abby has appealed, alleging that she repaid the note through the care she gave for Glen. The estate maintains that the instrument was a negotiable promissory note and that it is entitled to collect the amount due in cash. Who is correct and why? [*Gallwitz v. Novel*, 2011 WL 303253 (Ohio App.)]

3. Charter Bank of Gainesville had in its possession a note containing the following provision: "This note with interest is secured by a mortgage on real estate, of even date herewith, made by the maker hereof in favor of said payee…. The terms of said mortgage are by this reference made a part hereof." When the bank sued on the note, it said it was a holder of a negotiable instrument. Is this instrument negotiable? [*Holly Hill Acres, Ltd. v. Charter Bank of Gainesville*, 314 So.2d 209 (Fla. App.)]

4. On October 14, 1980, United American Bank of Knoxville made a $1,700,000 loan to Frederic B. Ingram. William F. Earthman, the president of the bank and a beneficiary of the loan, had arranged for the loan and prepared the loan documents. Mr. Ingram and Mr. Earthman were old friends, and Mr. Ingram had loaned Mr. Earthman money in the past. Mr. Ingram was in jail at the time of this loan and was unable to complete the documents for the loan. Mr. Earthman says that Mr. Ingram authorized him to do the loan so long as it did not cost him anything to do it.

Also on October 14, 1980, Mr. Earthman prepared and executed a personal $1,700,000 note to Mr. Ingram, using a standard Commerce Union Bank note form. Mr. Earthman wrote "Frederic B. Ingram" in the space for identifying the lending bank and also filled in another blank stating that the note would be due "Eighteen

Months after Date." With regard to the interest, Mr. Earthman checked a box signifying that the interest would be "At the Bank's 'Prime Rate' plus % per year."

Mr. Earthman then sold both of the notes, which ended up in the hands of third parties (holders in due course) who demanded payment. Mr. Ingram raised the defense that he had not authorized Mr. Earthman to handle the transactions. The third parties said the notes were negotiable instruments and they were entitled to payment without listening to Mr. Ingram's defenses. Mr. Earthman said his note to Mr. Ingram as well as the bank note from Mr. Ingram were not negotiable and that they could both raise defenses to the third parties seeking payment.

Who is correct? What do you think of Mr. Earthman's banking processes and procedures? What ethical issues do you see in these loan transactions? [*Ingram v. Earthman*, 993 S.W.2d 611 (Tenn.)]

5. The state of Alaska was a tenant in a large office building owned by Univentures, a partnership. The state made a lease payment of $28,143.47 to Univentures with state treasury warrant No. 21045102. Charles LeViege, the managing partner of Univentures, assigned the warrant to Lee Garcia. A dispute then arose among the Univentures partners, and the company notified the state that it should no longer pay LeViege the rent. The state placed a stop payment order on the warrant. Garcia claimed that he was a holder of a negotiable instrument and that the state owed him the money. The state claimed that a warrant did not qualify as a negotiable instrument. The warrant was in writing, was signed by the governor of the state, provided a definite sum of $28,143.47, and stated that "it will be deemed paid unless redeemed within two years after the date of issue." The warrant stated that it was "payable to the order of Univentures." Does the warrant meet the requirements for a negotiable instrument? [*National Bank v. Univentures*, 824 P.2d 1377 (Alaska)]

6. Nation-Wide Check Corp. sold money orders through local agents. A customer would purchase

a money order by paying an agent the amount of the desired money order plus a fee. The customer would then sign the money order as the remitter or sender and would fill in the name of the person who was to receive the money following the printed words "Payable to." In a lawsuit between Nation-Wide and Banks, a payee on some of these orders, the question was raised as to whether these money orders were checks and could be negotiable even though not payable to order or to bearer. Are the money orders negotiable instruments? [*Nation-Wide Check Corp. v. Banks*, 260 A.2d 367 (D.C.)]

7. George S. Avery signed a letter regarding the unpaid balance on a $20,000 promissory note owed to Jim Whitworth in the form of a letter addressed to Whitworth stating: "This is your note for $45,000.00, secured individually and by our Company for your security, due February 7, 1984." The letter was signed: "Your friend, George S. Avery." It was typed on stationery with the name of Avery's employer, V & L Manufacturing Co., Inc., printed at the bottom and the words "George Avery, President" printed at the top. Avery says he is not personally liable on the note. The court granted summary judgment for Whitworth and Avery appealed. Who is liable? [*Avery v. Whitworth*, 414 S.E.2d 725 (Ga. App.)]

8. Bellino made a promissory note that was payable in installments and contained the provision that on default of the payment of any installment, the holder had the option to declare the entire balance due and payable on demand. The note was negotiated to Cassiani, who sued Bellino for the full debt when there was a default on the installment. Is a note with an acceleration clause still negotiable? [*Cassiani v. Bellino*, 157 N.E.2d 409 (Mass.)]

9. Atlas Capital, LLC's sole member and manager was Weston Wade Sleater. Mr. Sleater signed two promissory notes totaling $4,000,000 as the maker of the notes. The signature blocks of the notes read, "Weston Wade Sleater & Atlas Marketing Group, L.C.," but the signature was only that of Mr. Sleater. Mr. Sleater is referred to as the maker of the note. Mr. Sleater failed to pay

the notes and a bankruptcy trustee brought suit to collect the remaining amount due. Mr. Sleater maintains that the notes are not his, but those of Atlas Capital. Is he correct? Is Mr. Sleater liable on the notes? Discuss the ambiguity issues as well as the way the notes were signed. [*In re Bedrock Marketing*, LLC, 404 B.R. 929 (D. Utah)]

10. Lloyd and Mario Spaulding entered into a contract to purchase property from Richard and Robert Krajcir. The two Spaulding brothers signed a promissory note to the Krajcir brothers with the following language: "The amount of $10,000 [is] to be paid sellers at the time of the initial closing [delivery of the deed]; plus, the principal amount payable to sellers at the time of the final indorsement of the subject H.U.D. loan." In litigation over the note, the Spauldings said it was not a negotiable instrument. The lower court found it to be a negotiable promissory note and the Spaulding partners appealed. Is the note negotiable? [*Krajcir v. Egid*, 712 N.E.2d 917 (Ill. App.)]

11. Is the following instrument negotiable?

I, Richard Bell, hereby promise to pay to the order of Lorry Motors Ten Thousand Dollars ($10,000) upon the receipt of the final distribution from the estate of my deceased aunt, Rita Dorn. This negotiable instrument is given by me as the down payment on my purchase of a 1986 Buick to be delivered in three weeks.

Richard Bell (signature).

12. Smith has in his possession the following instrument:

September 1, 2003
I, Selma Ray, hereby promise to pay Helen Savit One Thousand Dollars ($1,000) one year after date. This instrument was given for the purchase of Two Hundred (200) shares of Redding Mining Corporation, Interest 6%.

Selma Ray (signature).

What is this instrument? Is it negotiable?

13. Master Homecraft Co. received a promissory note with a stated face value from Sally and Tom Zimmerman. The note was payment for

remodeling their home and contained unused blanks for installment payments but contained no maturity date. When Master Homecraft sued the Zimmermans on the note, the couple argued that they should not be liable on the note because it is impossible to determine from its face the amount due or the date of maturity. Decide. [*Master Homecraft Co. v. Zimmerman*, 22 A.2d 440 (Pa.)]

14. A note from Mark Johnson with HealthCo International as payee for $28,979.15 included the following language:

[p]ayable in _____, Successive Monthly Installments of $ Each, and in 11 Successive Monthly Installments of $2,414.92 Each

thereafter, and in a final payment of $2,415.03 thereafter. The first installment being payable on the _____ day of _____ 20 _____, and the remaining installments on the same date of each month thereafter until paid.

Johnson signed the note. Is it negotiable? [*Barclays Bank, P.L.C. v. Johnson*, 499 S.E.2d 769 (N.C. App.)]

15. The text of a handwritten note stated simply that "'I Robert Harrison owe Peter Jacob $25,000 …,' /s/ Robert Harrison." Peter Jacob sought to use the handwritten note as a negotiable promissory note. Can he? [*Jacob v. Harrison*, 49 UCC Rep. Serv. 2d 554 (Del. Super.)]

CPA QUESTIONS

1. A company has in its possession the following instrument:

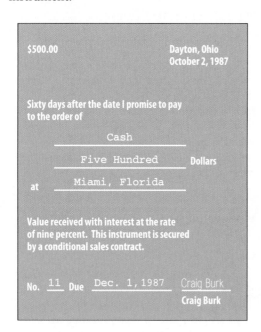

This instrument is:

a. Not negotiable until December 1, 1987.

b. A negotiable bearer note.

c. A negotiable time draft.

d. A nonnegotiable note because it states that it is secured by a conditional sales contract.

2. The instrument shown here is a:

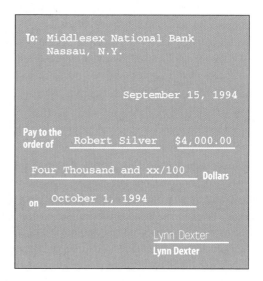

a. Draft

b. Postdated check

c. Trade acceptance

d. Promissory note

3. Under the commercial paper article of the UCC, for an instrument to be negotiable, it must:

a. Be payable to order or to bearer.

b. Be signed to the payee.

c. Contain references to all agreements between the parties.

d. Contain necessary conditions of payment.

4. An instrument reads as follows:

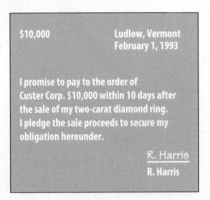

$10,000   Ludlow, Vermont
February 1, 1993

I promise to pay to the order of Custer Corp. $10,000 within 10 days after the sale of my two-carat diamond ring. I pledge the sale proceeds to secure my obligation hereunder.

R. Harris
R. Harris

Which of the following statements correctly describes this instrument?

a. The instrument is nonnegotiable because it is not payable at a definite time.

b. The instrument is nonnegotiable because it is secured by the proceeds of the sale of the ring.

c. The instrument is a negotiable promissory note.

d. The instrument is a negotiable sight draft payable on demand.

5. Which of the following instruments is subject to the provisions of the Negotiable Instruments Article of the UCC?

a. A bill of lading

b. A warehouse receipt

c. A certificate of deposit

d. An investment security

6. Under the Negotiable Instruments Article of the UCC, which of the following statements is correct regarding a check?

a. A check is a promise to pay money.

b. A check is an order to pay money.

c. A check does not need to be payable on demand.

d. A check does not need to be drawn on a bank.

© Manuel Gutjahr/iStockphoto.com

CHAPTER 29

Transfers of Negotiable Instruments and Warranties of Parties

learningoutcomes

After studying this chapter, you should be able to

LO.1 Explain the difference between negotiation of order paper and negotiation of bearer paper

LO.2 List the types of indorsements and describe their uses

LO.3 Determine the legal effect of forged and unauthorized indorsements

LO.4 Be familiar with the forged payee impostor exceptions

LO.5 List the indorser's warranties and describe their significance

M uch of the commercial importance of negotiable instruments lies in the ease with which they can be transferred. This chapter covers the requirements for, and issues in, the transfer or negotiation of negotiable instruments.

CPA   A. Transfer of Negotiable Instruments

Negotiable instruments are transferred by a process known as *negotiation.*

1. Effect of Transfer

When a contract is assigned, the transferee has the rights of the transferor. The transferee is entitled to enforce the contract but, as assignee, has no greater rights than the assignor. The assignee is in the same position as the original party to the contract and is subject to any defense that could be raised in a suit on an assigned contract.

When a negotiable instrument is transferred by negotiation, the transferee becomes the *holder of the paper.* A holder who meets certain additional requirements may also be a **holder in due course**. The status of holder in due course gives immunity from certain defenses that might have been asserted against the transferor (see Chapter 30 for a discussion of the rights and role of a holder in due course).

holder in due course – a holder who has given value, taken in good faith without notice of dishonor, defenses, or that instrument is overdue, and who is afforded special rights or status.

negotiation – the transfer of commercial paper by indorsement and delivery by the person to whom it is then payable in the case of order paper and by physical transfer in the case of bearer paper.

holder – someone in possession of an instrument that runs to that person (i.e., is made payable to that person, is indorsed to that person, or is bearer paper).

2. Definition of Negotiation

Under UCC §3-201(a), **negotiation** means "a transfer of possession … of an instrument by a person other than the issuer to a person who thereby becomes a holder."[1] Negotiation, then, is simply the transfer of a negotiable instrument in such a way that the transferee becomes a holder.[2] A **holder** is different from a possessor or an assignee of the paper. A holder is a transferee in possession of an instrument that runs to her. An instrument runs to a party if it is payable to her order, is indorsed to her, or is bearer paper.

3. How Negotiation Occurs: The Order or Bearer Character of an Instrument

The order or bearer character of the paper determines how it may be negotiated. The order or bearer character of an instrument is determined according to the words of negotiability used (see Chapter 28 for a complete discussion of order and bearer words of negotiation and more examples of bearer versus order instruments). The types of instruments that qualify as bearer paper include those payable to bearer as well as those payable to the order of "Cash" or payable in blank. The character of an instrument is determined as of the time negotiation takes place even though its character originally or at the time of prior transfers may have been different.

---

[1] Revised UCC §3-201(a).
[2] Revised UCC §3-201; *In re Kang Jin Hwang*, 396 B.R. 757 (Bkrtcy C.D. Cal. 2008); *In re Miller*, 666 F.3d 1255 (10th Cir. 2012).

CPA

B. How Negotiation Occurs: Bearer Instruments

UCC §3-201(b) provides, "If an instrument is payable to bearer, it may be negotiated by transfer of possession alone."[3] If an instrument qualifies for bearer status, then it is negotiated by **delivery** to another.[4] Delivery can be accomplished by actual transfer of possession wherein the transferee has possession of the instrument, or constructive transfer, whereby the transferee has exclusive access. **For Example,** when mortgage lenders finance a home mortgage, they often transfer the underlying promissory note on the mortgage several times through financial streams. Many of the underlying problems in the financial market's collapse in 2008 were the large bundles of the promissory notes tied to home mortgages that were in amounts above the value of the mortgaged properties. Who held the bearer promissory notes became a critical issue in foreclosures. Bearer paper is negotiated to a person taking possession of it without regard to whether such possession is lawful. Because delivery of a bearer instrument is effective negotiation, it is possible for a thief or an embezzling officer to transfer title to a bearer instrument. Such a person's presence in the chain of transfer does not affect the rights of those who have taken the bearer instrument in good faith.[5]

delivery – constructive or actual possession.

CASE SUMMARY

The Blank Indorsement Draws a Blank on Wrongful Foreclosure

FACTS: On September 22, 2006, Richard and Sabrina Emmons signed an adjustable rate promissory note and deed of trust with Chevy Chase Bank (now known as Capital One) for a property located in Vancleave, Mississippi. The note indicates that "[t]he Lender or anyone who takes this Note by Transfer and who is entitled to receive payments under this Note is called the 'Note Holder.'" According to the terms of the deed of trust, "MERS (Mortgage Electronic Recording System) is the beneficiary under this Security Instrument." Based on the assignment of deed of trust, executed on April 9, 2010, MERS then assigned the Emmons' deed of trust to U.S. Bank as trustee.

The deed of trust listed MERS and MERS' successors and assigns as beneficiary and nominee. On April 9, 2010, MERS assigned the deed of trust to U.S. Bank. The Emmons defaulted on their payments. The deed of trust provides for a power of sale in the event of the borrowers' default—a right which U.S. Bank then exercised through a non-judicial foreclosure (power of sale). The Emmons then filed suit alleging, among other things, wrongful foreclosure because they claimed U.S. Bank was not a holder of the promissory note.

DECISION: The court held that the Emmons' promissory note was a negotiable instrument that had been indorsed in blank and was therefore bearer paper. It could be further negotiated to a holder via the simple action of delivery. So the holder of the note (in this case, Capital One), would have the right to conduct a foreclosure sale should the parties fall into default on their payments. There was no wrongful foreclosure as long as the party foreclosing was a holder of the note and there had been a default. Capital One was a holder and the Emmons had defaulted. [*Emmons v. Capital One*, 2012 WL 773288 (S.D. Miss. 2012)]

---

[3] Revised UCC §3-201(b).
[4] If no payee is named, the instrument is bearer paper and is negotiated by delivery. *DCM Ltd. Partnership v. Wang*, 555 F. Supp. 2d 808 (E.D. Mich. 2008); *Waldron v. Delffs*, 988, S.W.2d 182 (Tenn. App. 1999).
[5] Revised UCC §§3-202 and 3-204; *Knight Pub. Co., Inc. v. Chase Manhattan Bank, N.A.*, 479 S.E.2d 478 (N.C. App. 1997); review denied 487 S.E.2d 548 (N.C. 1997); *In re Federal-Nogul Global, Inc.*, 319 B.R. 363 (D.Del. 2005).

Ethics & the Law

Having Your Mortgage Set Aside

In cases such as the *Emmons v. Capital One* case, the borrowers bring suit seeking to have their mortgage obligations set aside on the basis of technicalities in the paperwork or the separation of the paperwork. Generally, these borrowers owe far more on their mortgages than their homes are worth. In some cases, the mortgages have been deemed invalid or the courts have held there was no authority for foreclosure because of the problems with note transfers and the right of foreclosure. Evaluate the ethics of the borrowers in seeking to have their mortgages set aside.

Even though a bearer instrument may be negotiated by a mere transfer of possession, the one to whom the instrument is delivered may require the bearer to indorse the instrument. This situation most commonly arises when a check payable to "Cash" is presented to a bank for payment. The reason a transferee of bearer paper would want an indorsement is to obtain the protection of an indorser's warranties from the bearer.[6] The bank wants an indorsement on a check made payable to "Cash" so that it can turn to the check casher in the event payment issues arise.

CPA ## C. How Negotiation Occurs: Order Instruments

UCC §3-201(b) provides, "if an instrument is payable to an identified person, negotiation requires transfer of possession of the instrument and its indorsement by the holder."[7] A negotiable instrument that is payable to the order of a specific party is *order paper,* which can be negotiated only through indorsement and transfer of possession of the paper.[8] **Indorsement** and transfer of possession can be made by the person to whom the instrument is then payable or by an authorized agent of that person.[9]

indorsement – signature of the payee on an instrument.

CASE SUMMARY

The Tax Man Cometh, but He Can't Provide Your Indorsement

FACTS: Thorton Ring was behind on his property taxes for his property in Freeport, Maine. When he received a check payable to his order from Advest, Inc., in the amount of $11,347.09, he wrote the following on the back of the check: "Payable to Town of Freeport Property Taxes 2 Main St."; he sent it along with a letter to the town offices. The letter included the following: "I have paid $11,347.09 of real estate taxes and request the appropriate action to redeem the corresponding property." Ring did nothing further and his property was then liened by the tax clerk. Ring objected because he had paid the taxes. The town argued that the check was not indorsed and Ring thus had not paid the taxes in time to avoid the lien. The lower court found for the town and Ring appealed.

---

[6] The Uniform Electronic Transactions Act (UETA), promulgated by the National Conference of Commissioners on Uniform State Laws in July 1999 and enacted in 46 states, provides that the transfer of a note by electronic record affords the transferee the same rights as a tangible written note.
[7] Revised UCC §3-201(b). Although the modern spelling is "endorsement," the UCC has retained the British spelling of "indorsement."
[8] Revised UCC §3-204; *Unlimited Adjusting Group, Inc. v. Wells Fargo Bank, N.A.,* 94 Cal. Rptr. 3d 672 (Ca. App. 2009).
[9] Revised UCC §3-204. The UCC spellings are "indorse" and "indorser," the spellings used in this text. However, courts (including in some cases in this text) use the modern "endorse" and "endorser." *Jenkins v. Wachovia Bank,* 711 S.E.2d 80 (Ga. App. 2011).

CASE SUMMARY

Continued

DECISION: There was no indorsement. Ring's name must be signed for there to be negotiation of the instrument to the town. The check had only the first part of the necessary indorsement for order paper; Ring had to indorse the instrument for further negotiation. Indorsements vary according to the method of signing and the words used along with the signature. The nature of an indorsement also affects the future of the instrument in terms of its requirements for further negotiation. [*Town of Freeport v. Ring*, 727 A.2d 901 (Me. 1999)]

4. Blank Indorsement

blank indorsement – an indorsement that does not name the person to whom the paper, document of title, or investment security is negotiated.

When the indorser merely signs a negotiable instrument, the indorsement is called a **blank indorsement** (see Figure 29-1). A blank indorsement does not indicate the person to whom the instrument is to be paid, that is, the transferee. A blank indorsement turns an order instrument into a bearer instrument. A person who possesses an instrument on which the last indorsement is blank is the holder.[10] **For Example,** if a check is payable to the order of Jill Barnes and Ms. Barnes indorses the check on the back "Jill Barnes," then the check that was originally an order instrument is now a bearer instrument. The check can now be transferred as bearer paper, which requires only delivery of possession. Once Jill Barnes's signature appears as a blank indorsement on the back, the check becomes transferrable simply by delivery of possession to another party.

FIGURE 29-1	*Blank Indorsement*

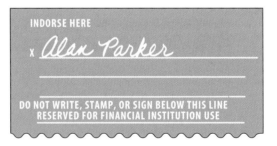

© Cengage Learning

5. Special Indorsement

special indorsement – an indorsement that specifies the person to whom the instrument is indorsed.

A **special indorsement** consists of the signature of the indorser and words specifying the person to whom the indorser makes the instrument payable, that is, the **indorsee** (see Figure 29-2).[11] **For Example,** if Jill Barnes wrote on the back of the check

indorsee – party to whom special indorsement is made.

---

[10] *Farmers Bank of Maryland v. Chicago Title Ins. Co.*, 877 A.2d 1145, aff'd 905 A.2d 366 (Md. 2005).
[11] Revised UCC §3-205; *Chicago Title Ins. Co. v. Allfirst Bank*, 905 A.2d 366, 60 UCC Rep. Serv. 2d 864 (Md. 2006).

E-Commerce & Cyberlaw

New Flexibility for Cyberspace Commercial Paper

The Check Clearing for the 21st Century Act (sometimes called "Check 21") allows banks to use images of checks as a substitute for paper checks. The substitute check is the legal equivalent of the paper check that has, for so long, dominated U.S. commerce. Under Check 21, the bank is also able to send you electronic copies of your canceled checks. Even if you still opt for paper summaries of your account activity each month, the bank need not return physical checks and can send small reproductions of your checks grouped together on the statement. Recently, you have been able to secure faster credits to your accounts for deposited checks because ATMs scan the checks in, checks that are recognized immediately as deposits. All the new regulations on check substitutes are known as Regulation CC and can be found at Regulation CC, 12 C.F.R. §229.2(zz)(2).

payable to her "Pay to Jack Barnes, /s/ Jill Barnes," the check could be negotiated further only through the signature and possession of Jack Barnes. A special indorsement in this case continues an order instrument as an order instrument. If, after receiving the check, Jack Barnes simply signed it on the back, the check would become bearer paper and could be transferred through possession only.

Although words of negotiability are required on the front of negotiable instruments, it is not necessary that indorsements contain the word *order* or *bearer*. Consequently, the paper indorsed as shown in Figure 29-2 continues to be negotiable and may be negotiated further.[12]

An indorsement of "Pay to account [number]" is a special indorsement. In contrast, the inclusion of a notation indicating the debt to be paid is not a special indorsement.

FIGURE 29-2	*Special Indorsement*

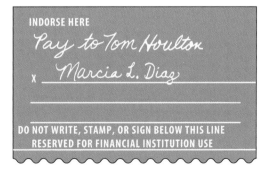

© Cengage Learning

---

[12] Only a check may use the phrase "Pay to" on its face and remain negotiable. All other instruments require words of negotiability on their face. Indorsements, on all instruments, need only "Pay to." UCC §3-110.

FIGURE 29-3 | *Qualified Indorsement*

© Cengage Learning

6. Qualified Indorsement

qualified indorsement – an indorsement that includes words such as "without recourse" that disclaims certain liability of the indorser to a maker or a drawee.

A **qualified indorsement** is one that qualifies the effect of a blank or a special indorsement by disclaiming certain liability of the indorser to a maker or a drawee. This disclaimer is given using the phrase "Without recourse" as part of the indorsement (see Figure 29-3). Any other words that indicate an intent to limit the indorser's secondary liability in the event the maker or the drawee does not pay on the instrument can also be used.[13]

The qualification of an indorsement does not affect the passage of title or the negotiable character of the instrument. It merely disclaims certain of the indorser's secondary liabilities for payment of the instrument in the event the original parties do not pay as the instrument provides.

This qualified form of indorsement is most commonly used when the indorser is a person who has no personal interest in the transaction. **For Example,** an agent or an attorney who is merely indorsing a check of a third person to a client might make a qualified indorsement because he is not actually a party to the transaction.

7. Restrictive Indorsement

restrictive indorsement – an indorsement that restricts further transfer, such as in trust for or to the use of some other person, is conditional, or for collection or deposit.

A **restrictive indorsement** specifies the purpose of the indorsement or the use to be made of the instrument (see Figure 29-4).[14] An indorsement is restrictive when it includes words showing that the instrument is to be deposited (such as "For deposit only"), when it is negotiated for collection or to an agent or a trustee, or when the negotiation is conditional.[15]

A restrictive indorsement does not prevent transfer or negotiation of the instrument once the initial restriction is honored. The indorsement "For deposit only" requires only that the first party who receives the instrument after the restriction is placed on it comply with that restriction. The indorsement "For deposit only" makes an instrument a bearer instrument for any bank. If the indorser's account number is added to a "For deposit only" indorsement, then the only party who can take the instrument after this restrictive indorsement is a bank with that account number. A restrictive indorsement reduces the risk of theft or unauthorized transfer by eliminating the bearer quality of a blank indorsement.

[13] *Antaeus Enterprises, Inc. v. SD-Barn Real Estate, LLC,* 480 F. Supp. 2d 734 (S.D.N.Y. 2007).
[14] Revised UCC §3-206.
[15] *Id. Travelers Cas. and Sur. Co. of America v. Bank of America,* 2009 WL 5176769 (Sup. Ct. N.Y.).

FIGURE 29-4	*Restrictive Indorsement*

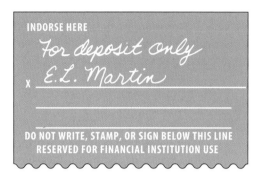

© Cengage Learning

8. Correction of Name by Indorsement

Sometimes the name of the payee or the indorsee of an instrument is spelled improperly. **For Example,** H. A. Price may receive a paycheck that is payable to the order of "H. O. Price." If this error in Price's name was a clerical one and the check is indeed intended for H. A. Price, the employee may ask the employer to write a new check payable to the proper name. However, under Article 3, a much simpler solution allows the payee or indorsee whose name is misspelled to indorse the wrong name, the correct name, or both. The person giving or paying value or taking it for collection for the instrument may require both forms of the signature.[16]

This correction of name by indorsement may be used only when it was intended that the instrument should be payable to the person making the corrective indorsement. If there were in fact two employees, one named H. A. Price and the other H. O. Price, it would be forgery for one to take the check intended for the other and, by indorsing it, obtain the benefit of the proceeds of the check.[17]

A fictitious, assumed, or trade name is treated the same as a wrong name. The same procedure for correction of a misspelled name with indorsement of both names applies to these forms of payee identification as well.[18]

9. Bank Indorsement

To simplify the transfer and collection of negotiable instruments from one bank to another, "any agreed method which identifies the transferor bank is sufficient for the item's further transfer to another bank."[19] A bank could simply indorse with its Federal Reserve System number instead of using its name.

Likewise, when a customer has deposited an instrument with a bank but has failed to indorse it, the bank may make an indorsement for the customer unless the instrument expressly requires the payee's personal indorsement. Furthermore, the mere stamping or marking on the item of any notation showing that it was deposited by the customer or credited to the customer's account is effective as an indorsement by the customer.

---

[16] Revised UCC §3-204(d).
[17] If a check is made payable to an individual "as guardian" for another, it cannot be negotiated until that individual is actually appointed as guardian. *Citibank v. Bank of Salem*, 35 UCC 2d 173 (W.D.N.Y. 1998).
[18] *DCM Ltd. Partnership v. Wang*, 555 F. Supp. 2d (E.D. Mich. 2008).
[19] Revised UCC §4-103.

10. Multiple Payees and Indorsements

Ordinarily, one person is named as the payee in the instrument, but two or more payees may be named. In that case, the instrument may specify that it is payable to any one or more of them or that it is payable to all jointly. **For Example,** if the instrument is made payable "to the order of Ferns and Piercy," then Ferns and Piercy are joint payees. The indorsements of both Ferns and Piercy are required to negotiate the instrument.

alternative payees –
those persons to whom a negotiable instrument is made payable, any one of whom may indorse and take delivery of it.

If the instrument is payable to **alternative payees** or if it has been negotiated to alternative indorsees, such as "Stahl or Glass" or "Stahl/Glass," it may be indorsed and delivered by either of them.

Under old Article 3, if the instrument was not clear on the relationship or types of multiple payees or indorsees, they were to be considered joint, and the signatures of all parties were required. Under Revised Article 3, when a court is faced with two or more payees who are separated by a comma or other symbol, for example, "Pay to the order of Jeff Bridges–Susan Sarandon," the court must first determine whether the symbols or separating marks are sufficiently clear to make the instrument payable jointly. If the court concludes that the instrument is ambiguous, then the preference is for alternative payees, which means that either Jeff or Susan could negotiate the instrument with one signature; they would not have to have the other's indorsement for negotiation. Under Revised Article 3, if the instrument is ambiguous, the payees or indorsees are considered payees in the alternative.

11. Agent or Officer Indorsement

An instrument may be made payable to the order of an officeholder. **For Example,** a check may read "Pay to the order of Receiver of Taxes." Such a check may be received and negotiated by the person who at the time is the receiver of taxes. This general identification of a payee is a matter of convenience, and the drawer of the check is not required to find out the actual name of the receiver of taxes at that time.

CASE SUMMARY

Checking Indorsements at Check City

FACTS: L & T Enterprises issued checks to one of L & T's subcontractors and one of that subcontractor's suppliers. Check City cashed the checks, but did so with the indorsement of only the subcontractor, not the supplier. The subcontractor had a long, positive history with Check City. Although the reverse side of the checks contained what at cursory glance might appear to be two signatures, even minimal attention to those signatures shows they are the subcontractor's business name and the signature of a presumably authorized employee, albeit in an order that is the opposite of what is customary. Both entries are in the same handwriting, and a prudent person cashing the checks could not possibly have mistaken the two entries for proper indorsements by both the subcontractor and the subcontractor's supplier.

Check City filed suit against L & T for negligence. The trial court held that L & T owed Check City a duty and that L & T breached that duty by failing to exercise ordinary care and substantially contributing to an alteration of an instrument or forged signature. L & T appealed.

DECISION: There is a difference between the liability for a forged indorsement and a missing indorsement. Here, Check City failed to obtain the necessary signatures for the two payees. The

CASE SUMMARY

Continued

result is that Check City has liability for the losses. Check City cannot hold L & T liable for opening the door to forgery when it failed to ensure that the signatures were there and genuine, a duty it holds as the first party to receive the check. The judgment in favor of Check City on its complaint is reversed. The parties will bear their own costs on appeal. [*Check City, Inc. v. L & T Enterprises*, 237 P.3d 910 (Utah App. 2010)]

If an instrument is drawn in favor of an officer of a named corporation, the instrument is payable to the corporation, the officer, or any successor to such officer. Any of these parties in possession of the instrument is the holder and may negotiate the instrument.[20]

Thinking Things Through

The Minor with an Embezzling Conservator

Steven Powell died in a tragic accident at work, entitling his minor son, Cody, to approximately $252,000 in life insurance proceeds. Karen Unrue, Steven's sister, approached Elizabeth Powell, Steven's widow, and offered to manage the insurance proceeds for Cody.

The probate court appointed Karen Unrue and Travis Powell (Steven's brother) as co-conservators. The probate court also waived the bond requirement and ordered "that the funds of the minor child, [Cody], be deposited in a restricted account and that no funds be withdrawn or transferred from such account without written [o]rder of [the probate court]." The certificate of appointment and fiduciary letter included the following restriction: "No withdrawals without court order."

On Cody's behalf, Unrue received seven checks totaling $252,447.51. Three of the checks were made payable to her and Travis jointly and included the designation "Co-conservators For [Cody], A Minor" or "Co–Cn For Minor, [Cody]." The other four checks were made payable to Unrue and included the designation "As Conservator Of [Cody], A Minor." Unrue endorsed the checks without including her title as co-conservator. Unbeknownst to Travis, Unrue forged his name on the three checks made payable to her and Travis as co-conservators and took all the checks to the Pawleys Island Bank of America (BOA). Unrue had Lee Ann Yourko, a personal banker, open a certificate of deposit (CD) account titled "Karen M. Unrue Guardian [Cody]." Yourko collected the checks and took them to a teller, who processed the checks and

deposited the proceeds into the CD account. Neither Yourko nor the teller questioned the conservator designation in the payee line of the checks.

A few days later, Unrue returned to the Pawleys Island BOA with a single check for $253.67 made payable to her "As Conservator For Cody A Minor." Unrue requested Meredith Lawrence, the branch manager, to open a Uniform Gift to Minors Act (UGMA) account titled, "Karen M. Unrue—cust [Cody]—UMGA [sic]." Lawrence did not question the conservator title on the payee line of the check. Lawrence also failed to notice that Unrue indorsed the check without including her title.

Approximately a month later, after the CD matured, Unrue withdrew 100% of the funds, $253,991.50, from the CD account. Unrue took the funds to the Pawleys Island BOA and deposited them in the UGMA savings account. Over the next several months, Unrue made seven online transfers totaling $258,500 from the UGMA savings account to her personal checking account.

Mrs. Powell brought suit against BOA for its negligence in managing the accounts and failing to notice the indorsement requirements and restrictions imposed on the conservator. Would Bank of America be liable? Be sure to discuss what you know about indorsement requirements and restrictive indorsements in formulating your answer. [*Cody P. v. Bank of America, N.A.*, 720 S.E.2d 473 (S.C. App. 2011)]

---

[20] Revised UCC §3-110(cc)(2)(li).

12. Missing Indorsement

When the parties intend to negotiate an order instrument but for some reason the holder fails to indorse it, there is no negotiation. The transfer without indorsement has only the effect of a contract assignment.[21] If the transferee gave value for the instrument (see Chapter 30 for more information on what constitutes giving value), the transferee has the right to require that the transferor indorse the instrument unqualifiedly and thereby negotiate the instrument.

CPA D. PROBLEMS IN NEGOTIATION OF INSTRUMENTS

The issues of signatures and requirements for negotiation can become quite complex when issues such as forgery, employee misconduct, and embezzlement arise.

13. Forged and Unauthorized Indorsements

forged or **unauthorized indorsement** – instrument indorsed by an agent for a principal without authorization or authority.

A **forged** or **unauthorized indorsement** is not a valid indorsement.[22] Accordingly, anyone who has possession of a forged instrument is not a holder because the indorsement of the person whose signature was forged was necessary for effective negotiation of the instrument to the possessor. However, proof of forgery requires expert testimony and a split from a pattern of payments is helpful.[23]

If payment of an instrument is made to one claiming under or through a forged indorsement, the payor ordinarily remains liable to the person who is the rightful owner of the paper. However, if the rightful owner has been negligent and contributed to the forgery or unauthorized signature problem, there are exceptions to these general rules on liability for forged indorsements (see Chapter 30 for more information on the rights and liabilities of the parties).

14. Quasi Forgeries: The Impostor Rule

impostor rule – an exception to the rules on liability for forgery that covers situations such as the embezzling payroll clerk.

The **impostor rule** provides three exceptions to the rule that a forged indorsement is not effective to validly negotiate an instrument. If one of the three impostor exceptions applies, the instrument is still effectively negotiated, even though there may have been a forgery of an indorsement.

(A) WHEN THE IMPOSTOR RULE APPLIES. The impostor rule applies in cases where an indorser is impersonating a payee and in two cases where the indorser is a dummy payee.[24]

(1) Impersonating Payee.
The impersonation of a payee in the impostor rule exception includes impersonation of the agent of the person who is named as payee. **For Example,** if Jones pretends to be the agent of Brown Corporation and thereby obtains a check payable to the order of the corporation, the impostor exception applies.

---

[21] Revised UCC §3-204(d).
[22] Revised UCC §3-403(2); Steven B. Dow, "Imposter Rule and the Problem of Agency under the Revised Uniform Commercial Code: New Risks for Bank Customers?" 16 Comm. L.J. 199 (2001); *Bloom v. G.P.F.,* 588 So.2d 607 (Fla. App. 1991).
[23] *Wagner v. Bank of America,* 51 UCC Rep. Serv. 2d 781 (Cal. App. 2003).
[24] Revised UCC §3-405; *Mills v. U.S. Bank,* 83 Cal. Rptr. 146 (Cal. App. 2008).

(2) Dummy Payee.

Another impostor scenario arises when the preparer of the instrument intends that the named payee will never benefit from the instrument. Such a "dummy" payee may be an actual or a fictitious person. This situation arises when the owner of a checking account wishes to conceal the true purpose of taking money from the account at the bank. The account owner makes out a check purportedly in payment of a debt that in fact does not exist.[25]

(3) Dummy Payee Supplied by Employee.

The third impostor situation arises when an agent or employee of the maker or the drawer has supplied the name to be used for the payee, intending that the payee should not have any interest in the paper.[26] This last situation occurs when an employee fraudulently causes an employer to sign a check made to a customer or another person, whether existing or not. The employee does not intend to send it to that person but rather intends to forge the latter's indorsement, cash the check, and keep the money. This exception to the impostor rule imposes responsibility on employers to have adequate internal controls to prevent employees from taking advantage of an accounting system with loopholes so that others are not required to bear the cost of the employer's lack of appropriate precautions.

(B) EFFECT OF IMPOSTOR RULE. When the impostor rule is applicable, any person may indorse the name of the payee. This indorsement is treated as a genuine indorsement by the payee and cannot be attacked on the ground that it is a forgery. This recognition of the fictitious payee's signature as valid applies even though the dummy payee of the paper is a fictitious person.[27]

(C) LIMITATIONS ON IMPOSTOR RULE. The impostor rule does not apply when there is a valid check to an actual creditor for a correct amount owed by the drawer and someone later forges the payee's name. The impostor rule does not apply in this situation even if the forger is an employee of the drawer.

Even when the unauthorized indorsement of the payee's name is effective by virtue of the impostor rule, a person forging the payee's name is subject to civil and criminal liability for making such an indorsement.

For the impostor rule to apply, the holders or the takers of the instrument must show that they took the instrument (1) in good faith and (2) for payment or collection.

CASE SUMMARY

Sorry, Charlie Walks Away with the $6.3 Million

FACTS: Won Charlie Yi solicited money from investors in the Korean–American community (plaintiffs) by representing that he would invest their money in brokerage accounts at Carlin Equities Corporation, a nationally recognized broker-dealer based in New York. Yi, however, did

[25] *State Sec. Check Cashing, Inc. v. American General Financial Services (DE)*, 972 A.2d 882 (Md. 2009).
[26] *Advocate Health and Hospitals Corp. v. Bank One*, 810 N.E.2d 962 (Ill. App. 2004).
[27] *Bank of Nichols Hills v. Bank of Oklahoma*, 196 P.3d 984 (Okla. App. 2008). *Bank of Glen Burnie v. Elkridge Bank*, 707 A.2d 438 (Md. App. 1988), *State Sec. Check Cashing, Inc. v. American General Financial Services*, 972 A.2d 882 (Md. 2009).

CASE SUMMARY

Continued

not invest the money he received from plaintiffs at all. Instead, Yi registered the name "Carlin Co." as a fictitious name under which he did business. He opened a bank account at Wells Fargo in the name of "Won Charlie Yi dba Carlin Co." Between January and September of 2003, Yi received eight checks, totaling $6.3 million, payable to "Carlin Co.," "Carlin Corp.," or "Carlin Corporation." Yi deposited the checks into his Wells Fargo account and absconded with plaintiffs' money. He was later apprehended by federal authorities and convicted of a variety of criminal fraud charges.

The defrauded investors filed suit against Wells Fargo to recover their losses for the bank's lack of ordinary care in being certain that the checks deposited were deposited with the intended payee. A jury found in favor of Wells Fargo and the investors appealed.

DECISION: The court affirmed the lower court's decision because the checks were made out to an intended payee. Although there were differing names on the check and the indorsements were not always precise, the parties intended the checks to go to Charlie's company and Charlie's account. Charlie was a fraudster and they lost their money, but Wells Fargo is not liable for losses when customers write legitimate checks to those whom they later realize cannot be trusted. Losses are absorbed by banks when they fail to act in a commercially reasonable manner in honoring checks. In this situation, there were no signals that there was anything wrong with the checks because, indeed, the checks were written by the account holders. [*Unlimited Adjusting Group Inc. v. Wells Fargo Bank,* **94 Cal. Rptr. 3d. 672 (2009)**]

(D) NEGLIGENCE OF DRAWEE NOT REQUIRED. The impostor rule applies without regard to whether the drawee bank acted with reasonable care.

CASE SUMMARY

The Great Rite-Aid Heist

FACTS: B.D.G.S., Inc., a New York corporation with headquarters in Washington, owns a warehouse in Utica, New York. In 1991, B.D.G.S. entered into an oral agreement with two local men, Anthony Balio and his employee, Peter Duniec, to manage the warehouse. Their responsibilities included finding tenants and collecting rent, which was then to be forwarded to B.D.G.S. and deposited into its bank account in Washington. Balio and Duniec formed the Beechgrove Warehouse Corporation and maintained a business account in that name at Savings Bank of Utica (SBU).

Between 1996 and 2000, B.D.G.S. believed that one of its tenants, Rite-Aid, had been falling behind and failing to make its rent payments. B.D.G.S. later discovered that Rite-Aid had been making the payments, but 16 checks had been indorsed to Beechgrove Warehouse and deposited into Beechgrove's SBU account. The checks had been made payable to DBGS (an apparent typographical error). There was a handwritten indorsement on the back of each check stating:

> *DBGS, Inc.*
>   *Pay to the order of*
>   *Beechgrove Warehouse*
>   *For Deposit [followed by Beechgrove's SBU account number]*

CASE SUMMARY

Continued

A refund check from Niagara Mohawk for $427,781.82 had similarly been indorsed and deposited in the SBU account. B.D.G.S. filed suit against SBU, Balio, Duniec, and Beechgrove Warehouse. B.D.G.S. also brought a claim against SBU. The jury found that SBU had not followed reasonable commercial standards by accepting the checks for deposit. The appellate court affirmed and SBU appealed.

DECISION: The court affirmed noting that SBU was dealing with a payee forgery and it was SBU's responsibility to verify that the party with the checks was actually the payee and was authorized to deposit the checks. Because SBU was the one that had contact with Balio and Duniec it had a chance to prevent the embezzlement but its practices were not detailed enough to catch payee forgeries. [***B.D.G.S., Inc. v. Balio***, 861 N.E.2d 813 (N.Y. 2006)]

15. Effect of Incapacity or Misconduct on Negotiation

A negotiation is effective even though (1) it was made by a minor or any other person lacking capacity; (2) it was an act beyond the powers of a corporation; (3) it was obtained by fraud, duress, or a mistake of any kind; or (4) the negotiation was part of an illegal transaction or was made in breach of duty. The rights of the parties in these types of negotiations depends on who holds the instrument (see Chapter 30).

16. Lost Instruments

The liability on lost instruments depends on who is demanding payment from whom and on whether the instrument was order or bearer paper when it was lost.

(A) ORDER INSTRUMENTS. If the lost instrument is order paper, the finder does not become the holder because the instrument has not been indorsed and delivered by the person to whom it was then payable. The former holder who lost it is still the rightful owner of the instrument.

(B) BEARER INSTRUMENTS. If the lost instrument is in bearer form when it is lost, the finder, as the possessor of a bearer instrument, is the holder and is entitled to enforce payment.

CPA E. WARRANTIES IN NEGOTIATION

When a negotiable instrument is transferred by negotiation, the transferors give certain implied warranties.

17. Warranties of Unqualified Indorser

When the transferor receives consideration for the indorsement and makes an unqualified indorsement, the warranties stated in this section are given by the transferor by implication. No distinction is made between an unqualified blank indorsement and an unqualified special indorsement.

(A) SCOPE OF WARRANTIES. The warranties of the unqualified indorser are found in §3-416 of the Revised UCC and provide that the warrantor is a person entitled to enforce the instrument; that all signatures on the instrument are authentic and authorized; that the instrument has not been altered; that the instrument is not subject to a defense or claim; that the drawer of the draft has authorized the issuance of the item in the amount for which the item is drawn; and that the warrantor has no knowledge of any insolvency proceeding with respect to the maker or acceptor.[28]

Those who present an instrument for payment (see Chapter 30), or the last party in line before the payor, make three warranties: that the warrantor is entitled to enforce the draft or authorized to obtain payment or acceptance of the draft; that the draft has not been altered; and that the warrantor has no knowledge that the signature of the drawer of the draft is unauthorized.[29]

If a forged indorsement has appeared during the transfer of the instrument, and there is a refusal to pay because of that problem, the last party who is a holder may turn to her transferor to recover on the basis of these implied warranties. These warranties give those who have transferred and held the instrument recourse against those parties who were involved in the transfer of the instrument, although they were not parties to the original instrument.

(b) **What Is not Warranted.** The implied warranties stated here do not guarantee that payment of the instrument will be made. Similarly, the holder's indorsement of a check does not give any warranty that the account of the drawer in the drawee bank contains funds sufficient to cover the check. However, implied warranties do, for example, promise that the signatures on the instrument are not forged. Likewise, they promise that no one has altered the amount on the instrument. The warranties are not warranties of payment or solvency. They are simply warranties about the nature of the instrument. A holder may not be paid the amount due on the instrument, but if the lack of payment results from a forgery, the holder has rights against those who transferred the instrument with a forged signature.

(c) **Beneficiary of Implied Warranties.** The implied warranties of the unqualified indorser pass to the transferee and any subsequent transferees. There is no requirement that subsequent transferees take the instrument in good faith to be entitled to the warranties. Likewise, the transferee need not be a holder to enjoy warranty protections.

(d) **Disclaimer of Warranties.** Warranties may be disclaimed when the instrument is not a check. A disclaimer of warranties is ordinarily made by adding "Without warranties" to the indorsement.

(e) **Notice of Breach of Warranty.** To enforce an implied warranty of an indorser, the party claiming under the warranty must give the indorser notice of the breach. This notice must be given within 30 days after the claimant learns or has reason to know of the breach and the identity of the indorser. If proper notice is not given, the warranty claim is reduced by the amount of the loss that could have been avoided had timely notice been given.

18. Warranties of Other Parties

Warranties are also made by the indorser who indorses "Without recourse" and by one who transfers by delivery only.

(a) **Qualified Indorser.** The warranty liability of a qualified indorser is the same as that of an unqualified indorser.[30] A qualified indorsement means that the indorser does not

---

[28] Revised UCC §3-416 (1990).
[29] Revised UCC §3-417. These warranties are for consumer accounts.
[30] Revised UCC §3-416(a).

assume liability for the payment of the instrument as written. (See §3-416(4).) However, a qualified indorsement does not eliminate the implied warranties an indorser makes as a transferor of an instrument. The implied warranty that is waived by a qualified indorsement is the fourth warranty on defenses. A qualified indorser still makes the other warranties on signatures and alteration but waives the warranty on defenses.

(B) TRANSFER BY DELIVERY. When the negotiable instrument is negotiated by delivery without indorsement, the warranty liability of the transferor runs only to the immediate transferee. In all other respects, the warranty liability is the same as in the case of the unqualified indorser. **For Example,** Thomas, a minor, gives Craig his note payable to bearer. Craig transfers the note for value and by delivery only to Walsh, who negotiates it to Hall. Payment is then refused by Thomas, who chooses to disaffirm his contract. Hall cannot hold Craig liable. Craig, having negotiated the instrument by delivery only, is liable on his implied warranties only to his immediate transferee, Walsh. Likewise, because Craig did not indorse the note, he is not secondarily liable for payment of the note.

MAKE THE CONNECTION

SUMMARY

Negotiation is the transferring of a negotiable instrument in such a way as to make the transferee the holder. When a negotiable instrument is transferred by negotiation, the transferee becomes the holder of the instrument. If such a holder becomes a holder in due course, the holder will be immune to certain defenses.

An *order instrument* is negotiated by an indorsement and delivery by the person to whom it is then payable. A bearer instrument is negotiated by delivery alone. The order or bearer character of an instrument is determined by the face of the instrument as long as the instrument is not indorsed. If the instrument has been indorsed, the character is determined by the last indorsement.

A number of different kinds of indorsements can be made on negotiable instruments. When an indorser merely authenticates the instrument, the indorsement is called a *blank indorsement*. If the last indorsement is a blank indorsement, the instrument is bearer paper, which may be negotiated by change of possession alone. A special indorsement consists of

the authentication by the indorser and words specifying the person to whom the indorser makes the instrument payable. If the last indorsement is a special indorsement, the instrument is order paper and may be negotiated only by an indorsement and delivery. A qualified indorsement eliminates the liability of the indorser to answer for dishonor of the paper by the maker or the drawee. A restrictive indorsement specifies the purpose of the instrument or its use.

A forged or unauthorized indorsement is no indorsement, and the possessor of the instrument cannot be a holder. The impostor rule makes three exceptions to this rule: dummy payee; employee fraud; and impersonating a payee.

A negotiation is effective even though (1) it is made by a minor, (2) it is an act beyond the powers of a corporation, (3) it is obtained by fraud, or (4) the negotiation is part of an illegal transaction. However, the transferor may be able to set aside the negotiation under general legal principles apart from the UCC. The negotiation cannot be set aside if the instrument is held by a person paying it in good faith and without knowledge of the facts on which the rescission claim is based.

The warranties of the unqualified indorser are as follows: (1) the warrantor is a person entitled to enforce the instrument; (2) all signatures on the instrument are authentic and authorized; (3) the instrument has not been altered; (4) the instrument is not subject to a defense or claim in recoupment of any party that can be asserted against the warrantor;

with respect to any item drawn on a consumer account, which does not bear a handwritten signature purporting to be the signature of the drawer, that the purported drawer of the draft has authorized the issuance of the item in the amount for which the item is drawn; and (5) the warrantor has no knowledge of any insolvency proceeding commenced with respect to the maker or acceptor or, in the case of an unaccepted draft, the drawer.

LEARNING OUTCOMES

After studying this chapter, you should be able to clearly explain:

A. Transfer of Negotiable Instruments

B. How Negotiation Occurs: Bearer Instruments

C. How Negotiation Occurs: Order Instruments

L0.1 Explain the difference between negotiation of order paper and negotiation of bearer paper

See *Emmons v. Capital One* on p. 602.

L0.2 List the types of indorsements and describe their uses

See *Check City v. L & T Enterprises* on pp. 608–609.

D. Problems in Negotiation of Instruments

L0.3 Determine the legal effect of forged and unauthorized indorsements

See Thinking Things Through on p. 609.

L0.4 Be familiar with the forged payee impostor exceptions

See *B.D.G.S., Inc. v. Balio* on pp. 612–613.
See *Unlimited Adjusting Group, Inc. v. Wells Fargo Bank* on pp. 611–612.

E. Warranties in Negotiation

L0.5 List the indorser's warranties and describe their significance

See the discussion of warranties on p. 613.

KEY TERMS

alternative payees
blank indorsement
delivery
forged or unauthorized
  indorsement

holder
holder in due course
impostor rule
indorsee
indorsement

negotiation
qualified indorsement
restrictive indorsement
special indorsement

QUESTIONS AND CASE PROBLEMS

1. Corey Brandon Bumgarner, who was separated from his wife, Crystal, had an accident caused by Donald Wood that resulted in $2,164.46 in damages to Corey's vehicle. Wood's insurance carrier mailed a draft in the amount of $2,164.46 drawn on Fleet Bank of Hartford, Connecticut, payable to Corey, to his box at P.O. Box 153,

Hillsboro, North Carolina. The draft was negotiated at Community Bank and Trust, and the name, "Crystal Bumgarner," was handwritten on the back of the draft. Corey's name was written below Crystal Bumgarner's name. Crystal Bumgarner's driver's license number was handwritten on the front of the draft.

Corey Bumgarner filed suit to have the insurer pay him the $2,164.46. The insurer indicated that it had sent order paper, that it had been delivered, and that there was, therefore, no claim against it or Wood. The trial court found that there had been no delivery and that Bumgarner was entitled to another check. Wood and his insurer appealed. Who is correct about delivery and why? [*Bumgarner v. Wood*, 563 S.E.2d 309, 47 UCC Rep. Serv. 2d 1099 (N.C. App.)]

2. How could a check made out to "Joseph Klimas and his Attorney Fritzshall & Gleason & Blue Cross Blue Shield Company and Carpenters Welfare Fund" be negotiated further? What would be required? [*Chicago District Council of Carpenters Welfare Fund v. Gleason's Fritzshall*, 693 N.E.2d 412 (Ill. App.)]

3. An insurer issued a settlement check on a claim brought by an injured minor that was payable to "Trudy Avants attorney for minor child Joseph Walton, mother Dolores Carpenter 11762 S. Harrells Ferry Road #E Baton Rouge LA 70816." The lawyer indorsed the check. Two unknown individuals forged indorsements for the other two names and obtained payment of the check. The insurer sued the payor bank claiming the instruments were not properly payable because of the forged indorsements. The court is unclear whether the indorsement required is one for an either/or payee or joint payee. What advice can you offer the court as it faces this issue? [*Coregis Insurance Co. v. Fleet National Bank*, 793 A.2d 254 (Conn. App.)]

4. ABCO (Abbott Development Company) made a note payable to Western State Bank of Midland. The FDIC took over Western State's operations after it failed. ABCO had defaulted on the note, after which the FDIC permitted ABCO Homes to refinance the note, making its refinancing note payable to the FDIC. The FDIC indorsed its note to SMS Financial and inadvertently sent it to SMS as part of a large batch of documents. When litigation resulted on the note, SMS claimed it was the holder. Others challenged its status, saying that SMS never had the instrument delivered to it. The lower court held SMS was not a holder and SMS appealed. Is SMS a holder? Why or why not? [*SMS Financial,*

L.L.C. v. ABCO Homes, Inc., 167 F.3d 235 (5th Cir.)]

5. Jerry O. Peavy, Jr., who did not have a bank account of his own, received a draft from CNL Insurance America in the amount of $5,323.60. The draft was drawn on CNL's account at Bank South, N.A., and was "payable to the order of Jerry Peavy and Trust Company Bank." Jerry O. Peavy, Sr., allowed his son Peavy, Jr., to deposit the draft in his account at Bank South, N.A. Bank South accepted the draft and deposited it on December 29, 1992, with only the signature of Jerry Peavy, Jr. Both Mr. and Mrs. Peavy, Sr., then wrote checks on the amount of the draft using the full amount to benefit their son.

On March 30, 1993, Bank South realized that it had improperly deposited the draft because it was lacking an indorsement from Trust Company Bank and reversed the transaction by debiting Mr. and Mrs. Peavy's account for the full amount of the draft. A bank officer then called Mr. and Mrs. Peavy, told them what had happened with the draft, and "threatened to send them to jail if they did not immediately deposit the sum of $5,323.60." The Peavys deposited that amount from the sale of some stock they owned and then filed suit against Bank South for its conversion of their son's draft and funds. Do the Peavys have a case? [*Peavy v. Bank South*, 474 S.E. 2d 690 (Ga. App.)]

6. Getty Petroleum distributes gasoline through dealer-owned stations. Customers who buy gas at a Getty station can pay by cash or credit card. When a customer uses a credit card, Getty processes the transactions, receives payment from the credit card company, and then issues computer-generated checks payable to dealers to reimburse them for their credit card sales. Many checks, however, are not intended for negotiation and are never delivered to the payees. Instead, Getty uses these checks for bookkeeping purposes, voiding them and then crediting the check amount toward the dealer's future purchases of gasoline from Getty.

Lorna Lewis, a supervisor in Getty's credit processing department, stole over 130 checks, forged the indorsements of the payees by hand or rubber stamp, and then submitted the checks to

American Express and other credit card companies to pay her own debts. The credit card companies then forwarded the checks through ordinary banking channels to Chemical Bank, where Getty had its checking account. Chemical Bank honored the checks Lewis had forged.

Getty, on discovering the larceny of Lewis, sought recovery of the amounts from the credit card companies. Getty sought payment on 31 of the checks from American Express (which had been paid by Chemical Bank). At trial, a judge held American Express liable to Getty for $58,841.60. The appeals court found that American Express was grossly negligent in taking and cashing the checks and also held it liable. American Express appealed. Who wins and why? [*Getty Petroleum Corp. v. American Exp. Travel Related Services Co., Inc.*, 683 N.E.2d 311 (N.Y.)]

7. Snug Harbor Realty Co. had a checking account in First National Bank. When construction work was obtained by Snug Harbor, its superintendent, Magee, would examine the bills submitted for labor and materials. He would instruct the bookkeeper which bills were approved, and the bookkeeper then prepared the checks in accordance with his instructions. After the checks were signed by the proper official of Snug Harbor, Magee picked them up for delivery. Instead of delivering certain checks, he forged the signatures of the respective payees as indorsers and cashed the checks. The drawee bank then debited the Snug Harbor account with the amount of the checks. Snug Harbor claimed this was improper and sued the bank for the amount of the checks. The bank claimed it was protected by the impostor rule. Will the bank be successful? Explain. [*Snug Harbor Realty Co. v. First National Bank*, 253 A.2d 581 (N.J. Super.)]

8. Benton, as agent for Savidge, received an insurance settlement check from Metropolitan Life Insurance Co. He indorsed it "For deposit" and deposited it in Bryn Mawr Trust Co. in Savidge's account. What were the nature and effect of this indorsement? [*Savidge v. Metropolitan Life Ins. Co.*, 110 A.2d 730 (Pa.)]

9. Allstate Insurance Company issued a check payable to "Chuk N. Tang & Rosa C. Tang

HWJT" with "Bank of America" on the second line and the following explanation on the front of the check: "Settlement of our rental dwelling loss caused by fire on 11/21/93." The Tangs indorsed the check and forged the indorsement of Bank of America. When Bank of America objected, the Tangs claimed that only they needed to sign the instrument for further negotiations. The check was intended as a joint payment for Bank of America as the mortgagee on the Tangs' rental property because the insurance policy required that the mortgagee be paid first before any proceeds went to the property owners. Bank of America sued Allstate. Is Bank of America entitled to recover for the lack of its indorsement? Was its indorsement necessary for further negotiation? [*Bank of America Nat'l Trust & Savings Ass'n v. Allstate Insurance Co.*, 29 F. Supp. 2d 1129 (C.D. Cal.)]

10. When claims filed with an insurance company were approved for payment, they were given to the claims clerk, who would prepare checks to pay those claims and then give the checks to the treasurer to sign. The claims clerk of the insurance company made a number of checks payable to persons who did not have any claims and gave them to the treasurer with the checks for valid claims, and the treasurer signed all of the checks. The claims clerk then removed the false checks, indorsed them with the names of their respective payees, and cashed them at the bank where the insurance company had its account. The bank debited the account of the insurance company with the amount of these checks. The insurance company claimed that the bank could not do this because the indorsements on the checks were forgeries. Was the insurance company correct? [*General Accident Fire & Life Assur. Corp. v. Citizens Fidelity Bank & Trust Co.*, 519 S.W. 2d 817 (Ky.)]

11. Eutsler forged his brother Richard's indorsement on certified checks and cashed them at First National Bank. When Richard sought to recover the funds from the bank, the bank stated that it would press criminal charges against Eutsler. Richard asked the bank to delay prosecution to give him time to collect directly from his brother. His brother promised to repay him the money but vanished some six months later without

having paid any money. Richard sued the bank. What result? [*Eutsler v. First Nat'l Bank, Pawhuska*, 639 P.2d 1245 (Okal.)]

12. Michael Sykes, the president of Sykes Corp., hired Richard Amelung to handle the company's bookkeeping and deal with all of its vendors. Amelung entered into an agreement with Eastern Metal Supply to help reduce Sykes's debt to Eastern. Whenever Sykes received a check, Amelung would sign it over to Eastern and allow it to keep 30 percent of the check amount. On 28 checks that totaled $200,000, Amelung indorsed the back as follows: "Sykes & Associates or Sykes Corporation, Richard Amelung." Amelung then turned the checks over to Eastern, and Eastern deposited them into its account at Barnett Bank. Eastern would then write one of its checks to Sykes Corp. for the 70 percent remaining from the checks. When Michael Sykes learned of the arrangement, he demanded the return of the 30 percent from Barnett Bank, claiming that it had paid over an unauthorized signature and that the indorsement was restricted and had been violated by the deposit into Eastern's account. What type of indorsement did Amelung make? Did he have the authority to do so? Should Sykes be reimbursed by Barnett? [*Sykes Corp. v. Eastern Metal Supply, Inc.*, 659 So. 2d 475 (Fla. App.)]

13. In January 1998, Allied Capital Partners, L.P. and American Factors Corporation were in the business of factoring accounts receivable for third-party clients. Allied assigned its factoring contract with Complete Design, Inc. to American but retained an interest in the factoring of Complete Design's invoices. On January 25, 1998, in payment of invoices issued by Complete Design, Clark Wilson Homes, Inc., issued a check for $6,823.15. The check was payable to:

> *Complete Design*
> *Allied Capital Partners, L.P.*
> *2340 E. Trinity Mills Ste. 300*
> *Carrollton, Texas 75006*

On February 10, 1998, Clark Wilson issued another check for $26,329.32 made payable to:

> *Complete Design*
> *Allied Capital Partners, L.P.*
> *2340 E. Trinity Mills Ste. 300*
> *Carrollton, Texas 75006*

Complete Design deposited both checks in its account at Bank One. However, Allied and American received none of the proceeds of the checks.

Complete Design subsequently declared bankruptcy, and Allied and American made demand on Bank One for damages resulting from Bank One's conversion of the two checks. Bank One denied all liability for conversion of the checks. Allied and American subsequently sued Bank One, asserting conversion. Bank One filed a motion for summary judgment asserting that, because it was ambiguous to whom the checks at issue were payable, they were payable upon a single indorsement. The trial court granted Bank One's motion. Allied and American appealed. Who is correct here? Were both signatures necessary for a proper indorsement, or will one do? [*Allied Capital Partners, L.P. v. Bank One, Texas, N.A.*, 68 S.W. 3d 51 (Tex. App.)]

14. Would a bank be liable to a customer who indorsed a check "For deposit only into account #071698570" if that check were deposited into the wrong account? What if the customer's indorsement was "For deposit only"? Would any account qualify? Would any bank qualify? [*Qatar v. First American Bank of Virginia*, 885 F. Supp. 849 (E.D. Va.)]

15. Two employees of the state of New Mexico fraudulently procured and indorsed a warrant (a draft drawn against funds of the state) made out to the Greater Mesilla Valley Sanitation District. There was no such sanitation district. The employees obtained payment from Citizens Bank. Western Casualty, the state's insurer, reimbursed the state for its loss and then brought suit against the bank for negligently paying the warrant. Is the bank liable for its payment? Discuss your answer. [*Western Casualty & Surety Co. v. Citizens Bank of Las Cruces*, 676 F.2d 1344 (10th Cir.)]

CPA QUESTIONS

1. Hand executed and delivered to Rex a $1,000 negotiable note payable to Rex or bearer. Rex then negotiated it to Ford and indorsed it on the back by merely signing his name. Which of the following is a correct statement?

   a. Rex's indorsement was a special indorsement.

   b. Rex's indorsement was necessary to Ford's qualification as a holder.

   c. The instrument initially being bearer paper cannot be converted to order paper.

   d. The instrument is bearer paper, and Ford can convert it to order paper by writing "pay to the order of Ford" above Rex's signature.

2. Jane Lane, a sole proprietor, has in her possession several checks that she received from her customers. Lane is concerned about the safety of the checks since she believes that many of them are bearer paper that may be cashed without endorsement. The checks in Lane's possession will be considered order paper rather than bearer paper if they were made payable (in the drawer's handwriting) to the order of:

   a. Cash

   b. Ted Tint, and indorsed by Ted Tint in blank

   c. Bearer, and indorsed by Ken Kent making them payable to Jane Lane

   d. Bearer, and indorsed by Sam Sole in blank

3. West Corp. received a check that was originally made payable to the order of one of its customers, Ted Burns. The following indorsement was written on the back of the check:

   Ted Burns, without recourse, for collection only

   Which of the following describes the indorsement?

	Special	Restrictive
a.	Yes	Yes
b.	No	No
c.	No	Yes
d.	Yes	No

4. An instrument reads as follows:

   $250.00 Chicago, Illinois April 1, 1992

   Thirty days after date I promise to pay to the order of ___Cash___

   Two hundred and fifty_____ Dollars at

   New York City

   Value received with interest at the rate of six percent per annum. This agreement arises out of a separate agreement.

   No. 20 Due May 1, 1992   Robert Smith

   Answer "Yes" or "No" for the following questions about the previous item.

   a. The instrument is a draft.

   b. The instrument is order paper.

   c. This is a negotiable instrument.

   d. Robert Smith is the maker.

   e. The instrument may be negotiated without indorsement.

5. Ashley needs to endorse a check that had been endorsed by two other individuals prior to Ashley's receipt of the check. Ashley does not want to have surety liability, so Ashley endorses the check "without recourse." Under the Negotiable Instruments Article of the UCC, which of the following types of endorsement did Ashley make?

   a. Blank.

   b. Special.

   c. Qualified.

   d. Restrictive.

CHAPTER 30

Liability of the Parties under Negotiable Instruments

© Manuel Gutjahr/iStockphoto.com

learningoutcomes

After studying this chapter, you should be able to

LO.1 Distinguish between an ordinary holder and a holder in due course

LO.2 List the requirements for becoming a holder in due course

LO.3 Explain the rights of a holder through a holder in due course

LO.4 List and explain the limited defenses not available against a holder in due course

LO.5 List and explain the universal defenses available against all holders

LO.6 Describe how the rights of a holder in due course have been limited by the Federal Trade Commission

621

C hapters 28 and 29 introduced the requirements for negotiable instruments and the methods for transfer of those instruments. However, the requirements of negotiability and transfer are simply preliminary steps for the discovery of the real benefit of using negotiable instruments in commerce, which is to streamline payment in commercial transactions. This chapter explains the streamlined protected status and rights of these special parties to negotiable instruments. The extent of the parties' rights and protections is covered in this chapter.

assignee–third party to whom contract benefits are transferred.

holder–someone in possession of an instrument that runs to that person (i.e., is made payable to that person, is indorsed to that person, or is bearer paper).

holder in due course–holder who has given value, taken in good faith without notice of dishonor, defenses, or that instrument is overdue, and who is afforded special rights or status.

A. Parties to Negotiable Instruments: Rights and Liabilities

The rights and defenses of the parties to negotiable instruments are determined by the types of parties involved.

1. Types of Parties

Parties with rights in a negotiable instrument can be **assignees** or **holders**. A holder may be an ordinary holder or a **holder in due course**. As noted in Chapter 28, a holder in due course is a special party to an instrument with special rights beyond those of the ordinary holder.

CPA

2. Ordinary Holders and Assignees

A holder is a party in possession of an instrument that runs to him. An instrument "runs" to a party if it is payable to his order, is bearer paper, or is indorsed to him (see Chapter 29). Any holder has all of the rights given through and under the negotiable instrument. The holder may demand payment or bring suit for collection on the instrument. A holder can give a discharge or release from liability on the instrument.

A holder who seeks payment of the instrument is required only to produce the instrument and show that the signature of the maker, drawer, or indorser is genuine. If the party obligated to pay under the instrument has no valid defense (such as forgery, which was discussed in Chapter 29), the holder is entitled to payment of the instrument.

The holder can recover from any of the parties who are liable on the instrument, regardless of the order of the signatures on the instrument. A holder could recover from the first indorser on an instrument or from the last party to indorse the instrument.

The rights of a holder are no different from the rights of a contract assignee (see Chapter 18). The assignee of a contract is in the same position and has the same rights as an ordinary holder. **For Example,** if a farmer who signed a note to pay for his tractor has a warranty problem with the tractor, he has a defense to payment on the note. Anyone who is assigned that note as an assignee or holder is also subject to the farmer's defense. (See Figure 30-1 and also the provisions on consumer credit protection under the discussion of the Federal Trade Commission rule in Chapter 33 and later in this chapter.)

CPA

3. The Holder-in-Due-Course Protections

The law gives certain holders of negotiable instruments special rights by protecting them from certain defenses. This protection makes negotiable instruments more attractive and allows greater ease of transfer. Unlike ordinary holders or assignees,

FIGURE 30-1	*Assignee, Holder, and Holder-in-Due-Course Rights*

Suppose that Farmer Fred signs an installment contract to purchase a tractor from John Deere for $153,000. John Deere assigns the contract to Finance Co.

Suppose that Farmer Fred signs a negotiable promissory note for $153,000 and John Deere then transfers it to Finance Co., a holder in due course.

Suppose that Farmer Fred has a roofing company replace the roof on his home, and he signs a negotiable promissory note for $5,000. Roofing Co. transfers the note to Finance Co.

© Cengage Learning

holders in due course take free of contract assignment defenses that are good against ordinary holders or assignees. Figure 30-1 shows the different rights of holders, assignees, and holders in due course.

(A) HOLDER IN DUE COURSE (HDC). To obtain the preferred status of a holder in due course,[1] a person must first be a holder. However, the preferred status of HDC requires additional standards. Those holders who do not meet the standards for an HDC have all the rights of a holder. However, HDCs enjoy additional protections beyond those basic holder rights. Under UCC.§3-302(a), there are four requirements for becoming an HDC.[2]

---

[1] Revised UCC.§3-302 Adam J. Levitin, "Finding Nemo: Rediscovering the Virtues of Negotiability in the Wake of Enron," 2007 Columbia L. Rev. 83 (2007).
[2] Revised UCC.§3-302(a).

CPA

(1) Value.

value – consideration or antecedent debt or security given in exchange for the transfer of a negotiable instrument or creation of a security interest.

Value is similar to consideration (see Chapter 15). **For Example,** a person who receives a negotiable note as a gift does not give value because gifts are not supported by consideration or value.[3]

A transferee takes an instrument for value when (1) the holder has promised to do something in exchange (such as update a Web site); (2) the transferee takes the instrument as security for a loan (such as when a debtor transfers a promissory note payable to him to the transferee); or (3) the transferee receives the instrument as payment for a debt already due.[4] As with consideration, the courts do not consider whether the value is enough; they determine only whether some value has been given.[5]

Under Revised Article 3, the original payee of a note is not an HDC unless that note is transferred to others and then back to the payee.[6]

A bank does not give value for a deposited check when it credits the depositor's account with the amount of the deposit. The bank gives value to the extent that the depositor is permitted to withdraw funds against that deposit.[7] **For Example,** if Janice deposits a $300 check into her account, which already has $400 in it, Janice's bank does not give value until Janice has written checks or withdrawn funds beyond the existing $400. The code follows FIFO (first in, first out) for drawing on funds. A bank that lets the customer draw on the funds deposited gives value.[8]

CPA

(2) Good Faith.

The element of **good faith** for becoming an HDC requires that a holder of a negotiable instrument act honestly in acquiring the instrument. In addition, the taker must follow reasonable standards of fair dealing.[9] Karl Llewellyn, one of the key drafters of the UCC, said that to comply with reasonable standards and good faith, the party must act with a "pure heart and an empty head."

good faith – absence of knowledge of any defects in or problems; "pure heart and an empty head."

Bad faith sometimes exists just because the transferee takes the instrument under such odd circumstances. **For Example,** if transferee buys a note made payable to an estate from an accountant in a bar at midnight, suspicion prevents HDC status.

close-connection doctrine – circumstantial evidence, such as an ongoing or a close relationship, that can serve as notice of a problem with an instrument.

The **close-connection doctrine** applies in circumstances that indicate a problem with the instrument. Under this doctrine, the holder has taken so many instruments from its transferor or is so closely connected with the transferor that any knowledge the transferor has is deemed transferred to the holder, preventing holder-in-due-course status. Examples include consumer transactions where the holder in due course is a company that regularly does business with a company that has continual problems with consumer complaints.[10]

---

[3] However, if the donor of the negotiable instrument were a holder in due course, it might be possible under a special Article 3 protection for the heir to also be a holder in due course despite the gift acquisition. UCC.§3-302(c)(iii). This protection for gift transfers by holders in due course is called the *shelter provision* (and is covered later in this chapter).

[4] Revised UCC.§3-303.

[5] Revised UCC.§3-303; *United Catholic Parish Schools of Beaver Dam Educational Ass'n v. Card Services Center*, 636 N.W.2d 206 (Wis App 2001). *Agriliance, LLC v. Farmpro Services, Inc.*, 328 F. Supp. 2d 958 (S.D. Iowa 2003).

[6] Revised UCC.§3-302(c).

[7] Revised UCC.§4-211 (2002).

[8] Allowing a deposit of a check with provisional credit does not make a bank a holder in due course, but on a cashier's check, when the bank becomes both the drawer and the drawee, the bank is obligated to pay on the instrument. *Flatiron Linen, Inc. v. First American State Bank*, 23 P.3d 1209 (Colo. 2011), If the bank does not impose provisional credit and makes the funds available immediately for the customer, it gives value and qualifies as a holder in due course. *Maine Family Federal Credit Union v. Sun Life Assur. Co. of Canada*, 727 A.2d 335 (Maine 1999), but see *Travelers Cas. and Sur. Co. of America v. Wells Fargo Bank N.A.*, 374 F.3d 521 (7th Cir. 2004).

[9] Revised UCC.§3-103(a)(4); issue of whether a party is a holder in due course is always an issue of fact. *Pasack Community Bank, Inc. v. Universal Funding, LLP*, 16 A.3d 1097 (N.J. App. 2011).

[10] *Associates Home Equity Services, Inc. v. Troup*, 778 A.2d 529 (N.J. Super. AD 2001); *Gonzalez v. Old Kent Mortgage Co.*, 2000 WL 1469313 (E.D. Pa. 2000).

CASE SUMMARY

Embezzling $29,000 and Having an HDC Cash Your Check

FACTS: Regent served as a settlement agent for closing real estate transactions. Regent cut checks to distribute funds to all the parties to such transactions. On December 23, 2005, New Randolph cashed a check from Regent, which was made out to Charae Pearson, for $1,945.99. Four days later, New Randolph cashed another check for Pearson, again from Regent, this time for $2,500. On January 11, 2006, Pearson brought Regent's check number 22221 for $29,588.31 to New Randolph. Unlike the prior checks, which spelled Pearson's name correctly, this check showed the payee as "CHAREA PAERSON." The check indicated that Pearson received it as a "LOAN PAYOFF." Pearson presented the check to Patrice Keys, manager of New Randolph. Pearson showed Keys her state identification card, which had been issued on December 30, 2005. Pearson told Keys that Regent issued the check to her to pay her a commission she earned from the sale of property.

PLS Check Cashers, which owned New Randolph, did not authorize Keys to cash checks in excess of $5,000 without approval from her supervisor. Keys contacted Sandra Arizaga of PLS. Arizaga authorized Keys to cash the check. Arizaga, who worked as director of operations for PLS, testified that she approved about three checks each week for amounts exceeding the amount of Regent's check number 22221. She spoke with Keys about the check, and then she looked up the phone number for Regent at Regent's Web site. Arizaga testified that she called the number and asked to speak with someone about verifying a check. The woman with whom she spoke confirmed that Regent issued the check to Pearson in the amount shown. Arizaga then contacted American Chartered Bank, which confirmed that the check came from a valid account with sufficient funds to cover the check, and that Regent had not stopped payment on the check.

Arizaga admitted that according to PLS's manual, the misspelling of Pearson's name could signal fraud. Pearson's recent identification card should also raise suspicion. Arizaga did not remember whether she noticed that the check indicated its purpose as "LOAN PAYOFF," instead of listing the payment as a commission.

Regent introduced PLS's manual into evidence. The manual emphasizes that PLS earns its fees by cashing checks, so the employee should "[s]pend * * * time proving that the check can be cashed and not looking for excuses not to cash it." The manual identifies several signs that a check might not be valid, including several of the factors present in this case. According to the manual, the employee should "verify that the check is good" by "phoning the maker."

Police arrested Pearson, charging her with check fraud. Two days later, police arrested Tatiana Auson, an employee of Regent, on the same charge. Regent had hired Auson to work as a funder, meaning that Regent authorized Auson to cut checks for the parties to real estate transactions. According to Regent's investigator, Auson cancelled checks intended for parties to real estate transactions, then issued new checks to different payees for the amounts of the original checks. Pearson admitted that Auson gave her the three checks that New Randolph cashed for Pearson. Pearson kept about $5,000 of the proceeds from the checks, and she gave the remainder to Auson. All three checks appeared to bear the signature of Karen Hendricks, who had authority to sign checks on behalf of Regent.

Regent told its bank to stop payment on the check. New Randolph sued Regent for payment of the check, claiming that its status as a holder in due course entitled it to payment, despite the evidence that Auson and Pearson conspired to defraud Regent.

New Randolph appealed.

DECISION: Notice that disqualifies a party from being an HDC is something more than a suspicion. The verification call made in this situation showed the good faith of New Randolph. It checked to be sure that the check was good and was entitled to payment regardless of the embezzlement and breaches of fiduciary duties of their respective employees in working through the transactions. [*New Randolph Halsted Currency Exchange, Inc. v. Regent Title Insurance Co.*, 939 N.E.2d 1024 (Ill. App. 2011)]

(3) Ignorance of the Instrument's Being Overdue or Dishonored.

An instrument can be negotiated even though it has been dishonored, it is overdue,[11] or it is demand paper, such as a check, that has been outstanding for more than a reasonable time.[12] These instruments can still be transferred and the transferee is still a holder. However, the fact that the instrument is circulating at a late date or after it has been dishonored is suspicious and results in notice from the circumstances that there may be some adverse claim or defense. A person who acquires title to the instrument under such circumstances can be a holder but cannot be a holder in due course. **For Example,** buying a discounted note after its due date is notice that something may be wrong with the instrument.

(4) Ignorance of Defenses and Adverse Claims.

Prior parties on an instrument may have defenses that entitle them to withhold payment from a holder of an instrument. **For Example,** the drawer of a check, upon demand for payment by the payee, could assert as a defense to payment that the merchandise the payee delivered under the terms of their underlying contract was defective. A person who acquires an instrument with notice or knowledge that there is a defense that a party may have or that there are claims of ownership of the instrument from different parties cannot be an HDC. In general, transferees who are aware of facts that would make a reasonable person ask questions are deemed to know what they would have learned if they had asked questions.[13] Such knowledge and the failure to ask questions will cost them their special status of holder in due course; they remain simply holders.

Knowledge acquired by a holder after the instrument was acquired does not prevent the holder from being a holder in due course. The fact that a holder, after acquiring the instrument, learns of a defense does not work retroactively to destroy the holder's character as an HDC.

CASE SUMMARY

Cashing a Postdated Check from an Embezzler: HDC?

FACTS: A check dated August 10, 2007, was made payable to one of Liccardi's employees, Charles Stallone, Jr. Liccardi withheld the check from Stallone because he suspected him of embezzlement. However, the check still disappeared from the company offices, and when the disappearance was discovered, Liccardi immediately placed a stop payment on the check. JCNB Check Cashing, Inc. (JCNB), cashed the check for Stallone before the issue date (the check was postdated) and JCNB then deposited the check in its own bank account on August 9, 2007. However, the issuing bank refused to honor the check. On February 11, 2009, Robert Triffin acquired the dishonored payroll check from JCNB and sued Liccardi and Stallone for the amount of the check plus interest. Triffin's business is buying dishonored checks and attempting to collect on them.

The trial court dismissed Triffin's complaint on the grounds that he was not a holder in due course. Triffin appealed.

DECISION: The Court held that Triffin was not a holder in due course because he had taken a check that was already dishonored. In addition, Triffin could not be a holder in due course

---

[11] *St. Bernard Savings & Loan Ass'n v. Cella*, 826 F. Supp. 985 (E.D. La. 1993); *Cadle Co. v. DeVincent*, 781 N.E.2d 817 (Mass. App. 2003); *Interim Capital LLC v. Herr Law Group, Ltd.*, 2011 WL 7047062 (D. Nev. 2011).

[12] *Max Duncan Family Investments, Ltd. v. NTFN Inc.*, 267 S.W.3d 447 (Tex. 2008).

[13] *Unr-Rohn, Inc. v. Summit Bank*, 687 N.E.2d 235 (Ind. App. 1997); but see contra view, *Pero's Steak and Spaghetti House v. Lee*, 90 S.W.3d 614 (Tenn. 2002).

CASE SUMMARY

Continued

through JCNB being a holder in due course, because JCNB did not follow reasonable commercial standards when it cashed the postdated check. New Jersey's statute that regulates check cashing services requires those services to at least examine the face of the instrument before cashing it. JCNB, thus, was not a holder in due course and Triffin could not step into its shoes as an HDC. [*Triffin v. Liccardi Ford, Inc.,* **10 A.3d 227 (N.J. Super. 2011)**]

Ethics & the Law

The Corner Check Cashing Company and Good Faith

Some public policy experts have argued that no check cashing company, defined as one that takes a portion of the amount of the check as a fee for cashing checks for individuals who cannot get them cashed at banks and credit unions, should ever be allowed holder in due course status. Do you agree with this argument? Are check cashing companies ethical in their behavior? Do you believe that the state laws on check cashing firms are a means of mandating ethical conduct?

CPA

holder through a holder in due course – holder of an instrument who attains holder-in-due-course status because a holder in due course has held it previous to him or her.

(B) HOLDER THROUGH A HOLDER IN DUE COURSE. Those persons who become holders of the instrument after an HDC has held it are given the same protection as the HDC, provided they are not parties to any fraud or illegality that affects the instrument. This status of **holder through a holder in due course** is given in these circumstances even if the transferee from a holder in due course does not satisfy the requirements for holder-in-due-course status. This elevated or protected status is called Article 3's "shelter rule," and it allows a person who is not an HDC to hide under the "umbrella" with a holder in due course and be sheltered from claims and defenses as if actually being an HDC. **For Example,** a person who acquires an instrument as an inheritance from an estate does not give value and is missing one of the requirements for being a holder in due course. However, if the estate was an HDC, that status does transfer to the heir. Furthermore, suppose that Avery is a holder in due course of a $5,000 promissory note due May 31, 2012. Avery gives the note to his nephew Aaron for Aaron's birthday on June 1, 2012. Aaron did not give value because the note was a gift, and he has taken the note as a holder after it has already become due. Nonetheless, because Avery was a holder in due course, Aaron assumes that status under Article 3's shelter provision.

B. DEFENSES TO PAYMENT OF A NEGOTIABLE INSTRUMENT

One of the key reasons for attaining HDC status is to be able to obtain payment on the negotiable instrument free of any underlying problems between the original parties to the instrument. An HDC takes an instrument free from certain types of defenses to payment. Whether a defense may be raised against an HDC claiming under a negotiable instrument depends on the nature of the defense.

CPA

4. Classification of Defenses

The importance of being a holder in due course or a holder through an HDC is that such holders are not subject to certain defenses called *limited defenses.* Another class of defenses, *universal defenses,* may be asserted against any party, whether an assignee, an ordinary holder, an HDC, or a holder through an HDC.[14]

5. Defenses against Assignee or Ordinary Holder

Assignees of negotiable instruments are subject to every defense raised. Similarly, a holder who does not become an HDC is subject to every payment defense just as though the instrument were not negotiable.

6. Limited Defenses Not Available against a Holder in Due Course

HDCs are not subject to any of the following defenses.

CPA

(A) ORDINARY CONTRACT DEFENSES. In general terms, the defenses that could be raised in a breach of contract claim cannot be raised against an HDC. The defenses of lack, failure, or illegality of consideration with respect to the instrument's underlying transaction cannot be asserted against the holder in due course. Misrepresentation about the goods underlying the contract is also not a defense. **For Example,** a businessperson cannot refuse to pay a holder in due course on the note used to pay for her copy machine just because her copy machine does not have the speed she was promised.

(B) INCAPACITY OF MAKER OR DRAWER. Ordinarily, the maker's or drawer's lack of capacity (except minors) may not be raised as a defense to payment to a holder in due course. Such incapacity is a defense, however, if the incapacity is at a legal level that makes the instrument a nullity. **For Example,** a promissory note made by an insane person for whom a court has appointed a guardian is void. In the case of a claim on the note by an HDC, the incapacity of the maker would be a defense.

CPA

fraud in the inducement – fraud that occurs when a person is persuaded or induced to execute an instrument because of fraudulent statements.

(C) FRAUD IN THE INDUCEMENT. If a person is persuaded or induced to execute the instrument because of fraudulent statements, such **fraud in the inducement** cannot be raised against a party with holder-in-due-course status. **For Example,** suppose Mills is persuaded to purchase an automobile because of Pagan's statements that the car was a demonstrator for the dealership and in good mechanical condition with a certification from the dealership's head mechanic. Mills, a car dealer, gives Pagan a note, which is negotiated until it reaches Han, who is a holder in due course. Mills meanwhile learns that the car has been in an accident and has a cracked engine block, that the head mechanic was paid to sign the certification, and that Pagan's statements were fraudulent. When Han demands payment of the note, Mills cannot refuse to pay on the ground of Pagan's fraud. Mills must pay the note because Han,

---

[14] Under the pre-Code law and under the 1952 Code, the universal defense was called a *real defense,* and the limited defense was called a *personal defense.* These terms have now been abandoned, but some licensing and CPA examinations may continue to use these pre-Code terms.

as an HDC, does not take the note subject to any fraud or misrepresentation in the underlying transaction. Mills is left with the remedy of recovering from Pagan for misrepresentation or fraud.

(D) **MISCELLANEOUS DEFENSES.**[15] The limited defenses listed in the preceding three subsections are those most commonly raised against demands by holders in due course for payment. The following are additional limited defenses that may be asserted: (1) prior payment or cancellation of the instrument, (2) nondelivery, (3) conditional or special-purpose delivery, (4) breach of warranty, (5) duress consisting of threats, (6) unauthorized completion, and (7) theft of a bearer instrument. These defenses, however, have a very limited effect in defending against an HDC's demand for payment.

7. Universal Defenses Available against All Holders

universal defenses – defenses that are regarded as so basic that the social interest in preserving them outweighs the social interest of giving negotiable instruments the freely transferable qualities of money; accordingly, such defenses are given universal effect and may be raised against all holders.

Certain defenses are regarded as so basic that the social interest in preserving them outweighs the social interest of giving negotiable instruments the freely transferable qualities of money. Accordingly, such defenses are given universal effect and may be raised against all holders, whether ordinary holders, HDCs, or holders through a holder in due course. These defenses are called **universal defenses**.[16]

CPA (A) **FRAUD AS TO THE NATURE OR ESSENTIAL TERMS OF THE INSTRUMENT.** The fact that a person signs an instrument because the person is fraudulently deceived as to its nature or essential terms is a defense available against all holders.[17] When one person induces another to sign a note by falsely representing that, for example, it is a contract for repairs or that it is a character reference, the note is invalid, and the defense of the misrepresentation of the character of the instrument can be used against a holder in due course. **For Example,** suppose that two homeowners are asked to sign a statement for a sales person that he was in their home and did a demonstration of a new solar water heater. Just as the homeowners are about to sign the verification statement, the salesman distracts them and then switches the verification for a purchase contract and promissory note for a $5,000 solar water heating system that the owners declined to purchase. The owners would have a defense of fraud in factum against a holder in due course of this note. The difference between fraud in the inducement—a personal defense—and fraud in factum—a universal defense—is that fraud in factum involves deception as to the documents themselves, not as to the underlying goods, services, or property.

CPA (B) **FORGERY OR LACK OF AUTHORITY.** The defense that a signature was forged or signed without authority can be raised by a drawer or maker against any HDC unless the drawer or maker whose name was signed has ratified it or is estopped by conduct or negligence from denying it.[18] The fact that the negligence of the drawer helped the wrongdoer does not prevent the drawee from raising the defense of forgery. (See Chapters 29 and 31 for more discussion of the impact of forgery on liability.)

---

[15] Revised UCC.§3-305.
[16] *City Rentals, Inc. v. Kessler*, 946 N.E. 2d 785 (Ohio App. 2010).
[17] Revised UCC.§3-305(a)(1)(iii).
[18] *Bank of Hoven v. Rausch*, 382 N.W.2d 39 (S.D. 1986); for general discussion of estoppel and ratification, see *Ziegler Furniture and Funeral Home, Inc. v. Cicmanec*, 209 N.W.2d 350 (S.D. 2006).

(c) Duress Depriving Control. A party may execute or indorse a negotiable instrument in response to a force of such a nature that, under general principles of law, duress makes the transaction void rather than merely voidable. Duress of this type and level may be raised as a defense against any holder. Economic duress, in the form of a reluctance to enter into a financially demanding instrument, is not a universal defense.[19] Duress that is attempted murder is a universal defense.

(d) Incapacity. The fact that the defendant is a minor who under general principles of contract law may avoid the obligation is a matter that may be raised against any kind of holder. Other kinds of incapacity may be raised as a defense if the effect of the incapacity is to make the instrument void, as when there has been a formal declaration of insanity.[20]

(e) Illegality. If an instrument is void by law when executed in connection with certain conduct, such as a note for gambling or one that involves usury, such defenses may be raised against an HDC.

CPA

(f) Alteration. An **alteration** is an unauthorized change or completion of a negotiable instrument designed to modify the obligation of a party to the instrument.[21] **For Example,** changing the amount of an instrument from $150 to $450 is an alteration.[22]

> **alteration** – unauthorized change or completion of a negotiable instrument designed to modify the obligation of a party to the instrument.

(1) Person Making Alteration.

An alteration is a change made by a party to the instrument. Recovery on the instrument is still possible under the terms of the instrument as it originally existed, if proof of the original terms is possible.

(2) Effect of Alteration.

If the alteration to the instrument was made fraudulently, the person whose obligations under the instrument are affected by that alteration is discharged from liability on the instrument. The instrument, however, can be enforced according to its original terms or its terms as completed. This right of enforcement is given to holders in due course who had no notice of such alteration.[23] While a holder in due course would come within the protected class on alteration, such status is not required for this recovery provision in the event of alteration. **For Example,** Ryan signed a negotiable demand note for $100 made payable to Long. A subsequent holder changed the amount from $100 to $700. A later holder in due course presented the note to Ryan for payment. Ryan would still be liable for the original amount of $100.

A summary of the universal and limited defenses is presented in Figure 30-2.

---

[19] *Miller v. Calhoun/Johnson Co.,* 497 S.E.2d 397 (Ga. App. 1998); *Smith v. Gordon,* 598 S.E.2d 92 (Ga. App. 2004).
[20] Revised UCC.§3-305(a)(1)(ii). *Erkins v. Alaska Trustee LLC,* 265 P.3d 292 (Alaska 2011).
[21] Revised UCC.§3-407(a); *Stahl v. St. Elizabeth Medical Center,* 948 S.W.2d 419 (Ky. App. 1997). *Farmers Deposit Bank v. Bank One,* 2005 WL 3453979 (E.D. Ky. 2005). A material alteration made based on the parties' negotiations (a 13 percent versus an 18 percent interest rate) is not fraudulent. *Darnall v. Petersen,* 592 N.W.2d 505 (Neb. App. 1999); *Knoefler v. Wojtalewicz,* 2003 WL 21496933 (Neb App 2003) (difference between bank interest rate and judgment interest rate is not material).
[22] However, if an instrument, such as a note, has been altered and the maker continues to pay without objection to the alteration, the alteration does not discharge the maker's liability. *Stahl v. St. Elizabeth Medical Center,* 948 S.W.2d 419 (Ky. App. 1997); again, for a general discussion of continuing payment as estoppel, see *Ziegler Furniture and Funeral Home, Inc. v. Cicmanec,* 709 N.W.2d 350 (S.D. 2006).
[23] Revised UCC.§3-407(b), (c).

FIGURE 30-2	*Defenses to Payment of Negotiable Instrument*

UNIVERSAL (AVAILABLE AGAINST ASSIGNEES, HOLDERS, AND HOLDERS IN DUE COURSE)(REAL)	LIMITED (AVAILABLE AGAINST ASSIGNEES AND HOLDERS BUT NOT AGAINST HOLDERS IN DUE COURSE) (PERSONAL)	MIXED (CIRCUMSTANCES VARY THE AVAILABILITY OF THESE DEFENSES)
FRAUD AS TO THE NATURE OF THE INSTRUMENT (FRAUD IN FACTUM)	FRAUD IN THE INDUCEMENT	DURESS
FORGERY	MISREPRESENTATION	INCAPACITY
UNAUTHORIZED SIGNATURE	LACK OF CONSIDERATION	
INCAPACITY (DECLARATION)	BREACH OF WARRANTY	
ILLEGALITY	CANCELLATION	
ALTERATION	FAILURE OF DELIVERY	
CONSUMER CREDIT CONTRACTS WITH FTC NOTICE	UNAUTHORIZED COMPLETION	
	ALL ORDINARY CONTRACT DEFENSES	

© Cengage Learning

8. Denial of Holder-in-Due-Course Protection

In certain situations, the taker of a negotiable instrument is denied the status and protections of an HDC.

(A) PARTICIPATING TRANSFEREE. When the transferee is working with the lender or seller to obtain a negotiable instrument from the buyer/borrower, the transferee's holder-in-due-course status comes into question. This close-connection doctrine (discussed earlier in this chapter as an issue in the good-faith requirement for becoming a holder in due course) prevents a transferee with intimate knowledge of the transferor's business practices from becoming an HDC.[24]

(B) THE FEDERAL TRADE COMMISSION RULE. In 1976, the Federal Trade Commission (FTC) adopted a rule that limits the rights of a holder in due course in a consumer credit transaction. The rule protects consumers who purchase goods or services for personal, family, or household use on credit.[25] When the note the buyer gave the seller as payment for the consumer goods is transferred to even a holder in due course, the consumer buyer may raise any defense that could have been raised against

---

[24] *In re Neals*, 459 B.R. 612 (D.S.C. 2011). *AIG Global Securities Lending Corp. v. Banc of America Securities LLC*, 2006 WL 1206333 (S.D.N.Y. 2006).

[25] The regulation does not cover purchases of real estate, securities, or consumer goods or services for which the purchase price is more than $25,000. *Fifth Third Bank v. Jones*, 168 P.3d 1 (Colo. App. 2007).

the seller. The FTC regulation requires that the following notice be included in boldface type at least 10 points in size in consumer credit contracts covered under the rule:

> *Notice*
> *Any holder of this consumer credit contract is subject to all claims and defenses which the debtor could assert against the seller of goods or services obtained with the proceeds hereof. Recovery hereunder by the debtor shall not exceed amounts paid by the debtor hereunder.*[26]

When a notice preserving consumer defenses is included in a negotiable instrument, no subsequent person can be a holder in due course of the instrument.[27]

C. LIABILITY ISSUES: HOW PAYMENT RIGHTS ARISE AND DEFENSES ARE USED

In this chapter and in Chapters 28 and 29, issues surrounding the types of instruments, transfers, holders, and holders in due course have been covered. However, there are procedures under Article 3 for bringing together all of the parties, instruments, and defenses so that ultimate liability and, hopefully, payment can be determined and achieved.

CPA

primary party – party to whom the holder or holder in due course must turn first to obtain payment.

maker – party who writes or creates a promissory note.

drawee – person to whom the draft is addressed and who is ordered to pay the amount of money specified in the draft.

secondary parties – called *secondary obligors* under Revised Article 3; parties to an instrument to whom holders turn when the primary party, for whatever reason, fails to pay the instrument.

CPA

indorser – secondary party (or obligor) on a note.

drawer – person who writes out and creates a draft or bill of exchange, including a check.

presentment – formal request for payment on an instrument.

9. The Roles of Parties and Liability

Every instrument has primary and secondary parties. The **primary party** is the party to whom the holder or holder in due course must turn first to obtain payment. The primary party on a note or certificate of deposit is the **maker**. The primary party on a draft is the **drawee**, assuming that the drawee has accepted the draft. Although a check must first be presented to the drawee bank for payment, the bank is not primarily liable on the instrument because the bank has the right to refuse to pay the check (see following and Chapter 31). The drawee bank on a check is the party to whom a holder or holder in due course turns first for payment despite the lack of primary-party status on the part of that drawee bank. The maker of a note is the party to whom holders and holders in due course must turn first for payment.

The **secondary parties** (or *secondary obligors,* as they are now called under Revised Article 3) to an instrument are those to whom holders turn when the primary party, for whatever reason, fails to pay the instrument. Secondary parties on notes are **indorsers**, and secondary parties on checks and drafts are **drawers** and **indorsers.**

10. Attaching Liability of the Primary Parties: Presentment

Presentment occurs when the holder or HDC of an instrument orally, in writing, or by electronic communication to the primary party requests that the instrument be

---

[26] One of the controversial changes to Article 3 is found in subsections 3-305(e) and (f). This change provides that if the Federal Trade Commission requires a notice to be included, but it is not, the instrument is deemed to have included it implicitly.

[27] Revised UCC.§3-106(d). This goes beyond the scope of the FTC regulation. The latter merely preserves the defenses of the consumer but does not bar holder-in-due-course protection for other parties, such as an accommodation party to a consumer's note. Also, the FTC regulation does not change the common law and permits the maker to bring contract actions against the holder of the note for contract breaches committed by the maker's original contract party. The rule changes the status of the parties as holders in due course. It does not change contract rights. *Pennsylvania Dept. of Banking v. NCAS of Delaware, LLC*, 931 A.2d 771 (Pa. 2007).

paid according to its terms. The primary party has the right to require that the presentment be made in a "commercially reasonable manner," which would include reasonable times for presentment, such as during business hours. The primary party can also require identification, authorization, and even a signature of receipt of the funds due under the instrument. In addition, the primary party can demand a valid indorsement on the instrument prior to making payment. Upon presentment, the primary party is required to pay according to the terms of the instrument unless there are defenses such as forgery, any of the other universal defenses for HDCs, or any defenses for holders.

If the primary party refuses to pay the instrument according to its terms, there has been a *dishonor,* and the holder is then left to turn to the secondary parties.

CPA | 11. Dishonor and Notice of Dishonor

dishonor – status when the primary party refuses to pay the instrument according to its terms.

notice of dishonor – notice that an instrument has been dishonored; such notice can be oral, written, or electronic but is subject to time limitations.

Dishonor occurs when the primary party refuses to pay the instrument according to its terms. The primary party is required to give **notice of dishonor**. The notice that the instrument has been dishonored can be oral, written, or electronic. That notice is subject to time limitations. **For Example,** a bank must give notice of dishonor by midnight of the next banking day. Nonbank primary parties must give notice of dishonor within 30 days following their receipt of notice of dishonor. Returning the dishonored check is sufficient notice of dishonor. (See Chapter 31 for more discussion of liability issues on dishonor of checks.) Upon dishonor, the holder must then turn to the secondary parties for payment.

E-Commerce & Cyberlaw

Electronic Presentment: One Fell Swoop, All Rights, All Payments, New Laws

Because we now use debit cards, some of the UCC. Article 3 provisions on checks are used far less, and the rights of the merchants and the buyers are covered under various federal and state laws on electronic funds transfers (covered in Chapter 31). Issues continue to evolve, such as the protections on debit cards, including the use of personal identification numbers (PINs) as a way of ensuring identity. Electronic technology requires that we change laws and grow into the new systems.

limited defenses – defenses available to secondary parties if the presenting party is a holder in due course.

The obligation of the secondary parties in these situations is to pay according to the terms of the instrument. These secondary parties will have **limited defenses** if the presenting party is a holder in due course. **For Example,** suppose that a check drawn on First Interstate Bank is written by Ben Paltrow to Julia Sutherland as payment for Julia's Bentley auto that Ben purchased. Julia deposits Ben's check into her account at AmeriBank, and AmeriBank sends the check to First Interstate to present it for payment. First Interstate finds that Ben's account has insufficient funds and dishonors the check. AmeriBank must notify First Interstate by midnight of the next banking day that the check has been dishonored, and then First Interstate must notify Julia by midnight of the next banking day that Ben's check was dishonored. Julia then has 30 days to notify Ben and turn to him as a drawer, or secondary party, for payment on the check.

Thinking Things Through

The Corner Check Cashing Company and Thieves—Who Wins?

Now is an ideal time to bring together all of the concepts you have learned in Chapters 27, 28, and 29. Analyzing this problem will help you integrate your knowledge about negotiable instruments. Sid's Salmon has purchased salmon from Fred's Fisheries. Sid wrote a check for $22,000 to Fred's. A thief broke into Fred's offices and took the cash on hand as well as the unindorsed check from Sid's. The thief took the check to the Corner Check Cashing Company (CCCC) and received

$22,000 less the cashing fee of $2,000. Fred notified Sid who then notified First Commerce Bank, the drawee of the check, of the theft. CCCC has presented the check for payment, and First Commerce refuses to pay. CCCC says it is a holder in due course. Are you able to help First Commerce Bank develop its response to CCCC?

Suppose that Fred had already indorsed the check when the thief stole it. Would CCCC be a holder in due course?

LawFlix

Ghost (1990) PG 13

Whoppi Goldberg plays a psychic who is asked by a deceased (the late Patrick Swayze) to help get back at his murderer (a co-worker at his finance firm) by posing as a character to obtain a check made payable to her, a fictitious character, who uses a bank account created through computer hacking. The check-cashing scenes are priceless, and, legally, far foreign to normal bank practices employed to prevent forgery.

MAKE THE CONNECTION

SUMMARY

A holder of a negotiable instrument can be either an ordinary holder or an HDC. The ordinary holder has the same rights that an assignee would have. Holders in due course and holders through an HDC are protected from certain defenses. To be an HDC, a person must first be a holder—that is, the person must have acquired the instrument by a proper negotiation. The holder must then also take for value, in good faith, without notice that the paper is overdue or dishonored, and without notice of defenses and adverse claims. Those persons who become holders of the instrument after an HDC are given the same protection as the HDC through the shelter provision, provided they are not parties to any fraud or illegality affecting the instrument.

The importance of being an HDC is that those holders are not being subject to certain defenses when demand for payment is made. These defenses are limited defenses and include ordinary contract

defenses, incapacity unless it makes the instrument void, fraud in the inducement, prior payment or cancellation, nondelivery of an instrument, conditional delivery, duress consisting of threats, unauthorized completion, and theft of a bearer instrument. Universal defenses may be asserted against any assignee, an ordinary holder, or HDC. Universal defenses include fraud as to the nature or essential terms of the paper, forgery or lack of authority, duress depriving control, incapacity, illegality that makes the instrument void, and alteration. Alteration is only a partial defense; an HDC may enforce the instrument according to its original terms.

The Federal Trade Commission rule on consumer credit contracts limits the immunity of an HDC from defenses of consumer buyers against their sellers. Immunity is limited in consumer credit transactions if the notice specified by the FTC regulation is included in the sales contract. When a notice preserving consumer defenses is stated in a negotiable instrument, no subsequent person can be an HDC.

Holders and HDCs are required to present instruments for payment to primary parties. Primary parties are makers and drawees. If the primary party refuses to pay, or dishonors, the instrument, it must give notice of dishonor in a timely fashion. The holder can then turn to secondary parties, drawers, and indorsers (secondary obligors) for payment.

LEARNING OUTCOMES

After studying this chapter, you should be able to clearly explain:

A. Parties to Negotiable Instruments: Rights and Liabilities

L0.1 Distinguish between an ordinary holder and a holder in due course
> See Sections 2 and 3 on p. 625 for examples of distinction.

L0.2 List the requirements for becoming a holder in due course
> See *Triffin v. Liccardi Ford, Inc.* on pp. 626–627.

B. Defenses to Payment of a Negotiable Instrument

L0.3 Explain the rights of a holder through a holder in due course
> See *New Randolph Halsted Currency Exchange, Inc. v. Regent Title Insurance Co.* on p. 625.

L0.4 List and explain the limited defenses not available against a holder in due course
> See the list of defenses in Figure 30-2 on p. 631.

L0.5 List and explain the universal defenses available against all holders
> See the Thinking Things Through discussion of the Corner Check Cashing Company on p. 634.

C. Liability Issues: How Payment Rights Arise and Defenses are Used

L0.6 Describe how the rights of a holder in due course have been limited by the Federal Trade Commission
> See the language of the rule on p. 632.

KEY TERMS

alteration
assignees
close-connection doctrine
dishonor
drawee
drawers
fraud in the inducement

good faith
holders
holder in due course
holder through a holder in
 due course
indorsers
limited defenses

maker
notice of dishonor
presentment
primary party
secondary parties
universal defenses
value

QUESTIONS AND CASE PROBLEMS

1. Randy Bocian had a bank account with First of America-Bank (FAB). On October 8, Bocian received a check for $28,800 from Eric Christenson as payment for constructing a pole barn on Christenson's property. Bocian deposited the check at FAB on October 9 and was permitted to draw on the funds through October 12. Bocian wrote checks totaling $12,334.21, which FAB cleared. On October 12, Christenson stopped payment on the check as the result of a contract dispute over the pole barn. Bocian's account was then overdrawn once the check was denied clearance by Christenson's bank. FAB brought suit against both Bocian and Christenson to collect its

loss. Christenson counterclaimed against Bocian for his contract breach claims on the pole barn construction. FAB maintained that it had given value and was a holder in due course and that, as such, it was not required to be subject to the pole barn issues or the stop payment order. Is FAB right? [*First of America-Bank Northeast Illinois v. Bocian*, 614 N.E.2d 890 (Ill. App.)]

2. Cronin, an employee of Epicycle, cashed his final paycheck at Money Mart Check Cashing Center. Epicycle had issued a stop payment order on the check. Money Mart deposited the check through normal banking channels. The check was returned to Money Mart marked "Payment Stopped." Money Mart brought an action against Epicycle, claiming that, as a holder in due course, it was entitled to recover against Epicycle. Epicycle argued that Money Mart could not be a holder in due course because it failed to verify the check as good prior to cashing it. Is Money Mart a holder in due course? [*Money Mart Check Cashing Center, Inc. v. Epicycle Corp.*, 667 P.2d 1372 (Colo.)]

3. Halleck executed a promissory note payable to the order of Leopold. Halleck did not pay the note when due, and Leopold brought suit on the note, producing it in court. Halleck admitted that he had signed the note but claimed plaintiff Leopold was required to prove that the note had been issued for consideration and that the plaintiff was in fact the holder. Are these elements of proof required as part of the case? [*Leopold v. Halleck*, 436 N.E.2d 29 (Ill. App.)]

4. Calhoun/Johnson Company d/b/a Williams Lumber Company (Williams) sold building materials to Donald Miller d/b/a Millercraft Construction Company (Millercraft) on credit. Miller had signed a personal guaranty for the materials. Miller requested lien waivers from Williams for four of his projects and asked for them from Fabian Boudreau, Williams's credit manager. Fabian refused to grant the waivers because Miller was $28,000 delinquent on his account. Miller agreed to bring his account current with the exception of $11,000 for which he signed a no-interest promissory note. Miller obtained the lien waivers and then defaulted on the note. Williams brought suit for payment, and

Williams said there was lack of consideration and that the note was not valid. He said he must give value to be able to recover on the note. Was he correct? [*Miller v. Calhoun/Johnson Co.*, 497 S.E.2d 397 (Ga. App.)]

5. Statham drew a check. The payee indorsed it to Kemp Motor Sales. Statham then stopped payment on the check on the grounds that there was a failure of consideration for the check. Kemp sued Statham on the check. When Statham raised the defense of failure of consideration, Kemp replied that he was a holder in due course. Statham claimed that Kemp could not recover because Statham learned of his defense before Kemp deposited the check in its bank account. Discuss the parties' arguments and rights in this situation. [*Kemp Motor Sales v. Statham*, 171 S.E.2d 389 (Ga. App.)]

6. Can check cashing companies be holders in due course? What arguments can you make for and against their holder-in-due-course status? [*Dal-Tile Corp. v. Cash N' Go*, 487 S.E.2d 529 (Ga. App.)]

7. Jones, wishing to retire from a business enterprise that he had been conducting for a number of years, sold all of the assets of the business to Jackson Corp. Included in the assets were a number of promissory notes payable to the order of Jones that he had taken from his customers. Upon the maturity of one of the notes, the maker refused to pay because there was a failure of consideration. Jackson Corp. sued the maker of the note. Who should succeed? Explain.

8. Elliot, an officer of Impact Marketing, drew six postdated checks on Impact's account. The checks were payable to Bell for legal services to be subsequently performed for Impact. Financial Associates purchased them from Bell and collected on four of the checks. Payment was stopped on the last two when Bell's services were terminated. Financial argued that it was a holder in due course and had the right to collect on the checks. Impact claimed that because the checks were postdated and issued for an executory promise, Financial could not be a holder in due course. Who was correct? Why? [*Financial Associates v. Impact Marketing*, 394 N.Y.S.2d 814]

9. *D* drew a check to the order of *P*. *P* took the check postdated. *P* knew that *D* was having financial difficulties and that the particular checking account on which this check was drawn had been frequently overdrawn. Do these circumstances prevent *P* from being a holder in due course? [*Citizens Bank, Booneville v. National Bank of Commerce,* 334 F.2d 257 (10th Cir.); *Franklin National Bank v. Sidney Gotowner,* 4 UCC. Rep. Serv. 953 (N.Y. Supp.)]

10. Daniel, Joel, and Claire Guerrette are the adult children of Elden Guerrette, who died on September 24, 1995. Before his death, Elden purchased a life insurance policy from Sun Life Assurance Company of Canada through a Sun Life agent, Steven Hall, and named his children as his beneficiaries. Upon his death, Sun Life issued three checks, each in the amount of $40,759.35, to each of Elden's children. The checks were drawn on Sun Life's account at Chase Manhattan Bank in Syracuse, New York. The checks were given to Hall for delivery to the Guerrettes. Hall and an associate, Paul Richard, then fraudulently induced the Guerrettes to indorse the checks in blank and to transfer them to Hall and Richard, purportedly to be invested in HER, Inc., a corporation formed by Hall and Richard. Hall took the checks from the Guerrettes and turned them over to Richard, who deposited them in his account at the Credit Union on October 26, 1995. The Credit Union immediately made the funds available to Richard.

The Guerrettes quickly regretted having negotiated their checks to Hall and Richard, and they contacted Sun Life the next day to request that Sun Life stop payment on the checks. Sun Life immediately ordered Chase Manhattan to stop payment on the checks. When the checks were ultimately presented to Chase Manhattan for payment, Chase refused to pay the checks, and they were returned to the Credit Union. The Credit Union received notice that the checks had been dishonored on November 3, 1995, the sixth business day following their deposit. By the time the Credit Union received notice, however, Richard had withdrawn from his account all of the funds represented by the three checks. The Credit Union was able to recover almost $80,000 from Richard, but there remained an unpaid balance of $42,366.56.

The Credit Union filed suit against Sun Life, and all of the parties became engulfed in litigation. The Credit Union indicated it was a holder in due course and was entitled to payment on the instrument. Sun Life alleged fraud. Is the Credit Union a holder in due course? Can the parties allege the fraud defense against it? [*Maine Family Federal Credit Union v. Sun Life Assur. Co. of Canada,* 727 A.2d 335 (Maine)]

11. G.C. Vincent was an employee of Porter County Development Corporation (PCDC). Vincent had three personal credit cards through Citibank. Vincent diverted checks to the PCDC, deposited them into his personal checking account, and issued checks drawn upon that personal account to pay part of the outstanding balance of his three Citibank-held credit card accounts. Citibank was unaware that Vincent used misappropriated funds to pay his credit card balance. PCDC filed suit to have Citibank return the embezzled funds. Citibank moved for summary judgment on the grounds that it was an HDC. The trial court granted summary judgment and PCDC appealed. Who should prevail on appeal and why? [*Porter County Development Corp. v. Citibank (South Dakota),* N.A., 855 N.E. 2d 306 (Ind. App.)]

12. Sanders gave Clary a check but left the amount incomplete. The check was given as advance payment on the purchase of 100 LT speakers. The amount was left blank because Clary had the right to substitute other LT speakers if they became available and the substitution would change the price. It was agreed that in no event would the purchase price exceed $5,000. Desperate for cash, Clary wrongfully substituted much more expensive LT speakers, thereby increasing the price to $5,700. Clary then negotiated the check to Lawrence, one of his suppliers. Clary filled in the $5,700 in Lawrence's presence, showing him the shipping order and the invoice applicable to the sale to Sanders. Lawrence accepted the check in payment of $5,000 worth of overdue debts and $700 in cash. Can Lawrence recover the full amount? Why or why not?

13. GRAS is a Michigan corporation engaged in the business of buying and selling cars. Between 1997 and 2000, Katrina Stewart was employed as a manager by GRAS. During that period, Stewart wrote checks, without authority, on GRAS's corporate account payable to MBNA and sent them to MBNA for payment of her husband's MBNA credit card account. MBNA accepted the checks and credited the proceeds to Stewart's husband's credit card debt. MBNA accepted and processed the GRAS checks in its normal manner through electronic processing. When MBNA receives a check for a credit card payment, the envelope containing the check and the payment slip is opened by machine and the check and the payment slip are electronically processed and credited to the cardholder's account balance. MBNA does not normally review checks for credit card payments. After crediting a payment check to the cardholder's account, MBNA transfers it to the bank on which it is written for collection. Pursuant to its standard practice, MBNA did not review the checks it received from Stewart. GRAS did not have a customer relationship with MBNA during the relevant time period.

GRAS sought a refund of the amounts Stewart embezzled via the MBNA application of the checks to Stewart's husband's credit card account. MBNA said it was a holder in due course. Was MBNA a holder in due course? Was MBNA subject to GRAS's defense of unauthorized instruments? [*Grand Rapids Auto Sales, Inc. v. MBNA America Bank,* 227 F. Supp. 2d 721 (W.D. Mich.)]

14. William Potts, was employed by Jemoli Holdings, Inc., to liquidate assets of defunct companies. Potts had the authority to sign checks for Jemoli. Potts had a personal investment account with Raymond James Financial Services.

When the stock market had its 2000 crash due to the dot-com bubble, Potts had difficulty meeting his margin calls. He began giving checks from Jemoli to Raymond James to cover the margin calls. When a representative questioned Mr. Potts about the Jemoli checks, he assured the representative that Jemoli was him, and that it was his firm. Over four months, Potts wrote checks totaling $1.5 million to Raymond James to cover loans and to make more investments. When Jemoli's principals discovered the embezzlement they brought suit to recover the funds from Raymond James. Raymond James says it was an HDC of the checks and not subject to Jemoli's claims for breach of fiduciary duty by its agent, Potts. Who is correct about the HDC status of Raymond James and why? [*Jemoli Holding, Inc. v. Raymond James Financial, Inc.,* 470 F.3d 14 (1st Cir.)]

15. Omni Trading issued two checks totaling $75,000 to Country Grain Elevators for grain it had purchased. Country Grain indorsed the checks over to the law firm of Carter & Grimsley as a retainer. Country Grain then collapsed as a business, and Omni stopped payment on the checks because all of its grain had not been delivered. Carter & Grimsley claimed it was a holder in due course and entitled to payment. However, the Department of Agriculture claimed its interest in the checks for liens and maintained that Carter & Grimsley was not a holder in due course because it had not given value. The trial court granted summary judgment for the Department of Agriculture because the checks were indorsed as a retainer for future legal work and Carter & Grimsley had not given value. Is Carter & Grimsley a holder in due course? [*Carter & Grimsley v. Omni Trading, Inc.,* 716 N. E.2d 320 (Ill. App.)]

CPA QUESTIONS

1. Under the Commercial Paper Article of the UCC, which of the following requirements must be met for a person to be a holder in due course of a promissory note?

   a. The note must be payable to bearer.

   b. The note must be negotiable.

   c. All prior holders must have been holders in due course.

   d. The holder must be the payee of the note.

2. A maker of a note will have a real defense against a holder in due course as a result of any of the following conditions except:

   a. Discharge in bankruptcy

   b. Forgery

   c. Fraud in the execution

   d. Lack of consideration

3. Under the commercial paper article of the UCC, in a nonconsumer transaction, which of the following are real (universal) defenses available against a holder in due course?

	Material Alteration	Discharge in Bankruptcy	Discharge in Bankruptcy
a.	No	Yes	Yes
b.	Yes	Yes	No
c.	No	No	Yes
d.	Yes	No	No

4. A holder in due course will take free of which of the following defenses?

   a. Infancy, to the extent that it is a defense to a simple contract

   b. Discharge of the maker in bankruptcy

   c. A wrongful filling-in of the amount payable that was omitted from the instrument

   d. Duress of a nature that renders the obligation of the party a nullity

5. Mask stole one of Bloom's checks. The check was already signed by Bloom and made payable to Duval. The check was drawn on United Trust Company. Mask forged Duval's signature on the back of the check at the Corner Check Cashing Company, which in turn deposited it with its bank, Town National Bank of Toka. Town National proceeded to collect on the check from United. None of the parties mentioned were negligent. Who will bear the loss, assuming the amount cannot be recovered from Mask?

   a. Bloom

   b. Duval

   c. United Trust Company

   d. Corner Check Cashing Company

6. Robb stole one of Markum's blank checks, made it payable to himself, and forged Markum's signature to it. The check was drawn on the Unity Trust Company. Robb cashed the check at the Friendly Check Cashing Company, which in turn deposited it with its bank, Farmer's National. Farmer's National proceeded to collect on the check from Unity Trust. The theft and forgery were quickly discovered by Markum, who promptly notified Unity. None of the parties mentioned were negligent. Who will bear the loss, assuming the amount cannot be recovered from Robb?

   a. Markum

   b. Unity Trust Company

   c. Friendly Check Cashing Company

   d. Farmer's National

7. For a person to be holder in due course of a promissory note

   a. The note must be payable in U.S. currency to the holder.

   b. The holder must be the payee of the note.

   c. The note must be negotiable.

   d. All prior holders must have been holders in due course.

© Manuel Gutjahr/iStockphoto.com

CHAPTER 31

Checks and Funds Transfers

learningoutcomes

After studying this chapter, you should be able to

LO.1 List and explain the duties of the drawee bank

LO.2 Explain the methods for, and legal effect of, stopping payment

LO.3 Describe the liability of a bank for improper payment and collection

LO.4 Discuss the legal effect of forgeries and material alterations

LO.5 Specify the time limitations for reporting forgeries and alterations

LO.6 Describe the electronic transfer of funds and laws governing it

T he three previous chapters have focused on the characteristics, parties, and transfer of all negotiable instruments. This chapter covers checks as negotiable instruments, the issues related to their transfer and payment because of the involvement of banks, and special rules applicable to banks as drawees. New technology has enhanced the ability of banks and consumers to make rapid commercial transactions through the use of electronic funds transfers. Special rules and rights have developed to govern these forms of payment that serve to facilitate everything from a consumer's withdrawing money from an automated teller machine to a buyer's wiring money to a seller whose business is located continents away.

A. Checks

check – order by a depositor on a bank to pay a sum of money to a payee; a bill of exchange drawn on a bank and payable on demand.

As discussed in Chapter 28, a **check** is, under Uniform Commercial Code (UCC) §3-104(f), "(i) a draft … payable on demand and drawn on a bank or (ii) a cashier's check or teller's check. An instrument may be a check even though it is described on its face by another term, such as 'money order.'"[1] The distinguishing characteristics of checks[4] and drafts are summarized in Figure 31-1. Under Revised Article 4, the change in consumer payment patterns away from formal, signed checks is reflected with the addition of "remotely-created consumer item," which are items directing payment that are drawn on a consumer account but do not carry a handwritten signature of the drawer.[2] Consumer account is defined as a bank account used for household, family, or personal purposes.[3] These types of payments include PayPal authorizations to pay from consumer checking accounts and automatic bill payments that consumers direct remotely.

1. Nature of a Check

(A) Sufficient Funds on Deposit. As a practical matter, a check is drawn on the assumption that the bank has on deposit in the drawer's account an amount sufficient to pay the check. In the case of other drafts, there is no assumption that the drawee has any of the drawer's money with which to pay the instrument. In international transactions, sellers may require buyers not only to accept a draft agreeing to pay but also to back up that draft with a line of credit from the buyer's bank. That line of credit is the backup should the funds for the draft not be forthcoming from the buyer.

If a draft is dishonored, the drawer is civilly liable. If a check is drawn with intent to defraud the person to whom it is delivered, the drawer is also subject to criminal

---

[1] Revised UCC §3-104(f).
[2] Revised UCC §3-104(16).
[3] Revised UCC §3-104(2).
[4] Checks are governed by both Article 3 of the UCC and Article 4 governing bank deposits and collections. The 2001 and 2002 versions of Article 4 are covered in this chapter, along with notations of the changes since the 1990 version. The new versions of Article 4 incorporate provisions in the American Bankers Association Bank Collection Code, enacted in 18 states, and followed in many other states. The purpose of the code was to introduce clarity into the processing of millions of electronic and paper transactions that banks must handle and to recognize the reality of electronic payments.

FIGURE 31-1	*Differences between a Check and a Draft*

Check	Draft
1. Drawee is always a bank. 2. Check is drawn on assumption money is in bank to cover check. 3. Check is payable on demand. 4. Drawee bank only accepts check through certification.	1. Drawee is not necessarily a bank. 2. No assumption drawee has any of drawer's money to pay instrument. 3. Draft may be payable on demand or at future date. 4. Acceptance is required for liability of drawee.

bad check laws – laws making it a criminal offense to issue a bad check with intent to defraud.

prosecution in most states. The laws under which such drawers are prosecuted are known as **bad check laws**. Most states provide that if the check is not made good within a stated period, such as 10 days, there is a presumption that the drawer originally issued the check with the intent to defraud.

CPA

demand draft – draft that is payable upon presentment.

postdate – to insert or place on an instrument a later date than the actual date on which it was executed.

time draft – bill of exchange payable at a stated time after sight or at a definite time.

(b) DEMAND PAPER. A draft may be payable either on demand or at a future date. A check is a form of **demand draft**. The standard form of check does not specify when it is payable, and it is therefore automatically payable on demand.

One exception arises when a check is **postdated**—that is, when the check shows a date later than the actual date of execution. Postdating a check means that the check is not payable until the date arrives, and it changes the check from a demand draft to a **time draft**.[5] However, banks are not obligated to hold a postdated check until the time used on the check unless the drawer has filed the appropriate paperwork with the bank for such a delay. Because of electronic processing, banks are not required to examine each instrument and honor postdated instrument requests unless the hold is placed into the bank's processing system by the customer.

(c) FORM OF THE CHECK. A check can be in any form of writing.[6] However, bank customers may agree, as part of the contract with their bank, to use certain forms for check writing. A remotely created consumer item need only be evidenced by a *record*, not by a written document. Under Revised UCC §3-104(a)(14), a *record* is defined as "information that is inscribed on a tangible medium or which is stored in an electronic or other medium and is retrievable in perceivable form."[7]

(d) DELIVERY NOT ASSIGNMENT. The delivery of a check is not an assignment of the money on deposit, so it does not automatically transfer the rights of the depositor against the bank to the holder of the check. A check written by a drawer on his drawee bank does not result in a duty on the part of the drawee bank to the holder to pay the holder the amount of the check.[8] An ordinary check drawn on a

---

[5] A bank is required to comply with a postdate on a check only if it is notified of the postdate in the same way the customer issues a stop payment order.
[6] Although not required for negotiation or presentment, a printed bank check, when the customer is using a written form, is preferable because it generally carries magnetic ink figures that facilitate sorting and posting.
[7] *Smith v. Farmers Union Mut. Ins. Co.* 260 P.3d 163 (Mont. 2011).
[8] *Crawford v. J.P. Morgan Chase Bank, NA*, 425 Fed. Appx. 445 (6th Cir. 2011).

customer's account is direction from a customer to the bank for payment, but it does not impose absolute primary liability on the bank at the time the check is written.

Banks assume more responsibility for some types of checks than for the ordinary customer's check. **For Example,** a bank **money order** payable to John Jones is a check and has the bank as both the drawer and the drawee.[9]

UCC §3-104(g) defines a cashier's check as "a draft with respect to which the drawer and drawee are the same bank or branches of the same bank."[10] In other words, a **cashier's check** is a check or draft drawn by a bank again on itself. If a cashier's check is drawn on another bank in which the drawer bank has an account, it is a **teller's check**. Although the drawer and drawee may be the same on a money order or a cashier's check, the instrument does not lose its three-party character or its status as a check.

Under new federal laws that Revised Article 4 recognizes, there is the new term **substitute check**, which is an electronic image or paper printout of an electronic image of a check. A substitute check has the same legal effect as a paper check. The bank that converts the paper check into electronic form, called the *reconverting bank*, has certain duties imposed by federal regulations to be certain that the electronic version or substitute check has all of the necessary legal information such as visible indorsements, magnetic bank code strip, payee, and signature of drawer.

money order – draft issued by a bank or a nonbank.

cashier's check – draft drawn by a bank on itself.

teller's check – draft drawn by a bank on another bank in which it has an account.

substitute check – electronic image of a paper check that a bank can create and that has the same legal effect as the original instrument.

2. Certified Checks

The drawee bank may *certify* or accept a check drawn on it. Under UCC §3-409(d), a certified check is "a check accepted by the bank on which it is drawn."[11] While a bank is under no obligation to certify a check, if it does so, the certification has the effect of the bank accepting primary liability on the instrument. Check certification requires that the actual certification be written on the check and authenticated by the signature of an authorized representative of the bank.[12] Upon certification, the bank must set aside, in a special account maintained by the bank, the amount of the certified check taken from the drawer's account. The certification is a promise by the bank that when the check is presented for payment, the bank will make payment according to the terms of the check. Payment is made regardless of the status of the drawer's account at that time.

A holder or drawer may request that a check be certified by a bank. When certification is at the request of the holder, all prior indorsers and the drawer are released from liability. When certification is at the request of the drawer, the indorsers and drawer, as secondary parties, are not released. Unless otherwise agreed, the delivery of a certified check, a cashier's check, or a teller's check discharges the debt for which the check is given, up to the amount of that check.[13]

---

[9] Revised UCC §3-104(f).

[10] Revised UCC §3-104(g). *Lerner v. First Commerce Bank*, 302 S.W.2d 16 (Tex. App. 2009).

[11] Revised UCC §3-409(d).

[12] Many courts treat cashier's checks and certified checks as the same because of their uniform commercial acceptability. See *Jones v. Wells Fargo Bank, N.A.*, 666 F.3d 955 (5th Cir. 2012). However, the rights of the parties are different because certification discharges all other parties to the instrument. A cashier's check does not result in the discharge of other parties on the instrument.

[13] Revised UCC §3-104(h) defines a traveler's check as "a draft drawn by a bank (i) on another bank, or (ii) payable at or through a bank."

CASE SUMMARY

A Double-Wide, a Cashier's Check, and a Little Fraud

FACTS: On May 7, 2004, Bryan K. and Lisa C. Fisher purchased a manufactured home at the sales lot of the Landmark Housing Center, Inc. Landmark was a registered dealer for a Texas company called Patriot Homes, Inc. until May 20, 2004.

On June 1, 2004, the Fishers borrowed $31,917.55 from Lynnville National Bank to make a down payment of one-half of the home's purchase price to Landmark. Lynnville issued a cashier's check made payable to Landmark. The same day, the Fishers delivered the cashier's check to Landmark and Landmark deposited the cashier's check into its business checking account with South Central Bank.

South Central's branch manager telephoned Lynnville and confirmed the date, amount, and payee of the cashier's check. The Lynnville employee explained that the funds were for the purchase of a manufactured home. South Central's branch manager later attested that the Lynnville employee said that the cashier's check was "good" or "fine," but the employee denied making such a statement. On the same day—June 1, 2004—South Central gave unfettered and immediate cash and credit to Landmark after the cashier's check was deposited into Landmark's account.

On June 3, 2004, an employee of Patriot called the Fishers and informed them that Landmark was no longer a dealer for Patriot. Lisa Fisher then called Lynnville to report that Landmark could not fulfill its contract and that it had misrepresented itself as a dealer for Patriot. The Fishers directed Lynnville to inform South Central of Landmark's suspected fraud and to stop or refuse payment on the cashier's check.

At approximately 10:00 a.m. on June 3, 2004, South Central paid a check for $24,000, which was written to South Central in exchange for a $24,000 cashier's check made payable to James Rice, a Landmark principal. South Central received the phone call from Lynnville regarding Landmark's suspected fraud and Lynnville's refusal to honor the Fishers' cashier's check at approximately 1:45 p.m., after the proceeds of the Fishers' check had already been paid out of Landmark's account. After notification of Lynnville's refusal to pay, South Central took no steps to retrieve or halt the withdrawal of any funds by Landmark. The following day, on June 4, 2004, South Central paid the $24,000 cashier's check upon presentment by Rice. South Central said it cleared the $24,000.00 cashier's check it issued after Lynnville's notice.

Rice and Landmark declared bankruptcy. With few alternatives as a result, South Central filed suit against Lynnville, alleging that Lynnville had wrongfully refused payment on the $31,917.35 cashier's check payable to Landmark, and sought to recover the amount of the check plus prejudgment interest, attorney fees, and costs. The trial court found for Lynnville and South Central appealed.

DECISION: Only under certain, very specific circumstances is a bank entitled to stop payment on a cashier's check: first, if the bank suspends payments—becomes insolvent; second, if the bank has its own defense—as distinguished from its customer's defense—against the person entitled to enforce the instrument; third, if the bank has a reasonable doubt about the identity of the person demanding payment; and finally, if the payment is prohibited by law. None of those circumstances occurred in this case. Lynnville's obligation to pay was clear and it was able to pay, but it refused payment on the check as an accommodation to the Fishers, who had no right to make that request. Reversed. [***South Central Bank of Daviess County v. Lynnville Nat. Bank***, 901 N.E.2d 576 (Ind. App. 2009)]

E-Commerce & Cyberlaw

The Nigerian "I Need Your Help" E-Mails

They are quite common, those e-mails that come into our accounts asking for help in transferring funds in exchange for a percentage of those funds. They only ask that they be able to use our bank accounts in the United States so that they are able to collect the money owed to them, with your 12 to 15 percent service fee for use of your account deducted.

These are scams, accomplished by simple means. The scammers do indeed have their alleged creditors furnish large checks initially to be deposited in your account. Those checks do seem to clear. They then have you write checks in the amount deposited (less your percentage fee) to them. However, subsequent problems develop with those initially deposited checks and your bank wants you to now cover the overdraft created by the scammers cashing your check. You end up owing the money to your bank. You have no claim based on forgery because it was your check. In short, the Nigerians win. There is no remedy under Article 3 or 4 for you. Fraud is the answer, but finding the scammers is a tall order. The federal government works tirelessly to alert people to the scams because it is nearly impossible for them to locate the scammers. Beware of e-mails coming your way from folks from Nigeria, Malaysia, and, well, any other country who wish to use your bank account for processing their payments. [*Chino Commercial Bank, N.A., v. Peters*, 118 Cal. Rptr. 3d 866 (Cal. App. 2010)]

CPA

3. Presentment for Obtaining Payment on a Check

A holder of a check must take required steps to obtain payment. As discussed in Chapter 30, there are primary and secondary parties for every negotiable instrument. Primary parties are makers and drawees. Under Revised Article 3, secondary parties are referred to as *secondary obligors* and are defined to include "an indorser, a drawer, an accommodation party, or any other party to the instrument that has a right of recourse against another party to the instrument."[14]

presentment – formal request for payment on an instrument.

The process for a holder to be paid on an instrument involves mandatory steps with time limitations. The holder must first seek payment from the drawee through **presentment**. No secondary obligor is liable on an instrument until presentment has been made. Presentment is required for checks, and presentment is made first to the drawee bank.[15]

(A) PRESENTMENT REQUIREMENTS. Presentment occurs when the holder of a check or other consumer transaction authorization demands payment.[16] Under Revised Article 3, the party presents either the check or a record for payment. If the presentment is done in person, the party to whom presentment is made can require that the presenter exhibit identification. The holder who is presenting the instrument must present the check or record for payment in a commercially reasonable manner; banks can treat the transaction as having occurred the following day when presentment is made after *the close of the business day*.[17] In the case of electronic banking, banks are permitted to impose times after which posting will occur the next day. If a check is presented to the drawee bank for payment and paid, the drawer has no liability because payment has been made. (For more details on presentment, generally, of instruments, see Chapter 30.)

[14] Revised UCC §3-104(12).

[15] It is important to note that the bank is unique as a drawee because its contract as a primary party is limited by its right to dishonor a check and its right to give only provisional credit.

[16] In addition to the UCC restrictions on times for presentment, banks must comply with federally imposed time constraints. Under the Expedited Funds Availability Act, 12 U.S.C. §4001 *et seq.*, banks are required to lift provisional credits on customer accounts.

[17] Revised UCC §4-107(1). *Rogers v. Bank of America, N.A.*, 73 UCC Rep. Serv. 2d 47 (S.D. Ill. 2010).

CPA

(B) TIME FOR PRESENTMENT OF A CHECK FOR PAYMENT.[18] Under the UCC, presentment must be made within a reasonable time after the drawers and indorsers have signed the check. What constitutes a reasonable time is determined by the nature of the instrument, by commercial usage, and by the facts of the particular case.

Failure to make timely presentment discharges all secondary obligors (prior indorsers) of the instrument. It also discharges the drawer to the extent that the drawer has lost, through the bank's failure, money that was on deposit at the bank to make the payment due under the check.[19]

The UCC establishes two presumptions as to what is a reasonable time for presentment of checks. If the check is not certified and is both drawn and payable within the United States, it is presumed that 90 days after the date of the check or the date of its issuance, whichever is later, is the reasonable period in which to make presentment for payment in order to attach secondary liability to the drawer.[20] With respect to attachment of the liability of an indorser, 30 days after indorsement is the presumed reasonable time.[21]

If a check is dated with the date of issue, it may be presented immediately for payment. If it is postdated, ordinarily it may not be presented until that date arrives. However, as noted earlier, the bank need not honor the date on the postdated instrument. If the holder delays in making presentment, the delay discharges the drawer if the bank itself fails during such delay.[22] If the holder of the check does not present it for payment or collection within 90 days after an indorsement was made, the secondary obligors (indorsers) are discharged from liability to the extent that the drawer has lost, through the bank's failure, money that was on deposit at the bank to meet the payment under the check.

Under Revised Articles 3 and 4, agreeing to honor an instrument beyond this time limit changes the obligation of the primary obligor and, as a result, changes the obligation of the secondary obligors. Such changes in the terms and conditions of payment serve to discharge the secondary obligors, a change that brings UCC Articles 3 and 4 in line with the principles of surety law (see Chapter 33).

A bank may continue to honor checks presented for payment after the 90-day period, but it does so with understanding of the discharge of liability for the primary and secondary obligors. A bank honoring a check that is overdue subjects the bank to questions about whether it exercised good faith and reasonable care in honoring it.[23]

4. Dishonor of a Check

If the bank refuses to make payment, the drawer is then subject to the same secondary liability as the drawer of an ordinary draft.[24] To be able to attach that secondary liability, the holder of the instrument must notify the drawer of the dishonor by the drawee. The notice of dishonor may be oral, written, or electronic.

CPA

(A) TIME FOR NOTICE OF DISHONOR. Banks in the chain of collection for a check must give notice of dishonor by midnight of the next banking day. Others, including the payee or holder of the check, must give notice of dishonor within 30 days after learning

---

[18] Revised UCC §3-501. *Whooping Creek Const., LLC v. Bartow County Bank*, 713 S.E.2d 871 (Ga. App. 2011)
[19] Revised UCC §3-605.
[20] Under the previous versions of Articles 3 and 4, the time was six months.
[21] Revised UCC §3-304.
[22] Revised UCC §4-208(c).
[23] Revised Article 3 changed the "negligence" of the bank to the "failure to exercise ordinary care" in §3-406. A bank need not pay a check that is presented to it after six months from the date of issue (except for certified checks), but it can honor such a check and charge the customer's account if it does so in good faith.
[24] Revised UCC §3-414. PayPal is not considered a bank for purposes of Articles 3 and 4. *Zepeda v. PayPal, Inc.*, 777 F. Supp. 2d 1215 (N.D. Cal. 2011).

that the instrument has been dishonored.[25] If proper notice of dishonor is not given to the drawer of the check, the drawer will be discharged from liability to the same extent as the drawer of an ordinary draft.[26]

CPA

(B) OVERDRAFT. If the bank pays the check but the funds in the account are not sufficient to cover the amount, the excess of the payment over the amount on deposit is an **overdraft**. This overdraft is treated as a loan from the bank to the customer, and the customer must repay that amount to the bank.

overdraft – negative balance in a drawer's account.

If the bank account from which the check is drawn is one held by two or more persons, the joint account holder who does not sign the check that creates an overdraft is not liable for the amount of the overdraft if she received no benefit from the proceeds of that check.[27] Additional issues on overdrafts and dishonor of checks are covered in Section 5.

Ethics & the Law

Getting Hit For SOOO Many Overdraft Fees

On August 28, 2008, Cortney Hassler had a balance of $112.35 in his checking account. He made a $39.58 payment in the morning and a $140.00 debit in the afternoon. Sovereign Bank did not post the transactions in the order that they occurred but, rather, rearranged the debits so that Cortney had to pay two $33 overdraft fees on his account. A provision in his checking account agreement indicated that Sovereign had the right to pay the withdrawals in any order. Cortney filed a class action suit against the bank for unfair trade practices and unjust enrichment. Evaluate the legal rights of the bank to post the transactions as it did. Evaluate the ethical issues in the changes in posting order so as to maximize the overdraft fees. [*Hassler v. Sovereign Bank*, 374 Fed. Appx. 341 (3rd Cir. 2010). See also *In re Checking Account Overdraft Litigation*, 694 F. Supp. 2d 1032 (S.D. Fla. 2010).]

5. The Customer-Bank Relationship

The relationship between banks and customers is governed by Articles 3 and 4 of the UCC as well as by several federal statutes. These laws impose duties and liabilities on both banks and customers.

(A) PRIVACY. The bank owes its customer the duty of maintaining the privacy of the information that the bank acquires in connection with its relationship with the customer. Law enforcement officers and administrative agencies cannot require the disclosure of information relating to a customer's account without first obtaining the customer's consent or a search warrant or without following the statutory procedures designed to protect customers from unreasonable invasions of privacy.[28] The **USA Patriot Act** does impose certain reporting requirements on banks, financial institutions, and businesses with regard to deposits of cash and large cash payments. These reporting requirements were imposed to be able to track money laundering efforts as well as possible funding of terrorist activities.[29] For example, checks that involve amounts of more than $10,000 generally trigger the bank reporting systems under the USA Patriot Act.

USA Patriot Act – federal law that, among other things, imposes reporting requirements on banks.

---

[25] The former time frame for nonbanks was midnight of the third business day.

[26] Revised UCC §4-213. Under Federal Reserve regulations, notice of dishonor may be given by telephone. *Security Bank and Trust Co. v. Federal Nat'l Bank*, 554 P.2d 119 (Okla. Ct. App. 1976). But see *City Check Cashing, Inc. v. Manufacturers Hanover Trust Co.*, 764 A.2d 411, 43 UCC Rep. Serv. 2d 768 (N.J. 2001). See also *JP Morgan Chase Bank, N.A. v. Cohen*, 907 N.Y.S.2d 101 (N.Y. Sup. 2009).

[27] Revised UCC §§4-214 and 4-401(b).

[28] Right to Financial Privacy Act of 1978, 12 U.S.C. §3401 *et seq.*

[29] 12 U.S.C. §5311 *et seq.* 2001.

With the advent of the Internet and other electronic exchanges of information, it has become much easier for businesses, including banks, to exchange information about customers. All businesses are subject to federal constraints on the use of customer information. (See Chapter 33 for more information.)

(B) PAYMENT. A bank is under a general contractual duty to its customers to pay on demand all checks to the extent of the funds in a depositor's account.

C P A

(1) Stale Checks.

stale check–a check whose date is longer than six months ago.

A bank acting in good faith may pay a check presented more than six months after its date (commonly known as a **stale check**), but unless the check is certified, the bank is not required to do so.[30] The fact that a bank may refuse to pay a check that is more than six months old does not mean that it must pay a check that is less than six months old or that it is not required to exercise reasonable care in making payment on any check.

CASE SUMMARY

The Nine-Year-Old Check Racing through the System

FACTS: On July 15, 1986, IBP, Inc., issued and delivered to Meyer Land & Cattle Company a $135,234.18 check for the purchase of cattle. IBP wrote the check on its account at Mercantile Bank of Topeka.

In the fall of 1995, Meyer's president, Tim Meyer, found the 1986 undeposited check behind a desk drawer in his home. Meyer indorsed the check with the corporation's authorized and accepted indorsement stamp and deposited the check at Sylvan State Bank. Sylvan then forwarded the check through the Federal Reserve System for collection from Mercantile. Mercantile, on receipt of the check, checked its computers for any stop payment orders and, finding none, paid the check.

IBP issues thousands of checks on its account every month. For example, between July 1995 and December 1995, IBP drew 73,769 checks on its account at Mercantile. The amount of the Meyer check was not unusual; many checks issued by IBP exceed the Meyer check amount.

IBP claimed that Mercantile had improperly honored a stale check and demanded that its account be credited with the amount of the Meyer check. IBP also said that it had issued a stop payment order, although it did not provide evidence and there were no computer records of it at the bank. Mercantile moved for summary judgment.

DECISION: The bank used an automated check cashing system and acted in good faith by hand-checking for stop payment orders before cashing the check. Furthermore, the debt had not been satisfied and Meyer was entitled to payment, so there was no unjust enrichment. Stop payment orders last only six months, and it is the customer's obligation to renew such stop payment orders. [*IBP, Inc. v. Mercantile Bank of Topeka*, 6 F. Supp. 2d 1258 (D. Kan. 1998)]

(2) Payment after Depositor's Death.

From the time of death, the bank can continue paying items until it actually knows of the customer's death.[31] The bank has the right, even with notice of the death, to continue to pay items for 10 days unless, for example, an heir or a government agency halts the payments.[32]

[30] Revised UCC §§3-304 and 4-404; *Commerce Bank, N.A. v. Rickett*, 748 A.2d 111 (N.J. Super. 2000).
[31] Revised UCC §4-405(2).
[32] Revised UCC §4-405(b); *Hieber v. Uptown Nat'l Bank of Chicago*, 557 N.E.2d 408 (Ill. App. 1990).

CPA

6. Stopping Payment of a Check

stop payment order – order by a depositor to the bank to refuse to make payment of a check when presented for payment.

A drawer may stop payment of a check by notifying the drawee bank in the required manner.[33] **Stop payment orders** are often used when a check is lost or mislaid. The drawer can always write a duplicate check but wants assurance that the original lost or misplaced check will not then also be presented for payment. The drawer can stop payment on the first check to prevent double-dipping. A drawer can also use a stop payment order on a check if the payee has not kept his end of the contract or has failed to provide assurances (see Chapter 26). However, the drawer must keep in mind that if a holder in due course has the check, the holder in due course can demand payment because she would not be subject to the personal defenses of breach of contract or nonperformance of contract. (See Chapter 30 and the rights of holders in due course.)

Stop payment orders are invalid for some forms of checks even when properly executed. Neither the drawer nor a bank customer can stop payment of a **certified check**. A bank customer cannot stop payment of a cashier's check.

CPA

certified check – check for which the bank has set aside in a special account sufficient funds to pay it; payment is made when check is presented regardless of amount in drawer's account at that time; discharges all parties except certifying bank when holder requests certification.

(A) Form of Stop Payment Order. The stop payment order may be either oral or by record (written or evidence of electronic order). If oral, however, the order is binding on the bank for only 14 calendar days unless confirmed in writing within that time. A record of the stop payment order or confirmation is effective for six months. A stop payment order can be renewed for an additional six months if the customer provides the bank a written extension.

(B) Liability to Holder for Stopping Payment. The act of stopping payment may in some cases make the drawer liable to the holder of the check. If the drawer has no proper ground for stopping payment, the drawer is liable to the holder of the check. In any case, the drawer is liable for stopping payment with respect to any holder in due course or any other party having the rights of a holder in due course unless payment was stopped for a reason that may be asserted as a defense against a holder in due course (see Chapter 30). The fact that payment of a check has been stopped does not affect its negotiable character.[34]

7. Wrongful Dishonor of a Check

wrongfully dishonored – error by a bank in refusing to pay a check.

A check is **wrongfully dishonored** by the drawee bank if the bank refuses to pay the amount of the check although (1) it is properly payable and (2) the account on which it is drawn is sufficient to pay the item. Dishonor for lack of funds can be a breach of contract if the customer has an agreement with the bank that it will pay overdraft items.

CPA

(A) Bank's Liability to Drawer of Check. If the bank improperly refuses to make payment, it is liable to the drawer for damages sustained by the drawer as a consequence of such dishonor.

(B) Bank's Liability to Holder. If a check has not been certified, the holder has no claim against the bank for the dishonor of the check regardless of the fact that the bank was wrong in its dishonor. The bank that certifies a check is liable to the holder when it dishonors the check.

---

[33] Revised UCC §4-403.
[34] *Seigel v. Merrill Lynch, Pierce, Fenner & Smith*, 745 A.2d 301 (D.C. 2000).

(c) Holder's Notice of Dishonor of Check. When a check is dishonored by nonpayment, the holder must follow the procedure for notice to the secondary parties. Notice of dishonor need not be given to the drawer who has stopped payment on a check or to drawers and indorsers who are aware that there are insufficient funds on deposit to cover the check. In those circumstances, no party has reason to expect that the check will be paid by the bank.

8. Agency Status of Collecting Bank

agent – person or firm who is authorized by the principal or by operation of law to make contracts with third persons on behalf of the principal.

When a customer deposits negotiable instruments in a bank, the bank is regarded as being merely an **agent**, even though the customer may be given the right to make immediate withdrawals against the deposited item. Because of the bank's **agency** status, the customer remains the owner of the item and is subject to the risks of ownership involved in its collection.

agency – the relationship that exists between a person identified as a principal and another by virtue of which the latter may make contracts with third persons on behalf of the principal. (Parties–principal, agent, third person)

When a bank cashes a check deposited by its customer or cashes a check drawn by its customer based on an amount from a deposited check, it is a holder of the check deposited by its customer. The bank may still collect from the parties on the check even though the bank is an agent for collection and has the right to charge back the amount of the deposited check if it cannot be collected.

9. Bank's Duty of Care

A bank is required to exercise ordinary care in the handling of items. The liability of a bank is determined by the law of the state where the bank, branch, or separate office involved is located.

CPA

(a) Modification of Bank Duties. The parties in the bank collection process may modify their rights and duties by agreement. However, a bank cannot disclaim liability for lack of good faith or failure to exercise ordinary care, nor can it limit the measure of damages for such lack of care.

When a bank handles checks by automated processes, the standard of ordinary care does not require the bank to make a physical examination of each item. Banks must use the ordinary care standard of the industry.

encoding warranty – warranty made by any party who encodes electronic information on an instrument; a warranty of accuracy.

(b) Encoding Warranty and Electronic Presentment. In addition to transfer and presentment warranties, an **encoding warranty** is also given by those who transfer instruments. Under this warranty, anyone placing information on an item or transmitting the information electronically warrants that the information is correct. When there is an agreement for electronic presentment, the presenter warrants that the transfer is made properly for transmissions.[35]

(c) Counterfeit Checks. One of the problems that banks now experience is the use of counterfeit checks. Because of automated processing, these checks can sail through bank systems and seemingly are cleared. Customers, in reliance on the check clearing, use those funds only to be told later that the check was a counterfeit and the funds credited to their account are then debited. The liability for the losses resulting from counterfeit checks will depend on whether the bank acted reasonably in its processing systems in clearing checks (particularly those for large amounts) and whether it complied with the time requirements for notifying customers of a dishonor of a deposited counterfeit check.

[35] Revised UCC §§4-207 to 4-209.

CASE SUMMARY

The Lawyers Who Got Taken by Their Counterfeit Clients

FACTS: Greenberg, Trager & Herbst, LLP (GTH), is a law firm specializing in construction litigation law. In September 2007, a partner at GTH received an e-mail from a representative of Northlink Industrial Limited, a Hong Kong company. Northlink was looking for legal representation to assist it in the collection of debts owed by its North American customers. Through a series of e-mails GTH agreed to represent Northlink and requested a $10,000 retainer. GTH then received a Citibank check for $197,750 from a Northlink customer and was told that it could take its retainer from those funds. On Friday, September 21, 2007, GTH deposited the check into its account at HSBC.

The next business day, Monday, September 24, HSBC processed the check through the Federal Reserve Bank of Philadelphia (FRBP) and because of the federal funds availability law, provisionally credited GTH's account for $197,750. FRBP presented an image replacement document (IRD) of the check to Citibank that same day.

Because the routing number was not recognized by Citi's processing system, the automated sorting system directed the IRD to the reject pocket.

HSBC received the IRD with the notation "sent wrong" the next day, September 25, 2007. Because the check was marked "sent wrong," HSBC assumed that there was a problem with the routing number that required sending the check to a different Federal Reserve bank. On September 26, 2007, HSBC sent the check to the Federal Reserve Bank, San Francisco (FRBS). HSBC never informed GTH of the "administrative return" of the check.

On September 27, 2007, a GTH partner called HSBC to determine whether the check had "cleared" and if the funds were available for disbursement. GTH was informed that the funds were available. Later that day, GTH wired $187,750 from its account to Hong Kong as Northlink instructed.

On October 2, 2007, HSBC received Citibank's notice that the check was being dishonored as "RTM [return to maker] Suspect Counterfeit." HSBC contacted GTH to inform them that the check had been dishonored. HSBC then revoked its provisional settlement and charged back GTH's account.

GTH filed suit against HSBC and Citibank for failure to inform GTH that the check had been returned and dishonored on September 25, and for informing GTH over the phone that the funds had "cleared" and were available for disbursement. HSBC and Citibank moved for summary judgment.

The trial court found that HSBC had no duty under the UCC to inform GTH that the check had been returned "sent wrong" on September 25, but rather that the dishonor actually took place when HSBC discovered that the check was "Suspect Counterfeit," and dismissed the complaint.

DECISION: The bank did not owe duty to GTH to have effective procedures in place to detect counterfeit checks. The bank is only required to present the check for payment to the drawee bank and the drawee bank and its customer are charged with the duty of monitoring properly payable items. The bank's alleged oral statement that the check had "cleared" and the funds were available for transfer was not a misrepresentation because banking rules do not allow reliance on oral representations. A check is not cleared until it actually goes through the banking system. The bank exercised ordinary care in handling the check and did not breach any duty to GTH and its alleged oral representations could not be a basis for GTH's reliance. [*Greenberg, Trager & Herbst, LLP v. HSBC Bank USA,* **934 N.Y.S.2d 43 75 UCC Rep. Serv.2d 775 (Sup. Ct. 2011)**]

CPA ## B. Liability of a Bank

Banks can make mistakes in the payment and collection of items presented to them by their customers. **For Example,** a check may slip through and be cashed over a customer's properly executed stop payment order. The bank would be liable for this improper payment and may also be liable for improperly collecting, paying, or refusing to pay a check.

10. Premature Payment of a Postdated Check

A check may be postdated, but the bank is not liable for making payments on the check before the date stated unless the drawer has given the bank prior notice. Such a notice is similar to a stop payment order; it must provide sufficient information so that the bank is moved to action by the trigger that comes from the orderly processing of the check as it flows through its electronic processing system.[36]

11. Payment Over a Stop Payment Order

A bank must be given a reasonable time in which to put a stop payment order into effect. However, if the bank makes payment of a check after it has been properly notified to stop payment, and there has been sufficient time for the order to be put into the system, the bank is liable to the drawer (customer) for the loss the drawer sustains in the absence of a valid limitation of the bank's liability.[37] The bank must have complete information on a stop payment order, such as the payee, check number, and amount, to be held responsible for the failure to stop payment.

CASE SUMMARY

The Double-Dipping Detective Agency: No Stopping Payment without Details

FACTS: Michael Rovell, a lawyer, wrote a check for $38,250 to the Pretty Eyes Detective Agency. After sending the check to Patricia O'Connor, the owner of Pretty Eyes, Rovell discovered that he had overpaid the invoice by more than $10,000. Rovell asked Lisa Fair, one of his employees and another lawyer, to contact American National Bank and make sure the check had not cleared.

Fair phoned Linda Williams, the law firm's account representative at the bank, and explained that if the check had not cleared, she wanted to stop payment and issue a new check for the correct amount. However, Fair did not know the check number, date of issue, the check amount, or the payee. Fair gave Williams check numbers 1084 and 1086 and, finding that they had not cleared, issued stop payment orders. Despite Williams's warning about waiting to issue a new check to Pretty Eyes, Fair issued a new check for $27,284.50. The original check had already cleared, and Pretty Eyes also cashed the second check. Rovell's account went into overdraft, and he sued for the bank's failure to honor a stop payment order.

DECISION: The bank has a duty to inform its customers of the requirements for a stop payment order. Once informed, the customer has the duty to provide the necessary information, including the check number. The customer did not provide the correct check number, the check in question had already cleared the day before, and the bank was not liable for both checks being paid. The customer here must bear the loss for the failure to provide all necessary information for a stop payment order. [*Rovell v. American Nat'l Bank*, 232 B.R. 381, 38 UCC2c 896 (N.D. Ill. 1998)]

---

[36] Note that a "postdated check" is not a check but a time draft. UCC §§4-401 to 4-402.
[37] Revised UCC §4-403(c); *Lombino v. Bank of America, N.A.*, 797 F. Supp. 2d 1078 (D. Nev. 2011).

CPA 12. Payment on a Forged Signature of Drawer

A forgery of the signature of the drawer occurs when the name of the drawer has been signed by another person without authority to do so with the intent to defraud by making it appear that the drawer signed the check. The bank is liable to the drawer if it pays a check on which the drawer's signature has been forged because a forgery ordinarily has no effect as a signature. The risk of loss caused by the forged signature of the drawer is placed on the bank without regard to whether the bank could have detected the forgery.[38] The reasoning behind the bank's liability for a forged drawer's signature is that the bank is presumed to know its own customers' signatures even if it does not regularly review checks for authenticity of the signature.

A bank's customer whose signature has been forged may be barred from holding the bank liable if the customer's negligence substantially contributed to the making of the forgery. This preclusion rule prevents or precludes the customer from making a forgery claim against the bank. However, to enjoy the protection of the preclusion rule, the bank, if negligent in its failure to detect the forgery or alteration, must have cashed the check in good faith or have taken it for value or collection.[39]

Article 4 of the UCC extends forgery protections and rights to alterations and unauthorized signings. When an officer with authority limited to signing $5,000 checks signs a check for $7,500, the signature is unauthorized. If the principal for the drawer account is an organization and has a requirement that two or more designated persons sign negotiable instruments on its behalf, signatures by fewer than the specified number are also classified as unauthorized signatures.

CPA 13. Payment on a Forged or Missing Indorsement

A drawee bank that honors a customer's check bearing a forged indorsement must recredit the customer's account upon the drawer's discovery of the forgery and notification to the bank. A drawee bank is liable for the loss when it pays a check that lacks an essential indorsement.[40] In such a case, the instrument is not properly payable. Without proper indorsements for an order instrument and special indorsements, the person presenting the check for payment is not the holder of the instrument and is not entitled to demand or receive payment. However, the bank can then turn to the indorsers and transferors of the instrument for breach of warranty liability in that all signatures were not genuine or authorized and they did not have title. All transferors can turn to their previous transferor until liability ultimately rests with the party who first accepted the forged indorsement. This party had face-to-face contact and could have verified signatures.

When a customer deposits a check but does not indorse it, the customer's bank may make an indorsement on behalf of the depositor unless the check expressly requires the customer's indorsement. A bank cannot add the missing indorsement of

---

[38] *Lynch v. Bank of America, N.A.*, 493 F. Supp. 2d 265 (D.R.I. 2007). Some states allow for an action for conversion of funds by the customer. *300 Broadway Healthcare Center, LLC v. Wachovia Bank, N.A.*, 39 A.3d 248 (N.J. App. 2012).

[39] Revised UCC §4-406(e); *Bucci v. Wachovia Bank, N.A.*, 591 F. Supp. 2d 773 (E.D. Pa. 2008); *Rodgeres v. Bank of America, N.A.*, 73 UCC Rep. Serv. 2d 47 (S.D. Ill. 2011).

[40] *Bank of Nichols Hills v. Bank of Oklahoma*, 196 P.3d 984 (Ok. App. 2008); *VIP Mortg. Corp. v. Bank of America, N.A.*, 769 F. Supp. 2d 20 (D. Mass. 2011).

a person who is not its customer when an item payable is deposited in a customer's bank account.[41]

14. Alteration of a Check

If the face of a check has been altered so that the amount to be paid has been increased, the bank is liable to the drawer for the amount of the increase when it makes payment of the greater amount.

The drawer may be barred from claiming that there was an alteration if there was negligence in writing the check or reporting its alteration. A drawer is barred from claiming alteration if the check was written negligently, the negligence substantially contributed to the making of the material alteration, and the bank honored the check in good faith and observed reasonable commercial standards in doing so.

For Example, the drawer is barred from claiming alteration when the check was written with blank spaces that readily permitted a change of "four" to "four hundred" and the drawee bank paid out the latter sum because the alteration was not obvious. A careful drawer will write figures and words close together and run a line through or cross out any blank spaces.

15. Unauthorized Collection of a Check

A collecting bank, or a bank simply collecting an item for a customer, is protected from liability when it follows its customer's instructions. It is not required to inquire or verify that the customer had the authority to give such instructions. In contrast, instructions do not protect a payor bank. It has an absolute duty to make proper payment. If it does not do so, it is liable unless it is protected by estoppel or by the preclusion rule. The person giving wrongful instructions is liable for the loss caused by those instructions.

16. Time Limitations

The liability of the bank to its depositor is subject to certain time limitations.

CPA **(A) FORGERY AND ALTERATION REPORTING TIME.** A customer must examine with reasonable care and promptness a bank statement and relevant checks that are paid in good faith and sent to the customer by the bank and must try to discover any unauthorized signature or alteration on the checks. The customer must notify the bank promptly after discovering either a forgery or an alteration. If the bank exercises ordinary care in paying a forged or an altered check and suffers a loss because the customer fails to discover and notify the bank of the forgery or alteration, the customer cannot assert the unauthorized signature or alteration against the bank.[42]

Under the Check Truncation Act (CTA—which is part of the Check 21 statute covered in Chapter 28), banks now have the right to substitute electronic images of checks for customer billing statements. The CTA is largely implemented through Federal Reserve Board regulations found at 12 CFR §229.2. Banks do not need to

---

[41] *Smith v. Farmers Union Mut. Ins. Co.*, 260 P.3d 163 (Mont. 2011).

[42] *Quilling v. National City Bank of Michigan/Illinois.* Not reported in F. Supp. 2d 2001, 2001 WL 1516732 (N.D. Ill.), 46 UCC Rep. Serv. 2d 207 (N.D. Ill. 2001).

provide the original check to their customers and can simply send copies of electronic images so long as the image provides enough clarity for the customer to see payee, encoding, indorsements, and so on.

With the use of substituted checks and online banking, consumers now have additional rights and time limits with substituted checks. Under the Check 21 statute, consumers have a new right to an expedited recredit to their account if a substitute check was charged improperly to their account. They have the right to see the original check if they can explain why it is necessary and that they are suffering a loss as a result of the improper charge of a substitute check to their account. Consumers have 40 calendar days from whichever of the following is later: (1) the delivery of their monthly bank statements or (2) that date on which the substitute check was made available to them for examination and/or review. If a consumer has been traveling or been ill, the rules permit the extension of the deadline for purposes of challenging a substitute check. Consumers can even call their bank and challenge a payment, but they will not then get the benefit of all the rights and protections under Check 21 and its regulations if they choose to proceed without a written demand on a substitute check.[43] Once the demand is made, the bank must either recredit the consumer's account within one business day or explain why it believes the substitute check was charged properly to the consumer's account. The oral demand does not start this clock running for the consumer's protection. There are also fines and overdraft protections provided while the substitute check issue is in the dispute/investigation stage.

Some cases of forgery are the result of a customer's lack of care, such as when an employee is given too much authority and internal controls are lacking with the result that the employee is able to forge checks on a regular basis not easily detected by the bank. Referred to as the *fictitious payee and impostor exceptions*, this issue was covered in Chapter 29.

Customers are precluded from asserting unauthorized signatures or alterations if they do not report them within one year from the time the bank statement is received.[44] A forged indorsement must be reported within three years.

(B) UNAUTHORIZED SIGNATURE OR ALTERATION BY SAME WRONGDOER. If there is a series of improperly paid items and the same wrongdoer is involved, the customer is protected only as to those items that were paid by the bank before it received notification from the customer and during that reasonable amount of time that the customer has to examine items or statements and to notify the bank. If the customer failed to exercise reasonable promptness and failed to notify the bank but the customer can show that the bank failed to exercise ordinary care in paying the items, the loss will be allocated between the customer and the bank.[45]

(C) STATUTE OF LIMITATIONS. An action to enforce a liability imposed by Article 4 must be commenced within three years after the cause of action accrued.

---

[43] 12 C.F.R. 229.54(b)(1)(iii).
[44] Revised UCC §4-406.
[45] Revised UCC §4-406 (2002); *J. Walter Thompson, U.S.A., Inc. v. First BankAmericano*, 518 F.3d 128 (2nd Cir. 2008), and *Dean v. Commonwealth Bank & Trust Co.*, 2012 WL 1137907 (Ky. App. 2012).

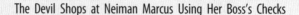

CASE SUMMARY

The Devil Shops at Neiman Marcus Using Her Boss's Checks

FACTS: Carol Young was employed as Brian P. Burns's secretary at a salary that never exceeded $75,000. Between 1995 and 2000, Young opened several credit card accounts with Neiman Marcus. In the three-year period prior to 2006, Young spent approximately $1 million at Neiman Marcus, and "the balance on [one] credit card, as of January 10, 2006, was in excess of $242,000." Young was offered entrée into Neiman Marcus's exclusive INCIRCLE® rewards program—a loyalty incentive program. Young had a personal shopper who knew of her annual salary of less than $75,000. However, the personal shopper repeatedly contacted and encouraged Young to make excessive purchases with her various Neiman Marcus cards.

Young would personally deliver on a regular basis fraudulent and forged checks drawn on Burns's Union Bank of California checking account to pay down her various [Neiman Marcus] credit card bills at the Customer Service Center in Neiman's San Francisco store. Young used three different methods for presenting Burns's checks: (a) stealing checks and forging Burns's signature; (b) stealing checks with no signature whatsoever; and (c) stealing checks with Burns's signature—checks that Burns presumed were for payments towards his own Neiman Marcus credit card account, but which were diverted to Young's credit card accounts.

Because Young managed all of Burns's accounts, the reconciliations she made had fake ledger entries for payment to third parties to cover her payments to Neiman Marcus. Burns did not detect Young's activities for three years because he did not see the bank statements, only Young did. A serendipitous examination of the ledger and canceled checks resulted in the discovery. Burns recovered what he could from his bank, an amount limited by UCC Article 4. Burns filed suit against Neiman Marcus, seeking to recover the funds paid on the checks and claiming that Neiman Marcus was subject to the defenses of forgery and unauthorized payments. The trial court granted Neiman Marcus's motion for demurrer and Burns appealed.

DECISION: The court affirmed the lower court's dismissal because it was unwilling to impose a broad duty on third parties to verify that every third-party check it receives is legitimate. Such a requirement would significantly slow down the flow and use of negotiable instruments and defeat both the purposes of Articles 3 and 4 as well as the well-defined rules for responsibility and liability when there are drawer and drawee forgeries. [***Burns v. Neiman Marcus Group, Inc.,*** **173 Cal. App. 4th 479 (Cal. App. 1st Dist. 2009)**]

Thinking Things Through

The Embezzling Home Health Care Worker Helped Along by Bank of America

Nancy Z. Paley opened a money market bank account in 1977 at a bank that subsequently was acquired by Bank of America (BOA). BOA was unable to locate Mrs. Paley's signature card, but never told Mrs. Paley to come in and sign a new card. At the time of the BOA acquisition, Mrs. Paley had $45,000 in her interest-bearing, money market account. Mrs. Paley rarely wrote checks on the account because of the restrictions on the number of checks allowed each month.

After losing a leg to diabetes at age 74 in 2002, Mrs. Paley hired Angela Sentore, a home health aide. In 2005, Mrs. Paley wrote a check to her husband that bounced due to insufficient funds. Puzzled because of the small amount of the check, Mrs. Paley checked the account and discovered that Ms. Sentore had negotiated 188 checks from the account, totaling $48,931.83, either by making them payable to herself, or by making them payable to third parties. Sixty-two of the checks were presented in person by Sentore to a teller at a BOA branch office.

Mrs. Paley demanded that BOA credit her account for the amount that had been paid over a forged signature. BOA pointed out that the time for claiming forgeries on the account had expired in 2002 and refused to credit the account.

Thinking Things Through

Continued

Mrs. Paley had never received the bank statements and had called once to ask that the statements be sent, but, again, she never received them. Mrs. Paley acknowledged that Ms. Sentore intercepted all of her mail and that the statements could have been destroyed by her.

BOA never questioned Sentore and the checks because they were for such small amounts that it was not bank policy to compare signatures. BOA followed reasonable commercial standards in its signature comparison practices and used automated processing that would only raise questions for checks written for amounts over $500, the BOA trigger for a signature comparison.

Mrs. Paley claimed that the bank should have known because of the differences in her signature. She always signed her checks with the middle initial "Z" in her name. None of the forged checks had the "Z" in the signature.

Mrs. Paley (who passed away before the case was decided) brought suit against BOA for payment over a forged signature as well as violation of New Jersey's consumer fraud statute. BOA defended on the grounds that Mrs. Paley's rights to claim the funds back ended when she did not check her statements. Analyze the claims of both sides and determine whether Mrs. Paley's estate should recover the embezzled funds. [***Estate of Paley v. Bank of America,*** **18 A.3d 1033 (N.J. App. 2011)**]

C. CONSUMER FUNDS TRANSFERS

Consumers are using electronic methods of payment at an increasing rate. From the swipe of the card at the grocery store checkout to the retrieval of funds from the local automated teller machine, *electronic funds transfers* represent a way of life for many consumers. A federal statute protects consumers making electronic funds transfers.

17. Electronic Funds Transfer Act

Electronic Funds Transfer Act (EFTA)–federal law that provides consumers with rights and protections in electronic funds transfers.

electronic funds transfer (EFT)–any transfer of funds (other than a transaction originated by a check, draft, or similar paper instrument) that is initiated through an electronic terminal, telephone, computer, or magnetic tape so as to authorize a financial institution to debit or credit an account.

Congress passed the **Electronic Funds Transfer Act (EFTA)** to protect consumers making electronic transfers of funds.[46] **Electronic funds transfer (EFT)** means any transfer of funds (other than a transaction originated by check, draft, or similar paper instrument) that is initiated through an electronic terminal, telephone, computer, or magnetic tape that authorizes a financial institution to debit or credit an account. The service available from an automated teller machine is a common form of EFT.

18. Types of Electronic Funds Transfer Systems

Currently, five common types of EFT systems are in use. In some of these systems, the consumer has a card to access a machine. The consumer usually has a private code that prevents others who wrongfully obtain the card from using it.

(A) AUTOMATED TELLER MACHINE. The *automated teller machine (ATM)* performs many of the tasks once performed exclusively by bank employees. Once a user activates an ATM, he can deposit and withdraw funds from his account, transfer funds between accounts, make payments on loan accounts, and obtain cash advances from bank credit cards.

---

[46] 15 U.S.C. §1693 *et seq.*

(B) Pay-by-Phone System. This system facilitates paying telephone, mortgage, utility, and other bills without writing checks. The consumer calls the bank and directs the transfer of funds to a designated third party.

(c) Direct Deposit and Withdrawal. Employees may authorize their employers to deposit wages directly to their accounts. A consumer who has just purchased an automobile on credit may elect to have monthly payments withdrawn from a bank account to be paid directly to the seller.

(d) Point-of-Sale Terminal. The *point-of-sale terminal* allows a business with such a terminal to transfer funds from a consumer's account to the store's account. The consumer must be furnished in advance with the terms and conditions of all EFT services and must be given periodic statements covering account activity. Any automatic EFT from an individual's account must be authorized in writing in advance.

Financial institutions are liable to consumers for all damages proximately caused by the failure to make an EFT in accordance with the terms and conditions of an account. Exceptions include insufficient funds, funds subject to legal process, exceeding an established credit limit, or insufficient cash is available in an ATM.

(e) Internet Banking. Internet banking is the customer use of computer access to bank systems to pay bills, balance accounts, transfer funds, and even obtain loans. Increasing in popularity, this form of banking still suffers from concerns about privacy and security. However, the revisions to Articles 3 and 4 recognize electronic records as valid proof of payment.

CPA 19. Consumer Liability

A consumer who notifies the issuer of an EFT card within two days after learning of a loss or theft of the card can be held to a maximum liability of $50 for unauthorized use of the card. Failure to notify within this time will increase the consumer's liability for losses to a maximum of $500.

Consumers have the responsibility to examine periodic statements provided by their financial institution. If a loss would not have occurred but for the failure of a consumer to report within 60 days of the transmittal of the statement any unauthorized transfer, then the loss is borne by the consumer.

CPA D. FUNDS TRANSFERS

The funds transfers made by businesses are governed by the UCC and Federal Reserve regulations.

20. What Law Governs?

In states that have adopted Article 4A of the Uniform Commercial Code, that article governs funds transfers.[47] In addition, whenever a Federal Reserve Bank is involved, the provisions of Article 4A apply by virtue of Federal Reserve regulations.

---

[47] The majority of the states have adopted the 1990 version of Article 4A.

21. Characteristics of Funds Transfers

The transfers regulated by Article 4A are characteristically made between highly sophisticated parties dealing with large sums of money. Speed of transfer is often an essential ingredient. An individual transfer may involve many millions of dollars, and the national total of such transfers on a business day can amount to trillions of dollars.

22. Pattern of Funds Transfers

In the simplest form of funds transfer, both the debtor and the creditor have separate accounts in the same bank.[48] In this situation, the debtor can instruct the bank to pay the creditor a specified sum of money by subtracting that amount from the debtor's account and adding it to the creditor's account. As a practical matter, the debtor merely instructs the bank to make the transfer.

A more complex situation is involved if each party has an account in a different bank. In that case, the funds transfer could involve only these two banks and no clearinghouse. The buyer can instruct the buyer's bank to direct the seller's bank to make payment to the seller. There is direct communication between the two banks. In a more complex situation, the buyer's bank may relay the payment order to another bank, called an **intermediary bank**, and that bank, in turn, transmits the payment order to the seller's bank. Such transactions become even more complex when two or more intermediary banks or a clearinghouse is involved.

intermediary bank – bank between the originator and the beneficiary bank in the transfer of funds.

23. Scope of UCC Article 4A

Article 4A applies to all funds transfers except as expressly excluded because of their nature or because of the parties involved.

(A) EFTA AND CONSUMER TRANSACTIONS. Article 4A does not apply to consumer transaction payments to which the EFTA applies. If any part of the funds transfer is subject to the EFTA, the entire transfer is expressly excluded from the scope of UCC Article 4A.[49]

(B) CREDIT AND DEBIT TRANSFERS. When the person making payment, such as the buyer, requests that payment be made to the beneficiary's bank, the transaction is called a **credit transfer**. If the beneficiary entitled to money goes to the bank according to a prior agreement and requests payment, the transaction is called a **debit transfer**. The latter transfer type is not regulated by Article 4A. Article 4A applies only to transfers begun by the person authorizing payment to another.

credit transfer – transaction in which a person making payment, such as a buyer, requests payment be made to the beneficiary's bank.

debit transfer – transaction in which a beneficiary entitled to money requests payment from a bank according to a prior agreement.

24. Definitions

Article 4A employs terms that are peculiar to that article or are used in a very different context from the contexts in which they appear elsewhere.

---

[48] The text refers to *debtor* and *creditor* in the interest of simplicity and because that situation is the most common in the business world. However, a gift may be made by a funds transfer. Likewise, a person having separate accounts in two different banks may transfer funds from one bank to another.
[49] UCC §4A-108 (1990). This exclusion applies when any part of the transaction is subject to Regulation E adopted under the authority of that statute.

funds transfer– communication of instructions or requests to pay a specific sum of money to the credit of a specified account or person without an actual physical passing of money.

originator– party who originates the funds transfer.

beneficiary– person to whom the proceeds of a life insurance policy are payable, a person for whose benefit property is held in trust, or a person given property by a will; the ultimate recipient of the benefit of a funds transfer.

beneficiary's bank– the final bank, which carries out the payment order, in the chain of a transfer of funds.

payment order– direction given by an originator to his or her bank or by any bank to a subsequent bank to make a specified funds transfer.

(A) FUNDS TRANSFER. A **funds transfer** is more accurately described as a communication of instructions or a request to pay a specific sum of money to, or to the credit of, a specified account or person. There is no actual physical transfer or passing of money.

(B) ORIGINATOR. The person starting the funds transfer is called the **originator** of the funds transfer.[50]

(C) BENEFICIARY. The **beneficiary** is the ultimate recipient of the benefit of the funds transfer. Whether the recipient is the beneficiary personally, an account owned by the beneficiary, or a third person to whom the beneficiary owes money is determined by the payment order.

(D) BENEFICIARY'S BANK. The **beneficiary's bank** is the final bank in the chain of transfer that carries out the transfer by making payment or application as directed by the payment order.

(E) PAYMENT ORDER. The **payment order** is the direction the originator gives to the originator's bank or by any bank to a subsequent bank to make the specified funds transfer. Although called a *payment order*, it is in fact a request. No bank is required or obligated to accept a payment order unless it is so bound by a contract or a clearinghouse rule that operates independently of Article 4A.

25. Manner of Transmitting Payment Order

Article 4A makes no provisions for the manner of transmitting a payment order. As a practical matter, most funds transfers under Article 4A are controlled by computers, and payment orders are electronically transmitted. Article 4A, however, applies to any funds transfer payment order even if made orally, such as by telephone, or in writing. Also, the agreement of the parties or the clearinghouse and funds transfer system rules may impose some restrictions on the methods for communicating orders.

26. Regulation by Agreement and Funds Transfer System Rules

Article 4A, with minor limitations, permits the parties to make agreements that modify or change the provisions of Article 4A that would otherwise govern. Likewise, the rules of a clearinghouse or a funds transfer system through which the banks operate may change the provisions of the Code.

(A) CHOICE OF LAW. When the parties enter into an agreement for a funds transfer, they may designate the law that is to apply in interpreting the agreement.

(B) CLEARINGHOUSE RULES. The banks involved in a particular funds transfer may be members of the same clearinghouse. In such a case, they will be bound by the lawful rules and regulations of the house. The rights of the parties involved in a funds transfer may be determined by the rules of FedWire, a clearinghouse system operated by the Federal Reserve System, or by CHIPS, which is a similar system operated by the New York clearinghouse.

27. Reimbursement of the Bank

After the beneficiary's bank accepts the payment order, it and every bank ahead of it in the funds transfer chain is entitled to reimbursement of the amount paid to or for

[50] UCC §4A-201.

the beneficiary. This reimbursement is due from the preceding bank. By going back along the funds transfer chain, the originator's bank, and ultimately the originator, makes payment of this reimbursement amount.

28. Error in Funds Transfer

There may be an error in a payment order. The effect of an error depends on its nature.

(A) TYPE OF ERROR. The error in a payment order may consist of a wrong identification or a wrong amount.

(1) Wrong Beneficiary or Account Number.

The payment order received by the beneficiary's bank may contain an error in the designation of the beneficiary or in the account number. This error may result in payment being made to or for the wrong person or account.

(2) Excessive Amount.

The payment order may call for the payment of an amount that is larger than it should be. For example, the order may wrongly add an additional zero to the specified amount.

(3) Duplicating Amount.

The payment order may be issued after a similar payment order has already been transferred, so that the second order duplicates the first. This duplication would result in doubling the proper amount paid by the beneficiary's bank.

(4) Underpayment.

The payment order may call for the payment of a smaller sum than was ordered. For example, the order may drop off one of the zeros from the amount ordered by the originator.

(B) EFFECT OF ERROR. When the error falls under one of the first three classes just discussed, the bank committing the error bears the loss because it caused the item to be wrongfully paid. In contrast, when the error is merely underpayment, the bank making the mistake can cure the fault by making a supplementary order for the amount of the underpayment. If verification by the agreed-upon security procedure would disclose an error in the payment order, a bank is liable for any loss caused by the error if it failed to verify the payment order by such a procedure. In contrast, if the security procedure followed did not reveal any error, there is no liability for accepting the payment order.

When an error of any kind is made, there may be liability under a collateral agreement of the parties, a clearinghouse or funds transfer system rule, or general principles of contract law. However, these rights may be lost in certain cases by failure to notify the involved bank that the mistake has been made.

29. Liability for Loss

Unless otherwise regulated by agreement or clearinghouse rule, banks have little or no liability in the funds transfer chain if they have followed the agreed-upon security procedure.

(A) UNAUTHORIZED ORDER. If a bank executes or accepts an unauthorized payment order, it is liable to any prior party in the transfer chain for the loss caused. If a bank acts on the basis of an unauthorized order that nevertheless is verified by the security procedure, the bank is not liable for the loss that is caused.

(B) FAILURE TO ACT. A bank that fails to carry out a payment order is usually liable, at the most, for interest loss and expenses. There is no liability for the loss sustained by the originator or for consequential damages suffered because payment was not made to satisfy the originator's obligation to the beneficiary.

LawFlix

French Kiss (1995)(PG-13)

Meg Ryan is able to have funds transferred from her account in Canada to an account in France to Cartier (the jewelers) so that Cartier can issue a check to her friend. The set-up as well as the execution involve both paper and wire transactions.

MAKE THE CONNECTION

SUMMARY

A *check* is a particular kind of draft; it is drawn on a bank and is payable on demand. A delivery of a check is not an assignment of money on deposit with the bank on which it is drawn. A check does not automatically transfer the rights of the depositor against the bank to the holder of the check, and there is no duty on the part of the drawee bank to the holder to pay the holder the amount of the check.

A check may be an *ordinary check*, a *cashier's check*, or a *teller's check*. The name on the paper is not controlling. Unless otherwise agreed, the delivery of a certified check, a cashier's check, or a teller's check discharges the debt for which it is given, up to the amount of the check.

Certification of a check by the bank is the acceptance of the check—the bank becomes the primary party. Certification may be at the request of the drawee or the holder. Certification by the holder releases all prior indorsers and the drawer from liability.

Notice of nonpayment of a check must be given to the drawer of a check. If no notice is given, the drawer is discharged from liability to the same extent as the drawer of an ordinary draft.

A depositor may stop payment on a check. However, the depositor is liable to a holder in due course unless the stop payment order was for a reason that may be raised against a holder in due course. The stop payment order may be made orally (binding for 14 calendar days) or with a record (effective for six months).

The depository bank is the agent of the depositor for the purpose of collecting a deposited item. The bank may become liable when it pays a check contrary to a stop payment order or when there has been a forgery or an alteration. The bank is not liable, however, if the drawer's negligence has substantially contributed to the forgery. A bank that pays on a forged instrument must recredit the drawer's account. A depositor is subject to certain time limitations to enforce liability of the bank. Banks are subject to reporting requirements under the USA Patriot Act.

A customer and a bank may agree that the bank should retain canceled checks and simply provide the customer with a list of paid items. The customer must examine canceled checks (or their electronic images) or paid items to see whether any were improperly paid.

An *electronic funds transfer (EFT)* is a transfer of funds (other than a transaction originated by check, draft, or other commercial paper) that is initiated through an electronic terminal, telephone, computer, or magnetic tape to authorize a financial institution to debit or credit an account. The Electronic Funds Transfer Act requires that a financial institution furnish consumers with specific information containing all the terms and conditions of all EFT services. Under certain conditions, the financial institution will bear the loss for unauthorized

transfers. Under other circumstances, the consumer will bear the loss.

Funds transfers regulated by UCC Article 4A are those made between highly sophisticated parties that deal with large sums of money. If any part of the funds transfer is subject to the EFTA, such as consumer transactions, the entire transfer is expressly excluded from the scope of Article 4A. A funds transfer is simply a request or an instruction to pay a specific sum of money to, or to the credit of, a specified person.

LEARNING OUTCOMES

After studying this chapter, you should be able to clearly explain:

A. Checks

L0.1 List and explain the duties of the drawee bank

See *IBP, Inc. v. Mercantile Bank of Topeka* on p. 648.

L0.2 Explain the methods for, and legal effect of, stopping payment

See *South Central Bank of Daviess County v. Lynnville Nat. Bank* on p. 644.

B. Liability of a Bank

L0.3 Describe the liability of a bank for improper payment and collection

See Thinking Things Through on pp. 656–657.

See Ethics & the Law on p. 647 for a discussion of overdraft fees issues.

L0.4 Discuss the legal effect of forgeries and material alterations

See *Rovell v. American Nat'l Bank* on p. 652.

See *Greenberg, Trager & Herbst v. HSBC Bank USA* on p. 651.

L0.5 Specify the time limitations for reporting forgeries and alterations

See *Burns v. Neiman Marcus* on p. 656.

C. Consumer Funds Transfers

See the EFTA discussion on p. 657.

D. Funds Transfers

L0.6 Describe the electronic transfer of funds and laws governing it

See the discussion of Article 4A on p. 659.

KEY TERMS

agency
agent
bad check laws
beneficiary
beneficiary's bank
cashier's check
certified check
check
credit transfer
debit transfer

demand draft
Electronic Funds Transfer Act (EFTA)
electronic funds transfer (EFT)
encoding warranty
funds transfer
intermediary bank
money order
originator
overdraft

payment order
postdated
presentment
stale check
stop payment orders
substitute check
teller's check
time draft
USA Patriot Act
wrongfully dishonored

QUESTIONS AND CASE PROBLEMS

1. William Elias was the former owner of Direct Lending, a subprime mortgage company purchased by EA Management. Sometime after the sale, Elias went to Chase Bank and had three cashier's checks drawn to third parties and payable out of Direct Lending accounts in the amount of $191,251.31. When the new owners of Direct Lending checked their account balances online, they discovered the withdrawal for the three cashier's checks. The treasurer went to the bank and stopped payment on all three cashier's checks. Elias brought suit against the bank for wrongful dishonor and consequential damages to his businesses as a result of the dishonor. Can Elias recover? Be sure to explain which Article 4 provisions apply and why. [*EA Management v. JP Morgan Chase, N.A.*, 655 F.3d 573 (6th Cir.)]

2. Helen was a very forgetful person, so she had placed her bank code (PIN number) on the back of her debit card. A thief stole Helen's card and was able to take $100 from an ATM on the day of the theft. That same day, Helen realized that the card was gone and phoned her bank. The following morning, the thief withdrew another $100. For how much, if anything, is Helen responsible? Why?

3. Adam Paul Strege (APS) opened a checking account at U.S. Bank. Just below his signature card for the account, he wrote, "Call if I bounce a check." APS bounced several checks and each time U.S. Bank covered those checks, but it did not notify APS of the bounced check status. The result was that APS continued to write checks and U.S. Bank had to request funds from him to cover the overdrafts in his account. APS refused to pay the amount due because he argued that U.S. Bank had breached its agreement with him to report all bounced checks. Discuss whether U.S. Bank had the obligation to notify APS of the bounced checks. [*APS v. U.S. Bank*, 2009 WL 4723311 (D. Minn.)]

4. Arthur Odgers died, and his widow, Elizabeth Odgers (Elizabeth Salsman by remarriage), retained Breslow as the attorney for her husband's estate. She received a check payable to her drawn on First National City Bank. Breslow told her to deposit it in her husband's estate. She signed an indorsement "Pay to the order of Estate of Arthur J. Odgers." Breslow deposited this check in his trustee account in National Community Bank, which collected the amount of the check from the drawee, First City National Bank. Thereafter, Elizabeth, as administratrix of the estate of Arthur J. Odgers, sued National Community Bank for collecting this check and crediting Breslow's trustee account with the proceeds. Was National Community Bank liable? Explain. [*Salsman v. National Community Bank*, 246 A.2d 162 (N.J. Super.)]

5. Shipper was ill for 14 months. His wife did not take care of his affairs carefully, nor did she examine his bank statements as they arrived each month. One of Shipper's acquaintances had forged his name to a check in favor of himself for $10,000. The drawee bank paid the check and charged Shipper's account. Shipper's wife did not notify the bank for 13 months after she received the statement and the forged check. Can she compel the bank to reverse the charge? Why or why not?

6. Ann Weldon maintained an account at Trust Company Bank. James Weldon, her son and a garment broker, purchased textile goods from Sportswear Services for resale to another corporation known as Thicket Textiles. Sportswear demanded certified funds from James Weldon before it would ship the goods. When James Weldon requested a certified check from Trust Company, Trust Company officer Sweat informed James that if it issued a certified check, payment could not be stopped even if the merchandise delivered was not as promised under the terms of the contract.

   Ann Weldon then obtained a $16,319.29 cashier's check drawn on her account and payable to Sportswear. James had deposited his funds into her account to cover the check. The check was delivered to Sportswear, and the goods were shipped the next day, but they were defective.

   Ann Weldon went to Trust Company Bank to issue a stop payment order, and the bank, believing that the check had not yet been delivered to Sportswear, did so for $25. James Weldon then notified Sportswear of the stop payment order. After Trust Company dishonored the cashier's check, Sportswear's bank was in contact with the bank and informed it that the check had already been delivered to Sportswear. Trust Company honored the check and credited Ann Weldon's account with the $25 stop payment fee. Ann filed suit because Trust Company did not stop payment. Should payment have been stopped? Why or why not? [*Weldon v. Trust Co. Bank of Columbus*, 499 S.E.2d 393 (Ga. App.)]

7. Gloria maintains a checking account at First Bank. On the third day of January, the bank sent her a statement of her account for December accompanied by the checks that the bank had paid. One of the checks had her forged signature, which Gloria discovered on the 25th of the month when she prepared a bank reconciliation. On discovering this, Gloria immediately notified the bank. On January 21, the bank had paid another check forged by the same party who had forged the December item. Who must bear the loss on the forged January check?

8. Dean bought a car from Cannon. As payment, Dean gave him a check drawn on South Dorchester Bank of Eastern Shore Trust Co. Cannon cashed the check at the Cambridge Bank of Eastern Shore Trust Co. The drawee bank refused payment when the check was presented on the ground that Dean had stopped payment because of certain misrepresentations made by Cannon. Will Eastern Shore Trust Co. succeed in an action against Dean for payment? [*Dean v. Eastern Shore Trust Co.*, 150 A. 797 (Md.)]

9. A depositor drew a check and delivered it to the payee. Fourteen months later, the check was presented to the drawee bank for payment. The bank had no knowledge that anything was wrong and paid the check. The depositor then sued the person receiving the money and the bank. The depositor claimed that the bank could not pay a stale check without asking the depositor whether payment should be made. Was the depositor correct? [*Advanced Alloys, Inc. v. Sergeant Steel Corp.*, 340 N.Y.S.2d 266 (Queens Co. Civ. Ct.)]

10. John G. Vowell and his wife, now deceased, had a checking account and a savings/money-market account with Mercantile Bank of Arkansas. In June 1997, Dr. Vowell and his wife allowed their daughter, Suzan Vowell, now also deceased, and her boyfriend to move in with them at their home. At that time, they knew that Suzan and her boyfriend had been involved with drugs, alcohol, writing bad checks, and stealing. They also knew that Suzan had stolen checks from them in the past and forged either Dr. Vowell's or his wife's signatures. They took precautions by hiding Mrs. Vowell's purse, which contained their checkbook, under the kitchen sink.

Beginning in June 1997, Suzan forged Mrs. Vowell's signature on 42 checks, drawn on both accounts, and committed nine unauthorized ATM withdrawals in the aggregate amount of $12,028.75. Suzan found her mother's purse hidden under the kitchen sink and stole the checkbooks and ATM card from the purse. She apparently had access to the personal identification number (PIN) for the accounts because the number was identical to the home security system code.

The Vowells received the following statements from the bank for the checking and savings accounts:

Date of Transaction	Amount	Statement date covering
July 9, 1997	$230.00	June 6–July 7, 1997
August 8, 1997	$1,235.25	July 8–August 6, 1997
August 23, 1997	$5,140.00	July 23–Aug 21, 1997
September 9, 1997	$1,423.50	Aug 7–Sept 7, 1997
September 26, 1997	$4,000.00	Aug 22–Sept 22, 1997

On September 15, 1997, Dr. Vowell had Mercantile freeze their accounts and begin investigating the alleged forgeries and other unauthorized transactions pursuant to its policy. Suzan was arrested subsequently when she tried to use the ATM card again.

The bank refused to credit the Vowells' account because it maintained that their negligence in handling their daughter caused the losses. The court found that the bank was liable for only $6,014.38, one-half of the entire sum of Suzan Vowell's unauthorized bank transactions and forgeries. The bank appealed. Can the Vowells recover? How much and why? [*Mercantile Bank of Arkansas v. Vowell*, 117 S.W.3d 603 (Ark. App.)]

11. Bogash drew a check on National Safety Bank and Trust Co. payable to the order of Fiss Corp. At the request of Fiss Corp., the bank certified the check. The bank later refused to make payment on the check because of a dispute between Bogash and the corporation over the amount due the corporation. Fiss sued the bank on the check. Can Fiss recover? [*Fiss Corp. v. National Safety Bank and Trust Co.*, 77 So.2d 293 (N.Y. City Ct.)]

12. David Marx was a gentleman in his 90s and a longtime customer of Whitney National Bank. His account had been in his name only until April 24, 1995, when he added his son, Stanley Marx, and his daughter, Maxine Marx Goodman, as joint owners and signatories on the account. The account names read: "David Marx or Maxine M. Goodman or Stanley B. Marx." At that time, the bank began sending the statements to Stanley Marx.

Joel Goodman, David Marx's grandson, visited his grandfather often and had access to his grandfather's checkbook. Joel forged 22 checks on his grandfather's account for a total of $22,834. The first 10 checks went unnoticed because they were cleared and the bank statement David Marx received during this time was never reviewed. The last five checks, which appeared on the May 16, 1995, bank statement, were

discovered when Stanley Marx reviewed the statement. David and Stanley notified the bank and completed the appropriate forms for the five checks, which totaled $10,000. Whitney National Bank refused to pay the $10,000, and David and Stanley filed suit. The trial court granted summary judgment for David and Stanley, and Whitney appealed. Who is liable on the checks? Did David and Stanley wait too long or are they protected because they let the bank know when they did? [*Marx v. Whitney National Bank*, 713 So.2d 1142 (La.)]

13. Norris, who was ill in the hospital, was visited by his sister during his last days. Norris was very fond of his sister and wrote a check to her that she deposited in her bank account. Before the check cleared, Norris died. Could the sister collect on the check even though the bank knew of the depositor's death? Explain. [*In re Estate of Norris*, 532 P.2d 981 (Colo.)]

14. Scott D. Leibling gave his bank, Mellon Bank, an oral stop payment order. Nineteen months later, the check emerged and Mellon Bank honored it. Leibling has filed suit against Mellon Bank for acting unreasonably under the circumstances. Is Mellon Bank liable to Leibling for paying the 19-month-old check when there was an oral stop payment order? Discuss your reasons for your answer. [*Leibling, P.C. v. Mellon, PSFS (NJ) N.A.*, 710 A.2d 1067, 35 UCC 2d 590 (N.J. Super.)]

15. Hixson paid Galyen Petroleum Co. money he owed by issuing three checks to Galyen. The bank refused to cash the three checks because of insufficient funds in the Hixson account to pay all three. Galyen sued the bank. What was the result? Why? [*Galyen Petroleum Co. v. Hixson*, 331 N.W.2d 1 (Neb)]

CPA QUESTIONS

1. A check has the following endorsements on the back:

    (1) Paul Frank **"without recourse"**

    (2) George Hopkins **"payment guaranteed"**

    (3) Ann Quarry **"collection guaranteed"**

    (4) Rachell Ott

Which of the following conditions occurring subsequent to the endorsements would discharge all of the endorsers?

a. Lack of notice of dishonor

b. Late presentment

c. Insolvency of the maker

d. Certification of the check

2. Blare bought a house and provided the required funds in the form of a certified check from a bank. Which of the following statements correctly describes the legal liability of Blare and the bank?

a. The bank has accepted; therefore, Blare is without liability.

b. The bank has not accepted; therefore, Blare has primary liability.

c. The bank has accepted, but Blare has secondary liability.

d. The bank has not accepted, but Blare has secondary liability.

3. In general, which of the following statements is correct concerning the priority among checks drawn on a particular account and presented to the drawee bank on a particular day?

a. The checks may be charged to the account in any order convenient to the bank.

b. The checks may be charged to the account in any order provided no charge creates an overdraft.

c. The checks must be charged to the account in the order in which the checks were dated.

d. The checks must be charged to the account in the order of lowest amount to highest amount to minimize the number of dishonored checks.

PART 5

Debtor-Creditor Relationships

© Manuel Gutjahr/iStockphoto.com

669

CHAPTER 32

© Manuel Gutjahr/iStockphoto.com

Nature of the Debtor-Creditor Relationship

learningoutcomes

After studying this chapter, you should be able to

LO.1 Distinguish a contract of suretyship from a contract of guaranty

LO.2 Define the parties to a contract of suretyship and a contract of guaranty

LO.3 List and explain the rights of sureties to protect themselves from loss

LO.4 Explain the defenses available to sureties

LO.5 Explain the nature of a letter of credit and the liabilities of the various parties to a letter of credit

T his section of the book deals with all aspects of debt: the creation of the debtor-creditor relationship, the statutory requirements for disclosure in those credit contracts, the means by which creditors can secure repayment of debt, and finally, what happens when debtors are unable to repay their debts. This chapter covers the creation of the debtor-creditor relationship, as well as two means of ensuring payment: the use of a surety or guarantor and the creation of a line of credit.

A. Creation of the Credit Relationship

A debtor-creditor relationship consists of a contract that provides for the creditor to advance funds to the debtor and requires the debtor to repay that principal amount with specified interest over an agreed-upon time. The credit contract, so long as it complies with all the requirements for formation and validity covered in Chapters 12 through 17, is enforceable just like any other contract. However, credit contracts often have additional statutory obligations and relationships that provide assurances on rights and collection for both the debtor and the creditor. Chapter 33 covers the rights of both debtors and creditors in consumer credit relationships. Chapter 34 covers the additional protection that creditors enjoy when debtors offer security interests in collateral. This chapter covers the additional relationships for securing repayment of debt known as *suretyships* and *lines of credit*.

suretyship – pledge or guaranty to pay the debt or be liable for the default of another.

B. Suretyship and Guaranty

A debtor can make a separate contract with a third party that requires the third party to pay the debtor's creditor if the debtor does not pay or defaults in the performance of an obligation. This relationship, in which a third party agrees to be responsible for the debt or other obligation, is used most commonly to ensure that a debt will be paid or that a contractor will perform the work called for by a contract. **For Example,** a third-party arrangement occurs when a corporate officer agrees to be personally liable if his corporation does not repay funds received through a corporate note. Contractors are generally required to obtain a surety bond in which a third party agrees to pay damages or complete performance of the construction project in the event the contractor fails to perform in a timely manner or according to the contract terms.

obligor – promisor.

surety – obligor of a suretyship; primarily liable for the debt or obligation of the principal debtor.

guaranty – agreement or promise to answer for a debt; an undertaking to pay the debt of another if the creditor first sues the debtor.

1. Definitions

One type of agreement to answer for the debt or default of another is called a **suretyship**. The **obligor** or third party who makes good on a debtor's obligation is called a **surety**. The other kind of agreement is called a **guaranty**, and the obligor

guarantor – one who undertakes the obligation of guaranty.

principal – person or firm who employs an agent; the person who, with respect to a surety, is primarily liable to the third person or creditor; property held in trust.

principal debtor – original borrower or debtor.

debtor – buyer on credit (i.e., a borrower).

obligee – promisee who can claim the benefit of the obligation.

creditor – person (seller or lender) who is owed money; also may be a secured party.

is called a **guarantor**. In both cases, the person who owes the money or is under the original obligation to pay or perform is called the **principal**, **principal debtor**, or **debtor**.[1] The person to whom the debt or obligation is owed is the **obligee** or **creditor**.

As discussed in Chapters 28 and 31, the revisions to Articles 3 and 4 put accommodation parties (now secondary obligors) in the same legal status as those in a surety/guarantor relationship. The revisions place secondary obligors in the position of a surety.

Suretyship and guaranty undertakings have the common feature of a promise to answer for the debt or default of another. The terms are often used interchangeably. However, certain forms of guaranty are qualified by one distinction. A surety is liable from the moment the principal is in default. The creditor or obligee can demand performance or payment from the surety without first proceeding against the principal debtor. A **guaranty of collection** is one in which the creditor generally cannot proceed directly against the guarantor and must first attempt to collect from the principal debtor. An exception is an **absolute guaranty**, which creates the same obligation as a suretyship. A **guaranty of payment** creates an absolute guaranty and requires the guarantor to pay upon default by the principal debtor.

CPA

guaranty of collection – form of guaranty in which creditor cannot proceed against guarantor until after proceeding against debtor.

absolute guaranty – agreement that creates the same obligation for the guarantor as a suretyship does for the surety; a guaranty of payment creates an absolute guaranty.

guaranty of payment – absolute promise to pay when a debtor defaults.

indemnity contract – agreement by one person, for consideration, to pay another person a sum of money in the event that the other person sustains a specified loss.

2. Indemnity Contract Distinguished

Both suretyship and guaranty differ from an **indemnity contract**. An indemnity contract is an undertaking by one person, for a consideration, to pay another person a sum of money in the event that the other person sustains a specified loss. **For Example,** a fire insurance policy is an indemnity contract. The insurance you obtain when you use a rental car is also an example of an indemnity contract.

3. Creation of the Relationship

Suretyship, guaranty, and indemnity relationships are based on contract. The principles relating to capacity, formation, validity, and interpretation of contracts are applicable. Generally, the ordinary rules of offer and acceptance apply. Notice of acceptance usually must be given by the obligee to the guarantor.

In most states, the statute of frauds requires that contracts of suretyship and guaranty be evidenced by a record to be enforceable. No record is required when the promise is made primarily for the promisor's benefit.

When the suretyship or guaranty is created at the same time as the original transaction, the consideration for the original promise that is covered by the guaranty is also consideration for the promise of the guarantor. When the suretyship or guaranty contract is entered into after and separate from the original transaction, there must be new consideration for the promise of the guarantor.

---

[1] Unless otherwise stated, *surety* as used in the text includes guarantor as well as surety. Often, the term *guarantee* is used for guaranty. In law, guarantee is actually one who benefits from the guaranty.

CASE SUMMARY

Are You Sure You're My Surety?

FACTS: James Feigenbaum, Sam Feigenbaum, and the Syma Feigenbaum Testamentary Trust own Lincoln Shopping Center. In 1996, the Feigenbaums leased 25,500 square feet in the Center to Guaracini Supermarkets, Inc. (GSI) for 10 years at a fixed rent of $7,500 per month and taxes, maintenance costs, and insurance. The lease did not impose an obligation on GSI to pay the Feigenbaums' legal expenses and costs if legal proceedings resulted.

The Guaracinis unconditionally guaranteed GSI's performance under the lease to the Feigenbaums (the guaranty) for the full term of the lease.

In 1998, GSI assigned the lease to Wakefern. Wakefern agreed to indemnify GSI against any claims or damages, including "reasonable legal fees and disbursements," arising from its default under the lease; however, Wakefern did not agree to indemnify the Guaracinis personally. Later in 1998, with the consent of the Feigenbaums, Wakefern reassigned the lease to Vineland Supermarket, Inc. Under the assignment, Vineland agreed to indemnify Wakefern and GSI from and against any claims or damages, including reasonable legal fees and disbursements, arising from Vineland's failure to perform under the lease. Vineland subsequently became insolvent.

In July 2003, Vineland failed to pay the monthly rent. The Feigenbaums filed suit claiming that the Guaracinis were primarily liable as guarantors of the lease, and Wakefern was liable as assignee of the lease from GSI (GSI had failed financially). The Feigenbaums' damages through August 31, 2006 were $616,815.66, which included attorneys' fees and costs. The trial court held the Guaracinis liable to the Feigenbaums and Wakefern liable to the Guaracinis. An appeal followed.

DECISION: The Guaracinis did not have a right of subrogation against Wakefern. Wakefern did not know of the Guaracinis' guaranty to the Feigenbaums when Wakefern contracted with GSI. The lease assignment only bound Wakefern to indemnify GSI for damages caused by a default under the lease. The Guaracinis, the owners of GSI, had the opportunity to negotiate from Wakefern a promise to indemnify them from any demand by the Feigenbaums on their personal guaranty, but did not do so. Reversed. [*Feigenbaum v. Guaracini*, 952 A.2d 511 (N.J. Super. 2008)]

exoneration – agreement or provision in an agreement that one party shall not be held liable for loss; the right of the surety to demand that those primarily liable pay the claim for which the surety is secondarily liable.

4. Rights of Sureties

Sureties have a number of rights to protect them from loss, to obtain their discharge because of the conduct of others that would be harmful to them, or to recover money that they were required to pay because of the debtor's breach.

(A) EXONERATION. A surety can be exonerated from liability, a means of discharging or relieving liability, if the creditor could have taken steps to stop or limit the surety's exposure for the debt. **For Example,** suppose that the surety learns that a debtor is about to leave the state, an act that makes it more difficult to collect debts. The surety may call on the creditor to take action against the debtor to provide a literal and figurative roadblock to the debtor's planned departure. If the creditor could proceed against the debtor who is about to leave and thereby protect the repayment and fails to do so, the surety is released or **exonerated** from liability to the extent that the surety has been harmed by such failure.

subrogation – right of a party secondarily liable to stand in the place of the creditor after making payment to the creditor and to enforce the creditor's right against the party primarily liable to obtain indemnity from such primary party.

(B) SUBROGATION. When a surety pays a claim that it is obligated to pay, it automatically acquires the claim and the rights of the creditor. This stepping into the shoes or position of another is known as **subrogation**.[2] That is, once the creditor is

---

[2] *Middlesex Mut. Assur. Co. v. Vaszil*, 873 A.2d 1030 (Conn. App. 2005); insurer had right of subrogation where guarantor had signed for tenant's liability for causing damage to the landlord's property once the insurer had paid the landlord.

paid in full, the surety stands in the same position as the creditor and may collect from the debtor or enforce any rights the creditor had against the debtor to recover the amount it has paid. The effect is the same as if the creditor, on being paid, made an express assignment of all rights to the surety. Likewise, the surety acquires any rights the debtor has against the creditor. **For Example,** if the creditor has not complied with statutory requirements, the surety can enforce those rights against the creditor just as the original debtor could.

CASE SUMMARY

The Dead-Beat Automotive Shop and the Owners' Guaranty

FACTS: Man-Data is a collection agency that sued Cheryl Mulhall and Robert Gonzales (defendants) to recover legal fees charged pursuant to a fee agreement between defendant B & A Automotive, Inc., and its former attorney, Scott Bassinger. Gonzales and Mulhall, both of whom were associated with B & A, signed a guaranty that they, in their individual capacities, would pay legal fees incurred by B & A. Bassinger was not paid and assigned his claim to Man-Data (plaintiff) for collection. Man-Data filed this suit and B & A failed to appear in the case; a bench trial resulted in a judgment against the defendants. The court prevented the individual defendants from attacking the validity of the fees charged under the fee agreement. The defendants appealed.

DECISION: The legal question here is whether the law precludes the individual defendants from challenging the amount of the obligation incurred by B & A. As a general rule, with exceptions that do not apply to this case, "the secondary obligor may raise as a defense to the secondary obligation any defense of the principal obligor to the underlying obligation[.]" The defendants had the right to raise any contract defenses that B & A had and also had the right to introduce evidence to establish their questions about and challenges to the legal bills they were being required to pay.

Reversed and remanded. [*Man-Data, Inc. v. B & A Automotive, Inc.*, 270 P.3d 318 (Or. App. 2011)]

CPA **(c) INDEMNITY.** A surety that has made payment of a claim for which it was liable as surety is entitled to **indemnity** from the principal debtor; that is, it is entitled to demand from the principal reimbursement of the amount that it has paid.

CPA **(d) CONTRIBUTION.** If there are two or more sureties (known as co-sureties), each is liable to the creditor or claimant for the full amount of the debt until the claim or debt has been paid in full. Between themselves, however, each co-surety is liable only for a proportionate share of the debt. Accordingly, if a surety has paid more than its share of the debt, it is entitled to demand **contribution** from its **co-sureties**. In the absence of a contrary agreement, co-sureties must share the debt repayment on a *pro rata* basis. **For Example,** Aaron and Bobette are co-sureties of $40,000 and $60,000, respectively, for Christi's $60,000 loan. If Christi defaults, Aaron owes $24,000 and Bobette owes $36,000.

indemnity – right of a person secondarily liable to require that a person primarily liable pay for loss sustained when the secondary party discharges the obligation that the primary party should have discharged; the right of an agent to be paid the amount of any loss or damage sustained without fault because of obedience to the principal's instructions; an undertaking by one person for a consideration to pay another person a sum of money to indemnify that person when a specified loss is incurred.

5. Defenses of Sureties

The surety's defenses include those that may be raised by a party to any contract and special defenses that are peculiar to the suretyship relationship.

Thinking Things Through

Pro Rata Shares for Co-Sureties

AFC Corporation borrowed $90,000 from First Bank and demanded three sureties for the loan. Anna Flynn agreed to be a surety for $45,000 for AFC's debt. Frank Conlan agreed to be a surety for $60,000, and Charles Aspen agreed to be a surety for $75,000. When AFC owed $64,000, it defaulted on the loan and demanded payment from the co-sureties. However, Frank Conlan was in bankruptcy. How much would Anna and Charles have to pay to First Bank?

CPA

contribution–right of a co-obligor who has paid more than a proportionate share to demand that the other obligor pay the amount of the excess payment made.

co-sureties–sureties for the same debtor and obligator.

(A) ORDINARY CONTRACT DEFENSES. Because the relationship of suretyship is based on a contract, the surety may raise any defense that a party to an ordinary contract may raise. For example, a surety may raise the defense of lack of capacity of parties, absence of consideration, fraud, or mistake.

Fraud and **concealment** are common defenses. Fraud on the part of the principal that is unknown to the creditor and in which the creditor has not taken part does not ordinarily release the surety.

Because the risk of the principal debtor's default is thrown on the surety, it is unfair for a creditor to conceal from the surety facts that are material to the surety's risk. Under common law, the creditor was not required to volunteer information to the surety and was not required to disclose that the principal was insolvent. A modern view that is receiving increased support is that the creditor should be required to inform the surety of matters material to the risk when the creditor has reason to believe that the surety does not possess such information.

CPA

fraud–act of making of a false statement of a past or existing fact, with knowledge of its falsity or with reckless indifference as to its truth, with the intent to cause another to rely thereon, and such person does rely thereon and is harmed thereby.

concealment–failure to volunteer information not requested.

pledge–bailment given as security for the payment of a debt or the performance of an obligation owed to the pledgee. (Parties–pledgor, pledgee)

(B) SURETYSHIP DEFENSES. Perhaps the most important thing for a surety to understand is the type of defense that does not result in a discharge of her obligation in the suretyship. The insolvency or bankruptcy of the principal debtor does not discharge the surety. The financial risk of the principal debtor is the reason that a surety was obtained from the outset. The lack of enforcement of the debt by the creditor is not a defense to the surety's obligation or a discharge. The creditor's failure to give the surety notice of default is not a defense. The creditor's right, without a specific guaranty of collection, is simply to turn to the surety for payment.[3]

In some cases, the creditor may have also taken a **pledge** of collateral for the debt in addition to the commitment of a surety. It is the creditor's choice as to whether to proceed against the collateral or the surety. If, however, the creditor proceeds first against the surety, the surety then has the right of exoneration and can step into the shoes of the creditor and repossess that collateral.

Changes in the terms of the loan agreement do not discharge a compensated surety. A surety who is acting gratuitously, however, would be discharged in the event of such changes. Changes in the loan terms that would discharge a gratuitous

---

[3] *Rossa v. D.L. Falk Const., Inc.,* 266 P.3d 1022 (Cal. 2012).

surety's obligation include extension of the loan terms and acceptance of late payments.[4]

A surety is discharged when the principal debtor performs his obligations under the original debt contract. If a creditor refuses to accept payment from a debtor, a surety is discharged.

A surety is also discharged, to the extent of the value of the collateral, if a creditor releases back to the debtor any collateral in the creditor's possession. **For Example,** suppose that Bank One has in its possession $10,000 in gold coins as collateral for a loan to Janice in the amount of $25,000. Albert has agreed to serve as a surety for the loan to Janice in the amount of $25,000. If a Bank One manager returns the $10,000 in coins to Janice, then Albert is discharged on his suretyship obligation to the extent of that $10,000. Following the release of the collateral, the most that Albert could be held liable for in the event of Janice's default is $15,000.

A surety is also discharged from her obligation if the creditor substitutes a different debtor. A surety and a guarantor make a promise that is personal to a specific debtor and do not agree to assume the risk of an assignment or a delegation of that responsibility to another debtor. A surety also enjoys the discharge rights afforded all parties to contracts, such as the statute of limitations. If the creditor does not enforce the suretyship agreement within the time limits provided for such contract enforcement in the surety's jurisdiction, the obligation is forever discharged.[5]

Figures 32-1 and 32-2 provide summaries of the defenses and release issues surrounding suretyship and guaranty relationships.

FIGURE 32-1	*No Release of Surety*

1. Fraud by debtor
2. Misrepresentation by debtor
3. Changes in loan terms (e.g., Extension of payment)—compensated surety only
4. Release of principal debtor
5. Bankruptcy of principal debtor
6. Insolvency of principal debtor
7. Death of principal debtor
8. Incapacity of principal debtor
9. Lack of enforcement by creditor
10. Creditor's failure to give notice of default
11. Failure of creditor to resort to collateral

© Cengage Learning

[4] *In re Chemtura Corp.*, 448 B.R. 635 (S.D.N.Y. 2011).
[5] *The Clark Const. Group, Inc. v. Wentworth Plastering of Boca Raton, Inc.*, 840 So.2d 357 (Fla. App. 2002); *The Clark Const. Group, Inc. v. Wentworth*, 840 So.2d 357 (Fla. App. 2003).

FIGURE 32-2	*Release of Surety*

> 1. Proper performance by debtor
> 2. Release, surrender, or destruction of collateral (to extent of value of collateral)
> 3. Substitution of debtor
> 4. Fraud/misrepresentation by creditor
> 5. Refusal by creditor to accept payment from debtor
> 6. Change in loan terms—uncompensated surety only
> 7. Statute of frauds
> 8. Statute of limitations

© Cengage Learning

C. LETTERS OF CREDIT

letter of credit – commercial device used to guarantee payment to a seller, primarily in an international business transaction.

issuer – party who issues a document such as a letter of credit or a document of title such as a warehouse receipt or bill of lading.

A **letter of credit** is a three-party arrangement with a payor, a beneficiary, and a party on whom the letter of credit is drawn, or **issuer**. A letter of credit is an agreement that the issuer of the letter will pay drafts drawn by the beneficiary of the letter. Letters of credit are a form of advance arrangement for financing. Sellers of goods, for example, know in advance how much money may be obtained from the issuer of the letter. A letter of credit may also be used by a creditor as a security device because the creditor knows that the drafts that the creditor draws will be accepted or paid by the issuer of the letter.[6]

The use of letters of credit arose in international trade. While international trade continues to be the primary area of use, there is a growing use of letters in domestic sales and in transactions in which the letter of credit takes the place of a surety bond. A letter of credit has been used to ensure that a borrower would repay a loan, that a tenant would pay the rent due under a lease, and that a contractor would properly perform a construction contract. This kind of letter of credit is known as a **standby letter**.

standby letter – letter of credit for a contractor ensuring he will complete the project as contracted.

There are few formal requirements for creating a letter of credit. Although banks often use a standardized form for convenience, they may draw up individualized letters of credit for particular situations (see Figure 32-3).

In international letters of credit, there are several sources of recognized standards that businesses use for the creation and execution of letters of credit. Along with the UCC, there is the Uniform Customs and Practice for Documentary Credits (or UCP), something that reflects ordinary international banking operational practices on letters of credit. The UCP is revised, generally, about every 10 years by the International Chamber of Commerce (ICC, see Chapter 7).

6. Definition

A letter of credit is an engagement by its issuer that it will pay or accept drafts when the conditions specified in the letter are satisfied. The issuer is usually a bank.

---

[6] *U.S. Material Supply, Inc. v. Korea Exchange Bank*, 417 F. Supp. 2d 652 (D.N.J. 2006), discussing the character and purpose of letters of credit. See also *City of Maple Grove v. Marketline Const. Capital, LLC*, 802 N.W. 2d 809 (Minn. App. 2011) for discussion of fact that a document is not a letter of credit if it requires verification of an outside event, as opposed to submission of documents.

FIGURE 32-3 **Letter of Credit**

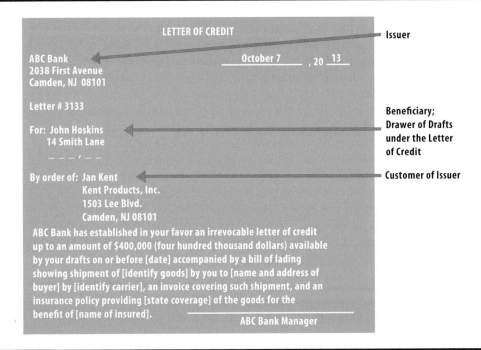

LETTER OF CREDIT — Issuer

ABC Bank
2038 First Avenue
Camden, NJ 08101

October 7 , 20 13

Letter # 3133

For: John Hoskins
    14 Smith Lane
— — — , — —

— Beneficiary; Drawer of Drafts under the Letter of Credit

By order of: Jan Kent
       Kent Products, Inc.
       1503 Lee Blvd.
       Camden, NJ 08101

— Customer of Issuer

ABC Bank has established in your favor an irrevocable letter of credit up to an amount of $400,000 (four hundred thousand dollars) available by your drafts on or before [date] accompanied by a bill of lading showing shipment of [identify goods] by you to [name and address of buyer] by [identify carrier], an invoice covering such shipment, and an insurance policy providing [state coverage] of the goods for the benefit of [name of insured].

ABC Bank Manager

© Cengage Learning

Three contracts are involved in letter-of-credit transactions: (1) the contract between the issuer and the customer of the issuer, (2) the letter of credit itself, and (3) the underlying agreement, often a contract of sale, between the beneficiary and the customer of the issuer of the letter of credit (see Figure 32-4). The letter of credit is completely independent from the other two contracts. Consideration is not required to establish or modify a letter of credit.

FIGURE 32-4 **The Contracts Involved in Letter-of-Credit Transactions**

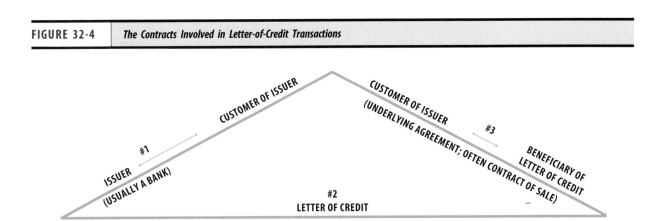

CUSTOMER OF ISSUER

CUSTOMER OF ISSUER
(UNDERLYING AGREEMENT; OFTEN CONTRACT OF SALE)

#3

BENEFICIARY OF LETTER OF CREDIT

#1

ISSUER
(USUALLY A BANK)

#2
LETTER OF CREDIT

© Cengage Learning

The issuer of the letter of credit is, in effect, the obligor on a third-party-beneficiary contract made for the benefit of the beneficiary of the letter. The key to the commercial success of letters of credit is their independence. **For Example,** a bank obligated to issue payment under a letter of credit "when the goods are delivered" must honor that obligation even if the buyer has complaints about the goods. It is the terms of the letter of credit that control the payment, not the relationship, contract, or problems of the beneficiary or issuer of the letter of credit.

The key to the commercial vitality and function of a letter of credit is that the issuing bank's promise is independent of the underlying contracts and the bank should not resort to them in interpreting a letter of credit. Sometimes called *the strict compliance rule,* banks must honor the letter of credit terms using strict interpretation. The respective parties are protected by a careful description of the documents that will trigger payment. The claim of a beneficiary of a letter of credit is not subject to defenses normally applicable to third-party contracts. Known as the *independence rule,* banks cannot, except in limited circumstances, delve into the underlying contract issues; the focus of the bank is only on the terms of the letter of credit.

CASE SUMMARY

The Letter of Credit and the Shoddy Mall

FACTS: In 2007, Wood Center Properties (WCP) entered into a Purchase and Sale Agreement to buy five shopping centers from Robert B. Greene (Greene) and Louisville Mall Associates, LP, and several other mall property groups (collectively, the "Mall Appellants"). While performing its due diligence, WCP discovered environmental contamination at the Crestwood Shopping Center, one of the shopping centers it intended to purchase. A prior shopping center tenant, Crestwood Coin Laundry (Tenant), spilled hazardous chemicals used in its dry cleaning business. As a result of the contamination, WCP chose not to purchase Crestwood Shopping Center, and the parties amended the Purchase and Sale Agreement to reflect WCP's decision.

Shortly thereafter, Greene offered to provide WCP with an irrevocable Letter of Credit, issued by M & T Bank, in the amount of $200,000.00. The Letter of Credit's purpose was to insulate WCP from liability and fund the environmental cleanup if the Tenant failed to do so. With that inducement, Crestwood Shopping Center was put back in the contract as one of the properties being purchased by WCP. Paragraph two of the amended contract provided:

> *At closing, Robert M. Greene, individually, shall deliver an irrevocable letter of credit for the benefit of Wood Center Properties, LLC in the amount of Two Hundred Thousand Dollars ($200,000.00) drawn on M & T Bank. This letter of credit shall extend for one (1) year from the date of Closing, and shall automatically renew for one (1) additional year unless Notice of non-renewal is given to [WCP] at least 60 days prior to the expiration date on the face of the Greene Letter of Credit.*

On June 13, 2007, M & T Bank issued the Letter of Credit for the benefit of WCP. The Letter of Credit contained an original expiration date of June 12, 2008 that provided:

> *It is a condition of this credit that it shall be deemed automatically extended without amendment for one (1) year from the expiration date hereof, or any future expiration date [emphasis added],*

CASE SUMMARY

Continued

unless sixty (60) days prior to any expiration date M & T Bank notifies [WCP] in writing that M & T Bank elects not to consider this credit renewed for any such additional period.

On April 7, 2008, M & T Bank automatically renewed the Letter of Credit for a second year and provided WCP and Greene with a letter of renewal, notifying them that the Letter of Credit's new expiration date was June 12, 2009. On March 6, 2009, M & T Bank sent a second renewal letter to WCP and Greene, again giving notice that it was automatically extending the Letter of Credit for a third year and its new expiration date was June 12, 2010.

After receiving M & T Bank's March 6, 2009, letter, Greene told M & T Bank his view that the Letter of Credit was only valid for two years and should expire on June 12, 2009. Greene requested that M & T Bank not renew the credit. Despite Greene's request, M & T Bank did not send a nonrenewal notification to WCP. WCP sought payment under the Letter of Credit and submitted the documents to M & T that were necessary for payment.

On July 27, 2009, Greene contacted WCP claiming the Letter of Credit had expired on June 12, 2009, and requested that it be returned. WCP filed a declaratory judgment action seeking the court's ruling that WCP was entitled to draw on the Letter of Credit. The court entered summary declaratory judgment in WCP's favor. Greene appealed.

DECISION: The issue of whether WCP was entitled to draw on the Letter of Credit had to be resolved by interpreting the Letter of Credit without reference to the parties' underlying purchase agreement. The Letter of Credit had a continuously renewing expiration date until M & T notified the purchaser that it elected to not renew the credit. However, the purchaser was entitled to draw on the Letter of Credit when it submitted documentation required by the Letter of Credit, regardless of where the parties were in their performance of the contract.

The Letter of Credit allowed payment based on the submission of the documents noted in the Letter of Credit regardless of renewals. The parties were at a different place in terms of their performance of their contract, but the Letter of Credit allowed payment, and M & T had no choice but to pay on the Letter of Credit once the terms for submission were met. [*Louisville Mall Associates, LP v. Wood Center Properties, LLC*, 361 S.W.3d 323 (Ky. App. 2012)]

7. Parties

The parties to a letter of credit are (1) the issuer; (2) the customer who makes the arrangements with the issuer; and (3) the beneficiary, who will be the drawer of the drafts that will be drawn under the letter of credit. There may also be (4) an **advising bank**[7] if the local issuer of the letter of credit requests its **correspondent bank**, where the beneficiary is located, to notify or advise the beneficiary that the letter has been issued. **For Example,** a U.S. merchant may want to buy goods from a Spanish merchant. There may have been prior dealings between the parties so that the seller is willing to take the buyer's commercial paper as payment or to take trade acceptances drawn on the buyer. If the foreign seller is not willing to do this, the U.S. buyer, as customer, may go to a bank, the issuer, and obtain a letter of credit naming the Spanish seller as beneficiary. The U.S. bank's correspondent or advising bank in Spain will notify the Spanish seller that this has been done. The Spanish seller will then draw drafts on the U.S. buyer. Under the letter of credit, the issuer is required to accept or pay these drafts.

advising bank – bank that tells beneficiary that letter of credit has been issued.

correspondent bank – will honor the letter of credit from the domestic bank of the buyer.

[7] See UCC §5-107; *Speedway Motorsports Intern. Ltd. v. Bronwen Energy Trading, Ltd.*, 706 S.E.2d 262 (N.C. 2011).

8. Duration

A letter of credit continues for any length of time it specifies. Generally, a maximum money amount is stated in the letter, so that the letter is exhausted or used up when the issuer has accepted or paid drafts aggregating that maximum. A letter of credit may be used in installments as the beneficiary chooses. The issuer or the customer cannot revoke or modify a letter of credit without the consent of the beneficiary unless that right is expressly reserved in the letter.

9. Form

A letter of credit must be in writing and signed by the issuer. If the credit is issued by a bank and requires a documentary draft or a documentary demand for payment[8] or if the credit is issued by a nonbank and requires that the draft or demand for payment be accompanied by a document of title, the instrument is presumed to be a letter of credit (rather than a contract of guaranty). Otherwise, the instrument must conspicuously state that it is a letter of credit.

Ethics & the Law

When the Creditors Rule the Debtor

Very often the creditors of a business can exercise a great deal of authority over the operation of the business when it has missed a payment on its debt or has experienced some business or market setbacks. Without owning any stock in a corporation, creditors will, in more than 50 percent of all cases in which they express concern about repayment, succeed in having both boards and officers replaced in part or in toto. **For Example,** Worlds of Wonder, Inc., a creative and innovative toy manufacturer that was responsible for the first talking toy, Teddy Ruxpin, was required by demands from its secured and unsecured creditors to obtain the resignation of its founder and CEO, Donald Kingsborough. Kingsborough was paid $212,500 at his departure for "emotional distress."* In 2009, the federal government, as a lender, required that the CEO of General Motors resign as a condition to receiving additional funds from the government to cover debt payments. In addition, the federal government negotiated the positions of union workers, investors, and hedge funds in the Chrysler Corporation restructuring as a condition of its receipt of federal funds.

Studies show** that creditors also have input on the following corporate actions:

Type of Decision	Percentage of Creditors with Vote
Declaration of dividends	48
Increased security	73
Restructuring of debt	55
Cap on borrowing	50
Cap on capital expenses	25
Restrictions on investment	23

Is it fair to have creditors control corporate governance? What are the risks for shareholders when creditors control the management of a company?

*"Toymaker Has Financing Pact," *New York Times*, April 2, 1988, C1 (Reuters item).
See Tim Reason, "Keeping Skin in the Game, *CFO Magazine*, February 1, 2005, **www.cfo.com, for a discussion of why creditors are involved and what they can do to help manage a debtor.

---

[8] A *documentary draft* or a *documentary demand for payment* is one for which honor is conditioned on the presentation of one or more documents. A document could be a document of title, security, invoice, certificate, notice of default, or other similar paper. UCC §5-103(1)(b).

10. Duty of Issuer

The issuer is obligated to honor drafts drawn under the letter of credit if the conditions specified in the letter have been satisfied. The issuer takes the risk that the papers submitted are the ones required by the letter. If they are not, the issuer cannot obtain reimbursement for payment made in reliance on such documents. The issuer has no duty to verify that the papers are properly supported by facts or that the underlying transaction has been performed. It is immaterial that the goods sold by the seller in fact do not conform to the contract so long as the seller tenders the documents specified by the letter of credit. If the issuer dishonors a draft without justification, it is liable to its customer for breach of contract.[9]

11. Reimbursement of Issuer

When the issuer of a letter of credit makes proper payment of drafts drawn under the letter of credit, it may obtain reimbursement from its customer for such payment. Examples of improper payment include payment made after the letter has expired or a payment that is in excess of the amount authorized by the letter. No reimbursement is possible if the payment is made without the proper presentation of required documents or if the payment is made in violation of a court injunction against payment.

MAKE THE CONNECTION

SUMMARY

Suretyship and guaranty undertakings have the common feature of a promise to answer for the debt or default of another. The terms are used interchangeably, but a guarantor of collection is ordinarily only secondarily liable, which means that the guarantor does not pay until the creditor has exhausted all avenues of recovery. If the guarantor has made an absolute guaranty, then its status is the same as that of a surety, which means that both are liable for the debt in the event the debtor defaults, regardless of what avenues of collection, if any, the creditor has pursued.

Surety and guaranty relationships are based on contract. Sureties have a number of rights to protect them. They are exoneration, subrogation, indemnity, and contribution. In addition to those rights, sureties also have certain defenses. They include ordinary contract defenses as well as some defenses peculiar to the suretyship relationship, such as release of collateral, change in loan terms, substitution of debtor, and fraud by the creditor.

A letter of credit is an agreement that the issuer of the letter will pay drafts drawn on the issuer by the beneficiary of the letter. The issuer of the letter of credit is usually a bank. There are three contracts involved in letter-of-credit transactions: (1) the contract between the issuer and the customer of the issuer, (2) the letter of credit itself, and (3) the underlying agreement between the beneficiary and the customer of the issuer of the letter of credit.

The parties to a letter of credit are the issuer, the customer who makes the arrangement with the issuer, and the beneficiary who will be the drawer of the drafts to be drawn under the letter of credit. The letter of credit continues for any time it specifies. The letter of credit must be in writing and signed by the issuer. Consideration is not required to establish or modify a letter of credit. If the conditions in the letter of credit have been complied with, the issuer is obligated to honor drafts drawn under the letter of credit.

---

[9] *CRM Collateral II, Inc. v. TriCounty Metropolitan Transp. Dist of Oregon,* 669 F.3d 963 (9th Cir. 2012). In some cases, letters of credit are so poorly drafted that payment must be made despite evolving concerns by the parties. *Nissho Iwai Europe PLC v. Korea First Bank,* 782 N.E.2d 55 (N.Y. 2002).

LEARNING OUTCOMES

After studying this chapter, you should be able to clearly explain:

A. Creation of the Credit Relationship
B. Suretyship and Guaranty

L0.1   Distinguish a contract of suretyship from a contract of guaranty
>   See the definitions on p. 672 and discussion of the terms related to surety and guaranty on p. 673.

L0.2   Define the parties to a contract of suretyship and a contract of guaranty
>   See the example on corporate officers and their relationship with company debt on p. 672.

L0.3   List and explain the rights of sureties to protect themselves from loss
>   See the *Feigenbaum v. Guaracini* case on p. 674.
>   See *Man-Data, Inc. v. B & A Automotive, Inc.*, on p. 675.

L0.4   Explain the defenses available to sureties

C. Letters of Credit

L0.5   Explain the nature of a letter of credit and the liabilities of the various parties to a letter of credit
>   See *Louisville Mall Associates, LP v. Wood Center Properties, LLC*, on pp. 680–681.

KEY TERMS

absolute guaranty	fraud	obligee
advising bank	guarantor	obligor
concealment	guaranty	pledge
contribution	guaranty of collection	principal
correspondent bank	guaranty of payment	principal debtor
co-sureties	indemnity	standby letter
creditor	indemnity contract	subrogation
debtor	issuer	surety
exoneration	letter of credit	suretyship

QUESTIONS AND CASE PROBLEMS

1. First Interstate Bank issued a letter of credit in favor of Comdata Network. Comdata is engaged in money transfer services. It provides money to truckers on the road by way of cash advances through form checks written by truckers. When Comdata enters into a business relationship with a trucking company, it requires a letter of credit. This requirement is to secure advances made on behalf of the trucking company. One of the trucking companies defrauded the bank that issued the letter of credit. Comdata demanded that the bank make payment to it under the letter of credit for cash advances that the trucking company had not repaid. The bank, alleging fraud by the trucking company, refused. Comdata filed suit. Can Comdata force payment? [*Comdata Network, Inc. v. First Interstate Bank of Fort Dodge*, 497 N.W.2d 807 (Iowa App.)]

2. LaBarge Pipe & Steel Company agreed to sell PVF $143,613.40 of 30-inch pipe provided that PVF obtain a letter of credit for $144,000, with the letter of credit entitling LaBarge to payment if PVF did not pay for the pipe within 30 days of invoice. PVF obtained the letter of credit from First Bank but received only a facsimile copy of it. The letter of credit required LaBarge to submit the original of the letter of credit for a demand of payment.

    PVF did not pay within 30 days and LaBarge submitted a facsimile copy of the letter of credit and requested payment. First Bank denied the request for payment and LaBarge filed suit against First Bank for failure to pay. LaBarge argued that it was not disputed that PVF had not paid on the contract and First Bank was required to pay on the letter of credit. How would you

explain First Bank's rights to LaBarge?
[*LaBarge Pipe & Steel Co. v. First Bank*, 550 F.3d
442 (5th Cir.)]

3. On August 1, 1987, Dori Leeds signed a
"guarantee of credit" with Sun Control Systems,
which guaranteed "the prompt payment, when
due, of every claim of [Sun Control Systems]
against [Dori Leeds dba 'Blind Ambitions']." At the
time she signed the guarantee of credit, Blind
Ambitions was in the business of installing window
treatments and installed only Faber brand blinds,
which were purchased from Sun Control Systems.
In 1991, Sun Control Systems sold and assigned all
of its assets to Faber. Shortly thereafter, Dori
assigned her interest in Blind Ambitions to David
and Judith Leeds, who continued to do business as
Blind Ambitions. In 1994 and 1995, Blind
Ambitions made credit purchases from Faber and
did not pay under the terms of those contracts.
Faber brought suit against Dori Leeds as the
guarantor of credit for Blind Ambitions. Dori
refused to pay on the grounds that she was acting
as a personal guarantor for her business, not for
Blind Ambitions. Is she correct? [*Faber
Industries, Ltd. v. Dori Leeds Witek*, 483 S.E.2d
443 (N.C. App.)]

4. Fern Schimke's husband, Norbert, was obligated
on two promissory notes in favor of Union
National Bank. Some time prior to his death,
Union National Bank prepared a guaranty
contract that was given to Norbert for his wife to
sign. She signed the guaranty at the request of
her husband without any discussion with him
about the provisions of the document she was
signing. On Norbert's death, the bank brought
suit against Fern on the basis of the guaranty.
Fern argued that because there was no
consideration for the guaranty, she could not
be liable. Is Fern correct? Must there be
consideration for a guarantor to be responsible for
payment? [*Union Nat'l Bank v. Fern Schimke*,
210 N.W.2d 176 (N.D.)]

5. In May 1989, Alma Equities Corp., owned by its
sole shareholder and president, Lewis Futterman,
purchased a hotel and restaurant in Vail,
Colorado, from Alien for $3,900,000. Alma paid
$600,000 in cash to Alien, and Alien provided a

purchase money loan to Alma for the remaining
amount of the sale price, with the loan secured
by a deed of trust on the hotel and restaurant.
The hotel and restaurant did not do well, and
Futterman negotiated a friendly foreclosure on
the property in 1991, whereby Alma would
continue to operate the hotel and restaurant on a
lease basis, with Futterman providing a personal
guaranty for the lease. Alma failed to make the
lease payments for the months of November and
December 1991 and, following an unlawful
detainer action filed by Alien for possession of
the hotel and restaurant, was forced into
bankruptcy. Alien turned to Futterman for
satisfaction on the lease payments. Futterman
said he should not have been forced to pay
because Alien's unlawful detainer forced Alma
into bankruptcy. Was Futterman correct? Did he
have a defense? [*Alien, Inc. v. Futterman*, 924
P.2d 1063 (Colo.)]

6. Charles Fontaine completed a form for Gordon
Contractors in which he signed that portion of
the form labeled "Name of Guarantor." His
signature followed immediately after a paragraph
beginning, "[I]n consideration of the extension of
credit by Gordon Building Supply Inc. the
undersigned customer hereby agrees that the
terms and conditions of all sales are as follows."
There was also a blank following this paragraph
for "Customer Name," and it was signed by a
Robert Schlaefli, although it is unclear whether
he signed it individually or as an agent. At the
beginning of the application, the blank for
"Name of Individual Applying" was filled in with
both Fontaine's and Schlaefli's names, and the
blank for "Name of Company or Business" bore
the words "McIntyre Development, Inc." Finally,
the blank for "Names of People Authorized to
Purchase" was filled in with Schlaefli's name and
that of a Glen Bush.

Upon default of the debtor (never clearly
identified in the agreement), Gordon Contractors
filed suit to collect from Fontaine as a guarantor.
Fontaine moved for summary judgment because
he was not identified on the contract as a
guarantor. The trial court granted Gordon
Contractors a summary judgment against
Fontaine, and Fontaine appealed. Determine the

parties' relationships and who is liable to whom. [*Fontaine v. Gordon Contractors Building Supply, Inc.*, 567 S.E.2d 324 (Ga. App.)]

7. Tri County Truck & Diesel borrowed $165,000 from Security State Bank and pledged its inventory as security for the loan. In addition, Fred and Randelle Burk agreed to act as sureties for the loan. Tri County defaulted on the loan and Security Bank repossessed the collateral. The inventory was damaged while Security Bank held it, and as a result, the sale of the inventory brought only $5,257.50 at a public auction. The Burks raised the defense of the damages as a setoff to their surety amount for the remainder of the loan. Security Bank said the Burks could not raise the damages as a defense because the Burks were sureties and had guaranteed the full amount of the loan. The trial court granted summary judgment for Security Bank, and the Burks appealed. What should the court do? [*Security State Bank v. Burk*, 995 P.2d 1272 (Wash App.)]

8. UPS Capital Business Credit agreed to loan Ashford International, Inc, an American company based in Atlanta, Georgia, for the sale of computers to the Ministry of Education in Jordan. Ashford was required to obtain a letter of credit from United California Discount Corporation (UCDC) for the loan. Ashford filed for bankruptcy and UPS submitted documentation for payment on the letter of credit. UCDC responded to the payment demand with a list of requirements for compliance with the letter of credit demands. UPS satisfied all the demands and UCDC then refused to pay because UPS did not submit original documents as required by the letter of credit. UPS maintains that UCDC waived that requirement by not listing it in its demands. Who is correct and why? [*Export-Import Bank of the U.S. v. United Cal. Discount Corp.*, 738 F. Supp. 2d 1047 (C.D. Cal. 2010)]

9. Ribaldgo Argo Consultores entered into a contract with R. M. Wade & Co. for the purchase of irrigation equipment. Ribaldgo obtained a letter of credit from Banco General, a bank with its principal place of business in Quito, Ecuador. The letter of credit required that Wade submit certain documents to obtain payment. The documents were submitted through Citibank as correspondent bank for Banco General. However, the documents were incomplete, and Citibank demanded additional information as required under the letter of credit. By the time Wade got the documents to Citibank, more than 15 days had expired, and the letter of credit required that Wade submit all documentation within 15 days of shipping the goods to obtain payment. Citibank refused to authorize the payment. Wade filed suit. Must Citibank pay? Why or why not? [*Banco General Runinahui, S.A. v. Citibank International*, 97 F.3d 480 (11th Cir.)]

10. Hugill agreed to deliver shingles to W. I. Carpenter Lumber Co. and furnished a surety bond to secure the faithful performance of the contract on his part. After a breach of the contract by Hugill, the lumber company brought an action to recover its loss from the surety, Fidelity & Deposit Co. of Maryland. The surety denied liability on the grounds that there was concealment of (a) the price to be paid for the shingles and (b) the fact that a material advance had been made to the contractor equal to the amount of the profit that he would make by performing the contract. Decide. [*W. I. Carpenter Lumber Co. v. Hugill*, 270 P.94 (Wash.)]

11. Donaldson sold plumbing supplies. The St. Paul-Mercury Indemnity Co., as surety for him, executed and delivered a bond to the state of California for the payment of all sales taxes. Donaldson failed to pay, and the surety paid the taxes that he owed and then sued him for the taxes. What was the result? [*St. Paul-Mercury Indemnity Co. v. Donaldson*, 83 S.E.2d 159 (S.C.)]

12. Paul owed Charles a $1,000 debt due September 1. On August 15, George, for consideration, orally promised Charles to pay the debt if Paul did not. On September 1, Paul did not pay, so Charles demanded $1,000 from George. Is George liable? Why or why not?

13. First National Bank hired Longdon as a secretary and obtained a surety bond from Belton covering the bank against losses up to $100,000 resulting from Longdon's improper conduct in the performance of his duties. Both Longdon and the

bank signed the application for the bond. After one year of service, Longdon was promoted to teller, and the original bond remained in effect. Shortly after Longdon's promotion, examination showed that Longdon had taken advantage of his new position and stolen $50,000. He was arrested and charged with embezzlement. Longdon had only $5,000 in assets at the time of his arrest. (a) If the bank demands a payment of $50,000 from Belton, what defense, if any, might Belton raise to deny any obligation to the bank? (b) If Belton fully reimburses the bank for its loss, under what theory or theories, if any, may Belton attempt to recover from Longdon?

14. Jack Smith was required by his bank to obtain two sureties for his line of credit of $100,000. Ellen Weiss has agreed to act as a surety for $50,000, and Allen Fox has agreed to act as a surety for $75,000. Smith has used the full $100,000 in the line of credit and is now in bankruptcy. What is the maximum liability of Weiss and Fox if the bank chooses to collect from them for Smith's default? How should the $100,000 be allocated between Weiss and Fox?

15. Industrial Mechanical had a contract with Free Flow Cooling, Ltd., a British company. Free Flow owed Industrial $171,974.44 for work Industrial had performed on a construction project in Texas. Free Flow did not pay Industrial, and Industrial filed suit against Siemens Energy & Automation as a guarantor or surety on the debt. Industrial alleges that Siemens is a surety based on a fax it received from Siemens on January 27, 1994. The fax is handwritten and states: "We have received preliminary notices and we like [*sic*] to point out that the contract we have signed does not allow for such action to recourse [*sic*] with the customer. Please advise all subcontractors and suppliers that the only recourse that they will have is against Siemens." The fax was signed "kind regards" by Arnold Schultz, Siemens's senior project manager for the Texas construction project. Nowhere in the fax did Siemens guarantee the debt of any specified entity or state that Siemens was agreeing to indemnify anyone or pay the obligations on behalf of anyone else. The fax failed to identify the principal debtor whom Siemens purportedly agreed to indemnify and failed to state that Siemens agreed to answer for that entity's debt. Can Industrial collect the amount of Free Flow's debt from Siemens? Why or why not? [*Industrial Mechanical, Inc. v. Siemens Energy & Automation, Inc.*, 495 S.E.2d 103 (Ga. App.)]

CPA QUESTIONS

1. Marbury Surety, Inc., agreed to act as a guarantor of collection of Madison's trade accounts for one year beginning on April 30, 1980, and was compensated for same. Madison's trade debtors are in default in payment of $3,853 as of May 1, 1981. As a result:

   a. Marbury is liable to Madison without any action on Madison's part to collect the amounts due.

   b. Madison can enforce the guaranty even if it is not in writing because Marbury is a del credere agent.

   c. The relationship between the parties must be filed in the appropriate county office because it is a continuing security transaction.

   d. Marbury is liable for those debts for which a judgment is obtained and returned unsatisfied.

2. Queen paid Pax and Co. to become the surety on a loan that Queen obtained from Squire. The loan is due, and Pax wishes to compel Queen to pay Squire. Pax has not made any payments to Squire in its capacity as Queen's surety. Pax will be most successful if it exercises its right to

   a. Reimbursement (indemnification)

   b. Contribution

   c. Exoneration

   d. Subrogation

3. Which of the following defenses by a surety will be effective to avoid liability?

   a. Lack of consideration to support the surety undertaking

   b. Insolvency in the bankruptcy sense of the debtor

   c. Incompetency of the debtor to make the contract in question

   d. Fraudulent statements by the principal debtor that induced the surety to assume the obligation and that were unknown to the creditor

4. For each of the numbered words or phrases, select the one best phrase from the list a through j. Each response may be used only once.

   (1) Indemnity contract

   (2) Suretyship contract

   (3) Surety

   (4) Third-party beneficiary

   (5) Co-surety

   (6) Statute of frauds

   (7) Right of contribution

   (8) Reimbursement

   (9) Subrogation

   (10) Exoneration

      a. Relationship whereby one person agrees to answer for the debt or default of another

      b. Requires certain contracts to be in writing to be enforceable

      c. Jointly and severally liable to creditor

   d. Promises to pay debt on default of principal debtor

   e. One party promises to reimburse debtor for payment of debt or loss if it arises

   f. Receives intended benefits of a contract

   g. Right of surety to require the debtor to pay before surety pays

   h. Upon payment of more than his/her proportionate share, each co-surety may compel other co-sureties to pay their shares

   i. Upon payment of debt, surety may recover payment from debtor

   j. Upon payment, surety obtains same rights against debtor that creditor had

4. When a principal debtor defaults and a surety pays the creditor the entire obligation, which of the following remedies gives the surety the best method of collecting from the debtor?

   a. Exoneration

   b. Contribution

   c. Subrogation

   d. Attachment

5. Which of the following bonds are an obligation of a surety?

   a. Convertible bonds.

   b. Debenture bonds.

   c. Municipal bonds.

   d. Official bonds.

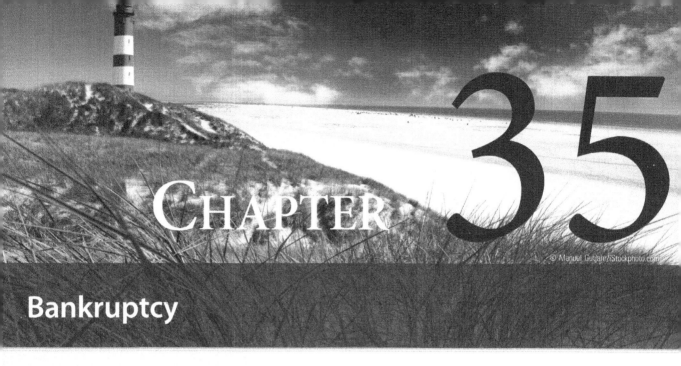

CHAPTER 35

Bankruptcy

© Manuel Gutjahr/iStockphoto.com

learningoutcomes

After studying this chapter, you should be able to

LO.1 List the requirements for the commencement of a voluntary bankruptcy case and an involuntary bankruptcy case

LO.2 Explain the procedure for the administration of a debtor's estate

LO.3 List a debtor's duties and exemptions

LO.4 Explain the significance of a discharge in bankruptcy

LO.5 Explain when a business reorganization plan or an extended-time payment plan might be used

W hat can a person or business do when overwhelmed by debts? Bankruptcy proceedings can provide temporary and sometimes permanent relief from those debts.

A. BANKRUPTCY LAW

Bankruptcy is a statutory proceeding with detailed procedures and requirements.

1. The Federal Law

Bankruptcy law is based on federal statutes that have been refined over the years. In October 2005, the Bankruptcy Abuse Prevention and Consumer Protection Act of 2005 (BAPCPA) took effect.[1] The BAPCPA was passed more than 10 years after the Bankruptcy Reform Commission was created, and the changes in bankruptcy law reflect an expressed congressional desire to curb a 15-year trend of increases in the number of bankruptcies.

Jurisdiction over bankruptcy proceedings is vested in the federal district courts. The district courts have the authority to transfer such matters to courts of special jurisdiction called **bankruptcy courts**.

bankruptcy courts – court of special jurisdiction to determine bankruptcy issues.

2. Types of Bankruptcy Proceedings

The three types of bankruptcy proceedings that existed before the 2005 reforms are still available to individuals and businesses.

CPA

Chapter 7 bankruptcy – liquidation form of bankruptcy under federal law.

liquidation – process of converting property into money whether of particular items of property or of all the assets of a business or an estate.

(A) LIQUIDATION OR CHAPTER 7 BANKRUPTCY. A **Chapter 7 bankruptcy** is one in which all of the debtor's assets (with some exemptions) will be **liquidated** to pay debts. Those debts that remain unpaid or are paid only partially are discharged, with some exceptions. The debtor who declares Chapter 7 bankruptcy begins again with a nearly clean slate.

Chapter 7 bankruptcy is available to individuals, partnerships, and corporations. However, farmers, insurance companies, savings and loans, municipalities, Small Business Administration companies, and railroads are not entitled to declare Chapter 7 bankruptcy because they are specifically governed by other statutes or specialized sections of the Bankruptcy Code.[2]

Under the BAPCPA, consumers generally cannot go directly to a Chapter 7 liquidation bankruptcy because they must demonstrate that they do not have the means to repay the debts before they can do a Chapter 7 liquidation.[3] The means test, which is discussed later, considers the disposable income that is available after the bankruptcy court has deducted allowable expenses that are listed as part of the means section of the BAPCPA, including items such as health insurance and child support.

---

[1] Pub. L. No. 109-8, 119 Stat. 23 (2005); the act is codified at 11 U.S.C. §101 *et seq.*

[2] For example, the Small Business Investment Act governs the insolvency of small business investment companies, 11 U.S.C. §109(b). Municipalities' bankruptcies are governed by Chapter 9 of the Bankruptcy Code, and farmers' bankruptcies are covered under Chapter 12. Following the 2008 market collapse, there were a series of municipal bankruptcies because of excessive debt and pension obligations.

[3] 11 U.S.C. §707(C)(2)(a). There are exceptions to the requirements of establishing no means, such as those who incurred their debts while on active military service.

Ethics & the Law

Bankruptcy Records

According to **www.bankruptcydata.com**, the following are the largest bankruptcies in the history of the United States:

Company	Date	Amount
Lehman Brothers	09/15/2008	$691,000,000 billion
Washington Mutual (WaMu)	09/26/2008	$327,900,000 billion
WorldCom	07/21/2002	$103,900,000 billion
General Motors	06/01/2009	$91,000,000 billion
CIT	11/01/2009	$80,400,000 billion
Enron	12/02/2001	$65,500,000 billion
Conseco	12/02/2002	$61,300,000 billion
MF Global	10/31/2011	$40,500,000 billion
Chrysler	04/20/2009	$39,300,000 billion
Thornburg Mortgage	05/05/2009	$36,500,000 billion

Total bankruptcy filings in the United States from 2005 to 2011 were as follows. Note the significant drop following the 2005 reforms, followed by the spike in 2008 because of the economic crisis.

Year	Total	Nonbusiness	Business
2011	1,410,653	1,362,847	47,806
2010	1,593,081	1,536,799	56,282
2009	1,473,675	1,412,838	60,837
2008	1,117,641	1,074,108	43,533
2007	850,912	822,590	28,322
2006	617,660	597,965	19,695
2005	2,078,415	2,039,214	39,201

Is there an ethical component to declaring bankruptcy? For example, actor Gary Busey's agent referred to bankruptcy as a business strategy. What are the risks of using bankruptcy as a business strategy?

CPA

Chapter 11 bankruptcy – reorganization form of bankruptcy under federal law.

(B) REORGANIZATION OR CHAPTER 11 BANKRUPTCY. Chapter 11 bankruptcy is a way for a debtor to reorganize and continue a business with protection from overwhelming debts and without the requirement of liquidation. Chrysler, General Motors, United Airlines, and Delta are all examples of companies that have gone through Chapter 11 bankruptcies. Stockbrokers, however, are not eligible for Chapter 11 bankruptcy.

CPA

Chapter 13 bankruptcy – proceeding of consumer debt readjustment plan bankruptcy.

(C) CHAPTER 13 BANKRUPTCY OR PAYMENT PLANS OR CONSUMER DEBT ADJUSTMENT PLANS. Chapter 13 of the federal Bankruptcy Code provides consumers an individual form of reorganization. Chapter 13 works with consumer debtors to develop a plan to repay debt. To be eligible for **Chapter 13 bankruptcy**, the individual must owe unsecured debts of less than $360,475 and secured debts of less than $1,081,400 and have regular income.[4] Chapter 13 plays an expanded role in bankruptcy because reforms require debtors with the means to pay their debts to go first into Chapter 13 bankruptcy rather than automatically declaring Chapter 7 bankruptcy.

B. HOW BANKRUPTCY IS DECLARED

Bankruptcy can be declared in different ways. The federal Bankruptcy Code spells out the requirements and process for declaration.

---

[4] 11 U.S.C. §109(e).

3. Declaration of Voluntary Bankruptcy

voluntary bankruptcy – proceeding in which the debtor files the petition for relief.

A **voluntary bankruptcy** is begun when the debtor files a petition with the bankruptcy court. A joint petition may be filed by a husband and wife. When a voluntary case is begun, the debtor must file a schedule of current income and current expenditures unless the court excuses this filing.

Under the 2005 reforms, a court can dismiss an individual debtor's (consumer's) petition for abuse if the debtor does not satisfy the **means test**, which measures the debtor's ability to pay by computing the debtor's disposable income. Only those debtors who fall below their state's median disposable income will be able to continue in a Chapter 7 proceeding. Individual debtors who meet the means test are required to go into Chapter 13 bankruptcy because they have not qualified for Chapter 7 bankruptcy. The formula for applying the means test is as follows:

means test – new standard under the Reform Act that requires the court to find that the debtor does not have the means to repay creditors; goes beyond the past requirement of petitions being granted on the simple assertion of the debtor saying, "I have debts."

Debtor's current monthly income less
Allowable expenses under the Bankruptcy Code = Disposable income
Disposable income × 60

The debtor commits bankruptcy abuse if this number is not less than the lower of the following:

- 25 percent of the debtor's unsecured claims or $7,025, whichever is greater; or

- $11,725

A finding of abuse means that the debtor's Chapter 7 voluntary petition is dismissed. Previously, the law required the judge to find "substantial abuse" before dismissing the petition; now the standard reads only "abuse."[5]

Under the BAPCPA, the bankruptcy judge also has the discretion to order the debtor's lawyer to reimburse the trustee for costs and attorney's fees and to assess a civil penalty against the lawyer if the court finds that the lawyer has not acted in good faith in filing the debtor's bankruptcy petition.[6] As part of this change, lawyers must declare themselves (in public ads as well as in any individual meetings with clients) to be "debt relief agencies" or state that they "help people file for relief under the Bankruptcy Code." The Code now requires those who help consumers deal with their creditors to disclose that part of the assistance could include filing for bankruptcy. Lawyers who advertise their credit/bankruptcy expertise are subject to the laws and regulations that apply to debt relief agencies. If the agency/lawyer advises them to do something that causes the court to declare that there has been bankruptcy abuse, the lawyer/debt relief agency is responsible as well. As part of their role as debt counselors, lawyers are prohibited under the changes in the law from advising clients to undertake more debt in contemplation of filing bankruptcy.[7]

Debtors are required to undergo credit counseling (from an approved nonprofit credit counseling agency) within the 180 days prior to declaring a bankruptcy. In addition, the court applies the means test described earlier to determine whether the debtor qualifies for bankruptcy.[8]

---

[5] 11 U.S.C. §707(b). *In re Lapke*, 428 B.R. 839 (8th Cir. 2010). A debtor who increased his federal income tax withholding to 85% prior to filing bankruptcy and earned over $200,000 per year as a pathologist was guilty of bad faith. *In re Laine*, 383 B.R. 166 (D. Kan. 2008).

[6] 11 U.S.C. §707(b)(4).

[7] 11 U.S.C. §§526–528. *Milavetz, Gallop & Milavetz, P.A. v. U.S.*, 130 S.Ct. 1324 (2010).

[8] 11 U.S.C. §109(h)(2). There are exceptions to the counseling requirements; for example, active military duty, disability, and emergencies. 11 U.S.C. 111(a) is the counseling provision. The counseling must be completed prior to filing for bankruptcy or the petition can be dismissed, *In re Ingram*, 460 B.R. 904 (6th Cir. 2011).

There is significant disagreement among the bankruptcy courts about the meaning of "projected income." The disagreement results from the differing situations of the debtors. **For Example,** how do courts deal with debtors who are about to experience a large drop in disposable income? And do courts then consider what happens when debtors' incomes are expected to go up? If the projected income test used is applied, the bankruptcy could be dismissed. Debtors and creditors take different positions depending on which way the income goes, and the courts continue to debate the definition of projected income.[9]

CASE SUMMARY

Disposable Income and Predisposed Not to Pay

FACTS: The Jasses filed for Chapter 13 bankruptcy relief. Their Form B22C indicated that their yearly household aggregate income was $143,403.96 based on income they received during the six-month period before filing. After deducting allowed expenses and deductions from their income, the Jasses' Statement of Current Monthly Income showed a "disposable income" of $3,625.63 per month.

The Jasses filed a Chapter 13 plan, which proposed to return $790.00 per month to unsecured creditors. At the hearing, the trustee objected to confirmation because the Jasses' "disposable income," as calculated on their Form B22C, was $3,625.63, and they proposed to pay only $790.00 to unsecured creditors. The trustee argued that because the Jasses were not proposing to pay their full disposable income of $3,625.63 to unsecured creditors, their plan did not comply with this "disposable income test."

The Jasses argued that the word "projected" in the statute modifies the definition of "disposable income." Mrs. Jass testified that beginning in December 2005, her husband experienced serious medical problems involving injuries to his intestines. She testified that her family incurred $12,000 in medical expenses. In light of these expenses and medical problems, the Jasses argued that their income in the future would not be commensurate with the "disposable income" shown on Form B22C. They argued that the changes under the BAPCPA did not require them to pay unsecured creditors the amount resulting from their Form B22C, so long as they could show that the income and expenses reported on the Form were inadequate representations of their future budget.

DECISION: The court held that the word *projected* modifies *disposable income* and that the Code intended that the disposable income figure be based on "projected income." The court acknowledged that the debtor would need to provide testimony regarding the change in circumstances that would result in a reduction of the income but also noted that without the word *projected* being used, the parties to a bankruptcy would be deprived of the fresh-start purpose the laws were intended to provide. They could not pay more money to creditors than they would be earning and their change in health and financial circumstances meant that they would simply not have the funds available to pay all that the form computed. [*In re Jass,* 340 B.R. 411 (Utah 2006)]

---

[9] *In re Turner,* 425 B.R. 918 (S.D. Ga. 2010); *In re Hilton,* 395 B.R. 433 (E.D. Wis. 2008); *In re Anstett,* 383 B.R. 380 (D.S.C. 2008); *In re Colclasure,* 383 B.R. 463 (E.D. Ark. 2008); and *In re Justice,* 418 B.R. 342 (W.D. Mo. 2009).

Thinking Things Through

Means Test Justifying the End of Debt

The following excerpt is a hypothetical case an experienced bankruptcy attorney worked through to illustrate the application of the means test.

The Brokes, a married couple in their early 40s, have two children in private schools. They are residents of Memphis, Shelby County, Tennessee; their annual gross income is $86,496. Like many debtors, the Brokes lost their home following an unsuccessful Chapter 13 case three years ago. They now rent a house for $2,000 a month. They owe back federal taxes in the amount of $9,000. They have secured debt on two cars with remaining balances of $10,000 and $6,000 and unsecured, consumer debt totaling $28,000. They desire to seek relief under Chapter 7 of the Bankruptcy Code.

The Brokes' gross monthly income is $7,208. After deducting taxes and other mandatory payroll deductions of $1,509, the couple has $5,699 in monthly income. The means test requires several additional deductions from the Brokes' gross monthly income. Section 707(b)(A)(2)(ii) provides a deduction for living and housing expenses using National Standards and Local Standards and additional Internal Revenue Service (IRS) figures. Allowable living expenses for a family of four in Ura and Ima Brokes' income bracket, based on national standards, total $1,564, while housing and utility figures for Shelby County, Tennessee, allow $1,354. In addition, there are allowable expenses for transportation. Based on IRS figures, the Brokes can subtract national ownership costs of $475 for the first car and $338 for the second, as well as regional operating and public transportation costs of $242 and $336, respectively. They can also deduct their

reasonably necessary health insurance costs, here the sum of $600, and $250 a month for private school tuition. Subtracting all of these figures from the Brokes' monthly income leaves $540.

Under §707(b)(2)(A)(iii), the Brokes can subtract payments on secured debt. The amount contractually due on their two automobiles over the next 60 months is $16,000. After dividing this total by 60 and rounding to the nearest dollar, the monthly allowable deduction for secured debt is $267. Subtracting this amount from $540 leaves $273.

Next come priority claim deductions. The Brokes are not subject to any child support or alimony claims, but they do owe $9,000 in back taxes. Again, dividing this amount by 60 yields a deductible amount of $150. Subtracting this from $273 leaves $123 in disposable monthly income. This figure would be multiplied by 60, amounting to a total of $7,380 in disposable income over the five-year period. Abuse is thus statutorily presumed because the debtors' current monthly income reduced by allowable amounts is not less than either $7,000 (25 percent of their nonpriority unsecured claims of $28,000) or $6,000. The Brokes' Chapter 7 case will therefore be dismissed (or they will be allowed voluntarily to convert their Chapter 7 case to a case under Chapter 13).

Does the means test make it more difficult for debtors to declare bankruptcy?*

*Robert J. Landry III and Nancy Hisey Mardis, "Consumer Bankruptcy Reform: Debtors' Prison without Bars or 'Just Desserts' for Deadbeats?" 36 *Golden Gate U. L. Rev.* 91 (2006). Reprinted with permission.

CPA

4. Declaration of Involuntary Bankruptcy

involuntary bankruptcy – proceeding in which a creditor or creditors file the petition for relief with the bankruptcy court.

(A) ELIGIBILITY. An **involuntary bankruptcy** is begun when creditors file a petition with the bankruptcy court. An involuntary case may be commenced against any individual, partnership, or corporation, except those excluded from filing voluntary petitions. Nonprofit corporations are also exempt from involuntary proceedings.[10]

CPA

(B) NUMBER AND CLAIMS OF PETITIONING CREDITORS. If there are 12 or more creditors, at least 3 of those creditors whose unsecured and undisputed claims total $14,425 or more must sign the involuntary petition.[11] If there are fewer than 12 creditors, excluding employees or insiders (that is, the debtor's relatives, partners, directors, and controlling

---

[10] 11 U.S.C. §303(a). *In re C.W. Min. Co.*, 431 B.R. 307 (Utah 2009). These amounts are adjusted periodically by statutory formulas.
[11] 11 U.S.C. §303. The term "undisputed" was added to this section. *In re Memorial Medical Center, Inc.*, 337 B.R. 388 (D.N.M. 2005).

persons), any creditor whose unsecured claim is at least $14,425 may sign the petition. In the case of involuntary consumer petitions, there is disagreement as to whether the debtor will still be required to complete the credit counseling requirement prior to the granting of the automatic stay.

bona fide–in good faith; without any fraud or deceit.

If a creditor holds security for a claim, only the amount of the claim in excess of the value of the security is counted. The holder of a claim that is the subject of a **bona fide** dispute may not be counted as a petitioning creditor.[12] **For Example,** David, a CPA, is an unsecured creditor of Arco Company for $15,000. Arco has a total of 10 creditors, all of whom are unsecured. Arco has not paid any of the creditors for three months. The debtor has fewer than 12 creditors. Any one of the creditors may file the petition if the unsecured portion of the amount due that creditor is at least $14,425.[13] Because David is owed $15,000 in unsecured debts, he may file the petition alone.

CPA

(C) **GROUNDS FOR RELIEF FOR INVOLUNTARY CASE.** The mere filing of an involuntary case petition does not result in an order of relief. The debtor may contest the bankruptcy petition. If the debtor does not contest the petition, the court will enter an order of relief if at least one of the following grounds exists: (1) The debtor is generally not paying debts as they become due or (2) within 120 days before the filing of the petition, a custodian has been appointed for the debtor's property.

FIGURE 35-1	*Declaration of Bankruptcy*

	Chapter 7	Chapter 11	Chapter 13
Trustee	Yes	No	Yes
Eligible persons: Individuals Partnerships Corporations	Yes (consumer restrictions) yes Yes	Yes (individual restrictions) yes Yes	Yes (consumer restrictions) No No
Voluntary	Yes	Yes	Yes
Involuntary	Yes, except for farmers and nonprofits**	Yes, except for farmers and nonprofits	No
Exemptions	S & L's, credit unions, SBA, railroads, municipalities	Same as chapter 7 plus stockbrokers*	Only individuals allowed
Requirements-Voluntary	Debts; means test applies to consumers	Debts; means test applies to consumers	Income plus<$360,475 unsecured debt; <$1,081,400 secured debt
Requirements-Involuntary	<12 = 1/$14,425 ≥12 = 3/$14,425	<12 = 1/$14,425 ≥12 = 3/$14,425	N/a

*Railroads are eligible
**Chapter 9 — Municipalities; Chapter 12 — Farmers

[12] 11 U.S.C. §303(b)(1). *In re Ballato*, 252 B.R. 553 (M.D. Fla. 2000).
[13] The amount was $10,000 originally, but the bankruptcy reforms had a built-in clause for increases in this figure.

CPA

automatic stay – order to prevent creditors from taking action such as filing suits or seeking foreclosure against the debtor.

5. Automatic Stay

Just the filing of either a voluntary or an involuntary petition operates as an **automatic stay**, which prevents creditors from taking action, such as filing suits or foreclosure actions, against the debtor.[14] The stay freezes all creditors in their filing date positions so that no one creditor gains an advantage over other creditors. This automatic stay ends when the bankruptcy case is closed or dismissed (for example, on a finding of abuse by the debtor who has failed to survive the means-to-pay test) or when the debtor is granted a discharge. An automatic stay means that all activity by creditors with respect to collection must stop, with some exceptions incorporated for child support and other family support issues under the 2005 reforms. All litigation with the debtor is halted, and any judgments in place cannot be executed.[15]

6. If the Creditors Are Wrong: Rights of Debtor in an Involuntary Bankruptcy

If an involuntary petition is dismissed other than by consent of all petitioning creditors and the debtor, the court may award costs, reasonable attorney fees, or damages to the debtor. The damages are those that were caused by taking possession of the debtor's property. The debtor may also recover damages against any creditor who filed the petition in bad faith.[16]

Figure 35-1 provides a summary of the requirements for declaration of bankruptcy and the standards for relief.

C. ADMINISTRATION OF THE BANKRUPTCY ESTATE

The administration of the bankruptcy estate varies according to the type of bankruptcy declared. This section of the chapter focuses on the process for liquidation or Chapter 7 bankruptcy. Figure 35-2 provides a flowchart view of the Chapter 7 liquidation process.

7. The Order of Relief

order of relief – the order from the bankruptcy judge that starts the protection for the debtor; when the order of relief is entered by the court, the debtor's creditors must stop all proceedings and work through the bankruptcy court to recover debts (if possible). Court finding that creditors have met the standards for bankruptcy petitions.

The **order of relief** is granted by the bankruptcy court and is the procedural step required for the case to proceed in bankruptcy court.[17] An order of relief is entered automatically in a voluntary case and in an involuntary case when those filing the petition have established that the debtor is unable to pay his, her, or its debts as they become due. In consumer cases and Chapter 11 cases that involve an individual, the bankruptcy court must apply the means test to determine whether the individual is eligible for declaring bankruptcy or whether there has been an abuse of the bankruptcy court and system.

---

[14] 11 U.S.C. §362. *In re Webb*, 2012 WL 1150139 (Ohio) and *In re Wolverine Fire Apparatus Co. of Sherwood Michigan*, 465 B.R. 808 (E.D. Wis. 2012). Proceeding with the foreclosure on a home after a stay is entered is a violation of the stay order. *In re Gonzalez*, 456 B.R. 429 (C.D. Cal. 2011).

[15] The reforms exempt dissolution, custody, child support, and other related litigation from the stay.

[16] *Arizona Public Service v. Apache County*, 857 P. 2d 1339 (Ariz. App. 1993).

[17] 11 U.S.C. §301.

Sports & Entertainment Law

From Millions to Nada: Celebrity Bankruptcies

- Michael Vick, who was one of the highest paid NFL players, filed for bankruptcy in 2008, from prison. Mr. Vick could not afford to pay his bills as well as the fines that were imposed when he entered a guilty plea on charges related to a dog-fighting operation. The former Atlanta Falcons player would not have the fines discharged in bankruptcy, but he was relieved of his other debts related to his personal property.

- MC Hammer, the "Hammer Time" mega star of the early 1990s declared bankruptcy in 1996 with $9.6 million in assets and $13.7 million in debts. Mr. Hammer's problem was that he had salary costs of $500,000 per month in order to maintain his entourage.

- Mike Tyson, the champ, facing sexual harassment charges, and the lawyer fees that go with them, declared bankruptcy in 2003. Today, Mr. Tyson says that he is broke but happy.

- Willie Nelson, Country Western singer, declared bankruptcy in 1990, a necessary result of his owing $16.7 million in taxes because the IRS won its case on Nelson's tax shelters, which were fraudulent. Mr. Nelson also said that he had too many hangers-on that he was supporting. Mr. Nelson was not able to get all of his tax debt discharged because the last three years survive bankruptcy. That is, not all tax debts are fully dischargeable and there is no discharge allowed for tax debts that resulted from fraud.

- Walt Disney, the founder of Disney Films, Disneyland, Disney World, and Disney Entertainment, declared bankruptcy in Kansas City before he moved to Hollywood. Mr. Disney ran a small animation studio there and when his only customer went bankrupt, Mr. Disney tried to continue on, living in his office and eating only canned beans. He eventually gave up, declared bankruptcy, and moved to Hollywood, where his animation skills were welcomed and, as a result, he founded an empire.

- Sir Elton John is the quintessential profligate spender whose purchases landed him in bankruptcy. By the time he declared bankruptcy in 2002, Sir Elton had credit card charges of $400,000 per month. His total debt per month was $2,000,000. He was discharged from most of his credit card and contract debt.

- Sinbad, the comedian, failed to pay taxes on his earnings from *Jingle All the Way*. California's Department of Revenue filed a $2.5 million lien on his home and he and his wife declared bankruptcy shortly after in 2009. Again, California will be paid, but the comedian and his spouse are relieved of other debts.

- Gary Coleman, the 4'8" comedian/actor, simply could not pay all the medical bills related to his various health problems. He was once worth $7,000,000 but declared bankruptcy with $72,000 in debt and no assets. The actor passed away in 2010 and there is an ongoing dispute among relatives over his estate, which grew after his bankruptcy.

What are the causes of bankruptcy? What advice would you give to celebrities and athletes about management of their income and bills?

8. List of Creditors

It is the debtor's responsibility to furnish the bankruptcy court with a list of creditors. Although imposing the responsibility for disclosing debts on the debtor may not seem to be effective, the debtor has an incentive for full disclosure. Those debts not disclosed by the debtor will not be discharged in bankruptcy.

9. Trustee in Bankruptcy

trustee in bankruptcy – impartial person elected to administer the debtor's estate.

The **trustee in bankruptcy** is elected by the creditors. The court or the U.S. trustee will appoint an interim trustee if the creditors do not elect a trustee.

The trustee is the successor to the property rights of the debtor. By operation of law, the trustee automatically becomes the owner of all of the debtor's property in excess of the property to which the debtor is entitled under exemption laws. The trustee holds all of the rights formerly owned by the debtor.

FIGURE 35-2	*Anatomy of Bankruptcy Case*

© Cengage Learning

CPA ## 10. The Bankrupt's Estate

All of the debtor's property, with certain exceptions discussed later, is included in the *bankrupt's estate*. Property inherited by the debtor within six months after the filing of the petition also passes to the trustee.

In many cases, when a debtor knows that insolvency is a problem and bankruptcy is imminent, the debtor attempts to hang onto property or reputation by making transfers of assets to friends, relatives, and creditors. However, trustees have the authority to set aside or void (1) transfers by the debtor that a creditor holding a valid claim under state law could have avoided at the commencement of the bankruptcy case, (2) **preferences**, that is, transfers of property by the debtor to a creditor, the effect of which is to enable the creditor to obtain payment of a higher

preferences – transfers of property by a debtor to one or more specific creditors to enable these creditors to obtain payment for debts owed.

percentage of the creditor's claim than the creditor would have received if the debtor's assets had been liquidated in bankruptcy, and (3) statutory liens that became effective against the debtor at the commencement of the bankruptcy.

11. Voidable Preferences

A debtor may not transfer property to prevent creditors from satisfying their legal claims. The trustee may void any such transfer, known as a *fraudulent transfer,* made or obligation incurred by the debtor within two years of bankruptcy when the debtor's actual intent was to hinder, delay, or defraud creditors by doing so.[18]

The trustee may also void certain transfers of property made by a debtor merely because their effect is to make the debtor insolvent or to reduce the debtor's assets to an unreasonably low amount.[19]

(A) THE INSOLVENT DEBTOR. A debtor is insolvent for purposes of determining voidable transfers when the total fair value of all of the debtor's assets does not exceed the debts owed by the debtor. This test for **insolvency** under voidable transfers is commonly called the **balance sheet test** because it is merely a comparison of assets to liabilities without considering whether the debtor will be able to meet future obligations as they become due. The debtor is presumed to be insolvent in the 90 days prior to declaration of bankruptcy.

(B) PREFERENTIAL TRANSFERS. A transfer of property by the debtor to a creditor may be set aside as **preferential transfers** and the property recovered by the debtor's trustee in bankruptcy if (1) the transfer was made to pay a debt incurred at some earlier time, (2) the transfer was made when the debtor was insolvent and within 90 days before the filing of the bankruptcy petition, and (3) the transfer resulted in the creditor receiving more than the creditor would have received in a liquidation of the debtor's estate. A debtor is presumed to be insolvent on and during the 90 days immediately preceding the date of the filing of the bankruptcy petition.[20]

Transfers made to **insiders** within the 12 months prior to the filing of the petition may be set aside.[21] **For Example,** if a building contractor transferred title to one of his model homes to the company accountant just six months before declaring bankruptcy, the transfer would be a preferential one that would be set aside. However, a transfer by an insider to a noninsider is not subject to recovery by the trustee. The sale of that same model home to a good faith buyer just three days before bankruptcy would be valid. **For Example,** the trustee in the Bernie Madoff case sought to set aside several transfers made to companies and individuals just prior to the time Mr. Madoff admitted that he had an insolvent, $50-billion Ponzi scheme. The trustee used several of the voidable preferences theories to seek a return of funds.

The trustee may not set aside certain transfers by a debtor as preferences. A transaction for present consideration, such as a cash sale, is not set aside.[22] A payment by a debtor in the ordinary course of business, such as the payment of a utility bill, will not be set aside. Under the prior bankruptcy law, a payment was not

CPA

insolvency—excess of debts and liabilities over assets, or inability to pay debts as they mature.

balance sheet test—comparison of assets to liabilities made to determine solvency.

preferential transfers—certain transfers of money or security interests in the time frame just prior to bankruptcy that can be set aside if voidable.

insider—full-time corporate employee or a director or their relatives.

[18] Prior to the reforms, the time period for fraudulent transfers was one year. *Grochocinski v. Schlossberg*, 402 B.R. 825 (N.D. Ill. 2009).
[19] 11 U.S.C. §548.
[20] 11 U.S.C. §547(f).
[21] 11 U.S.C. §547(b)(4)(B). *In re Manhattan Inv. Fund Ltd.*, 421 B.R. 613 (S.D.N.Y. 2009).
[22] *In re Smith Min. and Material, LLC*, 405 B.R. 589 (W.D. Ky. 2009).

a voidable preference if it was made in the ordinary course of business and it was made according to industry terms and practices. Under the 2005 reforms, the *and* is changed to *or,* and it is now easier for creditors to show that they were not the recipients of a voidable preference. Also under the 2005 reforms, nonconsumer debt payments that have a value of less than $5,850 are not subject to the voidable preference standards. The expectation is that the time and effort spent by bankruptcy trustees and courts will be reduced because of the minimum amount required before a challenge can be made. In nonconsumer debts, transfers of less than $5,850 within the voidable preference period are not considered voidable preferences.

CASE SUMMARY

Favoring Friends and Paying Early and Often

FACTS: Ames Department Stores operated over 400 retail stores throughout the northeastern United States. Promotions and advertising were crucial to Ames' business strategy, and Ames attributed over 50 percent of store revenue to advertised sales. Cellmark was Ames' principal paper supplier for all of these circulars, including the Home Book. Ames was also one of Cellmark's largest customers and top credit exposures.

Between June 1, 2000, and the beginning of the preference period —90 days before Ames filed for Chapter 11 bankruptcy on August 20, 2001—Ames employed an automated accounts payable system created by Oracle to track orders and generate payments to all of its domestic merchandise vendors. During that same period, Ames paid invoices in full at or around the invoice due date, because its computerized payables system automatically printed checks according to payment due date without regard to the identity of the vendor. The computer-generated checks were routinely mailed to vendors within a day or two of being printed. In the three years of the parties' prior dealings, Cellmark issued approximately 300 invoices to Ames.

In May 2001, as Ames' cash was becoming increasingly tight, Ames executives, including CFO Rolando de Aguiar, began holding regular meetings to decide which vendors should be paid. The decisions were based on the identity of the vendor and the needs of Ames' business. By August 2001, in the last three weeks before Ames' Chapter 11 filing, Ames was not issuing any checks to its creditors through a general check run. Instead, Ames issued checks only to pay invoices specifically selected out of the Oracle database and based on specific requests.

Eugene Bankers, Ames' Senior Vice President of Marketing and Advertising, repeatedly inquired about the status of payments to Cellmark.

Bankers communicated to others at Ames that if Ames did not send payment to Cellmark, Ames would not get the circular out, and it would go out of business. Bankers told Cellmark CEO Joe Hoffman that he was "aggressive with [Ames'] finance department to make sure that checks sent were being sent on a continuity [sic] basis to them."

The bankruptcy trustee sought to recover approximately $1.9 million that Ames had made by three checks to Cellmark for four invoices in the two weeks before filing for bankruptcy:

1. a check for $700,000.00 (the "$700,000 Check"), issued on August 6, 2001, that cleared on August 10, 2001;

2. a check for $690,690.52 (the "$691,000 Check"), issued on August 9, 2001, that cleared on August 13, 2001; and

3. a check for $764,918.81 (the "$765,000 Check"), issued on August 13, 2001, that cleared on August 15, 2001.

CASE SUMMARY

Continued

As of the Petition Date, Ames did not owe Cellmark anything.

DECISION: The court applied the test for voidable preferences and concluded that the payments made to Cellmark were not in the ordinary course of business and were made while Ames was insolvent. The court noted that the checks were issued immediately, rather than according to the pattern of the parties over the past few years; that Ames executives overrode their payment system to issue the checks early; and that the executives were aware of how critical Cellmark was to the company continuing to operate. The court noted that Ames did not disclose $200 million in debt on its financial statement and that its assets were not properly valued so that there was little chance it was solvent at the time the payments to Cellmark occurred. [*In re Ames Dept. Stores, Inc.*, 450 B.R. 24 (S.D.N.Y. 2011)]

(c) **SELF-SETTLED TRUST.** Under the Reform Act, the trustee has the ability to set aside the transfer of property into a "self-settled" (a self-created personal trust) any time within the past 10 years if the trustee can establish that the trust was created with actual intent to hinder, delay, or defraud existing or future creditors.[23] This section was added to address the problem of the many assets of individuals being in personal trusts for which those individuals serve as trustees.

12. Proof of Claim

Bankruptcy law regulates the manner in which creditors present their claims and the way in which the debtor's assets are distributed in payment of these claims.

After the debtor has filed a list of creditors, the court then sends a notice of the bankruptcy proceedings to listed creditors. The creditors who wish to participate in the distribution of the proceeds of the liquidation of the debtor's estate must file a proof of claim. A **claim** is a right to payment, whether liquidated (certain and not disputed), unliquidated, contingent, unmatured, disputed, legal, or equitable. A **proof of claim** is a written statement, signed by the creditor or an authorized representative, setting forth any claim made against the debtor and the basis for it. It must ordinarily be filed within 90 days after the first meeting of creditors.[24] A creditor must file within that time even though the trustee in bankruptcy in fact knows of the existence of the creditor's claim.

claim – creditor's right to payment.

proof of claim – written statement, signed by the creditor or an authorized representative, setting forth any claim made against the debtor and the basis for it.

CPA

13. Priority of Claims

Creditors who hold security for payment, such as a lien or a mortgage on the debtor's property, are less affected by the debtor's bankruptcy. Secured creditors may enforce their security interest to obtain payment of their claims up to the value of their security, the collateral in which they hold an interest. **For Example,** suppose that First Bank holds a mortgage on a company's office building. The mortgage amount is $750,000. The building is sold for $700,000. First Bank is entitled to the $700,000 from the sale. For the remaining portion of the debt, First Bank drops

[23] 11 U.S.C. §548(e).
[24] 11 U.S.C. §302(c).

down in priority to wait with the other unsecured creditors for its remaining $50,000. Unsecured creditors with unsecured debts have a statutory order of priority following the secured creditors' rights in their collateral as outlined in the list that appears below.[25] Once the bottom of the priority list is reached, any remaining unsecured creditors share on a *pro rata* basis any remaining assets of the debtor. Any balance remaining after all creditors have been paid goes to the debtor. However, in 98 to 99 percent of all bankruptcies, no unsecured creditors receive any payments, so it is highly unlikely that the debtor would ever receive anything from the bankruptcy litigation of the debtor's property and funds.

The list below is the statutory one for priorities of the unsecured creditors following the payment to any secured creditors from the debtors' pledged property:[26]

1. Allowed claims for debts to a spouse, former spouse, or child of the debtor and for alimony to, maintenance for, or support of such spouse or child (that were obligations at the time of the filing of the bankruptcy petition).

2. Costs and expenses of administration of the bankruptcy case, including fees to trustees, attorneys, and accountants, and the reasonable expenses of creditors in recovering property transferred or concealed by the debtor.

3. Claims arising in the ordinary course of a debtor's business or financial affairs after the commencement of the case but before the order of relief (involuntary).

4. Claims for wages, salaries, or commissions, including vacation, severance, or sick leave pay earned within 180 days before the filing of the petition or the date of cessation of the debtor's business, whichever occurred first, limited, however, to $11,725 for each person.[27]

5. Claims arising for contributions to employee benefit plans, based on services rendered within 180 days before the filing of the petition or when the debtor ceased doing business, whichever occurred first; the maximum amount is $11,725. Under the 2005 reforms (especially in Chapter 11 reorganizations), payments of key-employee retention plans are not permitted unless the plans are "essential" to keeping the key employee at the company that is in bankruptcy. Proving that they are essential requires the key employee actually to have a "bona fide" offer of employment from another company. In addition, there are limits on how much can be paid under key-employee retention plans.

6. Farm producers (up to $5,775) and fishers against debtors who operate grain storage facilities or fish storage or processing facilities, up to $5,775 per claim.

7. Claims by consumer creditors, not to exceed $2,600 for each claimant, arising from the purchase of consumer goods or services when such property or services were not delivered or provided.

8. Certain taxes and penalties due government, such as income and property taxes (there are time limits, for example, three years is the general time limit, with exceptions for fraud).

---

[25] 11 U.S.C. §507(1)–(6). Secured creditors' priority is determined by the priority rules related to Article 9, liens, and mortgages. *In re Black Angus Holdings, LLC*, 434 B.R. 612 (D. Kan. 2010).

[26] 11 U.S.C. §507. *In re Penaran*, 424 B.R. 868 (D. Kan. 2010). Debts owed to government agencies for unlawful receipt of food stamps are grouped in with alimony and support payments. *Wisconsin Dept. of Workforce Development v. Ratliff*, 390 B.R. 607 (E.D. Wis. 2008).

[27] Claims involving wage disputes or discrimination are treated as the claims of unsecured creditors. *In re Trans World Airlines, Inc.*, 322 F.3d 283 (3rd Cir. 2003).

9. All other unsecured creditors.

10. Tort claims for death or personal injury resulting from operation of a vehicle or vessel while intoxicated from alcohol, drug, and other substances.

11. Remainder (if any) to debtor.

Each claim must be paid in full before any lower claim is paid anything. If a class of claims cannot be paid in full, the claims in that case are paid on a *pro rata* basis. **For Example,** suppose that following the payment of all secured creditors, $10,000 is left to be distributed. The accountants who performed work on the bankruptcy are owed $15,000, and the lawyers who worked on it are owed $10,000. Because there is not enough to pay two parties in the same priority ranking, the $10,000 is split proportionately. The accountants will receive 15/25, or 3/5, of the $10,000, or $6,000, and the lawyers will receive 10/25, or 2/5, of the $10,000, or $4,000.

D. DEBTOR'S DUTIES AND EXEMPTIONS

Bankruptcy law imposes certain duties on the debtor and provides for specific exemptions of some of the debtor's estate from the claims of creditors.

14. Debtor's Duties

A debtor must file with the court a list of creditors, a schedule of assets and liabilities, and a statement of her financial affairs. The debtor must also appear for examination under oath at the first meeting of creditors.

CPA

15. Debtor's Exemptions

A debtor is permitted to claim certain property of the estate in the trustee's possession and keep it free from claims of creditors. Exemptions are provided under federal law, but state laws also provide for exemptions. In 14 states (examples are Massachusetts, New Jersey, Pennsylvania, and Connecticut), debtors can elect either federal or state exemption. In the other states (New York, California, Florida, and Delaware are examples), debtors are permitted to use only the state exemptions.[28] Examples of exempt property from the federal code include wedding rings, property used to earn a living, one VCR, and one car. New York exemptions include "all stoves in the home, one sewing machine, the family Bible, a pew in a public house of worship, enough food for sixty days, a wedding ring, and a watch not exceeding thirty-five dollars in value."[29] California exempts tools of the trade and the family cemetery plot.[30]

The principal exemptions provided by the Bankruptcy Code are the debtor's interest in real or personal property used as a residence.[31] The Reform Act has greatly limited the homestead exemption and, in effect, preempts state law on this debtor exemption. Debtors are required to have lived in the home for two years prior to bankruptcy, and the amount of the homestead exemption would be limited to $146,450.[32] To be able to

---

[28] 11 U.S.C. §522.

[29] N.Y. C.P.L.R. §5205 (2010).

[30] Cal. Civ. Proc. Code §704.010-704.210 (2009).

[31] A married couple gets a single homestead exemption. Gay couples who have registered under state domestic partner rights statutes are also entitled to only one homestead exemption. *In re Rabin*, 359 B.R. 242 (2007).

[32] The time requirement is at 11 U.S.C. §522(b)(3)(A), and the amount limitation is at 11 U.S.C. §522(o)(1). This amount refers to those who elect state exemptions. In the absence of state exemptions, the federal maximum is $21,625.

use a higher state homestead exemption, the debtor must have lived in the home for 1215 days (40 months).[33] Labeled as the most flagrant abuse of the existing bankruptcy system, debtors have used the homestead exemption to shift their assets into expensive homes to shield everything from bankruptcy. Known as the "mansion loophole," the changes in the Reform Act related to the homestead exemption were among the most debated and the most dramatic.[34] **For Example,** prior to the reforms actor Burt Reynolds declared bankruptcy in Florida and was relieved of millions in debt, but he was able to keep his $2.5 million Valhalla estate there. Corporate raider Paul Bilzerian, who was convicted of securities fraud, also declared bankruptcy in Florida but kept his mansion, the largest home in Hillsborough County, Florida. Former WorldCom CFO Scott Sullivan (who entered a guilty plea to fraud and other charges and is serving a five-year sentence) built a multimillion-dollar home in Florida to gain homestead protections. Wendy Gramm, who sat on Enron's board, purchased 200 acres of land in Texas and constructed a large home with her husband, former senator Phil Gramm, to take advantage of homestead exemptions then available in Texas. However, the Reform Act closed this corporate executive loophole by requiring that the $146,450 exemption apply to debtors who are convicted of securities fraud or bankruptcy fraud.[35]

Other exemptions include payments under a life insurance contract, alimony and child support payments, and awards from personal injury litigation.[36] Under the Reform Act, college savings accounts and IRAs are exempt property under the federal exemptions and can be used even by those debtors who are using state exemptions. The IRA exemption is limited to $1,171,650.[37]

CASE SUMMARY

Setting Aside Money for the Kids Before the Bankruptcy

FACTS: Michael and Alice Werth (debtors) filed a Chapter 7 petition on April 14, 2011, and received a discharge on January 23, 2012. On December 2, 2010, the Werths had opened two 529 accounts for the benefit of Michael Werth's two children by a previous marriage. They deposited $6,000.00 into each account. The accounts are owned by Alice Werth. By the petition date, the accounts held $12,197.12.

Michael Werth is responsible for one-half of the postsecondary educational expenses for his two children pursuant to a 2002 Separation Agreement, subject to certain limitations. As of the petition date, neither of Werth's children had yet graduated from high school.

The bankruptcy trustee moved for an order directing the debtors to turn over the balances in the two 529 education savings accounts.

DECISION: The court held that 529 accounts are exempt property under bankruptcy laws if they were started earlier than a year before the bankruptcy petition is filed. The court also held that even if the obligation to save is part of a divorce decree, the terms of which require the debtor/ex-spouse to provide support for his or her children, it is still not entitled to exemption from creditors' claims unless the obligation was undertaken sooner than one year before bankruptcy. [*In re Werth*, 468 B.R. 412 (D.Kan. 2012)]

[33] 11 U.S.C. §522(p)(2)(B).
[34] 11 U.S.C. §522(p).
[35] 11 U.S.C. §522(q).
[36] 11 U.S.C. §522(d) (including automatic adjustments).
[37] 11 U.S.C. §522(n). There are time requirements on college savings (529) accounts in order to obtain the exemption.

Businesses that declare bankruptcy would not have employee pension plan contributions included in their bankruptcy estates. Those contributions would be returned to the employees. The proposed changes are the result of the numerous large corporate bankruptcies, such as the one involving United Airlines and the pensions of its employees.[38]

16. Debtor's Protection against Discrimination

Federal, state, and local law may not discriminate against anyone on the basis of a discharge in bankruptcy. For example, a state cannot refuse to issue a new license to an individual if the license fees on a previous one have been discharged as a debt in the individual's declaration of bankruptcy.

E. DISCHARGE IN BANKRUPTCY

discharge in bankruptcy –
order of the bankruptcy court relieving the debtor from obligation to pay the unpaid balance of most claims.

The main objectives of a bankruptcy proceeding are to collect and distribute the debtor's assets and then issue a **discharge in bankruptcy** of the debtor from obligations. The decree terminating the bankruptcy proceeding is generally a discharge that releases the debtor from most debts. Under the BAPCPA, a discharge is available only once every eight years.

17. Denial of Discharge

The court will refuse to grant a discharge if the debtor has (1) within one year of the filing of the petition fraudulently transferred or concealed property with intent to

---

Ethics & the Law

The Skies Are Not So Friendly to Employee Pensions

As part of its Chapter 11 bankruptcy, United Airlines was relieved of its pension liabilities. Employees and unions wonder how a company can be permitted to renege on those benefits when so many protections were built into the law under ERISA. Congressional hearings now reveal that there were loopholes in the accounting processes for pension fund reporting that permitted United, and many others, to report pension numbers that made the pension funds look healthy when they really were not. The loopholes were Enronesque in nature. Companies could spin the pension obligations off the books so that the existing levels of obligations of the plan looked small and the assets very rich. Because of United's pension bailout, Congress changed the accounting for pension plans to avoid the problem of the rosy picture when the funds really need further funding. One interesting approach to protecting pension

plans is to require companies to fund the pension plans according to the numbers they have reported to the SEC in their financials. The numbers reported to the SEC for company pensions are accurate whereas the numbers reported for ERISA purposes are inflated. If United had funded its plans when its SEC numbers indicated it needed to (e.g., in 1998), the plan would have been sufficiently funded. Under ERISA guidelines, it was not required to kick in funds until 2002 when it was grossly underfunded.

Were companies acting ethically on their pension accounting? Were they acting legally?*

*Marry Williams Walsh, "Pension Law Loopholes Helped United Hide Its Troubles," *New York Times*, June 7, 2005, C1.

---

[38] 11 U.S.C. §541(b).

hinder, delay, or defraud creditors, (2) failed to keep proper financial records, (3) made a false oath or account,[39] (4) failed to explain satisfactorily any loss of assets, (5) refused to obey any lawful order of the court or refused to testify after having been granted immunity, (6) obtained a discharge within the last eight years,[40] (7) filed a written waiver of discharge that is approved by the court,[41] or (8) in the case of a consumer debtor, has failed to complete a personal financial management instructional course.[42]

A discharge releases the debtor from the unpaid balance of most debts except for taxes, customs duties, child support obligations, and tax penalties.[43] Student loan obligations are not discharged in bankruptcy unless the loan first became due more than seven years before bankruptcy or unless not allowing a discharge would impose undue hardship on the debtor.

CASE SUMMARY

Your Living Expenses Are Fairly Minimal in Maximum Security

FACTS: Bryan Anthony Looper had over $300,000 in student loans that were used to finance his education at Mercer University where he obtained an A.B., an M.B.A, and another unspecified graduate degree as well as a large number of courses toward his J.D. degree. He did not make payments on these student loans.

In 1996, he was elected assessor for Putnam County, Tennessee, a position he held for two years and four months. He was then convicted of the first-degree murder of state senator Tommy Burks. He exhausted all of his appeals and is currently serving a life sentence without the possibility of parole. The debtor has one dependent, a son born in August 1998. The circuit court for Putnam County, Tennessee, ordered Looper to pay child support of $161.00 per month plus $7,254.20 in medical expenses. Looper did not make any of the court-ordered child support payments and was in arrears by more than $23,515.00.

Looper asked to have his student loans discharged on the basis of his hardship.

DECISION: The court refused to discharge the student loans. Looper had all of his living expenses covered by the Tennessee Department of Corrections. Looper had made no effort to make any payments on any of his student loans and had also not made attempts to try and work with his lenders or apply to programs set up to help with student loans. The court also noted that Looper's circumstances were the result of his choices and conduct, not the result of unforeseen and uncontrollable events. He had three degrees and the capability of earning a living but, through poor choices, produced his own difficult circumstances. [*In re Looper*, **2007 WL 1231700 (Bankr. E.D. Tenn. 2007)**]

In addition, the following debts are not discharged by bankruptcy: (1) loans obtained by use of a false financial statement made with intent to deceive and on which the creditor reasonably relied, (2) debts not scheduled or listed with the

---

[39] The debtor must actually make a false statement. In *In re Mercer*, 211 F.3d 214 (5th Cir. 2000), the debtor ran up $3,186.82 on a credit card she was given by AT&T with a $3,000 credit limit. The credit card was issued to the debtor on a preapproved basis, so there was no fraud, just a great deal of spending. See also *In re Carver*, 418 B.R. 734 (C.D. Ill. 2009) that did not punish a debtor because he was mixed up when he began paying his attorney.

[40] 11 U.S.C. §727(a)(8).

[41] 11 U.S.C. §523.

[42] 11 U.S.C. §727(a)(11). The financial management course requirement applies to both Chapter 7 and Chapter 13 consumer bankruptcies.

[43] Child support obligations enjoy additional protections and priorities in bankruptcy. 11 U.S.C. §507(a).

FIGURE 35-3	*Nondischargeable Debts in Bankruptcy*

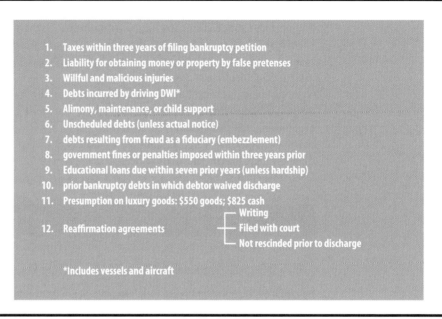

1. Taxes within three years of filing bankruptcy petition
2. Liability for obtaining money or property by false pretenses
3. Willful and malicious injuries
4. Debts incurred by driving DWI*
5. Alimony, maintenance, or child support
6. Unscheduled debts (unless actual notice)
7. debts resulting from fraud as a fiduciary (embezzlement)
8. government fines or penalties imposed within three years prior
9. Educational loans due within seven prior years (unless hardship)
10. prior bankruptcy debts in which debtor waived discharge
11. Presumption on luxury goods: $550 goods; $825 cash
12. Reaffirmation agreements — Writing / Filed with court / Not rescinded prior to discharge

*Includes vessels and aircraft

© Cengage Learning

court in time for allowance, (3) debts arising from fraud while the debtor was acting in a fiduciary capacity or by reason of embezzlement or larceny, (4) alimony and child support, (5) a judgment for willful and malicious injury, (6) a consumer debt to a single creditor totaling more than $5775 for luxury goods or services (within 90 days of the order of relief) and cash advances exceeding $825 based on consumer open-end credit, such as a credit card (within 70 days of the order of relief),[44] (7) damages arising from drunk driving or the operation of vessels and aircrafts by people who are inebriated,[45] (8) loans used to pay taxes (including credit cards),[46] (9) taxes not paid as a result of a fraudulent return, although other unpaid taxes beyond the past three years can be discharged,[47] (10) prebankruptcy fees and assessments owed to homeowners associations, and (11) debts owed to tax-qualified retirement plans. **For Example,** in regard to (5), the finding of malice in *Goldman v. O. J. Simpson* precluded the discharge by bankruptcy of the $8.5 million damage award from Simpson to the families of his murder victims, the Goldmans and Browns. Figure 35-3 has a listing of nondischargeable debts.

F. REORGANIZATION PLANS UNDER CHAPTER 11

In addition to liquidation under Chapter 7, the Bankruptcy Code permits debtors to restructure the organization and finances of their businesses so that they may continue to operate. In these rehabilitation plans, the debtor keeps all of the assets

[44] 11 U.S.C. §523(a)(2)(c)(i). (Amounts are adjusted each year).
[45] 11 U.S.C. §523(a)(9).
[46] 11 U.S.C. §523(a)(14A),(14B).
[47] 11 U.S.C. §§1129(a)(9)(c), (D), 1129(b)(2)(B), 1141(d)(6)(B).

(exempt and nonexempt), continues to operate the business, and makes a settlement that is acceptable to the majority of the creditors. This settlement is binding on the minority creditors.

Individuals, partnerships, and corporations in business may all be reorganized under the Bankruptcy Code. The first step is to file a plan for the debtor's reorganization. This plan may be filed by the debtor, any party in interest, or a committee of creditors. If the debtor wishes to move from a Chapter 11 proceeding (in the case of an individual debtor), the debtor must survive the means test that is now a requirement for determining eligibility for bankruptcy.

18. Contents of the Plan

The plan divides ownership interests and debts into those that will be affected by the adoption of the plan and those that will not be. It then specifies what will be done to those interests and claims that are affected. **For Example,** when mortgage payments are too high for the income of a corporation, a possible plan would be to reduce the mortgage payments and give the mortgage holder preferred stock to compensate for the loss sustained.

All creditors, shareholders, and other interest holders within a particular class must be treated the same way. **For Example,** the holders of first mortgage bonds must all be treated similarly. The treatment of the bondholders in the Chrysler and GM bankruptcies was a point of contention and negotiation in those reorganizations.

A plan can also provide for the assumption, rejection, or assignment of executory contracts. The trustee or debtor can, under certain circumstances, suspend performance of a contract not yet fully performed. **For Example,** collective bargaining agreements may be rejected with the approval of the bankruptcy court.[48]

19. Confirmation of the Plan

After the plan is prepared, the court must approve or confirm it. A plan will be confirmed if it has been submitted in good faith and if its provisions are reasonable.[49] After the plan is confirmed, the owners and creditors of the enterprise have only the rights that are specified in the plan. They cannot go back to their original contract positions.

CPA ## G. Payment Plans under Chapter 13

The Bankruptcy Code also provides for the adoption of extended-time payment plans for individual debtors who have regular income. These debtors must owe unsecured debts of less than $360,475 and secured debts of less than $1,081,400.

An individual debtor who has a regular income may submit a plan for the installment payment of outstanding debts. If the court approves it, the debtor may then pay the debts in the installments specified by the plan even if the creditors had not originally agreed to such installment payments.

---

[48] 11 U.S.C. §1113.
[49] 11 U.S.C. §1129.

20. Contents of the Plan

The individual debtor plan is, in effect, a budget of the debtor's future income with respect to outstanding debts. The plan must provide for the eventual payment in full of all claims entitled to priority under the Bankruptcy Code. All creditors holding the same kind or class of claim must be treated the same way.

21. Confirmation of the Plan

The plan has no effect until the court approves or confirms it. A plan will be confirmed if it was submitted in good faith and is in the best interests of the creditors.[50] When the plan is confirmed, debts are payable in the manner specified in the plan.

22. Discharge of the Debtor

After all of the payments called for by the plan have been made, the debtor is given a discharge. The discharge releases the debtor from liability for all debts except those that would not be discharged by an ordinary bankruptcy discharge.[51] Under the bankruptcy reforms, the court cannot grant a discharge until the debtor has completed an instructional course concerning personal financial management.[52] If the debtor does not perform under the plan, the creditors can move to transfer the debtor's case to a Chapter 7 proceeding, but they would still face the means test in qualifying for this move to Chapter 7.

MAKE THE CONNECTION

SUMMARY

Jurisdiction over bankruptcy cases is in U.S. district courts, which may refer all cases and related proceedings to adjunct bankruptcy courts.

Three bankruptcy proceedings are available: liquidation (Chapter 7), reorganization (Chapter 11), and extended-time payment (Chapter 13). A liquidation proceeding under Chapter 7 may be either voluntary or involuntary.

A *voluntary case* is commenced by the debtor's filing a petition with the bankruptcy court. A voluntary petition is subject to the means test to determine if the debtor meets the standard for declaring bankruptcy. An involuntary case is commenced by the creditors' filing a petition with the bankruptcy court. If there are 12 or more creditors, at least 3 whose unsecured claims total $14,425 or more must sign the involuntary petition. If there are fewer than 12 creditors, any creditor whose unsecured claim is at least $14,425 may sign the petition. If the debtor contests the bankruptcy petition, it must be shown that the debtor is not paying debts as they become due.

Eligibility for Chapters 7 and 11 bankruptcy excludes railroads, municipalities, and Small Business Administration companies. Individual debtors are restricted on Chapters 7 and 11 filings by their ability to repay. If found to have the means to pay, they go into a Chapter 13 proceeding. Chapter 13 eligibility is limited to consumers with $360,475 in unsecured debt and $1,081,400 in secured debt.

[50] 11 U.S.C. §1325.
[51] 11 U.S.C. §1328.
[52] 11 U.S.C. §1328(g)(1).

An automatic stay prevents creditors from taking legal action against the debtor after a bankruptcy petition is filed. The trustee in bankruptcy is elected by the creditors and is the successor to, and acquires the rights of, the debtor. In certain cases, the trustee can avoid transfers of property to prevent creditors from satisfying their claims. Preferential transfers may be set aside. A transfer for a present consideration, such as a cash sale, is not a preference.

Bankruptcy law regulates the way creditors present their claims and how the assets of the debtor are to be distributed in payment of the claims. Some assets of the debtor are exempt from the bankruptcy estate, such as a portion of the value of the debtor's home.

Secured claims are not affected by the debtor's bankruptcy. Unsecured claims are paid in the following order of priority:

1. Support or maintenance for a spouse, former spouse, or child.

2. Costs and expenses of administration of the bankruptcy case.

3. Claims arising in the ordinary course of a debtor's business or financial affairs after the commencement of the case but before the order of relief (involuntary).

4. Claims for wages, salaries, or commissions, including vacation, severance, or sick leave pay earned within 180 days before the filing of the petition or the date of cessation of the debtor's business, limited to $11,725 for each person.

5. Claims arising for contributions (up to $5,850) to employee benefit plans based on services

rendered within 180 days before the filing of the petition or when the debtor ceased doing business.

6. Farm producers (up to $5,775) and fishers against debtors who operate grain storage facilities or fish produce storage or processing facilities, up to $5,775 per claim.

7. Claims by consumer creditors, not to exceed $2,600 for each claimant.

8. Certain taxes and penalties due government units, such as income and property taxes.

9. All other unsecured creditors.

10. Remainder (if any) to debtor.

The decree terminating bankruptcy proceedings is generally a discharge that releases the debtor from most debts. Certain debts, such as income taxes, student loans, loans obtained by use of a false financial statement, alimony, and debts not listed by the debtor, are not discharged.

Under Chapter 11 bankruptcy, individuals, partnerships, and corporations in business may be reorganized so that the business can continue to operate. A plan for reorganization must be approved by the court. Under a Chapter 13 bankruptcy proceeding, individual debtors with a regular income may adopt extended-time payment plans for the payment of debts. A plan for extended-time payment must also be confirmed by the court. Federal, state, and local law may not discriminate against anyone on the basis of a discharge in bankruptcy.

LEARNING OUTCOMES

After studying this chapter, you should be able to clearly explain:

A. Bankruptcy Law

B. How Bankruptcy Is Declared

LO.1 List the requirements for the commencement of a voluntary bankruptcy case and an involuntary bankruptcy case
See the Sports & Entertainment Law discussion of celebrity bankruptcies on p. 754.

See discussion of Chapters 7, 11, and 13 on pp. 747–748 and chart on p. 752.

C. Administration of the Bankruptcy Estate

LO.2 Explain the procedure for the administration of a debtor's estate
See the list of priorities on p. 758.
See *In re Ames Dept. Stores* on pp. 757–758.

D. Debtor's Duties and Exemptions

L0.3 List a debtor's duties and exemptions
See the discussion of the homestead
exemptions on p. 760.
See *In re Werth* case on p. 761.

E. Discharge in Bankruptcy

L0.4 Explain the significance of a discharge in
bankruptcy
See *In re Looper* on p. 763.

F. Reorganization Plans under Chapter 11

See Ethics & the Law, The Skies Are Not So
Friendly on p. 762.

G. Payment Plans under Chapter 13

L0.5 Explain when a business reorganization
plan or an extended-time payment plan might be used
See the Ethics & the Law discussion of
United Airlines on p. 762.
See the discussion of Chrysler and GM on
p. 765.

KEY TERMS

automatic stay
balance sheet test
bankruptcy courts
bona fide
Chapter 7 bankruptcy
Chapter 11 bankruptcy
Chapter 13 bankruptcy

claim
discharge in bankruptcy
insiders
insolvency
involuntary bankruptcy
liquidated
means test

order of relief
preferences
preferential transfers
proof of claim
trustee in bankruptcy
voluntary bankruptcy

QUESTIONS AND CASE PROBLEMS

1. Hall-Mark regularly supplied electronic parts to
Peter Lee. On September 11, 1992, Lee gave
Hall-Mark a $100,000 check for parts it had
received. Hall-Mark continued to ship parts to
Lee. On September 23, 1992, Lee's check was
dishonored by the bank. On September 25,
1992, Lee delivered to Hall-Mark a cashier's
check for $100,000. Hall-Mark shipped nothing
more to Lee after receipt of the cashier's check.
On December 24, 1992, Lee filed a voluntary
petition for bankruptcy. The trustee filed a
complaint to have the $100,000 payment to
Hall-Mark set aside as a voidable preference.
Hall-Mark said it was entitled to the payment
because it gave value to Lee. The trustee said that
the payment was not actually made until the
cashier's check was delivered on September 25,
1992, and that Hall-Mark gave no further value
to Lee after that check was paid. Who was
correct? [*In re Lee*, 108 F.3d 239 (9th Cir.)]

2. Orso, who had declared bankruptcy, received a
structured tort settlement in a personal injury
claim he had pending. The settlement would pay
him an annuity each year for 30 years because
the claim was the result of an auto accident that
left him permanently and severely brain damaged
with an IQ of about 70. His ex-wife had a
pending claim for $48,000 in arrearages on
Orso's $1,000 per month child support
payments. His ex-wife wanted the annuity
included in the bankruptcy estate. Would this
property have been included in Orso's
bankruptcy estate? [*In re Orso*, 214 F.3d 637
(5th Cir.)]

3. Harold McClellan sold ice-making machinery to
Bobbie Cantrell's brother for $200,000 to be
paid in installment payments. McClellan took a
security interest in the ice machine but did not
perfect it by filing a financing statement. The
brother defaulted when he owed $100,000, and
McClellan brought suit. With the suit pending,
the brother "sold" the ice machine to Bobbie
Cantrell for $10. Bobbie then sold the machine
to someone for $160,000 and refused to explain
what happened to that money. McClellan added
Bobbie as a defendant in his suit against her
brother. Bobbie then declared bankruptcy.
McClellan sought to have the various transfers set
aside. The trial court refused to do so, and
McClellan appealed. Should the transfers be set

aside? Why or why not? [*McClellan v. Cantrell*, 217 F.3d 890 (7th Cir.)]

4. Okamoto owed money to Hornblower & Weeks-Hemphill, Noyes (a law firm and hereafter Hornblower). Hornblower filed an involuntary bankruptcy petition against Okamoto, who moved to dismiss the petition on the ground that he had more than 12 creditors and the petition could not be filed by only one creditor. Hornblower replied that the other creditors' claims were too small to count and, therefore, the petition could be filed by one creditor. Decide. [*In re Okamoto*, 491 F.2d 496 (9th Cir.)]

5. Jane Leeves declared voluntary Chapter 7 bankruptcy. The trustee included the following property in her bankruptcy estate:

   - Jane's wedding ring

   - Jane's computer for her consulting business that she operated from her home

   - Jane's car payment from a client in the amount of $5,000 that was received 91 days after Jane filed bankruptcy

   After collecting all of Jane's assets, the bankruptcy trustee was trying to decide how to distribute the assets. Jane had the following creditors:

   - Mortgage company—owed $187,000 (the trustee sold Jane's house for $190,000)

   - Expenses of the bankruptcy—$3,000

   - Federal income taxes—$11,000

   - Utility bills—$1,000

   - Office supply store open account—$1,000

   The trustee had $11,500 in cash, including the $3,000 additional cash left from the sale of the house after the mortgage company was paid. How should the trustee distribute this money? What if the amount were $14,500; how should that be distributed?

6. Kentile sold goods over an extended period of time to Winham. The credit relationship began without Winham's being required to furnish a financial statement. After a time, payments were not made regularly, and Kentile requested a financial statement. Winham submitted a statement for the year just ended. Kentile requested a second statement. The second statement was false. Kentile objected to Winham's discharge in bankruptcy because of the false financial statement. Should the discharge be granted? Why or why not?

7. D. Erik Von Kiel obtained loans from the U.S. Department of Health & Human Services so that he could complete his education as an osteopathic physician. He works at the International Academy of Life (IAL) in Orem, Utah, for no salary but receives gifts from IAL that total $150,000 per year, or about $12,787 per month. He pays no taxes on these "gifts" and has received them since 2005. Dr. Von Kiel pays all but $1,000 to his ex-wife and nine children for their support. He has given up his practice, taken a vow of poverty, and works at IAL to concentrate on alternative medicine. He has signed over full authority for the management of his financial affairs to two individuals, who apparently failed to manage wisely. As a result, Dr. Von Kiel filed for bankruptcy in order to be discharged from his HHS loans. HHS says that Dr. Von Kiel should not be discharged because of bad faith. Who is correct and why? [*In re Von Kiel*, 461 B.R. 323 (E.D. Pa.)]

8. Sonia, a retailer, has the following assets: a factory worth $1 million; accounts receivable amounting to $750,000, which fall due in four to six months; and $20,000 cash in the bank. Sonia's sole liability is a $200,000 note falling due today, which she is unable to pay. Can Sonia be forced into involuntary bankruptcy under the Bankruptcy Code?

9. Samson Industries ceased doing business and is in bankruptcy proceedings. Among the creditors are five employees seeking unpaid wages. Three of the employees are owed $3,500 each, and two are owed $1,500 each. These amounts became due within 90 days preceding the filing of the petition. Where, in the priority of claims, will the employees' wage claims fall?

10. Carol Cott, doing business as Carol Cott Fashions, is worried about an involuntary bankruptcy proceeding being filed by her creditors. Her net worth, using a balance sheet

approach, is $8,000 ($108,000 in assets minus $100,000 in liabilities). However, her cash flow is negative, and she has been hard pressed to meet current obligations as they mature. She is in fact some $12,500 in arrears in payments to her creditors on bills submitted during the past two months. Will the fact that Cott is solvent in the balance-sheet sense result in the court's dismissing the creditors' petition if Cott objects to the petition? Explain.

11. On July 1, Roger Walsh, a sole proprietor operating a grocery, was involuntarily petitioned into bankruptcy by his creditors. At that time, and for at least 90 days prior to that time, Walsh was unable to pay current obligations. On June 16, Walsh paid the May electric bill for his business. The trustee in bankruptcy claimed that this payment was a voidable preference. Was the trustee correct? Explain.

12. Steven and Teresa Hornsby are married and have three young children. On May 25, 1993, the Hornsbys filed a voluntary Chapter 7 petition. They had by that date accumulated more than $30,000 in debt, stemming almost entirely from student loans. They wanted a discharge of their student loans on grounds of undue hardship. The Hornsbys attended a succession of small Tennessee state colleges. Both studied business and computers, but neither graduated. Although they received several deferments and forbearances on the loans, they ultimately defaulted before making any payments. Interest had accumulated on the loans to the extent that Steven was indebted to the Tennessee Student Assistance Corporation (TSAC) for $15,058.52, and Teresa was indebted to TSAC for $18,329.15.

Steven was working for AT&T in Dallas, Texas; he made $6.53 per hour, occasionally working limited overtime hours. Teresa was employed by KinderCare Learning Center. Although she had begun work in Tennessee, she had transferred to become the director of a child care facility in Dallas. Teresa was earning $17,500 per year with medical benefits at the time of the hearing. In monthly net income, Steven earned approximately $1,083.33, and Teresa earned

$1,473.33, amounting to $2,556.66 of disposable income per month. The Hornsbys' reported monthly expenses came to $2,364.90. They operated with a monthly surplus of $191.76 to $280.43, depending on whether Steven earned overtime for a particular month. Under the federal bankruptcy laws, are the Hornsbys entitled to a discharge on their student loans? Explain your answer. [*In re Hornsby*, 144 F.3d 433 (6th Cir.)]

13. TLC was an Atlanta rhythm, blues, and hip-hop band that performed at clubs in 1991. The three-woman group signed a recording contract with LaFace Records. The group's first album that LaFace produced, *Oooooooohhh on the TLC Tip*, sold almost 3 million albums in 1992. The group's second album, *Crazysexycool*, also produced by LaFace, sold 5 million albums through June 1996. The two albums together had six top-of-the-chart singles.

LaFace had the right to renew TLC's contract in 1996 following renegotiation of the contract terms. In the industry, royalty rates for unknown groups, as TLC was in 1991, are generally 7 percent of the revenues for the first 500,000 albums and 8 percent for sales on platinum albums (albums that sell over 1 million copies). The royalty rate increases to 9.5 percent for all sales on an eighth album. Established artists in the industry who renegotiate often have royalty rates of 13 percent, and artists with two platinum albums can command an even higher royalty.

The three women in TLC—Tionne Watkins (T-Boz), Lisa Lopes (Left-Eye, who has since died), and Rozonda Thomas (Chili)—declared bankruptcy in July 1995. All three listed debts that exceeded their assets, which included sums owed to creditors for their cars and to Zale's and The Limited for credit purchases. Lopes was being sued by Lloyd's of London, which claimed she owed it $1.3 million it had paid on a policy held by her boyfriend on his home that was destroyed by fire. Lopes pleaded guilty to one count of arson in the destruction of the home but denied that she intended to destroy it. She was sentenced to five years probation and treatment at a halfway house.

Lopes asked that the Lloyd's claim be discharged in her bankruptcy. All three members of TLC asked that their contract with LaFace be discharged in bankruptcy because being bound to their old contract could impede their fresh financial starts.

Did the three women meet the standards for declaring bankruptcy? Evaluate whether Lopes's Lloyd's claim should be discharged. Determine whether the record contract should be discharged.

14. Place the following in order for a bankruptcy proceeding:
    a. Order of relief
    b. Collection of bankrupt's estate
    c. List of creditors
    d. Petition
    e. Evaluation of claims
    f. Voidable preferences
    g. Discharge

15. Three general unsecured creditors are owed $45,000 as follows: *A,* $15,000; *B,* $5,000; and *C,* $25,000. After all other creditors were paid, the amount left for distribution to general unsecured creditors was $9,000. How will the $9,000 be distributed?

CPA QUESTIONS

1. Which of the following statements is correct concerning the voluntary filing of a petition of bankruptcy?
   a. If the debtor has 12 or more creditors, the unsecured claims must total at least $13,475.
   b. The debtor must be solvent.
   c. If the debtor has less than 12 creditors, the unsecured claims must total at least $13,475.
   d. The petition may be filed jointly by spouses (AICPA adapted).

2. On February 28, Master, Inc., had total assets with a fair market value of $1,200,000 and total liabilities of $990,000. On January 15, Master made a monthly installment note payment to Acme Distributors Corp., a creditor holding a properly perfected security interest in equipment having a fair market value greater than the balance due on the note. On March 15, Master voluntarily filed a petition in bankruptcy under the liquidation provisions of Chapter 7 of the federal Bankruptcy Code. One year later, the equipment was sold for less than the balance due on the note to Acme.

   If a creditor challenged Master's right to file, the petition would be dismissed:
   a. If Master had less than 12 creditors at the time of filing.
   b. Unless Master can show that a reorganization under Chapter 11 of the federal Bankruptcy Code would have been unsuccessful.
   c. Unless Master can show that it is unable to pay its debts in the ordinary course of business or as they come due.
   d. If Master is an insurance company.

3. A voluntary petition filed under the liquidation provisions of Chapter 7 of the federal Bankruptcy Code:
   a. Is not available to a corporation unless it has previously filed a petition under the reorganization provisions of Chapter 11 of the federal Bankruptcy Code.
   b. Automatically stays collection actions against the debtor except by secured creditors for collateral only.
   c. Will be dismissed unless the debtor has 12 or more unsecured creditors whose claims total at least $13,475.
   d. Does not require the debtor to show that the debtor's liabilities exceed the fair market value of assets.

4. Which following conditions, if any, must a debtor meet to file a voluntary bankruptcy

petition under Chapter 7 of the federal Bankruptcy Code?

	Insolvency	Three or More Creditors
a.	Yes	Yes
b.	Yes	No
c.	No	Yes
d.	No	No

5. On July 15, 1988, White, a sole proprietor, was involuntarily petitioned into bankruptcy under the liquidation provisions of the Bankruptcy Code. White's nonexempt property has been converted to $13,000 cash, which is available to satisfy the following claims:

Unsecured claim for 1986 state income tax	$10,000
Fee owed to Best & Co., CPAs, for services rendered from April 1, 1988, through June 30, 1988	$6,000
Unsecured claim by Stieb for wages earned as an employee of White during March 1988	$3,000
There are no other claims.	

What is the maximum amount that will be distributed for the payment of the 1986 state income tax?

a. $4,000   c. $7,000

b. $5,000   d. $10,000

6. On May 1, 1997, two months after becoming insolvent, Quick Corp., an appliance wholesaler, filed a voluntary petition for bankruptcy under the provisions of Chapter 7 of the federal Bankruptcy Code. On October 15, 1996, Quick's board of directors had authorized and paid Erly $50,000 to repay Erly's April 1, 1996, loan to the corporation. Erly is a sibling of Quick's president. On March 15, 1996, Quick paid Kray $100,000 for inventory delivered that day. Which of the following is not relevant in determining whether the repayment of Erly's loan is a voidable preferential transfer?

a. That Erly is an insider.

b. That Quick's payment to Erly was made on account of an antecedent debt.

c. Quick's solvency when the loan was made by Erly.

d. That Quick's payment to Erly was made within one year of the filing of the bankruptcy petition.

© Manuel Gutjahr/iStockphoto.com

CHAPTER 36

Insurance

learningoutcomes

After studying this chapter, you should be able to

LO.1 Explain the necessity of having an insurable interest to obtain an insurance policy

LO.2 Recognize that the formation of a contract is governed by the general principles of contract law

LO.3 Explain why courts strictly construe insurance policies against insurance companies

LO.4 List and explain the five major categories of insurance

LO.5 Explain coinsurance and its purpose

LO.6 Explain incontestability clauses

B

y means of insurance, protection from loss and liability may be obtained.

A. The Insurance Contract

insurance – a plan of security against risks by charging the loss against a fund created by the payments made by policyholders.

Insurance is a contract by which one party for a stipulated consideration promises to pay another party a sum of money on the destruction of, loss of, or injury to something in which the other party has an interest or to indemnify that party for any loss or liability to which that party is subjected.

1. The Parties

insurer – promisor in an insurance contract.

underwriter – insurer.

insured – person to whom the promise in an insurance contract is made.

policy – paper evidencing the contract of insurance.

insurance agent – agent of an insurance company.

insurance broker – independent contractor who is not employed by any one insurance company.

The promisor in an insurance contract is called the **insurer** or **underwriter**. The person to whom the promise is made is the **insured** or the policyholder. The promise of the insurer is generally set forth in a written contract called a **policy**.

Insurance contracts are ordinarily made through an agent or broker. The **insurance agent** is an agent of the insurance company, often working exclusively for one company. For the most part, the ordinary rules of agency law govern the dealings between this agent and the applicant for insurance.[1]

An **insurance broker** is generally an independent contractor who is not employed by any one insurance company. When a broker obtains a policy for a customer, the broker is the agent of the customer for the purpose of that transaction. Under some statutes, the broker is made an agent of the insurer with respect to transmitting the applicant's payments to the insurer.

2. Insurable Interest

A person obtaining insurance must have an insurable interest in the subject matter insured. If not, the insurance contract cannot be enforced.

(a) Insurable Interest in Property. A person has an insurable interest in property whenever the destruction of the property will cause a direct pecuniary loss to that person.[2]

It is immaterial whether the insured is the owner of the legal or equitable title, a lienholder, or merely a person in possession of the property.[3] **For Example,** Vin Harrington, a builder, maintained fire insurance on a building he was remodeling under a contract with its owner, Chestnut Hill Properties. The building was destroyed by fire before renovations were completed. Harrington had an insurable interest in the property to the extent of the amount owed him under the renovation contract.

To collect on property insurance, the insured must have an insurable interest at the time the loss occurs.

---

[1] *Tidelands Life Ins. Co. v. France*, 711 So.2d 728 (Tex. App. 1986).
[2] *Plaisance v. Scottsdale Insurance Co.*, 2008 WL 4372888 (E.D. La. Sept. 22, 2008).
[3] *Gorman v. Farm Bureau Town & Country Insurance Co.*, 977 S.W.2d 519 (Mo. App. 1998).

(B) INSURABLE INTEREST IN LIFE. A person who purchases life insurance can name anyone as beneficiary regardless of whether that beneficiary has an insurable interest in the life of the insured. A beneficiary who purchases a policy, however, must have an insurable interest in the life of the insured. Such an interest exists if the beneficiary can reasonably expect to receive pecuniary gain from the continued life of the other person and, conversely, would suffer financial loss from the latter's death. Thus, a creditor has an insurable interest in the life of the debtor because he may not be paid the amount owed upon the death of the debtor.

CASE SUMMARY

She Lost Interest When He Got the House

FACTS: While Dorothy and James Morgan were still married, Dorothy purchased insurance on their home from American Security Insurance Company. The policy was issued on November 3, 1981, listing the "insured" as Dorothy L. Morgan. Shortly thereafter the Morgans entered into a separation agreement under which Dorothy deeded her interest in the house to James. The Morgans were divorced on August 26, 1982. On November 28, 1982, the house was destroyed by fire. American Security refused to pay on the policy, claiming that Dorothy had no insurable interest in the property at the time of the loss. The Morgans sued the insurer, contending that they were entitled to payment under the policy issued to Dorothy.

DECISION: Judgment for American Security. In the case of property insurance, the insurable interest must exist at the time of the loss. If the insured parts with all interest in the property prior to the loss, that individual is not covered. Dorothy had conveyed her interest in the property prior to the loss. She did not have an insurable interest at the time of the loss and therefore could not recover on the policy. James Morgan was not insured under the policy. [*Morgan v. American Security Ins. Co.*, 522 So.2d 454 (Fla. App. 1998)]

A partner or partnership has an insurable interest in the life of each of the partners because the death of any one of them will dissolve the firm and cause some degree of loss to the partnership. A business enterprise has an insurable interest in the life of an executive or a key employee because that person's death would inflict a financial loss on the business to the extent that a replacement might not be readily available or could not be found.

In the case of life insurance, the insurable interest must exist at the time the policy is obtained. It is immaterial that the interest no longer exists when the loss is actually sustained.[4] Thus, the fact that a husband (insured) and wife (beneficiary) are divorced after the life insurance policy was procured does not affect the validity of the policy. Also, the fact that a partnership is terminated after a life insurance policy is obtained by one partner on another does not invalidate the policy.

---

[4] One who obtains insurance on his own life may legally name a beneficiary without an insurable interest or later assign the policy to one without an insurable interest. Stranger-owned life insurance policies, or "STOLI" plans, are a growing concern for insurers in the life insurance industry. Under STOLI schemes elderly individuals are able to obtain third-party financing to purchase a life insurance policy and to fund the premiums owed under that policy, with some understanding or expectation that the policy will be assigned to an individual lacking an insurable interest, following the expiration of the policy's two-year contestability period. And, these policies may be sold on the Secondary Life Insurance Market. Although an insured may generally purchase life insurance in good faith, intending to keep it for himself and later assign it to a third party, regardless of whether the third party has an insurable interest, where a person who has an interest "lends himself to one without any, as a cloak to what is, in its inception, a wager" then the contract is void as against public policy. See *Carton v. B&B Equities Group, LLC*, 827 F. Supp. 2d 1235 (D. Nev. 2011). STOLI arrangements are in violation of public policy in most states that have addressed the issue.

CASE SUMMARY

Proceeds to the Surviving Partner or the Deceased Partner's Wife?

FACTS: Jewell Norred's husband, James Norred, was the business partner of Clyde Graves for 10 years. On May 7, 1979, Graves and Norred took out life insurance policies, with Graves being the beneficiary of Norred's policy and Norred being the beneficiary of Graves's policy. Premiums were paid out of partnership funds. On February 28, 1983, Graves and Norred divided the partnership assets, but they did not perform the customary steps of dissolving and winding up the partnership. Graves became the sole owner of the business and continued to pay the premiums on both insurance policies until James Norred died on December 5, 1983. Jewell Norred sued Graves, seeking the proceeds of the insurance policy for herself, alleging that Graves had no insurable interest in the life of James Norred at the time of his death. From a judgment on behalf of the estate, Graves appealed.

DECISION: Judgment for Graves. A partner or partnership has an insurable interest in the life of one of the partners. This interest continues even if the partnership is discontinued prior to the death of one of the partners. Thus, Graves was entitled to the proceeds of the policy. [*Graves v. Norred*, 510 So.2d 816 (Ala. 1987)]

3. The Contract

The formation of a contract of insurance is governed by the general principles applicable to contracts. By statute, an insurance policy must be written. To avoid deception, many state statutes also specify the content of certain policies, in whole or in part. Some statutes specify the size and style of type to be used in printing the policies. Provisions in a policy that conflict with statutory requirements are generally void.

(A) THE APPLICATION AS PART OF THE CONTRACT. The application for insurance is generally attached to the policy when issued and is made part of the contract of insurance by express stipulation of the policy.

The insured is bound by all material statements in the attached application. **For Example,** insurers seek to stop the issuance of stranger-owned life insurance policies or "STOLI" plans by amending their application process to require all applicants and their brokers to fill out Policy Owner Intent Forms, requiring disclosures that, if answered honestly, will indicate a STOLI scheme and rejection of the application. And, if not answered honestly, the policy can be voided during the two-year contestability period because of the material misrepresentations.[5]

(B) STATUTORY PROVISIONS AS PART OF THE CONTRACT. When a statute requires that insurance contracts contain certain provisions or cover certain specified losses, a contract of insurance that does not comply with the statute will be interpreted as though it contained all the provisions required by the statute. **For Example,** Louisiana law clearly requires liability insurance coverage on all rental vehicles to protect the victims injured due to the fault of the drivers of the rental vehicles. Avis did provide liability protection for the vehicle it rented to White. However, the

---

[5] See *Principal Life Insurance Co. v. DeRose*, 2011 WL 4738114 (M.D. Pa. Oct. 5, 2011).

E-Commerce & Cyberlaw

Insurance Contracts & E-Sign

The Electronic Signatures in Global and National Commerce Act (E-Sign) applies broadly to the insurance business.* Thus, with consent of the consumer, contracts may be executed with electronic signatures and documents may be delivered by electronic means. E-Sign also provides protections for insurance agents against liability resulting from any deficiencies in the electronic procedures set forth in an electronic contract, provided the agent did not engage in tortious conduct and was not involved in the establishment of the electronic procedures.

Insurance providers are precluded from canceling health insurance or life insurance protection by means of electronic notices.

*15 U.S.C. §7001(i).

terms of the car rental agreement provided for termination of liability coverage in wide-ranging circumstances. White injured Terence Czop while driving intoxicated, one of the causes set forth in the rental agreement for termination of liability coverage. Because state law requires coverage on rental vehicles, the court determined that to allow termination of coverage based on a violation of the rental agreement is against public policy.[6]

4. Antilapse and Cancellation Statutes and Provisions

If the premiums are not paid on time, the policy under ordinary contract law would lapse because of nonpayment. However, with life insurance policies, by either policy provision or statute, the insured is allowed a grace period of 30 or 31 days in which to make payment of the premium due. When there is a default in the payment of a premium by the insured, the insurer may be required by statute to (1) issue a paid-up policy in a smaller amount, (2) provide extended insurance for a period of time, or (3) pay the cash surrender value of the policy.

The contract of insurance may expressly declare that it may or may not be canceled by the insurer's unilateral act. By statute or policy provision, the insurer is commonly required to give a specific number of days' written notice of cancellation.[7]

5. Modification of Contract

As is the case with most contracts, a contract of insurance can be modified if both insurer and insured agree to the change. The insurer cannot modify the contract without the consent of the insured when the right to do so is not reserved in the insurance contract.

To make changes or corrections to the policy, it is not necessary to issue a new policy. An endorsement on the policy or the execution of a separate rider is effective for the purpose of changing the policy. When a provision of an endorsement conflicts with a provision of the policy, the endorsement controls because it is the later document.

---

[6] *Czop v. White*, 80 So.3d 1255 (La. App. 2011).
[7] *Transamerican Ins. Co. v. Tab Transportation*, 906 P.2d 1341 (Cal. 1995).

6. Interpretation of Contract

A contract of insurance is interpreted by the same rules that govern the interpretation of ordinary contracts. Words are to be given their plain and ordinary meaning and interpreted in light of the nature of the coverage intended. However, an insurance policy is construed strictly against the insurer, who chooses the language of the policy, and if a reasonable construction may be given that would justify recovery, a court will do so. **For Example,** Dr. Kolb consented to an elective surgical procedure on his right eye after which "something happened that caused the wound to start leaking" and resulted in loss of vision in his eye. This forced him to retire as an orthopedic surgeon. His Paul Revere Life Insurance disability income insurance policy provided income for life for a disability due to "accidental bodily injury." The policy provided benefits for a shorter duration if the disability was caused by "sickness." Dr. Kolb's vision loss was not expected and proceeded from an unidentified postsurgical cause. Applying the plain and ordinary meaning of "accidental" and "injury," the court decided that Dr. Kolb was entitled to income for life under the "injury" provision of the policy.[8]

If there is an ambiguity in the policy, the provision is interpreted against the insurer.[9] **For Example,** on August 29, 2005, the Buentes' residence in Gulfport, Mississippi, was damaged during Hurricane Katrina. Allstate tendered a check for $2,600.35 net after the deductible, under its Deluxe Homeowner's Policy. The Buentes contend their covered losses are between $50,000 and $100,000. They brought suit against Allstate. The trial judge denied Allstate's motion to dismiss, finding the two provisions of the policy that purport to exclude coverage for wind and rain damage were ambiguous in light of other policy provisions granting coverage for wind and rain damage and in light of the inclusion of a "hurricane deductible" as part of the policy. The court found that because the policy was ambiguous, its weather exclusion was unenforceable in the context of losses attributable to wind and rain that occur in a hurricane.[10]

7. Burden of Proof

When an insurance claim is disputed by the insurer, the person bringing suit has the burden of proving that there was a loss, that it occurred while the policy was in force, and that the loss was of a kind that was within the coverage or scope of the policy.[11]

A policy will contain exceptions to the coverage. This means that the policy is not applicable when an exception applies to the situation. Exceptions to coverage are generally strictly interpreted against the insurer. However, insurance policies are contracts and the plain and unambiguous language of the contract will apply. **For Example,** Aroa Marketing, Inc., purchased a commercial general liability (CGL) policy from Hartford Midwest Insurance Co. The policy covered any damages that Aroa became legally obligated to pay because of "bodily injury," "property damage," or "personal and advertising injury" arising out of Aroa's business. Coverage was excluded, however, for "personal and advertising injury" arising out of "any violation of any intellectual property rights, such as copyright, patent, trademark, trade name, trade secret, service mark, or other destination of origin or authenticity." Aroa hired

[8] *Kolb v. Paul Revere Life Insurance Co.,* 355 F.3d 1132 (8th. Cir. 2004).
[9] See *Arrowood Indemnity Co. v. King,* 39 A.3d 712 (Conn. 2012); *Koziol v. Peerless Insurance Co.,* 41 A.3d 647 (R.I. 2012).
[10] *Buente v. Allstate Ins. Co.,* 422 F. Supp. 2d 690 (S.D. Miss. 2006).
[11] *Koslik v. Gulf Insurance Co.,* 673 N.W.2d 343 (Wis. App. 2003).

Tara Radcliffe to appear in and film an exercise video for its business to be used at a consumer electronics show and on a client's Internet site. Aroa used her images to sell other products, and she sued for misappropriation of her image and violation of her right of publicity. The court found that Hartford had no duty to defend or indemnify Aroa because the model's claim fell within the intellectual property exclusion.[12]

8. Insurer Bad Faith

As is required in the case of all contracts, an insurer must act in good faith in processing and paying claims under its policy. In some states, laws have been enacted making an insurer liable for a statutory penalty and attorney fees in case of a bad-faith failure or delay in paying a valid claim within a specified period of time. A bad-faith refusal is generally considered to be any frivolous or unfounded refusal to comply with the demand of a policyholder to pay according to the policy.[13]

CASE SUMMARY

Ruining General Lafayette's* Good Name

*Check him out online.

FACTS: Don and Myna Leland owned rental property in Lake Charles, Louisiana, that was damaged by a tree falling into the building, shearing off a portion of the facade during Hurricane Rita in September 2005. By October 7, 2005, they notified their insurer, Lafayette Insurance Co., of the damages to this property. In September 2007, two years after the hurricane, the Lelands filed a lawsuit against the issuer for breach of the insurer's duty of good faith and fair dealing in adjusting losses associated with the hurricane. The jury found in favor of the Lelands, concluding that the plaintiffs sustained losses in excess of the amount paid under the defendant's policy in the amount of $144,800.00. Further, the jury concluded that the defendant: (1) failed to initiate a loss adjustment to the property within 30 days after notification of loss; (2) was arbitrary, capricious, or without probable cause in failing to pay any claim due within 60 days after receipt of satisfactory proof of loss; (3) failed to make an offer to settle the property damage within 30 days of receipt of satisfactory proof of loss; and (4) misrepresented pertinent facts or insurance policy provisions related to coverage at issue. From a judgment for the Lelands, Lafayette appealed.

DECISION: Judgment for the Lelands. The court of appeals affirmed the trial court's damages as amended as follows: $5,000 for loss of rental income, $53,000 for loss of personal income, $30,000 in interest and $45,000 each for the Lelands for mental anguish and emotional distress for a total of $178,000 in damages attributable to the insurer's breach of its duties. State law added a penalty of two times these damages, or $356,000. The insurer was also obligated to pay $144,800 in contractual damages for repairs owed under the insurance contract and $226,266 in attorneys' fees. In particular the court determined that the evidence was sufficient to support the awards for mental anguish. Mr. Leland testified extensively regarding the frustrations encountered in pursuing the multiyear claim and making little progress toward a conclusion, including a record of repeated and persisted demands to the insurers regarding his property, which remained unrepaired, causing him to borrow more than $142,000 for repairs in order to avoid the city's pending action to demolish the property. Both Lelands testified to the negative impact the multiyear process had taken on their personal relationship. [*Leland v. Lafayette Insurance Co.*, **77 So.3d 1078 (La. App. 2011)**]

---

[12] *Aroa Marketing, Inc. v. Hartford Insurance Co.*, 130 Cal. Rptr.3d 466 (Cal. App. 2011).
[13] *Uberti v. Lincoln National Life Ins. Co.*, 144 F. Supp. 2d 90 (D. Conn. 2001).

When it is a liability insurer's duty to defend the insured and the insurer wrongfully refuses to do so, the insurer is guilty of breach of contract and is liable for all consequential damages resulting from the breach. In some jurisdictions, an insured can recover for an excess judgment rendered against the insured when it is proven that the insurer was guilty of negligence or bad faith in failing to defend the action or settle the matter within policy limits.

If there is a reasonable basis for the insurer's belief that a claim is not covered by its policy, its refusal to pay the claim does not subject it to liability for a breach of good faith or for a statutory penalty.[14] This is so even though the court holds that the insurer is liable for the claim.

For Example, the following illustrates an insurer's bad-faith failure to pay a claim, as opposed to an insurer's reasonable basis for failure to pay. Carmela Garza's home and possessions were destroyed in a fire set by an arsonist on August 19. Carmela's husband, Raul, who was no longer living at the home, had a criminal record. An investigator for the insurer stated that while he had no specific information to implicate the Garzas in the arson, Carmela may have wanted the proceeds to finance relocation to another city. By October, however, Aetna's investigators ruled out the possibility that Garza had the motive or the opportunity to set the fire. The insurer thus no longer had a reasonable basis to refuse to pay the claim after this date. Yet it took over a year and a half and court intervention for Aetna to allow Carmela to see a copy of her policy, which had been destroyed in the fire. Two years after the fire, Aetna paid only $28,624.55 for structural damage to the fire-gutted home, which was insured for $111,000. The court held that Aetna's actions constituted a bad-faith failure to pay by the insurer.[15]

9. Time Limitations on Insured

The insured must comply with a number of time limitations in making a claim. For example, the insured must promptly notify the insurer of any claim that may arise, submit a proof-of-loss statement within the time set forth in the policy, and bring any court action based on the policy within a specified time period.[16]

10. Subrogation of Insurer

subrogation – right of a party secondarily liable to stand in the place of the creditor after making payment to the creditor and to enforce the creditor's right against the party primarily liable in order to obtain indemnity from such primary party.

In some instances, the insured has a claim against a third person for the harm covered by the insurance policy. **For Example,** *A* sells an automobile insurance policy that provides collision coverage to *B*. *C* "rear-ends" *B*'s car at a traffic rotary in the city. *A* pays *B* the full amount of the property damage repair costs. *A* is then **subrogated** to *B*'s claim against *C*, the person who caused the harm. See Figure 36-1. When the insurer is subrogated to the insured's claim, the insurer may enforce that claim against the third person.[17]

---

[14] *Shipes v. Hanover Ins. Co.*, 884 F.2d 1357 (11th Cir. 1989).

[15] See *Aetna Casualty & Surety Co. v. Garza*, 906 S.W.2d 543 (Tex. App. 1995).

[16] But see *Seeman v. Sterling Ins. Co.*, 699 N.Y.S.2d 542 (A.D. 1999), where the insured's four-month delay in notifying the insurer was excused because of his belief that only on-premises injuries were covered by his homeowners insurance policy and thus the policy would not cover an injury in which a paintball he fired at work struck his coworker in the eye.

[17] *Stratus Services Group, Inc. v. Kash 'N Gold Ltd.*, 935 N.Y.S.2d 302 (A.D. 2011).

| FIGURE 36-1 | *Subrogation* |

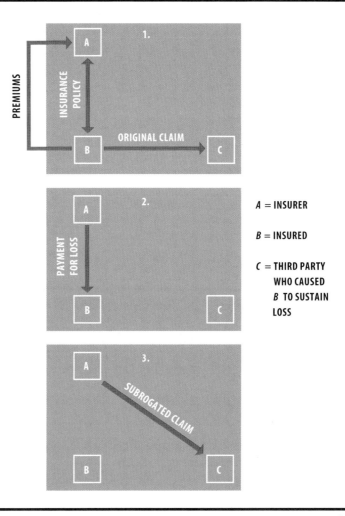

A = INSURER

B = INSURED

C = THIRD PARTY
WHO CAUSED
B TO SUSTAIN
LOSS

© Cengage Learning

B. KINDS OF INSURANCE

risk – peril or contingency against which the insured is protected by the contract of insurance.

Businesses today have specialized **risk** managers who identify the risks to which individual businesses are exposed, measure those risks, and purchase insurance to cover those risks (or decide to self-insure in whole or in part).

Insurance policies can be grouped into certain categories. Five major categories of insurance are considered here: (1) business liability insurance, (2) marine and inland marine insurance, (3) fire and homeowners insurance, (4) automobile insurance, and (5) life insurance.

11. Business Liability Insurance

Businesses may purchase Commercial General Liability (CGL) policies. This insurance is a broad, "all-risk" form of insurance providing coverage for mostly all

Ethics & the Law

On September 11, 2001, terrorist attacks killed 3,119 persons, devastated the U.S. airline industry, and had a severe impact on the U.S. insurance industry. In New York City, several office buildings, including One and Two World Trade Center, were destroyed, and other businesses in lower Manhattan were forced to shut down.

Business interruption insurance coverage is usually written as part of a company's commercial property insurance package. It not only covers policyholders for their lost profits and fixed charges and expenses for interruption to their business caused by physical damage or destruction to the insured's own property, but it may also cover "contingent business interruption" resulting from suspension of operations caused by damages to the property of a key supplier, distributor, or manufacturer. Such coverage, however, contains an exclusion for "war or military action." Are the September 11, 2001, terrorist attacks an "act of war" such that insurers are not responsible for business interruption claims? Can the president's words regarding war with al Qaeda be used to prove an "act of war" exclusion?

A court called upon to interpret an "act of war" exclusion will apply the plain and ordinary meaning of the policy's terms, and any ambiguity will be construed against the insurer. In *Pan American World Airways, Inc., v. Aetna Casualty & Surety Co.,** the Second Circuit Court

of Appeals held that an air carrier was entitled to recover for the destruction of its plane by terrorists in Cairo, Egypt, and the damage was not excluded under the policy's "act of war" exclusion. The court reasoned in part that there was no existing "war" between recognized sovereign states.

Pressured by historic losses as a result of "9/11," insurance companies in certain areas excluded perils resulting from "terrorism" in new commercial property insurance policies. Is it fair for insurers to exclude coverage altogether for losses due to acts of terrorism? Is it best to have the community absorb the losses? Is it best to have individuals and individual businesses cover the losses? See the Terrorism Risk Insurance Program Reauthorization Act of 2007, which extends the Terrorism Risk Insurance Act through December 31, 2014. The law extends the temporary federal program of shared public and private compensation for insured losses resulting from acts of terrorism. The 2007 law eliminates the requirement that the terrorist(s) are acting on behalf of any foreign person or foreign interest, and increases the program trigger to $110 million. The Secretary of State, in concurrence with the Attorney General of the United States, has authority to certify an event as an act of terrorism, thereby initiating the provisions and benefits of the act.

*See *Pan American World Airways, Inc. v. Aetna Casualty & Surety Co.*, 505 F.2d 989 (2d Cir. 1974).

sums that the insured may become legally obligated to pay as damages because of "bodily injury" or "property damage" caused by an "occurrence." The insurer is obligated to defend the insured business and pay damages under CGL policies for product liability cases, actions for wrongful termination of employees, sexual harassment cases, damages caused by business advertising or employee dishonesty, and trademark infringement suits.[18] The insurer may also be obligated to pay for damages in the form of cleanup costs imposed for contamination of land, water, and air under environmental statutes.[19]

CASE SUMMARY

EPA's PRP Suits the Court Just Fine

FACTS: Anderson Development Company (ADC) manufactures and sells specialty organic materials in Adrian, Michigan. It built a lagoon to handle the occasional accidental discharge of Curene 442 process water, believing it to be insoluble in water. Curene 442, which it

---

[18] *Charter Oak Fire Ins. Co. v. Heedon & Cos.*, 280 F.3d 730 (7th Cir. 2002).

[19] *Chemical Leaman Tank Lines, Inc. v. Aetna Casualty Co.*, 788 F. Supp. 846 (D.N.J. 1992); *United States v. Pepper's Steel, Inc.*, 823 F. Supp. 1574 (S.D. Fla. 1993). But see *Northville Industries v. National Union Fire and Ins. Co.*, 636 N.Y.S.2d 359 (A.D. 1995); *Aydin Corp. v. First State Ins. Co.*, 62 Cal. Rptr. 2d 825 (A.D. 1997).

CASE SUMMARY

Continued

manufactured between 1970 and 1979, was a known animal carcinogen, and it turned out to be soluble. The lagoon's discharge piping was connected to the sewer system, and the Curene 442 found its way to the city's sewage treatment plant. In 1985, the Environmental Protection Agency (EPA) sent ADC a formal notification that it was considered a "potentially responsible party" (PRP) for the release of hazardous substances into the soil and groundwater. This notice was called a *PRP letter.* ADC notified Travelers Indemnity Company, its insurer, of the letter, and Travelers contended that it was not prepared to defend or cover ADC in the matter. ADC did a study that revealed contamination on its property. The EPA and ADC entered a consent decree wherein ADC agreed to the cleanup activities required by the EPA, spending more than $6 million on the cleanup. ADC brought an action against its insurer, seeking coverage under its general liability insurance policies for the cost of its defense and the cost of the cleanup. Travelers alleged that it was not liable under the policies.

DECISION: Judgment for insured. The state's highest court has held that a PRP letter issued by the EPA is the functional equivalent of a "suit" brought in a court of law because the EPA's extensive authority to determine and apportion liability allows it to essentially usurp the traditional role of a court. Thus, Travelers had an obligation to defend the insured under the contractual terms used in the policy: "defend any suit." Travelers is also liable for "damages" as that term is used in the insurance contract because state court decisions hold that EPA-mandated cleanup costs constitute damages. [**Anderson Development Co. v. Travelers Indemnity Co., 49 F.3d 1128 (6th Cir. 1995)**]

The insurer must defend when coverage is a "close issue" regarding whether the policy would provide indemnity. The duty to defend does not depend on the truth or falsity of the allegations made against the insured by a third party; rather, the factual allegations in the complaint that potentially support a covered claim are all that is needed to invoke the insurer's duty to defend.[20] It is common for the insurer to seek a declaratory judgment if it believes the policy does not call for either a defense or indemnity. **For Example,** State Automobile Mutual Insurance Co. brought an action for declaratory judgment that it had no duty to defend and indemnify Flexdar, Inc., for the cost of cleanup of a chemical solvent discovered in the soil of Fexdar's manufacturing site, referencing its "pollution exclusion" language in its policies. The court found the language in the CGL policy in question was ambiguous, and thus ruled against the insurer.[21]

Businesses may purchase policies providing liability insurance for their directors and officers. Manufacturers and sellers may purchase product liability insurance. Professional persons, such as accountants, physicians, lawyers, architects, and engineers, may obtain liability insurance protection against malpractice suits. **For Example,** the architects of the MCI Center, a sports arena in Washington, D.C., were entitled under their professional liability insurance coverage to be defended by their insurer in a lawsuit seeking only injunctive relief for the firm's

[20] *Mid Continent Casualty Co. v. JHP Development Inc.,* 557 F.3d 207 (6th Cir. 2009).
[21] *State Automobile Mutual Insurance Co. v. Flexdar, Inc.,* 964 N.E.2d 845 (Ind. 2012). The court majority stated:

> After all, "[t]he insurance companies write the policies; we buy their forms or we do not buy their insurance." By more careful drafting State Auto has the ability to resolve any question of ambiguity. And in fact it has done so. In 2005 State Auto revised its policies to add an "Indiana Changes—Pollution Exclusion" endorsement. Id. At 852.

alleged failure to comply with the Americans with Disabilities Act's enhanced sightline requirements.[22]

12. Marine Insurance

marine insurance – policies that cover perils relating to the transportation of goods.

ocean marine – policies that cover transportation of goods in vessels in international and coastal trade.

inland marine – insurance that covers domestic shipments of goods over land and inland waterways.

hull insurance – insurance that covers physical damage on a freight-moving vessel.

cargo insurance – insurance that protects a cargo owner against financial loss if goods being shipped are lost or damaged at sea.

Marine insurance policies cover perils relating to the transportation of goods. **Ocean marine** insurance policies cover the transportation of goods in vessels in international and coastal trade. **Inland marine** insurance principally covers domestic shipments of goods over land and inland waterways.

(A) OCEAN MARINE. Ocean marine insurance is a form of insurance that covers ships and their cargoes against "perils of the sea." Four classes of ocean marine insurance are generally available: (1) hull, (2) cargo, (3) liability, and (4) freight. **Hull insurance** covers physical damage to the vessel.[23] **Cargo insurance** protects the cargo owner against financial loss if the goods being shipped are lost or damaged at sea.[24]

CASE SUMMARY

This Coverage Is Worth a Hill of Beans

FACTS: Commodities Reserve Company (CRC) contracted to sell 1,008 tons of beans and 50 tons of seed to purchasers in Venezuela. CRC purchased the beans and seeds in Turkey and chartered space on the ship *MV West Lion*. The cargo was insured under an ocean marine policy issued by St. Paul Fire & Marine Insurance Company. The Sue and Labor Clause in CRC's ocean marine policy with St. Paul provided: "In case of any loss or misfortune, it shall be lawful and necessary to and for the Assured … to sue, labor and travel for, in and about the defense, safeguard and recovery of the said goods and merchandise … to the charges whereof, the [insurer] will contribute according to the rate and quantity of the sum hereby insured." While the ship was sailing through Greek waters, Greek authorities seized the vessel for carrying munitions. CRC had to go to the expense of obtaining an order from a court in Crete to release the cargo. When St. Paul refused to pay the costs of the Cretan litigation to release the cargo, CRC brought suit against St. Paul.

DECISION: Judgment for CRC. The Sue and Labor Clause required CRC to sue for "recovery of the said goods and merchandise." The clause also requires the insurer to reimburse the insured for those expenses. [*Commodities Reserve Co. v. St. Paul Fire & Marine Ins. Co.*, 879 F.2d 640 (9th Cir. 1998)]

Cargo insurance does not cover risks prior to the loading of the insured cargo on board the vessel. An additional warehouse coverage endorsement is needed to insure merchandise held in a warehouse prior to import or export voyages.

liability insurance – covers the shipowner's liability if the ship causes damage to another ship or its cargo.

freight insurance – insures that shipowner will receive payment for transportation charges.

Liability insurance covers the shipowner's liability if the ship causes damage to another ship or its cargo. **Freight insurance** ensures that the shipowner will receive payment for the transportation charges. "All-risk" policies consolidate coverage of all four classes of ocean marine insurance into one policy.[25]

[22] *Washington Sports and Entertainment, Inc. v. United Coastal Ins.*, 7 F. Supp. 2d 1 (D.D.C. 1998).
[23] *Lloyd's v. Labarca*, 260 F.3d 3 (1st Cir. 2001).
[24] *Kimta, A. S. v. Royal Insurance Co., Inc.*, 9 P.3d 239 (Wash. App. 2001).
[25] *Transamerican Leasing, Inc. v. Institute of London Underwriters*, 7 F. Supp. 2d 1340 (S.D. Fla. 1998).

(B) INLAND MARINE. Inland marine insurance evolved from marine insurance. It protects goods in transit over land; by air; or on rivers, lakes, and coastal waters. Inland marine insurance can be used to insure property held by a bailee. Moreover, it is common for institutions financing automobile dealers' new car inventories to purchase inland marine insurance policies to insure against damage to the automobiles while in inventory.

13. Fire and Homeowners Insurance

fire insurance policy – a contract that indemnifies the insured for property destruction or damage caused by fire.

homeowners insurance policy – combination of standard fire insurance and comprehensive personal liability insurance.

A **fire insurance policy** is a contract to indemnify the insured for property destruction or damage caused by fire. In almost every state, the New York standard fire insurance form is the standard policy. A **homeowners insurance policy** is a combination of the standard fire insurance policy and comprehensive personal liability insurance. It thus provides fire, theft, and certain liability protection in a single insurance contract.

(A) FIRE INSURANCE. For fire insurance to cover fire loss, there must be an actual hostile fire that is the immediate cause of the loss. A *hostile fire* is one that becomes uncontrollable, burns with excessive heat, or escapes from the place where it is intended to be. To illustrate, when soot is ignited and causes a fire in the chimney, the fire is hostile. On the other hand, if a loss is caused by the smoke or heat of a fire that has not broken out of its ordinary container or become uncontrollable, the loss results from a friendly fire. The policy does not cover damage from a friendly fire.

By policy endorsement, however, the coverage may be extended to include loss by a friendly fire.

CASE SUMMARY

Excuse Me? The Fire Wasn't Hostile?

FACTS: Youse owned a ring that was insured with the Employers Fire Insurance Company against loss, including "all direct loss or damage by fire." Youse accidentally threw the ring into a trash burner, and it was damaged when the trash was burned. He sued the insurer.

DECISION: Judgment for insurer. A fire policy covers only loss caused by a hostile fire. The fire was not hostile because it burned in the area in which it was intended to burn. [*Youse v. Employers Fire Ins. Co.*, 238 P.2d 472 (Kan. 1951)]

(1) Coinsurance.

coinsurance clause – clause requiring the insured to maintain insurance on property up to a stated amount and providing that to the extent that this is not done, the insured is to be deemed a coinsurer with the insurer, so that the latter is liable only for its proportionate share of the amount of insurance required to be carried.

The insurer is liable for the actual amount of the loss sustained up to the maximum amount stated in the policy. An exception exists when the policy contains a coinsurance clause. A **coinsurance clause** requires the insured to maintain insurance on the covered property up to a certain amount or a certain percentage of the value (generally 80 percent). Under such a provision, if the policyholder insures the property for less than the required amount, the insurer is liable only for the proportionate share of the amount of insurance required to be carried. **For Example,** suppose that the owner of a building with a value of $400,000 insures it against loss to the extent of $240,000. The policy contains a coinsurance clause requiring that insurance of 80 percent of the value of the property be carried (in this case, $320,000). Assume that a $160,000 loss is then sustained. The insured would receive not $160,000 from the insurer but only three-fourths of that amount, which is $120,000, because the amount of the insurance carried ($240,000) is only three-fourths of the amount required ($360,000).

Some states prohibit the use of a coinsurance clause.

(2) Assignment.

Fire insurance is a personal contract, and in the absence of statute or contractual authorization, it cannot be assigned without the consent of the insurer.

(3) Occupancy.

Provisions in a policy of fire insurance relating to the use and occupancy of the property are generally strictly construed because they relate to the hazards involved.

(B) HOMEOWNERS INSURANCE. In addition to providing protection against losses resulting from fire, the homeowners policy provides liability coverage for accidents or injuries that occur on the premises of the insured. Moreover, the liability provisions provide coverage for unintentional injuries to others away from home for which the insured or any member of the resident family is held responsible, such as injuries caused to others by golfing, hunting, or fishing accidents.[26] Generally, motor vehicles, including mopeds and recreational vehicles, are excluded from such personal liability coverage.

A homeowners policy also provides protection from losses caused by theft. In addition, it provides protection for all permanent residents of the household, including all family members living with the insured. Thus, a child of the insured who lives at home is protected under the homeowners policy for the value of personal property lost when the home is destroyed by fire.

14. Automobile Insurance

Associations of insurers, such as the National Bureau of Casualty Underwriters and the National Automobile Underwriters Association, have proposed standard forms of automobile insurance policies. These forms have been approved by the association members in virtually all states. The form used today by most insurers is the Personal Auto Policy (PAP).

(A) PERILS COVERED. Part A of the policy provides liability coverage that protects the insured driver or owner from the claims of others for bodily injuries or damage to their property. Part B of the policy provides coverage for medical expenses sustained by a covered person or persons in an accident. Part C of the PAP provides coverage for damages the insured is entitled to recover from an *uninsured motorist*.[27] Part D provides coverage for loss or damage to the covered automobile. Coverage under Part D includes collision coverage and coverage of "other than collision" losses, such as fire and theft.

(B) COVERED PERSONS. Covered persons include the named insured or any family member (a person related by blood, marriage, or adoption or a ward or foster child

[26] *American Concept Ins. Co. v. Lloyds of London*, 467 N.W.2d 480 (S.D. 1991).
[27] *Montano v. Allstate Indemnity*, 211 F.3d 1278 (10th Cir. 2002).

who is a resident of the household). If an individual is driving with the permission of the insured, that individual is also covered.

(c) Use and Operation. The coverage of the PAP policy is limited to claims arising from the "use and operation" of an automobile. The term *use and operation* does not require that the automobile be in motion. Thus, the term embraces loading and unloading as well as actual travel.[28]

(d) Notice and Cooperation. The insured is under a duty to give notice of claims, to inform, and to cooperate with the insurer. Notice and cooperation are conditions precedent to the liability of the insurer.

CASE SUMMARY

Is Carrying a Transmission Down a Driveway "Loading or Unloading" a Truck? A Liberal Interpretation

FACTS: Gerhard Schillers was assisting his friend J. L. Loethen in removing a transmission from the bed of the Loethens' truck on the Loethens' property. While Schillers was carrying the transmission down a driveway, he fell and was seriously injured. J. L. was insured under his parents' automobile insurance policy with Shelter Mutual Insurance Company, which insured for liability, including "the loading and unloading" of the vehicle.

DECISION: Schillers's injuries were incidental to, and a consequence of, the unloading of the Loethens' pickup truck. The injuries would not have occurred if the men had not been unloading the truck. The unloading activity continued until the removed property was put in the place to which it was to be taken. Therefore, Schillers's injury was covered by the motor vehicle liability policy issued by Shelter Mutual. [*American Family Mutual Ins. Co. v. Shelter Mutual Ins. Co.*, 747 S.W.2d 174 (Mo. App. 1988)]

(e) No-Fault Insurance. Traditional tort law (negligence law) placed the economic losses resulting from an automobile accident on the one at fault. The purpose of automobile liability insurance is to relieve the wrongdoer from the consequences of a negligent act by paying defense costs and the damages assessed. Under no-fault laws, injured persons are barred from suing the party at fault for ordinary claims. When the insured is injured while using the insured automobile, the insurer will make a payment without regard to whose fault caused the harm. However, if the automobile collision results in a permanent serious disablement or disfigurement, or death, or if the medical bills and lost wages of the plaintiff exceed a specified amount, suit may be brought against the party who was at fault.

15. Life Insurance

There are three basic types of life insurance: term insurance, whole life insurance, and endowment insurance.

term insurance – policy written for a specified number of years that terminates at the end of that period.

Term insurance is written for a specified number of years and terminates at the end of that period. If the insured dies within the time period covered by the policy,

---

[28] See *American Home Insurance Co. v. First Speciality Insurance Corp.*, 894 N.E.2d 1167 (Mass. App. 2008).

the face amount is paid to the beneficiary. If the insured is still alive at the end of the time period, the contract expires, and the insurer has no further obligation. Term policies have little or no cash surrender value.

Whole life insurance (or ordinary life insurance) provides lifetime insurance protection. It also has an investment element.

Part of every premium covers the cost of insurance, and the remainder of the premium builds up a **cash surrender value** of the policy.

An **endowment insurance** policy is one that pays the face amount of the policy if the insured dies within the policy period. If the insured lives to the end of the policy period, the face amount is paid to the insured at the end of the period.

Many life insurance companies pay double the amount of the policy, called **double indemnity**, if death is caused by an accident and death occurs within 90 days afterward. A comparatively small additional premium is charged for this special protection.

In consideration of an additional premium, many life insurance companies also provide insurance against total permanent disability of the insured. **Disability** is usually defined in a life insurance policy as any "incapacity resulting from bodily injury or disease to engage in any occupation for remuneration or profit."

(A) EXCLUSIONS. Life insurance policies frequently provide that death is not within the protection of the policy and that a double indemnity provision is not applicable when death is caused by (1) suicide,[29] (2) narcotics, (3) the intentional act of another, (4) execution for a crime, (5) war activities, or (6) operation of aircraft.

(B) THE BENEFICIARY. The recipient of life insurance policy proceeds that are payable upon the death of the insured is called the **beneficiary**. The beneficiary may be a third person or the estate of the insured, and there may be more than one beneficiary.

The beneficiary named in a policy may be barred from claiming the proceeds of the policy. It is generally provided by statute or stated by court decision that a beneficiary who has feloniously killed the insured is not entitled to receive the proceeds of the policy.

The customary policy provides that the insured reserves the right to change the beneficiary without the latter's consent. When the policy contains such a provision, the beneficiary cannot object to a change that destroys all of that beneficiary's rights under the policy and that names another person as beneficiary.

An insurance policy will ordinarily state that to change the beneficiary, the insurer must be so instructed in writing by the insured and the policy must then be endorsed by the company with the change of the beneficiary. These provisions are construed liberally. If the insured has notified the insurer but dies before the endorsement of the change by the company, the change of beneficiary is effective.[30] However, if the insured has not taken any steps to comply with the policy requirements, a change of beneficiary is not effective even though a change was intended.

(C) INCONTESTABILITY CLAUSE. Statutes commonly require the inclusion of an **incontestability clause** in life insurance policies. Ordinarily, this clause states that after the lapse of two years, the policy cannot be contested by the insurance company.[31]

---

whole life insurance – ordinary life insurance providing lifetime insurance protection.

cash surrender value – sum paid the insured upon the surrender of a policy to the insurer.

endowment insurance – insurance that pays the face amount of the policy if the insured dies within the policy period.

double indemnity – provision for payment of double the amount specified by the insurance contract if death is caused by an accident and occurs under specified circumstances.

disability – any incapacity resulting from bodily injury or disease to engage in any occupation for remuneration or profit.

beneficiary – person to whom the proceeds of a life insurance policy are payable, a person for whose benefit property is held in trust, or a person given property by a will; the ultimate recipient of the benefit of a funds transfer.

incontestability clause – provision that after the lapse of a specified time the insurer cannot dispute the policy on the ground of misrepresentation or fraud of the insured or similar wrongful conduct.

[29] *Mirza v. Maccabees Life and Annuity Co.*, 466 N.W.2d 340 (Mich. App. 1991).

[30] *Zeigler v. Cardona*, 830 F. Supp. 1395 (M.D. Ala. 1993).

[31] The two-year period runs from the policy's date of issue to the date the suit is filed in court. See *PHL Variable Insurance Co. v. The Sheldon Hathaway Family Insurance Trust*, 2011 WL 703839 (D. Utah Feb. 20, 2011).

The insurer is free to contest the validity of the policy at any time during the contestability period. Once the period has expired, the insurer must pay the stipulated sum upon the death of the insured and cannot claim that in obtaining the policy, the insured had been guilty of misrepresentation, fraud, or any other conduct that would entitle it to avoid the contract of insurance.[32]

CASE SUMMARY

The Impostor Defense: Dealing with Substitutes with Different Attributes

FACTS: The Allstate life insurance policy on which this case centers went into effect on September 20, 2000, insuring the life of John Miller. The policy stated that if the insured died while the policy was in force, Allstate would pay a death benefit to the policy beneficiaries upon receiving proof of death. As required by Fla. Stat. §627.455, the policy further provided that it would become incontestable after remaining in force during the lifetime of the insured for a period of two years from its effective date. John Miller died on April 20, 2003—more than two years after the policy went into effect. The beneficiaries accordingly filed statements seeking to collect benefits under the policy. Rather than disburse the benefits, Allstate sought a declaratory judgment that the policy was void, alleging that the application was completed using fraudulent information and that an imposter had appeared at the medical exam in place of John Miller. The beneficiaries counterclaimed, alleging breach of contract based on Allstate's failure to pay benefits upon proof of death in accordance with the insurance policy's terms. Allstate appealed a judgment in favor of the beneficiaries.

DECISION: Judgment for the beneficiaries. The incontestability clause works to the mutual advantage of the insured, giving the insured a guarantee against expensive litigation to defeat the policy after it has been in effect during the lifetime of the insured for a period of two years from its date of issue and giving the company a reasonable time to ascertain whether the insurance contract should remain in force. Under Florida law where the insured's death occurred after the contestability period, Allstate could not void the policy on the ground that an imposter had undergone the precoverage physical examination in the insured's place. [***Allstate Life Ins. Co. v. Miller*, 424 F.3d 1113 (11th Cir. 2005)**]

Courts and legislatures have addressed the issue of "imposter fraud." In *Amex Life Assurance Co. v. Superior Court,* the California Supreme Court concluded that after the contestability period had expired, an insurer may not assert the defense that an imposter took the medical examination. Jose Morales had applied for a life insurance policy from Amex. A paramedic working for Amex met a man claiming to be Morales and took blood and urine samples, listing him as 5'10" and weighing 172 pounds. His blood sample was HIV negative. The individual did not provide identification. Some two years later, Morales died of AIDS–related causes. Morales had listed his height as 5'6" and his weight as 142 on his insurance application. The California Supreme Court stated that Amex, which had done nothing to protect its interest but collect premiums, could not challenge coverage based on the imposter defense.[33] Subsequent to the court's decision, the California legislature amended state insurance law to provide for an

[32] *Amica Life Insurance Co. v. Barbor,* 488 F. Supp. 2d 750 (N.D. Ill. 2007).
[33] *Amex Life Assurance Co. v. Superior Court,* 930 P.2d 1264 (Cal. 1997).

"imposter defense" in that state. As set forth in the *Miller* case, Florida does not recognize an imposter defense to incontestability. The legislative purpose of such clauses is to protect beneficiaries from an insurer's refusal to honor policies by asserting pre-existing conditions, leaving beneficiaries in the untenable position of having to battle with powerful insurance companies in court.

LawFlix

Double Indemnity (1944)

In this Billy Wilder film, Fred MacMurray is an insurance salesman coerced into a murder plot. The movie provides good coverage of insurable interest in life.

MAKE THE CONNECTION

SUMMARY

Insurance is a contract called a *policy*. Under an insurance policy, the insurer provides in consideration of premium payments, to pay the insured or beneficiary a sum of money if the insured sustains a specified loss or is subjected to a specified liability. These contracts are made through an insurance agent, who is an agent for the insurance company, or through an insurance broker, who is the agent of the insured when obtaining a policy for the latter.

The person purchasing an insurance contract must have an insurable interest in the insured's life or property. An insurable interest in property exists when the damage or destruction of the property will cause a direct monetary loss to the insured. In the case of property insurance, the insured must have an insurable interest at the time of loss. An insurable interest in the life of the insured exists if the purchaser would suffer a financial loss from the insured's death. This interest must exist as of the time the policy is obtained.

Ocean marine policies insure ships and their cargoes against the perils of the sea. Inland marine policies insure goods being transported by land, by air, or on inland and coastal waterways.

For fire insurance to cover a fire loss, there must be an actual hostile fire that is the immediate cause

of the loss. The insurer is liable for the actual amount of the loss sustained up to the maximum amount stated in the policy. An exception exists when the policy contains a coinsurance clause requiring the insured to maintain insurance up to a certain percentage of the value of the property. To the extent this is not done, the insured is deemed a coinsurer with the insurer, and the insurer is liable for only its proportional share of the amount of insurance required to be carried. A homeowners insurance policy provides fire, theft, and liability protection in a single contract.

Automobile insurance may provide protection for collision damage to the insured's property and injury to persons. It may also cover liability to third persons for injury and property damage as well as loss by fire or theft.

A life insurance policy requires the insurer to pay a stated sum of money to a named beneficiary upon the death of the insured. It may be a term insurance policy, a whole life policy, or an endowment policy. State law commonly requires the inclusion of an incontestability clause, whereby at the conclusion of the contestability period, the insurer cannot contest the validity of the policy.

LEARNING OUTCOMES

After studying this chapter, you should be able to clearly explain:

A. The Insurance Contract

LO.1   Explain the necessity of having an insurable interest to obtain an insurance policy
> See the Vin Harrington example of insurable interest in property, p. 774. See the discussion of a creditor's insurable interest in the life of a debtor, p. 775.

LO.2   Recognize that the formation of a contract is governed by the general principles of contract law
> See how insurers stop "STOLI" schemes through the application process where false answers to material questions make the insurance contract voidable by insurer, p. 776.

LO.3   Explain why courts strictly construe insurance policies against insurance companies
> See the discussion and examples in which the courts awarded coverage for the insured because the insurers chose the ambiguous language of the policies, p. 778.

B. Kinds of Insurance

LO.4   List and explain the five major categories of insurance
> See the description on business liability insurance, marine and inland insurance, fire and homeowners insurance, automobile insurance, and life insurance, beginning on p. 781.

LO.5   Explain coinsurance and its purpose
> See the example of the homeowner who underinsured his property, resulting in the insurer paying a claim at a proportionate share of the amount of insurance required, pp. 785–786.

LO.6   Explain incontestability clauses
> See the example of the handling of imposter fraud after the incontestability period has run out, p. 789.

KEY TERMS

beneficiary	homeowners insurance policy	liability insurance
cargo insurance	hull insurance	marine insurance
cash surrender value	incontestability clause	ocean marine
coinsurance clause	inland marine	policy
disability	insurance	risk
double indemnity	insurance agent	subrogated
endowment insurance	insurance broker	term insurance
fire insurance policy	insured	underwriter
freight insurance	insurer	whole life insurance

QUESTIONS AND CASE PROBLEMS

1. Mr. Keyes was injured on April 30, 2010, when he fell off Ms. Thibodeaux's roof. Mr. Keyes was cleaning and measuring the roof in preparation for painting when, unbeknownst to him, Ms. Thibodeaux sprayed a section of the metal roof with water. Mr. Keyes slipped on the wet roof and fell, seriously injuring himself. He filed the lawsuit under Ms. Thibodeaux's homeowner's policy against Lighthouse Property Insurance. Mr. Keyes and Ms. Thibodeaux married in August of 2008 but physically separated four months into the marriage. Mr. Keyes and Ms. Thibodeaux have not divorced. Mr. Keyes testified that he lives in a home he owns with his grandmother and aunt. He stated that he lived in that house prior to

marrying Ms. Thibodeaux and returned there after he was kicked out of her home 15 months prior to the accident. The homeowners policy precluded coverage for bodily injury to the named insured and relatives "who are residents of the insured's household." The definitions section of the policy states that the spouse of the name insured is treated as the named insured, if a resident of the same household. Lighthouse has refused coverage for Keyes under its reading of the policy. Keyes disagrees. Decide. [*Keyes v. Thibodeaux*, 85 So.3d 1284 (La. App.)]

2. Cecil Usher owned Belize NY, Inc. (Belize), a small construction company doing business in New York City. Belize purchased a commercial general liability insurance policy from Mount Vernon Fire Insurance Co. The policy's first page, entitled "Policy Declarations," describes the insured as "Belize N.Y., Inc."; it classifies the "Form of Business" as "Corporation," the "Business Description" as "Carpentry," and indicates that Belize was afforded commercial liability insurance in the amount of $1,000,000 per occurrence and $2,000,000 in the aggregate for the period June 1, 1995, to June 1, 1996. Two classifications are listed under "Premium Computation" on the Declarations page: "Carpentry—Interior—001" and "Carpentry—001." The policy makes no further mention of these two terms. Belize performed some $60,000 of demolition work on the United House of Prayer's renovation project on 272 West 125th Street in New York City. Belize was thereafter hired to supervise subcontractors working on the job. During that period of time, a person entered the building, shot several people with a firearm, and started a fire. Seven people died and several others were injured. The estates of the victims sued Belize, Inc., for "negligence, carelessness and recklessness" regarding the fire, and Belize notified Mount Vernon of the lawsuit. Mount Vernon refused to defend or indemnify Belize because Belize was not engaging in its carpentry operations in the building at the time of the incident. It asserted that its risk is limited to carpentry operations in accordance with the classifications set forth in the policy. Belize contended that the language of the policy did not provide that the classification "Carpentry" defined covered risks, and exclusions should have been stated in the contract. Decide. [*Mount Vernon Fire Insurance Co. v. Belize NY, Inc.*, 227 F.3d 232 (2d Cir.)]

3. On April 6, 1988, Luis Serrano purchased for $75,000 a 26'8"–long Carrera speedboat named *Hot Shot*. First Federal Savings Bank provided $65,000 financing for this purchase. Serrano obtained a marine yacht policy for hull insurance on the boat for $75,000 from El Fenix, with First Federal being named as payee under the policy.

   On May 2, 1988, Serrano sold the boat to Reinaldo Polito, and Serrano furnished First Federal with documents evidencing the sale. Polito assumed the obligation to pay off the balance due First Federal. On October 6, 1989, Serrano again applied to El Fenix for a new yacht policy, covering the period from October 6, 1989, through October 6, 1990, and the coverage extended to peril of confiscation by a governmental agency. Serrano did not have ownership or possession of the boat on October 6, 1989. First Federal, the named payee, had not perfected or recorded a mortgage on *Hot Shot* until July 5, 1990.

   On November 13, 1989, in the waters off Cooper Island in the British Virgin Islands (BVI), *Hot Shot* was found abandoned after a chase by governmental officials. A large shipment of cocaine was recovered, although no one was arrested. When Serrano and First Federal were informed that *Hot Shot* was subject to mandatory forfeiture under BVI law, they both filed claims under the October 6, 1989, insurance policy. What defenses would you raise on behalf of the insurer in this case? Decide. [*El Fenix v. Serrano Gutierrez*, 786 F. Supp. 1065 (D.P.R.)]

4. From the United Insurance Co., Rebecca Foster obtained a policy insuring the life of Lucille McClurkin and naming herself as beneficiary. McClurkin did not live with Foster, and Foster did not inform McClurkin of the existence of the policy. Foster paid the premiums on the policy and upon the death of McClurkin sued the United Insurance Co. for the amount of the

insurance. At the trial, Foster testified vaguely that her father had told her that McClurkin was her second cousin on his side of the family. Was Foster entitled to recover on the policy? [*Foster v. United Ins. Co.*, 158 S.E.2d 201 (S.C.)]

5. Dr. George Allard and his brother-in-law, Tom Rowland, did not get along after family land that was once used solely by Rowland was partitioned among family members after the death of Rowland's father. Rowland had a reputation in the community as a bully and a violent person. On December 17, Allard was moving cattle down a dirt road by "trolling" (leading the cattle with a bucket of feed, causing them to follow him). When he saw a forestry truck coming along the road, he led the cattle off the road onto Rowland's land to prevent frightening the cattle. When Rowland saw Allard, Rowland ran toward him screaming at him for being on his land. Allard, a small older man, retreated to his truck and obtained a 12-gauge shotgun. He pointed the gun toward the ground about an inch in front of Rowland's left foot and fired it. He stated that he fired the shot in this fashion to bring Rowland to his senses and that Rowland stepped forward into the line of fire. Allard claimed that if Rowland had not stepped forward, he would not have been hit and injured. Allard was insured by Farm Bureau homeowners and general liability policies, which did not cover liability resulting from intentional acts by the insured. Applying the policy exclusion to the facts of this case, was Farm Bureau obligated to pay the $100,000 judgment against Allard? [*Southern Farm Bureau Casualty Co. v. Allard*, 611 So.2d 966 (Miss.)]

6. Arthur Katz testified for the U.S. government in a stock manipulation case. He also pled guilty and testified against three of his law partners in an insurance fraud case. He received a six-month sentence in a halfway house and a $5,000 fine. Katz was placed in the Federal Witness Protection Program. He and his wife changed their names to Kane and moved to Florida under the program. Both he and his wife obtained new driver's licenses and Social Security numbers. Using his new identity, "Kane" obtained two life insurance

policies totaling $1.5 million. He named his wife beneficiary. A routine criminal background check on Kane found no criminal history.

From 1984 to 1987, Kane invested heavily in the stock market. On October 17, 1987, the day the stock market crashed, Kane shot and wounded his stockbroker, shot and killed the office manager, and then committed suicide. The insurers refused to pay on the policies, claiming that they never insure persons with criminal records. Mrs. Kane contended that the policies were incontestable after they had been in effect for two years. Decide. [*Bankers Security Life Ins. Society v. Kane*, 885 F.2d 820 (11th Cir.)]

7. Linda Filasky held policies issued by Preferred Risk Mutual Insurance Co. Following an injury in an automobile accident and storm damage to the roof of her home, Filasky sustained loss of income, theft of property, and water damage to her home. These three kinds of losses were covered by the policies with Preferred, but the insurer delayed unreasonably in processing her claims and raised numerous groundless objections to them. Finally, the insurer paid the claims in full. Filasky then sued the insurer for the emotional distress caused by the bad-faith delay and obstructive tactics of the insurer. The insurer defended that it had paid the claims in full and that nothing was owed Filasky. Decide. [*Filasky v. Preferred Risk Mut. Ins. Co.*, 734 P.2d 76 (Ariz.)]

8. Baurer purchased a White Freightliner tractor and agreed that his son-in-law, Britton, could use it in the trucking business. In return, Britton agreed to haul Baurer's hay and cattle, thus saving Baurer approximately $30,000 per year. Baurer insured the vehicle with Mountain West Farm Bureau Insurance Company. The policy contained an exclusionary clause that provided: "We don't insure your [truck] while it is rented or leased to others.... This does not apply to the use of your [truck] on a share expense basis." When the vehicle was destroyed, Mountain West refused to pay on the policy, contending that the arrangement between Baurer and Britton was a lease of the vehicle, which was excluded under the policy. Baurer sued, contending that it was a "share expense basis" allowed under the policy.

Is the insurance policy ambiguous? What rule of contract construction applies in this case? Decide. [*Baurer v. Mountain West Farm Bureau Ins.*, 695 P.2d 1307 (Mont.)]

9. Collins obtained from South Carolina Insurance Co. a liability policy covering a Piper Colt airplane he owned. The policy provided that it did not cover loss sustained while the plane was being piloted by a person who did not have a valid pilot's certificate and a valid medical examination certificate. Collins held a valid pilot's certificate, but his medical examination certificate had expired three months before. Collins was piloting the plane when it crashed, and he was killed. The insurer denied liability because Collins did not have a valid medical certificate. It was stipulated by both parties that the crash was in no way caused by the absence of the medical certificate. Decide. [*South Carolina Ins. Co. v. Collins*, 237 S.E.2d 358 (S.C.)]

10. Marshall Produce Co. had insured its milk- and egg-processing plant against fire. When smoke from a fire near its plant permeated the environment and was absorbed into the company's egg powder products, cans of powder delivered to the U.S. government were rejected as contaminated. Marshall Produce sued the insurance company for a total loss, but the insurer contended there had been no fire involving the insured property and no total loss. Decide. [*Marshall Produce Co. v. St. Paul Fire & Marine Ins. Co.*, 98 N.W.2d 280 (Minn.)]

11. Amador Pena, who had three insurance policies on his life, wrote a will in which he specified that the proceeds from the insurance policies should go to his children instead of to Leticia Pena Salinas and other beneficiaries named in the policies. He died the day after writing the will. The insurance companies paid the proceeds of the policies to the named beneficiaries. The executor of Pena's estate sued Salinas and the other beneficiaries for the insurance money. Decide. [*Pena v. Salinas*, 536 S.W.2d 671 (Tex. App.)]

12. Spector owned a small automobile repair garage in rural Kansas that was valued at $80,000. He purchased fire insurance coverage against loss to the extent of $48,000. The policy contained an 80 percent coinsurance clause. A fire destroyed a portion of his parts room, causing a loss of $32,000. Spector believes he is entitled to be fully compensated for this loss, as it is less than the $48,000 of fire protection that he purchased and paid for. Is Spector correct?

13. Carman Tool & Abrasives, Inc., purchased two milling machines, FOB Taiwan, from the Dah Lih Machinery Co. Carman obtained ocean marine cargo insurance on the machines from St. Paul Fire and Marine Insurance Co. and authorized Dah Lih to arrange for the shipment of the two machines to Los Angeles, using the services of Evergreen Lines. Dah Lih booked the machinery for shipment onboard Evergreen's container ship, the *M/V Ever Giant;* arranged for the delivery of the cargo to the ship; provided all of the shipping information for the bill of lading; and was the party to whom the bill was issued. Dah Lih then delivered the bill of lading to its bank, which in turn negotiated it to Carman's bank to authorize payment to Dah Lih. After the cargo was removed from the vessel in Los Angeles but before it was delivered to Carman, the milling machines were damaged to the extent of $115,000. Is the insurer liable to Carman? Can the insurer recover from Evergreen? [*Carman Tool & Abrasives, Inc. v. Evergreen Lines*, 871 F.2d 897 (9th Cir.)]

14. Vallot was driving his farm tractor on the highway. It was struck from the rear by a truck, overturned, exploded, and burned. Vallot was killed, and a death claim was made against All American Insurance Co. The death of Vallot was covered by the company's policy if Vallot had died from "being struck or run over by" the truck. The insurance company claimed that the policy was not applicable because Vallot had not been struck; the farm tractor had been struck, and Vallot's death occurred when the overturned tractor exploded and burned. The insurance company also claimed that it was necessary that the insured be both struck and run over by another vehicle. Decide. [*Vallot v. All American Ins. Co.*, 302 So.2d 625 (La. App.)]

15. When Jorge de Guerrero applied for a $200,000 life insurance policy with John Hancock Mutual Life Insurance Co., he stated on the insurance application that he had not seen a physician within the past five years. In fact, he had had several consultations with his physician, who three weeks prior to the application had diagnosed him as overweight and suffering from goiter. His response to the question on drug and alcohol use was that he was not an alcoholic or user of drugs. In fact, he had been an active alcoholic since age 16 and was a marijuana user. De Guerrero died within the two-year contestability period included in the policy, and John Hancock refused to pay. The beneficiary contended that all premiums were fully paid on the policy and that any misstatements in the application were unintentional. John Hancock contended that if the deceased had given the facts, the policy would not have been issued. Decide. [*de Guerrero v. John Hancock Mutual Life Ins. Co.*, 522 So.2d 1032 (Fla. App.)]

PART 6

Agency and Employment

© Manuel Gutjahr/iStockphoto.com

797

© Manuel Gutjahr/iStockphoto.com

CHAPTER 37

Agency

learningoutcomes

After studying this chapter, you should be able to

LO.1 Explain the difference between an agent and an independent contractor

LO.2 Explain three methods of creating an agency relationship

LO.3 Recognize that third persons who deal with an agent are required to take notice of acts contrary to the interests of the principal

LO.4 List and explain the duties an agent owes the principal

LO.5 Explain how the Uniform Durable Power of Attorney Act changes the common law rule on incapacity of the principal ne of the most common business relationships is that of agency. By virtue of the agency device, one person can make contracts at numerous places with many different parties at the same time.

A. Nature of the Agency Relationship

Agency is ordinarily based on the consent of the parties, and for that reason is called a *consensual relationship*. However, the law sometimes imposes an agency relationship. If consideration is present, the agency relationship is contractual.

1. Definitions and Distinctions

agency – relationship that exists between a person identified as a principal and another by virtue of which the latter may make contracts with third persons on behalf of the principal. (Parties—principal, agent, third person)

agent – person or firm who is authorized by the principal or by operation of law to make contracts with third persons on behalf of the principal.

principal – person or firm who employs an agent; person who, with respect to a surety, is primarily liable to the third person or creditor; property held in trust.

Agency is a relationship based on an express or implied agreement by which one person, the **agent**, is authorized to act under the control of and for another, the **principal**, in negotiating and making contracts with third persons.[1] The acts of the agent obligate the principal to third persons and give the principal rights against third persons. (See Figure 37-1.)

The term *agency* is frequently used with other meanings. It is sometimes used to denote the fact that one has the right to sell certain products, such as when a dealer is said to possess an automobile agency. In other instances, the term is used to mean an exclusive right to sell certain articles within a given territory. In these cases, however, the dealer is not an agent in the sense of representing the manufacturer.

It is important to be able to distinguish agencies from other relationships because certain rights and duties in agencies are not present in other relationships.

(A) Employees and Independent Contractors. Control and authority are characteristics that distinguish ordinary employees and independent contractors from agents.

(1) Employees.
An agent is distinguished from an ordinary employee who is not hired to represent the employer in making contracts with third persons. It is possible, however, for the same person to be both an agent and an employee. **For Example,** the driver for a spring water delivery service is an agent in making contracts between the company and its customers but is an employee with respect to the work of delivering products.

(2) Independent Contractors.
An **independent contractor** is bound by a contract to produce a certain result—for example, to build a house. The actual performance of the work is controlled by the contractor, not the owner. An agent or employee differs from an independent contractor in that the principal or employer has the right to control the agent or employee, but not the contractor, in the performance of the work. **For Example,** Ned and Tracy Seizer contract with Fox Building Company to build a new home on Hilton Head Island, South Carolina, according to referenced plans and specifications. Individuals hired by Fox to work on the home are subject to the authority and control of Fox, the independent contractor, not the Seizers.

independent contractor – contractor who undertakes to perform a specified task according to the terms of a contract but over whom the other contracting party has no control except as provided for by the contract.

---

[1] Restatement (Second) of Agency §1; *Union Miniere, S.A. v. Parday Corp.*, 521 N.E.2d 700 (Ind. App. 1988).

FIGURE 37-1 | *Agency Relationships*

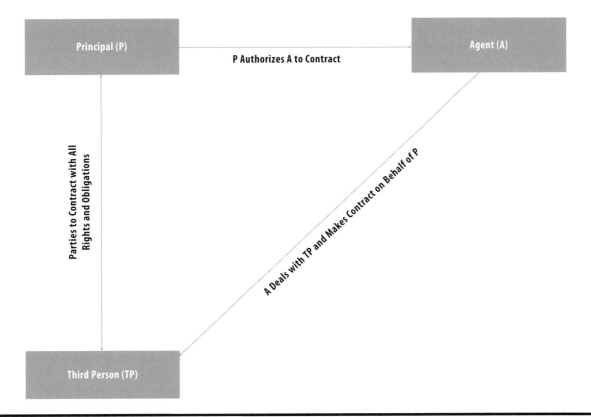

© Cengage Learning

However, Ned and Tracy could decide to build the home themselves, hiring two individuals from nearby Beaufort, Ted Chase and Marty Bromley, to do the work the Seizers will direct each day. Because Ted and Marty would be employees of the Seizers, the Seizers would be held responsible for any wrongs committed by these employees within the scope of their employment. As a general rule, on the other hand, the Seizers are not responsible for the torts of Fox, the independent contractor, and the contractor's employees. A "right to control" test determines whether an individual is an agent, an employee, or an independent contractor.[2]

CASE SUMMARY

Why Some Businesses Use Independent Agents Rather than Employees!

FACTS: Patricia Yelverton died from injuries sustained when an automobile owned and driven by Joseph Lamm crossed the center line of a roadway and struck the automobile driven by Yelverton. Yelverton's executor brought suit against Lamm and Lamm's alleged employer,

---

[2] *NE Ohio College of Massotherapy v. Burek*, 759 N.E.2d 869 (Ohio App. 2001).

CASE SUMMARY

Continued

Premier Industrial Products Inc. The relationship between Lamm and Premier was governed by a written contract entitled "Independent Agent Agreement," in which Lamm, as "Independent Agent," was given the right to sell Premier's products in a designated territory. The agreement provided that all orders were subject to acceptance by Premier and were not binding on Premier until so accepted. Lamm was paid by commission only. He was allowed to work on a self-determined schedule, retain assistants at his own expense, and sell the products of other companies not in competition with Premier. The executor claimed Lamm was an agent or employee of Premier. Premier stated Lamm was an independent contractor.

DECISION: Judgment for Premier. Lamm had no authority to make contracts for Premier but simply took orders. Therefore, he was not an agent. Lamm was not an employee of Premier. Premier had no right to control the way he performed his work and did not in fact do so. Lamm was an independent contractor. [*Yelverton v. Lamm*, 380 S.E.2d 621 (N.C. App. 1989)]

A person who appears to be an independent contractor may in fact be so controlled by the other party that the contractor is regarded as an agent of, or employee of, the controlling person. **For Example,** Pierce, who was under contract to Brookville Carriers, Inc., was involved in a tractor-trailer/car collision with Rich and others. Pierce owned the tractor involved in the accident on a lease from Brookville but could use it only to haul freight for Brookville; he had no authority to carry freight on his own, and all of his operating authority belonged to Brookville. The "owner/operator" was deemed an employee rather than independent contractor for purposes of assessing the liability of the employer.[3] The separate identity of an independent contractor may be concealed so that the public believes that it is dealing with the principal. When this situation occurs, the principal is liable as though the contractor were an agent or employee.

2. Classification of Agents

special agent – agent authorized to transact a specific transaction or to do a specific act.

A **special agent** is authorized by the principal to handle a definite business transaction or to do a specific act. One who is authorized by another to purchase a particular house is a special agent.

general agent – agent authorized by the principal to transact all affairs in connection with a particular type of business or trade or to transact all business at a certain place.

A **general agent** is authorized by the principal to transact all affairs in connection with a particular type of business or trade or to transact all business at a certain place. To illustrate, a person who is appointed as manager by the owner of a store is a general agent.

universal agent – agent authorized by the principal to do all acts that can lawfully be delegated to a representative.

A **universal agent** is authorized by the principal to do all acts that can be delegated lawfully to a representative. This form of agency arises when a person absent because of being in the military service gives another person a blanket power of attorney to do anything that must be done during such absence.

---

[3] *Rich v. Brookville Carriers, Inc.*, 256 F. Supp. 2d 26 (D. Me. 2003).

3. Agency Coupled with an Interest

interest in the authority – form of agency in which an agent has been given or paid for the right to exercise authority.

An agent has an **interest in the authority** when consideration has been given or paid for the right to exercise the authority. To illustrate, when a lender, in return for making a loan of money, is given, as security, authority to collect rents due the borrower and to apply those rents to the payment of the debt, the lender becomes the borrower's agent with an interest in the authority given to collect the rents.

interest in the subject matter – form of agency in which an agent is given an interest in the property with which that agent is dealing.

An agent has an **interest in the subject matter** when, for a consideration, she is given an interest in the property with which she is dealing. Hence, when the agent is authorized to sell property of the principal and is given a lien on such property as security for a debt owed to her by the principal, she has an interest in the subject matter.

B. Creating the Agency

An agency may arise by appointment, conduct, ratification, or operation of law.

4. Authorization by Appointment

express authorization – authorization of an agent to perform a certain act.

The usual method of creating an agency is by **express authorization**; that is, a person is appointed to act for, or on behalf of, another.

In most instances, the authorization of the agent may be oral. However, some appointments must be made in a particular way. A majority of the states, by statute, require the appointment of an agent to be in writing when the agency is created to acquire or dispose of any interest in land. A written authorization of agency is called a **power of attorney**. An agent acting under a power of attorney is referred to as an **attorney in fact**.[4]

power of attorney – written authorization to an agent by the principal.

attorney in fact – agent authorized to act for another under a power of attorney.

5. Authorization by Conduct

Conduct consistent with the existence of an agency relationship may be sufficient to show authorization. The principal may have such dealing with third persons as to cause them to believe that the "agent" has authority. Thus, if the owner of a store places another person in charge, third persons may assume that the person in charge is the agent for the owner in that respect. The "agent" then appears to be authorized and is said to have *apparent authority*, and the principal is estopped from contradicting the appearance that has been created.[5]

CASE SUMMARY

The "Bulletproof against Rust" Case. Oops! Now What?

FACTS: While constructing a hotel in Lincoln City, Oregon, the owner, Todd Taylor, became concerned about possible rusting in the exterior stucco system manufactured by ChemRex that was being installed at the hotel. The general contractor Ramsay-Gerding arranged a meeting with

---

[4] *Lamb v. Scott*, 643 So.2d 972 (Ala. 1994).
[5] *Intersparex Leddin KG v. AL-Haddad*, 852 S.W.2d 245 (Tenn. App. 1992).

CASE SUMMARY

Continued

the owner, the installer, and ChemRex's territory manager for Oregon, Mike McDonald, to discuss Mr. Taylor's concerns. McDonald told those present that the SonoWall system was "bulletproof against rust," and stated that "you're getting a five-year warranty." He followed up with a letter confirming the five-year warranty on parts and labor. A year later rust discoloration appeared, and no one from ChemRex ever fixed the problem. Taylor sued ChemRex for breach of warranty. ChemRex defended that McDonald did not have actual or apparent authority to declare such a warranty.

DECISION: Judgment for Taylor. The evidence indicated that ChemRex clothed Mike McDonald with the title of "territory manager" and gave him the actual authority to visit job sites and resolve problems. Although it denies he had actual authority, ChemRex took sufficient steps to create apparent authority to provide the five-year warranty on the stucco system. [*Taylor v. Ramsay-Gerding Construction Co.*, 196 P.3d 532 (Or. 2008)]

The term *apparent authority* is used when there is only the appearance of authority but no actual authority, and that appearance of authority was created by the principal. The test for the existence of apparent authority is an objective test determined by the principal's outward manifestations through words or conduct that lead a third person reasonably to believe that the "agent" has authority. A principal's express restriction on authority not made known to a third person is no defense.

Apparent authority extends to all acts that a person of ordinary prudence, familiar with business usages and the particular business, would be justified in believing that the agent has authority to perform. It is essential to the concept of apparent authority that the third person reasonably believe that the agent has authority. The mere placing of property in the possession of another does not give that person either actual or apparent authority to sell the property.

CPA ## 6. Agency by Ratification

An agent may attempt, on behalf of the principal, to do an act that was not authorized, or a person who is not the agent of another may attempt to act as such an agent. Very generally, notification may be express, where the principal explicitly approves the contract, or implied, where the principal does not object to the contract and accepts the contract's benefits. **For Example,** homeowners Schafstall and Alexander went to Lowe's Home Center to purchase a water system. Schafstall completed the purchase and signed the warranty contract for the installation service. The installation failed and resulted in over $100,000 in water damages to the property. Lowe's warranty limited its liability to just the cost of the reinstallation and repair parts for the system. Not only was Schafstall bound by the terms of the contract with its warranty, but Alexander ratified the contract by his presence at the transaction and is thus bound by its terms.[6]

---

[6] *Guideone Insurance Co. v. U.S. Water Systems, Inc. and Lowe's Home Centers*, 950 N.E.2d 1236 (Ind. App. 2011).

(a) Intention to Ratify. Initially, ratification is a question of intention. Just as in the case of authorization, when there is a question of whether the principal authorized the agent, there is a question of whether the principal intended to approve or ratify the action of the unauthorized agent.

The intention to ratify may be expressed in words, or it may be found in conduct indicating an intention to ratify. **For Example,** James Reiner signed a five-year lease of commercial space on 320 West Main Street in Avon, Connecticut, because his father Calvin was away on vacation, and the owner, Robert Udolf, told James that if he did not come in and sign the lease, his father would lose the opportunity to rent the space in question. James was aware that his father had an interest in the space, and while telling Robert several times that he had no authority, James did sign his name to the lease. In fact, his father took occupancy of the space and paid rent for three years and then abandoned the space. James is not liable on the remainder of the lease because the owner knew at the time of signing that James did not have authority to act. Although he did not sign the lease, Calvin ratified the lease signed by James by his conduct of moving into the space and doing business there for three years with full knowledge of all material facts relating to the transaction. The owner, therefore, had to bring suit against Calvin, not James.[7]

CPA **(b) Conditions for Ratification.** In addition to the intent to ratify, expressed in some instances with a certain formality, the following conditions must be satisfied for the intention to take effect as a ratification:

1. The agent must have purported to act on behalf of or as agent for the identified principal.

2. The principal must have been capable of authorizing the act both at the time of the act and at the time it was ratified.

3. The principal must have full knowledge of all material facts.

It is not always necessary, however, to show that the principal had actual knowledge. Knowledge will be imputed if a principal knows of other facts that would lead a prudent person to make inquiries or if that knowledge can be inferred from the knowledge of other facts or from a course of business. **For Example,** Stacey, without authorization but knowing that William needed money, contracted to sell one of William's paintings to Courtney for $298. Stacey told William about the contract that evening; William said nothing and helped her wrap the painting in a protective plastic wrap for delivery. A favorable newspaper article about William's art appeared the following morning and dramatically increased the value of all of his paintings. William cannot recover the painting from Courtney on the theory that he never authorized the sale because he ratified the unauthorized contract made by Stacey by his conduct in helping her wrap the painting with full knowledge of the terms of the sale. The effect is a legally binding contract between William and Courtney.

(c) Effect of Ratification. When an unauthorized act is ratified, the effect is the same as though the act had been originally authorized. Ordinarily, this means that the

---

[7] *Udolf v. Reiner*, 2000 WL 726953 (Conn. Super. May 19, 2000).

principal and the third party are bound by the contract made by the agent.[8] When the principal ratifies the act of the unauthorized person, such ratification releases that person from the liability that would otherwise be imposed for having acted without authority.

CPA

7. Proving the Agency Relationship

The burden of proving the existence of an agency relationship rests on the person who seeks to benefit by such proof. The third person who desires to bind the principal because of the act of an alleged agent has the burden of proving that the latter person was in fact the authorized agent of the principal and possessed the authority to do the act in question.[9]

C. Agent's Authority

When there is an agent, it is necessary to determine the scope of the agent's authority.

8. Scope of Agent's Authority

The scope of an agent's authority may be determined from the express words of the principal to the agent or it may be implied from the principal's words or conduct or from the customs of the trade or business.

(A) Express Authority. If the principal tells the agent to perform a certain act, the agent has express authority to do so. Express authority can be given orally or in writing.

incidental authority—
authority of an agent that is reasonably necessary to execute express authority.

(B) Incidental Authority. An agent has implied **incidental authority** to perform any act reasonably necessary to execute the express authority given to the agent. **For Example,** if the principal authorizes the agent to purchase goods without furnishing funds to the agent to pay for them, the agent has the implied incidental authority to purchase the goods on credit.[10]

customary authority—
authority of an agent to do any act that, according to the custom of the community, usually accompanies the transaction for which the agent is authorized to act.

(C) Customary Authority. An agent has implied **customary authority** to do any act that, according to the custom of the community, usually accompanies the transaction for which the agent is authorized to act. An agent who has express authority to receive payments from third persons, for example, has the implied customary authority to issue receipts.

apparent authority—
appearance of authority created by the principal's words or conduct.

(D) Apparent Authority. A person has **apparent authority** as an agent when the principal's words or conduct leads a third person to reasonably believe that the person has that authority and the third person relies on that appearance.[11]

---

[8] *Bill McCurley Chevrolet v. Rutz*, 808 P.2d 1167 (Wash. App. 1991).
[9] *Cummings, Inc. v. Nelson*, 115 P.3d 536 (Alaska 2005).
[10] *Badger v. Paulson Investment Co.*, 803 P.2d 1178 (Or. 1991).
[11] *Alexander v. Chandler*, 179 S.W.2d 385 (Mo. App. 2005).

CASE SUMMARY

CSX Gets Railroaded by Albert Arillotta

FACTS: Recovery Express and Interstate Demolition (IDEC) are two separate corporations located at the same business address in Boston. On August 22, 2003, Albert Arillotta, a "partner" at IDEC, sent an e-mail to Len Whitehead, Jr. of CSX Transportation expressing an interest in buying "rail cars as scrap." Arillotta represented himself to be "from interstate demolition and recovery express" in the e-mail. The e-mail address from which he sent his inquiry was **albert@recoveryexpress.com**. Arillotta went to the CSX rail yard, disassembled the cars, and transported them away. Thereafter CSX sent invoices for the scrap rail cars totaling $115,757.36 addressed to IDEC at its Boston office shared with Recovery Express. Whitehead believed Arillotta was authorized to act for Recovery Express, based on the e-mail's domain name, recoveryexpress.com. Recovery claims that Arillotta never worked for it. Recovery's president Thomas Trafton allowed the "fledgling" company to use telephone, fax, and e-mail services at its offices but never shared anything—assets, funds, books of business, or financials with IDEC—CSX sued Recovery for the invoice amount on the doctrine of "apparent authority." IDEC is now defunct. Recovery claims that Arillotta never worked for it and that it is not liable.

DECISION: Judgment for Recovery. Issuance of an e-mail address with Recovery's domain name to an individual who shared office space with Recovery did not give the individual, Albert Arillotta, apparent authority to enter contracts on Recovery's behalf. No reasonable person could conclude that Arillotta had apparent authority on the basis of an e-mail domain name by itself. Given the anonymity of the Internet, the court warned businesses to take additional action to verify a purported agent's authority to make a deal. [*CSX Transportation, Inc. v. Recovery Express, Inc.*, 415 F. Supp. 2d 6 (D. Mass. 2006)]

9. Effect of Proper Exercise of Authority

When an agent with authority properly makes a contract with a third person that purports to bind the principal, there is by definition a binding contract between the principal and the third person. The agent is not a party to this contract. Consequently, when the owner of goods is the principal, the owner's agent is not liable for breach of warranty with respect to the goods "sold" by the agent. The owner-principal, not the agent, was the "seller" in the sales transaction.

CPA

10. Duty to Ascertain Extent of Agent's Authority

A third person who deals with a person claiming to be an agent cannot rely on the statements made by the agent concerning the extent of authority.[12] If the agent is not authorized to perform the act or is not even the agent of the principal, the transaction between the alleged agent and the third person will have no legal effect between the principal and the third person.

Third persons who deal with an agent whose authority is limited to a special purpose are bound at their peril to find out the extent of the agent's authority. An attorney is such an agent. Unless the client holds the attorney out as having greater

[12] *Breed v. Hughes Aircraft Col.*, 35 Fed. App. 864 (Fed. Cir. 2002).

authority than usual, the attorney has no authority to settle a claim without approval from the client.

(A) AGENT'S ACTS ADVERSE TO PRINCIPAL. The third person who deals with an agent is required to take notice of any acts that are clearly adverse to the interest of the principal. Thus, if the agent is obviously using funds of the principal for the agent's personal benefit, persons dealing with the agent should recognize that the agent may be acting without authority and that they are dealing with the agent at their peril.

The only certain way that third persons can protect themselves is to inquire of the principal whether the agent is in fact the agent of the principal and has the necessary authority. **For Example,** Ron Fahd negotiated the sale of a fire truck to the Edinburg Volunteer Fire Company, on behalf of the manufacturer, Danko Company, at a price of $158,000. On Danko forms and letterhead Fahd drafted a "Proposal for Fire Apparatus" and it was signed by the president of the Fire Company and Fahd, as a dealer for Danko. Fahd gave a special $2,000 discount for prepayment of the cost of the chassis. Fahd directed that the prepayment check of $55,000 be made payable to "Ron Fahd Sales" in order to obtain the discount. The Fire Company's treasurer inquired of Fahd why the prepayment check was being made out to Fahd rather than Danko, and he accepted Fahd's answer without contacting Danko to confirm this unusual arrangement. Fahd absconded with the proceeds of the check. The Fire Company sued Danko claiming Fahd had apparent authority to receive the prepayment. While there was some indicia of agency, the court found that the Fire Company had failed to make reasonable inquiry with Danko to verify Fahd's authority to receive the prepayment in Fahd's name, and it rejected the claim that Fahd had apparent authority to accept the prepayment check made out to Fahd as opposed to Danko.[13]

11. Limitations on Agent's Authority

A person who has knowledge of a limitation on the agent's authority cannot ignore that limitation. When the third person knows that the authority of the agent depends on whether financing has been obtained, the principal is not bound by the act of the agent if the financing in fact was not obtained. If the authority of the agent is based on a writing and the third person knows that there is such a writing, the third person is charged with knowledge of limitations contained in it.

(A) "OBVIOUS" LIMITATIONS. In some situations, it may be obvious to third persons that they are dealing with an agent whose authority is limited. When third persons know that they are dealing with a representative of a government agency, they should recognize that such a person will ordinarily have limited authority. Third persons should recognize that a contract made with such an officer or representative may not be binding unless ratified by the principal.

The federal government places the risk on any individual making arrangements with the government to accurately ascertain that the government agent is within the bounds of his or her authority.

---

[13] *Edinburg Volunteer Fire Company v. Danko,* 867 N.Y.S.2d 547 (A.D. 2008).

CASE SUMMARY

Humlen Was Had?

FACTS: The FBI approached Humlen for assistance in securing the conviction of a drug trafficker. Humlen executed an agreement with the FBI to formalize his status as an informant. The agreement he signed contained compensation figures significantly less than those he had been promised by the FBI agents with whom he was dealing. Humlen claims that five agents repeatedly assured him that he would receive the extra compensation they had discussed with him, despite the wording of the contract. It was explained that the agreement had to be "couched" in that way because it was a discoverable document in any future criminal prosecution and thus could be used to destroy his credibility. Based on the information provided by Humlen, an arrest was made, and Humlen sought the remainder of his promised monetary reward from the FBI. The FBI refused to pay him any more than the contract stipulated. When no additional payment was forthcoming, Humlen sued the U.S. government.

DECISION: Judgment for the United States. The government, unlike private parties, cannot be bound by the apparent authority of its agents. When an agent exceeds his or her authority, the government can disavow the agent's words and is not bound by an implied contract. As a general rule, FBI agents lack the requisite actual authority—either express or implied—to contractually bind the United States to remit rewards to confidential informants. Moreover, Humlen's claims directly collide with the plain language of the agreement. [*Humlen v. United States,* **49** Fed. Cl. **497** (2001)]

(B) SECRET LIMITATIONS. If the principal has clothed an agent with authority to perform certain acts but the principal gives secret instructions that limit the agent's authority, the third person is allowed to take the authority of the agent at its face value. The third person is not bound by the secret limitations of which the third person has no knowledge.

D. DUTIES AND LIABILITIES OF PRINCIPAL AND AGENT

The creation of the principal-agent relationship gives rise to duties and liabilities.

12. Duties and Liabilities of Agent during Agency

While the agency relationship exists, the agent owes certain duties to the principal.

(A) LOYALTY. An agent must be loyal or faithful to the principal.[14] The agent must not obtain any secret benefit from the agency. If the principal is seeking to buy or rent property, the agent cannot secretly obtain the property and then sell or lease it to the principal at a profit.

An agent who owns property cannot sell it to the principal without disclosing that ownership to the principal. If disclosure is not made, the principal may avoid the

---

[14] *Patterson Custom Homes v. Bach,* 536 F. Supp. 2d 1026 (E.D. Ill. 2008).

contract even if the agent's conduct did not cause the principal any financial loss. Alternatively, the principal can approve the transaction and sue the agent for any secret profit obtained by the agent.

A contract is voidable by the principal if the agent who was employed to sell the property purchases the property, either directly or indirectly, without full disclosure to the principal.

An agent cannot act as agent for both parties to a transaction unless both know of the dual capacity and agree to it. If the agent does act in this capacity without the consent of both parties, any principal who did not know of the agent's double status can avoid the transaction.

An agent must not accept secret gifts or commissions from third persons in connection with the agency. If the agent does so, the principal may sue the agent for those gifts or commissions. Such practices are condemned because the judgment of the agent may be influenced by the receipt of gifts or commissions.

It is a violation of an agent's duty of loyalty to make and retain secret profits.

CASE SUMMARY

Was Grappolini a "Bad Boy"?

FACTS: Arthur Frigo, an adjunct professor at the Kellogg Graduate School of Management, formed Lucini Italia Co. (Lucini) to import and sell premium extra virgin olive oil and other products from Italy. Lucini's officers hired Guiseppe Grappolini as their olive oil supplier. They also hired him as their consultant. Grappolini signed an exclusivity agreement and a confidentiality agreement acknowledging the confidential nature of Lucini's product development, plans, and strategies. Grappolini was "branded" as a "master cultivator" in Lucini's literature and commercials.

In 1998, Lucini and Grappolini, as his consultant, discussed adding a line of extra virgin olive oils blended with "essential oils," for example, natural extracts such as lemon and garlic. It spent more than $800,000 developing the market information, testing flavors, designing labels and packaging, creating recipes, and generating trade secrets for the new products. Vegetal-Progress s.r.l. (Vegetal) was identified as the only company in Italy that was capable of producing the superior products Lucini sought, and Grappolini was assigned responsibility to obtain an exclusive supply contract with Vegetal.

In direct contravention of his representations to Lucini, Grappolini secretly negotiated an exclusive supply contract for the Grappolini Co., not for Lucini. Moreover, Grappolini Co. began to sell flavored olive oils in the United States, which coincided with Lucini's market research and recipe development that had been disclosed to Grappolini. When Lucini officers contacted Vegetal, they acknowledged that Grappolini was a "bad boy" in procuring the contract for his own company rather than for Lucini, but they would not renege on the contract. Lucini sued Grappolini.

DECISION: Judgment for Lucini. Grappolini was Lucini's agent and owed Lucini a duty to advance Lucini's interests, not his own. When he obtained an exclusive supply agreement with Vegetal for the Grappolini Co. instead of Lucini, he was disloyal and breached his fiduciary duties. As a result, Lucini suffered lost profits and damages of $4.17 million. In addition to these damages, Grappolini was ordered to pay $1,000,000 in punitive damages to deter similar acts in the future. Additionally, a permanent injunction was issued prohibiting Grappolini from using Lucini's trade secrets. [*Lucini Italia Co. v. Grappolini*, 2003 WL 1989605 (N.D. Ill. 2003)]

An agent is, of course, prohibited from aiding the competitors of a principal or disclosing to them information relating to the business of the principal. It is also a breach of duty for the agent to knowingly deceive a principal.[15]

(B) OBEDIENCE AND PERFORMANCE. An agent is under a duty to obey all lawful instructions.[16] The agent is required to perform the services specified for the period and in the way specified. An agent who does not do so is liable to the principal for any harm caused. For example, if an agent is instructed to take cash payments only but accepts a check in payment, the agent is liable for the loss caused the principal if a check is dishonored by nonpayment.

(C) REASONABLE CARE. It is the duty of an agent to act with the care that a reasonable person would exercise under the circumstances. **For Example,** Ethel Wilson applied for fire insurance for her house with St. Paul Reinsurance Co., Ltd., through her agent Club Services Corp. She thought she was fully covered. Unbeknown to her, however, St. Paul had refused coverage and returned her premium to Club Services, who did not refund it to Ms. Wilson or inform her that coverage had been denied. Fire destroyed her garage and St. Paul denied coverage. Litigation resulted, and St. Paul ended up expending $305,406 to settle the Wilson matter. Thereafter, St. Paul successfully sued Club Services Corp. under basic agency law principles that an agent (Club Services) is liable to its principal for all damages resulting from the agent's failure to discharge its duties.[17] In addition, if the agent possesses a special skill, as in the case of a broker or an attorney, the agent must exercise that skill.

(D) ACCOUNTING. An agent must account to the principal for all property or money belonging to the principal that comes into the agent's possession. The agent must, within a reasonable time, give notice of collections made and render an accurate account of all receipts and expenditures. The agency agreement may state at what intervals or on what dates such accountings are to be made. An agent must keep the principal's property and money separate and distinct from that of the agent.

(E) INFORMATION. It is the duty of an agent to keep the principal informed of all facts relating to the agency that are relevant to protecting the principal's interests.[18]

13. Duties and Liabilities of Agent after Termination of Agency

When the agency relationship ends, the duties of the agent continue only to the extent necessary to perform prior obligations. For example, the agent must return to the former principal any property that had been entrusted to the agent for the purpose of the agency. With the exception of such "winding-up" duties, the agency relationship is terminated, and the former agent can deal with the principal as freely as with a stranger.[19]

---

[15] *Koontz v. Rosener,* 787 P.2d 192 (Colo. App. 1990).
[16] *Stanford v. Neiderer,* 341 S.E.2d 892 (Ga. App. 1986).
[17] *St. Paul Reinsurance Co., Ltd. v. Club Services Corp.,* 30 Fed. Appx. 834 (10th Cir. 2002).
[18] Restatement (Second) of Agency §381; *Lumberman's Mutual Ins. Co. v. Franey Muha Alliant Ins.,* 388 F. Supp. 2d 292 (S.D.N.Y. 2005).
[19] *Corron & Black of Illinois, Inc. v. Magner,* 494 N.E.2d 785 (Ill. App. 1986).

14. Duties and Liabilities of Principal to Agent

The principal must perform the contract, compensate the agent for services, make reimbursement for proper expenditures and, under certain circumstances, must indemnify the agent for loss.

(A) EMPLOYMENT ACCORDING TO TERMS OF CONTRACT. When the contract is for a specified time, the principal is obligated to permit the agent to act as agent for the term of the contract. Exceptions are made for just cause or contract provisions that permit the principal to terminate the agency sooner. If the principal gives the agent an exclusive right to act in that capacity, the principal cannot give anyone else the authority to act as agent, nor may the principal do the act to which the exclusive agent's authority relates. **For Example,** if Jill Baker gives Brett Stamos the exclusive right for six months to sell her house, she cannot give another real estate agent the right to sell it during the six-month period or undertake to sell the house herself. If the principal or another agent sells the house, the exclusive agent is entitled to full compensation just as though the act had been performed by the exclusive agent.

(B) COMPENSATION. The principal must pay the agent the agreed compensation.[20] If the parties have not fixed the amount of the compensation by their agreement but intended that the agent should be paid, the agent may recover the customary compensation for such services. If there is no established compensation, the agent may recover the reasonable value of the services rendered.

(1) Repeating Transactions.

In certain industries, third persons make repeated transactions with the principal. In these cases, the agent who made the original contract with the third person commonly receives a certain compensation or percentage of commissions on all subsequent renewal or additional contracts. In the insurance business, for example, the insurance agent obtaining the policyholder for the insurer receives a substantial portion of the first year's premiums and then receives a smaller percentage of the premiums paid by the policyholder in subsequent years.

(2) Postagency Transactions.

An agent is not ordinarily entitled to compensation in connection with transactions, such as sales or renewals of insurance policies, occurring after the termination of the agency even if the postagency transactions are the result of the agent's former activities. However, if the parties' employment contract calls for such compensation, it must be paid. **For Example,** real estate agent Laura McLane's contract called for her to receive $1.50 for every square foot the Atlanta Committee for the Olympic Games, Inc. (ACOG), leased at an Atlanta building; and even though she had been terminated at the time ACOG executed a lease amendment for 164,412 additional square feet, she was contractually entitled to a $246,618 commission.[21]

[20] *American Chocolates, Inc. v. Mascot Pecan Co., Inc.*, 592 So.2d 93 (Miss. 1992).
[21] *McLane v. Atlanta Market Center Management Co.*, 486 S.E.2d 30 (Ga. App. 1997).

E. Termination of Agency

An agency may be terminated by the act of one or both of the parties to the agency agreement or by operation of law. When the authority of an agent is terminated, the agent loses all right to act for the principal.

15. Termination by Act of Parties

The duration of the agency relationship is commonly stated in the contract creating the relationship. In most cases, either party has the power to terminate the agency relationship at any time. However, the terminating party may be liable for damages to the other if the termination is in violation of the agency contract.

When a principal terminates an agent's authority, it is not effective until the agent receives the notice. Because a known agent will have the appearance of still being an agent, notice must be given to third persons of the termination, and the agent may have the power to bind the principal and third persons until this notice is given.

16. Termination by Operation of Law

The agency relationship is a personal one, and anything that renders one of the parties incapable of performing will result in the termination of the relationship by operation of law. The death of either the principal or the agent ordinarily terminates the authority of an agent automatically even if the death is unknown to the other.[22]

An agency is also terminated by operation of law on the (1) insanity of the principal or agent, (2) bankruptcy of the principal or agent, (3) impossibility of performance, such as the destruction of the subject matter, or (4) when the country of the principal is at war with that of the agent.

CASE SUMMARY

Missing Out by Minutes

FACTS: William Moore, a fire chief for the city of San Francisco, suffered severe head injuries in a fall while fighting a fire. Moore sued the building owner, Lera, for negligence. The attorneys for the parties held a conference and reached a settlement at 5:15 P.M. Unknown to them, Moore had died at 4:50 P.M. on that day. Was the settlement agreement binding?

DECISION: No. The death of either the principal or the agent terminates the agency. Thus, the death of a client terminates the authority of his agent to act on his behalf. Because Moore died at 4:50 P.M., his attorney no longer had authority to act on his behalf, and the settlement was not enforceable. [***Moore v. Lera Development Inc.,*** **274 Cal. Rptr. 658 (Cal. App. 1990)**]

---

[22] *New York Life Ins. Co. v. Estate of Haelen,* 521 N.Y.S.2d 970 (N.Y. Civ. Ct.1987).

17. Disability of the Principal under the UDPAA

The Uniform Durable Power of Attorney Act (UDPAA) permits the creation of an agency by specifying that "this power of attorney shall not be affected by subsequent disability or incapacity of the principal." Alternatively, the UDPAA permits the agency to come into existence upon the disability or incapacity of the principal. For this to be effective, the principal must designate the attorney in fact in writing. The writing must contain words showing the intent of the principal that the authority conferred shall continue notwithstanding the disability or incapacity of the principal. The UDPAA, which has been adopted by most states,[23] changes the common law and the general rule that insanity of the principal terminates the agent's authority to act for the principal. Society today recognizes that it may be in the best interest of a principal and good for the business environment for a principal to designate another as an attorney in fact to act for the principal when the principal becomes incapacitated.[24] It may be prudent to grant durable powers of attorney to different persons for property matters and for health care decisions.

Durable powers of attorney grant only those powers that are specified in the instrument. A durable power of attorney may be terminated by revocation by a competent principal and by the death of the principal.

CASE SUMMARY

Broad Powers ... But There Is a Limit, Lucille

FACTS: On May 31, 2000, Thomas Graham made his niece Lucille Morrison his attorney in fact by executing a durable power of attorney. It was notarized and filed at the Registry of Deeds. The power of attorney granted Lucille broad powers and discretion in Graham's affairs. However, it did not contain express authority to make gifts. On October 26, 2000, Lucille conveyed 11.92 acres of property valued at between $400,000 and $700,000 to herself based on consideration of services rendered to the principal, Thomas Graham. On June 5, 2001, Lucille, as attorney in fact for Graham, conveyed Graham's house in Charlotte to her son Ladd Morrison. On June 20, 2001, she conveyed Graham's Oakview Terrace property to her brother John Hallman for $3,000 to pay for an attorney to defend Graham in a competency proceeding. Thomas Graham died on August 7, 2001, and his estate sued to set aside the deeds, alleging Lucille's breach of fiduciary duties. After a judgment for the defendants, the estate appealed.

DECISION: Judgment for the estate regarding the 11.92 acre parcel of land Lucille conveyed to herself. When an attorney in fact conveys property to herself based on consideration of services rendered to the principal, the consideration must reflect a fair and reasonable price when compared with the market value of the property. There was no testimony regarding the value of Lucille's services compared with the value of the real property. The deed must be set aside. The conveyance of Graham's home to Ladd Morrison was a gift that was not authorized by her power

---

[23] The Uniform Durable Power of Attorney Act has been adopted in some fashion in all states except Connecticut, Florida, Georgia, Illinois, Indiana, Kansas, Louisiana, and Missouri.

[24] The Uniform Probate Code and the Uniform Durable Power of Attorney Act provide for the coexistence of durable powers and guardians or conservators. These acts allow the attorney in fact to continue to manage the principal's financial affairs while the court-appointed fiduciary takes the place of the principal in overseeing the actions of the attorney in fact. See *Rice v. Flood*, 768 S.W.2d 57 (Ky. 1989).

CASE SUMMARY

Continued

of attorney and must be set aside. Lucille had authority to sell the principal's property to John Hallman to obtain funds to pay an attorney to represent the principal. The estate's claim of conversion regarding this sale was denied. [***Estate of Graham v. Morrison*, 607 S.E.2d 295 (N.C. App. 2005)**]

18. Termination of Agency Coupled with an Interest

An agency coupled with an interest is an exception to the general rule as to the termination of an agency. Such an agency cannot be revoked by the principal before the expiration of the interest. It is not terminated by the death or insanity of either the principal or the agent.

19. Protection of Agent from Termination of Authority

The modern world of business has developed several methods of protecting an agent from the termination of authority for any reason.[25]

These methods include the use of an exclusive agency contract, a secured transaction, an escrow deposit, a standby letter of agreement, or a guarantee agreement.

20. Effect of Termination of Authority

If the principal revokes the agency, the authority to act for the principal is not terminated until the agent receives notice of revocation. As between the principal and the agent, the right of the agent to bind the principal to third persons generally ends immediately upon the termination of the agent's authority. This termination is effective without giving notice to third persons.

When the agency is terminated by the act of the principal, notice must be given to third persons. If this notice is not given, the agent may have the power to make contracts that will bind the principal and third persons. This rule is predicated on the theory that a known agent will have the appearance of still being the agent unless notice to the contrary is given to third persons.[26] **For Example,** Seltzer owns property in Boca Raton that he uses for the month of February and leases the remainder of the year. O'Neil has been Seltzer's rental agent for the past seven years, renting to individuals like Ed Tucker under a power of attorney that gives him authority to lease the property for set seasonal and off-season rates.

---

[25] These methods generally replace the concept of an agency coupled with an interest because of the greater protection given to the agent. Typically, the rights of the agent under these modern devices cannot be defeated by the principal, by operation of law, or by claims of other creditors.

[26] See *Stout Street Funding, LLC v. Johnson*, 2012 WL 1994800 (E.D. Pa. June 1, 2012). TRGC terminated its contract with Mabstract to serve as TRGC's closing agent on July 12, 2010, and obtained a court injunction barring Mabstract from engaging in any business on behalf of TRGC on July 15. Stout asserts that it had no actual notice of Mabstract's termination nor were there any red flags when it transmitted $480,000 into an escrow account held by Mabstract for a July 19 real estate transaction, which funds were misappropriated by Mabstract. It asserts that apparent authority lasts until a third party has actual notice of an agent's termination or until the third party has enough information to put that individual on inquiry.

O'Neil's right to bind Seltzer on a rental agreement ended when Seltzer faxed O'Neil a revocation of the power of attorney on March 1. A rental contract with Ed Tucker signed by O'Neil on behalf of Seltzer on March 2 will bind Seltzer, however, because O'Neil still appeared to be Seltzer's agent and Tucker had no notice to the contrary.

When the law requires giving notice in order to end the power of the agent to bind the principal, individual notice must be given or mailed to all persons who had prior dealings with the agent. In addition, notice to the general public can be given by publishing in a newspaper of general circulation in the affected geographic area a statement that the agency has been terminated.

If a notice is actually received, the power of the agent is terminated without regard to whether the method of giving notice was proper. Conversely, if proper notice is given, it is immaterial that it does not actually come to the attention of the party notified. Thus, a member of the general public cannot claim that the principal is bound on the ground that the third person did not see the newspaper notice stating that the agent's authority had been terminated.

MAKE THE CONNECTION

SUMMARY

An agency relationship is created by an express or implied agreement by which one person, the agent, is authorized to make contracts with third persons on behalf of, and subject to, the control of another person, the principal. An agent differs from an independent contractor in that the principal, who controls the acts of an agent, does not have control over the details of performance of work by the independent contractor. Likewise, an independent contractor does not have authority to act on behalf of the other contracting party.

A special agent is authorized by the principal to handle a specific business transaction. A general agent is authorized by the principal to transact all business affairs of the principal at a certain place. A universal agent is authorized to perform all acts that can be lawfully delegated to a representative.

The usual method of creating an agency is by express authorization. However, an agency relationship may be found to exist when the principal causes or permits a third person to reasonably believe that an agency relationship exists. In such a case, the

"agent" appears to be authorized and is said to have apparent authority.

An unauthorized transaction by an agent for a principal may be ratified by the principal.

An agent acting with authority has the power to bind the principal. The scope of an agent's authority may be determined from the express words of the principal to the agent; this is called express authority. An agent has incidental authority to perform any act reasonably necessary to execute the authority given the agent. An agent's authority may be implied so as to enable the agent to perform any act in accordance with the general customs or usages in a business or an industry. This authority is often referred to as customary authority.

The effect of a proper exercise of authority by an agent is to bind the principal and third person to a contract. The agent, not being a party to the contract, is not liable in any respect under the contract.

A third person dealing with a person claiming to be an agent has a duty to ascertain the extent of the agent's authority and a duty to take notice of any acts that are clearly adverse to the principal's interests. The third person cannot claim that apparent authority existed when that person has notice that the agent's conduct is adverse to the interests of the principal. A third person who has knowledge of limitations on an agent's authority is bound by those limitations. A third person is not bound by secret limitations.

While the agency relationship exists, the agent owes the principal the duties of (1) being loyal, (2) obeying all lawful instructions, (3) exercising reasonable care, (4) accounting for all property or money belonging to the principal, and (5) informing the principal of all facts relating to the agency that are relevant to the principal's interests. An agency relationship can be terminated by act of either the principal or the agent. However, the terminating party may be liable for damages to the other if the termination is in violation of the agency contract.

Because a known agent will have the appearance of still being an agent, notice must be given to third persons of the termination, and the agent may have the power to bind the principal and third persons until this notice is given.

An agency is terminated by operation of law upon (1) the death of the principal or agent, (2) insanity of the principal or agent, (3) bankruptcy of the principal or agent, (4) impossibility of performance, caused, for example, by the destruction of the subject matter, or (5) war.

In states that have adopted the Uniform Durable Power of Attorney Act (UDPAA), an agency may be created that is not affected by subsequent disability or incapacity of the principal. In UDPAA states, the agency may also come into existence upon the "disability or incapacity of the principal." The designation of an attorney in fact under the UDPAA must be in writing.

LEARNING OUTCOMES

After studying this chapter, you should be able to clearly explain:

A. Nature of the Agency Relationship

L0.1   Explain the difference between an agent and an independent contractor
See the Ned and Tracy Seizer example and the "right to control" test, beginning on p. 800.

B. Creating the Agency

L0.2   Explain three methods of creating an agency relationship
See the discussion on the usual method of creating an agency (which is by express authorization), p. 803.
See the *Taylor* case where actual authority to perform some tasks created apparent authority to perform other related tasks, pp. 803–804.
See the agency by ratification example of James and Calvin Reiner on p. 805.

C. Agent's Authority

L0.3   Recognize that third persons who deal with an agent are required to take notice of acts contrary to the interests of the principal

See the example of the Fire Company that failed to verify with the principal an agent's authority to receive a prepayment check of $55,000 made out in the agent's name, p. 808.

D. Duties and Liabilities Of Principal and Agent

L0.4   List and explain the duties an agent owes the principal
See the discussion concerning an agent's duty of loyalty, obedience, reasonable care, accounting, and information beginning on p. 809.

E. Termination of Agency

L0.5   Explain how the Uniform Durable Power of Attorney Act changes the common law rule on incapacity of the principal
See the *Estate of Graham* case on the limits of a durable power of attorney, pp. 814–815.

KEY TERMS

agency

agent

apparent authority

attorney in fact

customary authority

express authorization

general agent

incidental authority

independent contractor

interest in the authority

interest in the subject matter

power of attorney

principal

special agent

universal agent

QUESTIONS AND CASE PROBLEMS

1. How does an agent differ from an independent contractor?

2. Compare authorization of an agent by (a) appointment and (b) ratification.

3. Ernest A. Kotsch executed a durable power of attorney when he was 85 years old, giving his son, Ernie, the power to manage and sell his real estate and personal property "and to do all acts necessary for maintaining and caring for [the father] during his lifetime." Thereafter, Kotsch began "keeping company" with a widow, Margaret Gradl. Ernie believed that the widow was attempting to alienate his father from him, and he observed that she was exerting a great deal of influence over his father. Acting under the durable power of attorney and without informing his father, Ernie created the "Kotsch Family Irrevocable Trust," to which he transferred $700,000, the bulk of his father's liquid assets, with the father as grantor and initial beneficiary and Ernie's three children as additional beneficiaries. Ernie named himself trustee. His father sued to avoid the trust. Ernie defended his action on the ground that he had authority to create the trust under the durable power of attorney. Decide. [*Kotsch v. Kotsch*, 608 So.2d 879 (Fla. App.)]

4. Ken Jones, the number-one-ranked prizefighter in his weight class, signed a two-year contract with Howard Stayword. The contract obligated Stayword to represent and promote Jones in all business and professional matters, including the arrangement of fights. For these services, Jones was to pay Stayword 10 percent of gross earnings. After a year, when Stayword proved unsuccessful in arranging a title match with the champion, Jones fired Stayword. During the following year, Jones earned $4 million. Stayword sued Jones for $400,000. Jones defended himself on the basis that a principal has the absolute power at any time to terminate an agency relationship by discharging the agent, so he was not liable to Stayword. Was Jones correct?

5. Paul Strich did business as an optician in Duluth, Minnesota. Paul used only the products of the Plymouth Optical Co., a national manufacturer of optical products and supplies with numerous retail outlets and some franchise arrangements in areas other than Duluth. To increase business, Paul renovated his office and changed the sign on it to read "Plymouth Optical Co." Paul did business this way for more than three years—advertised under that name, paid bills with checks bearing the name of Plymouth Optical Co., and listed himself in the telephone and city directories by that name. Plymouth immediately became aware of what Paul was doing. However, because Paul used only Plymouth products and Plymouth did not have a franchise in Duluth, it saw no advantage at that time in prohibiting Paul from using the name and losing him as a customer. Paul contracted with the *Duluth Tribune* for advertising, making the contract in the name of Plymouth Optical Co. When the advertising bill was not paid, the *Duluth Tribune* sued Plymouth Optical Co. for payment. Plymouth's defense was that it never authorized Paul to do business under the name, nor authorized him to make a contract with the newspaper. Decide.

6. Record owned a farm that was managed by his agent, Berry, who lived on the farm. Berry hired

Wagner to bale the hay and told him to bill Record for this work. Wagner did so and was paid by Record. By the summer of the following year, the agency had been terminated by Record, but Berry remained in possession as tenant of the farm and nothing appeared changed. Late in the summer, Berry asked Wagner to bale the hay as he had done the previous year and bill Record for the work. He did so, but Record refused to pay on the ground that Berry was not then his agent. Wagner sued him. Decide. [*Record v. Wagner*, 128 A.2d 921 (N.H.)]

7. Gilbert Church owned Church Farms, Inc., in Manteno, Illinois. Church advertised its well-bred stallion Imperial Guard for breeding rights at $50,000, directing all inquiries to "Herb Bagley, Manager." Herb Bagley lived at Church Farms and was the only person available to visitors. Vern Lundberg answered the ad, and after discussions in which Bagley stated that Imperial Guard would remain in Illinois for at least a two-year period, Lundberg and Bagley executed a two-year breeding rights contract. The contract was signed by Lundberg and by Bagley as "Church Farms, Inc., H. Bagley, Mgr." When Gil Church moved Imperial Guard to Oklahoma prior to the second year of the contract, Lundberg brought suit for breach of contract. Church testified that Bagley had no authority to sign contracts for Church Farms. Decide. [*Lundberg v. Church Farms, Inc.*, 502 N.E.2d 806 (Ill.)]

8. The Holzmans signed an exclusive listing agreement with the Blum real estate brokerage firm. The contract provided that the Holzmans had an obligation to pay a commission "if they enter into a written agreement to sell the property to any person during the term of this exclusive listing agreement." The Holzmans entered into a written agreement to sell their house for $715,000 to the Noravians. On the advice of their attorney, the Holzmans included a default provision in this contract stating that in the event of default by the Holzmans, the Noravians' only remedy would be a refund of their deposit. Subsequently, the Sterns offered $850,000 for the property and the Holzmans

canceled their contract with the Noravians and returned their deposit. After the exclusive listing period expired, the Holzmans executed a contract to sell their property to the Sterns at the offered price of $850,000—with the contract calling for the Holzmans to pay half the real estate fee to Blum and half to a cooperating broker. Blum was paid this fee of $21,500. Blum brought suit against the Holzmans seeking the full commission for the Noravian contract under the exclusive listing agreement. Did Blum have a legal obligation or ethical duty to advise the Holzmans when considering the Sterns' offer that he believed they were obligated to him for the full commission under the Novarian contract? Decide. [*Holzman v. Blum*, 726 A.2d 818 (Md. App.)]

9. Tillie Flinn properly executed a durable power of attorney designating her nephew James C. Flanders and/or Martha E. Flanders, his wife, as her attorney in fact. Seven months later, Martha Flanders went to the Capitol Federal Savings and Loan Association office. She had the durable power of attorney instrument, five certificates of deposit, and a hand-printed letter identifying Martha as an attorney in fact and stating that Tillie wished to cash her five CDs that Martha had with her. At approximately 10:31 A.M., five checks were given to Martha in the aggregate amount of $135,791.34, representing the funds in the five CDs less penalties for early withdrawal. Some of the checks were drawn to the order of Martha individually and some to the order of James and Martha, as individuals. Tillie was found dead of heart disease later that day. The time of death stated on her death certificate was 11:30 A.M. The Flanderses spent the money on themselves. Bank IV, as administrator of Tillie's estate, sued Capitol Federal to recover the amount of the funds paid to the Flanderses. It contended that Capitol Federal breached its duty to investigate before issuing the checks. Capitol Federal contended that it did all that it had a duty to do. Decide. [*Bank IV v. Capitol Federal Savings and Loan Ass'n*, 828 P.2d 355 (Kan.)]

10. Lew owns a store on Canal Street in New Orleans. He paid a person named Mike and

other individuals commissions for customers brought into the store. Lew testified that he had known Mike for less than a week. Boulos and Durso, partners in a wholesale jewelry business, were visiting New Orleans on a business trip when Mike brought them into the store to buy a stereo. While Durso finalized the stereo transaction with the store's manager, Boulos and Mike negotiated to buy 2 cameras, 3 videos, and 20 gold Dupont lighters. Unknown to the store's manager, Mike was given $8,250 in cash and was to deliver the merchandise later that evening to the Marriott Hotel, where Boulos and Durso were staying. Mike gave a receipt for the cash, but it showed no sales tax or indication that the goods were to be delivered. Boulos testified that he believed Mike was the store owner. Mike never delivered the merchandise and disappeared. Boulos and Durso contended that Lew is liable for the acts of his agent, Mike. Lew denied that Mike was his agent, and the testimony showed that Mike had no actual authority to make a sale, to use a cash register, or even to go behind a sales counter. What ethical principle applies to the conduct of Boulos and Durso? Decide. [*Boulos v. Morrison*, 503 So.2d 1(La.)]

11. Martha Christiansen owns women's apparel stores bearing her name in New Seabury, Massachusetts; Lake Placid, New York; Palm Beach, Florida; and Palm Springs, California. At a meeting with her four store managers, she discussed styles she thought appropriate for the forthcoming season, advised them as always to use their best judgment in the goods they purchased for each of their respective stores, and cautioned "but no blue jeans." Later, Jane Farley, the manager of the Lake Placid store, purchased a line of high-quality blue denim outfits (designer jeans with jacket and vest options) from Women's Wear, Inc., for the summer season. The outfits did not sell. Martha refused to pay for them, contending that she had told all of her managers "no blue jeans" and that if it came to a lawsuit, she would fly in three managers to testify that Jane Farley had absolutely no authority to purchase denim outfits and was, in fact, expressly forbidden to do so. Women's Wear sued Martha,

and the three managers testified for her. Is the fact that Martha had explicitly forbidden Farley to purchase the outfits in question sufficient to protect her from liability for the purchases made by Farley?

12. Fred Schilling, the president and administrator of Florence General Hospital, made a contract, dated August 16, 1989, on behalf of the hospital with CMK Associates to transfer the capacity to utilize 25 beds from the hospital to the Faith Nursing Home. Schilling, on behalf of the hospital, had previously made a contract with CMK Associates on May 4, 1987. Schilling had been specifically authorized by the hospital board to make the 1987 contract. The hospital refused to honor the 1989 contract because the board had not authorized it. CMK contended that Schilling had apparent authority to bind the hospital because he was president and administrator of the hospital and he had been the person who negotiated and signed a contract with CMK in 1987. Thus, according to CMK, the hospital had held out Schilling as having apparent authority to make the contract. The hospital disagreed. Decide. [*Pee Dee Nursing Home v. Florence General Hospital*, 419 S.E.2d 843 (S.C. App.)]

13. Barbara Fox was the agent of Burt Hollander, a well-known athlete. She discovered that Tom Lanceford owned a 1957 Chevrolet convertible, which had been stored in a garage for the past 15 years. After demonstrating to Lanceford that she was the authorized agent of Hollander, she made a contract with Lanceford on behalf of Hollander to purchase the Chevrolet. Lanceford later discovered that the car was much more valuable than he originally believed, and he refused to deliver the car to Fox. Fox sued Lanceford for breach of contract. Can she recover?

14. Francis Gagnon, an elderly gentleman, signed a power of attorney authorizing his daughter, Joan, "to sell any of my real estate and to execute any document needed to carry out the sale… and to add property to a trust of which I am grantor or beneficiary." This power was given in case Gagnon was not available to take care of

matters personally because he was traveling. When Joan learned that Gagnon intended to sell his Shelburne property to Cosby for $750,000, she created an irrevocable trust naming Gagnon as beneficiary and herself as trustee. Acting then on the basis of the authority set forth in the power of attorney, she conveyed the Shelburne property to herself as trustee of the irrevocable trust, thus blocking the sale to Cosby. When Gagnon learned of this, he demanded that Joan return the Shelburne property to him, but she refused, saying she had acted within the authority set forth in the power of attorney. Did Joan violate any duty owed to Gagnon? Must she reconvey the property to Gagnon? [*Gagnon v. Coombs*, 654 N.E.2d 54 (Mass. App.)]

15. Daniels and Julian were employed by the Marriott Hotel in New Orleans and were close personal friends. One day after work, Daniels and Julian went to Werlein's music store to open a credit account. Julian, with Daniels's authorization and in her presence, applied for credit using Daniels's name and credit history. Later, Julian went to Werlein's without Daniels and charged the purchase of a television set to Daniels's account, executing a retail installment contract by signing Daniels's name. Daniels saw the new television in Julian's home and was informed that it was charged to the Werlein's account. Daniels told Julian to continue making payments. When Werlein's credit manager first contacted Daniels to inform her that her account was delinquent, she claimed that a money order for the television was in the mail. On the second call, she asked for a "payment balance." Some four months after the purchase, she informed Werlein's that she had not authorized the purchase of the television nor ratified the purchase. Werlein's sued Daniels for the unpaid balance. Decide. [*Philip Werlein, Ltd. v. Daniels*, 536 So.2d 722 (La. App.)]

CPA QUESTIONS

1. Generally, an agency relationship is terminated by operation of law in all of the following situations except the:

   a. Principal's death

   b. Principal's incapacity

   c. Agent's renunciation of the agency

   d. Agent's failure to acquire a necessary business license

2. Able, on behalf of Pix Corp., entered into a contract with Sky Corp., by which Sky agreed to sell computer equipment to Pix. Able disclosed to Sky that she was acting on behalf of Pix. However, Able had exceeded her actual authority by entering into the contract with Sky. If Pix wishes to ratify the contract with Sky, which of the following statements is correct?

   a. Pix must notify Sky that Pix intends to ratify the contract.

   b. Able must have acted reasonably and in Pix's best interest.

   c. Able must be a general agent of Pix.

   d. Pix must have knowledge of all material facts relating to the contract at the time it is ratified.

3. Which of the following actions requires an agent for a corporation to have a written agency agreement?

   a. Purchasing office supplies for the principal's business

   b. Purchasing an interest in undeveloped land for the principal

   c. Hiring an independent general contractor to renovate the principal's office building

   d. Retaining an attorney to collect a business debt owed the principal

4. Simmons, an agent for Jensen, has the express authority to sell Jensen's goods. Simmons also has the express authority to grant discounts of up to 5 percent of list price. Simmons sold Hemple a 10 percent discount. Hemple had not

previously dealt with either Simmons or Jensen. Which of the following courses of action may Jensen properly take?

a. Seek to void the sale to Hemple

b. Seek recovery of $50 from Hemple only

c. Seek recovery of $50 from Simmons only

d. Seek recovery of $50 from either Hemple or Simmons

5. Ogden Corp. hired Thorp as a sales representative for nine months at a salary of $3,000 per month plus 4 percent of sales. Which of the following statements is correct?

a. Thorp is obligated to act solely in Ogden's interest in matters concerning Ogden's business.

b. The agreement between Ogden and Thorp formed an agency coupled with an interest.

c. Ogden does not have the power to dismiss Thorp during the nine-month period without cause.

d. The agreement between Ogden and Thorp is not enforceable unless it is in writing and signed by Thorp.

6. Frost's accountant and business manager has the authority to:

a. Mortgage Frost's business property

b. Obtain bank loans for Frost

c. Insure Frost's property against fire loss

d. Sell Frost's business

CHAPTER 38

Third Persons in Agency

© Manuel Gutjahr/iStockphoto.com

learningoutcomes

After studying this chapter, you should be able to

LO.1 Explain when an agent is and is not liable to a third person as a party to a contract

LO.2 Describe how to execute a contract as an agent on behalf of a principal

LO.3 Explain the legal effect of a payment made by a third person to an authorized agent

LO.4 Explain the doctrine of *respondeat superior*

LO.5 Distinguish between the authority of a soliciting agent and that of a contracting agent

T he rights and liabilities of the principal, the agent, and the third person with whom the agent deals are generally determined by contract law. In some cases, tort or criminal law may be applicable.

A. Liability of Agent to Third Person

The liability of the agent to the third person depends on the existence of authority and the manner of executing the contract.

1. Action of Authorized Agent of Disclosed Principal

If an agent makes a contract with a third person on behalf of a disclosed principal and has proper authority to do so and if the contract is executed properly, the agent has no personal liability on the contract. Whether the principal performs the contract or not, the agent cannot be held liable by the third party. **For Example,** Lincoln Apartment Management, LP, required a vendor to sign a form before commencing work renovating Woodchase Village Apartments, which stated:

> *"Vendor understands and agrees that the legal Owner of the community is responsible for the payments of any services or materials performed or delivered, and not Lincoln, which is the property management company and Agent for the Owner of the community."*

The contractor's field manager, Jane Yang, signed the form before commencing work. After the work was performed the apartment complex was foreclosed, with the contractor still owed $59,758 for unpaid services. In a lawsuit against Lincoln by the contractor, the court determined that the owner, not the property manager, was solely liable for the debt.[1]

In speaking of an agent's action as authorized or unauthorized, it must be remembered that *authorized* includes action that, though originally *unauthorized*, was subsequently ratified by the principal. Once there is an effective ratification, the original action of the agent is no longer treated as unauthorized.

2. Unauthorized Action

If a person makes a contract as agent for another but lacks authority to do so, the contract does not bind the principal. When a person purports to act as agent for a principal, an implied warranty arises that that person has authority to do so. If the agent lacks authority, there is a breach of this warranty.

If the agent's act causes loss to the third person, that third person may generally hold the agent liable for the loss.

---

[1] *Grand Master Contracting, LLC v. Lincoln Apartment Management, LP,* 724 S.E.2d 456 (Ga. App. 2012).

CASE SUMMARY

The Company President Was Personally Liable When the Charcoal Plant Deal Did Not Ignite

FACTS: Craig Industries was in the business of manufacturing charcoal. Craig, the corporation's president, contracted in the name of the corporation to sell the company's plants to Husky Industries. Craig did not have authority from the board of directors to make the contract, and later the board of directors voted not to accept it. Husky Industries sued Craig on the theory that he, as agent for the corporation, exceeded his authority and should be held personally liable for damages.

DECISION: Judgment for Husky Industries. An agent who purports to contract in the name of a principal without, or in excess of, authority to do so is personally liable to the other contracting party for the agent's breach of implied warranty of authority. This liability is implied unless the agent manifests that no warranty of authority is made or the other contracting party knows the agent is not authorized. There was no discussion by the contracting parties concerning a limitation of Craig's warranty of authority to contract for the corporation, and Husky Industries was not aware that Craig was not authorized to make the contract. [***Husky Industries v. Craig,*** **618 S.W.2d 458 (Mo. App. 1981)**]

It is no defense for the agent in such a case that she acted in good faith or misunderstood the scope of authority. The purported agent is not liable for conduct in excess of authority when the third person knows that she is acting beyond the authority given by the principal.

An agent with a written authorization may avoid liability on the implied warranty of authority by showing the written authorization to the third person and permitting the third person to determine the scope of the agent's authority.

3. Disclosure of Principal

There are three degrees to which the existence and identity of the principal may be disclosed or not disclosed. An agent's liability as a party to a contract with a third person is affected by the degree of disclosure.

(A) DISCLOSED PRINCIPAL. When the agent makes known the identity of the principal and the fact that the agent is acting on behalf of that principal, the principal is called a **disclosed principal**. The third person dealing with an agent of a disclosed principal ordinarily intends to make a contract with the principal, not the agent. Consequently, the agent is not a party to, and is not bound by, the contract that is made.[2] **For Example,** Biefeld Jewelers was the trade name of Bie-Jewel Corp., a closely held corporation of which Margie Biefeld was one of several employees. The plaintiff sought to hold her personally liable on a contract for advertising services. While Ms. Biefeld signed a contract for advertising services without reference to holding a corporate office, the plain language of the agreement established that she was acting as an agent for a disclosed principal and that the plaintiff had notice of her status.[3]

disclosed principal – principal whose identity is made known by the agent as well as the fact that the agent is acting on the principal's behalf.

[2] *Stinchfield v. Weinreb,* 797 N.Y.S.2d 521 (A. D. 2005).
[3] *CBS Outdoor Group, Inc. v. Biefeld,* 836 N.Y.S.2d 497 (Civ. Ct. 2007).

partially disclosed principal – principal whose existence is made known but whose identity is not.

undisclosed principal – principal on whose behalf an agent acts without disclosing to the third person the fact of agency or the identity of the principal.

(B) **PARTIALLY DISCLOSED PRINCIPAL.** When the agent makes known the existence of a principal but not the principal's identity, the principal is a **partially disclosed principal**. Because the third party does not know the identity of the principal, the third person is making the contract with the agent, and the agent is therefore a party to the contract.

(C) **UNDISCLOSED PRINCIPAL.** When the third person is not told or does not know that the agent is acting as an agent for anyone else, the unknown principal is called an **undisclosed principal**.[4] In this case, the third person is making the contract with the agent, and the agent is a party to that contract.

CASE SUMMARY

You've Got to Tell Them You're Contracting on Behalf of the Named Principal, Silly

FACTS: In 2003, Philip Steen formed Nashville Sports Leagues, LLC, for the purpose of providing a recreational sports league for a growing demographic of active adults in Middle Tennessee. Mr. Steen served as the managing member of Nashville Sports until the LLC was administratively dissolved in 2004. Three years later, in January 2007, Mr. Steen registered TN Sports, LLC, with the Tennessee Secretary of State. TN Sports performed the same functions as Nashville Sports, and Mr. Steen continued to serve as the managing member. Mr. Steen also continued to do business under the name "Nashville Sports Leagues." In correspondence, he identified himself as an executive of Nashville Sports Leagues and used an "@nashvillesports.com" e-mail address. By spring 2007, the popularity of TN Sports had grown considerably with 11,000 members on more than 175 teams. Players had their choice of six different sports with options year-round. The success of TN Sports was due at least in part to the ease of finding willing players and forming teams on the TN Sports Web site. In addition to its essential networking function, the Web site provided users with game schedules and venue information, among other details about leagues and events. In the spring of 2007, Mr. Steen moved his TN Sports Web site to ICG Link, Inc., and it recommended that Mr. Steen build a new Web site to improve functionality. However, problems existed with the new Web site. Mr. Steen had not paid invoices from March to October, and ICG employees were instructed to "slow walk" the TN Sports Web site. The parties were unable to resolve their differences, and ICG Link filed a lawsuit against the LLC, and Mr. Steen personally, for breach of contract. The trial court found there was quasi-contract liability, less the cost to repair defects in the new Web site. It found Mr. Steen personally liable for the judgment and he appealed.

DECISION: In order for an agent to avoid personal liability on a contract, the agent must disclose the facts of the agency and the identity of the principal. Mr. Steen is the managing member of TN Sports LLC. However, in his transactions with ICG he failed to disclose that TN Sports LLC was his principal, identifying himself as an executive of Nashville Sports Leagues. Thus he is personally liable for the judgment for ICG on its quasi-contract claim in the amount of $13,952, which consists of amounts owed for Web site development and hosting services, with an offset for the cost of completion of the new Web site. [*ICG Link, Inc. v. Steen*, 363 S.W.3d 533 (Tenn. App. 2011)]

4. Assumption of Liability

Agents may intentionally make themselves liable on contracts with third persons.[5] This situation frequently occurs when the agent is a well-established local brokerage

---

[4] See *Castle Cheese Inc. v. MS Produce Inc.*, 2008 WL 4372856 (W.D. Pa. Sept. 19, 2008), where the court held that an agent must disclose both the identity of the principal and the fact of the agency relationship to avoid liability under a contract. One of the defendants, CVS Foods, did not establish that it had disclosed the fact it was acting as an agent, and it was held liable for breach of contract.

[5] *Fairchild Publications v. Rosston*, 584 N.Y.S.2d 389 (N.Y. County Sup. 1992).

house or other agency and when the principal is located out of town and is not known locally.

In some situations, the agent makes a contract that will be personally binding. If the principal is not disclosed, the agent is necessarily the other contracting party and is bound by the contract. Even when the principal is disclosed, the agent may be personally bound if it was the intention of the parties that the agent assume a personal obligation even though this was done to further the principal's business.[6]

CASE SUMMARY

The Thanks I Get for Being a Nice Person

FACTS: Grant Colledge was the managing member of A.T. Masterpiece Homes, a limited liability company. The trial court concluded that Colledge had assumed personal responsibility regarding the quality of work during the construction of the Bennetts' and the Hoefferles' homes. When the construction finished, the homes were in various stages of disrepair and structural failure. Judgment was issued against Colledge personally for $173,250 for the Bennetts and $55,250 for the Hoefferles. On appeal, Colledge contended that he should be shielded from personal liability because he was at all times acting only as an agent on behalf of a limited liability company, A.T. Masterpiece; and, he contends, any statements attributed to him where he said "I will take care of it" or "I guarantee it" were simply figures of speech and did not amount to an express assumption of personal liability.

DECISION: Judgment against Colledge. A person acting as an agent may assume personal liability on a business contract where he voluntarily undertakes a personal responsibility. For example, Colledge's statements to the Hoefferles had the effect of personally obligating himself for the structural integrity of the dormer because he made the statements with the goal of securing the Hoefferles' continuing performance on the contract. And his statements to the Bennetts led them to believe that he would personally ensure that the completed home was built properly. [*Bennett v. A.T. Masterpiece Homes at Broadsprings, LLC*, 40 A.3d 145 (Pa. Super. 2012)]

5. Execution of Contract

A simple contract that would appear to be the contract of the agent can be shown by other evidence, if believed, to have been intended as a contract between the principal and the third party.

CASE SUMMARY

If You Sign as an Agent, You Don't Have to Pay

FACTS: Audrey Walton was transferred from a hospital to Mariner Health Nursing Home on January 26, 2001. Her daughter Patricia Walton signed a 30-page document, "Resident's Agent Financial Agreement." Patricia indicated in that agreement that the only method of payment would be Medicare or Medical Assistance. Medicare assistance stopped in February 2001. On

---

[6] See *Boros v. Carter*, 537 So.2d 1134 (Fla. App. 1989).

CASE SUMMARY

Continued

January 10, 2003, Mariner Health sued both Audrey and Patricia for unpaid monthly bills amounting to $86,235. From a judgment for Mariner Health against both the patient and her daughter, Patricia appealed.

DECISION: Judgment for Patricia. As an agent, Patricia entered into the contract only for the benefit of Audrey and is personally insulated from liability by virtue of her status as an agent. *Note:* A state Nursing Home Bill of Rights did not authorize a nursing home to bring a private cause of action against a patient's agent for breach of contract unless the agent voluntarily and knowingly agreed to pay for the care with her or his own funds. [***Walton v. Mariner Health,*** **894 A.2d 584 (Md. 2006)**]

To avoid any question of interpretation, an agent should execute an instrument by signing the principal's name and either *by* or *per* and the agent's name. **For Example,** if Jane R. Craig is an agent for B. G. Gray, Craig should execute instruments by signing either "B.G. Gray, by Jane R. Craig" or "B. G. Gray, per Jane R. Craig." Such a signing is in law a signing by Gray, and the agent is therefore not a party to the contract. The signing of the principal's name by an authorized agent without indicating the agent's name or identity is likewise in law the signature of the principal.

If the instrument is ambiguous as to whether the agent has signed in a representative or an individual capacity, parol evidence is admissible as between the original parties to the transaction for establishing the character in which the agent was acting.

6. Torts and Crimes

Agents are liable for harm caused third persons by the agents' fraudulent, intentional, or negligent acts.[7] The fact that persons were acting as agents at the time or that they acted in good faith under the directions of a principal does not relieve them of liability if their conduct would impose liability on them when acting for themselves.

CASE SUMMARY

Employees Are Not Personally Liable for Roadway Accidents While at Work, Are They?

FACTS: Ralls was an employee of the Arkansas State Highway Department. While repairing a state highway, he negligently backed a state truck onto the highway, causing a collision with Mittlesteadt's car. Mittlesteadt sued Ralls, who raised the defense that, because he was acting on behalf of the state, he was not liable for his negligence.

---

[7] *Mannish v. Lacayo,* 496 So.2d 242 (Fla. App. 1986).

CASE SUMMARY

Continued

DECISION: The fact that an employee or agent is acting on behalf of someone else does not excuse or exonerate the agent or employee from liability for torts committed by the agent or employee. Ralls was therefore liable for his negligence even though it occurred within the scope of his employment by the state. [***Ralls v. Mittlesteadt*, 596 S.W.2d 349 (Ark. 1980)**]

If an agent commits a crime, such as stealing from a third person or shooting a third person, the agent is liable for the crime without regard to the fact of acting as an agent. The agent is liable without regard to whether the agent acted in self-interest or sought to advance the interest of the principal.

B. LIABILITY OF PRINCIPAL TO THIRD PERSON

The principal is liable to the third person for the properly authorized and executed contracts of the agent and, in certain circumstances, for the agent's unauthorized contracts.

7. Agent's Contracts

The liability of a principal to a third person on a contract made by an agent depends on the extent of disclosure of the principal and the form of the contract that is executed.

Ethics & the Law

Some time ago, dairy farmers owned large tracts of land in south Tempe, Arizona. The farmers used the land for grazing animals. Economic growth in this suburb of Phoenix was limited because of the state's inability at that time to attract large businesses to the area for relocation or location of new facilities.

In 1973, three farmers who owned adjoining parcels of land in the south Tempe area were approached by a local real estate agent with an offer for the purchase of their property. The amount of the offer was approximately 10 percent above the property's appraised value. The three farmers discussed the offer and concluded that with their need to retire, it was best to accept the offer and sell the land. All three signed contracts for the sale of their land.

After the contracts were entered into but before the transactions had closed, the three farmers learned that the land was being purchased by a real estate development firm from southern California.

The development firm had planned, and would be proposing to the Tempe City Council, a residential community, the Lakes. The Lakes would consist of upper-end homes in a community laced with parks, lakes, and ponds, with each house in the developed area backing up to its own dock and water recreation. The development firm had begun the project because it had learned of the plans of American Express, Rubbermaid, and Dial to locate major facilities in the Phoenix area.

The three farmers objected to the sale of their land when they learned the identity of the buyer. "If we had known who was coming in here and why, we never would have sold for such a low price." Were the farmers' contracts binding?

Is it ethical to use the strategy of an undisclosed principal? What is the role of an agent in a situation in which the third party is making a decision not as beneficial to him or her as it could or should be? Can the agent say anything?

CPA

(a) Simple Contract with Principal Disclosed. When a disclosed principal with contractual capacity authorizes or ratifies an agent's transaction with a third person and when the agent properly executes a contract with the third person, a binding contract exists between the principal and the third person. The principal and the third person may each sue the other in the event of a breach of the contract. The agent is not a party to the contract, is not liable for its performance, and cannot sue for its breach.[8]

The liability of a disclosed principal to a third person is not discharged by the fact that the principal gives the agent money with which to pay the third person. Consequently, the liability of a buyer for the purchase price of goods is not terminated by the fact that the buyer gave the buyer's agent the purchase price to remit to the seller.

(b) Simple Contract with Principal Partially Disclosed. A partially disclosed principal is liable for a simple contract made by an authorized agent. The third person may recover from either the agent or the principal.

(c) Simple Contract with Principal Undisclosed. An undisclosed principal is liable for a simple contract made by an authorized agent. Although the third person initially contracted with the agent alone, the third person, on learning of the existence of the undisclosed principal, may sue that principal.[9] In most jurisdictions, third persons can sue and collect judgments from the agent or principal, or both, until the judgment is fully satisfied (joint and several liability).[10]

8. Payment to Agent

When the third person makes payment to an authorized agent, the payment is deemed made to the principal. Even if the agent never remits or delivers the payment to the principal, the principal must give the third person full credit for the payment so long as the third person made the payment in good faith and had no reason to know that the agent would be guilty of misconduct.[11]

CASE SUMMARY

But We Already Paid!

FACTS: E.I. duPont de Nemours & Company licensed Enjay Chemical Company (now Exxon) and Johnson & Johnson to use certain chemical processes in return for which royalty payments by check were to be made to duPont. By agreement between the companies, the royalty payments to be made to duPont were to be made by check sent to a specified duPont employee, C.H.D., in its Control Division. These checks were sent during the next nine years. C.H.D. altered some of them so that he was named thereon as the payee. He then cashed them and used the money for his own purposes. Liberty Mutual Insurance Company, which insured the fidelity

---

[8] *Levy v. Gold & Co., Inc.*, 529 N.Y.S.2d 133 (A.D. 1988).

[9] *McDaniel v. Hensons, Inc.*, 493 S.E.2d 529 (Ga. App. 1997).

[10] *Crown Controls, Inc. v. Smiley*, 756 P.2d 717 (Wash. 1988).

[11] This general rule of law is restated in some states by Section 2 of the Uniform Fiduciaries Act, which is expressly extended by Section 1 of the act to agents, partners, and corporate officers. Similar statutory provisions are found in a number of other states.

CASE SUMMARY

Continued

of duPont's employees, and duPont sued Enjay and Johnson & Johnson on the basis that they still owed the amounts embezzled by C.H.D.

DECISION: Judgment for Enjay and Johnson & Johnson. Payment to an authorized agent has the legal effect of payment to the principal regardless of whether the agent remits the payment to the principal or embezzles it. C.H.D. was the agent authorized to receive the royalty checks. Therefore, the defendants had effectively paid the royalties when they sent C.H.D. the checks. His misconduct did not revive the debts that were paid by sending him the checks. [*Liberty Mutual Ins. Co. v. Enjay Chemical Co.*, 316 A.2d 219 (Del. Super. 1974)]

Because apparent authority has the same legal effect as actual authority, a payment made to a person with apparent authority to receive the payment is deemed a payment to the apparent principal.

When a debtor makes payment to a person who is not the actual or apparent agent of the creditor, such a payment does not discharge the debt unless that person in fact pays the money to the creditor.

CASE SUMMARY

But We Already Paid!
No You Didn't.

FACTS: Basic Research, LLC, ran advertisements on Rainbow Media Holdings' cable television networks from January to March 2008. Basic used an advertising agency named Icebox to place advertisements for its products. It paid Icebox up front for all of this advertising. Icebox went into bankruptcy, and it was discovered Icebox had not paid Rainbow Networks for three months of advertising, worth $590,000. Rainbow Networks obtained a $132,000 payment from the Icebox bankruptcy estate. Rainbow, now seeks payment from Basic for the remaining $406,000. Basic contends that Rainbow's only remedy was through the bankruptcy estate.

DECISION: Basic Research was a disclosed principal with whom Rainbow Networks had a credit agreement. Basic chose Icebox as its agent to place its advertisements and to make payments. Icebox didn't pay. It is Basic who is liable for the actions of its agent, and Basic is responsible for the $406,000 owed Rainbow Networks. [*Basic Research v. Rainbow Media Holdings, Inc.*, 2011 WL 2636833 (D. Utah July 6, 2011)]

9. Agent's Statements

A principal is bound by a statement made by an agent while transacting business within the scope of authority. This means that the principal cannot later contradict the statement of the agent and show that it is not true. Statements or declarations of an agent, in order to bind the principal, must be made at the time of performing the act to which they relate or shortly thereafter.

10. Agent's Knowledge

The principal is bound by knowledge or notice of any fact that is acquired by an agent while acting within the scope of actual or apparent authority. When a fact is known to the agent of the seller, the sale is deemed made by the seller with knowledge of that fact.

The rule that the agent's knowledge is imputed to the principal is extended in some cases to knowledge gained prior to the creation of the agency relationship. The notice and knowledge in any case must be based on reliable information. Thus, when the agent hears only rumors, the principal is not charged with notice.

If the subject matter is outside the scope of the agent's authority, the agent is under no duty to inform the principal of the knowledge, and the principal is not bound by it. The principal is not charged with knowledge of an agent when (1) the agent is acting adversely to the principal's interest or (2) the third party acts in collusion with the agent for the purpose of cheating the principal.

C. LIABILITY OF PRINCIPAL FOR TORTS AND CRIMES OF AGENT

Under certain circumstances, the principal may be liable for the torts or crimes of the agent or the employee.

CPA

11. Vicarious Liability for Torts and Crimes

Assume that an agent or an employee causes harm to a third person. Is the principal or the employer liable for this conduct? If the conduct constitutes a crime, can the principal or the employer be criminally prosecuted? The answer is that in many instances, the principal or the employer is liable civilly and may also be prosecuted criminally. That is, the principal or the employer is liable although personally free from fault and not guilty of any wrong. This concept of imposing liability for the fault of another is known as **vicarious liability**.

vicarious liability – imposing liability for the fault of another.

This situation arises both when an employer's employee or a principal's agent commits the wrong. The rules of law governing the vicarious liability of the principal and the employer are the same. In the interest of simplicity, this section is stated in terms of employees acting in the course of employment. Remember that these rules are equally applicable to agents acting within the scope of their authority. As a practical matter, some situations will arise only with agents. **For Example,** the vicarious liability of a seller for the misrepresentations made by a salesperson arise only when the seller appointed an agent to sell. In contrast, both the employee hired to drive a truck and an agent driving to visit a customer could negligently injure a third person with their vehicles. In many situations, a person employed by another is both an employee and an agent, and the tort is committed within the phase of "employee work."

respondeat superior – doctrine that the principal or employer is vicariously liable for the unauthorized torts committed by an agent or employee while acting within the scope of the agency or the course of the employment, respectively.

The rule of law imposing vicarious liability on an innocent employer for the wrong of an employee is also known as the doctrine of ***respondeat superior***. In modern times, this doctrine can be justified on the grounds that the business should pay for the harm caused in the doing of the business, that the employer will be more careful in the selection of employees if made responsible for their actions, and that the employer may obtain liability insurance to protect against claims of third persons.

(A) NATURE OF ACT. The wrongful act committed by an employee may be a negligent act, an intentional act, a fraudulent act, or a violation of a government regulation. It may give rise only to civil liability of the employer, or it may also subject the employer to prosecution for crime.

(1) Negligent Act.

Historically, the act for which liability would be imposed under the doctrine of *respondeat superior* was a negligent act committed within the scope of employment.

(2) Intentional Act.

Under the common law, a master was not liable for an intentional tort committed by a servant. The modern law holds that an employer is liable for an intentional tort committed by an employee for the purpose of furthering the employer's business.[12] **For Example,** Crane Brothers, Inc., drilled a well for Stephen May. When May did not pay his bill, two Crane Brothers' employees went to May's workplace, and an altercation ensued in which May was injured. Crane Brothers, Inc., was held vicariously liable for the torts of the employees, not because the employer itself committed the wrongful acts but because it was answerable for the manner in which its agents, the two employees, conducted themselves in doing the business of the employer.[13]

(3) Fraud.

Modern decisions hold the employer liable for fraudulent acts or misrepresentations. The rule is commonly applied to a principal-agent relationship. To illustrate, when an agent makes fraudulent statements in selling stock, the principal is liable for the buyer's loss. In states that follow the common law rule of no liability for intentional torts, the principal is not liable for the agent's fraud when the principal did not authorize or know of the agent's fraud.

(4) Government Regulation.

The employer may be liable because of the employee's violation of a government regulation. These regulations are most common in the areas of business and of protection of the environment. In such cases, the employer may be held liable for a penalty imposed by the government. In some cases, the breach of the regulation will impose liability on the employer in favor of a third person who is injured as a consequence of the violation.

(B) COURSE OF EMPLOYMENT. The mere fact that a tort or crime is committed by an employee does not necessarily impose vicarious liability on the employer. It must also be shown that the individual was acting within the scope of authority if an agent or in the course of employment if an employee. If an employee was not acting within the scope of employment, there is no vicarious liability.[14] **For Example,** after Rev. Joel Thomford accidentally shot and killed his parishioner during a deer

---

[12] Restatement (Second) of Agency §231.
[13] *Crane Brothers, Inc. v. May,* 556 S.E.2d 865 (Ga. App. 2001).
[14] *Young v. Taylor-White LLC,* 181 S.W.2d 324 (Tenn. 2005).

hunting trip, the parishioner's wife brought a wrongful death action against the pastor and the church. Because the accident occurred on the pastor's day off and the trip was not sponsored by the church, the pastor was not acting within the course of his employment at the time of the accident, and the church was not liable.[15]

CASE SUMMARY

He Was Back to Nettie's Business When He Hit the Studebaker

FACTS: Judith Studebaker was injured when a van owned and driven by James Ferry collided with her vehicle. On the morning of the incident, Ferry made his usual runs for the florist for whom he delivered flowers, Nettie's Flower Garden. Studebaker brought an action against Nettie's on a *respondeat superior* theory on the belief that Ferry was Nettie's employee at the time of the accident. Nettie's defended that Ferry was an independent contractor, not an employee. From a judgment in favor of Studebaker for $125,000, Nettie's appealed.

DECISION: Judgment against Nettie's. Applying a "right to control" test, it is clear that Nettie's controlled or had the right to control Ferry at the time of the collision. Nettie's set standards for Ferry's dress and conduct, determined his territory, and set standards for his van. Although Ferry made a slight detour prior to the accident to conduct personal business at a pawnshop, this did not relieve the employer from liability because he was clearly back to Nettie's business at the time of the accident. [***Studebaker v. Nettie's Flower Garden Inc.*, 842 S.W.2d 227 (Mo. App. 1992)**]

(c) Employee of the United States. The Federal Tort Claims Act (FTCA) declares that the United States shall be liable vicariously whenever a federal employee driving a motor vehicle in the course of employment causes harm under such circumstances that a private employer would be liable. Contrary to the general rule, the statute exempts the employee driver from liability.[16]

Thinking Things Through

Rule No. 1: Take the Safe Course

The National Safety Council estimates that one quarter of all automobile and truck accidents involve cell phone use or texting. In fatality and injury vehicle accidents, plaintiffs' attorneys subpoena cell phone records, which often form the basis of compelling liability cases against driver-employees *and* their employers. It is a near automatic conclusion by jurors that the operator using a cell phone or texting caused the accident. Thinking Things Through, for the safety of employees and the public, as well as the extraordinary liability risks for employers, it may well be a sound business practice to ban all cell phone usage while driving on company business.

---

[15] *Hentges v. Thomford*, 569 N.W.2d 424 (Minn. App. 1997).
[16] Claims of negligent hiring are not permissible under the FTCA. See *Tonelli v. United States*, 60 F.3d 492 (8th Cir. 1995).

12. Negligent Hiring and Retention of Employees

In addition to a complaint against the employer based on the doctrine of *respondeat superior*, a lawsuit may often raise a second theory, that of negligent hiring or retention of an employee.[17] Unlike the *respondeat superior* theory by which the employer may be vicariously liable for the tort of an employee, the negligent hiring theory is based on the negligence of the employer in the hiring process. Under the *respondeat superior* rule, the employer is liable only for those torts committed within the scope of employment or in the furtherance of the employer's interests. The negligent hiring theory has been used to impose liability in cases when an employee commits an intentional tort, almost invariably outside the scope of employment, against a customer or the general public, and the employer knew or should have known that the employee was incompetent, violent, dangerous, or criminal.[18]

(A) NEED FOR DUE CARE IN HIRING. An employer may be liable on a theory of negligent hiring when it is shown that the employer knew, or in the exercise of ordinary care should have known, that the job applicant would create an undue risk of harm to others in carrying out job responsibilities. Moreover, it must also be shown that the employer could have reasonably foreseen injury to the third party. Thus, an employer who knows of an employee's preemployment drinking problems and violent behavior may be liable to customers assaulted by that employee.

Employers might protect themselves from liability in a negligent hiring case by having each prospective employee fill out an employment application form and then checking into the applicant's work experience, background, character, and qualifications. This would be evidence of due care in hiring. Generally, the scope of a preemployment investigation should correlate to the degree of opportunity the prospective employee would have to do harm to third persons. A minimum investigation consisting of filling out an application form and conducting a personal interview would be satisfactory for hiring an outside maintenance person, but a full background inquiry would be necessary for hiring a security guard. However, such inquiry does not bar *respondeat superior* liability.

(B) EMPLOYEES WITH CRIMINAL RECORDS. The hiring of an individual with a criminal record does not by itself establish the tort of negligent hiring.[19] An employer who knows that an applicant has a criminal record has a duty to investigate to determine whether the nature of the conviction in relationship to the job to be performed creates an unacceptable risk to third persons.

(C) NEGLIGENT RETENTION. Courts assign liability under negligent retention on a basis similar to that of negligent hiring. That is, the employer knew, or should have known, that the employee would create an undue risk of harm to others in carrying out job responsibilities.

A hospital is liable for negligent retention when it continues the staff privileges of a physician that it knew or should have known had sexually assaulted a female patient in the past.[20]

---

[17] *Medina v. Graham's Cowboys, Inc.*, 827 P.2d 859 (N.M. App. 1992).

[18] *Rockwell v. Sun Harbor Budget Suites*, 925 P.2d 1175 (Nev. 1996).

[19] *Connes v. Molalla Transportation Systems*, 831 P.2d 1316 (Colo. 1992).

[20] *Capithorne v. Framingham Union Hospital*, 520 N.E.2d 139 (Mass. 1988). A hospital may also be vicariously liable for the negligent credentialing of its physicians, as determined in *Larson v. Wasemiller*, 738 N.W.2d 300 (Minn. 2007).

CASE SUMMARY

(1) Alcohol, (2) Battery, and (3) Negligent Retention: Three Strikes and You're Out!

FACTS: Mark Livigni was manager of the National Super Markets store in Cahokia, Illinois. After drinking alcoholic beverages one evening, he stopped by the store to check the premises when he observed a 10-year-old boy's unacceptable behavior outside the store. Livigni chased the boy to a car, where he pulled another child, a 4-year-old named Farris Bryant, from the car and threw him through the air. A multicount lawsuit was brought against National and Livigni. The evidence revealed that some eight years before the incident with Farris Bryant, Livigni had thrown an empty milk crate at a subordinate employee, striking him on the arm and necessitating medical treatment, and that some two years before the incident, he threw his 13-year-old son onto a bed while disciplining him, causing the boy to sustain a broken collarbone. Livigni was promoted to store manager subsequent to the milk crate incident, and he pled guilty to aggravated battery to his child and was sentenced to two years' probation. A verdict was rendered against National for $20,000 under a *respondeat superior* theory for the battery of Farris Bryant. A verdict was also rendered against National for $15,000 for negligent retention of Livigni and for $115,000 in punitive damages for willful and wanton retention. National appealed the trial court's denial of its motions for directed verdicts on these counts.

DECISION: Judgment for Bryant. Employers that wrongfully hire or retain unfit employees expose the public to the acts of these employees, and it is not unreasonable to hold the employer accountable when the employee causes injury to another. The principle is not *respondeat superior;* rather, it is premised on the wrongful conduct of the employer itself. In addition, the employer in this case is responsible under *respondeat superior* because Livigni was prompted to act, in part, to protect store property. A dissenting opinion stated that the decision would send the wrong message to employers on the negligent retention issue and cause them to terminate any employee who has ever had an altercation on or off company premises, which is contrary to the state's public policy of rehabilitating criminal offenders. [*Bryant v. Livigni*, **619 N.E.2d 550 (Ill. App. 1993)**]

13. Negligent Supervision and Training

A separate theory of liability in addition to the doctrine of *respondeat superior* is that of negligent supervision and training, that holds the principal directly liable for its negligence in regard to training and supervision of its employees and agents. **For Example,** Monadnock Training Council, Inc., certified Robert Hebert as an "authorized Monadnock instructor" and granted him actual authority to market and promote its PR-24 police baton. In a training session run by Hebert at the Chesire County House of Corrections in New Hampshire, Charles Herman suffered severe head trauma when training with Hebert without protective headgear in a room with unpadded cement walls. Monadnock was held directly liable for Herman's injuries based on its negligent supervision and training of Hebert.[21]

---

[21] *Herman v. Monadnock PR-24 Training Council, Inc.,* 802 A.2d 1187 (N.H. 2002).

FIGURE 38-1 | *Liability for Torts of Agent or Employee*

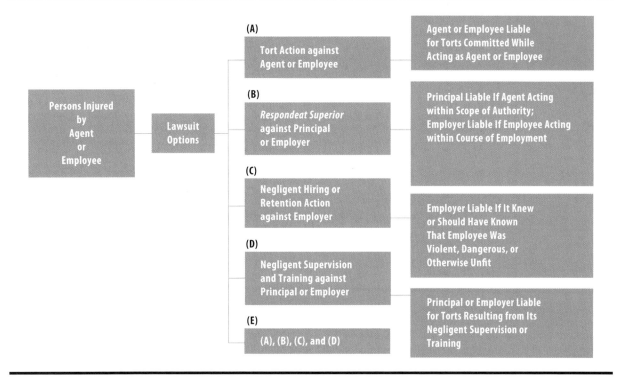

© Cengage Learning

14. Agent's Crimes

A principal is liable for the crimes of an agent committed at the principal's direction. When not authorized, however, the principal is ordinarily not liable for an agent's crime merely because it was committed while the agent was otherwise acting within the scope of the latter's authority or employment. **For Example,** the owner of the Main Tower Cafe in Hartford, Connecticut, was not vicariously liable for injuries sustained by a patron who was shot by a bouncer while attempting to enter the bar because the bouncer's intentional and willful act was motivated by his own spleen and malevolence against the victim in clear departure from his employment.[22] As an exception to the rule of nonliability just stated, courts now hold an employer criminally liable when the employee has in the course of employment violated environmental protection laws, liquor sales laws, pure food laws, or laws regulating prices or prohibiting false weights. **For Example,** an employer may be held criminally responsible for an employee's sale of liquor to a minor in violation of the liquor law even though the sale was not known to the employer and violated instructions given to the employee.

---

[22] *Pruitt v. Main & Tower, Inc.,* 2002 WL 532467 (Conn. Super. March 14, 2002); see also *Burgess v. Lee Acceptance Corp.,* 2008 WL 5111905 (E.D. Mich. Dec. 4, 2008).

15. Owner's Liability for Acts of an Independent Contractor

If work is done by an independent contractor rather than by an employee, the owner is not liable for harm caused by the contractor to third persons or their property. Likewise, the owner is not bound by the contracts made by the independent contractor. The owner is ordinarily not liable for harm caused to third persons by the negligence of the employees of the independent contractor.[23]

CASE SUMMARY

Plaintiffs' Attorneys Whine, "Why Do Courts Keep on Applying the 'Right to Control Test'?"

FACTS: Mark McLaurin was employed as a carpenter by Friede Goldman Offshore, Inc. Noble Drilling Inc. contracted with Friede Goldman (FG) to refit one of the offshore drilling rigs, the "Noble Clyde Boudreaux," at FG's Jackson County, Mississippi, facility. On July 30 and 31, 2002, McLaurin was assigned by Friede Goldman to construct scaffolding inside one of the pontoon extensions. A crane, operated by Friede Goldman employees, was in the process of lowering the roof structure of the pontoon for final placement. McLaurin was injured when he placed his hand in a "pinch point"—a space between two objects—while the roof was being lowered. McLaurin suffered a severely crushed left hand and arm. He received medical benefits and disability compensation from FG under the Longshore and Harbor Workers' Compensation Act. Maritime workers are also allowed to pursue separate claims against third parties responsible for their injuries, and McLaurin sued Noble Drilling for negligence. Noble Drilling sought the dismissal of the case asserting that it was not responsible for the negligence of the employees of an independent contractor.

DECISION: Judgment for Noble Drilling. McLaurin testified that no one from Noble instructed him to work inside the pontoon extension or on how to do his work. McLaurin's supervisor testified that Noble never told any member of his crew what to do and that he had "total control over my crew." Only FG employees were involved in the fitting work at the time of McLaurin's injury. And no Noble employee was present to observe the unsafe placement of McLaurin's hand in the pontoon extension. The mere fact that Noble could observe, inspect, and make recommendations does not establish that it had substantial control over the operation. [*McLaurin v. Noble Drilling Inc.*, 2009 WL 367401 (S.D. Miss. Feb. 10, 2009)]

(A) EXCEPTIONS TO OWNER'S IMMUNITY. There is a trend toward imposing liability on the owner when work undertaken by an independent contractor is inherently dangerous.[24] That is, the law is taking the position that if the owner wishes to engage in a particular activity, the owner must be responsible for the harm it causes. The owner cannot be insulated from such liability by the device of hiring an independent contractor to do the work.

Regardless of the nature of the activity, the owner may be liable for the torts and contracts of the independent contractor when the owner controls the conduct of the independent contractor.

---

[23] *King v. Lens Creek, Ltd., Partnership*, 483 S.E.2d 265 (W. Va. 1996).
[24] *Hinger v. Parker & Parsley Petroleum Co.*, 902 P.2d 1033 (N.M. App. 1995).

In certain circumstances, such as providing security for a business, collecting bills, and repossessing collateral, there is an increased risk that torts may be committed by the individuals performing such duties. The trend of the law is to refuse to allow the use of an independent contractor for such work to insulate the employer.

(B) UNDISCLOSED INDEPENDENT CONTRACTOR. In some situations, the owner appears to be doing the act in question because the existence of the independent contractor is not disclosed or apparent. This situation occurs most commonly when a franchisee does business under the name of the franchisor; when a concessionaire, such as a restaurant in a hotel, appears to be the hotel restaurant, although in fact it is operated by an independent concessionaire; or when the buyer of a business continues to run the business in the seller's name. In such cases of an undisclosed independent contractor, it is generally held that the apparent owner (that is, the franchisor, the grantor of the concession, or the seller) is liable for the torts and contracts of the undisclosed independent contractor.

16. Enforcement of Claim by Third Person

A lawsuit may be brought by a third person against the agent or the principal if each is liable. In most states and in the federal courts, the plaintiff may sue either or both in one action when both are liable. If both are sued, the plaintiff may obtain a judgment against both, although the plaintiff is allowed to collect the full amount of the judgment only once.

D. TRANSACTIONS WITH SALES PERSONNEL

Many transactions with sales personnel do not result in a contract with the third person with whom the salesperson deals.

17. Soliciting and Contracting Agents

soliciting agent – salesperson.

Giving an order to a salesperson often does not give rise to a contract. Ordinarily, a salesperson is a **soliciting agent**, whose authority is limited to soliciting offers from third persons and transmitting them to the principal for acceptance or rejection. Such an agent does not have authority to make a contract that will bind the principal to the third person. The employer of the salesperson is not bound by a contract until the employer accepts the order, and the third person (customer) may withdraw the offer at any time prior to acceptance.

contracting agent – agent with authority to make contracts; person with whom the buyer deals.

In contrast, if the person with whom the buyer deals is a **contracting agent** with authority to make contracts, by definition a binding contract exists between the principal and the customer from the moment that the agent agrees with the customer. In other words, the contract arises when the agent accepts the customer's order.[25]

---

[25] But see the complications that developed in *Ferris v. Tennessee Log Homes, Inc.*, 2009 WL 1506724, (W.D. Ky. May 27, 2009), where Tennessee Log Homes (TLH) had a licensing agreement that explicitly granted authority to its "agent" to generate contracts for the sale of log home packages on behalf of TLH.

MAKE THE CONNECTION

SUMMARY

An agent of a disclosed principal who makes a contract with a third person within the scope of authority has no personal liability on the contract. It is the principal and the third person who may each sue the other in the event of a breach. A person purporting to act as an agent for a principal warrants by implication that there is an existing principal with legal capacity and that the principal has authorized the agent to act. The person acting as an agent is liable for any loss caused the third person for breach of these warranties. An agent of a partially disclosed or an undisclosed principal is a party to the contract with the third person. The agent may enforce the contract against the third person and is liable for its breach. To avoid problems of interpretation, an agent should execute a contract "Principal, by Agent." Agents are liable for harm caused third persons by their fraudulent, malicious, or negligent acts.

An undisclosed or a partially disclosed principal is liable to a third person on a simple contract made by an authorized agent. When a third person makes payment to an authorized agent, it is deemed paid to the principal.

A principal or an employer is vicariously liable under the doctrine of *respondeat superior* for the torts of an agent or an employee committed within the scope of authority or the course of employment. The principal or the employer may also be liable for some crimes committed in the course of employment. An owner is not liable for torts caused by an independent contractor to third persons or their property unless the work given to the independent contractor is inherently hazardous.

A salesperson is ordinarily an agent whose authority is limited to soliciting offers (orders) from third persons and transmitting them to the principal. The principal is not bound until he or she accepts the order. The customer may withdraw an offer at any time prior to acceptance.

LEARNING OUTCOMES

After studying this chapter, you should be able to clearly explain:

A. Liability of Agent to Third Person

LO.1   Explain when an agent is and is not liable to a third person as a party to a contract

> See the Biefeld Jewelers example in which Margie Biefeld was acting as an agent for a disclosed principal when she signed the contract and was not a party to the contract, p. 825.

LO.2   Describe how to execute a contract as an agent on behalf of a principal

> See the "B. G. Gray, by Jane R. Craig" example on p. 828.
> Learn from the mistake of Philip Steen's insufficient disclosure of his principal in the *ICG Link case*, p. 826.

B. Liability of Principal to Third Person

LO.3   Explain the legal effect of a payment made by a third person to an authorized agent

> See the discussion of a third party's payment to an authorized agent who absconds with the payment, starting on p. 830.
> But see the effect of a payment by a disclosed principal to its agent who fails to pay the third party in the *Rainbow Networks* case, p. 831.

C. Liability of Principal for Torts and Crimes of Agent

LO.4   Explain the doctrine of *respondeat superior*

> See the Crane Brothers, Inc. example of employer liability for torts of the employees, p. 833.
> See the Rev. Joel Thomford example in which Rev. Thomford's employer, the church, was not liable for the pastor's accidental shooting of a parishioner on a hunting trip not sponsored by the church, pp. 833–834.

D. Transactions with Sales Personnel

L0.5 Distinguish between the authority of a soliciting agent and that of a contracting agent

See the discussion of the soliciting and contracting of agents, p. 839.

KEY TERMS

contracting agent
respondeat superior
disclosed principal

partially disclosed
  principal
soliciting agent

undisclosed principal
vicarious liability

QUESTIONS AND CASE PROBLEMS

1. Richard Pawlus was an owner of Dutch City Wood Products, Inc., which did business as "Dutch City Marketing." Pawlus purchased merchandise from Rothschild Sunsystems from April 24 to June 24 using the designation "Richard Pawlus Dutch City Marketing" on orders and correspondence. In October, Rothschild was notified that Pawlus was acting on behalf of the corporation when the merchandise was purchased. Rothschild sued Pawlus for payment for the merchandise. Pawlus contended that he was an agent of the corporation and was thus not personally liable. Decide. [*Rothschild Sunsystems, Inc. v. Pawlus*, 514 N.Y.S.2d 572 (A.D.)]

2. Myles Murphy was appointed by Cy Sinden, a famous developer, to purchase land for a shopping center near the intersection of I-95 and Route 1. Mary Mason, the property owner, contracted with Murphy for the sale of the property. Because of an economic downturn, Sinden was unable to provide the planned behind-the-scenes financing for the venture, and the contract was not performed. Mason's real estate experts determined that she lost $2 million because of the breach of contract. Mason also discovered that Sinden was "behind the deal." If Mason elects to sue Sinden, who turns out to be unable to pay the judgment because of the collapse of his business "empire," can she later bring suit against Murphy?

3. Lowell Shoemaker, an architect, was hired by Affhouse to work on a land development project. In September Shoemaker contacted Central Missouri Professional Services about providing engineering and surveying services for the project. Central submitted a written proposal to Shoemaker in October. About a week later, Shoemaker orally agreed that Central should proceed with the work outlined in the proposal. When the first phase of the work was completed, a bill of $5,864.00 was sent to Shoemaker. Shoemaker called Central and requested that all bills be sent directly to the owner/developer, Affhouse. When the bills were not paid, Central sued Shoemaker and Affhouse. The trial court entered a judgment against Shoemaker for $5,864 and he appealed. Shoemaker acknowledged that he did not disclose the identity of the principal to Central at the time the transaction was conducted, and explained:

   Q. You never told Mike Bates or Central Missouri Professional Services that you were an agent for Affhouse or any other undisclosed principal?
   A. That's correct. I never did.

   Q. Another note I wrote down was that the subject of Affhouse came up in your conversations with Mike Bates of Central Missouri Professional Services after he sent the bill to you?
   A. The early part of the year, yes.

   Shoemaker contends that since he made clear to Central that he was an architect and not the developer, there was no binding oral contract between Central and him. Decide. [*Central Missouri Professional Services v. Shoemaker*, 108 S.W.3d 6 (Mo. App.)]

4. Beverly Baumann accompanied her mother to Memorial Hospital, where her mother was placed in intensive care for heart problems. A nurse asked Baumann to sign various documents, including one that authorized the hospital to release medical information and to receive the mother's insurance benefits directly. This form stated: "I understand I am financially responsible to the hospital for charges not covered by this authorization." Baumann's mother died during the course of her hospitalization. The hospital later sued Baumann to recover $19,013.42 in unpaid hospital charges based on the form she signed, which the hospital called a "guarantee of payment." Baumann contended that she signed the document as an agent for her mother and was thus not personally liable. Decide. [*Memorial Hospital v. Baumann*, 474 N.Y.S.2d 636 (A.D.)]

5. Mills Electric Co. signed a contract with S&S Horticulture Architects, a two-person landscaping partnership operated by Sullivan and Smyth, to maintain the grounds and flowers at the Mills Electric Co. plant in Jacksonville, Florida. Mills checked references of S&S and found the company to be highly reputable. The contract set forth that S&S would select the flowers for each season and would determine when to maintain the lawns so long as they were properly maintained. The contract called for payments to be made to S&S on the first workday of each month, and the contract stipulated that "nothing herein shall make S&S an agent of the company." The contract also required that S&S personnel wear uniforms identifying them as employees of S&S. S&S had other accounts, but the large Mills Electric plant took up most of its time. While working on a terraced area near the visitors' entrance to the plant, Sullivan lost control of his large commercial mower, and the mower struck Gillespie, a plant visitor, causing her serious injury. A witness heard Sullivan apologizing to Gillespie and saying that "running that mower on the terrace is a two-person job." Gillespie brought suit against Mills Electric Co., contending Mills should be held vicariously liable. Decide.

6. Leo Bongers died intestate. Alfred Bongers and Delores Kuhl, Leo's nephew and niece, were appointed personal representatives of his estate. Leo left more than 120 antique cars, trucks, and motorcycles. The estate hired Bauer-Moravec to sell the vehicles at auction. Auctioneer Russ Moravec suggested that the vehicles be sold at an airstrip auction in May, June, or July. The estate rejected this recommendation and insisted that the sale be conducted in January on a farm owned by the estate. On January 30, the auction took place beginning at 9:30 A.M. with temperatures below freezing and some 800 people jammed into the bid barn. One auctioneer had purchased Putnam hitch balls to be used with mylar-type ropes so that small farm tractors could tow the vehicles into and out of the bid barn. One hour into the auction, Joseph Haag was seriously injured when a hitch ball came loose from the drawbar of the tractor towing an antique Studebaker truck. Haag sued the estate, claiming that Bauer-Moravec was acting as agent for the estate and that its negligence in not properly attaching the hitch ball and in using mylar-type tow rope rather than chains should be imputed to the estate under the doctrine of *respondeat superior*. The estate defended that it was not liable for the torts of the auctioneer and its employees because the auctioneer was an independent contractor. Decide. [*Haag v. Bongers*, 589 N.W.2d 318 (Neb.)]

7. On July 11, 1984, José Padilla was working as a vacation-relief route salesperson for Frito-Lay. He testified that he made a route stop at Sal's Beverage Shop, where he was told by Mrs. Ramos that she was dissatisfied with Frito-Lay service and no longer wanted its products in the store. He asked if there was anything he could do to change her mind. She said no and told him to pick up his merchandise. He took one company-owned merchandise rack to his van and was about to pick up another rack when Mr. Ramos said that the rack had been given to him by the regular route salesperson. Padilla said the route salesperson had no authority to give away Frito-Lay racks. A confrontation

occurred over the rack, and Padilla pushed Mr. Ramos against the cash register, injuring Ramos's back. Frito-Lay has a company policy, clearly communicated to all employees, that prohibits them from getting involved in any type of physical confrontation with a customer. Frito-Lay contended that Padilla was not acting within the course and scope of his employment when the pushing incident took place and that the company was therefore not liable to Ramos. Ramos contended that Frito-Lay was responsible for the acts of its employee Padilla. Decide. [*Frito-Lay, Inc. v. Ramos*, 770 S.W.2d 887 (Tex. App.)]

8. Jason Lasseigne, a Little League baseball player, was seriously injured at a practice session when he was struck on the head by a poorly thrown baseball from a team member, Todd Landry. The league was organized by American Legion Post 38. Claude Cassel and Billy Johnson were the volunteer coaches of the practice session. The Lasseignes brought suit on behalf of Jason against Post 38, claiming that the coaching was negligent and that Post 38 was vicariously liable for the harm caused by such negligence. Post 38 contended that it had no right to control the work of the volunteer coaches or the manner in which practices were conducted and as a result should not be held vicariously liable for the actions of the coaches. Decide. [*Lasseigne v. American Legion Post 38*, 543 So.2d 1111 (La. App.)]

9. Moritz, a guest at Pines Hotel, was sitting in the lobby when Brown, a hotel employee, dropped a heavy vacuum cleaner on her knee. When Moritz complained, the employee insulted her and hit her with his fist, knocking her unconscious. She sued the hotel for damages. Was the hotel liable? [*Moritz v. Pines Hotel, Inc.*, 383 N.Y. S.2d 704 (A.D.)]

10. Steve Diezel, an employee of Island City Flying Service in Key West, Florida, stole a General Electric Credit Corp. (GECC) aircraft and crashed the plane while attempting to take off. GECC brought suit against Island City on the theory that it had negligently hired Diezel as an employee and was therefore legally responsible for Diezel's act of theft. Diezel had a military prison record as a result of a drug offense and had been fired by Island City twice previously but had been immediately reinstated each time. Island City claimed that the evidence was insufficient to establish that it had been negligent in employing Diezel. Decide. [*Island City Flying Service v. General Electric*, 585 So.2d 274 (Fla.)]

11. The Bay State Harness Horse Racing and Breeding Association conducted horse races at a track where music for patrons was supplied by an independent contractor hired by the association. Some of the music played was subject to a copyright held by Famous Music Corp. The playing of that music was a violation of the copyright unless royalties were paid to Famous Music. No royalties were paid, and Famous Music sued the association, which raised the defense that the violation had been committed by an independent contractor specifically instructed not to play Famous Music's copyrighted material. Decide. [*Famous Music Corp. v. Bay State Harness Horse Racing and Breeding Association, Inc.*, 554 F.2d 1213 (1st Cir.)]

12. Steven Trujillo, told by the assistant door manager of Cowboys Bar "to show up to work tonight in case we need you as a doorman," came to the bar that evening wearing a jacket with the bar logo on it. Trujillo "attacked" Rocky Medina in the parking lot of the bar, causing him serious injury. Prior to working for Cowboys, Trujillo was involved in several fights at that bar and in its parking lot, and Cowboys knew of these matters. Medina sued Cowboys on two theories of liability: (1) *respondeat superior* and (2) negligent hiring of Trujillo. Cowboys's defense was that *respondeat superior* theory should be dismissed because the assault was clearly not within the course of Trujillo's employment. Concerning the negligent hiring theory, Cowboys asserted that Trujillo was not on duty that night as a doorman. Decide. [*Medina v. Graham's Cowboys, Inc.*, 827 P.2d 859 (N.M. App.)]

13. Neal Rubin, while driving his car in Chicago, inadvertently blocked the path of a Yellow Cab Co. taxi driven by Robert Ball, causing the taxi to swerve and hit Rubin's car. Angered by Rubin's driving, Ball got out of his cab and hit Rubin on the head and shoulders with a metal pipe. Rubin sued Yellow Cab Co. for the damages caused by this beating, contending that the employer was vicariously liable for the beating under the doctrine of *respondeat superior* because the beating occurred in furtherance of the employer's business, which was to obtain fares without delay. The company argued that Ball's beating of Rubin was not an act undertaken to further the employer's business. Is the employer liable under *respondeat superior*? [*Rubin v. Yellow Cab Co.*, 507 N.E.2d 114 (Ill. App.)]

14. Brazilian & Colombian Co. (B&C), a food broker, ordered 40 barrels of olives from Mawer-Gulden-Annis (MGA). MGA's shipping clerk was later told to make out the bill of lading to B&C's customer Pantry Queen; the olives were shipped directly to Pantry Queen. Eight days after delivery, the president of B&C wrote MGA to give it the name of its principal, Pantry Queen, and advised MGA to bill the principal directly. Pantry Queen was unable to pay for the olives, and MGA sued B&C for payment. B&C contended that it was well known to MGA that B&C was a food broker (agent) and the olives were shipped directly to the principal by MGA. It stated that as an agent, it was not a party to the contract and was thus not liable. Decide. [*Mawer-Gulden-Annis, Inc. v. Brazilian & Colombian Coffee Co.*, 199 N.E.2d 222 (Ill. App.)]

CPA QUESTIONS

1. Frey entered into a contract with Cara Corp. to purchase televisions on behalf of Lux, Inc. Lux authorized Frey to enter into the contract in Frey's name without disclosing that Frey was acting on behalf of Lux. If Cara repudiates the contract, which of the following statements concerning liability on the contract is *not* correct?

   a. Frey may not hold Cara liable and obtain money damages.

   b. Frey may hold Cara liable and obtain specific performance.

   c. Lux may hold Cara liable upon disclosing the agency relationship with Frey.

   d. Cara will be free from liability to Lux if Frey fraudulently stated that he was acting on his own behalf.

2. A principal will *not* be liable to a third party for a tort committed by an agent:

   a. Unless the principal instructed the agent to commit the tort

   b. Unless the tort was committed within the scope of the agency relationship

   c. If the agency agreement limits the principal's liability for the agent's tort

   d. If the tort is also regarded as a criminal act

3. Cox engaged Datz as her agent. It was mutually agreed that Datz would *not* disclose that he was acting as Cox's agent. Instead, he was to deal with prospective customers as if he were a principal acting on his own behalf. This he did and made several contracts for Cox. Assuming Cox, Datz, or the customer seeks to avoid liability on one of the contracts involved, which of the following statements is correct?

   a. Cox must ratify the Datz contracts in order to be held liable.

   b. Datz has *no* liability once he discloses that Cox was the real principal.

   c. The third party can avoid liability because he believed he was dealing with Datz as a principal.

   d. The third party may choose to hold either Datz or Cox liable.

4. Which of the following statements is (are) correct regarding the relationship between an agent and a nondisclosed principal?

   I. The principal is required to indemnify the agent for any contract entered into by the agent within the scope of the agency agreement.

II. The agent has the same actual authority as if the principal had been disclosed.

   a. I only

   b. II only

   c. Both I and II

   d. Neither I nor II

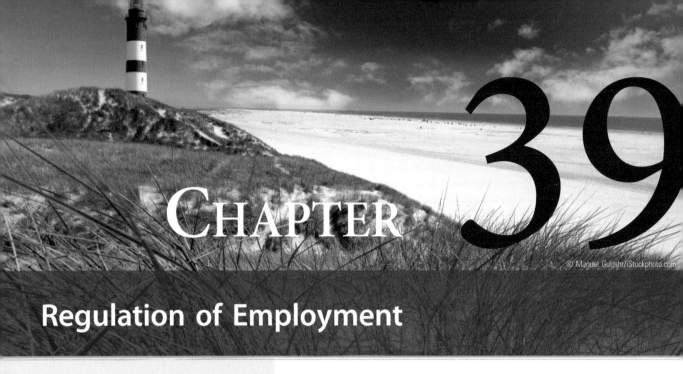

© Manuel Gutjahr/iStockphoto.com

CHAPTER 39

Regulation of Employment

learningoutcomes

After studying this chapter, you should be able to

LO.1 Explain the contractual nature of the employment relationship

LO.2 Explain how whistleblower protection under Sarbanes-Oxley is limited to conduct in violation of fraud or securities laws

LO.3 Explain how Dodd-Frank expands whistleblower protection to a wide range of financial services employees and provides incentives for whistleblowers

LO.4 Explain how the National Labor Relations Act prohibits employers from firing employees attempting to form a union, and requires employers to bargain with unions in good faith over wages, hours, and working conditions

LO.5 Explain how ERISA protects employee pensions and benefits

LO.6 Explain the essentials of unemployment benefits, family and medical leaves, military leaves, and social security benefits

LO.7 Explain how OSHA is designed to ensure workers safe and healthful working conditions

LO.8 Explain the three types of benefits provided by Workers' Compensation statutes

LO.9 Explain the sources of privacy rights, and applications to telephone, e-mail, text-messaging, and property searches

LO.10 Explain an employer's verification obligations when hiring new employees and discuss special hiring programs allowing aliens to work in the United States

E mployment law involves the law of contracts and the law established by lawmakers, courts, and administrative agencies.

A. THE EMPLOYMENT RELATIONSHIP

The relationship of an employer and an employee exists when, pursuant to an express or implied agreement of the parties, one person, the employee, undertakes to perform services or to do work under the direction and control of another, the employer, for compensation. In older cases, this relationship was called the *master-servant relationship.*

1. Characteristics of Relationship

An employee is hired to work under the control of the employer. An employee differs from an agent, who is to negotiate or make contracts with third persons on behalf of, and under the control of, a principal. However, a person may be both an employee and an agent for the other party. An employee also differs from an independent contractor, who is to perform a contract independent of, or free from, control by the other party.[1]

2. Creation of Employment Relationship

The relationship of employer and employee can be created only with the consent of both parties.

(A) INDIVIDUAL EMPLOYMENT CONTRACTS. As in contracts generally, both parties must assent to the terms of an employment contract. Subject to statutory restrictions, the parties are free to make a contract on any terms they wish.

(B) COLLECTIVE BARGAINING CONTRACTS. Collective bargaining contracts govern the rights and obligations of employers and employees in many private and public areas of employment. Under collective bargaining, representatives of the employees bargain with a single employer or a group of employers for an agreement on wages, hours, and working conditions. The agreement worked out by the representatives of the employees, usually union officials, is generally subject to a ratification vote by the employees. Terms usually found in collective bargaining contracts are (1) identification of the work belonging exclusively to designated classes of employees, (2) wage and benefits clauses, (3) promotion and layoff clauses, which are generally tied in part to seniority, (4) a management's rights clause, and (5) a grievance procedure. A grievance procedure provides a means by which persons claiming that the contract was violated or that they were disciplined or discharged without just cause may have their cases decided by impartial labor arbitrators.

3. Duration and Termination of Employment Contract

In many instances, the employment contract does not state any time or duration. In such a case, it may be terminated at any time by either party. In contrast, the employment

---

[1] *Ost v. West Suburban Travelers Limousine, Inc.,* 88 F.3d 435 (7th Cir. 1996).

contract may expressly state that it shall last for a specified period of time; an example would be an individual's contract to work as general manager for five years.

(A) Employment-at-Will Doctrine and Developing Exceptions. Ordinarily, a contract of employment may be terminated in the same manner as any other contract. If it is to run for a definite period of time, the employer cannot terminate the contract at an earlier date without justification. If the employment contract does not have a definite duration, it is terminable at will. Under the **employment-at-will doctrine** the employer has historically been allowed to terminate the employment contract at any time for any reason or for no reason.[2] Gradually, federal and state statutes were enacted to provide certain individual rights to workers, protecting them from workplace exploitation and discrimination by employers. And, in most states, courts have carved out narrow exceptions to the employment-at-will doctrine when the discharge violates an established public policy.[3] **For Example,** home health care nurse Eugene Patterson continued to provide wound care to a patient after he was directed to cease the care by his employer, and he was discharged for insubordination. Patterson did so because the physician's order for the care remained in place, and he believed that state law governing the practice of nursing required him to complete the physician directed care. The court held Patterson could sue his employer Gentiva Health Services for wrongful termination in violation of public policy. Absent statutory protection, or a court-created contract or tort exception, the employment-at-will doctrine is still the basic default rule governing employment in the United States.

Public policy exceptions are often made to the employment-at-will doctrine when an employee is discharged in retaliation for insisting that the employer comply with the state's food and drug act or for filing a workers' compensation claim.[4] In some states, so-called whistleblower laws have been enacted to protect employees who disclose employer practices that endanger public health or safety. Also, a statutory right exists for at-will employees who are terminated in retaliation for cooperating with a federal criminal prosecution or are terminated in violation of the public policy to provide truthful testimony.[5]

employment-at-will doctrine – doctrine in which the employer has historically been allowed to terminate the employment contract at any time for any reason or for no reason.

CASE SUMMARY

Pretext at the Pizzeria

FACTS: While working his nighttime cooking shift at Pizzeria Uno, Gerald Adams noticed that the restaurant's kitchen floor was saturated with a foul-smelling liquid coming from the drains. Adams left work, complaining of illness, and contacted the Department of Health about the drainage problem in the restaurant's kitchen. Upon returning to the restaurant a few days later, Adams was ordered into his manager's office. He was accused of stealing a softball shirt and taking home a work schedule. A shouting match ensued, and Adams was later arraigned on a criminal charge of disorderly conduct. The charges were eventually dropped and have since been expunged from his record. Adams contends that he was unlawfully terminated in violation of the state's whistleblower

---

[2] *Payne v. Western & Atlantic Railroad Co.*, 82 Tenn. 507, 518–519 (1884).
[3] *Patterson v. Gentiva Health Services, Inc.*, 2011 WL 3235466 (D. S.C. July 25, 2011).
[4] *Brigham v. Dillon Companies, Inc.*, 935 P.2d 1054 (Kan. 1997).
[5] *Fitzgerald v. Salsbury Chemical, Inc.*, 613 N.W.2d 275 (Iowa 2000). In *Garcetti v. Ceballos*, 547 U.S. 410 (2006), the U.S. Supreme Court held that when public employees make statements pursuant to their official duties, the First Amendment of the Constitution does not insulate their communications from employer discipline because the employees are not speaking as citizens for First Amendment purposes. In his dissent, Justice Souter argued that a public employee should have constitutional protection when the employee acts as a whistleblower.

CASE SUMMARY

Continued

act because he notified the Board of Health regarding the unsanitary kitchen conditions. Uno contends he was fired for threatening the supervisor, which is an untenable act.

DECISION: Judgment for Adams in the amount of $7,500. The confrontation between Adams and his employer was calculated by the employer to provoke a reaction from Adams that would serve as an excuse to fire him, a pretext for the real reason—Adam's phone call to the Board of Health. The wrongful termination and criminal charges that ensued from the verbal altercation were sufficient to establish damages for emotional distress. Adams's loss of security clearance in the National Guard, which prevented him from participating in an overseas mission in Germany, also supported the jury's finding of compensable emotional distress. [*Adams v. Uno Restaurants, Inc.*, 794 A.2d 489 (R.I. 2002)]

The contract of employment may be construed to bar a discharge of the employee except for cause. If so construed, good cause would then be required for the discharge of an at-will employee. Written personnel policies used as guidelines for supervisors have also been interpreted as being part of the employment contract. These policies have thus been held to restrict the employer's right to discharge at-will employees without proof of good or just cause. Moreover, employee handbooks that provide for "proper notice and investigation" before termination may bar employers from terminating employees without providing such notice and an investigation.[6]

Other courts still follow the common law at-will rule because they believe that a court should not rewrite the contract of the parties to provide employee protection that was never intended.[7]

(B) EMPLOYER REACTIONS. Employers have revised their personnel manuals and employee handbooks and have issued directives to all employees that no assurance of continued employment exists—that the employers are not obligated to have good cause to terminate employees, just as employees are free to leave their positions with the employers. While simultaneously reserving their at-will termination powers, many employers also may design specific, apparently fair termination procedures and promulgate antiharassment policies and procedures, as seen in the *Semple v. FedEx* decision.

CASE SUMMARY

It's Not Easy to Get Around the Employment-at-Will Doctrine, Mr. Semple

FACTS: John Semple was terminated from his employment with FedEx for falsification of company documents. He appealed his termination through internal FedEx procedures without success and thereafter sued the employer in federal court, contending that his termination was in

---

[6] *Carlson v. Lake Chelan Community Hospital*, 66 P.3d 1080 (Wash. App. 2003); but see *Trabing v. Kinko's, Inc.*, 57 P.3d 1248 (Wyo. 2002); *Williams v. First Tennessee National Corp.*, 97 S.W.3d 798 (Tex. App. 2003).
[7] See *Texas Farm Bureau Mutual Insurance Co. v. Sears*, 84 S.W.3d 604 (Tex. 2002).

CASE SUMMARY

Continued

violation of the "public policy exception" to the employment-at-will doctrine in that his termination resulted from his filing internal grievances regarding harassment by his superiors and that he was protected by the employee handbook exception to the at-will doctrine. The employer disagreed.

DECISION: Judgment for FedEx. When he was hired, John Semple signed an employment contract that included the following statement:

> I also agree that my employment and compensation can be terminated with or without cause and without notice or liability whatsoever, at any time, at the option of either the company or myself.

The employee handbook stated in part:

> The employment relationship between the Company and employee may be terminated at the will of either party as stated in the employment agreement signed upon application for employment. As described in that agreement, the policies and procedures set forth in this manual provide guidelines for management and employees during employment, but do not create contractual rights regarding termination otherwise.

Semple was an employee at-will. No public policy prevented FedEx from terminating Semple's employment. Moreover, FedEx had not surrendered its statutory right to terminate at-will employees based on its employee handbook. [*Semple v. Federal Express Corp.,* **2008 WL 1793481 (D. S.D. April 17, 2008); affirmed 566 F.3d 788 (8th Cir. 2009)**]

Most employers have no interest in terminating employees without good and sufficient cause. They have taken steps to ensure that terminations are in fact for good cause and that a solid case exists for each termination should the employee in question sue on an unjust dismissal theory. Employers have standardized their termination methods. Employers often require that every disciplined employee be advised in writing of the infraction, informed of the expected corrective action, and informed of the fact that further misconduct could lead to additional discipline up to and including discharge. When a termination appears to be warranted, most employers require that at least two supervisors be involved and that they take care to ensure that the reasons for the termination are accurate and consistent with the documentation concerning the employee's deficiencies. Moreover, employers should inform the employee of the basis of the proposed termination and give the employee an opportunity to be heard before the dismissal notice is issued.

(c) JUSTIFIABLE DISCHARGE. An employer may be justified in discharging an employee because of the employee's (1) nonperformance of duties, (2) misrepresentation or fraud in obtaining the employment, (3) disobedience of proper directions, (4) disloyalty, (5) theft or other dishonesty, (6) possession or use of drugs or intoxicants, (7) misconduct, or (8) incompetence.

Employers generally have the right to lay off employees because of economic conditions, including a lack of work. Such actions are sometimes referred to as *reductions in force (RIFs).*

Employers, however, must be very careful not to make layoffs based on age, for that is a violation of the Age Discrimination in Employment Act.

In some states, a "service letter" statute requires an employer on request to furnish to a discharged employee a letter stating the reason for the discharge.

4. Whistle Blower Protection under the Sarbanes-Oxley and Dodd-Frank Acts

The Sarbanes-Oxley Act (SOX) of 2002 was enacted to restore investor confidence in financial markets following the exposure in 2001–2002 of widespread misconduct by directors and officers of publicly held companies. SOX contains reforms regarding corporate accountability, enhanced disclosure requirements, and enforcement and liability provisions. Title VIII of the Act contains protections for corporate whistleblowers.[8]

(A) PROTECTION PROVIDED. SOX prohibits a publicly traded company or any agent of it from taking an adverse employment action against an employee who provides information, testifies, or "otherwise assists" in proceedings regarding (1) mail, wire, bank, or securities fraud, (2) any violation of an SEC rule or regulation, or (3) any federal law protecting shareholders against fraud. The Act sets forth the types of adverse employment actions that qualify for protection, specifically protecting employees from discharge, demotion, suspension, threats, harassment, failure to hire or rehire, blacklisting, or action otherwise discriminatory against employees in their terms and conditions of employment.

The Act protects employees who provide information or assistance to supervisors, or a federal regulatory or law enforcement agency, or to members of Congress or a congressional committee. The Act does not protect employees who provide information to the world, however. **For Example,** Nicholas Tides and Matthew Neumann were not protected under SOX when they provided a newspaper reporter information and documents about the questionable integrity of Boeing's data storage system and were fired for violating company confidentiality rules.[9]

Case law cautions that SOX whistleblower protection provisions do not provide "whistleblower protection for all employee complaints about how a public company spends it money and pays its bills."[10]

(B) PROCEDURES. An individual who believes that she or he has been subject to an adverse employment action because of whistleblowing activities must file a complaint with the Department of Labor's Occupational Safety and Health Administration (OSHA) within 90 days after the asserted adverse employment action. OSHA administers 13 other federal whistleblower laws and has experienced investigators to facilitate its responsibilities under the SOX.

(C) THE DODD-FRANK EXPANSION. The Dodd-Frank Wall Street Reform and Consumer Protection Act of 2010 (Dodd-Frank)[11] expands whistleblower protections to a

---

[8] 18 U.S.C. §1514A (2005).
[9] *Tides v. Boeing Co.*, 644 F.3d 809 (9th Cir. 2011).
[10] *Platone v. Flyi, Inc.*, 2006 WL 3246910 (Dept. of Labor Sept. 29, 2006). See also *Welch v. Choa*, 536 F.3d 269 (4th Cir. 2008), in which CFO Welch had refused to certify an SEC quarterly report as required by SOX because of accounting irregularities and thus was fired. The court of appeals held that the conduct in question was not shown to be in violation of any fraud or securities laws listed in SOX; thus, Welch was not protected. However, in *Sylvester v. Parexel International LLC*, 2011 WL 2165854 (DOL Adm. Rev. Bd. May 25, 2011) the DOL's Administrative Review Board subsequently held that its prior ruling in *Platone v. Flyi, Inc.*—that an employee's complaint must "definitely and specifically" relate to the categories of fraud or securities violations listed in Section 806—"has evolved into an inappropriate test and is often applied too strictly."
[11] The whistleblower protection provisions are codified at 15 U.S.C. §78u-6.

wide range of financial services employees and provides expanded protections and incentives for whistleblowers.

Dodd-Frank covers almost any employee working in the financial services industry related to the extension of credit, including employees of privately held companies, and protects them from retaliation for disclosing information about fraud or unlawful conduct related to consumer financial products. It covers employees who extend credit, service loans, provide real estate settlement services, and provide financial advice, including credit counseling to consumers.

Dodd-Frank requires the Securities and Exchange Commission to pay whistleblowers bounties of between 10 and 30 percent on monetary sanctions that aggregate to at least $1 million. To recover an award, a whistleblower must provide the SEC (1) voluntarily (2) with original information (3) that leads to a successful enforcement action or actions in federal court or before an agency (4) in which overall recovery totals over $1,000,000.[12]

Dodd-Frank expands on the SOX cause of action as follows:

1. Dodd-Frank expands the SOX statute of limitations from 90 to 180 days. The Dodd-Frank limitations period is six years.

2. Whistleblowers must exhaust administrative remedies under SOX at OSHA and DOL's Administrative Review Board before court review. Dodd-Frank allows an immediate lawsuit in federal district court.

3. SOX provides for actual back pay lost, as part of make whole relief, while Dodd-Frank allows recovery of double back pay as liquidated damages.

Dodd-Frank exempts whistleblower claims from predispute arbitration agreements. And it provides a burden-shifting framework for a private cause of action for employees who are retaliated against for protected activity so that once an employee has shown by a preponderance of the evidence that the protected activity was a contributing factor in an adverse employment action, the employer must show by clear and convincing evidence that it would have taken the same action in the absence of the employee's whistleblowing activities to avoid liability.

5. Duties of the Employee

The duties of an employee are determined primarily by the contract of employment with the employer. The law also implies certain obligations.

(A) SERVICES. Employees are under the duty to perform such services as may be required by the contract of employment.

(B) TRADE SECRETS. An employee may be given confidential trade secrets by the employer but must not disclose this knowledge to others. An agreement by the employee to refrain from disclosing trade secrets is binding. If the employee violates

---

[12] 17 C.F.R. §240.21F-1, *et seq.* To start an action a whistleblower must file a complaint with the SEC's Office of the Whistleblower, which includes a description of the misconduct, demonstrates eligibility, and declares under penalty of perjury that the information is true and accurate. Whistleblowers may submit a claim anonymously through an attorney.

this obligation, the employer may enjoin the use of the information by the employee and by any person to whom it has been disclosed by the employee.

Former employees who are competing with their former employer may be enjoined from using information about suppliers and customers that they obtained while employees when this information is of vital importance to the employer's business. Injunctive relief is denied, however, if the information is not important or not secret.

(c) INVENTIONS. Employment contracts commonly provide that an employer will own any invention or discovery made by an employee, whether during work hours, after work hours, or for a period of one or two years after leaving the employment. In the absence of an express or implied agreement to the contrary, the inventions of an employee usually belong to the employee. This is true even though the employee used the time and property of the employer in the discovery. In this case, however, the employer has what is known as a **shop right** to use the invention without cost in its operations.

> **shop right** – right of an employer to use in business without charge an invention discovered by an employee during working hours and with the employer's material and equipment.

6. Rights of the Employee

The rights of an employee are determined by the contract of employment and by the law as declared by courts, lawmakers, and administrative agencies.

(A) COMPENSATION. The rights of an employee with respect to compensation are governed in general by the same principles that apply to the compensation of an agent. In the absence of an agreement to the contrary, when an employee is discharged, whether for cause or not, the employer must pay wages to the expiration of the last pay period. State statutes commonly authorize employees to sue employers for wages improperly withheld and to recover penalties and attorney fees. In addition to hourly wages, payments due for vacations and certain bonuses are considered "wages" under state statutes.[13] **For Example,** Diane Beard worked for Summit Institute as a licensed practical nurse for 13 months when she walked off the job and terminated her employment. She requested her accrued vacation pay of $432, but Summit refused to pay her, claiming she had abandoned her job and thus forfeited her right to vacation pay under company policy. Accrued vacation qualifies as "wages," and she was entitled to the $432 vacation pay plus a penalty equal to 90 days' wages at the employee's rate of pay or $9,720, plus $2,400 in attorneys' fees for the trial and an additional $2,600 in attorneys' fees for the appeal. These statutes with their penalty provisions are designed as a coercive means to compel employers to promptly pay their employees.[14]

(B) FEDERAL WAGE AND HOUR LAW. Workers at enterprises engaged in interstate commerce are covered by the Fair Labor Standards Act (FLSA),[15] popularly known as the Wage and Hour Act. These workers cannot be paid less than a specified minimum wage.

---

[13] *Knutson v. Snyder Industries, Inc.*, 436 N.W.2d 496 (Neb. 1989).
[14] *Beard v. Summit Institute of Pulmonary Medicine and Rehabilitation, Inc.*, 707 So.2d 1233 (La. 1998); see also *Beckman v. Kansas Dep't. of Human Resources*, 43 P.3d 891 (Kan. App. 2002).
[15] P.L. 75-718, 52 Stat. 1060, 29 U.S.C. §201 *et seq.*

CASE SUMMARY

What Is a "Willful" Violation?

FACTS: An action against an employer for violating the Fair Labor Standards Act must be brought within two years unless the violation was willful, in which case it may be brought within three years. McLaughlin, the secretary of labor, brought suit against Richland Shoe Company for failing to pay the minimum wage. Richland claimed that the suit was barred because more than two years had elapsed. McLaughlin claimed that the violation was willful, in which case the action was properly brought because three years had not expired. The parties disagreed as to what proof was required to establish that the violation was "willful."

DECISION: To be "willful" within the statute, the violation must be intentional or made with reckless indifference to whether the statute has been satisfied. Because the case had not been tried on the basis of this standard, the case was remanded to the lower court to determine the matter in the light of the new definition of *willful*. [*McLaughlin v. Richland Shoe Co.*, 486 U.S. 128 (1998)]

The FLSA has been amended to cover domestic service workers, including housekeepers, cooks, and nannies. Executive, administrative, and professional employees and outside salespersons are exempt from both the minimum wage and overtime provisions of the law.[16] Students "working" at internships *may* be covered by the FLSA.[17]

(1) Subminimum Wage Provisions.

The FLSA allows for the employment of full-time students at institutions of higher education at wage rates below the statutory minimum. Also, individuals whose productive capacity is impaired by age, physical or mental deficiency, or injury may be employed at less than the minimum wage to prevent the curtailment of work opportunities for these individuals. In these cases, however, a special certificate is needed by the employer from the Department of Labor's (DOL) Wage and Hour Division, which has offices throughout the United States.

(2) Wage Issues.

Deductions made from wages as a result of cash or merchandise shortages and deductions for tools of the trade are not legal if they reduce wages below the minimum wage. An employer's requirement that employees provide uniforms or tools of their own is a violation of the law to the extent that the expenses for these items reduce wages below the minimum wage.[18]

---

[16] In *Christopher v. SmithKline Beecham Corp.*, 132 S. Ct. 2156 (2012), the U.S. Supreme Court determined that pharmaceutical representatives, whose primary duty is to obtain nonbinding commitments from physicians to prescribe their drugs, are "outside salesmen" excluded from overtime pay requirements of the FLSA.

[17] A developing issue in our society is the utilization of unpaid interns—generally high school or college students—and their coverage, if any, under the FLSA and other employment laws. The FLSA does not define the terms *intern* or *trainee*. The Act broadly defines the word "employee" as "to suffer or permit to work." The DOL utilizes a six-factor test for determining whether an individual is a trainee (intern) or an employee under the FLSA. In *Solis v. Laurelbrook Sanitarium and School, Inc.*, 642 F.3d 518 (6th Cir. 2011), the U.S. Court of Appeals for the Sixth Circuit determined that the DOL's test was overly rigid, and applied a "primary benefit of the relationship test" deciding that the primary benefit in that case ran to the students. Unpaid interns not considered employees are not entitled to the protections of the FLSA and Title VII of the Civil Rights Act of 1964. Practically speaking, it is up to the high schools and colleges to make sure that the internships they arrange are for the primary benefit of their students, and not substitutes for regular, paid employees.

[18] See Gayle Cinqugrani, "Uniform Deductions, Low Commissions Lead to DOL Penalties for FLSA Violations," *107 D.L.R. A-10* (June 6, 2012), where an investigation by the Wage and Hour Division of the DOL between November 2008 and November 2010 found that Vizza Wash LP, doing business as Wash-Tub, made illegal deductions from employees' paychecks for items such as uniforms, insurance claims, and cash register shortages, which caused the employees' pay to fall below the federal minimum wage of $7.25 per hour.

Job-related training generally is compensable under the FLSA. However, an exception exists for voluntary training not directly related to an employee's job when the employee does not perform productive work. **For Example,** Hogar, Inc., operates a nursing home and required new employees to undergo two days of unpaid training before assuming paid duties as nurses' aides, maintenance/laundry workers, and kitchen workers. Little or no instruction was offered to these "trainees," and each individual would perform the regular duties of the position for the two-day period. Hogar's practices did not fall within the training exception because the trainees performed productive work with little or no actual training during a regular shift. In a lawsuit brought by the Secretary of Labor, Hogar was ordered by the court to pay 14 hours' pay (two days' pay) for each employee so "trained," plus liquidated damages of an additional 14 hours pay. [19]

A large Pennsylvania landscape contractor whose cash wages appeared to comply with all applicable laws was found to be in violation of the FLSA because his Guatemalan and Mexican seasonal workers were required to pay employment-related costs, such as point-of-hire transportation costs, visa costs, and recruiter's fees, which reduced their real wages to below the minimum wage. [20]

(3) Overtime Pay.

Overtime must be paid at a rate of one and a half times the employee's regular rate of pay for each hour worked in excess of 40 hours in a workweek. [21]

(4) Child Labor Provisions.

The FLSA child labor provisions are designed to protect educational opportunities for minors and prohibit their employment in occupations detrimental to their health and well-being. The FLSA restricts hours of work for minors under 16 and lists hazardous occupations too dangerous for minors to perform.

B. LABOR RELATIONS LAWS

Even if employers are not presently unionized, they are subject to certain obligations under federal labor relations law. It is important to both unionized and nonunionized employers to know their rights and obligations under the National Labor Relations Act (NLRA). [22] Employee rights and obligations are also set forth in this act. The Labor-Management Reporting and Disclosure Act regulates internal union affairs. [23]

7. The National Labor Relations Act

The National Labor Relations Act (NLRA), passed in 1935, was based on the federal government's power to regulate interstate commerce granted in Article 1, Section 8, of the Constitution. Congress, in enacting this law, explained that its purpose was to remove obstructions to commerce caused by employers who

---

[19] *Herman v. Hogar Praderas De Amor, Inc.,* 130 F. Supp. 2d 257 (S.D. P.R. 2001).

[20] *Rivera v. Brickman Group, Ltd.,* 2008 WL 81570 (E.D. Pa. Jan. 7, 2008).

[21] DOL regulations, referred to as the *white collar exemptions* from the overtime requirements of the FLSA, took effect on August 23, 2004. Generally, executive, administrative, professional, outside sales, computer professional, and certain "highly compensated employees" are exempt from the overtime requirements if they meet the "tests" set forth in the new regulations.

[22] 29 U.S.C. §§141–169. Note that in the *Lechmere* and *Transportation Management* cases presented in this section, the employers were not unionized.

[23] 29 U.S.C. §§401–531.

denied their employees the right to join unions and refused to accept collective bargaining.[24] Congress stated that these obstructions resulted in depression of wages, poor working conditions, and diminution of purchasing power.

Section 7 of the amended NLRA is the heart of the act, stating in part that "[e]mployees shall have the right to self-organization … to bargain collectively through representatives of their own choosing and to engage in other concerted activities for the purpose of collective bargaining or other mutual aid or protection … and shall have the right to refrain from such activities…."

Section 8 of the NLRA contains employer and union unfair labor practices, set forth in Figure 39-1, and authorizes the National Labor Relations Board to conduct proceedings to stop such practices.

The act applies to private-sector employers with gross incomes of $500,000 or more. The Railway Labor Act applies to employees of railroad and air carriers.

8. National Labor Relations Board

Administration of the NLRA is entrusted to the five-member National Labor Relations Board (NLRB, or Board) and the general counsel of the Board. The general counsel is responsible for investigating and prosecuting all unfair labor practice cases. The five-member Board's major function is to decide unfair labor practice cases brought before it by the general counsel.

The Board is also responsible for conducting representation and decertification elections. This responsibility is delegated to the regional directors of the 32 regional offices located throughout the United States who (1) determine the appropriateness of each proposed bargaining unit for the purpose of collective bargaining, (2) investigate petitions for the certification or decertification of unions, and (3) conduct elections to determine the choice of the majority of those employees voting in the election. Should a majority of the employees voting select a union, the NLRB will certify that union as the exclusive representative of all employees within the unit for the purpose of bargaining with the employer to obtain a contract with respect to wages, hours, and other conditions of employment.

9. Election Conduct

The Board of the NLRB has promulgated preelection rules restricting electioneering activities so that the election will express the true desire of employees. The NLRA prohibits employer interference or coercion during the preelection period. The act also prohibits during this period employer statements that contain threats of reprisal or promises of benefits. **For Example,** it is a violation of section 8(c) of the NLRA for a Southern California manufacturer to make implied threats to relocate its plant to Mexico if the employees choose union representation. Furthermore, when the company announced its intent to move to Mexico one day after the union won a representation election, the Labor Board obtained an injunction against the move.[25]

The Board prohibits all electioneering activities at polling places and has formulated a "24-hour rule," which prohibits both unions and employers from making speeches to captive audiences within 24 hours of an election. The rationale is to preserve free elections and prevent any party from obtaining undue advantage.

---

[24] N.L.R.A. §1; 29 U.S.C. §141.
[25] See *Quadrtech Corp.*, N.L.R.B., No. 21–CA–33997 (settlement Dec. 11, 2000).

FIGURE 39-1 | *Employer and Union Unfair Labor Practices Charge*

UNFAIR LABOR PRACTICES CHARGES AGAINST EMPLOYERS	SECTION OF THE NLRA*
1. Restrain or coerce employees in the exercise of their rights under section 7; threat of reprisals or promise of benefits	8(a)(1); 8(c)
2. Dominate or interfere with the formation or administration of a labor organization or contribute financial or other support to it	8(a)(2)
3. Discriminate in regard to hire or tenure of employment or any term or condition of employment in order to encourage or discourage membership in any labor organization	8(a)(3)
4. Discharge or otherwise discriminate against employees because they have given testimony under the act	8(a)(4)
5. Refuse to bargain collectively with representatives of its employees	8(a)(5)

UNFAIR LABOR PRACTICES CHARGES AGAINST UNIONS	SECTION OF THE NLRA
1. Restrain or coerce employees in the exercise of their rights under section 7	8(b)(1)(A)
2. Restrain or coerce an employer in the selection of its representatives	8(b)(1)(B)
3. Cause or attempt to cause an employer to discriminate against an employee	8(b)(2)
4. Refuse to bargain collectively with the employer	8(b)(3)
5. Require employees to pay excessive fees for membership	8(b)(5)
6. Engage in "featherbed practices" of seeking pay for services not performed	8(b)(6)
7. Use secondary boycotts (banned, except for publicity proviso)	8(b)(4)
8. Allow recognitional and organizational picketing by an uncertified union	8(b)(7)
9. Enter into "hot cargo" agreements, except for construction and garment industries	8(e)

* 29 U.S.C. §151.

10. Union Activity on Private Property

Although section 7 of the NLRA gives employees the statutory right to self-organization, employers have the undisputed right to make rules to maintain discipline in their establishments. Generally speaking, employers may prohibit union solicitation by employees during work periods. During nonworking time, employers may prohibit activity and communications only for legitimate efficiency and safety reasons and only if the prohibitions are not manifestly intended to impede employees' exercise of their rights under the law. Nonunion employers, moreover, may not refuse to interview or retain union members because of their union membership. And even if a union pays an individual working for a nonunion employer to help organize the company, that individual is still protected under the NLRA.[26]

An employer may validly post its property against all nonemployee solicitations, including distribution of union literature, if reasonable efforts by the union through other available channels of communication would enable it to reach the employees with its message.

CASE SUMMARY

The Supreme Court Is Always Right

FACTS: Lechmere, Inc., owned and operated a retail store located in a shopping plaza in Newington, a suburb of Hartford, Connecticut. Lechmere was also part owner of the plaza's parking lot, which was separated from a public highway by a 46-foot-wide grassy strip. Almost all of the strip was public property. In a campaign to organize Lechmere employees, nonemployee union organizers from Local 919 of the United Food and Commercial Workers placed handbills on the windshields of cars parked in the employees' part of the parking lot. After Lechmere denied the organizers access to the lot, they picketed from the grassy strip. In addition, they were able to contact directly some 20 percent of the employees. The union filed an unfair labor practice charge with the Board, alleging that Lechmere had violated the NLRA by barring the organizers from its property. An administrative law judge ruled in the union's favor. The Board affirmed, and the Court of Appeals enforced the Board's order. The matter was heard by the Supreme Court.

DECISION: Judgment for Lechmere. A two-stage test is used in evaluating the accommodation between the employees' right to learn of the advantages of unionization from outside union organizers and an employer's property rights. Stage 1 considers whether the outsiders have reasonable access to employees off the employer's property. Stage 2 applies if the access is infeasible. In such a case, the employer's property rights must yield to the extent needed to communicate information on organizational rights. The Court majority determined that the outsiders had reasonable access from the grassy strip. The dissent believed that holding up signs from the grassy strip was not sufficient to learn of advantages of unionization. [*Lechmere, Inc. v. NLRB*, 502 U.S. 527 (1992)]

10a. Social Media and Section 7: Protected Activity for Union and Nonunion Workers

Section 7 of the NLRA grants all employees—union and nonunion—the right to engage in protected concerted activities pertaining to self-organization, forming,

[26] *N.L.R.B. v. Town & Country Electric, Inc.*, 516 U.S. 85 (1995).

joining, or assisting a union or "for other mutual aid or protection."[27] Under Section 7, employees have a right to discuss their terms and conditions of employment with coworkers. Some employers' Internet and social media policies may be overly broad in that they may tend to chill employees' exercise of their Section 7 rights. **For Example,** American Medical Response of Connecticut (AMR), an ambulance service, terminated an employee in part for posting unfavorable remarks about her supervisor on Facebook page. The employee, Ms. Souza, had mocked her supervisor on Facebook; when she received supportive comments from some coworkers, she posted additional remarks about the supervisor and was terminated. AMR's company handbook contained several policy provisions about blogging and Internet postings, including prohibiting employees from making "disparaging, discriminatory or defamatory comments when discussing the company or the employee's supervisors, co-workers and/or competitors." The acting Regional Director issued an unfair labor practice complaint against AMR, asserting that AMR enforced an overly broad policy on blogging and Internet posting. The matter settled before the scheduled hearing before the ALJ. Other Facebook firing cases are in the settlement, complaint, or ALJ stages of Board procedures.[28]

Though employees retain the right to talk about working conditions on social media, including discussing treatment by a supervisor in blunt language, case law will develop that not only protects Section 7 rights, but also protects employer rights to make rules to maintain discipline in the workplace and to protect the employer's reputation when a Facebook conversation on a page set to allow access to "friends of friends" involves very offensive, insulting, and disrespectful comments about supervisors or managers. The latter situation is not like a conversation between employees at a water cooler, where there is an expectation of privacy, but is more like calling the boss names on the plant floor in front of multiple employees and the public, as there is no expectation of privacy. This conduct does not involve protected concerted activity. Although discussion of grievances in the context of "mutual aid or protection" is protected under Section 7, an individual's personal griping is not.

11. Firing Employees for Union Activity

Although employers and supervisors often feel betrayed by individual employees who take leadership roles in forming organizations, the NLRA prohibits discrimination against such employees because of their union activity.

The NLRB has found evidence of discrimination against active union supporters when the employer

1. Discharges on the strength of past misdeeds that were condoned;

2. Neglects to give customary warnings prior to discharge;

---

[27] On June 18, 2012, the NLRB announced that it has launched a Web page describing the rights of employees to engage in concerted activity, even if they do not belong to a union. It is available at **http://www.nlrb.gov/concerted-activity.**

[28] *See* the ALJ's ruling in *Hispanics United of Buffalo*, 2011 WL 3894520 (N.L.R.B. Div. of Judges Sept. 2, 2011), where the ALJ followed the Board's *Parexel International LLC* "concerted activity" precedent, 356 N.L.R.B. No. 82 (Jan. 28, 2011), finding that the nonunion nonprofit organization unlawfully terminated five employees who had posted comments on Facebook, some of which were profane and sarcastic, in response to a complaint by a coworker, Cruz-Moore, about their job performance. The ALJ stated in part:

> ... The discriminates herein were taking a first step towards taking group action to defend themselves against the accusations they could reasonably believe Cruz-Moore was going to make to management. By discharging the discriminates on October 12, Respondent prevented them from taking any further group action vis-à-vis Cruz-Moore's criticisms. Moreover, the fact that Respondent lumped the discriminates together in terminating them, established that Respondent viewed the five as a group and that their activity was concerted ....

3. Discharges for a rule generally unenforced;

4. Applies disproportionately severe punishment to union supporters; or

5. Effects layoffs in violation of seniority status with disproportionate impact on union supporters.

The NLRA preserves the right of the employer to maintain control over the workforce in the interest of discipline, efficiency, and pleasant and safe customer relations. Employees, on the other hand, have the right to be free from coercive discrimination resulting from union activity.

At times these two rights may collide. For example, an employee may be discharged for apparently two reasons: (1) violation of a valid company rule and (2) union activity. The employer gives the former as the reason for termination; the latter remains unstated on the employer's part, causing the filing of a section 8(a)(3) unfair labor practice charge against the employer. These are known as *dual motive cases.* The general counsel must present on behalf of the dismissed employee a prima facie case that such protected conduct as union activity was a motivating factor in the dismissal. After this showing, the burden shifts to the employer, who must prove that the employee would have been dismissed for legitimate business reasons even absent the protected conduct.

CASE SUMMARY

The Sam Santillo Story

FACTS: Prior to his discharge, Sam Santillo was a bus driver for Transportation Management Corporation. On March 19, Santillo talked to officials of the Teamsters Union about organizing the drivers who worked with him. Over the next four days, Santillo discussed with his fellow drivers the possibility of joining the Teamsters and distributed authorization cards. On the night of March 23, George Patterson, who supervised Santillo and the other drivers, told one of the drivers that he had heard of Santillo's activities. Patterson referred to Santillo as two-faced and promised to get even with him. Later that evening, Patterson talked to Ed West, who was also a bus driver. Patterson asked, "What's with Sam and the Union?" Patterson said that he took Santillo's actions personally, recounted several favors he had done for Santillo, and added that he would remember Santillo's activities when Santillo again asked for a favor. On Monday, March 26, Santillo was discharged. Patterson told Santillo that he was being fired for leaving his keys in the bus and taking unauthorized breaks. Santillo filed charges with the Board, and the general counsel issued a complaint, contending that Santillo was discharged because of his union activities in distributing authorization cards to fellow employees. The evidence revealed that the practice of leaving keys in buses was commonplace among company employees and the company tolerated the practice of taking coffee breaks. The company had never taken disciplinary action against an employee for the behavior in question.

DECISION: Judgment for Santillo and the NLRB. The general counsel established a prima facie case by showing that Santillo was involved in union-organizing activities just prior to his discharge. The employer did not meet its burden of proving that Santillo was fired for a legitimate business reason. The infractions involved were commonplace, and no discipline had ever been issued to any employee previously. The reasons given by the company were pretextual. Santillo would not have been fired had the employer not considered his effort to establish a union. [*NLRB v. Transportation Management Corp.,* 462 U.S. 393 (1983)]

12. Duty of Employer to Bargain Collectively

Once a union wins a representative election, the Board certifies the union as the exclusive bargaining representative of the employees. The employer then has the obligation under the NLRA to bargain with the union in good faith over wages, hours, and working conditions. These matters are *mandatory subjects of bargaining* and include seniority provisions, promotions, layoff and recall provisions, no-strike no-lockout clauses, and grievance procedures. Employers also have an obligation to bargain about the "effects" of the shutdown of a part of a business[29] and may have an obligation to bargain over the decision to relocate bargaining unit work to other plants.[30] Absent clearly expressed consent by a union, an employer violates its duty to bargain by changing a term or condition of employment without first bargaining to impasse with a union. **For Example,** Aramark Educational Services violated the NLRA when it unilaterally implemented a new, strict "Social Security no-match" policy of suspending employees with uncorrected discrepancies in their social security numbers prior to any discussion and impasse in bargaining with UNITE HERE Local 26.[31]

Permissive subjects of bargaining are those over which an employer's refusal to bargain is not a section 8(a)(5) unfair labor practice. Examples are the required use of union labels, internal union affairs, union recognition clauses, and benefits for already retired workers.

CASE SUMMARY

To Bargain or Not To Bargain?

FACTS: Four subsidiaries of the Southern Company made modifications to the health care and life insurance benefits of their future retirees without negotiating with their employees' unions. The unions filed unfair labor practice charges with the NLRB claiming violations of Section 8(a)(5), refusal to bargain over mandatory subjects of bargaining. The employer defended that retirees are not employees under NLRA and such benefits are permissive subjects of bargaining.

DECISION: Judgment against the employer. While benefits of workers who have already retired are not mandatory subjects of bargaining, retirement benefits for current employees are mandatory subjects of bargaining. [*Southern Nuclear Operating Co. v. NLRB*, 524 F.3d 1350 (D.C. Cir. 2008)]

13. Right to Work

right-to-work laws – laws restricting unions and employees from negotiating clauses in their collective bargaining agreements that make union membership compulsory.

The NLRA allows states to enact **right-to-work laws**. These laws restrict unions and employers from negotiating clauses in their collective bargaining agreements that make union membership compulsory.[32]

Advocates of such laws contend that compulsory union membership is contrary to the First Amendment right of freedom of association. Unions have attacked these laws as unfair because unions must represent all employees, and in right-to-work

---

[29] *First National Maintenance v. N.L.R.B.*, 452 U.S. 666 (1981).
[30] *Dubuque Packing Co. and UFCWIU, Local 150A*, 303 N.L.R.B. 66 (1991).
[31] *Aramark Educational Services, Inc.*, 335 N.L.R.B. No. 11 (Feb. 18, 2010).
[32] Right-to-work statutes declare unlawful any agreement that denies persons the right to work because of nonmembership in a union or the failure to pay dues to a union as a condition of employment. These laws have been adopted in Alabama, Arizona, Arkansas, Florida, Georgia, Idaho, Indiana Iowa, Kansas, Louisiana, Mississippi, Nebraska, Nevada, North Carolina, North Dakota, Oklahoma, South Carolina, South Dakota, Tennessee, Texas, Utah, Virginia, and Wyoming.

states where a majority of employees vote for union representation, nonunion employees receive all of the benefits of collective bargaining contracts without paying union dues.

14. Strike and Picketing Activity

economic strikers – union strikers trying to enforce bargaining demands when an impasse has been reached in the negotiation process for a collective bargaining agreement.

If the parties reach an impasse in the negotiation process for a collective bargaining agreement, a union may call a strike and undertake picketing activity to enforce its bargaining demands. Strikers in such a situation are called **economic strikers**. Although the strike activity is legal, the employers may respond by hiring temporary or permanent replacement workers.

(A) Rights of Strikers. Economic strikers who unconditionally apply for reinstatement when their positions are filled by permanent replacements are not entitled to return to work at the end of the economic strike. They are, however, entitled to full reinstatement when positions become available.

CASE SUMMARY

Avoiding the Sack—The Pilots Returned before Their Positions Were Filled

FACTS: Striking pilots of Eastern Airlines made an unconditional offer to return to work on November 22, 1989. As of that date, some 227 new-hire replacement pilots were in training but had not obtained certificates from the Federal Aviation Administration permitting them to fly revenue flights. The striking pilots contended that the trainees were not permanent replacement pilots on the date they offered to go back to work because the trainees could not lawfully fly revenue flights. Eastern contended that the new-hire pilots were permanent employees and as such should not be displaced.

DECISION: The pilots' positions were not filled by permanent replacements at the time the striking pilots unconditionally applied to return to work. The new-hire replacement pilots were not qualified to fill the positions at that time. Giving preference to trainees over returning strikers would discourage employees from exercising their right to strike. [*Eastern Airlines Inc. v. Airline Pilots Association Int'l*, **970 F.2d 722 (11th Cir. 1990)**]

Strikers responsible for misconduct while out on strike may be refused reemployment by the employer.

When employees strike to protest an employer's unfair labor practice, such as firing an employee for union-organizing activity, these unfair labor practice strikers have a right to return to their jobs immediately at the end of the strike. This right exists even if the employer has hired permanent replacements.[33]

primary picketing – legal presentations in front of a business notifying the public of a labor dispute.

(B) Picketing. Placing persons outside a business at the site of a labor dispute so that they may, by signs or banners, inform the public of the existence of a labor dispute is called **primary picketing** and is legal. Should the picketing employees mass together in great numbers in front of the gates of the employer's facility to

---

[33] *Poly America, Inc. v. N.L.R.B.*, 260 F.3d 465 (5th Cir. 2001).

mass picketing – illegal tactic of employees massing together in great numbers to effectively shut down entrances of the employer's facility.

secondary picketing – picketing an employer with which a union has no dispute to persuade the employer to stop doing business with a party to the dispute; generally illegal under the NLRA.

effectively shut down the entrances, such coercion is called **mass picketing**; it is illegal. **Secondary picketing** is picketing an employer with whom a union has no dispute to persuade the employer to stop doing business with a party to the dispute. Secondary picketing is generally illegal under the NLRA. An exception exists for certain product picketing at supermarkets or other multiproduct retail stores provided that it is limited to asking customers not to purchase the struck product at the neutral employer's store.[34]

15. Regulation of Internal Union Affairs

To ensure the honest and democratic administration of unions, Congress passed the Labor-Management Reporting and Disclosure Act (LMRDA).[35] Title IV of the LMRDA establishes democratic standards for all elections for union offices, including

1. Secret ballots in local union elections;

2. Opportunity for members to nominate candidates;

3. Advance notice of elections;

4. Observers at polling and at ballot-counting stations for all candidates;

5. Publication of results and preservation of records for one year;

6. Prohibition of any income from dues or assessments to support candidates for union office; and

7. Advance opportunity for each candidate to inspect the membership name and address lists.

C. Pension Plans and Federal Regulation

The Employee Retirement Income Security Act (ERISA)[36] was adopted in 1974 to protect employee pensions and benefits.

16. ERISA

The act sets forth fiduciary standards and requirements for administration, vesting, funding, and termination insurance.

(A) Administration. Commonly a "benefits claims committee" is set up under the plan to make determinations about coverage issues, and courts will not disturb the finding of a benefits committee unless the determinations are "arbitrary and capricious." **For Example,** Joe Gustafson, who provided chauffeur services for senior executives at NYNEX for a number of years while classified as an independent contractor, sought benefits under ERISA because he asserted he was a common law employee of NYNEX. While the court determined he was in fact an employee entitled to overtime compensation under the Fair Labor Standards Act, the court was compelled to defer to the benefits committee's determination that Gustafson was

---

[34] N.L.R.B. v. Fruit and Vegetable Packers, Local 760 (Tree Fruits, Inc.), 377 U.S. 58 (1964); but see N.L.R.B. v. Retail Clerks, Local 1001 (Safeco Title Ins. Co.), 477 U.S. 607 (1980).
[35] 29 U.S.C. §§401–531.
[36] P.L. 93-406, 88 Stat. 829, 29 U.S.C. §§1001–1381.

not an employee under the NYNEX plan because he was not "on the payroll" as required by the plan guidelines. The court found that such a determination was not arbitrary or capricious.[37] Nevertheless, individuals may successfully challenge determinations of the plan administrators. **For Example,** Bell South denied ERISA-covered benefits to Suzanne Lee under both its Short Term Disability Plan and its Long Term Disability Plan. She suffered from chronic pain syndrome, and the administrator determined that she had failed to submit "objective medical evidence" of her condition. The U.S. Court of Appeals reviewed the extensive medical record of pain care specialists supporting her diagnosis and determined that Bell South had acted arbitrarily and capriciously in denying Lee's claim of benefits.[38]

(B) Fiduciary Standards and Reporting. Persons administering a pension fund must handle it to protect the interest of employees.[39]

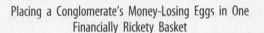

CASE SUMMARY

Placing a Conglomerate's Money-Losing Eggs in One Financially Rickety Basket

FACTS: Charles Howe and others worked for Massey-Ferguson, a wholly owned subsidiary of Varity Corporation. These employees were beneficiaries of Massey-Ferguson's self-funded employee welfare benefit plan, an ERISA-protected plan that Massey-Ferguson itself administered. Varity became concerned that some of Massey-Ferguson's money-losing divisions were losing too much money, and it developed a business plan to deal with the problem that amounted to placing many of Varity's money-losing eggs in one financially rickety basket. It called for a transfer of Massey-Ferguson's money-losing divisions, along with other debts, to a newly created, separately incorporated subsidiary called Massey Combines. The plan foresaw the possibility that Massey Combines would fail, but it viewed such a failure, from Varity's business perspective, as closer to a victory than to a defeat because failure would eliminate several poorly performing divisions and eradicate various debts that Varity would transfer to Massey Combines. Among the obligations that Varity hoped the reorganization would eliminate were those arising from the benefit plan's promises to pay medical and other nonpension benefits to employees of Massey-Ferguson's money-losing divisions. Varity called employees together at a special meeting. The thrust of Varity's remarks was that the employees' benefits would remain secure if they voluntarily transferred to Massey Combines. As Varity knew, however, the reality was very different. The evidence showed that Massey Combines was insolvent from the day of its creation and that it hid its $46 million negative net worth by overvaluing its assets and underestimating its liabilities. After Massey Combines went into receivership, the employees lost their benefits, and Howe and others sued for reinstatement of the old plan. Varity's defense was that individuals did not have a right to bring an ERISA lawsuit for individual relief.

DECISION: Judgment for Howe and the other employees restoring plan benefits. When an employer runs a benefits plan and its managers or agents, regardless of their job titles, talk about those benefits to employees, painting a false picture of security to induce them to transfer to a new company by saying "your benefits are secure," they are fiduciaries, and their breach of fiduciary duties in making false and misleading statements is binding on the employer. ERISA §502(a)(3) authorizes lawsuits for individual equitable relief for breach of fiduciary duties. [*Varity Corp. v. Howe,* **516 U.S. 489 (1996)**]

---

[37] *Gustafson v. Bell Atlantic Corp.*, 171 F. Supp. 2d 311 (S.D.N.Y. 2001).
[38] *Lee v. Bell South Telecommunications Inc.*, 318 Fed. Appx. 829 (11th Cir. 2009).
[39] *John Hancock Mutual Life Ins. Co. v. Harris Trust*, 510 U.S. 86 (1993).

The fact that an employer contributed all or part of the money to the pension fund does not entitle it to use the fund as though the employer still owned it. Persons administering pension plans must make detailed reports to the Secretary of Labor.

(c) Vesting. *Vesting* is the right of an employee to pension benefits paid into a pension plan in the employee's name by the employer. Prior to ERISA, many pension plans did not vest accrued benefits until an employee had 20 to 25 years of service. Thus, an employee who was forced to terminate service after 18 years would have no pension rights or benefits. Under ERISA, employees' rights must be fully vested within five or seven years in accordance with the two vesting options available under the law.

In the past, it had been common for pension plans to contain break-in-service clauses, whereby employees who left their employment for a period longer than one year for any reason other than an on-the-job injury lost pension eligibility rights. Under the Retirement Equity Act of 1984,[40] an individual can leave the workforce for up to five consecutive years and still retain eligibility for pension benefits.

(d) Funding. Pension funds may be broadly classified as "defined contribution plans" and "defined benefit plans."

A **defined contribution plan** is one that provides for an individual account for each plan participant and for benefits based solely on the amount contributed to the participant's account. It is also known as an *individual account plan.* These plans include 401(k) plans, employee stock option plans (ESOPs), profit-sharing plans, and stock bonus plans. Commonly, the employer establishes these plans and defines its own contributions to be matched by contributions from plan participants.

A **defined benefit plan** is an employer commitment to make specified future payments to participants upon retirement. The employer establishes a pension fund for this purpose, and the employer is contractually obligated to make those payments even if the assets set aside to finance the plan turn out to be inadequate. ERISA established an insurance plan, called the **Pension Benefit Guaranty Corporation (PBGC)**, to protect employees covered under defined benefit plans should the employer go out of business.

In the case of defined benefit plans, the entire investment risk is on the employer who sponsors the plan. The employer must cover any underfunding that may result from the plan's poor performance. However, if the plan becomes overfunded, the employer may reduce or suspend its contributions.[41]

Defined contribution plans are the ones most frequently offered by employers today, in part because of the employers' risk of underfunding defined benefit plans. Defined contribution plans are not insured by the PBGC.

(e) Enforcement. ERISA authorizes the Secretary of Labor and employees to bring court actions to compel the observance of statutory requirements.

defined contribution plan—a plan providing individual accounts for each employee participant with benefits defined solely on the amounts contributed by each employee with matching contributions by the employer.

defined benefit plan—an employer established pension fund obligating the employer to make specified future payments to participants upon retirement.

Pension Benefit Guaranty Corporation (PBGC)—an insurance plan to protect employees covered by defined benefit plans in case an employer is unable to meet its payment obligations from the employer's pension fund.

[40] P.L. 98-397, 29 U.S.C. §1001.
[41] *Hughes Aircraft Co. v. Jacobson,* 523 U.S. 1093 (1998).

D. Unemployment Benefits, Family Leaves, and Social Security

Generally, when employees are without work through no fault of their own, they are eligible for unemployment compensation benefits. Twelve-week maternity, paternity, or adoption leaves and family and medical leaves are available for qualifying employees. Social Security provides certain benefits, including retirement and disability benefits.

17. Unemployment Compensation

Unemployment compensation today is provided primarily through a federal-state system under the unemployment insurance provisions of the Social Security Act of 1935.[42] All states have laws that provide similar benefits, and the state agencies are loosely coordinated under the federal act. Agricultural employees, domestic employees, and state and local government employees are not covered by this federal-state system. Federal programs of unemployment compensation exist for federal civilian workers and former military service personnel. A separate federal unemployment program applies to railroad workers.

(A) Eligibility. In most states, an unemployed person must be available for placement in a similar job and willing to take such employment at a comparable rate of pay. Full-time students generally have difficulty proving that they are available for work while they are still going to school.

CASE SUMMARY

Priority of Necessity: Work Comes before School

FACTS: Robert Evjen was a full-time employee of Boise Cascade. At the same time, he was a full-time student at Chemata Community College. He was laid off as part of a general economy move by the employer. He applied for unemployment compensation. His claim was opposed on the ground that he was not available for work because he was going to school. The referee found that Evjen never missed work to go to classes, that he could not afford to go to school without working, and that, in case of any conflict between work and school, work came first.

DECISION: Judgment for Evjen. To obtain unemployment benefits, an unemployed individual must prove, among other things, that she or he is "available for work" and is unable to obtain suitable work. A student's unavailability for work during school hours is contrary to the concept of "available for work," which requires availability for all shifts of suitable work. However, Evjen's uncontroverted testimony that his education was secondary to his employment was sufficient to overcome either an inference or a presumption of nonavailability. He was available for work and therefore entitled to unemployment compensation. [*Evjen v. Employment Agency,* **539 P.2d 662 (Or. App. 1975)**]

If an employee quits a job without cause or is fired for misconduct, the employee is ordinarily disqualified from receiving unemployment compensation benefits.

[42] 42 U.S.C. §§301–1397e.

For Example, stealing property from an employer constitutes misconduct for which benefits will be denied. Moreover, an employee's refusal to complete the aftercare portion of an alcohol treatment program has been found to be misconduct connected with work, disqualifying the employee from receiving benefits.

(B) **FUNDING.** Employers are taxed for unemployment benefits based on each employer's "experience rating" account. Thus, employers with a stable workforce with no layoffs, who therefore do not draw on the state unemployment insurance fund, pay lower tax rates. Employers whose experience ratings are higher pay higher rates. Motivated by the desire to avoid higher unemployment taxes, employers commonly challenge the state's payment of unemployment benefits to individuals who they believe are not properly entitled to benefits.

18. Family and Medical Leaves of Absence

The Family and Medical Leave Act of 1993 (FMLA)[43] entitles an eligible employee, whether male or female, to a total of 12 workweeks of unpaid leave during any 12-month period (1) because of the birth or adoption of the employee's son or daughter, (2) to care for the employee's spouse, son, daughter, or parent with a serious health condition, or (3) because of a serious health condition that makes the employee unable to perform the functions of his or her position. Notice should be given by the employer to an employee that the leave he or she is taking will count against FMLA entitlement in order to comply with the Secretary of Labor's regulations.[44] In the case of an employee's serious health condition or that of a covered family member, an employer may require the employee to use any accrued paid vacation, personal, medical, or sick leave toward any part of the 12-week leave provided by the act. When an employee requests leave because of the birth or adoption of a child, the employer may require the employee to use all available paid personal, vacation, and medical leave, but not sick leave, toward any FMLA leave.

To be eligible for FMLA leave, an employee must have been employed by a covered employer for at least 12 months and have worked at least 1,250 hours during the 12-month period preceding the leave. Covered employers are those that employ 50 or more employees.[45] Upon return from FMLA leave, the employee is entitled to be restored to the same or an equivalent position with equivalent pay and benefits. **For Example,** when Magda Brenlla returned to her position at LaSorsa Buick in the Bronx, New York, after quadruple bypass surgery, she was terminated by the owner who told her he had decided to consolidate the positions of office manager and controller, even though he had no business plan for restructuring, and soon thereafter had to hire additional help in the office. The judge upheld a jury verdict of $320,000, finding that the jury had ample evidence to conclude that the real reason for her termination was her FMLA leave.[46]

The FMLA provides specific statutory relief for violations of the provisions of the act, including pay to the employee for damages equal to lost wages and benefits or any actual monetary losses, plus interest, plus an equal amount in liquidated damages.[47]

---

[43] 29 U.S.C. §§2601–2654.

[44] See *Ragsdale v. Wolverine World Wide, Inc.,* 535 U.S. 81 (2002).

[45] *Bellum v. PCE Constructors Inc.,* 407 F.3d 734 (5th Cir. 2005). Joint employers are obligated to honor FMLA-qualifying leaves. See *Grace v. USCAR,* 521 F.3d 655 (6th Cir. 2008).

[46] *Brenlla v. LaSorsa Buick,* 2002 WL 1059117 (S.D.N.Y. May 28, 2002).

[47] See *Arban v. West Publishing Co.,* 345 F.3d 390 (6th Cir. 2003), in which the U.S. Court of Appeals required the doubling of a jury verdict of $130,000 under the FMLA provision providing for liquidated damages unless the employer is able to prove that it acted "in good faith …" and had reasonable grounds to believe it was not in violation of the FMLA. 29 U.S.C. §2617(a)(iii).

19. Leaves for Military Service under USERRA

The Uniformed Services Employment and Re-Employment Rights Act (USERRA) was enacted in 1994 to encourage noncareer service in the armed services, minimize the disruption experienced in the civilian careers of reservists, and promote prompt reemployment of reservists upon return from military leave.[48] In the context of mobilizing more than 500,000 reservists between September 11, 2001, and the summer of 2006, the USERRA has and will have a broad impact on U.S. employers as it provides reemployment and benefit protection rights for returning military personnel and prohibits discrimination against individuals because of their application for or performance of military service.[49]

(A) PROTECTIONS. Section 4312 of the USERRA generally requires returning reservists to be "promptly reemployed" and returned to the same or comparable positions of like seniority, status, and pay they would have had if they had not been activated. Moreover, Section 4316(c) provides that persons reemployed under the act shall not be discharged from employment within a year of their reemployment if their period of service was more than 180 days. For service of more than 30 days, the protective period is 180 days. However, the employer may terminate an individual for cause regardless of the duration of service.

Sections 4312(a)(3) and (4) provide protection for those disabled while in the service and requires employers to make reasonable efforts to accommodate each employee's disability so that each individual may return to the same or comparable positions or, if no longer qualified for the position, allow for the transfer to a position the disabled individual can perform closest to the prior position in terms of seniority, status, and pay.

Section 4323 of the act provides a full range of remedies, including back pay for loss of wages and benefits as well as liquidated damages in an amount equal to the actual damages when the employer's failure to comply with the act was willful. The Department of Labor has issued USERRA regulations.[50] The act's enforcement is performed by the U.S. Justice Department's Division of Civil Rights.

CASE SUMMARY

USSERA—Because It's the Right Thing to Do!

FACTS: Michael Serricchio, an Air Force reservist, was employed as a financial advisor at Wachovia Securities and called up to active duty in the wake of September 11, 2001. Upon completion of his active duty, he sought to return to Wachovia with comparable earnings potential and opportunity for advancement. In the year prior to his activation for military duty, Mr. Serricchio was personally responsible for servicing in excess of 130 accounts, was responsible for managing in excess of $9 million dollars with his partner, and was earning $6,500 per month based on those assets. If Serricchio accepted Wachovia's reemployment offer, he would have been managing a handful of accounts, generating, according to Wachovia's own documents, a small amount in monthly commissions that had to be repaid to Wachovia to offset his monthly draw.

[48] 38 U.S.C.§4301 (2005).
[49] 38 U.S.C. §§4312, 4316, and 4317 (2005).
[50] 30 Federal Register Vol. 70 No. 242 (Dec. 19, 2005).

CASE SUMMARY

Continued

The employer argued that it provided the same draw and commission structure to the plaintiff and this was sufficient to fulfill its reemployment obligations under Section 4316. Serricchio contended that Wachovia's offer did not satisfy its obligation to reemploy him in a position of like pay; and the employer's failure to comply with the USERRA was willful, entitling him to double back pay as liquidated damages.

DECISION: Judgment for Serricchio. Wachovia understood that Serricchio had a right to be reinstated to his previous position as if he had never left. But even though Wachovia had a military-leave policy that expressly included that provision, the company did not offer Serricchio a position comparable to the one he held before leaving for military service. The court upheld an award of $389,453 in back pay, $389,453 in liquidated damages, $830,107 in attorneys' fees and costs, and $36,567 in interest for a total of $1.64 million. [*Serricchio v. Wachovia Securities, LLC,* 685 F.3d 169 (2d Cir. 2011)]

(B) **DEFENSES.** In addition to an employer's right to terminate a reemployed service-person for cause, employers may be excused from reemploying or continuing employment of persons under §4312(d)(1) of the act when the employer's circumstances have so changed as to make reemployment impossible, unreasonable, or an undue hardship. The burden of proof on the matter is on the employer.
For Example, Joseph Duarte was called to active duty in the Marine Corps Reserve to serve nine months' active duty from November to July. On his return in July he was given his same pay but diminished status by being assigned a temporary assignment rather than acting as a primary consultant to one of the employer's business groups. Faced with financial need to reduce its payroll, the employer eliminated Duarte's temporary assignment and terminated him four months later for what it believed was economic "cause." Duarte believed that his termination violated the USERRA. The court disagreed with the employer and determined that Duarte was within the act's one-year protective period and had been returned to work in the diminished status of a temporary assignment that was a direct result of his military service. Duarte was awarded back pay of $114,500 and front pay of $324,000, less $55,000 in severance benefits already paid him, for a total of $384,000 in damages.[51] Liquidated damages equal to $384,000 were declined because the employer's actions were not deemed willful.

(C) **DISCRIMINATION AND RETALIATION PROTECTION.** As opposed to the protections contained in Section 4312, the act's Section 4311 provides separate and distinct statutory protection against discrimination of employees on the basis of military service and retaliation against individuals, whether military or not, who give testimony or statements on behalf of a USERRA claimant. **For Example,** a Section 4311 discrimination violation is made out that bakery driver Robert Mills was terminated by Multigrain Baking Co. because of his need to have time off for reserve duty training after the personnel director, Marsha Coyle, testified on cross-examination,

---

[51] *Duarte v. Agilent Technologies, Inc.,* 366 F. Supp. 2d 1039 (D. Colo. 2005).

"If we knew Bobby Mills was in the Guard, we would not have hired him. These drivers have to be available to protect their territories or we lose business."

20. Social Security

Employees and employers are required to pay Social Security taxes, which provide employees with four types of insurance protection: retirement benefits, disability benefits, life insurance benefits, and health insurance (Medicare). The federal Social Security Act established a federal program of aid for the aged, the blind, and the disabled. This is called the Supplemental Security Income (SSI) program. Payments are administered directly by the Social Security Administration, which became an independent government agency in 1995.

E. EMPLOYEES' HEALTH AND SAFETY

The Occupational Safety and Health Act of 1970 (OSHA) was passed to assure every worker, so far as possible, safe and healthful working conditions and to preserve the country's human resources.[52] OSHA provides for (1) the establishment of safety and health standards and (2) effective enforcement of these standards and the other employer duties required by OSHA.

21. Standards

The Secretary of Labor has broad authority under OSHA to promulgate occupational safety and health standards.[53] Except in emergency situations, public hearings and publication in the *Federal Register* are required before the secretary can issue a new standard. Any person adversely affected may then challenge the validity of the standard in a U.S. Court of Appeals. The secretary's standards will be upheld if they are reasonable and supported by substantial evidence. The secretary must demonstrate a need for a new standard by showing that it is reasonably necessary to protect employees against a "significant risk" of material health impairment. The cost of compliance with new standards may run into billions of dollars. The secretary is not required to do a cost-benefit analysis for a new standard but must show that the standard is economically feasible.

22. Employer Duties

Employers have a "general duty" to furnish each employee a place of employment that is free from hazards that are likely to cause death or serious physical injuries.

OSHA requires employers to maintain records of occupational illness and injuries if they result in death, loss of consciousness, or one or more lost workdays or if they require medical treatment other than first aid. Such records have proven to be a valuable aid in recognizing areas of risk. They have been especially helpful in identifying the presence of occupational illnesses.

---

[52] 29 U.S.C. §651 *et seq.*
[53] *Martin v. OSHRC*, 499 U.S. 144 (1991).

23. Enforcement

The Occupational Safety and Health Administration (also identified as OSHA) is the agency within the Department of Labor that administers the act. OSHA has authority to conduct inspections and to seek enforcement action when noncompliance has occurred. Worksite inspections are conducted when employer records indicate incidents involving fatalities or serious injuries.[54] These inspections may also result from employee complaints. The act protects employees making complaints from employer retaliation. Employers have the right to require an OSHA inspector to secure a warrant before inspecting the employer's plant.

If OSHA issues a citation for a violation of workplace health or safety standards, the employer may challenge the citation before the Occupational Safety and Health Review Commission (OSHRC). Judicial review of a commission ruling is obtained before a U.S. Court of Appeals. **For Example,** after an accident at Staley Manufacturing Company's Decatur, Illinois, plant in which an employee was fatally asphyxiated, OSHA inspectors issued citations for multiple violations of the OSH Act. The employer challenged the citations before the OSHRC. Upon review by the U.S. Court of Appeals, the court affirmed OSHRC's decision, finding

Thinking Things Through

Taking Chances or Shortcuts in Violation of OSHA Standards Is Bad Management

John Carlo, Inc. (JCI) was installing a sewer line down the middle of an existing roadway in Jacksonville, Florida. The new line crossed under an existing gas line that was perpendicular to the proposed sewer line. The JCI crew worked in two stacked trench boxes, laying pipe up to the location where the pipeline crossed the trench for the sewer line. OSHA regulations require protection of employees from cave-ins; trench boxes and sloping of trench walls provide this protection. The following day, the crew removed the top trench box because both boxes would not fit under the perpendicular gas line. The crew pulled the bottom box under the perpendicular gas line and prepared the bottom of the trench to lay one joint of the sewer pipe. Project superintendent Cox had discussed this move with his foreman Jacobs. Jacobs reminded Cox that this move would leave the top portion of the trench unprotected. Cox explained that he realized the problem, but because JCI had bid the project based on 6-foot-wide trenches, they could not slope the trenches. The supervisors anticipated that just 15 minutes was needed to lay the one joint of pipe. Two crew members entered the trench to lay the pipe. The trench walls above the box (approximately 6 feet) were not sloped or otherwise protected. A large clay ball dislodged, fell into the trench, and struck one employee, who eventually died as a result.

Thinking Things Through, was it a reasonable risk for the employer to utilize the two employees in the trench for just 15 minutes to lay one joint of pipe? Of course not! The ALJ found that both supervisors "knowingly and deliberately" violated the OSHA standard because it was "more expedient to place employees in an unprotected trench... than to take the time to adequately shore up or slope the trench to protect the employees." The $50,000 willful violation penalty was upheld by the U.S. Court of Appeals.*

In 1970, the year that OSHA became law, the American population was approximately 204,000,000; over 14,000 workers were killed in industrial accidents. In 2009, with the U.S. population at an estimated 307,000,000, some 4,551 workers were killed in work-related incidents. OSHA has drastically improved the safety and health of workers. OSHA standards are commonly devised as corrective responses to the occurrence of previous fatalities or injuries on often similarly situated work sites. Employees are empowered to refuse to expose themselves to dangerous duties under the *Whirlpool v. Marshall* U.S. Supreme Court decision.** Management and employees must always be encouraged to take the safe course!

*John Carlo, Inc. v. Secretary of Labor, 2008 CCH OSHD ¶ 32,929.
**445 U.S. 1 (1980).

---

[54] *Chao v. Mallard Bay Drilling Co.,* 534 U.S. 235 (2002).

that the company's "plain indifference" to act on the hazards at the workplace and train employees how to handle the hazards was a willful violation of the act, allowing for civil penalty of no more than $70,000 for each violation.[55]

The Occupational Safety and Health Act provides that no employer shall discharge or in any manner discriminate against employees because they filed a complaint with OSHA, testified in any OSHA proceeding, or exercised any right afforded by the act. A regulation issued by the Secretary of Labor under the act provides that if employees with no reasonable alternative refuse in good faith to expose themselves to a dangerous condition, they will be protected against subsequent discrimination. The Secretary of Labor may obtain injunctive and other appropriate relief in a U.S. district court against an employer who discriminates against employees for testifying or exercising any right under the act.

24. State "Right-to-Know" Legislation

Laws that guarantee individual workers the "right to know" if there are hazardous substances in their workplaces have been enacted by many states in recent years. These laws commonly require an employer to make known to an employee's physician the chemical composition of certain workplace substances in connection with the employee's diagnosis and treatment by the physician. Furthermore, local fire and public health officials, as well as local neighborhood residents, are given the right to know if local employers are working with hazardous substances that could pose health or safety problems.

F. COMPENSATION FOR EMPLOYEES' INJURIES

For most kinds of employment, workers' compensation statutes govern compensation for injuries. These statutes provide that an injured employee is entitled to compensation for accidents occurring in the course of employment from a risk involved in that employment.

25. Common Law Status of Employer

In some employment situations, common law principles apply. Workers' compensation statutes commonly do not apply to employers with fewer than a prescribed minimum number of employees or to agricultural, domestic, or casual employment. When an exempted area of employment is involved, it is necessary to consider the duties and defenses of employers apart from workers' compensation statutes.

(A) DUTIES. The employer is under the common law duty to furnish an employee with a reasonably safe place in which to work, reasonably safe tools and appliances, and a sufficient number of competent fellow employees for the work involved. The employer is also under the common law duty to warn the employee of any unusual dangers particular to the employer's business.

---

[55] *A. E. Staley Manufacturing Co. v. Chao*, 295 F.3d 1341 (D.C. Cir. 2002).

(B) **DEFENSES.** At common law, the employer is not liable to an injured employee if the employee is harmed by the act of a fellow employee. Similarly, an employer is not liable at common law to an employee harmed by an ordinary hazard of the work because the employee assumed such risks. If the employee is guilty of contributory negligence, regardless of the employer's negligence, the employer is not liable at common law to an injured employee.

26. Statutory Changes

The rising incidence of industrial accidents resulting from the increasing use of more powerful machinery and the growth of the industrial labor population led to a demand for statutory modification of common law rules relating to the liability of employers for industrial accidents.

(A) **MODIFICATION OF EMPLOYER'S COMMON LAW DEFENSES.** One type of change by statute was to modify the defenses that an employer could assert when sued by an employee for damages. **For Example,** under the Federal Employer's Liability Act (FELA), which covers railroad workers, the injured employee must still bring an action in court and prove the negligence of the employer or other employees. However, the burden of proving the case is made lighter by limitations on employers' defenses. Under FELA, contributory negligence is a defense only in mitigation of damages; assumption of the risk is not a defense.[56]

(B) **WORKERS' COMPENSATION.** A more sweeping development was made by the adoption of workers' compensation statutes in every state. In addition, civil employees of the U.S. government are covered by the Federal Employees' Compensation Act. When an employee is covered by a workers' compensation statute and the injury is job connected, the employee's remedy is limited to that provided in the workers' compensation statute.[57]

Workers' compensation proceedings are brought before a special administrative agency or workers' compensation board. In contrast, a common law action for damages or an action for damages under an employer's liability statute is brought in a court of law.

CASE SUMMARY

Locked in

FACTS: Bryant is the administrator of the estate of the deceased and the guardian of the deceased's minor child. Bryant sued Wal-Mart for damages following the death of the deceased based on the theory of false imprisonment. While working on the night restocking crew, the deceased suffered a stroke. Medical personnel arrived six minutes later but could not enter the store because management had locked all doors of the store for security reasons and no manager was present to open a door. By the time the medical crew entered the store to assist her, they were

---

[56] 45 U.S.C. §1 *et seq.*
[57] In *Fu v. Owens*, 622 F.3d 880 (8th Cir. 2010), Helen Fu's injuries, incurred when a coworker assaulted her at work at a Target-owned clinic in Minnesota, occurred because she was at the job, in touch with associations and conditions inseparable from it. The injuries occurred because she was on the job and thus she was subject to the exclusivity provision of the Workers' Compensation Act.

CASE SUMMARY

Continued

unable to revive her, and she died 15 hours later. Bryant contended that the false imprisonment occurred between the time the deceased became ill and the time the medical team was unable to enter the store. Wal-Mart contended that Bryant's exclusive remedy is the Workers' Compensation Act.

DECISION: Judgment for Wal-Mart. It is well settled that a claim under the Workers' Compensation Act is the sole and exclusive remedy for injury or occupational disease incurred in the course of employment. In exchange for the right to recover scheduled compensation without proof of negligence on the part of the employer, employees forgo other rights and remedies they once had. Injuries to an employee's peace, happiness, and feelings are not compensable under the act. [*Bryant v. Wal-Mart Stores, Inc.*, 417 S.E.2d 688 (Ga. Ct. App. 1922)]

For injuries arising within the course of the employee's work from a risk involved in that work, workers' compensation statutes usually provide (1) immediate medical benefits, (2) prompt periodic wage replacement, often computed as a percentage of weekly wages (ranging from 50 percent to 80 percent of the injured employee's wage) for a specified number of weeks, and (3) a death benefit of a limited amount.[58] In such cases, compensation is paid without regard to whether the employer or the employee was negligent. However, no compensation is generally allowed for a willful, self-inflicted injury or one sustained while intoxicated.[59]

There has been a gradual widening of the workers' compensation statutes, so compensation today is generally recoverable for both accident-inflicted injuries and occupational diseases.

G. Employee Privacy

Employers may want to monitor employee telephone conversations in the ordinary course of their business to evaluate employee performance and customer service; to document business transactions between employees and customers; or to meet special security, efficiency, or other needs. Employers may likewise want to monitor e-mail for what they perceive to be sound business reasons. Employers also may seek to test employees for drug use or search employee lockers for illicit drugs. Litigation may result because employees may believe that such activities violate their right to privacy.

27. Source of Privacy Rights

The Bill of Rights contained in the U.S. Constitution, including the Fourth Amendment, which protects against unreasonable search and seizure, provides a philosophical and legal basis for individual privacy rights for federal employees. The Fourteenth Amendment applies this privacy protection to actions taken by state and local governments that affect their employees. The privacy rights of individuals

---

[58] *Union Light & Power Co. v. DC Department of Employment Services*, 796 A.2d 665 (D.C. App. 2002).
[59] See *Beck v. Newt Brown Contractors, LLC*, 72 So.3d 982 (La. App. 2011).

working in the private sector are not directly controlled by the Bill of Rights, however, because challenged employer actions are not government actions. Limited employee privacy rights in the private sector are provided by statute, case law, and collective bargaining agreements.

28. Monitoring Employee Telephone Conversations

The Federal Wiretapping Act[60] makes it unlawful to intercept oral and electronic communications and provides for both criminal liability and civil damages against the violator. There are two major exceptions, however. The first allows an employer to monitor a firm's telephones in the "ordinary course of business" through the use of extension telephones; a second exception applies when there is prior employee consent to the interception. If employer monitoring results in the interception of a business call, it is within the ordinary-course-of-business exception. Personal calls can be monitored, however, only to the extent necessary to determine that the call is personal, and the employer must then cease listening. **For Example,** Newell Spears taped all phone conversations at his store in trying to find out if an employee was connected to a store theft. He listened to virtually all 22 hours of intercepted and recorded telephone conversations between his employee Sibbie Deal and her boyfriend Calvin Lucas without regard to the conversations' relation to Spears's business interest. While Spears might well have legitimately monitored Deal's calls to the extent necessary to determine that the calls were personal and made or received in violation of store policy, the scope of the interception in this case was well beyond the boundaries of the ordinary-course-of-business exception and in violation of the act.[61]

Employer monitoring of employee phone calls can be accomplished without fear of violating the act if consent is established. Consent may be established by prior written notice to employees of the employer's monitoring policy. It is prudent, as well, for the employer to give customers notice of the policy through a recorded message as part of the employer's phone-answering system.

29. E-Mail Monitoring

Electronic mail (e-mail) is a primary means of communication in many of today's businesses, serving for some employers as an alternative to faxes, telephones, or the U.S. Postal Service. Employers may want to monitor employees' e-mail messages to evaluate the efficiency and effectiveness of their employees or for corporate security purposes, including the protection of trade secrets and other intangible property interests. When employees are disciplined or terminated for alleged wrongful activities discovered as a result of e-mail searches, however, the issue of privacy may be raised. (See Chapter 2 for a discussion of use of e-mail in litigation and discovery.)

The Electronic Communications Privacy Act of 1986 (ECPA)[62] amended the federal wiretap statute and was intended in part to apply to e-mail. However, ordinary-course-of-business and consent exceptions apply to e-mail, and it would appear that employers have broad latitude to monitor employee e-mail use. **For Example,** the e-mails that Gina Holmes sent to her personal attorney on a company-issued computer regarding litigation with the company were not protected

---

[60] Title III of the Omnibus Crime Control and Safe Streets Act of 1968, 28 U.S.C. §§2510–2520.
[61] *Deal v. Spears*, 580 F.2d 1153 (8th Cir. 1992); *Arias v. Mutual Central Alarm Services, Inc.*, 182 F.R.D. 407 (S.D.N.Y. 1998).
[62] 18 U.S.C. §§2510–2520.

by the attorney-client privilege because the company handbook stated that employees were prohibited from using the computer to send or receive personal e-mails. Moreover, the company warned that it would monitor its technology resources for compliance with its computer policy, and that employees "have no rights of privacy" with respect to information on the computers.[63] Very few cases involving e-mail and Web site issues have been adjudicated so far under the ECPA. It has been held that for an employee's secure Web site to be "intercepted" in violation of the wiretap act, the electronic documents acquired must be acquired during transmission, not while in electronic storage.[64]

An employer can place itself within the consent exception of the act by issuing a policy statement to all employees that informs them of the monitoring program and its purposes and justification.

30. Property Searches

Protected by the Fourth Amendment, public-sector employees have a reasonable expectation of privacy with respect to their desks and file cabinets. However, depending on the fact-specific purpose, justification, and scope of the search, the balance of interest should favor the public employer because its interests in supervision, control, and the efficient operation of the workplace outweigh a public employee's privacy interests.[65] Search of a postal service employee's locker was held not to be a Fourth Amendment violation because well-publicized regulations informed employees that their lockers were subject to search to combat pilferage and stealing. However, the warrantless search of the desk and files of a psychiatrist employed by a state hospital was found to be a Fourth Amendment violation, exceeding the scope of a reasonable work-related search when the search examined his private possessions, including purely personal belongings, and management sought to justify the search on false grounds.[66]

In the private sector, employers may create a reasonable expectation of privacy by providing an employee a locker and allowing the employee to provide his or her own lock. A search of that locker could be an invasion of privacy.[67] If, however, the employer provides a locker and lock but retains a master key and this is known to employees, the lockers may be subject to legitimate reasonable searches by the employer. If a private-sector employer notifies all employees of its policy on lockers, desks, and office searches and the employer complies with its own policy, employees will have no actionable invasion of privacy case.

Many businesses use overt or hidden video cameras as a security method in the workplace to enhance worker safety and to prevent and/or detect theft or other criminal conduct. To avoid state constitutional or statutory claims for invasion of privacy, employers should not set up video cameras in areas where employees have a reasonable expectation of privacy.[68] Utilizing signs to notify employees and members of the

---

[63] *Holmes v. Petrovich Development Co.*, 191 Cal. App. 4th 1047 (3d Dist. 2011).

[64] *Konop v. Hawaiian Airlines, Inc.*, 302 F.3d 868 (9th Cir. 2002); *Fraser v. Nationwide Mutual Insurance Co.*, 352 F.3d 107 (3d Cir. 2003) (court held that the wiretaps act was not violated because the employer did not "intercept" the e-mail but retrieved it after it had been sent and received).

[65] *O'Connor v. Ortega*, 480 U.S. 709 (1987).

[66] *Ortega v. O'Connor*, 146 F.3d 1149 (9th Cir. 1998).

[67] *Kmart Corp. v. Trotti*, 677 S.W.2d 632 (Tex. App. 1984).

[68] See *Kline v. Security Guards, Inc.*, 386 F.3d 246 (3rd Cir. 2004). Some 370 employees of Dana Corporation's Reading, Pennsylvania, facility sued the corporation and its security guard company after employees learned that a new audio and video surveillance system at the entrance of the facility allowed what was said in the area where employees "punch in" for work to be observed and heard in the guard booth. The Third Circuit Court of Appeals rejected the employer's preemption claims and remanded the matter to the state court to handle the invasion of privacy and other tort claims.

public that certain areas are under video surveillance is a common business practice not likely to initiate privacy claims. Additionally, employers should disseminate their written policy on surveillance and obtain a consent form from employees acknowledging that they received this notice to preserve their consent defense.

31. Drug and Alcohol Testing

Drug and alcohol testing is an additional source of privacy concerns for employees. Public-sector employees may see drug and alcohol testing as potentially infringing on their Fourth and Fifth Amendment rights, although they may be subject to this testing on the basis of reasonable suspicion. In ordinary circumstances, however, random drug testing is not permissible in the public sector except for mass transit workers and some safety-sensitive positions. The Federal Omnibus Transportation Employee Testing Act,[69] which covers certain classes of employees working in the airline, railroad, and trucking industries, makes covered employees subject to random drug and alcohol testing. Random drug and alcohol testing of employees working in safety-sensitive positions in the private sector also is permissible, as is the testing of private-sector employees on the basis of reasonable suspicion.

H. Employer-Related Immigration Laws

The Immigration and Naturalization Act (INA), the Immigration Reform and Control Act of 1986 (IRCA), and the Immigration Act of 1990[70] are the principal employer-related immigration laws. Administration of these laws was formerly under the Immigration and Naturalization Service, and is now reorganized under the Department of Homeland Security (DHS) as the United States Bureau of Citizenship and Immigration Services (USCIS).

32. Employer Liability

The IRCA sets criminal and civil penalties against employers who knowingly hire aliens who have illegally entered the United States. The IRCA was designed to stop illegal immigration by eliminating job opportunities for these aliens.

33. Employer Verification and Special Hiring Programs

Upon hiring a new employee, an employer must verify that the employee is authorized to work in the United States. USCIS has designated Form I-9, Immigration Eligibility Verification Form, as the official verification form to comply with the IRCA.

The prospective employee must complete the initial portion of Form I-9, attesting under the penalty of perjury that he or she is a U.S. citizen or is authorized to work in the United States, and that the verification document(s) presented to the employer are genuine and relate to the signer. The employer must then review the documents that support the individual's right to work in the United States.

---

[69] P.L. 102-143, 105 Stat. 952, 49 U.S.C. §1301 nt.
[70] P.L. 101-649, 8 U.S.C. §1101.

In April 2011, USCIS issued a final rule on acceptable identity documents for the I-9 employment eligibility process, divided into three sections.[71] List A documents verify identity and employment authorization and include a U.S. passport, the new U.S. passport card, and the temporary Form I-551 (permanent resident card) or a permanent resident card that includes a machine-readable immigrant visa. List B documents verify only identity; an example is a state-issued driver's license. List C documents, such as a Social Security card or official birth certificate, verify employment authorization. The employer is prohibited from requiring other documentation.[72]

(A) E-VERIFY. Employers may verify new employee eligibility status through the federal government's mostly voluntary employment verification program called E-Verify. The E-Verify system is an Internet-based voluntary system that electronically compares information on I-9 forms with records at the Social Security Administration and the Department of Homeland Security (DHS). In 2010, DHS instituted a U.S. passport photo matching program by comparing E-Verify data with State Department records. Employers that use E-Verify must notify applicants that they use E-Verify and cannot use the program as a prescreening tool. USCIS statistics for FY 2010 on E-Verify use showed that 98.3 percent of new hires surveyed were confirmed "work authorized" in three to five seconds.

Executive Order 12989 was amended in 2008 to require federal contractors to use E-Verify to confirm the employment eligibility of their workforce.

Under the Legal Arizona Workers Act, upheld by the Supreme Court, all an Arizona employer is required to do to avoid sanctions is to use the I-9 system and E-Verify.[73]

(B) SPECIAL HIRING PROGRAMS. Congress has provided increases in visas for entrepreneurs and those aliens with the greatest skills who could stimulate the American economy through their employment and job-creating investments.[74] H-1 classification visas allow aliens of "distinguished merit and ability" to enter and work in the United States on a temporary basis. These people include architects, engineers, lawyers, physicians, and teachers. An annual cap of 65,000 visas is applied to the H-1B visa classification (the regular cap). An advanced degree exception (ADE) cap provides for an additional 20,000 annual visas for individuals who have obtained master's degrees or higher at U.S. universities. The hiring employer must attest that it will not lay off an American employee 90 days before or after filing a petition to employ a foreign worker regarding any position to be filled by the foreign worker. H-1B professionals must be paid the higher of the actual or prevailing wage for each position in order to eliminate economic incentives to use this foreign workers' program.

---

[71] *See Federal Register* (Apr. 15, 2011). USCIS stated that concerns about document fraud were among the most important reasons for this rulemaking.
[72] 8 U.S.C. §1324B (a)(b).
[73] *Chamber of Commerce of the United States v. Whiting*, 131 S. Ct. 624 (2011).
[74] In a report released by the Fiscal Policy Institute of Albany, New York, on November 16, 2007, entitled "Working for A Better Life: A Profile of Immigrants in the New York State Economy," the whole range of immigrants in the state, both documented and undocumented, was studied. The report found that immigrants constitute 37 percent of the population of New York City and 46 percent of its labor force. They make up 25 percent of the city's CEOs; 50 percent of accountants; and 33 percent of clerks, receptionists, and cleaners. In upstate areas, immigrants constitute 5 percent of the population and labor force, 20 percent of professors, 35 percent of physicians, 20 percent of software engineers, and 80 percent of seasonal farm workers. All told, they contributed an estimated $229 billion in economic output in the state in 2006. Basically, there are rich, poor, and middle-class immigrants, like everyone else. See 227 DLR A-9 (Nov. 27, 2007). The Fiscal Policy Institute's 2010 report found that immigrants constituted 37 percent of New York City's population and 48 percent of its workforce. 147 DLR A-9 (Aug. 2, 2010).

L-1 visas allow qualifying multinational businesses to make intracompany transfers of foreign persons to the United States when the individuals are employed in management or have "specialized knowledge." L-1 visas are good for up to seven years for executives and managers. "Specialized knowledge" personnel may stay for five years. There are no annual caps on the number of L-1 visas issued, and the employer is not required to attest that no American worker will be laid off.

Many technology companies are utilizing L-1 visas as an alternative to the H-1B visas. Although the H-1B visa program requires employers to pay foreign workers the prevailing U.S. wage for a particular job, the L-1 visa has no such requirement. **For Example,** an engineer on an L-1 visa from India may be paid the same wage rate as paid in India, rather than the much higher prevailing rate for U.S. engineers. USCIS requires each transferee, or his or her employer, to demonstrate that the transferee's responsibilities are "primarily managerial."

For Example, Brazilian corporation Granite Ebenezer established a U.S.-based affiliate, Brazil Quality Stones, Inc. (BQS), as a California corporation. Eugene dos Santos, a Brazilian citizen, served as President and CEO of both entities and owned 99 percent of the corporation's stock. Citizenship and Immigration Services determined that he was not entitled to an L-1 visa. Although BQS submitted an organizational chart with him at the top supervising five employees, only three had received pay during the quarter. The USCIS determined that BQS had not reached the level of development in which dos Santos could devote his primary attention to managerial duties as opposed to operational ones.[75]

MAKE THE CONNECTION

SUMMARY

The relationship of employer and employee is created by the agreement of the parties and is subject to the principles applicable to contracts. If the employment contract sets forth a specific duration, the employer cannot terminate the contract at an earlier date unless just cause exists. If no definite time period is set forth, the individual is an at-will employee. Under the employment-at-will doctrine, an employer can terminate the contract of an at-will employee at any time for any reason or for no reason. Courts in many jurisdictions, however, have carved out exceptions to this doctrine when the discharge violates public policy or is contrary to good faith and fair dealing in the employment relationship. The Fair Labor Standards Act regulates minimum wages, overtime hours, and child labor.

Under the National Labor Relations Act, employees have the right to form a union to obtain a collective bargaining contract or to refrain from organizational activities. The National Labor Relations Board conducts elections to determine whether employees in an appropriate bargaining unit desire to be represented by a union. The NLRA prohibits employers' and unions' unfair labor practices and authorizes the NLRB to conduct proceedings to stop such practices. Economic strikes have limited reinstatement rights. Federal law sets forth democratic standards for the election of union offices.

The Employees Retirement Income Security Act (ERISA) protects employees' pensions by requiring (1) high standards of those administering

---

[75] *Brazil Quality Stones, Inc. v. Chertoff,* 531 F.3d 1063 (9th Cir. 2008).

the funds, (2) reasonable vesting of benefits, (3) adequate funding, and (4) an insurance program to guarantee payments of earned benefits.

Unemployment compensation benefits are paid to persons for a limited period of time if they are out of work through no fault of their own. Persons receiving unemployment compensation must be available for placement in a job similar in duties and comparable in rate of pay to the job they lost. Twelve-week maternity, paternity, and adoption leaves are available under the Family and Medical Leave Act. Employers and employees pay Social Security taxes to provide retirement benefits, disability benefits, life insurance benefits, and Medicare.

The Occupational Safety and Health Act provides for the (1) establishment of safety and health standards and (2) effective enforcement of these standards. Many states have enacted "right-to-know" laws, which require employers to inform their employees of any hazardous substances present in the workplace.

Workers' compensation laws provide for the prompt payment of compensation and medical benefits to persons injured in the course of employment without regard to fault. An injured employee's remedy is generally limited to the remedy provided by the workers' compensation statute. Most states also provide compensation to workers for occupational diseases.

The Bill of Rights is the source of public-sector employees' privacy rights. Private-sector employees may obtain limited privacy rights from statutes, case law, and collective bargaining agreements. Employers may monitor employee telephone calls, although once it is determined that the call is personal, the employer must stop listening or be in violation of the federal wiretap statute. The ordinary-course-of-business and consent exceptions to the Electronic Communications Privacy Act of 1986 (ECPA) give private employers a great deal of latitude to monitor employee e-mail. Notification to employees of employers' policies on searching lockers, desks, and offices reduces employees' expectations of privacy, and a search conducted in conformity with a known policy is generally not an invasion of privacy. Drug and alcohol testing is generally permissible if it is based on reasonable suspicion; random drug and alcohol testing may also be permissible in safety-sensitive positions.

Immigration laws prohibit the employment of aliens who have illegally entered the United States.

LEARNING OUTCOMES

After studying this chapter, you should be able to clearly explain:

A. The Employment Relationship

LO.1 Explain the contractual nature of the employment relationship

See the *FedEx* case in which the employment contract and the employee handbook both preserved the employer's at-will termination powers, pp. 849–850. See the example of the public policy exception to the employment-at-will doctrine protecting home health care nurse Eugene Patterson, p. 848.

LO.2 Explain how whistleblower protection under Sarbanes-Oxley is limited to conduct in violation of fraud or securities laws

See the example involving whistleblowers Tides and Neumann who were not protected under SOX because they disclosed information and documents to a newspaper and not a regulatory or law enforcement agency on p. 851.

LO.3 Explain how Dodd-Frank expands whistleblower protection to a wide range of financial services employees and provides incentives for whistleblowers

See what a whistleblower must do to recover a bounty under Dodd-Frank on p. 852.

B. Labor Relations Laws

LO.4 Explain how the National Labor Relations Act prohibits employers from firing employees attempting to form a union, and requires employers to bargain with unions in good faith over wages, hours, and working conditions

See the *Sam Santillo* case on wrongful termination of an employee because of his union activity, p. 860.

See the role that the National Labor Relations Board plays in regulating employers' overly broad social media policies that are in violation of Section 7 of the NLRA, starting on p. 858. See the discussion of mandatory and permissive subjects of bargaining, p. 861.

C. Pension Plans and Federal Regulation

L0.5 Explain how ERISA protects employee pensions and benefits

See the Bell South example in which Ms. Lee successfully sued for disability benefits, p. 864.

See the discussion of defined contribution plans and defined benefit plans on p. 865.

D. Unemployment Benefits, Family Leaves, and Social Security

L0.6 Explain the essentials of unemployment benefits, family and medical leaves, military leaves, and social security benefits

E. Employees' Health and Safety

L0.7 Explain how OSHA is designed to ensure workers safe and healthful working conditions

See the Thinking Things Through discussion for reasons why taking chances or shortcuts in violation of OSHA standards is bad management, p. 871.

F. Compensation for Employees' Injuries

L0.8 Explain the three types of benefits provided by Workers' Compensation statutes

G. Employee Privacy

L0.9 Explain the sources of privacy rights, and applications to telephone, e-mail, text-messaging, and property searches

H. Employer-Related Immigration Laws

L0.10 Explain an employer's verification obligations when hiring new employees and discuss special hiring programs allowing aliens to work in the United States

See the Brazilian Quality Stones example of a CEO who did not meet his burden of proof that his responsibilities were "primarily managerial," p. 879.

KEY TERMS

defined benefit plan
defined contribution plan
economic strikers
employment-at-will doctrine

mass picketing
Pension Benefit Guaranty
  Corporation (PBGC)
primary picketing

right-to-work laws
secondary picketing
shop right

QUESTIONS AND CASE PROBLEMS

1. What remedies does an employee who has been wrongfully discharged have against an employer?

2. Michael Smyth was an operations manager at Pillsbury Co., and his employment status was that of an employee at will. Smyth received certain e-mail messages at home, and he replied to his supervisor by e-mail. His messages contained some provocative language including the phrase "kill the backstabbing bastards" and a reference to an upcoming company party as the "Jim Jones Koolaid affair." Later, Smyth was given two weeks' notice of his termination, and he was told that his e-mail remarks were inappropriate and unprofessional. Smyth believes that he is the victim of invasion of privacy because the e-mail messages caused his termination, and the company had promised that e-mail communications would not be intercepted and used as a basis for discipline or discharge. The company denies that it intercepted the e-mail messages and points out that Smyth himself sent the unprofessional comments to his supervisor. Is Smyth entitled to reinstatement and back pay because of the invasion of privacy? [*Smyth v. Pillsbury Co.*, 914 F. Supp. 97 (E.D. Pa.)]

3. Michael Hauck claimed that he was discharged by his employer, Sabine Pilot Service, because he refused its direction to perform the illegal act of pumping the bilges of the employer's vessel into the waterways. Hauck was an employee at will, and Sabine contends that it therefore had the right to discharge him without having to show cause. Hauck brought a wrongful discharge action against Sabine. Decide. [*Sabine Pilot Service, Inc., v. Hauck*, 687 S.W.2d 733 (Tex.)]

4. Jeanne Eenkhoorn worked as a supervisor at a business office for the New York Telephone Co. While at work, she invented a process for terminating the telephone services of delinquent subscribers. The telephone company used the process but refused to compensate her for it, claiming a shop right. Eenkhoorn then sued for damages on a quasi-contract theory. Decide. [*Eenkhoorn v. New York Telephone Co.*, 568 N.Y. S.2d 677]

5. One Monday, a labor organization affiliated with the International Ladies Garment Workers Union began an organizational drive among the employees of Whittal & Son. On the following Monday, six of the employees who were participating in the union drive were discharged. Immediately after the firings, the head of the company gave a speech to the remaining workers in which he made a variety of antiunion statements and threats. The union filed a complaint with the NLRB, alleging that the six employees were fired because they were engaging in organizational activity and were thus discharged in violation of the NLRA. The employer defended its position, arguing that it had a business to run and that it was barely able to survive in the global economy against cheap labor from third-world countries. It asserted that the last thing it needed was "union baloney." Was the NLRA violated?

6. David Stark submitted an application to the maintenance department of Wyman-Gordon Co. Stark was a journeyman millwright with nine years' experience at a neighboring company at the time of his application to Wyman-Gordon. Stark was vice president of the local industrial workers' union. In his preliminary interview with

the company, Ms. Peevler asked if Stark was involved in union activity, and Stark detailed his involvement to her. She informed Stark that Wyman-Gordon was a nonunion shop and asked how he felt about this. Peevler's notes from the interview characterize Stark's response to this question as "seems to lean toward third-party intervention." Company officials testified that Stark's qualifications were "exactly what we were looking for," but he was not hired. Stark claimed that he was discriminated against. Wyman-Gordon denied that any discrimination had occurred. Is a job applicant (as opposed to an employee) entitled to protection from antiunion discrimination? On the facts of this case, has any discrimination taken place? [*Wyman-Gordon Co. v. N.L.R.B.*, 108 L.R.R.M. 2085 (1st Cir.)]

7. Armenda Malone and Stephen Krantz were induced to leave other employment and join ABI's CD-ROM division as national account managers in part because of a favorable commission agreement at ABI. Their employment relationship with ABI had no set duration, and as such they were employees at will. For the first two quarters of their employment, their commission reports were approved by the president of the division and paid without incident. Thereafter, a new management team took over the division. When the mid-level manager presented third quarter commission reports based on the prior practice to the new vice president, Bruce Lowry, for approval, he was told, "You got to learn how to f— these people." Lowry then utilized severable variables—some of which the mid-level manager found "ridiculous"—to reduce the commission figures. After much discourse that carried on well into the fourth quarter, Lowry announced that a new model for determining commissions would be implemented. Commissions for both the third and fourth quarters, ending in December, were then calculated based on this model. ABI asserts that because Malone and Krantz were employees at will, the employer had the right to interpret or alter how it pays employees as it sees fit. Krantz and Malone left ABI and have sued for what they believe are the full commissions earned in the third and fourth quarters. Present a legal theory

on behalf of Malone and Krantz for the payment of back commissions. Assess the strengths and weaknesses of Lowry's approach to employee relations. How would you decide this case? [*Malone v. American Business Information, Inc.*, 647 N.W.2d 569 (Neb.)]

8. Jane Richards was employed as the sole crane operator of Gale Corp. and held the part-time union position of shop steward for the plant. On May 15, Richards complained to OSHA concerning what she contended were seven existing violations of the Occupational Safety and Health Act that were brought to her attention by members of the bargaining unit. On May 21, she stated to the company's general manager at a negotiating session: "If we don't have a new contract by the time the present one expires on June 15, we will strike." On May 22, an OSHA inspector arrived at the plant, and Richards told her supervisor, "I blew the whistle." On May 23, the company rented and later purchased two large electric forklifts that were used to do the work previously performed by the crane, and the crane operator's job was abolished. Under the existing collective bargaining contract, the company had the right to lay off for lack of work. The contract also provided for arbitration, and it prohibited discipline or discharge without "just cause." On May 23, Richards was notified that she was being laid off "for lack of work" within her classification of crane operator. She was also advised that the company was not planning on using the crane in the future and that, if she were smart, she would get another job. Richards claimed that her layoff violated the National Labor Relations Act, the Occupational Safety and Health Act, and the collective bargaining agreement. Was she correct?

9. Virgil Deemer and Thomas Cornwell, employees at a Whirlpool Corporation plant, refused to comply with a supervisor's order that they perform maintenance work on certain mesh screens located some 20 feet above the plant floor. Twelve days before a fellow employee had fallen to his death from the screens. Because they refused to do the work assigned them, they were told to punch out and go home; reprimands were placed in their files. Should employees be able to

pick and choose what work they will perform? Do Deemer and Cornwell have any recourse? [*Whirlpool v. Marshall*, 445 U.S. 1]

10. In May, the nurses union at Waterbury Hospital went on strike, and the hospital was shut down. In mid-June, the hospital began hiring replacements and gradually opened many units. To induce nurses to take employment during the strike, the hospital guaranteed replacement nurses their choice of positions and shifts. If a preferred position was in a unit that was not open at that time, the hospital guaranteed that the individual would be placed in that position at the end of the strike. The strike ended in October and as the striking workers returned to work, the hospital began opening units that had been closed during the strike. It staffed many of these positions with replacement nurses. The nurses who had the positions prior to the strike and were waiting to return to work believed that they should have been called to fill these positions rather than the junior replacements who had held other positions during the strike. Decide. [*Waterbury Hospital v. NLRB*, 950 F.2d 849 (2d Cir.)]

11. Buffo was employed by the Baltimore & Ohio Railroad. Along with a number of other workers, he was removing old brakes from railroad cars and replacing them with new brakes. In the course of the work, rivet heads and scrap from the brakes accumulated on the tracks under the cars. This debris was removed only occasionally when the workers had time. Buffo, while holding an air hammer in both arms, was crawling under a car when his foot slipped on scrap on the ground, causing him to strike and injure his knee. He sued the railroad for damages under the Federal Employers Liability Act. Decide. [*Buffo v. Baltimore & Ohio Railroad Co.*, 72 A.2d 593 (Pa.)]

12. Mark Phipps was employed as a cashier at a Clark gas station. A customer drove into the station and asked him to pump leaded gasoline into her 1976 Chevrolet, an automobile equipped to receive only unleaded gasoline. The station manager told Phipps to comply with the request, but he refused, believing that his dispensing leaded gasoline into the gas tank was a

violation of law. Phipps stated that he was willing to pump unleaded gas into the tank, but the manager immediately fired him. Phipps sued Clark for wrongful termination. Clark contended that it was free to terminate Phipps, an employee at will, for any reason or no reason. Decide. [*Phipps v. Clark Oil & Refining Corp.*, 396 N.W.2d 588 (Minn. App.)]

13. Reno, Nevada, police officers John Bohach and Jon Catalano communicated with each other on the Alphapage computer system, typing messages on a keyboard and sending them to each other by use of a "send" key. The computer dials a commercial paging company, which receives the message by modem, and the message is then sent to the person paged by radio broadcast. When the system was installed, the police chief warned that every Alphapage message was logged on the network, and he barred messages that were critical of department policy or discriminatory. The two police officers sought to block a department investigation into their messages and prevent disclosure of the messages' content. They claimed that the messages should be treated the same as telephone calls under federal wiretap law. The department contended that the system was essentially a form of e-mail whose messages are by definition stored in a computer, and the storage was itself not part of the communication. Was the federal wiretap law violated? [*Bohach v. City of Reno*, 932 F. Supp. 1232 (D. Nev.)]

14. Michael Kittell was employed at Vermont Weatherboard. While operating a saw at the plant, Kittell was seriously injured when a splinter flew into his eye and penetrated his head. Kittell sued Vermont Weatherboard, seeking damages under a common law theory. His complaint alleged that he suffered severe injuries solely because of the employer's wanton and willful acts and omissions. The complaint stated that he was an inexperienced worker, put to work without instructions or warning on a saw from which the employer had stripped away all safety devices. Vermont Weatherboard made a motion to dismiss the complaint on the ground that the Workers' Compensation Act provided the exclusive remedy for his injury. Decide. [*Kittell v. Vermont Weatherboard, Inc.*, 417 A.2d 926 (Vt.)]

© Manuel Gutjahr/iStockphoto.com

CHAPTER 40

Equal Employment Opportunity Law

learningoutcomes

After studying this chapter, you should be able to

LO.1 Explain the difference between the *disparate treatment* theory of employment discrimination and the *disparate impact* theory of employment discrimination

LO.2 List and explain the categories of individuals protected against unlawful employment discrimination under Title VII

LO.3 Recognize, and know the remedies for, sexual harassment in the workplace

LO.4 Explain the antiretaliation provision of Title VII

LO.5 List and explain the laws protecting equal pay for women and men for equal work, as well as the laws forbidding discrimination on the basis of age and against individuals with disabilities

LO.6 Explain how both Title VII of the Civil Rights Act and the ADA protect from discrimination U.S. citizens working in foreign countries for American-owned and American-controlled businesses

L aws of the United States reflect our society's concern that all Americans, including minorities, women, and persons with disabilities, have equal employment opportunities and that the workplace is free from discrimination and harassment. Title VII of the Civil Rights Act of 1964, as amended in 1972, 1978, and 1991, is the principal law regulating equal employment opportunities in the United States. Other federal laws require equal pay for men and women doing substantially the same work and forbid discrimination because of age or disability.

CPA A. Title VII of the Civil Rights Act of 1964, as Amended

Title VII of the Civil Rights Act of 1964[1] seeks to eliminate employer and union practices that discriminate against employees and job applicants on the basis of race, color, religion, sex, or national origin. The law applies to the hiring process and to discipline, discharge, promotion, and benefits.

1. Theories of Discrimination

The Supreme Court has created, and the Civil Rights Act of 1991 has codified, two principal legal theories under which a plaintiff may prove a case of unlawful employment discrimination: disparate treatment and disparate impact.

A *disparate treatment* claim exists where an employer treats some individuals less favorably than others because of their race, color, religion, sex, or national origin. Proof of the employer's discriminatory motive is essential in a disparate treatment case.[2]

Disparate impact exists when an employer's facially neutral employment practices, such as hiring or promotion examinations, although neutrally applied and making no adverse reference to race, color, religion, sex, or national origin, have a significantly adverse or disparate impact on a protected group. In addition, the employment practice in question is not shown by the employer to be job related and consistent with business necessity. Under the disparate impact theory, it is not a defense for an employer to demonstrate that it did not intend to discriminate.

For Example, if plant manager Jones is heard telling the personnel director that the vacant welder's position should be filled by a male because "this is man's work," a qualified female applicant turned down for the job would prevail in a *disparate treatment* theory case against the employer because she was not hired because of her gender. Necessary evidence of the employer's discriminatory motive would be satisfied by testimony about the manager's "this is man's work" statement.

If the policy for hiring new pilots at Generic Airlines, Inc., required a minimum height of 5 feet 7 inches, and no adverse reference to gender was stated in this

---

[1] 42 U.S.C. §2000(e) *et seq.*
[2] *Woodson v. Scott Paper Co.,* 109 F.3d 913 (3d Cir. 1997).

employment policy, nevertheless, the 5-feet-7-inch minimum height policy has an adverse or disparate impact on women because far fewer women than men reach this height. Such an employment policy would be set aside on a *disparate impact* theory, and a minimum height for the position would be established by the court based on evidence of job-relatedness and business necessity. A 5-feet-5-inch height requirement was set by one court for pilots.

CASE SUMMARY
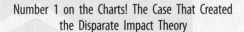

Number 1 on the Charts! The Case That Created the Disparate Impact Theory

FACTS: Griggs and other black employees of the Duke Power Company's Dan River Station challenged Duke Power's requirement of a high school diploma and passing standardized general intelligence tests for transfer to more desirable "inside" jobs. The district court and Court of Appeals found no violation of Title VII because the employer did not adopt the diploma and test requirements with the purpose of intentionally discriminating against black employees. The Supreme Court granted *certiorari*.

DECISION: Judgment for Griggs. The absence of any intent on the part of the employer to discriminate was not a defense. Title VII prohibits not only overt discrimination but also practices that are fair in form but discriminatory in operation. If any employment practice, such as a diploma or testing requirement, that operates to exclude minorities at a substantially higher rate than white applicants cannot be shown to be "job-related" and consistent with "business necessity," the practice is prohibited. [*Griggs v. Duke Power Co.*, 401 U.S. 424 (1971)]

"Disparate treatment" and "disparate impact" may both be at issue in the same case. **For Example,** as required by the city charter, the city of New Haven used objective examinations to identify those firefighters best qualified for promotion to fill vacant lieutenant and captain positions. On the basis of the examinations' results, no black candidates were eligible for immediate promotion. A rancorous public debate ensued. The city threw out the results based on the statistical racial disparity to avoid potential liability in a lawsuit based on *disparate impact* against the black candidates. White and Hispanic firefighters who passed the exams but were denied a chance for promotion by the city's refusal to certify the test results, sued the city, alleging a *disparate treatment* (intentional discrimination) case—that discarding the test results discriminated against them based on their race in violation of Title VII. The Supreme Court determined that the city rejected the test results because the higher-scoring candidates were white and that without some other justification this express race-based decision making is prohibited. The Court stated that "a strong basis in evidence" standard was necessary before the city could make an employment decision based on fear of liability under Title VII—and the Court held that the city did not meet this standard. The statistical disparity by itself was insufficient to constitute a strong basis in evidence of unlawful disparate impact. The examinations were job related and consistent with business necessity. And there was no strong basis in evidence of an equally valid, less-discriminating testing alternative. Thus, in a 5-4 decision, the U.S. Supreme Court ruled that the city had violated the civil rights of the white and Hispanic firefighters and remanded the case for further proceedings.[3]

2. The Equal Employment Opportunity Commission

The Equal Employment Opportunity Commission (EEOC) is a five-member body appointed by the president to establish equal employment opportunity policy under the laws it administers. The EEOC supervises the agency's conciliation and enforcement efforts.

The EEOC administers Title VII of the Civil Rights Act, the Equal Pay Act (EPA), the Age Discrimination in Employment Act (ADEA), Section 501 of the Rehabilitation Act (which prohibits federal-sector discrimination against persons with disabilities), and Title I (the employment provisions) of the Americans with Disabilities Act (ADA).

(A) PROCEDURE. Where a state or local EEO agency with the power to act on claims of discriminatory practices exists, the charging party must file a complaint with that agency. The charging party must wait 60 days or until the termination of the state proceedings, whichever occurs first, before filing a charge with the EEOC. If no state or local agency exists, a charge may be filed directly with the EEOC so long as it is filed within 180 days of the occurrence of the discriminatory act. The commission conducts an investigation to determine whether reasonable cause exists to believe that the charge is true. If such cause is found to exist, the EEOC attempts to remedy the unlawful practice through conciliation. If the EEOC does not resolve the matter to the satisfaction of the parties, it may decide to litigate the case when systemic or unusual circumstances exist, including a "pattern or practice of discrimination." In most instances, however, the EEOC issues the charging party a *right-to-sue letter*. Thereafter, the individual claiming a violation of EEO law has 90 days to file a lawsuit in a federal district court.[4]

(1) Pattern-or-Practice Cases.

Section 707 of Title VII permits the EEOC to sue employers when it has reasonable cause to believe they are engaged in a *pattern or practice* of unlawful employment discrimination. It must establish that intentional discrimination was the defendant employer's "standard operating procedure." A first phase focuses on the employer's policy or practice, not on individual charges. Once the pattern or practice of discrimination is established, the process moves to the individual relief phase, where individual claims may be presented. The purpose of Section 707 is to provide the government with a swift and effective weapon to eliminate unlawful practices.[5]

---

[3] *Ricci v. DeStefano*, 557 U.S. 557 (2009). Contrary to the extensive presentation in the majority decision of the detailed steps taken to develop and administer the examinations, the dissent asserted that the Court had ignored substantial evidence of multiple flaws in the tests and that the Court had failed to acknowledge that better tests used in other cities have yielded less racially skewed outcomes. The decision, the dissent, and two concurrences provide an insight into the complexities of our judicial process.

[4] An individual who misses the filing deadline of Title VII may be able to bring a race discrimination case under the two-year time limit allowed under Section 1981 of the Civil Rights Act of 1964, codified at 42 U.S.C. §1981, and sometimes called a *Section 1981 lawsuit*. In the *Edelman v. Lynchburg College* decision, 535 U.S. 106 (2002), the U.S. Supreme Court approved an EEOC regulation that allows certain defective charges to be cured, with the cured charge relating back to the date the EEOC first received the initial charge, which was within the 300-day filing period.

[5] See *EEOC v. Mitsubishi Motor Manufacturing of America*, 102 F.3d 869 (7th Cir. 1996).

(2) Systemic "Class Action" Cases.

The EEOC has placed renewed focus on identifying, developing, and litigating discrimination cases involving employment policies affecting large classes of individuals in every statute enforced by the agency. When an individual files a discrimination charge with the EEOC, it now may expand its investigation into that employer's related employment practices involving similarly situated individuals. Possible statutory violations discovered during the course of the investigation of the initial individual charge may lead to the EEOC bringing a "systemic" case on behalf of a number of employees against the employer under Section 706 of the Act. However, before bringing the action to court under Section 706 the EEOC itself must conduct an investigation of each individual charge that is filed and if reasonable cause is found, the agency must provide the employer an opportunity to conciliate each individual case.[6]

(B) **DAMAGES.** Title VII sets damages available to victims of discrimination (see Figure 40-1).

Section 706(k) of Title VII provides that the court in its discretion allow the prevailing party, other than the EEOC and the United States, a reasonable attorneys' fee. Thus, a court may award a prevailing individual in a Civil Rights Act lawsuit against an employer reasonable attorney fees and costs. It also may award attorneys' fees against the EEOC itself if the agency's lawsuit is without foundation.

For Example, in *EEOC v. Peoplemark*, the federal district court awarded a temporary staffing firm, Peoplemark, the prevailing party in a lawsuit initiated by the EEOC, attorneys' fees, expert witness fees, and other expenses totaling $751,942.48, because the EEOC should have known at a certain point that there was no evidence supporting its complaint that the company maintained a policy adversely affecting a class of African Americans of denying employment to any person with a criminal record.[7]

(C) **THE ARBITRATION OPTION.** With the exception of transportation employees, employers can craft arbitration agreements that require employees to arbitrate any employment dispute, including statutory discrimination claims, and these mandatory arbitration clauses can be enforced in federal courts under the Federal Arbitration Act.[8] Courts do, however, require that the arbitration clauses be "fair." Moreover, a party agreeing to arbitration does not forgo substantive rights afforded by Title VII or alter federal antidiscrimination statutes. A fair arbitration clause requires adequate discovery, mandates that the arbitrator have authority to apply the same types of relief available from a court, and should not preclude an employee from vindicating statutory rights because of arbitration costs.[9]

A union may negotiate a provision in a collective bargaining agreement requiring all employment-related discrimination claims to be resolved in arbitration.[10]

[6] See *EEOC v. CRST Van Expedited, Inc.*, 679 F.3d 657 (8th Cir. 2012).
[7] *EEOC v. Peoplemark*, 2010 WL 748250 (W.D. Mich. Feb. 26, 2010).
[8] *Circuit City Stores, Inc. v. Adams*, 532 U.S. 105 (2001).
[9] See *Circuit City II*, 279 F.3d 889 (9th Cir. 2002).
[10] For some 35 years it was widely understood that an individual may prospectively waive his or her own statutory right to a judicial forum and be compelled to resolve a statutory discrimination claim in arbitration, but a union may not prospectively waive that right for the individual in a collective bargaining agreement. See *Alexander v. Gardner-Denver Co.*, 485 U.S. 36 (1974) and *Gilmer v. Interstate/Johnson Lane Corp.*, 500 U.S. 20 (1991). In *14 Penn Plaza, LLC v. Pyett*, 556 U.S. 247 (2009), the U.S. Supreme Court, in a 5-4 decision, held that a provision in a collective bargaining agreement (CBA) negotiated under the National Labor Relations Act between a union and employer group that requires union members to arbitrate Age Discrimination in Employment Act (ADEA) claims is enforceable as a matter of federal law. Thus, the petitioner union members were precluded from bringing their ADEA case in federal court and the matter had to be resolved under the arbitration provisions of the CBA.

| FIGURE 40-1 | *Unlawful Discrimination under Title VII of the Civil Rights Act of 1964 as Amended by the Civil Rights Act of 1991* |

DISCRIMINATORY TREATMENT IN EMPLOYMENT DECISIONS ON THE BASIS OF RACE, COLOR, RELIGION, SEX, OR NATIONAL ORIGIN

DISPARATE TREATMENT THEORY	DISPARATE IMPACT THEORY
NONNEUTRAL PRACTICE OR NONNEUTRAL APPLICATION	FACIALLY NEUTRAL PRACTICE AND NEUTRAL APPLICATION
REQUIRES PROOF OF DISCRIMINATORY INTENT	DOES NOT REQUIRE PROOF OF DISCRIMINATORY INTENT REQUIRES PROOF OF ADVERSE EFFECT ON PROTECTED GROUP AND EMPLOYER IS UNABLE TO SHOW THAT THE CHALLENGED PRACTICE IS JOB RELATED FOR THE POSITION IN QUESTION AND IS CONSISTENT WITH BUSINESS NECESSITY
EITHER PARTY HAS A RIGHT TO REQUIRE A JURY TRIAL WHEN SEEKING COMPENSATORY OR PUNITIVE DAMAGES	NO RIGHT TO A JURY TRIAL
REMEDY REINSTATEMENT, HIRING, OR PROMOTION BACK PAY LESS INTERIM EARNINGS RETROACTIVE SENIORITY ATTORNEY AND EXPERT WITNESS FEES PLUS COMPENSATORY* AND PUNITIVE DAMAGES DAMAGES CAPPED FOR CASES OF SEX AND RELIGIOUS DISCRIMINATION DEPENDING ON SIZE OF EMPLOYER:	REMEDY REINSTATEMENT, HIRING, OR PROMOTION BACK PAY LESS INTERIM EARNINGS RETROACTIVE SENIORITY ATTORNEY AND EXPERT WITNESS FEES

NUMBER OF EMPLOYEES	DAMAGES CAP
100 OR FEWER	$ 50,000
101 TO 200	100,000
201 TO 500	200,000
OVER 500	300,000
NO CAP ON DAMAGES FOR RACE CASES	

* COMPENSATORY DAMAGES INCLUDE FUTURE PECUNIARY LOSSES AND NONPECUNIARY LOSSES SUCH AS EMOTIONAL PAIN AND SUFFERING.

B. Protected Classes and Exceptions

To successfully pursue a Title VII lawsuit, an individual must belong to a protected class and meet the appropriate burden of proof. Exceptions exist for certain employment practices.

3. Race and Color

The legislative history of Title VII of the Civil Rights Act demonstrates that a primary purpose of the act is to provide fair employment opportunities for black Americans. The protections of the act are applied to blacks based on race or color.

The word *race* as used in the act applies to all members of the four major racial groupings: white, black, Native American, and Asian-Pacific. Native Americans can file charges and receive the protection of the act on the basis of national origin, race, or, in some instances, color. Individuals of Asian-Pacific origin may file discrimination charges based on race, color, or, in some instances, national origin. Whites are also protected against discrimination because of race and color.

For Example, two white professors at a predominately black university were successful in discrimination suits against the university when it was held that the university had discriminated against them on the basis of race and color in tenure decisions.[11]

4. Religion

Title VII requires employers to accommodate their employees' or prospective employees' religious practices. Most cases involving allegations of religious discrimination revolve around the determination of whether an employer has made reasonable efforts to accommodate religious beliefs.

If an employee's religious beliefs prohibit working on Saturday, an employer's obligation under Title VII is to try to find a volunteer to cover for the employee on Saturdays. The employer would not have an obligation to violate a seniority provision of a collective bargaining agreement or call in a substitute worker if such accommodation would require more than a *de minimis* or very small cost.

(A) GARMENTS WORN FOR RELIGIOUS REASONS. Ordinarily employers have little reason to be informed or concerned about the religious practices of individual employees. However, because many Muslim women wear special clothing as part of their religious observances, which may conflict with an employer's safety or grooming standards, employers should develop appropriate and justifiable policies for their business and provide training for supervisors on how to properly handle requests for religious accommodations. **For Example,** a federal district court ruled in favor of a Muslim employee who was terminated for refusal to remove her head scarf when dealing with customers, where the employer did not strictly enforce its "company uniform policy" until after September 11, 2001. The court did not accept the employer's argument that allowing an exception for the employee would lead to the need for many other exceptions, making its company uniform policy meaningless.[12]

Safety risks may provide a justifiable basis for a dress code. **For Example,** a court ruled that Kelly Services did not discriminate against a Muslim woman when it decided not to refer her to a client company, Nahan Printing, because she wears a khimar. She had been informed by a Kelly staffing supervisor that "you would have to take your scarf off—you cannot cover your hair," and the applicant replied that she could not remove her khimar because her religion required her to wear it. The EEOC asserted that the employer could have reasonably accommodated her by

[11] *Turgeon v. Howard University*, 571 F. Supp. 679 (D.D.C. 1983).
[12] *EEOC v. Alamo Rent-A-Car*, 432 F. Supp. 2d 1006 (D. Ariz. 2006).

allowing her to tie her khimar back like people with long hair are allowed to do. However, the Nahan Printing executive explained that hair is permanent; a khimar is different from hair because of the risk that the khimar—like a hat—could fall off into the machinery; and the safety risk would be the worker reaching in and trying to grab it, pulling an individual into a piece of equipment or damaging equipment, or other individuals who are trying to help could potentially be hurt as well.[13]

(B) BODY ART WORK RULES AND RELIGIOUS BELIEFS. Employees have challenged employer bans on body art as religious discrimination, asserting that the employers have not made reasonable efforts to accommodate religious beliefs. EEOC's 1980 Guidelines broadly define religion "to include moral or ethical beliefs as to what is right and wrong which are sincerely held with the strength of traditional religious views."[14] The Guidelines do not limit religion to theistic practices or to beliefs professed by organized religions. **For Example,** Kimberly Cloutier was a member of the Church of Body Modification. Costco's grooming policy prohibited any "visible facial or tongue jewelry" in order to present a professional image to its customers. Ms. Cloutier wore an eyebrow ring as a religious practice. Ms. Cloutier rejected Costco's offer to return her to work if she wore a bandage or plastic retainer over the jewelry because it would violate her religious beliefs. The U.S. Court of Appeals determined that her refusal to accept an accommodation short of an exemption was an undue hardship for the employer because an exemption would negatively impact the company's policy of professionalism.[15]

Some courts, however, look for actual proof of harm to the employer in assessing whether undue hardship exists for an employer. **For Example,** the EEOC brought an action against Red Robin Gourmet Burgers, Inc., for failure to provide an exemption from its grooming policy for an employee's religious tattoos surrounding his wrists. The federal district court looked for actual proof of the restaurant's assertion that the tattoos contravened the company's "family-oriented image," such as customer complaints or other evidence, as opposed to the mere assertion. The court concluded that the employer failed to provide sufficient evidence of undue hardship in accommodating an exemption for the employee.[16]

Title VII permits religious societies to grant hiring preferences in favor of members of their religion. It also provides an exemption for educational institutions to hire employees of a particular religion if the institution is owned, controlled, or managed by a particular religious society. The exemption is a broad one and is not restricted to the religious activities of the institution.

5. Sex

Employers who discriminate against female or male employees because of their sex are held to be in violation of Title VII. The EEOC and the courts have determined that the word *sex* as used in Title VII means a person's gender, not the person's sexual orientation. State and local legislation, however, may provide specific protection against discrimination based on sexual orientation.

---

[13] *EEOC v. Kelly Services, Inc.*, 598 F.3d 1022 (8th Cir. 2010).
[14] 29 C.F.R. §1605.1 (1980). The EEOC's definition of religion was derived from early Selective Service cases that moved beyond institutional religions and theistic belief structures in handling exemptions to the draft and military service. See *Welsh v. U.S.*, 398 U.S. 333, 343-44 (1970), which allows for expansion of belief systems to include nonreligious ethical or moral codes.
[15] *Cloutier v. Costco*, 390 F.3d 126 (1st Cir. 2004).
[16] *EEOC v. Red Robin Gourmet Burger, Inc.*, 2005 WL 2090677 (W.D. Wash. Aug. 29, 2005).

(A) Height, Weight, and Physical Ability Requirements. Under the *Griggs v. Duke Power* precedent, an employer must be able to show that criteria used to make an employment decision that has a disparate impact on women, such as minimum height and weight requirements, are in fact job related. All candidates for a position requiring physical strength must be given an opportunity to demonstrate their capability to perform the work. Women cannot be precluded from consideration just because they have not traditionally performed such work.

(B) Pregnancy-Related Benefits. Title VII was amended by the Pregnancy Discrimination Act (PDA) in 1978. The amendment prevents employers from treating pregnancy, childbirth, and related medical conditions in a manner different from the manner in which other medical conditions are treated. Thus, women unable to work as a result of pregnancy, childbirth, or related medical conditions must be provided the same benefits as all other workers. These include temporary and long-term disability insurance, sick leave, and other forms of employee benefit programs. An employer who does not provide disability benefits or paid sick leave to other employees is not required to provide them for pregnant workers.[17]

The PDA also protects women from termination or other employment actions because of pregnancy. **For Example,** a catering manager who informed her employer that she would be taking a 12-week leave after childbirth, during the busiest time of the year, and was subsequently fired by her employer for "customer complaints," was able to bring suit against the employer under the PDA, where the employer's reason was a "pretext."[18]

6. Sexual Harassment

Tangible employment action and hostile work environment are two classifications of sexual harassment.

(A) Tangible Employment Action. Sexual harassment classified as *tangible employment action* involves situations in which a supervisor performs an "official act" of the enterprise, such as discharge, demotion, or undesirable reassignment against a subordinate employee because of the employee's refusal to submit to the supervisor's demand for sexual favors. The employer is always vicariously liable for this harassment by a supervisor under the so-called aided-in-the-agency-relation standard. That is, the supervisor is aided in accomplishing the wrongful objective by the existence of the agency relationship. The employer empowered the supervisor as a distinct class of agent to make economic decisions affecting other employees under the supervisor's control. The employer can raise no affirmative defense based on the presence of an employer's antiharassment policy in such a case.

(B) Hostile Work Environment. A second type of sexual harassment classified as *hostile work environment* occurs when a supervisor's conduct does not affect an employee's economic benefits but causes anxiety and "poisons" the work environment for the employee. Such conduct may include unwelcome sexual flirtation, propositions, or

[17] In *AT&T Corporation v. Hulteen*, 556 U.S. 701 (2009), the U.S. Supreme Court addressed a current effect of a pre-PDA personnel policy. Prior to the PDA of 1978, AT&T employees on "disability" leave received full-service credit towards retirement benefits for the entire period of absence. Pregnancy at that time was considered a "personal" leave of absence and women on this leave received a maximum service credit of 30 days. Upon retirement, Noreen Hulteen received seven months less service credit for the pre-PDA leave for a pregnancy than she would have had for the same leave time for a disability, and it resulted in a smaller pension benefit. The Court decided against Ms. Hulteen, determining that there was no intent to apply the PDA retroactively, and that AT&T's pre-PDA leave policy was not discriminatory when adopted.
[18] *Newman v. Deer Path Inn*, 1999 WL 1129105 (N.D. Ill. Nov. 7, 1999).

other abuses of a sexual nature, including the use of degrading words or the display of sexually explicit pictures.[19] This type of sexual harassment applies to all cases involving supervisors in which the enterprise takes no official act, including constructive discharge cases. The plaintiff must prove severe and pervasive conduct on the supervisor's part to meet the plaintiff's burden of proof.[20] The employer may raise an affirmative defense to liability for damages by proving that (1) it exercised reasonable care to prevent and promptly correct any sexually harassing behavior at its workplace and (2) the plaintiff employee unreasonably failed to take advantage of corrective opportunities provided by the employer. The existence of an employer's sexual harassment policy and notification procedures (see Figure 40-2) will aid the employer in proving the affirmative defense in hostile working environment cases.

(c) RATIONALE. The "primary objective of Title VII, like that of any statute meant to influence primary conduct, is not to provide redress but to avoid harm."[21] When there is no "official act" of the employer, the employer may raise an affirmative defense. This approach fosters the preventative aspect of Title VII, encouraging employers to exercise reasonable care to prevent and correct sexual harassment while providing damages only when the conduct is clearly attributed to an official action of the enterprise or when the employer has not exercised reasonable care to prevent and correct misconduct. **For Example,** Kim Ellerth alleged that she was subject to constant sexual harassment by her supervisor, Ted Slowik, at Burlington Industries. Slowik made comments about her breasts, told her to "loosen up," and warned, "You know, Kim, I could make your life very hard or very easy at Burlington." When Kim was being considered for promotion, Slowik expressed reservations that she was not "loose enough" and then reached over and rubbed her knee. She received the promotion, however. After other such incidents, she quit and filed charges alleging that she was constructively discharged because of the unendurable working conditions resulting from the hostile work environment created by Slowik. She did not use Burlington's sexual harassment internal complaint procedures. Because she was not a victim of a tangible employment action involving an official act of the enterprise, because she received the promotion sought, the employer will be able to raise an affirmative defense. She will be able to prove severe and pervasive conduct on the part of a supervisor under a hostile work environment theory. However, the employer may defeat liability by proving both that it exercised reasonable care to prevent and correct sexual harassing behavior through its internal company complaint policies and that Kim unreasonably failed to take advantage of the company procedures.[22]

(d) NONSUPERVISORS. An employer is liable for the sexual harassment caused its employees by coworkers or customers only when it knew or should have known of the misconduct and failed to take prompt remedial action.

---

[19] According to EEOC Guidelines §1604.11(f), unwelcome sexual advances, requests for sexual favors, and other verbal or physical conduct of a sexual nature constitute sexual harassment when (1) submission to or rejection of such conduct has the purpose or effect of unreasonably interfering with an individual's work performance or creating an intimidating, hostile, or offensive working environment.

[20] *Oncale v. Sundowner Offshore Services, Inc.,* 523 U.S. 75 (1998). The Supreme Court stated in *Oncale* that it did not intend to turn Title VII into a civility code, and the Court set forth the standard for judging whether the conduct in question amounted to sexual harassment requiring that the conduct be judged from the perspective of a reasonable person in the plaintiff's position, considering all circumstances. The Court warned that "common sense" and "context" must apply in determining whether the conduct was hostile or abusive.

[21] *Faragher v. City of Boca Raton,* 524 U.S. 775, 805 (1998) (citing *Albemale Paper Co. v. Moody,* 422 U.S. 405, 418 (1975)).

[22] *Burlington Industries, Inc. v. Ellerth,* 524 U.S. 742 (1998); see also *Faragher v. City of Boca Raton,* 524 U.S. 775 (1998). In *Pennsylvania v. Suders,* 542 U.S. 129 (2004), the U.S. Supreme Court reviewed a decision of the Third Circuit Court of Appeals that held that a "constructive discharge," if proved, constituted a "tangible employment action" that renders the employer liable for damages and precludes an affirmative defense. The Supreme Court disagreed with the Third Circuit's reading of its *Ellerth/Faragher* decisions, and made it very clear that "an official act of the enterprise" is necessary for the plaintiff to defeat the employer's right to raise an affirmative defense.

FIGURE 40-2	*Employer Procedure—Sexual Harassment*

A. DEVELOP AND IMPLEMENT AN EQUAL EMPLOYMENT POLICY THAT SPECIFICALLY PROHIBITS SEXUAL HARASSMENT AND IMPOSES DISCIPLINE UP TO AND INCLUDING DISCHARGE. SET FORTH SPECIFIC EXAMPLES OF CONDUCT THAT WILL NOT BE TOLERATED SUCH AS:

  • UNWELCOME SEXUAL ADVANCES, WHETHER OR NOT THEY INVOLVE PHYSICAL TOUCHING

  • SEXUAL EPITHETS AND JOKES; WRITTEN OR ORAL REFERENCES TO SEXUAL CONDUCT; GOSSIP REGARDING ONE'S SEX LIFE; COMMENTS ON AN INDIVIDUAL'S BODY; AND COMMENTS ABOUT AN INDIVIDUAL'S SEXUAL ACTIVITY, DEFICIENCIES, OR PROWESS

  • DISPLAY OF SEXUALLY SUGGESTIVE OBJECTS, PICTURES, AND CARTOONS

  • UNWELCOME LEERING, WHISTLING, BRUSHING AGAINST THE BODY, SEXUAL GESTURES, AND SUGGESTIVE OR INSULTING COMMENTS

  • INQUIRIES INTO ONE'S SEXUAL EXPERIENCES

  • DISCUSSION OF ONE'S SEXUAL ACTIVITIES

B. ESTABLISH ONGOING EDUCATIONAL PROGRAMS, INCLUDING ROLE-PLAYING AND FILMS TO DEMONSTRATE UNACCEPTABLE BEHAVIOR.

C. DESIGNATE A RESPONSIBLE SENIOR OFFICIAL TO WHOM COMPLAINTS OF SEXUAL HARASSMENT CAN BE MADE. AVOID ANY PROCEDURE THAT REQUIRES AN EMPLOYEE TO FIRST COMPLAIN TO THE EMPLOYEE'S SUPERVISOR, BECAUSE THAT INDIVIDUAL MAY BE THE OFFENDING PERSON. MAKE CERTAIN COMPLAINANTS KNOW THAT THERE WILL BE NO RETALIATION FOR FILING A COMPLAINT.

D. INVESTIGATE ALL COMPLAINTS PROMPTLY AND THOROUGHLY.

E. KEEP COMPLAINTS AND INVESTIGATIONS AS CONFIDENTIAL AS POSSIBLE AND LIMIT ALL INFORMATION TO ONLY THOSE WHO NEED TO KNOW.

F. IF A COMPLAINT HAS MERIT, IMPOSE APPROPRIATE AND CONSISTENT DISCIPLINE.

7. Protection against Retaliation

Section 704(a) sets forth Title VII's antiretaliation provision in the following terms:

> It shall be an unlawful practice for an employer to discriminate against any of his employees or applicants for employment … because he has opposed any practice made an unlawful employment practice by this subchapter [*the opposition clause*], or because he has made a charge, testified, assisted, or participated in any manner in an investigation, proceeding, or hearing under this subchapter [*the participation clause*].

Some U.S. courts of appeals had held that the retaliation provisions set forth in Section 704(a) of Title VII apply only to retaliation that takes the form of "ultimate employment actions" such as demotions, suspensions, and terminations and do not apply to ministerial matters such as reprimands and poor evaluations. The EEOC believed that the statute prohibits any adverse treatment that is based on a retaliatory motive and is reasonably likely to deter the charging party or others from engaging in protected activity. In *Burlington Northern v. White* (*Burlington*) the Supreme Court held that a plaintiff may pursue a retaliation claim under Title VII if the "employer's challenged action would have been material to a reasonable employee" and likely would have "dissuaded a reasonable worker from making or supporting a charge of discrimination."[23] By focusing on the materiality of the challenged action and the perspective of a reasonable person, this standard was designed to screen out trivial conduct while capturing those acts that are likely to dissuade employees from complaining or assisting in complaints about discrimination.

CASE SUMMARY
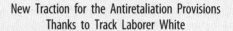

New Traction for the Antiretaliation Provisions
Thanks to Track Laborer White

FACTS: BNSF Railway hired Shelia White as a track laborer at its Tennessee Yard. She was the only woman in the track department. When hired, she was given the job of operating forklifts as opposed to doing ordinary track labor tasks. Three months after being hired, she complained to the roadmaster that her foreman treated her differently than male employees and had twice made inappropriate remarks. The foreman was suspended without pay for 10 days and ordered to attend training on sexual harassment. Also at that time, the roadmaster reassigned the forklift duties to the former operator who was "senior" to White and assigned White to track labor duties. Six months into her employment, White refused to ride in a truck as directed by a different foreman, and she was suspended for insubordination. Thirty-seven days later, she was reinstated with full back pay, and the discipline was removed from her record. She filed a complaint with the EEOC, claiming that the reassignment to track laborer duties was unlawful gender discrimination and retaliation for her complaint about her treatment by the foreman. The 37-day suspension led to a second retaliation charge. A jury rejected her gender discrimination claim and awarded her compensatory damages for her retaliation claims. BNSF appealed, contending that Ms. White had been hired as a track laborer and it was not retaliatory to assign her to do the work she was hired to do. It also asserted that the 37-day suspension had been corrected and she had been made whole for her loss.

DECISION: Judgment for White. The Supreme Court held that the jury could reasonably conclude that the reassignment from forklift operator to track laborer duties would have been materially adverse to a reasonable employee, thus constituting retaliatory discrimination. Moreover, the Court held that an indefinite suspension without pay for a month, even if the employee later received back pay, could well act as a deterrent to filing a discrimination complaint. [*Burlington Northern Santa Fe Railway Co. v. White*, **548 U.S. 53 (2006)**]

Subsequent to the *Burlington* decision, the Supreme Court has settled the broad legal issues regarding retaliation claims under federal antidiscrimination laws, including protection of an employee who speaks out about discrimination not of her own initiative, but in answering questions during an internal investigation into rumors of sexual harassment by her supervisor[24] and also providing a "zone of interest" standard for determining whether third parties' retaliation claims are protected under Title VII.[25]

---

[23] *Burlington Northern Santa Fe Railway Co. v. White*, 548 U.S.133 (2006).
[24] *Crawford v. Metropolitan Government of Nashville*, 555 U.S. 271 (2009).
[25] *Thompson v. North American Stainless, LP*, 131 S.Ct. 863 (2011).

Thinking Things Through

Retaliation – The Number One Risk for Employers

Since the Supreme Court's adoption of a broader definition of retaliation than was used in some judicial circuits prior to the *Burlington* decision, the number of retaliation charges filed with the EEOC has risen dramatically. Management-side employment lawyers see "retaliation as the number one risk for employers today." The litigation costs involved in a single retaliation case are substantial.

The source of unlawful retaliation can emanate from a CEO and other top executives down through middle managers or first-level managers, and it can also originate from organizational tolerance of coworker retaliation. Retaliation occurs in all types and sizes of organizations in all employment sectors of society.

(A) NEED FOR A COMPREHENSIVE PROGRAM. Employers must develop and implement effective antiretaliation and educational policies and procedures for their top executives, middle managers, and first-level supervisors. Additionally, each organization's highest human resource (HR) officer must have authority to independently investigate and report directly to the CEO, and have authority as well to report to an appropriate board of directors' committee regarding the business justification for proposed or actual employer actions with potential retaliation liability.*

(B) EDUCATIONAL DISCUSSION OF HUMAN NATURE AND THE COSTS OF RETALIATION. Employers must recognize that the educational effort is going to be challenging in some cases because of the "human nature" of the controversy. For instance, an employee has gone to a supervisor's supervisor, the HR department, or the EEOC, and has charged his or her

*Some employees with poor records believe that if they have filed complaints with the EEOC, they are immune from all discipline. However, these "protected" employees are not immune from discipline or discharge. The *Burkhart v. American Railcar Industries Inc.* decision, 603 F.3d 472 (8th Cir. 2010), can be used in an educational program for executives, managers, and staff to demonstrate that employees who have engaged in protected activities under Title VII are not immune from discipline or discharge for major performance issues.

supervisor with discrimination based on race, color, religion, sex, national origin, age, or disability. If the complaint is valid, the supervisor should be appropriately disciplined. It may well be that the complaint is perceived by management or coworkers as lacking merit. How can the accused supervisor or coworkers treat the complainant as though nothing has happened? Is it not human nature for the supervisor to want to take materially adverse action against that individual? Would not the ideal solution for the supervisor be to "come up with" a business basis for terminating the complainant?

The adverse economic consequences of such an action to the employer could be severe. For Example, in the Supreme Court's *Crawford v. Metropolitan Government of Nashville*** case, on remand to the district court, the employer contended that it fired Crawford for irregularities in the school system's payroll office for which Crawford was responsible. Crawford testified that she had never previously been disciplined during her 30 years of service with Metro, and local officials did not begin to investigate her job performance until after she disclosed the alleged sexual harassment by the school district's employee relations coordinator. The jury found that the reasons for firing Crawford were pretextual and awarded Crawford $420,000 in compensatory damages, $408,762 in back pay, and $727,496 in front pay, for a total monetary award of approximately $1.56 million.

THINKING THINGS THROUGH, all employees at all levels should be instructed that because of the adverse impact on the complainant-victim, the potential adverse economic consequence to the employer, and the distraction and disruption to the workforce caused by ongoing litigation, violations of the employer's no-discrimination and no-retaliation policy will been enforced with major discipline—up to and including discharge!

**555 U.S. 271 (2009).

The EEOC takes the position that claims can be filed for retaliation not only under Title VII but also under the Americans with Disabilities Act, the Age Discrimination in Employment Act, and the Equal Pay Act.

8. National Origin

Title VII protects members of all nationalities from discrimination. The judicial principles that have emerged from cases involving race, color, and gender employment discrimination are generally applicable to cases involving allegations of discrimination related to national origin. Thus, physical standards, such as minimum height requirements, that tend to exclude persons of a particular national origin because of the physical stature of the group have been found unlawful when these standards cannot be justified by business necessity.

Adverse employment action based on an individual's lack of English language skills violates Title VII when the language requirement bears no demonstrable relationship to the successful performance of the job to which it is applied.

CASE SUMMARY

A Close Call

FACTS: Manuel Fragante applied for a clerk's job with the city and county of Honolulu. Although he placed high enough on a civil service eligibility list to be chosen for the position, he was not selected because of a perceived deficiency in oral communication skills caused by his "heavy Filipino accent." Fragante brought suit, alleging that the defendants had discriminated against him on the basis of his national origin in violation of Title VII of the Civil Rights Act.

DECISION: Judgment for the city and county of Honolulu. Accents and national origin are inextricably intertwined in many cases. Courts look carefully at nonselection decisions based on foreign accents because an employer may unlawfully discriminate against someone based on national origin by falsely stating that it was the individual's inability to measure up to the communication skills demanded of the job. Because the record showed that the ability to speak clearly was one of the most important skills required for the clerk's position and because the judge confirmed that Fragante was difficult to understand, the court dismissed his complaint. [*Fragante v. City and County of Honolulu*, **888 F.2d 591 (9th Cir. 1989)**]

---

9. Title VII Exceptions

Section 703 of Title VII defines which employment activities are unlawful. This same section, however, also exempts several key practices from the scope of Title VII enforcement. The most important are the bona fide occupational qualification exception, the testing and educational requirement exception, and the seniority system exception.

(A) BONA FIDE OCCUPATIONAL QUALIFICATION EXCEPTION. It is not an unlawful employment practice for an employer to hire employees on the basis of religion, sex, or national origin in those certain instances where religion, sex, or national origin is a bona fide occupational qualification (BFOQ) reasonably necessary to the normal operation of a particular enterprise. **For Example,** a valid BFOQ is a men's clothing store's policy of hiring only males to do measurements for suit alterations. An airline's policy of hiring only female flight attendants is not a valid BFOQ because such a policy is not reasonably necessary to safely operate an airline.

CASE SUMMARY

It's a Woman's Choice

FACTS: Johnson Controls, Inc. (JCI), manufactures batteries. A primary ingredient in the battery-manufacturing process is lead. Occupational exposure to lead entails health risks, including the risk of harm to any fetus carried by a female employee. After eight of its employees became pregnant

CASE SUMMARY

Continued

while maintaining blood lead levels exceeding those set by the Centers for Disease Control as dangerous for a worker planning to have a family, respondent JCI announced a policy barring all women, except those whose infertility was medically documented, from jobs involving lead exposure exceeding the OSHA standard. The United Auto Workers (UAW) brought a class action in the district court, claiming that the policy constituted sex discrimination violative of Title VII of the Civil Rights Act of 1964, as amended. The court granted summary judgment for JCI based on its BFOQ defense, and the Court of Appeals affirmed. The Supreme Court granted *certiorari*.

DECISION: Judgment for the UAW. JCI's fetal protection policy discriminated against women because the policy applied only to women and did not deal with the harmful effect of lead exposure on the male reproductive system. JCI's concerns about the welfare of the next generation do not suffice to establish a BFOQ of female sterility. Title VII, as amended, mandates that decisions about the welfare of future children be left to the parents who conceive, bear, support, and raise them rather than to the employers who hire those parents or to the courts. Moreover, an employer's tort liability for potential fetal injuries does not require a different result. If, under general tort principles, Title VII bans sex-specific fetal-protection policies, the employer fully informs the woman of the risk, and the employer has not acted negligently, the basis for holding an employer liable seems remote at best. [*UAW v. Johnson Controls*, 499 U.S. 187 (1991)]

(B) TESTING AND EDUCATIONAL REQUIREMENTS. Section 703(h) of the act authorizes the use of "any professionally developed ability test [that is not] designed, intended, or used to discriminate." Employment testing and educational requirements must be "job related"; that is, the employers must prove that the tests and educational requirements bear a relationship to job performance.

Courts will accept prior court-approved validation studies developed for a different employer in a different state or region so long as it is demonstrated that the job for which the test was initially validated is essentially the same job function for which the test is currently being used. **For Example,** a firefighters' test that has been validated in a study in California will be accepted as valid when later used in Virginia. Such application is called *validity generalization.*

The Civil Rights Act of 1991 makes it an unlawful employment practice for an employer to adjust scores or use different cutoff scores or otherwise alter the results of employment tests to favor any race, color, religion, sex, or national origin. This provision addresses the so-called race-norming issue, whereby the results of hiring and promotion tests are adjusted to ensure that a minimum number of minorities are included in application pools.

(C) SENIORITY SYSTEM. Section 703(h) provides that differences in employment terms based on a bona fide seniority system are sanctioned so long as the differences do not stem from an intention to discriminate. The term *seniority system is* generally understood to mean a set of rules that ensures that workers with longer years of continuous service for an employer will have a priority claim to a job over others with fewer years of service. Because such rules provide workers with considerable job security, organized labor has continually and successfully fought to secure seniority provisions in collective bargaining agreements.

10. Affirmative Action and Reverse Discrimination

Employers have an interest in affirmative action because it is fundamentally fair to have a diverse and representative workforce. Moreover, affirmative action is an effective means of avoiding litigation costs associated with discrimination cases while at the same time preserving management prerogatives and preserving rights to government contracts. Employers, under **affirmative action plans (AAPs)**, may undertake special recruiting and other efforts to hire and train minorities and women and help them advance within the company. However, the plan may also provide job preferences for minorities and women. Such aspects of affirmative action plans have resulted in numerous lawsuits contending that Title VII of the Civil Rights Act of 1964, the Fourteenth Amendment, or collective bargaining contracts have been violated. The Supreme Court has not been able to settle the many difficult issues before it with a clear and consistent majority. The Court has decided cases narrowly, with individual justices often feeling compelled to speak in concurring or dissenting opinions.

> **affirmative action plan (AAP)** – plan to have a diverse and representative workforce.

(A) **AFFIRMATIVE ACTION PROGRAMS.** In its 1995 *Adarand Constructors, Inc. v. Pena*[26] decision, the Supreme Court placed significant limits on the federal government's authority to implement programs favoring businesses owned by racial minorities over white-owned businesses. The decision reinstated a reverse discrimination challenge to a federal program designed to provide highway construction contracts to "disadvantaged" subcontractors in which race-based presumptions were used to identify such individuals. The Court found the program to be violative of the equal protection component of the Fifth Amendment's due process clause and announced a strict scrutiny standard for evaluating the racial classifications used in the federal government's Disadvantaged Business Enterprise (DBE) program. This standard can be satisfied only by narrowly tailored measures that further compelling governmental interests. The Court stated that programs based on disadvantage rather than race are subject only to the most relaxed judicial scrutiny. Six additional years of litigation ensued before the case involving Adarand Constructors, Inc., was finally concluded on procedural and jurisdictional grounds. *Adarand I*, as it is now called, is now the landmark Supreme Court decision setting forth the legal principles for evaluating affirmative action programs involving race and remedies.

Following the Court's *Adarand I* decision, the EEOC issued a statement on affirmative action, stating, in part:

> *Affirmative action is lawful only when it is designed to respond to a demonstrated and serious imbalance in the workforce, is flexible, is time limited, applies only to qualified workers, and respects the rights of nonminorities and men.*[27]

(B) **REVERSE DISCRIMINATION.** When an employer's AAP is not shown to be justified or "unnecessarily trammels" the interests of nonminority employees, it is often called *reverse discrimination.* **For Example,** a city's decision to rescore police promotional tests to achieve specific racial and gender percentages unnecessarily trammeled the interests of nonminority police officers.[28]

---

[26] 515 U.S. 200 (1995).
[27] *The Steelworkers v. Weber*, 443 U.S. 193 (1979), and *Johnson v. Santa Clara Transportation Agency*, 480 U.S. 617 (1987), are very important U.S. Supreme Court decisions in the developing law on permissible affirmative action plans.
[28] *San Francisco Police Officers Ass'n v. San Francisco*, 812 F.2d 1125 (9th Cir. 1987).

(c) Executive Order. Presidential Executive Order 11246 regulates contractors and subcontractors doing business with the federal government. This order forbids discrimination against minorities and women and in certain situations requires affirmative action to be taken to offer better employment opportunities to minorities and women. The Secretary of Labor has established the Office of Federal Contract Compliance Programs (OFCCP) to administer the order.

C. Other Equal Employment Opportunity (EEO) Laws

Major federal laws require equal pay for men and women doing equal work and forbid discrimination against older people and those with disabilities.

11. Equal Pay

The Equal Pay Act prohibits employers from paying employees of one gender a lower wage rate than the rate paid employees of the other gender for equal work, or substantially equal work, in the same establishment for jobs that require substantially equal skill, effort, and responsibility and that are performed under similar working conditions.[29]

CASE SUMMARY

I Do the Same Job as Two Male Colleagues. Doesn't the Equal Pay Act Require That I Get Equal Pay?

FACTS: Jeannette Renstrom was the head grocery buyer at wholesale food distributor Nash Finch Co. at its St. Cloud, Minnesota, distribution center. She sued her employer under the Equal Pay Act because Nash Finch paid her less than two male employees who performed equal work—Bill Crosier, the head grocery buyer for the Omaha distribution center, and Dale Ebensteiner, the head grocery buyer for the Fargo and Minot distribution centers. Nash Finch seeks summary judgment.

DECISION: The term *establishment* refers to a distinct physical place of business rather than an entire business or enterprise, which may include several places of business. Each of Nash Finch's distribution centers is a separate "establishment." Because Renstrom did not work at the same establishment as the two comparators that she has identified (Crosier and Ebensteiner), her claim under the EPA must be dismissed.

Additionally, in order for the equal pay standard to apply, Ms. Renstrom needed to show that the Head Grocery Buyer jobs required equal skill, equal effort, and equal responsibility. There is little question that the job involved equal skill and responsibility. In light of the undisputed evidence that both Crosier and Ebensteiner had essentially "double work"—Crossier, because he handled 18 military facilities, and Ebensteiner, because he handled two distribution centers—Renstrom cannot meet her burden to show that the jobs required equal effort. Judgment for Nash Finch. [*Renstrom v. Nash Finch Co.*, 787 F. Supp. 2d 961 (D. Minn. 2011)]

[29] 29 U.S.C. §206 (d)(1).

The Equal Pay Act does not prohibit all variations in wage rates paid men and women but only those variations based solely on gender. The act sets forth four exceptions. Variances in wages are allowed where there is (1) a seniority system, (2) a merit system, (3) a system that measures earnings by quantity or quality of production, or (4) a differential based on any factor other than gender.

12. Age Discrimination

The Age Discrimination in Employment Act (ADEA) forbids discrimination by employers, unions, and employment agencies against persons over 40 years of age.[30] Section 4(a) of the ADEA sets forth the employment practices that are unlawful under the act, including the failure to hire because of age and the discharge of employees because of age. Section 7(b) of the ADEA allows for doubling the damages in cases of willful violations of the act. Consequently, an employer who willfully violates the ADEA is liable not only for back wages and benefits but also for an additional amount as liquidated damages.[31]

CASE SUMMARY

Miffed at Being RIF-ed

FACTS: Calvin Rhodes began his employment with Dresser Industries in 1955 as an oil industry salesman. In the throes of a severe economic downturn, Rhodes took a job selling oil field equipment at another Dresser company that became Guiberson Oil Tools. After seven months, he was discharged and told that the reason was a reduction in force (RIF) but that he would be eligible for rehiring. At that time, he was 56 years old. Within two months, Guiberson hired a 42-year-old salesperson to do the same job. Rhodes sued Guiberson for violating the ADEA. At the trial, Lee Snyder, the supervisor who terminated Rhodes, testified in part that Jack Givens, Snyder's boss who instructed Snyder to fire Rhodes, once said that he could hire two young salesmen for what some of the older salesmen were costing.

DECISION: Judgment for Rhodes. The official reason given Rhodes, that he was being terminated under a RIF, was false. Every other reason given by the employer was countered with evidence that Rhodes was an excellent salesman. Based on all of the evidence, including the statement about hiring two young salesmen for what some of the older salesmen were costing, a reasonable jury could find that Guiberson Oil discriminated against Rhodes on the basis of age. [**Rhodes v. Guiberson Oil Tools, 75 F.3d 989 (5th Cir. 1996)**]

The Older Workers Benefit Protection Act (OWBPA) of 1990[32] amends the ADEA by prohibiting age discrimination in employee benefits and establishing minimum standards for determining the validity of waivers of age claims. The OWBPA amends the ADEA by adopting an "equal benefit or equal cost" standard, providing that older workers must be given benefits at least equal to those provided for younger workers unless the employer can prove that the cost of providing an equal benefit would be more for an older worker than for a younger one.

Employers commonly require that employees electing to take early retirement packages waive all claims against their employers, including their rights or claims under the ADEA. The OWBPA requires that employees be given a specific period of time to evaluate a proposed package.

Enforcement of the ADEA is the responsibility of the EEOC. Procedures and time limitations for filing and processing ADEA charges are the same as those under Title VII.[33] However, Title VII is materially different from the ADEA with respect to burdens of persuasion, and Supreme Court decisions construing Title VII do not control the construction of the ADEA. Rather, in all cases of disparate treatment, including mixed-motive cases, the plaintiff has to prove, by a preponderance of the evidence, that age was the "but for" cause of the challenged adverse employment action.[34]

13. Discrimination against Persons with Disabilities

The right of persons with disabilities to enjoy equal employment opportunities was established on the federal level with the enactment of the Rehabilitation Act of 1973.[35]

Although not specifically designed as an employment discrimination measure but as a comprehensive plan to meet many of the needs of persons with disabilities, the act contains three sections that provide guarantees against discrimination in employment. Section 501 is applicable to the federal government itself, Section 503 applies to federal contractors, and Section 504 applies to the recipients of federal funds.

Title I of the Americans with Disabilities Act of 1990 extends employment protection for disabled persons beyond the federal level to state and local governmental agencies and to all private employers with 15 or more employees. The ADA refers to the term *qualified individuals with disabilities* rather than the term *handicapped persons*, which is used in the Rehabilitation Act. In drafting the ADA, Congress relied heavily on the language of the Rehabilitation Act and its regulations. It was anticipated that the body of case law developed under the Rehabilitation Act would provide guidance in the interpretation and application of the ADA. However, protections for individuals were eroded by U.S. Supreme Court decisions in 1999 and 2002. Under these precedents, numerous claims of ADA plaintiffs were extinguished at the threshold stage of proving the plaintiff had a disability. With the cooperation and agreement of both the employer and disability communities, the ADA Amendments Act of 2008 (ADAAA) became law (effective January 1, 2009), effectively overturning the Supreme Court decisions and restoring the original congressional intent of providing broad coverage to protect individuals who face discrimination on the basis of disability.[36] Under Title I of the ADA, an employer may make preemployment inquiries into the ability of a job applicant to perform job-related functions. Under "user-friendly" EEOC guidelines on preemployment

[33] In *Smith v. City of Jackson, Mississippi*, 544 U.S. 228 (2005), the U.S. Supreme Court determined that disparate impact claims of age discrimination are permitted under the ADEA. The Court relied on its Title VII *Griggs v. Duke Power Co.* precedent, which interpreted text identical to that in the ADEA, with the substitution of the word "age" for the words "race, color, religion, sex or national origin," the narrowing of the coverage of the ADEA, which permits employers to take actions that would otherwise be prohibited based on "reasonable factors other than age" (called the *RFOA provision*) and the EEOC regulations permitting disparate impact claims. The dissenting justices asserted that in the nearly four decades since the law's enactment, the Court had never read it to impose liability on an employer without proof of discriminatory intent. The *Smith v. City of Jackson* court decided the disparate impact case before it against the petitioning police officers, finding that the City's larger pay raises to younger employees were based on an RFOA that responded to the City's legitimate goal of retaining its new police officers.

[34] *Gross v. FBL Financial Services, Inc.*, 557 U.S. 167 (2009).

[35] 42 U.S.C. §§701–794.

[36] 42 U.S.C. §§12101-12117; P.L. 110-325, S3406 (Sept. 25, 2008).

inquiries under the ADA, an employer may ask applicants whether they will need reasonable accommodations for the hiring process. If the answer is yes, the employer may ask for reasonable documentation of the disability. In general, the employer may not ask questions about whether an applicant will need reasonable accommodations to do the job. However, the employer may make preemployment inquiries regarding the job applicant's ability to perform job-related functions.

After making a job offer (contingent upon the applicant's passing a medical examination), the employer may rescind the offer if the position in question poses a direct threat to the worker's health or safety. **For Example,** Mario Echazabal was initially offered a job at Chevron's El Segundo, California, oil refinery but the offer was rescinded when the company doctors determined that exposure to chemicals on the job would further damage his already-reduced liver functions (due to hepatitis C) and might potentially kill him. An affirmative defense then exists for employers—not only in cases where hiring an individual poses a direct threat to the health or safety of other employees in the workplace, but also when there is a direct threat to the employee in question. However, the employer must make an individualized medical risk assessment of the employee's condition.[37]

(A) PROVING A CASE. The Americans with Disabilities Act, as amended in 2008, prohibits employers from discriminating "against a qualified individual on the basis of a disability." A qualified individual with a disability is one "who, with or without reasonable accommodation, can perform the essential functions of the employment position." To establish a viable claim under the act, a plaintiff must prove that (1) he or she has a disability; (2) he or she is qualified for the position; and (3) an employer has discriminated against him or her because of a disability.

The ADAAA defines the term "disability" in a three-pronged definition as follows:

> 1. *DISABILITY: The term "disability" means, with respect to an individual—*
>
>   A. *a physical or mental impairment that substantially limits one or more major life activities of such individual;*
>   B. *a record of such an impairment; or*
>   C. *being regarded as having such an impairment.*

The ADAAA sets forth in unmistakable language that the definition of disability "shall be construed in favor of broad coverage of individuals under this Act" and mandates that the term "substantially limits" be construed accordingly. Moreover, the determination of whether an impairment substantially limits a major life activity must be made without regard to the ameliorative effects of mitigating measures (with the exception that ameliorative effects of ordinary eyeglasses or contact lenses are considered in determinations of whether an impairment substantially limits a major life activity).

The ADAAA includes an expansive compilation of major life activities to confirm the congressional purpose of providing a broad scope of protection to individuals under the ADA.[38]

---

[37] *Chevron v. Echazabal*, 536 U.S. 73 (2002).
[38] Section 3(2) of the act provides:
MAJOR LIFE ACTIVITIES—

    A. IN GENERAL.—For purposes of paragraph (1), major life activities include, but are not limited to, caring for oneself; performing manual tasks; seeing, hearing, eating, sleeping, walking, standing, lifting, bending, speaking, breathing, learning, reading, concentrating, thinking, communicating, and working.

    B. MAJOR BODILY FUNCTIONS.—For purposes of paragraph (1), a major life activity also includes the operation of major bodily functions, included but not limited to, functions of the immune system; normal cell growth; digestive, bowel, bladder, neurological, brain, respiratory, circulatory, endocrine, and reproductive functions.

(B) REASONABLE ACCOMMODATIONS UNDER THE ADA. Section 101(9) of the ADA defines an employer's obligation to make "reasonable accommodations" for individuals with disabilities to include (1) making existing facilities accessible to and usable by individuals with disabilities and (2) restructuring jobs, providing modified work schedules, and acquiring or modifying equipment or devices.[39] An employer is not obligated under the ADA to make accommodations that would be an "undue hardship" on the employer.

For Example, before passage of the ADA, a supermarket meatcutter unable to carry meat from a refrigerator to a processing area might have been refused clearance to return to work after a back injury until he was able to perform all job functions. Today, under the ADA, it would be the employer's obligation to provide that worker with a cart to assist him in performing the job even if the cart cost $500. However, if the meatcutter was employed by a small business with limited financial resources, an "accommodation" costing $500 might be an undue hardship that the employer could lawfully refuse to make.

Seniority systems provide for a fair and uniform method of treating employees whereby employees with more years of service have a priority over employees with less years of service when it comes to layoffs, job selection, and other benefits such as days off and vacation periods. Seniority rules apply not only under collective bargaining agreements but also to many nonunion job classifications and to nonunion settings. An employer's showing that a requested accommodation conflicts with seniority rules is ordinarily sufficient to show that the requested "accommodation" is not "reasonable." **For Example,** Robert Barnett, a cargo handler for U.S. Airways, Inc., sought a less physically demanding job in the mailroom due to a back injury. Because a senior employee bid the job, U.S. Airways refused Barnett's request to accommodate his disability by allowing him to work the mailroom position. Barnett filed suit under the ADA, and the case progressed to the U.S. Supreme Court, which determined that ordinarily such a requested accommodation is not "reasonable." On remand to the trial court, Barnett was given the opportunity to show that the company allowed exceptions to the seniority rules and he fit within such exceptions.[40]

(C) FAILURE TO TAKE ACTION. With courts applying a less-demanding standard for coverage under the amended ADA, employers are finding requests to provide "reasonable accommodations" more common. Employers are liable for failure to take appropriate action regarding requests for reasonable accommodations. **For Example,** Jane Gagliardo had been diagnosed with multiple sclerosis that began affecting her work. The most severe symptom was fatigue, which affected her ability to think, focus, and remember. All of her symptoms were subject to being exacerbated by stress. She sought a "reasonable accommodation" under the ADA of having one major client removed from her job responsibilities. The employer took no action on this request. Moreover, while she continued to seek accommodation to no avail, the employer began disciplining her for poor job performance and ultimately fired her. She was awarded $2.3 million in compensation and punitive damages.[41]

---

[39] A reasonable accommodation may also include "reassignment to a vacant position." In *Duvall v. Georgia-Pacific Consumer Products L.P.*, 607 F.3d 1255 (10th Cir. 2010), the Tenth Circuit Court of Appeals was called upon to decide when a position is "vacant" for the purpose of the ADA. It determined that when a disabled employee seeks the reasonable accommodation of reassignment to a vacant position, positions within the company are "vacant" for the purpose of the ADA when they would be available to similarly suited nondisabled employees to apply for and obtain. Duvall, the employee in question, did not meet his burden of showing that the jobs he sought were available within GP, as they were occupied by a contractor service, and no GP employee had been given a contractor-filled position during the time in question.

[40] *U.S. Airways v. Barnett*, 535 U.S. 391 (2002).

[41] *Gagliardo v. Connaught Laboratories, Inc.*, 311 F.3d 565 (3d Cir. 2008). See also *Tobin v. Liberty Mutual Insurance Co.*, 553 F.3d 121 (1st Cir. 2009).

Where a disability is obvious and known to the employer, an employee is obligated to engage in an "interactive process" regarding accommodation of a disability, even when a formal request for accommodation is not made.

For Example, 19-year-old Patrick Brady, who has cerebral palsy, was hired to work as a Wal-Mart pharmacy aide. After "a few days" on the job with no training, he was transferred to the job of collecting shopping carts and garbage in the parking lot. His supervisor, Ms. Chin, regarded Brady as "too slow" and stated that "she knew there was something wrong with him." While Brady did not request reasonable accommodations because his disability was obvious and known to the employer, Wal-Mart was found to be in violation of the ADA, and a judgment of $900,000—including $300,000 in punitive damages—was upheld by the U.S. Court of Appeals.[42]

(D) EXCLUSIONS FROM COVERAGE OF THE ACT. The act excludes from its coverage employees or applicants who are "currently engaging in the illegal use of drugs." The exclusion does not include an individual who has been successfully rehabilitated from such use or is participating in or has completed supervised drug rehabilitation and is no longer engaging in the illegal use of drugs.

Title V of the act states that behaviors such as transvestitism, transsexualism, pedophilia, exhibitionism, compulsive gambling, kleptomania, pyromania, and psychoactive substance use disorders resulting from current illegal use of drugs are not in and of themselves considered disabilities.

D. EXTRATERRITORIAL EMPLOYMENT

The Civil Rights Act of 1991 amended both Title VII and the ADA to protect U.S. citizens employed in foreign countries by American-owned or American-controlled companies against discrimination based on race, color, religion, national origin, sex, or disability.[43] The 1991 act contains an exemption if compliance with Title VII or the ADA would cause a company to violate the law of the foreign country in which it is located.

LawFlix

Parenthood (1989) (PG)

A candid movie about raising children that has the added bonus of a scene involving Steve Martin (Gil) and his boss, Dave, in which the two cross quite a few Title VII lines in their discussion about Gil's job and future at the company.

---

[42] *Brady v. Wal-Mart Stores, Inc.*, 531 F.3d 127 (2d Cir. 2008).
[43] Section 109 of the Civil Rights Act of 1991, P.L. 102-166, 105 Stat. 1071.

MAKE THE CONNECTION

SUMMARY

Title VII of the Civil Rights Act of 1964, as amended, forbids discrimination on the basis of race, color, religion, sex, or national origin. The EEOC administers the act. Intentional discrimination is unlawful when there is disparate treatment of individuals because of their race, color, religion, gender, or national origin. Also, employment practices that make no reference to race, color, religion, sex, or national origin, but that nevertheless have an adverse or disparate impact on the protected group, are unlawful. In disparate impact cases, the fact that an employer did not intend to discriminate is no defense. The employer must show that there is a job-related business necessity for the disparate impact practice in question. Employers have several defenses they may raise in a Title VII case to explain differences in employment conditions: (1) bona fide occupational qualifications reasonably necessary to the normal operation of the business, (2) job-related professionally developed ability tests,

and (3) bona fide seniority systems. If a state EEO agency or the EEOC is not able to resolve the case, the EEOC issues a right-to-sue letter that enables the person claiming a Title VII violation to sue in a federal district court. An affirmative action plan is legal under Title VII provided there is a voluntary "plan" justified as a remedial measure and provided it does not unnecessarily trammel the interests of whites.

Under the Equal Pay Act (EPA), employers must not pay employees of one gender a lower wage rate than the rate paid to employees of the other gender for substantially equal work. Workers over 40 years old are protected from discrimination by the Age Discrimination in Employment Act (ADEA). Employment discrimination against persons with disabilities is prohibited by the Americans with Disabilities Act (ADA). Under the ADA, employers must make reasonable accommodations without undue hardship on them to enable individuals with disabilities to work.

LEARNING OUTCOMES

After studying this chapter, you should be able to clearly explain:

A. Title VII of the Civil Rights Act of 1964, as Amended

LO.1 Explain the difference between the *disparate treatment* theory of employment discrimination and the *disparate impact* theory of employment discrimination

See the discussion of the New Haven Firefighters case in which the city relied on a disparate impact theory and the firefighters asserted disparate treatment, pp. 887–888.

B. Protected Classes and Exceptions

LO.2 List and explain the categories of individuals protected against unlawful employment discrimination under Title VII

See the discussion and examples of protections under Title VII applied to the categories of race and color, religion, sex, and national origin, beginning on p. 891.

LO.3 Recognize, and know the remedies for, sexual harassment in the workplace

See the Ellerth example and the employer's affirmative defense on p. 894. See Figure 40-2 for a presentation of an employer sexual harassment policy, p. 895.

LO.4 Explain the antiretaliation provision of Title VII

See the *White* case, which sets forth the elements of retaliatory discrimination and the remedy provided, p. 896.
See why retaliation is the number one employment liability risk for employers and the antiretaliation actions proposed for employers, p. 897.

C. Other Equal Employment Opportunity (EEO) Laws

LO.5 List and explain the laws protecting equal pay for women and men for equal work, as well as the laws forbidding discrimination on the basis of age and against individuals with disabilities

> See the *Renstrom* case with the narrow meaning of the word "establishment" making her EPA case without merit, p. 901.
>
> See the *Rhodes* case with facts and a remedy applicable to age discrimination on p. 902.
>
> See the Patrick Brady example of the attention-getting judgment in a case where the employer failed to recognize its

obligation to make a reasonable accommodation, p. 906.

D. Extraterritorial Employment

LO.6   Explain how both Title VII of the Civil Rights Act and the ADA protect from discrimination U.S. citizens working in foreign countries for American-owned and American-controlled businesses

> See the discussion of the exemption for employers where compliance would cause a company to violate the law of the country in which it is located, p. 906.

KEY TERM

affirmative action plans (AAPs)

QUESTIONS AND CASE PROBLEMS

1. List the major federal statutes dealing with the regulation of equal rights in employment.

2. The EEOC notified North American Stainless (NAS) in February 2003 that Miriam Regalado had filed a charge of sex discrimination against the company. Three weeks later NAS fired her coworker Eric Thompson, a person to whom Ms. Regalado was engaged. Thompson had worked for NAS for seven years as a metallurgical engineer. Thompson filed his own charge with the EEOC and a subsequent lawsuit under Title VII of the Civil Rights Act, claiming that NAS fired him to retaliate against Regalado for filing her charge with the EEOC.

   The employer contended that because Thompson did not "engag[e] in any statutorily protected activity, either on his own behalf or on behalf of Miriam Regalado," he is not included in the class of persons for whom Congress created a retaliation cause of action. Thompson argued that the Supreme Court adopted a broad standard in its *Burlington* decision because Title VII's antiretaliation provision is worded broadly, and that there is no textual basis for making an exception to it for third-party reprisals. Decide. [*Thompson v. North American Stainless Steel, LP*, 131 S.Ct. 863]

3. Dial Corp. implemented a "work tolerance test," which all new employees were required to pass to obtain employment in its Armour Star brand

sausage-making department. Of the applicants who passed the test, 97 percent were male and 38 percent were female. The EEOC "demonstrated" that the facially neutral work tolerance test "caused" a disparate impact on women. The defending employer did not deny that the employment practice in question caused the disparate impact. Rather, the employer responded that the test was "job related" and "necessary" to reduce job-related injuries at the plant and submitted evidence that the number of job injuries had been reduced after implementation of the testing program. The evidence showed that the company had initiated numerous other safety initiatives that had an impact on reducing injuries at the plant. After they failed the test, 52 women were denied jobs. Decide this case. [*EEOC v. Dial Corp.*, 2005 WL 2839977 (S.D. Iowa)]

4. Continental Photo, Inc., is a portrait photography company. Alex Riley, a black man, applied for a position as a photographer with Continental. Riley submitted an application and was interviewed. In response to a question on a written application, Riley indicated that he had been convicted for forgery (a felony) six years before the interview, had received a suspended sentence, and was placed on five-year probation. He also stated that he would discuss the matter with his

interviewer if necessary. The subject of the forgery conviction was subsequently not mentioned by Continental's personnel director in his interview with Riley. Riley's application for employment was eventually rejected. Riley inquired about the reason for his rejection. The personnel director, Geuther, explained to him that the prior felony conviction on his application was a reason for his rejection. Riley contended that the refusal to hire him because of his conviction record was actually discrimination against him because of his race in violation of Title VII. Riley felt that his successful completion of a five-year probation without incident and his steady work over the years qualified him for the job. Continental maintained that because its photographers handle approximately $10,000 in cash per year, its policy of not hiring applicants whose honesty was questionable was justified. Continental's policy excluded all applicants with felony convictions. Decide. Would the result have been different if Riley had been a convicted murderer? [*Continental Photo, Inc.*, 26 Fair Empl. Prac. Cas. (B.N.A.) 1799 (E.E.O.C.)]

5. Beth Faragher worked part-time and summers as an ocean lifeguard for the Marine Safety Section of the city of Boca Raton, Florida. Bill Terry and David Silverman were her supervisors over the five-year period of her employment. During this period, Terry repeatedly touched the bodies of female employees without invitation and would put his arm around Faragher, with his hand on her buttocks. He made crudely demeaning references to women generally. Silverman once told Faragher, "Date me or clean the toilets for a year." She was not so assigned, however. The city adopted a sexual harassment policy addressed to all employees. The policy was not disseminated to the Marine Safety Section at the beach, however. Faragher resigned and later brought action against the city, claiming a violation of Title VII and seeking nominal damages, costs, and attorneys' fees. The city defended that Terry and Silverman were not acting within the scope of their employment when they engaged in harassing conduct, and the city should not be held liable for their actions. Are part-time employees covered by Title VII? Was Silverman's threat, "Date me or clean toilets for a year,"

a basis for *quid pro quo* vicarious liability against the city? Decide this case. [*Faragher v. City of Boca Raton*, 524 U.S. 775]

6. Mohen is a member of the Sikh religion whose practice forbids cutting or shaving facial hair and requires wearing a turban that covers the head. In accordance with the dictates of his religion, Mohen wore a long beard. He applied for a position as breakfast cook at the Island Manor Restaurant. He was told that the restaurant's policy was to forbid cooks to wear facial hair for sanitary and good grooming reasons and that he would have to shave his beard or be denied a position. Mohen contended that the restaurant had an obligation to make a reasonable accommodation to his religious beliefs and let him keep his beard. Is he correct?

7. Sylvia Hayes worked as a staff technician in the radiology department of Shelby Memorial Hospital. On October 1, Hayes was told by her physician that she was pregnant. When Hayes informed the doctor of her occupation as an X-ray technician, the doctor advised Hayes that she could continue working until the end of April so long as she followed standard safety precautions. On October 8, Hayes told Gail Nell, the director of radiology at Shelby, that she had discovered she was two months pregnant. On October 14, Hayes was discharged by the hospital. The hospital's reason for terminating Hayes was its concern for the safety of her fetus given the X-ray exposure that occurs during employment as an X-ray technician. Hayes brought an action under Title VII, claiming that her discharge was unlawfully based on her condition of pregnancy. She cited scientific evidence and the practice of other hospitals where pregnant women were allowed to remain in their jobs as X-ray technicians. The hospital claimed that Hayes's discharge was based on business necessity. Moreover, the hospital claimed that the potential for future liability existed if an employee's fetus was damaged by radiation encountered at the workplace. Decide. [*Hayes v. Shelby Memorial Hospital*, 546 F. Supp. 259 (N.D. Ala.)]

8. Overton suffered from depression and was made sleepy at work by medication taken for this

condition. Also, because of his medical condition, Overton needed a work area away from public access and substantial supervision to complete his tasks. His employer terminated him because of his routinely sleeping on the job, his inability to maintain contact with the public, and his need for supervision. Overton argued that he is a person with a disability under the ADA and the Rehabilitation Act, fully qualified to perform the essential functions of the job, and that the employer had an obligation to make reasonable accommodations, such as allowing some catnaps as needed and providing some extra supervision. Decide. [*Overton v. Reilly*, 977 F.2d 1190 (7th Cir.)]

9. A teenage female high school student named Salazar was employed part-time at Church's Fried Chicken Restaurant. Salazar was hired and supervised by Simon Garza, the assistant manager of the restaurant. Garza had complete supervisory powers when the restaurant's manager, Garza's roommate, was absent. Salazar claimed that while she worked at the restaurant, Garza would refer to her and all other females by a Spanish term that she found objectionable. According to Salazar, Garza once made an offensive comment about her body and repeatedly asked her about her personal life. On another occasion, Garza allegedly physically removed eye shadow from Salazar's face because he claimed it was unattractive. Salazar also claimed that one night she was restrained in a back room of the restaurant while Garza and another employee fondled her. Later that night, when Salazar told a customer what had happened, she was fired. Salazar brought suit under Title VII against Garza and Church's Fried Chicken, alleging sexual harassment. Church's, the corporate defendant, maintained that it should not be held liable under Title VII for Garza's harassment. Church's based its argument on the existence of a published fair treatment policy. Decide. [*Salazar v. Church's Fried Chicken, Inc.*, 44 Fair Empl. Prac. Cas. (B.N.A.) 472 (S.D. Tex.)]

10. John Chadbourne was hired by Raytheon on February 4, 1980. His job performance reviews were uniformly high. In December 1983, Chadbourne was hospitalized and diagnosed with AIDS. In January 1984, his physician informed Raytheon that Chadbourne was able to return to work. On January 20, 1984, Chadbourne took a return-to-work physical examination required by Raytheon. The company's doctor wrote the County Communicable Disease Control Director, Dr. Juels, seeking a determination of the appropriateness of Chadbourne's returning to work. Dr. Juels informed the company that "contact of employees to an AIDS patient appears to pose no risk from all evidence accumulated to date." Dr. Juels also visited the plant and advised the company doctor that there would be no medical risk to other employees at the plant if Chadbourne returned to work. Raytheon refused to reinstate Chadbourne to his position until July 19, 1984. Its basis for denying reinstatement was that coworkers might be at risk of contracting AIDS. Was Raytheon entitled to bar Chadbourne from work during the six-month period of January through July? [*Raytheon v. Fair Employment and Housing Commission*, 261 Cal. Rptr. 197 (Ct. App.)]

11. Connie Cunico, a white woman, was employed by the Pueblo, Colorado, School District as a social worker. She and other social workers were laid off in seniority order because of the district's poor financial situation. However, the school board thereafter decided to retain Wayne Hunter, a black social worker with less seniority than Cunico because he was the only black on the administrative staff. No racial imbalance existed in the relevant workforce with black persons constituting 2 percent. Cunico, who was rehired over two years later, claimed that she was the victim of reverse discrimination. She stated that she lost $110,361 in back wages plus $76,000 in attorneys' fees and costs. The school district replied that it was correct in protecting with special consideration the only black administrator in the district under the general principles it set forth in its AAP. Did the employer show that its affirmative action in retaining Hunter was justified as a remedial measure? Decide. [*Cunico v. Pueblo School District No. 6*, 917 F.2d 431 (10th Cir.)]

12. Della Janich was employed as a matron at the Yellowstone County Jail in Montana. The duties of the position of matron resemble those of a

parallel male position of jailer. Both employees have the responsibility of booking prisoners, showering and dressing them, and placing them in the appropriate section of the jail depending on the offender's sex. Because 95 percent of the prisoners at the jail were men and 5 percent were women, the matron was assigned more bookkeeping duties than the jailer. At all times during Janich's employment at the jail, her male counterparts received $125 more per month as jailers. Janich brought an action under the Equal Pay Act, alleging discrimination against her in her wages because of her sex. The county sheriff denied the charge. Decide. [*Janich v. Sheriff*, 29 Fair Empl. Prac. Cas. (B.N.A.) 1195 (D. Mont.)]

13. Following a decline in cigarette sales, L & M, Inc., hired J. Gfeller as vice president of sales and charged him to turn around the sales decline. After receiving an analysis of the ages of sales personnel and first-line management, Gfeller and his assistant, T. McMorrow, instituted an intensive program of personnel changes that led to the termination of many older managers and sales representatives. A top manager who sought to justify keeping an older manager was informed that he was "not getting the message." Gfeller and McMorrow emphasized that they wanted young and aggressive people and that the older people were not able to conform or adapt to new procedures. R. E. Moran, who had been rated a first-rate division manager, was terminated and replaced by a 27-year-old employee. Gfeller and McMorrow made statements about employees with many years' experience: "It was not 20 years' experience, but rather 1 year's experience 20 times." The EEOC brought suit on behalf of the terminated managers and sales representatives. The company vigorously denied any discriminatory attitude with regard to age. Decide. [*EEOC v. Liggett and Meyers, Inc.*, 29 F.E.P. 1611 (E.D.N.C.)]

14. Mazir Coleman had driven a school bus for the Casey County, Kentucky, Board of Education for four years. After that time, Coleman's left leg had to be amputated. Coleman was fitted with an artificial leg and underwent extensive rehabilitation to relearn driving skills. When his driving skills had been sufficiently relearned over the course of four years, Coleman applied to the county board of education for a job as a school bus driver. The board refused to accept Coleman's application, saying that it had no alternative but to deny Coleman a bus-driving job because of a Kentucky administrative regulation. That regulation stated in part: "No person shall drive a school bus who does not possess both of these natural bodily parts: feet, legs, hands, arms, eyes, and ears. The driver shall have normal use of the above named body parts." Coleman brought an action under the Rehabilitation act, claiming discrimination based on his physical handicap. The county board of education denied this charge, claiming that the reason they rejected Coleman was because of the requirement of the state regulation. Could Coleman have maintained an action for employment discrimination in light of the state regulation on natural body parts? Decide. [*Coleman v. Casey County Board of Education*, 510 F. Supp. 301 (N.D. Ky.)]

15. Marcia Saxton worked for Jerry Richardson, a supervisor at AT&T's International Division. Richardson made advances to Saxton on two occasions over a three-week period. Each time Saxton told him she did not appreciate his advances. No further advances were made, but thereafter Saxton felt that Richardson treated her condescendingly and had stopped speaking to her on a social basis at work. Four months later, Saxton filed a formal internal complaint, asserting sexual harassment, and went on "paid leave." AT&T found inconclusive evidence of sexual harassment but determined that the two employees should be separated. Saxton declined a transfer to another department, so AT&T transferred Richardson instead. Saxton still refused to return to work. Thereafter, AT&T terminated Saxton for refusal to return to work. Saxton contended she had been a victim of hostile working environment sexual harassment. AT&T argued that while the supervisor's conduct was inappropriate and unprofessional, it fell short of the type of action necessary for sexual harassment under federal law (the *Harris* case). Decide. [*Saxton v. AT&T Co.*, 10 F.3d 526 (7th Cir.)]

PART 7

Business Organizations

© Manuel Gutjahr/iStockphoto.com

913

CHAPTER 41

Types of Business Organizations

© Manuel Gutjahr/iStockphoto.com

learningoutcomes

After studying this chapter, you should be able to

LO.1 Explain the advantages and disadvantages of the three principal forms of business organizations

LO.2 Recognize that the rules of law governing the rights and liabilities of joint ventures are substantially the same as those that govern partnerships

LO.3 Evaluate whether a business arrangement is a franchise protected under state or federal law

LO.4 Explain how the rights of the parties to a franchise agreement are determined by their contract

LO.5 Explain why freedom from vicarious liability is a reason for franchisors to use the franchise format

LO.6 Recognize the implications of the misclassifications of employees as franchisee-independent contractors

W hat form of legal organization should you have for your business? The answer will be found in your needs for money, personnel, control, tax and estate planning, and protection from liability.

A. PRINCIPAL FORMS OF BUSINESS ORGANIZATIONS

The law of business organizations may be better understood if the advantages and disadvantages of proprietorships, partnerships, and corporations are first considered.

1. Individual Proprietorships

A **sole or individual proprietorship** is a form of business ownership in which one individual owns the business. The owner may be the sole worker of the business or employ as many others as needed to run the concern. Individual proprietorships are commonly used in retail stores, service businesses, and agriculture.

(A) ADVANTAGES. The proprietor or owner is not required to expend resources on organizational fees. The proprietor, as the sole owner, controls all decisions and receives all profits. The net earnings of the business are not subject to corporate income taxes but are taxed only as personal income.

(B) DISADVANTAGES. The proprietor is subject to unlimited personal liability for the debts of the business and cannot limit this risk. The investment capital in the business is limited by the resources of the sole proprietor. Because all contracts of the business are made by the owner or in the owner's name by agents of the owner, the authority to make contracts terminates on the death of the owner, and the business is subject to disintegration.

2. Partnerships, LLPs, and LLCs

A **partnership** involves the pooling of capital resources and the business or professional talents of two or more individuals whose goal is making a profit. Law firms, medical associations, and architectural and engineering firms may operate under the partnership form. Today, however, these firms may convert to a **limited liability partnership (LLP)**. A wide range of small manufacturing, retail, and service businesses operate as partnerships. These businesses may operate under the form of organization called **limited liability company (LLC)**, which allows tax treatment as a partnership with limited liability for the owners.

(A) ADVANTAGES. The partnership form of business organization allows individuals to pool resources and then initiate and conduct their business without the requirement of a formal organizational structure.

(B) DISADVANTAGES. Major disadvantages of a partnership are the unlimited personal liability of each partner and the uncertain duration of the business because the partnership is dissolved by the death of one partner. Unlimited personal liability is remedied by the LLC form of business organization. Professional partnerships that convert to an LLP shield innocent partners from personal liability beyond their investment in the firm.

sole or individual proprietorship – form of business ownership in which one individual owns the business.

partnership – pooling of capital resources and the business or professional talents of two or more individuals (partners) with the goal of making a profit.

limited liability partnership (LLP) – partnership in which at least one partner has a liability limited to the loss of the capital contribution made to the partnership.

limited liability company (LLC) – a partnership for federal tax treatment and the limited liability feature of the corporate form of business organization.

3. Corporations

corporation – artificial being created by government grant, which for many purposes is treated as a natural person.

Business **corporations** exist to make a profit and are created by government grant. State statutes regulating the creation of corporations require a corporate structure consisting of shareholders, directors, and officers. The shareholders, as the owners of the business, elect a board of directors, which is responsible for managing the business. The directors employ officers, who serve as the agents of the business and run day-to-day operations. Corporations range in size from incorporated one-owner enterprises to large multinational concerns.

(A) ADVANTAGES. The major advantage to the shareholder, or investor, is that the shareholder's risk of loss from the business is limited to the amount of capital she invested in the business or paid for shares. This factor, coupled with the free transferability of corporate shares, makes the corporate form of business organization attractive to investors.

By purchasing shares, a large number of investors may contribute the capital assets needed to finance large business enterprises. As the capital needs of a business expand, the corporate form becomes more attractive.

A corporation is a separate legal entity capable of owning property, contracting, suing, and being sued in its own name. It has perpetual life. In other words, a corporation is not affected by the death of any of its shareholders or the transfer of their shares. In contrast to the case of a partnership or proprietorship, the death of an owner has no legal effect on the corporate entity.

(B) DISADVANTAGES. A corporation is required to pay corporate income taxes. Shareholders are required to pay personal income taxes on the amount received when they receive a distribution of profits from the corporation. This is a form of double taxation.

Incorporation involves the expenditure of funds for organizational expenses. Documents necessary for the formation of a corporation, which are required by state law, must be prepared, and certain filing fees must be paid. State corporation laws may also require filing an annual report and other reports.

B. SPECIALIZED FORMS OF ORGANIZATIONS

CPA

4. Joint Ventures

joint venture – relationship in which two or more persons or firms combine their labor or property for a single undertaking and share profits and losses equally unless otherwise agreed.

A **joint venture**, or joint adventure, is a relationship in which two or more persons or entities combine their labor or property for a single business undertaking and share profits and losses equally or as otherwise agreed.[1] **For Example,** Front-Line Promotions and Insights Promotions formed a "joint venture" to produce two events with musical and celebrity talent at the Sugar Mill in New Orleans on February 16 and February 17, 2008, the NBA All-Star Weekend in New Orleans. The entities agreed to split the costs and revenues from the events.[2]

---

[1] See *Abeles Inc. v. Creekstone Farms Premium Beef*, LLC, 2009 WL 2495802 (E.D.N.Y. March 30, 2009), for an in-depth discussion of the law of joint ventures. The court referenced a precedent, stating: "A joint venture has been described as a nebulous concept whose boundaries are not precisely drawn. Defining a joint venture is easier than identifying it, for each case depends upon its own facts."

[2] Boxer Floyd "Money Mayweather" was to appear at the event on February 17, 2008, and be paid $25,000, but he did not appear. The joint venture sued him for breach of contract and consequential damages. In *Front-Line Inc. v. Mayweather Promotions, LLC*, 2009 U.S. Lexis 27136 (E.D.N.Y. April 2, 2009), the U.S. District Court allowed Front-Line Promotions to pursue its claim against Mayweather Promotions, LLC.

A joint venture is similar in many respects to a partnership. It differs primarily in that the joint venture typically involves the pursuit of a single enterprise or transaction, although its accomplishment may require several years. A partnership is generally a continuing business or activity but may be expressly created for a single transaction. Because the distinction is so insubstantial, most courts hold that joint ventures are subject to the same principles of law as partnerships. **For Example,** the Virginia Uniform Partnership Act was utilized to enable PGI, Inc., to sue Rathe Productions, Inc., for conversion of its share of a settlement agreement with the Smithsonian Institute because PGI/Rathe was involved in a joint venture and the "rules of law governing the rights, duties and liabilities of joint ventures are substantially the same as those which govern partnerships."[3]

CASE SUMMARY

Unilateral Action: Years of Litigation

FACTS: Prior to 1992, Drs. Kurwa and Kislinger maintained their own ophthalmologist practices in the San Gabriel Valley. They subsequently agreed to pursue a new business model at that time by creating a joint venture where, under what is called a "capitation agreement," HMOs would pay the joint venture a monthly fee based on the number of members of the HMO in exchange for their ophthalmologist services. They signed a handwritten "Agreement between Bud and Mark" in which they outlined the structure within which they would solicit business and share profits. They agreed to incorporate as a professional medical corporation to operate their joint venture business. Thus, Trans Valley Eye Associates, Inc., was formed. The joint venture had capitation agreements with three HMOs serving some 200,000 patients in the year before its demise and earned revenues of $2 million. Beginning September 26, 2003, Dr. Kurwa was suspended from the practice of medicine for 60 days, and placed on five years' probation by the California Medical Board. The doctors also discovered at that time that their corporation did not contain a specific statement in its Articles of Incorporation that it was a professional medical corporation, thus making it an ordinary for-profit corporation. In this setting Dr. Kislinger unilaterally terminated the joint venture and appropriated for himself, without any compensation to Dr. Kurwa, the very successful 11-year venture. Dr. Kislinger contended that Dr. Kurwa had no standing to bring an action against him on behalf of Trans Valley. From adverse decisions in the trial court, Dr. Kurwa appealed.

DECISION: Courts in other states have recognized that joint ventures may choose to operate their venture in the corporate form without divesting themselves of the rights and obligations of joint venturers. The factual allegations in the complaint state a cause of action against Dr. Kislinger for breach of his fiduciary duty as a director of Trans Valley for misappropriating assets of the corporation. While Dr. Kurwa may have been precluded from owning shares in a professional corporation during his suspension, that does not mean Dr. Kislinger is not required to account to Dr. Kurwa for his interest in the joint enterprise or allow Dr. Kurwa to sell his shares in Trans Valley to an eligible licensed person. [*Kurwa v. Kislinger*, 138 Cal. Rptr. 3d 610 (Cal. App. 2012)]

(A) DURATION OF JOINT VENTURE. A joint venture continues for the time specified in the agreement of the parties. In the absence of a fixed-duration provision, a joint venture is ordinarily terminable at the will of any participant. When the joint venture clearly relates to a particular transaction, such as the construction of a

---

[3] *PGI, Inc. v. Rathe Productions, Inc.*, 576 S.E.2d 438 (Va 2003). See also *Pugliese v. Mandello*, 871 N.Y.S.2d 174 (A.D. 2008).

specified bridge, the joint venture ordinarily lasts until the particular transaction or project is completed or becomes impossible to complete.

(B) LIABILITY TO THIRD PERSONS. The conclusion that persons are joint venturers is important when a suit is brought by or against a third person for personal injuries or property damage. If there is a joint venture, the fault or negligence of one venturer will be imputed to the other venturers.[4]

5. Unincorporated Associations

An **unincorporated association** is a combination of two or more persons for the furtherance of a common purpose.[5] No particular form of organization is required. Any conduct or agreement indicating an attempt to associate or work together for a common purpose is sufficient.[6]

The authority of an unincorporated association over its members is governed by ordinary contract law. Except when otherwise provided by statute, an unincorporated association does not have any legal existence apart from its members. Thus, an unincorporated association cannot sue or be sued in its own name.

Generally, the members of an unincorporated association are not liable for the debts or liabilities of the association by the mere fact that they are members. It must usually be shown that they authorized or ratified the act in question. If either authorization or ratification by a particular member can be shown, that member has unlimited liability for the act.

unincorporated association – combination of two or more persons for the furtherance of a common nonprofit purpose.

CASE SUMMARY

Batters with Two Strikes Should Never Trust the Umpire, and Their Parents Should Have Little Faith That the Association Will Pay the Bills

FACTS: Golden Spike Little League was an unincorporated association of persons who joined together to promote a Little League baseball team in Ogden, Utah. They sent one of their members to arrange for credit at Smith & Edwards, a local sporting goods store. After getting credit, various members went to the store and picked up and signed for different items of baseball equipment and uniforms, at a total cost of $3,900. When Smith, the owner, requested payment, the members arranged a fundraising activity that produced only $149. Smith sued the Golden Spike Little League as an entity and the members who had picked up and signed for the equipment individually. The individual defendants denied that they had any personal liability, contending that only the Golden Spike Little League could be held responsible.

DECISION: Judgment for Smith against the individual members. The association could not be held liable because it did not have any legal existence. The persons who purchased the goods from the seller were personally liable as buyers even though they had purported to act on behalf of the unincorporated association. [*Smith & Edwards v. Golden Spike Little League*, **577 P.2d 132 (Utah 1978)**]

---

[4] *Kim v. Chamberlain*, 504 So.2d 1213 (Ala. App. 1987).

[5] The National Conference of Commissioners on Uniform State Laws has adopted a Uniform Unincorporated Nonprofit Association Act. In addition, community associations are being formed, primarily for the purpose of community planning and environmental protection.

[6] Under a policy of minimizing judicial involvement in private organizations, courts ordinarily will refrain from reviewing decisions on the internal-governance issues of unincorporated private associations where the organization's own adjudicatory procedures are followed. In *Tackney v. United States Naval Academy Alumni Association Inc.*, 971 A.2d 309 (Md. App. 2009), involving an incorporated private association, the court found that judicial intervention was not warranted regarding the election of trustees in 2006, because the alumni board's actions were not fraudulent or arbitrary.

6. Cooperatives

cooperative – group of two or more persons or enterprises that acts through a common agent with respect to a common objective, such as buying or selling.

A **cooperative** consists of a group of two or more independent persons or enterprises that cooperate for a common objective or function. Thus, farmers may pool their farm products and sell them. Consumers may likewise pool their orders and purchase goods in bulk.

(A) INCORPORATED COOPERATIVES. Statutes commonly provide for the special incorporation of cooperative enterprises. Such statutes often provide that any excess of payments over the cost of operation shall be refunded to each participant member in direct proportion to the volume of business that the member has done with the cooperative. This contrasts with the payment of a dividend by an ordinary business corporation in which the payment of dividends is proportional to the number of shares held by the shareholder and is unrelated to the extent of the shareholder's business activities with the enterprise.

(B) ANTITRUST LAW EXEMPTION. The agreement by the members of sellers' cooperatives that all products shall be sold at a common price is an agreement to fix prices. Therefore, the sellers' cooperative is basically an agreement in restraint of trade and a violation of antitrust laws. The Capper-Volstead Act of 1922 expressly exempts normal selling activities of farmers' and dairy farmers' cooperatives from the operation of the federal Sherman Antitrust Act so long as the cooperatives do not conspire with outsiders to fix prices.

C. THE FRANCHISE BUSINESS FORMAT

In individual situations, *franchising* is a *method* of doing business, not a *form* of business organization. A franchisor or franchisee could be a sole proprietor, a partnership, a limited liability company, or a corporation. It is a *business format*, as opposed to a business organization. Franchising relies on contract law to set forth the rights and obligations of the parties. However, the Federal Trade Commission Act and certain state laws require disclosure. Any federal and/or state laws regulating securities, intellectual property, antitrust violations, sales, agency, employment, and tort law apply to franchises.

Section 5 of the Federal Trade Commission Act prohibits deceptive, manipulative, or unfair business practices,[7] and state deceptive trade practices acts similarly prohibit such practice.

franchise – privilege or authorization, generally exclusive, to engage in a particular activity within a particular geographic area, such as a government franchise to operate a taxi company within a specified city, or a private franchise as the grant by a manufacturer of a right to sell products within a particular territory or for a particular number of years.

As defined by the Federal Trade Commission (FTC) a commercial business arrangement is a **franchise** if it satisfies three definitional elements: the franchisor must (1) promise to provide a trademark or other commercial symbol; (2) promise to exercise significant control or provide significant assistance in the operation of the business; and (3) require a minimum payment of at least $500 during the first six months of operations.[8]

---

[7] 15 U.S.C. §45.

[8] Many business opportunities are not franchises and are subject to federal and state "business opportunity" laws. Companies that market and sell products to persons to enable them to start a business may be subject to these laws. The FTC issued a new "business opportunity rule" effective March 1, 2012, 12 C.F.R. Part 437. It exempts franchisors covered by the FTC Franchise Rule from the new rule.

7. Definition and Types of Franchises

franchisor – party granting the franchise.

franchisee – person to whom franchise is granted.

The **franchisor** is the party granting the franchise, and the **franchisee** is the person to whom the franchise is granted. There are three principal types of franchises. The first is a *manufacturing* or *processing franchise*, in which the franchisor grants the franchisee authority to manufacture and sell products under the trademark(s) of the franchisor. The franchisor may supply an essential ingredient in a processing franchise, such as the syrup for an independent regional Coca-Cola bottling company. The second type of franchise is a *service franchise*, whereby the franchisee renders a service to customers under the terms of a franchise agreement. The drain-cleaning service provided by Roto-Rooter is an example of a service franchise. The third type is a *distribution franchise*, in which the franchisor's products are sold to a franchisee, who then resells to customers in a geographical area. Exxon Mobil Oil Company's products are often sold to retail customers through independent distribution franchises.

A common issue in litigation under state laws protecting franchisees or dealers is whether the business arrangement is a franchise or dealership under the applicable state law.[9] The *Girl Scouts of Manitou* case dealt with such a question.

CASE SUMMARY

Are Girl Scouts "Dealers"?

FACTS: The Girl Scouts of the United States of America (GSUSA) is led by the National Council. Local councils are governed by their own independent boards of directors, and employ their own officers and professional staff and are responsible for their own financial health. For a nominal fee, GSUSA issues a charter to the local council, which grants to that council "the right to develop, manage, and maintain Girl Scouting throughout the areas of its jurisdiction, including the right to use GSUSA's names and protected marks." Plaintiff Manitou Council is one of GSUSA's local councils. It employs a full-time staff of 17 people. It owns significant real property, including two large Girl Scout camps and a corporate office building. Manitou asserts that nearly 100 percent of its annual revenues derive from the sale of Girl Scout merchandise and services, private donations, and investment income from Manitou's reserve funds. Girl Scout cookie sales alone generate more than $1 million in revenue each year. While the charter was still in effect, Manitou rejected the GSUSA merger directive, and GSUSA sought to unilaterally remove more than half of Manitou's jurisdiction. Manitou sued GSUSA under the Wisconsin Fair Dealership Law (WFDL), seeking a preliminary injunction. From a ruling in favor of GSUSA, Manitou appealed.

DECISION: GSUSA was enjoined from making any changes to Manitou's jurisdiction pending final resolution on the merits. Under the WFDL, it is illegal for any grantor to "terminate, cancel, fail to renew, or substantially change the competitive circumstances of a dealership agreement without good cause." GSUSA's argument that the Girl Scouts "are not 'dealers' of anything," emphasizing the word "dealer" as if its members are accused of selling drugs on the street corner, is unavailing. It matters not whether we would call the Girl Scouts "dealers" in everyday conversation; what matters is only how the statute defines the term, and the activities of Manitou clearly fall within its definition. Manitou is a business. It sells and distributes goods.

[9] *Missouri Beverage Co., Inc. v. Sheldon Brothers, Inc.,* 669 F.3d 873 (8th Cir. 2012).

CASE SUMMARY

Continued

It distributes services. It makes extensive use of GSUSA's marks and names. These requirements satisfy the statutes' plain language, which the Wisconsin Supreme Court has recognized was designed "to encompass an extraordinarily diverse set of business relationships not limited to the traditional franchise." [***Girl Scouts of Manitou v. GSUSA***, 549 F.3d 1079 (7th Cir. 2008)]

8. The Franchise Agreement

The relationship between the franchisor and the franchisee is ordinarily an arm's-length relationship between two independent contractors. Their respective rights are determined by the contract existing between them, called the **franchise agreement**.[10] The agreement sets forth the rights of the franchisee to use the **trademarks**, **trade name**, **trade dress**, and **trade secrets** of the franchisor. **For Example,** Burger King Corporation licenses franchisees to use the trademarks Burger King, Whopper, Croissanwich, and Whopper Jr.[11] The franchise agreement commonly requires the franchisor to provide training for the franchisee's employees, including processing or repair training. Thus, a new Chili's Bar and Grill franchise can expect to have its employees taught how to prepare and serve the food on its menu. In a distribution franchise, an Acura dealer can expect the franchisor to train its mechanics to repair the automobiles it sells. The franchise agreement also deals with terms for payment of various fees by the franchisee and sets forth compliance requirements for quality control set by the franchisor.

The duration of a franchise is a critical element of the franchise agreement. The franchise may last for as long as the parties agree. The laws in some states may require advance written notice of cancellation.[12] Franchise contracts generally specify the causes for which the franchisor may terminate the franchise, such as the franchisee's death, bankruptcy, failure to make payments, or failure to meet sales quotas.[13] **For Example,** Burger King Corp. (BKC) instituted a required new item, value meals, "which must be sold in all U.S. restaurants … and failure to comply will be considered a default under the applicable franchise agreement." After due notice to franchisees Elizabeth and Luan Sadik and no compliance by the Sadiks with regard to the directive to sell the new value meal items, BKC cancelled the franchise, and the courts upheld BKC's action as proper under the franchise contract.[14]

Franchise agreements frequently contain an arbitration provision under which a neutral party is to make a final and binding determination whether there has been a breach of the contract sufficient to justify cancellation of the franchise.[15] The arbitration provision may provide that the franchisor can appoint a trustee to run the business of the franchisee while arbitration proceedings are pending.

franchise agreement – sets forth rights of franchisee to use trademarks, etc., of franchisor.

trademark – mark that identifies a product.

trade name – name under which a business is carried on and, if fictitious, must be registered.

trade dress – product's total image including its overall packaging look.

trade secret – formula, device, or compilation of information that is used in one's business and is of such a nature that it provides an advantage over competitors who do not have the information.

---

[10] *See American Standard Inc. v. Meehan*, 517 F. Supp. 2d 976 (N.D. Ohio 2007).
[11] *Burger King Corp. v. Hinton, Inc.*, 203 F. Supp. 2d 1357 (S.D. Fla. 2002).
[12] See, for example, Mo. Rev. Stat. §407.405.
[13] *Smith's Sports Cycles, Inc. v. American Suzuki*, 82 So.3d 682 (Ala. 2011).
[14] *Burger King Corp. v. E-Z Corporations*, 572 F.3d 1306 (11th Cir. 2009).
[15] *Central New Jersey Freightliner, Inc., v. Freightliner Corp.*, 987 F. Supp. 289 (D.N.J. 1998).

9. Special Protections under Federal Laws

Holders of automobile dealership franchises are protected from bad-faith termination of their dealerships by the federal Automobile Dealers' Day in Court Act (ADDCA).[16] **For Example,** Anthony Arciniaga was allowed to proceed with his ADDCA lawsuit against General Motors. The court refused to allow GM to create and apply a corporate structure that evades the ADDCA. Collectively, the court looked to the Dealer Sales and Service Agreement, the Shareholders' Agreement, and other documents that together made up the understanding between Arciniaga and GM, which made it possible for Arciniaga to become an automobile dealer. The court concluded that all of the agreements viewed together constituted a "motor vehicle franchise contract." The court refused to focus on just one document as asserted by GM because doing so would negate the protective features of the ADDCA.[17]

When an automobile manufacturer makes arbitrary and unreasonable demands and then terminates a dealer's franchise for failure to comply with the demands, the manufacturer is liable for the damages caused. The right of a franchisee to transfer its contractual rights in the franchise is protected by the state law subject to notice and approval by the franchisor.[18]

CASE SUMMARY

An Associate of Tony and Carmella Soprano? Prove It

FACTS: After a fire at its Audi dealership, Coast Automotive Group, Ltd., sought to transfer its contractual rights in the franchise to Aspen Knolles, Ltd. Applications were submitted to Volkswagen of America (VOA) and Audi of America (AOA), the franchisors, for approval. Under state law, a franchisor can reject a proposed transferee by giving material reasons relating to the character, financial ability, or business experience of the proposed transferee. However, it may not unreasonably withhold consent. VOA and AOA rejected the proposed corporate transferee, Aspen Knolles, Inc., because a principal of the group, Mr. Mazzuoccola, a race car enthusiast who sponsored a professional racing team and owned a Jeep dealership, was said by an individual to have associated with known organized crime figures. Coast sued VOA and AOA for specific performance. At the trial, Mr. Mazzuoccola took the witness stand to testify about his business experience.

DECISION: Judgment for Coast. The right of a franchisee to transfer its contractual rights in the franchise is protected by state law subject to notice and approval by the franchisor. The burden of proof is on the franchisor to present credible reasons for the refusal to consent. It is not a credible reason to turn down a transferee because of association with automobile racing. Association with organized crime figures is a valid reason to turn down a transferee; but there was no credible evidence presented to support such a contention at the trial. Indeed, Mr. Mazzuoccola took the stand giving VOA and AOA an opportunity to question him on character issues, and none were raised. Specific performance is the appropriate remedy. [*VW Credit, Inc. v. Coast Automobile Group, Ltd.*, 787 A.2d 950 (N.J. Super. 2002)]

---

[16] 15 U.S.C. §§1221–1225.
[17] *Arciniaga v. General Motors Corp.*, 418 F. Supp. 2d 374 (S.D.N.Y. 2005).
[18] *KMS Restaurant Corp. v. Wendy's International*, 361 F.3d 1321 (11th Cir. 2004).

The Petroleum Marketing Practices Act (PMPA) gives gas station franchisees the opportunity to continue in business by purchasing the entire premises used in selling motor fuel when the franchisor decides to sell the property and not renew a lease. In some instances, the franchisor's intentions are unclear and its actions may be perceived as contrary to the PMPA. Litigation may be necessary to resolve the matter. **For Example,** eight independent gas station operators who leased stations from Shell Oil Co. and sold Shell products were successful in their PMPA lawsuit against Shell when Shell phased out rental subsidies provided franchisees under the parties' lease agreements and set the wholesale prices it charged dealers for gasoline so high that the increase would squeeze dealers' profits or force them to raise prices that competition could undercut. The dealers argued this was done to reduce the number of independent gas stations in the region. A jury awarded $3.3 million in compensatory damages.[19]

The PMPA prohibits early termination of a franchise, except when the franchisee's failure to comply with a provision of the franchise is so serious as to undermine the entire relationship.[20]

10. Disclosure

The offer and sale of a franchise requires compliance with both federal and state laws.

Franchise Rule – FTC rule requiring detailed disclosures and prohibiting certain practices.

(A) FEDERAL LAW. Franchisors must comply with the FTC's amended **Franchise Rule**, which supplanted the FTC's Uniform Franchise Offering Circular (UFOC) disclosure format in 2008. The amended Rule updates the UFOC to address utilization of new technologies, like the Internet; requires more disclosure about the nature of the franchisor franchisee relationship; exempts certain entities like large franchisees; and prohibits certain practices not addressed in the UFOC. The Franchise Rule requires a franchisor to provide each prospective franchisee with a detailed franchise disclosure document ("FDD") at least 14 calendar days before the prospective franchisee signs a binding agreement or makes any payment to the franchisor. This ensures that prospective franchisees have sufficient time in which to review the disclosures. The FDD requires some 23 items of disclosure, including topics such as: (1) the business experience of the franchisor and its brokers, (2) any current and past litigation against the franchisor, (3) any previous bankruptcy, (4) the material terms of the franchise agreement, (5) initial and recurring payments, (6) restrictions on territories, (7) grounds for termination of the franchise, and (8) actual, average, or projected sales, profits, or earnings.[21]

(B) STATE LAWS. Some 35 states allow franchisors who utilize properly prepared FDDs and comply with the FTC's Franchise Rule 14-day reflection period to enter franchise agreements with franchisees. The remaining 15 states have franchising laws of their own, often requiring franchisors to file a franchise offering circular with a state agency. These states, referred to as "registration

---

[19] Kimberly Blanton, "Jury Rules for Franchisees in Shell Trial," *Boston Globe*, December 9, 2004, at C-3.

[20] In *Chevron v. El-Khoury*, 285 F.3d 1159 (9th Cir. 2002), the Court of Appeals remanded a franchise termination case for trial on the materiality of a franchisee's failure to pay $15,000 in California sales taxes when the oil company had unsuccessfully attempted to buy out the dealer and, when the last buyout offer was rejected, had selected him to be audited. The dealer eventually paid all taxes due. One of Chevron's executives testified that the failure to pay taxes was between "the dealer and the state" rather than the dealer and Chevron. However, Chevron contended that the failure to pay all taxes when due was a violation of the franchise agreement and tarnished the company's image.

[21] See the Federal Trade Commission, *Franchise Rule Compliance Guide*, 16 C.F.R. Part 436, for details on the other disclosure items required by the FDD. For FTC staff opinions, see **http://www.ftc.gov/bcp/franchise/netadopin.shtm**.

states," seek to protect citizens from fraudulent schemes and provide recourse in state court if a franchisor violates state laws.[22]

11. Vicarious Liability Claims against Franchisors

In theory, a franchisor is not liable to a third person dealing with or affected by the franchise holder. This freedom from liability is one of the main reasons franchisors use franchises. If the negligence of the franchisee causes harm to a third person, the franchisor is not liable because the franchisee is an independent contractor. However, franchisors continue to be subject to lawsuits based on the wrongful conduct of their franchisees under the theory of either actual authority or apparent authority.[23]

CASE SUMMARY

Why Franchisors Use Franchises!

FACTS: William Roberts operated a McDonald's restaurant in Newcastle, Washington, under a franchise agreement with McDonald's Corporation. A thriving drug scene existed among employees and assistant managers at the restaurant. In May 2000, the restaurant hired 15-year-old D.L.S., and within weeks, she was part of the drug scene there. Thereafter, she left home to live with an assistant manager and use drugs. Her father, Clifford Street, and D.L.S. sued McDonald's Corp. and Roberts for introducing D.L.S. to drugs and sex. The trial court dismissed the claims against McDonald's Corp., and D.L.S. and her father appealed. Mr. Street testified that "no person in their right mind would believe that McDonald's did not control what happened at the individual restaurants."

DECISION: The franchise agreement clearly provided that Roberts was not an agent of McDonald's Corporation and that McDonald's had no control over the daily operations of the restaurant. Thus, McDonald's has no liability as Roberts' actual principal. The court next considered an apparent authority theory to determine whether McDonald's created apparent authority that it operated the Newcastle restaurant and would ensure a safe working environment for young workers there. Beyond the general impression created by advertising that McDonald's restaurants offer a wholesome environment, no representations or acts of McDonald's existed to create an apparent employment relationship between McDonald's and D.L.S. She and her parents must pursue their claims against the franchisee. [**D.L.S. v. Maybin**, 121 P.3d 1210 (Wash. App. 2005)]

To maintain uniform systems for processing or distributing goods or rendering services, franchisors often place significant controls on their franchisees' businesses. These controls are set forth in franchise agreements and operating manuals. In a lawsuit brought against a franchisor for the wrongful conduct of its franchisee, the franchise agreement and operations manuals may be used as evidence of the franchisor's right to control the franchisee and the existence of an agency relationship rather than an independent contractor relationship.[24]

---

[22] The registration states are California, Hawaii, Illinois, Indiana, Maryland, Michigan, Minnesota, New York, North Dakota, Oregon, Rhode Island, South Dakota, Virginia, Washington, and Wisconsin.
[23] *Ketterling v. Burger King Corporation*, 272 P.3d 527 (Idaho 2012).
[24] *J. M. v. Shell Oil Co.*, 1996 Bus. Franchise Guide (C.C.H.) ¶ 10,817 (Mo. App.).

Thinking Things Through

Don't Finagle the Bagel!

Ken Miyamoto was president and a shareholder of Bixby's Food Systems, Inc. (Bixby's), a franchisor of bagel restaurants. The business is incorporated and provides limited liability to Miyamoto and its other corporate investors. Bixby's hired a lawyer familiar with franchise disclosure laws in Illinois and drafted a franchise offering circular (FOC) in accordance with state laws. Jan and Phillip McKay attended a meeting of existing and prospective franchisees where Miyamoto spoke and said that prospective franchisees had signed and paid for 340 development agreements; a similar statement also appeared in a Bixby's newsletter. The McKays soon thereafter executed a franchise agreement. Based on Miyamoto's view that a lease of larger retail space than recommended in Bixby's circular would bring in larger revenues, the McKays executed the larger-than-recommended lease and spent $400,000 making their restaurant operational, which was a much higher investment than projected in the FOC. When the restaurant opened, sales did not come close to the figures estimated in the FOC. After eight months of operations, Bixby's terminated the McKays' franchise for their inability to pay Bixby's franchise royalty fees. Bixby's sued the McKays for continuing to use its trademark, and the McKays counterclaimed against Bixby's, Inc. and Miyamoto as an individual for violation of the state Franchise Disclosure Act and the state Deceptive Business Practices Act.

Bixby's FOC was not shown to contain material misstatements of fact. However, the McKays listed a number of statements made by Miyamoto that were untrue concerning future events regarding costs, profitability, and financial success, like his encouraging them to rent larger-than-

recommended retail space to bring in larger revenues, which did not materialize. The court held that such statements about future events, costs, and profitability are not actionable misrepresentations under the state Franchise Disclosure Act. Corporate executives selling franchises have latitude to take the facts set forth in franchise offering circulars and project a bright future in most respects. That is, they have a legal right to put their "spin" on the facts, just as society does in governmental and personal affairs. Of course, buyers must beware and view assertions about future events, costs, and profitability with critical analysis and informed skepticism.

With his business incorporated and his circulars drafted by competent counsel, was Miyamoto immune from personal liability in this case? The answer is no. When Miyamoto told the group of prospective franchisees that some 340 development agreements had been signed and paid for and later repeated this statement in a newsletter, he was not Thinking Things Through. Through the discovery process that preceded a trial, the McKays' attorney "discovered" that Bixby's had just 15 agreements executed and paid for at the time of Miyamoto's assertion that 340 agreements were executed and paid for. Such a material misstatement of fact was a violation of the state franchising and deceptive practices laws.

The economic resources expended by Bixby's, Inc., to provide limited liability could not shield its shareholder-president from the consequences of his enormous lie. Along with Bixby's, Inc., Miyamoto was held personally liable to the McKays under the state statutes.*

---

*Bixby's Food Systems, Inc. v. McKay, 193 F. Supp. 2d 1053 (N.D. Ill. 2002).

To avoid negating its franchisees' independent contractor status and being liable for the wrongful conduct of a franchisee, the franchisor should make certain that the franchise agreement minimizes the number and kind of provisions that authorize the franchisor to control the "means" of operating the business. **For Example,** the franchisor should not exercise control over employment-related matters.[25]

Franchisors may also insulate themselves from liability by requiring individual franchisees to take steps to publicly maintain their own individual business identities.

---

[25] Consider the degree of control exercised by McDonald's Corp. over its franchises. Only designated food and beverages may be served, and franchisees are required to use prescribed buildings and equipment. The franchisor dictates the level of quality, service, and cleanliness. All franchisees' employees must wear the uniforms designated by the franchisor with McDonald's logos. McDonald's dictates management, advertising, and personnel policies and requires that managers be trained at its "Hamburger University." The Illinois Court of Appeals held that the question of whether a franchise was an apparent agent of McDonald's was an issue of material fact that should go to a jury in a lawsuit involving a customer's slip and fall on ice in the franchised restaurant's bathroom. The court stated that the employees responsible for maintaining the bathroom wore "McDonald's uniforms" and were required to follow McDonald's standards of "quality, service, and cleanliness." *O'Banner v. McDonald's Corp.*, 653 N.E.2d 1267 (Ill. App. 1995). On further appeal to the Supreme Court of Illinois, the Court of Appeals was reversed because in order to recover on an apparent agency theory, the customer had to show that he actually relied on the apparent agency in going to the restaurant where he was injured. The customer failed to do so, thus losing the right to hold McDonald's Corp. liable for his injuries. *O'Banner v. McDonald's Corp.*, 670 N.E.2d 632 (Ill. 1996). See *Husain v. McDonald's Corp.*, 140 Cal. Rptr. 3d 370, 377 (Cal. App. 2012), where the form license agreement between McDonald's and the franchisor explains the essence of the "McDonald's system" is to ensure comprehensive control by McDonald's over every material aspect of the restaurant's operations so the uniformity of the McDonald's customer experience could be assured in every one of its locations.

For Example, a gas station may post a sign stating that it is "dealer owned and operated," or a real estate franchise may list on its business sign the franchise name and the name of the local owner, such as Century 21, L & K Realty Co. All invoices, purchase orders, paychecks, and notices to employees should contain notice of the independent ownership and operation of the business. Finally, franchisors should require their franchisees to maintain appropriate comprehensive general liability insurance, workers' compensation insurance, and other appropriate insurance.

12. Franchises and Employee Misclassifications

Whether someone is a franchisee-independent contractor or an employee is determined by the actual relationship between the individual and the business, and not by a label or a franchise agreement. **For Example,** Coverall North American Inc. is one of the largest global commercial cleaning franchisors in North America, with over 9,000 franchise owners and 50,000 customers. Each individual who purchases a janitorial cleaning franchise must enter a standard unit agreement with Coverall. The agreement gives Coverall the exclusive rights to perform all billing and collection services provided by franchisees and to deduct fees before remitting payments. State law deals with whether an individual who is performing services is an independent contractor or an employee. Under one prong of the Massachusetts law, the burden is placed on Coverall to establish that the individual "is performing services that are part of an independent, separate, and distinct business from that of the employer." Coverall trains its franchisees and provides them with uniforms and identification badges; it contracted with all customers, with limited exceptions, until May 2009; and Coverall is the party billing all customers for cleaning services performed and receives a percentage of the revenues earned on every cleaning service. Accordingly, Coverall sells cleaning services, the same services provided by the "franchisees." Because the franchisees did not perform services outside the usual course of Coverall's business, Coverall failed to establish that franchisees were independent contractors.[26]

The U.S. Labor Secretary stated that misclassification has saved some employers as much as 20 to 30 percent on their labor costs, which allows them to gain business by underbidding employers that obey the rules and causes a downward pressure on wages and a loss in government revenues.[27]

LawFlix

Good Burger (1997) (PG)

This film is a story of the competition, mass marketing, and secret sauce issues in franchising. The movie provides a look at liability, product quality, and espionage.

---

[26] *Awauh v. Coverall North America, Inc.* 707 F. Supp. 2d 80 (D. Mass. 2010).

[27] Misclassification deprives employees of the protection of wage and hour laws and time-and-one-half rates for overtime work; it also denies them eligibility for unemployment insurance coverage, workers' compensation protection, and other statutory right under the antidiscrimination and labor laws.

Employers who pay workers' compensation and unemployment insurance premiums for their employees as required by law and pay overtime rates under the Fair Labor Standards Act are placed at a competitive disadvantage compared to employers who misclassify their employees. States are deprived of payroll taxes and unemployment and workers' compensation taxes.

MAKE THE CONNECTION

SUMMARY

The three principal forms of Business Organizations are sole proprietorships, partnerships, and corporations. A *sole proprietorship* is a form of business organization in which one person owns the business, controls all decisions, receives all profits, and has unlimited liability for all obligations and liabilities. A *partnership* involves the pooling of capital resources and talents of two or more persons whose goal is making a profit; the partners are subject to unlimited personal liability. However, newly created forms of Business Organizations—the *limited liability company* and the *limited liability partnership*—allow for tax treatment as a partnership with certain limited liability for the owners.

A business *corporation* exists to make a profit. It is created by government grant, and its shareholders elect a board of directors whose members are responsible for managing the business. A shareholder's liability is limited to the capital the shareholder invested in the business or paid for shares. Corporate existence continues without regard to the death of shareholders or the transfer of stock by them.

The selection of the form of organization is determined by the nature of the business, tax considerations, the financial risk involved, the importance of limited liability, and the extent of management control desired.

A *joint venture* exists when two or more persons combine their labor or property for a single business undertaking and share profits and losses as agreed. An unincorporated association is a combination of two or more persons for the pursuit of a common purpose.

A *cooperative* consists of two or more persons or enterprises, such as farmers, who cooperate to achieve a common objective, such as the distribution of farm products.

By a franchise, the owner of a trademark, trade name, or copyright licenses others to use the mark or copyright in selling goods or services. To protect against fraud, the FTC requires that franchisors provide prospective franchisees with a disclosure statement 10 days prior to any transaction. The Automobile Dealers' Day in Court Act and the Petroleum Marketing Practices Act are federal laws that provide covered franchisees with protection from bad-faith terminations. State laws also protect franchisees in a wide range of businesses. A franchisor is not liable to third persons dealing with its franchisees. Liability of the franchisor may, however, be imposed on the ground of the apparent authority of the franchisee or the latter's control by the franchisor. Liability of the franchisor may also arise in cases of product liability.

LEARNING OUTCOMES

After studying this chapter, you should be able to clearly explain:

A. Principal Forms of Business Organizations

L0.1   Explain the advantages and disadvantages of the three principal forms of business organizations
    See the discussion on proprietorships, partnerships (LLPs and LLCs), and corporations beginning on p. 916.

B. Specialized Forms of Organizations

L0.2   Recognize that the rules of law governing the rights and liabilities of joint ventures are substantially the same as those that govern partnerships
    See the *PGI/Rathe* joint venture remedy on p. 918.

See the *Kurwa* case and the joint venture remedy while operating in the corporate form on p. 918.

C. The Franchise Business Format

L0.3   Evaluate whether a business arrangement is a franchise protected under state or federal law
    See the *Girl Scouts of Manitou* case applying a state's fair dealership law, pp. 921–922.
    See the example where Mr. Arciniaga was allowed to proceed with his federal ADDCA lawsuit against General Motors on p. 923.

LO.4 Explain how the rights of the parties to a franchise agreement are determined by their contract
> See the *Burger King* example involving cancellation of franchises, p. 922.

LO.5 Explain why freedom from vicarious liability is a reason for franchisors to use the franchise format
> See the *McDonald's* case in which only the franchisee was liable for the torts to the

minor emanating from the McDonald's restaurant, p. 925.

LO.6 Recognize the implications of the misclassifications of employees as franchisee-independent contractors
> See the *Coverall* misclassification scheme on p. 927.

KEY TERMS

cooperative	franchisor	trade dress
corporations	joint venture	trade name
franchise	limited liability company (LLC)	trade secrets
franchise agreement	limited liability partnership (LLP)	trademarks
franchise rule	partnership	unincorporated association
franchisee	sole or individual proprietorship	

QUESTIONS AND CASE PROBLEMS

1. In July 2008 Miller Brewing Co. and Coors Brewing Co. formed a joint venture to better compete with the dominant beer manufacturer, Anheuser Busch. The venture was named "MillerCoors LLC." Under the joint venture Miller Brewing Co. and Coors Brewing Company have a 50 percent voting interest in the entity, and each appoints half of the directors. Moreover, the CEOs of Miller and Coors resolve disputes, and all revenues are distributed directly to Miller and Coors, with cash returned to meet the operating needs of the joint venture. Ohio law requires just cause for the termination of beer distributors but allows a "successor manufacturer" to terminate existing distributorships without proving just cause so long as the predecessor does not exercise control over the successor. In accordance with the "successor manufacturer" exception, MillerCoors LLC notified Ohio wholesale beer distributors that it was terminating their distributorships. The distributorships sought injunctive relief. MillerCoors LLC moved for summary judgment. Decide. [*Beverage Distributors, Inc. v. Miller Brewing Co.*, 803 F. Supp. 2d 765 (S.D. Ohio)]

2. Jerome, Sheila, Gary, and Ella agreed to purchase a tract of land and make it available for use as a free playground for neighborhood children. They called the enterprise Meadowbrook Playground. Jerome and Gary improperly hung one of the playground swings, and a child was injured. Suit was brought against Meadowbrook Playground. Can damages be recovered?

3. Morris Friedman was president of Tiny Doubles International, Inc. He sold business opportunities for Tiny Doubles Studios, which made small photographic statues of people for customers. Friedman was the primary negotiator with prospective buyers of these studio business opportunities. He advised buyers up front that the opportunities were not franchises, and accordingly, he did not provide all of the information set forth in the disclosure rule on franchising, although he did provide full answers to all questions asked. Many businesses closed, however, because of lack of success. The FTC claims Friedman violated its disclosure rule. Friedman disagrees. Decide. [*FTC v. Tiny Doubles Int'l, Inc.*, 1996 Bus. Franchise Guide (C.C.H.) ¶ 10,831]

4. Wolf, King, and others sold business "opportunities" in vending machines by taking out ads in newspapers throughout the country.

When individuals responded, telemarketers called "fronters" would tell them of false earnings estimates, and those who could afford $16,000 to $25,000 for vending machines were turned over to "closers" who promised wonderful results. References were provided who were "shills"— they did not own vending machines but were paid to tell "stories" that were monitored by Wolf, King, and other supervisors. None of the individuals was given franchise disclosure documents. King induced one investor to mortgage her house so that she could pay $70,000 for a number of vending machines. In three years Wolf, King, and others took in some $31.3 million. The FTC alleged that the defendants violated the FTC franchise disclosure rule.

Is there a franchise disclosure rule violation if Wolf and King were merely selling vending machines? What if Wolf and King promised exclusive territories for the machines? Why would a franchise disclosure rule be necessary in this case? Decide. [*FTC v. Wolf*, Bus. Franchise Guide ¶ 27,655 (C.C.H. D. Fla.)]

5. Katherine Apostoleres owned the rights to Dunkin Donuts franchises in Brandon and Temple Terrace, Florida. The franchisor offered all its franchisees the right to renew their existing franchise agreements if they agreed to abide by advertising decisions favored by two-thirds of the local franchise owners in a given television market. Apostoleres refused the offer because she did not want to be bound by the two-thirds clause. Soon thereafter, Dunkin Donuts audited her two stores, and using a "yield and usage" analysis, it concluded that gross sales were being underreported. Based on these audits and a subsequent audit, Dunkin Donuts gave notice of immediate termination of Apostoleres's franchises, contending that the franchise agreement had been violated. Apostoleres stated that an implied obligation of good faith exists by operation of law in every contract, and she asserted that the audits were in retaliation for her refusal to accept the renewal agreement. The yield and usage test used in the audit was not specified in the franchise agreement as a measure to be used to enforce the franchisor's rights, and certain accounting experts testified as to the unreliability of this test. Was Dunkin Donuts

liable for breach of its implied obligation of good faith in this case? [*Dunkin Donuts of America v. Minerva, Inc.*, 956 F.2d 1566 (11th Cir.)]

6. To establish that a business is a "franchisee" qualifying for protection under the Illinois Franchise Disclosure Act, the business must demonstrate that it paid a franchise fee either directly or indirectly to the "franchisor" to enter the business. To-Am Equipment Company believed it had paid an implied fee in excess of $500 to enter the forklift business as a dealer for Mitsubishi-Caterpillar Forklift of America (MCFA) when it paid $1,658 for service manuals, which MCFA had commanded it to possess. MCFA denied that it had charged To-Am a franchise fee and asserted that it was not obligated to To-Am under the state Franchise Disclosure Act. Decide. [*To-Am Equipment Co. v. Mitsubishi-Caterpillar Forklift of America*, 853 Supp. 987 (N.D. Ill.)]

7. For a five-year period, Laurie Henry worked for James Doull, the owner of four Taco Bell franchises. During that time, she had an affair with Doull. He was the father of her two illegitimate children. Enraged over a domestic matter, Doull physically assaulted her at the Taco Bell Restaurant and then fired her and ordered her off the premises. Later, on Doull's recommendation, she was hired by a "company store" in an adjoining state. Henry brought suit against Doull, his corporate entity Taco Tia, Inc., and the Taco Bell Corporation (TBC). She did not characterize her suit as a case of sexual harassment. Rather, she contended that TBC was responsible for Doull's actions because he was TBC's agent. She sought damages for the loss of romantic and material satisfactions a person might expect from a traditional courtship and wedding. TBC denied that Doull was its employee or agent. The evidence showed that Henry knew that Doull's stores differed from TBC "company" stores. She insisted, having worked for four years for Doull at stores adorned with Taco-Bell signs, that Taco Bell was responsible for Doull's actions. Decide. [*Henry v. Taco Tia, Inc.*, 606 So.2d 1376 (La. App.)]

8. The Armory Committee was composed of officers from various National Guard units.

It organized a New Year's Eve dance at a charge of $2 per person to defray costs. Perry, along with others, was a member of the Armory Committee. Libby was a paying guest at the dance who was injured by slipping on frozen ruts in the immediate approaches to the steps leading to the armory building where the dance was held. He sued Perry, Turner, and the other committee members. The evidence showed that every member of the committee had taken some part in planning or running the dance with the exception of Turner. Was the Armory Committee an unincorporated association or a joint venture? Decide. [*Libby v. Perry*, 311 A.2d 527 (Me.)]

9. The Kawasaki Shop of Aurora, Illinois (dealer), advised Kawasaki Motors Corp. (manufacturer) that it intended to move its Kawasaki franchise from New York Street to Hill Avenue, which was in the same market area. The Hill Avenue location was also the site of a Honda franchise. The manufacturer's sales manager advised the dealer that he did not want the dealer to move in with Honda at the Hill Avenue site. In February, the dealer moved to the Hill Avenue location. Effective May 1, the manufacturer terminated the dealer's franchise. The dealer brought suit against the manufacturer under the state's Motor Vehicle Franchise Act, which made it unlawful to terminate franchises for site control (requiring that the dealer's site be used exclusively as a Kawasaki dealership). The manufacturer argued that it had a right to have its products sold by a dealer who was not affiliated with a competitor. Decide. [*Kawasaki Shop v. Kawasaki Motors Corp.*, 544 N.E.2d 457 (Ill. App.)]

10. Goodward, a newly hired newspaper reporter for the *Cape Cod News*, learned that the local cranberry growers had made an agreement under which they pooled their cranberry crops each year and sold them at what they determined to be a fair price. Goodward believes that such an agreement is in restraint of trade and a violation of the antitrust laws. Is he correct?

11. Food Caterers of East Hartford, Connecticut, obtained a franchise from Chicken Delight to use that name at its store. Food Caterers agreed to the product standards and controls specified by the franchisor. The franchise contract required the franchisee to maintain a free delivery service to deliver hot, freshly prepared food to customers. The franchisee used a delivery truck that bore no sign or name. Its employee Carfiro was driving the truck in making a food delivery when he negligently struck and killed McLaughlin. The victim's estate sued Chicken Delight on the theory that Carfiro was its agent because he was doing work that Chicken Delight required and that benefited Chicken Delight. Was Carfiro the agent of Chicken Delight? [*McLaughlin's Estate v. Chicken Delight, Inc.*, 321 A.2d 456 (Conn.)]

12. Groseth had the International Harvester (IH) truck franchise in Yankton, South Dakota. The franchise agreement Groseth signed required dealers to "cooperate with the Company by placing orders for goods in accordance with advance ordering programs announced by the Company." IH wanted to terminate Groseth's franchise because he refused to comply with IH's requirement that a computerized "dealer communication network" (DCN) be set up. Under the DCN, each dealer was required to obtain a computer terminal, display screen, and software. The DCN was initially used for ordering parts and allowed IH to reduce the number of employees needed for manual processing of "parts" orders. Groseth refused to set up the DCN because of the expense. Moreover, he contended that the task of ordering parts was easily accomplished by telephone or written orders. Did IH have good cause to terminate Groseth's franchise? [*Groseth International Harvester, Inc. v. International Harvester*, 442 N.W.2d 229 (S.D.)]

13. Brenner was in the scrap iron business. Almost daily, Plitt lent Brenner money with which to purchase scrap iron. The agreement of the parties was that when the scrap was sold, Plitt would be repaid and would receive an additional sum as compensation for making the loans. The loans were to be repaid in any case without regard to whether Brenner made a profit. A dispute arose over the nature of the relationship between the

two men. Plitt claimed that it was a joint venture. Decide. [*Brenner v. Plitt*, 34 A.2d 853 (Md.)]

14. Donald Salisbury, William Roberts, and others purchased property from Laurel Chapman, a partner of Chapman Realty, a franchisee of Realty World. The purchasers made payments directly to Laurel Chapman at the Realty World office, and Chapman was to make payments on the property's mortgage. However, Chapman did not make the payments and absconded with the funds. Salisbury and Roberts sued the franchisor, Realty World, claiming that Realty World was liable for the wrongful acts of the apparent agent, Chapman. Realty World and Chapman Realty were parties to a franchise agreement stating that the parties were franchisor and franchisee. The agreement contained a clause that required Chapman to prominently display a certificate in the office setting forth her status as an independent franchisee. Chapman displayed such a sign, but the plaintiffs did not recall seeing it. Chapman Realty hires, supervises, and sets the compensation for all of its employees. The plaintiffs pointed out that Chapman Realty used the service mark Realty World on its signs, both outside and inside its offices. They pointed out

that a Realty World manual sets forth the general standards by which franchisees must run their businesses and that this represents clear control over the franchise. They contended that, all things considered, Realty World held out Chapman Realty as having authority to bind Realty World. Realty World disagreed, stating that both were independent businesses. Decide. [*Salisbury v. Chapman and Realty World, Inc.*, 65 N.E.2d 127 (Ill. App.)]

15. H.C. Blackwell Co. held a franchise from Kenworth Truck Co. to sell its trucks. After 12 years, the franchise was nearing expiration. Kenworth notified Blackwell that the franchise would not be renewed unless Blackwell sold more trucks and improved its building and bookkeeping systems within the next 90 days. Blackwell spent $90,000 attempting to meet the demands of Kenworth but could not do so because a year was required to make the specified changes. Kenworth refused to renew the franchise. Blackwell sued Kenworth for damages under the federal Automobile Dealers' Day in Court Act. Blackwell claimed that Kenworth had refused to renew in bad faith. Decide. [*Blackwell v. Kenworth Truck Co.*, 620 F.2d 104 (5th Cir.)]

CPA QUESTIONS

1. A joint venture is a(an):

   a. Association limited to no more than two persons in business for profit

   b. Enterprise of numerous co-owners in a nonprofit undertaking

   c. Corporate enterprise for a single undertaking of limited duration

   d. Association of persons engaged as co-owners in a single undertaking for profit

© Manuel Gutjahr/iStockphoto.com

CHAPTER 42

Partnerships

learningoutcomes

After studying this chapter, you should be able to

LO.1 Explain how partnerships are created by agreement, and understand that only when the partners' partnership agreement does not resolve an issue does partnership law apply

LO.2 Understand that no writing is needed to form a partnership, nor a tax ID number, nor a partnership name. All that is needed is clear evidence that the partners carried on as co-owners of a business for profit

LO.3 Distinguish between express authority and customary authority of a partner to act for a partnership

LO.4 List the duties of partners to one another

LO.5 Explain the nature and extent of a partner's liability on firm contracts and torts

LO.6 Describe how a partnership may be dissolved by the acts of partners, by operation of law, and by order of the court

933

P artnerships may be created without the formality of even a written partnership agreement when two or more individuals simply operate a business for a profit as co-owners. In July 2008 Paula Balzer was recruited to work for Blue Flame, a firm specializing in the business of marketing and live promotions. As of October 1, 2008, she states she was made a partner. Two firm e-mails reference her as a partner, and she was paid a monthly $15,000 draw. The firm's 2008 and 2009 tax returns listed her as a partner of Blue Flame. In October 2010, the partners had a falling-out with Paula. She disengaged from the firm on November 12, 2010, upon completion of two events she was committed to staging. The partners never executed a written partnership agreement with Paula and as a result did not believe she had partnership rights. When the firm failed to pay her certain money and expenses the court reverted to basic partnership law that a written contract of partnership is not necessary to the formation of a partnership and concluded that a partnership existed on the basis of the facts before the court.[1] Partnership relations are not narrowly governed by partnership law but are governed by the partners' partnership agreement. Only when the partnership agreement does not resolve an issue does partnership law apply. In many instances, individuals do not obtain legal advice in choosing the partnership form of business organization. Properly informed individuals today will probably not choose the partnership form of organization because partners are open to unlimited personal liability; they may choose a limited liability company to insulate the members from personal liability.

A. NATURE AND CREATION

Partnerships are created by agreement. A codification of general partnership law is found in the Uniform Partnership Act (UPA), which has been revised (Revised Uniform Partnership Act, or RUPA). Together, the UPA and the RUPA are in effect in 49 states.[2] Limited partnerships (LPs) and limited liability partnerships (LLPs) differ significantly from general partnerships and are discussed in the next chapter. The 1994 or 1997 versions of the Revised Uniform Partnership Act apply in 38 states.[3] Like the UPA, most of the provisions of the RUPA apply only when the partners do not have partnership agreement language that deals with the matter at issue.[4] Certain features of the RUPA that differ from those of the UPA are identified in the text.

---

[1] *Balzer v. Millward*, 2011 WL 1547211 (D. Conn. April 21, 2011).

[2] The UPA or the RUPA is in effect in all states except Louisiana.

[3] The RUPA or versions of it have been adopted by Alabama, Alaska, Arizona, Arkansas, California, Colorado, Connecticut, Delaware, District of Columbia, Florida, Hawaii, Idaho, Illinois, Iowa, Kansas, Kentucky, Maine, Maryland, Minnesota, Mississippi, Montana, Nebraska, Nevada, New Jersey, New Mexico, North Dakota, Ohio, Oklahoma, Oregon, Puerto Rico, South Dakota, Tennessee, Texas, Utah, Vermont, Virginia, Washington, West Virginia, and Wyoming. The RUPA was approved in 1992 and amended in 1993, 1994, and 1997. It provides for a transition period after passage, during which only newly created partnerships come under the new law, with all partnerships in the state eventually being governed by the RUPA (see R.U.P.A. §1206(a)).

[4] See *Mission West v. Republic*, 873 A.2d 372 (Md. App. 2005).

1. Definition

partnership – pooling of capital resources and the business or professional talents of two or more individuals (partners) with the goal of making a profit.

A **partnership** (also called a **general partnership**) is a relationship created by the voluntary "association of two or more persons to carry on as co-owners a business for profit."[5] The persons so associated are called **partners** or **general partners**. A partner is the agent of the partnership and of each partner with respect to partnership matters. A partner is not an employee of the partnership even when doing work that would ordinarily be done by an employee.

general partnership – partnership in which the partners conduct as co-owners a business for profit, and each partner has a right to take part in the management of the business and has unlimited liability.

CASE SUMMARY

A Partner Is Not an Employee

partner – one of two or more persons who jointly own and carry on a business for profit.

FACTS: Ford and Mitcham were partners engaged in construction. Ford was killed at work. His widow made a claim for workers' compensation against the partnership. Mitcham opposed the claim on the ground that Ford was a partner, not an employee.

general partners – partners who publicly and actively engage in the transaction of firm business.

DECISION: Workers' compensation denied. While a working partner does work, a partner is not an employee. The essential element of an employment relationship is the right of the employer to control the employee. Although a partner is required to act in a proper manner, a partner is not subject to the control of the partnership in the same sense as an employee and therefore is not an "employee" of the partnership for the purpose of workers' compensation. [***Ford v. Mitcham***, **298 So.2d 34 (Ala. App. 1974)**]

2. Characteristics of a Partnership

A partnership has distinguishing characteristics:

1. A partnership is a voluntary, consensual relationship.

2. A partnership involves partners' contributions of capital, services, or a combination of these.

3. The partners are associated as co-owners to transact the business of the firm for profit.

unincorporated association – combination of two or more persons for the furtherance of a common nonprofit purpose.

If profit is not the object, the group will commonly be an **unincorporated association**.

The UPA does not make the partnership a separate entity, and, therefore, suit cannot be brought by the firm in its name in the absence of a special statute or procedural rule so providing. However, in RUPA states, partnerships are recognized as "entities."

3. Rights of Partners

The rights of partners are determined by the partnership agreement. If written, this agreement is interpreted by the same rules that govern the interpretation of any other written document. Any matter not covered by the partnership agreement may be covered by a provision of the applicable UPA or RUPA.

[5] U.P.A. §6(1).

4. Partnership Agreement

Because of the complexity of the problems involved, *partnership agreements* are typically written. However, there is no requirement that they be in writing unless compliance with a statute of frauds is required. **For Example,** the world's highest-paid performers in the early 1990s, the New Kids on the Block, who grossed $74.1 million in one year, were a group started by promoter Maurice Starr. He obtained $60,000 from James Martorano, who was connected with organized crime, and $50,000 from businessman Jeffrey Furst to finance the initial recording and promotion of the group. Martorano and Furst testified that ultimately all three agreed with a handshake that 50 percent of the profits from the group would be shared between Martorano as a silent partner and Furst, who would also provide limousine service and security. They testified that Starr would keep half of the profits. Starr denied that a partnership existed because he believed that such an alleged business arrangement would have had to be reduced to writing with great detail. However, based on the evidence, which included damaging testimony that Starr tried to buy some witnesses' silence, a jury decided that a binding oral partnership agreement existed.[6]

To reduce or avoid disputes and litigation, partnership agreements should be in writing. Courts will enforce partnership agreements, under the standards of the law of contracts, according to the agreements' terms.[7] **For Example,** dentist Steven Schwartz was terminated from a three-dentist practice "without cause" by vote of his two other partners. The partnership agreement allowed for termination of a partner as long as either party gave the other 90 days notice. The appeals court interpreted the partnership agreement as written, finding that the provision was entered into by sophisticated and highly educated professionals, and not in violation of public policy.[8]

partnership agreement—document prepared to evidence the contract of the parties. (Parties—partners or general partners)

articles of partnership—See *Partnership Agreement.*

articles of copartnership—See *Partnership Agreement.*

The formal document that is prepared to evidence the contract of the parties is termed a **partnership agreement**, **articles of partnership**, or **articles of copartnership**. The partnership agreement governs the partnership during its existence and may contain provisions relating to dissolution. (See Figure 42-1.)

CPA ## 5. Determining the Existence of a Partnership

If the parties agree that the legal relationship between them shall be such that they in fact operate a business for profit as co-owners, a partnership is created even though the parties may not have labeled their new relationship as such.[9] The law is concerned with the substance of what is done rather than the name. Conversely, a partnership does not arise if the parties do not agree to the elements of a partnership even though they call it one.[10]

---

[6] *Boston Globe*, November 13, 1995, 13. For an example of a situation in which no oral partnership was found to exist, see *Prince v. O'Brien*, 683 N.Y.S.2d 504 (A.D. 1998). Marvin Prince and Darren O'Brien met and became friends while living in Toronto. Prince, a Jamaican native, helped O'Brien refine his reggae-singing ability and knowledge of Jamaican dialect, and participated in the coining of O'Brien's stage name "Snow." Before O'Brien became a success with his debut reggae album *12 Inches of Snow*, the friends may have casually discussed splitting their hypothetical profits equally but never agreed to share losses. Later, when Marvin Prince toured with O'Brien, he was designated and paid as an employee of O'Brien's corporation. The court found that Prince failed to prove the existence of an oral partnership agreement.
[7] *Krajacich v. Great Falls Clinic*, 276 P.3d 922 (Mont. 2012).
[8] *Schwartz v. Family Dental Group*, P.C., 943 A.2d 1122 (Conn. App. 2008).
[9] *Swecker v. Swecker*, 360 S.W.3d 422 (Tenn. App. 2011).
[10] See *Cleland v. Thirion*, 704 N.Y.S.2d 316 (A.D. 2000).

CASE SUMMARY

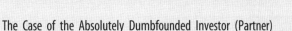

The Case of the Absolutely Dumbfounded Investor (Partner)

FACTS: David Byker, an accountant, and Tom Mannes, a real estate professional, agreed to engage in an ongoing business enterprise to raise investment funds for separate real estate–related ventures and to share equally in the profits, losses, and expenses. Over the years, the parties pursued various individual limited partnerships, sharing equally in commissions, financing fees, and termination costs. Byker and Mannes then created a subsequent entity, Pier 1000, Ltd., to own and manage a marina. This venture was not successful, and they took profits from a prior entity and borrowed money to continue operations. The unsuccessful marina was later returned to its previous owners in exchange for assumption of Byker's and Mannes's direct obligations to that business. The nine-year business relationship between them ceased. Later, Byker approached Mannes and requested that he share in the payments resulting from losses that were incurred from their various entities. Mannes was, in his words, "absolutely dumbfounded" by the request, and he refused payment. Byker sued, contending that a general partnership was underlying all their business affairs. Mannes asserted that he merely invested in separate business ventures with Byker and that there were no other understandings between them.

DECISION: Judgment for David Byker. Partnership law does not require that individuals be aware of their status as "partners" to have a legal partnership. The intent to create a partnership is not required if the acts and the conduct of the parties otherwise evidence that the parties carried on as co-owners of a business for profit. No writing is needed to form a partnership. No name or tax ID number is necessary to attain legal status as a partnership, nor is it required that the parties must aggregate all entities under a general partnership tax return. Mannes filed his tax returns based on his share of the income and expense from the individual legal entities that existed with the legal status of each entity controlling his tax obligations. However, additional evidence indicated that a partnership existed, including the general agreement in principle from the beginning that they would share profits and losses together in their real estate investment business. While they should have created a legal entity to address the situation that precipitated the lawsuit, because they did not, partnership law applies. [***Byker v. Mannes*, 641 N.W.2d 210 (Mich. 2002)**]

A partnership is shown to exist when it is established that the parties have agreed to the formation of a business organization that has the characteristics of a partnership. The burden of proving the existence of a partnership is on the person who claims that one exists.[11]

When the nature of the relationship is not clear, the following rules aid in determining whether the parties have created a partnership.

CPA (A) **CONTROL.** The presence or absence of control of a business enterprise is significant in determining whether there is a partnership and whether a particular person is a partner.

CPA (B) **SHARING PROFITS AND LOSSES.** The fact that the parties share profits and losses is strong evidence of a partnership.[12]

CPA (C) **SHARING PROFITS.** An agreement that does not provide for sharing losses but does provide for sharing profits is evidence that the parties are partners. If the partners

---

[11] *MacArthur v. Stein*, 934 P.2d 214 (Mont. 1997).
[12] *Botsee Gates v. Houston*, 897 N.E.2d 532 (Ind. App. 2008).

| FIGURE 42-1 | *Partnership Agreement* |

PARTNERSHIP AGREEMENT

THIS IS A PARTNERSHIP AGREEMENT EXECUTED AT CINCINNATI, OHIO, THIS 9TH DAY OF SEPTEMBER, 1998, BY AND AMONG LOUIS K. HALL, SHARON B. YOUNG, AND C. LYNN MUELLER, INDIVIDUALS RESIDING IN CINCINNATI, OHIO, HEREINAFTER SOMETIMES REFERRED TO INDIVIDUALLY AS "PARTNER" AND COLLECTIVELY AS "PARTNERS."

RECITALS

THE PARTNERS TO THIS AGREEMENT DESIRE TO ACQUIRE A CERTAIN PARCEL OF REAL ESTATE AND TO DEVELOP SUCH REAL ESTATE FOR LEASE OR SALE, ALL FOR INVESTMENT PURPOSES. THIS AGREEMENT IS BEING EXECUTED TO DELINEATE THE BASIS OF THEIR RELATIONSHIP.

PROVISIONS

1. NAME; AND PRINCIPAL OFFICES. THE NAME OF THE PARTNERSHIP SHALL BE: HALL, YOUNG AND MUELLER, ASSOCIATES. ITS PRINCIPAL PLACE OF BUSINESS SHALL BE AT: 201 RIVER ROAD, CINCINNATI, OHIO 45238.

2. PURPOSE. THE PURPOSE OF THE PARTNERSHIP SHALL BE TO PURCHASE AND OWN FOR INVESTMENT PURPOSES, A CERTAIN PARCEL OF REAL ESTATE LOCATED AT 602 SIXTH STREET, CINCINNATI, OHIO, AND TO ENGAGE IN ANY OTHER TYPE OF INVESTMENT ACTIVITIES THAT THE PARTNERSHIP MAY FROM TIME TO TIME HEREINAFTER UNANIMOUSLY AGREE UPON.

3. CAPITAL CONTRIBUTIONS. THE CAPITAL OF THE PARTNERSHIP SHALL BE THE AGGREGATE AMOUNT OF CASH AND PROPERTY CONTRIBUTED BY THE PARTNERS. A CAPITAL ACCOUNT SHALL BE MAINTAINED FOR EACH PARTNER.

A. CAPITAL CONTRIBUTIONS. ANY ADDITIONAL CAPITAL WHICH MAY BE REQUIRED BY THE PARTNERSHIP SHALL BE CONTRIBUTED TO THE PARTNERSHIP BY THE PARTNERS IN THE SAME RATIO AS THAT PARTNER'S ORIGINAL CONTRIBUTION TO CAPITAL AS TO THE TOTAL OF ALL ORIGINAL CAPITAL CONTRIBUTIONS TO THE PARTNERSHIP UNLESS OTHERWISE AGREED BY THE PARTNERS.

share profits, it is assumed that they will also share losses. Sharing profits is prima facie evidence of a partnership. However, a partnership is not to be inferred when profits are received in payment (1) of a debt, (2) of wages, (3) of an annuity to a deceased partner's surviving spouse or representative, (4) of interest, or (5) for the goodwill of the business.[13] **For Example,** the fact that one doctor receives one-half of the net income does not establish that doctor as a partner of another doctor when the former was guaranteed a minimum annual amount. Also, federal income tax and Social Security contributions were deducted from the payments to the doctor, thus indicating that the relationship was employer and employee. If there is no evidence of the reason for receiving the profits, a partnership of the parties involved exists.

CPA (D) GROSS RETURNS. The sharing of gross returns is itself very slight, if any, evidence of partnership. **For Example,** in a case in which one party owned a show that was exhibited on land owned by another under an agreement to divide the gross proceeds, no partnership was proven. There was no co-ownership or community of interest in the business.

CPA (E) CONTRIBUTION OF SKILL OR LABOR. The fact that all persons have not contributed capital to an enterprise does not establish that the enterprise is not a partnership. A partnership may be formed even though some of its members furnish only skill or labor.

---

[13] U.P.A. §7(4).

CASE SUMMARY

Can You Fire Your Partner?

FACTS: On graduating from Vanderbilt University with a degree in economics, James Pettes began working for Video Magic, a video rental business. In 1987, Dr. Gordon Yukon, a pediatrician, wanted to invest in a two-store video business called Rent-a-Flick, with one store located on Quince Road and the other in Germantown. Pettes testified that Yukon paid $42,000 for the business. Pettes testified that they agreed they would be partners, with Pettes managing the two stores and earning the same amount he earned at Video Magic. Pettes testified that he worked 70 to 80 hours a week and his capital contribution was "sweat equity." He also testified that many times Yukon told him and others that Pettes and Yukon were partners. Pettes testified that in the middle of 1992, the parties agreed to divide the business so that the Germantown store would go to Yukon and the Quince Road store would go to Pettes. In December 1992, Pettes made a written demand for an accounting. On January 5, 1993, Dr. Yukon "fired" Pettes. Sutherland, an employee, testified that she questioned Yukon about this action because Pettes was a partner, and Yukon's reply was not a denial of the partnership but rather a claim that in the absence of written proof, Pettes could not prove such an arrangement. Pettes sued for breach of an oral partnership agreement and an accounting.

DECISION: Judgment for Pettes. From the totality of the proof in this case, the parties intended a partnership and co-ownership to the extent that a dissolution agreement would result in Yukon's acquiring the Germantown store and Pettes's acquiring the Quince Road store. The implied partnership and agreed dissolution of the partnership are binding on the parties, and Pettes is entitled to the value of the Quince Road store as of January 3, 1993. [*Pettes v. Yukon*, 912 S.W.2d 709 (Tenn. App. 1995)]

CPA **(F) FIXED PAYMENT.** When a person who performs continuing services for another receives a fixed payment that does not depend on the existence of profit and is not affected by losses, that person is not a partner.

CPA ## 6. Partners as to Third Persons

In some instances, persons who are in fact not partners may be held liable to third persons as though they were partners. This liability arises when they conduct themselves in such a manner that others are reasonably led to believe that they are partners and to act in reliance on that belief to their injury.[14] A person who is held liable as a partner under such circumstances is termed a *nominal partner*, a *partner by estoppel*, or an *ostensible partner*.

Partnership liability may arise by estoppel when a person who in fact is not a partner is described as a partner in a document filed with the government provided the person so described has in some way participated in the filing of the document and the person claiming the benefit of the estoppel had knowledge of that document and relied on the statement. **For Example,** Jean Collins allowed the partnership of Holt and Schwark to use her name to help the partnership get started. A business name registration certificate filed at city hall and signed by all of the individuals specifies Holt, Schwark, and Collins as partners. If a creditor who sees this registration statement extends credit to the firm in reliance in part on the fact that

[14] U.P.A. §16(1); *Andrews v. Elwell*, 367 F. Supp. 2d 35 (D. Mass. 2005).

Collins is a partner, Collins is estopped from denying that she is a partner. She has a partner's liability along with the other partners insofar as that creditor is concerned.

Under the RUPA, an apparent partnership or partnership by estoppel is called a *purported* partnership, and a third person who relies on the partnership's representations that the purported partner had authority to bind the partnership can hold it liable as if the purported partner were an actual partner with authority.[15] Under the RUPA, a partnership can limit potential liability with a publicly recorded statement of partnership authority or limitation on partner authority.[16]

CPA

7. Partnership Property

In general, partnership property consists of all property contributed by the partners or acquired for the firm or with its funds.

There is usually no limitation on the type and amount of property that a partnership may acquire. The firm may own real as well as personal property unless it is prohibited from doing so by statute or by the partnership agreement.

The parties may agree that real estate owned by one of the partners should become partnership property. When this intent exists, the particular property constitutes partnership property even if it is still in the name of the original owner.

Article 2 of the RUPA recognizes that partnerships are "entities" that can acquire and own property in the partnership's name. If a partner desires to retain an interest in property contributed to the partnership in RUPA states, the partner must condition the transfer of the property to the partnership to reflect this interest or set forth the condition in the partnership agreement. Otherwise, the property becomes partnership property under the entity theory, and the contributing partner has no right to get it back, even in liquidation.[17]

8. Tenancy in Partnership

tenancy in partnership – ownership relationship that exists between partners under the Uniform Partnership Act.

Under the UPA, partners hold title to firm property by **tenancy in partnership**.[18] The characteristics of such a tenancy are as follows:

1. Each partner has an equal right to use firm property for partnership purposes in the absence of a contrary agreement.

2. A partner possesses no divisible interest in any specific item of partnership property that can be voluntarily sold, assigned, or mortgaged by a partner.

3. A creditor of a partner cannot proceed against any specific items of partnership property. The creditor can proceed only against the partner's interest in the partnership. This is done by applying to a court for a **charging order**. By this procedure, the share of any profits that would be paid to the debtor-partner is paid to a receiver on behalf of the creditor, or the court may direct the sale of the interest of the debtor-partner in the partnership.

charging order – order by a court, after a business partner's personal assets are exhausted, requiring that the partner's share of the profits be paid to a creditor until the debt is discharged.

4. Upon the death of a partner, the partnership property vests in the surviving partners for partnership purposes and is not subject to the rights of the surviving spouse of the deceased partner.

[15] R.U.P.A. §308.
[16] R.U.P.A. §303.
[17] R.U.P.A. §204.
[18] U.P.A. §25(1); *Krause v. Vollmar*, 614 N.E.2d 1136 (Ohio App. 1992).

CPA

9. Assignment of a Partner's Interest

Although a partner cannot transfer specific items of partnership property in the absence of authority to so act on behalf of the partnership, a partner's interest in the partnership may be voluntarily assigned by the partner. The assignee does not become a partner without the consent of the other partners. Without this consent, the assignee is entitled to receive only the assignor's share of the profits during the continuance of the partnership and the assignor's interest upon the dissolution of the firm. The assignee has no right to participate in the management of the partnership or to inspect the books of the partnership.

B. AUTHORITY OF PARTNERS

The scope of a partner's authority is determined by the partnership agreement and by the nature of the partnership.

10. Authority of Majority of Partners

When there are more than two partners in a firm, the decision of the majority prevails in matters involving how the ordinary functions of the business will be conducted. To illustrate, a majority of the partners of a firm decide to increase the firm's advertising. They subsequently enter into a contract for that purpose. The transaction is valid and binds the firm and all of the partners.

Majority action is not binding if it contravenes the partnership agreement. For such matters, unanimous action is required.[19] Thus, the majority of the members cannot change the nature of the business against the protests of the minority.

When there are an even number of partners, an even division on a matter that requires majority approval is always a possibility. In such a case, the partnership is deadlocked. When the partners are evenly divided on any question, one partner has no authority to act.

CASE SUMMARY

Strictly Business, or Trashing Your Partner?

FACTS: Summers and Dooley formed a partnership to collect trash. Summers became unable to work, and he hired a third man to do his work and paid him out of his personal funds. Summers suggested to Dooley that the third man be paid from the partnership funds, but Dooley refused to do so. Finally, Summers sued Dooley for reimbursement for the money he had spent to pay the third man.

DECISION: Judgment for Dooley. Summers had no authority to employ the third man at the expense of the firm. Because the partners were evenly divided on the question of such employment, Summers had no authority to act. [*Summers v. Dooley*, **481 P.2d 318 (Idaho 1971)**]

---

[19] U.P.A. §18(h).

If the division is over a basic issue and the partners persist in the deadlock so that it is impossible to continue the business, any one of the partners may petition the court to order the dissolution of the firm.

11. Express Authority of Individual Partners

express authority – authority of an agent to perform a certain act.

An individual partner may have **express authority** to perform certain acts either because the partnership agreement provides for this or because a sufficient number of partners have agreed to it.

A partner's authority to act for the firm is similar to that of an agent to act for a principal. Thus, in addition to express authority, a partner has the authority to do those acts that are customary for a member of a partnership conducting the particular business of that partnership.[20] As in the case of an agent, the acts of a partner in excess of authority do not ordinarily bind the partnership.

12. Customary Authority of Individual Partners

A partner, by virtue of being a comanager of the business, customarily has certain powers necessary and proper for carrying out that business. The scope of such powers varies with the nature of the partnership and with the business customs and usages of the area in which the partnership operates.

A partner may make any contract necessary to transact the firm's business.

CASE SUMMARY

"Jerry Should Have Run It by Me," Silvio Seethed

FACTS: Silvio Giannetti and his daughter and son-in-law, Anne Marie and Jerry Pruzinsky, are partners in a general partnership known as Giannetti Investment Company (GIC), which owns and operates Brougham Manor Apartments. Jerry entered into an access agreement with Omnicom, a provider of cable television services, giving Omnicom the right to enter Brougham Manor for purposes of installing, maintaining, and promoting cable service. Some time later, when he learned of the contract, Silvio denied Omnicom access to the property. Omnicom was unable to repair a signal leakage problem and was forced to discontinue cable service. Omnicom sued GIC for breach of contract. GIC contended that Jerry did not sign the agreement in the partnership name and thereby failed to bind GIC.

DECISION: Judgment for Omnicom. A contract executed in the name of a partner is binding on the partnership. Jerry executed the contract in the usual course of GIC's business, for it is a typical activity for an apartment complex to contract for cable television. [***Omnicom v. Giannetti Investment Co.,*** **561 N.W.2d 138 (Mich. App. 1997)**]

A partner can sell the firm's goods in the regular course of business, make purchases within the scope of the business, and borrow money for firm purposes. When borrowing money, a partner may execute commercial paper in the firm's name or give security such as a mortgage.[21] A partner may purchase insurance, hire

---

[20] *Ball v. Carlson*, 641 P.2d 303 (Colo. App. 1981).
[21] *U.S. Leather v. H&W Partnership*, 60 F.3d 222 (5th Cir. 1995).

employees, and adjust claims for or against the firm. Notice given to a partner is effective notice to the partnership.[22]

13. Limitations on Authority

The partners may agree to limit the powers of each partner. When a partner, contrary to such an agreement, executes a contract on behalf of the firm with a third person, the firm is bound if the third person was unaware of the limitation. In this case, the partner violating the agreement is liable to the other partners for any loss caused by the breach of the limitation. Under the UPA, if the third person knew of the limitation, the firm would not be bound.[23] Under the RUPA, the term *knew* is confined to actual knowledge,[24] which is cognitive awareness. Under the RUPA, a partnership may file a statement of partnership authority setting forth any restrictions on a general partner's authority.[25] **For Example,** Bernard Roeger was general partner of RNR, with three limited partners. Restrictions were clearly set forth in the partnership agreement limiting Roeger's borrowing authority to no more than $650,000 for the construction of a building on partnership property. Roeger on behalf of RNR entered a construction loan agreement with People's Bank with a note and mortgage in the amount of $990,000, and over an 18-month period, the bank disbursed an aggregate sum of $952,699. The bank did not request a written consent from any of the other partners or review the partnership agreement. When the loan was not paid, the bank foreclosed on the property. RNR defended on behalf of the partnership that the bank negligently failed to investigate and discover the limitation on Roeger's authority to borrow. The case was decided for the bank because it had no actual knowledge or notice of the restriction on the general partner's authority. The court also pointed out that the partnership could have protected itself by filing a statement of partnership authority setting forth the restrictions on the general partner under RUPA section 303.[26]

A third person must not assume that a partner has all of the authority that the partner purports to have. If there is anything that would put a reasonable person on notice that the partner's powers are limited, the third person is bound by that limitation.

The third person must be on the alert for the following prohibited transactions because they warn that the partner with whom the third person deals has either restricted authority or no authority at all. (See Figure 42-2.)

14. Prohibited Transactions

A partner cannot enter into certain transactions on behalf of the partnership unless expressly authorized to do so. A third person entering into such a transaction does so at the risk that the partner has not been authorized. The following are prohibited transactions.

(A) Cessation of Business. A partner cannot bind the firm by a contract that would make it impossible for the firm to conduct its usual business.[27]

[22] *Cham, Hill, Inc., v. Block & Veatch*, 557 N.W.2d 829 (Wis. App. 1996).
[23] U.P.A. §9(4).
[24] R.U.P.A. §102(a).
[25] R.U.P.A. §303.
[26] *RNR Investments, Ltd. v. People's First Community Bank*, 812 So.2d 561 (Fla. App. 2002).
[27] *Wales v. Roll*, 769 P.2d 899 (Wyo. 1989).

| FIGURE 42-2 | *Limitations on Authority of Individual Partner to Bind Partnership* |

© Cengage Learning

CASE SUMMARY

Family Feud

FACTS: The Patel family, consisting of parents and a son, was a partnership that owned and operated a motel. The parents made a contract to sell the motel, but thereafter the son refused to sell. He claimed that the contract of sale was not binding.

DECISION: Judgment for the son. The motel was not an asset held by the partnership for sale. It was an asset that was essential for the running of the partnership/business. Accordingly, neither one partner nor a majority had implied authority to sell the motel. To the contrary, the unanimous consent of all partners was required for the sale of the motel because such a sale would make it impossible to continue the partnership business. [*Patel v. Patel*, 260 Cal. Rptr. 255 (Cal. App. 1989)]

(B) SURETYSHIP. A partner has no implied authority to bind the firm by contracts of surety, guarantee, or indemnity for purposes other than firm business.[28]

(C) ARBITRATION. A partner cannot submit controversies of the firm to arbitration "unless authorized by the other partners or unless they have abandoned the business."[29]

(D) CONFESSION OF JUDGMENT. All partners should have an opportunity to defend in court. Because of this, a partner cannot confess judgment against the firm on one of its obligations. Exceptions exist when the other partners consent or when they have abandoned the business.

---

[28] *First Interstate Bank of Oregon v. Bergendahl*, 723 P.2d 1005 (Or.App. 1986).
[29] U.P.A. §9(3)(e).

(E) Assignment for Creditors. A partner cannot make a general assignment of firm property for the benefit of creditors unless authorized by the other partners or unless they have abandoned the business.

(F) Personal Obligations. A partner cannot discharge personal obligations or claims of the firm by interchanging them in any way.

C. Duties, Rights, and Liabilities of Partners

The rights and duties of partners are based on their dual capacity of agent and co-owner.

15. Duties of Partners

In many respects, the duties of a partner are the same as those of an agent.

(A) Loyalty and Good Faith. Each partner must act in good faith toward the partnership. One partner must not take any advantage over the other(s) by the slightest misrepresentation or concealment.[30] Each partner owes a duty of loyalty to the firm. This duty requires a partner's devotion to the firm's business and bars making any secret profit at the expense of the firm.[31]

Moreover, the duty of loyalty bars the use of the firm's property for personal benefit or the exploitation of a business opportunity of the partnership for personal gain. **For Example,** when one partner renewed the lease of the building occupied by the firm but the lease was renewed in the name of that partner alone, that partner was compelled to hold the lease for the firm. The failure to renew the lease in the name of the firm was a breach of the duties of good faith and loyalty owed to the firm.

A partner cannot promote a competing business. A partner who does so is liable for damages sustained by the partnership.

Each partner also owes a fiduciary duty of good faith to all other partners. This duty extends to any transaction connected with the formation, conduct, or liquidation of the partnership.

A breach of fiduciary duty requires the complete forfeiture of all compensation during the period of the breach. **For Example,** general partners Michael Morton and Scott DeGraff breached their fiduciary duty to their partners when they did not disclose the parts of a deal they were keeping for themselves relating to a proposed relocation of the partnership's Las Vegas nightclub, Drink. Morton and DeGraff had been paid $833,190 in management fees during the period of time they were found to be in breach of their fiduciary duty to the partnership, and the court ordered them to return these funds to the partnership. [32]

(B) Obedience. Each partner is obligated to perform all duties and to obey all restrictions imposed by the partnership agreement or by the vote of the required number of partners.[33] **For Example,** when the partnership agreement required that each partner in an insurance sales firm give his "entire time" to the business and

---

[30] *Brosseau v. Ranzau*, 81 S.W.3d 381 (Tex. App. 2002).
[31] Under R.U.P.A. 404(e), partners may pursue their own interests without automatically violating their fiduciary duties to the firm.
[32] *Caparos v. Morton*, 845 N.E.2d 773 (Ill. App. 2006).
[33] *Cobin v. Rice*, 823 F. Supp. 1419 (D. Ind. 1993).

"not engage in any other business that would work to the disadvantage of the partnership," Richard Levatino's engaging in an insurance-related business outside the firm was a breach of the partnership agreement and was a proper basis for the assessment of punitive damages.[34]

(c) Other Duties. A partner must refrain from engaging in grossly negligent or intentional misconduct in transacting firm business under the RUPA.[35] Partners are accountable as a fiduciary and must hold as trustee for the firm any profits derived by a partner without the consent of the other partners.[36]

CPA

16. Rights of Partners as Owners

Each partner, in the absence of a contrary agreement, has the following rights. These rights stem from the fact that the partner is a co-owner of the partnership business.

CPA

(a) Management. Each partner has a right to take an equal part in transacting the business of the firm. It is immaterial that one partner contributed more than another or that one contributed only services.

Incidental to the right to manage the partnership, each partner has the right to possession of the partnership property for the purposes of the partnership.

CPA

(b) Inspection of Books. All partners are equally entitled to inspect the books of the firm. "The partnership books shall be kept, subject to any agreement between the partners, at the principal place of business of the partnership, and every partner shall at all times have access to and may inspect and copy any of them."[37]

CPA

(c) Share of Profits. Each partner is entitled to a share of the profits. The partners may provide, if they so wish, that profits shall be shared in unequal proportions. In the absence of such a provision in the partnership agreement, each partner is entitled to an equal share of the profits without regard to the amount of capital contributed or services performed for the partnership.

CPA

(d) Compensation. In the absence of a contrary agreement, a partner is not entitled to compensation for services performed for the partnership. There is no right to compensation even if the services are unusual or more extensive than the services rendered by other partners. Consequently, when one partner becomes seriously ill and the other partners transact all of the firm's business, they are not entitled to compensation for those services. The sickness of a partner is considered a risk assumed in the relationship. No agreement can be inferred that the active partners are to be compensated even though the services rendered by them are such that they would ordinarily be rendered in the expectation of receiving compensation. As an exception, "a surviving partner is entitled to reasonable compensation for services performed in winding up the partnership affairs."[38]

Contrary to the preceding, the partners may agree that one of the partners will devote full time as manager of the business and receive for such services a salary in addition to the managing partner's share of the profits.

---

[34] *Gates, Duncan, and VanCamp v. Levatino*, 962 S.W.2d 21 (Tenn. App. 1997).
[35] R.U.P.A. §404(c).
[36] U.P.A. §21; R.U.P.A. §404(b)(1).
[37] U.P.A. §19. See *Smith v. Brown & Jones*, 633 N.Y.S.2d 436 (Sup. Ct. 1995).
[38] U.P.A. §18(f).

(E) REPAYMENT OF LOANS. A partner is entitled to the return of any money advanced to or for the firm. Such amounts must be separate and distinct from original or additional contributions to the capital of the firm.

CPA

(F) PAYMENT OF INTEREST. In the absence of an agreement to the contrary, contributions to capital do not draw interest. The theory is that the profits constitute sufficient compensation. Advances by a partner in the form of loans are treated as if they were made by a stranger and bear interest from the date the advance is made. When the partnership business continues after dissolution, a retiring partner is entitled to interest on the value of her interest in the partnership.[39]

CPA

(G) CONTRIBUTION AND INDEMNITY. A partner who pays more than a proportionate share of the debts of the firm has a right to contribution from the other partners. Under this principle, if an employee of a partnership negligently injures a third person while acting within the scope of employment and if the injured party collects damages from one partner, the latter may enforce contribution from the other partners to divide the loss proportionately among them.

The partnership must indemnify every partner for payments made and personal liabilities reasonably incurred in the ordinary and proper conduct of its business or for the preservation of its business or property. A partner has no right, however, to indemnity or reimbursement if the partner has (1) acted in bad faith, (2) negligently caused the necessity for payment, or (3) previously agreed to assume the expense alone.[40]

CPA

(H) DISTRIBUTION OF CAPITAL. After the payment of all creditors and the repayment of loans made to the firm by partners, every partner is entitled to receive a share of the firm property upon dissolution. Unless otherwise stated in the partnership agreement, all partners are entitled to the return of their capital contributions.

After such distribution is made, each partner is the sole owner of the fractional part distributed to that partner rather than a co-owner of all the property as during the existence of the partnership.

CPA

17. Liability of Partners and Partnership

The liability of a partnership and of the partners for the acts of individual partners and of employees is governed by the same principles that apply to the liability of an employer or a principal for the acts of an employee or agent.

CPA

(A) NATURE AND EXTENT OF PARTNER'S LIABILITY. Partners are **jointly liable** on all firm contracts. They are **jointly and severally liable** for all torts committed by an employee or one of the partners in the scope of the partnership business.[41] When partners are liable for the wrongful injury caused a third person, the latter may sue all or any of the members of the firm.

Partners who have satisfied a claim against the partnership have the right to contribution from the other partners, whereby the liability is apportioned among

joint liability – apportions partners' responsibility for partnership debt equally.

joint and several liability – disproportionate satisfaction of partnership debt rendering each partner liable for the entire debt with the right to contribution from other partners.

---

[39] *Lewis v. Edwards*, 554 S.E.2d 17 (N.C. App. 2001).
[40] *Gramacy Equities Corp. v. DuMont*, 531 N.E.2d 629 (N.Y. A.D.1988).
[41] See *Wayne Smith Construction v. Wolman, Durberstein*, 604 N.E.2d 157 (Ohio 1992), where the Ohio Supreme Court described joint liability and joint and several liability as follows: Joint liability apportions responsibility for a contractual debt equally, in the absence of a partnership agreement to the contrary, among the partners and thereby limits the creditor's execution on one individual partner's personal property to a *pro rata* share of the debt. Joint and several liability, on the other hand, allows for disproportionate satisfaction of the partnership obligation by rendering each general partner responsible for the entire amount of the partnership debt.

all partners. Unlike the UPA, partners under the Revised Uniform Partnership Act (RUPA) are jointly and severally liable for both tort and contract obligations of the firm.[42] However, the RUPA alters the traditional applications of "joint and several" liability by requiring that the creditors and tort victims satisfy their claims against the partnership before pursuing the personal assets of a partner.

CASE SUMMARY

"Joint Liability" and "Joint and Several Liability": A Big Difference

FACTS: PNC Bank sued two of the eight general partners of Washington Square Enterprises, Farinacci and Gruttadauria, for the unpaid balance of their partnership's business line of credit. The trial court entered judgment in the amount of $4,190.33 plus interest against each of the two partners. The trial court determined that the eight general partners were jointly liable, not jointly and severally liable, for the debt to PNC. In addition, it issued a separate judgment against Farinacci and Gruttadauria in the amount of one-eighth each of the entire debt of $33,522. PNC appealed, contending that the trial court should have found the partners jointly and severally liable or that the trial court should have apportioned the debt according to the percentages of each partner's ownership interest in the partnership, rather than dividing the debt equally among the eight partners.

DECISION: The trial court properly decided the case, holding the two partners jointly liable. In 2007 Ohio adopted the Revised Uniform Partnership Act (RUPA) effective January 1, 2010, which provides that all partners are liable jointly and severally for all obligations of the partnership unless otherwise agreed by the claimant or provided by law. However, the new law states that the RUPA language does not apply to partnerships formed prior to January 1, 2009. The Washington Square Partnership was formed in 1978. "Joint liability" apportions responsibility for a contractual debt equally among all general partners in the absence of a partnership agreement to the contrary. PNC Bank's contention that the judgment be apportioned according to the percentage of the partners' ownership interests is without legal precedent. [*PNC Bank N.A. v. Farinacci*, 964 N.E.2d 1124 (Ohio App. 2011)]

CPA

(B) LIABILITY OF NEW PARTNERS. A person admitted as a partner into an existing partnership has *limited liability* for all obligations of the partnership arising before such admission. This is a limited liability in that the preadmission claim may be satisfied only out of partnership property and does not extend to the individual property of the newly admitted partner.[43] **For Example,** Citizens Bank was unsuccessful in its attempt to satisfy part of a $1.2 million deficiency judgment against the Parkham-Woodman Medical partnership from the individual property of Dr. Hunley, who had joined the practice after the underlying obligation leading to the deficiency judgment was assumed.[44]

(C) EFFECT OF DISSOLUTION ON PARTNER'S LIABILITY. A partner remains liable after dissolution of the partnership unless expressly released by the creditors or unless all claims against the partnership have been satisfied. The dissolution of the partnership does not of itself discharge the existing liability of any partner. The individual

[42] R.U.P.A. §307(d).
[43] U.P.A. §17; see also U.P.A. §41(1), (7).
[44] *Citizens Bank v. Parkman Woodman Medical Associates*, 874 F. Supp. 705 (D. Mass. 1995).

property of a deceased partner is liable for the obligations of the partnership that were incurred while the deceased partner was alive. However, the individual creditors of the deceased partner have priority over the partnership creditors with respect to such property.[45]

18. Enforcement and Satisfaction of Creditors' Claims

The firm may have been sued in the name of all individual partners doing business as the partnership, as in the case of "*Plaintiff v. A, B, C, doing business as the Ajax Warehouse.*" The partners named are bound by the judgment against the firm if they have been properly served in the suit.

If a debt is contractual in origin, common law requires that the partnership's assets be resorted to and exhausted before partnership creditors can reach a partner's individual assets.[46]

Personal creditors of a partner must first pursue the assets of that partner for satisfaction of their claims. After a partner's personal assets are exhausted, the creditor may enforce the unpaid portion of a judgment by obtaining a charging order against the partner's interest in the partnership. Under such an order, a court requires that the partner's share of the profits be paid to the creditor until the debt is discharged.

D. Dissolution and Termination

The end of a partnership's existence is marked by dissolution and termination.

CPA 19. Effect of Dissolution

Dissolution is the "change in the relationship of the partners caused by any partner ceasing to be associated in the carrying on as distinguished from the winding-up of the business."[47] Dissolution does not necessarily mean that the business has ended. If the partnership agreement provides that the business is to be continued by the remaining partner(s), it will continue without a winding up, and the former partner's interest will be bought out according to the partnership agreement. Also, when breach of the partnership agreement causes dissolution, innocent partners may continue the business, provided they pay the breaching partner the value of his or her interest.[48]

If no legal basis exists to continue the business, dissolution ends the right of the partnership to exist as a going concern, but it does not end the existence of the partnership.[49] Dissolution is followed by a winding-up period at the conclusion of which the partnership's legal existence terminates.

Dissolution reduces the authority of the partners. From the moment of dissolution, the partners lose authority to act for the firm "except so far as may be necessary to wind up partnership affairs or to complete transactions begun but not then finished."[50] The vested rights of the partners are not extinguished by dissolving the firm, and the existing liabilities remain.

[45] U.P.A. §36.
[46] *McCune & McCune v. Mountain Bell Tel. Co.*, 758 P.2d 914 (Utah 1988).
[47] U.P.A. §29.
[48] U.P.A. §38 (2)(b).
[49] *Sheppard v. Griffin*, 776 S.W.2d 119 (Tenn. App. 1989).
[50] U.P.A. §33.

20. Dissolution by Act of the Parties

A partnership may be dissolved by action of the parties. However, certain acts of the parties do not cause a dissolution.

(A) AGREEMENT. A partnership may be dissolved in accordance with the terms of the original agreement of the parties. This may be by the expiration of the period for which the relationship was to continue or by the performance of the object for which the partnership was organized.[51] The relationship may also be dissolved by subsequent agreement. The partners may agree to dissolve the firm before the lapse of the time specified in the articles of partnership or before the attainment of the object for which the firm was created.

(B) EXPULSION. A partnership is dissolved by the expulsion of any partner from the business, whether or not authorized by the partnership agreement.[52]

(C) ALIENATION OF INTEREST. Neither a voluntary sale of a partner's interest nor an involuntary sale for the benefit of creditors works a dissolution of the partnership.

(D) WITHDRAWAL. A partner has the power to withdraw from the partnership at any time. However, if the withdrawal violates the partnership agreement, the withdrawing partner becomes liable to the copartners for damages for breach of contract.[53] When the relationship is for no definite purpose or time, a partner may withdraw without liability at any time. **For Example,** a partner, Mary Harshman, was able to bring about the dissolution of a family partnership that held and managed 1,879 acres of land in New York state and force the distribution of the partnership assets because it was an at-will partnership with no definite term or particular objective to be achieved.[54] Restrictive provisions on later employment are commonly found in professional and marketing partnership agreements.

21. Dissolution by Operation of Law

operation of law – attaching of certain consequences to certain facts because of legal principles that operate automatically, as contrasted with consequences that arise because of the voluntary action of a party designed to create those consequences.

A partnership is dissolved by **operation of law** in the following instances.

(A) DEATH. A partnership is dissolved immediately upon the death of any partner. Thus, when the executor of a deceased partner carries on the business with the remaining partner, there is legally a new firm.

(B) BANKRUPTCY. Bankruptcy of the firm or of one of the partners causes the dissolution of the firm; insolvency alone does not.

(C) ILLEGALITY. A partnership is dissolved by an event that makes it unlawful for the business of the partnership to be carried on or for the members to carry it on in partnership. To illustrate, when it is made unlawful by statute for judges to engage in the practice of law, a law firm is dissolved when one of its members becomes a judge.

22. Dissolution by Decree of Court

A court may decree the dissolution of a partnership for proper cause. A court will not order the dissolution for trifling causes or temporary grievances that do not involve a permanent harm or injury to the partnership.

---

[51] U.P.A. §31(1)(a).
[52] *Susman v. Cypress Venture*, 543 N.E.2d 184 (Ill. App. 1989).
[53] *BPR Group v. Bendetson*, 906 N.E.2d 956 (Mass. 2009).
[54] *Harshman v. Pantaleoni*, 741 N.Y.S.2d 348 (A.D. 2002).

The filing of a complaint seeking a judicial dissolution does not in itself cause a dissolution of the partnership; it is the decree of the court that has that effect.

A partner may obtain a decree of dissolution for any of the following reasons.

(A) INSANITY. A partner has been judicially declared insane or of unsound mind.

(B) INCAPACITY. One of the partners has become incapable of performing the terms of the partnership agreement.

(C) MISCONDUCT. One of the partners has been guilty of conduct that substantially prejudices the continuance of the business. The habitual drunkenness of a partner is a sufficient cause for judicial dissolution.

(D) IMPRACTICABILITY. One of the partners persistently or willfully acts in such a way that it is not reasonably practicable to carry on the partnership business. Dissolution will be granted when dissensions are so serious and persistent that continuance is impracticable or when all confidence and cooperation between the partners have been destroyed.

CASE SUMMARY

Strategy = Squeeze Out Dyas
Ethics (Trust, Fairness, Loyalty, Doing No Harm) = None
Law = Dissociation, Dissolution

FACTS: Edward Dyas and Joseph Della Ratta were equal owners of two hotels in Ocean City, Maryland. The "old" hotel was completed in 1988 and the "new" hotel was completed in 2006, with both properties owned under their Spa Motel General Partnership (Spa). They were also developers and equal owners of the Maresol Condominium project in Ocean City, which was completed in 2004 and held under Dyas's and Della Ratta's Bay View Limited Liability Company (Bay View). Della Ratta owned the construction company that built these projects, "DRI," and he also owned "CMC," the company that managed the two hotels. Dyas believed that Della Ratta was attempting to squeeze him out from ownership of Spa and Bay View. Under Dyas's analysis, Della Ratta's strategy in the general partnership, Spa, was to call for a very substantial capital contribution to pay claims asserted by CMC for alleged advances made by it to pay for operational expenses and to pay claims to DRI for the new hotel's construction costs. Dyas contended those calls were unauthorized because the underlying claims could not be substantiated and the partnership agreement required that the developers first seek a commercial loan.

With respect to Bay View, Dyas's theory of Della Ratta's squeeze-out strategy involved two ploys. First, that Della Ratta sought personally to purchase the loan from Severn Bank and obtain from it an assignment of the security instrument, on which Della Ratta then would foreclose, so that he could buy in at the foreclosure sale. Severn Bank, however, would not assign the loan to Della Ratta. Dyas further alleged that, as an alternate squeeze-out strategy, Della Ratta wrongfully refused to sell condominium units in Maresol. The resulting illiquidity would deprive Bay View of the cash needed to repay Severn Bank, so that Della Ratta could buy Maresol at a foreclosure sale conducted by Severn Bank. After a 10-day trial, the circuit court concluded that Dyas had proven these allegations. The ultimate findings of the trial court were that it was "no longer reasonably practicable to carry on the business" of Spa or of Bay View and that Dyas "had proved to the court's satisfaction facts sufficient for the court to grant a dissolution" of the entities. The court further ordered dissociation of Della Ratta as a partner in Spa. The court supervised the winding up of the general partnership. Della Ratta appealed.

CASE SUMMARY

Continued

DECISION: Judgment for Dyas. A review of Della Ratta's activities while a partner in Spa demonstrates satisfactory grounds for the dissociation and dissolution determinations of the trial court since his conduct was such that it was "not reasonably practicable to carry on the business in partnership with him." [*Della Ratta v. Dyas*, 961 A.2d 629 (Md. App. 2008)]

(E) **Lack of Success.** The partnership cannot continue in business except at a loss.

(F) **Equitable Circumstances.** A decree of dissolution will be granted under any other circumstances that equitably call for a dissolution. Such a situation exists when one partner was induced by fraud to enter into the partnership.

CPA

23. Dissociation under the RUPA

Under the RUPA and its "entity" concept, a partner can leave the firm and not disrupt the partnership's legal existence. The RUPA uses the term *dissociation* for the departure of a partner[55] and reserves the term *dissolution* for those instances when a partner's departure results in the winding up and termination of the business.[56]

A partner has the absolute power to dissociate at will, just as a partner has the power to withdraw under the UPA, even if it is wrongful.[57] If wrongful, the partner is liable for damages for breach of contract.

A partner's dissociation from a firm ends the individual's right to participate in the management of the business.[58] It also ends the duty of loyalty owed the firm, and the individual may compete with the firm once dissociated.[59] If the partnership business continues after a partner dissociates from a firm, the partnership must buy out the dissociated partner's interest based on his share of the higher of the liquidation value of the firm or the value of the firm's business as a going concern on the date of dissociation, with interest.[60]

The RUPA created "notices" to deal with lingering authority of a dissociated partner based on apparent authority. To avoid liability, notice of lack of authority or liability should be given to customers and creditors regarding the dissociation of a partner. A filing with the Secretary of State limits liability and authority to 90 days after filing.[61] If no notice is given or filed, the partnership may be bound by the acts of a dissociated partner for up to two years after dissociation based on apparent authority.[62]

---

[55] R.U.P.A. §601 cmt 1.
[56] R.U.P.A. §801.
[57] R.U.P.A. §601(1), 602(a).
[58] In a two-person partnership, when one partner withdraws, the partnership is dissolved by operation of law because there cannot be a one-person partnership. The buyout rule of RUPA §701(b) does not apply, and the dissolution procedures take over. See *Corrales v. Corrales*, 129 Cal. Rptr. 3d 428 (Cal. App. 2011).
[59] R.U.P.A. §404(2).
[60] R.U.P.A. §701(b). In *Rapport v. Gelfand*, 129 Cal. Rptr. 3d 670, 680 (Cal. App. 2011), the court interprets the term *liquidation value* as used in RUPA §701(b) to mean the sale price of the separate assets based on their market value as determined by a willing and knowledgeable buyer and a willing and knowledgeable seller, neither of whom is under any compulsion to buy or sell. Thus, for purposes of section 701, subdivision (b), "liquidation value" does not incorporate the common definition of "liquidation," which generally implies some urgency for immediate cash.
[61] R.U.P.A. §704.
[62] R.U.P.A. §702.

CPA   ## 24. Notice of Dissolution

Under some circumstances, one partner may continue to possess the power to make a contract that binds the partnership even though the partnership has been dissolved.

(A) NOTICE TO PARTNERS. When the firm is dissolved by the act of a partner, notice must be given to the other partners unless that partner's act clearly shows an intent to withdraw from or to dissolve the firm. If the withdrawing partner acts without notice to the other partners, that partner is bound by contracts created for the firm.

When the dissolution is caused by the act, death, or bankruptcy of a partner, each partner is liable to the copartners for a share of any liability created by any other partner acting for the partnership without knowledge or notice of the act, death, or bankruptcy of the partner who caused the dissolution.

CPA   **(B) NOTICE TO THIRD PERSONS.** When dissolution is caused by the act of a partner or of the partners, notice must be given to third parties. A notice should expressly state that the partnership has been dissolved. Circumstances from which a termination may be inferred are generally not sufficient notice.

Thus, the fact that the partnership checks added the abbreviation *Inc.* after the partnership name was not sufficient notice that the partnership did not exist and that the business had been incorporated.

Actual notice of dissolution must be given to persons who have dealt with the firm.

CASE SUMMARY

Notice Necessary!

FACTS: Paul Babich ran a business under the name of House of Paul. The business became a partnership between Babich, Dyson, and Schnepp but continued under the same name. The partners arranged for printing advertising material with Philipp Lithographing Company, making contracts on three separate occasions for such printing. During the course of these dealings, the House of Paul became a corporation. When the printing bills were not paid in full, Philipp sued the partners as individuals. They claimed they were not liable because the corporation had made the contracts.

DECISION: Whether or not the House of Paul was a corporation with respect to a particular contract was not important because no notice had been given of its change from a partnership to a corporation. Having originally done business with the defendant as a partnership, Philipp could hold the individual persons liable as partners until notice to the contrary was given to Philipp. [*Philipp Lithographing Co. v. Babich*, 135 N.W.2d 343 (Wis. 1965)]

For persons who have had no dealings with the firm, a publication of the fact of dissolution is sufficient. Such notice may be by newspaper publication, by posting a placard in a public place, or by any similar method. Failure to give proper notice continues the power of each partner to bind the others with respect to third persons on contracts within the scope of the business.

When dissolution has been caused by operation of law, notice to third persons is not required. As between the partners, however, the UPA requires knowledge or notice of dissolution by death and bankruptcy.

25. Winding up Partnership Affairs

Most established partnerships deal with the question of how to proceed with the business upon the death of a partner in the written partnership agreement. The agreement may set forth a method for establishing the value of the deceased partner's interest as of the date of death or allow for the remaining partners to purchase the deceased partner's interest. The agreement may also allow for the continuation of the business as usual while the valuation process is completed. However, in the absence of an agreement, either express or implied, permitting the surviving partners to continue the business, the partners must wind up the business and account for the share of the deceased partner.[63]

When dissolution is obtained by court decree, the court may appoint a receiver to conduct the winding up of the partnership business. This may be done in the usual manner, or the receiver may sell the business as a going concern to those partners who wish to continue its operation.

With a few exceptions, all partners have the right to participate in the winding up of the business.[64]

CPA

26. Distribution of Assets

Creditors of the firm have first claim on the assets of the partnership.[65] Difficulty arises when there is a contest between the creditors of the firm and the creditors of the individual partners. The general rule is that firm creditors have first claim on assets of the firm. The individual creditors share in the remaining assets, if any.

After the firm's liabilities to nonpartners have been paid, the assets of the partnership are distributed as follows: (1) each partner is entitled to a refund of advances made to or for the firm, (2) contributions to the capital of the firm are then returned, and (3) the remaining assets, if any, are divided equally as profits among the partners unless there is some other agreement. A partner who contributes only services to the partnership is not considered to have made a capital contribution, absent an agreement to the contrary.

CASE SUMMARY

Are Time and Labor Capital Contributions? Fred Ott Says They Ought to Be

FACTS: Fred Ott and Charles Corley were partners doing business as "Lakewood Associates, a general partnership." Corley provided the capital to purchase the land to be sold by the partnership, called Lakewood Estates. Corley brought suit for the dissolution of the partnership, and Ott contended that his contributions of time and labor in improving Lakewood Estates should be credited to him as capital contributions in the distribution of assets.

DECISION: Judgment for Corley. There was no evidence of any agreement between the partners that Ott's services should be credited as capital contributions. Therefore, the value of the services could not be credited as capital contributions in the distribution of assets. [**Corley v. Ott, 485 S.E.2d 97 (S.C. 1997)**]

---

[63] *Chaney v. Burdett*, 560 S.E.2d 21 (Ga. 2002); *King v. Stoddard*, 104 Cal.Rptr. 903 (Cal. App. 1972).
[64] U.P.A. §37.
[65] *Holmes v. Holmes*, 849 P.2d 1140 (Or. App. 1993).

KEY TERMS

articles of copartnership
articles of partnership
charging order
express authority
general partnership

general partners
jointly and severally liable
jointly liable
operation of law
partners

partnership
partnership agreement
tenancy in partnership
unincorporated
 association

QUESTIONS AND CASE PROBLEMS

1. Ray, Linda, and Nancy form a partnership. Ray and Linda contribute property and cash. Nancy contributes only services. Linda dies, and the partnership is liquidated. After all debts are paid, the surplus is not sufficient to pay back Linda's estate and Ray for the property and cash originally contributed by Linda and Ray. Nancy claims that the balance should be divided equally among Ray, Linda's estate, and Nancy. Is she correct?

2. Baxter, Bigelow, Owens, and Dailey were partners in a New York City advertising agency. Owens, who was in poor health and wanted to retire, advised the partners that she had assigned her full and complete interest in the partnership to her son, Bartholomew, a highly qualified person with 10 years of experience in the advertising business. Baxter, Bigelow, and Dailey refused to allow Bartholomew to attend management meetings and refused his request to inspect the books. Bartholomew pointed out that his mother had invested as much in the firm as any other partner. He believed, as assignee of his mother's full and complete partnership interest, that he is entitled to (a) inspect the books as he sees fit and (b) participate fully in the management of the firm. Was Bartholomew correct?

3. Amy Gargulo and Paula Frisken operated as a partnership Kiddies Korner, an infants' and children's clothing store. They operated the business very successfully for three years, with both Paula and Amy doing the buying and Paula keeping the books and paying the bills. Amy and Paula decided to expand the business when an adjoining store became vacant. At the same time, they incorporated the business. Children's Apparel, Inc., was a major supplier to the business before the expansion. After the expansion, business did not increase as

anticipated, and when a nationally known manufacturer of children's apparel opened a factory outlet nearby, the business could no longer pay its bills. Children's Apparel, which had supplied most of the store's stock after expansion, sued Amy and Paula as partners for bills due for expansion stock. Children's Apparel did not know that Amy and Paula had incorporated. Amy and Paula contended that the business was incorporated and that they therefore were not liable for business debts occurring after incorporation. Were Amy and Paula correct?

4. Calvin Johnson and Rudi Basecke did business as the Stockton Cheese Co., a partnership, which owned a building and equipment. The partners agreed to dissolve the partnership but never got around to completing the winding-up process. Calvin continued to use the building and to pay insurance on it but removed Rudi's name as an insured on the policy. When the building was later destroyed by fire, Calvin claimed the proceeds of the fire insurance policy because he and his wife were the named insureds on the policy and they had paid the premiums. Rudi claimed that although the partnership was dissolved before the fire, the winding up of the partnership was not completed at the time of the fire. He therefore claimed that he was entitled to half of the net proceeds of the policy. Decide. [*State Casualty v. Johnson*, 766 S.W.2d 113 (Mo. App.)]

5. Samuel Shaw purchased a ticket through Delta Airlines to fly a "Delta Connection" flight on SkyWest Airlines to Elko, Nevada. He was seriously injured when the SkyWest plane crashed near Elko. SkyWest's relationship with Delta was a contractual business referral arrangement, whereby Delta benefits through its charges for issuing tickets to connecting

passengers to and from smaller communities, and SkyWest benefits from revenue generated by passengers sent to it by Delta. Both firms make a profit from this arrangement. SkyWest and Delta are often mentioned together by Delta in national print advertisements. Shaw believed that regardless of how the airlines characterize themselves, these airlines are in fact partners because they share profits from their combined efforts. Delta contended that it had no control over SkyWest's airplane operations and that sharing profits as compensation for services does not create a partnership. Decide. [*Shaw v. Delta Airlines, Inc.*, 798 F. Supp. 1453 (D. Nev.)]

6. Larson entered into a Special Manager Incentive Agreement (SMIA) with Tandy Corp. He agreed to manage a Radio Shack store for compensation equal to one-half of the adjusted gross profit of the store as computed by a specific formula and to provide the company with a $20,000 "security deposit" on equipment used to set up the store. The agreement was for a period of two years, automatically renewable annually until either party gave notice of termination 30 days prior to the end of a fiscal year. After some eight and one-half years of operating under renewed agreements, Tandy gave Larson notice of his termination. Larson sued Tandy, claiming that the SMIA was a partnership agreement because there were shared risks, expenses, profits, and losses. He sought an accounting for his reasonable share in the value of the store. Tandy argued that under the SMIA, Larson was an employee-manager, not a partner, and that the ultimate decision making on all matters was Tandy's. Decide. [*Larson v. Tandy Corp*, 371 S.E.2d 663 (Ga. App.)]

7. Two brothers, Eugene and Marlowe Mehl, formed a partnership to operate the family farm. One year, Eugene Mehl withdrew $7,200 from the partnership account and bought the Dagmar Bar. The warranty deed and the liquor license to the bar were obtained in the names of Eugene Mehl and his wife, Bonnie. In a subsequent lawsuit, Marlowe claimed that the bar was a partnership asset. Decide. [*Mehl v. Mehl*, 786 P.2d 1173 (Mont.)]

8. Daniel Zuckerman, a minor, and Elaine, his mother, brought a medical malpractice action against Dr. Joseph Antenucci and Dr. Jose Pena. Although the summons did not state that the two defendants were partners, the undisputed evidence at the trial established that this was their relationship and that the alleged acts of malpractice were done in the course of partnership business. The jury returned a verdict finding that Dr. Pena was guilty of malpractice but that Dr. Antenucci was not guilty of malpractice. The amount of the verdict was $4 million. Antenucci contended that he cannot be held liable on a partnership theory for the act of his partner. Is he correct? [*Zuckerman v. Antenucci*, 748 N.Y.S.2d 578 (A.D.)]

9. Thomas Bartomeli decided to leave his employment to join his brother Raymond full-time in a small construction company. The brothers each contributed individual assets to the company and worked together to acquire equipment with both signing notes jointly to acquire certain equipment. Thomas considered himself a partner in the company; Raymond often referred to Thomas as his partner. It was the practice of the company to garage the equipment at Thomas's house. In 1983, the company was incorporated, but Thomas never held any shares in the company. On several occasions, Thomas's careless operation of equipment resulted in loss or damage to the company. Raymond became dissatisfied with Thomas's work performance, and on January 17, 1991, Thomas was removed as secretary of the corporation.

On April 19, 1991, Thomas went to the company office and demanded a blank check from the secretary. Raymond found out about this demand and fired him. On April 20, 1991, Thomas demanded from Raymond either 50 percent of the company or certain equipment owned by the company. On April 22, 1991, Thomas was removed as vice president of the company. Raymond attempted to reach an agreement with Thomas on a division of company assets at that point but was not successful. Thereafter, Thomas sued his brother, alleging that Raymond had breached the brothers' contract of partnership. Because the company was a corporation, is it legally inconsistent for Thomas to contend that there was a contract for partnership in the company? How would you decide this case? [*Bartomeli v. Bartomeli*, 783 A.2d 1050 (Ct. App.)]

10. Friedman, the "O" Street Carpet Shop, Inc., and Langness formed a partnership known as NFL Associates. "O" Street Carpet's net contribution to capital was $5,004; Langness contributed $14,000 in cash; and Friedman contributed his legal services, on which no value was placed by the articles of partnership. The articles stated that Friedman was entitled to 10 percent of the profits and that Langness was to receive payments of $116.66 per month. The partnership's accountant treated the payments to Langness as a return of her capital. Years later, the partnership sold the rental property owned by the partnership, and the partnership was wound up. Friedman claimed that he was entitled to 10 percent of the partnership capital upon dissolution. Langness claimed that Friedman was not entitled to a capital distribution and that the monthly payments to her should not have been treated as a return of capital. Decide. [*Langness v. "O" Street Carpet, Inc.*, 353 N.W.2d 709 (Neb.)]

11. Ross, Marcos, and Albert are partners. Ross and Marcos each contributed $60,000 to the partnership; Albert contributed $30,000. At the end of the fiscal year, distributable profits total $150,000. Ross claims $60,000 as his share of the profits. Is he entitled to this sum?

12. Leland McElmurry was one of three partners of MHS Enterprises, a Michigan partnership. Commonwealth Capital Investment Corp. sued the partnership and obtained a judgment of $1,137,285 against it, but the partnership could not pay the judgment. Commonwealth then sued McElmurry for the entire debt on the theory that, as a partner of MHS, he was liable for its debts. What, if any, is McElmurry's liability? [*Commonwealth Capital Investment Corp. v. McElmurry*, 302 N.W.2d 222 (Mich. App.)]

13. Thomas Smith and Jackie Lea were partners in the logging business. In January 1981, they joined Gordon Redd and went into business running a sawmill, calling the business Industrial Hardwood Products (IHP). Smith and Lea used their logging equipment at the mill site. Smith hauled 400 loads of gravel, worth some $26,000, from his father's land for the mill yard in the process of getting the mill operational. Smith and Lea received $300 a week compensation for their work, which was reported on federal W-2 forms. They worked up to 65 hours per week and were not paid overtime. All three discussed business decisions. Smith and Lea had the authority to write checks and to hire and fire employees. Lea left the business in 1983 and was paid $20,000 by Redd. The testimony indicated that the three individuals agreed in January 1981 that as soon as the bank was paid off and Redd was paid his investment, Lea and Smith would be given an interest in the mill. No written agreement existed. Redd invested $410,452 in the business and withdrew $500,475 from it. As of December 31, 1986, IHP had sufficient retained earnings to retire the bank debt. In April 1987, Smith petitioned the Chancery Court for dissolution of the "partnership" and an accounting. Redd denied that any partnership agreement was formed and asserted that Smith was an employee because he was paid wages. He offered to pay Smith $50,000 for the gravel and use of his equipment. Decide. [*Smith v. Redd*, 593 So.2d 989 (Miss.)]

14. Mason and Phyllis Ledbetter operated a business in Northbrook, Illinois, as a partnership called Ledbetters' Nurseries that specialized in the sale of garden lilies. The grounds of the nurseries were planted with numerous species of garden lilies, and hundreds of people toured the Ledbetters' gardens every day. After a tour, Sheila Clark offered to buy the facilities at a "top-notch price." Mason felt he could not refuse the high offer, and he signed a contract to sell all the facilities, including all flowers and the business name. When Phyllis refused to go along with the contract, Clark sued the Ledbetters' Nurseries partnership, seeking to obtain specific performance of the sales contract. Decide.

15. St. John Transportation Co., a corporation, made a contract with the partnership of Bilyeu and Herstel, contractors, by which the latter was to construct a ferryboat. Herstel, a member of the firm of contractors, executed a contract in the firm name with Benbow for certain materials and labor in connection with the construction of the ferryboat. In an action brought by Benbow to enforce a lien against the ferryboat, the *James Johns*, it was contended that all members of the firm were bound by the contract made by Herstel. Do you agree? [*Benbow v. The Ferryboat James Johns*, 108 P. 634 (Or.)]

CPA QUESTIONS

1. Acorn and Bean were general partners in a farm machinery business. Acorn contracted, on behalf of the partnership, to purchase 10 tractors from Cobb Corp. Unknown to Cobb, Acorn was not authorized by the partnership to make such contracts. Bean refused to allow the partnership to accept delivery of the tractors, and Cobb sought to enforce the contract. Cobb will:

    a. Lose, because Acorn's action was beyond the scope of Acorn's implied authority.

    b. Prevail, because Acorn had implied authority to bind the partnership.

    c. Prevail, because Acorn had apparent authority to bind the partnership.

    d. Lose, because Acorn's express authority was restricted, in writing, by the partnership agreement.

2. Upon dissolution of a general partnership, distributions will be made on account of:

    I. Partners' capital accounts.

    II. Amounts owed partners with respect to profits.

    III. Amounts owed partners for loans to the partnership in the following order:

        a. III, I, II

        b. I, II, III

        c. II, III, I

        d. III, II, I

3. Which of the following statements is correct with respect to a limited partnership?

    a. A limited partner may *not* be an unsecured creditor of the limited partnership.

    b. A general partner may *not* also be a limited partner at the same time.

    c. A general partner may be a secured creditor of the limited partnership.

    d. A limited partnership can be formed with limited liability for all partners.

4. When a partner in a general partnership lacks actual or apparent authority to contract on behalf of the partnership, and the party contracted with is aware of this fact, the partnership will be bound by the contract if the other partners:

	Ratify the Contract	Amend the Partnership Agreement
a.	Yes	Yes
b.	Yes	No
c.	No	Yes
d.	No	No

CHAPTER 43

LPs, LLCs, and LLPs

learningoutcomes

After studying this chapter, you should be able to

LO.1   Explain the history of making limited liability available to general partnerships

LO.2   Explain the extent of a founding general partner's liability for the debts of the firm, and how unlimited liability can be avoided by utilization of a corporate general partner

LO.3   Explain the nature and extent of a limited partner's liability for the debts of the firm

LO.4   Explain the advantages of a limited liability company

LO.5   Understand that unless modified in an operating agreement, managers of LLCs owe member-investors the traditional duties of loyalty and care

LO.6   Explain how a limited liability partnership "shields" innocent partners from liability to third parties

A. The Arrival of Partnership Limited Liability

Individuals owning businesses or professional firms are concerned about exposing their personal wealth to liability beyond that invested in their businesses or firms. As discussed previously, limited liability is not a feature of general partnership law. The concept of making limited liability available to general partnerships was considered by the RUPA Drafting Committee when it began its work to revise the Uniform Partnership Act in 1987, but the concept was rejected. A limited partnership form of business organization had existed since 1916 under the Uniform Limited Partnership Act with limited partners (investors) having limited liability, but the firms' general partners were exposed to personal liability for firm debts under this act. The concept of full limited liability for partnerships began to take hold in 1986 when businesses forming limited partnerships under the Revised Uniform Limited Partnership Act utilized corporate general partners, with the general partners avoiding personal liability by the simple expedient of incorporating.

An IRS ruling classifying a Wyoming limited liability company (LLC) as a partnership for tax purposes led to the rapid spread of LLC statutes to every state within six years of the IRS ruling.[1] As part of the limited liability trend established by the swift enactment of LLC laws throughout the country, most states have also enacted limited liability partnership (LLP) acts. Like LLCs, they provide businesses and those offering professional services the benefit of single taxation as a partnership as well as limited liability.

B. Limited Partnership

A limited partnership is a special kind of partnership.

1. Formation of Limited Partnerships

The Uniform Limited Partnership Act (ULPA) was approved by the National Conference of Commissioners on Uniform State Law in 1916. It was revised in 1976 (RULPA), and this RULPA was amended in 1985. All states except Louisiana have adopted a version of the RULPA.

limited partnership – partnership that can be formed by "one or more general partners and one or more limited partners."

CPA

limited partner – partner who neither takes part in the management of the partnership nor appears to the public to be a general partner.

general partner – partnership in which **CPA** the partners conduct as co-owners a business for profit, and each partner has a right to take part in the management of the business and has unlimited liability; general partners publicly and actively engage in the transaction of firm business.

(A) Members of a Limited Partnership. In a **limited partnership** certain members contribute capital but have limited liability for firm debts. The most these members can lose is their investment. These members are known as **limited partners.** The partners who manage the business and are personally liable for the firm debts are **general partners.**[2] A limited partnership can be formed by "one or more general partners and one or more limited partners."[3]

(B) Certificate of Limited Partnership. Unlike a general partnership, a limited partnership can be created only by executing a certificate of limited partnership.

Under the 1985 amendments to the RULPA, the certificate requires the following information: (1) the limited partnership's name, (2) the address of the partnership's

---

[1] Rev. Rul. 88-76, 1988—2 C.B. 360.
[2] *Brooke v. Mt. Hood Meadows, Ltd.,* 725 P.2d 925 (Or. App. 1986).
[3] R.U.L.P.A. §101(7).

registered office and the name and business address of its agent for service of process, (3) the name and business address of each general partner, (4) the partnership's mailing address, and (5) the latest date on which the limited partnership is to dissolve. The names of the limited partners (the investors) are not required. This allows for the preservation of the confidentiality of the investors' names from competitors. Moreover, new investors may be admitted as limited partners without the significant administrative burden involved in amending the certificate, as was required under the ULPA. The RULPA provides for filing the certificate with the office of the secretary of state, as opposed to the local filing required under the ULPA.

When there is no filing of the limited partnership certificate, all participants have the status and liability of general partners in a general partnership. However, technical defects in the certificate do not prevent formation of a limited partnership if there has been substantial, good-faith compliance with the filing requirements.[4]

CPA **(c) LIMITED PARTNERSHIP AGREEMENT.** The RULPA embodies the policy of freedom of contract and maximum flexibility regarding the limited partnership agreement.[5] Most limited partnership agreements are drafted almost exclusively by their founding general partners, and courts resolve ambiguities against the drafting general partners and in favor of the reasonable expectations of the limited partners. **For Example,** when the general partners of the Nantucket Island Associates Limited Partnership unilaterally amended the limited partnership agreement to add a new class of preferred limited partnership units with superior rights to existing unit holders, ambiguous agreement language was construed against the general partners by the court, and the general partners were found to be in breach of the agreement by adding the new class of units.[6]

2. Characteristics of Limited Partnerships

A limited partnership has the following characteristics.

CPA **(A) CAPITAL CONTRIBUTIONS.** Under the ULPA, a limited partner contributed either cash or property but not services. Under the RULPA, however, a limited partner may contribute services.

CPA **(B) FIRM NAME.** With certain exceptions, a limited partner's name cannot appear in the firm name. Under the RULPA, the words *limited partnership* must appear without abbreviation in the firm name.

CPA **(C) MANAGEMENT AND CONTROL OF THE FIRM.** The general partners manage the business and are personally liable for firm debts. However, general partners may avoid personal liability by incorporating. Limited partners (the investors) have the right to a share of the profits and a return of capital upon dissolution and have limited liability. The limitation of liability is lost, however, if they participate in the control of the business, as seen in the *Gilroy, Sims & Associates Ltd.* case.

---

[4] R.U.L.P.A. §201(b); *Fabry Partnership v. Christensan,* 794 P.2d 719 (Nev. 1990).
[5] See *Gotham Partners, L.P. v. Hallowood Realty Partners, L.P.,* 817 A.2d 160 (Del. 2002).
[6] *In re Nantucket Island Associates Limited Partnership Unit Holders Litigation,* 810 A.2d 351 (Del. Ch. 2002).

CASE SUMMARY

The Problem of Limited Partners in Control

FACTS: Gilroy, Sims & Associates, Ltd., was a limited partnership engaged in real estate development whose original general partners were Richard Gilroy and William Sims. Thomas Green and John Murphy, Jr., were listed as limited partners along with certain other individuals on the certificate of limited partnership. Green and Murphy took an active role in the day-to-day operations of the real estate developed by the limited partnership. Financing was obtained to construct the venture's building in St. Louis in 1968, and a mortgage was payable to American National Insurance Company over 27 years. In 1976, the partnership executed a Restated Agreement, and Green and Murphy became general partners of Gilroy, Sims, agreeing to "unlimited liability for the debts of the partnership." In the fall of 1990, the partnership stopped making mortgage payments. After foreclosure by American National, a deficiency of $1,437,840 was outstanding. Green and Murphy believed that as limited partners when the debt was incurred in 1968, they were absolved from any personal liability beyond the assets of the firm. American National disagreed.

DECISION: Judgment for American National Insurance Company. Green and Murphy expressly adopted the partnership obligation in the Restated Agreement executed in 1976. Moreover, although Green's and Murphy's limited partner status would ordinarily limit their personal liability to creditors to the amount of their investment, their active roles in taking part in the control of the business subjected them to potential general partner liability. [*American National Ins. Co. v. Gilroy, Sims & Associates, Ltd.*, 874 F. Supp. 971 (E.D. Mo. 1995)]

The RULPA lists a number of "safe harbor" activities in which limited partners may engage without losing their protection from liability. These activities include

1. Being a contractor for, or an agent or employee of, the limited partnership or of a general partner;

2. Consulting with and advising a general partner regarding the partnership business;

3. Acting as a surety for the limited partnership; and

4. Voting on partnership matters, such as dissolving and winding up the limited partnership or removing a general partner.

(D) RIGHT TO SUE. A limited partner may bring a derivative action on behalf of the limited partnership to enforce a claim that the limited partnership possesses against others but that the partnership refuses to enforce.[7] This derivative suit is filed in the name of the limited partner, and the partnership is named as a defendant, with the limited partnership deriving the benefits of the action.

Limited partners may sue their partnership's general partner to protect the limited partners' interest. General partners today are commonly corporations with their own boards of directors and management teams, with the limited partnership format providing investment and tax incentives for investor–limited partners and the general partners reserving to themselves broad authority to act in the general partners' sole

---

[7] *Garber v. Stevens*, 941 N.Y.S.2d 127 (A.D. 2012).

discretion and often in the general partners' own best interest. **For Example,** Donald Weedon and others formed a limited partnership under Delaware law to raise capital for the securities broker–dealer business. The partnership agreement, as allowed by Delaware law, gave the corporate general partners and its directors the right to restrict their fiduciary duties in managing the partnership and gave the general partner broad power to act, even in conflicted situations, subject only to very loose constraints of a subjective bad-faith standard. Nonemployee limited partners referred to by the court as the "outside investors" brought suit against the corporate general partners and members of the general partner's board of directors and top management for squeezing out all nonemployee limited partners and paying less than the fair value for their units in violation of fiduciary duties and the partnership agreement. The trial court decided in favor of the plaintiffs, stating in part:

> … *Even given the wide discretion the partnership agreement gives to the defendants to issue new units without fear of liability, the defendants managed to step out of bounds in one important respect. By deciding to permit the general partner's outside directors to acquire new units at a favorable price and by denying the same opportunity to Outside Investors, the defendants breached their contractual duties. This decision, I find, was not undertaken in good faith but instead as quid pro quo for the outside directors' willing assent to the issuance of a large number of new units to management and employees.…*

The plaintiffs received a make-whole remedy from the court with monetary damages tied to fair market values.[8]

(E) Dissolution. The dissolution and winding up of limited partnerships is governed by the same principles applicable to general partnerships.

C. Limited Liability Companies

Limited liability company (LLC) acts were rapidly adopted by state legislatures throughout the country following a favorable tax ruling on this form of organization by the Internal Revenue Service.[9] This corporate-sounding entity is considered in this chapter because it is a form of limited partnership.

CPA

3. Characteristics of LLCs

The IRS has determined that an LLC may qualify for partnership federal tax treatment. Unlike a corporation, an LLC pays no federal taxes on its income as an entity. Instead, the income (or losses, deductions, and credits) flows through to the LLC's owners (called *members*) based on their proportionate interest in the company. The members report the income on their personal tax returns. The LLC combines this tax advantage with the limited liability feature of the corporate form of business organization. The owners and managers are not personally liable for the debts and obligations of the entity, provided that these individuals fulfill their common law duty to disclose that they are acting as agents for the limited liability company.

[8] *Gelfman v. Weeden Investors, L.P.*, 859 A.2d 89 (Del. Ch. 2004).
[9] IRS Rev. Rul. 88-76. LLCs have been adopted by every state and the District of Columbia. A Uniform Limited Liability Company Act was approved by the National Conference of Commissioners on Uniform State Law.

CPA　(A) **FORMATION.** As set forth previously, general partnerships may be created without the formality of even a written partnership agreement when two individuals simply operate a business for profit as co-owners. LLCs, however, require a formal filing of articles of organization with the secretary of state in a manner similar to a filing of articles of incorporation by a corporation or a certificate of limited partnership for a limited partnership.

The articles for an LLC must contain the name, purpose, duration, registered agent, and principal office of the LLC. An LLC must use the words *limited liability company* or *LLC* in the company's name. The LLC is a legal entity with authority to conduct business in its own name.[10] LLC acts are characterized as "flexible statutes" because they generally permit owners to engage in the private ordering of relationships, with broad freedom of contract to govern these relationships as set forth in their operating agreements.[11]

CPA　(B) **CAPITAL CONTRIBUTIONS.** An ownership interest in an LLC may be issued for cash, property, or services. The owners of the entity are known as *members*.

Capital contributions must comply with the "operating agreement" as discussed in the following paragraph. **For Example,** William Eichengrun claims his capital contribution to the LLC was in services, not cash, because he was the LLC's managing member. However, in proceedings to dissolve the LLC and distribute its assets, Eichengrun was not allowed to participate in the distribution because the operating agreement required that "initial capital contributions" of members be in cash or the fair market value of property.[12]

CPA　(C) **MANAGEMENT.** Management of an LLC is vested in its members. An *operating agreement*, equivalent to the bylaws of a corporation or a partnership agreement, sets forth the specific management authority of members and managers.

The operating agreement need not be in writing. All amendments must be unanimous unless otherwise agreed to by the members. Oral amendments may modify written terms unless otherwise set forth in the operating agreement. To promote certainty in management, it is recommended that the operating agreement be in writing and that it be changed only by written amendments adopted by a specified percentage or number of members.

The management structure created in the operating agreement may provide for the company to be member managed. However, members commonly delegate authority to run the entity to managers who may or may not be required to be members of the LLC. A member is not entitled to compensation for services performed by an LLC unless it is stipulated in the operating agreement. (Members receive profits and losses according to the terms of the operating agreement.)

In a member-managed company, each member has equal rights in management, with decisions made by a majority vote of the members.[13] In a manager-managed company, nonmanager members have no rights in management except for extraordinary matters, such as amending the operating agreement or consenting to merge with another entity.

---

[10] An individual has a right to appear before a court and represent himself or herself. However, a member of an LLC who as such is not personally liable for the LLC's actions cannot appear before a court on behalf of the LLC entity. The LLC may appear in court only through counsel. Thus, a nonattorney member of an LLC was not allowed to represent the LLC in a court case. *Collier v. Cobalt, LLC,* 2002 WL 726640 (E.D. La. April 22, 2002). See also *Gobe Media Group, LLC v. Cisneros,* 959 A.2d 892 (N.J. Super. 2008).

[11] *Elf Atochem N. America, Inc. v. Jaffari,* 727 A.2d 286 (Del. Super. Ct. 1999).

[12] *KSI Rockville, LLC v. Eichengrun,* 760 N.Y.S.2d 520 (A. D. 2003).

[13] *IIC Holdings, LLC v. HR Software Acquisition Group, Inc.,* 750 N.Y.S.2d 425 (Sup. Ct. 2002).

Managers have the same fiduciary duties to the entity as corporate officers have to a corporation. LLC acts are characterized as "flexible statutes" allowing broad freedom of contract to govern relationships, as spelled out in detail in operating agreements. The parties are free to waive or modify in their operating agreements the duties of loyalty and care owed by managers to members. Unless modified, however, state LLC acts may apply fiduciary duties to managers who would qualify as fiduciaries under traditional equitable principles.

CASE SUMMARY

Golf Course Owner Out of Bounds

FACTS: Minority members in a Delaware limited liability company, Peconic Bay, LLC, brought a breach of fiduciary duty action against the LLC's manager and its majority interest holder regarding the sale of the LLC at an auction, in which the LLC was purchased by the manager. The "manager" is Gatz Properties, LLC, which is managed and partially owned by William Gatz. Peconic Bay, LLC, held a long-term lease on valuable property in New York that allowed the LLC to operate a first-rate Robert Trent Jones, Jr. designed golf course, called Long Island National Golf Course. The golf management company, American Golf, held a sublease on the property after it opened in 1999, never made a profit, and let the course fall into disrepair. Gatz knew in 2004 that American Golf would exercise its early termination option in 2010, yet he did nothing to plan for its exit. Rather, Gatz made a series of decisions that placed Peconic Bay in an economically vulnerable position. Then Gatz decided to put Peconic Bay on the auction block without engaging an experienced broker to market it to golf course managers or owners. Gatz, on behalf of Gatz Properties, was the only bidder to show up. Knowing this fact before formulating his bid, Gatz purchased Peconic Bay for a nominal value over the debt and merged Peconic Bay into Gatz Properties.

DECISION: Judgment for the minority members. The LLC agreement makes clear that the manager could only enter into a self-dealing transaction, such as its purchase of the LLC, if it proves that the terms were fair. The LLC agreement essentially incorporates a core element of the traditional fiduciary duty of loyalty. The manager's defense that his voting power gave him a license to exploit the minority fundamentally misunderstands Delaware law. The manager was free not to vote his membership interest for a sale. But he was not free to create a situation of distress by failing to cause the LLC to explore its market alternatives and then to buy the LLC for a nominal price. The purpose of the duty of loyalty is in large measure to prevent the exploitation by a fiduciary of his self-interest to the disadvantage of the minority. The fair price requirement of that duty, which is incorporated in the LLC agreement here, makes sure that if the conflicted fiduciary engages in self-dealing, he pays a price that is as much as an arms-length purchaser would pay. [*Auriga Capital Corp. v. Gatz Properties, LLC*, 40 A.3d 839 (Del. Ch. 2012)]

In some states, members of manager-managed LLCs owe no fiduciary duty to the LCC unless a member exercises some or all of the authority of a manager pursuant to the operating agreement.[14]

---

[14] In *Remora Investments, LLC v. Orr*, 673 S.E.2d 845 (Va. 2009), the Virginia Supreme Court held that nothing in the statutory provisions relating to LLCs provides for fiduciary duties between members of an LLC or between a member and a manager of an LLC. The statutory standard of conduct for a manager of an LLC is to discharge duties in accordance with his or her good-faith business judgment of the best interests of the company, rather than by imposing fiduciary duties on members. In contrast, the Uniform Limited Liability Act of 2006, which has been adopted in Idaho, Iowa, Nebraska, Utah, and Wyoming, states that members of an LLC owe each other the fiduciary duties of loyalty and care. See *Bush v. Sage Health Care, LLC*, 203 P.3d 694 (Idaho 2009). See also *Melcher v. Apollo Medical Fund Management*, 208 N.Y.S.2d 207 (A. D. 2006), referencing Delaware Code, Title 6 §18-110(c).

CPA   **(D) Distributions.** Profits and losses are shared according to the terms of the operating agreement.

Liquidating distributions must first be applied to return all contributions not previously returned, and the remainder is distributed per capita to members unless members alter these rules in the operating agreement.

Any distribution made when the company is insolvent is unlawful. Each member or manager who votes to make an unlawful distribution is in violation of his or her fiduciary duty to the firm and is personally liable for the amount of distribution improperly paid.[15] However, the individual may compel contribution from all other responsible members and managers.

(E) LLC Property. The LLC is an independent entity separate and distinct from the members. The LLC owns and holds property in its own name.[16]

CASE SUMMARY

"Another Person": The Unintended Consequences of an LLC Transaction

FACTS: In 1998, Shell and Texaco combined their retail marketing and refining activities into a limited liability company called Equilon Enterprises, LLC. They contributed all their western refining and marketing assets and assigned gas station leases and dealer agreements to the new LLC. Shell and Texaco, as the sole members of the LLC, received 100 percent of the ownership. The individual gas stations continued to sell Shell and Texaco products under their same leases and agreements. California law, identical in relevant part to the federal Petroleum Marketing Practices Act, states that a franchisor *"shall not sell, transfer, or assign to another person"* unless it first makes a bona fide offer to sell that interest to the franchisee. Forty-three independent Shell and Texaco dealers in southern California who leased from Shell and Texaco claimed that Shell and Texaco violated the California law by transferring the gas stations to the new LLC, Equilon, without offering them a chance to purchase the stations. Shell and Texaco contend that the law does not apply because they merely contributed their assets to an LLC that they controlled.

DECISION: Judgment for the independent dealers. What is the meaning of "another person" under the law in question? LLCs are distinct legal entities, separate from their members just as corporations are separate and distinct from their shareholders. Both corporations and LLCs are included within the definition of "person" under the state law. Because Equilon is an LLC, it is distinct from its members Shell and Texaco and is "another person" under the statute. The gas stations that were previously owned by the individual oil companies are now owned by "another person," Equilon.

Because Shell and Texaco relinquished title, possession, and control of the gas stations to Equilon, they "transferred" the properties to Equilon. Once members contribute assets to an LLC, those assets become capital of the LLC and the members lose any interest they had in the assets.

Under the plain language of the statute, the transaction at issue was a transfer to another person, Equilon, which triggered the duty to offer the gas stations to the franchisees first. [*Abrahim & Sons, Inc. v. Equilon Enterprises, LLC*, 252 F.3d 958 (9th Cir. 2002)]

(F) Assignment. An interest in an LLC is personal property and is generally assignable. However, LLC members cannot transfer the right to participate in management without the consent of the other members of the LLC.

---

[15] *Florence Cement Co. v. Vitttaino*, 807 N.W.2d 461 (Mich. App. 2011).
[16] *Northeast Realty, LLC v. Misty Bayou, LLC*, 920 So.2d 938 (La. App. 2006).

CASE SUMMARY

"I'm in Charge," said the Admiral's Daughter. "No, You're Not," said the Admiral's New Wife.

FACTS: Admiral Dewey Monroe and his wife Lou Ann Monroe formed an LLC in 2003, with Dewey holding an 80% membership interest and Lou Ann a 20% membership interest, respectively. The LLC provided that Lou Ann would be the managing member. Dewey died in 2004 and bequeathed his entire estate to his daughter, Janet Ott. Janet called a meeting of the company, seeking to remove Lou Ann and elect herself as the company's new managing member, asserting that she had inherited her father's full LLC membership upon his death under his will. The LLC asserted that Janet had inherited only Dewey's right to share profits and losses and to receive distributions but did not inherit a right to the management and control of the company.

DECISION: Judgment for the LLC and Lou Ann. Dewey Monroe was dissociated from the company upon his death by operation of law, terminating all his rights as a member to participate in the management and control of the company, and only the right to share profits and losses and to receive distributions survived to be inherited by Janet under his will. [*Ott v. Monroe*, 719 S.E. 2d 309 (Va. 2011)]

A creditor's right against a member's interest in an LLC is limited to a *charging order*. The creditor with such an order has only the rights of an assignee of an interest in an LLC.

(G) DISSOLUTION. Most LLC statutes provide that an LLC will dissolve by the consent of the members or upon the death, retirement, resignation, expulsion, or bankruptcy of a member. Statutes also provide, however, that the business of the LLC may be continued with the consent of all of the remaining members. With a change in IRS regulations away from its four-factor corporate characteristics test, discussed in the following section, some states have begun to amend LLC laws to give limited liability companies the option of perpetual existence.

Situations in which it is not reasonably practicable to carry on the business in conformity with the operating agreement may arise. The LLC statute commonly permits a court to decree dissolution of the LLC when such a situation occurs.[17] **For Example,** Haley and Talcott each had a 50 percent interest in a real estate LLC. They had a falling out. The operating agreement contained an exit mechanism to buy out Haley's share, but the mechanism could not relieve Haley of his obligation as a personal guarantor for the LLC's mortgage. Because the LLC was deadlocked and the exit mechanism was not an adequate remedy, the court ordered the dissolution of the LLC and the sale of its property.[18]

Upon the winding up of an LLC, the assets are distributed according to the operating agreement. Should the agreement fail to provide for this event, the assets will be distributed according to the state's LLC statute.

(H) TAX CLASSIFICATION. The IRS applied a four-factor corporate characteristics test in determining whether an LLC would be taxed as a partnership or a corporation, allowing no more than two characteristics to exist to qualify for taxation as a partnership. The factors were continuity of life, centralized management, limited liability, and free transferability of interest. The four-factor test became obsolete on

---

[17] *Venture Sales, LLC v. Perkins*, 86 So.3d 910 (Miss. 2012).
[18] *Haley v. Talcott*, 864 A.2d 86 (Del. Ch. 2004).

FIGURE 43-1 | *Comparison of General Partnership, Limited Partnership, Limited Liability Company, and Limited Liability Partnership*

	General Partnership	**Limited Partnership**	**Limited Liability Company (LLC)**	**Limited Liability Partnership (LLP)**
Creation	No formality required.	Filing a certificate of limited partnership with appropriate state office.	Filing articles of organization with secretary of state.	Registration of LLP filed with state government.
Liability	Unlimited liability of each partner for firm debts.	General partners: unlimited liability for firm debts. Limited partners: no liability beyond loss of investment.	All members are liable for LLC debts to the extent of their capital contributions and equity in firm. No personal liability beyond this.	No liability for partners beyond their contributions and equity in firm, except unlimited personal liability for their own wrongful acts and those of persons whom they supervise.
Management	All partners according to their partnership agreement or the UPA or RUPA.	General partners according to their partnership agreement or the UPA or RUPA. Limited partners excluded.	By members of firm, who may delegate authority to managers.	All partners according to partnership agreement or the UPA.
Dissolution	As set forth in the partnership agreement or the UPA or RUPA.	As set forth in the partnership agreement or the ULPA or RULPA.	As set forth in LLC statute or articles of organization.	As set forth in partnership agreement or the UPA or RUPA.

© Cengage Learning

the implementation by the IRS of its so-called check-the-box entity classification election procedure available to unincorporated associations that are not publicly traded.[19] Now, if an LLC wants to be classified as a partnership, all it needs to do is make that election by checking the box on the appropriate IRS form.

[19] Treas. Reg. 301.7701 *et seq.*

(i) **Disregarding the LLC Entity.** Some LLC statutes provide that courts may disregard the LLC entirely and hold the owners personally liable beyond their investments to the same extent as done in corporate law when exceptional circumstances demand.[20]

CASE SUMMARY

Piercing the LLC Veil

FACTS: Kaycee Land and Livestock entered into a contract with Flahive Oil and Gas, LLC, allowing it to use the surface of its real property. Kaycee alleges that Flahive Oil and Gas caused environmental contamination of its real property. Because the LLC has no assets at this time, Kaycee seeks to pierce the limited liability company veil and disregard the LLC entity of Flahive Oil and Gas and hold Roger Flahive, the managing member of the LLC who directed all operations on the property, individually liable for the contamination. The question presented to the court is, "In the absence of fraud, is the remedy of piercing the veil available against a company formed under the Wyoming Limited Liability Company Act?"

DECISION: The equitable remedy of piercing the corporate veil is an available remedy under the Wyoming Limited Liability Company Act. When corporations fail to follow the statutorily mandated formalities, comingle funds, or ignore restrictions in their articles of incorporation regarding separate treatment of the corporate property, the courts deem it appropriate to disregard the separate identity and do not permit shareholders to be sheltered from liability to third parties for damages caused by the corporation's acts. No public policy exists to treat LLCs differently than corporations regarding veil piercing. [***Kaycee Land and Livestock v. Flahive***, 46 P.3d 323 (Wyo. 2002)]

4. LLCs and Other Entities

LLCs are distinguishable from Subchapter S corporations and limited partnerships.

(A) **LLC Distinguished from a Subchapter S Corporation.** Under a Subchapter S corporation (so named from Subchapter S of the Internal Revenue Code), shareholders of a close corporation may be treated as partners for tax purposes and retain the benefit of limited liability under the corporate form. An S corporation is limited to 75 shareholders who must be U.S. citizens or resident aliens. Although partnerships and corporations may generally not be shareholders, employee stock ownership plans (ESOPs) and nonprofit entities may be. In contrast, an LLC has no limit on the number of owners, and there is no restriction on the types of entities or persons that may own an LLC. Thus, partnerships, corporations, and foreign investors may be owners of an LLC. Because substantial taxes on appreciated assets are payable on the liquidation of an S corporation, it is generally not feasible to convert an existing S corporation to an LLC.

CPA

(B) **LLC Distinguished from a Limited Partnership.** Limited partners in a limited partnership have the advantage of limited liability. However, every limited partnership must have a general partner who manages the business, and this partner can be subject to unlimited liability. This structural feature is a major disadvantage of the limited partnership form that does not exist in a limited liability company (LLC). Also,

---

[20] *Net Jets Aviation, Inc. v. LHC Communications, LLC,* 537 F.3d 168 (2d Cir. 2008); but see *Serio v. Baystate Properties, LLC,* 39 A.3d 131 (Md. App. 2012).

individual limited partners may lose their limited liability if they participate in the control of the business. Under an LLC, the members may actively participate in the control of the business and still receive limited liability protection. As stated previously in this chapter, a general partner may avoid unlimited liability on a sizeable limited partnership project by incorporating.

(c) USAGE. It is expected that the LLC will in many instances replace general and limited partnerships as well as close corporations and S corporations. The LLC will not replace the publicly traded corporation, however, because publicly traded partnerships and LLCs must be classified as corporations for tax purposes.[21]

D. LIMITED LIABILITY PARTNERSHIPS

As part of the limited liability trend established by the swift enactment of LLC laws throughout the country, most states have recently enacted limited liability partnership (LLP) acts. Like LLCs, they provide businesses and those offering professional services the benefit of single taxation as a partnership as well as limited liability.[22]

CPA

5. Extent of Limited Liability

In a general partnership, partners are jointly liable for partnership debts and jointly and severally liable for partnership torts. LLP statutes were initially drafted to shield innocent partners from vicarious negligence or malpractice liability of their partners. Some states now provide "full shields" for innocent partners that eliminate the vicarious personal liability of these partners for the obligations of the partnership and free them from any obligation to contribute personal assets beyond their investments in the partnership. However, the "liability shield" of a registered limited liability partnership only applies to a partner's liability to third parties and does not shield against breaches of the partnership's or partners' obligations to each other. In every state, however, LLP partners remain fully liable for their own negligence and continue to have unlimited liability for the wrongful acts of those whom they directly supervise and control.

CASE SUMMARY

A Limited Shield

FACTS: Phillip Kuslansky sued his former law partners for breach of contract for failure to pay him the value of his interest in the registered limited liability partnership upon his withdrawal from the partnership. His former partners moved to dismiss the complaint, contending that they were shielded from liability with respect to the plaintiff partner who had withdrawn from the partnership. From a judgment for the defendant former partners, Kuslansky appealed.

---

[21] See IRS Notice 88-75, 1988, 1988-2 CB 386. The traditional corporation retains many advantages, such as the low corporate income tax on corporate profits, which allows accumulation of capital for expansion or the distribution of all corporate earnings as compensation as well as providing fringe benefits for employee-owners with pretax dollars (IRC §§79, 119, 162).

[22] The 1994 Revised Uniform Partnership Act (RUPA) was amended in 1996 to include two new articles: Article 10, dealing with limited liability partnerships, and Article 11, dealing with foreign limited liability partnerships. Articles 1 through 11 constitute the Uniform Limited Liability Partnership Act.

CASE SUMMARY

Continued

DECISION: Judgment for Kuslansky. The state LLP law does not shield general partners in registered limited liability partnerships from personal liability for breaches of the partnership's or partners' obligations to each other. [*Kuslansky v. Kuslansy, Robbins, Stechel and Cunningham, LLP*, 858 N.Y.S.2d 213 (A.D. 2008)]

Professional LLPs continue to be subject to professional regulations, and the appropriate regulating boards set the amount and type of malpractice insurance firms must carry to operate as an LLP.

For Example, to illustrate the effects of a change from a general partnership to an LLP, surgeons Jones, Smith, and Gray are partners. Jones inadvertently removed Miller's healthy kidney rather than his diseased kidney, and a jury returned a verdict of $2 million. Smith and Gray, although innocent partners, are jointly and severally liable along with Jones under general partnership law, and their personal assets can be reached to pay the judgment if necessary. Under an LLP, only partnership assets and the personal assets of Jones are available to pay the judgment. Smith's and Gray's personal assets cannot be reached.

CPA

6. Registration and Usage

LLP statutes are designed to permit the conversion of existing general partnerships into limited liability partnerships. The statutes require registration with the secretary of state, and the name of the partnership must contain the term *limited liability partnership* or *LLP*.

Traditional partnership agreements, like those used by many accounting and law firms and other professional partnerships, can be converted into limited liability partnership agreements without major redrafting or renegotiating of the underlying agreements. It is thus expected that many of these professional firms will organize under this new form of partnership.

Ethics & the Law

The S & L Crisis

When the Office of the Special Counsel concluded its work in both civil and criminal litigation against officers, directors, and consultants involved with failed savings and loan institutions in the late 1980s, it released a report on its work. On the civil side, the Office of the Special Counsel had obtained settlements from defendants in civil suits of $2.9 billion in restitution. Accounting firms, along with lawyers and consultants, comprised 71 percent of the defendants.

Because most accounting firms were organized as partnerships, the result was that many partners were required to dig into their personal assets to meet the restitution requirements imposed by the federal government. Since the creation of LLPs, all of the largest accounting

firms in the United States have restructured, with most choosing the LLP for conducting business. All forms of restructuring will ensure limited personal liability for their principals.

Was the restructuring undertaken to avoid liability? Does limited liability insulate those who make decisions from liability for those decisions? Financiers attempt to determine what stake the officers in a corporation have in the corporation. Stock ownership and exposure to losses through the value of those shares are seen as a positive influence. Do liability limitations reduce the stake a principal has? Is it good to have decision makers separated from the costs of those decisions?

MAKE THE CONNECTION

SUMMARY

A limited partnership consists of one or more limited partners who contribute cash, property, or services without liability for losses beyond their investment, and one or more general partners, who manage the business and have unlimited personal liability. A limited partner's protection from unlimited liability may be lost if the partner participates in the control of the business. "Safe harbor" activities for limited partners are set forth in the RULPA. General partners may avoid personal liability by incorporating. A certificate of limited partnership must be filed when the partnership is formed for the law to apply. Otherwise, general partnership law applies.

A limited liability company is a hybrid form of business organization that combines the tax advantages of a partnership with the limited liability feature of the corporation. It must be formed in accordance with

state law in order to have effect, and the designation LLC must appear with the company's name. Management of an LLC is vested in its members, and members can delegate authority to run the entity to managers, the terms of which are set forth in the company's operating agreement. Members receive profits and losses according to the operating agreement. A member's interest in an LLC is assignable, but consent of the other members is needed for the assignee to participate in the firm's management.

A limited liability partnership is a new form of business organization that allows existing partnerships to convert to this form without major renegotiation of the underlying partnership agreement. Innocent partners in a limited liability partnership are not personally liable for the torts of other partners beyond their investment in the firm.

LEARNING OUTCOMES

After studying this chapter, you should be able to clearly explain:

A. The Arrival of Partnership Limited Liability

L0.1   Explain the history of making limited liability available to general partnerships

> See the presentation of the developing law of partnership limited liability on p. 962.

B. Limited Partnership

L0.2   Explain the extent of a founding general partner's liability for the debts of the firm, and how unlimited liability can be avoided by utilization of a corporate general partner

> See the discussion of general partners' avoidance of personal liability through incorporation, p. 962.

L0.3   Explain the nature and extent of a limited partner's liability for the debts of the firm

> See the *Gilroy* case in which limited partners (investors) lost their limitation of liability by participating in the control of the business, p. 964.

C. Limited Liability Companies

L0.4   Explain the advantages of a limited liability company

> See the discussion of the advantages of an LLC, including the tax advantages of treatment as a partnership with the limited liability feature of a corporation, beginning on p. 965.

L0.5   Understand that unless modified in an operating agreement, managers of LLCs owe member-investors the traditional duties of loyalty and care

> See the *Gatz* case, where the manager's conduct breached his fiduciary duties to minority members, on p. 967.

D. Limited Liability Partnerships

L0.6   Explain how a limited liability partnership "shields" innocent partners from liability to third parties

> See the example involving Dr. Jones's removal of the wrong kidney, with innocent partners Smith's and Grey's personal assets being shielded from liability from a large judgment beyond partnership and Dr. Jones' assets, p. 973.

KEY TERMS

general partners   limited partners   limited partnership

QUESTIONS AND CASE PROBLEMS

1. What is the principal advantage of an LLP over an LLC?

2. Alan Waung, a Hong Kong businessperson, purchased a golf course in Saginaw, Michigan, as an investment. As an avid golfer, Alan anticipates spending several weeks during the year at his "Northern Pines" course. He has been informed that a Subchapter S corporation would allow him and his family-member shareholders to be treated as partners for U.S. tax purposes while retaining the limited liability of the corporate form. Advise Mr. Waung on this matter. What form of business organization would you recommend?

3. Kate Haley, an experienced builder, formed a limited partnership in August 2011, along with two limited partners, Drs. Growbioski and Gailen, who each provided $100,000 to the partnership for initial capital for the construction of a medical office building near Stowe, Vermont. With the bustle of getting building and environmental permits and placating abutters to the property, as well as lining up suppliers and subcontractors and getting the job started, Kate simply did not find an opportunity to take the long drive to file the certificate of limited partnership with the secretary of state's office in Montpelier. A confluence of bad weather, an accident causing serious personal injury, financing disappointments, labor difficulties, design problems, and some personal problems resulted in the project being stopped before completion with some $550,000 in overdue bills. Dr. Growbioski has been approached by several suppliers and craftsmen seeking payment for supplies and work performed. As a limited partner, he believes that he is not liable for firm debts beyond his investment, which was $100,000. Explain to Dr. Growbioski his obligations at this point.

4. Alice Meyers, Monroe Moylan, and Bart Means practice medicine as Bay Area Anesthetics Associates (BAAA), a limited liability partnership. A newly certified nurse anesthesiologist, Mary Noyes, working with Dr. Means and not realizing a patient's allergy condition set forth on her chart, inadvertently administered the wrong anesthesia, which resulted in the patient's death. In a malpractice suit against Bay Area Anesthetics Associates, LLP, is the partnership liable for Mary Noyes's actions if she was employed by the hospital? What if she was employed by the partnership? Explain in detail.

5. Sabastian Hafner joined a start-up business with a business plan focused on making breads without common food allergens, such as wheat, yeast, dairy, and gluten, to be marketed in a major metropolitan area. The five founders of the business, including Sabastian, selected the limited liability company (LLC) as their form of business organization. The Articles of Organization for the limited liability company were duly filed with the secretary of state. The Operating Agreement simply provided that founding member Jillian Lopez would be the sole manager of the firm, and it set a salary for her at $40,000 per year. She hired employees to perform production, delivery, and sales work. Sebastian and the other three members spent time nights and early mornings "pitching in" at the bakery. After two months of diligent work, Sabastian, a second-year MBA student, sought back pay for the 40 hours each week he spent at the bakery during the previous eight weeks. He pointed out to the other members of the LLC that state law authorizes employees to sue for their wages. What are Sabastian's rights regarding pay for the service he performed for the LLC?

6. Hurwitz and Padden practiced law as equal partners for a short period of time before converting to an LLC. Some three years later, Padden informed Hurwitz that he intended to leave the firm. When they could not agree on how to divide $200,000 in fees relating to work acquired before the dissolution of the LLC,

Hurwitz filed suit seeking an equal division of the fees under partnership principles. Padden contended that partnership principles should not apply to the dissolution of an LLC even though the state's LLC law incorporated the definition and use of the term *dissolution* from the UPA. Decide. [*Hurwitz v. Padden*, 581 N.W.2d 359 (Minn. App.)]

7. Don Mason and Beth Daley were managers and members of Pacific Beach Developers, LLC (PBD), a start-up real estate development company focusing on rehabilitating older properties for increased rental values and possible resale. Daley made a contract with San Diego Architects Associates (SDAA) to provide plans for the rehabilitation of a 60-unit building on Ingraham Street for $97,000, signing the contract "Beth Daley, manager P.B.D. LLC." Financing for the Ingraham Street property fell through, and PBD's option on the property expired. Although Daley notified SDAA that the "Ingraham Street deal was off," SDAA had nearly completed its work, and SDAA brought suit for the contract price against both the LLC and Beth Daley. At the point the lawsuit was initiated, PBD had no working capital remaining, and Don and Beth had "moved on," having taken jobs as mutual fund salespersons. Advise Beth of her legal obligations to SDAA.

8. John and Amelia have general commitments from a number of individuals to invest in their Sproondrift Cove Club golf course and distinctive residential community in Duval County. John wants to form a limited partnership. He realizes that every limited partnership must have a general partner who manages the business and is subject to unlimited liability for all debts and liabilities of the limited partnership. But he says that is no problem because the general partner can be a corporation and can limit its liability exposure by simply creating a "shell" corporation. John stated to Amelia, "As officers of the corporate general partner, you and I can operate the business without the limited partners interfering … we run the show!" Amelia responded, "John, what you propose seems so very complicated, risky, and expensive. A number of our investors are

relatives who may want to be listened to, and some of our investors are professionals who could give us some valuable advice. Maybe a limited liability company would be a better entity for us." Compare the advantages and disadvantages of an LLC with a limited partnership and recommend the most appropriate form of business organization for this venture.

9. Hacienda Farms, Ltd., was organized as a limited partnership with Ricardo de Escamilla as the general partner and James L. Russell and H. W. Andrews as limited partners. The partnership raised vegetables and truck crops that were marketed principally through a produce concern controlled by Andrews. All three individuals decided which crops were to be planted. The general partner had no power to withdraw money from the partnership's two bank accounts without the signature of one of the limited partners. After operating for some seven and one-half months under these procedures, the limited partners demanded that the general partner resign as farm manager, which he did. Six weeks later, the partnership went into bankruptcy. Laurance Holzman, as trustee in bankruptcy, brought an action against Russell and Andrews, claiming that they had become liable to the creditors of the partnership as general partners because they had taken part in the control of the partnership business. How would you decide the case under the ULPA? Would the outcome be different under the RULPA? [*Holzman v. de Escamilla*, 195 P.2d 833 (Cal. App.)]

10. Jerome Micco was a major shareholder and corporate officer of Micco and Co., Inc., which was a limited partner in Harbor Creek, Ltd., a limited partnership formed to build a condominium complex. Hommel, an electrical contractor, was the successful bidder on certain electrical work for the project. For several months, Hommel worked under the direction of the construction supervisor and was paid by the limited partnership for his work. Because of financial difficulties, the supervisor was released. Thereafter, Jerome Micco played a major role in the building of the project, directing what work was to be performed. Hommel submitted payment invoices directly to Micco. When Hommel was

not paid, he sued Micco, contending that Micco was a limited partner who ran the operation personally and was personally responsible for the debt. Micco argued that he was an employee or agent of a corporation (Micco and Co., Inc.) and thus could not be held liable for the debt. The evidence reveals that Micco had no occasion to tell Hommel that he was acting as a corporate officer. Is it ethical for a corporate officer and shareholder to seek to avoid individual liability in this case? How would you decide the case? [*Hommel v. Micco*, 602 N.E.2d 1259 (Ohio App.)]

11. Ralph and Maureen K. Hagan (collectively "Hagan") owned the Stuart Court Apartments in Richmond, Virginia. On April 30, 1994, Hagan executed an agreement with Adams Property Associates, Inc. (Adams), giving Adams the exclusive right to sell the property for $1,600,000. The agreement provided that if the property was "sold or exchanged" within one year, with or without Adams's assistance, Hagan would pay Adams a fee of 6 percent of the "gross sales amount." Seven days before the year expired, Hagan, Roy T. Tepper, and Lynn Parsons formed a limited liability company, Hagan, Parsons, & Tepper, LLC (HPT). By deed dated April 23, 1995, Hagan transferred the property to HPT. Adams contends it is entitled to a commission from Hagan pursuant to the April 1994 agreement. Hagan contends the transaction was just a contribution of capital to a new company, not a sale. Decide. [*Hagan v. Adams Property Associates, Inc.*, 482 S.E.2d 805 (Va. 1997)]

12. Peter Kertesz formed an LLC and operated it in South Florida under the business name "Mourning Flowers." The LLC specialized in the sale of flowers to funeral homes. Although

Kertesz was initially the only member and manager, he ultimately granted ownership interests totaling 55 percent of the LLC to six individuals. In mid-2007, the members had a falling out that culminated in the majority removing Kertesz as managing member. Kertesz alleged that shortly after this, the LLC's distributors and clients "threatened to terminate their relationship with the LLC if Kertesz was not brought back into the operations of the LLC." These actions, Kertesz claimed, caused the LLC to suffer irreparable harm. Kertesz sought the judicial dissolution of the LLC on the basis of these circumstances and an alleged deadlock in management of the LLC, and sought the appointment of a receiver to protect the assets and goodwill of the LLC. What relief, if any, is Kertesz entitled to? [*Kertesz v. The Spa Floral, LLC*, 994 So.2d 473 (Fla. App.)]

13. Thomas Banner assigned his voting rights and his right to receive distributions in the Hut at Avon, LLC, to Elizabeth Condo as part of a divorce settlement. When the other members of the Hut Group, Thomas Connors and George Roberts, learned of the unapproved assignment, they contacted Banner and expressed the view that the assignment violated the antiassignment clause of the operating agreement, which required the primary consent of all the members. After some negotiations, Banner agreed to sell his entire rights to Connors and Roberts for $125,000. Condo sued these members in court for the destruction of the value of the assignment. The LLC defended that the assignment was in violation of the operating agreement and thus was void. Decide. [*Condo v. Connors*, 266 P.3d 1110 (Colo. 2011)]

CPA QUESTIONS

1. Which of the following statements is correct with respect to a limited partnership?

   a. A limited partner may *not* be an unsecured creditor of the limited partnership.

   b. A general partner may *not* also be a limited partner at the same time.

   c. A general partner may be a secured creditor of the limited partnership.

   d. A limited partnership can be formed with limited liability for all partners.

CHAPTER 44

Corporation Formation

© Manuel Gutjahr/iStockphoto.com

learningoutcomes

After studying this chapter, you should be able to

LO.1 Recognize that a corporation is a separate legal entity, distinct and apart from its stockholders

LO.2 Explain the wide range of power given to corporations under modern corporate codes

LO.3 Understand that the promoter is personally liable for preincorporation contracts

LO.4 Understand that after a corporate charter has been dissolved the owners and officers may be personally responsible for contracts made in the corporate name if they knew or should have known of the dissolution

LO.5 Explain a stockholder's option when he or she objects to a proposed consolidation or merger of the corporation

LO.6 Recognize that liabilities of predecessor corporations can be imposed on successor corporations when the transaction is a de facto merger or a continuation of the predecessor

The corporation is one of the most important forms of business organization.

A. NATURE AND CLASSES

A *corporation* is an artificial person that is created by government action.

1. The Corporation as a Person

A **corporation** is an artificial person created by government action and granted certain powers. It exists in the eyes of the law as a person, separate and distinct from the persons who own the corporation.

The concept that the corporation is a distinct legal person means that the corporation's property is owned not by the persons who own shares in the corporation but by the corporation. Debts of the corporation are debts of this artificial person, not of the persons running the corporation or owning shares of stock in it.[1] The corporation can sue and be sued in its own name, but shareholders cannot be sued or held liable for corporate actions or obligations.[2]

CASE SUMMARY

Collins Claims Cardinal Rule

FACTS: Lisa Hayes sued Jennifer Collins seeking the repayment of a loan issued by her deceased husband to Collins's corporation. After her husband's death, Hayes learned that her husband had been having an affair with Collins and filed suit against Collins individually for the failure to repay the loan to the corporation. Collins filed an answer denying individual liability for the corporate debt.

DECISION: Judgment for Collins. The cardinal rule of corporate law is that a corporation possesses a legal existence separate and apart from its officers and shareholders; therefore, the mere operation of corporate business does not render one personally liable for corporate acts, including a corporate loan. [*Hayes v. Collins*, 538 S.E.2d 785 (Ga. App. 2000)]

A corporation is formed by obtaining approval of a **certificate of incorporation**, **articles of incorporation**, or a **charter** from the state or national government.[3]

---

[1] *American Truck Lines, Inc. v. Albino*, 424 S.E.2d 367 (Ga. App. 1992).

[2] Also, a corporation does not have standing to pursue a claim on behalf of its sole shareholders. See *Accurate Printers, Inc. v. Stark*, 671 S.E.2d 228 (Ga. App. 2008).

[3] *Charter*, *certificate of incorporation*, and *articles of incorporation* are all terms used to refer to the documents that serve as evidence of a government's grant of corporate existence and powers. Most state incorporation statutes now provide for a certificate of incorporation issued by the secretary of state, but a Revised Model Business Corporation Act (RMBCA) has done away with the certificate of incorporation. Under the RMBCA, corporate existence begins when articles of incorporation are filed with the secretary of state. An endorsed copy of the articles together with a fee, receipt, or acknowledgment replaces the certificate of incorporation. See RMBCA §§1.25 and 2.03 and footnote 8 in this chapter.

2. Classifications of Corporations

Corporations may be classified in terms of their relationship to the public, the source of their authority, and the nature of their activities.

(A) PUBLIC, PRIVATE, AND QUASI-PUBLIC CORPORATIONS. A **public corporation** is one established for governmental purposes and for the administration of public affairs. A city is a public or municipal corporation acting under authority granted to it by the state.

A **private corporation** is one organized for charitable and benevolent purposes or for purposes of finance, industry, and commerce. Private corporations are often called *public* in business circles when their stock is sold to the public.

A **quasi-public corporation**, sometimes known as a public service corporation or a public utility, is a private corporation furnishing services on which the public is particularly dependent. An example of a quasi-public corporation is a gas and electric company.

(B) PUBLIC AUTHORITIES. The public increasingly demands that government perform services. Some of these are performed directly by government. Others are performed by separate corporations or **authorities** created by government. **For Example,** a city parking facility may be organized as a separate municipal parking authority, or a public housing project may be operated as an independent housing authority.

(C) DOMESTIC AND FOREIGN CORPORATIONS. A corporation is called a **domestic corporation** with respect to the state under whose law it has been incorporated. Any other corporation going into that state is called a **foreign corporation**. Thus, a corporation holding a Texas charter is a domestic corporation in Texas but a foreign corporation in all other states.[4]

(D) SPECIAL SERVICE CORPORATIONS. Corporations formed for transportation, banking, insurance, and savings and loan operations and similar specialized functions are subject to separate codes or statutes with regard to their organization. In addition, federal and state laws and administrative agencies regulate in detail the way these businesses are conducted.

(E) CLOSE CORPORATIONS. A corporation whose shares are held by a single shareholder or a small group of shareholders is known as a **close corporation**. Its shares are not traded publicly. Many such corporations are small firms that are incorporated to obtain either the advantage of limited liability or a tax benefit, or both.

Many states have statutes that have liberalized corporation law as it applies to close corporations. **For Example,** Nancy Davis Judson and Hall Davis IV are siblings who inherited their parents' stock in a domestic close corporation, Hall's Mortuary, Inc., a prominent and successful funeral home in Port Allen, Louisiana. Nancy was the secretary-treasurer, a director, and shareholder of 50 percent of the corporation's stock. Hall was president, a director, and the shareholder of the other 50 percent of the corporation's stock. The siblings had a falling out. Nancy filed a

---

*Sidebar definitions:*

public corporation – corporation that has been established for governmental purposes and for the administration of public affairs.

private corporation – corporation organized for charitable and benevolent purposes or for purposes of finance, industry, and commerce.

quasi-public corporation – private corporation furnishing services on which the public is particularly dependent, for example, a gas and electric company.

authorities – corporations formed by government that perform public service.

domestic corporation – corporation that has been incorporated by the state in question as opposed to incorporation by another state.

foreign corporation – corporation incorporated under the laws of another state.

close corporation – corporation whose shares are held by a single shareholder or a small group of shareholders.

---

[4] Failure of a foreign corporation to obtain a certificate of authority to do intrastate business in the state, under that state's door-closing statute, may mean that the foreign corporation cannot enforce a contract entered into in the state. **For Example,** TradeWinds Environmental Restoration, Inc., a New York–based company, entered into a contract with Alabama contractor BBC to do structural-drying services at a number of coastal condominiums after Hurricane Ivan in 2004. TradeWinds performed the work under the contract valued at $400,000. When TradeWinds sued for the money owed under the contract, the court determined that the "labor" performed is not an article of commerce, nor is the agreement to supply it an act of commerce. And the court determined that TradeWinds' business was intrastate, rather than interstate, and without a certificate of authority to perform the work, TradeWinds could not enforce the contract. *TradeWinds Environmental Restoration, Inc. v. Brown Brothers Construction, LLC,* 999 So.2d 875 (Ala. 2008).

court action to compel Hall to comply with the bylaws regarding her participation in the management of the business and to allow her access to all corporate records. Hall responded with accusations of his own. Thereafter, Hall alleged that he and Nancy were deadlocked in the management of corporate affairs and petitioned the court for involuntary dissolution and the appointment of a liquidator. Nancy objected and wanted a jury trial on a number of issues. The court applied a statute, nearly identical to a Delaware statute, "designed to obviate a deadlocked vote of two equal shareholders" of a close corporation and ordered the dissolution of the corporation.[5]

CPA

(F) Subchapter S Corporations. Subchapter S is a subdivision of the Internal Revenue Code. If corporate shareholders meet the requirements of this subdivision, they may elect Subchapter S status, which allows the shareholders to be treated as partners for tax purposes and retain the benefit of limited liability under the corporate form. A Subchapter S corporation is limited to 75 shareholders.

Under the Small Business Job Protection Act of 1996, employee stock ownership plans (ESOPs) and tax-exempt entities may be shareholders subject to certain special taxation rules.[6] Other reforms in this act make it easier for small businesses to comply with S corporation rules.

(G) Professional Corporations. A corporation may be organized for the purpose of conducting a profession. Each officer, director, and shareholder of a professional corporation must be licensed to practice the profession. Professional incorporation does not shield a practitioner from personal liability relating to the professional services rendered.

eleemosynary corporation – corporation organized for a charitable or benevolent purpose.

(H) Nonprofit Corporations. A *nonprofit corporation* (or an **eleemosynary corporation**), is one that is organized for charitable or benevolent purposes. Nonprofit corporations include hospitals, nursing homes, and universities.[7] Special procedures for incorporation are prescribed, and provision is made for a detailed examination of and hearing regarding the purpose, function, and methods of raising money for the enterprise.

3. Corporations and Governments

Problems arise about the power of governments to create and regulate corporations.

(A) Power to Create. Because by definition a corporation is created by government, the right to be a corporation must be obtained from the proper governmental agency. The federal government may create corporations whenever appropriate to carry out the powers granted to it.

police power – power to govern; the power to adopt laws for the protection of the public health, welfare, safety, and morals.

general corporation code – state's code listing certain requirements for creation of a corporation.

Generally, a state by virtue of its **police power** may create any kind of corporation for any purpose. Most states have a **general corporation code**, which lists certain requirements, and anyone who satisfies the requirements and files the necessary papers with the government may automatically become a corporation. In 1950, the American Bar Association (ABA) published a Model Business Corporation Act (MBCA) to assist legislative bodies in the modernization of state corporation laws. An updated version was published in 1969. Statutory language similar to that

---

[5] *Judson v. Davis*, 916 So.2d 1106 (La. App. 2005).
[6] Pub. L. No. 104-188 (August 20, 1996).
[7] The Committee on Corporate Laws of the American Bar Association has prepared a Model Nonprofit Corporation Act. A revised Model Nonprofit Corporation Act was approved in 1986.

contained in the 1969 version of the MBCA has been adopted in whole or in part by 35 states. A complete revision of the model act was approved in 1984 (RMBCA).[8] Updates to the model act have been approved subsequent to the scandals involving public corporations in recent years.[9] Jurisdictions following the model act have made numerous modifications to reflect their differing views about balancing the interests of public corporations, shareholders, and management. Caution must therefore be exercised in making generalizations about model act jurisdictions. There is no *uniform* corporation act.

(B) POWER TO REGULATE. Subject to constitutional limitations, corporations may be regulated by statutes.

(1) Protection of the Corporation as a Person.
The Constitution of the United States prohibits the national government and state governments from depriving any person of life, liberty, or property without due process of law. Many state constitutions contain a similar limitation on their respective state governments. A corporation is regarded as a "person" within the meaning of such provisions.

The federal Constitution prohibits a state from denying to any person within its jurisdiction the equal protection of the laws. No such express limitation is placed on the federal government, although the due process clause binding the federal government is liberally interpreted so that it prohibits substantial inequality of treatment.

(2) Protection of the Corporation as a Citizen.
For certain purposes, such as determining the right to bring a lawsuit in a federal court, a corporation is a citizen of any state in which it has been incorporated and of the state where it has its principal place of business.

B. CORPORATE POWERS

Except for limitations in the federal Constitution or the state's own constitution, a state legislature may give corporations any lawful powers. The RMBCA contains a general provision on corporate powers granting a corporation "the same powers as an individual to do all things necessary or convenient to carry out its business and affairs."[10]

4. Particular Powers
Modern corporation codes give corporations a wide range of powers.

(A) PERPETUAL LIFE. One of the distinctive features of a corporation is its perpetual or continuous life—the power to continue as an entity forever or for a stated period of time regardless of changes in stock ownership or the death of any shareholders.

---

[8] The Revised Model Business Corporation Act (1984) was approved by the Committee on Corporate Laws Section of Business Law of the American Bar Association. The committee approved revisions to sections 6.40 and 8.33 on March 27, 1987, and to section 7.08 on June 16, 1996; changes to Subchapters B and D of Chapter 1 of the model act, which accommodate the use of electronic means for transmitting and filing required corporate documents with the secretary of state, were approved on September 20, 1997. Model act citations are to the 1984 Revised Model Business Corporation Act (RMBCA) unless designated otherwise.

[9] Revisions included in the 2005 edition of the act apply to directors' conflicting interest transactions, provisions relating to directors' involvement with corporate opportunities, and updates on the role and responsibilities of corporate directors and officers.

[10] RMBCA §3.02. State statutes generally contain similar broad catchall grants of powers.

(B) Corporate Name. A corporation must have a name to identify it. As a general rule, it may select any name for this purpose. Most states require that the corporate name contain some word indicating the corporate character[11] and that the name not be the same as, or deceptively similar to, the name of any other corporation. Some statutes prohibit the use of a name that is likely to mislead the public.

(C) Corporate Seal. A corporation may have a distinctive seal. However, a corporation need not use a seal in the transaction of business unless this is required by statute or a natural person in transacting that business would be required to use a seal.

bylaws—rules and regulations enacted by a corporation to govern the affairs of the corporation and its shareholders, directors, and officers.

(D) Bylaws. Bylaws are the rules and regulations enacted by a corporation to govern the affairs of the corporation and its shareholders, directors, and officers.

Bylaws are adopted by shareholders, although in some states they may be adopted by the directors of the corporation. Approval by the state or an amendment of the corporate charter is not required to make the bylaws effective.

The bylaws are subordinate to the general law of the state, the statute under which the corporation is formed, and the charter of the corporation.[12] Bylaws that conflict with such superior authority or that are in themselves unreasonable are invalid. Bylaws that are valid are binding on all shareholders regardless of whether they know of the existence of those bylaws or were among the majority that consented to their adoption. Bylaws are not binding on third persons, however, unless they have notice or knowledge of them.

(E) Stock. A corporation may issue certificates representing corporate stock. Under the RMBCA, authorized, but unissued, shares may be issued at the price set by the board of directors. Under UCC Article 8 (1978 and 1994 versions), securities may be "uncertificated," or not represented by an instrument.

(F) Making Contracts. Corporation codes give corporations the power to make contracts.

(G) Borrowing Money. Corporations have the implied power to borrow money in carrying out their authorized business purposes.

(H) Executing Negotiable Instruments. Corporations have the power to issue or indorse negotiable instruments and to accept drafts.

(I) Issuing Bonds. A corporation may exercise its power to borrow money by issuing bonds.

(J) Transferring Property. The corporate property may be leased, assigned for the benefit of creditors, or sold. In many states, however, a solvent corporation may not transfer all of its property without the consent of all or a substantial majority of its shareholders.

A corporation, having power to incur debts, may mortgage or pledge its property as security for those debts. This rule does not apply to public service companies, such as street transit systems and gas and electric companies.

(K) Acquiring Property. A corporation has the power to acquire and hold such property as is reasonably necessary for carrying out its express powers.

---

[11] RMBCA §4.01(a) declares that the corporate name must contain the word *corporation, company, incorporated,* or *limited* or an abbreviation of one of these words.
[12] *Roach v. Bynum,* 403 So.2d 187 (Ala. 1981).

treasury stock – corporate stock that the corporation has reacquired.

(L) BUYING BACK STOCK. Generally, a corporation may purchase its own stock if it is solvent at the time and the purchase does not impair capital. Stock that is reacquired by the corporation that issued it is commonly called **treasury stock**.

Although treasury stock retains the character of outstanding stock, it has an inactive status while it is held by the corporation.[13] Thus, the treasury shares cannot be voted, nor can dividends be declared on them.

(M) DOING BUSINESS IN ANOTHER STATE. A corporation has the power to engage in business in other states. However, this does not exempt the corporation from satisfying valid restrictions imposed by the foreign state in which it seeks to do business.

(N) PARTICIPATING IN AN ENTERPRISE. Corporations may generally participate in an enterprise to the same extent as individuals. Not only may they enter into joint ventures, but also the modern statutory trend is to permit a corporation to be a member of a partnership, and a corporation may be a limited partner. The RMBCA authorizes a corporation "to be a promoter, partner, member, associate, or manager of any partnership, joint venture, trust, or other entity."[14]

(O) PAYING EMPLOYEE BENEFITS. The RMBCA empowers a corporation "to pay pensions and establish pension plans, pension trusts, profit-sharing plans, share bonus plans, share option plans, and benefit or incentive plans for any or all of its current or former directors, officers, employees, and agents."[15]

(P) CHARITABLE CONTRIBUTIONS. The RMBCA authorizes a corporation, without any limitation, "to make donations for the public welfare or for charitable, scientific, or educational purposes."[16] In some states, a limitation is imposed on the amount that can be donated for charitable purposes.

5. *Ultra Vires* Acts

ultra vires – act or contract that the corporation does not have authority to do or make.

When a corporation acts in excess of or beyond the scope of its powers, the corporation's act is described as ***ultra vires***. Such an action is improper in the same way that it is improper for an agent to act beyond the scope of the authority given by the principal. It is also improper with respect to shareholders and creditors of the corporation because corporate funds have been diverted to unauthorized uses.

The modern corporation statute will state that every corporation formed under it will have certain powers unless the articles of incorporation expressly exclude some of the listed powers, and then the statute will list every possible power that is needed to run a business. In some states, the legislature makes a blanket grant of all power that a natural person running the business would possess.[17] The net result is that the modern corporation possesses such a broad scope of powers that it is difficult to find an action that is *ultra vires*. If a mining corporation should begin to manufacture television sets, that might be an *ultra vires* transaction, but such an extreme departure rarely happens.

---

[13] When a corporation reacquires its own shares, it has the choice of retiring them and thus restoring them to the status of authorized, but unissued, shares or of treating them as still issued and available for transfer. The latter are described as treasury shares.

[14] RMBCA §3.02(9).

[15] RMBCA §3.02(12).

[16] RMBCA §3.02(13).

[17] Note the broad powers granted under RMBCA §3.02; see also Cal Corp Code §§202(b), 207, 208 for an all-purpose clause granting all of the powers of a natural person in carrying out business activities. See *MIC v. Battle Mountain Corp.*, 70 P.3d 1176 (Colo. 2003), where Colorado's *ultra vires* statute prohibits claims that a corporation is acting beyond the scope of its powers.

Because nonprofit corporations have a more restricted range of powers than business corporations, actions not authorized by the charters of nonprofit corporations are more likely to be found *ultra vires.*[18]

C. Creation and Termination of the Corporation

All states have general laws governing the creation of corporations.

CPA

6. Promoters

promoters – persons who plan the formation of the corporation and sell or promote the idea to others.

Corporations come into existence as the result of the activities of one or more persons known as **promoters** who bring together persons interested in the enterprise, aid in obtaining subscriptions to stock, and set in motion the machinery that leads to the formation of the corporation itself.

A corporation is not liable on a contract made by its promoter for its benefit unless the corporation takes some affirmative action to adopt such a contract. This action may be express words of adoption, or it may be acceptance of the contract's benefits. A corporation may also become bound by such contracts through assignment or novation.

The promoter is personally liable for all contracts made on behalf of the corporation before its existence unless the promoter is exempted by the terms of the agreement or by the circumstances surrounding it.[19]

CASE SUMMARY

The Promoter Is Personally Liable

FACTS: Clinton Investors Company, as landlord, entered into a three-year lease with the Clifton Park Learning Center as tenant. The lease was executed by Bernie Watkins, who represented himself to be the treasurer of the Learning Center. On May 31, 1984, the day before the lease term began, Watkins signed a rider to the lease. He again signed as treasurer of the tenant but identified the tenant as "the Clifton Park Learning Center, Inc." Watkins had not consulted an attorney regarding the formation of the corporation. He mistook the reservation of the business name with the secretary of state for the filing of a certificate of incorporation. On February 11, 1985, a certificate of incorporation was filed. By March 1986, the Learning Center had become delinquent in rental payments and other fees in the amount of $18,103. Clinton sued Watkins and the Learning Center for the amounts due. Watkins claimed that only the corporation was liable.

DECISION: Judgment against Watkins. Because no corporation existed when Watkins signed the lease with Clinton, his legal status was that of a promoter. The subsequent formation of a corporation and adoption of the lease did not relieve Watkins from liability in addition to his individual liability as a promoter. [*Clinton Investors Co. v. Watkins*, **536 N.Y.S.2d 270 (A.D. 1989)**]

---

[18] *Lovering v. Seabrook Island Property Owners Ass'n,* 344 S.E.2d 862 (S.C. App. 1986). But see *St. Louis v. Institute of Med. Ed. & Res.,* 786 S.W.2d 885 (Mo. App. 1990).
[19] See *GS Petroleum, Inc. v. R and S Fuel, Inc.,* 2009 WL 1554680 (Del. Super. June 4, 2009), where the court found that the promoters were not liable on the preincorporation contract for the sale of a Shell gas station. The court reasoned that the terms of the contract did not intend promoter liability, and the business was incorporated by the buyer before taking possession of the business.

A promoter is liable for all torts committed in connection with the promoter's activities. The corporation is not ordinarily liable for the torts of the promoter, but it may become liable by its conduct after incorporation. If a promoter induces making a contract by fraud, the corporation is liable for the fraud if it assumes or ratifies the contract with knowledge or notice of such fraud.

A promoter stands in a fiduciary relation to the corporation and to stock subscribers and cannot make secret profits at their expense. Accordingly, if a promoter makes a secret profit on a sale of land to the corporation, the promoter must surrender the profit to the corporation.

The corporation is not liable in most states for the expenses and services of the promoter unless it subsequently promises to pay for them, or the corporation's charter or a statute imposes such liability on it.

7. Incorporation

incorporator – one or more natural persons or corporations who sign and file appropriate incorporation forms with a designated government official.

One or more natural persons or corporations may act as **incorporators** of a corporation by signing and filing appropriate forms with a designated government official.[20] These papers are filed in duplicate, and a filing fee must be paid. The designated official (usually the secretary of state), after being satisfied that the forms conform to statutory requirements, stamps "Filed" and the date on each copy. The official then retains one copy and returns the other copy, along with a filing fee receipt, to the corporation.[21]

Statutes may require incorporators to give some form of public notice, such as by advertising in a newspaper, of their intention to form a corporation, stating its name, address, and general purpose.

8. Application for Incorporation

In most states, the process of forming a corporation is begun by filing an application for a certificate of incorporation. This application contains or is accompanied by articles of incorporation. The instrument is filed with the secretary of state and sets forth certain information about the new corporation. The articles of incorporation must contain (1) the name of the corporation, (2) the number of shares of stock the corporation is authorized to issue, (3) the street address of the corporation's initial registered office and the name of its initial registered agent, and (4) the name and address of each incorporator.[22] The articles of incorporation may also state the purpose or purposes for which the corporation is organized. If there is no "purpose clause," the corporation automatically has the purpose of engaging in any lawful business.[23] Also, if no reference is made to the duration of the corporation in the articles of incorporation, it will automatically have perpetual duration.[24]

9. The Certificate of Incorporation

Most state incorporation statutes now provide for a certificate of incorporation to be issued by the secretary of state after articles of incorporation that conform to state requirements have been filed. The Revised Model Business Corporation Act (RMBCA)

---

[20] RMBCA §2.01.
[21] RMBCA §1.25.
[22] RMBCA §2.02.
[23] RMBCA §3.01.
[24] RMBCA §3.02.

has eliminated the certificate of incorporation in an effort to reduce the volume of paperwork handled by the secretary of state.

Under the RMBCA, corporate existence begins when the articles are filed with the secretary of state.[25] In some states, corporate existence begins when the proper government official issues a certificate of incorporation. In other states, it does not begin until an organizational meeting is held by the new corporation.

10. Proper and Defective Incorporation

If the procedure for incorporation has been followed, the corporation has a legal right to exist. It is then called a **corporation de jure**, meaning that it is a corporation by virtue of law.

Assume that there is some defect in the corporation that is formed. If the defect is not a material one, the law usually overlooks the defect and holds that the corporation is a corporation de jure.

The RMBCA abolishes objections to irregularities and defects in incorporating. It provides that the

> *secretary of state's filing of the articles of incorporation is conclusive proof that the incorporators satisfied all conditions precedent to incorporation. ...*[26]

Many state statutes follow this pattern. Such an approach is based on the practical consideration that when countless persons are purchasing shares of stock and entering into business transactions with thousands of corporations, it becomes an absurdity to expect that anyone is going to make the detailed search that would be required to determine whether a given corporation is a corporation de jure.[27]

(A) DE FACTO CORPORATION. The defect in the incorporation may be so substantial that it cannot be ignored, and the corporation will not be accepted as a corporation de jure, yet compliance may be sufficient for recognizing that there is a corporation. When this occurs, the association is called a **de facto** corporation.

Although conflict exists among authorities, the traditional elements of a de facto corporation are that (1) a valid law exists under which the corporation could have been properly incorporated, (2) an attempt to organize the corporation has been made in good faith, (3) a genuine attempt to organize in compliance with statutory requirements has been made, and (4) corporate powers have been used.

(B) CORPORATION BY ESTOPPEL. The defect in incorporation may be so great that by law the association cannot be accepted as a de facto corporation. In such a case then, there is no corporation. If the individuals involved proceed to run the business in spite of such irregularity, they may be held personally liable as partners for the business's debts.[28] This rule is sometimes not applied when a person has dealt with the business as though it were a corporation.[29] In such instances, the party is estopped from denying that the "corporation" had legal existence. In effect, there is **corporation by estoppel** with respect to that party.

corporation de jure – corporation with a legal right to exist by virtue of law.

de facto – existing in fact as distinguished from as of right, as in the case of an officer or a corporation purporting to act as such without being elected to the office or having been properly incorporated.

corporation by estoppel – corporation that comes about when parties estop themselves from denying that the corporation exists.

---

[25] RMBCA §2.03(a).
[26] RMBCA §2.03(b).
[27] This trend and the reasons for it may be compared to those involved in the concept of the negotiability of commercial paper. Note the similar protection from defenses given to the person purchasing shares of stock for value and without notice. U.C.C. §8–202.
[28] In a minority of states, a court will not hold individuals liable as partners but will hold liable the person who committed the act on behalf of the business on the theory that that person was an agent who acted without authority and is therefore liable for breach of the implied warranties of the existence of a principal possessing capacity and of proper authorization.
[29] *Am. South Bank v. Holland*, 669 So.2d 151 (Ala. Civ. App. 1994).

Several jurisdictions that follow the 1969 MBCA have expressly retained the doctrines of corporation by estoppel and de facto corporations.[30] Other courts interpreting the language of the 1969 MBCA, however, have held that the doctrines of de facto corporation and corporation by estoppel no longer exist.

The language of the 1984 version allows some jurisdictions sufficient room for the de facto and estoppel doctrines to operate through Section 2.04 of the MBCA. The *First Community Bank* case applied the corporation by estoppel doctrine in a 1984 MBCA jurisdiction.

CASE SUMMARY

Corporation by Estoppel Is Still Good Law under the 1984 MBCA

FACTS: The Community Youth Center (CYC) corporation failed to pay its annual registration fee in 2000 and was automatically dissolved by the State Corporation Commission. CYC continued to operate and held itself out as a corporation well into 2005 when it obtained a loan from the First Community Bank to finance a swimming pool at its facility. The loan was secured by the CYC property. After the corporation defaulted on its loan payments the bank foreclosed and subsequently purchased the property at a foreclosure sale. CYC contended that the president, vice president, and treasurer of CYC had no standing to make the 2005 loan transaction because CYC's corporate status had been terminated. The bank contended that under the doctrine of corporation by estoppel, CYC continued to exist in 2005, and consequently the officer-directors had authority to borrow money and grant a deed of trust, thereby giving the bank a valid lien on the property.

DECISION: Judgment for the bank. A corporation acting and carrying on its corporate business under its corporate name for more than five years after termination of its corporate existence should be deemed a corporation by estoppel. CYC may not have been a de jure corporation, but the court cannot reasonably ignore the actual existence of such a corporation. CYC obtained a loan from First Community Bank and made numerous payments toward that loan before ultimately defaulting on the loan. In order to relieve CYC of its loan obligations, the corporation must have ceased to exist in 2000 both in law and in fact. CYC ceased to exist only in law, not in fact. CYC's directors failed to wind up the corporate business as was their duty. The corporation cannot be relieved from liability for acts done in its name and during its actual existence as a corporation by estoppel. [*First Community Bank, N.A. v. Community Youth Center*, 2010 WL 8696179 (Va. Cir. Ct. Dec. 20, 2010)]

With respect to preincorporation debts, the 1984 act imposes liability only on persons who act as, or on behalf of, a corporation while knowing that no corporation exists.[31]

11. Insolvency, Bankruptcy, and Reorganization

When a corporation has financial troubles so serious that it is insolvent, the best thing may be to go through bankruptcy or reorganization proceedings. The law with respect to bankruptcy and reorganizations is discussed in Chapter 35.

12. Forfeiture of Charter

In states that have adopted the RMBCA, the secretary of state may commence proceedings to administratively dissolve a corporation if (1) the corporation does not

---

[30] See Ga. Bus. Corp Code §22–5103; Minn. Bus Corp Act §301:08. See also *H. Rich Corp. v. Feinberg*, 518 So.2d 377 (Fla. App. 1987).
[31] RMBCA §2.04.

pay franchise taxes within 60 days after they are due, (2) the corporation does not file its annual report within 60 days after it is due, or (3) the corporation is without a registered agent or registered office for 60 days or more.[32] After a corporate charter has been dissolved, the owners and officers of the dissolved corporation are not shielded from personal liability by using the corporate name when making contracts if they knew or should have known of the dissolution. **For Example,** on October 2, 2004, Dinky, Inc., was involuntarily dissolved for failure to file an annual report and pay an annual franchise tax. Elaine Kostopulos, the president and sole shareholder of Dinky, Inc., had incorporated her business in 1989 and regularly purchased products manufactured by Benetton USA, Inc., since that time. During the five years after Dinky was dissolved, she continued to operate as a corporation, ordering and making payments to Benetton through June 7, 2009. Between June and November 2009, Benetton sought payment of over $200,000 owed by Dinky. Ms. Kostopulos claims she was unaware of the dissolution until late 2009, when payment problems arose. Dinky applied for reinstatement at that time. With corporate status reinstated, Ms. Kostopulos contends that she is not personally liable for the debts incurred by the dissolved corporation during the time of its dissolution. The court determined that Ms. Kostopulos cannot escape personal liability by reinstating her corporation, holding that "she should have known" about the dissolution of Dinky, over such a long period of time.[33]

After a corporation is dissolved, a contract made by an officer of the dissolved corporation cannot be enforced against the other party to the contract. **For Example,** a lucrative contract with Florio Entertainment, Inc., was signed "Louis Lofredo, LL Associates as company president" using a letterhead "LL Associates, Inc." In fact, the corporation "LL Associates, Inc." had been dissolved years before the contract was negotiated and signed, and Lofredo had made no effort to reinstate the corporation. LL Associates, Inc., had no legal existence and thus could not be a party to the contract and could not enforce the contract.[34]

A corporation whose powers are suspended for nonpayment of taxes cannot sue or defend a lawsuit while its taxes remain unpaid.[35]

13. Judicial Dissolution

Judicial dissolution of a corporation may be decreed when its management is deadlocked and the deadlock cannot be broken by the shareholders.[36] In some states, a "custodian" may be appointed for a corporation when the shareholders are unable to break a deadlock in the board of directors and irreparable harm is threatened to, or sustained by, the corporation because of the deadlock.

D. Consolidations, Mergers, and Conglomerates

Two or more corporations may be combined to form a new structure or enterprise.

---

[32] RMBCA §14.20.

[33] *Benetton U.S.A. Corp. v. Dinky, Inc.*, 2011 WL 5024549 (N.D. Ill. Oct. 19, 2011). But see section 2.04 of the 1984 RMBCA, which provides that all persons purporting to act for or on behalf of a corporation "knowing that there was no incorporation" under the Act are jointly and severally liable for all liabilities while so acting. There would be no liability for an individual that did not and should not have known of the dissolution.

[34] *Animazing Entertainment, Inc. v. Louis Lofredo Associates, Inc.*, 88 F. Supp. 2d 265 (S.D.N.Y. 2000).

[35] *Kaufman, Inc. v. Performance Plastering, Inc.*, 39 Cal.Rptr. 3d 33 (Cal. App. 2006).

[36] After a shareholder has requested dissolution of a corporation, a state statute may offer an option to the corporation or other existing shareholders to purchase shares owned by the petitioning shareholder(s) for "fair value" in lieu of dissolution. See *Dawkins v. Hickman Family Corp.*, 2010 WL 4683472 (N.D. Miss. Nov. 10, 2010).

FIGURE 44-1 | *Consolidation*

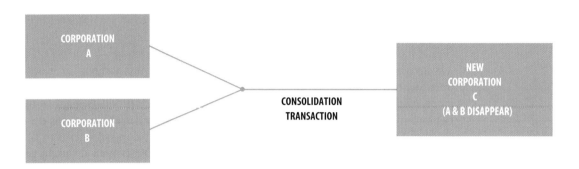

© Cengage Learning

CPA

14. Definitions

Enterprises may be combined by a consolidation or merger of corporations or by the formation of a conglomerate.

CPA

consolidation (of corporations) – combining of two or more corporations in which the corporate existence of each one ceases and a new corporation is created.

(A) CONSOLIDATION. In a **consolidation** of two or more corporations, their separate existences cease, and a new corporation with the property and assets of the old corporations comes into being (see Figure 44-1).

When a consolidation occurs, the new corporation ordinarily succeeds to the rights, powers, and immunities of its component parts. However, limitations may be imposed by constitution, statute, or certificate of incorporation.

CPA

merger (of corporations) – combining of corporations by which one absorbs the other and continues to exist, preserving its original charter and identity while the other corporation ceases to exist.

(B) MERGER. When two corporations **merge**, one absorbs the other. One corporation retains its original charter and identity and continues to exist; the other disappears, and its corporate existence terminates (see Figure 44-2).

A stockholder who objects to a proposed consolidation or merger or who fails to convert existing shares into stock of the new or continuing corporation may apply to a court to appraise the value of the stock that she holds.[37] Should either party act arbitrarily, vexatiously, or not in good faith in the appraisal process, the courts have the right to assess court costs and attorney fees. The new or continuing corporation is then required to pay the "fair value" of the stock to the stockholder.[38]

CASE SUMMARY

The Sound of Music: $63.44 per Share

FACTS: The Trapp Family Lodge, Inc. (TFL), was incorporated in 1962 as a holding company for certain assets of the Von Trapp family, including the Trapp Family Lodge, a resort hotel complex located in Stowe, Vermont, and other assets, including certain royalty rights related to the family's story as portrayed in a Broadway musical and a movie. A majority of TFL

---

[37] *Delaware Open MRI Radiology v. Kessler*, 898 A.2d 290 (Del. Ch. 2006).

[38] See *Spenlinhauer v. Spencer Press Inc.*, 959 N.E.2d 436 (Mass. App. 2011), where a minority shareholder dissented to a proposed merger, and after executing a cash-out merger, the court determined the "fair value" of the minority shares as the pro rata percentage of the net selling price.

CASE SUMMARY

Continued

shareholders approved a merger with a new corporation in 1994, and the merger took place on January 28, 1995. The dissenting shareholders, holding 76,529 of the corporation's 198,000 outstanding shares, were paid $33.84 per share as fair value by the TFL board of directors. The dissenting shareholders brought suit seeking a higher price as fair value. After the trial court set the fair value of $63.44, TFL appealed.

DECISION: Judgment for the dissenting shareholders. Dissenters' rights statutes were enacted in response to the common law rule that required unanimous consent from shareholders to make fundamental changes in a corporation. Under this rule minority shareholders could block corporate change by refusing to cooperate in hope of establishing a nuisance value for their shares. In response, legislatures enacted statutes authorizing corporate changes by majority vote. To protect the interests of minority shareholders, statutes generally permit a dissenting minority to demand that the corporation buy back shares at fair value. The basic concept of fair value is that the stockholder is entitled to be paid for his or her "proportionate interest in a going concern." The trial court properly rejected the fact-specific appraisal made on behalf of the majority shareholders because it lacked thoroughness and credibility, unjustifiably reducing the value of the lodge operations and overstating income taxes to reduce after-tax cash flows. The court accepted the appraisal made on behalf of the minority shareholders that utilized the average of a net asset value method of evaluation and a discounted cash flow method of evaluation, and yielded a value of $63.44 per share. [*In re 75,629 Shares of Common Stock of Trapp Family Lodge, Inc.,* **725 A.2d 927 (Vt. 1999)**]

conglomerate – relationship of a parent corporation to subsidiary corporations engaged in diversified fields of activity unrelated to the field of activity of the parent corporation.

(c) CONGLOMERATE. Conglomerate describes the relationship of a parent corporation to subsidiary corporations engaged in diversified fields of activity unrelated to the parent corporation's field of activity. **For Example,** a wire-manufacturing corporation that owns all stock of a newspaper corporation and of a drug-manufacturing corporation would be described as a conglomerate. In contrast, if the wire-manufacturing company owned a mill that produced the metal used in making the wire and a mine that produced the ore that was used by the mill, the relationship would probably be described as an *integrated industry* rather than as a conglomerate. This term is merely a matter of usage rather than of legal definition. Likewise, when

FIGURE 44-2	*Merger*

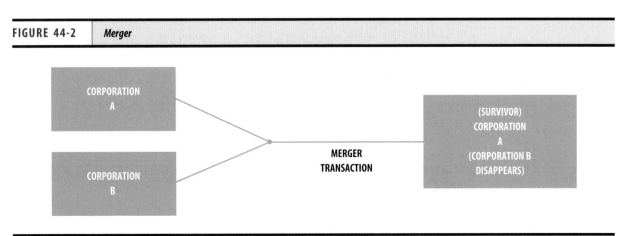

the parent company is not engaged in production or the rendering of services, it is customary to call it a *holding company*.

Without regard to whether the enterprise is a holding company or whether the group of corporations constitutes a conglomerate or an integrated industry, each part is a distinct corporation to which ordinary corporation law applies. In some instances, additional principles apply because of the nature of the relationships existing among the several corporations involved.

15. Legality

Consolidations, mergers, and asset acquisitions between enterprises are prohibited by federal antitrust legislation when the effect is to lessen competition in interstate commerce. A business corporation may not merge with a charitable corporation because this combination would divert the assets of the respective corporations to purposes not intended by their shareholders.

16. Liability of Successor Corporations

When corporations are combined in any way, the question of who is liable for the debts and obligations of the predecessor corporation arises.

(A) MERGERS AND CONSOLIDATIONS. Generally, the enterprise engaging in or continuing the business after a merger or consolidation succeeds to all of the rights and property of the predecessor, or disappearing, corporation.[39]

CASE SUMMARY

A Marshmallow of a Case for the Plaintiff Marsh USA

FACTS: The Orleans Parish School Board ("School Board") in New Orleans, Louisiana, hired Johnson & Higgins, Inc. (J&H), in 1996, creating an ongoing insurance consulting agreement between them. The terms of the agreement provided that the School Board would pay J&H, Inc. for its consulting services and would later be reimbursed by the insurance carrier eventually selected by the School Board. Pursuant to their agreement, over the next few years, J&H's Mrs. Ippolito prepared several Requests for Proposals ("RFP") on behalf of the School Board. The School Board paid its fees for this consulting work without complaint. During this time, Johnson & Higgins merged with Marsh McLennan, a company that thereafter merged into Marsh USA, Inc. In 2001, Mrs. Ippolito prepared, at the request of the School Board, two more requests for proposals. Per the terms of the RFPs, Marsh was to receive $70,000 as its consulting fee under NO. 7656 and a $5,000 consulting fee under NO. 7657. Mrs. Ippolito and her staff spent several months working on the project for the School Board. The School Board never paid Marsh for the services and Marsh USA, Inc., sued the School Board for breach of contract, seeking payment of $75,000. The School Board asserted that Marsh USA was not a proper party to the lawsuit and that no contract had existed with it. From a judgment for Marsh USA, Inc., the School Board appealed.

DECISION: Judgment for Marsh USA, Inc. When two corporations merge or consolidate, the new successor corporation acquires all of the assets and rights of the former corporation. The minutes of a School Board meeting reflect the School Board's awareness of the merger in this case as well as its continuing contract with the firm. [**Marsh Advantage America v. Orleans Parish School Board**, 995 So.2d 53 (La. App. 2008)]

---

[39] *Corporate Express Office Products, Inc. v. Phillips*, 847 So.2d 406 (Fla. 2003).

The enterprise continuing the business is also subject to all of the debts and liabilities of the predecessor corporation.[40]

Liabilities of predecessor corporations can be imposed on a successor corporation when the transaction is a de facto merger[41] or the successor is a mere continuation of the predecessor. **For Example,** Steven Stepp manufactured pleasure boats through Thoroughbred Power Boats, Inc., until August 1996 at which time Thoroughbred Power Boats, Inc., ceased manufacturing and selling boats. In August 1996, Velocity Power Boats, Inc., began manufacturing and selling pleasure boats at the same location. Stephen Stepp and his wife were the only officers and board members of both corporations. Finding that Velocity was merely a "new hat" for Thoroughbred Power Boats, Inc., with the same or similar management and ownership, Velocity Power Boats, Inc., was held liable as a successor corporation for damages for a May 6, 1995, boating accident caused by a defective Thoroughbred Power Boats, Inc., manufactured boat.[42]

(B) Asset Sales. In contrast with a merger or consolidation, a corporation may merely purchase the assets of another business. In that case, the purchaser does not become liable for the obligations of the predecessor business. **For Example,** Hull Corporation sold one of its operating divisions to SP Industries, Inc. (SPI) for $6 million under an asset purchase agreement (APA) that stated that the buyer SPI assumed no liability for preclosing claims against Hull. In fact as Hull and SPI were negotiating the APA, Hull was having difficulties regarding engineering and installation work the division had performed in China for Berg Chilling Systems, Inc. Berg Chilling sued SPI under the doctrine of successor liability for the payment of a $1,650,000 arbitration award because of the defective work done by Hull in China. The court held that SPI did not assume Hull's contractual liability to Berg under any exception to the traditional corporate rule of successor nonliability.[43]

Corporations may seek to avoid liability for the obligations of a predecessor corporation by attempting to disguise a consolidation or merger as being merely a sale of assets. Courts will not recognize such a transaction and will impose a successor's liability on the successor corporation.[44] In addition, even when the old corporate entity is not formally dissolved, a finding of a de facto merger resulting in successor liability may occur. **For Example,** "old" Duro Industries, Inc., owed its supplier, Milliken & Co., $8,754,680 for raw materials and Milliken obtained a judgment for this amount from a New York court. Investors and related entities executed a plan acquiring the assets of old Duro, while shedding old Duro's debts to Milliken and establishing "new" Duro Textiles, LLC. New Duro had the same CEO as old Duro, continued to sell the same product line, and employed all of old Duro's employees. The court found successor liability for the Milliken debt against new Duro.[45]

[40] *Beck v. Roper Whitney, Inc.,* 190 F. Supp. 2d 524 (W.D.N.Y. 2001).
[41] *Ulanet v. D'Artagnan, Inc.,* 170 F. Supp. 2d 356 (E.D.N.Y. 2001); see *Callahan & Sons, Inc. v. Dykeman Electric Co. Inc.,* 266 F. Supp. 2d 208 (D. Mass 2003).
[42] *Paten v. Thoroughbred Power Boats, Inc.,* 294 F.3d 640 (5th Cir. 2002).
[43] *Berg Chilling Systems Inc. v. Hull Corp.,* 435 F.3d 455 (3d Cir. 2006).
[44] *State v. Westwood Squibb Pharmaceutical Co., Inc.,* 981 F. Supp. 760 (W.D.N.Y. 1997).
[45] *Milliken & Co. v. Duro Textiles, LLC,* 887 N.E.2d 244 (Mass. 2008).

CASE SUMMARY

Corporate Shell Games Not Allowed

FACTS: Since 1976, McGhan/Cal. Inc., a manufacturer of prostheses used in breast augmentation surgery, and later McGhan/Del., received numerous complaints about its implants. It also received inquiries from the Food and Drug Administration. In April 1977, Mary Marks had surgery; two McGhan implants were used. Because of defects in the McGhan implants, Marks underwent three additional operations, eventually having the McGhan products replaced with implants manufactured by another company. In June 1977, McGhan/Cal. was acquired by a Delaware subsidiary of 3M, called McGhan/Del. Inc. McGhan/Del. removed the implants from the market in April 1979. On January 1, 1981, 3M's wholly owned subsidiary McGhan/Del. Inc. was reorganized as a division of 3M and dissolved. In January 1982, following her fourth surgery, Marks brought a product liability suit against 3M. 3M contended that it was not liable for the actions of the predecessor corporation.

DECISION: The transaction between the 3M subsidiary McGhan/Del. Inc. and McGhan/Cal. Inc. amounted to a de facto merger of the seller and the purchaser. McGhan/Cal. changed its name, distributed 3M stock to its shareholders, and dissolved, and all key employees signed employment contracts to work for the purchaser. No cash was paid for the business. The transaction was not an assets sale. The second reorganization amounted to a continuation of the de facto merger. Public policy requires that 3M, having accepted the benefits of a going concern, should also assume the costs that all other going concerns must bear. It should not be allowed to avoid liability to an injured person by merely shuffling paper and manipulating corporate entities. [***Marks v. Minnesota Mining and Manufacturing Co.,* 232 Cal. Rptr. 594 (Cal. App. 1986)**]

LawFlix

Barbarians at the Gate (1996) (R)

In this movie that focuses on the law and ethics of takeovers, you can see the manipulation that occurs and the impact greed has on the companies themselves.

MAKE THE CONNECTION

SUMMARY

A *corporation* is an artificial person created by government action. It exists as a separate and distinct entity possessing certain powers. In most states, the corporation comes into existence when the secretary of state issues a certificate of incorporation. The most

common forms of corporations are private business corporations whose stock is sold to the public (publicly held) and close corporations, which are business firms whose shares are not traded publicly. Corporations may be formed for purposes other than conducting a business. For example, there are nonprofit corporations, municipal corporations, and public authorities for governmental purposes.

An *ultra vires* act occurs when a corporation acts beyond the scope of the powers given it. Because states now grant broad powers to corporations, it is unlikely that a modern corporation would act beyond the scope of its powers.

A *promoter* is a person who brings together the persons interested in the enterprise and sets in motion all that must be done to form a corporation. A corporation is not liable on contracts made by its promoter for the corporation unless it adopts the contracts. The promoter is personally liable for contracts made for the corporation before its existence. A promoter stands in a fiduciary relation to the corporation and stockholders.

The procedures for incorporation are set forth in the statutes of each state. In most states, the corporation comes into existence on issuance of the certificate of incorporation. When all requirements have been satisfied, the corporation is a corporation de jure. When there has not been full compliance with all requirements for incorporation, a de facto corporation may be found to exist. Or when sufficient compliance

for a de facto corporation does not exist, in some jurisdictions a third person may be estopped from denying the legal existence of the "corporation" with which it did business (corporation by estoppel).

A corporation has the power to continue as an entity forever or for a stated period of time regardless of changes in the ownership of the stock or the death of a shareholder. It may make contracts, issue stocks and bonds, borrow money, execute commercial paper, transfer and acquire property, acquire its own stock if it is solvent and the purchase does not impair capital, and make charitable contributions. Subject to limitations, a corporation has the power to do business in other states. A corporation may also participate in a business enterprise to the same extent as an individual; that is, it may be a partner in a partnership, or it may enter a joint venture or other enterprise. Special service corporations, such as banks, insurance companies, and railroads, are subject to separate statutes governing their organization and powers.

Two or more corporations may be combined to form a new enterprise. This combination may be a consolidation, with a new corporation coming into existence, or a merger, in which one corporation absorbs the other.

LEARNING OUTCOMES

After studying this chapter, you should be able to clearly explain:

A. Nature and Classes

LO.1 Recognize that a corporation is a separate legal entity, distinct and apart from its stockholders
See the *Collins* case in which Ms. Collins was not liable for a loan to her corporation, p. 979.

B. Corporate Powers

LO.2 Explain the wide range of power given to corporations under modern corporate codes
See the RMBCA general provision granting corporations "the same powers as an individual to do all things necessary or convenient to carry out its business and affairs," p. 982.

C. Creation and Termination of the Corporation

LO.3 Understand that the promoter is personally liable for preincorporation contracts

See the *Clinton Investors Co.* case in which Watkins, a promoter, was held personally liable for a preincorporation lease, p. 985.

LO.4 Understand that after a corporate charter has been dissolved the owners and officers may be personally responsible for contracts made in the corporate name if they knew or should have known of the dissolution
See the example where Ms. Kostopulos was personally liable for debts incurred during the time of dissolution because she should have known about the dissolution, p. 989.

D. Consolidations, Mergers, and Conglomerates

LO.5 Explain a stockholder's option when he or she objects to a proposed consolidation or merger of the corporation

L0.6   Recognize that liabilities of predecessor corporations can be imposed on successor corporations when the transaction is a de facto merger or a continuation of the predecessor

See the example of Velocity Power Boats, Inc., which became essentially a "new hat" for Thoroughbred Power Boats, Inc., with liability as a corporate successor for a defective Thoroughbred boat, p. 993.

KEY TERMS

articles of incorporation
authorities
bylaws
certificate of
  incorporation
charter
close corporation
conglomerate
consolidation

corporation
corporation by estoppel
corporation de jure
de facto
domestic corporation
eleemosynary corporation
foreign corporation
general corporation code
incorporators

merge
police power
private corporation
promoters
public corporation
quasi-public corporation
treasury stock
ultra vires

QUESTIONS AND CASE PROBLEMS

1. Edwin Edwards and Karen Davis owned EEE, Inc., which owned three convenience stores, all of which sold gasoline. Reid Ellis delivered to the three convenience stores $26,675.02 worth of gasoline for which he was not paid. Ellis proved that Edwards and Davis owned the business, ran it, and in fact personally ordered the gasoline. He claimed that they were personally liable for the debt owed him by EEE, Inc. Decide. [*Ellis v. Edwards*, 348 S.E.2d 764 (Ga. App.)]

2. Graham and Black were each 50 percent shareholders of a building supply business. When Graham filed a petition to dissolve the corporation under RMBCA §14.30, the court appointed a custodian with full powers to run the corporation's day-to-day operations. Subsequently, the court concluded that Black and Graham functioned as directors, they were deadlocked within the meaning of RMBCA §14.30(2)(1), and adequate grounds existed to dissolve the corporation because of the lack of cooperation between Black and Graham and its probable irreparable harm to the business. The court entered an order directing that within one week of receiving an expected appraisal, each would submit a sealed bid in writing for the other's stock. The custodian was to accept the high bid, and the purchaser was to immediately tender the purchase price. In the event that neither stockholder made a bona fide offer, the custodian would be redesignated the receiver and proceed to dissolve the corporation (RMBCA §14.32 [c]-[e]). The sale was unsuccessful, and by subsequent order, the court converted the custodianship into a receivership, directing that the receiver wind up and liquidate the business affairs of the corporation. Black did not believe that the successful business should be liquidated, and he directed his attorney to appeal. Decide. [*Black v. Graham*, 464 S.E.2d 814 (Ga.)]

3. Compare and contrast consolidations, mergers, and conglomerates.

4. On January 27, 1982, Joe Walker purchased a wheel-loader machine from Thompson & Green Machinery Co. (T&G). Walker signed a promissory note for $37,886.30 on behalf of "Music City Sawmill, Inc., by Joe Walker, President." When Sawmill was unable to make payments on the loader, the machine was returned to T&G. T&G brought suit against Sawmill and subsequently discovered that Sawmill had not been incorporated on January 27, 1982, when the machine was purchased but had been incorporated the next day. T&G then sued Walker individually. The lawsuit was

Walker's first notice that Sawmill was not incorporated on the date of the sale. Walker's defense was that T&G dealt with Sawmill as a corporation and did not intend to bind him personally on the note and therefore was estopped to deny Sawmill's corporate existence. Decide based on the 1969 MBCA. What would be the result if the RMBCA applied? [*Thompson & Green Machinery Co. v. Music City Lumber Co., Inc., Music City Sawmill Co., Inc.,* 683 SW.2d 340 (Tenn. App.)]

5. North Pole, Inc., approved a plan to merge with its subsidiary, Santa's Workshop, Inc. The merger plan provided that certain of Workshop's shareholders would receive $3.50 per share. The highest independent appraisal of the stock was $4.04 per share. Hirschfeld, Inc., a shareholder, claimed the fair value was $16.80 per share. Workshop offered to make its corporate books and records available to Hirschfeld to assess the validity of the $16.80 demand. This offer was declined. Hirschfeld did not attempt to base the $16.80 demand on any recognizable method of stock valuation. Hirschfeld contended it had a right to get the asking price. Refer to RMBCA §§13.02, 13.28, and 13.31. Could Hirschfeld have blocked the merger until Workshop paid the $16.80? Decide. [*Santa's Workshop v. Hirschfeld, Inc.,* 851 P.2d 265 (Colo. App.)]

6. Richard Ramlall was hired by CloseCall (MD) Inc. to negotiate a billing dispute with Verizon involving some $2 million in asserted overcharges. CloseCall (MD) agreed to a contingent fee "bonus" for its negotiators of 10 percent of the refund. The negotiations were successful. However, before he could collect his fee CloseCall (MD) merged with MVCC Acquisition Corp., a wholly owned subsidiary of MobilePro Corp., which was created for the express purpose of merging with CloseCall (MD). MVCC survived and CloseCall (MD) dissolved. MVCC then changed its name to CloseCall (DE). The merger agreement between CloseCall and MVCC referenced the 10 percent bonus due on the Verizon billing dispute. The surviving Delaware corporation created by the merger of CloseCall (MD) into MVCC is CloseCall (DE). Ramlall sued CloseCall (DE) for

the bonus as the successor corporation of CloseCall (MD). CloseCall (DE) contends that after the merger CloseCall (DE) did not owe any money to Ramlall. Is CloseCall (DE) a successor corporation? Is it liable to Ramlall for the "bonus fee"? [*Ramlall v. Mobile Pro Corp.,* 30 A.2d 1003 (Md. App.)]

7. Morris Gray leased waterfront property on the Ross Barnett Reservoir to a restaurant, Edgewater Landing, Inc., for a 10-year term. After a year and a half, Edgewater's original shareholder, Billy Stegall, sold all of his shares in the corporation to Tom Bradley and Bradley's bookkeeper, Sandra Martin. Gray visited the property in the ninth year of the lease and found many problems with the condition of the property. He claimed that the lease required the tenant to make necessary repairs. Gray sued Edgewater Landing, Inc., and Tom Bradley and Sandra Martin individually for breach of the lease. Bradley and Martin replied that they were not liable for the debt of the corporation. Decide. [*Gray v. Edgewater Landing, Inc.,* 541 So.2d 1044 (Miss.)]

8. Emmick was a director and shareholder of Colonial Manors, Inc. (CM). He organized another corporation named Oahe Enterprises, Inc. To obtain shares of the Oahe stock, Emmick transferred CM shares arbitrarily valued by him at $19 per share to Oahe. The CM shares had a book value of $.47 per share, but Emmick believed that the stock would increase to a value of $19. The directors of Oahe approved Emmick's payment with the valuation of $19 per share. Golden sued Emmick on the ground that he had fraudulently deceived Oahe Corp. about the value of the CM shares and thus had made a secret profit when he received the Oahe shares that had a much greater value than the CM shares he gave in exchange. Emmick contended that his firm opinion was that the future potential value of CM shares would surely reach $19 per share. Decide. [*Golden v. Oahe Enterprises, Inc.,* 295 N.W.2d 160 (S.D.)]

9. Madison Associates purchased control of the majority of shares of 79 Realty Corp. from the Kimmelmans and the Zauders, who then resigned as directors. The Alpert group, which

owned the remaining 26 percent of 79 Realty refused to sell their shares. Partners of Madison Associates replaced the Kimmelmans and Zauders as directors of 79 Realty Corp., and as controlling directors, they approved a plan to merge 79 Realty Corp. with the Williams Street Corp., which was owned by Madison Associates. A shareholders' meeting was called, and the merger was approved by two-thirds of the shareholders. The Alpert group's shares were then forcibly canceled, with the price paid for these shares determined at their fair market value. The Alpert group brought suit contending the merger was unlawful because the sole purpose was to benefit the Madison Associates. Decide. [*Alpert v. 28 Williams Street Corp.*, 473 N.E.2d 19 (N.Y.)]

10. The Seabrook Island Property Owners Association, Inc., is a nonprofit corporation organized under state law to maintain streets and open spaces owned by property owners of Seabrook Island. Seabrook Island Co. is the developer of Seabrook Island and has majority control of the board of directors of the association. The association's bylaws empower the board of directors to levy an annual maintenance charge. Neither the association's charter nor its bylaws authorize the board to assess any other charges. When the board levied, in addition to the annual maintenance charge, an emergency budget assessment on all members to rebuild certain bridges and to revitalize the beach, the Loverings and other property owners challenged in court the association's power to impose the assessment. Decide. [*Lovering v. Seabrook Island Property Owners Ass'n*, 344 S.E.2d 862 (S.C. App.)]

11. Adams and two other persons were promoters for a new corporation, Aldrehn Theaters Co. The promoters retained Kridelbaugh to perform legal services in connection with the incorporation of the new business and promised to pay him $1,500. Aldrehn was incorporated through Kridelbaugh's services, and the promoters became its only directors. Kridelbaugh attended a meeting of the board of directors at which he was told that he should obtain a permit for the corporation to sell stock because the directors

wished to pay him for his previous services. The promoters failed to pay Kridelbaugh, and he sued the corporation. Was the corporation liable? [*Kridelbaugh v. Aldrehn Theaters Co.*, 191 N.W. 803 (Iowa)]

12. On August 19, 1980, Joan Ioviero injured her hand when she slipped and fell while leaving the dining room at the Hotel Excelsior in Venice, Italy. This hotel was owned by an Italian corporation, Cigahotels, S.p.A. (The designation *S.p.A.* stands for *Societa per Azionean*, the Italian term for *corporation*.) In 1973, a firm called Ciga Hotels, Inc., was incorporated in New York. Its certificate of incorporation was amended in 1979, changing the name of the firm to Landia International Services, Inc. This New York corporation was employed by the Italian corporation Cigahotels, S.p.A., to provide sales and promotional services in the United States and Canada. Ioviero sought to hold the New York corporation liable for her hand injury at the Venice hotel. She pointed to the similarity of the first corporate name used by the New York firm to the name Cigahotels, S.p.A., and the fact that the New York firm represented the interests of the Italian firm in the United States as clear evidence that the two firms were the same single legal entity. She asked that the court disregard the separate corporate entities. The New York corporation moved that the case be dismissed because it was duly incorporated in New York and did not own the Excelsior Hotel in which Ioviero was injured. Decide. [*Ioviero v. CigaHotel, Inc., aka Landia I.S., Inc.*, 475 N.Y.S.2d 880 (A.D.)]

13. William Sullivan was ousted from the presidency of the New England Patriots Football Club, Inc. Later, he borrowed $5,348,000 to buy 100 percent control of the voting shares of the corporation. A condition of the loan was that he reorganize the Patriots so that the income from the corporation could be devoted to repayment of the personal loan and the team's assets could be used as collateral. Sullivan, therefore, arranged for a cash freeze-out merger of the holders of the 120,000 shares of nonvoting stock. David Coggins, who owned 10 shares of nonvoting

stock and took special pride in the fact that he was an owner of the team, refused the $15-a-share buyout and challenged the merger in court. He contended that the merger was not for a legitimate corporate purpose but to enable Sullivan to satisfy his personal loan. Sullivan contended that legitimate business purposes were given in the merger proxy statement, such as the National Football League's policy of discouraging public ownership of teams. Coggins responded that before the merger, Sullivan had 100 percent control of the voting stock and thus control of the franchise, and that no legal basis existed to eliminate public ownership. Decide. [*Coggins v. New England Patriots Football Club*, 492 N.E.2d 1112 (Mass.)]

CPA QUESTIONS

1. Which of the following statements is correct concerning the similarities between a limited partnership and a corporation?

   a. Each is created under a statute and must file a copy of its certificate with the proper state authorities.

   b. All corporate stockholders and all partners in a limited partnership have limited liability.

   c. Both are recognized for federal income tax purposes as taxable entities.

   d. Both are allowed statutorily to have perpetual existence.

2. Rice is a promoter of a corporation to be known as Dex Corp. On January 1, 1985, Rice signed a nine-month contract with Roe, a CPA, which provided that Roe would perform certain accounting services for Dex. Rice did not disclose to Roe that Dex had not been formed. Prior to the incorporation of Dex on February 1, 1985, Roe rendered accounting services pursuant to the contract. After rendering accounting services for an additional period of six months pursuant to the contract, Roe was discharged without cause by the board of directors of Dex. In the absence of any agreements to the contrary, who will be liable to Roe for breach of contract?

   a. Both Rice and Dex

   b. Rice only

   c. Dex only

   d. Neither Rice nor Dex

3. In general, which of the following must be contained in articles of incorporation?

   a. The names of the states in which the corporation will be doing business

   b. The name of the state in which the corporation will maintain its principal place of business

   c. The names of the initial officers and their terms of office

   d. The classes of stock authorized for issuance

Chapter 45

Shareholder Rights in Corporations

© Manuel Gutjahr/iStockphoto.com

learningoutcomes

After studying this chapter, you should be able to

LO.1 Explain how to calculate the book value of a share of stock

LO.2 Distinguish between stocks and bonds

LO.3 Distinguish between subscriptions for and transfers of stock

LO.4 Explain the rights of shareholders

LO.5 Explain the nature of a shareholder derivative lawsuit

LO.6 Explain the exceptions to the limited liability of shareholders

T he two most common instruments used to provide funds for a corporation are stocks and bonds.

A. Corporate Stocks and Bonds

Ownership of a corporation is represented by stock. A *bond* is a corporate debt.

1. Nature of Stock

An interest in a corporation is based on ownership of one or more shares of stock of the corporation. Each share represents a fractional interest in the total property of the corporation. The shareholder does not own or have an interest in any specific property of the corporation; the corporation is the owner of all of its property. The terms *share, stock,* and *share of stock* mean the same thing.

outstanding – name for shares of a company that have been issued to stockholders.

(a) Capital and Capital Stock. *Capital* refers to the net assets of the corporation. Shares that have been issued to holders are said to be **outstanding**. **Capital stock** refers to the value received by the corporation for its outstanding stock.

capital stock – declared money value of the outstanding stock of the corporation.

(b) Valuation of Stock. Corporate stock may have a specified **par value**. This means that the person subscribing to the stock and acquiring it from the corporation must pay that amount.

par value – specified monetary amount assigned by an issuing corporation for each share of its stock.

Shares may be issued with no par value. In that case, no amount is stated in the certificate, and the amount that the subscriber pays the corporation is determined by the board of directors. The Revised Model Business Corporation Act (RMBCA) eliminates the concept of par value, so stock issued by corporations in states following the RMBCA is always no par.

book value – value found by dividing the value of the corporate assets by the number of shares outstanding.

The value found by dividing the value of the net corporate assets by the number of shares outstanding is the **book value** of the shares. **For Example,** Roger Eggett entered a Shareholder Agreement in 1995 with Todd Cusick and Curtis Chisholm, forming the Wasatch Energy Corporation. The terms of the Shareholder Agreement provided that should a shareholder separate from the corporation, the remaining shareholders would have the option to purchase that shareholder's corporate stock. The remaining shareholders, as per the Shareholder Agreement, would either purchase the stock for book value, if the separating shareholder voluntarily left the corporation, or for par value if the shareholder was terminated for cause. The Shareholder Agreement defined *book value* as the shareholder's net equity in the corporation, which would be determined by Wasatch's certified year-end financial statements. The Shareholder Agreement defined *par value* as the original price the shareholder paid for the stock. Egget tendered his resignation two years later, and offered to sell his stock according to the Shareholder Agreement "for the audited book value of the corporation as of June 30, 1997 divided by the number of shares he owned." Wasatch Corp. responded by firing Egget, wrongly asserting the firing was for cause, and tendered him a check for the par value of his stock, $1,217, Eggett's original investment. Eggett sued and was awarded the book value of his shares, $135,671, plus $60,000 in attorney fees.[1] The **market value** of a share of

market value – price at which a share of stock can be voluntarily bought or sold in the open market.

[1] *Eggett v. Wasatch Energy Corp.,* 29 P.3d 668 (Utah App. 2001).

stock is the price at which that stock can be voluntarily bought or sold in the open market.

2. Certificates of Stock and Uncertificated Shares

certificate of stock – document evidencing a shareholder's ownership of stock issued by a corporation.

A corporation ordinarily issues a **certificate of stock** or *share certificate* as evidence of the shareholder's ownership of stock. The issuance of such certificates is not essential either to the existence of a corporation or to the ownership of its stock.

In states that have adopted the 1978 and 1994 amendments to Article 8 of the U.C.C., uncertificated shares may be issued. Uncertificated shares are not represented by instruments. Their ownership and transfer are registered on the books maintained by, or on behalf of, the issuer corporation.[2]

3. Kinds of Stock

common stock – stock that has no right or priority over any other stock of the corporation as to dividends or distribution of assets upon dissolution.

The stock of a corporation may be divided into two or more classes.

CPA

(A) Classification by Preferences. **Common stock** is ordinary stock that has no preferences. Each share usually entitles the holder to have one vote, to receive a share of the profits in the form of dividends when declared, and to participate in the distribution of capital upon dissolution of the corporation. **Preferred stock** has a priority over common stock. The priority may be with respect to either dividends or the distribution of capital upon dissolution of the corporation, or both. Preferred stock is ordinarily nonvoting.

preferred stock – stock that has a priority or preference as to payment of dividends or upon liquidation, or both.

CPA

(1) Cumulative Preferred Stock.
The right to receive dividends depends on the declaration of dividends by the board of directors for a particular period of time. If there is no fund from which the dividends may be declared or if the directors do not declare them from an available fund, the shareholder has no right to dividends. The fact that a shareholder has not received dividends for the current year does not in itself give the right to accumulate or carry over into the next year a claim for those dividends. However, in the absence of a statement that the right to dividends is noncumulative, courts frequently hold that preferred stock has the right to accumulate dividends for each year in which there was a surplus available for dividend payment but dividends were not declared.

CPA

(2) Participating Preferred Stock.
Sometimes the preferred stock is given the right of participation. If it is, then after the common shares receive dividends or a capital distribution is made equal to that first received by the preferred stock, both kinds participate or share equally in the balance.

(B) Duration of Shares. Ordinarily, shares continue to exist for the life of the corporation. However, any kind of share, whether common or preferred, may be made terminable at an earlier date.

(c) Fractional Shares. A corporation may issue fractional shares or scrip or certificates representing fractional shares. These can be sold or combined for the acquisition of whole shares.

---

[2] U.C.C. §8-102(1)(b). The 1978 and 1994 amendments to Article 8 of the U.C.C. have been adopted in all of the states except Alabama.

4. Characteristics of Bonds

bond – obligation or promise in writing and sealed, generally of corporations, personal representatives, and trustees; fidelity bonds.

A **bond** is an instrument promising to repay a loan of money to a corporation. Typically, the loan is for a relatively long period of time, generally five years or longer. A bond obligates the corporation to pay the bondholder the amount of the loan, called the *principal*, at a stated time, called the **maturity date**, and to pay a fixed amount of *interest* at regular intervals, commonly every six months. The relationship between the bondholder and the issuing corporation is that of creditor and debtor. Unlike dividends, which are discretionary, bond interest must be paid. A bond may be secured by a mortgage or lien on corporate property. A **debenture** is an unsecured bond of the corporation with no specific corporate assets pledged as security for payment.

maturity date – date that a corporation is required to repay a loan to a bondholder.

debenture – unsecured bond of a corporation, with no specific corporate assets pledged as security for payment.

Bonds are negotiable securities.[3] Bonds held by owners whose names and addresses are registered on the books of the corporation are called **registered bonds.**

registered bonds – bonds held by owners whose names and addresses are registered on the books of the corporation.

5. Terms and Control

bond indenture – agreement setting forth the contractual terms of a particular bond issue.

The contractual terms of a particular bond issue are set forth in an agreement called a **bond indenture** or **deed**. An **indenture trustee**, usually a commercial banking institution, represents the interests of the bondholders in making sure that the corporation meets the terms and covenants of the bond issue.[4] For example, the terms of the bond indenture may require a **sinking fund**, by which the borrowing corporation is required to set aside a fixed amount of money each year toward the ultimate payment of the bonds. The indenture trustee makes certain that such terms are complied with in accordance with its responsibilities set forth in the bond indenture.

deed – instrument by which the grantor (owner of land) conveys or transfers the title to a grantee.

indenture trustee – usually a commercial banking institution, to represent the interests of the bondholders and ensure that the terms and covenants of the bond issue are met by the corporation.

Bondholders do not vote for directors or have the right to vote on matters on which shareholders vote. However, when the debt is risky, it is highly likely that significant restraints on the corporation's freedom of action will be imposed by the terms of the indenture.

sinking fund – fixed amount of money set aside each year by the borrowing corporation toward the ultimate payment of bonds.

B. ACQUISITION OF SHARES

Shares may be acquired from the corporation or from an existing shareholder.

6. Nature of Acquisition

Shares of stock may be acquired (1) from the corporation by subscription, either before or after the corporation is organized, or (2) by transfer of existing shares from a shareholder or from the corporation. The transfer may be voluntary, as by a sale, gift, or bequest by will, or involuntary, as by an execution sale to pay the judgment of a creditor. The transfer may also take place by operation of law—as when the stock of a shareholder passes to the shareholder's trustee in bankruptcy.

---

[3] U.C.C. §8-105.
[4] *Lorenc v. CSX Corp.*, CCH Sec. L. Rep. 95298 (W.D. Pa. 1990).

7. Statute of Frauds

Under the 1978 version of Article 8, a contract for the sale of corporate shares must be evidenced by a writing, or it cannot be enforced.[5] The 1994 version of Article 8 renders the statute of frauds inapplicable to contracts for the sale or purchase of securities.[6] The commentary notes explain that the 1978 statute's potential for filtering out fraudulent claims is outweighed by the obstacles the statute presents to the development of modern commercial practices in the securities business.

No writing is required for a contract by which a broker agrees with a customer to buy or sell securities for the customer. That is an agency agreement, not a sale made between the customer and the broker.

8. Subscription

stock subscription – contract or agreement to buy a specific number and kind of shares when they are issued by the corporation.

A **stock subscription** is a contract or an agreement to buy a specific number and kind of shares when the corporation issues them. As in the case of any other contract, the agreement to subscribe to shares of a corporation may be avoided for fraud.

(A) Subscription before Incorporation. In many states, a preincorporation subscription of shares is an offer to the corporation. According to this view, it is necessary for the corporation to accept the subscription offer either expressly or by conduct. A few states hold that subscriptions automatically become binding contracts when the organization of the corporation has been completed. In some states, the preincorporation subscription is irrevocable for a stated period. The RMBCA provides that "a subscription for shares entered into before incorporation is irrevocable for six months unless the subscription agreement provides a longer or shorter period or all the subscribers agree to revocation."[7]

acceptance – unqualified assent to the act or proposal of another; as the acceptance of a draft (bill of exchange), of an offer to make a contract, of goods delivered by the seller, or of a gift or deed.

(B) Subscription after Incorporation. Subscriptions may be made after incorporation. In that event, the transaction is like any other contract with the corporation. The offer of the subscription may come from the subscriber or from the corporation. In either case, there must be an **acceptance**. Upon acceptance, the subscriber immediately becomes a shareholder with all the rights, privileges, and liabilities of a shareholder even though she has not paid any of the purchase price. Moreover, the subscriber is a shareholder even though no share certificate has been issued. In contrast with a contract for immediate subscription to shares, the contract may be one for the future issue of shares. In that case, the contracting party has only a contract and is not a shareholder as of the formation of the contract.

9. Transfer of Shares

In the absence of a valid restriction, a shareholder may transfer shares to anyone.

(A) Restrictions on Transfer. Restrictions on the transfer of stock are valid if they are not unreasonable. It is lawful to require that the corporation or other stockholders be given the first right to purchase stock before a shareholder may sell stock to an outsider.

---

[5] U.C.C. §8-319(a); *Goldfinger v. Brown*, 564 N.Y.S.2d 461 (A.D. 1991).
[6] U.C.C. §8-113.
[7] RMBCA §6.20(a).

Such restrictions are widely used, particularly in close corporations, so current shareholders can control the ownership and management of the corporation and prevent outsiders from "invading the business"; also, restrictions serve to maintain parity among shareholders.

CASE SUMMARY

Restrictions on Transfer of Stock Are Legal, Morris

FACTS: In 1974 Billy Fought, Brady Morris, Clayton Strong, and John Peyton organized Vicksburg Mold and Die, Inc., for the purpose of designing and manufacturing plastic and metal products. Each individual was issued 25 shares of stock. The shareholders entered into a stock redemption agreement requiring a stockholder wishing to sell his stock to offer proportionate shares to each stockholder. Morris was elected president and Fought vice president, and all four individuals worked at the plant. Strong retired in 1979 and sold his shares in accordance with the stock redemption plan. In 1983, Peyton decided to sell his shares and agreed to sell them all to Morris, thus giving Morris control of the corporation. Fought sued Morris for breach of his fiduciary duty to Fought and for the value of Fought's pro rata share of Peyton's stock.

DECISION: Judgment for Fought. Section 2 of the stock redemption agreement was designed to maintain a balance of power in the four-person close corporation. Before stock could be sold to others, it had to be offered to each shareholder on a pro rata basis. Each individual had an opportunity to maintain the initial balance of power. By purchasing all of Peyton's stock, Morris bought control of the corporation. In doing so, he violated the stock redemption agreement and thus breached his fiduciary duty as a director, officer, and shareholder. [*Fought v. Morris*, **543 So.2d 167 (Miss. 1989)**]

A provision giving a corporation the right to purchase a shareholder's shares on the death of the shareholder is valid.[8]

A restriction on the right of a certificate's purchaser to transfer his stock is not valid unless the restriction is conspicuously noted on the certificate or the transferee had actual knowledge of the restriction. A restriction on the transfer of stock is strictly interpreted.[9]

When no restrictions exist, the issuer has a duty to register the transfer.

For Example, Richard Jones purchased 1,000 certificated shares of International Generic Corporation (IGC) from Madison Tucker on March 30, 2013, at fair market value. Tucker properly indorsed the certificates to Jones on that date, and her signatures were duly notarized. On September 15, 2013, Jones presented the securities to IGC to register the transfer of shares and to collect dividends for the second quarter (April 1 through June 30) and the third quarter (July 1 through September 30). IGC refused to register the shares in Jones's name, believing him to be a person of questionable integrity that it did not want as an "owner" of IGC. Under either the 1978 or 1994 version of Article 8 of the U.C.C., it was improper for IGC to fail to register the stock that had been transferred to a bona fide purchaser, Jones.[10] No restrictions existed on the certificate, and IGC had a duty to

---

[8] See *Puritas Metal Products v. Cook*, 972 N.E2d 615 (Ohio 2012), where a trial court incorrectly determined that the decedent's death resulted in a "transfer" under the corporation's code of regulation. In fact, the decedent's shares were in a marital trust, and upon his death the shares were retained by the trustee of the trust, his wife, to administer and vote as she saw fit.

[9] *Capano v. Wilmington Country Club, Inc.*, 2001 WL 1359254 (Del. Ch. Nov. 1, 2001).

[10] U.C.C. §8-401 (1978); U.C.C. §8-401 (1994).

register the transfer and was liable for its failure to do so. Jones was entitled to the dividends from the date of presentation of the stock for transfer. Prior to that date, the issuer, IGC, was entitled to treat the registered owner, Madison Tucker, as exclusively entitled to exercise the rights of ownership, including the right to dividends.[11] Thus, IGC was not liable to Jones for the second-quarter dividends. However, dividends declared after the date of presentment, which included the third-quarter dividend declared in October 2013 with a record date in October, must be paid to Jones by IGC.

(B) INTEREST TRANSFERRED. The transfer of shares may be absolute; that is, it may divest all ownership and make the transferee the full owner. The transfer may be of only a partial interest in the stock, or the transfer may be for security, such as when stock is pledged to secure the repayment of a loan.

10. Mechanics of Transfer

When stock is represented by a certificate, the ownership of shares is transferred by the delivery of the certificate of stock, indorsed by its owner in blank or to a specified person. Ownership may also be transferred by the delivery of the certificate accompanied by a separate assignment or power of attorney executed by the owner.[12]

A delivery from the owner of the shares directly to the transferee is not required. It can be made to an intermediary. When there is no delivery of the share certificate to anyone, however, there is no transfer of ownership of the shares.

A physical transfer of the certificate without a necessary indorsement is effective as between the parties. Thus, a gift of shares is binding even though no indorsement has been made. An indorsement is required to make the transferee a bona fide purchaser.

11. Effect of Transfer

The transfer of existing shares of stock may raise questions between the parties to the transfer and between them and the corporation.

(A) VALIDITY OF TRANSFER. Because a transfer of shares is a transfer of ownership, the transfer must satisfy the requirements governing any other transfer of property or agreement to transfer property.[13] As between the parties, a transfer may be set aside for any ground that would warrant similar relief under property law. If the transfer has been obtained by duress, the transferor may obtain a rescission of the transfer.

(B) NEGOTIABILITY. Under common law, the transferee of shares of stock had no greater right than the transferor because the certificate and the shares represented by the certificate were nonnegotiable. By statute, the common law rule has been changed by imparting negotiability to certificated stock. Just as various defenses cannot be asserted against the holder in due course of a commercial paper, statutory law provides that similar defenses cannot be raised against the person acquiring the certificate in good faith and for value. Against such a person, the defense cannot be raised that the transferor did not own the shares or did not have authority to deliver

[11] U.C.C. §8-207(1) (1978); U.C.C. §8-207(a) (1994).
[12] U.C.C. §8-309. See *Kesling v. Kesling*, 967 N.E.2d 66, 68 (Ind. App. 2012), where the corporate bylaws set forth the two methods of transferring stock in TP Orthodontics, Inc.
[13] *Gallant v. Kanterman*, 671 N.Y.S.2d 50 (A.D. 1998).

the certificate or that the transfer was made in violation of a restriction on transfer not known to the person and not noted conspicuously on the certificate.

Statements sent by the issuer identifying the ownership of uncertificated securities are neither certificated securities nor negotiable instruments. Although certificated securities have the quality of negotiability, they are not commercial paper within Article 3 of the U.C.C.

(c) SECURED TRANSACTION. Corporate stock is frequently delivered to a creditor as security for a debt owed by the shareholder. Thus, a debtor borrowing money from a bank may deliver shares of stock to the bank as collateral security for the repayment of the loan. A broker's customer purchasing stock on margin may leave the stock in the possession of the broker as security for the payment of any balance due. The delivery of the security to the creditor is a pledge. This gives rise to a perfected security interest without any filing by the creditor. In itself, the pledge does not make the pledgee of the corporate stock the owner of the stock.

(d) EFFECT OF TRANSFER ON CORPORATION. The corporation is entitled to treat as the owner of shares the person whose name is on the corporation's books as the owner. Therefore, until there is a transfer on its books, the corporation may still treat a transferor of shares as the owner. The corporation may properly refuse to recognize a transferee when the corporation is given notice or has knowledge that the transfer is void or in breach of trust. In such a case, the corporation properly refuses to register a transfer until the rights of the parties have been determined. The corporation may also refuse to register the transfer of shares when the outstanding certificate is not surrendered to it or there is a lack of satisfactory proof that the certificate has been lost, destroyed, or stolen.

CASE SUMMARY

U.C.C. Rules!

FACTS: Equivest Associates, a partnership, owned 10,000 shares of Altec International Inc. Equivest pledged these shares to secure loans by Lloyds Bank. Sometime after pledging the stock, Equivest transferred beneficial ownership of 350 shares of Altec stock to Thorn Hoffman and 350 shares to John Erikson. Thereafter, in 1988, Altec elected to be treated as a Subchapter S corporation, which necessitated that shareholders return their old stock certificates and be issued new certificates. Neither Erikson nor Hoffman had certificates to return because their stock had been pledged by Equivest to Lloyds Bank. Altec had knowledge that Erikson and Hoffman were the beneficial owners of 700 shares of Altec stock. However, Altec distributed cash dividends to Equivest, the registered owner of the 10,000 shares during the period from 1988 until March 14, 1990, when Equivest defaulted on its loan to Lloyds Bank and Lloyds sold all of the pledged stock, including Hoffman's and Erikson's 700 shares, at public auction. Hoffman and Erikson contend that Altec should have made all cash distributions to them as shareholders, not Equivest. Altec contends it complied with the U.C.C. by making distributions to the owner of record.

DECISION: Judgment for Altec. U.C.C. §8-207(1) permitted Altec to treat Equivest as the owner of the 700 shares because it was the registered owner according to Altec's corporate books and Hoffman and Erikson had not made the due presentment to Altec for registration of the transfer of the 700 shares. [*Hoffman v. Altec Int'l Inc.*, **546 N.W.2d 162 (Wis. App. 1996)**]

12. Lost, Destroyed, and Stolen Share Certificates

The owner of a lost, destroyed, or stolen share certificate is entitled to a replacement if the owner files a sufficient indemnity bond and requests the new certificate within a reasonable time before the issuer has notice that the original certificate has been acquired by a bona fide purchaser. **For Example,** if established by clear and convincing evidence, Linda Rosso would be entitled to the replacement of damaged jointly held stock certificates that her late husband Richard disposed of and never replaced. The court pointed out that there is a distinction between certificates issued a shareholder and the "shares" issued the shareholder. A *share* is the actual property of the shareholder while the *certificate* is merely the authentic evidence of the stockholder's ownership of shares.[14] If, after the new security is issued, a bona fide purchaser appears with the original certificate, the corporation must register a transfer of the security to that person and accept that person as the owner of the shares.

CPA ## C. Rights of Shareholders

The rights of shareholders stem from their status as owners.

CPA ## 13. Ownership Rights

Shareholder control over the corporation is indirect. Periodically (ordinarily once a year), the shareholders elect directors and by this means control the corporation. At other times, however, the shareholders have no right or power to control corporate activity so long as it is conducted within lawful channels.

CPA **(A) CERTIFICATES OF STOCK.** A shareholder has the right to have a properly executed certificate as evidence of ownership of shares. An exception is made when the corporation is authorized to issue uncertificated securities.

CPA **(B) TRANSFER OF SHARES.** Unless limited by a valid restriction, a shareholder has the right to transfer her shares. The shareholder may sell the shares at any price or transfer them as a gift. The fact that the seller sells at a price higher than the market price is not unlawful even if the seller is a director or an officer.

CASE SUMMARY

It's the Real Thing, Controlling Shares in Coke-Anderson, and You Have to Pay a Premium

FACTS: Paul Warlick, Jr., was the president and chief executive officer and a stockholder of Coca-Cola Bottling Company of Anderson, S.C. (Coke-Anderson). He controlled a majority of the shares of stock of the company. Warlick agreed to sell this controlling interest in Coke-Anderson to Coke-Asheville for a price greater than the market value of the shares. Wayne Shoaf, a

---

[14] *Rosso v. Rosso*, 701 N.W.2d 355 (Neb. 2005).

CASE SUMMARY

Continued

minority shareholder, brought suit against Warlick, contending that Warlick had violated his fiduciary duty to the corporation by receiving an unlawful premium for the sale of the majority interest in Coke-Anderson.

DECISION: Judgment for Warlick. Paying or receiving a premium for the controlling shares of stock in a corporation is not unlawful. A majority shareholder who is also a director and an officer is generally under no duty to minority shareholders to refrain from receiving a premium on the sale of the controlling stock. [*Shoaf v. Warlick*, 380 S.E.2d 865 (S.C. App. 1989)]

CPA

14. Right to Vote

The right to vote means the right to vote at shareholders' meetings for the election of directors and on other special matters that shareholders must vote on. **For Example,** a proposal to change the capital structure of the corporation or a proposal to sell all or substantially all assets of the corporation must be approved by the shareholders.

CPA

(A) WHO MAY VOTE. Ordinarily, only shareholders of record—those common shareholders in whose name the stock appears on the books of the corporation—are entitled to vote. The board of directors may fix a date for closing the corporate books for this purpose.

CPA

(B) NUMBER OF VOTES. Unless there is a provision to the contrary, for each share owned, each shareholder is entitled to one vote on each matter to be voted. This procedure is called *straight voting*, and it is the normal method for shareholder voting on corporate matters. However, in the case of voting to elect directors only, **cumulative voting** is mandatory in nearly half of the states. This requirement is imposed by either state constitution or state statute. Cumulative voting is permitted by law in other states when provided for in the articles of incorporation or bylaws.

cumulative voting – system of voting for directors in which each shareholder has as many votes as the number of voting shares owned multiplied by the number of directors to be elected, and such votes can be distributed for the various candidates as desired.

Cumulative voting is a form of voting that is designed to give proportional representation on the board of directors to minority shareholders. Under a cumulative voting plan, each shareholder has as many votes as the number of shares owned multiplied by the number of directors to be elected. A shareholder may cast all of these votes for one candidate or may divide the votes between two or more candidates. This system enables minority shareholders to cast all of their votes for a candidate who will represent their interests on the board of directors.

Under straight voting, minority shareholders would always be outvoted. **For Example,** assume that minority shareholder Tyler Feldberg owned 400 shares of stock and majority shareholder C. J. Jones controlled the remaining 600 shares. Also assume that five directors are to be elected to the board. If straight voting were used for the election of directors, C. J., with 600 shares, would always outvote Tyler's 400 shares. However, under cumulative voting, Tyler would be allowed 2,000 votes (400 shares times five directors), and C. J. would be allowed 3,000 votes (600 shares times five directors). The five candidates with the highest number of votes will be elected. If Tyler casts 1,000 votes for each of two directors and C. J. casts 1,000 votes for each of three directors, Tyler, who owns 40 percent of the stock, is able to elect two-fifths of the board to represent his interests.

voting by proxy – authorizing someone else to vote the shares owned by the shareholder.

proxy – written authorization by a shareholder to another person to vote the stock owned by the shareholder; the person who is the holder of such a written authorization.

voting trust – transfer by two or more persons of their shares of stock of a corporation to a trustee who is to vote the shares and act for such shareholders.

(C) VOTING BY PROXY. A shareholder has the right to authorize another to vote the shares owned by the shareholder. This procedure is known as **voting by proxy**. In the absence of restrictions to the contrary, any person, even someone who is not a shareholder, may act as a proxy. The authorization from the shareholder may be made by any writing.[15] The authorization is also commonly called a **proxy**.

(D) VOTING AGREEMENTS AND TRUSTS. Shareholders, as a general rule, are allowed to enter into an agreement by which they concentrate their voting strength for the purpose of electing directors or voting on any other matter.

A **voting trust** is created when by agreement a group of shareholders or all of the shareholders transfer their shares in trust to one or more persons as trustees. The trustees are authorized to vote the stock during the life of the trust agreement.[16] In general, such agreements are upheld if their object is lawful. In some jurisdictions, such trusts cannot run beyond a stated number of years. There are some signs of a relaxation as to time. Several states have abandoned all time limitations, several have extended the time limitation, and many provide for an extension or renewal of the agreement.

CPA

15. Preemptive Offer of Shares

preemptive right – shareholder's right upon the increase of a corporation's capital stock to be allowed to subscribe to such a percentage of the new shares as the shareholder's old shares bore to the former total capital stock.

If the capital stock of a corporation is increased, shareholders ordinarily have the **preemptive right** to subscribe to the same percentage of the new shares that their old shares represented of the former total of capital stock. This right is given to enable shareholders to maintain their relative interests in the corporation.

The existence of a preemptive right may make it impossible to conclude a transaction in which the corporation is to transfer a block of stock as consideration. Moreover, practical difficulties arise as to how stock should be allocated among shareholders of different classes.

The RMBCA provides that shareholders do not have preemptive rights unless the articles of incorporation provide for them.

CPA

16. Inspection of Books

A shareholder has the right to inspect the books of the shareholder's corporation. In some states, there are no limitations on this right. In most states, the inspection must be made in good faith, for proper motives, and at a reasonable time and place.[17] In many states, a shareholder must own a certain percentage of the outstanding stock of a corporation (commonly 5 percent) or must own at least one share of stock for a minimum amount of time (commonly six months) to have the right to inspect the books. A shareholder is not relegated to accepting opinions and numbers offered by a company's auditor and may employ an expert accountant of his own to review and analyze the books and records of the corporation.[18]

The purpose of inspection must be reasonably related to the shareholder's interest as a shareholder. **For Example,** minority shareholder Julio Herencia was entitled access to corporate books and records and an accounting when the majority shareholders of Centercut Restaurant Corp. did not follow the shareholders agreement's method of valuation for the repurchase of his shares.[19] A shareholder is

---

[15] RMBCA §7.07.
[16] *Bettner Trust v. Bettner*, 495 N.E.2d 194 (Ind. App. 1986).
[17] RMBCA §16.02(c); *Leary v. Foley*, 884 So.2d 655 (La. App. 2004).
[18] *Missouri v. III Investments, Inc.*, 80 S.W.3d 855 (Mo. App. 2002).
[19] *Herencia v. Centercut Restaurant Corp.*, 938 N.Y.S.2d 286 (A. D. 2012). See also *Feil v. Greater Lakeside Corp.*, 81 So.3d 178 (La. App. 2011).

entitled to inspect the records to determine the financial condition of the corporation, the quality of its management, and any matters relating to rights or interests in the corporate business, such as the value of stock.[20]

CASE SUMMARY

... No Fury Like a Stockholder Scorned

FACTS: U.S. Die Casting, Inc., is a closely held Ohio corporation that owns 5 percent of Security First Corporation, a Delaware corporation, which owns an Ohio savings and loan bank. David Slyman is the president of U.S. Die and its sole stockholder. The defendant, Security First, entered into a merger agreement with Mid Am, Inc., a large regional bank holding company; and after the announcement of the merger, Security First's stock increased significantly. The merger agreement required Security First to pay a termination fee of $2 million plus third-party expenses not to exceed $250,000 contingent on the occurrence of certain events within one year after termination, should Security First pull out of the merger. The merger did not go through, and the market price for Security First stock dropped significantly. Security First gave as a reason for failing to go through with the merger "the realization that Mid Am's management philosophy and direction were fundamentally different from its own." Security First paid Mid Am $275,000 in expenses and agreed to pay an additional $2 million if a certain event occurred within one and one-half years after termination. U.S. Die submitted a written demand to Security First pursuant to section 220 to inspect all of its books and records related to the Mid Am merger and its termination. Security First refused to comply. The Court of Chancery granted U.S. Die's demand, and Security First appealed.

DECISION: Judgment for U.S. Die. Section 220 proceedings are an important part of the corporate governance landscape in Delaware. Stockholders have a right to at least a limited inquiry into books and records when they have established some credible basis to believe that there has been wrongdoing. Concerning the purpose for the inspection, Slyman testified:

> I would like to make my own decision as to why the merger was not completed. Telling me that it was a difference of philosophies didn't get me to understand why it was not completed. The philosophy was there prior to it....

Slyman's testimony does call into question the defendant's purported reason for abrogating the merger agreement—namely, "the realization that Mid Am's management philosophy and direction were fundamentally different from its own." The Court of Chancery found the defendant's reason suspect because management philosophies could have been researched before entering into the agreement. Expense payments made to Mid Am in excess of the stipulation in the merger agreement and payment of a termination fee for a period beyond the time period set forth in the agreement are a basis for U.S. Die to inspect books and records, subject to remand on the scope of the inspection. [*Security First v. U.S. Die Casting, Inc.*, 687 A.2d 563 (Del. Super. 1997)]

A shareholder is entitled to inspect the books to obtain information needed for a lawsuit against the corporation or its directors or officers, to organize the other shareholders into an "opposition" party to remove the board of directors at the next election, or to buy the shares of other shareholders.[21]

[20] *Ihrig v. Frontier Equity Exchange*, 128 P.3d 993 (Kan. App. 2006).
[21] See *Kelley Manufacturing Co. v. Martin*, 674 S.E.2d 92 (Ga. App. 2009), where the court determined that two shareholders showed a proper purpose for seeking inspection of books: to enforce the company's bylaws; to ensure proper corporate governance and to determine if corporate waste, mismanagement, and other breaches of fiduciary duty were occurring; to inspect corporate records to protect the shareholders' substantial ownership interest; and to inspect records related to the shareholders' removal as trustees, directors, officers, and employees of the corporation.

Inspection has frequently been refused when it was sought merely from idle curiosity or for "speculative purposes." Inspection has sometimes been denied on the ground that it was sought merely to obtain a mailing list of persons who would be solicited to buy products of another enterprise. Inspection has also been refused when the object of the shareholder was to advance political or social beliefs without regard to the welfare of the corporation. Cases that deny the right of inspection do so when it would be harmful to the corporation[22] or is sought only for the purpose of annoying, harassing, or causing vexation or of aiding competitors of the corporation.

(A) FORM OF BOOKS. There are generally no requirements regarding the form of corporate books and records. The RMBCA recognizes that corporate books and records may be stored in modern data storage systems. "A corporation shall maintain its records in written form or in any other form capable of conversion into written form within a reasonable time."[23]

(B) FINANCIAL STATEMENTS. The RMBCA requires a corporation to furnish annual financial statements. These statements include a balance sheet as of the end of the fiscal year, an income statement for that year, and a statement of changes in shareholders' equity for that year.[24] A number of state statutes contain similar provisions and set forth a statutory penalty for any officer responsible for providing the financial statements who fails to perform such duties after written request.

CPA

17. Dividends

A shareholder has the right to receive a proportion of dividends as they are declared, subject to the relative rights of other shareholders to preferences, accumulation of dividends, and participation. There is no absolute right that dividends be declared, but dividends, when declared, must be paid in the manner indicated.

CPA

(A) FUNDS AVAILABLE FOR DECLARATION OF DIVIDENDS. Statutes commonly provide that no dividends may be declared unless there is an "earned surplus" for their payment. Earned surplus, also known as *retained earnings*, consists of the accumulated profits earned by the corporation since its formation less prior dividend distributions. Dividend payments are prohibited if the corporation is insolvent or would be rendered insolvent by the payment of the dividend.

As an exception to these rules, a wasting assets corporation may pay dividends out of current net profits without regard to the preservation of the corporate assets. **Wasting assets corporations** are those designed to exhaust or use up the assets of the corporation (for example, by extracting oil, coal, iron, and other ores) as compared with manufacturing plants whose object is to preserve the plant as well as to continue to manufacture. A wasting assets corporation may also be formed for the purpose of buying and liquidating a stock of merchandise from a company that has received a discharge in bankruptcy court.

In some states, statutes provide that dividends may be declared from earned surplus or from current net profits without regard to the existence of a deficit from former years.

wasting assets corporation – corporation designed to exhaust or use up the assets of the corporation, such as by extracting oil, coal, iron, and other ores.

---

[22] *Retail Property Investors, Inc., v. Skeens*, 471 S.E.2d 181 (Va. 1996).
[23] RMBCA §16.01(d).
[24] RMBCA §16.20. See *Troccoli v. Lab Contract Industries, Inc.*, 687 N.Y.S.2d 400 (A.D. 1999).

CPA **(B) DISCRETION OF DIRECTORS.** Assuming that a fund is available for the declaration of dividends, it is then a matter primarily within the discretion of the board of directors whether a dividend shall be declared. The fact that there is an earned surplus that could be used for dividends does not mean that they must be declared. This rule is not affected by the nature of the shares. Thus, the fact that the shareholders hold cumulative preferred shares does not give them any right to demand a declaration of dividends or to interfere with an honest exercise of discretion by the directors.

Maintaining an adequate cash and working capital position is an important practical consideration in determining whether to declare a cash dividend. In general, courts refuse to substitute their judgment for the judgment of the directors of the corporation and interfere with their decision on dividend declaration only when it is shown that their conduct is harmful to the welfare of the corporation or its shareholders.[25]

(C) FORM OF DIVIDENDS. Customarily, a dividend is paid in money. However, it may be paid in property, such as a product manufactured by the corporation; in shares of other corporations held by the corporation; or in shares of the corporation itself.

(D) EFFECT OF TRANSFER OF SHARES. When a corporation declares a cash or property dividend, the usual practice is for the board of directors to declare a dividend as of a certain date—the *declaration date*—payable to shareholders of record on a stated future date—the *record date*—with a *payment date* following the record date, usually by some 30 days. The person who is the owner of the shares on the record date is entitled to the dividend even if the shares are transferred prior to the payment date.

If the dividend consists of shares in the corporation declaring the dividend, ownership of the dividend is determined by the date of distribution. Whoever is the owner of the shares when the stock dividend is distributed is entitled to the stock dividend. The reason for this variation from the cash dividend rule is that the declaration of a stock dividend has the effect of diluting the existing corporate assets among a larger number of shares. The value of the holding represented by each share is diminished as a result. Unless the person who owns the stock on the distribution date receives a proportionate share of the stock dividend, the net effect will be to lessen that person's holding.

18. Capital Distribution

Upon dissolution of the corporation, shareholders are entitled to receive any balance of the corporate assets that remains after the payment of all creditors. Certain classes of stock may have a preference or priority in this distribution.

CPA ## 19. Shareholders' Actions

When the corporation has the right to sue its directors, officers, or third persons for damages caused by them to the corporation or for breach of contract, one or more shareholders may bring such action if the corporation refuses to do so. This is a **derivative (secondary) action** in that the shareholder enforces only the cause of action of the corporation and any money recovery is paid into the corporate treasury.

derivative (secondary) action – secondary action for damages or breach of contract brought by one or more corporate shareholders against directors, officers, or third persons.

[25] *Gabelli & Co. v. Liggett Group, Inc.,* 479 A.2d 276 (Del. Super. 1984).

In a derivative action, when a corporation has failed to enforce a right, a shareholder bringing such a suit must show that a demand was made on the directors to enforce the right in question. The shareholder must show (1) that the directors refused to enforce the right[26] or (2) that a demand that the directors enforce the right is excused because the directors are deemed incapable of making an impartial decision regarding the pursuit of the litigation. Additionally, where a special litigation committee (SLC) is formed by the board of directors with full authority to decide what position to take with regard to a derivative lawsuit, demand on the entire board may be excused on a case-by-case basis, as exemplified in the *AIG, Inc.*, case.

CASE SUMMARY

"Curb Your Enthusiasm," Defendants Greenberg and Smith Argue

FACTS: Plaintiff stockholders sued derivatively CEO Maurice Greenberg, CFO Howard Smith, and other former officers who had served on American Insurance Group's (AIG's) board of directors. The plaintiffs took this action on behalf of the corporation for damages the former officers had caused AIG by having the corporation engage in illegal acts. In one example, it was asserted by the plaintiffs that AIG had created a fictional reinsurance business transaction with General Reinsurance Corp. to inflate loss reserves, thus making AIG appear to be a healthier company than it actually was and inflating AIG's stock price. AIG's board of directors formed a special litigation committee (SLC) to look into the stockholder plaintiffs' allegations, giving full authority to the SLC to address the litigation. The SLC investigated all matters and decided to join this action as a direct plaintiff on behalf of the corporation, asserting breach of fiduciary duty and indemnification claims against former CEO Greenberg and former CFO Smith. The defendants, Greenberg and Smith, contended that the stockholder plaintiffs must make a demand on the full board. Moreover, they asserted that under procedural law, boards of directors should not be lightly bypassed by derivative plaintiffs.

DECISION: Judgment for the stockholder plaintiffs. Corporation law seeks to ensure that boards are not lightly bypassed by derivative plaintiffs and not allowed to usurp the board's right to manage the affairs of the corporation. AIG's board's primacy in decision making has been fully honored. The SLC chose to have AIG sue Greenberg and Smith itself, to seek dismissal of certain defendants and to otherwise take no position on the plaintiffs' claims. The board gave the SLC full authority to make this decision, and through the SLC the board asserted control over the lawsuit. Demand is thus excused and the plaintiffs are free to proceed against the defendants. [*AIG, Inc. v. Greenberg*, 965 A.2d 763 (Del. Ch. 2009)]

A special litigation committee is vested with enormous power to pursue a corporate claim or seek dismissal of a derivative suit. But courts will defer to the business judgment and conclusions of the SLC only if the directors involved possess a disinterested independence and do not have relationships that prevent an unprejudicial exercise of judgment.[27]

---

[26] *Marx. v. Akers*, 666 N.E.2d 1034 (N.Y. 1996). But see *Potter v. Hughes*, 546 F.3d 1051 (9th Cir. 2008).
[27] *In re Comverse Technology, Inc.*, 766 N.Y.S.2d 10 (A.D. 2008).

CASE SUMMARY

It's Not Good Retailing to Publicly Tout "Low Cost Manufacturing – High Retail Pricing" on Wall Street: Wall Street Abuts Main Street

FACTS: Shareholders of Abercrombie & Fitch Co. filed a derivative suit on behalf of the company against several officers and directors alleging that the defendants caused Abercrombie to make misleading public statements between June 2 and August 18, 2005, which caused stock prices to rise and then fall once the falsity of the statements were revealed. According to the complaint, Abercrombie adopted a business model of selling products with a low manufacturing cost at high retail prices, resulting in a high per-unit margin. The company sought to create such a desired brand that it could "train" its customers to not expect a sale or markdowns and instead just pay the high price. This approach manifested itself most particularly in Abercrombie's denim products. Abercrombie issued reports indicating that its denim sales were strong and that its high gross margin business strategy was working. The shareholders allege that these statements were misleading because company insiders knew that Abercrombie was amassing a large surplus of inventory such that there would have to be dramatic markdowns to clear out the inventory, causing a negative correction in the company's stock price. The stock price eventually did fall, which kicked off a spate of lawsuits and regulatory investigations. During this time, when the insiders are alleged to have known that the price would soon fall, five of the defendants—Singer, Jeffries, Bachmann, Kessler, and Griffin—sold a large number of their personally owned shares of Abercrombie stock. The corporation formed an SLC, consisting of board members Allan Tuttle and Lauren Brisky. During the investigation Mr. Tuttle recused himself from considering claims against Mr. Singer, Abercrombie's president, COO, and CFO, due to a prior relationship at the Gucci company. The SLC recommended that the corporation seek dismissal of the suit, and the district court granted a motion to dismiss. The shareholders appealed.

DECISION: The court of appeals reversed the district court, having serious doubts about Mr. Tuttle's independence because he recused himself from considering the claims against the person at the very center of the alleged improper activity. When Tuttle recused himself from considering the claims against Singer, he essentially launched a signal flare that he was not independent. Mr. Singer, as the COO, appears to have been heavily involved in the strategy of touting the success of the business model to the market. He was also alleged to have engaged in insider trading. Without a demonstration that its SLC was independent, the corporation's motion to dismiss based on the SLC's recommendation could not be granted. [*Booth Family Trust v. Jeffries,* **640 F.3d 134 (6th Cir. 2011)**]

Mere allegations that a director and other directors move in the same social circles or are characterized as close friends is not enough to negate a director's independence for presuit demand excusal purposes.

Lawsuits may be brought by minority shareholders against majority shareholders who are oppressive toward minority shareholders. Oppressive conduct may include payment of grossly excessive salaries and fringe benefits to the majority stockholders who are also officers of the corporation. Shareholders may bring a derivative action to obtain a dissolution of the corporation by judicial decree.[28]

D. LIABILITY OF SHAREHOLDERS

A shareholder is ordinarily protected from the liabilities of the corporation. Some exceptions exist, however.

---

[28] *Miller v. Up In Smoke, Inc.,* 738 F. Supp.2d 878 (N.D. Ind. 2010). But see *Whithorn v. Whithorn Farms, Inc.,* 195 P.3d 836 (Mont. 2008).

20. Limited Liability

The liability of a shareholder is generally limited. This means that the shareholder is not personally liable for the debts and liabilities of the corporation. The capital contributed by shareholders may be exhausted by the claims of creditors, but there is no personal liability for any unpaid balance.

21. Ignoring the Corporate Entity

Ordinarily a corporation is regarded and treated as a separate legal entity, and the law does not look behind a corporation to see who owns or controls it.

The fact that two corporations have identical shareholders does not justify a court's regarding the two corporations as one. Similarly, the fact that there is a close working relationship between two corporations does not in itself constitute any basis for ignoring their separate corporate entities when they in fact are separately run enterprises.

(A) "PIERCING THE CORPORATE VEIL." A court may disregard the corporate entity, or figuratively "pierce the corporate veil," when exceptional circumstances warrant. The decision whether to disregard the corporate entity is made on a case-by-case basis, weighing all factors before the court. Factors that may lead to piercing the corporate veil and imposing liability on its owners (the shareholders) are (1) the failure to maintain adequate corporate records and the commingling of corporate and other funds,[29] (2) grossly inadequate capitalization,[30] (3) the diversion by shareholders of corporate funds or assets,[31] (4) the formation of the corporation to evade an existing obligation, (5) the formation of the corporation to perpetrate a fraud or conceal illegality, and (6) a determination that injustice and inequitable consequences would result if the corporate entity were recognized.[32]

CASE SUMMARY

Sometimes "Parents" Have to Pay the Rent in Business, Too

FACTS: Inter-Tel is an Arizona corporation that designs, manufactures, and sells telecommunication services primarily to businesses. Inter-Tel Technology Inc. (Technologies) operates Inter-Tel's retail division. On July 2, 1998, Technologies purchased Integrated Telecom

---

[29] *East Market v. Tycorp Pizza IV, Inc.,* 625 S.E.2d 191, 198 (N.C. App. 2006).

[30] In *Trevino v. MERSCORP, Inc.,* 583 F. Supp. 2d 521 (D. Del. 2008), the court determined that a shortage of capital is not per se a reason to pierce the corporate veil; rather, a more relevant inquiry would be "Was the entity established to defraud its creditors?" An example of grossly inadequate capitalization is found in *Klokke Corp. v. Classic Exposition, Inc.,* 912 P.2d 929 (Or. App. 1996), in which Classic's two shareholders invested $1,000 of capital to start a business and immediately took out a $200,000 loan. The business remained undercapitalized until part of it was sold. However, the two shareholders effectively withdrew all of the proceeds of the sale in October 1991, and the business was again without sufficient capital, leaving it unable to meet its financial obligations. The court held that the shareholders were personally liable up to the amount withdrawn in October 1991 after the partial sale of the business.

[31] See *Trustees of the National Elevator Industry Pension Fund v. Lutyk,* 332 F.3d 188 (3d Cir. 2003), in which the Court of Appeals found the equitable remedy of piercing the corporate veil justified. The sole shareholder, Andrew Lutyk, siphoned funds over the final months of the corporation's operations while it was known to be deeply insolvent, used corporate funds to pay entertainment expenses without an identifiable business purpose, and commingled corporate assets with his own. Personal liability was imposed on Lutyk to make unpaid payments to a union's benefit plans.

[32] *Barton v. Moore,* 558 N.W.2d 746 (Minn. 1997).

CASE SUMMARY

Continued

Services Corp. (ITS), with Inter-Tel, the Arizona parent, paying for the stock. ITS was Inter-Tel's first retail branch in Kentucky, selling Inter-Tel's products from an office building in Louisville it leased from Linn Station Properties. After ITS was acquired by Technologies, ITS no longer possessed any financial independence. ITS could not maintain a bank account, hold any funds, or pay any bills. All of ITS's regional offices were transformed from independent dealers of communications equipment into direct sales "branches" of Inter-Tel. ITS employees became employees of Inter-Tel and were paid by Inter-Tel from its headquarters in Arizona. When a customer purchased a telecommunications system from ITS the payment went directly into a "lock box" or depository account controlled by Inter-Tel. Once the funds were placed in this account, they belonged to Inter-Tel. Inter-Tel paid all the vendors who provided ITS with goods and services. Inter-Tel paid ITS's rent for the Linn Station Road property from the time Technologies acquired ITS until ITS abandoned the premises in 2002. Linn Properties sued ITS for unpaid rent and failure to maintain the property, and a default judgment was entered against ITS for $332,900. ITS was a defunct corporation without any assets, so Linn Properties brought a breach of corporate veil action against Technologies and Inter-Tel.

DECISION: Judgment for Linn Properties. Limited liability for corporate entities is described by some scholars as springing from both democratic and economic principles in the early days of the United States. The "imposition of limited liability was perceived as a means of encouraging the small-scale entrepreneur, and of keeping entry into business markets competitive and democratic," assuring that the corporate world was not dominated by industrialists who had the immense personal wealth to withstand any business risk. The economic rationale was that the public would benefit from investment by shareholders who would be willing to take risks in industry, manufacturing, and general commercial development if personal liability could be avoided should their ventures not succeed. By the twentieth century, deliberate misuse of the corporate form by shareholders who were either individuals or other corporations had led courts to authorize piercing the corporate veil. The equitable doctrine of veil piercing cannot be thwarted by having two entities, rather than one, dominate the subsidiary and dividing the conduct between the two so that each can point the finger to some extent at the other. Inter-Tel and Technologies together exercised complete control and dominion over ITS, causing it to lose any semblance of separate corporate existence. Technologies and Inter-Tel transferred all of ITS's income and assets to themselves, thus deriving all of the benefits from the business while leaving behind a shell entity from which a legitimate creditor could recover nothing. Under these circumstances there was the requisite domination and injustice to justify piercing ITS's corporate veil to hold both Technologies and Inter-Tel responsible for the default judgment previously obtained by Linn Station against ITS. [*Inter-Tel Technologies Inc. v. Linn Station Properties, LLC*, 360 S.W.3d 152 (Ky. 2012)]

(B) **"ALTER EGO" THEORY.** Some courts express their reasons for disregarding the corporate entity by stating that the corporation is the *"alter ego"* of the wrongdoer. A corporation is a separate and distinct person from the person or persons who own the corporation. However, when a corporation is so dominated and controlled by a shareholder(s), officer(s), or director(s) that the separate personalities of the individual and the corporation no longer exist and there is a wrongful use of that control, the courts will disregard the corporate entity so as not to sanction a fraud or injustice.[33] **For Example,** V&M Industries, Inc., owned land on which some 40,000 plus used tires caught fire. It took nearly a week to extinguish the fire and caused severe air pollution in the St. Louis area. Vernon Leirer originally owned 99 percent of V&M corporate stock; all corporate officers other than Leirer were nonfunctioning; the corporation was inadequately capitalized; no stock certificates were issued; and corporate records were generally not kept. At a time just before the fire, when Leirer was no longer a shareholder or officer, he exercised total direction and control over the corporation and "ran the show." The court held that to adhere to the fiction of separate corporate existence would sanction fraud. It concluded that V&M, Inc., was the *alter ego* for Leirer, and Leirer was personally responsible for civil penalties under the Environmental Protection Act.[34]

Limited liability is important to our economy because it encourages investors to make investments in high-risk ventures. It should be disregarded only in exceptional circumstances. When fraud or deceit is absent, other circumstances for piercing the corporate veil must be so strong as to clearly indicate that the corporation is the alter ego of the controlling person.

(c) OBTAINING ADVANTAGES OF CORPORATE EXISTENCE. Courts will not go behind the corporate identity merely because the corporation has been formed to obtain tax savings or to obtain limited liability for its shareholders. Similarly, the corporate entity will not be ignored merely because the corporation does not have sufficient assets to pay the claims against it.

One-person, family, and other closely held corporations are permissible and entitled to all of the advantages of corporate existence. The fact that the principal shareholder runs or oversees the day-to-day operations does not justify ignoring the corporate entity.

22. Other Exceptions to Limited Liability

Liability may be imposed on a shareholder as though there were no corporation when the court ignores the corporate entity either because of the particular circumstances of the case or because the corporation is so defectively organized that it is deemed not to exist.

(a) WAGE CLAIMS. Statutes sometimes provide that the shareholders shall have unlimited liability for the wage claims of corporate employees. This exception has been abandoned in some states in recent years or has been confined to corporate officers who are active in corporate decision making.[35]

(b) UNPAID SUBSCRIPTIONS. Most states prohibit the issuance of par value shares for less than par or except for "money, labor done, or property actually received." Whenever shares issued by a corporation are not fully paid for, the original subscriber receiving the shares, or any transferee who does not give value or who knows that the shares were not fully paid for, is liable for the unpaid balance if the corporation is insolvent and the money is required to pay its creditors.[36]

[33] *Dishon v. Ponthie,* 918 So.2d 1132 (La. App. 2005).
[34] *Illinois v. V&M Industries,* 700 N.E.2d 746 (Ill. App. 1998).
[35] *Cusimano v. Metro Auto, Inc.,* 860 P.2d 532 (Colo. App. 1993).
[36] *Frasier v. Trans-Western Land Corp.,* 316 N.W.2d 612 (Neb. 1982). But see *Brunfield v. Horn,* 547 So.2d 415 (Ala. 1989).

CASE SUMMARY

You've Got to Pay for Your Stock, Silly

FACTS: On July 19, 1984, Keith and Joan Bryan incorporated Bryan's Inc. The corporation was authorized to issue 100 shares of stock with a par value of $1,000 per share. The corporation issued 50 shares to Keith and 50 shares to Joan, although it did not receive any payment in labor, services, money, or property for the stock. On August 30, 1984, Bryan's Inc. bought Hanewald's dry goods store, giving Hanewald a promissory note for part of the purchase price. The business was not successful, and after four months, Keith and Joan Bryan decided to close the store. They disbursed all of the corporation's funds in payment of all bills except for the debt owed Hanewald. No corporate funds were available to pay this debt. Hanewald sued the Bryans individually for the amount owed. The Bryans contended that they were not personally liable for the corporation's debts.

DECISION: Judgment for Hanewald. Organizing a corporation to avoid personal liability is legitimate and a primary advantage to doing business in the corporate form. But proper capitalization is the principal prerequisite for this limited liability. Keith and Joan Bryan's failure to pay for their stock makes them liable to Hanewald, the corporate creditor, to the extent that the stock was not paid for. Because the debt to Hanewald, $36,000, was less than the par value of their stock, $100,000, the Bryans are personally liable for the entire corporate debt owed to Hanewald. [*Hanewald v. Bryan's, Inc.*, 429 N.W.2d 414 (N.D. 1988)]

If the corporation has issued the shares as fully paid for, has given them as a bonus, or has agreed to release the subscriber for the unpaid balance, the corporation cannot recover that balance. The fact that the corporation is thus barred does not prevent creditors of the corporation from bringing an action to compel payment of the balance. The same rules are applied when stock is issued as fully paid for in return for property or services that were overvalued so that the stock is not actually paid for in full. A conflict of authority exists, however, as to whether the shareholder is liable from the mere fact that the property or service given for the shares was in fact overvalued by the directors or whether it must also be shown that the directors acted in bad faith in making the erroneous valuation. The trend of modern statutes is, in the absence of proof of fraud, to prohibit disputing the valuation placed by the corporation on services or property.

(c) UNAUTHORIZED DIVIDENDS. If dividends are improperly paid out of capital, shareholders are generally liable to creditors to the extent of such depletion of capital. In some states, the liability of a shareholder depends on whether the corporation was insolvent at the time and whether debts were existing at the time.

23. The Professional Corporation

The extent to which incorporation limits the liability of shareholders of a professional corporation depends on the interpretation of the statute under which the corporation was formed.

(A) ACT OF SHAREHOLDER IN CREATING LIABILITY. The statutes that authorize the formation of professional corporations usually require that share ownership be limited to duly licensed professionals. If a shareholder in a professional corporation, such as a corporation of physicians, negligently drives the professional corporation's automobile in going to attend a patient or is personally obligated on a contract made for the corporation or is guilty of malpractice, the physician-shareholder is liable without limit for the liability that has been created. This is the same rule of law that applies in the case of the ordinary business corporation.

Professional corporation statutes generally repeat the rule governing malpractice liability by stating that the liability of a shareholder for malpractice is not affected by the fact of incorporation.

(B) MALPRACTICE LIABILITY OF AN ASSOCIATE. The liability of a shareholder in a professional corporation for the malpractice of an associate varies from state to state depending on the language of the professional corporation statute in effect and on the court decisions under the statute.[37]

If the statute provides for limited liability, as in a business corporation, then where doctors *A, B,* and *C* are a professional corporation, *A* and *B* will not be liable for the malpractice of *C* beyond the extent of corporate assets. If the statute provides for vicarious personal liability, as in a partnership, and doctors *A, B,* and *C* are a professional corporation, each will have unlimited liability for any malpractice liability incurred by the others. Often the statutory reference to malpractice liability is not very clear, and the courts are called on to resolve the question of the liability of a professional shareholder for the malpractice of an associate.

LawFlix

Meet Joe Black (1998) (PG-13)

A transfer of corporate control and the role of shareholder control is at the heart of this film about a corporation under takeover fire.

---

[37] ABA Model Professional Corporation Act Amendments (1984) §34 offers three alternative positions regarding the liability of shareholders: (1) limited liability, as in a business corporation, (2) vicarious personal liability, as in a partnership, and (3) personal liability limited in amount and conditioned on financial responsibility in the form of insurance or a surety bond.

MAKE THE CONNECTION

SUMMARY

The ownership of a corporation is evidenced by a holder's shares of stock that have been issued by the corporation. Common stock is ordinary stock that has no preferences but entitles the holder to (1) participate in the control of the corporation by exercising one vote per share of record, (2) share in the profits in the form of dividends, and (3) participate, upon dissolution, in the distribution of net assets after the satisfaction of all creditors (including bondholders). Other classes of stock exist, such as preferred stock, that have priority over common stock with regard to distribution of dividends and/or assets upon liquidation. Shares may be acquired by subscription of an original issue or by transfer of existing shares.

Bonds are debt securities, and a bondholder is a creditor rather than an owner of the corporation. Bondholders' interests are represented by an indenture trustee who is responsible for ensuring that the corporation complies with the terms of the bond indenture.

Shareholders control the corporation, but this control is indirect. Through their voting rights, they elect directors, and by this means, they can control the corporation. *Preemptive rights*, if they exist, allow shareholders to maintain their voting percentages when the corporation issues additional shares of stock. Shareholders have the right to inspect the books of the corporation unless it would be harmful to the corporation. Shareholders also have the right to receive dividends when declared at the discretion of

the directors. Shareholders may bring a derivative action on behalf of the corporation for damages to the corporation. Shareholders are ordinarily protected from liability for the acts of the corporation.

Ordinarily, each corporation is treated as a separate person, and the law does not look beyond the corporate identity merely because the corporation was formed to obtain tax savings or limited liability. The fact that two corporations have the same shareholders does not justify disregarding the separate corporate entities. However, when a corporation is formed to perpetrate a fraud, a court ignores the corporate form, or "pierces the corporate veil." The corporate form is also ignored to prevent injustice or because of the functional reality that the two corporations in question are one.

LEARNING OUTCOMES

After studying this chapter, you should be able to clearly explain:

A. Corporate Stocks and Bonds

L0.1 Explain how to calculate the book value of a share of stock
See the example in which Roger Eggett was awarded the book value of his stock, p. 1001.

L0.2 Distinguish between stocks and bonds
See the discussion of stocks as an ownership interest in a corporation and bonds as a corporate debt, beginning on p. 1002.

B. Acquisition of Shares

L0.3 Distinguish between subscriptions for and transfers of stock
See the discussion of stock subscriptions for new issues of stock on p. 1004.
See the discussion of transfers of shares and the impact of restrictions, beginning on p. 1004.

C. Rights of Shareholders

L0.4 Explain the rights of shareholders
See the discussion of shareholder ownership rights, including the right to

vote, inspect books and records, and receive dividends when declared, beginning on p. 1008.

L0.5 Explain the nature of a shareholder derivative lawsuit
See the *AIG* case, where stockholder plaintiffs were excused from making a demand on the full board, p. 1014.
See the Abercrombie & Fitch Co. litigation where the court did not defer to the special litigation committee (SLC) because one of the two members was not "independent," p. 1015.

D. Liability of Shareholders

L0.6 Explain the exceptions to the limited liability of shareholders
See the *Inter-Tel* case where "grandparent" and "parent" corporations transferred all income and assets to themselves, and as a result the corporate entities were disregarded to accomplish justice, pp. 1016–1017.

KEY TERMS

acceptance
bond
bond indenture
book value
capital stock
certificate of stock
common stock
cumulative voting
debenture

deed
derivative (secondary)
  action
indenture trustee
market value
maturity date
outstanding
par value
preemptive right

preferred stock
proxy
registered bonds.
sinking fund
stock subscription
voting by proxy
voting trust
wasting assets
  corporations

QUESTIONS AND CASE PROBLEMS

1. Monica Beam, a shareholder of Martha Stewart Living Omnimedia, Inc. (MSO), filed a derivative action against Martha Stewart and the other MSO board of directors, alleging that Stewart breached her duties to MSO by illegally selling ImClone stock and mishandling media attention, thereby jeopardizing the financial future of MSO. Ms. Beam asserted that it would be a futile act to make a demand on the corporation because a majority of the outside directors were not independent of Stewart. Ms. Beam pleaded the particularized facts that director Darla Moore attended a wedding reception hosted by Stewart's personal lawyer for his daughter and was a longtime friend of Stewart; and that director Naomi Seligman made a phone call to publisher John Wiley, Inc., to express concern over a planned book critical of Stewart. Should Ms. Beam be excused from making a demand on the board of directors to pursue the derivative action because the outside directors were not independent of Stewart? [*Beam v. Stewart*, 845 A.2d 1040 (Del)]

2. Six members of the Weston family, who owned 6.8 percent of the stock of Weston Paper and Manufacturing Company, brought suit against three corporate directors and CFIS, a firm hired by the company to make the annual evaluation of the company's stock for allocating stock options to its employees. The Westons stated that their claims against the defendants were personal claims, alleging that they were injured by CFIS and the three directors who kept the price of the stock low to obtain more shares of stock through the stock option plan. From an adverse ruling on their right to maintain a direct action against the directors, the Westons appealed. How would you decide this case? [*Weston v. Weston Paper and Manufacturing Co.*, 74 Ohio 377]

3. Tomlinson and Hubbard were two of five shareholders in Multimedia Software Distributors, a corporation. The corporation was formed in 1992 and filed for bankruptcy in 1994. In 1996, Tomlinson filed a claim in his own name, alleging that Hubbard had breached his fiduciary duties to Tomlinson by diverting proceeds owned by Multimedia to another business owned by Hubbard. Hubbard contends that Tomlinson is an improper plaintiff. Decide. [*Hubbard v. Tomlinson*, 747 N.E.2d 69 (Ind. App.)]

4. Russell Nugent was involved in the roofing business in Kansas City, incorporating his business as Russell Nugent Roofing, Inc. In 1985, the name was changed to On Top Roofing, Incorporated. On August 27, 1987, On Top, Inc., ceased to exist, and RNR, Inc., was incorporated. RNR, Inc., went out of business in 1988, and RLN Construction, Inc., was incorporated. In 1989, the business was organized as Russell Nugent, Inc. Nugent and his wife had been sole shareholders, officers, and directors of each corporation. When one roofing company was incorporated, the prior roofing company ceased doing business. All of the companies were located at the same business address and used the same telephone number. Nugent paid himself and his wife more than $100,000 in salaries in 1986. In 1986, the

corporation paid $99,290 in rent for property that the Nugents owned. Nugent testified that he changed to a new corporation every time he needed to get a "fresh start." The evidence showed that he used the On Top Roofing logo on his trucks and Yellow Pages advertisements throughout the period of the successive corporations. Suppliers who were not paid for materials in 1986 and 1987 by the insolvent corporations sought to pierce the corporate veils and hold Nugent personally liable. Nugent defended that as a shareholder, he had no personal liability. Decide. [*K.C. Roofing Center v. On Top Roofing, Inc.*, 807 S.W.2d 545 (Mo. App.)]

5. The stock of West End Development Co. was subject to a transfer restriction. This restriction required that any shareholder selling shares first offer every other shareholder the right to purchase a proportion of the shares being sold. The proportions were to be the same as the percentages of the outstanding shares that the other shareholders already owned. This restriction was stated in the articles of incorporation but was not stated on the stock certificate of the corporation. The Taylors owned stock in the company and sold their stock to Vroom, an officer of the corporation, without first offering any stock to the other shareholders, as required by the restriction. The other shareholders brought an action against Vroom to recover from him the percentages of the shares they would have been entitled to if the Taylors had followed the transfer restriction. Decide. [*Irwin v. West End Development Co.*, 481 F.2d 34 (10th Cir.)]

6. Siebrecht organized Siebrecht Realty Co., a corporation, and then transferred his building to the corporation in exchange for its stock. The corporation rented different parts of the building to different tenants. Elenkrieg, an employee of one of the tenants, fell and was injured because of the defective condition of a stairway. She sued Siebrecht individually on the ground that the corporation had been formed by him for the purpose of securing limited liability. Decide. [*Elenkrieg v. Siebrecht*, 144 N.E. 519 (N.Y.)]

7. William Carter, a former officer and employee of Wilson Construction Co., Inc., owned 317

shares of stock in Wilson. Carter left Wilson to become part owner and employee of C&L Contracting Co., which was a direct competitor of Wilson. Carter requested access to Wilson's corporate books to determine the value of his shares. Wilson refused, not wanting to divulge its business practices to a direct competitor. Decide. [*Carter v. Wilson Construction Co., Inc.*, 348 S.E.2d 830 (N.C. App.)]

8. Ken and Charlotte Maschmeier were the majority shareholders of Southside Press; each owned 1,300 shares. Marty and Larry Maschmeier, who each owned 1,200 shares of the corporation, had a falling out with Ken and Charlotte and were terminated as employees of the business. Ken and Charlotte started a new corporation, which employed most of the employees of the old corporation and which took most of its former customers. Gross receipts of Southside Press went from $613,258 down to $18,172 two years later. The $18,172 figure was from the lease of equipment. Ken and Charlotte continued to draw from Southside annual salaries of $20,000, which were in excess of the gross receipts of the business. Marty and Larry brought suit against Ken and Charlotte, alleging "oppressive" conduct. Ken and Charlotte stated that they had paid Marty and Larry excellent salaries when they were employed by the corporation. Ken and Charlotte contended they had a right to start a new corporation as they saw fit. Decide. [*Maschmeier v. Southside Press, Inc.*, 435 N.W.2d 377 (Iowa App.)]

9. Gladys Boles and 28 other owners of property at Hidden Valley Lakes Development sued the corporate developer, National Development Co. Inc. (NDC); NDC's parent, Sunstates Corporation; and the individual behind both corporations, Clyde Engle, for breach of contract and fraud. The centerpiece of this development, Crystal Lake, a 30-acre recreational lake, failed to hold water; and it was determined that it could never do so. Instead of having a 30-acre lake as the centerpiece, the plaintiffs had a 30-acre hole in the ground. While the controversy over NDC's breach of contract was pending, Engle made a "proposal" to the CEO of NDC to transfer

$2.4 million in receivables to Sunstates in exchange for an unsecured promissory note. Evidence showed that all of Sunstates' assets thereafter were transferred to Engle, making the note NDC held from Sunstates worthless. Sunstates purchased approximately $1.9 million of oriental art, antique jewelry, rare books, and other collectibles, which were maintained in Engle's home in Illinois. Likewise, Sunstates purchased a Rolls Royce from Libco, a corporation in which Engle was the majority shareholder. This automobile also appeared to be in Engle's possession or control. Engles regrets that the lake did not work out, a risk that the developer and the homeowners have to live with, and points out that NDC is a separate legal entity with limited liability for its shareholders. Engle asserts that he is not personally liable for damages in this case. Decide. [*Boles v. National Development Co., Inc.*, 175 N.W.3d 226 (Tenn. App.)]

10. Ed Klein was the sole shareholder, director, and chief executive officer of The Gun Exchange, Inc., a retail firearms dealership. The inventory of The Gun Exchange had been pledged as security for a $622,500 debt owed to InterFirst Bank. It also owed $231,484.60 to Sporting Goods, Inc.; this debt was unsecured. On May 20, InterFirst Bank notified Klein of its intention to foreclose on the inventory and sell it at public auction. InterFirst Bank further advised Klein that, pursuant to his personal guarantee, he would be responsible for any deficiency following the sale. Klein immediately incorporated The Gun Store, Inc., for the purpose of purchasing the assets of The Gun Exchange at the foreclosure sale. Before the foreclosure sale, Klein obtained a $650,000 line of credit from CharterBank on behalf of The Gun Store. At the sale, Klein purchased the assets of The Gun Exchange for $650,000 even though the highest prior bid was $175,000. (Had the $175,000 bid been accepted, Klein would have been personally liable for the deficiency to InterFirst Bank.)

After the foreclosure sale, no funds existed to pay the unsecured creditors of The Gun Exchange. Following the sale, The Gun Store began operating as a retail firearms dealer with the inventory purchased from the foreclosure

sale. It operated in the same location and with the same personnel as The Gun Exchange. Sporting Goods, Inc., sued Klein individually for the $231,484.60. Klein contended that the corporate form under which he did business insulated him as a shareholder from liability for corporate obligations. Decide. Is it ethical to seek limited liability under the corporate form, as Klein did in this case? [*Klein v. Sporting Goods, Inc.*, 772 S.W.2d 173 (Tex. Civ. App.)]

11. Ibanez owned shares of stock in Farmers Underwriters. He left the stock certificate lying on top of his desk in his office. Many persons continually passed through the office, and one day Ibanez realized that someone had taken the certificate from the top of his desk. Ibanez applied to Farmers Underwriters for a duplicate stock certificate. The corporation refused to issue a duplicate on the ground that it was Ibanez's own fault that the original certificate had been stolen. Ibanez claimed that he was entitled to a new certificate even though he had been at fault. Was he correct? [*Ibanez v. Farmers Underwriters Ass'n*, 534 P.2d 1336 (Cal.)]

12. On March 3, 2002, pursuant to a public offering, First All State Trucking Corp. (FAST) issued securities to investors in denominations of $1,000. The interest rate was 7 percent per year payable semiannually, and the maturity date was March 3, 2010. The rights and obligations of the issuer, FAST, and the holders of the securities were set forth in an indenture agreement. Because the securities were not secured by a mortgage or lien on corporate property, Alec believes they are shares of preferred stock. Is Alec correct? Fully explain the type of security involved, and discuss the extent of the holders' voting rights.

13. Linhart owned shares of stock in First National Bank. She borrowed money from the bank and pledged the stock as security. She later decided to transfer 70 head of cattle and the shares of stock to her son, but she could not deliver the share certificate to him because it was held by the bank. She therefore executed a bill of sale reciting the transfer of the cattle and the stock to the son. She gave him the bill of sale, and he had the bill recorded. After her death, the son brought an

action to determine the ownership of the stock. Was the son the owner of the shares?

14. Birt was a hospital patient. The doctor who treated him was a shareholder of a professional corporation organized under the Indiana Medical Professional Corporation Act. Birt claimed that the doctor who treated him was guilty of malpractice, and he sued the doctor. He also sued the professional corporation and all of its officers, directors, and shareholders. These other defendants asserted that they were not liable because the corporate entity shielded them. The plaintiff claimed that the corporation was not a shield because in fact all of the persons were rendering medical services and should be held liable as in a partnership. The statute did not expressly regulate the matter of limited liability beyond declaring that it did not change the law between a person supplying medical services and the patient. Decide. [*Birt v. St. Mary Mercy Hospital*, 370 N.E.2d 379 (Ind. App.)]

15. Ronald Naquin, an employee of Air Engineered Systems & Services, Inc., owned one-third of its outstanding shares. After six years, he was fired and an offer was made to buy out his interest in Air Engineered at a price that Naquin thought inadequate. He then formed a competing business and made a written request to examine the corporate records of Air Engineered. This request was denied. Naquin filed suit to require Air Engineered to allow him to examine the books. Air Engineered raised the defense that he was a competitor seeking to gain unfair competitive advantage. Decide. [*Naquin v. Air Engineered Systems & Services, Inc.*, 463 So.2d 992 (La. App.)]

CPA QUESTIONS

1. A stockholder's right to inspect books and records of a corporation will be properly denied if the stockholder:

   a. Wants to use corporate stockholder records for a personal business

   b. Employs an agent to inspect the books and records

   c. Intends to commence a stockholder's derivative suit

   d. Is investigating management misconduct

2. The limited liability of a stockholder in a closely held corporation may be challenged successfully if the stockholder:

   a. Undercapitalized the corporation when it was formed

   b. Formed the corporation solely to have limited personal liability

   c. Sold property to the corporation

   d. Was a corporate officer, director, or employee

3. Price owns 2,000 shares of Universal Corp.'s $10 cumulative preferred stock. During its first year of operations, cash dividends of $5 per share were declared on the preferred stock but were never paid. In the second year, dividends on the preferred stock were neither declared nor paid. If Universal is dissolved, which of the following statements is correct?

   a. Universal will be liable to Price as an unsecured creditor for $10,000.

   b. Universal will be liable to Price as a secured creditor for $20,000.

   c. Price will have priority over the claims of Universal's bond owners.

   d. Price will have priority over the claims of Universal's unsecured judgment creditors.

4. Under the Revised Model Business Corporation Act, a dissenting stockholder's appraisal right generally applies to which of the following corporate actions?

	Consolidations	Shares from mergers
a.	Yes	Yes
b.	Yes	No
c.	No	Yes
d.	No	No

© Manuel Gutjahr/iStockphoto.com

CHAPTER 46

Securities Regulation

learningoutcomes

After studying this chapter, you should be able to

LO.1 Explain the meaning of state "blue sky laws"

LO.2 Define "security"

LO.3 Compare and distinguish between the Securities Act of 1933 and the Securities Exchange Act of 1934

LO.4 Explain how the 1934 Act's policy of fostering reliance on market integrity is served by Rule 10b-5 private investor lawsuits when injured by material misstatements by the issuer

LO.5 Explain the factors that subject an individual to liability for insider trading

LO.6 Explain how securities firms regulate themselves and provide a process to resolve controversies relating to the sale of securities

I s there anything that protects you when you buy corporate securities?

A. STATE REGULATION

To protect the public from the sale of fraudulent securities, many states have adopted statutes regulating the intrastate sale of securities.

CPA

blue sky laws – state statutes designed to protect the public from the sale of worthless stocks and bonds.

1. State Blue Sky Laws

State laws regulating securities are called **blue sky laws**. The term *blue sky* is derived from the purpose of such laws, which is to prevent the sale of speculative schemes that have no more value than the blue sky. The state statutes vary in detail. They commonly contain (1) an antifraud provision prohibiting fraudulent practices and imposing criminal penalties for violations, (2) broker-dealer licensing provisions regulating the persons engaged in the securities business, and (3) provisions for the registration of securities, including disclosure requirements, with a designated government official.

A Uniform Securities Act, covering the foregoing three categories of regulations, exists to provide guidance to states in updating their securities laws. This act also contains alternative regulations that can be adopted by states with different regulatory philosophies.

2. National Securities Markets Improvement Act

Congress reallocated responsibility between state and federal security regulators in the National Securities Markets Improvement Act (NSMIA) of 1996,[1] recognizing that the dual system of state and federal regulation of securities resulted in duplicative regulation and expenses. Title I of the act exempts from state review and registration securities offered by mutual funds and stocks listed on the New York Stock Exchange, the NASDAQ National Market system, and other stock exchanges identified by the Securities and Exchange Commission (SEC). The act preserves the states' authority to investigate and bring enforcement actions for fraud or deceit or for unlawful conduct by a broker or dealer in connection with securities transactions.[2] Also, the states may continue to collect filing fees for securities in effect as of October 25, 1996. The act also eliminates duplicative registration requirements for investment advisors by dividing regulatory authority between the SEC, which exclusively regulates investment advisors with assets under management of $25 million or more, and the states, which have the responsibility to regulate all investment advisors managing lower sums of money.[3]

B. FEDERAL REGULATION

The stock market crash of 1929 and the Great Depression that followed led to the enactment of federal legislation to regulate the securities industry.

---

[1] P.L. 104-290, 110 Stat 3416, 15 U.S.C. §78a nt.
[2] The 1996 Act amends §18(c) of the 1933 Securities Act to accomplish this result.
[3] NSMIA §303(a), which adds a new §203A to the Investment Advisors Act of 1940.

3. Federal Laws Regulating the Securities Industry

Six federal securities regulation laws were passed between 1933 and 1940. The two principal laws that provide the basic framework for the federal regulation of the sale of securities in interstate commerce are the Securities Act of 1933 and the Securities Exchange Act of 1934.

The 1933 act deals with the original distribution of securities by the issuing corporations. It is a disclosure statute designed to secure essential facts for the investor. The 1934 act is concerned with the secondary distribution of securities in the national securities exchanges and in the over-the-counter markets. That is, the 1933 act regulates the issuance of securities by a corporation to the first owner. The 1934 act regulates the sale of securities from one owner to another. Four other federal laws deal with specific aspects of the securities industry.[4] These aspects include holding companies in utility businesses, trustees for debt securities, mutual funds, and investment advisors.

The Securities Enforcement Remedies and Penny Stock Reform Act of 1990[5] (Remedies Act) expands the enforcement remedies of the SEC to reduce fraudulent financial reporting and financial fraud. Under the Remedies Act, the SEC may start administrative proceedings against any person or entity, whether regulated by the SEC or not, and may issue a temporary cease-and-desist order prior to notice and a hearing. The SEC may also order an accounting and disgorgement of ill-gotten gains. In addition, the Remedies Act authorizes courts to bar individuals who have engaged in fraudulent activities from serving as officers and directors of public corporations.

The Securities Acts Amendments of 1990[6] authorize sanctions against SEC-regulated persons for violation of foreign laws. The amendments facilitate the ability of the SEC and foreign regulators to exchange information and cooperate in international securities law enforcement.

The Market Reform Act of 1990[7] was enacted to provide the SEC with powers to deal with market volatility. Under the law, the SEC has the power to suspend all trading when markets are excessively volatile. Also, the SEC may require "large traders" to identify themselves and provide information concerning their trading.

The Private Securities Litigation Reform Act (PSLRA) of 1995[8] was passed to alleviate abuses in private securities litigation. The intent of the act is to reduce the number of lawsuits brought against issuers of securities and accounting firms. This law applies only to private securities litigation, and the SEC's enforcement activities are not affected by the act.

The NSMIA, previously referred to in regard to the allocation of responsibility for securities regulation between the states and the federal government, also provides for national standards allowing brokers and dealers to improve their ability to borrow funds to finance market-making and underwriting activities.[9] This act also provides new national standards regulating margin restriction.

---

[4] The Public Utility Holding Company Act of 1935 (15 U.S.C. §79 *et seq.*) provides comprehensive regulation of holding companies and their subsidiaries in interstate gas and electric utilities businesses. The Trust Indenture Act of 1939 (15 U.S.C. §§77aaa to 77bbb) was enacted to protect the interests of the holders of bonds and other debt securities offered to the public in interstate commerce by requiring the appointment of independent institutional trustees. The Investment Company Act of 1940 (15 U.S.C. §§80a-1 to 80a-52) provides for the registration and comprehensive regulation of mutual funds and all other investment companies. The Investment Advisors Act of 1940 (15 U.S.C. §§80b-1 to 80b-21) requires registration with the Securities and Exchange Commission of all persons engaged in the business of providing investment advice in interstate commerce. In 1970, the Securities Investors Protection Act was enacted to protect investors from the business failures of brokers and dealers.

[5] P.L. 101-429, 104 Stat. 931, 15 U.S.C. §77g.

[6] P.L. 101-550, 104 Stat. 2713, 15 U.S.C. §78a.

[7] P.L. 101-432, 104 Stat. 963, 15 U.S.C. §78a.

[8] P.L. 104-67, 109 Stat. 737, 15 U.S.C. §78a nt.

[9] NSMIA §104 P.L. 104-290, 110 Stat. 3416, 15 U.S.C. §776.

E-Commerce & Cyberlaw

Facilitation of the Use of Electronic Record Keeping

Under the Electronic Signatures in Global and National Commerce Act (E-Sign), brokerage firms and mutual funds may avoid the expense of paper mailings of legally required documents, such as monthly statements, trade confirmations, prospectuses, and financial reports, and deliver these documents or "records" by electronic means. The consumer must, however, consent to receiving these electronic records, and the consumer must consent electronically or confirm the consent electronically. Moreover, firms must inform consumers of their right to receive hard copy documents.

The Sarbanes-Oxley Act of 2002[10] contains numerous reforms regarding corporate accountability, enhanced disclosure requirements, auditor- and accounting-related provisions, and enforcement and liability provisions, which will be discussed in this chapter and the subsequent chapter on accountants' liability.

The Dodd-Frank Wall Street Reform and Consumer Protection Act of 2010[11] contains numerous reforms and initiatives to create a sound economic foundation to grow jobs, protect consumers, and reform Wall Street to protect the economy, American consumers, investors, and businesses. To prevent another financial crisis the Act created the Financial Stability Oversight Council to oversee the various government agencies responsible for regulating financial institutions. Many sections of the Act require various studies to be undertaken and mandate or permit rulemaking by the Commodity Futures Trading Commission and the SEC. The impact of this comprehensive law will become increasingly apparent as rulemaking advances.[12]

CPA

4. Definition of Security

securities – stocks and bonds issued by a corporation. Under some investor protection laws, the term includes any interest in an enterprise that provides unearned income to its owner.

For the securities acts to apply, the transaction must involve a "security" within the meaning of the acts.[13] Congress adopted a definition of **security** sufficiently broad to encompass virtually any instrument that might be sold as an investment.

The definition of *security* includes not only investment instruments such as stocks and bonds but also "investment contracts." The definition of an *investment contract*, developed by the Supreme Court, is sufficiently broad to allow the securities acts to apply to a wide range of investment transactions or schemes, including the sale of bottled whiskey, cattle-breeding programs, and a limited liability partnership to

---

[10] P.L. 107-204, 116 Stat. 745.

[11] P.L. 111-203, 124 Stat. 1376, 15 U.S.C. §8305 (2012).

[12] See, for example, *Statement of General Policy on the Sequencing of the Compliance Dates for Final Rules Applicable to Security-Based Swaps Adopted Pursuant to the Securities Exchange Act of 1934* and the *Dodd-Frank Wall Street Reform and Consumer Protection Act*, 77 F.R. 35625 (June 14, 2012).

    Political considerations may also impede the rulemaking process. For example, Sections 1502 and 1504 of the Act required the SEC to produce final rules mandating disclosures relating to conflict minerals and payments made by U.S. oil, gas, and mining companies to foreign government for projects in their countries, such as money for production licenses, taxes, and royalties. Congress required disclosure of payments for conflict minerals being used to finance the war in the Democratic Republic of the Congo or a neighboring country. Moreover, the nontransparent payments weigh on developing nations' growth and are a risk to investors and the public. Major oil companies believe that the proposed rules by the SEC will provide a competitive advantage to Russian and Chinese firms not bound by the Dodd-Frank mandates. The SEC is well past the April 17, 2011, statutory deadline for a final rule.

[13] The Supreme Court has consistently held that the definition of a security set forth in §3(a)(10) of the 1934 Act is identical to the definition set forth in §2(1) of the 1933 Act. The definition of security under these acts is not to be confused with the narrower definition in Article 8 of the Uniform Commercial Code. See *SEC v. Infinity Group Co.*, 993 F. Supp. 321 (E.D. Pa. 1998).

operate local telephone companies.[14] Under the Supreme Court's definition, an investment contract exists if the following elements are present: (1) an investment of money, (2) a common enterprise, and (3) an expectation of future profits from the efforts of others. **For Example,** the sale of citrus groves to investors, coupled with the execution of service contracts to plant, harvest, and sell the fruit and the distribution of the profits of the venture to the investors, is an investment contract. An instrument denominated as a "note" may in fact be a "security" subject to regulation under the 1934 act.[15]

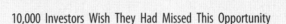

CASE SUMMARY

10,000 Investors Wish They Had Missed This Opportunity

FACTS: "Opportunity doesn't always knock ... sometimes it rings" (ETS Payphones promotional brochure). And sometimes it hangs up. So it did for the 10,000 people who invested a total of $300 million in the payphone sale-and-leaseback arrangements touted by ETS under that slogan. Charles Edwards was the chairman, chief executive officer, and sole shareholder of ETS Payphones, Inc. Acting partly through a subsidiary, ETS sold payphones to the public via independent distributors. The payphones were offered packaged with a site lease, a five-year leaseback and management agreement, and a buyback agreement. The purchase price for the payphone packages was approximately $7,000. Under the leaseback and management agreement, purchasers received $82 per month, a 14 percent annual return. Purchasers were not involved in the day-to-day operation of the payphones they owned. ETS selected the site for the phones, installed the equipment, arranged for connection and long distance service, collected coin revenues, and maintained and repaired the phones. Under the buyback agreement, ETS promised to refund the full purchase price of the package at the end of the lease or within 180 days of the purchaser's request. The payphones did not generate enough revenue for ETS to make the payments required by the leaseback agreements, so the company depended on funds from new investors to meet its obligations. In September 2000, ETS filed for bankruptcy protection. The SEC brought this civil enforcement action alleging that Edwards and ETS had violated the registration requirements and antifraud provisions of the 1933 act. The district court concluded the arrangement was an "investment contract" subject to the securities laws. The Eleventh Circuit Court of Appeals reversed the lower court because the scheme offered a contractual entitlement to a fixed rather than a variable return.

DECISION: Judgment for the SEC. Congress's purpose in enacting the securities laws was to regulate investments in whatever form they are made and by whatever name they are called. To that end, it enacted a broad definition of "security" sufficient to encompass virtually any instrument that might be sold as an investment. The U.S. Supreme Court applied the *Hovey* test for an investment contract finding (1) an investment of money, (2) a common enterprise, and (3) an expectation of future "profits" from the efforts of others, including fixed returns based on contracts. The Court determined that the ETS investment scheme can be an "investment contract" and thus a "security" under the securities laws. It reversed and remanded the case to the Court of Appeals. [*SEC v. Edwards*, **540** U.S. 389 (2004)]

5. Securities Act of 1933

The 1933 act deals with the original issue of securities. It prohibits the offer or sale of securities to the public in interstate commerce before a registration statement is

---

[14] *SEC v. Shiner*, 268 F. Supp. 2d 1333 (S.D. Fla. 2003).
[15] *SEC v. Wallenbrock*, 313 F.3d 532 (9th Cir. 2002).

Thinking Things Through

Problem: Conflicts of Interest—Remedy: Commonsense Rules

Full-service brokerage firms serve both retail and corporate clients. On the retail side, brokers buy and sell stocks and bonds for retail clients from all walks of life. The firms' research analysts perform the very important function of studying the performance of companies listed on the major stock exchanges, and the analysts make recommendations on these companies' securities, such as "buy," "hold," or "sell," for the benefit of their brokers and clients. Brokerage firms also serve corporate clients by underwriting and distributing new issues of stocks and bonds. This is called the INVESTMENT BANKING function of the firm. When a manufacturing or service company issues securities for the first time, the transaction is called an INITIAL PUBLIC OFFERING or IPO. Lucrative fees are earned by brokerage firms from the successful placement of such issues. These securities are sold to retail clients and the public by the brokerage firms, with firm analysts' recommendations being an important element in the success of the placements and the overall profitability of the brokerage firms.

An investigation into Merrill Lynch by the New York Attorney General's Office revealed that while certain Merrill analysts were publicly recommending certain technology companies that were investment banking clients of the firm, internal e-mails indicated that these analysts believed the same companies were "crap" and "junk." One wrote to a colleague questioning his "positive" recommendation of a company whose numbers seemed weak to her, and his response to her was, he had written "pos," in place of [expletive deleted].

The public and retail clients believed that the firm's analysts were independent of the investment banking function of the firm and that

the recommendations were made solely with retail clients' interests in mind. The New York Attorney General's Office concluded, however, that analysts and investment bankers were closely involved in each other's work and were not independent; that the analyst department's compensation was tied to the results of the investment banking department's results; and that analysts were negotiating with investment banking clients for ratings.

Now the SEC has rules that eliminate this type of blatant conflict of interest at full-service brokerage firms. These rules are based on management common sense. The rules include the following: (1) Investment banking divisions may not supervise firms' analysts, (2) compensation for analysts may not be linked to specific investment banking transactions, (3) analysts must disclose whether they own shares in a company they recommend and certify that their recommendations are their true opinions, (4) analysts appearing in public forums before the media must disclose whether they have an interest in the company being discussed, and (5) firms must make comprehensive disclosures about their rating systems and the firms they represent as investment banking clients.*

*Section 501(a) of the Sarbanes-Oxley Act required the SEC to adopt rules that address potential conflicts of interest in securities research. Regulation Analyst Certification ("Regulation AC") requires certification of any research report by an analyst that the views expressed accurately reflect the analyst's personal views. Moreover, the written certification requires disclosure of any compensation received by the analyst that was either directly or indirectly paid in relation to the views or recommendations expressed in the report or the views expressed in any public appearance. The SEC has approved National Association of Securities Dealers (NASD) and New York Stock Exchange (NYSE) rule changes relating to research analyst conflicts of interest.

registration statement—document disclosing specific financial information regarding the security, the issuer, and the underwriter.

prospectus—information provided to each potential purchaser of securities setting forth the key information contained in the registration statement.

filed with the SEC. A **registration statement** is a document disclosing specific financial information regarding the security, the issuer, and the underwriter. The seller must also provide a prospectus to each potential purchaser of the securities. The **prospectus** sets forth the key information contained in the registration statement. The object is to provide the interested investor detailed information about the security and the enterprise. The SEC does not approve or disapprove the securities as being good or bad investments but only reviews the form and content of the registration statement and the prospectus to ensure full disclosure. The requirements of advance disclosure to the public through the filing of the registration statement with the SEC and the sending of a prospectus to each potential purchaser are commonly referred to as the **registration requirements** of the 1933 act.

CPA (A) **APPLICABILITY.** The 1933 act applies to (1) stocks, (2) corporate bonds, and (3) any conceivable type of corporate interest or instrument that has the characteristics of an investment security, including convertible securities and variable annuities. The act applies to all such instruments that have investment characteristics.

CPA

registration requirements –
provisions of the Securities Act
of 1933 requiring advance
disclosure to the public of a
new securities issue through
filing a statement with the SEC
and sending a prospectus to
each potential purchaser.

(B) THE REGISTRATION PROCESS. Section 5 of the 1933 act provides for the division of the registration process into three time periods: (1) the prefiling period, (2) the waiting period, from the date of filing with the SEC to the date the registration statement becomes effective (a minimum of 20 days but commonly extended for additional 20-day periods after each amendment by the issuer in compliance with SEC requirements for additional information), and (3) the posteffective period. The time divisions allow the public an opportunity to study the information disclosed in the registration process before a sale can be made. Permissible, required, and prohibited activities during these time periods are set forth in Figure 46-1.

CPA

(C) REGULATION A OFFERINGS. Regulation A provides a simplified registration process for small issues of securities by small businesses. Although technically exempt from the 1933 act registration requirements, a Regulation A offering involves a "mini-registration" with the SEC. Under the SEC's Small Business Initiative, Regulation A applies to the offerings of securities up to $5 million in a 12-month period. Disclosure requirements are simplified by the use of the small corporate offerings registration (SCOR) form, with its question-and-answer, "fill-in-the-blank" format. Also, the financial statements required in a Regulation A offering are less extensive than those required for a registered public offering.

Issuers may broadly solicit indications of interest from prospective investors before filing an *offering statement* with the SEC. This allows the issuer to "test the waters" and explore investor interest before incurring the expenses associated with a Regulation A offering. Solicitation-of-interest documents must be factual and comply with the antifraud provisions of the securities acts. No sales may be made until the SEC qualifies the offering statement and the seller delivers the final-offering circular, including the offering price, to the investor.

CPA

(D) REGISTRATION EXEMPTIONS. Certain private and limited offerings of securities are exempt from the registration requirements of the act under SEC Regulation D.

Offerings of securities restricted to residents of the state in which the issuing corporation is organized and doing business are exempt from federal regulation. This intrastate offering exemption is applied very narrowly by the SEC and the courts, and such offerings are subject to state laws.

CPA

(1) Rule 506 Exemption.

The most important exemption under Regulation D is SEC Rule 506. This rule provides general permission to offer and sell to a potentially indefinite number of individuals who meet the definition of accredited investor.[16] It is commonly referred to as the *private placement exemption*. There is no limitation on the amount of money that can be raised by the offering.[17] Specific information must be provided to all buyers if any buyers are nonaccredited investors; the number of nonaccredited investors is limited to no more than 35.

CPA

(2) Rule 505 Exemption.

SEC Rule 505 of Regulation D exempts from registration offerings of less than $5 million to no more than 35 nonaccredited purchasers over a 12-month period.

---

[16] The term *accredited investor* is defined to include virtually every type of institution that participates in the private placement market such as banks, stock brokerage firms, insurance companies, mutual fund companies, retirement plans with assets in excess of $5 million, and so on as well as individual investors with substantial income or large net worth.

[17] *Kunz v. SEC*, 2003 WL 1605865, 64 Fed. Appx. 659 (10th Cir. 2003).

FIGURE 46-1	*Registration Periods*

	PROHIBITED OR REQUIRED ACTIVITIES	PERMITTED ACTIVITIES
PREFILING PERIOD	ISSUER MUST NOT SELL OR OFFER FOR SALE A SECURITY BEFORE REGISTRATION STATEMENT IS FILED.	ISSUER MAY PLAN WITH UNDERWRITERS THE DISTRIBUTION OF THE SECURITY.
WAITING PERIOD	NO FINAL SALE OF A SECURITY PERMITTED DURING THIS PERIOD.	PRELIMINARY PROSPECTUS* CONTAINING INFORMATION FROM THE REGISTRATION STATEMENT BEING REVIEWED BY THE SEC MAY BE DISTRIBUTED TO INVESTORS, WHO MAY MAKE OFFERS. ADVERTISEMENTS MAY BE PLACED IN FINANCIAL PUBLICATIONS, IDENTIFYING PARTICULARS OF THE SECURITY, FROM WHOM A PROSPECTUS CAN BE OBTAINED, AND BY WHOM ORDERS WILL BE EXECUTED.**
POSTEFFECTIVE PERIOD	MUST PROVIDE A COPY OF FINAL PROSPECTUS WITH EVERY WRITTEN OFFER, CONFIRMATION OF SALE, OR DELIVERY OF SECURITY. MUST UPDATE PROSPECTUS WHENEVER IMPORTANT NEW DEVELOPMENTS OCCUR OR AFTER NINE MONTHS.	SALES OF THE SECURITY MAY BE COMPLETED.

*The preliminary prospectus is commonly called the *red herring* prospectus because of the red ink caption required by the SEC, informing the public that a registration statement has been filed but is not yet effective and that no final sale can be made until after the effective date.

**These advertisements are sometimes called *tombstone ads* because they are commonly framed by a black ink border.

© Cengage Learning

No limit exists on the number of accredited investors who may participate. No general solicitation or general advertising is permitted under Rule 505. If any prospective investors are nonaccredited, the issuer must furnish all investors specific information on the issuer, its business, and the securities offered for sale.

CPA

(3) Rule 504 Exemption.

Under SEC Rule 504 of Regulation D, as amended in 1999, an issuer can offer and sell securities up to $1 million within a 12-month period without registration and without most of the restrictions contained in Rules 505 and 506.

CPA

(4) Restrictions.

Securities acquired under Rules 506, 505, and 504 exemptions from registration are considered restricted securities. Their resale may require registration. Rules requiring registration of these Regulation D securities prior to resale ensure that investors purchase these securities as an investment rather than for public distribution. When there is no attempt to make public distributions, investors ordinarily fit within one of several exemptions to registration upon resale. Generally, all restrictions expire after two years.

CPA **(E) LIABILITY.** Issuers, sellers, and "aiders and abettors" may be subject to civil and criminal liability under the 1933 act.

CPA ***(1) Issuer's Civil Liability for False or Misleading Statements.***
The Securities Act of 1933 imposes civil liability under section 11 for making materially false or misleading statements in a registration statement and for omitting any required material fact. An issuing company has virtually no defense if there has been a false statement and a loss.

CPA ***(2) Civil Liability of Sellers of Securities.***
Section 12 of the 1933 act applies to those who "offer or sell" securities and employ any device or scheme to defraud or obtain money by means of untrue statements of material facts. This section makes such persons or firms liable to purchasers for damages sustained.

CPA ***(3) Criminal Liability.***
Section 24 of the 1933 act imposes criminal penalties on anyone who willfully makes untrue statements of material facts or omits required material facts from a registration statement. Section 17 of the act makes it unlawful for any person to employ any device, scheme, or artifice to defraud in the offer or sale of securities.

6. Securities Exchange Act of 1934

The 1934 act deals with the secondary distribution of securities. It was designed to prevent fraudulent and manipulative practices on the security exchanges and in over-the-counter markets. The act requires the disclosure of information to buyers and sellers of the securities. Furthermore, the act controls credit in these markets.

CPA **(A) REGISTRATION AND REPORTING REQUIREMENTS.** Exchanges, brokers, and dealers who deal in securities traded in interstate commerce or on any national security exchange must register with the SEC unless exempted by it.

Companies whose securities are listed on a national securities exchange and unlisted companies with assets in excess of $10 million and 500 or more shareholders are subject to the reporting requirements of the act.[18]

CPA ***(1) Principal Reports.***
Form 10-K is the principal annual report form used by commercial and industrial companies required to file under the 1934 act. The reports require nonfinancial information about the registrant's activities during the year, such as the nature of the firm's business, the property or businesses it owns, and a statement concerning legal proceedings by or against the company. The report requires the submission of financial statements with management's analysis of the financial condition of the company as well as a report and analysis of the performance of corporate shares. It requires a listing of all directors and executive officers and disclosure of executive compensation information.

---

[18] 61 F.R. 21354, 21356 (May 9, 1996).

Registrants who are required to file 10-K reports must also file quarterly reports, called *10-Q reports*. The 10-Q reports are principally concerned with financial information relevant to the quarterly period.

The SEC requires that annual shareholder reports be submitted to shareholders in any proxy solicitation on behalf of management. These reports contain essentially the same information as the 10-K.

CPA *(2) Certifications and Disclosure Controls.*

The Sarbanes-Oxley Act of 2002 requires written certification of the 10-K and 10-Q reports by each company's CEO and CFO, as set forth in section 302(a) of the act and shown in the following excerpt. A "knowing" misrepresentation in connection with the certification process is punishable by fine up to $1 million and imprisonment of up to 10 years. A "willful" misrepresentation in connection with the certification process is punishable by fine up to $5 million and imprisonment of up to 20 years.[19]

Moreover, under Section 304 of the Act, if an issuer is required to prepare an accounting restatement due to the material noncompliance of the issuer as a result of misconduct concerning any reporting requirement under the Securities laws, the CFO shall reimburse the issuer for any bonus received within a 12-month period. **For Example,** Carl Jasper, the CFO of semiconductor manufacturer Maxim Integrated Products, back-dated stock options granted employees and directors, concealing millions of dollars in expenses from investors. Maxim was required to restate its financial statements for 2002, 2003, 2004, and 2005. In addition to a civil fine, Jasper was ordered in accordance with SOX Section 304 to reimburse Maxim for $1.8 million in bonuses and profits he received from the sale of Maxim stocks.[20]

Section 302(a) of the act requires CEOs and CFOs to certify that:

   (1) *the signing officer has reviewed the report;*
   (2) *based on the officer's knowledge, the report does not contain any untrue statement of a material fact or omit to state a material fact necessary in order to make the statements made, in light of the circumstances under which such statements were made, not misleading;*
   (3) *based on such officer's knowledge, the financial statements, and other financial information included in the report, fairly present in all material respects the financial condition and results of operations of the issuer as of, and for, the periods presented in the report;*
   (4) *the signing officers—*
     (A) are responsible for establishing and maintaining internal controls....

The SEC considers information "material" if there is a substantial likelihood that it would have been viewed by a reasonable investor as having significantly altered the total mix of information made available and if a reasonable investor would have considered the fact important in making an investment decision. The SEC has recommended that each company organize key employees into a "disclosure committee" responsible for considering the "materiality" of information and the company's disclosure obligations. For example, any transactions with insiders should be carefully considered for SEC filings.

[19] 18 U.S.C. §1350(c).
[20] *SEC v. Jasper*, 678 F.2d 1116 (9th Cir. 2012).

Before Sarbanes-Oxley, many public companies published pro forma (provided in advance) financial results in press releases before filing their official quarterly reports with the SEC. This approach allowed these companies to cast their "financials" in a favorable light. The SEC financial statements are prepared under a set of accounting conventions called *generally accepted accounting principles*, or GAAP. Pro forma financial results are not prepared using GAAP, and they may not provide a true and accurate picture of a company's financial status. Section 401 of the Sarbanes-Oxley Act instructed the SEC to issue rules requiring the presentation of pro forma financial statements in a manner that does not contain material misstatements or omit material facts and can be reconciled with financial results using GAAP. SEC Regulation G imposes a broad range of limitations on the use of pro forma results. If a company issues a press release saying that its pro forma earnings will be $5 million for the quarter when its official GAAP earnings will be just $4 million, the company will have to disclose both figures and explain what expenses were excluded from the pro forma figures and why.

CPA **(B) ANTIFRAUD PROVISION.** Section 10(b) of the 1934 act makes it unlawful for any person to use any manipulative or deceptive device in contravention of SEC rules. Under the authority of Section 10(b) of the 1934 act, the SEC has promulgated *Rule 10b-5*. This rule is the principal antifraud rule relating to the secondary distribution of securities. The rule states:

> *It shall be unlawful for any person, directly or indirectly, by use of any means or instrumentality of interstate commerce, or of the mails or of any facility of any national securities exchange,*
>
> *(a) To employ any device, scheme, or artifice to defraud,*
> *(b) To make any untrue statement of a material fact or to omit to state a material fact necessary in order to make the statements made, in the light of the circumstances under which they were made, not misleading, or*
> *(c) To engage in any act, practice, or course of business that operates or would operate as a fraud or deceit upon any person, in connection with the purchase or sale of any security.*[21]

CPA **(1) Private Actions.**
Rule 10b-5 applies to all securities, whether registered or not, as long as use is made of the mail, interstate commerce, or a national stock exchange. Subject to the safe harbor provisions of the Private Securities Litigation Reform Act as discussed in the following section, under Rule 10b-5, a civil action for damages may be brought by any private investor who purchased or sold a security and was injured because of false, misleading, or undisclosed information.[22]

CPA **(2) Liability for "Material Misstatements or Omissions of Fact."**
Rule 10b-5 prohibits the making of any untrue statement of a "material" fact or the omission of a material fact necessary to render statements made not misleading. In every Rule 10b-5 case, the plaintiff must show "reliance" on the misrepresentation and resulting injury.

[21] 17 C.F.R. §240.10b-5.
[22] *Miller v. Thane International, Inc.,* 519 F.3d 879 (9th Cir. 2008).

In *Basic, Inc. v. Levinson*, the Supreme Court dealt with the question of what should be the standard of "materiality" in merger cases.

CASE SUMMARY

Why Silence Is Golden

FACTS: In December 1978, Combustion Engineering, Inc., and Basic Inc. agreed to merge. During the preceding two years, representatives of the two companies had meetings regarding the possibility of a merger. During this time, Basic made three public statements denying that any merger negotiations were taking place or that it knew of any corporate developments that would account for the heavy trading activity in its stock. Certain former shareholders who sold this stock between Basic's first public denial of merger activity and the public announcement of the merger brought a section 10(b) and Rule 10b-5 action against Basic and some of its directors. The former shareholders contended that Basic had made material misrepresentations in its public statements denying merger activity. Basic raised the defense that the alleged misrepresentations were not material and that there was no showing of reliance by the shareholders on Basic's statements.

DECISION: The standard for materiality applicable to preliminary merger discussions is to be decided on a case-by-case basis depending on the probability that the transaction will be consummated and on its significance to the issuer. There is a presumption of reliance by the shareholders on the misstatements of the corporations. This presumption is supported by the policy of the 1934 act, which is to foster reliance on market integrity. However, the presumption may be rebutted by showing that the market price was not affected by the misrepresentation. The case is remanded for further proceedings consistent with this opinion. [*Basic, Inc. v. Levinson*, 485 U.S. 224 (1988)]

In the pharmaceutical industry "materiality" of adverse event reports is a "fact-specific" inquiry. It requires consideration of the source and content and context of the reports, as set forth in the *Matrixx Initiatives* case.

CASE SUMMARY

Rule No. 1 For Corporate Finance Executives: Be Very Careful About What You Say

FACTS: Matrixx develops, manufactures, and markets over-the-counter pharmaceutical products. Its core product, Zicam Cold Remedy, with its active ingredient zinc gluconate, accounted for approximately 70 percent of Matrixx's sales. Individuals who purchased Matrixx securities between October 22, 2003, and February 6, 2004, filed a securities fraud class action against Matrixx under Section 10(b) of the 1934 Act. In October 2003 Matrixx made a statement to the market that Zicam was "poised for growth in the upcoming cold and cough season." It expressed its expectations that revenues would "be up in excess of 50%." In January 2004 it raised its revenue guidance, predicting an 80 percent increase.

On January 30, 2004, Dow Jones Newswires reported that the Food and Drug Administration (FDA) was "'looking into complaints that an over-the-counter common-cold medicine manufactured by a unit of Matrixx Initiatives, Inc. may be causing some users to lose their sense of smell'" in light of at least three product liability lawsuits. Matrixx's stock fell from

CASE SUMMARY

Continued

$13.55 to $11.97 per share after the report. In response, on February 2, Matrixx issued a press release that stated in part:

> *Matrixx believes statements alleging that intranasal Zicam products caused anosmia (loss of smell) are completely unfounded and misleading. In no clinical trial of intranasal zinc gluconate gel products has there been a single report of lost or diminished olfactory function (sense of smell). Rather, the safety and efficacy of zinc gluconate for the treatment of symptoms related to the common cold have been well established ...*

The day after Matrixx issued this press release, its stock price bounced back to $13.40 per share. On February 6, 2004, *Good Morning America*, a nationally broadcast morning news program, reported that Dr. Jafek had discovered more than a dozen patients suffering from anosmia after using Zicam. It also noted that four lawsuits had been filed against Matrixx. The price of Matrixx stock plummeted to $9.94 per share that same day. Zicam again issued a press release largely repeating its February 2 statement.

Prior to these public statements, between October 2003 and February 2004, medical experts had revealed to Matrixx a plausible causal relationship between Zicam Cold Remedy and anosmia. For example, Dr. Linschoten sent abstracts of studies to Matrixx that had confirmed "zinc's toxicity." In September 2003 Matrixx learned of a planned national medical conference presentation by Dr. Jafek of the University of Colorado finding that 10 patients suffered loss of smell after Zicam use. The investors claim that the information the company had about the causal relationship between Zicam and anosmia were material facts necessary in order to make the statements made by Matrixx to the market not misleading. Matrixx defended that the investors had not alleged a statistically significant correlation between the use of Zicam and anosmia so as to make failure to publicly disclose complaints and the University of Colorado study a material omission.

DECISION: The "materiality" requirement of a Section 10(b) claim by investors that Matrixx made statements that were misleading as to material facts was satisfied in this case. There is a substantial likelihood that the disclosure of the omitted facts asserted in this case would have been viewed by a reasonable investor as having significantly altered the "total mix" of information made available by the company. Section 10(b) and Rule 10b-5 do not create an affirmative duty to disclose any and all material information (silence, absent a duty to disclose, is not misleading under Rule 10b-5). However, disclosure is required in order to make the statements made by Matrixx to the market not misleading. Matrixx told the market that revenues were going to rise 50 then 80 percent, yet it had information that its leading revenue product caused loss of the sense of smell. Matrixx also stated that reports its product caused anosmia were "completely unfounded and misleading," yet it had contrary information that a reasonable investor would deem material. The FDA and medical professionals do not limit the evidence considered for assessing causation to statistically significant data nor should investors be so limited. [*Matrixx Initiatives, Inc. v. Siracusano*, **131 S. Ct. 1309 (2011)**]

CPA   **(c) LITIGATION REFORM ACT.** The Private Securities Litigation Reform Act (PSLRA, or the Litigation Reform Act) of 1995 was passed because of (1) congressional concern over an excess of frivolous private securities lawsuits, (2) the financial burdens placed on accountants and other professional advisors by such litigation, and (3) concern that the investors in a class-action lawsuit have their interests fairly represented. Important features of the act are as follows.

CPA

(1) Safe Harbor Rules.

Issuers of securities frequently believed that lawsuits against them under Rule 10b-5 occurred simply because the corporation made a projection that failed to materialize. The Litigation Reform Act provides shelter for issuers from private liability for forward-looking statements that were not known to be false when made and that were accompanied by meaningful cautionary statements informing investors of contingencies that could cause results to differ from projected results.

To preserve the protections of the PSLRA, quarterly and annual reports to the SEC (Forms 10-Q and 10-K) and quarterly and annual reports to stockholders, as well as corporate press releases on financial matters, now commonly utilize the expression *forward-looking statements* regarding corporate statements that estimate or project the short-term and long-term outlook for a business. Moreover, these reports typically include a section entitled "Cautionary Statements" or "Risk Factors," and contain a statement such as:

> *Forward-looking statements as contained in this report involve a number of risks, including but not limited to product demand, pricing, market acceptance, supply problems, intellectual property rights and litigation, and risks in product and technology development.*

Corporations do not have to caution against every conceivable factor that may cause results to differ from the issuer's forward-looking statements. **For Example,** Ivax Corporation, a drug company, issued a press release including optimistic assumptions about future events. Attached to the release was an italicized warning that stated in specific detail the kinds of misfortunes that could befall Ivax and could cause results to differ from its forward-looking statements. This cautionary statement did not mention that a large goodwill writedown could occur; and when a writedown did occur, Ivax stock declined sharply. Harris, Wolpin, and others brought a Rule 10b-5 fraud suit against Ivax based on the omission of a warning about the writedown risk. The court held that the cautionary statements were sufficient to warn an investor of risks similar to that actually realized and the statements satisfied Ivax's burden to warn under the statute. Ivax was not required to list all risk factors, and the failure to mention one risk that in fact occurred did not "blow Ivax out of the safe harbor."[23]

CPA

(2) Litigation Reform.

The Litigation Reform Act places a heightened pleading requirement on plaintiffs attempting to plead fraud in securities cases, and requires not only that the plaintiffs specify each statement alleged to have been false or misleading and the reason for the belief but also that the plaintiffs plead "scienter"—the mental state embracing intent to deceive, manipulate, or defraud.[24] In the *Matrixx Initiatives* case, the Supreme Court held that the investors adequately pleaded scienter, where the allegations give rise to the compelling inference that Matrixx elected not to disclose the reports of adverse events not because it believed they were meaningless, but because it understood their likely effect on the market.[25]

---

[23] *Harris v. Ivax Corp.*, 182 F.3d 799 (11th Cir. 1999).

[24] In an October 26, 1999, Bloomberg Forum conference call, Lucent Technologies' CEO, McGinn, characterized Lucent as a market "leader" reaping "exceptionally strong growth in... optical networking" and described Lucent as growing at the same rate as the market (40 to 50 percent). After the conference call, Lucent stock moved from $59 per share to $80.62. The following year, however, the stock "tanked" to $2.19 a share, and investors who had purchased stock in 1999 and 2000 sued. In the fall of 1999, management e-mails acknowledged that the optical networking group was in "serious disrepair" and was up against a "revenue wall." The court determined that the plaintiffs were in compliance with the PSLRA and that McGinn's October 26, 1999, statement had not been "forward looking"—and that there were sufficient allegations to demonstrate that his statements had been misleading. Subsequently, the court approved a $610 million settlement of the case. *In re Lucent Technologies Inc., Securities Litigation*, 307 F. Supp. 2d 633 (D. N.J. 2004).

[25] *Matrixx Initiatives, Inc. v. Siracusano*, 131 S. Ct. 1309, 1324 (2011); see also *Frank v. Dana Corp.*, 646 F.3d 954 (6th Cir. 2011).

The Litigation Reform Act also provides for *proportionate liability*, as opposed to joint and several liability, for defendants who are found not to have knowingly committed a violation of the security laws. In addition, securities fraud is eliminated as a predicate for private RICO actions absent a prior criminal conviction. Under the act, frivolous private securities lawsuits require payment of the defendant's reasonable attorney fees.

CPA

(3) Class-Action Reforms.

Reforms were necessary to protect against "lawyer-driven lawsuits" in which a class-action counsel would direct a "professional" plaintiff to buy a security to have standing to bring a class-action lawsuit. Thereafter, the class-action counsel would race to the courthouse to file before any other plaintiff and thus be able to claim enhanced standing to represent the class. The Litigation Reform Act provides that the status of lead plaintiff is offered to the person with the largest financial interest in the case, who then selects the lead counsel.

(4) Aiders and Abettors.

In its *Central Bank of Denver*[26] decision, the U.S. Supreme Court ruled that a private investor may not bring an action under Section 10(b) of the 1934 act against "aiders and abettors" such as accountants, lawyers, and investment bankers who provide assistance to the primary violator. In enacting the Litigation Reform Act, Congress did not follow the then–SEC Chairman's recommendation that aiding and abetting liability in private claims be established in the act. Instead, Congress directed the SEC's prosecution of aiders and abettors. Courts, however, have affirmed a private cause of action under Section 10(b) with a rebuttable presumption of reliance on the defendant's deceptive acts (1) where there is an omission of a material fact by one who has a duty to disclose, or (2) under the **fraud-on-the-market** doctrine where reliance is presumed when the statements in question become public.[27] The *Stoneridge Investments*[28] case is an example of "aiding and abetting" and the reluctance of the U.S. Supreme Court to expand the Section 10(b) private right of action where there was no duty to disclose and the deceptive acts were not communicated to the public. In its *Janus Capital Group, Inc.*, decision, the U.S. Supreme Court considered whether a mutual fund investment advisor, Janus Capital Management LLC (JCM), can be held liable in a private cause of action under Section 10(b) for false statements included in its client mutual funds' prospectuses, the client being Janus Investment Fund (JIF), a separate legal entity owned entirely by mutual fund investors. The court majority determined that JCM was not the "maker" of the false statement in the JIF prospectuses, just as one who prepares or publishes a statement on behalf of another is not its maker. It stated that a broader reading of "make," including persons or entities without ultimate control over the content of the statement, would substantially undermine the Court's *Central Bank* decision.[29]

fraud-on-the-market – a theory that in an open and developed securities market, the price of a stock is determined by the information on the company available to the public, and misleading statements will defraud purchasers of stock even if they do not directly rely on these statements.

---

[26] *Central Bank of Denver v. First Interstate Bank of Denver*, 611 U.S. 164 (1994).
[27] In *Connecticut Retirement Plans and Trust Funds v. Amgen Inc.*, 660 F.3d 1170 (9th Cir. 2011), the Ninth Circuit held that at the class certification stage of a securities fraud lawsuit, proof of the materiality of an allegedly fraudulent statement or omission is not a precondition to invoking the fraud-on-the-market presumption of reliance. The U.S. Supreme Court granted *certiorari* and will address this matter in the fall of 2012.
[28] *Stoneridge Investment Partners, LLC v. Scientific Atlanta, Inc.*, 552 U.S. 148 (2008).
[29] *Janus Capital Group v. First Derivative Traders*, 131 S. Ct. 2296 (2011).

CPA

(5) Auditor Disclosure.

The Litigation Reform Act amends the 1934 act by requiring auditors who discover illegal acts to notify management and the board of directors and, in some cases, to notify the SEC if the issuer does not.[30] Auditors are relieved from liability for any such disclosure to the SEC.

CPA

(6) Lawyer Reporting of Wrongdoing.

The ABA Model Rules of Professional Conduct, which serve as a basis for most states' ethics rules for lawyers, were revised to free lawyers from their duty of confidentiality to those clients who use the lawyers' advice to commit a crime or fraud.[31] The ABA also revised its Model Rules to allow a lawyer who knows that an officer or employee of a corporation will likely harm the company to refer the matter to higher-up officials of the organization.[32]

7. Trading on Insider Information

Section 10(b) and Rule 10b-5 form a basis for imposing sanctions for trading on **insider information**. The Insider Trading and Securities Fraud Enforcement Act of 1988, which amended the 1934 act, gave the SEC authority to bring an action against an individual purchasing or selling a security while in possession of material inside information. The court may impose a civil penalty of up to three times the profit gained or loss avoided as a result of the unlawful sale. Persons who "aid or abet" in the violation may also be held liable under the act.

insider information – privileged information on company business only known to employees.

Under the 1988 insider trading act, "controlling persons," including employers whose lax supervision may allow employees to commit insider trading violations, are subject to civil penalties.[33] The SEC must prove "knowing" or "reckless" behavior by the controlling person. The 1988 law establishes bounty programs that allow the SEC to reward informants giving information on insider trading activity. The reward is up to 10 percent of any penalty imposed.

insider – full-time corporate employee or a director.

temporary insider – someone retained by a corporation for professional services on an as-needed basis, such as an attorney, accountant, or investment banker.

tippee – individual who receives information about a corporation from an insider or temporary insider.

(A) TRADING BY INSIDERS AND TIPPEES. An **insider** may be a director or corporate employee. A **temporary insider** is someone retained by the corporation for professional services, such as an attorney, accountant, or investment banker. Insiders and temporary insiders are liable for inside trading when they fail to disclose material nonpublic information before trading on it and thus make a secret profit. A **tippee** is an individual who receives information from an insider or a temporary insider. A tippee is subject to the insider's fiduciary duty to shareholders when the insider has breached the fiduciary duty to shareholders by improperly disclosing the information to the tippee and when the tippee knows or should know there has been a breach.[34] Such a breach occurs when an insider benefits personally from her disclosure. When the insider does not breach a fiduciary duty, a tippee does not violate the securities laws.

---

[30] P.L. 104-671, 109 Stat. 763, 15 U.S.C. §78j-l nt.
[31] Model Rule 1.6, "Confidentiality of Information."
[32] Model Rule 1.13, "Organization as Client."
[33] P.L. 100-704, 102 Stat. 4677, 15 U.S.C. §78u-1(a)(2).
[34] *United States v. Chestman*, 974 F.2d 564 (2d Cir. 1991).

CASE SUMMARY

No Secrets from Secrist!

FACTS: On March 6, 1973, Dirks, an investment analyst, received information from Secrist, a former officer of Equity Funding of America, alleging that the assets of Equity Funding were vastly overstated as the result of fraudulent corporate practices. On investigation by Dirks, certain corporation employees corroborated the charges of fraud. Neither Dirks nor his firm owned or traded any Equity Funding stock, but throughout his investigation, he openly discussed the information he had obtained with a number of clients and investors. The information from Dirks induced them to sell Equity Funding stock in excess of $16 million. On March 27, the New York Stock Exchange halted trading of Equity Funding stock, and a subsequent investigation revealed the vast fraud that had taken place. The SEC, investigating Dirks's role in the exposure of the fraud, claimed that Dirks had aided and abetted violations of the Securities Act of 1933, the Securities Exchange Act of 1934, and SEC Rule 10b-5 by repeating the allegations of fraud to members of the investment community who later sold their Equity Funding stock.

DECISION: Judgment for Dirks. Secrist, the insider, did not violate any fiduciary duty to shareholders when he disclosed information about the fraudulent practices to the tippee, Dirks. Secrist received no monetary or personal benefit for the information but was motivated by the desire to expose the fraud. Because the insider did not breach his fiduciary duty when he gave nonpublic information to Dirks, Dirks breached no duty when he passed the information on to investors. [***Dirks v. SEC*, 463 U.S. 646 (1983)]**

(B) **MISAPPROPRIATORS.** Individuals who misappropriate or steal valuable nonpublic information in breach of a fiduciary duty to their employer and trade in securities on that information are guilty of insider trading as "misappropriators."

For Example, an employee working for a financial printing firm was found guilty of insider trading under section 10(b) and Rule 10b-5.[35] While proofreading a financial document being prepared for a client firm, he figured out the identity of tender offer targets. Soon after that, he traded on this valuable nonpublic information to his advantage.

It is no defense to a section 10(b) and Rule 10b-5 criminal charge of participating in a "scheme to defraud" that the victim of the fraud (an employer) had no economic interest in the securities traded. The convictions of a stockbroker and a columnist for the *Wall Street Journal* were upheld under section 10(b) of the 1934 act. The columnist violated his fiduciary duty to his employer by revealing prepublication information about his column to the stockbroker. The stockbroker then used the information to trade in the securities identified in the column.[36]

Where an individual misappropriates confidential information for security trading purposes in breach of a fiduciary duty owed to the source of the information rather than to the shareholders who sold securities to the individual, that individual may be convicted of security fraud in violation of section 10(b) and Rule 10b-5.

[35] *SEC v. Materia*, 745 F.2d 197 (2d Cir. 1984).
[36] *Carpenter v. United States*, 484 U.S. 19 (1987).

CASE SUMMARY

The Case of the Dastardly Misappropriator

FACTS: James O'Hagan was a partner in the law firm of Dorsey & Whitney in Minneapolis, Minnesota. In July 1988, Grand Metropolitan PLC, a company based in London, England, retained Dorsey & Whitney as local counsel to represent Grand Met regarding a potential tender offer for the common stock of the Pillsbury Company headquartered in Minneapolis. O'Hagan did no work on the Grand Met representation. Dorsey & Whitney withdrew from representing Grand Met on September 9, 1988. Less than a month later, on October 4, 1988, Grand Met publicly announced its tender offer for Pillsbury stock. Previously, on August 18, 1988, while Dorsey & Whitney was still representing Grand Met, O'Hagan began purchasing call options for Pillsbury stock. Each option gave him the right to purchase 100 shares of Pillsbury stock by a specified date in September 1988. Later in August and September, O'Hagan purchased additional Pillsbury call options. By the end of September, he owned 2,500 unexpired Pillsbury options, apparently more than any other individual investor. O'Hagan also purchased, in September 1988, some 5,000 shares of Pillsbury common stock at a price just under $39 per share. When Grand Met announced its tender offer in October, the price of Pillsbury stock rose to nearly $60 per share. O'Hagan then sold his Pillsbury call options and common stock, making a profit of more than $4.3 million. O'Hagan was charged and convicted of securities fraud in violation of section 10(b) and Rule 10b-5. On appeal, he claimed that he was not a "misappropriator," for he had no fiduciary duty to the Pillsbury shareholders from whom he purchased calls and stock; in fact, he had not even worked on the transaction at the law firm.

DECISION: Judgment against O'Hagan. "Misappropriation" requires that there be "deceptive" conduct "in connection with" a securities transaction. A fiduciary who pretends loyalty to the principal while secretly converting the principal's information for personal gain dupes or defrauds the principal. O'Hagan's failure to disclose his personal trading to his law firm and its client, Grand Met, was a breach of his fiduciary duty and was "deceptive" conduct "in connection with" a securities transaction. The misappropriation theory is designed to protect the integrity of the securities market against "outsiders" like O'Hagan, who have access to confidential information that will affect a company's stock price when revealed but have no fiduciary or other duty to the company's shareholders. [*United States v. O'Hagan*, 521 U.S. 657 (1997)]

(c) REGULATION FD. The SEC adopted Regulation FD (Fair Disclosure) to end the practice of selective disclosure by issuers of securities to security analysts and selected institutional investors of important nonpublic information, such as advance warnings of negative or positive earnings results, before disclosing the information to the general public. Those privy to the early release of the information had been able to make a profit or avoid a loss at the expense of the uninformed general public. For example, uninformed investors may have watched the price of XYZ Corporation fall from $47 a share to $32 a share over two days only to find out later in a subsequently disseminated general press release by the corporation that "earnings will not meet street estimates." Analysts with prior knowledge of the negative earnings reports were able to take action before the public was informed. Regulation FD requires that any disclosure be a public disclosure by filing Form 8-K or other disclosures to the public, including use of the Internet to broadly disseminate information.[37] **For Example,** when Brian

---

[37] 17 C.F.R. §240.10b5-1.

Moynihan, CEO of Bank of America, speaks to a group of investment analysts about his company at a Wall Street meeting, Bank of America may broadcast the talk over the Web and issue a press release summarizing Moynihan's comments to comply with Regulation FD.

(D) REMEDY FOR INVESTORS. Investors who lack the inside information possessed by the insider and sell their stock during the relevant time period may recover damages from any insider who made use of undisclosed information. Recovery is by a civil action based on Rule 10b-5.

8. Disclosure of Ownership and Short-Swing Profits

Corporate directors and officers owning equity securities in their corporation and any shareholder owning more than 10 percent of any class of the corporation's equity securities are statutorily defined as insiders and must file with the SEC a disclosure statement regarding such ownership and all related transactions. This is required under section 16(a) of the 1934 act. Under section 403(a) of the Sarbanes-Oxley Act, these individuals must electronically report transactions in company stock to the SEC by the second business day after the transaction. Moreover, the transaction must be posted on the SEC's and the company's Web sites within one day after the filing date.

Section 16 is designed to prevent the unfair use of information available to these corporate insiders. This section prevents insiders from participating in short-term trading in their corporation's securities.

short-swing profit – profit realized by a corporate insider from selling securities less than six months after purchase.

If such a person sells at a profit any of these securities less than six months after their purchase, the profit is called a **short-swing profit**. Under section 16(b), the corporation may sue a director, officer, or major stockholder for a short-swing profit.[38] The corporation may recover that profit even without a fraudulent intent in acquiring and selling the securities. However, the corporation must bring the lawsuit within two years after the date the profit was realized.[39]

9. Tender Offers

A corporation or group of investors may seek to acquire control of another corporation by making a general offer to all shareholders of the target corporation to purchase their shares for cash at a specified price. This is called a **cash tender offer**. The offer to purchase is usually contingent on the tender of a fixed number of shares sufficient to ensure takeover. The bid price is ordinarily higher than the prevailing market price. Should more shares be tendered than the offeror is willing to purchase, the tender offeror must purchase shares from each shareholder on a pro rata basis.

cash tender offer – general offer to all shareholders of a target corporation to purchase their shares for cash at a specified price.

The Williams Act, which amended the 1934 act,[40] was passed to ensure that public shareholders who are confronted with a cash tender offer will not be required to act without adequate information. Under section 14(d) of the Williams Act, a person making a tender offer must file appropriate SEC forms. These forms provide information about the background and identity of the person filing, the source of funds used to make stock purchases, the amount of stock beneficially owned, the

---

[38] *Levy v. Southbrook International Investments, Ltd.*, 263 F.3d 10 (2d Cir. 2001); *Donaghue v. Natural Microsystems Corp.*, 198 F. Supp. 2d 487 (S.D.N.Y. 2002).
[39] *Credit Suisse Securities (USA) LLC v. Simmons*, 132 S. Ct. 1414 (2012).
[40] P.L. 90-439, 82 Stat. 454, 15 U.S.C. §78m(d), (e).

purpose of the purchases, any plan the purchaser proposes to follow if it gains control over the target corporation, and any contracts or understandings that it has with other persons concerning the target corporation.[41]

Section 14(e) of the Williams Act is the antifraud section. It prohibits fraudulent, deceptive, or manipulative practices. SEC Rule 14e-1 requires any tender offer to remain open for a minimum of 20 business days from the date it is first published or given to security holders. Federal and state legislation, as well as administrative regulation, is aimed at requiring disclosure of information and allowance of a reasonable length of time for consideration of the facts. These requirements are designed to make agreement to takeovers the result of voluntary action based on full knowledge of material facts.

As far as the courts are concerned, takeovers must be regarded with a neutral eye. If there is misrepresentation or other misconduct, the law will interfere. Otherwise, freedom of contract requires that courts not interfere with the judgment of the contracting parties.

10. Regulation of Accountants and Attorneys by the SEC

Accountants play a vital role in financial reporting under the federal securities laws administered by the SEC. Sections 1, 12, 17, and 24 of the 1933 act and section 10(b) of the 1934 act are the sections under which accountants may be subject to liability.

An accountant who prepares any statement, opinion, or other legal paper filed with the SEC with the preparer's consent is deemed to be practicing before the SEC. Because it relies so heavily on accountants, the SEC has promulgated Rule 2(e), which regulates and provides the basis for discipline of accountants, attorneys, and

E-Commerce & Cyberlaw

Douglas Colt was a second-year law student who developed a way to make money from the Internet. He set up a free Web site promising folks hot tips on stocks. However, Colt bought the stocks himself at low prices before pumping them up at his Web site. Once the shares were pumped up to a high enough price from the users of his Web site buying the shares, he would then sell all of his shares (i.e., dump them). Colt made more than $345,000 using the old tool of "pump-and-dump."

Colt had attracted 9,000 investors to his Web site (Fast-Trades .com). One of his shares, American Education Corporation, climbed 700 percent before he sold his holdings.

Those who participated in the pump-and-dump scam, including Colt's mother, a councilwoman from Colorado, agreed to a consent decree settlement. None will pay a fine and none will repay their profits. They have simply agreed not to violate federal securities laws in the future. Georgetown University, Colt's law school, said there will be no disciplinary action.

Did Colt violate insider trading laws or any federal securities laws? Was Colt's conduct ethical?

Enforcement on insider trading has been on the increase. The SEC has created a new group, called its Cyberforce, to deal specifically with insider trading over the Internet.

[41] Section 14(d) requires a filing by any person making a tender offer that, if successful, would result in the acquisition of 5 percent of any class of an equity security required to be registered under the 1934 Act. Section 13(d) of the Act requires disclosure to the issuer, the SEC, and the appropriate stock exchange when a person acquires 5 percent of a class of equity security through stock purchases on exchanges or through private purchases. The person may have acquired the stock for investment purposes, not for control, but must still file disclosure forms under §13(d). See *SEC v. Bilzerian*, 814 F. Supp. 116 (D. D.C. 1993). Section 14(d) applies only to shares to be acquired by tender offer.

consultants who practice before the SEC.[42] Under Rule 2(e), the SEC may suspend or disbar from practice before it those who are unqualified or unethical or who have violated federal securities laws or SEC rules.[43]

Section 307 of the Sarbanes-Oxley Act explicitly requires the SEC to establish minimum standards of professional conduct for attorneys practicing before the SEC in the representation of publicly held companies. The act and SEC rules require that attorneys report evidence of material violations of securities laws, up the chain of command, to the companies' general counsel, CEO, audit committees, or the full board of directors.

CPA C. INDUSTRY SELF-REGULATION

The National Association of Securities Dealers (NASD) is a self-regulatory organization guided by procedural and conduct rules. It seeks to detect misconduct of regulated persons and firms, and may issue appropriate sanctions as a means of protecting investors. The sanctions are subject to SEC review and thereafter review by the U.S. Court of Appeals. **For Example,** PAZ Securities, Inc., and its president, Joseph Mizrachi, repeatedly failed to provide information requested by the NASD under its rules. The SEC affirmed the NASD's default judgment expelling PAZ and also barring Mizrachi from ever associating with an NASD member. The U.S. Court of Appeals ultimately upheld the SEC's sanctions since failure to respond is a significant harm to the self-regulatory system because it undermines the NASD's ability to detect misconduct.[44] Subsequently, the NASD and the New York Stock Exchange merged their member regulation functions into one self-regulatory organization, the Financial Industry Regulatory Authority (FINRA). FINRA is the largest independent regulator for all securities firms doing business in the United States, registering industry participants, enforcing rules, and administering the largest dispute resolution forum for investors and registered firms.[45] It provides a BrokerCheck system, which allows investors to check out the professional and disciplinary backgrounds of firms and brokers online.[46]

11. Arbitration of Securities Disputes

Both NASD and securities firms with seats on the New York Stock Exchange have adopted codes of arbitration that allow customers and members to submit disputes to arbitration. The arbitration rights are contractual and are set forth in writing when opening an account with the securities firms. Investors who have agreed to arbitrate their securities disputes can be compelled to arbitrate, rather than sue, in courts.[47] NASD and NYSE arbitrations are now administered by FINRA. Courts are very reluctant to vacate an arbitration award.

---

[42] 17 C.F.R. §201.2e.

[43] Rule 2(e) provides: "Suspension and disbarment. (1) The Commission may deny, temporarily or permanently, the privilege of appearing or practicing before it in any way to any person who is found by the Commission after notice of an opportunity for hearing in the matter (i) not to possess the requisite qualifications to represent others, or (ii) to be lacking in character or integrity or to have engaged in unethical or improper professional conduct, or (iii) to have willfully violated, or willfully aided and abetted, the violation of any provision of the federal securities laws (15 U.S.C. §§77a to 80B-20), or the rules and regulations thereunder." 17 C.F.R. §201.2e.

[44] *PAZ Securities, Inc. v. SEC*, 566 F.3d 1172 (D.C. Cir. 2009).

[45] FINRA oversees some 629,640 registered securities representatives. In 2011, it barred 329 individuals and suspended 475 brokers from association with FINRA-regulated firms, levied fines totaling more than $63 million, and ordered more than $19 million in restitution to harmed investors. See http://www.finra.org/ABOUTFINRA.

[46] http://www.finra.org/brokercheck.

[47] *99 Commercial Street, Inc. v. Goldberg*, 811 F. Supp. 900 (S.D.N.Y.1992).

CASE SUMMARY

The Sting of Justice—Punitive Damages

FACTS: In 1985, petitioners Antonio Mastrobuono, then an assistant professor of medieval literature, and his wife, Diane Mastrobuono, an artist, opened a securities trading account with respondent Shearson Lehman Hutton, Inc. (SLH), by executing Shearson's standard client's agreement form. Respondent Nick DiMinico, a vice president of SLH, managed the Mastrobuonos' account until they closed it. The Mastrobuonos sued SLH for the fraudulent conduct of DiMinico, and the matter was referred to arbitration under NASD rules. A panel of three arbitrators convened hearings in Chicago, Illinois, where the Mastrobuonos lived, and the panel awarded them $115,274 for commissions and $44,053 for margin interest "as satisfaction for their claims." The panel also awarded them $400,000 as punitive damages. SLH refused to pay the punitive damages and was able to get this portion of the award vacated in a federal court action that was affirmed on appeal to the U.S. Court of Appeals for the Seventh Circuit. Under the terms of the customer agreement, the agreement was to be "governed by the laws of the State of New York," and disputes between the broker-dealer and the customer were to be "settled by arbitration" conducted under NASD rules. New York decisional law follows the "*Garrity* rule," which prohibits arbitrators from awarding punitive damages even in cases when courts may award such damages. By contrast, NASD arbitration rules anticipate that arbitrators will award a broad range of relief, including punitive damages. The Supreme Court decided to hear the case because of differing views held by the courts of appeals.

DECISION: Judgment for the Mastrobuonos. NASD's Code of Arbitration Procedure indicated that arbitrators may award "damages and other relief," and a manual provided to NASD arbitrators recognizes that "arbitrators may consider punitive damages as a remedy." The arbitration award should have been fully enforced, including the award for punitive damages. [***Mastrobuono v. Shearson Lehman Hutton*, 514 U.S. 52 (1995)**]

LawFlix

Wall Street (1987) (R)

This movie will walk you through not just the evolution of greed but the evolution of a young broker moving from gathering information to stealing it to obtaining it through insiders. The movie chronicles the market's regulations as well as an individual's loss of values.

MAKE THE CONNECTION

SUMMARY

State blue sky laws, which apply only to intrastate transactions, protect the public from the sale of fraudulent securities. The term *security* is defined sufficiently broadly to encompass not only stocks and bonds but also any conceivable type of corporate interest that has investment characteristics.

Two principal laws provide the basic framework for federal regulation of the sale of securities in interstate commerce. The Securities Act of 1933 deals with the issue or original distribution of securities by issuing corporations. The Securities Exchange Act of 1934 regulates the secondary distribution or sale of securities on exchanges. These acts are administered by the Securities and Exchange Commission. Except for certain private and limited offerings, the 1933 act requires that a registration statement be filed with the SEC and that a prospectus be provided to each potential purchaser. Criminal and civil penalties exist for fraudulent statements made in this process. The 1934 act provides reporting requirements for companies whose securities are listed on a national exchange and unlisted companies that have assets in excess of $10 million and 500 or more shareholders.

Rule 10b-5 is the principal antifraud rule under the 1934 act. Trading on "inside information" is unlawful and may subject those involved to a civil penalty of three times the profit made on the improperly disclosed information. Cash tender offers are regulated by the SEC under authority of the Williams Act. The securities industry provides arbitration procedures to resolve disputes between customers and firms.

LEARNING OUTCOMES

After studying this chapter, you should be able to clearly explain:

A. State Regulation

LO.1   Explain the meaning of state "blue sky laws"

See the discussion of the common-content features of state securities laws such as antifraud provisions, licensing provisions, and regulation of securities on p. 1027.

B. Federal Regulation

LO.2   Define "security"
See the *Edwards* case as an example of the broad definition of *security* sufficient to encompass virtually any instrument that might be sold as an investment, p. 1030.

LO.3   Compare and distinguish between the Securities Act of 1933 and the Securities Exchange Act of 1934

See the discussion regarding the regulation of the original issue of securities, beginning on p. 1030.
See the discussion regarding the secondary distribution of securities designed to prevent fraudulent and manipulative practices on the securities exchanges, beginning on p. 1034.

LO.4   Explain how the 1934 Act's policy of fostering reliance on market integrity is served by Rule 10b-5 private investor lawsuits when injured by material misstatements by the issuer

See the *Basic Inc.* case on "materiality" in merger cases on p. 1037.
See the *Matrixx* case on "materiality" in the pharmaceutical industry on pp. 1037–1038.

LO.5   Explain the factors that subject an individual to liability for insider trading

See the *Dirks* case that illustrates the rule that when the insider does not breach a fiduciary duty, a tippee does not violate securities laws, p. 1042.
See the *O'Hagan* case regarding outsiders who have access to confidential information that will affect a company's stock price, p. 1043.

LO.6   Explain how securities firms regulate themselves and provide a process to resolve controversies relating to the sale of securities

See the regulatory functions performed by the Financial Industry Regulatory Authority on p. 1046.
See the discussion on the NASD and NYSE regulatory procedures and arbitration codes beginning on p. 1046.

KEY TERMS

blue sky laws	insider information	security
cash tender offer	prospectus	short-swing profit
fraud-on-the-market	registration requirements	temporary insider
insider	registration statement	tippee

QUESTIONS AND CASE PROBLEMS

1. Cable operator Charter Communications Inc. arranged to overpay Scientific Atlanta and Motorola $20 for each set-top box it purchased—with the understanding that they would return the overpayment by purchasing cable advertising from Charter. The transactions, it was alleged, had no economic substance; but because Charter would then record the advertising purchases as revenue and capitalize its purchases of the set-top boxes—in violation of generally accepted accounting principles—the transactions would enable Charter to fool its auditor into approving a financial statement showing it met projected Wall Street revenue and operating cash-flow numbers. The suppliers agreed to the arrangement. Charter used the inflated number of $17 million on its financial statements that were filed with the SEC and reported to the public. The suppliers had no role in preparing or disseminating Charter's financial statements, and their own statements booked the transactions as a wash. A private right of action was brought against the cable box suppliers by investors for damages under Section 10(b) of the 1934 Act as "aiders and abettors." Decide. [*Stoneridge Investment Partners, LLC v. Scientific Atlantic, Inc.*, 552 U.S. 148]

2. Corporation A was involved in merger discussions with Corporation B. During this time, Corporation A made public statements denying that any merger negotiations were taking place or that it knew of any corporate developments that would account for heavy trading activity in its stock. A class of former shareholders who sold Corporation A stock after the public denial of merger activity and the announcement of the merger some six weeks later sued Corporation A, contending it made material misrepresentations of fact in denying the merger activity. Corporation A stock increased 25% upon the merger announcement. Corporation A stated that at the time of its denial of merger activity it was just involved in preliminary negotiations and its actions were not material until negotiations reached an agreement in principle. Moreover, it asserted that the shareholders made no showing that they relied on the denial statement. Decide.

3. *Business Week* magazine is sent to a national distributor of magazines, Curtis Circulations Co., which sells the magazines to various wholesalers, including Hudson News. *Business Week* publishes a column entitled "Inside Wall Street," and the evidence shows that stocks discussed favorably in the column tend to increase in value after release to the public. *Business Week* has a strict confidentiality policy prior to release of the magazine to the public applicable to all employees involved in production and distribution. This policy also applies to Hudson News. Gregory Savage, an employee of Hudson News, and the "top person" in the delivery room area, arranged to have the "Inside Wall Street" column faxed to his neighbor, a stockbroker named Larry Strath, prior to the close of the market on Thursday and prior to release to the public that evening. Strath traded on the information and passed it on to Joseph Falcone, who likewise traded on the basis of this information. While Falcone paid Strath $200 for a copy of the column each week, he contends that the information he received was too remote from the *Business Week* confidentiality policy to be actionable by the SEC. What theory do you believe the SEC pursued against Falcone? What are the elements of the theory? How would you decide this case? [*United States v. Falcone.* 257 F.3d 226 (2d Cir.)]

4. Minnesota Prostate Research Labs, Inc. (MPRL), made an initial public offering of its shares in August 1998. It stated in its prospectus that research on laboratory animals indicated that the lab may have discovered a cure for prostate cancer in humans. MPRL pointed out as well that results in animal testing did not necessarily mean that the same positive result would occur in humans. MPRL shares initially traded at $10 per share in 1999 and rose to $18 in August 2001, when the MPRL prostate cancer drug was finally approved for sale to the public. Tuttle reviewed the initial prospectus and analysts' reports on the drug and purchased 10,000 shares at $18 per share on August 18, 2001. In September of 2002, an independent study of the four leading prostate medicines indicated that MPRL's product was as effective as sugar pills in curing prostate cancer and other prostate symptoms. The price of MPRL shares plummeted to $6 per share. Tuttle is contemplating a Rule 10b-5 securities fraud class-action lawsuit against MPRL. Advise him of his chances of success in this lawsuit and any expenses that he would be exposed to other than the cost of his attorney.

5. The following transactions in Heritage Cosmetics Co., Inc., stock took place: On January 21, Jones, the corporation's vice president of marketing, purchased 1,000 shares of stock at $25 per share. On January 24, Sylvan, a local banker and director of Heritage, purchased 500 shares of stock at $26 per share. On January 30, McCarthy, a secretary at Heritage, purchased 300 shares of stock at $26.50. On February 12, Winfried, a rich investor from New England, purchased 25,000 shares at an average price of $26 per share. At that time, Heritage had a total of 200,000 shares of stock outstanding. On June 14, Winfried sold his entire holding in Heritage at an average price of $35 per share. In a local newspaper interview, Winfried was quoted regarding his reasons for selling the stock: "I have not had the pleasure of meeting any person from Heritage, but I have the highest regard for the Heritage Company, … I sold my stock simply because the market has gone too high and in my view is due for a correction." After independently

reading Winfried's prediction on the stock market, Jones, Sylvan, and McCarthy sold their shares on June 15 for $33 per share. On June 20, Heritage Co. demanded that Jones, Sylvan, McCarthy, and Winfried pay the corporation the profits made on the sale of the stock. Was the corporation correct in making such a demand on each of these people?

6. Dorozhko hacked into the corporate network of Thomson Financial on October 17, 2007 at 2:15 P.M. and gained access to IMS Health's soon-to-be-released negative earnings announcement due out at 5:00 P.M. He purchased $41,670 worth of put options. IMS shares were trading at $29.56 at the close on October 17. On October 18, 2007, IMS Health's stock price plunged at the opening of trading to $21.20 per share, on the negative news issued at 5:00 P.M. on October 17. Within six minutes, Dorozhko sold the put options for a net profit of $286,456. Did Dorozhko's "hacking and trading" violate either the traditional or misappropriation theories of "insider trading"?

7. Mary Dale worked in the law office of Emory Stone, an attorney practicing securities law. While proofreading Mary's keying of a document relating to the merger of two computer software companies, Emory joked to her, "If I weren't so ethical, I could make a few bucks on this info. Nomac Software stock prices are going to take off when this news hits 'The Street.'" That evening, Mary told her friend Rick Needleworth, a stockbroker, what her boss had said. Needleworth bought 500 shares of Nomac Software stock the next day and sold it three days later when the news of the merger was made public. He made a profit of $3,500. Did Dale, Stone, or Needleworth violate any securities law(s) or ethical principles with respect to the profit made by Needleworth?

8. International Advertising, Inc. (IA), would like to raise $10 million in new capital to open new offices in eastern Europe. It believes it could raise the capital by selling shares of stock to its directors and executive officers as well as to its bank and a large insurance company whose home office is located near IA's headquarters. Opposition to the

financing plan exists because of the trouble, time, and cost involved with registering with the SEC. Advise IA how best to proceed with the registration of the new issue of stock.

9. Dubois sold Hocking a condominium that included an option to participate in a rental pool arrangement. Hocking elected to participate in the arrangement. Under it, the rental pool's agent rented condominiums, pooled the income, and after deducting a management fee, distributed the income to the owners on a pro rata basis. Hocking brought a Rule 10b-5 fraud action against Dubois. Dubois contended that the sale of the condominium was not a security under the securities acts, so Hocking could not bring a securities suit against her. Was Dubois correct? [*Hocking v. Dubois*, 839 F.2d 290 (9th Cir.)]

10. William Rubin, president of Tri-State Mining Co., sought a loan from Bankers Trust Co. To secure the loan, he pledged worthless stock in six companies and represented that the stock was worth $1.7 million. He also arranged for fictitious quotations to appear in an investment reporting service used by the bank to value the pledged securities. The bank loaned Rubin $475,000 and took the securities as pledged collateral. In a criminal action against Rubin under section 17(a) of the 1933 act, Rubin's defense was that the pledging of securities did not constitute an offer or sale of securities under the act. Was Rubin correct? [*Rubin v. United States*, 449 U.S. 424]

11. J. C. Cowdin, a director of Curtis-Wright Co., phoned Robert Gintel, a partner of Cady, Roberts & Co., a stock brokerage house, and advised him that Curtis-Wright's quarterly dividend had been cut. Gintel immediately entered orders selling Curtis-Wright shares for his customers' accounts. The stock was selling at over $40 a share when the orders were executed but fell to $30 soon after the dividend cut was announced to the public. The SEC contended that the firm, Cady, Roberts & Co., and Gintel violated section 10(b) of the 1934 act, Rule 10b-5, and section 17(a) of the 1933 act. Gintel and Cady, Roberts & Co. disagreed. Decide. [*In re Cady, Roberts & Co.*, 40 SEC 907]

12. In a January 2000 prospectus for its initial public offering of shares, Apex Oil Discovery Co. (AODC) estimated a sizable volume of oil production based on the studies of two geologists and a test well at one of its Oklahoma properties. A cautionary statement advised that the projections were only estimates based on the opinion of the two experts and a test well, and that actual production could vary significantly. Lutz bought 10,000 shares of Apex in May 2000 for $20 per share. By October 2000, 12 of its 15 drilling operations under way that year turned out to be dry holes. On October 18, 2000, AODC stock fell to $6 per share. Lutz brought a private securities civil action under SEC Rule 10b-5 against AODC, alleging that the AODC oil production estimates that induced him to buy the stock were fraudulent as evidenced by the 80 percent failure rate of its drilling operations. What defense, if any, does AODC have in this case? Decide.

13. Douglas Hansen, Leo Borrell, and Bobby Lawrence were three psychiatrists who recognized the need for an inpatient treatment facility for adolescents and children in their community. They became limited partners in building a for-profit psychiatric facility. Each had a 6.25 percent interest in the partnership. Healthcare International, Inc., the general partner with a 75 percent interest, had expertise in hospital construction, management, and operation. Hansen, Borrell, and Lawrence asserted that the managerial control of the partnership was undertaken and operated by the general partner to the exclusion of the limited partners. The doctors claimed that their interest was a security—"an investment contract"—that gave them status to file a securities suit against the general partner under the 1934 act. The general partner disagreed. Decide. [*L & B Hospital Ventures, Inc. v. Health-care International, Inc.*, 894 F.2d 150 (5th Cir.)]

14. Texas International Speedway, Inc. (TIS), filed a registration statement and prospectus with the Securities and Exchange Commission offering a total of $4,398,900 in securities to the public. The proceeds of the sale were to be used to finance the construction of an automobile

speedway. The entire issue was sold on the offering date. TIS did not meet with success, and the corporation filed a petition for bankruptcy. Huddleston and Bradley instituted a class-action suit in U.S. district court on behalf of themselves and other purchasers of TIS securities. Their complaint alleged violations of section 10(b) of the 1934 act. The plaintiffs sued most of the participants in the offering, including the accounting firm of Herman & MacLean. Herman & MacLean had issued an opinion concerning certain financial statements and a pro forma balance sheet that were contained in the registration statement and prospectus. The plaintiffs claimed that the defendants had engaged in a fraudulent scheme to misrepresent or conceal material facts regarding the financial condition of TIS, including the costs incurred in building the speedway. Herman & MacLean contended that the case should be dismissed because section 11 of the 1933 act provides an express remedy for a misrepresentation in a registration statement, so an action under section 10(b) of the 1934 act is precluded. Decide. [*Herman & MacLean v. Huddleston*, 459 U.S. 375]

15. Melvin J. Ford, president of International Loan Network, Inc. (ILN), promoted ILN's financial enrichment programs to ILN members and prospective members with evangelical fervor at revival-style "President's Night" gatherings. His basic philosophy was this:

The movement of money creates wealth. What we believe is that if you organize people and get money moving, it can actually create wealth.

One ILN program was the Maximum Consideration Program, which, somewhat like a chain letter, provided $5,000 awards to members who sold $3,000 worth of new memberships called PRAs and made a deposit on the purchases of nonresidential real estate. According to Ford, an individual purchasing $16,000 worth of PRAs could receive an award of up to $80,000 because "all of a sudden the velocity of money increases to such a point, the ability to create wealth expands to such a degree, that we could come back and give somebody an award for up to $80,000." The SEC contended that ILN was selling unregistered investment contracts in violation of the 1933 act. ILN disagreed, contending that the program never guaranteed a return and was thus not an investment contract. Decide. Could ILN have provided full disclosure to investors concerning the program in a prospectus if required by the 1933 act? [*SEC v. ILN, Inc.*, 968 F.2d 1304 (D.C. Cir.)]

CPA QUESTIONS

1. Which of the following is least likely to be considered a security under the Securities Act of 1933?

   a. Stock options

   b. Warrants

   c. General partnership interests

   d. Limited partnership interests

2. Which of the following statements is correct regarding a common stock offering that requires registration under the Securities Act of 1933?

   a. The registration statement is automatically effective when filed with the SEC.

   b. The issuer would act unlawfully if it were to sell the common stock without providing the investor with a prospectus.

   c. The SEC will determine the investment value of the common stock before approving the offering.

   d. The issuer may make sales 10 days after filing the registration statement.

3. Hamilton Corp. is making a $4,500,000 securities offering under Rule 505 of Regulation D of the Securities Act of 1933. Under this regulation, Hamilton is:

   a. Required to provide full financial information to accredited investors only

   b. Allowed to make the offering through a general solicitation

   c. Limited to selling to no more than 35 nonaccredited investors

   d. Allowed to sell to an unlimited number of investors both accredited and nonaccredited

4. Under the liability provisions of Section 11 of the Securities Act of 1933, an auditor may help to establish the defense of due diligence if:

 I. The auditor performed an additional review of the audited statements to ensure that the statements were accurate as of the effective date of a registration statement.

 II. The auditor complied with GAAS.

   a. I only

   b. II only

   c. Both I and II

   d. Neither I nor II

5. Under the Securities Exchange Act of 1934, which of the following conditions generally will allow an issuer of securities to terminate the registration of a class of securities and suspend the duty to file periodic reports?

	The corporation has fewer than 300 shareholders	The securities are listed on a national securities exchange
a.	Yes	Yes
b.	Yes	No
c.	No	Yes
d.	No	No

CHAPTER

Accountants' Liability and Malpractice

© Manuel Gutjahr/iStockphoto.com

learningoutcomes

After studying this chapter, you should be able to

LO.1   Define *malpractice*

LO.2   Distinguish malpractice liability from breach of contract liability

LO.3   List which third parties may recover for the malpractice liability of accountants and when they may do so

LO.4   Discuss the difference between accounting malpractice and fraud

LO.5   Explain how Sarbanes-Oxley and Dodd-Frank have affected the accounting profession and accountants' liability

W hen is a professional, such as an accountant, liable for harm caused by improper performance?

A. GENERAL PRINCIPLES OF ACCOUNTANTS' LIABILITY

Whether an accountant can be held liable for malpractice requires a look at what constitutes malpractice, the effect of others' conduct on liability, whether there are limitations on such liability, and whether there are damages that resulted from malpractice.

1. What Constitutes Malpractice?

An accountant who makes a contract to perform services has a duty to exercise the skill and care that are common for the accounting profession.[1] If the services are not rendered in accordance with those standards, the result is **malpractice**, as it is commonly called, which is a tort and a form of negligence.

malpractice – practice that occurs when services are not properly rendered in accordance with commonly accepted standards; negligence by a professional in performing his or her skill.

Accountants are not insurers of the content of financial statements they prepare and, unless they agree to do so, are not normally liable for detecting fraud.[2] Changes made under Sarbanes-Oxley (covered later in the chapter) require accountants who perform audit work to undertake the role of certifying the internal controls of companies. This certification requirement was imposed with the hope that adequate internal controls can prevent fraud.[3] An accountant can, however, be held liable for turning a blind eye to suspicious issues and items.[4]

The standards for accountants' professional liability are found in state and federal statutes (see Chapter 46 for a discussion of federal securities issues, liabilities, and standards), court decisions, the actual contract with the client, generally accepted auditing standards (GAAS), and generally accepted accounting practices (GAAP).[5] Following GAAP and GAAS is persuasive but not conclusive evidence of meeting standards for the profession. Customs in any profession are persuasive but not conclusive evidence of professional performance.

Recovery from an accountant for malpractice requires proof of the elements of negligence (see Chapter 9 for more information). The duty and breach of duty elements are determined by the professional performance standards. The breach of professional standards must have caused the losses or damages, which must also be established.

Certified public accountants are liable for damages proximately caused by their negligence, or their failure to observe sound accounting practices. Accountants owe their clients a duty to exercise the degree of care, skill, and competence that reasonably competent members of their profession would exercise under similar circumstances.[6] Accountants are also liable if they fail to call attention to a condition

---

[1] *Thornton, LLP v. Federal Deposit Ins. Corp.*, 435 Fed. Appx. 188 (4th Cir. 2011).
[2] In re *Countrywide Litigation*, 588 F. Supp. 2d 1132 (C.D. Cal. 2009).
[3] Section 404 of Sarbanes-Oxley has become a day-to-day term in business language as companies work to obtain their "404 certifications" from auditors. Securities and Exchange Commission, *Management's Reports on Internal Controls over Financial Reporting and Certification in Exchange Act Periodic Reports,* Securities Act Release No. 33-8283 (June 5, 2003).
[4] In re *MoneyGram Intern., Inc. Securities Litigation*, 626 F. Supp. 2d 947 (W.D. Minn. 2009).
[5] In re *CBI Holding Co.*, 419 B.R. 553 (S.D.N.Y. 2009).
[6] *Greenstein, Logan & Co. v. Burgess Marketing, Inc.*, 744 S.W.2d 170 (Tex. 1987).

that causes losses if the client could have taken preventive steps following the accountant's warning.[7]

An accountant is liable to the client if the accountant negligently fails to detect or fraudulently conceals signs that an employee of the client is embezzling or the internal audit controls of the client's business are not being observed or are lax. An accountant who prepares tax returns and acts as tax manager for the client will be liable when additional taxes or penalties are assessed against the client as a result of the accountant's negligent advice. For example, a client may recover damages from the accountant when the accountant negligently fails to inform the client of the tax consequences of selling the business.[8]

CASE SUMMARY

This Is Interesting—You Owe Me

FACTS: Bruce Ashland is a certified public accountant. He began providing services for Doug O'Bryan Contracting in 1987–1988. From 1979 through the first quarter of 1995, O'Bryan operated as a sole proprietorship. O'Bryan's well-drilling business prospered and grew during the early 1990s. On several occasions over the years, Ashland recommended to O'Bryan that he incorporate. O'Bryan ultimately followed Ashland's advice and incorporated effective April 1, 1995.

For taxation purposes, incorporating in April meant that O'Bryan remained a cash basis taxpayer for the first quarter of the year, January 1, 1995, through March 31, 1995. Then, on incorporation, the business changed to accrual basis accounting for the last three quarters, April 1, 1995, through December 31, 1995. When Ashland prepared O'Bryan's 1995 tax return in October 1996, he mistakenly calculated O'Bryan's income for the first quarter using accrual based figures. As a result, Ashland understated, and consequently underreported, O'Bryan's realized income for the first quarter.

Another accountant discovered Ashland's mistake during O'Bryan's divorce proceedings in 1997. O'Bryan's divorce attorney hired a different accountant to review and amend the mistaken return, and, as of June 28, 1998, O'Bryan had $239,933 in additional tax liability for 1995 plus interest. O'Bryan brought suit against Ashland for accountant malpractice seeking the interest the IRS charged on his unpaid tax liability. At trial, Ashland admitted negligence. The jury held Ashland liable for, among other things, the interest the IRS had assessed against O'Bryan, $39,038.83.

DECISION: The court, after looking at differing views around the country on awarding interest, concluded that damages for accountant's malpractice should put the client in the same position that he or she would have been in had the accountant not been negligent. Here, O'Bryan would not have owed the interest if Ashland had computed his taxes properly. O'Bryan was able to establish that he could have paid the taxes when they were due. While he had the use of the money, that use did not change the fact that he had to pay an additional sum that would not have been owed if his accountant had computed his taxes correctly. [*O'Bryan v. Ashland*, 717 N.W.2d 632 (S.D. 2006)][9]

---

[7] *Ronson v. David S. Talesnick, CPA*, 33 F. Supp. 2d 347 (D.N.J. 1999).
[8] *Deloitte, Haskins, & Sells v. Green*, 403 S.E.2d 818 (Ga. 1991).
[9] Other courts have reached different results on the ability of the client to recover interest due the IRS. *Rosenbach v. Diversified Group, Inc.*, 819 N.Y.S. 2d 851 (N.Y. Sup. Ct. 2006). Some courts treat recovery as a jury issue. *Amato v. KPMG LLP*, 2006 WL 2376245 (M.D. Pa.).

2. Choice of Remedy

In addition to liability under tort law for malpractice, accountants may be held liable for breach of contract for their failure to meet professional standards.

(A) **BREACH OF CONTRACT.** An accountant breaches an audit contract if the audit work, for example, was not completed. In such a situation, the client need not pay the accountant's fee. If the work was complete, but there were minor errors, the damages caused by the error can be deducted from the fee.

Remedies for breach of contract are not available to third parties against accountants because they are not ordinarily considered third-party beneficiaries of contracts with accountants.

(B) **TORT LIABILITY.** A client or third party may be able to recover from an accountant on the basis of negligence, gross negligence, or fraud. These theories are covered in the remaining sections of the chapter.

Because malpractice is both a breach of contract and an independent tort, the client who is harmed has the choice of recovering for breach of contract or for the particular tort that is involved. Generally, the client will bring a tort action because there are higher damages under tort law than those afforded for a breach of contract. The statute of limitations on torts versus contracts may also influence the theory for liability. The statute of limitations begins to run on the tort of malpractice from the date the harm was discovered. The contract statute of limitations runs from the date the contract is breached. This time differential may be very important because in some cases, the client may not realize that there has been any harm until some time after a breach of the contract occurred.

3. The Environment of Accountants' Malpractice Liability

Accountants have moved from being primarily clerical business participants to being essential players in business strategies. In addition, accountants have moved from being employees of one employer to being independent contractors performing accounting services for many clients. Accountants are now employed to produce data that third parties use and rely on in making decisions about loans or investments. **For Example,** accountants prepare statements submitted to banks that will use those statements to determine whether to make a loan or extend a line of credit. Auditors' certifications of financial statements become part of the documents given to potential investors in companies. As these changes in the role of accountants took place, it became natural for courts to allow third parties relying on accountants' work and certifications to recover from the accountants when the accountants' and auditors' malpractice caused damages to them.

At the same time that these changes were taking place in the nature and role of accountants, changes were also taking place in other areas of the law. Manufacturers and parts suppliers were held liable to those who purchased the final products and were injured by defects in them. The rising tide of liability to third parties has naturally influenced the law regulating accountants.[10]

---

[10] The interplay between the various areas of malpractice liability and those of accountants is seen further in the fact that the Restatement (Second) of Torts does not contain a separate provision applicable only to accountants but deals with the subject of malpractice liability of accountants to third parties in a general section (§552). Section 552 provides that

> [O]ne who in the course of his business, profession or employment, or in any other transaction in which he has a pecuniary interest, supplies false information for the guidance of others in their business transactions, is subject to liability for pecuniary loss caused to them by their justifiable reliance on the information, if he fails to exercise reasonable care or competence in obtaining or communicating the information.

The section then defines which parties can enforce this liability.

4. Limitation of Liability

Can accountants protect themselves from liability for malpractice claims of clients and third parties? Because the law generally permits any contracting party to limit or disclaim liability for negligence, an accountant may exclude liability for malpractice on a theory of negligence. Influenced by the consumer protection movement and by the law governing product liability, courts will require such disclaimers to be (1) clear and unambiguous and (2) conspicuous. If these requirements are not met, the disclaimers are not enforceable.

(A) SCOPE OF LIMITATION. Disclaimers are valid in certain limited circumstances.[11] **For Example,** when a client owns land in a foreign country, it is reasonable for the accountant to accept the valuation placed on the land by someone in that foreign country. The accountant should, however, include in the financial statement prepared for the client a statement that the valuation of that land was obtained from an identified person in the foreign country and that the accountant assumes no responsibility for the accuracy of that valuation. If the accountant's work has been so restricted, the accountant is protected from claims of third parties because there has been full disclosure about the accountant's limited information and ability to verify the work of others. **For Example,** when the accountant is restricted from examining accounts receivable and the accountant's certification states that no opinion was expressed as to accounts receivable, the accountant cannot be held liable if the accounts receivable turn out to be overstated.[12]

(B) LIMITATIONS ON EXCULPATORY PROVISIONS. A disclaimer based on lack of knowledge does not protect the accountant from liability if the accountant knew or had reason to know that the statements made were false. If the accountant states that he had no personal knowledge, he impliedly represents that he did not have any knowledge or reason to know that the statements were not correct. A disclaimer that is made when the accountant has reason to suspect that underlying information is false would be **misrepresentation** and would result in the accountant's liability.[13]

In some states, a **limitation-of-liability** or **exculpatory clause** protects the accountant from a malpractice suit brought by a client only, not from a suit brought by a third party. In such cases, courts apply the general rule of contract law that only a party to a contract is bound by an exculpatory or limitation-of-liability clause.

misrepresentation – False statement of fact made innocently without any intent to deceive.

limitation-of-liability clause – Provision in a contract stating that one of the parties is not liable for damages in case of breach; also called *exculpatory clause.*

exculpatory clause – Provision in a contract stating that one of the parties is not liable for damages in case of breach; also called *limitation-of-liability clause.*

B. ACCOUNTANTS' LIABILITY TO THIRD PARTIES: BEYOND PRIVITY

Most accountants' malpractice litigation involves the question of whether third parties may recover from the accountants, not on what standards of conduct accountants should observe. Various issues and factors, covered in both judicial

[11] The American Institute of Certified Public Accountants has an ethics rule on liability limitations and indemnifications that took effect on July 1, 2009, and can be found at **www.aicpa.org/download/ethics/EDITED_Adopted_501_8_final.pdf.**
[12] *Stephans Industries, Inc. v. Haskins & Sells,* 438 F.2d 357 (10th Cir. 1971).
[13] However, an accountant can provide financial information on an employee's severance package and disclaim liability by advising the employee to obtain independent tax advice. *Buehner v. IBM Corp.,* 704 N.Y.S.2d 303 (2000).

decisions and statutes, determine whether accountants will be held liable to third parties.[14]

5. Status of the Accountant

An accountant may be a full-time employee of a company, an independent contractor doing regular work for a client, or an independent outside auditor. What constitutes negligence is the same for all three types of accountants. The liability of the accountant to the third party, when recognized, is based on the reliance of the third party on the work of the accountant.[15]

6. Conflicting Theories of Accountants' Third-Party Liability

There are a number of theories that have been developed for third parties to recover for an accountant's negligence. These views may be identified as (1) the privity rule, (2) the contact rule, (3) the known user rule, (4) the foreseeable user rule, and (5) the intended user rule. In addition, some courts follow (6) a flexible rule, deciding each case as it arises. Each of these views is an attempt to draw a boundary line between the interloper and a "proper" plaintiff with sufficient connection to the accountant for recovery for the accountant's negligence. In some states, statutes define when nonprivity plaintiffs may recover for an accountant's negligence.[16]

privity rule – Succession or chain of relationship to the same thing or right, such as privity of contract, privity of estate, privity of possession.

(A) THE PRIVITY RULE. The **privity rule** precludes a negligence malpractice suit by a third party. This rule holds that only the party in privity with the accountant—that is, the accountant's client—may recover from the accountant.[17] When the privity rule is applied, a bank lending money to the accountant's client cannot recover from the accountant for malpractice.

CASE SUMMARY

The Ear, Nose, and Throat Guy Who Took $1.4 Million to the Alps

FACTS: McGladrey conducted a financial audit of Subspecialty Centers of America, LLC (SCA). SCA is owned by Dr. Mark S. Weinberger, an ear, nose, and throat surgeon. The audit was for the year ending December 31, 2003. McGladrey issued its audit report in March 2004. The audit report indicated that SCA's "balance sheet presents fairly in all material respects to the financial position of SCA in conformity with generally accepted auditing standards." Citibank received the audit report and in June 2004 made a $1.4 million term loan to SCA. The term loan was a modification of a prior term loan that Citibank had made to SCA. Prior to 2004, Citibank had four outstanding loans to SCA: (1) a mortgage loan for its diagnostic surgery center; (2) a mortgage loan for its office condominium; (3) a revolving line of credit; and (4) a term loan. The 2004 term loan was an increase and an extension of the prior term loan.

---

[14] *Tricontinental Industries, Ltd. v. PricewaterhouseCoopers, LLP*, 475 F.3d 824 (8th Cir. 2007).
[15] *Brown v. KPMG Peat Marwick*, 856 S.W.2d 742 (Tex 1993) but see *Prospect High Income Fund v. Grant Thorton, LLP*, 203 S.W.3d 602 (Tex. App. 2006).
[16] See, e.g., Ark. Code Ann. §16–114–302 (2012); 225 Ill. Comp. Stat. 450/30.1 (2012); Kan. Stat. Ann. §1–402 (2012); La.Rev.Stat. Ann. §37:91 (2007); Mich. Comp. Laws §600.2962 (2012); N.J.S.A. 2A:53A–25(b)(2) (2012); Utah Code Ann. §58–26a-602 (2012); Wyo. Stat. Ann. §33–3–201 (2009).
[17] This rule was originally known as the New York rule, *Ultramares Corp. v. Touche*, 174 N.E. 441 (N.Y. 1931). Although it has been replaced in New York by the contact rule, the privity rule is still the law in many jurisdictions. *Solow v. Heard McElroy & Vestal, LLP*, 7 So.3d 1269 (La. App. 2009).

CASE SUMMARY

Continued

Dr. Weinberger took the $1.4 million and left for Europe. Dr. Weinberger was subsequently located residing in a tent in the Italian Alps and was brought back to the United States in 2010. Hundreds of malpractice suits were filed against him, and federal prosecutors charged him with multiple counts of health care fraud.

Citibank brought suit to recover from McGladrey the money that it loaned SCA on the grounds that it relied on McGladrey's negligent audit of Dr. Weinberger's surgical practice in making the $1.4 million term loan to SCA.

The trial court excluded testimony from Edward A. Bartko, an accountant and senior managing director in the corporate finance department of FTI Consulting, Inc., who was engaged by Citibank to offer a professional opinion regarding McGladrey's audit of SCA. Bartko opined that McGladrey's audit was deficient because McGladrey did not use health care specialists who possessed the expertise to analyze the medical files of SCA's patients, and who would have ultimately uncovered any medical fraud. Bartko's report indicated that FTI's team of health care specialists uncovered numerous red flags in SCA's patient files, which should have been discovered by McGladrey's audit.

The jury found for McGladrey and Citibank appealed.

DECISION: The court held that Mr. Bartko was not an expert and could not simply parrot the work of others, so his testimony was properly excluded. The court also held that Citibank had made many loans to SCA and that the $1.4 million loan was part of an entire package of lending agreements and that the jury was permitted to consider the relationship as part of its determination of whether McGladrey was responsible for the information that led to the loan, that is, the clean audit opinion. The court held that the decision to lend was based on other factors and not simply on the audit and financial report of McGladrey. [*Citibank, N.A. v. McGladrey and Pullen, LLP*, 953 N.E.2d 38 (Ill. App. 2011)]

(B) THE CONTACT RULE. In relaxing the privity requirement, New York now allows a third party to recover from a negligent accountant if there was some contact between the third party and the accountant. **For Example,** an accountant may go to a bank to see what information the bank requires for the accountant's client to obtain a loan. In this case, there is a sufficient "link" or "contact" between the bank and the accountant to allow the bank to recover from the accountant if it sustains a loss because of the accountant's negligence.[18] The New York *contact rule* requires that the accountant meet or communicate with the nonprivity party to establish a relationship equivalent to privity. The accountant must also know the purpose of the accounting work and foresee the nonprivity party's reliance on that work.[19]

There must be enough contact with, or dealings between, the third party and the accountant to give the accountant reason to know that the third party was relying for a particular purpose on the financial statements prepared by the accountant.[20]

[18] *Sykes v. RFD Third Ave.*, 938 N.E.2d 325 (N.Y. 2010); *Retirement Programs for Employees of Town of Fairfield v. NEPC, LLC*, 2011 WL 6934794, 53 Conn. L. Rptr. 194 (Conn. Super. 2011). Some courts are strict on the contact rule and describe the contact rule not as a different rule but as requiring "a relationship sufficiently intimate to be equated with privity." *Empire of American v. Arthur Andersen & Co.*, 514 N.Y.S.2d 578 (N.Y. 1987). The contact rule has been adopted by a minority of states. *Idaho Bank & Trust Co. v. First Bankcorp of Idaho*, 772 P.2d 720 (Idaho 1989).

[19] *Travelers Cas. and Sur. Co. of America v. Ernst & Young LLP*, 542 F.3d 475 (5th Cir. 2008).

[20] The contact rule applies to malpractice defendants generally. It is not limited to suits against accountants. *Ossining Union Free School District v. Anderson*, 539 N.E.2d 91 (N.Y. 1989), but see *Indianapolis-Marion County Public Library v. Charlier Clark & Linard, P.C.*, 900 N.E.2d 801 (Ind. App. 2009).

(c) THE KNOWN USER RULE. Under this rule for nonprivity parties, the accountant is liable to third parties who experience a loss as a result of the accountant's negligence when the accountant knew that the third party would be using the accountant's work product. **For Example,** a shareholder may recover from an accountant for negligently preparing and certifying an annual financial report that was prepared for distribution to shareholders.[21]

Under the known user rule, the fact that the nonprivity party's reliance on a financial statement was foreseeable does not entitle the third party to recover from the accountant for negligent preparation of the statement. The third party must show that the accountant knew the statement would be furnished to that plaintiff. Thus, under this rule, the plaintiff's reliance must thus be actually foreseen and not merely reasonably foreseeable.[22]

Under the known user rule, it is sufficient if the user or third party is a member of a known class even though the identity of the particular user is not known to the accountant. However, some states hold that when the identity of the intended user is known to the accountant, another party coming within the same class cannot recover from the accountant.[23] **For Example,** an accountant prepares a financial statement for a client with the knowledge that the client will take it to First National Bank to obtain a loan. First National Bank may recover from the accountant for negligent loss even though the bank never had any direct contact or dealings (that is, was never in privity) with the accountant. However, no one other than First National may seek recovery from the accountant for negligence.

The fact that the third party was a foreseeable user does not afford a basis for recovery in a "known user" state. When an accountant prepares a financial statement for the client and nothing is said about what further use of the statement will be made, creditors of the client cannot recover from the accountant for negligent preparation of the statement. The client would be the only known user.

If the court follows the privity rule or the contact rule described in the two preceding sections, the known user cannot seek recovery from the accountant for negligent malpractice. Moreover, some courts that follow the known user rule apply it so strictly that a substitute foreseeable user is not permitted to recover. To illustrate, assume that in the example just given, the client was refused the loan by First National Bank. The client might then make an application for a loan to Second National Bank. In known-user states, Second National Bank could not recover from the accountant because it was not a known user.

(d) THE FORESEEABLE USER RULE. The accountant may foresee that a particular class of unknown parties will rely on her work. **For Example,** when the accountant prepares a financial statement knowing that the client is going to use it to borrow money from some bank or finance company, the accountant foresees a class of lenders. Similarly, the accountant may know that the financial statement will be used to sell the stock of the client corporation. Here again, there is a foreseeable class consisting of unknown parties.

---

[21] *Altrust Financial Services, Inc. v. Adams*, 76 So.2d 228 (Ala. 2011).

[22] *Lindner Fund v. Abney*, 770 S.W.2d 437 (Mo. App. 1989). The rule that the nonprivity plaintiff may recover from the accountant for malpractice negligence only if the accountant's statement was furnished to that plaintiff, or the accountant knew that the client who was given the statement would in turn give the statement to the plaintiff, is often identified as "the Restatement rule." This rule is based on Restatement (Second) Torts §482 (1965). There is, however, some uncertainty as to the exact boundaries of the Restatement rule. See *Finderne Management Co. Inc. v. Barrett*, 809 A.2d 857 (N.J. Super. 2002).

[23] *In re Enron Corp. Securities, Derivatives, & ERISA Litigation*, 762 F. Supp. 2d 942 (S.D. Tex. 2010).

The *foreseeable user rule* imposes liability on the accountant for negligent malpractice when he can foresee the parties who will rely on his work in the financial statements. The foreseeable user rule allows these third parties to recover for their losses without regard to the lack of privity of contract between them and the accountant.[24]

CASE SUMMARY

The Merger of Art and Papel

FACTS: Cast Art Industries* produced and sold collectible figurines and giftware. Papel Giftware was in the same line of business as Cast Art, and in spring 2000 Cast Art explored acquiring Papel. Among the factors that made Papel attractive to Cast Art were Papel's large number of existing customer accounts, its existing sales force, and its production facilities. Eventually, Cast Art decided on a merger, rather than an acquisition. Cast Art negotiated a loan agreement with PNC Bank for $22 million to fund the venture. PNC's conditions included that it receive audited financial statements and that Cast Art's CEO, Scott Sherman, personally guarantee $3.3 million of the loan.

KPMG (defendant) had audited Papel's financial statements since 1997. KPMG was already in the process of auditing Papel's 1998 and 1999 financial statements when Cast Art and Papel began their merger discussions. In its letter to the chairman of Papel's audit committee dated November 17, 1999, in which it agreed to undertake these audits and report the results, KPMG noted the parameters of its work:

> An audit is planned and performed to obtain reasonable assurance about whether the financial statements are free of material misstatement, whether caused by error or fraud. Absolute assurance is not attainable because of the nature of audit evidence and the characteristics of fraud. Therefore, there is a risk that material errors, fraud (including fraud that may be an illegal act), and other illegal acts may exist and not be detected by an audit performed in accordance with generally accepted auditing standards. Also, an audit is not designed to detect matters that are immaterial to the financial statements.

The process of KPMG completing its audits of Papel's financial statements for the years 1998 and 1999 was protracted because of tensions between John Quinn, the KPMG partner responsible for the audit, and Frederick Wasserman, Papel's chief financial officer, resulting from slowness in providing KPMG with records as well as disagreements over adjustments that KPMG concluded had to be made to Papel's financial statements. Eventually, Wasserman agreed to certain adjustments, and KPMG concluded that the remainder were immaterial and waived their inclusion. In September 2000, KPMG delivered to Papel the completed audits for the years 1998 and 1999. KPMG included in its accompanying opinion letter, which again was addressed to the chairman of Papel's audit committee, that Papel "was not in compliance with certain financial covenants" with its lenders, which KPMG characterized as raising "substantial doubt about the Company's ability to continue as a going concern."

Cast Art obtained copies of the completed 1998 and 1999 audits and provided copies to PNC. Three months later, in December 2000, Cast Art and Papel consummated the merger. Shortly after the merger was finalized, Cast Art began to experience difficulty in collecting some of the accounts receivable that it had believed Papel had had outstanding prior to the merger. Cast Art began its own investigation and learned that the 1998 and 1999 financial statements prepared by Papel were inaccurate and that Papel had engaged regularly in accelerating revenue.

---

[24] *In re Washington Mut., Inc. Securities, Derivative & ERISA Litigation*, 2010 WL 2545415 (W.D. Wash. 2010). See also *Bank of America, N.A. v. BDO Seidman, LLP*, 2012 WL 806007 (Mass. Super. 2012).

CASE SUMMARY

Continued

Papel did not follow its stated policy to recognize revenue from sales when goods were shipped and invoices sent. Papel routinely booked revenue from goods that had not yet been shipped. For example, testimony at trial established that Papel would pack goods for shipment and book the revenue but then simply place the shipping cartons in trailers on its property and color code the invoices to note when the goods were, in fact, to be shipped and billed. There was also testimony that at certain points Papel would not close out its books at month's end. Rather, it would hold them open and book the improperly extended month revenue that was earned in the following period. There was also testimony that at least one transaction, referred to at trial as the "Bookman" transaction, was a fraudulent entry of a $121,244 sale that never occurred.

Although Cast Art knew at the time of the merger that Papel was carrying a significant amount of debt, it was unaware of those accounting irregularities until after the merger was complete. The surviving corporation was unable to generate sufficient revenue to carry its debt load and produce new goods, and it eventually failed.

Following a lengthy trial for KPMG's malpractice, a jury returned a verdict in favor of Cast Art and awarded damages totaling $31.8 million, which was amended to $38,096,902 by the trial court judge. The Appellate Division upheld the verdict on liability but vacated the damage award and remanded for a new trial on damages. The case was certified to the New Jersey Supreme Court.

DECISION: The court held that New Jersey was not a privity state, but it was also not a foreseeable user state, that its statute was somewhere in between. The New Jersey standard is that the auditor must be aware AT THE TIME OF THE ENGAGEMENT that a third party would be using the auditor's work for making decisions about loans, etc. Because KPMG had begun the work prior to the plans for the merger, it could not be held liable to PNC for its audit work. Further, KPMG had issued qualifications on its opinion that would cast doubt on the company as an ongoing entity. The court held that it could not be held liable for the demise of the business. The New Jersey Supreme Court reversed a $38,000,000 verdict and dismissed the case. [*Cast Art Industries, LLC v. KPMG LLP*, 36 A.3d 1049 (N.J. 2012)]

*The individual plaintiffs, Scott Sherman, Gary Barsellotti, and Frank Colapinto, were Cast Art's shareholders. Because the claims of Cast Art and the individual plaintiffs are inextricably intertwined, the court referred simply to Cast Art and plaintiff in the singular.

(E) THE INTENDED USER RULE. Fear that the foreseeability rule does not sufficiently restrict the number of potential claimants has led some courts to limit recovery to those nonprivity users who were not merely foreseeable but also expected or intended to rely on the work of the accountant in a particular transaction or another similar transaction.[25] In this view, the accountant must have furnished the information directly to the nonprivity user or to the client, knowing that the client would transmit the information to the nonprivity plaintiff.

(F) THE FLEXIBLE RULE. Some courts have rejected the requirement of privity for malpractice against accountants but have not adopted any of the rules discussed in the preceding sections. These courts prefer to keep the question open and to decide each case as it arises.

(G) UNKNOWN USER. When the accountant has no knowledge of, or reason to know of, any third party's use of the accountant's work, the third party is not able to come

[25] *Bay Harbour Management LLC v. Carothers*, 282 Fed. Appx. 71, 2008 WL 2566557 (2nd Cir.). Some courts regard this rule as representing the majority view. The foreseeable user rule brings the law with respect to accountants into harmony with the tort law relating to other parties and activities.

Thinking Things Through

How Many Plaintiffs Can There Be in a Class-Action Securities Litigation?
How Many Defendants?

With the collapse of companies such as Countrywide, New Century Financial, Lehman Brothers, and other firms affected by or involved in the subprime mortgage market, litigation against all of these firms' auditors is ongoing. The following is a list of all of the types of plaintiffs who have brought suit against auditors:

- Shareholders who purchased stock in the companies

- State pension funds with stock in their portfolios

- Banks and other institutions that lent money

- Banks and other institutions that accepted stock as collateral for loans

- Universities that received stock as endowment gifts

- Companies that contracted with the companies after having requested financial statements

Applying the various standards for accountant liability you have learned, discuss whether each of these groups will be able to recover from the auditors for these firms and why or why not.

---

within any exception to the requirement of privity. Consequently, a nonprivity party cannot recover for the accountant's negligence when the accountant had no knowledge of any use that could affect the party.[26]

7. Nonliability Parties

There are some third parties to whom accountants do not have liability.

(A) INTERLOPERS. No court imposes liability on the accountant to a total stranger who gets possession of the accountant's work and then sustains a loss because of a false statement in the work. This applies regardless of whether the statement was negligent or intentional. **For Example,** assume that a negligently prepared financial statement of a corporation is thrown in the wastepaper basket and is then retrieved by a security guard. If the guard thinks that the statement is a "hot tip" and invests in the stock of the corporation on the basis of the statement, the guard cannot recover from the accountant for negligence in preparing the statement. Accountants are not liable to interlopers, but courts continue to struggle with drawing the line between interlopers and rightful third parties.

(B) PARTIES AFFECTED BY THE DECISION OF ACCOUNTANT'S CLIENT. On the basis of information furnished by the accountant to a client, the client may make a decision that affects a third party. **For Example,** a report by an independent auditor may indicate that a fiscal officer of the client has not handled funds properly. The report may indicate that it is economically unsound to enter into a contract with a third party. Assume that the client relies on the accountant's report and fires the employee or refuses to make a contract with the third party. If the report of the accountant was negligently made and the true facts would not have justified the action taken by the client, most courts hold that third parties harmed in this indirect way have no cause of action.[27]

[26] *Sundamerican Bank & Trust Co. v. Harrison*, 851 S.W.2d 563 (Mo. App. 1993).
[27] *Harper v. Inkster Public Schools*, 404 N.W.2d 776 (Mich. App. 1987).

8. Defenses to Accountants' Liability: Contributory and Comparative Negligence of the Client or Third Party

contributory negligence –
Negligence of the plaintiff that contributes to injury and at common law bars recovery from the defendant although the defendant may have been more negligent than the plaintiff.

(A) CONTRIBUTORY NEGLIGENCE. When an accountant has been negligent, the client's negligence may reduce the accountant's liability. To establish client **contributory negligence**, the accountant must show that the client contributed to the accountant's failure or that the client ignored the accountant's instructions. **For Example,** when the financial statement indicates that it is merely a working examination and is not certified by the accountant, the third party is negligent in relying on the statement and has been contributorily negligent.

If those who are using a financial statement are highly sophisticated and have been warned by their advisers that the corporate assets have been overvalued, the users cannot hold the accountant who prepared the financial statement liable for negligence in overstating the value of the corporate assets. In such a case, the users ares contributorily negligent, something that reduces or eliminates the accountant's liability.[28]

Some states ignore the contributory negligence of clients except in two circumstances. One is if the client interfered with the accountant's audit. Client interference with the accountant's work will excuse the accountant's liability. Another is if the client's negligence contributed to the accountant's negligence, but such contribution is not a bar to recovery by the client. **For Example,** the negligence of the accountant's client in keeping records is not a bar to the accountants' liability to the client because the liability comes from the accountant's failure to discover the true facts.[29] The issue in these circumstances becomes not whether the accountant knew, but whether the accountant should have known.

comparative negligence –
Defense to negligence that allows plaintiff to recover reduced damages based on his level of fault.

(B) COMPARATIVE NEGLIGENCE. Some states apply the **comparative negligence** concept and permit proof of the client's negligence.[30] Under comparative negligence standards, the accountant and the client are assessed a percentage of blame for their respective levels of negligence in the use and preparation of the financial statements, and the client's recovery is reduced by its percentage of fault. **For Example,** if a jury finds that the client was responsible for 30 percent of the resulting loss, recovery from the accountant is reduced by 30 percent.

9. Accountants' Fraud Malpractice Liability to Third Parties

Society in general condemns fraud more strongly than it does negligence. There is greater liability of accountants for fraudulent malpractice.

(A) WHAT CONSTITUTES FRAUD BY ACCOUNTANTS. *Fraud* is defined as a false statement made with knowledge that it was false or with reckless indifference as to whether it was true[31] with the intent that the listener rely on it. A false statement in accounting typically occurs when the client's financial statements make it appear to be in a better financial position than is actually the case. **For Example,** in the case of Bernie Madoff Securities, the auditor signed off for years on financial statements that made the firm seem solvent when in fact the company had lost $50 billion.

---

[28] *Scottish Heritable Trust v. Peat Marwick Main & Co.,* 81 F.3d 606 (5th Cir. 1996).
[29] *World Radio Laboratories, Inc. v. Coopers & Lybrand,* 538 N.W.2d 501 (Neb. App. 1995).
[30] *American Nat'l Bank v. Touche Ross & Co.,* 659 N.E.2d 1276 (Ohio 1996).
[31] In re *Dell Securities Litigation,* 591 F. Supp. 2d 877 (W.D. Tex. 2009).

FIGURE 47-1	*Theories of Accountants' Liability to Third Parties*

THEORY	TYPE OF LIABILITY	THIRD PARTY LIABILITY	CLIENT LIABILITY
STATUTORY	1933 SECURITIES ACT— OMISSION OR MISSTATEMENT IN REGISTRATION STATEMENT 1934 SECURITIES EXCHANGE ACT—10b (SEE CHAPTER 46)	PURCHASERS OF SHARES SHAREHOLDERS; PURCHASER OF SHARES	COMPANY
CONTRACT	BREACH OF CONTRACT	NO—NOT CONSIDERED THIRD PARTY BENEFICIARIES	MATERIAL BREACH; MINOR BREACH DAMAGES
TORT	PRIVITY REQUIRED	NO RECOVERY	RECOVERY ALLOWED UNLESS DEFENSES APPLY
	CONTACT RULE REQUIRED	CAN RECOVER IF ACTUAL CONTACT WITH ACCOUNTANT	
	KNOWN USER RULE	CAN RECOVER IF ACCOUNTANT KNOWS THIRD PARTY WILL USE FINANCIALS/WORK	
	FORESEEABLE USER RULE	CAN RECOVER IF ACCOUNTANT CAN FORESEE UNKNOWN PERSONS RELYING ON FINANCIALS	
	INTENDED USER RULE	CAN RECOVER IF ACCOUNTANT KNOWS CLIENT WILL GIVE IT TO ANOTHER	
	UNKNOWN USER	NO RECOVERY	
FRAUD	KNOWN AND UNKNOWN	RECOVERY	RECOVERY

At times, falsified financial statements are used as a means to obtain a downgrade on the ratings for the financial condition of a corporation. Such undervaluation then induces shareholders to sell their stock to a dominant group of shareholders. The false financial statement purposely undervalues the corporation's assets to make the shareholders believe their stock has little value and that sale at the low price offered by the dominant group is a good buy.

(B) ACCOUNTANTS' FRAUD LIABILITY TO INTENDED VICTIMS. Fraud by an accountant typically misleads a third party or a class of parties, a group whose identity is known to the accountant. Any such victim, whether an identified party or member of a class of potential victims, may recover from the accountant for loss caused by fraud. Privity (relating to liability for negligence) is not required when the basis of the malpractice suit is fraud. The public policy of preventing fraud overrides the concern of holding accountants liable to third parties.

An accountant might certify a false financial statement for a corporate client with knowledge that it will be used to sell the corporation's securities to third parties.[32] If so, the third parties may recover from the accountant for the damages sustained. **For Example,** an accountant has been held liable for disguising the true character of a hoped-for profit from the sale and resale of real estate. The accountant described the sale and resale as "deferred income," although there was little reason to believe that the transaction could ever be completed because the buyer, who was obligated to pay $5 million for the property, had assets of only $100,000. The financial statement would have shown a loss instead of a substantial profit if the true character of this risky transaction had been disclosed.

CASE SUMMARY

When the Auditor Just Duplicates What Management Wants

FACTS: Throughout the early and mid-1990s, Xerox had a significant market share in the digital copying products industry, a financially healthy company with revenues rising at a double-digit rate.

However, to get these earnings, Xerox had to reallocate revenues from service to the equipment portion of sales-type leases by assuming an artificial gross margin differential between the two lease components (or an assumed profit margin) that had no basis in economic reality. Xerox used this method to pull forward $617 million of equipment revenues from 1997 to 2000. Internally, KPMG referred to this method as "half-baked revenue recognition." Xerox's earnings were inflated $43 million as a result.

In 1996, KPMG objected to this practice as violating GAAP but, after arguments with Xerox senior management, approved its implementation in 1998, while continuing to criticize its use. In 1999, KPMG informed Xerox that this practice violated GAAP, but Xerox refused to follow this advice. Nevertheless, KPMG certified Xerox's 1999 and 2000 financial statements.

In 2001, Xerox began issuing a series of earnings restatements that would total $11 billion. In late 2001, Xerox announced that PriceWaterhouseCoopers, LLP ("PwC") was replacing KPMG as the company's new auditor for the 2001 fiscal year. Xerox paid a $10 million fine to the SEC to settle civil charges and also agreed to complete its restatement of earnings for 1997 through 2001.

Investors such as the Florida State pension plan and other individual investors (plaintiffs) brought suit against the executive officers of Xerox as well as Xerox's external auditor, KPMG, for fraud.

KPMG moved to have the complaint against it dismissed because it was not a party to the accounting fraud.

DECISION: The court found that the facts showed that KPMG was aware of accounting issues, that it raised these issues and problems to managers, and that each time, KPMG backed down on its concerns. KPMG replaced the lead auditor on the Xerox account when Xerox requested that he be replaced. The court referred to the accounting firm as a "virtual pushover" for the client and that its complicity in the continuing misstatements was enough to have a case of fraud brought to

[32] In re *IMAX Securities Litigation*, 587 F. Supp. 2d 471 (S.D.N.Y. 2008).

CASE SUMMARY

Continued

trial. KPMG was aware of the accounting problems and allowed them to continue. Knowledge is the key element in fraud and the plaintiffs had included enough facts to show that knowledge. The court held that the complaint should not be dismissed because there was enough alleged, which, if proved, was enough to hold KPMG liable. [***Carlson v. Xerox Corp.*, 392 F. Supp. 2d 267 (D. Conn. 2005)**]

C. SARBANES-OXLEY AUDITOR AND ACCOUNTING-RELATED PROVISIONS

Following the collapses of Enron and WorldCom during 2001–2002, Congress quickly passed sweeping legislation (see Chapter 8 and Chapter 46) designed to increase the liability for securities violations, financial fraud, and obstruction of justice and to impose new responsibility and accountability with regard to financial reporting by companies. Called the *Sarbanes-Oxley Act* (SOX or SarBox), this legislation imposes substantial requirements on auditors and the standards and practices of the audit profession.

10. Auditor Independence

One of the concerns reflected in SOX was that auditors were not exercising sufficient discretion and independence in conducting audits of their clients. The act takes several steps to increase the auditor's independence as it conducts its audits of company financial records.

(A) PUBLIC COMPANY ACCOUNTING OVERSIGHT BOARD. The first section of SOX created a new Public Company Accounting Oversight Board (PCAOB, often referred to as *Peekaboo*) that is responsible for promoting high professional standards among auditors.[33] The board, which consists of five presidential appointees, is not a governmental body but a nonprofit organization with its own budgeting and staffing authority. No more than two members of the board can be CPAs, and members of the board operate on a full-time basis. The board has the following responsibilities:

- Operating a registration system for public accounting firms that prepare audit reports for companies that issue securities

- Enforcing and refining rules to ensure audit quality, ethics, and independence by auditors

- Conducting inspections of public accounting firms to determine their compliance with Sarbanes-Oxley requirements

- Investigating violations and imposing disciplinary sanctions where necessary for members of the profession

- Encouraging the highest professional standards among public accounting firms and auditors

[33] In the financial industry, professionals have translated the acronym for the new board, PCAOB, as *Peekaboo* because of the board's role in shedding light on financial systems and reporting.

Ethics & the Law

The Bernie Madoff Feeder Firm Auditor

Philip Stevenson's living trust had its assets invested in Greenwich Sentry, an investment advisor. Greenwich Sentry was a feeder fund for Madoff Securities, an investment firm run by Bernie Madoff that turned out to be a $50 billion Ponzi scheme. Mr. Madoff entered a guilty plea to charges of securities fraud and was sentenced to 150 years in prison.

PricewaterhouseCoopers was the auditor for Greenwich Sentry. When Mr. Stephenson first invested his trust's assets in Greenwich, he did very well. For example, in the initial five months, his $60 million investment grew to $62,540,565, despite the fact that the Dow Jones Industrial Average was going down during this period. As we now know, the gains were illusory, and when Madoff revealed his fraud on

December 8, 2008, Stephenson learned that his investment was gone, an investment that he has yet to recover.

Stephenson's suit against PricewaterhouseCoopers (PWC) alleged that there were red flags that should have alerted PWC to the fraud such as control problems at Greenwich as well as problems with risk management procedures at the firm. Also, Stephenson argued that the extraordinary returns were, in and of themselves, a red flag. Can PWC be held liable for the losses experienced with another firm? Discuss the ethical obligations of PWC. PWC's literature touts itself as an expert in auditing hedge funds. Does that claim make a difference in your answer? [*Stephenson v. PricewaterhouseCoopers, LLP*, 768 F. Supp. 2d 562 (S.D.N.Y.2011)]

(B) REGISTRATION WITH THE PCAOB. Any public accounting firm that conducts audits for companies that issue securities must file an annual registration statement with PCAOB. That registration requires the accounting firm to disclose all companies for which it has done audits and all the fees paid by those companies—both audit fees and nonaudit fees, commonly referred to as *consulting services*. The accounting firm is also required to disclose any sanctions and pending civil or criminal proceedings against it, along with its policies and procedures for quality control in audits. PCAOB then approves the accounting firm for continued work in the audit of issuers of securities. That approval or denial must be made within 45 days following the accounting firm's annual registration filing.

(C) MAINTAINING AUDITOR INDEPENDENCE. In many of the companies that experienced financial collapse prior to SOX, the companies' auditors had conflicts that may have tainted their independent judgment on accounting issues or even on whether the companies were viable entities. **For Example,** many of the audit firms received substantial fees from companies for management consulting services for which they were providing certified statements. Arthur Andersen received $21 million annually for its audit work with Enron and another $29 million for its consulting services. The consulting contract created a conflict that interfered with the audit firm's ability to make honest decisions in its audit work.

To help eliminate conflicts of interest, Sarbanes-Oxley prohibits certain activities by audit firms for their audit clients, including the following:

1. Bookkeeping and other services related to the accounting records or financial statements of the audit client

2. Design and implementation of financial information systems

3. Appraisal and valuation services, fairness opinions, and contribution-in-kind reports

4. Actuarial services

5. Internal audit outsourcing services

6. Management functions and human resources

7. Broker or dealer, investment adviser, and investment banking services

8. Legal services and expert services unrelated to the audit

9. Any other service that the board determines, by regulation, is impermissible[34]

All nonaudit services to be performed by the auditor for an audit client (except those listed above as expressly prohibited) require prior approval by the board.

In addition, to ensure that audit partners do not become entrenched, Sarbanes-Oxley requires audit firms to change audit partners at least once every five years.[35] The rotation of the audit partner in charge of a company account brings a new perspective to the issues in the financial systems and reports and helps to eliminate the bias of close, personal relationships that develop over longstanding working relationships.

SOX also requires accounting firms to set up internal systems for developing and monitoring professional ethics and for the discussion of ethical issues that arise during the course of the audits of clients.

11. Audit Committees

SOX also addresses issues on the corporate side of the interaction between auditors and companies—the audit committee of the company's board. Under the statute, audit committees must be composed of board members who are independent, defined in the statute as directors who do not accept consulting or other fees from the company and who are not affiliated with the company, certain of its employees, or any of its subsidiaries.[36]

E-Commerce & Cyberlaw

Destruction of Documents, Destruction of a Career, Destruction of a Firm

The congressional investigation into the Enron collapse uncovered the following e-mails:

- A May 28, 1999, e-mail to David Duncan from Benjamin Neuhausen, a member of Andersen's Professional Standards Group at its Chicago main office, evaluated the wisdom of having Enron's CFO Andrew Fastow as the principal in a company that was off the books and doing trades with Enron: "Setting aside the accounting, idea of a venture entity managed by CFO is terrible from a business point of view. Conflicts galore. Why would any director in his or her right mind ever approve such a scheme?"

- A June 1, 1999, e-mail from David Duncan responded: "[O]n your point 1 (i.e., the whole thing is a bad idea), I really couldn't agree more. Rest assured that I have already communicated and it has been agreed to by Andy that CEO, General [Counsel], and Board discussion and approval will be a requirement, on our part, for acceptance of a venture similar to what we have been discussing."

These e-mails are discoverable and admissible when litigation results from an auditor's work. The only protections are the privilege between lawyer and client, but these e-mails were between auditors who worked for the same audit firm.

---

[34] 15 U.S.C. §78j-1. *Baena v. KPMG LLP*, 389 F. Supp. 2d 112, affirmed 453 F.3d 1 (D. Mass. 2005).
[35] 15 U.S.C. §78j-1.
[36] 15 U.S.C. §1741.

Members of audit committees must also be allowed to interact with auditors without management being present and also be permitted to hire independent advisors. At least one member of the audit committee must be a financial expert or someone who understands financial reporting and audit work. The audit committee is now the central point for ensuring that SOX standards are being followed.

Audit committees are required to establish procedures whereby they can be notified of problems with the company's internal controls. Audit committees need to establish the means and mechanisms for monitoring the company's internal control systems so they can verify that financial reports are based on data generated by effective company reporting systems.

12. Records Retention

Accounting firm Arthur Andersen was convicted of one count of obstruction of justice for its destruction of Enron records while SEC investigations were pending. The conviction was later reversed because the court held that although there may have been sufficient evidence about individual Andersen employees' willful destruction of documents, the jury instructions were flawed in attributing that knowledge to the full Andersen firm automatically without proof of actual knowledge (an element required in all criminal cases; see Chapter 8).[37] The statute used for prosecution in that case was not specific enough to tie the firm to individual employee conduct. Furthermore, the penalties, even with such a conviction, were minimal. As discussed in Chapter 8, SOX substantially increased both the scope of and penalties for the obstruction of justice through accountants' and auditors' destruction of records. Under Sarbanes-Oxley, those who destroy, conceal, alter, or mutilate documents when either a civil or criminal investigation is pending are subject to up to 20 years' imprisonment as well as fines.[38]

13. Dodd-Frank and Accountants as Whistleblowers

Under the Dodd-Frank Act (see Chapter 47 for more information), accountants who work for audit firms are not permitted to use information obtained during the court of an audit for purposes of obtaining an award that comes from their reporting information to the SEC that results in an enforcement action. Auditors and audit firm responsibilities are to report any fraud at the company to management and the audit committee. If the board takes no action, the auditor must then go to the SEC. Auditors are only eligible for whistleblower rewards if they report conduct by the company that is intended to thwart an SEC investigation.

LawFlix

Midnight Run (1988) (R)

Charles Grodin plays an accountant who embezzles from his mafia boss but gives the money to charity.

---

[37] *Andersen, LLP v. U.S.*, 544 U.S. 696 (2005). David Duncan, the partner in charge of the Enron account, withdrew his guilty plea on obstruction when the court reversed the firm's verdict.
[38] 18 U.S.C. §1512. Persuading another to destroy documents is obstruction of justice. *U.S. v. Moyer*, 674 F.3d 192 (3rd Cir. 2012).

MAKE THE CONNECTION

SUMMARY

Professionals who agree to perform services for others must perform those services according to the standards of the profession. Accountants, as professionals, must perform their audit work at the levels and standards of competency and thoroughness established for their profession. If an accountant negligently fails to observe those standards, the accountant could be liable for breach of contract or negligence. This tort of negligent breach of contract constitutes malpractice, and the other party to the contract can recover from the accountant either for breach of contract or for the negligence involved.

In some circumstances, not only are accountants liable to their clients, they may also be liable for malpractice to certain third parties who have used or relied on the financial statement. States and courts differ as to when an accountant is liable to third parties. Some courts do not recognize accountant liability to third parties; these courts require privity between the parties. Most courts hold accountants liable to some third parties but differ as to which third parties and how far to extend the accountant's liability. The various rules that determine accountant liability to third parties are the contact rule, which requires that the third party must have had some contact with the accountant before there can be liability; the known user rule in which the accountant is aware of the third party who will use the accountant's information; the foreseeability rule in which the accountant is held liable if it was possible

to foresee that the third party would use the accountant's information; the intended user rule in which the client tells the accountant of the intended use of the audit work; the unknown user rule in which the accountant is not liable to third parties it could not have known would use the information or audit work; and the flexible rule that decides on a case-by-case basis.

Accountants guilty of fraud have liability to all third parties, even those not in privity of contract with the accountant.

To a limited degree, an accountant is protected from malpractice liability by a disclaimer of liability or by the contributory negligence of the plaintiff.

Sarbanes-Oxley (SOX) increases the penalties for accountants who destroy documents when civil or criminal investigations are pending. The act also prohibits conduct by accountants that creates a conflict of interest and requires audit firms to register for authorization to do audit work on public companies. Audit committees of boards are now required to work closely with auditors to make sure that the financial systems in the company and its reports are sound. A federal oversight board reviews the work of audit firms and is authorized to discipline audit firms and accountants for their failure to honor standards or comply with the law.

Dodd-Frank whistleblower provisions do not apply to auditors unless the company is obstructing an investigation.

LEARNING OUTCOMES

After studying this chapter, you should be able to clearly explain:

A. General Principles of Accountants' Liability

L0.1   Define *malpractice*
See Section 1 on p. 1055.

L0.2   Distinguish malpractice liability from breach of contract liability
See "Choice of Remedy" on p. 1057.
See *Cast Art Industries, LLC v. KPMG LLP* on pp. 1062–1063.

B. Accountants' Liability to Third Parties: Beyond Privity

L0.3   List which third parties may recover for the malpractice liability of accountants and when they may do so
See *Citibank, N.A. v. McGladrey and Pullen, LLP* on pp. 1059–1060.

L0.4   Discuss the difference between accounting malpractice and fraud

> See *Carlson v. Xerox Corp* on pp. 1067–1068.
>
> See Ethics & the Law on Bernie Madoff Feeder fund, p. 1069.

C. Sarbanes-Oxley Auditor, Dodd-Frank, and Accounting-Related Provisions

L0.5   Explain how Sarbanes-Oxley has affected the accounting profession and accountants' liability

> See E-Commerce & Cyberlaw on p. 1070.

KEY TERMS

comparative negligence
contributory negligence
exculpatory clause

limitation-of-liability
malpractice
misrepresentation

privity rule

QUESTIONS AND CASE PROBLEMS

1. The auditing firm of Timm, Schmidt & Co. prepared annual financial statements for Clintonville Fire Apparatus, Inc. (CFA). CFA showed these statements to Citizens State Bank and asked for loans. On the basis of the financial statements, Citizens loaned CFA approximately $380,000. Timm later discovered that the financial statements overvalued CFA by more than $400,000. Citizens demanded repayment of the loans. CFA could not pay the balance, and Citizens sued Timm and its malpractice liability insurer. They raised the defense that the suit was barred by lack of privity and the fact that no one in the Timm firm knew that CFA intended to use the financial statements to obtain loans from anyone. Is the lack of privity a defense? [*Citizens State Bank v. Timm, Schmidt & Co.*, 335 N.W.2d 361 (Wis.)]

2. Parente, Randolph, Orlando & Associates (Parente) is an accounting firm that had done auditing work for Sparkomatic for nearly 20 years. On June 14, 1993, Sparkomatic entered into a Memorandum of Intent with Williams Controls to sell Williams assets from Sparkomatic's Kenco division. The sale price was to be the "audited book value" of the assets, and the book value would be based on the June 30, 1993, balance sheet (which Parente did not prepare). Sparkomatic then engaged Parente to audit the financial statements for December 31, 1990, 1991, and 1992 and to prepare an interim balance sheet for 1993.

   On August 1, 1993, Sparkomatic and Williams Controls entered into an asset purchase agreement, which required that Williams be furnished financials through June 1993 as prepared by "Sparkomatic's independent public accountant." Parente was not identified by name in the agreement. Parente did review the asset purchase agreement with Williams prior to commencing its work and knew that Williams would be using the information Parente prepared.

   Following the closing, additional information came to light indicating that Williams had overpaid for the assets of Kenco, and Williams filed suit against Parente for negligence, negligent misrepresentation, and breach of contract. Parente moved for summary judgment. What should the decision be and why? Discuss several possible theories. [*Williams Controls v. Parente, Randolph, Orlando, & Associates*, 39 F. Supp. 2d 517 (M.D. Pa.)]

3. David S. Talesnick served as the accountant for Kenneth Ronson and his wife as well as for Ronson's company, performing accounting and tax services for all. From 1980 to 1983, Ronson, his wife, and his company invested in the White Rim Oil & Gas, Pine Coal, and Winchester Coal limited partnerships. During those years, the Ronsons and his company were able to report losses on their income tax returns because of these investments. However, the IRS determined that the limited partnerships were not qualified investments under the tax code and disallowed the loss deductions. The Ronsons and his company all owed back taxes, interest, and penalties as a result. The Ronsons disputed the

finding and asked Talesnick how they might appeal the ruling and not have the interest clock ticking on what they owed. Talesnick wrote a letter and advised them to post a bond of $91,300, the amount then due. Talesnick was incorrect in his advice on payment and accrual of interest, and by the time the final determination was made against the Ronsons and Ronson's company, they owed $235,063 with interest. The Ronsons sued Talesnick for malpractice. Could they recover? How much? [*Ronson v. David S. Talesnick, CPA*, 33 F. Supp. 2d 347 (D.N.J.)]

4. The certified public accounting partnership of James, Guinn, and Head prepared a certified audit report of four corporations, known as the Paschal Enterprises, with knowledge that their report would be used to induce Shatterproof Glass Corp. to lend money to those corporations. The report showed the corporations to be solvent when in fact they were insolvent. Shatterproof relied on the audit report, loaned approximately $500,000 to the four corporations, and lost almost all of it because the liabilities of the companies were in excess of their assets. Shatterproof claimed that James and other accountants had been negligent in preparing the report and sued them to recover the loss on the loan. The accountants raised the defense that they had been retained not by Shatterproof but by Paschal. Was this defense valid? [*Shatterproof Glass Corp. v. James*, 466 S.W.2d 873 (Tex. App.)]

5. AUSA Life Insurance Company and others were institutional investors in the securities of JWP, Inc., a company that went belly up, resulting in nearly a 100 percent loss of their investments. Ernst & Young served as auditor for JWP from 1985 to 1992. During most of that period, JWP was in a period of rapid expansion that was financed by private placements of debt securities, and it became increasingly leveraged. By 1991, it was losing an average of $10 million per month. Ernst & Young knew of "accounting irregularities" from at least 1988 through 1991 but did not insist on their correction. Ernst & Young issued unqualified financial opinions for all of those years. One of the irregularities was

recording anticipated future tax benefits of net operating loss in violation of GAAP. AUSA and its fellow investors sued Ernst & Young for their losses. The federal district court dismissed the case and AUSA appealed. Should AUSA be able to recover? Explain your answer. [*AUSA Life Insurance Co. v. Ernst & Young*, 206 F.3d 202 (2d Cir. 2000), 119 F. Supp. 2d 394 (S.D.N.Y. 2000), aff'd in unpublished opinion]

6. For almost 13 years, Touche Ross had prepared the annual audit of Buttes Gas and Oil Co. Buttes wanted to obtain a loan from Dimensional Credit Corp. (DCC) and showed DCC its most recent annual audit. DCC made the loan on the basis of what it learned from the audit. The loan was not repaid, and DCC then realized that it had been misled by negligent statements about Buttes's financial condition that appeared in the annual statement prepared by Touche Ross. Would DCC be able to recover against Touche Ross for its negligence in preparing this report?

7. Henry Hatfield, CPA, was hired to prepare audited financial statements for Happy Campers, a nonprofit organization providing summer camp scholarships for inner-city, low-income children. The executive director of Happy Campers was embezzling but falsified records that Hatfield used in his audit. First Bank gave Happy Campers a $100,000 loan based on Hatfield's certified financials. The embezzlement was discovered, and Happy Campers defaulted on the loan. Can First Bank recover its loss from Hatfield?

8. What is the difference between the standards for auditor liability in a civil action by investors against the auditor versus auditor liability for violation of securities laws?

9. Hicks, the president and manager of Intermountain Merchandising, wanted to sell the business to Montana Merchandising, Inc. To provide a basis for the transaction, he retained Bloomgren, an accountant, to conduct an audit of Intermountain. Bloomgren knew that Montana would use the audit report in making the purchase of the business from Intermountain.

Bloomgren's audit report showed the Intermountain business as profitable. Thayer, Montana's president, relied on this report in agreeing to purchase the business of Intermountain and in agreeing to the terms of the purchase. Sometime later, it was discovered that the accountant had made a number of mistakes and that the business that was sold was actually insolvent. Thayer and Montana Merchandising sued Hicks and Bloomgren for damages. The suit claimed that the accountant had negligently misrepresented the facts. The accountant defended on the basis that Thayer was not in privity of contract with him and therefore could not sue him. Was he right? [*Thayer v. Hicks*, 793 P.2d 784 (Mont.)]

10. Audit firm Grant Thornton had prepared financial reports for use by the board of directors of First National Bank of Keystone (Keystone) in response to an investigation by the Office of the Comptroller of the Currency (OCC) that raised questions about the value of Keystone's loan portfolio. Stan Quay, a partner at Grant Thornton, was in charge of the 1998 audit. On March 24, 1999, Quay presented several members and prospective members of Keystone's board and Keystone's shareholders with draft copies of Keystone's 1998 financial statements and told them that Keystone was going to get an unqualified or "clean" audit opinion on its 1998 financial statements.

In April 1999, and despite the fact that Keystone was in fact insolvent at the end of 1998, Grant Thornton issued a clean audit report for Keystone. The audit report contained the following statement: "This report is intended for the information and use of the Board of Directors and Management of The First National Bank of Keystone and its regulatory agencies and should not be used by third parties for any other purpose."

Gary Ellis, a president of another bank, was being recruited in early 1999 by the Keystone board to take the president's position at Keystone. Following the Keystone board meeting on March 24, 1999, Ellis met Quay and two other outside directors at a bar at the Fincastle Country Club. Quay spoke with Ellis and the

two outside directors because Keystone did not have a chief financial officer, thus making Quay the only person capable of going over the financial statements with the others. At the country club, Quay told Ellis and the two outside directors that Keystone was going to receive a "clean [audit]." Ellis also attended the March 25, 1999, shareholders' meeting at which Quay informed the group that Grant Thornton was going to give Keystone a clean audit opinion for 1998. On March 30, 1999, Ellis visited Keystone. During this visit, Quay told Ellis once again that Keystone would receive a clean audit opinion for 1998.

Ellis signed a two-year contract at a base salary of $375,000 plus benefits, including the use of a corporate vehicle and a country club membership. He also purchased $49,500 in Keystone stock. By September 1999, Keystone Bank was closed. Ellis filed suit against Grant Thornton. The district court ruled in favor of Ellis on his negligent misrepresentation claim and found that he was entitled to $2,419,233 in damages. Grant Thornton appealed. Is this verdict correct? Explain why or why not Grant Thornton is liable for the loss of the job. [*Ellis v. Grant Thornton LLP*, 530 F.3d 280 (4th Cir. 2008)]

11. Equisure, Inc., was required to file audited financial statements when it applied for a listing on the American Stock Exchange (AMEX). Stirtz, Equisure's auditor, issued a favorable audit opinion used for the AMEX application. Stirtz also issued "clean" opinions on Equisure's required SEC filings, such as its 10k.

Noram, a securities broker, loaned $900,000 in margin credit to purchasers of Equisure's stock based on the firm's audited financials. AMEX stopped trading on Equisure's stock because of allegations of insider trading and stock manipulation, and Noram was left without collateral for $2.5 million in loans. Stirtz resigned as Equisure's auditor, and Noram filed suit against Stirtz. The trial court granted Stirtz summary judgment. Noram appealed. Who is liable here? Was the court's decision correct? [*Noram Investment Services, Inc. v. Stirtz Bernards Boyden*, 611 N.W.2d 372 (Minn. App.)]

CPA QUESTIONS

1. In general, the third-party (primary) beneficiary rule as applied to a CPA's legal liability in conducting an audit is relevant to which of the following causes of action against a CPA?

	Fraud	Constructive Fraud	Negligence
a.	Yes	Yes	No
b.	Yes	No	No
c.	No	Yes	Yes
d.	No	No	Yes

2. Beckler & Associates, CPAs, audited and gave an unqualified opinion on the financial statements of Queen Co. The financial statements contained misstatements that resulted in a material overstatement of Queen's net worth. Queen provided the audited financial statements to Mac Bank in connection with a loan made by Mac to Queen. Beckler knew that the financial statements would be provided to Mac. Queen defaulted on the loan. Mac sued Beckler to recover for its losses associated with Queen's default. Which of the following must Mac prove in order to recover?

   I. Beckler was negligent in conducting the audit.

   II. Mac relied on the financial statements.

   a. I only

   b. II only

   c. Both I and II

   d. Neither I nor II

3. In a common law action against an accountant, lack of privity is a viable defense if the plaintiff:

   a. Is the client's creditor who sues the accountant for negligence.

   b. Can prove the presence of gross negligence that amounts to a reckless disregard for the truth.

   c. Is the accountant's client.

   d. Bases the action upon fraud.

4. Cable Corp. orally engaged Drake & Co., CPAs, to audit its financial statements. Cable's management informed Drake that it suspected the accounts receivable were materially overstated. Though the financial statements Drake audited included a materially overstated accounts receivable balance, Drake issued an unqualified opinion. Cable used the financial statements to obtain a loan to expand its operations. Cable defaulted on the loan and incurred a substantial loss.

   If Cable sues Drake for negligence in failing to discover the overstatement, Drake's best defense would be that Drake did *not*

   a. Have privity of contract with Cable.

   b. Sign an engagement letter.

   c. Perform the audit recklessly or with an intent to deceive.

   d. Violate generally accepted auditing standards in performing the audit.

5. Which of the following services is a CPA generally required to perform when conducting a personal financial planning engagement?

   a. Assisting the client to identify tasks that are essential in order to take action on planning decisions.

   b. Assisting the client to take action on planning decisions.

   c. Monitoring progress in achieving goals.

   d. Updating recommendations and revising planning decisions.

6. Which of the following statements is (are) correct regarding the common law elements that must be proven to support a finding of constructive fraud against a CPA misrepresentation?

   I. The plaintiff has justifiably relied on the CPA's misrepresentation.

   II. The CPA has acted in a grossly negligent manner.

   a. I only

   b. II only

   c. Both I and II

   d. Neither I nor II

CHAPTER 48

Management of Corporations

© Manuel Gutjahr/iStockphoto.com

learningoutcomes

After studying this chapter, you should be able to

LO.1 Explain how shareholders, as owners of the corporation, exercise limited control over management by voting at shareholders' meetings to elect directors

LO.2 Explain the qualifications and powers of directors

LO.3 Explain the liability of directors and the meaning of the business judgment rule (BJR)

LO.4 Explain the obligation of officers—who have access to corporate information and agency powers—to not violate their fiduciary duties to the corporation

LO.5 Explain the rationale for the "say-on-pay" provision of the Dodd-Frank Act

LO.6 Explain how directors, officers, and the corporation itself may be criminally liable for regulatory offenses

A corporation is managed, directly or indirectly, by its shareholders, board of directors, and officers.

A. SHAREHOLDERS

As owners, the shareholders have the right to control the corporation.

1. Extent of Management Control by Shareholders

As a practical matter, control of the shareholders is generally limited to voting at shareholders' meetings to elect directors. In this sense, shareholders indirectly determine the management policies of the business. At shareholders' meetings, they may also vote to amend bylaws, approve shareholder resolutions, or vote on so-called extraordinary corporate matters. *Extraordinary matters* include the sale of corporate assets outside the regular course of the corporation's business or the merger or dissolution of the corporation.

2. Meetings of Shareholders

To have legal effect, action by the shareholders must ordinarily be taken at a regular or special meeting.

(A) REGULAR MEETINGS. The time and place of regular or stated meetings are usually prescribed by the articles of incorporation or the bylaws. Notice to shareholders of such meetings is ordinarily not required, but it is usually given as a matter of good business practice. Some statutes require that notice of all meetings be given.

(B) SPECIAL MEETINGS. Generally, notice must be given specifying the subject matter of special meetings. Unless otherwise prescribed, special meetings are called by the directors. It is sometimes provided that a special meeting may be called by a certain percentage of shareholders.[1] Notice of the day, hour, and place of a special meeting must be given to all shareholders. The notice must include a statement of the nature of the business to be transacted, and no other business may be transacted at this meeting.

(C) QUORUM. A valid meeting requires the presence of a quorum of the voting shareholders. A **quorum** is the minimum number of persons (shareholders or persons authorized to vote a stated proportion of the voting stock) required to transact business. If a quorum is present, a majority of those present may act on any matter unless there is an express requirement of a higher affirmative vote.

When a meeting opens with a quorum, the quorum is generally not broken if shareholders leave the meeting and those remaining are not sufficient to constitute a quorum.

quorum – minimum number of persons, shares represented, or directors who must be present at a meeting in order to lawfully transact business.

---

[1] N.Y. Bus.Corp. Law §603.

3. Action without Meeting

A number of statutes provide for corporate action by shareholders without holding a meeting. The Revised Model Business Corporation Act (RMBCA) provides that "action required or permitted by this Act to be taken at a shareholders' meeting may be taken without a meeting if the action is taken by all shareholders entitled to vote on the action."[2] The action must be evidenced by a written consent describing the action taken, signed by all shareholders entitled to vote on the action, and delivered to the corporation for inclusion in the minutes.

B. Directors

The board of directors has oversight responsibility for a company's business affairs, including (1) approving strategic plans, (2) reviewing operating and financial results, (3) approving SEC filings, (4) approving the hiring of executives, (5) evaluating management's performance and approving executive compensation packages, (6) appointing and meeting with auditors, and (7) evaluating and acting on extraordinary matters, such as the merger, acquisition, or sale of the business.

Most states now permit the number of directors to be fixed by the bylaws. Many specify that the board of directors shall consist of not less than three directors; a few authorize one or more.[3] Professional corporation legislation often authorizes or is interpreted as authorizing a one- or two-person board of directors.

4. Qualifications

Eligibility for membership on a board of directors is determined by statute, articles of incorporation, or bylaws.[4] In the absence of a contrary provision, any person (including a nonresident, a minor, or a person who is not a shareholder) is eligible for membership. Bylaws may require that a director own stock in the corporation although this requirement is not ordinarily imposed.

CPA

5. Powers of Directors

The board of directors has authority to manage the corporation. Courts will not interfere with the board's discretion in the absence of (1) illegal conduct or (2) fraud harming the rights of creditors, shareholders, or the corporation.

The board of directors may enter into any contract or transaction necessary to carry out the business for which the corporation was formed. The board may appoint officers and other agents to act for the company, or it may appoint several of its own members as an executive committee to act for the board between board meetings. (See Figure 48-1.) Broad delegation of authority, however, may involve the risk of being treated as an unlawful abdication of the board's management power.

---

[2] RMBCA §7.04(a).
[3] Del. Code §141(b). See also RMBCA §8.03.
[4] In family-owned businesses, shareholder agreements are often utilized to impose restrictions on the voting of shares and eligibility standards for membership on the board of directors to maintain continuity of management, ownership, and control of a corporation. See *Miniat v. EMI*, 315 F.3d 712 (7th Cir. 2002).

CASE SUMMARY

The Case of Medoff, the Marathon Man

FACTS: The Boston Athletic Association (BAA) is a nonprofit corporation created to sponsor the annual Boston Marathon. The BAA authorized its president, William Cloney, to negotiate contracts for it. Cloney executed a contract with attorney Marshall Medoff, giving Medoff exclusive power to promote the marathon. The BAA transferred to Medoff all rights to use the marathon name and logos. The contract's financial terms were extremely favorable to Medoff, who could renew the contract from year to year. When the BAA's board members learned of the contract, they declared that it was beyond the authorization vested in Cloney. The board brought an action to have the contract set aside. Medoff contended that Cloney had authority to make the contract and that therefore the contract bound the corporation.

DECISION: Judgment for the BAA. It is the obligation of the board to direct the corporation. Consistent with this obligation, a board may delegate general managerial functions to corporate officers, but certain powers cannot be delegated. The contract made with Medoff surrendered virtually complete control of the marathon to Medoff. The board in this case improperly delegated to Cloney the authority to make such a contract, which prevented accomplishment of the BAA's corporate purpose, that of sponsoring the marathon. Authority to make such a contract was beyond the power of the board to delegate. [*Boston Athletic Association v. International Marathon, Inc.*, 467 N.E.2d 58 (Mass. 1984)]

CPA   6. Conflict of Interest

A director is disqualified from taking part in corporate action involving a matter in which the director has an undisclosed conflicting interest. Because it cannot be known how the other directors would have acted if they had known of the conflict of interest, the corporation generally may avoid any transaction because of a director's secret disqualification.

A number of states provide by statute that a director's conflict of interest does not impair the transaction or contract entered into or authorized by the board of directors if the disqualified director disclosed the interest and if the contract or transaction is fair and reasonable with respect to the corporation. Thus, a director may lend money to a corporation if the board of directors is informed of the transaction and the terms approximate the market rate for businesses with similar credit ratings. Some states simply require notice of the conflicting interests and abstaining from all participation in the transaction. **For Example,** Delos Yancey, Jr., and Delos Yancey III were directors of State Mutual Insurance Co. Subsequently, they formed North American Services, Inc., and served as directors of both companies. State Mutual decided to sell one of its companies, Atlas Life Insurance, Inc. North American expressed an interest in purchasing Atlas, and thereafter the Yanceys recused themselves from State Mutual's decision-making process in selling the company. State Mutual sold Atlas to North American at a $5.2 million loss. Some two years later, North American resold Atlas for a $22.6 million gain, and a shareholder derivative suit was brought against the Yanceys. The court decided the case in favor of the

FIGURE 48-1   *Powers of Directors*

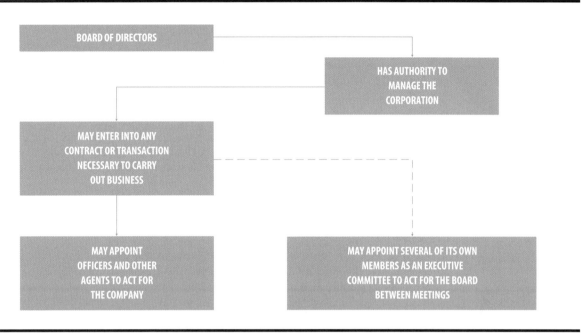

© Cengage Learning

Yanceys, holding that they complied with the state's "safe harbor" law by giving notice of their conflicting interest to State Mutual and thereafter abstaining from all participation in the corporate transaction.[5]

To prevent conflicts of interest and covert compensation schemes, section 402(a) of the federal Sarbanes-Oxley Act[6] prohibits all loans either directly or indirectly to directors and executive officers by their corporations, with an exception for companies in the consumer credit business, which may make loans to directors and officers on terms no more favorable than those offered to the general public.

Prior to Sarbanes-Oxley, it was a common practice for publicly traded companies to provide low-interest loans to company officers. **For Example,** Bernard Ebbers, while CEO of WorldCom, Inc., used company stock as collateral for bank loans used to buy additional shares of WorldCom stock. When WorldCom's share prices weakened in late 2000 and Ebbers needed to put up additional collateral to cover his loans, WorldCom's board of directors decided to lend him more than $400 million at just over 2 percent interest with no fixed due date. The company rate was far below the personal loan rate at banks near company headquarters of between 9.75 percent and 16.67 percent, and well below margin loan rates at 5 percent. Business conglomerate Tyco International Ltd. maintained a "key employee loan fund" that was used like a revolving line of

---

[5] *Fisher v. State Mutual Insurance Co.,* 290 F.3d 1256 (11th Cir. 2002).
[6] P.L. 107-204, 116 Stat. 745.

credit by Tyco executives Dennis Kozlowski and Martin Swartz to fund their lavish lifestyles. The language of Sarbanes-Oxley is broad and far reaching and prohibits all direct personal loans by public companies, such as relocation loans, tax loans, and loans to purchase securities.

7. Meetings of Directors

Action by directors is ordinarily taken at a meeting of the board of directors. Bylaws sometimes require the meeting to be held at a particular place. Generally, a director is not allowed to vote by proxy.

Most states permit action to be taken by the board of directors without holding an actual meeting. It is required when such action is taken that it be set forth in writing and signed by all directors.

8. Liability of Directors

In dealing with the corporation, the directors act in a fiduciary capacity. It is into their care that the stockholders have entrusted the control of the corporate property and the management of the business.

CPA

business judgment rule (BJR)–rule that allows management immunity from liability for corporate acts where there is a reasonable indication that the acts were made in good faith with due care.

(A) THE BUSINESS JUDGMENT RULE. Courts recognize that the decisions of corporate directors often involve weighing and balancing legal, ethical, commercial, promotional, public relations, and other factors. Accordingly, courts will not sit in judgment on the wisdom of decisions made by directors. If the directors have acted in good faith on the basis of adequate information, courts will not enjoin the course of action taken by the directors.[7] Moreover, even though such action causes loss to the corporation, the directors will not be held personally liable for it. This principle is called the **business judgment rule (BJR)**.

CPA

(1) The Traditional Rule.
Courts apply the business judgment rule as a presumption that in making a business decision, the directors acted (1) on an informed basis, (2) in good faith, and (3) in the honest belief that the action taken was in the best interest of the corporation. The party challenging the directors' actions has the burden of proving that they did not act on an informed basis or in good faith or in the best interest of the corporation.[8] (See the *Disney* case.)

CPA

(2) Application in Corporate Control Transactions.
When a corporation receives a takeover bid, the target board of directors may tend to take actions that are in their own interest and not in the interest of the shareholders. Courts have recognized the potential for director self-interest in this situation. (See the *Van Gorkom* case.)

---

[7] In discharging their duties, directors are not individually liable if, acting in good faith, they rely upon "the opinion of counsel for the corporation" or "written reports setting forth financial data concerning the corporation and prepared by an independent public accountant or certified public accountant or firm of such accountants"—which opinions or statements turn out to be flawed. *Casey v. Brennan*, 344 N.J. Super.83 (2002).

[8] *Huang Group v. LTI*, 760 N.E.2d 14 (Ohio App. 2002).

CASE SUMMARY

Problem: "A Mismatch of Cultures and Styles"
Solution: $140 Million Severance Payment
Shareholders: Not Happy!

FACTS: Michael Ovitz was a founder of Creative Artists Agency (CAA), an agency in 1995 with 1,400 of Hollywood's top actors, directors, writers, and musicians. Ovitz was considered one of the most powerful figures in Hollywood at that time. Because of the untimely death of Disney's prior president in a helicopter crash, Walt Disney Co. CEO Michael Eisner focused on hiring Ovitz as president. The chairman of Disney's compensation committee, Irwin Russell, in consultation with Eisner, negotiated the Ovitz employment agreement (OEA). As part of the OEA, if Disney fired Ovitz for any reason other than gross negligence or malfeasance, Ovitz would be entitled to a nonfault termination (NFT) package consisting of his remaining salary for the five-year period, bonuses, and the immediate vesting of stock options. Russell met with a compensation expert for advice on the contract and had telephone conversations with two compensation committee members, Sidney Poitier and Ignatio Lozano. CEO Eisner telephoned each member of the board of directors to inform them of his plan to hire Ovitz. On September 26, 1995, the Compensation Committee had a one-hour meeting to discuss several topics, including the OEA. Thereafter, the full board of directors met and elected Ovitz president of Disney. After he joined Disney, it soon became apparent that a "mismatch of cultures and styles" ensued and that Ovitz was not succeeding as president. The trial court gave an example as follows:

> *In January 1996, a corporate retreat was held at Walt Disney World in Orlando, Florida. At that retreat, Ovitz failed to integrate himself in the group of executives by declining to participate in group activities, insisting on a limousine, when the other executives, including Eisner, were taking a bus, and making inappropriate demands of the park employees. In short, Ovitz "was a little elitist for the egalitarian Walt Disney World cast members [employees]," and a poor fit with his fellow executives.*

When it became clear that Ovitz was not working out, Eisner considered his options. Sanford Litvak, Disney's general counsel, advised Eisner and other directors that Ovitz had not been shown to have been grossly negligent or malfeasant in his year at Disney, and no cause existed to avoid the NFT payments. Eisner decided it was necessary to terminate Ovitz on a nonfault basis and notified the board members. The board members supported this decision under the nonfault termination agreement. Ovitz was ultimately paid $140 million in severance pay. Stockholders brought a derivative suit, asserting that Eisner and the board of directors had breached their fiduciary duties in connection with Ovitz's hiring and termination. Years of litigation cumulated in a 37-day trial that ended on January 19, 2005.

DECISION: Judgment for the defendants. Eisner's actions should not serve as a model for directors and CEOs. By virtue of his imperial nature as CEO, he handicapped the board's decision-making abilities, stacking the board with his friends who, although not necessarily beholden to him in a legal sense, were more willing to support him unconditionally than truly independent directors. He failed to keep the board informed as he should have and failed to better involve the board in the process of hiring Ovitz, usurping the role for himself, although not a violation of law. Despite the legitimate criticisms leveled at Eisner, especially at having enthroned himself as the omnipotent and infallible monarch of his personal Magic Kingdom, Eisner's actions were taken in good faith and did not breach his fiduciary duty of care because he was not grossly negligent, nor was any other director in violation of a fiduciary duty. The redress for failures that arise from faithful management (not in violation of fiduciary duties) must come from the markets, not the courts. Corporate decisions are made, risks are taken, the results become apparent, capital flows accordingly, and shareholder value increases or decreases. [*In re Walt Disney Co. Derivative Litigation*, 907 A.2d 693 (Del. Ch. 2005)]

CASE SUMMARY

Directors—Independent Evaluators, Not Pawns

FACTS: Jerome Van Gorkom was chairman and chief executive officer of Trans Union Inc. On September 13, Van Gorkom arranged a meeting with Jay Pritzker, a well-known takeover specialist and a social acquaintance, to determine his interest in acquiring Trans Union. On Thursday, September 18, Pritzker made an offer of $55 per share (a price suggested by Van Gorkom). Pritzker wanted a decision to be made by the board no later than Sunday, September 21. On Friday, Van Gorkom called a special meeting of the board of directors for noon the following day; no agenda was announced. At the directors' meeting, Van Gorkom made a 20-minute oral analysis of the merger transaction. He showed that the company was having difficulty generating sufficient income to offset its increasingly large investment tax credits. Van Gorkom discussed his meeting with Pritzker and the reasons for the meeting. Copies of the proposed merger agreement were delivered too late to be studied before or during the meeting. No consultants or investment advisors were called on to support the merger price of $55 per share. The merger was approved at the end of the two-hour meeting. Certain shareholders brought a class-action suit against the directors, contending that the board's decision was not the product of informed business judgment. The directors responded that their good-faith decision was shielded by the business judgment rule.

DECISION: Judgment for the shareholders. Directors cannot claim the protection of the business judgment rule if they have been grossly negligent in exercising their judgment. The directors approved the merger based on a 20-minute oral analysis by the president, Van Gorkom, at a hastily called board meeting with no prior notice of its purpose. No investment consultants or other experts were employed to assess the intrinsic value of the company, nor were the merger documents containing the terms of the merger available for study by the directors. Deciding to sell the company without any information and deliberation was gross negligence. The directors therefore could not claim the protection of the business judgment rule when they voted to "sell" the company for $55 per share. The directors are personally liable for damages. [*Smith v. Van Gorkom*, **488 A.2d 858 (Del. 1985)**]

(3) Protection of Directors.

In the wake of court decisions holding directors personally liable for damages for gross negligence and in the wake of the resulting general reluctance of individuals to serve as directors, states have passed statutes to protect directors. The aim of the various state laws is essentially the same: to reduce the risk of personal liability for directors who act in good faith when their decisions are challenged. The laws permit a corporation, by a stockholder-approved amendment to its charter or certificate of incorporation, to protect its directors from monetary liability for duty-of-care violations (gross negligence) provided they have not acted in bad faith, breached their duty of loyalty, or gained an improper personal benefit.[9] The laws provide for indemnification and advancement of expenses. **For Example,** the certificate of incorporation of Jennifer Convertibles, Inc., a Delaware corporation, includes an exculpatory clause, pursuant to section 102(b)(7) of Delaware's General Corporate Law. The clause protects directors from liability for breach of fiduciary duty except

---

[9] See Del. Code §102(b)(7); N.Y. Bus. Corp. Law §§721–723; Ohio Gen. Corp. Law §1701.59; Ind. Bus. Corp. Law, ch. 35,§1(e); Mo. Gen. Bus. Corp. Law 351.355 §§2, 7.

in cases of breach of duty of loyalty, bad faith, knowing violation of the law, or improper personal benefit, as is appropriate under Delaware law.[10]

For Example, to avoid supervision by the Office of Thrift Supervision (OTS), the directors of Oak Tree Savings Bank, a subsidiary of Landmark Land Company, Inc., which had loaned subsidiary land development companies $986 million, placed the bank in bankruptcy. Because of this, director Bernard Ille resigned. In civil proceedings brought against all of the bank directors, Ille successfully defended himself against the OTS charges. He thus would be entitled to mandatory

Thinking Things Through

Are the Days of the Imperial CEO Over?

Many changes clarifying the role of corporate directors have occurred since the Enron and WorldCom debacles came to light in 2001. The Sarbanes-Oxley Act and its legal reforms followed. The financial crisis of 2008–2009 resulted in the Dodd-Frank Act and its legal reforms. The American Bar Association Committee on Corporate Laws published its *Corporate Director's Guidebook, Sixth Edition,* in 2012, which emphasizes themes arising out of these crises important to all directors. For example, consider this outline of a corporation's "risks" regarding its legal and regulatory compliance profile:

The board should ensure that employees of the corporation are informed and periodically reminded of corporate policies, including those pertaining to compliance with

   (i)   codes of business conduct and ethics;
  (ii)   anti-discrimination and employment laws;
 (iii)   environmental and health and safety laws;
  (iv)   anti-bribery laws;
   (v)   anti-trust and competition laws;
  (vi)   securities laws, particularly those addressing insider trading; and
 (vii)   laws and regulations of other countries as applicable.

The major securities markets require their listed companies to adopt codes of business conduct and ethics applicable to all employees, officers, and directors. The corporation should have appropriate controls throughout the organization for monitoring compliance with such laws and codes. Controls may include whistleblower and hotline policies. The corporation also must establish procedures for addressing violations.*

Michael Eisner, considered by many as the Imperial CEO, stacked the board with his friends and expected and received loyalty from them regarding all-important corporate decisions. Is it critical for a board's nominating/corporate governance committee to receive nomination from not only other directors but also institutional investors and other shareholders rather than just the CEO—as was the case at Disney with CEO Eisner?

The chairman of Disney's Compensation Committee hired a highly regarded consultant regarding Ovitz's employment contract and telephoned two members of the committee to inform them of progress. A vote was taken on September 26, after less than an hour of discussion by the committee, and, thereafter, Ovitz was elected president. As a best practice, should the entire compensation committee have been kept in the loop on this significant matter during negotiations by e-mail, executive summaries, and backup documentation? Should the Disney board have been given meaningful documentation on the appointment to study a week before the board meeting? Do you think it would have been good form for a Disney director back then to question "Mr." Eisner regarding the Ovitz appointment: "I don't think we are ready to vote … give us some more supporting documents"? Do you believe that members of a board of directors today feel entitled to have adequate and timely information and to ask, with civility, the tough questions? Has the private governance of a public corporation like Disney with CEO Eisner been supplanted in part by a layer of government governance of public corporations guided by Sarbanes-Oxley and Dodd-Frank regulations to protect public interests along with the very vital corporate interests?**

*Corporate Director's Guidebook, 7th ed. (ABA April 2012) p. 36, www.abanet.org/abastore.
**See Hillary A. Sale, "The New "Public" Corporation," 74 *Law and Contemporary Problems* 137 (Winter 2011).

[10] *KDW Restructuring & Liquidation Services LLC v. Greenfield*, 2012 WL 2125986 (S.D. N.Y. June 12, 2012). The court found that there was sufficient facts in the complaint against Harley Greenfield, Jennifer's CEO, to support claims for breach of duty of loyalty and breach of the duty to act in good faith regarding a 2009 transaction causing a net loss of $11 million at the end of the 2009 fiscal year.

indemnification from the bank. In addition, employees Trapani and Braun, who were subpoenaed and deposed under adversarial circumstances but were not charged, were deemed to have succeeded on the merits in their defense and were entitled to mandatory indemnification for legal expenses under state law. The other directors and employees charged were found not to have acted in good faith and were not entitled to indemnification.[11]

(B) ACTIONS AGAINST DIRECTORS. Actions against directors should be brought by the corporation. If the corporation fails to act, as is the case when the directors alleged to be liable control the corporation, shareholders may bring the action in a representative capacity for the corporation.[12] **For Example,** Risa Weinberger became concerned that the president and majority shareholder of American Composting Inc., James Willits, was using corporate funds for his own personal benefit. Corporate bank statements showed payments to his ex-wife of $283,068.48, payments to the law firm that represented him in his divorce of $145,789, and a "loans to shareholders" balance that increased from $21,075 in 2004 to $444,642 by September 2011. The court determined that Ms. Weinberger may pursue the shareholder derivative suit on behalf of American Composting Inc. because a demand on the board of directors controlled by Willets would be futile.[13]

(C) REMOVAL OF DIRECTOR. Ordinarily, directors are removed by vote of the shareholders. In some states, the board of directors may remove a director and elect a successor on the ground that the removed director (1) did not accept office, (2) failed to satisfy the qualifications for office, (3) was continually absent from the state without a leave of absence granted by the board, generally for a period of six months or more, (4) was discharged in bankruptcy, (5) was convicted of a felony, (6) was unable to perform the duties of director because of any illness or disability, generally for a period of six months or more, or (7) had been judicially declared of unsound mind.[14]

The RMBCA provides for removal of directors "with or without cause" by a majority vote of the shareholders unless the articles of incorporation provide that directors may be removed only for cause.[15] **For Example,** former Conseco, Inc., director Dennis Murray, Sr., was unsuccessful in his action against the board of directors challenging his removal from the board. The court held that the directors had unlimited authority to remove a fellow director without regard for the reasons why the other directors wished to remove him.[16] Directors may always be voted out of office at a regular meeting of shareholders held for the election of directors.

C. OFFICERS, AGENTS, AND EMPLOYEES

Corporations generally have a president, at least one vice president, a secretary, a treasurer, and, frequently, a chief executive officer (CEO). The duties of these officers are generally set forth in the corporation's bylaws. The duty of the secretary to keep minutes of the proceedings of shareholders and directors is commonly

---

[11] *In re Landmark Land Co. of California,* 76 F.3d 553 (4th Cir. 1996).
[12] *In re Abbott Laboratories Derivative Shareholder Litigation,* 325 F.3d 795 (7th Cir. 2003).
[13] *Weinberger v. American Composting, Inc.,* 2012 WL 1190970 (E.D. Ark. Apr. 9, 2012).
[14] See California Corp Code §807, recognizing grounds (1), (2), (5), and (7).
[15] RMBCA §8.08(a).
[16] *Murray v. Conseco, Inc.,* 766 N.E.2d 38 (Ind. App. 2002).

included. Corporation codes generally expressly permit the same person to be both secretary and treasurer. In large corporations, there is often a recording secretary and a corresponding secretary.

Sometimes the officers are elected by the shareholders, but usually they are appointed by the board of directors. The RMBCA follows the general pattern of providing for the appointment of officers by the board of directors.[17] Ordinarily, no particular formality is required to make such appointments. Unless prohibited, a director may hold an executive office.

Officers ordinarily hire the employees and agents of the corporation.

9. Powers of Officers

The officers of a corporation are its agents. Consequently, their powers are controlled by the laws of agency.[18] As in the case of any other agency, a third person has the burden of proving that a particular officer had the authority he or she purported to have.

The fact that the officer or employee acting on behalf of the corporation is a major shareholder does not give either any greater agency powers. Moreover, the person dealing with the officer or employee is charged with knowledge of any limitation on authority contained in the recorded corporate charter or articles of incorporation.

When the nature of the transaction is unusual, that unusual nature should alert a third person to the necessity of specific authorization from the corporation.

(A) PRESIDENT. It is sometimes held that, in the absence of some limitation on authority, the president of a corporation has by virtue of that office the authority to act as agent on behalf of the corporation within the scope of the business in which the corporation is empowered to engage. It has also been held, however, that the president has such broad powers only when the president is the general manager of the corporation. In instances in which a corporation has a president and chief executive officer, the CEO has authority to exercise personal judgment and discretion in the administrative and executive functions of the corporation as endowed by its bylaws and the resolutions of the board of directors. When a corporation has both a CEO and a president, the CEO is ordinarily the officer entrusted with the broader decisional powers, whereas the president is the executing officer. The president does not have authority by virtue of that office to make a contract that, because of its unusual character, would require action by the board of directors or shareholders.[19]

The president cannot make a contract to fix long-term or unusual contracts of employment, release a claim of the corporation, promise that the corporation will later repurchase shares issued to a subscriber, or mortgage a corporate property.[20]

It is ordinarily held that the president of a business corporation is not authorized to execute commercial paper in the name of the corporation. However, the president may do so when authorized by the board of directors to borrow money for the corporation.

---

[17] RMBCA §8.40(a).
[18] *IFC Credit Corp. v. Nuova Pasta Co.*, 815 F. Supp. 268 (N.D. Ill. 1993).
[19] *French v. Chosin Few, Inc.*, 173 F. Supp. 2d 451 (W.D.N.Y. 2001).
[20] *Schmidt v. Farm Credit Services*, 977 F.2d 511 (10th Cir. 1992).

(B) **OTHER OFFICERS AND EMPLOYEES.** The authority of corporate employees and other officers, such as the secretary or treasurer, is generally limited to the duties of their office. However, the authority may be extended by the conduct of the corporation in accordance with the general principles governing apparent authority based on the conduct of the principal. An unauthorized act may, of course, be ratified. The authority of the general manager of the corporation is determined by principles of ordinary agency law.

10. Liability Relating to Fiduciary Duties

The relationship of officers to the corporation, like that of directors, is a fiduciary one. Officers, because of their access to corporate information developed in the pursuit of their daily duties on behalf of the corporation, have an obligation to inform the directors of material information relating to the business. Officers have an obligation not to make any secret financial gain at the expense of the corporation. Because of their level of knowledge of the business, officer-directors have a high fiduciary duty to the corporation.

(A) **CORPORATE OPPORTUNITIES.** If an officer diverts a corporate opportunity, the corporation may recover from the officer the profits of which the corporation has been deprived.

CASE SUMMARY

Ruling Wisely and Decently?

FACTS: Demoulas Super Markets, Inc. (DSM), was owned by brothers George and Telemachus Demoulas, each owning an equal number of shares of stock. From 1964 through May 1971, the company grew from 5 stores to a chain of 14 supermarkets, including 2 stores in New Hampshire. George died suddenly on June 27, 1971, and, at his death, Telemachus assumed control of DSM under the terms of a voting trust. In 1990, George's son Arthur, age 22 and a shareholder of DSM, brought a shareholder derivative action on behalf of DSM, contending that since George's death, Telemachus had diverted business opportunities away from DSM into other businesses that were solely owned by Telemachus's branch of the family. The evidence showed that in the 1970s two new corporations were formed and operated supermarkets in New Hampshire; DSM supplied the financing and management, but ownership was held in the name of Telemachus's sister and daughter. By 1986, these stores grew into a single supermarket chain operating under the Market Basket name and entirely owned by members of Telemachus's branch of the family. The trial court judge determined that Telemachus had diverted these corporate opportunities from DSM, and the court ordered the transfer of the assets and liabilities of the new corporations back to DSM. In her decision, the judge cited lines from *Ulysses*, by Alfred Lord Tennyson, in which Ulysses speaks lovingly of his son, Telemachus, expressing the belief that he would rule wisely and decently after his death. Telemachus denied that any acts were improper or gave rise to liability and charged that the judge was not impartial, as evidenced by her quotation from Tennyson's poem.

DECISION: Judgment against Telemachus. Judicial bias was not present, and the literary reference was simply the judge's stylistic way of stating the theme of her decision against Telemachus, based on the facts she had found. Telemachus had a fiduciary duty to DSM. A fiduciary violates

CASE SUMMARY

Continued

his duty of loyalty by advancing the pecuniary interests of a child or a sibling in a manner that would constitute a breach if he had acted for himself. The record is clear that the New Hampshire companies were set up under Telemachus's direction and were independent in name only, with DSM managing and financing them. The return to DSM of the assets and liabilities of the diverted business was the proper remedy. [*Demoulas v. Demoulas Super Markets, Inc.*, 677 N.E.2d 159 (Mass. 1997); see also 787 N.E.2d 1059 (Mass. 2003)]

An opportunity that would be advantageous to the corporation must first be offered to the corporation before an officer or a director, who owes a fiduciary duty to the corporation, can take advantage of the opportunity. Full disclosure is required. Only if the opportunity is rejected by a majority of disinterested directors may the officer then take advantage of the opportunity. **For Example,** Nancy Harris was president of the Northeast Harbor Golf Club, Inc. In her capacity as club president, she learned of an opportunity to purchase the Gilpin property, which adjoined the golf club. Her private purchase of the property constituted the taking of a corporate opportunity and resulted in her liability to the club. Harris believed that her purchase, in a separate transaction, of the Smallidge land, which was adjacent to three of the golf club's holes and could be developed, was not usurpation of a corporate opportunity because she learned of the availability independently of the club. However, this also was a corporate opportunity because it was so closely related to the club's business. She was obligated to disclose the opportunity to the corporation and let it decide whether to pursue it.[21]

Officers may avail themselves of all opportunities lying outside the field of their duties as officers when business opportunities come to them in an individual capacity.[22]

(B) SECRET PROFITS. Officers are liable to the corporation for secret profits made in connection with, or at the expense of, the business of the corporation.

(C) DUTY OF LOYALTY. A corporate officer, while still employed by his or her firm, may be in breach of the officer's fiduciary duty of loyalty by recruiting key management employees to join a competing company by telling them about the competitor's beneficial compensation, signing bonuses, medical benefits, and superior computer systems. However, an officer may legally make arrangements before leaving the firm to compete in the future. The line separating mere preparation from active competition may be difficult to discern, and, if misjudged, may lead to significant liability for the officer and a competitor aider and abettor, as is evidenced by the *Security Title v. Pope* case.

---

[21] *Northeast Harbor Golf Club v. Harris*, 725 A.2d 1018 (Me. 1999); see *Anderson v. Bellino*, 658 N.W.2d 645 (Neb. 2003).
[22] *Hill v. Southeastern Floor Covering Co.*, 596 So.2d 874 (Miss. 1992).

CASE SUMMARY

Walkin' with Linda Pope

FACTS: Linda Pope ran one of the largest and most successful title insurance branches in the title insurance industry for Security Title Insurance. First American Title Insurance sought to regain its top position in title insurance sales through its Talon division by recruiting key people from other companies who had relationships with key customers and other key employees. Talon recruited Pope. While still employed by Security Title, Pope secretly solicited key management employees to join Talon–First American and planned to bring all 40 employees with her. She arranged for a Talon official, over drinks and dinners, to help with the recruiting by telling Security Title employees about Talon's beneficial compensation, signing bonuses, medical benefits, and superior computer system. Security Title asserted that Pope's actions, aided and abetted by Talon, resulted in $12,194,335 in lost profits after 35 employees walked out on October 20, which was when Security Title "walked her out"—fired Pope—having discovered her plans to leave. Security Title sued Pope for breach of fiduciary duty of loyalty and sued Talon–First American as an aider and abettor. Pope defended that she was merely making arrangements to compete in the future.

DECISION: Judgment for Security Title. Pope breached her fiduciary duty by improperly recruiting Security Title employees for Talon while she was still employed by Security Title. First American's argument that Pope had merely discussed her plans with the other employees and was only preparing to compete with Security Title flies in the face of a wealth of evidence presented to the jury. She secretly solicited key management employees to join a competitor and enticed employees to leave by telling them of bonuses and benefits. [*Security Title Agency, Inc. v. Pope*, 200 P.3d 977 (Ariz. App. 2008)]

11. Agents and Employees

The authority, rights, and liabilities of an agent or employee of a corporation are governed by the same rules as those applicable when the principal or employer is a natural person. The authority of corporate employees is also governed by general agency principles. **For Example,** R. Bryan Smith, president of Allstate Building Systems applied for a credit account with 84 Lumber Company. The first sentence of the application stated: "BY SIGNING BELOW I HEREBY CERTIFY THAT I AM THE OWNER, GENERAL PARTNER OR PRESIDENT OF THE ABOVE BUSINESS,..." The instructions on the first page of the contract state, "If the Applicant is a corporation, then President must sign the application." The language is a certification that the individual signing the contract has the authority to sign the contract in a representative capacity for the company. Immediately following this clause is the language, "I DO UNCONDITIONALLY ... PERSONALLY GUARANTEE THIS CREDIT ACCOUNT AND PAYMENTS OF ANY AND ALL AMOUNTS DUE BY THE ABOVE BUSINESS." Mr. Smith signed both in a representative capacity and personally guaranteed the contract. He agreed to be personally responsible for the $27,611 owed on the account and the court enforced the agreement as written.[23]

---

[23] *84 Lumber Co. v. Smith*, 356 S.W.3d 380 (Tenn. 2011); but see *Stamina Products, Inc. v. Zinctec USA Inc.*, 90 A.D.3d 1021 (A.D.2d 2011), where Anthyony Yau signed a contract on behalf of Zinctec, solely as a corporate officer, and did not bind himself individually under the agreement.

The fact that a person is acting on behalf of a corporation does not serve as a shield from the liability that would be imposed for acts done on behalf of a natural person.

D. LIABILITY

Limited liability is a major reason for incorporating. Management, however, is not free from all civil and criminal liability simply because the corporate form is used.

12. Liability of Management to Third Persons

Officers and managers of a corporation are not liable to third parties for the economic consequences of their advice so long as they acted in good faith to advance the interests of the corporation, even if they cause the corporation to refuse to deal with or break its contract with these third persons.

Ordinarily, the management of a corporation (its directors, officers, and executive employees) is not liable to third persons for the effect of its management or advice. The liability of a director or an officer for misconduct may usually be enforced only by the corporation or by shareholders bringing a derivative action on behalf of the corporation. Ordinarily, directors or officers are not liable to a third person for loss caused by the negligent performance of their duties as directors or officers even if, because of such negligence, the corporation is in turn liable to the third person to whom the corporation owed the duty to use care or was under a contract obligation to render a particular service.

However, in those rare cases when a director or an officer has in some way participated in or directed the tortious act, personal liability will attach. For example, a corporate officer and director may be held personally liable for the tort of fraud in the inducement regarding a false promise to grant an insurance agency an exclusive territory selling viatical settlements, by which life insurance policies of terminally ill people are purchased at a discount in exchange for an immediate cash settlement.[24]

13. Criminal Liability

Officers and directors, as well as the corporation itself, may be criminally accountable for business regulatory offenses.

(A) ACTIVE PARTICIPATION. Officers and directors, as in the case of agents, are personally responsible for any crimes committed by them even when they act on behalf of the corporation.[25] At the local level, they may be criminally responsible for violation of ordinances relating to sanitation, safety, and hours of closing.

At the state level, they may be criminally liable for conducting a business without obtaining necessary licenses or after the corporate certificate of incorporation has been forfeited.

At the federal level, officers and directors may be criminally liable for tax and securities law violations as well as egregious environmental protection law and worker safety law violations. International transactions may lead to potential criminal

[24] *First Financial USA, Inc. v. Steinger*, 760 So.2d 996 (Fla. App. 2000).
[25] *Joy Management Co. v. City of Detroit*, 455 N.W.2d 55 (Mich. App. 1990).

Ethics & the Law

Dodd-Frank "Say-on-Pay"!

For nearly a decade, one of the concerns that shareholders and others have raised about corporate officers is their level of compensation. Former Treasury Secretary Geithner identified executive compensation practices as a contributing factor to the financial crisis of 2008–2009, where incentives for short-term gains overwhelmed the checks and balances meant to mitigate the risk of excessive financial leverage. Some commentators are now identifying excessive executive compensation as the No. 1 problem in corporate governance. While private sector wages rose only 2 percent in 2010, the median compensation for CEOs at Standard & Poor's 500 index companies was up by 18 percent from 2009 to an average of 12 million. It is in this context that Congress passed the Dodd-Frank Wall Street Reform Act and included in it the "say-on-pay provision," whereby publicly traded companies must include a separate shareholder resolution to approve executive compensation in their proxies at least once every three years.* The Act states that the vote shall not be binding on the issuer or construed as overriding a decision of the board of directors. However, while a negative vote does not prove a breach of fiduciary duty, it is a contextual fact where other direct evidence of the directors' conduct may prove a violation of a corporate "pay-for-performance" policy and an abuse of discretion or bad faith.

For Example, a pension fund, as shareholders, sued derivatively on behalf of Cincinnati Bell, Inc., the directors of the company for breach of the duty of loyalty and the company's pay-for-performance policy, where the directors granted $4 million in bonuses, on top of $4.5 million in salary and other compensation to CEO Cassidy, in the same year the company incurred a $61.3 million decline in net income, a drop in earnings per share from $.37 to $.09, a reduction in share price from $3.45 to $2.80, and a negative 18.8 percent annual shareholder return. In compliance with Dodd-Frank the board included a shareholder resolution in its March 21, 2011, proxy seeking shareholder approval of the 2010 executive compensation. The board recommended that the shareholders vote in support of the resolution. On May 3, 2011, 66 percent of voting shareholders voted against the 2010 executive compensation. The directors filed a motion to dismiss the lawsuit. Normally, a board of directors is protected by the "business judgment rule" when making decisions about executive compensation, and courts will not inquire into the wisdom of actions taken by directors in the

absence of fraud, bad faith, or abuse of discretion. However, the business judgment rule is a presumption that may be rebutted at trial by a plaintiff with factual evidence that board members acted disloyally —that is, not in the best interests of the company or its shareholders. The court determined that the plaintiff had sufficiently pled facts of breach of fiduciary duty and unjust enrichment, and it denied the defendants' motion to dismiss, allowing the case to go to trial. At trial the defendants may offer the affirmative defense of the business judgment rule and the plaintiff will have to prove by clear and convincing evidence that the directors acted with reckless disregard for the best interests of the corporation.**

Most boards that faced "no" votes on compensation packages for their executive officers revised their compensation practices in response. **For Example,** Hewlett-Packard reconstructed the formula that had been used to provide its then CEO, Leo Apotheker, with a $30 million compensation package covering a period when its stock fell by almost half. The following figures are some examples of CEO total annual compensation packages for 2012.***

Company	CEO	Amount
McKesson	John H. Hammergren	$131,190,000
Ralph Lauren	Ralph Lauren	$66,650,000
Vornado Realty	Michael D. Fascitelli	$64,400,000
Kinder Morgan	Richard D. Kinder	$60,940,000
Honeywell	David M. Cote	$55,790,000
Express Scripts	George Paz	$51,520,000
Priceline.com	Jeffery H. Boyd	$50,180,000
United Health Group	Stephen J. Hemsley	$48,830,000
Marathon Oil	Clarence P. Cazalot Jr.	$43,710,000
Gilead Sciences	John C. Martin	$43,190,000

Is it troubling to shareholders and employees that outsourcing and cost-cutting occur but CEO salaries remain at the same or higher levels? Will the Dodd-Frank Say-on-Pay legislation impact boards of directors' responsiveness to their shareholders?

*15 U.S.C. §78n-1(a) (2010).
**NECA-IBEW Pension Fund v. Cox, 2011 WL 4383368 (S.D. Ohio, Sept. 20, 2011). But see Dennis v. Hart, 2012 WL 33199 (S.D. Cal. Jan. 6, 2012).
***forbes.com/lists/2012/12/ceo-compensation-12_rank.html.

exposure. Under the Foreign Corrupt Practices Act, it is a crime for a U.S. firm to make payments or gifts to a foreign officer to obtain business. Not only is the U.S. corporation subject to a fine but also the officers and individuals involved are subject to fine and imprisonment.

(B) RESPONSIBLE CORPORATE OFFICER DOCTRINE. Officers and directors may be criminally liable under a number of federal and state statutes for failure to prevent the commission of a crime if they are found to be the "responsible corporate officers." These statutes include the Food, Drug and Cosmetic Act, the Federal Hazardous Substances Act, the Occupational Safety and Health Act, the Federal Water Pollution Act, and, at the state level, the California Corporate Criminal Liability Act. **For Example,** Gary Lundgren was a shareholder and officer of KIE, Inc., which owned and operated a sewage treatment plant on Ketron Island. He knew of the facility's discharge of pollutants into Puget Sound without a permit. As the "responsible corporate officer," he was held personally liable for a $250,000 penalty because he controlled the facility with knowledge of the violations.[26] The California Corporate Criminal Liability Act requires managers in control of corporate operations who have knowledge of "serious concealed dangers" to employees or customers to notify the appropriate regulatory authority or be subject to criminal liability.[27]

(C) LIABILITY OF THE CORPORATION ITSELF. A corporation itself may be convicted of a criminal offense if its agent committed the offense acting within the scope of the agent's authority. **For Example,** Steenberg Homes, Inc., was convicted of negligent criminal homicide in the deaths of two cyclists who were killed when the company's trailer truck, loaded with timber, disengaged from the tractor. If safety chains had been properly attached, the accident would not have happened, and the corporation's failure to establish and enforce safety procedures was a cause of the deaths of the cyclists.[28]

(D) PUNISHMENT OF CORPORATIONS. Under the Organizational Federal Sentencing Guidelines, organizations, including corporations, trusts, pension funds, unions, and nonprofit organizations, are subject to greatly increased fines for criminal convictions. However, corporations and other covered organizations that implement an effective compliance program designed to prevent and detect corporate crimes and voluntarily disclose such crimes to the government will be subject to much lower fines under the guidelines.[29]

14. Indemnification of Officers, Directors, Employees, and Agents

While performing what they believe to be their duty, officers, directors, employees, and agents of corporations may commit acts for which they are later sued or criminally prosecuted. The RMBCA broadly authorizes the corporation to indemnify these persons if they acted in good faith and in a manner reasonably believed to be in, or not opposed to, the interests of the corporation and had no reason to believe that their conduct was unlawful.[30] In some states, statutory provision is made requiring the corporation to indemnify directors and officers for reasonable expenses incurred by them in defending unwarranted suits brought against them by shareholders.

---

[26] *State Department of Ecology v. Lundgren*, 971 P.2d 948 (Wash. App. 1999).
[27] Cal. Penal Code §387 (West 2006).
[28] *State v. Steenberg Homes, Inc.*, 859 N.W.2d 668 (Wis. App. 1998).
[29] U.S. Sentencing Commission Guidelines Manual §§8C2.5(f), 8C2.6. On April 8, 2004, the Commission adopted amendments to the Guidelines and requires a periodic assessment of the "risk of criminal conduct" by the corporation or organization.
[30] Subchapter 8E, added in 1980 and revised in 1994.

15. Liability for Corporate Debts

Because the corporation is a separate legal person, debts that it owes are ordinarily the obligations of the corporation only. Consequently, neither directors nor officers are individually liable for corporate debts, even though it may have been their acts that gave rise to the debts.

In some states, liability for corporate debts is imposed on the corporation's officers and directors when the corporation improperly engages in business.

16. Protection of Shareholders

Shareholders may obtain protection from misconduct by management and by the majority of the shareholders. Shareholders may protect themselves by voting at the next annual election for new directors and for new officers if the latter are elected. Shareholders may take remedial action at a special meeting called for that purpose. Objecting shareholders may bring a legal action when the management misconduct complained of constitutes a legal wrong.[31]

17. Civil Liability of the Corporation

A corporation is liable to third persons for the acts of its officers, employees, and agents to the same extent that a natural person is liable for the acts of agents and employees. This means that the ordinary rules of agency law determine the extent to which the corporation is liable to a third person for a contract made or a tort committed by management personnel, employees, and agents.

LawFlix

Smartest Guys in the Room (2005)(R)

The story of Enron executives and their ploys that duped creditors, analysts, shareholders, and employees. A look at what happens when a board is asleep at the wheel and the officers have unfettered authority.

[31] *Christner v. Anderson, Nietzke & Co.,* 444 N.W.2d 779 (Mich. 1989).

MAKE THE CONNECTION

SUMMARY

Ordinarily, stockholder action is taken at a regular or special meeting of the stockholders. The presence of a quorum of the voting shareholders is required.

Management of a corporation is under the control of a board of directors elected by the shareholders.

Courts will not interfere with the board's judgment in the absence of unusual conduct such as fraud. A director is disqualified from taking part in corporate action when the director has a conflict of interest. Action by directors is usually taken at a properly called meeting of the board. Directors act in a fiduciary capacity in dealing with the corporation. Directors who act in good faith and have exercised reasonable care are not liable for losses resulting from their management decisions. Ordinarily, directors are removed by shareholders.

Officers of a corporation, including a CEO, president, vice president, secretary, and treasurer, are usually selected and removed by the board of directors. Officers are agents of the corporation, and their powers are governed by the law of agency. Their relations with the corporation are fiduciary in nature,

and they are liable for any secret profits and for diverting corporate opportunities to their own advantage.

Directors and officers, as in the case of agents generally, are personally responsible for any torts or crimes they commit even if they act on behalf of the corporation. The corporation itself may be prosecuted for crimes and is subject to fines if convicted. The ordinary rules of agency law determine the extent to which a corporation is liable for a contract made or tort committed by a director, officer, corporate agent, or employee.

LEARNING OUTCOMES

After studying this chapter, you should be able to clearly explain:

A. Shareholders

LO.1 Explain how shareholders, as owners of the corporation, exercise limited control over management by voting at shareholders' meetings to elect directors

> See the discussion of shareholder voting and meetings beginning on p. 1078.

B. Directors

LO.2 Explain the qualifications and powers of directors

> See the discussion regarding the broad authority of directors to manage the corporation, beginning on p. 1079.

LO.3 Explain the liability of directors and the meaning of the business judgment rule (BJR)

> See the *Walt Disney* case in which an unsuccessful action taken by directors was protected by the BJR, p. 1083.
> See the *Van Gorkom* case in which directors were not protected by the BJR, because they were grossly negligent in their judgment, p. 1084.
> See the changes clarifying the role of corporate directors brought about by Sarbanes-Oxley and Dodd-Frank regulations, on p. 1085.

C. Officers, Agents, and Employees

LO.4 Explain the obligation of officers—who have access to corporate information and agency powers—to not violate their fiduciary duties to the corporation

> See the *Demoulas Super Markets* case regarding diverting corporate opportunities, pp. 1088–1089.
> See the *Security Title v. Pope* case regarding a manager's duty of loyalty, p. 1090.

LO.5 Explain the rationale for the "say-on-pay" provision of the Dodd-Frank Act

> See the examples of executive compensation practices leading to the financial crisis of 2008–2009 on p. 1092.
> See the *Cincinnati Bell* excessive compensation example on p. 1092.

D. Liability

LO.6 Explain how directors, officers, and the corporation itself may be criminally liable for regulatory offenses

> See the Gary Lundgren example in which, as a "responsible corporate officer," Gary was held personally liable for environmental law violations, p. 1093.

KEY TERMS

business judgment rule (BJR)   quorum

QUESTIONS AND CASE PROBLEMS

1. Shareholders of Bear Stearns sued the directors of the corporation for damages for violation of the directors' fiduciary duties in effecting a stock-for-stock merger with J. P. Morgan Chase for an implied value of $10 per share while the company's stock had previously reached a 15-month high of $160. On March 10, 2008, information began leaking into the market that Bear Stearns had a liquidity problem. On March 13, 2008, the company was forced to seek emergency financing from the Federal Reserve and J. P. Morgan Chase. By the weekend of March 14–16, the company could no longer operate without major financing. In an effort to preserve some shareholder value while averting the uncertainty of bankruptcy (where stockholders would likely receive nothing), and represented by teams of legal and financial experts and relying on their financial advisor Lazard Freres & Co.'s opinion that the "exchange ratio is fair, from a financial point of view, to the shareholders," the board of directors approved the initial merger agreement. The shareholder plaintiffs contended that the ultimate $10 share price paid was inadequate and they presented their experts who vigorously dissected the board's decisions. What defense, if any, would you raise on behalf of the Bear Stearns board of directors? [*In re Bear Stearns Litigation*, 870 N.Y.S.2d 709]

2. In 1996, Congress offered national banks the opportunity to become Subchapter S entities. Amboy Bancorporation was a small, highly profitable New Jersey Bank that was overcapitalized. Amboy's president and CEO utilized Bank Advisory Group, Inc. (BAG), to calculate the fair value of individual shares of Amboy stock. The board of directors approved a merger cash buy-out program designed to reduce the shareholder base to below the 75 qualified shareholders necessary to obtain Subchapter S status. BAG incorrectly applied a minority and marketability discount to its evaluation of the fair value of the stock, bringing it down from $110 per share to $70.13 per share. Casey and other shareholders who cashed out under the plan at $73 per share sued the board of directors individually for damages for approving such a flawed plan. Are directors personally liable when they act in reliance on a report by an outside expert whose advice is flawed? If a public accounting firm or an attorney gave the flawed advice, would the directors be personally liable? [*Casey v. Brennan*, 344 N.J. Super. 83]

3. The majority shareholder and president of Dunaway Drug Stores, Inc., William B. Dunaway, was structuring and executing the sale of virtually all of the corporation's assets to Eckerd Drug Co. While doing this, he negotiated a side noncompete agreement with Eckerd, giving Dunaway $300,000 plus a company car in exchange for a covenant not to compete for three years. He simultaneously amended two corporate leases with Eckerd, thereby decreasing the value of the corporation's leasehold estates. The board of directors approved the asset sale. Minority shareholders brought a derivative action against William Dunaway, claiming breach of his fiduciary duty in negotiating the undisclosed noncompete agreement, which did not require him to perform any service for buyer Eckerd Drug. Did William Dunaway make sufficient disclosure about all of the negotiations of the asset sale to Eckerd Drug? Did William Dunaway violate any fiduciary duty to the corporation? Decide. [*Dunaway v. Parker*, 453 S.E.2d 43 (Ga. App.)]

4. Larry Phillips was hired for a two-year period as executive secretary of the Montana Education Association (MEA). Six months later, he was fired. He then sued MEA for breach of contract and sued the directors and some of the other employees of MEA on the theory that they had caused MEA to break the contract with him and were therefore guilty of the tort of maliciously interfering with his contract with MEA. The evidence showed that the individual defendants, without malice, had induced the corporation to break the contract with Phillips but that this had been done to further the welfare of the corporation. Was MEA liable for breach of contract? Were the individual defendants

shielded from personal liability? [*Phillips v. Montana Education Ass'n*, 610 P.2d 154 (Mont.)]

5. Christy Pontiac, a corporation, was indicted for theft by swindle and forgery involving a GM cash rebate program. Hesli, a middle-management employee of Christy Pontiac, had forged the cash rebate applications for two cars so that the rebate money was paid to Christy Pontiac instead of its customers. When confronted by a customer who should have received a rebate, the president of the dealership attempted to negotiate a settlement. The president did not contact GM headquarters until after an investigation was begun by the state attorney general. Christy Pontiac argued that it could not be held responsible for a crime involving specific intent because only natural persons, as opposed to corporations, can form such intent. Decide. [*State v. Christy Pontiac-GMC, Inc.*, 354 N.W.2d 17 (Minn.)]

6. Larry G. Snodgrass and Mark Swinnea owned equal interests in two business entities, ERI Consulting Engineers, Inc. (ERI), and Malmeba Company, Ltd., which they operated together for approximately 10 years. ERI manages asbestos abatement projects for contractors. It leased office space from Malmeba, their partnership that owned the building. Snodgrass and ERI purchased Swinnea's interest in ERI in 2001. ERI paid Swinnea $497,500 to redeem Swinnea's ERI stock, and Snodgrass transferred his half-interest in Malmeba to Swinnea. ERI agreed to employ Swinnea for six years, and Swinnea agreed not to compete with ERI. At the same time, ERI agreed to continue leasing from Malmeba for six years. Unknown to Snodgrass, the wives of Swinnea and Chris Power, an ERI employee, had created a new company called Air Quality Associates a month before Swinnea and Snodgrass executed the buyout agreement. Air Quality Associates was created to perform mold abatement, but later engaged in asbestos abatement as a contractor even though neither wife had experience in the asbestos abatement field. Swinnea did not disclose the existence of Air Quality Associates to Snodgrass during the ERI buyout negotiations. Over a 33-month period Snodgrass suffered a total loss of profits of $178,000 for business lost to Swinnea. Was Swinnea free to outmaneuver Snodgrass in their buyout agreement as part of the competitive spirit of America? Do owners have a fiduciary duty to each other in negotiating a buyout agreement with a noncompete clause? Are Swinnea's action's so contrary to our public sense of justice and propriety to merit exemplary damages? [*ERI Consulting Engineers, Inc. v. Swinnea*, 318 S.W.3d 867 (Tex.); *Swinnea v. ERI Consulting Engineers*, 364 S.W.3d 421 (Tex. App.)

7. Discuss the power of a corporation president to employ a sales manager and to agree that the manager should be paid a stated amount per year plus a percentage of any increase in the dollar volume of sales that might take place.

8. Richard Grassgreen was executive vice president and then president and chief operating officer of Kinder-Care, Inc., the largest proprietary provider of child care in the country. The company was restructured in 1989 and changed its name to the Enstar Group, Inc. Between 1985 and 1990, while Grassgreen served as the corporation's investment manager, he invested millions of dollars of company money in junk bond deals with Michael Milken, and he secretly retained some $355,000 in commitment fees. When the corporation discovered this, Grassgreen repaid the corporation. It sued him to recover any compensation paid him over the five-year period during which the secret payments were made, some $5,197,663. Grassgreen defended that his conduct caused little, if any, damage to the corporation because the corporation did not lose any money on any of the investments for which he received personal fees. Decide. [*Enstar Group, Inc. v. Grassgreen*, 812 F. Supp. 1562 (M.D. Ala.)]

9. Danny Hill, the general manager of Southeastern Floor Covering Co., Inc. (SE), had full authority to run the business. His responsibilities included preparing and submitting bid proposals to general contractors for floor coverings and ceilings on construction projects. Hill prepared and submitted a bid for a job for Chata

Construction Co. for asbestos encapsulation, ceramic tile, ceilings, carpets, and vinyl tile flooring. However, because SE was not licensed by the EPA, the asbestos work was withdrawn. In the past, SE had used Larry Barnes's company, which was EPA licensed, to do asbestos work under a subcontract agreement. Hill did not pursue a subcontract with Barnes for the Chata job. Rather, Hill and Barnes worked up a bid together and submitted it to Chata for the asbestos work. The bid was accepted, and Hill made $90,000 from the Chata job. Two years later, SE found out about Hill's role in the asbestos work done for Chata, and the corporation sued him for the lost profits. Hill argued that SE was not licensed by the EPA to do asbestos work and thus could not claim a lost corporate opportunity when it was not qualified to do the work. Decide. Are any ethical principles applicable to this case? [*Hill v. Southeastern Floor Covering Co.*, 596 So.2d 874 (Miss.)]

10. A director of a corporation cannot lend money to the corporation because that would create the danger of a conflict of interest between the director's status as a director and as a creditor. Appraise this statement.

11. Hamway and other minority shareholders brought an action against majority shareholders of Libbie Rehabilitation Center, Inc., including Frank Giannotti, CEO-director; Alex Grossman, president-director; Henry Miller, vice president–director; Ernest Dervishian, secretary and corporate attorney; and Lewis Cowardin, treasurer-director. The minority shareholders contended that the corporation paid excessive salaries to these director-officers and was wasting corporate assets. Prior to coming to Libbie, Giannotti had been a carpet and tile retailer, Grossman a pharmacist, Miller a real estate developer, Dervishian a lawyer, and Cowardin a jeweler. The evidence showed that the extent of their work for the corporation was very limited. For example, Cowardin, Libbie's finance officer, who was paid $78,121, demonstrated no knowledge of the Medicare and Medicaid programs, the principal source of Libbie's income. Although he claimed to have spent 20 to 25 hours a week on corporate duties, he reported on the tax return for his jewelry business that he spent 75 percent of his working time in that business. One expert witness of the plaintiff testified that the five men were performing the management functions of one individual. The director-officers contended that the business was making a profit and that all salaries were approved by a board of directors that had extensive business experience. Were the directors within their rights to elect themselves officers and set pay for themselves as they saw fit? Did they violate any legal or ethical duty to their shareholders?

12. Anthony Yee was the president of Waipahu Auto Exchange, a corporation. As part of his corporate duties, he arranged financing for the company. Federal Services Finance Corp. drew 12 checks payable to the order of Waipahu Auto Exchange. These were then indorsed by its president, "Waipahu Auto Exchange, Limited, by Anthony Yee, President," and were cashed at two different banks. Bishop National Bank of Hawaii, on which the checks were drawn, charged its depositor, Federal Services, with the amount of the checks. Federal Services then sued Bishop National Bank to restore to its account the amount of the 12 checks on the ground that Bishop National Bank had improperly made payment on the checks because Anthony Yee had no authority to cash them. Did Yee have authority to indorse and cash the checks? [*Federal Services Finance Corp. v. Bishop Nat'l Bank of Hawaii*, 190 F.2d 442 (9th Cir.)]

13. Klinicki and Lundgren incorporated Berlinair, Inc., a closely held Oregon corporation. Lundgren was president and responsible for developing business. Klinicki served as vice president and director responsible for operations and maintenance. Klinicki owned one-third of the stock, and Lundgren controlled the rest. They both met with BFR, a consortium of Berlin travel agents, about contracting to operate some charter flights. After the initial meeting, all contracts with BFR were made by Lundgren, who learned that there was a good chance that

the BFR contract would be available. He incorporated Air Berlin Charter Co. (ABC) and was its sole owner. He presented BFR with a contract proposal, and it awarded the contract to ABC. Although Lundgren was using Berlinair's working time and facilities, he managed to keep the negotiations a secret from Klinicki. When Klinicki discovered Lundgren's actions, he sued him for usurping a corporate opportunity for Berlinair. Lundgren contended that it was not a usurpation of corporate opportunity because Berlinair did not have the financial ability to undertake the contract with BFR. Decide. Are any ethical principles applicable to this case? Consider the applicability of Chief Justice Cardozo's statement in *Meinhard v. Salmon*, 164 N.E. 545 (N.Y. 1928), concerning the level of conduct for fiduciaries: "A trustee is held to something stricter than the morals of the marketplace. Not honesty alone, but the punctillo of an honor the most sensitive is then the standard of behavior… ." [*Klinicki v. Lundgren*, 695 P.2d 906 (Or.)]

14. Rudolph Redmont, the president of Abbott Thinlite Corp., left Abbott to run Circle Corp. in competition with his former employer. It was claimed that he diverted contracts from his former employer to his new one, having gained the advantage of specific information about the deals in progress while employed by Abbott. Abbott sued Redmont and Circle Corp. to recover lost profits. Redmont contended that all of the contracts in question were made after he left Abbott, at which time his fiduciary duty to Abbott had ceased. Decide. [*Abbott Thinlite Corp. v. Redmont*, 475 F.2d 85 (2d Cir.)]

15. William Gurtler was president and a board member of Unichem Corp., which produced and sold chemical laundry products. While president of Unichem, he encouraged his plant manager to leave to join a rival business, which Gurtler was going to join in the near future. Moreover, Gurtler sold Unichem products to his son, G. B. Gurtler, at a figure substantially below their normal price and on credit even though G. B. had no credit history. Gurtler made the sales with full knowledge that G. B. was going to start a rival business. Also at that time, Gurtler was aware that his wife was soliciting Unichem employees to join the new Gurtler Chemical Co., and he helped her design Gurtler's label so that it would look like Unichem's. Gurtler guaranteed a $100,000 bank loan for the new Gurtler Chemical Co. with funds to be disbursed after he left Unichem. One month later, He became president of Gurtler Chemical Co. Unichem sued Gurtler for breach of fiduciary duty and for the loss of profits that resulted. Gurtler contended that his sales to G. B. guaranteed needed revenue to Unichem and constituted a sound business decision that should be applauded and that was protected under the business judgment rule. Decide. Are any ethical principles applicable to this case? [*Unichem Corp. v. Gurtler*, 498 N.E.2d 724 (Ill. App.)]

CPA QUESTIONS

1. Davis, a director of Active Corp., is entitled to:

   a. Serve on the board of a competing business

   b. Take sole advantage of a business opportunity that would benefit Active

   c. Rely on information provided by a corporate officer

   d. Unilaterally grant a corporate loan to one of Active's shareholders

2. Absent a specific provision in its articles of incorporation, a corporation's board of directors has the power to do all of the following *except*:

   a. Repeal the bylaws

   b. Declare dividends

   c. Fix compensation of directors

   d. Amend the articles of incorporation

3. Which of the following statements is correct regarding fiduciary duty?

   a. A director's fiduciary duty to the corporation may be discharged by merely disclosing his or her self-interest.

   b. A director owes a fiduciary duty to the shareholders but *not* to the corporation.

   c. A promoter of a corporation to be formed owes no fiduciary duty to anyone, unless the contract engaging the promoter so provides.

   d. A majority shareholder as such may owe a fiduciary duty to fellow shareholders.

Appendix 1

In order to determine what the law on a particular question or issue is, it may be necessary to examine (1) compilations of constitutions, treaties, statutes, executive orders, proclamations, and administrative regulations; (2) reports of state and federal court decisions; (3) digests of opinions; (4) treatises on the law; and (5) loose-leaf services. These sources can be either researched traditionally or using fee and/or non-fee-based computerized legal research, accessed through the World Wide Web.

A. COMPILATIONS

In the consideration of a legal problem in business it is necessary to determine whether the matter is affected or controlled by a constitution, national or state; by a national treaty; by an Act of Congress, a state legislature, or a city ordinance; by a decree or proclamation of the President of the United States, a governor, or a mayor; or by a regulation of a federal, state, or local administrative agency.

Each body or person that makes laws, regulations, or ordinances usually compiles and publishes at the end of each year or session all of the matter that it has adopted. In addition to the periodical or annual volumes, it is common to compile all the treaties, statutes, regulations, or ordinances in separate volumes. To illustrate, the federal Anti-Injunction Act may be cited as the Act of March 23, 1932, 47 Stat. 70, 29 U.S.C. § 101 et seq. This means that this law was enacted on March 23, 1932, and that it can be found at page 70 in Volume 47 of the reports that contain all of the statutes adopted by the Congress.

The second part of the citation, 29 U.S.C. § 101 et seq., means that in the collection of all of the federal statutes, which is known as the United States Code, the full text of the statute can be found in the sections of the 29th title beginning with Section 101.

B. COURT DECISIONS

For complicated or important legal cases or when an appeal is to be taken, a court will generally write an opinion, which explains why the court made the decision. Appellate courts as a rule write opinions. The great majority of these decisions, particularly in the case of the appellate courts, are collected and printed. In order to avoid confusion, the opinions of each court are ordinarily printed in a separate set of reports, either by official reporters or private publishers.

In the reference "*Pennoyer v. Neff*, 95 U.S. 714, 24 L. Ed. 565," the first part states the names of the parties. It does not necessarily tell who was the plaintiff and who was the defendant. When an action is begun in a lower court, the first name is that of the plaintiff and the second name that of the defendant. When the case is appealed, generally the name of the person taking the appeal appears on the records of the higher court as the first one and that of the adverse party as the second. Sometimes, therefore, the original order of the names of the parties is reversed.

The balance of the reference consists of two citations. The first citation, 95 U.S. 714, means that the opinion which the court filed in the case of *Pennoyer v. Neff* may be found on page 714 of the 95th volume of a series of books in which are printed officially the opinions of the United States Supreme Court. Sometimes the same opinion is printed in two different sets of volumes. In the example, 24 L.Ed. 565 means that in the 24th volume of another set of books, called Lawyer's Edition, of the United States Supreme Court Reports, the same opinion begins on page 565.

In opinions by a state court there may also be two citations, as in the case of *Morrow v. Corbin*, 122 Tex. 553, 62 S.W.2d 641. This means that the opinion in the lawsuit between Morrow and Corbin may be found in the 122nd volume of the reports of the highest court of Texas, beginning on page 553; and also in Volume 62 of the Southwestern Reporter, Second Series, at page 641.

The West Publishing Company publishes a set of sectional reporters covering the entire United States. They are called "sectional" because each reporter, instead of being limited to a particular court or a particular state, covers the decisions of the courts of a particular section of the country. Thus the decisions of the courts of Arkansas, Kentucky, Missouri, Tennessee, and Texas are printed by the West Publishing company as a group in a sectional reporter called the Southwestern Reporter.[1] Because of the large number of decisions involved, generally only the opinions of the state appellate courts are printed. A number of states[2] have discontinued publication of the opinions of their courts, and those opinions are now found only in the West reporters.

The reason for the "Second Series" in the Southwestern citation is that when there were 300 volumes in the original series, instead of calling the next volume 301, the publisher called it Volume 1, Second Series. Thus 62 S. W.2d Series really means the 362nd volume of the Southwestern Reporter. Six to eight volumes appear in a year for each geographic section.

In addition to these state reporters, the West Publishing Company publishes a Federal Supplement, which primarily reports the opinions of the Federal District Courts; the Federal Reporter, which primarily reports the decisions of the United States Courts of Appeals; and the Supreme Court Reporter, which reports the decisions of the United States Supreme Court. The Supreme Court decisions are also reported in a separate set called the Lawyers' Edition, published by the Lawyers Cooperative Publishing Company.

The reports published by the West Publishing Company and Lawyers Cooperative Publishing Company are unofficial reports, while those bearing the name or abbreviation of the United States or of a state, such as "95 U.S. 714" or "122 Tex. 553" are official reports. This means that in the case of the latter, the particular court, such as the United States Supreme Court, has officially authorized that its decisions be printed and that by federal statute such official printing is made. In the case of the unofficial reporters, the publisher prints the decisions of a court on its own initiative. Such opinions are part of the public domain and not subject to any copyright or similar restriction.

C. DIGESTS OF OPINIONS

The reports of court decisions are useful only if one has the citation, that is, the name and volume number of the book and the page number of the opinion one is seeking. For this reason, digests of the decisions have been prepared. These digests organize the entire field of law under major headings, which are then arranged in alphabetical order. Under each heading, such as "Contracts," the subject is divided into the different questions that can arise with respect to that field. A master outline is thus created on the subject. This outline includes short paragraphs describing what each case holds and giving its citation.

D. TREATISES AND RESTATEMENTS

Very helpful in finding a case or a statute are the treatises on the law. These may be special books, each written by an author on a particular subject, such as Williston on Contracts, Bogert on Trusts, Fletcher on Corporations, or they may be general encyclopedias, as in the case of *American Jurisprudence, American Jurisprudence, Second,* and *Corpus Juris Secundum.*

Another type of treatise is found in the restatements of the law prepared by the American Law Institute. Each restatement consists of one or more volumes devoted to a particular phase of the law, such as the Restatement of the Law of Contracts, Restatement of the Law of Agency, and Restatement of the Law of Property. In each restatement, the American Law Institute, acting through special committees of judges, lawyers, and professors of law, has set forth what the law is; and in many areas where there is no law or the present rule is regarded as unsatisfactory, the restatement specifies what the Institute deems to be the desirable rule.

E. LOOSE-LEAF SERVICES

A number of private publishers, notably Commerce Clearing House and Prentice-Hall, publish loose-leaf books devoted to particular branches of the law. Periodically, the publisher sends to the purchaser a number of pages that set forth any decision, regulation, or statute made or adopted since the prior set of pages was prepared. Such services are unofficial.

F. COMPUTERIZED LEGAL RESEARCH

National and local computer services are providing constantly widening assistance for legal research. The database in such a system may be opinions, statutes, or administrative regulations stored word for word; or the later history of a particular case giving its full citation and showing whether the case has been followed by other courts; or the text of forms and documents. By means of a

---

[1] The sectional reporters are: Atlantic—A. (Connecticut, Delaware, District of Columbia, Maine, Maryland, New Hampshire, New Jersey, Pennsylvania, Rhode Island, Vermont); Northeastern—N.E. (Illinois, Indiana, Massachusetts, New York, Ohio); N.W. (Iowa, Michigan, Minnesota, Nebraska, North Dakota, South Dakota, Wisconsin); Pacific—P. (Alaska, Arizona, California, Colorado, Hawaii, Idaho, Kansas, Montana, Nevada, New Mexico, Oklahoma, Oregon, Utah, Washington, Wyoming); Southeastern—S.E. (Georgia, North Carolina, South Carolina, Virginia, West Virginia); Southwestern— S.W. (Arkansas, Kentucky, Missouri, Tennessee, Texas); and Southern—So. (Alabama, Florida, Louisiana, Mississippi). There is also a special New York State reporter known as the New York Supplement and a special California State reporter known as the California Reporter.

[2] See, for example, Alaska, Florida, Iowa, Kentucky, Louisiana, Maine, Mississippi, Missouri, North Dakota, Oklahoma, Texas, and Wyoming.

terminal connected to the system, the user can retrieve the legal information at a great saving of time and with the assurance that it is up-to-date.

There are two leading, fee-based systems for computer-aided research. Listed alphabetically, they are LEXIS and WESTLAW.

A specialized service of legal forms for business is provided by Shepard's BUSINESS LAW CASE MANAGEMENT SYSTEM. A monthly fee is required for usage.

Numerous free, private sites offer a lot of legal resources. The federal government offers a variety of case law, regulations, and code enactments, either pending or newly promulgated. To find the most comprehensive source of government-maintained legal information, go to **http://www.house.gov**. The United States Supreme Court has information about both its current term and past terms at **www.supremecourt.gov**. Another website that provides excellent information about current controversies that reach the United States Supreme Court is **www.scotusblog.com**.

State governments provide access to regulations and codes online. As an example, go to the State of California's site, **www.leginfo.legislation.ca.gov**. You can access an array of information about both state and federal government through links at **www.USA.gov**.

We the people of the United States of America, in order to form a more perfect union, establish justice, insure domestic tranquility, provide for the common defense, promote the general welfare, and secure the blessings of liberty to ourselves and our posterity, do ordain and establish this Constitution for the United States of America.

Article I

SECTION 1

All legislative powers herein granted shall be vested in a Congress of the United States, which shall consist of a Senate and House of Representatives.

SECTION 2

1. The House of Representatives shall be composed of members chosen every second year by the people of the several States, and the electors in each State shall have the qualifications requisite for electors of the most numerous branch of the State legislature.

2. No person shall be a representative who shall not have attained to the age of twenty-five years, and been seven years a citizen of the United States, and who shall not, when elected, be an inhabitant of that State in which he shall be chosen.

3. Representatives and direct taxes shall be apportioned among the several States which may be included within this Union, according to their respective numbers, which shall be determined by adding to the whole number of free persons, including those bound to service for a term of years, and excluding Indians not taxed, three fifths of all other persons.[1] The actual enumeration shall be made within three years after the first meeting of the Congress of the United States, and within every subsequent term of ten years, in such manner as they shall by law direct. The number of representatives shall not exceed one for every thirty thousand, but each State shall have at least one representative; and until such enumeration shall be made, the State of New Hampshire shall be entitled to choose three, Massachusetts eight, Rhode Island and Providence Plantations one, Connecticut five, New York six, New Jersey four, Pennsylvania eight, Delaware one, Maryland six, Virginia ten, North Carolina five, South Carolina five, and Georgia three.

4. When vacancies happen in the representation from any State, the executive authority thereof shall issue writs of election to fill such vacancies.

5. The House of Representatives shall choose their speaker and other officers; and shall have the sole power of impeachment.

SECTION 3

1. The Senate of the United States shall be composed of two senators from each State, chosen by the legislature thereof, for six years; and each senator shall have one vote.

2. Immediately after they shall be assembled in consequence of the first election, they shall be divided as equally as may be into three classes. The seats of the senators of the first class shall be vacated at the expiration of the second year, of the second class at the expiration of the fourth year, and of the third class at the expiration of the sixth year, so that one third may be chosen every second year; and if vacancies happen by resignation, or otherwise, during the recess of the legislature of any State, the executive thereof may make temporary appointments until the next meeting of the legislature, which shall then fill such vacancies.[2]

3. No person shall be a senator who shall not have attained to the age of thirty years, and been nine years a citizen of the United States, and who shall not, when elected, be an inhabitant of that State for which he shall be chosen.

4. The Vice President of the United States shall be President of the Senate, but shall have no vote, unless they be equally divided.

5. The Senate shall choose their other officers, and also a president pro tempore, in the absence of the Vice President, or when he shall exercise the office of the President of the United States.

6. The Senate shall have the sole power to try all impeachments. When sitting for that purpose, they shall

[1] See the 14th Amendment.

[2] See the 17th Amendment.

be on oath or affirmation. When the President of the United States is tried, the chief justice shall preside: and no person shall be convicted without the concurrence of two thirds of the members present.

7. Judgment in cases of impeachment shall not extend further than to removal from office, and disqualification to hold and enjoy any office of honor, trust or profit under the United States: but the party convicted shall nevertheless be liable and subject to indictment, trial, judgment and punishment, according to law.

SECTION 4

1. The times, places, and manner of holding elections for senators and representatives, shall be prescribed in each State by the legislature thereof; but the Congress may at any time by law make or alter such regulations, except as to the places of choosing senators.

2. The Congress shall assemble at least once in every year, and such meeting shall be on the first Monday in December, unless they shall by law appoint a different day.

SECTION 5

1. Each House shall be the judge of the elections, returns and qualifications of its own members, and a majority of each shall constitute a quorum to do business; but a smaller number may adjourn from day to day, and may be authorized to compel the attendance of absent members, in such manner, and under such penalties as each House may provide.

2. Each House may determine the rules of its proceedings, punish its members for disorderly behavior, and, with the concurrence of two thirds, expel a member.

3. Each House shall keep a journal of its proceedings, and from time to time publish the same, excepting such parts as may in their judgment require secrecy; and the yeas and nays of the members of either House on any question shall, at the desire of one fifth of those present, be entered on the journal.

4. Neither House, during the session of Congress, shall, without the consent of the other, adjourn for more than three days, nor to any other place than that in which the two Houses shall be sitting.

SECTION 6

1. The senators and representatives shall receive a compensation for their services, to be ascertained by law, and paid out of the Treasury of the United States. They shall in all cases, except treason, felony, and breach of the peace, be privileged from arrest during their attendance at the session of their respective Houses, and in going to and returning from the same; and for any speech or debate in either House, they shall not be questioned in any other place.

2. No senator or representative shall, during the time for which he was elected, be appointed to any civil office under the authority of the United States, which shall have been created, or the emoluments whereof shall have been increased during such time; and no person holding any office under the United States shall be a member of either House during his continuance in office.

SECTION 7

1. All bills for raising revenue shall originate in the House of Representatives; but the Senate may propose or concur with amendments as on other bills.

2. Every bill which shall have passed the House of Representatives and the Senate, shall, before it becomes a law, be presented to the President of the United States; if he approves he shall sign it, but if not he shall return it, with his objections to that House in which it shall have originated, who shall enter the objections at large on their journal, and proceed to reconsider it. If after such reconsideration two thirds of that House shall agree to pass the bill, it shall be sent, together with the objections, to the other House, by which it shall likewise be reconsidered, and if approved by two thirds of that House, it shall become a law. But in all such cases the votes of both Houses shall be determined by yeas and nays, and the names of the persons voting for and against the bill shall be entered on the journal of each House respectively. If any bill shall not be returned by the President within ten days (Sundays excepted) after it shall have been presented to him, the same shall be a law, in like manner as if he had signed it, unless the Congress by their adjournment prevent its return, in which case it shall not be a law.

3. Every order, resolution, or vote to which the concurrence of the Senate and the House of Representatives may be necessary (except on a question of adjournment) shall be presented to the President of the United States; and before the same shall take effect, shall be approved by him, or being disapproved by him, shall be repassed by two thirds of the Senate and House of Representatives, according to the rules and limitations prescribed in the case of a bill.

SECTION 8

The Congress shall have the power

1. To lay and collect taxes, duties, imposts, and excises, to pay the debts and provide for the common defense and general welfare of the United States; but all duties, imposts, and excises shall be uniform throughout the United States;

2. To borrow money on the credit of the United States;

3. To regulate commerce with foreign nations, and among the several States, and with the Indian tribes;

4. To establish a uniform rule of naturalization, and uniform laws on the subject of bankruptcies throughout the United States;

5. To coin money, regulate the value thereof, and of foreign coin, and fix the standard of weights and measures;

6. To provide for the punishment of counterfeiting the securities and current coin of the United States;

7. To establish post offices and post roads;

8. To promote the progress of science and useful arts, by securing for limited times to authors and inventors the exclusive rights to their respective writings and discoveries;

9. To constitute tribunals inferior to the Supreme Court;

10. To define and punish piracies and felonies committed on the high seas, and offenses against the law of nations;

11. To declare war, grant letters of marque and reprisal, and make rules concerning captures on land and water;

12. To raise and support armies, but no appropriation of money to that use shall be for a longer term than two years;

13. To provide and maintain a navy;

14. To make rules for the government and regulation of the land and naval forces;

15. To provide for calling forth the militia to execute the laws of the Union, suppress insurrections and repel invasions;

16. To provide for organizing, arming, and disciplining the militia, and for governing such part of them as may be employed in the service of the United States, reserving to the States respectively, the appointment of the officers, and the authority of training the militia according to the discipline prescribed by Congress;

17. To exercise exclusive legislation in all cases whatsoever, over such district (not exceeding ten miles square) as may, by cession of particular States, and the acceptance of Congress, become the seat of the government of the United States, and to exercise like authority over all places purchased by the consent of the legislature of the State in which the same shall be, for the erection of forts, magazines, arsenals, dockyards, and other needful buildings; and

18. To make all laws which shall be necessary and proper for carrying into execution the foregoing powers, and all other powers vested by this Constitution in the government of the United States, or in any department or officer thereof.

SECTION 9

1. The migration or importation of such persons as any of the States now existing shall think proper to admit, shall not be prohibited by the Congress prior to the year one thousand eight hundred and eight, but a tax or duty may be imposed on such importation, not exceeding ten dollars for each person.

2. The privilege of the writ of habeas corpus shall not be suspended, unless when in cases of rebellion or invasion the public safety may require it.

3. No bill of attainder or ex post facto law shall be passed.

4. No capitation, or other direct, tax shall be laid, unless in proportion to the census or enumeration hereinbefore directed to be taken.[3]

5. No tax or duty shall be laid on articles exported from any State.

6. No preference shall be given by any regulation of commerce or revenue to the ports of one State over those of another: nor shall vessels bound to, or from, one State be obliged to enter, clear, or pay duties in another.

7. No money shall be drawn from the treasury, but in consequence of appropriations made by law; and a regular statement and account of the receipts and expenditures of all public money shall be published from time to time.

8. No title of nobility shall be granted by the United States: and no person holding any office of profit or trust under them, shall, without the consent of the Congress, accept of any present, emolument, office, or title, of any kind whatever, from any king, prince, or foreign State.

SECTION 10

1. No State shall enter into any treaty, alliance, or confederation; grant letters of marque and reprisal; coin money; emit bills of credit; make anything but gold and silver coin a tender in payment of debts; pass any bill of attainder, ex post facto law, or law impairing the obligation of contracts, or grant any title of nobility.

2. No State shall, without the consent of the Congress, lay any imposts or duties on imports or exports, except what may be absolutely necessary for executing its inspection laws: and the net produce of all duties and imposts laid by any State on imports or exports, shall be for the use of the treasury of the United States; and all such laws shall be subject to the revision and control of the Congress.

3. No State shall, without the consent of the Congress, lay any duty of tonnage, keep troops, or ships of war in time of peace, enter into any agreement or compact with another State, or with a foreign power, or engage in war, unless actually invaded, or in such imminent danger as will not admit of delay.

Article II

SECTION 1

1. The executive power shall be vested in a President of the United States of America. He shall hold his office during the term of four years, and, together with the Vice President, chosen for the same term, be elected as follows:

2. Each State shall appoint, in such manner as the legislature thereof may direct, a number of electors, equal to the whole number of senators and representatives to

---

[3] See the 16th Amendment.

which the State may be entitled in the Congress: but no senator or representative, or person holding an office of trust or profit under the United States, shall be appointed an elector.

The electors shall meet in their respective States, and vote by ballot for two persons, of whom one at least shall not be an inhabitant of the same State with themselves. And they shall make a list of all the persons voted for, and of the number of votes for each; which list they shall sign and certify, and transmit sealed to the seat of the government of the United States, directed to the president of the Senate. The president of the Senate shall, in the presence of the Senate and House of Representatives, open all the certificates, and the votes shall then be counted. The person having the greatest number of votes shall be the President, if such number be a majority of the whole number of electors appointed; and if there be more than one who have such majority, and have an equal number of votes, then the House of Representatives shall immediately choose by ballot one of them for President; and if no person have a majority, then from the five highest on the list the said House shall in like manner choose the President. But in choosing the President, the votes shall be taken by States, the representation from each State having one vote; a quorum for this purpose shall consist of a member or members from two thirds of the States, and a majority of all the States shall be necessary to a choice. In every case, after the choice of the President, the person having the greatest number of votes of the electors shall be the Vice President. But if there should remain two or more who have equal votes, the Senate shall choose from them by ballot the Vice President.[4]

3. The Congress may determine the time of choosing the electors, and the day on which they shall give their votes; which day shall be the same throughout the United States.

4. No person except a natural born citizen, or a citizen of the United States, at the time of the adoption of this Constitution, shall be eligible to the office of President; neither shall any person be eligible to that office who shall not have attained to the age of thirty-five years, and been fourteen years a resident within the United States.

5. In the case of removal of the President from office, or of his death, resignation, or inability to discharge the powers and duties of the said office, the same shall devolve on the Vice President, and the Congress may by law provide for the case of removal, death, resignation, or inability, both of the President and Vice President, declaring what officer shall then act as President, and such officer shall act accordingly, until the disability be removed, or a President shall be elected.

6. The President shall, at stated times, receive for his services a compensation, which shall neither be increased nor diminished during the period for which he shall have been elected, and he shall not receive within that period any other emolument from the United States, or any of them.

7. Before he enter on the execution of his office, he shall take the following oath or affirmation:—"I do solemnly swear (or affirm) that I will faithfully execute the office of President of the United States, and will to the best of my ability, preserve, protect and defend the Constitution of the United States."

SECTION 2

1. The President shall be commander in chief of the army and navy of the United States, and of the militia of the several States, when called into the actual service of the United States; he may require the opinion, in writing, of the principal officer in each of the executive departments, upon any subject relating to the duties of their respective office, and he shall have power to grant reprieves and pardons for offenses against the United States, except in cases of impeachment.

2. He shall have power, by and with the advice and consent of the Senate, to make treaties, provided two thirds of the senators present concur; and he shall nominate, and by and with the advice and consent of the Senate, shall appoint ambassadors, other public ministers and consuls, judges of the Supreme Court, and all other officers of the United States, whose appointments are not herein otherwise provided for, and which shall be established by law: but the Congress may by law vest the appointment of such inferior officers, as they think proper, in the President alone, in the courts of law, or in the heads of departments.

3. The President shall have power to fill up all vacancies that may happen during the recess of the Senate, by granting commissions which shall expire at the end of their next session.

SECTION 3

He shall from time to time give to the Congress information of the state of the Union, and recommend to their consideration such measures as he shall judge necessary and expedient; he may, on extraordinary occasions, convene both Houses, or either of them, and in case of disagreement between them with respect to the time of adjournment, he may adjourn them to such time as he shall think proper; he shall receive ambassadors and other public ministers; he shall take care that the laws be faithfully executed, and shall commission all the officers of the United States.

SECTION 4

The President, Vice President, and all civil officers of the United States, shall be removed from office on impeachment for, and conviction of, treason, bribery, or other high crimes and misdemeanors.

[4] Superseded by the 12th Amendment.

Article III

SECTION 1

The judicial power of the United States shall be vested in one Supreme Court, and in such inferior courts as the Congress may from time to time ordain and establish. The judges, both of the Supreme and inferior courts, shall hold their offices during good behavior, and shall, at stated times, receive for their services, a compensation, which shall not be diminished during their continuance in office.

SECTION 2

1. The judicial power shall extend to all cases, in law and equity, arising under this Constitution, the laws of the United States, and treaties made, or which shall be made, under their authority;—to all cases affecting ambassadors, other public ministers and consuls;—to all cases of admiralty and maritime jurisdiction;—to controversies to which the United States shall be a party;—to controversies between two or more States; between a State and citizens of another State;[5]—between citizens of different States;—between citizens of the same State claiming lands under grants of different States, and between a State, or the citizens thereof, and foreign States, citizens or subjects.

2. In all cases affecting ambassadors, other public ministers and consuls, and those in which a State shall be party, the Supreme Court shall have original jurisdiction. In all the other cases before mentioned, the Supreme Court shall have appellate jurisdiction, both as to law and to fact, with such exceptions, and under such regulations as the Congress shall make.

3. The trial of all crimes, except in cases of impeachment, shall be by jury; and such trial shall be held in the State where the said crimes shall have been committed; but when not committed within any State, the trial shall be at such place or places as the Congress may by law have directed.

SECTION 3

1. Treason against the United States shall consist only in levying war against them, or in adhering to their enemies, giving them aid and comfort. No person shall be convicted of treason unless on the testimony of two witnesses to the same overt act, or on confession in open court.

2. The Congress shall have power to declare the punishment of treason, but no attainder of treason shall work corruption of blood, or forfeiture except during the life of the person attainted.

Article IV

SECTION 1

Full faith and credit shall be given in each State to the public acts, records, and judicial proceedings of every other State. And the Congress may by general laws prescribe the manner in which such acts, records and proceedings shall be proved, and the effect thereof.

SECTION 2

1. The citizens of each State shall be entitled to all privileges and immunities of citizens in the several States.[6]

2. A person charged in any State with treason, felony, or other crime, who shall flee from justice, and be found in another State, shall on demand of the executive authority of the State from which he fled, be delivered up to be removed to the State having jurisdiction of the crime.

3. No person held to service or labor in one State under the laws thereof, escaping into another, shall in consequence of any law or regulation therein, be discharged from such service or labor, but shall be delivered up on claim of the party to whom such service or labor may be due.[7]

SECTION 3

1. New States may be admitted by the Congress into this Union; but no new State shall be formed or erected within the jurisdiction of any other State, nor any State be formed by the junction of two or more States, or parts of States, without the consent of the legislatures of the States concerned as well as of the Congress.

2. The Congress shall have power to dispose of and make all needful rules and regulations respecting the territory or other property belonging to the United States; and nothing in this Constitution shall be so construed as to prejudice any claims of the United States, or of any particular State.

SECTION 4

The United States shall guarantee to every State in this Union a republican form of government, and shall protect each of them against invasion; and on application of the legislature, or of the executive (when the legislature cannot be convened) against domestic violence.

Article V

The Congress, whenever two thirds of both Houses shall deem it necessary, shall propose amendments to this Constitution, or, on the application of the legislature of two thirds of the several States, shall call a convention for

---

[5] See the 11th Amendment.

[6] See the 14th Amendment, Sec. 1.
[7] See the 13th Amendment.

proposing amendments, which in either case, shall be valid to all intents and purposes, as part of this Constitution when ratified by the legislatures of three fourths of the several States, or by conventions in three fourths thereof, as the one or the other mode of ratification may be proposed by the Congress; provided that no amendment which may be made prior to the year one thousand eight hundred and eight shall in any manner affect the first and fourth clauses in the ninth section of the first article; and that no State, without its consent, shall be deprived of its equal suffrage in the Senate.

Article VI

1. All debts contracted and engagements entered into, before the adoption of this Constitution, shall be as valid against the United States under this Constitution, as under the Confederation.[8]

2. This Constitution, and the laws of the United States which shall be made in pursuance thereof; and all treaties made, or which shall be made, under the authority of the United States, shall be the supreme law of the land; and the judges in every State shall be bound thereby, anything in the Constitution or laws of any State to the contrary notwithstanding.

3. The senators and representatives before mentioned, and the members of the several State legislatures, and all executive and judicial officers, both of the United States and of the several States, shall be bound by oath or affirmation to support this Constitution; but no religious test shall ever be required as a qualification to any office or public trust under the United States.

Article VII

The ratification of the conventions of nine States shall be sufficient for the establishment of this Constitution between the States so ratifying the same.

Done in Convention by the unanimous consent of the States present the seventeenth day of September in the year of our Lord one thousand seven hundred and eighty-seven, and of the independence of the United States of America the twelfth. In witness whereof we have hereunto subscribed our names.

A. AMENDMENTS

First Ten Amendments passed by Congress Sept. 25, 1789.
Ratified by three-fourths of the States December 15, 1791.

[8] See the 14th Amendment, Sec. 4.

Amendment I

Congress shall make no law respecting an establishment of religion, or prohibiting the free exercise thereof; or abridging the freedom of speech, or of the press; or the right of the people peaceably to assemble, and to petition the government for a redress of grievances.

Amendment II

A well regulated militia, being necessary to the security of a free State, the right of the people to keep and bear arms, shall not be infringed.

Amendment III

No soldier shall, in time of peace be quartered in any house, without the consent of the owner, nor in time of war, but in a manner to be prescribed by law.

Amendment IV

The right of the people to be secure in their persons, houses, papers, and effects, against unreasonable searches and seizures, shall not be violated, and no warrants shall issue, but upon probable cause, supported by oath or affirmation, and particularly describing the place to be searched, and the person or things to be seized.

Amendment V

No person shall be held to answer for a capital, or otherwise infamous crime, unless on a presentment or indictment of a grand jury, except in cases arising in the land or naval forces, or in the militia, when in actual service in time of war or public danger; nor shall any person be subject for the same offense to be twice put in jeopardy of life or limb; nor shall be compelled in any criminal case to be a witness against himself, nor be deprived of life, liberty, or property, without due process of law; nor shall private property be taken for public use without just compensation.

Amendment VI

In all criminal prosecutions, the accused shall enjoy the right to a speedy and public trial, by an impartial jury of the State and district wherein the crime shall have been committed, which district shall have been previously ascertained by law, and to be informed of the nature and cause of the accusation; to be confronted with the witnesses against him; to have compulsory process for obtaining witnesses in his favor, and to have the assistance of counsel for his defense.

Amendment VII

In suits at common law, where the value in controversy shall exceed twenty dollars, the right of trial by jury shall be preserved, and no fact tried by a jury shall be otherwise reexamined in any court of the United States, then according to the rules of the common law.

Amendment VIII

Excessive bail shall not be required, nor excessive fines imposed, nor cruel and unusual punishments inflicted.

Amendment IX

The enumeration in the Constitution of certain rights shall not be construed to deny or disparage others retained by the people.

Amendment X

The powers not delegated to the United States by the Constitution, nor prohibited by it to the States, are reserved to the States respectively, or to the people.

Amendment XI

Passed by Congress March 5, 1794. Ratified January 8, 1798.

The judicial power of the United States shall not be construed to extend to any suit in law or equity, commenced or prosecuted against one of the United States by citizens of another State, or by citizens or subjects of any foreign State.

Amendment XII

Passed by Congress December 12, 1803. Ratified September 25, 1804.

The electors shall meet in their respective States, and vote by ballot for President and Vice President, one of whom, at least, shall not be an inhabitant of the same State with themselves; they shall name in their ballots the person voted for as President, and in distinct ballots, the person voted for as Vice President, and they shall make distinct lists of all persons voted for as President and of all persons voted for as Vice President, and of the number of votes for each, which lists they shall sign and certify, and transmit sealed to the seat of the government of the United States, directed to the President of the Senate;—The President of the Senate shall, in the presence of the Senate and House of Representatives, open all the certificates and the votes shall then be counted;—The person having the greatest number of votes for President, shall be the President, if such number be a majority of the whole number of electors appointed; and if no person have such majority, then from the persons having the highest numbers not exceeding three on the list of those voted for as President, the House of Representatives shall choose immediately, by ballot, the President. But in choosing the President, the votes shall be taken by States, the representation from each State having one vote; a quorum for this purpose shall consist of a member or members from two thirds of the States, and a majority of all the States shall be necessary to a choice. And if the House of Representatives shall not choose a President whenever the right of choice shall devolve upon them, before the fourth day of March next following, then the Vice President shall act as President, as in the case of the death or other constitutional disability of the President. The person having the greatest number of votes as Vice President shall be the Vice President, if such number be a majority of the whole number of electors appointed, and if no person have a majority, then from the two highest numbers on the list, the Senate shall choose the Vice President; a quorum for the purpose shall consist of two thirds of the whole number of Senators, and a majority of the whole number shall be necessary to a choice. But no person constitutionally ineligible to the office of President shall be eligible to that of Vice President of the United States.

Amendment XIII

Passed by Congress February 1, 1865. Ratified December 18, 1865.

SECTION 1

Neither slavery nor involuntary servitude, except as punishment for crime whereof the party shall have been duly convicted, shall exist within the United States, or any place subject to their jurisdiction.

SECTION 2

Congress shall have power to enforce this article by appropriate legislation.

Amendment XIV

Passed by Congress June 16, 1866. Ratified July 23, 1868.

SECTION 1

All persons born or naturalized in the United States, and subject to the jurisdiction thereof, are citizens of the

United States and of the State wherein they reside. No State shall make or enforce any law which shall abridge the privileges or immunities of citizens of the United States; nor shall any State deprive any person of life, liberty, or property, without due process of law; nor deny to any person within its jurisdiction the equal protection of the laws.

SECTION 2

Representatives shall be apportioned among the several States according to their respective numbers, counting the whole number of persons in each State, excluding Indians not taxed. But when the right to vote at any election for the choice of electors for President and Vice President of the United States, representatives in Congress, the executive and judicial officers of a State, or the members of the legislature thereof, is denied to any of the male inhabitants of such State, being twenty-one years of age, and citizens of the United States, or in any way abridged, except for participation in rebellion, or other crime, the basis of representation therein shall be reduced in the proportion which the number of such male citizens shall bear to the whole number of male citizens twenty-one years of age in such State.

SECTION 3

No person shall be a senator or representative in Congress, or elector of President and Vice President, or hold any office, civil or military, under the United States, or under any State, who having previously taken an oath, as a member of Congress, or as an officer of the United States, or as a member of any State legislature, or as an executive or judicial officer of any State, to support the Constitution of the United States, shall have engaged in insurrection or rebellion against the same, or given aid or comfort to the enemies thereof. But Congress may by a vote of two thirds of each House, remove such disability.

SECTION 4

The validity of the public debt of the United States, authorized by law, including debts incurred for payment of pensions and bounties for services in suppressing insurrection or rebellion, shall not be questioned. But neither the United States nor any State shall assume or pay any debt or obligation incurred in aid of insurrection or rebellion against the United States, or any claim for the loss or emancipation of any slave; but all such debts, obligations, and claims shall be held illegal and void.

SECTION 5

The Congress shall have power to enforce, by appropriate legislation, the provisions of this article.

Amendment XV

Passed by Congress February 27, 1869. Ratified March 30, 1870.

SECTION 1

The right of citizens of the United States to vote shall not be denied or abridged by the United States or by any State on account of race, color, or previous condition of servitude.

SECTION 2

The Congress shall have power to enforce this article by appropriate legislation.

Amendment XVI

Passed by Congress July 12, 1909. Ratified February 25, 1913.

The Congress shall have power to lay and collect taxes on incomes, from whatever source derived, without apportionment among the several States, and without regard to any census or enumeration.

Amendment XVII

Passed by Congress May 16, 1912. Ratified May 31, 1913.

The Senate of the United States shall be composed of two senators from each State, elected by the people thereof, for six years; and each senator shall have one vote. The electors in each State shall have the qualifications requisite for electors of the most numerous branch of the State legislature.

When vacancies happen in the representation of any State in the Senate, the executive authority of such State shall issue writs of election to fill such vacancies: Provided, That the legislature of any State may empower the executive thereof to make temporary appointments until the people fill the vacancies by election as the legislature may direct.

This amendment shall not be so construed as to affect the election or term of any senator chosen before it becomes valid as part of the Constitution.

Amendment XVIII

Passed by Congress December 17, 1917. Ratified January 29, 1919.

After one year from the ratification of this article, the manufacture, sale, or transportation of intoxicating liquors within, the importation thereof into, or the exportation thereof from the United States and all territory subject to the jurisdiction thereof for beverage purposes is hereby prohibited.

The Congress and the several States shall have concurrent power to enforce this article by appropriate legislation.

This article shall be inoperative unless it shall have been ratified as an amendment to the Constitution by the legislatures of the several States, as provided in the Constitution, within seven years from the date of the submission hereof to the States by Congress.

Amendment XIX

Passed by Congress June 5, 1919. Ratified August 26, 1920.

The right of citizens of the United States to vote shall not be denied or abridged by the United States or by any State on account of sex.

The Congress shall have power by appropriate legislation to enforce the provisions of this article.

Amendment XX

Passed by Congress March 3, 1932. Ratified January 23, 1933.

SECTION 1

The terms of the President and Vice President shall end at noon on the 20th day of January, and the terms of Senators and Representatives at noon on the 3d day of January, of the years in which such terms would have ended if this article had not been ratified; and the terms of their successors shall then begin.

SECTION 2

The Congress shall assemble at least once in every year, and such meeting shall begin at noon on the 3d day of January, unless they shall by law appoint a different day.

SECTION 3

If, at the time fixed for the beginning of the term of the President, the President-elect shall have died, the Vice President-elect shall become President. If a President shall not have been chosen before the time fixed for the beginning of his term, or if the President-elect shall have failed to qualify, then the Vice President-elect shall act as President until a President shall have qualified; and the Congress may by law provide for the case wherein neither a President-elect nor a Vice President-elect shall have qualified, declaring who shall then act as President, or the manner in which one who is to act shall be selected, and such person shall act accordingly until a President or Vice President shall have qualified.

SECTION 4

The Congress may by law provide for the case of the death of any of the persons from whom the House of Representatives may choose a President whenever the right of choice shall have devolved upon them, and for the case of the death of any of the persons from whom the Senate may choose a Vice President whenever the right of choice shall have devolved upon them.

SECTION 5

Sections 1 and 2 shall take effect on the 15th day of October following the ratification of this article.

SECTION 6

This article shall be inoperative unless it shall have been ratified as an amendment to the Constitution by the legislatures of three-fourths of the several States within seven years from the date of its submission.

Amendment XXI

Passed by Congress February 20, 1933. Ratified December 5, 1933.

SECTION 1

The eighteenth article of amendment to the Constitution of the United States is hereby repealed.

SECTION 2

The transportation or importation into any State, Territory, or possession of the United States for delivery or use therein of intoxicating liquors in violation of the laws thereof, is hereby prohibited.

SECTION 3

This article shall be inoperative unless it shall have been ratified as an amendment to the Constitution by conventions in the several States, as provided in the Constitution, within seven years from the date of the submission thereof to the States by the Congress.

Amendment XXII

Passed by Congress March 24, 1947. Ratified February 26, 1951.

SECTION 1

No person shall be elected to the office of the President more than twice, and no person who has held the office of President, or acted as President, for more than two years of a term to which some other person was elected President shall be elected to the office of the President more than once. But this article shall not apply to any person holding the office of President when this article was proposed by the Congress, and shall not prevent any person who may be holding the office of President, or acting as President, during the term within which this article becomes operative from holding the office of President or acting as President during the remainder of such term.

SECTION 2

This article shall be inoperative unless it shall have been ratified as an amendment to the Constitution by the legislatures of three-fourths of the several States within seven years from the date of its submission to the States by the Congress.

Amendment XXIII

Passed by Congress June 16, 1960. Ratified April 3, 1961.

SECTION 1

The District constituting the seat of Government of the United States shall appoint in such manner as the Congress may direct:

A number of electors of President and Vice President equal to the whole number of Senators and Representatives in Congress to which the District would be entitled if it were a State, but in no event more than the least populous State; they shall be in addition to those appointed by the States, but they shall be considered, for the purposes of the election of President and Vice President, to be electors appointed by a State; and they shall meet in the District and perform such duties as provided by the twelfth article of amendment.

SECTION 2

The Congress shall have power to enforce this article by appropriate legislation.

Amendment XXIV

Passed by Congress August 27, 1962. Ratified February 4, 1964.

SECTION 1

The right of citizens of the United States to vote in any primary or other election for President or Vice President, for electors for President or Vice President, or for Senator or Representative in Congress, shall not be denied or abridged by the United States or any State by reason of failure to pay any poll tax or other tax.

SECTION 2

The Congress shall have power to enforce this article by appropriate legislation.

Amendment XXV

Passed by Congress July 6, 1965. Ratified February 23, 1967.

SECTION 1

In case of the removal of the President from office or of his death or resignation, the Vice President shall become President.

SECTION 2

Whenever there is a vacancy in the office of the Vice President, the President shall nominate a Vice President who shall take office upon confirmation by a majority vote of both Houses of Congress.

SECTION 3

Whenever the President transmits to the President pro tempore of the Senate and the Speaker of the House of Representatives his written declaration that he is unable to discharge the powers and duties of his office, and until he transmits to them a written declaration to the contrary, such powers and duties shall be discharged by the Vice President as Acting President.

SECTION 4

Whenever the Vice President and a majority of either the principal officers of the executive departments or of such other body as Congress may by law provide, transmit to the President pro tempore of the Senate and the Speaker of the House of Representatives their written declaration that the President is unable to discharge the powers and duties of his office, the Vice President shall immediately assume the powers and duties of the office as Acting President.

Thereafter, when the President transmits to the President pro tempore of the Senate and the Speaker of the House of Representatives his written declaration that no inability exists, he shall resume the powers and duties of his office unless the Vice President and a majority of either the principal officers of the executive department or of such other body as Congress may by law provide, transmit within four days to the President pro tempore of the Senate and the Speaker of the House of Representatives their written declaration that the President is unable to discharge the powers and duties of his office. Thereupon Congress shall decide the issue, assembling within forty-eight hours for that purpose if not in session. If the Congress, within twenty-one days after receipt of the latter written declaration, or, if Congress is not in session, within twenty-one days after Congress is required to assemble, determines by two-thirds vote of both Houses that the President is unable to discharge the powers and duties of his office, the Vice President shall continue to discharge the same as Acting President; otherwise, the President shall resume the powers and duties of his office.

Amendment XXVI

Passed by Congress March 23, 1971. Ratified July 5, 1971.

SECTION 1

The right of citizens of the United States, who are eighteen years of age or older, to vote shall not be denied or abridged by the United States or by any State on account of age.

Amendment XXVII

Passed by Congress September 25, 1789. Ratified May 18, 1992.

No law, varying the compensation for the services of the Senators and Representatives, shall take effect, until an election of Representatives shall have intervened.

A

abate—put a stop to a nuisance; reduce or cancel a legacy because the estate of the decedent is insufficient to make payment in full.

absolute guaranty—agreement that creates an obligation for a guarantor similar to that promised by a surety in suretyship relationships. The ability to demand payment immediately from a guarantor in an absolute guaranty situation distinguishes it from suretyship.

absolute privilege—complete defense against the tort of defamation, as in the speeches of members of Congress on the floor and witnesses in a trial.

abstract of title—history of the transfers of title to a given piece of land, briefly stating the parties to and the effect of all deeds, wills, and judicial proceedings relating to the land.

acceptance—unqualified assent to the act or proposal of another; as the acceptance of a draft (bill of exchange), of an offer to make a contract, of goods delivered by the seller, or of a gift or deed.

acceptor—drawee who has accepted the liability of paying the amount of money specified in a draft.

accommodation party—person who signs an instrument to lend credit to another party to the paper.

accord and satisfaction—agreement to substitute for an existing debt some alternative form of discharging that debt, coupled with the actual discharge of the debt by the substituted performance.

acknowledgment—admission or confirmation, generally of an instrument and usually made before a person authorized to administer oaths, such as a notary public; used to establish that the instrument was executed by the person making the instrument, that it was a voluntary act, or that the instrument is recorded.

acquired distinctiveness—through advertising, use and association, over time, an ordinary descriptive word or phase has taken on a new source identifying meaning and functions as a mark in the eyes of the public.

act-of-state doctrine—doctrine whereby every sovereign state is bound to respect the independence of every other sovereign state, and the courts of one country will not sit in judgment of another government's acts done within its own territory.

adeemed—canceled; as in a specifically bequeathed property being sold or given away by the testator prior to death, thus canceling the bequest.

adjustable rate mortgage (ARM)—mortgage with variable financing charges over the life of the loan.

administrative agency—government body charged with administering and implementing legislation.

administrative law—law governing administrative agencies.

Administrative Procedure Act—federal law that establishes the operating rules for administrative agencies.

administrative regulations—rules made by state and federal administrative agencies.

administrator, administratrix—person (man, woman) appointed to wind up and settle the estate of a person who has died without a will.

admissibility—the quality of the evidence in a case that allows it to be presented to the jury.

adverse possession—hostile possession of real estate, which when actual, visible, notorious, exclusive, and continued for the required time, will vest the title to the land in the person in such adverse possession.

advising bank—bank that tells beneficiary that letter of credit has been issued.

affidavit—statement of facts set forth in written form and supported by the oath or affirmation of the person making the statement setting forth that such facts are true on the basis of actual knowledge or on information and belief. The affidavit is executed before a notary public or other person authorized to administer oaths.

affirm—action taken by an appellate court that approves the decision of the court below.

affirmative action plan (AAP)—plan to have a diverse and representative workforce.

after-acquired goods—goods acquired after a security interest has attached.

agency—the relationship that exists between a person identified as a principal and another by virtue of which the latter may make contracts with third persons on behalf of the principal. (Parties—principal, agent, third person) *agent*—person or firm who is authorized by the principal or by operation of law to make contracts with third persons on behalf of the principal.

airbill—document of title issued to a shipper whose goods are being sent via air.

alteration—unauthorized change or completion of a negotiable instrument designed to modify the obligation of a party to the instrument.

alternative payees—those persons to whom a negotiable instrument is made payable, any one of whom may indorse and take delivery of it.

ambiguous—having more than one reasonable interpretation.

answer—what a defendant must file to admit or deny facts asserted by the plaintiff.

anticipatory breach—promisor's repudiation of the contract prior to the time that performance is required.

anticipatory repudiation—repudiation made in advance of the time for performance of the contract obligations.

antilapse statutes—statutes providing that the children or heirs of a deceased beneficiary may take the legacy in the place of the deceased beneficiary.

apparent authority—appearance of authority created by the principal's words or conduct.

appeal—taking a case to a reviewing court to determine whether the judgment of the lower court or administrative agency was correct. (Parties—appellant, appellee)

appellate jurisdiction—the power of a court to hear and decide a given class of cases on appeal from another court or administrative agency.

appropriation—taking of an image, likeness, or name for commercial advantage.

arbitration—the settlement of disputed questions, whether of law or fact, by one or more arbitrators by whose decision the parties agree to be bound.

Article 2—section of the Uniform Commercial Code that governs contracts for the sale of goods.

articles of copartnership—See *Partnership Agreement.*

articles of incorporation—See *Certificate of Incorporation.*

articles of partnership—See *Partnership Agreement.*

assignee—third party to whom contract benefits are transferred.

assignment—transfer of a right. Generally used in connection with personal property rights, as rights under a contract, commercial paper, an insurance policy, a mortgage, or a lease. (Parties—assignor, assignee)

assignor—party who assigns contract rights to a third party.

association tribunal—a court created by a trade association or group for the resolution of disputes among its members.

assumption—mortgage transfers in which the transferee and mortgagor are liable and the property is subject to foreclosure by the mortgagee if payments are not made.

attestation clause—clause that indicates a witness has observed either the execution of the will or the testator's acknowledgment of the writing as the testator's will.

attorney in fact—agent authorized to act for another under a power of attorney.

attorney-client privilege—right of individual to have discussions with his/her attorney kept private and confidential.

attractive nuisance doctrine—a rule imposing liability upon a landowner for injuries sustained by small children playing on the land when the landowner permits a condition to exist or maintains equipment that a reasonable person should realize would attract small children who could not realize the danger. The rule does not apply if an unreasonable burden would be imposed upon the landowner in taking steps to protect the children.

authorities—corporations formed by government that perform public service.

automatic perfection—perfection given by statute without specific filing or possession requirements on the part of the creditor.

automatic stay—order to prevent creditors from taking action such as filing suits or seeking foreclosure against the debtor.

B

bad check laws—laws making it a criminal offense to issue a bad check with intent to defraud.

bailee—person who accepts possession of a property.

bailee's lien—specific, possessory lien of the bailee upon the goods for work done to them. Commonly extended by statute to any bailee's claim for compensation, eliminating the necessity of retention of possession.

bailment—relationship that exists when personal property is delivered into the possession of another under an agreement, express or implied, that the identical property will be returned or will be delivered in accordance with the agreement. (Parties—bailor, bailee)

bailment for mutual benefit—bailment in which the bailor and bailee derive a benefit from the bailment.

bailor—person who turns over the possession of a property.

balance sheet test—comparison of assets to liabilities made to determine solvency.

bankruptcy—procedure by which one unable to pay debts may surrender all assets in excess of any exemption claim to the court for administration and distribution to creditors, and the debtor is given a discharge that releases him from the unpaid balance due on most debts.

bankruptcy courts—court of special jurisdiction to determine bankruptcy issues.

battle of the forms—merchants' exchanges of invoices and purchase orders with differing boilerplate terms.

bearer—person in physical possession of commercial paper payable to bearer, a document of title directing delivery to bearer, or an investment security in bearer form.

bearer paper—instrument with no payee, payable to cash or payable to bearer.

bedrock view—a strict constructionist interpretation of a constitution.

beneficiary—person to whom the proceeds of a life insurance policy are payable, a person for whose benefit property is held in trust, or a person given property by a will; the ultimate recipient of the benefit of a funds transfer.

beneficiary's bank—the final bank, which carries out the payment order, in the chain of a transfer of funds.

bequest—gift of personal property by will.

best available treatment—in environmental law, a requirement that state-of-the-art methods be used for treating water.

best conventional treatment—in environmental law, a requirement that water be treated with the most commonly used method.

bicameral—a two-house form of the legislative branch of government.

bilateral contract—agreement under which one promise is given in exchange for another.

bill of lading—document issued by a carrier acknowledging the receipt of goods and the terms of the contract of transportation.

bill of sale—writing signed by the seller reciting that the personal property therein described has been sold to the buyer.

blackmail—extortion demands made by a nonpublic official.

blank indorsement—an indorsement that does not name the person to whom the paper, document of title, or investment security is negotiated.

blocking laws—laws that prohibit the disclosure, copying, inspection, or removal of documents located in the enacting country in compliance with orders from foreign authorities.

blue sky laws—state statutes designed to protect the public from the sale of worthless stocks and bonds.

bona fide—in good faith; without any fraud or deceit.

bond—obligation or promise in writing and sealed, generally of corporations, personal representatives, and trustees; fidelity bonds.

bond indenture—agreement setting forth the contractual terms of a particular bond issue.

book value—value found by dividing the value of the corporate assets by the number of shares outstanding.

breach—failure to act or perform in the manner called for in a contract.

breach of the peace—violation of the law in the repossession of the collateral.

brownfields—land that is a designated Superfund cleanup site but which lies fallow because no one is willing to risk

liability by buying the property, even when the hazardous waste has been removed or property no one is willing to spend the money to remove the hazardous waste.

bubble concept—method for determining total emissions in one area; all sources are considered in an area.

business ethics—balancing the goal of profits with values of individuals and society.

business judgment rule (BJR)—rule that allows board immunity from liability for corporate acts where there is a reasonable indication that the acts were made in good faith with due care.

bylaws—rules and regulations enacted by a corporation to govern the affairs of the corporation and its shareholders, directors, and officers.

C

cancellation provision—crossing out of a part of an instrument or a destruction of all legal effect of the instrument, whether by act of party, upon breach by the other party, or pursuant to agreement or decree of court.

capital stock—declared money value of the outstanding stock of the corporation.

cargo insurance—insurance that protects a cargo owner against financial loss if goods being shipped are lost or damaged at sea.

carrier—individual or organization undertaking the transportation of goods.

case law—law that includes principles that are expressed for the first time in court decisions.

cashier's check—draft (check) drawn by a bank on itself.

cash surrender value—sum paid the insured upon the surrender of a policy to the insurer.

cash tender offer—general offer to all shareholders of a target corporation to purchase their shares for cash at a specified price.

cause of action—right to damages or other judicial relief when a legally protected right of the plaintiff is violated by an unlawful act of the defendant.

cease-and-desist order—order issued by a court or administrative agency to stop a practice that it decides is improper.

certificate of deposit (CD)—promise to pay instrument issued by a bank.

certificate of incorporation—written approval from the state or national government for a corporation to be formed.

certificate of stock—document evidencing a shareholder's ownership of stock issued by a corporation.

certified check—check for which the bank has set aside in a special account sufficient funds to pay it; payment is made when check is presented regardless of amount in drawer's account at that time; discharges all parties except certifying bank when holder requests certification.

cestui que trust—beneficiary or person for whose benefit the property is held in trust.

CF—cost and freight.

Chapter 11 bankruptcy—reorganization form of bankruptcy under federal law.

Chapter 7 bankruptcy—liquidation form of bankruptcy under federal law.

Chapter 13 bankruptcy—proceeding of consumer debt readjustment plan bankruptcy.

charging order—order by a court, after a business partner's personal assets are exhausted, requiring that the partner's share of the profits be paid to a creditor until the debt is discharged.

charter—grant of authority from a government to exist as a corporation. Generally replaced today by a certificate of incorporation approving the articles of incorporation.

check—order by a depositor on a bank to pay a sum of money to a payee; a draft drawn on a bank and payable on demand.

choice-of-law clause—clause in an agreement that specifies which law will govern should a dispute arise.

chose in action—intangible personal property in the nature of claims against another, such as a claim for accounts receivable or wages.

CIF—cost, insurance, and freight.

civil disobedience—the term used when natural law proponents violate positive law.

civil law—the law that defines the rights of one person against another.

claim—right to payment.

Clayton Act—a federal law that prohibits price discrimination.

Clean Air Act—federal legislation that establishes standards for air pollution levels and prevents further deterioration of air quality.

Clean Water Act—federal legislation that regulates water pollution through a control system.

close corporation—corporation whose shares are held by a single shareholder or a small group of shareholders.

close-connection doctrine—circumstantial evidence, such as an ongoing or a close relationship, that can serve as notice of a problem with an instrument.

COD—cash on delivery.

coinsurance clause—clause requiring the insured to maintain insurance on property up to a stated amount and providing that to the extent that this is not done, the insured is to be deemed a coinsurer with the insurer, so that the latter is liable only for its proportionate share of the amount of insurance required to be carried.

collateral—property pledged by a borrower as security for a debt.

comity—principle of international and national law that the laws of all nations and states deserve the respect legitimately demanded by equal participants.

commerce clause—that section of the U.S. Constitution allocating the power for business regulation between the federal government and the states.

commercial impracticability—situation that occurs when costs of performance rise suddenly and performance of a contract will result in a substantial loss.

commercial lease—any nonconsumer lease.

commercial paper—written, transferable, signed promise or order to pay a specified sum of money; a negotiable instrument.

commercial unit—standard of the trade for shipment or packaging of a good.

commission merchant—bailee to whom goods are consigned for sale.

commission or factorage—consignee's compensation.

common carrier—carrier that holds out its facilities to serve the general public for compensation without discrimination.

common law—the body of unwritten principles originally based upon the usages and customs of the community that were recognized and enforced by the courts.

common stock—stock that has no right or priority over any other stock of the corporation as to dividends or distribution of assets upon dissolution.

community property—cotenancy held by husband and wife in property acquired during their marriage under the law of some of the states, principally in the southwestern United States.

comparative negligence—defense to negligence that allows plaintiff to recover reduced damages based on his level of fault.

compensatory damages—sum of money that will compensate an injured plaintiff for actual loss.

complaint—the initial pleading filed by the plaintiff in many actions, which in many states may be served as original process to acquire jurisdiction over the defendant.

composition of creditors—agreement among creditors that each shall accept a partial payment as full payment in consideration of the other creditors doing the same.

Comprehensive Environmental Response, Compensation, and Liability Act (CERCLA)—federal law that authorizes the president to issue funds for the cleanup of areas that were once disposal sites for hazardous wastes.

computer crimes—wrongs committed using a computer or with knowledge of computers.

concealment—failure to volunteer information not requested.

condition—stipulation or prerequisite in a contract, will, or other instrument.

condition precedent—event that must take place before the duty to perform under a contract arises.

condition subsequent—event whose occurrence or lack thereof terminates a contract.

condominium—combination of co-ownership and individual ownership.

confidential relationship—relationship in which, because of the legal status of the parties or their respective physical or mental conditions or knowledge,

one party places full confidence and trust in the other.

conflict of interest—conduct that compromises an employee's allegiance to that company.

conglomerate—relationship of a parent corporation to subsidiary corporations engaged in diversified fields of activity unrelated to the field of activity of the parent corporation.

consent decrees—informal settlements of enforcement actions brought by agencies.

consequential damages—damages the buyer experiences as a result of the seller's breach with respect to a third party; also called *special damages.*

consideration—promise or performance that the promisor demands as the price of the promise.

consignee—(1) person to whom goods are shipped, (2) dealer who sells goods for others.

consignment—bailment made for the purpose of sale by the bailee. (Parties —consignor, consignee)

consignor—(1) person who delivers goods to the carrier for shipment, (2) party with title who turns goods over to another for sale.

consolidation (of corporations)—combining of two or more corporations in which the corporate existence of each one ceases and a new corporation is created.

conspiracy—agreement between two or more persons to commit an unlawful act.

constitution—a body of principles that establishes the structure of a government and the relationship of the government to the people who are governed.

constructive bailment—bailment imposed by law as opposed to one created by contract, whereby the

bailee must preserve the property and redeliver it to the owner.

constructive delivery—See *symbolic delivery.*

constructive eviction—act or omission of the landlord that substantially deprives the tenant of the use and enjoyment of the premises.

consumer—any buyer afforded special protections by statute or regulation.

consumer credit—credit for personal, family, and household use.

consumer goods—goods used or bought primarily for personal, family, or household use.

consumer lease—lease of goods by a natural person for personal, family, or household use.

Consumer Product Safety Improvement Act—federal law that sets standards for the types of paints used in toys; a response to the lead paint found in toys made in China; requires tracking for international production; increases penalties.

contract—a binding agreement based on the genuine assent of the parties, made for a lawful object, between competent parties, in the form required by law, and generally supported by consideration.

contract carrier—carrier that transports on the basis of individual contracts that it makes with each shipper.

contract interference—tort in which a third party interferes with others' freedom to contract.

contract of adhesion—contract offered by a dominant party to a party with inferior bargaining power on a take-it-or-leave-it basis.

contract under seal—contract executed by affixing a seal or making an impression on the paper or on some adhering substance such as wax attached to the document.

contracting agent—agent with authority to make contracts; person with whom the buyer deals.

Contracts for the International Sale of Goods (CISG)—uniform international contract code contracts for international sale of goods.

contractual capacity—ability to understand that a contract is being made and to understand its general meaning.

contribution—right of a co-obligor who has paid more than a proportionate share to demand that the other obligor pay the amount of the excess payment made.

contributory negligence—negligence of the plaintiff that contributes to injury and at common law bars recovery from the defendant although the defendant may have been more negligent than the plaintiff.

conversion—act of taking personal property by a person not entitled to it and keeping it from its true owner or prior possessor without consent.

cooperative—group of two or more persons or enterprises that acts through a common agent with respect to a common objective, such as buying or selling.

copyright—exclusive right given by federal statute to the creator of a literary or an artistic work to use, reproduce, and display the work.

corporation—artificial being created by government grant, which for many purposes is treated as a natural person.

corporation by estoppel—corporation that comes about when parties estop themselves from denying that the corporation exists.

corporation de jure—corporation with a legal right to exist by virtue of law.

correspondent bank—will honor the letter of credit from the domestic bank of the buyer.

cost plus—method of determining the purchase price or contract price equal to the seller's or contractor's costs plus a stated percentage as the profit.

co-sureties—sureties for the same debtor and obligor.

cotenancy—when two or more persons hold concurrent rights and interests in the same property.

Council on Environmental Quality (CEQ)—federal agency that establishes national policies on environmental quality and then recommends legislation to implement these policies.

counterclaim—a claim that the defendant in an action may make against the plaintiff.

counteroffer—proposal by an offeree to the offeror that changes the terms of, and thus rejects, the original offer.

course of dealing—pattern of performance between two parties to a contract.

court—a tribunal established by government to hear evidence, decide cases brought before it, and provide remedies when a wrong has been committed.

covenant against encumbrances—guarantee that conveyed land is not subject to any right or interest of a third person.

covenant of further assurances—promise that the grantor of an interest in land will execute any additional documents required to perfect the title of the grantee.

covenant of quiet enjoyment—covenant by the grantor of an interest in land that the grantee's possession of the land shall not be disturbed.

covenant of right to convey—guarantee that the grantor of an interest in land, if not the owner, has the right or authority to make the conveyance to a new owner.

covenant of seisin—guarantee that the grantor of an interest in land owns the estate conveyed to a new owner.

covenants (or warranties) of title—grantor's covenants of a deed that guarantee such matters as the right to make the conveyance, to ownership of the property, to freedom of the property from encumbrances, or that the grantee will not be disturbed in the quiet enjoyment of the land.

credit transfer—transaction in which a person making payment, such as a buyer, requests payment be made to the beneficiary's bank.

creditor—person (seller or lender) who is owed money; also may be a secured party.

crime—violation of the law that is punished as an offense against the state or government.

criminal law—the law that defines wrongs against society.

cross-examination—the examination made of a witness by the attorney for the adverse party.

cumulative voting—system of voting for directors in which each shareholder has as many votes as the number of voting shares owned multiplied by the number of directors to be elected, and such votes can be distributed for the various candidates as desired.

customary authority—authority of an agent to do any act that, according to the custom of the community, usually accompanies the transaction for which the agent is authorized to act.

cyberlaw—laws and precedent applicable to Internet transactions and communications.

cyberspace—World Wide Web and Internet communication.

cybersquatters—term for those who register and set up domain names on the Internet for resale to the famous users of the names in question.

D

de facto—existing in fact as distinguished from as of right, as in the case of an officer or a corporation purporting to act as such without being elected to the office or having been properly incorporated.

debenture—unsecured bond of a corporation, with no specific corporate assets pledged as security for payment.

debit transfer—transaction in which a beneficiary entitled to money requests payment from a bank according to a prior agreement.

debtor—buyer on credit (i.e., a borrower).

decedent—upon death, person whose estate is being administered.

deed—instrument by which the grantor(owner of land) conveys or transfers the title to a grantee.

defamation—untrue statement by one party about another to a third party.

defendant—party charged with a violation of civil or criminal law in a proceeding.

defined benefit plan—an employer commitment to make specified future payments to participants upon retirement.

defined contribution plan—a plan that provides for an individual account for each plan participant and for benefits based solely on the amount contributed to the participant's account; also known as an *individual account plan*.

definite time—time of payment computable from the face of the instrument.

delegated powers—powers expressly granted the national government by the Constitution.

delegation—transfer to another of the right and power to do an act.

delegation of duties—transfer of duties by a contracting party to another person who is to perform them.

delivery—constructive or actual possession.

demand draft—draft that is payable upon presentment.

demurrer—a pleading to dismiss the adverse party's pleading for not stating a cause of action or a defense.

deposition—the testimony of a witness taken out of court but under oath.

depositor—person, or bailor, who gives property for storage.

derivative (secondary) action—secondary action for damages or breach of contract brought by one or more corporate shareholders against directors, officers, or third persons.

development statement—statement that sets forth significant details of a real estate or property development as required by the federal Interstate Land Sales Act.

devise—gift of real estate made by will.

devisee—beneficiary of a devise.

direct damages—losses that are caused by breach of a contract.

direct examination—examination of a witness by his or her attorney.

directed verdict—a direction by the trial judge to the jury to return a verdict in favor of a specified party to the action.

disability—any incapacity resulting from bodily injury or disease to engage in any occupation for remuneration or profit.

discharge in bankruptcy—order of the bankruptcy court relieving the debtor from obligation to pay the unpaid balance of most claims.

disclosed principal—principal whose identity is made known by the agent as well as the fact that the agent is acting on the principal's behalf.

discovery—procedures for ascertaining facts prior to the time of trial in order to eliminate the element of surprise in litigation.

dishonor—status when the primary party refuses to pay the instrument according to its terms.

disinherited—excluded from sharing in the estate of a decedent.

Dispute Settlement Body (DSB)—means, provided by the World Trade Organization, for member countries to resolve trade disputes rather than engage in unilateral trade sanctions or a trade war.

distinctiveness—capable of serving the source-identifying function of a mark.

distribution per stirpes—distribution of an estate made in as many equal parts as there are family lines represented in the nearest generation; also known as *stirpital distribution*.

distributor—entity that takes title to goods and bears the financial and commercial risks for the subsequent sale of the goods.

divestiture order—a court order to dispose of interests that could lead to a monopoly.

divisible contract—agreement consisting of two or more parts, each calling for corresponding performances of each part by the parties.

document of title—document treated as evidence that a person is entitled to receive, hold, and dispose of the document and the goods it covers.

domestic corporation—corporation that has been incorporated by the state in question as opposed to incorporation by another state.

dominant tenement—land that is benefited by an easement.

donee—recipient of a gift.

donor—person making a gift.

double indemnity—provision for payment of double the amount specified by the insurance contract if death is caused by an accident and occurs under specified circumstances.

draft or bill of exchange—an unconditional order in writing by one person upon another, signed by the person giving it, and ordering the person to whom it is directed to pay upon demand or at a definite time a sum certain in money to order or to bearer.

drawee—person to whom the draft is addressed and who is ordered to pay the amount of money specified in the draft.

drawer—person who writes out and creates a draft or bill of exchange, including a check.

due diligence—process of checking the environmental history and nature of land prior to purchase.

due process—the constitutional right to be heard, question witnesses, and present evidence.

due process clause—in the Fifth and Fourteenth Amendments, a guarantee of protection from unreasonable procedures and unreasonable laws.

dumping—selling goods in another country at less than their fair value.

duress—conduct that deprives the victim of free will and that generally gives the victim the right to set aside any transaction entered into under such circumstances.

duty—an obligation of law imposed on a person to perform or refrain from performing a certain act.

E

easement—permanent right that one has in the land of another, as the right to cross another's land or an easement of way.

easement by implication—easement not specifically created by deed that arises from the circumstances of the parties and the land location and access.

economic duress—threat of financial loss.

Economic Espionage Act (EEA)—federal law that makes it a felony to copy, download, transmit, or in anyway transfer proprietary files, documents, and information from a computer to an unauthorized person.

economic strikers—union strikers trying to enforce bargaining demands when an impasse has been reached in the negotiation process for a collective bargaining agreement.

effects doctrine—doctrine that U.S. courts will assume jurisdiction and will apply antitrust laws to conduct outside of the United States when the activity of business firms has direct and substantial effect on U.S. commerce; the rule has been modified to require that the effect on U.S. commerce also be foreseeable.

effluent guidelines—EPA standards for maximum ranges of discharge into water.

electronic funds transfer (EFT)—any transfer of funds (other than a transaction originated by a check, draft, or similar paper instrument) that is initiated through an electronic terminal, telephone, computer, or magnetic tape so as to authorize a financial institution to debit or credit an account.

Electronic Funds Transfer Act (EFTA)—federal law that provides consumers with rights and protections in electronic funds transfers.

eleemosynary corporation—corporation organized for a charitable or benevolent purpose.

embezzlement—statutory offense consisting of the unlawful conversion of property entrusted to the wrongdoer.

eminent domain—power of government and certain kinds of corporations to take private property against the objection of the owner, provided the taking is for a public purpose and just compensation is made for it.

emissions offset policy—controls whether new factories can be built in a nonattainment area.

employment-at-will doctrine—doctrine in which the employer has historically been allowed to terminate the employment contract at any time for any reason or for no reason.

en banc—the term used when the full panel of judges on the appellate court hears a case.

encoding warranty—warranty made by any party who encodes electronic information on an instrument; a warranty of accuracy.

Endangered Species Act (ESA)—federal law that identifies and protects species that are endangered from development or other acts that threaten their existence.

endowment insurance—insurance that pays the face amount of the policy if the insured dies within the policy period.

entitlement theory—also known as *rights theory*; Nozick's theory that (1) everyone has a set of rights, and (2) it is up to the governments to protect those rights.

environmental impact statement (EIS)—formal report prepared under NEPA to document findings on the impact of a federal project on the environment.

equitable title—beneficial interest in a trust.

equity—the body of principles that originally developed because of the inadequacy of the rules then applied by the common law courts of England.

escalation clause—provision for the automatic increase of the rent at periodic intervals.

escheat—transfer to the state of the title to a decedent's property when the owner of the property dies intestate and is not survived by anyone capable of taking the property as heir.

E-sign—signature over the Internet.

estate in fee—largest estate possible, in which the owner has absolute and entire interest in the land.

estoppel—principle by which a person is barred from pursuing a certain course of action or of disputing the truth of certain matters.

ethical egoism—Ayn Rand theory of ethics that we should all act in our own best interests.

ethics—a branch of philosophy dealing with values that relate to the nature of human conduct and values associated with that conduct.

ex post facto *law*—a law making criminal an act that was lawful when done or that increases the penalty when done. Such laws are generally prohibited by constitutional provisions.

exculpatory clause—provision in a contract stating that one of the parties is not liable for damages in case of breach; also called *limitation-of-liability clause*.

executed contract—agreement that has been completely performed.

execution—the carrying out of a judgment of a court, generally directing that property owned by the defendant be sold and the proceeds first be used to pay the execution or judgment creditor.

executive branch—the branch of government (e.g., the president) formed to execute the laws.

executor, executrix—person (man, woman) named in a will to administer the estate of the decedent.

executory contract—contract in which something remains to be done by one or both parties.

exhaustion of administrative remedies—requirement that an agency make its final decision before the issue can be taken to court.

existing goods—goods that physically exist and are owned by the seller at the time of a transaction.

exoneration—agreement or provision in an agreement that one party will not be held liable for loss; the right of the surety to demand that those primarily liable pay the claim for which the surety is secondarily liable.

expert witness—one who has acquired special knowledge in a particular field as through practical experience or study, or both, whose opinion is admissible as an aid to the trier of fact.

export sale—direct sale to customers in a foreign country.

express authority—authority of an agent to perform a certain act.

express authorization—authorization of an agent to perform a certain act.

express contract—agreement of the parties manifested by their words, whether spoken or written.

express warranty—statement by the defendant relating to the goods, which statement is part of the basis of the bargain.

extortion—illegal demand by a public officer acting with apparent authority.

F

facilitation payments—(or grease payments) legal payments to speed up or ensure performance of normal government duties.

factor—bailee to whom goods are consigned for sale.

false imprisonment—intentional detention of a person without that person's consent; called the shopkeeper's tort when shoplifters are unlawfully detained.

FAS—free alongside the named vessel.

federal district court—the general trial court of the federal system.

Federal Register—government publication issued five days a week that lists all administrative regulations, all presidential proclamations and executive orders, and other documents and classes of documents that the president or Congress direct to be published.

Federal Register Act—federal law requiring agencies to make public disclosure of proposed rules, passed rules, and activities.

Federal Sentencing Guidelines—federal standards used by judges in determining mandatory sentence terms for those convicted of federal crimes.

federal system—the system of government in which a central government is given power to administer to national concerns while individual states retain the power to administer to local concerns.

fee simple defeasibles—fee simple interest that can be lost if restrictions on its use are violated.

fee simple estate—highest level of land ownership; full interest of unlimited duration.

felony—criminal offense that is punishable by confinement in prison for more than one year or by death, or that is expressly stated by statute to be a felony.

field warehousing—stored goods under the exclusive control of a warehouse but kept on the owner's premises rather than in a warehouse.

Fifth Amendment—constitutional protection against self-incrimination; also guarantees due process.

finance lease—three-party lease agreement in which there is a lessor, a lessee, and a financier.

financing statement—brief statement (record) that gives sufficient information to alert third persons that a particular creditor may have a security interest in the collateral described.

fire insurance policy—a contract that indemnifies the insured for property destruction or damage caused by fire.

firm offer—offer stated to be held open for a specified time, which must be so held in some states even in the absence of an option contract, or under the UCC, with respect to merchants.

first-in-time provision—creditor whose interest attached first has priority in the collateral when two creditors have a secured interest.

first-to-perfect basis—rule of priorities that holds that first in time in perfecting a security interest, mortgage, judgment, lien, or other property attachment right should have priority.

fixture—personal property that has become so attached to or adapted to real estate that it has lost its character as personal property and is part of the real estate.

floating lien—claim in a changing or shifting stock of goods of the buyer.

FOB place of destination—shipping contract that requires seller to deliver goods to buyer.

FOB place of shipment—contract that requires the seller to arrange for shipment only.

forbearance—refraining from doing an act.

forcible entry and detainer—action by the landlord to have the tenant removed for nonpayment of rent.

foreclosure—procedure for enforcing a mortgage resulting in the public sale of the mortgaged property and, less commonly, in merely barring the right of the mortgagor to redeem the property from the mortgage.

foreign corporation—corporation incorporated under the laws of another state.

Foreign Corrupt Practices Act (FCPA)—federal law that makes it a felony to influence decision makers in other countries for the purpose of obtaining business, such as contracts for sales and services; also imposes financial

reporting requirements on certain U.S. corporations.

forged or unauthorized indorsement—instrument indorsed by an agent for a principal without authorization or authority.

forgery—fraudulently making or altering an instrument that apparently creates or alters a legal liability of another.

formal contracts—written contracts or agreements whose formality signifies the parties' intention to abide by the terms.

Fourth Amendment—privacy protection in the U.S. Constitution; prohibits unauthorized searches and seizures.

franchise—(1) privilege or authorization, generally exclusive, to engage in a particular activity within a particular geographic area, such as a government franchise to operate a taxi company within a specified city, or a private franchise as the grant by a manufacturer of a right to sell products within a particular territory or for a particular number of years; (2) right to vote.

franchise agreement—sets forth rights of franchisee to use trademarks, etc., of franchisor.

franchisee—person to whom franchise is granted.

Franchise Rule—rule requiring detailed disclosures and prohibiting certain practices.

franchising—granting of permission to use a trademark, trade name, or copyright under specified conditions; a form of licensing.

franchisor—party granting the franchise.

fraud—making of a false statement of a past or existing fact, with knowledge of its falsity or with reckless indifference as to its truth, with the intent to cause another to rely thereon, and such person does rely thereon and is harmed thereby.

fraud in the inducement—fraud that occurs when a person is persuaded or induced to execute an instrument because of fraudulent statements.

fraud-on-the-market—a theory that in an open and developed securities market, the price of a stock is determined by the information on the company available to the public, and misleading statements will defraud purchasers of stock even if they do not directly rely on these statements.

Freedom of Information Act—federal law permitting citizens to request documents and records from administrative agencies.

freight forwarder—one who contracts to have goods transported and, in turn, contracts with carriers for such transportation.

freight insurance—insures that ship owner will receive payment for transportation charges.

full warranty—obligation of a seller to fix or replace a defective product within a reasonable time without cost to the buyer.

funds transfer—communication of instructions or requests to pay a specific sum of money to the credit of a specified account or person without an actual physical passing of money.

fungible goods—homogeneous goods of which any unit is the equivalent of any other unit.

future goods—goods that exist physically but are not owned by the seller and goods that have not yet been produced.

G

garnishment—the name given in some states to attachment proceedings.

general agent—agent authorized by the principal to transact all affairs in connection with a particular type of business or trade or to transact all business at a certain place.

general corporation code—state's code listing certain requirements for creation of a corporation.

general jurisdiction—the power to hear and decide most controversies involving legal rights and duties.

general legacies—certain sums of money bequeathed to named persons by the testator; to be paid out of the decedent's assets generally without specifying any particular fund or source from which the payment is to be made.

general partnership—partnership in which the partners conduct as co-owners a business for profit, and each partner has a right to take part in the management of the business and has unlimited liability.

general partners—partners who publicly and actively engage in the transaction of firm business.

general partners—partnership in which the partners conduct as co-owners a business for profit, and each partner has a right to take part in the management of the business and has unlimited liability; general partners publicly and actively engage in the transaction of firm business.

gift—title to an owner's personal property voluntarily transferred by a party not receiving anything in exchange.

gift causa mortis—gift, made by the donor in the belief that death was immediate and impending, that is revoked or is revocable under certain circumstances.

good faith—absence of knowledge of any defects or problems; "pure heart and an empty head."

goods—anything movable at the time it is identified as the subject of a transaction.

grantee—new owner of a land conveyance.

grantor—owner who transfers or conveys an interest in land to a new owner.

gratuitous bailment—bailment in which the bailee does not receive any compensation or advantage.

gray market goods—foreign-made goods with U.S. trademarks brought into the United States by a third party without the consent of the trademark owners to compete with these owners.

grease payments—(or facilitation payments) legal payments to speed up or ensure performance of normal government duties.

guarantor—one who undertakes the obligation of guaranty.

guaranty—agreement or promise to answer for a debt; an undertaking to pay the debt of another if the creditor first sues the debtor.

guaranty of collection—form of guaranty in which creditor cannot proceed against guarantor until after proceeding against debtor.

guaranty of payment—absolute promise to pay when a debtor defaults.

guest—transient who contracts for a room or site at a hotel.

H

hearsay evidence—statements made out of court that are offered in court as proof of the information contained in the statements and that, subject to many exceptions, are not admissible in evidence.

holder—someone in possession of an instrument that runs to that person (i.e., is made payable to that person, is indorsed to that person, or is bearer paper).

holder in due course—a holder who has given value, taken in good faith without notice of dishonor, defenses, or that instrument is overdue, and who is afforded special rights or status.

holder through a holder in due course—holder of an instrument who attains holder-in-due-course status because a

holder in due course has held it previous to him or her.

holographic will—unwitnessed will written by hand.

homeowners insurance policy—combination of standard fire insurance and comprehensive personal liability insurance.

hotelkeeper—one regularly engaged in the business of offering living accommodations to all transient persons.

hull insurance—insurance that covers physical damage on a freight-moving vessel.

I

identification—point in the transaction when the buyer acquires an interest in the goods subject to the contract.

identified—term applied to particular goods selected by either the buyer or the seller as the goods called for by the sales contract.

identity theft—use of another's credit tools, social security number, or other IDs to obtain cash, goods, or credit without permission.

illusory promise—promise that in fact does not impose any obligation on the promisor.

impeach—using prior inconsistent evidence to challenge the credibility of a witness.

implied contract—contract expressed by conduct or implied or deduced from the facts.

implied warranty—warranty that was not made but is implied by law.

implied warranty of merchantability—group of promises made by the seller, the most important of which is that the goods are fit for the ordinary purposes for which they are sold.

impostor rule—an exception to the rules on liability for forgery that covers situations such as the embezzling payroll clerk.

in pari delicto—equally guilty; used in reference to a transaction as to which relief will not be granted to either party because both are equally guilty of wrongdoing.

incidental authority—authority of an agent that is reasonably necessary to execute express authority.

incidental damages—incurred by the nonbreaching party as part of the process of trying to cover (buy substitute goods) or sell (selling subject matter of contract to another); includes storage fees, commissions, and the like.

income—money earned by the principal, or property in trust, and distributed by the trustee.

incontestability clause—provision that after the lapse of a specified time the insurer cannot dispute the policy on the ground of misrepresentation or fraud of the insured or similar wrongful conduct.

incorporation by reference—contract consisting of both the original or skeleton document and the detailed statement that is incorporated in it.

incorporator—one or more natural persons or corporations who sign and file appropriate incorporation forms with a designated government official.

indemnity—right of a person secondarily liable to require that a person primarily liable pay for loss sustained when the secondary party discharges the obligation that the primary party should have discharged; the right of an agent to be paid the amount of any loss or damage sustained without fault because of obedience to the principal's instructions; an undertaking by one person for a consideration to pay another person a sum of money to indemnify that person when a specified loss is incurred.

indemnity contract—agreement by one person, for consideration, to pay another person a sum of money in the event that the other person sustains a specified loss.

indenture trustee—usually a commercial banking institution, to represent the interests of the bondholders and ensure that the terms and covenants of the bond issue are met by the corporation.

independent contractor—contractor who undertakes to perform a specified task according to the terms of a contract but over whom the other contracting party has no control except as provided for by the contract.

indorsee—party to whom special indorsement is made.

indorsement—signature of the payee on an instrument.

indorser—secondary party (or obligor) on a note.

informal contract—simple oral or written contract.

informal settlements—negotiated disposition of a matter before an administrative agency, generally without public sanctions.

injunction—order of a court of equity to refrain from doing (negative injunction) or to do (affirmative or mandatory injunction) a specified act.

inland marine—insurance that covers domestic shipments of goods over land and inland waterways.

insider—full-time corporate employee or a director or their relatives.

insider information—privileged information on company business only known to employees.

insolvency—excess of debts and liabilities over assets, or inability to pay debts as they mature.

instruction—summary of the law given to jurors by the judge before deliberation begins.

insurable interest—the right to hold a valid insurance policy on a person or property.

insurance—a plan of security against risks by charging the loss against a fund created by the payments made by policyholders.

insurance agent—agent of an insurance company.

insurance broker—independent contractor who is not employed by any one insurance company.

insured—person to whom the promise in an insurance contract is made.

insurer—promisor in an insurance contract.

integrity—the adherence to one's values and principles despite the costs and consequences.

intellectual property rights—trademark, copyright, and patent rights protected by law.

intended beneficiary—third person of a contract whom the contract is intended to benefit.

intentional infliction of emotional distress—tort that produces mental anguish caused by conduct that exceeds all bounds of decency.

intentional tort—civil wrong that results from intentional conduct.

intervivos gift—any transaction that takes place between living persons and creates rights prior to the death of any of them.

interest in the authority—form of agency in which an agent has been given or paid for the right to exercise authority.

interest in the subject matter—form of agency in which an agent is given an interest in the property with which that agent is dealing.

interlineation—writing between the lines or adding to the provisions of a document, the effect thereof depending upon the nature of the document.

intermediary bank—bank between the originator and the beneficiary bank in the transfer of funds.

interrogatories—written questions used as a discovery tool that must be answered under oath.

intestate—condition of dying without a will as to any property.

intestate succession—distribution, made as directed by statute, of a decedent's property not effectively disposed of by will.

invasion of privacy—tort of intentional intrusion into the private affairs of another.

invitee—person who enters another's land by invitation.

involuntary bankruptcy—proceeding in which a creditor or creditors file the petition for relief with the bankruptcy court.

issuer—party who issues a document such as a letter of credit or a document of title such as a warehouse receipt or bill of lading.

J

joint and several liability—disproportionate satisfaction of partnership debt rendering each partner liable for the entire debt with the right to contribution from other partners.

joint liability—apportions partners' responsibility for debt equally.

joint tenancy—estate held jointly by two or more with the right of survivorship as between them, unless modified by statute.

joint venture—relationship in which two or more persons or firms combine their labor or property for a single undertaking and share profits and losses equally unless otherwise agreed.

judge—primary officer of the court.

judgment lien—lien by a creditor who has won a verdict against the landowner in court.

judgment n.o.v. (or non obstante veredicto, *"notwithstanding the verdict"*)— a judgment entered after verdict upon the motion of the losing party on the ground that the verdict is so wrong that a judgment should be entered the opposite of the verdict.

judicial branch—the branch of government (courts) formed to interpret the laws.

judicial triage—court management tool used by judges to expedite certain cases in which time is of the essence, such as asbestos cases in which the plaintiffs are gravely ill.

jurisdiction—the authority of courts to hear and determine a given class of cases; the power to act over a particular defendant.

jurisdictional rule of reason—rule that balances the vital interests, including laws and policies, of the United States with those of a foreign country.

jury—a body of citizens sworn by a court to determine by verdict the issues of fact submitted to them.

K

Kant's categorical imperative—theory of ethical thought that asks individuals to be governed by the same set of rules in all circumstances; whether you are buyer or seller, the standards for full and fair disclosure are the same.

L

land—earth, including all things embedded in or attached thereto, whether naturally or by the act of humans.

landlord—one who leases real property to another.

law—the order or pattern of rules that society establishes to govern the conduct of individuals and the relationships among them.

lease—agreement between the owner of property and a tenant by which the former agrees to give possession of the property to the latter in consideration of the payment of rent. (Parties—landlord or lessor, tenant or lessee)

leasehold estate—interest of a tenant in rented land.

legacy—gift of money made by will.

legal title—title held by the trustee in a trust situation.

legatee—beneficiary who receives a gift of personal property by will.

legislative branch—the branch of government (e.g., Congress) formed to make the laws.

lessee—one who has a possessory interest in real or personal property under a lease; a tenant.

lessor—one who conveys real or personal property by a lease; a landlord.

letter of credit—commercial device used to guarantee payment to a seller, primarily in an international business transaction.

letters of administration—written authorization given to an administrator of an estate as evidence of appointment and authority.

letters testamentary—written authorization given to an executor of an estate as evidence of appointment and authority.

liability insurance—covers the ship owner's liability if the ship causes damage to another ship or its cargo.

libel—written or visual defamation without legal justification.

license—personal privilege to do some act or series of acts upon the land of another, as the placing of a sign there on, not amounting to an ease mentor a right of possession.

licensee—someone on another's premises with the permission of the occupier, whose duty is to warn the licensee of nonobvious dangers.

licensing—transfer of technology rights to a product so that it may be produced by a different business organization in a foreign country in exchange for royalties and other payments as agreed.

lien—claim or right, against property, existing by virtue of the entry of a judgment against its owner or by the entry of a judgment and a levy there under on the property, or because of the relationship of the claimant to the particular property, such as an unpaid seller.

life estate—an estate for the duration of a life.

limitation-of-liability clause—provision in a contract stating that one of the parties shall not be liable for damages in case of breach; also called an *exculpatory clause.*

limited covenant—any covenant that does not provide the complete protection of a full covenant.

limited defenses—defenses available to secondary parties if the presenting party is a holder in due course.

limited liability company (LLC)—a partnership for federal tax treatment and the limited liability feature of the corporate form of business organization.

limited liability partnership (LLP)—partnership in which at least one partner has a liability limited to the loss of the capital contribution made to the partnership.

limited partner—partner who neither takes part in the management of the partnership nor appears to the public to be a general partner.

limited partnership—partnership that can be formed by "one or more general partners and one or more limited partners."

limited (special) jurisdiction—the authority to hear only particular kinds of cases.

limited warranty—any warranty that does not provide the complete protection of a full warranty.

lineals—relationship that exists when one person is a direct descendant of the other; also called *lineal descendants.*

liquidated damages—damages established in advance of breach as an alternative to establishing compensatory damages at the time of the breach.

liquidated damages clause—specification of exact compensation in case of a breach of contract.

liquidation—process of converting property into money whether of particular items of property or of all the assets of a business or an estate.

living trust—trust created to take effect within the lifetime of the settlor; also called *inter vivos* trust.

living will—document by which individuals may indicate that if they become unable to express their wishes and are in an irreversible, incurable condition, they do not want life-sustaining medical treatments.

living-document view—the term when a constitution is interpreted according to changes in conditions.

lottery—any plan by which a consideration is given for a chance to win a prize; it consists of three elements: (1) there must be a payment of money or something of value for an opportunity to win, (2) a prize must be available, and (3) the prize must be offered by lot or chance.

M

mailbox rule—timing for acceptance tied to proper acceptance.

maker—party who writes or creates a promissory note.

malpractice—basis for liability when services are not properly rendered in accordance with commonly accepted standards; negligence by a professional in performing his or her skill.

marine insurance—policies that cover perils relating to the transportation of goods.

market power—the ability to control price and exclude competitors.

market value—price at which a share of stock can be voluntarily bought or sold in the open market.

mask work—specific form of expression embodied in a chip design, including the stencils used in manufacturing semiconductor chip products.

mass picketing—illegal tactic of employees massing together in great numbers to effectively shut down entrances of the employer's facility.

maturity date—date that a corporation is required to repay a loan to a bondholder.

means test—new standard under the Reform Act that requires the court to find that the debtor does not have the means to repay creditors; goes beyond the past requirement of petitions being granted on the simple assertion of the debtor saying, "I have debts."

mechanic's lien—protection afforded by statute to various kinds of laborers and persons supplying materials, by giving them a lien on the building and land that has been improved or added to by them.

mediation—the settlement of a dispute through the use of a messenger who carries to each side of the dispute the issues and offers in the case.

merchant—seller who deals in specific goods classified by the UCC.

merger (of corporations)—combining of corporations by which one absorbs the other and continues to exist, preserving its original charter and identity while the other corporation ceases to exist.

minitrial—a trial held on portions of the case or certain issues in the case.

Miranda warnings—warnings required to prevent self-incrimination in a criminal matter.

mirror image rule—common law contract rule on acceptance that requires language to be absolutely the same as the offer, unequivocal and unconditional.

misdemeanor—criminal offense with a sentence of less than one year that is neither treason nor a felony.

misrepresentation—false statement of fact made innocently without any intent to deceive.

mistrial—a court's declaration that terminates a trial and postpones it to a later date; commonly entered when evidence has been of a highly prejudicial character or when a juror has been guilty of misconduct.

money—medium of exchange.

money order—draft issued by a bank or a nonbank.

moral relativists—group of ethical theorists who believe that ethical choices are determined according to the circumstances and not according to any predetermined set of standards.

mortgage—interest in land given by the owner to a creditor as security for the payment of the creditor for a debt, the nature of the interest depending upon the law of the state where the land is located. (Parties—mortgagor, mortgagee)

most-favored-nation clause—clause in treaties between countries whereby any privilege subsequently granted to a third country in relation to a given treaty subject is extended to the other party to the treaty.

motion for summary judgment—request that the court decide a case on basis of law only because there are no material issues disputed by the parties.

motion to dismiss—a pleading that may be filed to attack the adverse party's pleading as not stating a cause of action or a defense.

N

National Environmental Policy Act (NEPA)—federal law that mandates study of a project's impact on the environment before it can be undertaken by any federal agency.

National Pollutant Discharge Elimination System (NPDES)—federal law that regulates discharge into bodies of water.

natural law—a system of principles to guide human conduct independent of, and sometimes contrary to, enacted law and discovered by man's rational intelligence.

necessaries—things indispensable or absolutely necessary for the sustenance of human life.

negligence—failure to exercise due care under the circumstances in consequence of which harm is proximately caused to one to whom the defendant owed a duty to exercise due care.

negotiability—quality of an instrument that affords special rights and standing.

negotiable bill of lading—document of title that by its terms calls for goods to be delivered "to the bearer" or "to the order of" a named person.

negotiable instruments—drafts, promissory notes, checks, and certificates of deposit that, in proper form, give special rights as "negotiable commercial paper."

negotiable warehouse receipt—receipt that states the covered goods will be delivered "to the bearer" or "to the order of."

negotiation—the transfer of commercial paper by indorsement and delivery by the person to whom it is then payable in the case of order paper and by physical transfer in the case of bearer paper.

Noise Control Act—federal law that controls noise emissions from low-flying aircraft.

nominal damages—nominal sum awarded the plaintiff in order to establish that legal rights have been violated although the plaintiff in fact has not sustained any actual loss or damages.

nonattainment areas—"dirty" areas that do not meet federal standards under the Clean Air Act.

nonconforming use—use of land that conflicts with a zoning ordinance at the time the ordinance goes into effect.

nonconsumer lease—lease that does not satisfy the definition of a consumer lease; also known as a *commercial lease.*

nonnegotiable bill of lading—See *straight bill of lading.*

nonnegotiable instrument—contract, note, or draft that does not meet negotiability requirements of Article 3.

nonnegotiable warehouse receipt—receipt that states the covered goods received will be delivered to a specific person.

notice of dishonor—notice that an instrument has been dishonored; such notice can be oral, written, or electronic but is subject to time limitations.

notice statute—statute under which the last good faith or bona fide purchaser holds the title.

notice-race statute—statute under which the first bona fide purchaser to record the deed holds the title.

novation—substitution for an old contract with a new one that either replaces an existing obligation with a new obligation or replaces an original party with a new party.

nuisance—conduct that harms or prejudices another in the use of land or that harms or prejudices the public.

O

obligee—promisee who can claim the benefit of the obligation.

obligor—promisor.

ocean marine—policies that cover transportation of goods in vessels in international and coastal trade.

offer—expression of an offeror's willingness to enter into a contractual agreement.

offeree—person to whom an offer is made.

offeror—person who makes an offer.

Oil Pollution Act—federal law that assigns cleanup liability for oil spills in U.S. waters.

open meeting law—law that requires advance notice of agency meeting and public access.

opening statements—statements by opposing attorneys that tell the jury what their cases will prove.

operation of law—attaching of certain consequences to certain facts because of legal principles that operate automatically as contrasted with consequences that arise because of the voluntary action of a party designed to create those consequences.

option contract—contract to hold an offer to make a contract open for a fixed period of time.

order of relief—the order from the bankruptcy judge that starts the protection for the debtor; when the order of relief is entered by the court, the debtor's creditors must stop all proceedings and work through the bankruptcy court to recover debts (if possible). Court finding that creditors have met the standards for bankruptcy petitions.

order paper—instrument payable to the order of a party.

original jurisdiction—the authority of courts to hear the original proceedings in a case.

originator—party who originates the funds transfer.

output contract—contract of a producer to sell its entire production or output to a buyer.

outstanding—name for shares of a company that have been issued to stockholders.

overdraft—negative balance in a drawer's account.

P

par value—specified monetary amount assigned by an issuing corporation for each share of its stock.

parol evidence rule—rule that prohibits the introduction into evidence of oral or written statements made prior to or contemporaneously with the execution of a complete written contract, deed, or instrument, in the absence of clear proof of fraud, accident, or mistake causing the omission of the statement in question.

partially disclosed principal—principal whose existence is made known but whose identity is not.

partner—one of two or more persons who jointly own and carry on a business for profit.

partnership—pooling of capital resources and the business or professional talents of two or more individuals (partners) with the goal of making a profit.

partnership agreement—document prepared to evidence the contract of the parties. (Parties—partners or general partners)

party—person involved in a legal transaction; may be a natural person, an artificial person (e.g., a corporation), or an unincorporated enterprise (e.g., a government agency).

past consideration—something that has been performed in the past and which, therefore, cannot be consideration for a promise made in the present.

payable to order—term stating that a negotiable instrument is payable to the order of any person described in it or to a person or order.

payee—party to whom payment is to be made.

payment order—direction given by an originator to his or her bank or by any bank to a subsequent bank to make a specified funds transfer.

Pension Benefit Guaranty Corporation (PBGC)—a federal insurance plan established by ERISA that protects employees covered under defined benefit plans should the employer go out of business.

per capita—method of distributing estate assets on an equal-per-person basis.

per stirpes—method for distribution of an estate that divides property equally down family lines.

perfected security interest—security interest with priority because of filing, possession, automatic or temporary priority status.

periodic tenancy—tenancy that continues indefinitely for a specified rental period until terminated; often called a month-to-month tenancy.

personal property—property that is movable or intangible, or rights in such things.

personal representative—administrator or executor who represents decedents under the UPC.

physical duress—threat of physical harm to person or property.

plaintiff—the party who initiates a lawsuit.

pleadings—the papers filed by the parties in an action in order to set forth the facts and frame the issues to be tried, although, under some systems, the pleadings merely give notice or a general indication of the nature of the issues.

pledge—bailment given as security for the payment of a debt or the performance of an obligation owed to the pledgee. (Parties—pledgor, pledgee)

police power—the power to govern; the power to adopt laws for the protection of the public health, welfare, safety, and morals.

policy—paper evidencing the contract of insurance.

positive law—law enacted and codified by governmental authority.

possession—exclusive dominion and control of property.

possibility of reverter—nature of the interest held by the grantor after conveying land outright but subject to a condition or provision that may cause the grantee's interest to become forfeited and the interest to revert to the grantor or heirs.

postdate—to insert or place on an instrument a later date than the actual date on which it was executed.

power of attorney—written authorization to an agent by the principal.

precedent—a decision of a court that stands as the law for a particular problem in the future.

predatory lending—a practice on the part of the subprime lending market whereby lenders take advantage of less sophisticated consumers or those who are desperate for funds by using the lenders' superior bargaining positions to obtain credit terms that go well beyond compensating them for their risk.

predicate act—qualifying underlying offense for RICO liability.

preemption—the federal government's superior regulatory position over state laws on the same subject area.

preemptive right—shareholder's right upon the increase of a corporation's capital stock to be allowed to subscribe to such a percentage of the new shares as the shareholder's old shares bore to the former total capital stock.

preferences—transfers of property by a debtor to one or more specific creditors to enable these creditors to obtain payment for debts owed.

preferential transfers—certain transfers of money or security interests in the time frame just prior to bankruptcy that can be set aside if voidable.

preferred stock—stock that has a priority or preference as to payment of dividends or upon liquidation, or both.

prescription—acquisition of a right to use the land of another, as an easement, by making hostile, visible, and notorious use of the land, continuing for the period specified by the local law.

presentment—formal request for payment on an instrument.

price discrimination—the charging practice by a seller of different prices to different buyers for commodities of similar grade and quality, resulting in reduced competition or a tendency to create a monopoly.

prima facie—evidence that, if believed, is sufficient by itself to lead to a particular conclusion.

primary party—party to whom the holder or holder in due course must turn first to obtain payment.

primary picketing—legal presentations in front of a business notifying the public of a labor dispute.

primum non nocere—"above all do no harm."

principal—person or firm who employs an agent; person who, with respect to a surety, is primarily liable to the third person or creditor; property held in trust.

principal debtor—original borrower or debtor.

prior art—a showing that an invention as a whole would have been obvious to a person of ordinary skill in the art when the invention was patented.

private carrier—carrier owned by the shipper, such as a company's own fleet of trucks.

private corporation—corporation organized for charitable and benevolent purposes or for purposes of finance, industry, and commerce.

private law—the rules and regulations parties agree to as part of their contractual relationships.

private nuisance—nuisance that affects only one or a few individuals.

privileges and immunities clause—a clause that entitles a person going into another state to make contracts, own property, and engage in business to the same extent as citizens of that state.

privity—succession or chain of relationship to the same thing or right, such as privity of contract, privity of estate, privity of possession.

privity of contract—relationship between a promisor and the promisee.

privity rule—succession or chain of relationship to the same thing or right, such as privity of contract, privity of estate, privity of possession.

pro rata—proportionately, or divided according to a rate or standard.

probate—procedure for formally establishing or proving that a given writing is the last will and testament of the person who purportedly signed it.

procedural law—the law that specifies the steps that must be followed in enforcing rights and liabilities.

process—paperwork served personally on a defendant in a civil case.

product disparagement—false statements made about a product or business.

profit—right to take a part of the soil or produce of another's land, such as timber or water.

promisee—person to whom a promise is made.

promisor—person who makes a promise.

promissory estoppel—doctrine that a promise will be enforced although it is not supported by consideration when the promisor should have reasonably expected that the promise would induce action or forbearance of a definite and substantial character on the part of the promised and injustice can be avoided only by enforcement of the promise.

promissory note—unconditional promise in writing made by one person to another, signed by the maker engaging to pay on demand, or at a definite time, a sum certain in money to order or to bearer. (Parties—maker, payee)

promoters—persons who plan the formation of the corporation and sell or promote the idea to others.

proof of claim—written statement, signed by the creditor or an authorized representative, setting forth any claim made against the debtor and the basis for it.

property report—condensed version of a property development statement filed with the secretary of HUD and given to a prospective customer at least 48 hours before signing a contract to buy or lease property.

prosecutor—party who originates a criminal proceeding.

prospectus—information provided to each potential purchaser of securities setting forth the key information contained in the registration statement.

proxy—written authorization by a shareholder to another person to vote the stock owned by the shareholder; the person who is the holder of such a written authorization.

public corporation—corporation that has been established for governmental purposes and for the administration of public affairs.

public nuisance—nuisance that affects the community or public at large.

public policy—certain objectives relating to health, morals, and integrity of government that the law seeks to advance by declaring invalid any contract that conflicts with those objectives even though there is no statute expressly declaring such a contract illegal.

public warehouses—entities that serve the public generally without discrimination.

punitive damages—damages, in excess of those required to compensate the plaintiff for the wrong done, that are imposed in order to punish the defendant because of the particularly wanton or willful character of wrongdoing; also called *exemplary damages*.

purchase money security interest (PMSI)—the security interest in the goods a seller sells on credit that become the collateral for the creditor/seller.

Q

qualified indorsement—an indorsement that includes words such as "without recourse" that disclaims certain liability of the indorser to a maker or a drawee.

qualified privilege—media privilege to print inaccurate information without liability for defamation, so long as a retraction is printed and there was no malice.

quantum meruit—"as much as deserved"; an action brought for the value of the services rendered the defendant when there was no express contract as to the purchase price.

quasi contract—court-imposed obligation to prevent unjust enrichment in the absence of a contract.

quasi-judicial proceedings—forms of hearings in which the rules of evidence and procedure are more relaxed but each side still has a chance to be heard.

quasi-public corporation—private corporation furnishing services on which the public is particularly dependent, for example, a gas and electric company.

quitclaim deed—deed by which the grantor purports to give up only whatever right or title the grantor may have in the property without specifying or warranting transfer of any particular interest.

quorum—minimum number of persons, shares represented, or directors who must be present at a meeting in order to lawfully transact business.

R

race statute—statute under which the first party to record the deed holds the title.

race-notice statute—See *notice-race statute*.

Racketeer Influenced and Corrupt Organizations (RICO) Act—federal law, initially targeting organized crime, that has expanded in scope and provides penalties and civil recovery for multiple criminal offenses, or a pattern of racketeering.

real property—land and all rights in land.

recognizance—obligation entered into before a court to do some act, such as to appear at a later date for a hearing. Also called a *contract of record*.

recorder—public official in charge of deeds.

recross-examination—an examination by the other side's attorney that follows the redirect examination.

redemption—buying back of one's property, which has been sold because of a default, upon paying the amount that had been originally due together with interest and costs.

redirect examination—questioning after cross-examination, in which the attorney for the witness testifying may ask the same witness other questions to overcome effects of the cross-examination.

reference to a third person—settlement that allows a nonparty to resolve the dispute.

reformation—remedy by which a written instrument is corrected when it fails to express the actual intent of both parties because of fraud, accident, or mistake.

registered bonds—bonds held by owners whose names and addresses are registered on the books of the corporation.

registration requirements—provisions of the Securities Act of 1933 requiring advance disclosure to the public of a new securities issue through filing a statement with the SEC and sending a prospectus to each potential purchaser.

registration statement—document disclosing specific financial information regarding the security, the issuer, and the underwriter.

remainder interest—land interest that follows a life estate.

remand—term used when an appellate court sends a case back to trial court for additional hearings or a new trial.

remedy—action or procedure that is followed in order to enforce a right or to obtain damages for injury to a right.

rent-a-judge plan—dispute resolution through private courts with judges paid to be referees for the cases.

representative capacity—action taken by one on behalf of another, as the act of a personal representative on behalf of a decedent's estate, or action taken both on one's behalf and on behalf of others, as a shareholder bringing a representative action.

repudiation—result of a buyer or seller refusing to perform the contract as stated.

request for production of documents—discovery tool for uncovering paper or electronic evidence in a case.

requirements contract—contract in which the buyer buys its needs (requirements) from the seller.

rescission—action of one party to a contract to set the contract aside when the other party is guilty of a breach of the contract.

reservation of rights—assertion by a party to a contract that even though a tendered performance (e.g., a defective product) is accepted, the right to damages for nonconformity to the contract is reserved.

Resource Conservation and Recovery Act (RCRA)—federal law that regulates the disposal of potentially harmful substances and encourages resource conservation and recovery.

Resource Recovery Act—early federal solid waste disposal legislation that provided funding for states and local governments with recycling programs.

respondeat superior—doctrine that the principal or employer is vicariously liable for the unauthorized torts committed by an agent or employee while acting within the scope of the agency or the course of the employment, respectively.

restrictive covenants—covenants in a deed by which the grantee agrees to refrain from doing specified acts.

restrictive indorsement—an indorsement that restricts further transfer, such as in trust for or to the use of

some other person, is conditional, or for collection or deposit.

reverse—the term used when the appellate court sets aside the verdict or judgment of a lower court.

reverse mortgage—mortgage in which the owners get their equity out of their home over a period of time and return the house to the lender upon their deaths.

reversible error—an error or defect in court proceedings of so serious a nature that on appeal the appellate court will set aside the proceedings of the lower court.

reversionary interest—interest that a lessor has in property that is subject to an outstanding lease.

revoke—testator's act of taking back his or her will and its provisions.

right—legal capacity to require another person to perform or refrain from an action.

right of escheat—right of the state to take the property of a decedent that has not been distributed.

right of first refusal—right of a party to meet the terms of a proposed contract before it is executed, such as a real estate purchase agreement.

right of privacy—the right to be free from unreasonable intrusion by others.

rights theory—Nozick's theory of ethics that (1) everyone has a set of rights, and (2) it is up to the governments to protect those rights.

right to cure—second chance for a seller to make a proper tender of conforming goods.

right-to-work laws—laws restricting unions and employees from negotiating clauses in their collective bargaining agreements that make union membership compulsory.

risk—peril or contingency against which the insured is protected by the contract of insurance.

risk of loss—in contract performance, the cost of damage or injury to the goods contracted for.

Robinson-Patman Act—a federal statute designed to eliminate price discrimination in interstate commerce.

run with the land—concept that certain covenants in a deed to land are deemed to run or pass with the land so that whoever owns the land is bound by or entitled to the benefit of the covenants.

S

Safe Drinking Water Act—a federal law that establishes national standards for contaminants in drinking water.

sale on approval—term indicating that no sale takes place until the buyer approves or accepts the goods.

sale or return—sale in which the title to the property passes to the buyer at the time of the transaction but the buyer is given the option of returning the property and restoring the title to the seller.

search engine—Internet service used to locate Web sites.

search warrant—judicial authorization for a search of property where there is the expectation of privacy.

seasonable—timely.

secondary meaning—a legal term signifying the words in question have taken on a new meaning with the public, capable of serving a source-identifying function of a mark.

secondary parties—called *secondary obligors* under Revised Article 3; parties to an instrument to whom holders turn when the primary party, for whatever reason, fails to pay the instrument.

secondary picketing—picketing an employer with which a union has no dispute to persuade the employer to stop doing business with a party to

the dispute; generally illegal under the NLRA.

secrecy laws—confidentiality laws applied to home-country banks.

secured party—person owed the money, whether as a seller or a lender, in a secured transaction in personal property.

secured transaction—credit sale of goods or a secured loan that provides special protection for the creditor.

securities—stocks and bonds issued by a corporation. Under some investor protection laws, the term includes any interest in an enterprise that provides unearned income to its owner.

security agreement—agreement of the creditor and the debtor that the creditor will have a security interest.

security interest—property right that enables the creditor to take possession of the property if the debtor does not pay the amount owed.

self-help repossession—creditor's right to repossess the collateral without judicial proceedings.

self-proved wills—wills that eliminate some formalities of proof by being executed according to statutory requirements.

selling on consignment—entrusting a person with possession of property for the purpose of sale.

semiconductor chip product—product placed on a piece of semiconductor material in accordance with a predetermined pattern that is intended to perform electronic circuitry functions.

service mark—mark that identifies a service.

servient tenement—land that is subject to an easement.

settlor—one who settles property in trust or creates a trust estate.

severalty—ownership of property by one person.

shared powers—powers that are held by both state and national governments.

Sherman Antitrust Act—a federal statute prohibiting combinations and contracts in restraint of interstate trade, now generally inapplicable to labor union activity.

shop right—right of an employer to use in business without charge an invention discovered by an employee during working hours and with the employer's material and equipment.

shopkeeper's privilege—right of a store owner to detain a suspected shoplifter based on reasonable cause and for a reasonable time without resulting liability for false imprisonment.

short-swing profit—profit realized by a corporate insider from selling securities less than six months after purchase.

sinking fund—fixed amount of money set aside each year by the borrowing corporation toward the ultimate payment of bonds.

situational ethics—a flexible standard of ethics that permits an examination of circumstances and motivation before attaching the label of right or wrong to conduct.

Sixth Amendment—the U.S. constitutional amendment that guarantees a speedy trial.

slander—defamation of character by spoken words or gestures.

slander of title—malicious making of false statements as to a seller's title.

small claims courts—courts that resolve disputes between parties when those disputes do not exceed a minimal level; no lawyers are permitted; the parties represent themselves.

social contract—theory of ethics that focuses on social norms; what is ethical is the standard set by implied agreement; for example, we disapprove of people who cut in line ahead of us.

sole or individual proprietorship—form of business ownership in which one individual owns the business.

soliciting agent—salesperson.

sovereign compliance doctrine—doctrine that allows a defendant to raise as an affirmative defense to an antitrust action the fact that the defendant's actions were compelled by a foreign state.

sovereign immunity doctrine—doctrine that states that a foreign sovereign generally cannot be sued unless an exception to the Foreign Sovereign Immunities Act of 1976 applies.

special agent—agent authorized to transact a specific transaction or to do a specific act.

special drawing rights (SDRs)—rights that allow a country to borrow enough money from other International Money Fund (IMF) members to permit that country to maintain the stability of its currency's relationship to other world currencies.

special indorsement—an indorsement that specifies the person to whom the instrument is indorsed.

specific legacies—identified property bequeathed by a testator; also called *specific devises.*

specific lien—right of a creditor to hold particular property or assert a lien on particular property of the debtor because of the creditor's having done work on or having some other association with the property, as distinguished from having a lien generally against the assets of the debtor merely because the debtor is indebted to the lien holder.

specific performance—action brought to compel the adverse party to perform a contract on the theory that merely suing for damages for its breach will not be an adequate remedy.

spendthrift trust—a trust that, to varying degrees, provides that creditors of the beneficiary shall not be able to reach the principal or income held by the trustee and that the beneficiary shall not be able to assign any interest in the trust.

spot zoning—allowing individual variation in zoning.

stakeholder analysis—the term used when a decision maker views a problem from different perspectives and measures the impact of a decision on various groups.

stakeholders—those who have a stake, or interest, in the activities of a corporation; stakeholders include employees, members of the community in which the corporation operates, vendors, customers, and any others who are affected by the actions and decisions of the corporation.

stale check—a check whose date is longer than six months ago.

standby letter—letter of credit for a contractor ensuring he will complete the project as contracted.

stare decisis—"let the decision stand"; the principle that the decision of a court should serve as a guide or precedent and control the decision of a similar case in the future.

status quo ante—original positions of the parties.

statute of frauds—statute that, in order to prevent fraud through the use of perjured testimony, requires that certain kinds of transactions be evidenced in writing in order to be binding or enforceable.

statute of limitations—statute that restricts the period of time within which an action may be brought.

statutory law—laws enacted by a legislative body.

stay (or delay) of foreclosure—delay of foreclosure obtained by the mortgagor to prevent undue hardship.

stirpes—family lines; distribution *per stirpes* refers to the manner in which descendants take property by right of representation.

stock subscription—contract or agreement to buy a specific number and kind of shares when they are issued by the corporation.

stop payment order—order by a depositor to the bank to refuse to make payment of a check when presented for payment.

straight (or nonnegotiable) bill of lading—document of title that consigns transported goods to a named person.

strict liability—civil wrong for which there is absolute liability because of the inherent danger in the underlying activity, for example, the use of explosives.

strict tort liability—product liability theory that imposes liability upon the manufacturer, seller, or distributor of goods for harm caused by defective goods.

subject matter jurisdiction—judicial authority to hear a particular type of case.

sublease—a transfer of the premises by the lessee to a third person, the sublessee or subtenant, for a period of less than the term of the original lease.

sublessee—person with lease rights for a period of less than the term of the original lease (also *subtenant*).

subprime lending market—a credit market that makes loans to high-risk consumers (those who have bankruptcies, no credit history, or a poor credit history), often loaning money to pay off other debts the consumer has due.

subrogation—right of a party secondarily liable to stand in the place of the creditor after making payment to the creditor and to enforce the creditor's right against the party primarily liable in order to obtain indemnity from such primary party.

substantial impairment—material defect in a good.

substantial performance—equitable rule that if a good-faith attempt to perform does not precisely meet the terms of the agreement, the agreement will still be considered complete if the essential purpose of the contract is accomplished.

substantive law—the law that creates, defines, and regulates rights and liabilities.

substitute check—electronic image of a paper check that a bank can create and that has the same legal effect as the original instrument.

substitution—substitution of a new contract between the same parties.

sum certain—amount due under an instrument that can be computed from its face with only reference to interest rates.

summary jury trial—a mock or dry-run trial for parties to get a feel for how their cases will play to a jury.

summation—the attorney address to a jury that is given after all the evidence is presented in court and sums up a case and urges the jury to reach a particular verdict.

Superfund Amendment and Reauthorization Act—federal law that authorizes the EPA to collect cleanup costs from those responsible for the ownership, leasing, dumping, or security of hazardous waste sites.

Superfund sites—areas designated by the EPA for cleanup of hazardous waste.

surety—obligor of a suretyship; primarily liable for the debt or obligation of the principal debtor.

suretyship—undertaking to pay the debt or be liable for the default of another.

symbolic delivery—delivery of goods by delivery of the means of control, such as a key or a relevant document of title, such as a negotiable bill of lading; also called *constructive delivery*.

T

takeover laws—laws that guard against unfairness in corporate takeover situations.

tariff—(1) domestically—government-approved schedule of charges that may be made by a regulated business, such as a common carrier or warehouser; (2) internationally—tax imposed by a country on goods crossing its borders, without regard to whether the purpose is to raise revenue or to discourage the traffic in the taxed goods.

tax lien—lien on property by a government agency for nonpayment of taxes.

teller's check—draft drawn by a bank on another bank in which it has an account.

temporary insider—someone retained by a corporation for professional services on an as-needed basis, such as an attorney, accountant, or investment banker.

temporary perfection—perfection given for a limited period of time to creditors.

tenancy at sufferance—lease arrangement in which the tenant occupies the property at the discretion of the landlord.

tenancy at will—holding of land for an indefinite period that may be terminated at any time by the landlord or by the landlord and tenant acting together.

tenancy by entirety or tenancy by entireties—transfer of property to both husband and wife.

tenancy for years—tenancy for a fixed period of time, even though the time is less than a year.

tenancy in common—relationship that exists when two or more persons own undivided interests in property.

tenancy in partnership—ownership relationship that exists between partners under the Uniform Partnership Act.

tenant—one who holds or possesses real property by any kind of right or title; one who pays rent for the temporary use and occupation of another's real property under a lease.

tender—goods have arrived, are available for pickup, and buyer is notified.

term insurance—policy written for a specified number of years that terminates at the end of that period.

termination statement—document (record), which may be requested by a debtor who has paid in full, stating that a security interest is no longer claimed under the specified financing statement.

testamentary capacity—sufficient mental capacity to understand that a writing being executed is a will and what that entails.

testamentary intent—designed to take effect at death, as by disposing of property or appointing a personal representative.

testamentary trust—trust that becomes effective only when the settlor's will takes effect after death.

testate—condition of leaving a will upon death.

testate distribution—distribution of an estate in accordance with the will of the decedent.

testator, testatrix—man, woman who makes a will.

third-party beneficiary—third person whom the parties to a contract intend to benefit by the making of the contract and to confer upon such person the right to sue for breach of contract.

time draft—bill of exchange payable at a stated time after sight or at a definite time.

tippee—individual who receives information about a corporation from an insider or temporary insider.

tort—civil wrong that interferes with one's property or person.

Toxic Substances Control Act (TOSCA)—first federal law to control the manufacture, use, and disposal of toxic substances.

trade dress—product's total image including its overall packaging look.

trade libel—written defamation about a product or service.

trade name—name under which a business is carried on and, if fictitious, must be registered.

trade secret—any formula, device, or compilation of information that is used in one's business and is of such a nature that it provides an advantage over competitors who do not have the information.

trademark—mark that identifies a product.

transferee—buyer or vendee.

traveler's check—check that is payable on demand provided it is countersigned by the person whose specimen signature appears on the check.

treasury stock—corporate stock that the corporation has reacquired.

treble damages—three times the damages actually sustained.

trespass—an unauthorized action with respect to person or property.

trial de novo—a trial required to preserve the constitutional right to a jury trial by allowing an appeal to proceed as though there never had been any prior hearing or decision.

tripartite—three-part division (of government).

trust—transfer of property by one person to another with the understanding or declaration that such property be held for the benefit of another; the holding of property by the owner in trust for another, upon a declaration of trust, without a transfer to another person. (Parties—settlor, trustee, beneficiary)

trust agreement—instrument creating a trust; also called *deed of trust*.

trust corpus—fund or property that is transferred to the trustee or held by the settlor as the body or subject matter of the trust; also called *trust fund, trust estate*, and *trust res*.

trustee—party who has legal title to estate and manages it.

trustee in bankruptcy—impartial person elected to administer the debtor's estate.

trustor—donor or settlor who is the owner of property and creates a trust in the property.

tying—the anticompetitive practice of requiring buyers to purchase one product in order to get another.

U

ultra vires—act or contract that the corporation does not have authority to do or make.

unconscionable—unreasonable, not guided or restrained by conscience and often referring to a contract grossly unfair to one party because of the superior bargaining powers of the other party.

underwriter—insurer.

undisclosed principal—principal on whose behalf an agent acts without disclosing to the third person the fact of agency or the identity of the principal.

undue influence—influence that is asserted upon another person by one who dominates that person.

Uniform Probate Code (UPC)—uniform statute on wills and administration of estates.

Uniform Simultaneous Death Act—law providing that when survivorship cannot be established, the property of each person shall be disposed of as though he or she had survived the other.

unilateral contract—contract under which only one party makes a promise.

unincorporated association—combination of two or more persons for the furtherance of a common nonprofit purpose.

universal agent—agent authorized by the principal to do all acts that can lawfully be delegated to a representative.

universal defenses—defenses that are regarded as so basic that the social interest in preserving them outweighs the social interest of giving negotiable instruments the freely transferable qualities of money; accordingly, such defenses are given universal effect and may be raised against all holders.

USA Patriot Act—federal law that, among other things, imposes reporting requirements on banks.

usage of trade—language and customs of an industry.

usury—lending money at an interest rate that is higher than the maximum rate allowed by law.

utilitarians—those who support the ethical theory of resolving dilemmas by doing the most good for the most people.

uttering—crime of issuing or delivering a forged instrument to another person.

V

valid—legal.

valid contract—agreement that is binding and enforceable.

value—consideration or antecedent debt or security given in exchange for the transfer of a negotiable instrument or creation of a security interest.

variance—permission of a landowner to use the land in a specified manner that is inconsistent with the zoning ordinance.

vicarious liability—imposing liability for the fault of another.

void agreement—agreement that cannot be enforced.

voidable contract—agreement that is otherwise binding and enforceable but may be rejected at the option of one of the parties as the result of specific circumstances.

voidable title—title of goods that carries with it the contingency of an underlying problem.

voir dire *examination*—the preliminary examination of a juror or a witness to ascertain fitness to act as such.

voluntary bankruptcy—proceeding in which the debtor files the petition for relief.

voting by proxy—authorizing someone else to vote the shares owned by the shareholder.

voting trust—transfer by two or more persons of their shares of stock of a corporation to a trustee who is to vote the shares and act for such shareholders.

W

waiver—release or relinquishment of a known right or objection.

warehouse—entity engaged in the business of storing the goods of others for compensation.

warehouse receipt—receipt issued by the warehouse for stored goods. Regulated by the UCC, which clothes the receipt with some degree of negotiability.

warranty—promise either express or implied about the nature, quality, or performance of the goods.

warranty against encumbrances—warranty that there are no liens or other encumbrances to goods except those noted by seller.

warranty deed—deed by which the grantor conveys a specific estate or interest to the grantee and makes one or more of the covenants of title.

warranty of habitability—implied warranty that the leased property is fit for dwelling by tenants.

warranty of title—implied warranty that title to the goods is good and transfer is proper.

wasting assets corporation—corporation designed to exhaust or use up the assets of the corporation, such as by extracting oil, coal, iron, and other ores.

way of necessity—grantee's right to use land retained by the grantor for going to and from the conveyed land.

White-Collar Crime Penalty Enhancement Act of 2002—federal reforms passed as a result of the collapses of companies such as Enron; provides for longer sentences and higher fines for both executives and companies.

white-collar crimes—crimes committed generally in the course of doing business and usually involving some form of deceit used to get gains.

whole life insurance—ordinary life insurance providing lifetime insurance protection.

will—instrument executed with the formality required by law by which a person makes a disposition of his or her property to take effect upon death.

writ of certiorari—order by the U.S. Supreme Court granting a right of review by the court of a lower court decision.

wrongfully dishonored—error by a bank in refusing to pay a check.

Z

zoning—restrictions imposed by government on the use of designated land to ensure an orderly physical development of the regulated area.

case index

Opinion cases are in boldface type at the case summary; cited cases are in Roman type.

1-800 Contacts, Inc. v. Weigner, 273
14 Penn Plaza, LLC v. Pyett, 889
84 Lumber Co. v. Smith, 1090
99 Commercial Street, Inc. v. Goldberg, 1046
300 Broadway Healthcare Center, LLC v. Wachovia Bank, N.A., 653

A

A. E. Staley Manufacturing Co. v. Chao, 872
A. L. Schutzman Company, Inc. v. Nutsco, Inc., 563–564
A.B. & S. Auto Service, Inc. v. South Shore Bank of Chicago, 705
Abbot v. Schnader, Harrison, Segal & Lewis, LLP, 350
Abbott Thinlite Corp. v. Redmont, 1099
ABC Metals & Recycling Co., Inc. v. Highland Computer Forms, Inc., 477
Abeles Inc. v. Creekstone Farms Premium Beef, LLC, 917
Abrahim & Sons, Inc. v. Equilon Enterprises, LLC, 968
Accurate Printers, Inc. v. Stark, 979
Ace American Ins. Co. v. Wendt, LLP, 470
Ackerley Media Group, Inc. v. Sharp Electronics Corp., 280
Adamar of New Jersey v. Luber, 289
Adams v. Lindsell, 274
Adams v. National Engineering Service Corp., 695
Adams v. Uno Restaurants, Inc., 848–849
Adams v. Wacaster Oil Co., Inc., 543
Adams Outdoor Adv., Ltd., Part. v. Long, 1126–1127
Adarand Constructors, Inc. v. Pena (Adarand I), 900
Adbar v. New Beginnings, 398
Adcock v. Ramtreat Metal Technology, Inc., 576
ADP Marshall, Inc. v. Brown University, 253, 254
Advanced Alloys, Inc. v. Sergeant Steel Corp., 665

Advanced Bodycare Solutions, LLC v. Thione International, Inc., 541
Advocate Health and Hospitals Corp. v. Bank One, 611
Aetna Casualty & Surety Co. v. Garza, 780
Aetna Chemical Co. v. Spaulding & Kimball Co., 553
Affiliated FM Ins. Co. v. Constitution Reinsurance Corp., 355
Affinity Internet v. Consolidated Credit, 351
AgGrow Oils, LLC v. National Union Fire Ins., 362
AIG Global Securities Lending Corp. v. Banc of America Securities LLC, 631
AIG, Inc. v. Greenberg, 1014
Akron v. Akron Center for Reproductive Health, Inc., 72
Alamance County Board of Education v. Bobby Murray Chevrolet, Inc., 552
Alamo Rent-A-Car v. Mendenhall, 511
Albemale Paper Co. v. Moody, 894
Aldrich & Co. v. Donovan, 301
Alexander v. Chandler, 806
Alexander v. Gardner-Denver Co., 889
Alfred v. Capital Area Soccer League, Inc., 181
Alien, Inc. v. Futterman, 685
Allegheny Ludlum Corp. v. United States, 131
Allied Capital Partners L.P. v. Bank One, Texas, N.A., 619
Allied Grape Growers v. Bronco Wine Co., 482
Allright, Inc. v. Schroeder, 441
Allstate Ins. Co. v. Winnebago County Fair Ass'n, Inc., 463
Allstate Life Ins. Co. v. Miller, 789
Alpert v. 28 Williams Street Corp., 997–998
Altera Corp. v. Clear Logic Inc., 216
Altrust Financial Services, Inc. v. Adams, 1061
Am. South Bank v. Holland, 987
Amato v. KPMG LLP, 1056
Ameral v. Pray, 180
American Bank & Trust Co. v. Koplik, 396

American Chocolates, Inc. v. Mascot Pecan Co., Inc., 812
American Concept Ins. Co. v. Lloyds of London, 786
American Cyanamid Co. v. New Penn Motor Express, Inc., 461–462
American Family Mutual Ins. Co. v. Shelter Mutual Ins. Co., 787
American Geophysical Union v. Texaco Inc., 204
American Home Insurance Co. v. First Speciality Insurance Corp., 787
American National Ins. Co. v. Gilroy, Sims & Associates, Ltd., 964
American Nat'l Bank v. Touche Ross & Co., 1065
American Power & Light Co. v. Securities and Exchange Commission, 65
American Security Services, Inc. v. Vodra, 336
American Society for the Prevention of Cruelty to Animals v. Ringling Brothers Barnum & Bailey Circus, 1136
American Standard Inc. v. Meehan, 922
American Telephone and Telegraph Co. v. Hitachi, 139
American Tempering, Inc. v. Craft Architectural Metals Corp., 473
American Truck Lines, Inc. v. Albino, 979
American Trucking Associations, Inc. v. Michigan Public Service Com'n, 75
American United Logistics, Inc. v. Catellus, 362
Amex Life Assurance Co. v. Superior Court, 789
Amezcua v. Los Angeles Harley-Davidson, 185
Amica Life Insurance Co. v. Barbor, 789
Amoco Oil Co. v. DZ Enterprises, Inc., 456
Amstar Corp. v. Domino's Pizza Inc., 197
Amtz v. Valdez, 587
Andersen v. Hunt, 1170
Andersen, LLP v. US, 1071
Anderson v. Bellino, 1089
Anderson v. City of Hermosa Beach, 1144
Anderson v. Little League Baseball, Inc., 1158